1997
Florida
Statistical Abstract

Thirty-first Edition

Susan S. Floyd, Editor
Eve M. Irwin, Managing Editor
Dorothy A. Evans, Publications Production Specialist

Bureau of Economic and Business Research
Warrington College of Business Administration

UNIVERSITY OF
FLORIDA

UNIVERSITY OF FLORIDA

John V. Lombardi, President

WARRINGTON COLLEGE OF BUSINESS ADMINISTRATION

John Kraft, Dean

BUREAU OF ECONOMIC AND BUSINESS RESEARCH

Stanley K. Smith, Director

1997 Abstract **Advisory Board**

Order books from Bureau of Economic and Business Research
College of Business Administration
221 Matherly Hall, Post Office Box 117145
Gainesville, Florida 32611-7145
phone (352) 392-0171
fax (352) 392-4739
email: bebr@bebr.cba.ufl.edu
http://www.cba.ufl.edu/bebr/

ISBN 0-930885-25-2

Printed in the United States of America on acid-free paper

Cover photograph of Pine Log Swamp in Washington County.
Courtesy of photographer James Valentine and
The Elizabeth Ordway Dunn Foundation

CONTENTS

PREFACE

Since 1967 the *Florida Statistical Abstract* has provided a comprehensive collection of the latest statistics available on the social, economic and political organization of Florida. This thirty-first edition continues the tradition. Most of the data is at the county level, although the *Abstract* also includes information about Florida Metropolitan Statistical Areas, cities, planning districts, and other substate units along with comparisons of Florida with other Sunbelt and other populous states and the United States as a whole. This volume contains a selection of data collected by public and private entities. Agencies of the State of Florida and the Federal Government contribute the majority of the data.

Every effort is made to publish the most up-to-date figures possible; however, these data cover a wide range of activities reported for different time periods so uniformity is impossible. Statistics in this edition are generally for the most recent year or period available by the summer of 1997. Each table title states the time period for data shown in the table and exceptions are footnoted. Sources are given at the bottom of each table. Usually more statistical detail and a more comprehensive discussion of methods and definitions than can be included in the *Abstract* are in the source. Data not available in publications at the time of printing are identified in the source notes as "unpublished data," "prepublication release," and/or with an address on the Internet. Some data are available both in print and on line or CD-ROM.

Each year all tables are reviewed: new tables of current interest are added, continuing series are updated or revised to reflect changes in source definitions or methods, and less timely data are eliminated. Some tables of "benchmark" data, although not timely, are repeated. The reader is encouraged to use tables in earlier editions.

Organization of the *Florida Statistical Abstract*. The *Abstract* is organized around five divisions, each of which is subdivided into sections. Table numbers correspond to the section numbers. The first division (Sections 1.00 through 7.00) generally includes tables presenting data on characteristics of the population: demographics, housing, education, income, employment, and welfare. Except for Section 8.00, which presents data on physical geography and the environment, the next three divisions (Sections 9.00 through 23.00) refer primarily to establishments engaged in economic, social, and political activities.

Establishments are classified in most sources according to the Standard Industrial Classification (SIC) system. Major industry divisions are assigned two-digit codes 01 through 99; subdivisions are classified by three- and four-digit codes. (See the Glossary, "Industrial Classification System, Standard," for more discussion and employment Table 6.03 for a two-digit industry listing.)

The last division of the *Abstract* contains tables of a comparative nature: economic and social trends. Time series showing the fluctuations of major economic indicators such as prices and employment are included in Section 24.00. Selected statistics of the economic, social, and physical environments of Florida, other Sunbelt and other populous states and the United States comprise Section 25.00.

Changes in this edition. As in any year, changes in the availability of various agency publications may necessitate revisions to the *Abstract.* There were a few table deletions and revisions to table formats throughout this volume, but they were minimal. Several new tables were added. Some of the new tables in this edition include apartment rent statistics, a time series of abortions by county since 1990, graduation and dropout rates, readiness for college indicators, students and families involved in home schooling, recently released median household income and poverty statistics, manufacturing pay and jobs, cattle and calves by county, voter turnout in the 1996 elections, prisoner demographics, violent juvenile offenders, and hate crime statistics.

Abstract diskettes. *Abstract* tables are available on microcomputer diskette. To order diskettes please contact the Bureau of Economic and Business Research, 221 Matherly Hall, P. O. Box 117145, Gainesville, Florida, 32611-7145, (352) 392-0171, or e-mail bebr@bebr.cba.ufl.edu.

Bureau of Economic and Business Research. The Bureau's mission is twofold: (1) to produce, collect, analyze, and disseminate economic and demographic data on Florida; and (2) conduct applied research and publish findings on topics relating to the state's ongoing economic growth and development. The Bureau's activities are organized around four research programs: forecasting, population, survey, and policy studies.

Acknowledgments. Again, it is with mixed emotions that we say goodbye to a very important *Abstract* staff member. As faithful readers may recall, former editor Ann Pierce retired prior to the 1996 edition of the *Abstract*. This year we bid farewell to former managing editor, Gayle Thompson, who also retired. Gayle served as an invaluable keyperson to the success of the *Abstract* since the 1991 edition. Her eye for detail and persistence for accuracy in the pursuit of a better product led to innovations in design and to implementation of the streamlined process that we now use in producing the *Abstract*, earning her a much deserved 1996 Davis Productivity Award. Amazingly, Gayle began at the Bureau with virtually no knowledge of computers and over the years became our "Excel Expert." Her talents and perseverance will be missed, along with her kind spirit and creativity. We'll also miss her holiday goodies and crafts. However, we know she is enjoying spending time with her children and grandson and we wish her a long, happy and fulfilling retirement.

This edition benefited from the advice the BEBR's Associate Director, John F. (Dick) Scoggins and of two outside reviewers; University Librarian Emeritus, Ray Jones, and Professor and Assistant Dean for Graduate Studies for the University of Florida's College of Journalism and Communications, Dr. John W. Wright.

The *Abstract* cover photograph of Pine Log Swamp in Washington County was taken by photographer James Valentine. I wish to thank Jim and the Elizabeth Ordway Dunn Foundation for allowing us to share this pristine view of Florida's panhandle.

As we bid farewell to Gayle, we welcome our newest *Abstract* staff member, Eve Irwin, as managing editor of this year's edition. Eve came on-board as we were beginning production of this year's volume and has jumped into the fire. Eve formerly worked for the Federal Deposit Insurance Corporation in a local field office, and is an Air Force Reservist. She brings with her an extensive computer background (that promises to be innovatively put to the test in future editions) and a good sense of humor. Other key personnel in the production of the 1997 *Abstract* were student statistical assistants Bradley Taylor (who has graduated and will leave us for the "real world" at the end of production) and Kerri Sass. Eve and her staff were completely responsible for table layout and design, data entry and proofing, quality control, and final printing of the tables. We utilized the experience Brad gained in working with Gayle on the previous volume to help orient Eve to the production process. Additionally, Brad assisted with final proofing of the text portions of the volume and with revisions made in the Census Index. Even though Kerri arrived later in the process, she managed to catch on quickly. We look forward to working with her on future volumes. A few of the most requested data series, including income and employment, were not available until near the end of scheduled production. This delay required us to seek additional in-house assistance. Joining the production staff on a part-time basis this year was Janet Rose, who performed data entry and proofed tables. Janet also ordered various sources and assisted with the publication and cover bid processes. Janet Fletcher also provided much needed proofing assistance. Dorothy Evans, publications production specialist, was responsible for the preparation of the section dividers and maps and for the conversion of all text material and the index again this year.

Many other members of the Bureau also contributed to this volume. June Nogle provided unpublished data from the BEBR Population Program. Ken Mease supplied data from the BEBR monthly Florida Economic and Consumer Survey. Pamela Middleton was in charge of distribution and filled all in-coming order requests. Pam, Janet Fletcher, and Janet Rose handled promotional mailings and were assisted by students Marian Vagle and Shannon Schatzle. Carol McLarty answered questions about the cover production process, supplied data from the BEBR Data Base, and marketed the volume. Clint Collins provided valuable computer support in our conversion to Windows 95.

We are always pleased to receive suggestions from users for improving the coverage and presentation of data in the *Florida Statistical Abstract*.

Susan S. Floyd
Editor

Gainesville, Florida
October 1997

Counties and Metropolitan Statistical Areas
Effective December 31, 1992 to present

Daytona Beach MSA
  Flagler County
  Volusia County

Ft. Lauderdale PMSA*
  Broward County

Ft. Myers-Cape Coral MSA
  Lee County

Ft. Pierce-Port St. Lucie MSA
  Martin County
  St. Lucie County

Ft. Walton Beach MSA
  Okaloosa County

Gainesville MSA
  Alachua County

Jacksonville MSA
  Clay County
  Duval County
  Nassau County
  St. Johns County

Lakeland-Winter Haven MSA
  Polk County

Melbourne-Titusville-
Palm Bay MSA
  Brevard County

Miami PMSA*
  Dade County

Naples MSA
  Collier County

Ocala MSA
  Marion County

Orlando MSA
  Lake County
  Orange County
  Osceola County
  Seminole County

Panama City MSA
  Bay County

Pensacola MSA
  Escambia County
  Santa Rosa County

Punta Gorda MSA
  Charlotte County

Sarasota-Bradenton MSA
  Manatee County
  Sarasota County

Tallahassee MSA
  Gadsden County
  Leon County

Tampa-St. Petersburg-
Clearwater MSA
  Hernando County
  Hillsborough County
  Pasco County
  Pinellas County

West Palm Beach-Boca Raton MSA
  Palm Beach County

* Miami-Ft. Lauderdale CMSA

Population

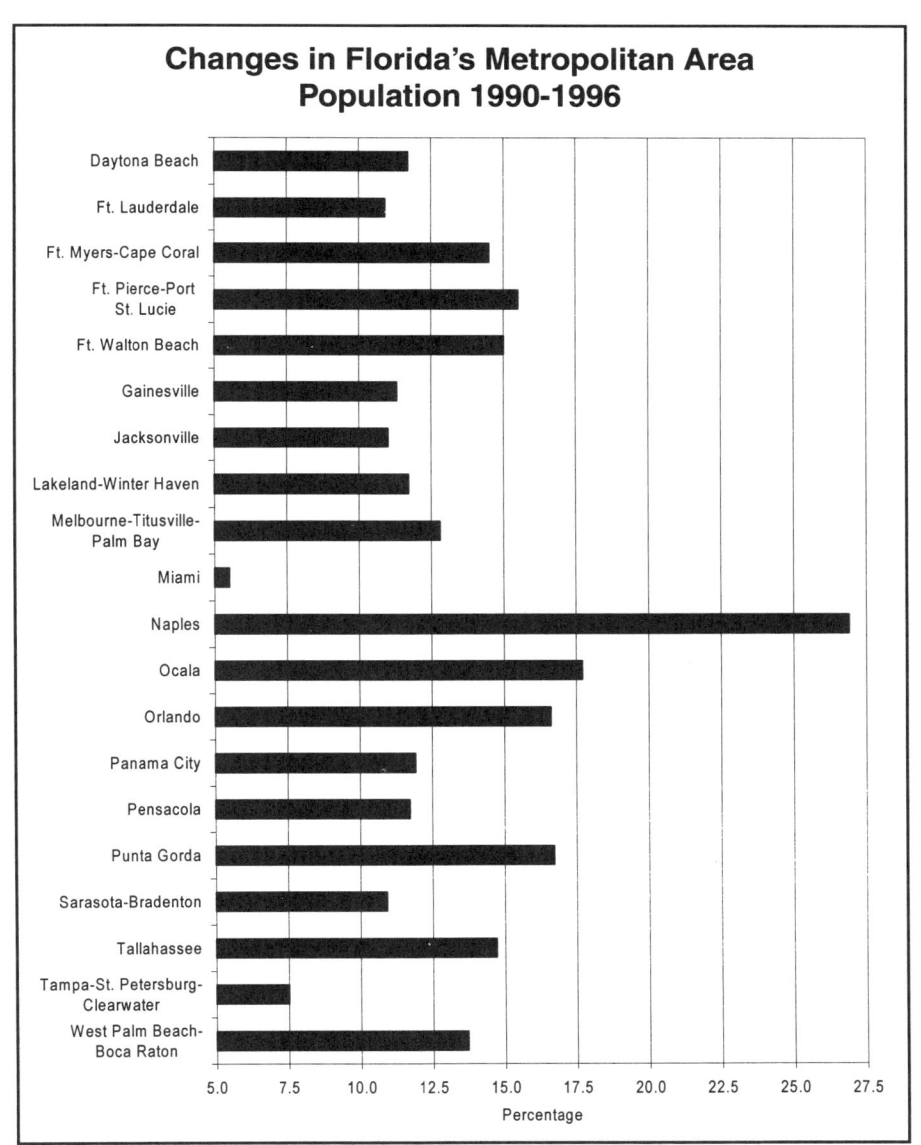

Changes in Florida's Metropolitan Area Population 1990-1996

Metropolitan Area	
Daytona Beach	
Ft. Lauderdale	
Ft. Myers-Cape Coral	
Ft. Pierce-Port St. Lucie	
Ft. Walton Beach	
Gainesville	
Jacksonville	
Lakeland-Winter Haven	
Melbourne-Titusville-Palm Bay	
Miami	
Naples	
Ocala	
Orlando	
Panama City	
Pensacola	
Punta Gorda	
Sarasota-Bradenton	
Tallahassee	
Tampa-St. Petersburg-Clearwater	
West Palm Beach-Boca Raton	

Percentage

5.0   7.5   10.0   12.5   15.0   17.5   20.0   22.5   25.0   27.5

Source: Table 1.65

SECTION 1.00
POPULATION

TABLES LISTED BY MAJOR HEADINGS

University of Florida   **Bureau of Economic and Business Research**

SECTION 1.00
POPULATION
(Continued)

TABLES LISTED BY MAJOR HEADINGS

Table 1.10. CENSUS COUNTS: TOTAL, URBAN, AND RURAL POPULATION
IN FLORIDA, CENSUS YEARS 1830 TO 1990

Census year and date	Total Number	Change from preceding census Number	Change from preceding census Percentage	Urban Number	Urban Percentage of total	Rural Number	Rural Percentage of total
Previous urban definition 1/							
1830 (June 1)	34,730	(X)	(X)	0	0.0	34,730	100.0
1840 (June 1)	54,477	19,747	56.9	0	0.0	54,477	100.0
1850 (June 1)	87,445	32,968	60.5	0	0.0	87,445	100.0
1860 (June 1)	140,424	52,979	60.6	5,708	4.1	134,716	95.9
1870 (June 1)	187,748	47,324	33.7	15,275	8.1	172,473	91.9
1880 (June 1)	269,493	81,745	43.5	26,947	10.0	242,546	90.0
1890 (June 1)	391,422	121,929	45.2	77,358	19.8	314,064	80.2
1900 (June 1)	528,542	137,120	35.0	107,031	20.3	421,511	79.7
1910 (April 15)	752,619	224,077	42.4	219,080	29.1	533,539	70.9
1920 (January 1)	968,470	215,851	28.7	353,515	36.5	614,955	63.5
1930 (April 1)	1,468,211	499,741	51.6	759,778	51.7	708,433	48.3
1940 (April 1)	1,897,414	429,203	29.2	1,045,791	55.1	851,623	44.9
1950 (April 1)	2,771,305	873,891	46.1	1,566,788	56.5	1,204,517	43.5
1960 (April 1)	4,951,560	2,180,255	78.7	3,077,989	62.2	1,873,571	37.8
Current urban definition 2/							
1950 (April 1)	2,771,305	873,891	46.1	1,813,890	65.5	957,415	34.5
1960 (April 1)	4,951,560	2,180,255	78.7	3,661,383	73.9	1,290,177	26.1
1970 (April 1)	6,791,418	1,839,858	37.2	5,544,551	81.6	1,244,892	18.3
1980 (April 1)	9,746,324	2,954,906	43.5	8,212,385	84.3	1,533,939	15.7
1990 (April 1)	12,937,926	3,191,602	32.8	10,970,445	84.8	1,967,481	15.2

(X) Not applicable.

1/ Figures have been adjusted to constitute a substantially consistent series
based on incorporated places of 2,500 or more persons with additional areas defined
as urban under special rules.

2/ The current urban definition defines the urban population as all persons living
in urbanized areas and in places of 2,500 or more persons outside urbanized areas.
An urbanized area comprises an incorporated place and adjacent densely settled surrounding area that together have a minimum population of 50,000. Population not
classified as urban constitutes the rural population. Rural classification need not
imply farm residence or a sparsely settled area because a small city is rural as long
as it is outside an urbanized area and has fewer than 2,500 persons.

Source: U.S., Department of Commerce, Bureau of the Census, *1990 Census of Population: General Population Characteristics, Florida,* 1990 CP-1-11, and previous census editions.

Table 1.12.   STATES: CENSUS COUNTS, APRIL 1, 1990, AND ESTIMATES, JULY 1, 1996
IN FLORIDA, OTHER STATES, AND THE UNITED STATES

State	Census April 1 1990 (1,000)	Estimates July 1 1996 (1,000)	Percentage change 1990 to 1996	State	Census April 1 1990 (1,000)	Estimates July 1 1996 (1,000)	Percentage change 1990 to 1996
Florida	12,938	14,400	11.3	Missouri	5,117	5,359	4.7
				Montana	799	879	10.1
Alabama	4,040	4,273	5.8	Nebraska	1,578	1,652	4.7
Alaska	550	607	10.4	Nevada	1,202	1,603	33.4
Arizona	3,665	4,428	20.8	New Hampshire	1,109	1,162	4.8
Arkansas	2,351	2,510	6.8	New Jersey	7,730	7,988	3.3
California	29,758	31,878	7.1	New Mexico	1,515	1,713	13.1
Colorado	3,294	3,823	16.0	New York	17,991	18,185	1.1
Connecticut	3,287	3,274	-0.4	North Carolina	6,632	7,323	10.4
Delaware	666	725	8.8	North Dakota	639	644	0.7
District of				Ohio	10,847	11,173	3.0
Columbia	607	543	-10.5	Oklahoma	3,146	3,301	4.9
Georgia	6,478	7,353	13.5	Oregon	2,842	3,204	12.7
Hawaii	1,108	1,184	6.8	Pennsylvania	11,883	12,056	1.5
Idaho	1,007	1,189	18.1	Rhode Island	1,003	990	-1.3
Illinois	11,431	11,847	3.6	South Carolina	3,486	3,699	6.1
Indiana	5,544	5,841	5.3	South Dakota	696	732	5.2
Iowa	2,777	2,852	2.7	Tennessee	4,877	5,320	9.1
Kansas	2,478	2,572	3.8	Texas	16,986	19,128	12.6
Kentucky	3,687	3,884	5.3	Utah	1,723	2,000	16.1
Louisiana	4,220	4,351	3.1	Vermont	563	589	4.6
Maine	1,228	1,243	1.3	Virginia	6,189	6,675	7.9
Maryland	4,781	5,072	6.1	Washington	4,867	5,533	13.7
Massachusett	6,016	6,092	1.3	West Virginia	1,793	1,826	1.8
Michigan	9,295	9,594	3.2	Wisconsin	4,892	5,160	5.5
Minnesota	4,376	4,658	6.4	Wyoming	454	481	6.1
Mississippi	2,575	2,716	5.5	United States	248,718	265,284	6.7

Note: Includes persons in the Armed Forces residing in each state. Some data may be revised.

Source: U.S., Department of Commerce, Bureau of the Census, Population Division, Internet site http://www.census.gov/.

University of Florida   **Bureau of Economic and Business Research**

Table 1.19. COUNTIES: CENSUS COUNTS IN THE STATE AND COUNTIES OF FLORIDA, 1940 THROUGH 1990

County	1940	1950	1960	1970	1980	1990	Percentage change				
							1940–1950	1950–1960	1960–1970	1970–1980	1980–1990
Florida	1,897,414	2,771,305	4,951,560	6,791,418	9,746,961	12,938,071	46.1	78.7	37.2	43.5	32.7
Alachua	38,607	57,026	74,074	104,764	151,369	181,596	47.7	29.9	41.4	44.5	20.0
Baker	6,510	6,313	7,363	9,242	15,289	18,486	-3.0	16.6	25.5	65.4	20.9
Bay	20,686	42,689	67,131	75,283	97,740	126,994	106.4	57.3	12.1	29.8	29.9
Bradford	8,717	11,457	12,446	14,625	20,023	22,515	31.4	8.6	17.5	36.9	12.4
Brevard	16,142	23,653	111,435	230,006	272,959	398,978	46.5	371.1	106.4	18.7	46.2
Broward	39,794	83,933	333,946	620,100	1,018,257	1,255,531	110.9	297.9	85.7	64.2	23.3
Calhoun	8,218	7,922	7,422	7,624	9,294	11,011	-3.6	-6.3	2.7	21.9	18.5
Charlotte	3,663	4,286	12,594	27,559	58,460	110,975	17.0	193.8	118.8	112.1	89.8
Citrus	5,846	6,111	9,268	19,196	54,703	93,513	4.5	51.7	107.1	185.0	70.9
Clay	6,468	14,323	19,535	32,059	67,052	105,986	121.4	36.4	64.1	109.2	58.1
Collier	5,102	6,488	15,753	38,040	85,971	152,099	27.2	142.8	141.5	126.0	76.9
Columbia	16,859	18,216	20,077	25,250	35,399	42,613	8.0	10.2	25.8	40.2	20.4
Dade	267,739	495,084	935,047	1,267,792	1,625,509	1,937,194	84.9	88.9	35.6	28.2	19.2
De Soto	7,792	9,242	11,683	13,060	19,039	23,865	18.6	26.4	11.8	45.8	25.3
Dixie	7,018	3,928	4,479	5,480	7,751	10,585	-44.0	14.0	22.3	41.4	36.6
Duval	210,143	304,029	455,411	528,865	571,003	672,971	44.7	49.8	16.1	8.0	17.9
Escambia	74,667	112,706	173,829	205,334	233,794	262,798	50.9	54.2	18.1	13.9	12.4
Flagler	3,008	3,367	4,566	4,454	10,913	28,701	11.9	35.6	-2.5	145.0	163.0
Franklin	5,991	5,814	6,576	7,065	7,661	8,967	-3.0	13.1	7.4	8.4	17.0
Gadsden	31,450	36,457	41,989	39,184	41,674	41,116	15.9	15.2	-6.7	6.4	-1.3
Gilchrist	4,250	3,499	2,868	3,551	5,767	9,667	-17.7	-18.0	23.8	62.4	67.6
Glades	2,745	2,199	2,950	3,669	5,992	7,591	-19.9	34.2	24.4	63.3	26.7
Gulf	6,951	7,460	9,937	10,096	10,658	11,504	7.3	33.2	1.6	5.6	7.9

Continued . . .

Table 1.19. COUNTIES: CENSUS COUNTS IN THE STATE AND COUNTIES OF FLORIDA, 1940 THROUGH 1990 (Continued)

County	1940	1950	1960	1970	1980	1990	Percentage change 1940-1950	1950-1960	1960-1970	1970-1980	1980-1990
Hamilton	9,778	8,981	7,705	7,787	8,761	10,930	-8.2	-14.2	1.1	12.5	24.8
Hardee	10,158	10,073	12,370	14,889	20,357	19,499	-0.8	22.8	20.4	36.7	-4.2
Hendry	5,237	6,051	8,119	11,859	18,599	25,773	15.5	34.2	46.1	56.8	38.6
Hernando	5,641	6,693	11,205	17,004	44,469	101,115	18.6	67.4	51.8	161.5	127.4
Highlands	9,246	13,636	21,338	29,507	47,526	68,432	47.5	56.5	38.3	61.1	44.0
Hillsborough	180,148	249,894	397,788	490,265	646,939	834,054	38.7	59.2	23.2	32.0	28.9
Holmes	15,447	13,988	10,844	10,720	14,723	15,778	-9.4	-22.5	-1.1	37.3	7.2
Indian River	8,957	11,872	25,309	35,992	59,896	90,208	32.5	113.2	42.2	66.4	50.6
Jackson	34,428	34,645	36,208	34,434	39,154	41,375	0.6	4.5	-4.9	13.7	5.7
Jefferson	12,032	10,413	9,543	8,778	10,703	11,296	-13.5	-8.4	-8.0	21.9	5.5
Lafayette	4,405	3,440	2,889	2,892	4,035	5,578	-21.9	-16.0	0.1	39.5	38.2
Lake	27,255	36,340	57,383	69,305	104,870	152,104	33.3	57.9	20.8	51.3	45.0
Lee	17,488	23,404	54,539	105,216	205,266	335,113	33.8	133.0	92.9	95.1	63.3
Leon	31,646	51,590	74,225	103,047	148,655	192,493	63.0	43.9	38.8	44.3	29.5
Levy	12,550	10,637	10,364	12,756	19,870	25,912	-15.2	-2.6	23.1	55.8	30.4
Liberty	3,752	3,182	3,138	3,379	4,260	5,569	-15.2	-1.4	7.7	26.1	30.7
Madison	16,190	14,197	14,154	13,481	14,894	16,569	-12.3	-0.3	-4.8	10.5	11.2
Manatee	26,098	34,704	69,168	97,115	148,445	211,707	33.0	99.3	40.4	52.9	42.6
Marion	31,243	38,187	51,616	69,030	122,488	194,835	22.2	35.2	33.7	77.4	59.1
Martin	6,295	7,807	16,932	28,035	64,014	100,900	24.0	116.9	65.6	128.3	57.6
Monroe	14,078	29,957	47,921	52,586	63,188	78,024	112.8	60.0	9.7	20.2	23.5
Nassau	10,826	12,811	17,189	20,626	32,894	43,941	18.3	34.2	20.0	59.5	33.6
Okaloosa	12,900	27,533	61,175	88,187	109,920	143,777	113.4	122.2	44.2	24.6	30.8
Okeechobee	3,000	3,454	6,424	11,233	20,264	29,627	15.1	86.0	74.9	80.4	46.2

Continued . . .

Table 1.19. COUNTIES: CENSUS COUNTS IN THE STATE AND COUNTIES OF FLORIDA, 1940 THROUGH 1990 (Continued)

County	1940	1950	1960	1970	1980	1990	Percentage change				
							1940–1950	1950–1960	1960–1970	1970–1980	1980–1990
Orange	70,074	114,950	263,540	344,311	470,865	677,491	64.0	129.3	30.6	36.8	43.9
Osceola	10,119	11,406	19,029	25,267	49,287	107,728	12.7	66.8	32.8	95.1	118.6
Palm Beach	79,989	114,688	228,106	348,993	576,758	863,503	43.4	98.9	53.0	65.3	49.7
Pasco	13,981	20,529	36,785	75,955	193,661	281,131	46.8	79.2	106.5	155.0	45.2
Pinellas	91,852	159,249	374,665	522,329	728,531	851,659	73.4	135.3	39.4	39.5	16.9
Polk	86,665	123,997	195,139	228,515	321,652	405,382	43.1	57.4	17.1	40.8	26.0
Putnam	18,698	23,615	32,212	36,424	50,549	65,070	26.3	36.4	13.1	38.8	28.7
St. Johns	20,012	24,998	30,034	31,035	51,303	83,829	24.9	20.1	3.3	65.3	63.4
St. Lucie	11,871	20,180	39,294	50,836	87,182	150,171	70.0	94.7	29.4	71.5	72.3
Santa Rosa	16,085	18,554	29,547	37,741	55,988	81,608	15.3	59.2	27.7	48.3	45.8
Sarasota	16,106	28,827	76,895	120,413	202,251	277,776	79.0	166.7	56.6	68.0	37.3
Seminole	22,304	26,883	54,947	83,692	179,752	287,521	20.5	104.4	52.3	114.8	60.0
Sumter	11,041	11,330	11,869	14,839	24,272	31,577	2.6	4.8	25.0	63.6	30.1
Suwannee	17,073	16,986	14,961	15,559	22,287	26,780	-0.5	-11.9	4.0	43.2	20.2
Taylor	11,565	10,416	13,168	13,641	16,532	17,111	-9.9	26.4	3.6	21.2	3.5
Union	7,094	8,906	6,043	8,112	10,166	10,252	25.5	-32.1	34.2	25.3	0.8
Volusia	53,710	74,229	125,319	169,487	258,762	370,737	38.2	68.8	35.2	52.7	43.3
Wakulla	5,463	5,258	5,257	6,308	10,887	14,202	-3.8	0.0	20.0	72.6	30.4
Walton	14,246	14,725	15,576	16,087	21,300	27,759	3.4	5.8	3.3	32.4	30.3
Washington	12,302	11,888	11,249	11,453	14,509	16,919	-3.4	-5.4	1.8	26.7	16.6

Source: University of Florida, Bureau of Economic and Business Research, *The Urbanization of Florida's Population*; *Historical Perspective of County Growth, 1830–1970*, and *Florida Estimates of Population, April 1, 1996*. Data from U.S. Bureau of the Census.

Table 1.20. COUNTIES: CENSUS COUNTS, APRIL 1, 1980 AND 1990, AND ESTIMATES, APRIL 1, 1987 THROUGH 1996 IN THE STATE AND COUNTIES OF FLORIDA

(in thousands, rounded to hundreds)

County	Census		Estimates								
	1980	1990	1987	1988	1989	1991	1992	1993	1994	1995	1996
Florida	9,747.0	12,938.1	12,000.2	12,327.6	12,650.9	13,196.0	13,424.4	13,608.6	13,878.9	14,149.3	14,411.6
Alachua	151.4	181.6	173.9	176.1	179.1	183.8	186.2	190.7	193.9	198.3	202.1
Baker	15.3	18.5	17.5	17.8	18.1	18.9	19.2	19.5	19.7	20.3	20.7
Bay	97.7	127.0	122.5	124.4	125.8	128.6	131.3	134.1	136.3	139.2	142.2
Bradford	20.0	22.5	22.8	23.0	23.0	22.7	23.1	23.3	24.2	24.3	25.0
Brevard	273.0	399.0	363.0	376.3	388.4	409.4	417.7	427.0	436.3	445.0	450.2
Broward	1,018.3	1,255.5	1,176.8	1,206.7	1,232.5	1,278.4	1,294.1	1,317.5	1,340.2	1,364.2	1,392.3
Calhoun	9.3	11.0	9.8	10.1	10.8	11.2	11.8	11.5	11.6	12.0	12.5
Charlotte	58.5	111.0	91.4	97.0	103.2	115.6	118.7	121.7	124.9	127.6	129.5
Citrus	54.7	93.5	81.7	85.9	90.4	95.9	98.6	100.8	102.8	105.5	107.9
Clay	67.1	106.0	95.7	98.5	103.0	108.2	113.4	114.9	117.8	120.9	125.4
Collier	86.0	152.1	127.7	135.3	143.7	161.6	168.5	174.7	180.5	186.5	193.0
Columbia	35.4	42.6	40.4	41.1	41.9	43.5	45.2	46.4	48.9	50.4	52.6
Dade	1,625.5	1,937.2	1,846.8	1,879.1	1,908.9	1,961.7	1,982.9	1,951.1	1,990.4	2,013.8	2,043.3
De Soto	19.0	23.9	22.4	22.9	23.5	24.5	24.8	25.5	26.3	26.6	26.7
Dixie	7.8	10.6	9.6	9.8	10.2	10.5	10.9	11.8	12.2	12.4	12.6
Duval	571.0	673.0	645.9	656.4	663.4	681.6	693.5	701.6	710.6	718.4	728.4
Escambia	233.8	262.8	259.0	260.4	261.6	265.1	267.8	272.1	277.1	282.7	286.3
Flagler	10.9	28.7	20.5	23.1	26.0	30.5	32.0	33.5	35.3	37.0	39.1
Franklin	7.7	9.0	8.6	8.7	8.8	9.2	9.4	9.8	10.0	10.2	10.4
Gadsden	41.7	41.1	41.4	41.4	41.1	42.2	42.5	43.2	44.9	44.7	46.3
Gilchrist	5.8	9.7	7.9	8.5	9.1	10.0	10.2	10.7	11.5	11.9	12.2
Glades	6.0	7.6	7.1	7.2	7.3	7.9	8.1	8.3	8.4	8.6	9.4
Gulf	10.7	11.5	11.2	11.2	11.3	11.6	11.7	12.4	13.3	13.3	13.5

See footnote at end of table.

Continued . . .

Table 1.20. COUNTIES: CENSUS COUNTS, APRIL 1, 1980 AND 1990, AND ESTIMATES, APRIL 1, 1987 THROUGH 1996 IN THE STATE AND COUNTIES OF FLORIDA (Continued)

(in thousands, rounded to hundreds)

County	Census 1980	Census 1990	1987	1988	1989	1991	1992	1993	1994	1995	1996
Hamilton	8.8	10.9	9.5	10.1	10.6	11.0	11.5	11.6	11.9	12.5	13.4
Hardee	20.4	19.5	20.0	19.9	19.7	19.8	21.1	22.0	22.5	22.9	22.5
Hendry	18.6	25.8	24.0	24.8	25.3	27.2	27.8	28.1	28.7	29.5	30.2
Hernando	44.5	101.1	83.4	90.5	95.5	104.4	108.1	111.7	114.9	117.9	119.9
Highlands	47.5	68.4	62.1	64.3	66.4	70.6	72.2	73.2	75.9	77.3	78.0
Hillsborough	646.9	834.1	792.2	809.5	822.6	843.2	854.0	866.1	879.1	892.9	910.9
Holmes	14.7	15.8	15.1	15.2	15.5	16.0	16.2	16.3	16.9	17.4	17.4
Indian River	59.9	90.2	80.2	83.7	86.8	92.4	94.1	95.6	97.4	100.3	102.2
Jackson	39.2	41.4	41.2	41.2	41.2	41.6	42.6	44.4	45.4	46.6	48.6
Jefferson	10.7	11.3	11.2	11.2	11.3	12.0	12.3	13.0	13.1	13.5	13.7
Lafayette	4.0	5.6	5.1	5.2	5.4	5.7	5.6	5.6	5.8	6.5	7.0
Lake	104.9	152.1	137.2	141.0	146.5	157.1	162.6	167.2	171.2	176.9	182.3
Lee	205.3	335.1	300.6	312.3	325.4	344.0	350.8	357.6	367.4	376.7	383.7
Leon	148.7	192.5	174.4	178.9	187.5	198.3	202.6	206.3	212.1	217.5	221.6
Levy	19.9	25.9	23.8	24.5	25.3	26.7	27.5	28.2	29.1	29.8	30.7
Liberty	4.3	5.6	4.6	4.7	4.7	5.6	5.5	5.7	6.5	6.9	7.4
Madison	14.9	16.6	15.4	15.4	15.8	16.5	17.0	17.3	17.8	18.3	18.7
Manatee	148.4	211.7	193.5	199.7	205.7	215.1	219.3	223.5	228.3	233.2	236.8
Marion	122.5	194.8	174.2	180.9	188.1	200.3	206.6	212.0	217.9	224.6	229.3
Martin	64.0	100.9	88.3	92.0	96.2	103.1	105.0	106.8	110.2	112.0	114.5
Monroe	63.2	78.0	73.1	75.5	76.8	79.5	81.0	81.8	82.3	83.4	83.8
Nassau	32.9	43.9	41.2	42.1	43.5	45.0	45.5	46.5	47.4	49.1	51.1
Okaloosa	109.9	143.8	137.5	139.8	141.6	146.1	150.0	154.5	158.3	162.7	165.3
Okeechobee	20.3	29.6	27.3	28.1	28.9	30.2	31.1	31.8	32.3	32.9	33.6

Continued . . .

See footnote at end of table.

Table 1.20. COUNTIES: CENSUS COUNTS, APRIL 1, 1980 AND 1990, AND ESTIMATES, APRIL 1, 1987 THROUGH 1996 IN THE STATE AND COUNTIES OF FLORIDA (Continued)

(in thousands, rounded to hundreds)

County	Census 1980	Census 1990	1987	1988	1989	Estimates 1991	1992	1993	1994	1995	1996
Orange	470.9	677.5	602.8	622.3	652.4	701.3	712.6	727.8	740.2	759.0	777.6
Osceola	49.3	107.7	87.6	95.2	101.0	114.4	119.8	125.7	131.1	136.6	139.7
Palm Beach	576.8	863.5	784.8	817.5	841.5	883.0	897.0	918.2	937.2	962.8	981.8
Pasco	193.7	281.1	258.2	267.0	274.4	285.4	290.3	294.0	298.9	305.6	309.9
Pinellas	728.5	851.7	825.7	834.0	844.6	855.8	860.7	865.0	870.7	876.2	881.4
Polk	321.7	405.4	383.0	391.6	399.0	414.7	420.9	429.9	437.2	443.2	452.7
Putnam	50.5	65.1	61.0	62.3	63.9	66.0	67.8	67.6	69.0	69.5	70.3
St. Johns	51.3	83.8	74.2	78.3	82.0	86.1	88.4	91.2	94.8	98.2	101.7
St. Lucie	87.2	150.2	129.5	136.3	144.1	155.1	158.9	163.2	166.8	171.2	175.5
Santa Rosa	56.0	81.6	73.3	75.6	79.1	83.9	88.0	90.3	93.8	96.1	98.5
Sarasota	202.3	277.8	258.1	264.3	271.4	283.1	287.2	290.6	296.0	301.5	305.8
Seminole	179.8	287.5	251.4	264.7	277.3	298.1	305.9	310.9	316.6	324.1	329.0
Sumter	24.3	31.6	29.3	29.8	30.9	32.0	33.1	33.8	35.2	36.5	40.6
Suwannee	22.3	26.8	25.3	25.7	26.3	27.4	27.6	28.6	29.3	30.5	31.4
Taylor	16.5	17.1	17.2	17.2	17.2	17.4	17.4	17.4	17.5	18.3	19.0
Union	10.2	10.3	10.6	10.1	10.3	10.6	11.4	12.0	12.5	12.6	13.0
Volusia	258.8	370.7	333.6	347.6	360.2	376.7	384.0	390.1	396.6	403.0	407.2
Wakulla	10.9	14.2	13.2	13.5	13.8	14.4	14.7	15.4	16.4	17.0	18.0
Walton	21.3	27.8	26.2	26.6	27.1	29.2	29.7	30.6	31.9	33.4	34.3
Washington	14.5	16.9	16.3	16.5	16.8	17.2	17.4	17.6	18.1	19.0	19.8

Note: These are revised intercensal estimates that incorporate the effects of 1990 census counts, all revisions to 1980 census counts, and any changes that may have occurred in the underlying base data. Estimates reflect changes to Dade and Broward counties as a result of Hurricane Andrew in August 1992.

Source: University of Florida, Bureau of Economic and Business Research, Population Program, *Special Population Reports*, May 1991, and *Florida Estimates of Population, April 1, 1996*. Census data from U.S. Bureau of the Census.

Table 1.31. COUNTIES AND CITIES: CENSUS COUNTS, APRIL 1, 1990, AND ESTIMATES
APRIL 1, 1996, IN THE STATE, COUNTIES, AND MUNICIPALITIES
OF FLORIDA

Area	Census 1990	Estimates 1996	Area	Census 1990	Estimates 1996
Florida	12,938,071	14,411,563	Brevard (Continued)		
Incorporated	6,415,302	7,116,696	Rockledge	16,023	18,434
Unincorporated	6,522,769	7,294,867	Satellite Beach	9,889	10,106
			Titusville	39,394	41,321
Alachua	181,596	202,140	West Melbourne	8,399	9,171
Alachua	4,547	5,882	Unincorporated	149,204	173,455
Archer	1,372	1,407			
Gainesville	85,075	97,693	Broward	1,255,531	1,392,252
Hawthorne	1,305	1,381	Coconut Creek	27,269	34,528
High Springs	3,144	3,571	Cooper City	21,335	27,686
LaCrosse	122	139	Coral Springs	78,864	98,553
Micanopy	626	645	Dania	13,183	17,320
Newberry	1,644	2,289	Davie	47,143	59,393
Waldo	1,017	1,042	Deerfield Beach	46,997	48,974
Unincorporated	82,744	88,091	Ft. Lauderdale	149,238	150,150
			Hallandale	30,997	31,458
Baker	18,486	20,709	Hillsboro Beach	1,748	1,753
Glen St. Mary	480	460	Hollywood	121,720	125,689
Macclenny	3,966	4,253	Lauderdale-by-the-		
Unincorporated	14,040	15,996	Sea	2,990	3,000
			Lauderdale Lakes	27,341	27,859
Bay	126,994	142,159	Lauderhill	49,015	50,020
Callaway	12,253	14,044	Lazy Lake Village	33	40
Cedar Grove	1,479	2,102	Lighthouse Point	10,378	10,470
Lynn Haven	9,298	11,353	Margate	42,985	48,168
Mexico Beach	992	973	Miramar	40,663	46,490
Panama City	34,396	37,236	North Lauderdale	26,473	27,354
Panama City Beach	4,051	4,554	Oakland Park	26,326	28,144
Parker	4,598	4,976	Parkland	3,773	10,378
Springfield	8,719	9,482	Pembroke Park	4,933	4,949
Unincorporated	51,208	57,439	Pembroke Pines	65,566	94,354
			Plantation	66,814	76,223
Bradford	22,515	24,983	Pompano Beach	72,411	74,271
Brooker	312	331	Sea Ranch Lakes	619	619
Hampton	296	312	Sunrise	65,683	74,766
Lawtey	676	668	Tamarac	44,822	50,051
Starke	5,226	5,163	Wilton Manors	11,804	11,886
Unincorporated	16,005	18,509	Unincorporated	154,408	157,706
Brevard	398,978	450,164	Calhoun	11,011	12,504
Cape Canaveral	8,014	8,375	Altha	497	604
Cocoa	17,722	17,874	Blountstown	2,404	2,484
Cocoa Beach	12,123	12,794	Unincorporated	8,110	9,416
Indialantic	2,844	2,938			
Indian Harbour			Charlotte	110,975	129,468
Beach	6,933	7,579	Punta Gorda	10,637	12,308
Malabar	1,977	2,364	Unincorporated	100,338	117,160
Melbourne	60,034	66,970			
Melbourne Beach	3,078	3,198	Citrus	93,513	107,889
Melbourne Village	591	612	Crystal River	4,050	4,072
Palm Bay	62,543	74,395	Inverness	5,797	6,741
Palm Shores	210	578	Unincorporated	83,666	97,076

See footnotes at end of table.   Continued . . .

University of Florida   **Bureau of Economic and Business Research**

Table 1.31. COUNTIES AND CITIES: CENSUS COUNTS, APRIL 1, 1990, AND ESTIMATES
APRIL 1, 1996, IN THE STATE, COUNTIES, AND MUNICIPALITIES
OF FLORIDA (Continued)

Area	Census 1990	Estimates 1996	Area	Census 1990	Estimates 1996
Clay	105,986	125,431	Dixie	10,585	12,602
Green Cove Springs	4,497	4,988	Cross City	2,041	2,070
Keystone Heights	1,315	1,340	Horseshoe Beach	252	194
Orange Park	9,488	9,508	Unincorporated	8,292	10,338
Penney Farms	609	636			
Unincorporated	90,077	108,959	Duval	672,971	728,437
			Atlantic Beach	11,636	13,116
Collier	152,099	193,036	Baldwin	1,450	1,560
Everglades	321	541	Jacksonville Beach	17,839	20,086
Naples	19,505	21,127	Neptune Beach	6,816	7,503
Unincorporated	132,273	171,368	Jacksonville (Duval)	635,230	686,172
Columbia	42,613	52,565	Escambia	262,798	286,301
Ft. White	468	517	Century	1,989	2,040
Lake City	9,626	10,049	Pensacola	59,198	60,658
Unincorporated	32,519	41,999	Unincorporated	201,611	223,603
Dade	1,937,194	2,043,316	Flagler	28,701	39,052
Aventura 1/	0	16,996	Beverly Beach	314	324
Bal Harbour	3,045	3,117	Bunnell	1,873	2,048
Bay Harbor Islands	4,703	4,663	Flagler Beach	3,818	4,225
Biscayne Park	3,068	3,030	Marineland (part)	21	12
Coral Gables	40,091	41,205	Unincorporated	22,675	32,443
El Portal	2,457	2,485			
Florida City	5,978	5,590	Franklin	8,967	10,378
Golden Beach	774	835	Apalachicola	2,602	2,798
Hialeah	188,008	206,500	Carrabelle	1,200	1,361
Hialeah Gardens	7,727	12,208	Unincorporated	5,165	6,219
Homestead	26,694	25,385			
Indian Creek Village	44	50	Gadsden	41,116	46,322
Islandia	13	13	Chattahoochee	4,382	4,104
Key Biscayne 1/	0	8,886	Greensboro	586	592
Medley	663	884	Gretna	1,981	2,841
Miami	358,648	365,127	Havana	1,717	1,864
Miami Beach	92,639	91,848	Midway	976	1,172
Miami Shores	10,084	10,162	Quincy	7,452	7,336
Miami Springs	13,268	13,358	Unincorporated	24,022	28,413
North Bay	5,383	5,894			
North Miami	50,001	50,757	Gilchrist	9,667	12,150
North Miami Beach	35,361	38,057	Bell	267	286
Opa-Locka	15,283	15,790	Fanning Springs		
Pinecrest 1/	0	18,988	(part)	230	237
South Miami	10,404	10,537	Trenton	1,287	1,346
Surfside	4,108	4,361	Unincorporated	7,883	10,281
Sweetwater	13,909	14,060			
Virginia Gardens	2,212	2,267	Glades	7,591	9,413
West Miami	5,727	5,832	Moore Haven	1,432	1,548
Unincorporated	1,036,902	1,064,431	Unincorporated	6,159	7,865
De Soto	23,865	26,716	Gulf	11,504	13,545
Arcadia	6,488	6,600	Port St. Joe	4,044	4,128
Unincorporated	17,377	20,116	Wewahitchka	1,779	1,830

See footnotes at end of table.   Continued . . .

University of Florida   **Bureau of Economic and Business Research**

Table 1.31. COUNTIES AND CITIES: CENSUS COUNTS, APRIL 1, 1990, AND ESTIMATES
APRIL 1, 1996, IN THE STATE, COUNTIES, AND MUNICIPALITIES
OF FLORIDA (Continued)

Area	Census 1990	Estimates 1996	Area	Census 1990	Estimates 1996
Gulf (Continued)			Jackson	41,375	48,629
Unincorporated	5,681	7,587	Alford	482	536
			Bascom	90	117
Hamilton	10,930	13,431	Campbellton	202	251
Jasper	2,099	2,075	Cottondale	900	1,079
Jennings	712	783	Graceville	2,675	2,688
White Springs	704	817	Grand Ridge	536	703
Unincorporated	7,415	9,756	Greenwood	474	627
			Jacob City	261	320
Hardee	19,499	22,519	Malone	765	2,205
Bowling Green	1,836	1,876	Marianna	6,292	6,546
Wauchula	3,243	3,573	Sneads	1,746	2,096
Zolfo Springs	1,219	1,247	Unincorporated	26,952	31,461
Unincorporated	13,201	15,823			
			Jefferson	11,296	13,713
Hendry	25,773	30,157	Monticello	2,603	2,884
Clewiston	6,085	6,349	Unincorporated	8,693	10,829
La Belle	2,703	3,125			
Unincorporated	16,985	20,683	Lafayette	5,578	7,012
			Mayo	917	930
Hernando	101,115	119,931	Unincorporated	4,661	6,082
Brooksville	7,589	7,794			
Weeki Wachee	11	11	Lake	152,104	182,309
Unincorporated	93,515	112,126	Astatula	981	1,175
			Clermont	6,910	7,291
Highlands	68,432	77,996	Eustis	12,856	14,286
Avon Park	8,078	8,110	Fruitland Park	2,715	2,981
Lake Placid	1,158	1,427	Groveland	2,300	2,487
Sebring	8,841	8,955	Howey-in-the-Hills	724	796
Unincorporated	50,355	59,504	Lady Lake	8,071	12,287
			Leesburg	14,783	15,352
Hillsborough	834,054	910,855	Mascotte	1,761	2,376
Plant City	22,754	26,081	Minneola	1,515	2,463
Tampa	280,015	289,337	Montverde	890	1,111
Temple Terrace	16,444	19,138	Mount Dora	7,316	8,483
Unincorporated	514,841	576,299	Tavares	7,383	8,233
			Umatilla	2,350	2,432
Holmes	15,778	17,412	Unincorporated	81,549	100,556
Bonifay	2,612	2,759			
Esto	253	321	Lee	335,113	383,706
Noma	207	219	Cape Coral	74,991	87,632
Ponce de Leon	406	466	Ft. Myers	44,947	46,328
Westville	257	292	Ft. Myers Beach 1/	0	6,039
Unincorporated	12,043	13,355	Sanibel	5,468	5,838
			Unincorporated	209,707	237,869
Indian River	90,208	102,211			
Fellsmere	2,179	2,412	Leon	192,493	221,621
Indian River Shores	2,278	2,640	Tallahassee	124,773	138,863
Orchid	10	29	Unincorporated	67,720	82,758
Sebastian	10,248	13,967			
Vero Beach	17,350	17,697	Levy	25,912	30,690
Unincorporated	58,143	65,466	Bronson	875	854

See footnotes at end of table.   Continued . . .

Table 1.31. COUNTIES AND CITIES: CENSUS COUNTS, APRIL 1, 1990, AND ESTIMATES
APRIL 1, 1996, IN THE STATE, COUNTIES, AND MUNICIPALITIES
OF FLORIDA (Continued)

Area	Census 1990	Estimates 1996	Area	Census 1990	Estimates 1996
Levy (Continued)			Nassau	43,941	51,097
Cedar Key	668	742	Callahan	946	1,018
Chiefland	1,917	1,989	Fernandina Beach	8,765	9,988
Fanning Springs			Hilliard	2,276	2,509
(part)	263	297	Unincorporated	31,954	37,582
Inglis	1,241	1,295			
Otter Creek	136	126	Okaloosa	143,777	165,319
Williston	2,168	2,269	Cinco Bayou	386	410
Yankeetown	635	612	Crestview	9,886	12,429
Unincorporated	18,009	22,506	Destin	8,090	9,802
			Ft. Walton Beach	21,407	22,037
Liberty	5,569	7,439	Laurel Hill	543	600
Bristol	937	1,130	Mary Esther	4,139	4,406
Unincorporated	4,632	6,309	Niceville	10,509	11,705
			Shalimar	341	630
Madison	16,569	18,745	Valparaiso	6,316	6,635
Greenville	950	1,010	Unincorporated	82,160	96,665
Lee	306	314			
Madison	3,345	3,463	Okeechobee	29,627	33,643
Unincorporated	11,968	13,958	Okeechobee	4,943	5,069
			Unincorporated	24,684	28,574
Manatee	211,707	236,778			
Anna Maria	1,744	1,843	Orange	677,491	777,556
Bradenton	43,769	48,031	Apopka	13,611	19,255
Bradenton Beach	1,657	1,682	Bay Lake	19	24
Holmes Beach	4,810	5,043	Belle Isle	5,272	5,596
Longboat Key			Eatonville	2,505	2,506
(part)	2,544	2,649	Edgewood	1,062	1,479
Palmetto	9,268	9,860	Lake Buena Vista	1,776	23
Unincorporated	147,915	167,670	Maitland	8,932	9,871
			Oakland	700	748
Marion	194,835	229,260	Ocoee	12,778	19,261
Belleview	2,678	3,307	Orlando	164,674	173,122
Dunnellon	1,639	1,785	Windermere	1,371	1,776
McIntosh	411	422	Winter Garden	9,863	12,413
Ocala	42,045	43,332	Winter Park	22,623	24,750
Reddick	554	570	Unincorporated	432,305	506,732
Unincorporated	147,508	179,844			
			Osceola	107,728	139,724
Martin	100,900	114,464	Kissimmee	30,337	38,175
Jupiter Island	549	581	St. Cloud	13,005	16,601
Ocean Breeze Park	519	510	Unincorporated	64,386	84,948
Sewall's Point	1,588	1,736			
Stuart	11,936	13,773	Palm Beach	863,503	981,793
Unincorporated	86,308	97,864	Atlantis	1,653	1,694
			Belle Glade	16,177	16,858
Monroe	78,024	83,789	Boca Raton	61,486	67,754
Key Colony Beach	977	1,048	Boynton Beach	46,284	50,940
Key West	24,832	27,009	Briny Breezes	400	398
Layton	183	200	Cloud Lake	121	121
Unincorporated	52,032	55,532	Delray Beach	47,184	52,039

See footnotes at end of table.   Continued . . .

University of Florida   **Bureau of Economic and Business Research**

Table 1.31. COUNTIES AND CITIES: CENSUS COUNTS, APRIL 1, 1990, AND ESTIMATES
APRIL 1, 1996, IN THE STATE, COUNTIES, AND MUNICIPALITIES
OF FLORIDA (Continued)

Area	Census 1990	Estimates 1996	Area	Census 1990	Estimates 1996
Palm Beach (Continued)			Pinellas (Continued)		
Glen Ridge	207	219	Indian Shores	1,405	1,473
Golf Village	184	195	Kenneth City	4,345	4,334
Golfview	153	153	Largo	65,910	67,798
Greenacres City	18,683	23,733	Madeira Beach	4,225	4,225
Gulf Stream	690	707	North Redington		
Haverhill	1,058	1,187	Beach	1,135	1,147
Highland Beach	3,209	3,264	Oldsmar	8,361	9,224
Hypoluxo	807	1,371	Pinellas Park	43,571	44,472
Juno Beach	2,172	2,659	Redington Beach	1,626	1,605
Jupiter	24,907	30,599	Redington Shores	2,366	2,411
Jupiter Inlet			Safety Harbor	15,120	16,750
Colony	405	421	St. Petersburg	240,318	241,276
Lake Clarke Shores	3,364	3,640	St. Petersburg Beach	9,200	9,589
Lake Park	6,704	6,887	Seminole	9,251	9,658
Lake Worth	28,564	29,844	South Pasadena	5,644	5,867
Lantana	8,392	8,477	Tarpon Springs	17,874	19,507
Manalapan	312	330	Treasure Island	7,266	7,347
Mangonia Park	1,453	1,392	Unincorporated	257,232	273,190
North Palm Beach	11,343	11,855			
Ocean Ridge	1,570	1,635	Polk	405,382	452,707
Pahokee	6,822	6,935	Auburndale	8,846	9,323
Palm Beach	9,814	9,790	Bartow	14,716	15,025
Palm Beach Gardens	22,990	31,909	Davenport	1,529	1,981
Palm Beach Shores	1,035	1,028	Dundee	2,335	2,572
Palm Springs	9,763	9,950	Eagle Lake	1,758	1,903
Riviera Beach	27,646	27,782	Ft. Meade	4,993	5,455
Royal Palm Beach	15,532	17,668	Frostproof	2,875	2,904
South Bay	3,558	3,329	Haines City	11,683	12,911
South Palm Beach	1,480	1,498	Highland Park	155	155
Tequesta Village	4,499	4,673	Hillcrest Heights	221	235
Wellington 1/	0	26,148	Lake Alfred	3,622	3,771
West Palm Beach	67,764	78,370	Lake Hamilton	1,128	1,137
Unincorporated	405,118	444,341	Lake Wales	9,670	9,928
			Lakeland	70,576	75,422
Pasco	281,131	309,936	Mulberry	2,988	3,314
Dade City	5,633	5,963	Polk City	1,439	1,644
New Port Richey	14,044	14,555	Winter Haven	24,725	25,485
Port Richey	2,521	2,629	Unincorporated	242,123	279,542
St. Leo	1,009	690			
San Antonio	776	831	Putnam	65,070	70,287
Zephyrhills	8,220	8,867	Crescent City	1,859	1,847
Unincorporated	248,928	276,401	Interlachen	1,160	1,390
			Palatka	10,444	10,685
Pinellas	851,659	881,383	Pomona Park	726	755
Belleair	3,963	4,080	Welaka	533	601
Belleair Beach	2,070	2,138	Unincorporated	50,348	55,009
Belleair Bluffs	2,234	2,221			
Belleair Shore	60	60	St. Johns	83,829	101,729
Clearwater	98,784	101,867	Hastings	595	648
Dunedin	34,027	35,104	Marineland (part)	0	0
Gulfport	11,709	11,871	St. Augustine	11,695	12,149
Indian Rocks Beach	3,963	4,169	St. Augustine Beach	3,657	4,116

See footnotes at end of table.   Continued . . .

Table 1.31. COUNTIES AND CITIES: CENSUS COUNTS, APRIL 1, 1990, AND ESTIMATES
APRIL 1, 1996, IN THE STATE, COUNTIES, AND MUNICIPALITIES
OF FLORIDA (Continued)

Area	Census 1990	Estimates 1996	Area	Census 1990	Estimates 1996
St. Johns (Continued)			Taylor (Continued)		
Unincorporated	67,882	84,816	Unincorporated	9,960	11,806
St. Lucie	150,171	175,458	Union	10,252	13,023
Ft. Pierce	36,830	37,273	Lake Butler	2,116	2,084
Port St. Lucie	55,761	74,894	Raiford	198	257
St. Lucie Village	584	633	Worthington Springs	178	178
Unincorporated	56,996	62,658	Unincorporated	7,760	10,504
Santa Rosa	81,608	98,491	Volusia	370,737	407,199
Gulf Breeze	5,530	5,959	Daytona Beach	61,991	63,796
Jay	666	683	Daytona Beach		
Milton	7,216	7,534	Shores	2,197	2,870
Unincorporated	68,196	84,315	DeBary 1/	(X)	11,568
			DeLand	16,622	18,000
Sarasota	277,776	305,848	Deltona 1/	(X)	56,148
Longboat Key (part)	3,393	3,907	Edgewater	15,351	17,761
North Port	11,973	15,905	Holly Hill	11,141	11,370
Sarasota	50,897	51,311	Lake Helen	2,344	2,435
Venice	17,052	18,619	New Smyrna Beach	16,549	18,239
Unincorporated	194,461	216,106	Oak Hill	917	1,083
			Orange City	5,347	6,137
Seminole	287,521	329,031	Ormond Beach	29,721	32,426
Altamonte Springs	35,167	38,200	Pierson	2,988	1,240
Casselberry	18,849	24,393	Ponce Inlet	1,704	2,232
Lake Mary	5,929	7,470	Port Orange	35,399	40,543
Longwood	13,316	13,598	South Daytona	12,488	12,910
Oviedo	11,114	19,247	Unincorporated	155,978	108,441
Sanford	32,387	35,279			
Winter Springs	22,151	26,474	Wakulla	14,202	18,022
Unincorporated	148,608	164,370	St. Marks	307	297
			Sopchoppy	367	385
Sumter	31,577	40,593	Unincorporated	13,528	17,340
Bushnell	1,998	2,358			
Center Hill	735	762	Walton	27,759	34,328
Coleman	857	847	DeFuniak Springs	5,200	5,511
Webster	746	854	Freeport	843	1,080
Wildwood	3,560	3,989	Paxton	600	625
Unincorporated	23,681	31,783	Unincorporated	21,116	27,112
Suwannee	26,780	31,424	Washington	16,919	19,751
Branford	670	659	Caryville	631	579
Live Oak	6,332	6,465	Chipley	3,866	4,110
Unincorporated	19,778	24,300	Ebro	255	269
			Vernon	778	849
Taylor	17,111	19,022	Wausau	313	332
Perry	7,151	7,216	Unincorporated	11,076	13,612

(X) Not applicable.   1/ Not incorporated in 1990.
Note: Census counts include all adjustments made through September 30, 1996.
Estimates reflect changes to Dade and Broward counties as a result of Hurricane
Andrew in August 1992.
Source: University of Florida, Bureau of Economic and Business Research, Popula-
tion Program, *Florida Estimates of Population, April 1, 1996.* Census data from U.S.
Bureau of the Census.

University of Florida   **Bureau of Economic and Business Research**

Table 1.34. AGE, RACE, AND SEX: CENSUS COUNTS, APRIL 1, 1990, AND ESTIMATES, APRIL 1, 1996, BY AGE, RACE, AND SEX IN FLORIDA

Age	All races Total	All races Male	All races Female	White Total	White Male	White Female	Black 1/ Total	Black 1/ Male	Black 1/ Female
Census, 1990									
All ages	12,937,926	6,261,770	6,676,156	10,971,995	5,323,424	5,648,571	1,772,356	845,923	926,433
0-14	2,428,671	1,243,364	1,185,307	1,860,162	955,468	904,694	523,856	265,194	258,662
15-24	1,682,627	859,036	823,591	1,343,380	691,738	651,642	305,932	150,087	155,845
25-44	3,920,704	1,954,702	1,966,002	3,290,085	1,658,800	1,631,285	555,627	261,562	294,065
45-64	2,549,998	1,201,564	1,348,434	2,259,374	1,068,506	1,190,868	258,632	118,670	139,962
65-69	737,129	331,267	405,862	689,346	310,846	378,500	44,214	18,850	25,364
70-74	627,699	279,758	347,941	592,046	265,200	326,846	33,373	13,561	19,812
75-79	483,532	204,877	278,655	456,675	194,660	262,015	25,375	9,572	15,803
80-84	302,099	118,468	183,631	286,770	112,991	173,779	14,592	5,145	9,447
85 and over	205,467	68,734	136,733	194,157	65,215	128,942	10,755	3,282	7,473
Estimates, 1996									
All ages	14,411,563	6,992,872	7,418,691	12,163,337	5,904,890	6,258,447	2,000,793	968,505	1,032,288
0-14	2,776,875	1,418,294	1,358,581	2,129,076	1,089,636	1,039,440	589,527	298,974	290,553
15-24	1,719,933	883,735	836,198	1,349,586	694,782	654,804	330,080	135,591	131,319
25-44	4,185,553	2,104,914	2,080,639	3,478,986	1,762,107	1,716,879	614,307	274,057	272,838
45-64	3,065,783	1,471,667	1,594,116	2,697,557	1,304,121	1,393,436	323,199	233,698	263,477
65-69	729,936	327,545	402,391	677,957	305,716	372,241	47,460	31,363	37,356
70-74	712,549	310,083	402,466	671,658	293,703	377,955	37,778	24,734	31,355
75-79	564,947	237,835	327,112	536,188	227,043	309,145	26,811	19,888	27,572
80-84	384,996	150,444	234,552	366,239	143,973	222,266	17,622	15,060	22,718
85 and over	270,991	88,355	182,636	256,090	83,809	172,281	14,009	9,963	16,848

1/ "Black" reflects the self-identification of respondents in the 1990 census.
Note: Data for age and race categories have been modified by the U.S. Bureau of the Census to account for misreporting. As a result, these numbers may differ from those found in other publications.

Source: University of Florida, Bureau of Economic and Business Research, Population Program, *Florida Population Studies*, July 1997, Volume 30, No. 3. Bulletin No. 118, and unpublished data.

Table 1.35. AGE AND SEX: ESTIMATES BY SEX AND AGE GROUP AND MEDIAN AGE IN THE STATE AND COUNTIES OF FLORIDA
APRIL 1, 1996

County	Total	Sex		Age					18 and over	Median 1/
		Male	Female	0-14	15-24	25-44	45-64	65 and over		
Florida	14,411,563	6,992,872	7,418,691	2,776,875	1,719,933	4,185,553	3,065,783	2,663,419	11,160,865	28.5
Alachua	202,140	99,845	102,295	37,925	50,790	63,323	31,338	18,764	157,770	31.6
Baker	20,709	11,071	9,638	4,682	3,517	6,887	3,862	1,761	14,944	35.3
Bay	142,159	69,968	72,191	30,581	18,823	43,675	30,688	18,392	106,063	35.0
Bradford	24,983	14,024	10,959	4,580	3,604	8,326	5,190	3,283	19,422	38.6
Brevard	450,164	220,964	229,200	85,624	50,144	133,066	100,482	80,848	349,906	38.9
Broward	1,392,252	668,386	723,866	265,257	140,037	426,695	289,071	271,192	1,086,127	35.3
Calhoun	12,504	6,636	5,868	2,327	1,929	3,906	2,530	1,812	9,658	52.0
Charlotte	129,468	62,101	67,367	17,146	10,870	26,930	31,622	42,900	108,869	51.8
Citrus	107,889	51,254	56,635	15,263	8,720	21,500	26,845	35,561	89,567	33.9
Clay	125,431	61,958	63,473	29,221	17,294	39,440	27,694	11,782	90,293	42.9
Collier	193,036	94,523	98,513	33,873	18,018	49,962	45,007	46,176	153,765	35.0
Columbia	52,565	26,749	25,816	11,830	7,372	15,075	11,259	7,029	38,349	35.2
Dade	2,043,316	985,827	1,057,489	448,284	259,819	618,760	435,292	281,161	1,520,403	37.5
De Soto	26,716	14,417	12,299	5,074	3,496	7,642	5,343	5,161	20,648	38.6
Dixie	12,602	6,624	5,978	2,329	1,662	3,360	3,010	2,241	9,803	33.0
Duval	728,437	356,125	372,312	164,777	100,474	242,765	139,288	81,133	538,081	33.6
Escambia	286,301	140,404	145,897	60,531	42,889	88,500	58,120	36,261	214,896	48.7
Flagler	39,052	18,653	20,399	5,785	3,556	8,418	10,012	11,281	32,109	43.5
Franklin	10,378	5,161	5,217	1,718	1,174	2,503	2,952	2,031	8,291	32.5
Gadsden	46,322	22,970	23,352	10,956	7,010	14,166	8,990	5,200	33,275	33.7
Gilchrist	12,150	6,450	5,700	2,331	2,464	3,130	2,598	1,627	9,244	40.8
Glades	9,413	4,758	4,655	1,698	1,179	2,363	2,236	1,937	7,324	36.1

See footnotes at end of table.

Continued . . .

Table 1.35. AGE AND SEX: ESTIMATES BY SEX AND AGE GROUP AND MEDIAN AGE IN THE STATE AND COUNTIES OF FLORIDA, APRIL 1, 1996 (Continued)

County	Total	Sex		Age						
		Male	Female	0-14	15-24	25-44	45-64	65 and over	18 and over	Median 1/
Gulf	13,545	7,394	6,151	2,380	1,903	4,286	3,047	1,929	10,591	32.7
Hamilton	13,431	7,306	6,125	2,667	2,369	4,304	2,598	1,493	10,054	33.1
Hardee	22,519	11,987	10,532	5,095	3,343	6,340	4,245	3,496	16,440	30.8
Hendry	30,157	15,579	14,578	7,969	4,540	8,787	5,579	3,282	20,803	50.3
Hernando	119,931	57,154	62,777	18,371	10,430	24,089	28,800	38,241	98,063	53.7
Highlands	77,996	36,690	41,306	11,708	6,695	14,337	16,781	28,475	64,037	35.0
Hillsborough	910,855	444,750	466,105	192,807	117,243	293,633	188,813	118,359	686,440	36.4
Holmes	17,412	9,111	8,301	3,245	2,660	4,895	3,876	2,736	13,434	45.4
Indian River	102,211	49,032	53,179	16,652	9,434	24,504	22,275	29,346	82,584	35.0
Jackson	48,629	25,997	22,632	8,597	7,876	15,293	10,268	6,595	38,008	35.5
Jefferson	13,713	6,133	7,580	2,821	1,932	4,112	2,912	1,936	10,290	33.0
Lafayette	7,012	4,095	2,917	1,227	1,165	2,485	1,341	794	5,502	46.7
Lake	182,309	87,003	95,306	30,024	16,532	41,075	41,934	52,744	147,070	43.6
Lee	383,706	184,823	198,883	65,826	36,101	97,349	88,819	95,611	307,039	29.2
Leon	221,621	106,706	114,915	40,831	56,013	68,223	38,837	17,717	172,514	41.3
Levy	30,690	14,696	15,994	5,833	3,532	7,449	7,194	6,682	23,714	34.6
Liberty	7,439	4,363	3,076	1,308	1,109	2,666	1,573	783	5,837	33.0
Madison	18,745	9,778	8,967	4,115	2,839	5,783	3,485	2,523	13,841	44.3
Manatee	236,778	112,294	124,484	39,696	22,234	58,733	51,088	65,027	190,537	43.0
Marion	229,260	109,919	119,341	41,547	24,108	54,655	52,232	56,718	179,968	45.2
Martin	114,464	55,770	58,694	17,589	10,069	29,246	25,617	31,943	93,798	40.2
Monroe	83,789	42,736	41,053	13,374	7,620	28,318	21,359	13,118	68,471	35.5
Nassau	51,097	25,278	25,819	11,247	6,825	15,425	12,097	5,503	37,603	33.3
Okaloosa	165,319	82,830	82,489	37,283	22,262	56,004	32,844	16,926	121,812	37.5

See footnotes at end of table.

Continued . . . .

Table 1.35. AGE AND SEX: ESTIMATES BY SEX AND AGE GROUP AND MEDIAN AGE IN THE STATE AND COUNTIES OF FLORIDA, APRIL 1, 1996 (Continued)

County	Total	Sex		Age						Median 1/
		Male	Female	0-14	15-24	25-44	45-64	65 and over	18 and over	
Okeechobee	33,643	17,018	16,625	7,444	4,319	8,314	7,195	6,371	24,783	32.9
Orange	777,556	385,410	392,146	163,858	115,141	267,206	147,392	83,959	587,531	35.5
Osceola	139,724	68,546	71,178	30,257	18,098	42,385	29,997	18,987	104,373	41.5
Palm Beach	981,793	470,752	511,041	174,425	93,650	272,867	207,216	233,635	779,878	48.5
Pasco	309,936	146,424	163,512	47,058	27,992	67,745	66,635	100,506	254,496	43.3
Pinellas	881,383	415,173	466,210	139,055	84,208	239,718	196,959	221,443	718,178	38.8
Polk	452,707	218,972	233,735	89,925	54,337	119,462	97,208	91,775	346,637	39.1
Putnam	70,287	34,134	36,153	14,586	8,545	17,655	15,784	13,717	52,857	39.3
St. Johns	101,729	49,489	52,240	18,146	12,383	29,649	23,825	17,726	80,149	40.3
St. Lucie	175,458	85,232	90,226	33,741	18,482	46,555	38,166	38,514	135,850	34.4
Santa Rosa	98,491	49,177	49,314	21,682	12,644	32,356	21,449	10,360	72,802	50.1
Sarasota	305,848	143,238	162,610	41,112	24,163	68,808	72,019	99,746	257,476	35.1
Seminole	329,031	161,633	167,398	68,612	41,684	112,482	72,231	34,022	247,487	41.5
Sumter	40,593	21,046	19,547	6,922	5,043	9,979	9,330	9,319	32,211	38.7
Suwannee	31,424	15,226	16,198	6,217	4,438	7,749	7,369	5,651	23,722	34.7
Taylor	19,022	9,618	9,404	4,196	2,649	5,420	3,999	2,758	14,003	33.8
Union	13,023	8,519	4,504	2,133	1,923	5,448	2,476	1,043	10,430	41.0
Volusia	407,199	196,746	210,453	69,687	46,832	109,746	88,556	92,378	325,580	36.3
Wakulla	18,022	8,961	9,061	3,823	2,585	5,292	4,155	2,167	13,325	39.8
Walton	34,328	17,364	16,964	6,060	4,301	9,175	8,407	6,385	26,921	36.9
Washington	19,751	9,902	9,849	3,932	2,841	5,159	4,372	3,447	14,919	38.1

1/ Estimates based on Bureau of the Census modified age, race, and sex data.
Note: Detail may not add to totals because of rounding.

Source: University of Florida, Bureau of Economic and Business Research, Population Program, *Florida Population Studies*, July 1997, Volume 30, No. 3. Bulletin No. 118, and unpublished data.

Table 1.36. HISPANIC POPULATION: ESTIMATES BY SEX AND AGE GROUP IN THE STATE AND COUNTIES OF FLORIDA APRIL 1, 1995

County	Total	Sex		Age					
		Male	Female	0-14	15-24	25-44	45-64	65 and over	
Florida	2,014,681	1,005,710	1,008,971	443,229	292,897	682,099	366,240	230,216	
Alachua	7,966	4,080	3,886	1,363	3,029	2,528	677	369	
Baker	216	153	63	29	23	104	42	18	
Bay	2,651	1,366	1,285	659	481	881	440	190	
Bradford	480	358	122	55	52	245	99	29	
Brevard	18,298	9,237	9,061	4,570	2,809	6,133	3,161	1,625	
Broward	170,656	85,289	85,367	39,442	25,393	65,635	27,551	12,635	
Calhoun	227	134	93	57	33	104	29	4	
Charlotte	3,738	1,986	1,752	760	644	1,107	686	541	
Citrus	2,539	1,192	1,347	463	270	484	676	646	
Clay	4,320	2,133	2,187	1,252	725	1,487	627	229	
Collier	26,129	14,492	11,637	7,801	4,722	8,808	3,524	1,274	
Columbia	888	429	459	239	156	259	124	110	
Dade	1,126,929	548,323	578,606	217,057	148,331	374,391	227,929	159,221	
De Soto	4,308	2,852	1,456	1,308	852	1,720	320	108	
Dixie	114	77	37	22	23	50	16	3	
Duval	21,765	11,211	10,554	5,953	3,223	8,242	2,939	1,408	
Escambia	6,052	3,068	2,984	1,537	949	2,172	927	467	
Flagler	2,119	1,005	1,114	495	347	497	459	321	
Franklin	69	30	39	17	10	21	13	8	
Gadsden	1,073	622	451	378	171	394	89	41	
Gilchrist	226	155	71	28	51	85	44	18	
Glades	985	569	416	326	172	313	123	51	

See footnotes at end of table.

Continued . . .

Table 1.36. HISPANIC POPULATION: ESTIMATES BY SEX AND AGE GROUP IN THE STATE AND COUNTIES OF FLORIDA
APRIL 1, 1995 (Continued)

County	Total	Sex		Age				
		Male	Female	0-14	15-24	25-44	45-64	65 and over
Gulf	256	207	49	28	42	135	36	15
Hamilton	459	300	159	125	88	179	61	6
Hardee	5,471	3,080	2,391	1,925	1,134	1,628	586	198
Hendry	7,988	4,456	3,532	2,685	1,435	2,618	883	367
Hernando	4,468	2,224	2,244	1,048	568	1,127	1,029	696
Highlands	4,394	2,277	2,117	1,353	712	1,274	608	447
Hillsborough	131,305	66,613	64,692	31,039	20,297	42,728	22,403	14,838
Holmes	240	165	75	45	40	109	33	13
Indian River	3,662	2,040	1,622	1,091	576	1,209	486	300
Jackson	1,394	1,081	313	91	166	794	296	47
Jefferson	279	218	61	25	43	152	49	10
Lafayette	316	271	45	31	37	192	48	8
Lake	5,826	3,015	2,811	1,692	916	1,819	953	446
Lee	22,213	11,763	10,450	6,317	4,008	7,125	3,179	1,584
Leon	7,034	3,932	3,102	1,123	2,377	2,598	709	227
Levy	649	301	348	155	110	167	126	91
Liberty	179	158	21	10	20	123	24	2
Madison	298	236	62	57	39	162	25	15
Manatee	13,555	7,385	6,170	4,559	2,525	4,399	1,441	631
Marion	10,182	5,122	5,060	2,631	1,378	3,063	1,894	1,216
Martin	7,025	4,008	3,017	2,203	1,143	2,558	743	378
Monroe	11,084	5,701	5,383	2,382	1,307	3,655	2,334	1,406
Nassau	607	301	306	188	88	186	99	46
Okaloosa	5,608	3,009	2,599	1,533	804	2,190	824	257

Continued . . .

See footnotes at end of table.

Table 1.36. HISPANIC POPULATION: ESTIMATES BY SEX AND AGE GROUP IN THE STATE AND COUNTIES OF FLORIDA APRIL 1, 1995 (Continued)

County	Total	Sex		Age				
		Male	Female	0-14	15-24	25-44	45-64	65 and over
Okeechobee	4,763	2,802	1,961	1,858	918	1,568	328	91
Orange	101,522	50,557	50,965	26,106	17,703	36,451	15,014	6,248
Osceola	23,778	11,912	11,866	6,504	4,594	7,462	3,899	1,319
Palm Beach	95,282	50,048	45,234	24,177	14,394	34,458	15,377	6,876
Pasco	14,999	7,663	7,336	4,242	2,273	4,260	2,567	1,657
Pinellas	28,262	14,114	14,148	6,100	4,155	9,649	4,959	3,399
Polk	21,036	11,224	9,812	7,297	3,687	6,051	2,651	1,350
Putnam	2,079	1,073	1,006	741	327	543	277	191
St. Johns	2,916	1,432	1,484	703	368	934	571	340
St. Lucie	10,107	5,483	4,624	2,755	1,662	3,376	1,377	937
Santa Rosa	1,730	885	845	533	277	608	223	89
Sarasota	8,579	4,385	4,194	1,927	1,216	2,791	1,610	1,035
Seminole	28,056	13,898	14,158	6,994	4,591	10,090	4,446	1,935
Sumter	1,053	644	409	333	190	357	120	53
Suwannee	927	521	406	235	171	288	142	91
Taylor	280	173	107	50	55	129	30	16
Union	376	302	74	39	40	225	60	12
Volusia	21,851	11,489	10,362	6,277	3,821	6,742	3,069	1,942
Wakulla	89	47	42	25	4	26	25	9
Walton	521	275	246	125	93	149	99	55
Washington	235	159	76	61	39	92	32	11

Note: Detail may not add to totals because of rounding.

Source: University of Florida, Bureau of Economic and Business Research, Population Program, *Special Population Reports: Hispanic Population Estimates by Age and Sex for Florida and Its Counties, April 1, 1995.* August 1996.

Table 1.37. PERSONS AGED 65 AND OVER: CENSUS COUNTS, APRIL 1, 1990, AND ESTIMATES, APRIL 1, 1996, BY AGE IN THE STATE AND COUNTIES OF FLORIDA

County	65-69 Census 1990	65-69 Esti- mates 1996	70-74 Census 1990	70-74 Esti- mates 1996	75-79 Census 1990	75-79 Esti- mates 1996	80-84 Census 1990	80-84 Esti- mates 1996	85 and over Census 1990	85 and over Esti- mates 1996	Percentage aged 65 and over 1990	Percentage aged 65 and over 1996
Florida	737,129	729,936	627,699	712,549	483,532	564,947	302,099	384,996	205,467	270,991	18.2	18.5
Alachua	5,652	5,487	4,256	5,082	3,176	3,711	2,064	2,478	1,594	2,006	9.2	9.3
Baker	475	594	391	455	284	326	181	225	119	161	7.8	8.5
Bay	5,673	6,124	4,040	5,064	2,799	3,539	1,611	2,220	1,019	1,445	11.9	12.9
Bradford	962	954	689	919	501	654	344	418	228	338	12.1	13.1
Brevard	24,416	24,503	18,598	23,457	12,108	16,988	6,697	9,811	4,265	6,089	16.6	18.0
Broward	66,625	62,240	66,832	66,043	61,690	60,683	39,750	48,592	24,398	33,634	20.7	19.5
Calhoun	481	478	374	473	342	362	237	270	158	229	14.5	14.5
Charlotte	12,517	12,298	10,563	12,153	7,375	9,236	4,281	5,713	2,570	3,500	33.6	33.1
Citrus	10,174	10,570	8,313	10,012	5,785	7,598	3,066	4,586	1,807	2,795	31.2	33.0
Clay	3,225	3,702	2,248	3,185	1,628	2,187	994	1,442	846	1,266	8.4	9.4
Collier	11,975	13,765	9,810	13,167	6,649	9,690	3,894	6,036	2,128	3,518	22.7	23.9
Columbia	2,063	2,188	1,533	2,005	1,047	1,405	597	843	380	588	13.2	13.4
Dade	80,679	80,696	64,600	70,320	55,537	54,412	38,461	41,718	29,145	34,015	13.9	13.8
De Soto	1,495	1,461	1,323	1,511	934	1,118	523	648	317	423	19.2	19.3
Dixie	612	798	406	632	278	408	139	257	97	146	14.5	17.8
Duval	25,010	24,504	18,494	21,674	13,599	16,305	8,314	10,830	5,985	7,820	10.6	11.1
Escambia	11,247	10,888	8,189	10,057	5,770	7,219	3,450	4,695	2,488	3,402	11.9	12.7
Flagler	3,275	3,913	2,180	3,439	1,048	2,157	482	1,100	303	672	25.4	28.9
Franklin	492	660	449	497	291	414	192	255	164	205	17.7	19.6
Gadsden	1,574	1,503	1,353	1,332	1,069	1,049	647	710	509	606	12.5	11.2
Gilchrist	482	539	384	468	202	325	136	164	113	131	13.6	13.4
Glades	549	604	424	552	296	420	120	240	79	121	19.3	20.6

Continued . .

Table 1.37. PERSONS AGED 65 AND OVER: CENSUS COUNTS, APRIL 1, 1990, AND ESTIMATES, APRIL 1, 1996, BY AGE IN THE STATE AND COUNTIES OF FLORIDA (Continued)

County	65-69 Census 1990	65-69 Esti-mates 1996	70-74 Census 1990	70-74 Esti-mates 1996	75-79 Census 1990	75-79 Esti-mates 1996	80-84 Census 1990	80-84 Esti-mates 1996	85 and over Census 1990	85 and over Esti-mates 1996	Percentage aged 65 and over 1990	Percentage aged 65 and over 1996
Gulf	601	596	449	516	338	383	224	247	136	187	15.2	14.2
Hamilton	376	483	324	357	271	289	171	209	100	155	11.4	11.1
Hardee	1,028	1,011	792	1,001	558	697	353	463	214	324	15.1	15.5
Hendry	1,023	1,046	712	888	540	622	323	425	203	301	10.9	10.9
Hernando	11,953	11,844	9,332	11,468	5,635	8,112	2,508	4,333	1,522	2,484	30.6	31.9
Highlands	7,403	7,516	6,572	8,338	4,654	6,281	2,557	4,050	1,558	2,290	33.2	36.5
Hillsborough	34,478	34,675	27,070	32,047	19,750	24,168	11,931	15,861	8,217	11,608	12.2	13.0
Holmes	804	795	629	742	501	520	330	387	216	292	15.7	15.7
Indian River	8,260	8,088	7,086	8,535	4,676	6,542	2,787	3,804	1,642	2,377	27.1	28.7
Jackson	1,841	1,840	1,548	1,597	1,310	1,323	887	993	568	842	14.9	13.6
Jefferson	516	559	416	505	335	402	226	261	175	209	14.8	14.1
Lafayette	227	252	167	219	109	160	74	101	38	62	11.0	11.3
Lake	13,461	14,538	11,212	15,065	8,506	11,315	5,248	7,237	3,239	4,589	27.4	28.9
Lee	27,822	27,793	23,435	27,016	16,350	20,350	9,343	12,762	5,648	7,690	24.6	24.9
Leon	5,325	5,500	4,246	4,661	2,910	3,711	1,880	2,263	1,340	1,582	8.2	8.0
Levy	1,758	1,982	1,415	1,898	904	1,469	513	829	296	504	18.8	21.8
Liberty	197	268	176	195	123	151	75	100	50	69	11.2	10.5
Madison	662	684	603	628	490	520	336	376	228	315	14.0	13.5
Manatee	17,136	16,196	15,799	17,151	12,396	14,247	8,090	9,948	5,761	7,485	28.0	27.5
Marion	15,556	16,834	12,415	16,658	8,170	12,274	4,222	6,841	2,534	4,111	22.0	24.7
Martin	8,985	8,596	7,772	8,904	5,600	7,141	3,267	4,426	1,898	2,876	27.3	27.9
Monroe	4,665	4,240	3,475	3,739	2,285	2,690	1,251	1,619	671	830	15.8	15.7

Continued . . .

Table 1.37. PERSONS AGED 65 AND OVER: CENSUS COUNTS, APRIL 1, 1990, AND ESTIMATES, APRIL 1, 1996, BY AGE IN THE STATE AND COUNTIES OF FLORIDA (Continued)

County	65-69 Census 1990	65-69 Estimates 1996	70-74 Census 1990	70-74 Estimates 1996	75-79 Census 1990	75-79 Estimates 1996	80-84 Census 1990	80-84 Estimates 1996	85 and over Census 1990	85 and over Estimates 1996	Percentage aged 65 and over 1990	Percentage aged 65 and over 1996
Nassau	1,612	1,905	1,220	1,475	837	1,027	489	641	285	455	10.1	10.8
Okaloosa	5,345	5,760	3,615	4,835	2,151	3,258	1,215	1,783	916	1,290	9.2	10.2
Okeechobee	1,763	1,982	1,364	1,906	906	1,307	448	723	262	453	16.0	18.9
Orange	25,045	25,842	18,745	22,924	13,071	16,776	8,238	10,812	6,419	7,605	10.6	10.8
Osceola	4,886	5,683	4,028	4,863	2,811	3,986	1,678	2,459	1,436	1,996	13.8	13.6
Palm Beach	58,699	57,130	57,252	61,164	46,390	52,797	28,697	37,961	17,932	24,583	24.2	23.8
Pasco	27,031	24,618	26,172	27,278	19,440	23,674	11,358	15,822	6,501	9,114	32.2	32.4
Pinellas	59,240	52,554	55,480	55,569	46,573	48,073	33,313	35,547	26,278	29,700	25.9	25.1
Polk	25,097	26,069	20,281	25,506	14,753	19,039	8,810	12,216	5,746	8,945	18.4	20.3
Putnam	4,303	4,307	3,211	3,975	2,172	2,724	1,198	1,633	730	1,078	17.8	19.5
St. Johns	4,964	5,383	3,709	4,962	2,475	3,663	1,413	2,192	1,131	1,526	16.3	17.4
St. Lucie	11,312	11,543	9,133	11,182	6,088	8,425	2,989	4,796	1,762	2,568	20.8	22.0
Santa Rosa	3,037	3,651	1,956	2,952	1,412	1,833	753	1,155	559	769	9.5	10.5
Sarasota	25,967	24,833	23,807	26,503	18,835	22,198	12,058	15,219	8,471	10,993	32.1	32.6
Seminole	10,357	10,564	7,697	9,166	5,482	6,702	3,509	4,253	2,515	3,337	10.3	10.3
Sumter	2,540	2,794	2,056	2,751	1,339	1,924	717	1,147	382	703	22.3	23.0
Suwannee	1,400	1,598	1,080	1,481	893	1,103	639	795	477	674	16.8	18.0
Taylor	769	880	615	747	459	545	269	373	164	213	13.3	14.5
Union	279	332	216	295	131	201	76	123	62	92	7.5	8.0
Volusia	26,578	24,991	22,608	25,164	16,707	19,769	10,369	12,972	7,735	9,482	22.7	22.7
Wakulla	573	688	404	584	328	417	194	286	137	192	11.5	12.0
Walton	1,678	2,102	1,173	1,756	850	1,215	500	784	338	528	16.4	18.6
Washington	924	922	783	886	610	718	393	518	263	403	17.6	17.5

Source: University of Florida, Bureau of Economic and Business Research, Population Program, unpublished data. Census data from U.S. Bureau of the Census.

Table 1.38. AGE AND SEX PROJECTIONS: CENSUS COUNTS, APRIL 1, 1990
ESTIMATES, APRIL 1, 1996, AND PROJECTIONS, APRIL 1, 2000, 2005
AND 2010, BY AGE AND SEX IN FLORIDA

Age	Census 1990	Estimates 1996	Projections 2000	Projections 2005	Projections 2010
Total	12,937,926	14,411,563	15,428,873	16,642,735	17,836,377
0-4	873,022	953,185	948,499	975,547	1,036,310
5-9	809,306	935,969	992,664	982,233	1,005,929
10-14	746,343	887,721	977,331	1,036,095	1,020,412
15-19	803,784	836,996	942,599	1,048,647	1,093,742
15-17	455,160	473,823	534,078	594,671	620,336
18-19	348,624	363,173	408,521	453,976	473,406
20-24	878,843	882,937	899,418	1,032,266	1,125,843
25-29	1,055,071	944,717	931,011	947,558	1,081,984
30-34	1,062,261	1,079,747	994,877	962,458	978,977
35-39	951,453	1,116,038	1,147,874	1,033,626	993,358
40-44	851,919	1,045,051	1,177,404	1,212,150	1,089,731
45-49	690,756	943,108	1,078,876	1,249,488	1,281,100
50-54	591,849	784,980	976,492	1,152,913	1,328,702
55-59	586,872	674,515	807,373	1,066,718	1,249,442
60-64	680,521	663,180	718,026	901,765	1,184,065
65-69	737,129	729,936	712,250	784,961	981,106
70-74	627,699	712,549	724,940	702,218	771,171
75-79	483,532	564,947	637,790	651,938	629,755
80-84	302,099	384,996	434,922	507,615	517,915
85 and over	205,467	270,991	326,527	394,539	466,835
Male	6,261,770	6,992,872	7,503,612	8,102,126	8,689,993
0-4	447,221	485,741	483,416	497,174	528,115
5-9	414,103	478,509	506,049	500,728	512,739
10-14	382,040	454,044	499,870	528,461	520,418
15-19	412,795	427,995	481,998	536,091	557,875
15-17	234,171	242,815	273,679	304,587	317,024
18-19	178,624	185,180	208,319	231,504	240,851
20-24	446,241	455,740	464,565	532,172	579,860
25-29	532,167	483,506	481,310	488,824	557,207
30-34	531,382	546,099	507,388	493,933	501,635
35-39	471,494	558,281	577,883	522,910	505,072
40-44	419,659	517,028	584,984	605,526	546,303
45-49	335,721	462,676	529,804	616,446	635,834
50-54	282,812	380,157	475,567	562,313	651,212
55-59	274,786	320,719	387,277	514,829	603,916
60-64	308,245	308,115	337,368	427,520	564,328
65-69	331,267	327,545	326,175	363,315	457,267
70-74	279,758	310,083	317,420	313,712	347,184
75-79	204,877	237,835	266,155	273,741	269,014
80-84	118,468	150,444	170,356	196,734	202,160
85 and over	68,734	88,355	106,027	127,697	149,854

See footnote at end of table.   Continued . . .

University of Florida   **Bureau of Economic and Business Research**

Table 1.38. AGE AND SEX PROJECTIONS: CENSUS COUNTS, APRIL 1, 1990
ESTIMATES, APRIL 1, 1996, AND PROJECTIONS, APRIL 1, 2000, 2005
AND 2010, BY AGE AND SEX IN FLORIDA (Continued)

Age	Census 1990	Estimates 1996	Projections 2000	Projections 2005	Projections 2010
Female	6,676,156	7,418,691	7,925,261	8,540,609	9,146,384
0-4	425,801	467,444	465,083	478,373	508,195
5-9	395,203	457,460	486,615	481,505	493,190
10-14	364,303	433,677	477,461	507,634	499,994
15-19	390,989	409,001	460,601	512,556	535,867
15-17	220,989	231,008	260,399	290,084	303,312
18-19	170,000	177,993	200,202	222,472	232,555
20-24	432,602	427,197	434,853	500,094	545,983
25-29	522,904	461,211	449,701	458,734	524,777
30-34	530,879	533,648	487,489	468,525	477,342
35-39	479,959	557,757	569,991	510,716	488,286
40-44	432,260	528,023	592,420	606,624	543,428
45-49	355,035	480,432	549,072	633,042	645,266
50-54	309,037	404,823	500,925	590,600	677,490
55-59	312,086	353,796	420,096	551,889	645,526
60-64	372,276	355,065	380,658	474,245	619,737
65-69	405,862	402,391	386,075	421,646	523,839
70-74	347,941	402,466	407,520	388,506	423,987
75-79	278,655	327,112	371,635	378,197	360,741
80-84	183,631	234,552	264,566	310,881	315,755
85 and over	136,733	182,636	220,500	266,842	316,981

Note: Medium projections are shown. High and low projections are available from the Bureau of Economic and Business Research, University of Florida.

Source: University of Florida, Bureau of Economic and Business Research, Population Program, unpublished data. Census data from U.S. Bureau of the Census.

University of Florida   **Bureau of Economic and Business Research**

Table 1.39. MEDIAN AGE: CENSUS, APRIL 1, 1990, AND PROJECTIONS, APRIL 1
2000, 2005, AND 2010, IN THE STATE AND COUNTIES OF FLORIDA

County	Census 1990	Projections 2000	2005	2010	County	Census 1990	Projections 2000	2005	2010
Florida	36.3	39.5	41.3	42.7	Lafayette	32.0	33.6	34.6	35.5
					Lake	44.6	48.3	50.4	52.7
Alachua	28.2	28.6	28.7	28.9	Lee	42.0	45.0	47.1	49.3
Baker	30.2	32.2	32.8	33.4	Leon	28.8	29.6	30.2	30.7
Bay	33.2	36.7	38.2	39.3	Levy	38.4	43.2	45.6	47.7
Bradford	33.6	36.1	37.3	38.2	Liberty	32.5	35.2	35.9	36.7
Brevard	36.1	40.4	42.4	44.2	Madison	32.2	33.4	33.8	34.2
Broward	37.6	40.1	41.6	42.9	Manatee	42.9	45.5	47.5	49.5
Calhoun	33.4	36.3	37.3	38.2	Marion	40.0	45.0	47.3	49.6
Charlotte	53.7	52.3	53.5	55.2	Martin	44.3	46.4	48.3	50.5
Citrus	50.8	52.9	54.6	56.4	Monroe	38.8	41.4	42.9	44.3
Clay	32.0	35.4	36.9	38.1	Nassau	33.3	36.9	38.7	39.9
Collier	40.6	44.5	46.8	49.2	Okaloosa	31.3	34.5	35.5	36.0
Columbia	33.6	36.0	36.9	37.7	Okeechobee	34.3	39.1	41.1	42.8
Dade	34.2	36.2	37.2	37.6	Orange	31.4	34.0	35.0	35.7
De Soto	36.4	38.2	39.5	40.3	Osceola	33.6	37.1	38.9	40.4
Dixie	36.8	39.8	41.5	43.1	Palm Beach	39.8	42.9	44.9	46.8
Duval	31.4	34.0	34.8	35.1	Pasco	47.9	49.5	51.0	52.9
Escambia	32.3	34.2	35.1	35.6	Pinellas	42.1	44.5	46.2	48.0
Flagler	46.4	50.3	52.7	55.1	Polk	36.4	40.6	42.6	44.4
Franklin	38.9	47.1	50.4	53.1	Putnam	37.2	40.7	42.5	44.2
Gadsden	31.8	33.5	34.6	35.7	St. Johns	36.9	41.1	43.2	45.3
Gilchrist	33.5	34.4	35.4	36.5	St. Lucie	37.7	42.3	44.8	47.0
Glades	40.0	40.6	42.2	43.8	Santa Rosa	32.4	35.7	37.3	38.6
Gulf	35.6	36.2	36.9	37.5	Sarasota	48.9	51.3	53.2	55.2
Hamilton	30.8	33.4	34.4	35.6	Seminole	33.2	36.6	38.2	39.5
Hardee	32.7	33.8	34.4	34.9	Sumter	40.1	41.6	44.1	46.6
Hendry	30.3	31.2	31.6	31.7	Suwannee	36.5	40.4	42.3	44.0
Hernando	49.4	51.3	53.0	55.0	Taylor	33.5	35.3	36.2	37.0
Highlands	51.4	54.9	56.3	57.9	Union	31.2	35.0	36.2	37.5
Hillsborough	33.0	36.4	37.9	38.9	Volusia	39.3	42.4	44.4	46.3
Holmes	35.5	37.5	38.8	39.8	Wakulla	34.2	37.1	38.4	39.4
Indian River	43.8	46.8	48.7	50.8	Walton	37.7	41.5	43.9	46.1
Jackson	34.3	35.9	37.0	38.0	Washington	37.2	36.7	37.3	37.8
Jefferson	33.8	36.7	38.3	39.7					

Note: Projections are based on Bureau of the Census modified age, race, and sex data.

Source: University of Florida, Bureau of Economic and Business Research, Population Program, unpublished data. Census data from U.S., Department of Commerce, Bureau of the Census, *1990 Census of Population: General Population Characteristics, Florida.*

University of Florida   **Bureau of Economic and Business Research**

Table 1.40. MALE AND FEMALE PROJECTIONS: PROJECTIONS, APRIL 1, 2000, 2005, AND 2010, BY SEX IN THE STATE AND COUNTIES OF FLORIDA

County	2000			2005			2010		
	Total	Male	Female	Total	Male	Female	Total	Male	Female
Florida	15,428,873	7,503,612	7,925,261	16,642,735	8,102,126	8,540,609	17,836,377	8,689,993	9,146,384
Alachua	214,902	106,603	108,299	229,403	114,083	115,320	243,601	121,336	122,265
Baker	22,197	11,937	10,260	23,697	12,698	10,999	25,197	13,448	11,749
Bay	151,296	74,468	76,828	162,497	79,934	82,563	173,604	85,339	88,265
Bradford	25,998	14,637	11,361	27,101	15,189	11,912	28,196	15,743	12,453
Brevard	486,503	238,314	248,189	530,500	259,431	271,069	573,599	280,273	293,326
Broward	1,477,997	711,722	766,275	1,581,097	763,853	817,244	1,681,700	814,255	867,445
Calhoun	13,099	6,949	6,150	13,795	7,303	6,492	14,404	7,612	6,792
Charlotte	144,598	69,414	75,184	162,901	78,224	84,677	181,001	87,019	93,982
Citrus	118,802	56,390	62,412	132,199	62,755	69,444	145,304	69,055	76,249
Clay	138,701	68,536	70,165	154,997	76,519	78,478	171,099	84,335	86,764
Collier	220,102	107,876	112,226	251,497	122,777	128,720	282,801	137,750	145,051
Columbia	57,303	29,117	28,186	62,897	31,836	31,061	68,599	34,600	33,999
Dade	2,134,700	1,033,937	1,100,763	2,245,097	1,090,646	1,154,451	2,352,995	1,145,049	1,207,946
De Soto	29,897	16,404	13,493	32,001	17,357	14,644	34,096	18,324	15,772
Dixie	14,103	7,408	6,695	15,602	8,133	7,469	17,200	8,905	8,295
Duval	763,398	373,747	389,651	805,501	394,864	410,637	846,701	415,457	431,244
Escambia	303,491	150,681	152,810	317,094	157,514	159,580	330,590	164,274	166,316
Flagler	46,300	22,101	24,199	55,299	26,340	28,959	64,305	30,596	33,709
Franklin	11,104	5,397	5,707	11,897	5,766	6,131	12,798	6,174	6,624
Gadsden	48,201	24,189	24,098	50,098	25,148	24,950	52,001	26,088	25,913
Gilchrist	13,802	7,323	6,479	15,599	8,208	7,391	17,502	9,143	8,359
Glades	10,067	5,354	4,713	10,766	5,667	5,099	11,570	6,040	5,530

Continued . . .

Table 1.40. MALE AND FEMALE PROJECTIONS: PROJECTIONS, APRIL 1, 2000, 2005, AND 2010, BY SEX IN THE STATE AND COUNTIES OF FLORIDA (Continued)

County	2000 Total	2000 Male	2000 Female	2005 Total	2005 Male	2005 Female	2010 Total	2010 Male	2010 Female
Gulf	15,196	8,783	6,413	15,803	9,072	6,731	16,299	9,312	6,987
Hamilton	15,302	8,660	6,642	16,602	9,297	7,305	17,900	9,924	7,976
Hardee	23,102	12,261	10,841	23,698	12,503	11,195	24,202	12,716	11,486
Hendry	32,597	16,833	15,764	35,499	18,258	17,241	38,303	19,639	18,664
Hernando	135,596	64,578	71,018	154,898	73,799	81,099	173,997	83,021	90,976
Highlands	84,499	39,679	44,820	92,400	43,377	49,023	100,099	47,093	53,006
Hillsborough	963,898	471,336	492,562	1,028,700	503,369	525,331	1,091,804	534,312	557,492
Holmes	17,999	9,470	8,529	18,602	9,776	8,826	19,095	10,025	9,070
Indian River	111,005	53,169	57,836	121,599	58,211	63,388	131,999	63,256	68,743
Jackson	51,202	27,372	23,830	53,899	28,777	25,122	56,603	30,155	26,448
Jefferson	14,596	6,523	8,073	15,402	6,922	8,480	16,200	7,317	8,883
Lafayette	7,800	4,620	3,180	8,598	4,999	3,599	9,300	5,333	3,967
Lake	201,204	95,985	105,219	224,300	106,962	117,338	247,100	117,915	129,185
Lee	419,602	202,134	217,468	463,195	223,245	239,950	506,102	244,173	261,929
Leon	238,099	114,987	123,112	257,798	124,784	133,014	277,199	134,333	142,866
Levy	33,201	15,918	17,283	36,496	17,508	18,988	39,798	19,109	20,689
Liberty	8,104	4,750	3,354	8,799	5,100	3,699	9,604	5,500	4,104
Madison	19,603	10,247	9,356	20,499	10,706	9,793	21,502	11,216	10,286
Manatee	254,999	121,303	133,696	276,905	132,185	144,720	298,497	142,945	155,552
Marion	252,299	120,861	131,438	280,300	134,192	146,108	308,099	147,565	160,534
Martin	125,302	61,031	64,271	138,002	67,111	70,891	150,500	73,172	77,328
Monroe	88,002	44,379	43,623	92,899	46,428	46,471	97,702	48,546	49,156
Nassau	55,396	27,406	27,990	60,607	29,970	30,637	65,800	32,502	33,298
Okaloosa	177,596	88,664	88,932	192,697	95,894	96,803	207,805	103,173	104,632

Continued . . .

Table 1.40. MALE AND FEMALE PROJECTIONS: PROJECTIONS, APRIL 1, 2000, 2005, AND 2010, BY SEX IN THE STATE AND COUNTIES OF FLORIDA (Continued)

County	2000 Total	2000 Male	2000 Female	2005 Total	2005 Male	2005 Female	2010 Total	2010 Male	2010 Female
Okeechobee	36,844	18,901	17,943	40,046	20,349	19,697	43,146	21,781	21,365
Orange	846,697	418,367	428,330	934,199	461,208	472,991	1,020,397	503,331	517,066
Osceola	160,601	78,872	81,729	186,302	91,524	94,778	211,801	103,998	107,803
Palm Beach	1,064,296	510,952	553,344	1,164,101	559,957	604,144	1,262,197	608,364	653,833
Pasco	332,102	157,059	175,043	358,798	170,155	188,643	384,904	183,207	201,697
Pinellas	905,299	429,077	476,222	934,301	445,461	488,840	962,799	461,172	501,627
Polk	481,401	232,775	248,626	516,002	249,415	266,587	549,802	265,748	284,054
Putnam	74,100	35,941	38,159	78,797	38,184	40,613	83,300	40,347	42,953
St. Johns	113,198	55,146	58,052	127,304	62,039	65,265	141,200	68,808	72,392
St. Lucie	194,101	94,111	99,990	216,900	105,054	111,846	239,400	115,930	123,470
Santa Rosa	110,407	55,568	54,839	123,402	61,887	61,515	136,198	68,071	68,127
Sarasota	325,704	152,885	172,819	349,602	164,602	185,000	372,801	176,146	196,655
Seminole	360,901	177,649	183,252	399,599	196,859	202,740	437,899	215,682	222,217
Sumter	46,002	25,026	20,976	50,801	27,227	23,574	55,502	29,429	26,073
Suwannee	33,900	16,450	17,450	36,899	17,911	18,988	40,001	19,405	20,596
Taylor	19,403	10,077	9,326	19,800	10,273	9,527	20,202	10,466	9,736
Union	13,996	8,975	5,021	14,999	9,448	5,551	16,101	9,967	6,134
Volusia	437,406	211,510	225,896	473,801	229,403	244,398	509,401	246,937	262,464
Wakulla	21,254	11,026	10,228	23,853	12,302	11,551	26,553	13,619	12,934
Walton	37,599	19,057	18,542	41,400	20,855	20,545	45,101	22,601	22,500
Washington	20,902	10,735	10,167	22,097	11,323	10,774	23,300	11,917	11,383

Source: University of Florida, Bureau of Economic and Business Research, Population Program, *Florida Population Studies*, July 1997, Volume 30, No. 3. Bulletin No. 118.

Table 1.41. AGE PROJECTIONS: PROJECTIONS, APRIL 1, 2000, 2005, AND 2010, BY AGE IN THE STATE AND COUNTIES OF FLORIDA

County	2000			2005			2010		
	0-24	25-64	65 and over	0-24	25-64	65 and over	0-24	25-64	65 and over
Florida	4,760,511	7,831,933	2,836,429	5,074,788	8,526,676	3,041,271	5,282,236	9,187,359	3,366,782
Alachua	94,328	100,854	19,720	100,308	108,266	20,829	104,925	115,687	22,989
Baker	8,546	11,659	1,992	8,914	12,567	2,216	9,203	13,488	2,506
Bay	51,838	79,204	20,254	54,878	85,137	22,482	57,104	91,209	25,291
Bradford	8,219	14,250	3,529	8,291	15,034	3,776	8,340	15,665	4,191
Brevard	144,829	252,080	89,594	155,292	276,853	98,355	161,652	301,879	110,068
Broward	433,321	769,283	275,393	465,105	832,933	283,059	484,842	891,024	305,834
Calhoun	4,288	6,895	1,916	4,341	7,376	2,078	4,357	7,774	2,273
Charlotte	31,027	66,849	46,722	34,246	77,649	51,006	36,382	87,297	57,322
Citrus	25,513	54,023	39,266	27,158	61,569	43,472	28,094	68,206	49,004
Clay	50,227	74,518	13,956	54,680	83,176	17,141	57,972	91,581	21,546
Collier	58,273	108,591	53,238	65,442	124,576	61,479	71,263	139,459	72,079
Columbia	20,807	28,695	7,801	22,625	31,529	8,743	24,003	34,496	10,100
Dade	742,040	1,103,105	289,555	783,724	1,159,046	302,327	809,095	1,220,565	323,335
De Soto	9,507	14,696	5,694	10,243	15,664	6,094	10,862	16,536	6,698
Dixie	4,329	7,058	2,716	4,669	7,750	3,183	4,966	8,487	3,747
Duval	275,563	402,415	85,420	290,139	425,485	89,877	299,281	449,682	97,738
Escambia	109,534	155,241	38,716	113,810	162,350	40,934	116,381	170,277	43,932
Flagler	10,676	21,822	13,802	12,178	26,208	16,913	13,351	30,432	20,522
Franklin	2,873	5,887	2,344	2,825	6,314	2,758	2,786	6,645	3,367
Gadsden	18,007	24,811	5,383	18,158	26,160	5,780	18,161	27,439	6,401
Gilchrist	5,342	6,607	1,853	5,890	7,629	2,080	6,396	8,661	2,445
Glades	2,947	5,156	1,964	3,053	5,602	2,111	3,155	6,076	2,339

Continued . . .

Table 1.41. AGE PROJECTIONS: PROJECTIONS, APRIL 1, 2000, 2005, AND 2010, BY AGE IN THE STATE AND COUNTIES OF FLORIDA (Continued)

County	2000 0-24	2000 25-64	2000 65 and over	2005 0-24	2005 25-64	2005 65 and over	2010 0-24	2010 25-64	2010 65 and over
Gulf	4,583	8,572	2,041	4,699	8,961	2,143	4,761	9,241	2,297
Hamilton	5,454	8,218	1,630	5,669	9,104	1,829	5,874	9,873	2,153
Hardee	8,487	11,016	3,599	8,574	11,413	3,711	8,602	11,681	3,919
Hendry	13,416	15,651	3,530	14,623	16,992	3,884	15,633	18,277	4,393
Hernando	31,868	60,877	42,851	35,409	71,294	48,195	37,743	80,688	55,566
Highlands	19,343	33,666	31,490	20,440	37,501	34,459	21,186	41,109	37,804
Hillsborough	323,386	512,696	127,816	341,065	548,056	139,579	352,306	582,267	157,231
Holmes	5,852	9,292	2,855	5,856	9,732	3,014	5,824	10,068	3,203
Indian River	27,749	51,111	32,145	29,758	57,056	34,785	31,056	62,550	38,393
Jackson	16,806	27,611	6,785	17,207	29,625	7,067	17,567	31,241	7,795
Jefferson	4,871	7,647	2,078	4,910	8,244	2,248	4,945	8,715	2,540
Lafayette	2,537	4,360	903	2,726	4,825	1,047	2,860	5,271	1,169
Lake	49,705	92,345	59,154	53,641	104,395	66,264	56,485	115,534	75,081
Lee	109,675	206,896	103,031	118,535	232,910	111,750	124,460	256,369	125,273
Leon	102,236	116,943	18,920	108,786	128,557	20,455	114,146	139,380	23,673
Levy	9,732	15,935	7,534	10,287	17,698	8,511	10,723	19,355	9,720
Liberty	2,558	4,697	849	2,718	5,157	924	2,911	5,610	1,083
Madison	7,130	9,929	2,544	7,416	10,490	2,593	7,659	11,119	2,724
Manatee	65,901	120,778	68,320	70,413	134,637	71,855	73,336	146,801	78,360
Marion	70,382	117,665	64,252	75,924	131,978	72,398	80,030	145,461	82,608
Martin	29,848	60,737	34,717	32,346	68,047	37,609	33,952	74,622	41,926
Monroe	22,086	52,546	13,370	23,306	55,927	13,666	23,880	58,969	14,853
Nassau	19,082	30,206	6,108	20,309	33,339	6,959	21,348	36,192	8,260
Okaloosa	63,539	94,730	19,327	68,611	102,536	21,550	72,392	111,315	24,098

Continued . . .

Table 1.41. AGE PROJECTIONS: PROJECTIONS, APRIL 1, 2000, 2005, AND 2010, BY AGE IN THE STATE AND COUNTIES OF FLORIDA (Continued)

County	2000			2005			2010		
	0-24	25-64	65 and over	0-24	25-64	65 and over	0-24	25-64	65 and over
Okeechobee	12,515	17,131	7,198	13,416	18,579	8,051	14,078	19,930	9,138
Orange	299,685	454,710	92,302	328,677	502,806	102,716	350,007	552,131	118,259
Osceola	54,558	84,217	21,826	61,991	98,731	25,580	68,309	112,555	30,937
Palm Beach	289,599	526,911	247,786	313,618	585,023	265,460	329,346	638,139	294,712
Pasco	79,252	147,147	105,703	84,198	163,767	110,833	87,003	177,948	119,953
Pinellas	228,162	456,755	220,382	233,377	481,416	219,508	233,085	501,560	228,154
Polk	148,839	232,449	100,113	155,688	251,562	108,752	159,894	269,580	120,328
Putnam	23,764	35,610	14,726	24,590	38,577	15,630	25,022	41,254	17,024
St. Johns	32,772	60,720	19,706	35,583	69,406	22,315	37,713	77,173	26,314
St. Lucie	56,012	95,226	42,863	60,440	108,797	47,663	63,550	121,555	54,295
Santa Rosa	37,325	60,781	12,301	40,573	67,875	14,954	43,137	74,762	18,299
Sarasota	67,903	152,312	105,489	70,700	167,043	111,859	71,573	179,165	122,063
Seminole	117,889	205,387	37,625	127,041	229,759	42,799	133,767	252,611	51,521
Sumter	13,329	22,467	10,206	14,292	24,889	11,620	14,981	27,056	13,465
Suwannee	11,044	16,589	6,267	11,555	18,317	7,027	12,021	19,949	8,031
Taylor	6,778	9,720	2,905	6,799	9,901	3,100	6,736	10,174	3,292
Union	4,140	8,591	1,265	4,208	9,286	1,505	4,273	9,971	1,857
Volusia	123,421	216,363	97,622	131,914	238,368	103,519	137,080	258,524	113,797
Wakulla	7,233	11,545	2,476	7,874	13,103	2,876	8,494	14,578	3,481
Walton	10,952	19,212	7,435	11,622	21,183	8,595	12,166	22,962	9,973
Washington	7,079	10,267	3,556	7,435	10,941	3,721	7,751	11,509	4,040

Source: University of Florida, Bureau of Economic and Business Research, Population Program, *Florida Population Studies*, July 1997, Volume 30, No. 3. Bulletin No. 118.

Table 1.42. PERSONS AGED 65 AND OVER: PROJECTIONS BY AGE IN THE STATE AND COUNTIES OF FLORIDA
APRIL 1, 2000, 2005, AND 2010

County	2000 65-74	2000 75-84	2000 85 and over	2005 65-74	2005 75-84	2005 85 and over	2010 65-74	2010 75-84	2010 85 and over
Florida	1,437,190	1,072,712	326,527	1,487,179	1,159,553	394,539	1,752,277	1,147,670	466,835
Alachua	10,315	7,077	2,328	10,364	7,728	2,737	12,159	7,571	3,259
Baker	1,182	615	195	1,258	721	237	1,407	818	281
Bay	11,661	6,801	1,792	12,450	7,797	2,235	14,325	8,194	2,772
Bradford	1,841	1,288	400	1,849	1,438	489	2,157	1,419	615
Brevard	48,728	33,120	7,746	50,722	37,323	10,310	58,944	37,875	13,249
Broward	123,580	111,243	40,570	125,994	111,231	45,834	149,866	106,000	49,968
Calhoun	945	703	268	1,015	766	297	1,170	752	351
Charlotte	24,706	17,644	4,372	25,899	19,514	5,593	30,898	19,566	6,858
Citrus	20,948	14,607	3,711	21,905	16,581	4,986	25,980	16,714	6,310
Clay	7,766	4,559	1,631	9,439	5,557	2,145	12,343	6,358	2,845
Collier	28,791	19,753	4,694	31,461	23,546	6,472	38,503	25,034	8,542
Columbia	4,343	2,718	740	4,726	3,074	943	5,687	3,213	1,200
Dade	150,302	101,261	37,992	153,242	108,087	40,998	171,614	106,469	45,252
De Soto	3,063	2,104	527	3,092	2,332	670	3,544	2,329	825
Dixie	1,640	870	206	1,779	1,123	281	2,097	1,269	381
Duval	45,038	31,009	9,373	45,038	33,550	11,289	51,762	32,530	13,446
Escambia	20,579	13,977	4,160	20,768	15,089	5,077	23,035	14,721	6,176
Flagler	8,067	4,703	1,032	9,028	6,176	1,709	11,067	6,859	2,596
Franklin	1,327	774	243	1,536	909	313	1,978	1,026	363
Gadsden	2,788	1,889	706	2,968	1,969	843	3,494	1,950	957
Gilchrist	1,091	615	147	1,179	703	198	1,421	772	252
Glades	1,070	735	159	1,083	815	213	1,264	801	274

Continued . . .

Table 1.42.   PERSONS AGED 65 AND OVER: PROJECTIONS BY AGE IN THE STATE AND COUNTIES OF FLORIDA, APRIL 1, 2000, 2005, AND 2010 (Continued)

County	2000			2005			2010		
	65-74	75-84	85 and over	65-74	75-84	85 and over	65-74	75-84	85 and over
Gulf	1,126	701	214	1,163	736	244	1,285	732	280
Hamilton	925	517	188	1,016	598	215	1,249	665	239
Hardee	1,845	1,358	396	1,749	1,481	481	2,013	1,322	584
Hendry	1,948	1,208	374	2,072	1,363	449	2,466	1,374	553
Hernando	23,683	15,695	3,473	25,158	18,079	4,958	30,680	18,344	6,542
Highlands	15,863	12,582	3,045	16,205	14,190	4,064	18,600	14,012	5,192
Hillsborough	67,057	46,399	14,360	70,566	51,146	17,867	84,256	51,232	21,743
Holmes	1,523	990	342	1,584	1,051	379	1,748	1,023	432
Indian River	16,551	12,618	2,976	16,782	14,029	3,974	19,469	13,898	5,026
Jackson	3,439	2,362	984	3,604	2,375	1,088	4,270	2,357	1,168
Jefferson	1,095	755	228	1,166	824	258	1,405	838	297
Lafayette	512	314	77	585	356	106	633	398	138
Lake	30,698	22,734	5,722	32,545	26,429	7,290	38,553	27,195	9,333
Lee	54,836	38,593	9,602	57,013	42,567	12,170	68,139	42,321	14,813
Leon	10,360	6,765	1,795	10,989	7,296	2,170	13,711	7,446	2,516
Levy	3,973	2,898	663	4,164	3,394	953	4,961	3,489	1,270
Liberty	514	257	78	534	295	95	634	346	103
Madison	1,264	921	359	1,255	945	393	1,397	902	425
Manatee	32,492	26,918	8,910	32,893	28,288	10,674	38,700	27,272	12,388
Marion	34,447	24,302	5,503	36,191	28,541	7,666	43,259	29,188	10,161
Martin	17,379	13,666	3,672	17,822	15,004	4,783	21,110	14,890	5,926
Monroe	7,571	4,807	992	7,530	4,941	1,195	8,796	4,669	1,388
Nassau	3,626	1,915	567	4,001	2,252	706	4,965	2,442	853
Okaloosa	11,350	6,370	1,607	12,007	7,381	2,162	13,211	8,026	2,861

Continued . . .

Table 1.42. PERSONS AGED 65 AND OVER: PROJECTIONS BY AGE IN THE STATE AND COUNTIES OF FLORIDA APRIL 1, 2000, 2005, AND 2010 (Continued)

County	2000 65-74	2000 75-84	2000 85 and over	2005 65-74	2005 75-84	2005 85 and over	2010 65-74	2010 75-84	2010 85 and over
Okeechobee	4,017	2,573	608	4,135	3,084	832	4,870	3,165	1,103
Orange	50,295	32,996	9,011	53,897	37,555	11,264	65,310	38,908	14,041
Osceola	11,546	7,772	2,508	13,223	9,022	3,335	16,909	9,863	4,165
Palm Beach	117,190	100,121	30,475	122,205	106,015	37,240	147,029	104,246	43,437
Pasco	49,778	44,364	11,561	50,154	45,908	14,771	58,880	43,718	17,355
Pinellas	101,026	87,067	32,289	98,644	85,751	35,113	111,654	78,787	37,713
Polk	51,623	37,142	11,348	52,567	41,696	14,489	61,026	41,280	18,022
Putnam	8,186	5,179	1,361	8,127	5,783	1,720	9,223	5,663	2,138
St. Johns	10,440	7,343	1,923	11,045	8,698	2,572	14,127	8,834	3,353
St. Lucie	23,194	16,222	3,447	24,445	18,453	4,765	29,383	18,753	6,159
Santa Rosa	7,467	3,838	996	8,749	4,927	1,278	10,861	5,682	1,756
Sarasota	50,221	42,131	13,137	51,345	44,617	15,897	60,311	43,114	18,638
Seminole	20,731	12,891	4,003	23,333	14,523	4,943	30,101	15,367	6,053
Sumter	5,614	3,674	918	6,065	4,291	1,264	7,287	4,500	1,678
Suwannee	3,231	2,240	796	3,468	2,619	940	4,128	2,750	1,153
Taylor	1,648	1,006	251	1,665	1,139	296	1,756	1,187	349
Union	717	423	125	815	511	179	1,017	593	247
Volusia	49,110	37,287	11,225	50,215	39,698	13,606	59,058	38,620	16,119
Wakulla	1,369	864	243	1,518	1,054	304	1,954	1,127	400
Walton	4,204	2,534	697	4,434	3,221	940	5,159	3,538	1,276
Washington	1,735	1,335	486	1,741	1,398	582	2,009	1,354	677

Source: University of Florida, Bureau of Economic and Business Research, Population Program, unpublished data.

Table 1.43. RACE PROJECTIONS: ESTIMATES, APRIL 1, 1996, AND PROJECTIONS, APRIL 1, 2000, 2005, AND 2010, BY RACE IN THE STATE AND COUNTIES OF FLORIDA

(rounded to thousands)

County	Estimates, 1996 Total	White	Black	Projections 2000 Total	White	Black	2005 Total	White	Black	2010 Total	White	Black
Florida	14,164	12,163	2,001	15,142	12,990	2,152	16,305	13,981	2,325	17,446	14,953	2,493
Alachua	196	158	38	208	167	41	221	178	44	235	188	47
Baker	21	18	3	22	19	3	24	21	3	25	22	3
Bay	138	123	15	147	131	16	158	141	17	168	151	18
Bradford	25	20	5	26	21	5	27	22	5	28	23	5
Brevard	442	407	35	477	440	38	520	480	41	562	519	43
Broward	1,364	1,120	243	1,443	1,169	274	1,538	1,227	311	1,630	1,283	347
Calhoun	12	10	2	13	11	2	14	11	2	14	12	2
Charlotte	128	123	5	143	137	6	161	154	7	179	170	8
Citrus	107	105	2	118	115	3	131	128	3	144	141	3
Clay	123	116	7	135	128	8	151	142	9	167	157	10
Collier	192	183	9	218	208	10	249	238	11	280	268	12
Columbia	52	42	10	57	46	10	62	51	11	68	56	12
Dade	2,004	1,556	449	2,088	1,602	486	2,188	1,659	530	2,285	1,713	572
De Soto	26	22	5	30	24	6	32	26	6	34	28	6
Dixie	13	11	1	14	13	1	15	14	1	17	16	2
Duval	709	532	178	742	556	186	780	585	196	818	613	205
Escambia	277	219	58	293	231	62	305	240	65	317	249	68
Flagler	39	36	3	46	42	4	55	50	4	63	59	5
Franklin	10	9	1	11	10	1	12	11	1	13	11	1
Gadsden	46	19	27	48	20	28	49	21	29	51	22	30
Gilchrist	12	11	1	14	13	1	15	14	1	17	16	1
Glades	9	8	1	9	8	1	10	9	1	11	9	2

Continued . . .

Table 1.43. RACE PROJECTIONS: ESTIMATES, APRIL 1, 1996, AND PROJECTIONS, APRIL 1, 2000, 2005, AND 2010, BY RACE IN THE STATE AND COUNTIES OF FLORIDA (Continued)

(rounded to thousands)

County	Estimates, 1996			2000			Projections 2005			2010		
	Total	White	Black	Total	White	Black	Total	White	Black	Total	White	Black
Gulf	13	11	3	15	11	4	16	12	4	16	13	3
Hamilton	13	8	5	15	9	6	16	10	6	18	11	7
Hardee	22	20	2	23	21	2	23	21	2	24	22	2
Hendry	29	25	5	32	27	5	35	30	5	37	32	5
Hernando	119	115	4	135	130	5	154	149	5	173	167	6
Highlands	77	70	7	84	77	7	91	84	7	99	92	7
Hillsborough	894	772	122	945	815	129	1,006	868	138	1,066	919	147
Holmes	17	16	1	18	16	1	18	17	1	19	17	1
Indian River	102	94	7	110	103	7	121	114	7	131	124	7
Jackson	48	34	14	51	36	14	53	38	15	56	40	16
Jefferson	14	8	6	14	9	6	15	9	6	16	10	6
Lafayette	7	6	1	8	6	1	9	7	1	9	8	1
Lake	181	166	15	200	184	15	223	207	16	245	229	16
Lee	380	356	25	416	390	26	459	430	28	501	471	30
Leon	217	162	55	233	175	58	251	189	62	270	203	67
Levy	30	27	3	33	30	3	36	33	3	39	36	3
Liberty	7	6	1	8	7	1	9	7	1	10	8	1
Madison	19	11	8	19	12	8	20	12	8	21	13	8
Manatee	235	217	18	253	234	19	274	254	20	295	274	21
Marion	227	200	27	250	221	29	277	246	31	304	272	33
Martin	113	107	7	124	117	7	137	129	7	149	141	8
Monroe	83	78	4	87	82	4	92	87	5	97	92	5
Nassau	51	46	5	55	50	5	60	56	5	65	61	5
Okaloosa	160	144	16	171	154	17	185	166	19	199	178	21

Continued . . .

Table 1.43. RACE PROJECTIONS: ESTIMATES, APRIL 1, 1996, AND PROJECTIONS, APRIL 1, 2000, 2005, AND 2010, BY RACE IN THE STATE AND COUNTIES OF FLORIDA (Continued)

(rounded to thousands)

County	Estimates, 1996			2000			Projections 2005			2010		
	Total	White	Black	Total	White	Black	Total	White	Black	Total	White	Black
Okeechobee	33	31	2	36	34	3	39	37	3	43	40	3
Orange	756	634	123	822	687	135	905	754	151	986	819	167
Osceola	137	129	8	157	148	9	182	172	10	207	195	12
Palm Beach	969	847	122	1,049	919	130	1,146	1,005	141	1,241	1,090	151
Pasco	307	301	6	329	322	7	355	348	7	381	373	8
Pinellas	868	797	70	890	817	74	918	840	77	944	863	81
Polk	448	390	58	476	416	60	510	447	63	542	477	66
Putnam	70	57	12	73	61	13	78	65	13	82	69	14
St. Johns	101	94	7	112	105	7	126	119	7	140	133	7
St. Lucie	174	146	27	192	163	29	214	183	31	236	203	33
Santa Rosa	96	92	4	108	103	5	120	115	6	133	127	6
Sarasota	304	291	13	323	310	13	347	333	14	370	355	14
Seminole	322	295	27	353	324	29	391	359	32	428	393	35
Sumter	40	33	7	46	37	8	50	42	9	55	46	9
Suwannee	31	27	4	34	29	4	37	32	4	40	35	4
Taylor	19	15	3	19	16	4	20	16	3	20	17	3
Union	13	10	3	14	11	3	15	12	3	16	13	3
Volusia	403	368	35	432	396	37	468	430	38	503	463	40
Wakulla	18	16	2	21	18	3	24	21	3	26	23	3
Walton	34	31	2	37	34	3	41	38	3	44	42	3
Washington	19	16	3	20	17	3	21	18	4	23	19	4

Source: University of Florida, Bureau of Economic and Business Research, Population Program, *Florida Population Studies*, July 1997, Volume 30, No. 3. Bulletin No. 118.

Table 1.65. METROPOLITAN AREAS: CENSUS COUNTS, APRIL 1, 1980 AND 1990, AND
ESTIMATES, APRIL 1, 1996, IN THE STATE AND
METROPOLITAN AREAS OF FLORIDA

Metropolitan area	Census 1980	Census 1990	Estimates 1996	Percentage change 1980-1990	Percentage change 1990-1996
Florida	9,746,961	12,938,071	14,411,563	32.7	11.4
Metropolitan areas, total	9,038,653	12,023,514	13,354,273	33.0	11.1
Daytona Beach	269,675	399,438	446,251	48.1	11.7
Flagler County	10,913	28,701	39,052	163.0	36.1
Volusia County	258,762	370,737	407,199	43.3	9.8
Ft. Lauderdale	1,018,257	1,255,531	1,392,252	23.3	10.9
Ft. Myers-Cape Coral	205,266	335,113	383,706	63.3	14.5
Ft. Pierce-Port St. Lucie	151,196	251,071	289,922	66.1	15.5
Martin County	64,014	100,900	114,464	57.6	13.4
St. Lucie County	87,182	150,171	175,458	72.3	16.8
Ft. Walton Beach	109,920	143,777	165,319	30.8	15.0
Gainesville	151,369	181,596	202,140	20.0	11.3
Jacksonville	722,252	906,727	1,006,694	25.5	11.0
Clay County	67,052	105,986	125,431	58.1	18.3
Duval County	571,003	672,971	728,437	17.9	8.2
Nassau County	32,894	43,941	51,097	33.6	16.3
St. Johns County	51,303	83,829	101,729	63.4	21.4
Lakeland-Winter Haven	321,652	405,382	452,707	26.0	11.7
Melbourne-Titusville-Palm Bay	272,959	398,978	450,164	46.2	12.8
Miami	1,625,509	1,937,194	2,043,316	19.2	5.5
Naples	85,971	152,099	193,036	76.9	26.9
Ocala	122,488	194,835	229,260	59.1	17.7
Orlando	804,774	1,224,844	1,428,620	52.2	16.6
Lake County	104,870	152,104	182,309	45.0	19.9
Orange County	470,865	677,491	777,556	43.9	14.8
Osceola County	49,287	107,728	139,724	118.6	29.7
Seminole County	179,752	287,521	329,031	60.0	14.4
Panama City	97,740	126,994	142,159	29.9	11.9
Pensacola	289,782	344,406	384,792	18.9	11.7
Escambia County	233,794	262,798	286,301	12.4	8.9
Santa Rosa County	55,988	81,608	98,491	45.8	20.7
Punta Gorda	58,460	110,975	129,468	89.8	16.7
Sarasota-Bradenton	350,696	489,483	542,626	39.6	10.9
Manatee County	148,445	211,707	236,778	42.6	11.8
Sarasota County	202,251	277,776	305,848	37.3	10.1
Tallahassee	190,329	233,609	267,943	22.7	14.7
Gadsden County	41,674	41,116	46,322	-1.3	12.7
Leon County	148,655	192,493	221,621	29.5	15.1
Tampa-St. Petersburg- Clearwater	1,613,600	2,067,959	2,222,105	28.2	7.5
Hernando County	44,469	101,115	119,931	127.4	18.6
Hillsborough County	646,939	834,054	910,855	28.9	9.2
Pasco County	193,661	281,131	309,936	45.2	10.2
Pinellas County	728,531	851,659	881,383	16.9	3.5
West Palm Beach-Boca Raton	576,758	863,503	981,793	49.7	13.7

Note: Data are for Metropolitan Statistical Areas (MSAs) and for Primary Metropolitan Statistical Areas (PMSAs) based on 1992 MSA designations. See Glossary for
definitions and map at the front of the book for area boundaries. Estimates reflect
changes to Dade and Broward counties as a result of Hurricane Andrew in August 1992.
    Source: University of Florida, Bureau of Economic and Business Research, Popula-
tion Program, *Florida Estimates of Population, April 1, 1996.* Census data from U.S.
Bureau of the Census.

University of Florida   **Bureau of Economic and Business Research**

Table 1.66. PLANNING DISTRICTS: CENSUS COUNTS, APRIL 1, 1990, AND ESTIMATES
APRIL 1, 1996, IN THE STATE, COMPREHENSIVE PLANNING
DISTRICTS, AND COUNTIES OF FLORIDA

District and county	Census 1990	Estimates 1996	Percentage change 1990 to 1996	District and county	Census 1990	Estimates 1996	Percentage change 1990 to 1996
Florida	12,938,071	14,411,563	11.4	District 5	446,952	528,363	18.2
				Citrus	93,513	107,889	15.4
District 1	675,633	763,761	13.0	Hernando	101,115	119,931	18.6
Bay	126,994	142,159	11.9	Levy	25,912	30,690	18.4
Escambia	262,798	286,301	8.9	Marion	194,835	229,260	17.7
Holmes	15,778	17,412	10.4	Sumter	31,577	40,593	28.6
Okaloosa	143,777	165,319	15.0	District 6	1,994,559	2,285,983	14.6
Santa Rosa	81,608	98,491	20.7	Brevard	398,978	450,164	12.8
Walton	27,759	34,328	23.7	Lake	152,104	182,309	19.9
Washington	16,919	19,751	16.7	Orange	677,491	777,556	14.8
District 2	337,533	392,173	16.2	Osceola	107,728	139,724	29.7
Calhoun	11,011	12,504	13.6	Seminole	287,521	329,031	14.4
Franklin	8,967	10,378	15.7	Volusia	370,737	407,199	9.8
Gadsden	41,116	46,322	12.7	District 7	546,805	613,581	12.2
Gulf	11,504	13,545	17.7	De Soto	23,865	26,716	11.9
Jackson	41,375	48,629	17.5	Hardee	19,499	22,519	15.5
Jefferson	11,296	13,713	21.4	Highlands	68,432	77,996	14.0
Leon	192,493	221,621	15.1	Okeechobee	29,627	33,643	13.6
Liberty	5,569	7,439	33.6	Polk	405,382	452,707	11.7
Wakulla	14,202	18,022	26.9	District 8	2,178,551	2,338,952	7.4
District 3	354,196	407,097	14.9	Hillsborough	834,054	910,855	9.2
Alachua	181,596	202,140	11.3	Manatee	211,707	236,778	11.8
Bradford	22,515	24,983	11.0	Pasco	281,131	309,936	10.2
Columbia	42,613	52,565	23.4	Pinellas	851,659	881,383	3.5
Dixie	10,585	12,602	19.1	District 9	909,327	1,051,628	15.6
Gilchrist	9,667	12,150	25.7	Charlotte	110,975	129,468	16.7
Hamilton	10,930	13,431	22.9	Collier	152,099	193,036	26.9
Lafayette	5,578	7,012	25.7	Glades	7,591	9,413	24.0
Madison	16,569	18,745	13.1	Hendry	25,773	30,157	17.0
Suwannee	26,780	31,424	17.3	Lee	335,113	383,706	14.5
Taylor	17,111	19,022	11.2	Sarasota	277,776	305,848	10.1
Union	10,252	13,023	27.0	District 10	1,204,782	1,373,926	14.0
District 4	1,018,984	1,136,742	11.6	Indian River	90,208	102,211	13.3
Baker	18,486	20,709	12.0	Martin	100,900	114,464	13.4
Clay	105,986	125,431	18.3	Palm Beach	863,503	981,793	13.7
Duval	672,971	728,437	8.2	St. Lucie	150,171	175,458	16.8
Flagler	28,701	39,052	36.1	District 11	3,270,749	3,519,357	7.6
Nassau	43,941	51,097	16.3	Broward	1,255,531	1,392,252	10.9
Putnam	65,070	70,287	8.0	Dade	1,937,194	2,043,316	5.5
St. Johns	83,829	101,729	21.4	Monroe	78,024	83,789	7.4

Note: Data are for planning district boundaries as defined in May 1984. See map.
Estimates reflect changes to Dade and Broward counties as a result of Hurricane
Andrew in August 1992.

Source: University of Florida, Bureau of Economic and Business Research,
Population Program, *Florida Estimates of Population, April 1, 1996.* Census data from
U.S. Bureau of the Census.

University of Florida   **Bureau of Economic and Business Research**

Planning Districts

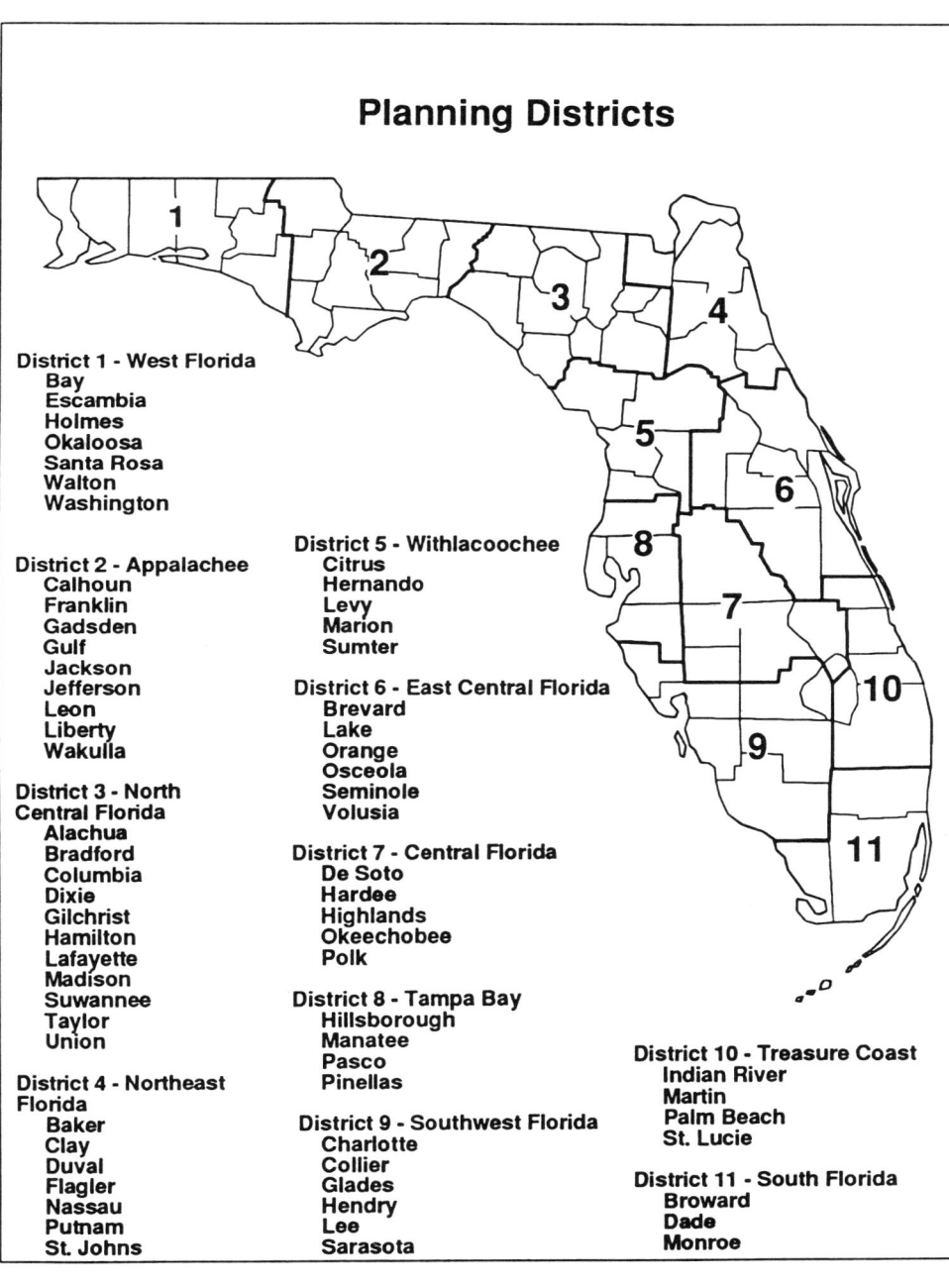

District 1 - West Florida
- Bay
- Escambia
- Holmes
- Okaloosa
- Santa Rosa
- Walton
- Washington

District 2 - Appalachee
- Calhoun
- Franklin
- Gadsden
- Gulf
- Jackson
- Jefferson
- Leon
- Liberty
- Wakulla

District 3 - North Central Florida
- Alachua
- Bradford
- Columbia
- Dixie
- Gilchrist
- Hamilton
- Lafayette
- Madison
- Suwannee
- Taylor
- Union

District 4 - Northeast Florida
- Baker
- Clay
- Duval
- Flagler
- Nassau
- Putnam
- St. Johns

District 5 - Withlacoochee
- Citrus
- Hernando
- Levy
- Marion
- Sumter

District 6 - East Central Florida
- Brevard
- Lake
- Orange
- Osceola
- Seminole
- Volusia

District 7 - Central Florida
- De Soto
- Hardee
- Highlands
- Okeechobee
- Polk

District 8 - Tampa Bay
- Hillsborough
- Manatee
- Pasco
- Pinellas

District 9 - Southwest Florida
- Charlotte
- Collier
- Glades
- Hendry
- Lee
- Sarasota

District 10 - Treasure Coast
- Indian River
- Martin
- Palm Beach
- St. Lucie

District 11 - South Florida
- Broward
- Dade
- Monroe

Table 1.67. HEALTH DISTRICTS: CENSUS COUNTS, APRIL 1, 1990, AND ESTIMATES
APRIL 1, 1996, IN THE STATE, DEPARTMENT OF HEALTH
DISTRICTS, AND COUNTIES OF FLORIDA

District and county	Census 1990	Esti-mates 1996	Per-cent-age change 1990 to 1996	District and county	Census 1990	Esti-mates 1996	Per-cent-age change 1990 to 1996
Florida	12,938,071	14,411,563	11.4	District 6	1,045,761	1,147,633	21.0
District 1	515,942	584,439	68.3	Hillsborough	834,054	910,855	9.2
Escambia	262,798	286,301	8.9	Manatee	211,707	236,778	11.8
Okaloosa	143,777	165,319	15.0	District 7	1,471,718	1,696,475	71.7
Santa Rosa	81,608	98,491	20.7	Brevard	398,978	450,164	12.8
Walton	27,759	34,328	23.7	Orange	677,491	777,556	14.8
District 2	530,904	609,262	237.5	Osceola	107,728	139,724	29.7
Bay	126,994	142,159	11.9	Seminole	287,521	329,031	14.4
Calhoun	11,011	12,504	13.6	District 8	933,192	1,078,344	121.1
Franklin	8,967	10,378	15.7	Charlotte	110,975	129,468	16.7
Gadsden	41,116	46,322	12.7	Collier	152,099	193,036	26.9
Gulf	11,504	13,545	17.7	De Soto	23,865	26,716	11.9
Holmes	15,778	17,412	10.4	Glades	7,591	9,413	24.0
Jackson	41,375	48,629	17.5	Hendry	25,773	30,157	17.0
Jefferson	11,296	13,713	21.4	Lee	335,113	383,706	14.5
Leon	192,493	221,621	15.1	Sarasota	277,776	305,848	10.1
Liberty	5,569	7,439	33.6	District 9	863,503	981,793	13.7
Madison	16,569	18,745	13.1	Palm Beach	863,503	981,793	13.7
Taylor	17,111	19,022	11.2	District 10	1,255,531	1,392,252	10.9
Wakulla	14,202	18,022	26.9	Broward	1,255,531	1,392,252	10.9
Washington	16,919	19,751	16.7	District 11	2,015,218	2,127,105	12.9
District 3	411,498	470,307	209.8	Dade	1,937,194	2,043,316	5.5
Alachua	181,596	202,140	11.3	Monroe	78,024	83,789	7.4
Bradford	22,515	24,983	11.0	District 12	399,438	446,251	45.9
Columbia	42,613	52,565	23.4	Flagler	28,701	39,052	36.1
Dixie	10,585	12,602	19.1	Volusia	370,737	407,199	9.8
Gilchrist	9,667	12,150	25.7	District 13	573,144	679,982	100.2
Hamilton	10,930	13,431	22.9	Citrus	93,513	107,889	15.4
Lafayette	5,578	7,012	25.7	Hernando	101,115	119,931	18.6
Levy	25,912	30,690	18.4	Lake	152,104	182,309	19.9
Putnam	65,070	70,287	8.0	Marion	194,835	229,260	17.7
Suwannee	26,780	31,424	17.3	Sumter	31,577	40,593	28.6
Union	10,252	13,023	27.0	District 14	493,313	553,222	41.2
District 4	925,213	1,027,403	76.2	Hardee	19,499	22,519	15.5
Baker	18,486	20,709	12.0	Highlands	68,432	77,996	14.0
Clay	105,986	125,431	18.3	Polk	405,382	452,707	11.7
Duval	672,971	728,437	8.2	District 15	370,906	425,776	57.1
Nassau	43,941	51,097	16.3	Indian River	90,208	102,211	13.3
St. Johns	83,829	101,729	21.4	Martin	100,900	114,464	13.4
District 5	1,132,790	1,191,319	13.7	Okeechobee	29,627	33,643	13.6
Pasco	281,131	309,936	10.2	St. Lucie	150,171	175,458	16.8
Pinellas	851,659	881,383	3.5				

Note: See map of districts in Section 7.00. Estimates reflect changes to Dade
and Broward counties as a result of Hurricane Andrew in August 1992.

Source: University of Florida, Bureau of Economic and Business Research, Population Program, *Florida Estimates of Population, April 1, 1996.* Census data from U.S.
Bureau of the Census.

University of Florida   **Bureau of Economic and Business Research**

Table 1.69. POPULOUS CITIES: CENSUS COUNTS, APRIL 1, 1980 AND 1990, AND ESTIMATES
APRIL 1, 1996, IN THE 1996 MOST POPULOUS CITIES OF FLORIDA

City	Total population Census 1980	Total population Census 1990	Total population Estimates 1996	Rank 1980	Rank 1990	Rank 1996	Percentage change 1990 to 1996
Jacksonville (Duval)	540,920	635,230	686,172	1	1	1	8.0
Miami	346,865	358,648	365,127	2	2	2	1.8
Tampa	271,577	280,015	289,337	3	3	3	3.3
St. Petersburg	238,647	240,318	241,276	4	4	4	0.4
Hialeah	145,254	188,008	206,500	6	5	5	9.8
Orlando	128,291	164,674	173,122	7	6	6	5.1
Ft. Lauderdale	153,279	149,238	150,150	5	7	7	0.6
Tallahassee	81,548	124,773	138,863	11	8	8	11.3
Hollywood	121,323	121,720	125,689	8	9	9	3.3
Clearwater	85,170	98,784	101,867	10	10	10	3.1
Coral Springs	37,349	78,864	98,553	27	13	11	25.0
Gainesville	81,371	85,075	97,693	12	12	12	14.8
Pembroke Pines	35,776	65,566	94,354	34	21	13	43.9
Miami Beach	96,298	92,639	91,848	9	11	14	-0.9
Cape Coral	32,103	74,991	87,632	41	14	15	16.9
West Palm Beach	63,305	67,764	78,370	13	17	16	15.7
Plantation	48,501	66,814	76,223	20	18	17	14.1
Lakeland	47,406	70,576	75,422	21	16	18	6.9
Port St. Lucie	14,690	55,761	74,894	72	27	19	34.3
Sunrise	39,681	65,683	74,766	25	20	20	13.8
Palm Bay	18,560	62,543	74,395	61	22	21	19.0
Pompano Beach	52,618	72,411	74,271	17	15	22	2.6
Largo	57,958	65,910	67,798	14	19	23	2.9
Boca Raton	49,447	61,486	67,754	18	24	24	10.2
Melbourne	46,536	60,034	66,970	22	25	25	11.6
Daytona Beach	54,176	61,991	63,796	16	23	26	2.9
Pensacola	57,619	59,198	60,658	15	26	27	2.5
Davie	20,515	47,143	59,393	58	32	28	26.0
Deltona 1/	(X)	(X)	56,148	(X)	(X)	29	(X)
Delray Beach	34,329	47,184	52,039	36	31	30	10.3
Sarasota	48,868	50,897	51,311	19	28	31	0.8
Boynton Beach	35,624	46,284	50,940	35	34	32	10.1
North Miami	42,566	50,001	50,757	24	29	33	1.5
Tamarac	29,376	44,822	50,051	45	36	34	11.7
Lauderhill	37,271	49,015	50,020	28	30	35	2.1

(X) Not applicable.
1/ Not incorporated in 1990.
Note: Data are for the 35 most populous cities in the state. Changes in city
populations include the effects of annexations. Estimates reflect changes to Dade
and Broward counties as a result of Hurricane Andrew in August 1992.
Source: University of Florida, Bureau of Economic and Business Research, Population Program, *Florida Estimates of Population, April 1, 1996*. Census data from U.S.
Bureau of the Census.

University of Florida   **Bureau of Economic and Business Research**

Table 1.72. COMPONENTS OF CHANGE: COMPONENTS OF POPULATION CHANGE IN THE STATE AND COUNTIES OF FLORIDA, APRIL 1, 1990 TO APRIL 1, 1996

	Total population		Popula-tion change	Components of change 1/			
	Census	Estimates		Natural increase		Net migration	
County	April 1 1990	April 1 1996	1990 to 1996	Number	Per-centage	Number	Per-centage
Florida	12,938,071	14,411,563	1,473,492	305,475	20.7	1,168,017	79.3
Alachua	181,596	202,140	20,544	8,096	39.4	12,448	60.6
Baker	18,486	20,709	2,223	870	39.1	1,353	60.9
Bay	126,994	142,159	15,165	5,543	36.6	9,622	63.4
Bradford	22,515	24,983	2,468	440	17.8	2,028	82.2
Brevard	398,978	450,164	51,186	8,713	17.0	42,473	83.0
Broward	1,255,531	1,392,252	136,721	23,088	16.9	113,633	83.1
Calhoun	11,011	12,504	1,493	18	1.2	1,475	98.8
Charlotte	110,975	129,468	18,493	-4,424	0.0	22,917	100.0
Citrus	93,513	107,889	14,376	-3,715	0.0	18,091	100.0
Clay	105,986	125,431	19,445	5,004	25.7	14,441	74.3
Collier	152,099	193,036	40,937	4,958	12.1	35,979	87.9
Columbia	42,613	52,565	9,952	1,436	14.4	8,516	85.6
Dade	1,937,194	2,043,316	106,122	88,251	83.2	17,871	16.8
De Soto	23,865	26,716	2,851	685	24.0	2,166	76.0
Dixie	10,585	12,602	2,017	216	10.7	1,801	89.3
Duval	672,971	728,437	55,466	38,012	68.5	17,454	31.5
Escambia	262,798	286,301	23,503	11,040	47.0	12,463	53.0
Flagler	28,701	39,052	10,351	-488	0.0	10,839	100.0
Franklin	8,967	10,378	1,411	-44	0.0	1,455	100.0
Gadsden	41,116	46,322	5,206	2,011	38.6	3,195	61.4
Gilchrist	9,667	12,150	2,483	142	5.7	2,341	94.3
Glades	7,591	9,413	1,822	-2	0.0	1,824	100.0
Gulf	11,504	13,545	2,041	58	2.8	1,983	97.2
Hamilton	10,930	13,431	2,501	307	12.3	2,194	87.7
Hardee	19,499	22,519	3,020	1,451	48.0	1,569	52.0
Hendry	25,773	30,157	4,384	2,193	50.0	2,191	50.0
Hernando	101,115	119,931	18,816	-3,415	0.0	22,231	100.0
Highlands	68,432	77,996	9,564	-1,658	0.0	11,222	100.0
Hillsborough	834,054	910,855	76,801	38,159	49.7	38,642	50.3
Holmes	15,778	17,412	1,634	72	4.4	1,562	95.6
Indian River	90,208	102,211	12,003	-949	0.0	12,952	100.0
Jackson	41,375	48,629	7,254	477	6.6	6,777	93.4
Jefferson	11,296	13,713	2,417	262	10.8	2,155	89.2
Lafayette	5,578	7,012	1,434	138	9.6	1,296	90.4
Lake	152,104	182,309	30,205	-1,372	0.0	31,577	100.0
Lee	335,113	383,706	48,593	1,651	3.4	46,942	96.6

See footnotes at end of table.   Continued . . .

University of Florida   **Bureau of Economic and Business Research**

Table 1.72. COMPONENTS OF CHANGE: COMPONENTS OF POPULATION CHANGE IN THE STATE
AND COUNTIES OF FLORIDA, APRIL 1, 1990 TO APRIL 1, 1996 (Continued)

County	Total population Census April 1 1990	Total population Estimates April 1 1996	Population change 1990 to 1996	Natural increase Number	Natural increase Per- centage	Net migration Number	Net migration Per- centage
Leon	192,493	221,621	29,128	9,423	32.4	19,705	67.6
Levy	25,912	30,690	4,778	72	1.5	4,706	98.5
Liberty	5,569	7,439	1,870	152	8.1	1,718	91.9
Madison	16,569	18,745	2,176	333	15.3	1,843	84.7
Manatee	211,707	236,778	25,071	-720	0.0	25,791	100.0
Marion	194,835	229,260	34,425	1,061	3.1	33,364	96.9
Martin	100,900	114,464	13,564	-660	0.0	14,224	100.0
Monroe	78,024	83,789	5,765	1,564	27.1	4,201	72.9
Nassau	43,941	51,097	7,156	1,904	26.6	5,252	73.4
Okaloosa	143,777	165,319	21,542	8,624	40.0	12,918	60.0
Okeechobee	29,627	33,643	4,016	1,378	34.3	2,638	65.7
Orange	677,491	777,556	100,065	40,374	40.3	59,691	59.7
Osceola	107,728	139,724	31,996	5,564	17.4	26,432	82.6
Palm Beach	863,503	981,793	118,290	9,728	8.2	108,562	91.8
Pasco	281,131	309,936	28,805	-8,381	0.0	37,186	100.0
Pinellas	851,659	881,383	29,724	-15,853	0.0	45,577	100.0
Polk	405,382	452,707	47,325	10,799	22.8	36,526	77.2
Putnam	65,070	70,287	5,217	1,036	19.9	4,181	80.1
St. Johns	83,829	101,729	17,900	1,517	8.5	16,383	91.5
St. Lucie	150,171	175,458	25,287	3,222	12.7	22,065	87.3
Santa Rosa	81,608	98,491	16,883	4,211	24.9	12,672	75.1
Sarasota	277,776	305,848	28,072	-9,672	0.0	37,744	100.0
Seminole	287,521	329,031	41,510	13,969	33.7	27,541	66.3
Sumter	31,577	40,593	9,016	-41	0.0	9,057	100.0
Suwannee	26,780	31,424	4,644	-58	0.0	4,702	100.0
Taylor	17,111	19,022	1,911	341	17.8	1,570	82.2
Union	10,252	13,023	2,771	18	0.6	2,753	99.4
Volusia	370,737	407,199	36,462	-2,491	0.0	38,953	100.0
Wakulla	14,202	18,022	3,820	397	10.4	3,423	89.6
Walton	27,759	34,328	6,569	286	4.4	6,283	95.6
Washington	16,919	19,751	2,832	154	5.4	2,678	94.6

1/ Natural increase is calculated as the difference between the number of births
and the number of deaths; net migration is calculated as the difference between total
population change and natural increase.
   Note: Vital statistics data for persons of unreported residence are included only
in the entries for the state. For this reason, natural increase and net migration
columns may not add to their state totals. Estimates reflect changes to Dade and
Broward counties as a result of Hurricane Andrew in August 1992.
   Source: University of Florida, Bureau of Economic and Business Research, Population Program, *Florida Estimates of Population, April 1, 1996.* Census data from U.S.
Bureau of the Census.

University of Florida   **Bureau of Economic and Business Research**

Table 1.73.   MIGRATION: NET MIGRATION OF THE TOTAL POPULATION AND OF PERSONS
AGED 65 AND OVER BY STATE OF EXCHANGE WITH FLORIDA
1985 THROUGH 1990

State	Total population	Aged 65 and over Total	Aged 65 and over Percentage	State	Total population	Aged 65 and over Total	Aged 65 and over Percentage
Alabama	5,151	1,108	21.5	Montana	1,736	-45	-2.6
Alaska	1,429	6	0.4	Nebraska	4,203	245	5.8
Arizona	75	-1,122	-1,496.0	Nevada	-775	-358	46.2
Arkansas	3,506	114	3.3	New Hampshire	11,127	2,970	26.7
California	23,174	3,041	13.1	New Jersey	120,962	26,130	21.6
Colorado	9,277	-210	-2.3	New Mexico	2,571	-10	-0.4
Connecticut	42,608	10,484	24.6	New York	297,081	67,343	22.7
Delaware	2,628	934	35.5	North Carolina	-17,224	-1,899	11.0
District of Columbia	2,238	470	21.0	North Dakota	1,895	19	1.0
				Ohio	68,332	11,953	17.5
Georgia	-27,182	-510	1.9	Oklahoma	10,530	186	1.8
Hawaii	3,015	201	6.7	Oregon	-278	-291	104.7
Idaho	800	46	5.8	Pennsylvania	60,603	14,421	23.8
Illinois	66,910	12,525	18.7	Rhode Island	10,189	2,254	22.1
Indiana	31,927	6,513	20.4	South Carolina	-3,536	-76	2.1
Iowa	9,017	977	10.8	South Dakota	1,380	67	4.9
Kansas	4,218	223	5.3	Tennessee	-1,844	-301	16.3
Kentucky	12,138	1,233	10.2	Texas	58,576	432	0.7
Louisiana	29,392	724	2.5	Utah	1,357	-87	-6.4
Maine	7,140	2,499	35.0	Vermont	3,162	1,067	33.7
Maryland	20,755	5,323	25.6	Virginia	11,788	4,070	34.5
Massachusetts	57,645	14,880	25.8	Washington	-192	-252	131.3
Michigan	61,951	15,560	25.1	West Virginia	12,220	1,300	10.6
Minnesota	8,804	1,485	16.9	Wisconsin	20,090	4,467	22.2
Mississippi	8,496	84	1.0	Wyoming	1,588	32	2.0
Missouri	11,029	1,441	13.1				

Note: Based on U.S. Bureau of the Census age, race, and sex data.

Source: University of Florida, Bureau of Economic and Business Research, unpublished data.

University of Florida   **Bureau of Economic and Business Research**

Table 1.74. MIGRATION: MIGRATION FLOWS IN THE STATE AND COUNTIES OF FLORIDA, 1991 THROUGH 1994

County	Net migration				In-migration				Out-migration			
	1991	1992	1993	1994	1991	1992	1993	1994	1991	1992	1993	1994
Florida 1/	99,683	94,230	108,462	101,017	436,574	428,329	429,374	437,102	336,891	334,099	320,912	336,085
Alachua	1,239	276	556	888	11,865	11,320	11,176	12,178	10,626	11,044	10,620	11,290
Baker	142	211	54	112	977	1,037	936	951	835	826	882	839
Bay	2,136	2,073	1,179	1,450	10,967	11,470	9,384	10,488	8,831	9,397	8,205	9,038
Bradford	28	130	-78	60	1,169	1,163	1,123	1,139	1,141	1,033	1,201	1,079
Brevard	6,884	7,343	4,595	5,020	25,807	26,557	23,749	25,097	18,923	19,214	19,154	20,077
Broward	11,825	22,377	16,337	13,343	67,150	76,319	75,028	75,477	55,325	53,942	58,691	62,134
Calhoun	101	52	147	40	582	516	584	489	481	464	437	449
Charlotte	3,050	3,210	3,214	3,533	8,944	8,887	8,985	9,670	5,894	5,677	5,771	6,137
Citrus	2,907	2,515	2,775	3,390	7,275	7,879	7,004	7,630	4,368	5,364	4,229	4,240
Clay	2,314	1,643	1,841	2,607	12,285	12,082	11,895	13,089	9,971	10,439	10,054	10,482
Collier	2,937	3,707	4,043	3,435	13,299	13,512	13,827	13,900	10,362	9,805	9,784	10,465
Columbia	272	515	879	791	2,620	2,798	2,945	3,149	2,348	2,283	2,066	2,358
Dade	-9,036	-36,814	-15,360	-21,363	49,396	46,199	46,606	44,799	58,432	83,013	61,966	66,162
De Soto	-43	-58	43	-96	1,759	1,747	1,752	1,580	1,802	1,805	1,709	1,676
Dixie	163	162	271	290	725	717	751	766	562	555	480	476
Duval	2,961	1,797	-2,063	126	44,745	44,966	38,968	41,658	41,784	43,169	41,031	41,532
Escambia	131	-441	-863	-501	19,073	18,757	16,059	17,699	18,942	19,198	16,922	18,200
Flagler	1,584	1,619	1,619	2,184	3,109	3,145	3,208	3,716	1,525	1,526	1,589	1,532
Franklin	71	124	70	83	499	503	470	500	428	379	400	417
Gadsden	-81	145	-76	131	1,921	2,165	2,064	2,093	2,002	2,020	2,140	1,962
Gilchrist	238	333	255	292	783	893	850	936	545	560	595	644
Glades	-49	-106	134	-56	512	513	697	554	561	619	563	610
Gulf	95	323	54	228	621	888	683	813	526	565	629	585
Hamilton	83	39	11	175	554	572	602	618	471	533	591	443

See footnotes at end of table.

Continued . . .

Table 1.74. MIGRATION: MIGRATION FLOWS IN THE STATE AND COUNTIES OF FLORIDA, 1991 THROUGH 1994 (Continued)

County	Net migration				In-migration				Out-migration			
	1991	1992	1993	1994	1991	1992	1993	1994	1991	1992	1993	1994
Hardee	-231	-244	-316	-429	1,675	1,597	1,491	1,376	1,906	1,841	1,807	1,805
Hendry	47	77	24	-497	2,828	3,006	2,783	2,460	2,781	2,929	2,759	2,957
Hernando	3,512	3,635	3,477	3,061	8,725	8,643	8,501	8,617	5,213	5,008	5,024	5,556
Highlands	1,019	1,666	1,347	1,390	5,127	5,482	5,196	5,215	4,108	3,816	3,849	3,825
Hillsborough	1,521	-218	-1,476	1,378	48,795	47,512	45,410	47,724	47,274	47,730	46,886	46,346
Holmes	289	159	203	353	1,038	1,019	1,028	1,085	749	860	825	732
Indian River	1,123	683	1,494	1,557	5,827	5,520	5,762	6,022	4,704	4,837	4,268	4,465
Jackson	555	253	5	275	2,342	2,149	2,000	2,158	1,787	1,896	1,995	1,883
Jefferson	75	17	93	45	675	655	667	648	600	638	574	603
Lafayette	60	-14	46	156	306	308	306	448	246	322	260	292
Lake	3,746	4,347	4,962	6,203	11,993	12,404	12,856	14,398	8,247	8,057	7,894	8,195
Lee	4,204	4,685	6,749	6,742	21,703	21,129	22,238	23,179	17,499	16,444	15,489	16,437
Leon	1,888	2,028	1,220	971	12,207	13,153	12,698	13,198	10,319	11,125	11,478	12,227
Levy	372	496	583	550	1,887	2,107	1,992	2,073	1,515	1,611	1,409	1,523
Liberty	23	113	129	59	283	319	326	288	260	206	197	229
Madison	-42	148	87	-5	671	711	720	665	713	563	633	670
Manatee	2,994	3,702	3,268	4,133	16,536	17,056	16,490	17,338	13,542	13,354	13,222	13,205
Marion	3,868	4,657	5,452	5,415	13,051	14,387	14,048	14,473	9,183	9,730	8,596	9,058
Martin	942	1,931	1,957	1,721	7,657	8,309	8,372	8,516	6,715	6,378	6,415	6,795
Monroe	190	1,556	-509	-145	7,294	8,400	6,985	6,822	7,104	6,844	7,494	6,967
Nassau	946	943	697	724	3,712	3,638	3,599	3,596	2,766	2,695	2,902	2,872
Okaloosa	3,128	2,536	1,055	963	16,779	17,209	13,241	15,155	13,651	14,673	12,186	14,192
Okeechobee	-130	231	-342	-142	2,339	2,532	2,291	2,228	2,469	2,301	2,633	2,370
Orange	2,762	4,196	2,025	365	54,805	54,331	51,843	54,365	52,043	50,135	49,818	54,000

See footnotes at end of table.

Continued . . .

Table 1.74. MIGRATION: MIGRATION FLOWS IN THE STATE AND COUNTIES OF FLORIDA, 1991 THROUGH 1994 (Continued)

County	Net migration				In-migration				Out-migration			
	1991	1992	1993	1994	1991	1992	1993	1994	1991	1992	1993	1994
Osceola	1,800	2,578	1,535	2,601	11,255	11,675	11,217	12,794	9,455	9,097	9,682	10,193
Palm Beach	10,905	14,251	15,031	11,529	49,418	50,739	53,062	53,807	38,513	36,488	38,031	42,278
Pasco	4,262	5,736	6,369	6,335	19,931	20,290	20,864	21,821	15,669	14,554	14,495	15,486
Pinellas	4,925	4,146	5,616	7,823	45,935	43,852	43,358	46,811	41,010	39,706	37,742	38,988
Polk	3,589	1,648	4,325	4,564	22,394	20,708	21,403	22,415	18,805	19,060	17,078	17,851
Putnam	270	530	408	395	3,302	3,206	3,048	3,166	3,032	2,676	2,640	2,771
St. Johns	1,603	2,710	2,030	1,974	7,349	8,126	7,980	8,076	5,746	5,416	5,950	6,102
St. Lucie	2,907	2,484	2,469	2,316	11,802	11,237	11,120	11,520	8,895	8,753	8,651	9,204
Santa Rosa	3,140	3,018	2,683	3,368	9,773	9,764	9,350	10,443	6,633	6,746	6,667	7,075
Sarasota	3,259	3,771	4,924	5,351	18,048	17,608	18,460	19,159	14,789	13,837	13,536	13,808
Seminole	3,943	3,450	3,451	2,678	28,685	28,363	28,457	28,731	24,742	24,913	25,006	26,053
Sumter	377	304	571	680	2,124	2,014	2,065	2,319	1,747	1,710	1,494	1,639
Suwannee	423	533	460	496	1,700	1,770	1,801	2,150	1,277	1,237	1,341	1,654
Taylor	-168	-109	-55	57	681	706	707	791	849	815	762	734
Union	53	108	23	33	528	590	544	558	475	482	521	525
Volusia	5,981	6,138	5,532	4,487	23,187	22,546	21,764	22,082	17,206	16,408	16,232	17,595
Wakulla	389	440	425	447	1,275	1,312	1,362	1,306	886	872	937	859
Walton	538	697	744	564	2,094	2,251	2,230	2,217	1,556	1,554	1,486	1,653
Washington	65	286	199	334	1,057	1,193	1,139	1,335	992	907	940	1,001

1/ County flow data will not add to state flow data due to the method in which the data are aggregated.
Note: Data are based on individual income tax returns filed by citizens and resident aliens with the IRS. Only returns for which the social security number matches from one year to the next are used. Data are affected by births, deaths, marriages, reporting error, and changes in tax filing status. IRS migration data tends to understate activity in Florida due to its large elderly population and foreign immigration.

Source: U.S., Department of the Treasury, Internal Revenue Service, unpublished data.

Table 1.75.   COUNTY RANKINGS AND DENSITY: ESTIMATES, RANK, PERCENTAGE DISTRIBUTION
LAND AREA, AND DENSITY IN THE STATE AND COUNTIES OF FLORIDA
APRIL 1, 1996

County	Estimates Number	Rank in state	Per- centage of state	Land area 1/ (square miles)	Density Persons per square mile	Rank in state
Florida	14,411,563	(X)	100.00	53,937.2	267	(X)
Alachua	202,140	19	1.40	874.3	231	20
Baker	20,709	51	0.14	585.3	35	49
Bay	142,159	24	0.99	763.7	186	26
Bradford	24,983	49	0.17	293.2	85	36
Brevard	450,164	9	3.12	1,018.5	442	11
Broward	1,392,252	2	9.66	1,208.9	1,152	2
Calhoun	12,504	62	0.09	567.4	22	61
Charlotte	129,468	26	0.90	693.7	187	25
Citrus	107,889	30	0.75	583.6	185	27
Clay	125,431	27	0.87	601.1	209	21
Collier	193,036	20	1.34	2,025.5	95	34
Columbia	52,565	37	0.36	797.2	66	42
Dade	2,043,316	1	14.18	1,944.5	1,051	4
De Soto	26,716	48	0.19	637.3	42	47
Dixie	12,602	61	0.09	704.1	18	64
Duval	728,437	7	5.05	773.9	941	5
Escambia	286,301	15	1.99	663.6	431	12
Flagler	39,052	42	0.27	485.0	81	38
Franklin	10,378	64	0.07	534.0	19	62
Gadsden	46,322	40	0.32	516.2	90	35
Gilchrist	12,150	63	0.08	348.9	35	51
Glades	9,413	65	0.07	773.5	12	66
Gulf	13,545	58	0.09	565.1	24	59
Hamilton	13,431	59	0.09	514.9	26	58
Hardee	22,519	50	0.16	637.4	35	50
Hendry	30,157	47	0.21	1,152.7	26	57
Hernando	119,931	28	0.83	478.3	251	18
Highlands	77,996	35	0.54	1,028.5	76	40
Hillsborough	910,855	4	6.32	1,051.0	867	6
Holmes	17,412	56	0.12	482.6	36	48
Indian River	102,211	31	0.71	503.3	203	23
Jackson	48,629	39	0.34	915.8	53	44
Jefferson	13,713	57	0.10	597.8	23	60
Lafayette	7,012	67	0.05	542.8	13	65
Lake	182,309	21	1.27	953.1	191	24
Lee	383,706	11	2.66	803.6	477	10

See footnotes at end of table.   Continued . . .

University of Florida   **Bureau of Economic and Business Research**

Table 1.75. COUNTY RANKINGS AND DENSITY: ESTIMATES, RANK, PERCENTAGE DISTRIBUTION
LAND AREA, AND DENSITY IN THE STATE AND COUNTIES OF FLORIDA
APRIL 1, 1996 (Continued)

County	Estimates			Land area 1/ (square miles)	Density	
	Number	Rank in state	Per-centage of state		Persons per square mile	Rank in state
Leon	221,621	18	1.54	666.8	332	15
Levy	30,690	46	0.21	1,118.4	27	55
Liberty	7,439	66	0.05	835.9	9	67
Madison	18,745	54	0.13	692.0	27	56
Manatee	236,778	16	1.64	741.2	319	16
Marion	229,260	17	1.59	1,579.0	145	30
Martin	114,464	29	0.79	555.7	206	22
Monroe	83,789	34	0.58	997.3	84	37
Nassau	51,097	38	0.35	651.6	78	39
Okaloosa	165,319	23	1.15	935.8	177	28
Okeechobee	33,643	44	0.23	774.3	43	46
Orange	777,556	6	5.40	907.6	857	7
Osceola	139,724	25	0.97	1,322.0	106	31
Palm Beach	981,793	3	6.81	1,974.2	497	9
Pasco	309,936	13	2.15	745.0	416	13
Pinellas	881,383	5	6.12	280.2	3,146	1
Polk	452,707	8	3.14	1,874.9	241	19
Putnam	70,287	36	0.49	722.2	97	32
St. Johns	101,729	32	0.71	609.0	167	29
St. Lucie	175,458	22	1.22	572.5	306	17
Santa Rosa	98,491	33	0.68	1,015.8	97	33
Sarasota	305,848	14	2.12	571.8	535	8
Seminole	329,031	12	2.28	308.2	1,068	3
Sumter	40,593	41	0.28	545.7	74	41
Suwannee	31,424	45	0.22	687.7	46	45
Taylor	19,022	53	0.13	1,042.0	18	63
Union	13,023	60	0.09	240.3	54	43
Volusia	407,199	10	2.83	1,105.9	368	14
Wakulla	18,022	55	0.13	606.7	30	54
Walton	34,328	43	0.24	1,057.7	32	53
Washington	19,751	52	0.14	579.9	34	52

(X) Not applicable.

1/ Land area figures as provided by the Geography division of the U.S. Bureau of
the Census represent the total area in the counties in 1990 and are not adjusted for
lands which cannot be developed (government-owned parks or reserves) or are uninhab-
itable (swamps or marshes).

Note: Estimates reflect changes to Dade and Broward counties as a result of Hurricane Andrew in August 1992.

Source: University of Florida, Bureau of Economic and Business Research, Population Program, *Florida Estimates of Population, April 1, 1996.* Census data from U.S.
Bureau of the Census.

University of Florida   **Bureau of Economic and Business Research**

Table 1.80.   INSTITUTIONAL POPULATION: ESTIMATED NUMBER OF INMATES AND PATIENTS
IN THE STATE, COUNTIES, AND MUNICIPALITIES
OF FLORIDA, APRIL 1, 1996

County or city	Total	County or city	Total
Florida	85,067	Gilchrist	898
Incorporated	14,467	Glades	729
Unincorporated	70,600	Gulf	1,326
Alachua	1,938	Hamilton	1,529
Gainesville	1,458	Hardee	1,329
Unincorporated	480	Hendry	1,286
Baker	1,805		
Bay	985	Hernando	462
Panama City	212	Highlands	74
Unincorporated	773	Hillsborough	1,389
		Tampa	861
Bradford	3,841	Unincorporated	528
Brevard	1,469		
Titusville	57	Holmes	1,224
Unincorporated	1,412	Indian River	281
Broward	1,517	Jackson	5,044
Cooper City	6	Malone	1,351
Davie	13	Marianna	141
Ft. Lauderdale	121	Unincorporated	3,552
Pembroke Pines	444		
Pompano Beach	79	Jefferson	820
Unincorporated	854	Lafayette	1,163
		Lake	879
Calhoun	1,198		
Charlotte	1,221	Lee	736
Punta Gorda	30	Cape Coral	30
Unincorporated	1,191	Ft. Myers	162
Citrus	70	Unincorporated	544
		Leon	1,057
Collier	98	Tallahassee	878
Columbia	1,832	Unincorporated	179
Lake City	469	Levy	237
Unincorporated	1,363		
Dade	7,774	Liberty	1,465
Miami	2,976	Bristol	80
North Miami	219	Unincorporated	1,385
Opa-Locka	24	Madison	1,470
Unincorporated	4,555	Madison	32
		Unincorporated	1,438
De Soto	1,641	Manatee	349
Dixie	994	Bradenton	179
Duval (Jacksonville)	566	Palmetto	25
		Unincorporated	145
Escambia	2,202		
Pensacola	198	Marion	2,337
Unincorporated	2,004	Ocala	66
Franklin	236	Unincorporated	2,271
Gadsden	2,617	Martin	1,422
Chatahoochee	1,498	Stuart	64
Gretna	740	Unincorporated	1,358
Unincorporated	379	Monroe	46

See footnote at end of table.   Continued . . .

Table 1.80. INSTITUTIONAL POPULATION: ESTIMATED NUMBER OF INMATES AND PATIENTS
IN THE STATE, COUNTIES, AND MUNICIPALITIES
OF FLORIDA, APRIL 1, 1996 (Continued)

County or city	Total	County or city	Total
Nassau	40	St. Lucie	167
Fernandina Beach	16	Ft. Pierce	83
Unincorporated	24	Unincorporated	84
Okaloosa	1,780	Santa Rosa	245
Okeechobee	642	Milton	61
		Unincorporated	184
Orange	2,587		
Eatonville	82	Sarasota	24
Orlando	58	Sarasota	6
Winter Park	30	Unincorporated	18
Unincorporated	2,417	Seminole	203
Osceola	203	Casselberry	6
Palm Beach	1,696	Sanford	69
Boca Raton	7	Unincorporated	128
Lantana	109	Sumter	3,397
West Palm Beach	232		
Unincorporated	1,348	Taylor	1,104
		Union	3,894
Pasco	820	Raiford	20
Pinellas	1,328	Unincorporated	3,874
Clearwater	38	Volusia	1,712
Largo	27	Daytona Beach	56
Pinellas Park	27	Ormond Beach	6
St. Petersburg	273	Unincorporated	1,650
Unincorporated	963		
Polk	2,961	Walton	1,165
Bartow	242	De Funiak Springs	40
Unincorporated	2,719	Unincorporated	1,125
Putnam	416	Washington	1,127

Note: Inmates and patients residing in federal and state government-operated
institutions and considered nonresidents of the local area for revenue-sharing purposes. Unless city data are specified separately for a county, county data are for
unincorporated areas.

Source: University of Florida, Bureau of Economic and Business Research, Population Program, *Florida Estimates of Population, April 1, 1996.*

University of Florida   **Bureau of Economic and Business Research**

Table 1.83. PLANNING DISTRICTS: ESTIMATES, APRIL 1, 1996, AND PROJECTIONS
SPECIFIED YEARS APRIL 1, 2000 THROUGH 2020, IN THE STATE
AND COMPREHENSIVE PLANNING DISTRICTS OF FLORIDA

(in thousands, rounded to hundreds)

District	Estimates 1996	Projections 2000	2005	2010	2015	2020
Florida	14,411.6					
Low		14,700.4	15,391.1	16,087.6	16,825.5	17,595.7
Medium		15,429.2	16,643.0	17,836.1	19,046.3	20,263.3
High		16,093.7	17,834.6	19,526.7	21,209.6	22,871.9
District 1	763.8					
Low		765.6	767.7	761.5	747.1	724.1
Medium		819.2	877.7	935.6	994.3	1,053.1
High		879.5	1,005.5	1,140.2	1,284.5	1,437.4
District 2	392.2					
Low		382.5	376.7	365.9	349.7	328.4
Medium		420.9	451.4	481.7	512.1	542.9
High		463.0	534.9	612.3	695.6	784.5
District 3	407.1					
Low		400.0	397.2	388.9	375.5	357.0
Medium		436.1	468.0	500.1	531.8	564.0
High		475.5	548.3	626.5	710.1	799.5
District 4	1,136.7					
Low		1,128.5	1,132.5	1,122.0	1,097.6	1,058.8
Medium		1,213.3	1,306.2	1,397.6	1,490.3	1,583.4
High		1,308.8	1,507.7	1,721.1	1,950.7	2,196.4
District 5	528.4					
Low		525.6	616.0	533.9	519.5	492.5
Medium		586.2	655.0	723.0	792.1	862.2
High		654.7	794.5	947.6	1,115.4	1,298.2
District 6	2,286.0					
Low		2,250.8	2,274.0	2,251.5	2,186.4	2,076.7
Medium		2,493.3	2,748.7	3,000.2	3,256.6	3,515.3
High		2,765.3	3,300.3	3,880.7	4,514.1	5,199.1
District 7	613.6					
Low		613.3	616.4	612.6	602.3	585.3
Medium		655.8	704.2	751.4	799.2	847.0
High		703.9	806.1	914.8	1,031.0	1,154.2
District 8	2,339.0					
Low		2,306.3	2,289.0	2,250.7	2,194.2	2,118.6
Medium		2,456.3	2,598.7	2,738.0	2,878.8	3,020.1
High		2,622.7	2,951.5	3,298.2	3,666.4	4,055.4
District 9	1,051.6					
Low		1,041.7	1,054.5	1,044.9	1,014.2	962.0
Medium		1,152.7	1,273.5	1,392.6	1,513.9	1,636.3
High		1,277.8	1,529.1	1,802.7	2,102.0	2,426.4
District 10	1,373.9					
Low		1,352.8	1,363.3	1,348.0	1,309.0	1,245.2
Medium		1,494.7	1,640.6	1,784.1	1,930.2	2,077.4
High		1,653.5	1,961.9	2,295.4	2,657.7	3,048.7
District 11	3,519.4					
Low		3,490.6	3,477.8	3,434.3	3,363.5	3,264.4
Medium		3,700.7	3,919.1	4,132.4	4,347.3	4,561.9
High		3,936.1	4,426.3	4,942.1	5,487.8	6,062.6

Note: See footnote on Table 1.84.

Source: University of Florida, Bureau of Economic and Business Research, Population Program, *Florida Population Studies,* February 1997, Volume 30, No. 2.   Bulletin No. 117.

University of Florida   **Bureau of Economic and Business Research**

Table 1.84. PROJECTIONS: ESTIMATES, APRIL 1, 1996, AND PROJECTIONS
SPECIFIED YEARS APRIL 1, 2000 THROUGH 2020, IN THE STATE
AND COUNTIES OF FLORIDA

County	Estimates 1996	Projections 2000	2005	2010	2015	2020
Florida	14,411.6					
Low		14,700.4	15,391.1	16,087.6	16,825.5	17,595.7
Medium		15,429.2	16,643.0	17,836.1	19,046.3	20,263.3
High		16,093.7	17,834.6	19,526.7	21,209.6	22,871.9
Alachua	202.1					
Low		202.7	203.5	202.3	199.3	194.5
Medium		214.9	229.4	243.6	257.8	272.1
High		228.5	259.0	291.1	325.2	361.2
Baker	20.7					
Low		20.0	19.6	18.9	18.0	16.7
Medium		22.2	23.7	25.2	26.7	28.2
High		24.5	28.2	32.2	36.5	41.0
Bay	142.2					
Low		142.8	144.5	144.8	143.7	141.0
Medium		151.3	162.5	173.6	185.0	196.2
High		161.1	183.9	208.3	234.5	261.9
Bradford	25.0					
Low		23.5	22.4	21.1	19.6	17.9
Medium		26.0	27.1	28.2	29.3	30.4
High		28.7	32.2	35.9	39.7	43.8
Brevard	450.2					
Low		440.2	440.4	432.8	418.0	395.7
Medium		486.5	530.5	573.6	617.3	661.4
High		538.0	633.8	736.9	848.7	968.7
Broward	1,392.3					
Low		1,395.0	1,405.1	1,400.6	1,383.1	1,352.1
Medium		1,478.0	1,581.1	1,681.7	1,782.9	1,883.8
High		1,573.0	1,788.3	2,015.5	2,256.6	2,511.0
Calhoun	12.5					
Low		11.3	10.5	9.7	8.6	7.4
Medium		13.1	13.8	14.4	15.1	15.8
High		15.0	17.2	19.6	22.1	24.8
Charlotte	129.5					
Low		125.3	125.9	122.6	115.5	104.6
Medium		144.6	162.9	181.0	199.6	218.4
High		166.0	205.4	248.9	297.1	350.0
Citrus	107.9					
Low		107.6	110.0	110.1	108.0	103.6
Medium		118.8	132.2	145.3	158.7	172.3
High		131.6	158.3	187.4	219.2	253.8
Clay	125.4					
Low		125.7	129.1	129.7	127.7	122.9
Medium		138.7	155.0	171.1	187.5	204.0
High		153.6	185.8	220.9	259.2	300.8
Collier	193.0					
Low		190.8	194.8	192.1	182.8	166.8
Medium		220.1	251.5	282.8	314.8	347.3
High		253.0	317.8	389.9	470.2	558.5

See footnote at end of table.   Continued . . .

University of Florida   **Bureau of Economic and Business Research**

Table 1.84. PROJECTIONS: ESTIMATES, APRIL 1, 1996, AND PROJECTIONS
SPECIFIED YEARS APRIL 1, 2000 THROUGH 2020, IN THE STATE
AND COUNTIES OF FLORIDA (Continued)

County	Estimates 1996	Projections 2000	2005	2010	2015	2020
Columbia	52.6					
Low		51.8	52.3	51.9	50.4	47.9
Medium		57.3	62.9	68.6	74.2	79.9
High		63.3	75.3	88.3	102.3	117.3
Dade	2,043.3					
Low		2,012.7	1,990.3	1,952.6	1,901.2	1,835.6
Medium		2,134.7	2,245.1	2,353.0	2,461.9	2,570.8
High		2,269.6	2,533.1	2,809.9	3,102.0	3,409.1
De Soto	26.7					
Low		28.2	28.4	28.4	28.1	27.5
Medium		29.9	32.0	34.1	36.2	38.3
High		31.8	36.2	40.9	45.9	51.2
Dixie	12.6					
Low		12.2	12.1	11.6	10.8	9.7
Medium		14.1	15.6	17.2	18.8	20.4
High		16.1	19.7	23.6	27.9	32.5
Duval	728.4					
Low		719.9	714.4	703.2	686.7	664.7
Medium		763.4	805.5	846.7	888.3	929.9
High		811.7	909.3	1,011.9	1,120.4	1,234.5
Escambia	286.3					
Low		285.9	280.8	273.9	265.3	255.1
Medium		303.4	317.0	330.5	344.1	357.9
High		322.5	357.4	394.1	432.9	473.7
Flagler	39.1					
Low		40.3	43.0	44.0	43.0	40.2
Medium		46.3	55.3	64.3	73.5	82.9
High		53.4	70.2	89.3	110.7	134.6
Franklin	10.4					
Low		10.0	9.9	9.6	9.2	8.6
Medium		11.1	11.9	12.8	13.6	14.5
High		12.2	14.2	16.4	18.7	21.1
Gadsden	46.3					
Low		45.5	44.4	43.1	41.5	39.7
Medium		48.2	50.1	52.0	53.9	55.8
High		51.3	56.5	62.0	67.7	73.8
Gilchrist	12.2					
Low		11.4	11.2	10.4	9.2	7.6
Medium		13.8	15.6	17.5	19.4	21.3
High		16.4	20.7	25.5	31.0	36.9
Glades	9.4					
Low		8.7	8.3	7.8	7.0	6.2
Medium		10.1	10.8	11.6	12.3	13.0
High		11.6	13.6	15.8	18.1	20.6
Gulf	13.5					
Low		13.8	13.0	12.2	11.2	10.2
Medium		15.2	15.8	16.3	16.8	17.4
High		16.8	18.7	20.7	22.8	25.0

See footnote at end of table.   Continued . . .

University of Florida   **Bureau of Economic and Business Research**

Table 1.84. PROJECTIONS: ESTIMATES, APRIL 1, 1996, AND PROJECTIONS
SPECIFIED YEARS APRIL 1, 2000 THROUGH 2020, IN THE STATE
AND COUNTIES OF FLORIDA (Continued)

County	Estimates 1996	Projections 2000	2005	2010	2015	2020
Hamilton	13.4					
Low		13.2	12.8	12.0	11.0	9.8
Medium		15.3	16.6	17.9	19.2	20.6
High		17.6	20.8	24.4	28.4	32.7
Hardee	22.5					
Low		20.8	19.5	18.0	16.4	14.8
Medium		23.1	23.7	24.2	24.7	25.2
High		25.5	28.0	30.6	33.4	36.2
Hendry	30.2					
Low		29.5	29.5	28.9	27.9	26.4
Medium		32.6	35.5	38.3	41.2	44.1
High		36.1	42.4	49.2	56.6	64.5
Hernando	119.9					
Low		117.6	199.9	118.1	112.4	102.5
Medium		135.6	154.9	174.0	193.5	213.4
High		155.9	195.6	239.8	289.0	343.1
Highlands	78.0					
Low		76.5	76.7	75.6	73.2	69.4
Medium		84.5	92.4	100.1	108.0	115.9
High		93.4	110.4	128.7	148.5	169.9
Hillsborough	910.9					
Low		909.6	913.9	908.9	895.8	874.5
Medium		963.9	1,028.7	1,091.8	1,155.5	1,219.1
High		1,025.7	1,163.1	1,307.9	1,461.6	1,624.1
Holmes	17.4					
Low		16.3	15.3	14.2	13.1	11.8
Medium		18.0	18.6	19.1	19.6	20.2
High		19.9	22.0	24.2	26.6	29.0
Indian River	102.2					
Low		100.4	101.0	99.7	96.7	91.9
Medium		111.0	121.6	132.0	142.7	153.4
High		122.8	145.4	169.8	196.4	225.0
Jackson	48.6					
Low		48.3	47.8	47.0	45.8	44.3
Medium		51.2	53.9	56.6	59.3	62.0
High		54.4	60.8	67.6	74.8	82.4
Jefferson	13.7					
Low		13.1	12.7	12.1	11.4	10.6
Medium		14.6	15.4	16.2	17.0	17.8
High		16.1	18.3	20.6	23.2	25.8
Lafayette	7.0					
Low		6.8	6.6	6.2	5.8	5.1
Medium		7.8	8.6	9.3	10.0	10.7
High		9.0	10.8	12.7	14.8	17.1
Lake	182.3					
Low		182.3	186.8	187.3	184.0	176.9
Medium		201.2	224.3	247.1	270.4	293.8
High		222.8	268.8	318.9	373.7	433.0

See footnote at end of table.   Continued . . .

University of Florida   **Bureau of Economic and Business Research**

Table 1.84. PROJECTIONS: ESTIMATES, APRIL 1, 1996, AND PROJECTIONS
SPECIFIED YEARS APRIL 1, 2000 THROUGH 2020, IN THE STATE
AND COUNTIES OF FLORIDA (Continued)

County	Estimates 1996	Projections 2000	2005	2010	2015	2020
Lee	383.7					
Low		379.9	385.2	382.8	373.3	356.5
Medium		419.6	463.2	506.1	549.7	593.8
High		464.4	554.3	651.8	758.0	872.8
Leon	221.6					
Low		215.3	213.6	208.5	200.2	188.5
Medium		238.1	257.8	277.2	296.8	316.5
High		263.1	307.4	355.0	406.4	461.4
Levy	30.7					
Low		30.3	30.6	30.3	29.4	28.0
Medium		33.5	36.8	40.1	43.4	46.7
High		37.0	44.0	51.6	59.7	68.6
Liberty	7.4					
Low		6.7	6.3	5.7	4.9	3.9
Medium		8.1	8.8	9.6	10.4	11.2
High		9.6	11.6	13.9	16.4	19.2
Madison	18.7					
Low		17.6	16.9	16.1	15.0	13.8
Medium		19.6	20.5	21.5	22.4	23.4
High		21.6	24.4	27.4	30.5	33.9
Manatee	236.8					
Low		230.6	229.8	225.0	216.6	204.5
Medium		255.0	276.9	298.5	320.3	342.2
High		281.9	330.7	383.2	439.9	500.7
Marion	229.3					
Low		228.5	233.3	233.4	228.8	219.4
Medium		252.3	280.3	308.1	336.3	364.8
High		279.3	335.8	397.4	464.5	537.2
Martin	114.5					
Low		113.4	114.7	113.8	110.8	105.7
Medium		125.3	138.0	150.5	163.3	176.2
High		138.6	165.1	193.8	225.0	258.8
Monroe	83.8					
Low		82.9	82.4	81.1	79.2	76.7
Medium		88.0	92.9	97.7	102.5	107.3
High		93.5	104.9	116.7	129.2	142.5
Nassau	51.1					
Low		50.1	50.4	49.7	48.1	45.7
Medium		55.4	60.6	65.8	71.0	76.2
High		61.3	72.5	84.6	97.7	111.8
Okaloosa	165.3					
Low		167.7	171.6	173.7	173.6	171.5
Medium		177.6	192.7	207.8	222.9	237.9
High		189.1	218.4	249.9	283.2	318.5
Okeechobee	33.6					
Low		33.4	33.2	32.5	31.3	29.6
Medium		36.9	40.1	43.2	46.3	49.5
High		40.8	47.8	55.4	63.6	72.3

See footnote at end of table.   Continued . . .

University of Florida   **Bureau of Economic and Business Research**

Table 1.84. PROJECTIONS: ESTIMATES, APRIL 1, 1996, AND PROJECTIONS
SPECIFIED YEARS APRIL 1, 2000 THROUGH 2020, IN THE STATE
AND COUNTIES OF FLORIDA (Continued)

County	Estimates 1996	Projections 2000	2005	2010	2015	2020
Orange	777.6					
Low		766.6	776.8	771.8	752.7	718.7
Medium		846.7	934.2	1,020.4	1,108.3	1,197.1
High		937.0	1,117.9	1,314.1	1,528.2	1,759.7
Osceola	139.7					
Low		139.4	144.5	144.2	138.7	127.6
Medium		160.6	186.3	211.8	238.1	264.7
High		184.7	235.8	292.8	356.6	427.2
Palm Beach	981.8					
Low		963.1	966.9	953.0	922.8	875.5
Medium		1,064.3	1,164.1	1,262.2	1,361.8	1,462.1
High		1,177.1	1,391.4	1,622.7	1,873.5	2,143.6
Pasco	309.9					
Low		313.6	319.3	321.2	319.9	315.1
Medium		332.1	358.8	384.9	411.2	437.7
High		353.7	406.4	462.2	521.9	585.2
Pinellas	881.4					
Low		852.5	826.0	795.6	761.9	724.5
Medium		905.3	934.3	962.8	991.8	1,021.1
High		961.4	1,051.3	1,144.9	1,243.0	1,345.4
Polk	452.7					
Low		454.4	458.6	458.1	453.3	444.0
Medium		481.4	516.0	549.8	584.0	618.1
High		512.4	583.7	659.2	739.6	824.6
Putnam	70.3					
Low		69.9	69.9	69.3	68.1	66.3
Medium		74.1	78.8	83.3	87.9	92.5
High		78.9	89.0	99.7	111.1	123.1
St. Johns	101.7					
Low		102.6	106.1	107.2	106.0	102.3
Medium		113.2	127.3	141.2	155.4	169.7
High		125.4	152.7	182.5	215.1	250.6
St. Lucie	175.5					
Low		175.9	180.7	181.5	178.7	172.1
Medium		194.1	216.9	239.4	262.4	285.7
High		215.0	260.0	309.1	362.8	421.3
Santa Rosa	98.5					
Low		100.1	102.8	103.3	101.7	97.8
Medium		110.4	123.4	136.2	149.3	162.4
High		122.3	147.9	175.8	206.4	239.5
Sarasota	305.8					
Low		307.5	310.8	310.7	307.7	301.5
Medium		325.7	349.6	372.8	396.3	419.7
High		346.7	395.6	447.1	502.0	560.0
Seminole	329.0					
Low		326.8	332.5	331.5	324.2	310.3
Medium		360.9	399.6	437.9	476.9	516.4
High		399.4	478.5	564.4	658.2	759.8

See footnote at end of table.   Continued . . .

University of Florida   **Bureau of Economic and Business Research**

Table 1.84. PROJECTIONS: ESTIMATES, APRIL 1, 1996, AND PROJECTIONS
SPECIFIED YEARS APRIL 1, 2000 THROUGH 2020, IN THE STATE
AND COUNTIES OF FLORIDA (Continued)

County	Estimates 1996	2000	2005	2010	2015	2020
Sumter	40.6					
Low		41.6	42.2	42.0	40.9	39.0
Medium		46.0	50.8	55.5	60.2	65.0
High		50.9	60.8	71.4	83.0	95.5
Suwannee	31.4					
Low		30.7	30.7	30.2	29.1	27.5
Medium		33.9	36.9	40.0	43.0	46.0
High		37.5	44.1	51.4	59.1	67.4
Taylor	19.0					
Low		17.5	16.3	15.0	13.7	12.3
Medium		19.4	19.8	20.2	20.6	20.9
High		21.4	23.4	25.6	27.7	30.0
Union	13.0					
Low		12.6	12.4	12.1	11.6	10.9
Medium		14.0	15.0	16.1	17.1	18.3
High		15.4	17.9	20.6	23.5	26.7
Volusia	407.2					
Low		395.5	393.0	383.9	368.8	347.5
Medium		437.4	473.8	509.4	545.6	581.9
High		483.4	565.5	653.6	748.7	850.7
Wakulla	18.0					
Low		18.5	18.5	18.0	16.9	15.2
Medium		21.3	23.9	26.6	29.2	31.9
High		24.5	30.2	36.5	43.5	51.0
Walton	34.3					
Low		34.0	34.4	34.1	33.2	31.6
Medium		37.6	41.4	45.1	48.9	52.7
High		41.6	49.6	58.1	67.4	77.4
Washington	19.8					
Low		18.8	18.3	17.5	16.5	15.3
Medium		20.9	22.1	23.3	24.5	25.8
High		23.0	26.3	29.8	33.5	37.4

Note: The medium projection is the one we believe is most likely to provide an accurate forecast of future population. The high and low projections indicate the range in which future populations are likely to fall. They do not represent absolute limits to growth; for any county, the future population may be above the high projection or below the low projection. If future distributions of errors are similar to past distributions, however, future populations will fall between high and low projections in approximately two-thirds of Florida's counties. Adjustments have been made to account for the effects of Hurricane Andrew on Dade county. For a detailed description of projection methodology, see the source.

Source: University of Florida, Bureau of Economic and Business Research, Population Program, *Florida Population Studies,* February 1997, Volume 30, No. 2. Bulletin No. 117.

University of Florida   **Bureau of Economic and Business Research**

Table 1.87. VETERANS: ESTIMATED NUMBER OF VETERANS IN CIVIL LIFE BY PERIOD
OF SERVICE IN FLORIDA AND THE UNITED STATES, JULY 1, 1995

(rounded to thousands)

Area	Total veterans	War veterans						Peacetime veterans		
		Total	World War I	World War II	Korea 1/	Viet-nam 1/	Per-sian Gulf 1/	Be-tween Korea and Viet-nam	Post-Viet-nam	Oth-er
Florida	1,709	1,343	1	613	316	484	82	154	200	12
United States	26,067	20,072	13	7,410	4,465	8,237	1,442	2,814	3,025	157

1/ No prior wartime service.
Source: U.S., Department of Veterans Affairs, *Annual Report of the Secretary of Veterans Affairs, Fiscal Year, 1995.*

Table 1.89. IMMIGRANTS: NEW ARRIVALS BY PORT OF ENTRY IN FLORIDA AND IN THE
UNITED STATES, FISCAL YEARS 1995 AND 1996

Port of entry	1995	1996	Port of entry	1995	1996
Florida	36,668	34,704	Florida (Continued)		
			Port Everglades	404	785
Jacksonville	6	7	Tampa	129	263
Miami	35,090	32,394	West Palm Beach	34	21
Orlando	1,005	1,234			
			United States	380,291	421,405

Note: Excludes legal immigrants admitted under "residency since 1982" and special agricultural workers. Data are for fiscal years ending September 30.

Table 1.90. IMMIGRANTS: NUMBER ADMITTED BY SPECIFIED COUNTRY OF BIRTH AND
RESIDENCE IN FLORIDA AND THE UNITED STATES, FISCAL YEAR 1996

Country of birth	Florida	United States	Country of birth	Florida	United States
Total 1/	79,461	915,900	India	1,393	44,859
Brazil	1,353	5,891	Jamaica	4,996	19,089
Canada	1,866	15,825	Mexico	3,155	163,572
Colombia	3,510	14,283	Nicaragua	3,480	6,903
Cuba	22,217	26,466	Peru	2,338	12,871
Dominican Republic	2,050	39,604	Philippines	1,796	55,876
Haiti	7,748	18,386	United Kingdom	1,501	13,548
Honduras	1,309	5,870	Venezuela	1,517	3,468

1/ Only admissions of 1,000 or more immigrants to Florida are shown separately by country of birth, therefore totals include other countries not shown separately.
Note: Data are for fiscal year ending September 30 and includes legalized aliens.
Source for Tables 1.89 and 1.90: U.S., Immigration and Naturalization Service, Statistics Division, unpublished data.

University of Florida   **Bureau of Economic and Business Research**

Table 1.91.   IMMIGRANTS: NUMBER ADMITTED BY COUNTRY OF BIRTH AND INTENDED
RESIDENCE IN THE METROPOLITAN AREAS OF FLORIDA, FISCAL YEAR 1996

County of birth	Daytona Beach	Ft. Lauderdale	Ft. Myers-Cape Coral	Ft. Pierce-Port St. Lucie	Ft. Walton Beach	Gainesville	Jacksonville	Lakeland-Winter Haven	Melbourne-Titusville-Palm Bay	Miami
Total 1/	694	10,290	677	634	178	317	1,526	722	667	41,527
Brazil	9	355	6	8	1	5	6	10	8	540
Canada	45	430	53	19	7	10	19	17	33	205
Colombia	12	651	28	6	1	5	13	4	16	2,054
Cuba	17	441	6	10	0	1	27	26	8	20,061
Dominican Republic	3	230	21	1	7	0	5	0	4	1,356
Haiti	4	1,659	74	127	1	2	16	103	0	3,139
Honduras	10	79	5	2	0	2	8	4	4	949
India	48	221	11	19	5	33	95	39	32	155
Jamaica	30	1,774	35	39	1	6	27	86	58	1,540
Mexico	116	159	97	141	4	5	30	188	10	396
Nicaragua	1	110	4	0	0	6	5	5	1	3,150
Peru	8	493	11	6	1	4	11	7	6	1,389
Philippines	44	156	21	23	35	10	269	22	55	337
United Kingdom	39	199	40	17	13	15	33	39	49	142

County of birth	Naples	Ocala	Orlando	Panama City	Pensacola	Punta Gorda	Sarasota-Bradenton	Tallahassee	Tampa-St. Petersburg-Clearwater	West Palm Beach-Boca Raton
Total 1/	933	193	5,517	105	281	241	958	292	5,010	6,553
Brazil	3	7	151	1	11	0	4	2	54	154
Canada	34	13	183	8	23	31	98	7	300	226
Colombia	20	9	253	0	2	6	8	1	137	226
Cuba	99	4	170	0	1	1	24	1	551	433
Dominican Republic	24	0	164	0	2	0	4	0	107	107
Haiti	245	0	494	0	0	52	46	2	91	1,611
Honduras	6	1	45	0	2	0	13	0	74	90
India	8	19	189	19	7	18	16	38	175	186
Jamaica	4	12	385	1	1	18	25	4	183	660
Mexico	219	16	324	3	0	12	128	4	392	358
Nicaragua	3	2	36	0	0	0	6	1	31	94
Peru	11	1	136	0	1	0	19	2	93	127
Philippines	9	13	226	12	63	16	38	9	242	103
United Kingdom	38	14	241	9	3	8	85	20	217	203

1/ Only admissions of 1,000 or more immigrants to Florida are shown separately by
country of birth, therefore totals include other countries not shown separately.
Note: Data are for fiscal year ending September 30 and includes legalized aliens.

Source: U.S., Immigration and Naturalization Service, Statistics Division, unpublished data.

University of Florida   **Bureau of Economic and Business Research**

HOUSING

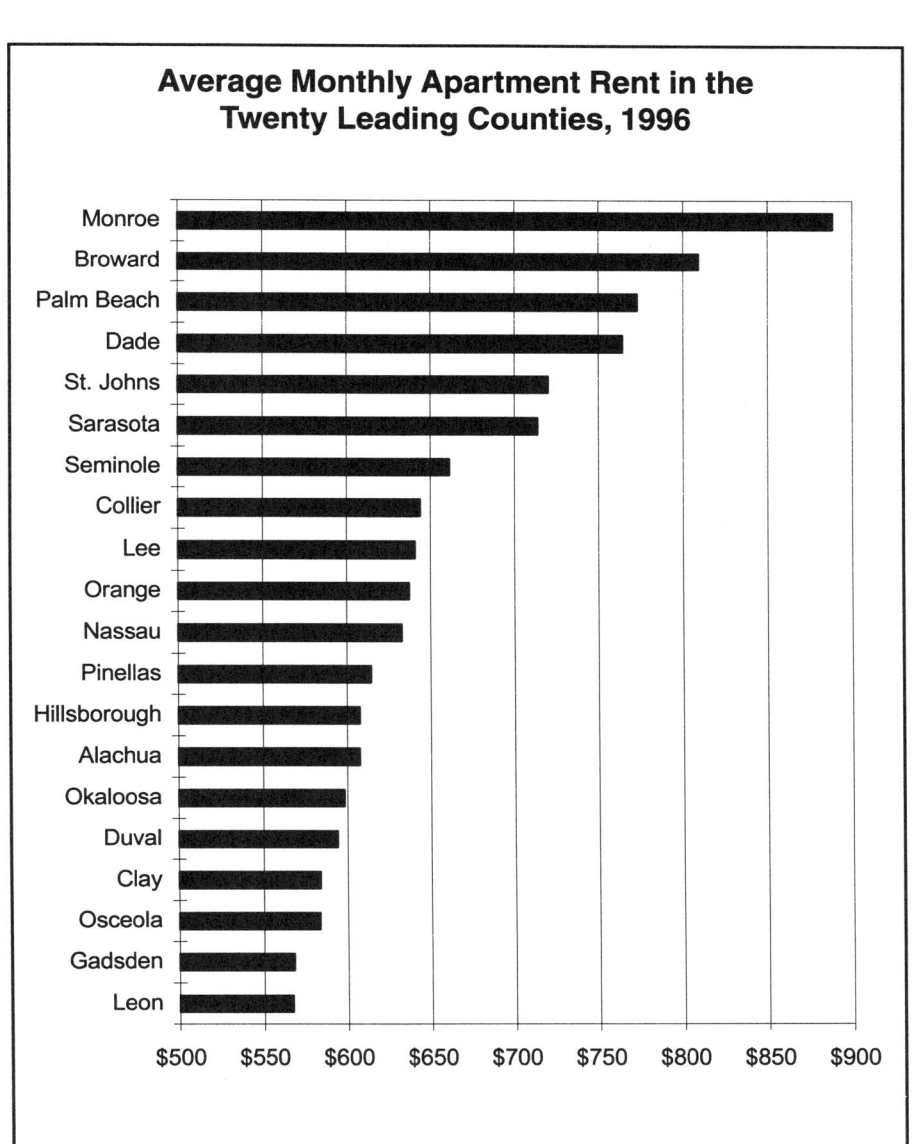

Average Monthly Apartment Rent in the Twenty Leading Counties, 1996

Source: Table 2.15

SECTION 2.00
HOUSING

TABLES LISTED BY MAJOR HEADINGS

Table 2.01.   STATES: ESTIMATES OF HOUSING UNITS AND HOUSEHOLDS IN FLORIDA, OTHER
STATES, AND THE UNITED STATES, JULY 1, 1995

(in thousands)

State	Total housing units	Households Total	Persons in--	State	Total housing units	Households Total	Persons in--
Florida	6,654	5,527	13,864	Missouri	2,337	2,031	5,179
				Montana	369	333	846
Alabama	1,783	1,602	4,160	Nebraska	690	621	1,588
Alaska	239	209	587	Nevada	646	587	1,502
Arizona	1,826	1,551	4,138	New Hampshire	524	429	1,118
Arkansas	1,059	938	2,425	New Jersey	3,155	2,861	7,783
California	11,727	10,925	30,848	New Mexico	684	602	1,655
Colorado	1,582	1,461	3,663	New York	7,332	6,672	17,592
Connecticut	1,353	1,223	3,177	North Carolina	3,119	2,730	6,968
Delaware	314	269	697	North Dakota	287	243	616
District of				Ohio	4,545	4,219	10,888
Columbia	271	232	514	Oklahoma	1,442	1,248	3,182
Georgia	2,929	2,645	7,025	Oregon	1,309	1,216	3,076
Hawaii	425	385	1,150	Pennsylvania	5,107	4,567	11,716
Idaho	463	415	1,141	Rhode Island	424	374	955
Illinois	4,679	4,335	11,543	South Carolina	1,567	1,351	3,580
Indiana	2,401	2,183	5,644	South Dakota	311	269	704
Iowa	1,186	1,090	2,742	Tennessee	2,184	2,003	5,126
Kansas	1,095	971	2,488	Texas	7,348	6,677	18,301
Kentucky	1,610	1,456	3,758	Utah	658	617	1,921
Louisiana	1,761	1,556	4,225	Vermont	285	223	563
Maine	620	476	1,206	Virginia	2,705	2,476	6,415
Maryland	2,023	1,852	4,930	Washington	2,250	2,084	5,312
Massachusetts	2,521	2,291	5,855	West Virginia	791	712	1,792
Michigan	4,021	3,539	9,342	Wisconsin	2,188	1,910	4,990
Minnesota	1,956	1,732	4,494	Wyoming	207	181	470
Mississippi	1,065	961	2,625	United States	108,026	97,061	256,079

Note: Detail may not add to totals because of rounding. See Glossary for definition of household.

Source: U.S., Department of Commerce, Bureau of the Census, Internet site http://
www.census.gov/.

University of Florida   **Bureau of Economic and Business Research**

Table 2.02. STATES: HOMEOWNERSHIP RATES IN THE STATE AND SPECIFIED METROPOLITAN
STATISTICAL AREAS (MSAS) OF FLORIDA AND IN OTHER STATES AND THE
UNITED STATES, 1994, 1995, AND 1996

State and MSA	1994	1995	1996	State and MSA	1994	1995	1996
Florida	65.7	66.6	67.1	Michigan	72.0	72.2	73.3
				Minnesota	68.9	73.3	75.4
Metropolitan Statistical				Mississippi	69.2	71.1	73.0
Area 1/				Missouri	68.4	69.4	70.2
Ft. Lauderdale	69.0	68.8	67.5	Montana	68.8	68.7	68.6
Jacksonville	63.9	66.6	66.6	Nebraska	68.0	67.1	66.8
Miami	51.4	50.9	51.9	Nevada	55.8	58.6	61.1
Orlando	59.6	61.7	66.5	New Hampshire	65.1	66.0	65.0
Tampa-St. Petersburg-				New Jersey	64.1	64.9	64.6
Clearwater	66.0	68.1	68.0	New Mexico	66.8	67.0	67.1
Alabama	68.5	70.1	71.0	New York	52.5	52.7	52.7
Alaska	58.8	60.9	62.9	North Carolina	68.7	70.1	70.4
Arizona	67.7	62.9	62.0	North Dakota	63.3	67.3	68.2
Arkansas	68.1	67.2	66.6	Ohio	67.4	67.9	69.2
California	55.5	55.4	55.0	Oklahoma	68.5	69.8	68.4
Colorado	62.9	64.6	64.5	Oregon	63.9	63.2	63.1
Connecticut	63.8	68.2	69.0	Pennsylvania	71.8	71.5	71.7
Delaware	70.5	71.7	71.5	Rhode Island	56.5	57.9	56.6
Georgia	63.4	66.6	69.3	South Carolina	72.0	71.3	72.9
Hawaii	52.3	50.2	50.6	South Dakota	66.4	67.5	67.8
Idaho	70.7	72.0	71.4	Tennessee	65.2	67.0	68.8
Illinois	64.2	66.4	68.2	Texas	59.7	61.4	61.8
Indiana	68.4	71.0	74.2	Utah	69.3	71.5	72.7
Iowa	70.1	71.4	72.8	Vermont	69.4	70.4	70.3
Kansas	69.0	67.5	67.5	Virginia	69.3	68.1	68.5
Kentucky	70.6	71.2	73.2	Washington	62.4	61.6	63.1
Louisiana	65.8	65.3	64.9	West Virginia	73.7	73.1	74.3
Maine	72.6	76.7	76.5	Wisconsin	64.2	67.5	68.2
Maryland	64.1	65.8	66.9	Wyoming	65.8	69.0	68.0
Massachusetts	60.6	60.2	61.7	United States	64.0	64.7	65.4

1/ Data for 1994 are based on 1980 metropolitan/nonmetropolitan definitions and
data for 1995 and 1996 are based on the 1990 definitions. Boundaries for the Orlando
MSA changed as a result of the 1990 decennial census.

Note: Data are based on the American Housing Survey (AHS) conducted by the Bureau
of the Census. Homeownership rates are computed by dividing the number of households
that are owners by the total number of households.

Source: U.S., Department of Commerce, Bureau of the Census, *Housing Vacancy Survey: Annual Statistics, 1996*. Data from Internet site http://www.census.gov/.

University of Florida   **Bureau of Economic and Business Research**

Table 2.05. HOUSEHOLDS AND AVERAGE HOUSEHOLD SIZE: ESTIMATES IN THE STATE
AND COUNTIES OF FLORIDA, APRIL 1, 1996

County	Households Esti-mates	Per-cent-age 1/	Average household size Esti-mates	Per-cent-age 1/	County	Households Esti-mates	Per-cent-age 1/	Average household size Esti-mates	Per-cent-age 1/
Florida	5,712,371	11.2	2.46	0.0	Lafayette	2,086	21.2	2.74	0.0
					Lake	76,059	19.6	2.35	0.0
Alachua	79,664	11.8	2.39	-0.4	Lee	160,629	14.6	2.35	0.0
Baker	6,259	12.7	2.99	-0.3	Leon	86,338	15.4	2.43	0.0
Bay	54,653	11.7	2.53	-0.4	Levy	11,978	18.8	2.51	-0.4
Bradford	7,884	9.6	2.68	0.0	Liberty	2,221	30.2	2.69	0.0
Brevard	182,091	12.8	2.43	0.0	Madison	6,169	11.7	2.75	0.0
Broward	588,336	11.3	2.36	0.4	Manatee	101,734	11.7	2.29	0.0
Calhoun	4,190	10.5	2.64	0.0	Marion	92,303	18.1	2.44	0.0
Charlotte	56,757	17.2	2.23	0.0	Martin	48,945	13.8	2.28	0.0
Citrus	46,820	15.4	2.27	0.0	Monroe	36,055	7.4	2.24	0.0
Clay	43,507	18.7	2.85	-0.3	Nassau	18,871	16.5	2.68	0.0
Collier	78,557	27.3	2.40	-0.4	Okaloosa	61,213	14.8	2.60	0.0
Columbia	18,813	20.5	2.66	-0.4	Okeechobee	11,458	12.2	2.75	0.0
Dade	724,487	4.6	2.77	0.7	Orange	295,691	16.0	2.56	0.0
De Soto	9,269	12.7	2.62	0.0	Osceola	50,801	29.8	2.68	0.0
Dixie	4,534	15.8	2.56	0.0	Palm Beach	413,778	13.2	2.33	0.4
Duval	278,674	8.3	2.54	0.0	Pasco	134,060	10.2	2.26	0.0
Escambia	106,699	8.2	2.57	0.0	Pinellas	394,256	3.6	2.18	0.0
Flagler	16,103	35.5	2.41	0.4	Polk	174,478	11.9	2.53	0.0
Franklin	4,098	13.0	2.42	0.0	Putnam	27,048	7.9	2.55	0.0
Gadsden	14,912	11.2	2.90	0.0	St. Johns	40,516	21.2	2.44	0.0
Gilchrist	4,087	24.5	2.65	0.0	St. Lucie	67,951	16.8	2.54	0.0
Glades	3,316	14.9	2.56	-0.4	Santa Rosa	36,147	20.9	2.68	0.0
Gulf	4,685	8.3	2.56	0.0	Sarasota	137,891	9.9	2.18	0.0
Hamilton	4,146	18.9	2.81	0.0	Seminole	122,926	14.2	2.65	0.4
Hardee	6,953	8.8	2.95	0.0	Sumter	14,824	22.3	2.46	0.0
Hendry	9,656	14.9	2.99	0.0	Suwannee	11,795	17.6	2.61	0.0
Hernando	49,988	18.2	2.37	0.0	Taylor	6,690	4.5	2.67	0.0
Highlands	33,683	14.0	2.28	0.0	Union	3,135	17.9	2.91	0.0
Hillsborough	354,902	9.2	2.51	0.0	Volusia	168,476	9.8	2.33	0.0
Holmes	6,253	7.8	2.56	0.0	Wakulla	6,600	26.7	2.70	0.0
Indian River	43,174	13.4	2.33	0.0	Walton	13,481	19.4	2.44	0.0
Jackson	16,901	16.8	2.56	0.0	Washington	7,180	11.4	2.54	-0.4
Jefferson	4,537	13.9	2.79	0.0					

1/ Percentage change 1990 to 1996.
Note: The occurrence of Hurricane Andrew in August 1992 created significant prob-
lems in south Florida for the usual estimation methodology. The hurricane destroyed
thousands of housing units and forced many residents to move to other locations. In
order to obtain information on these population movements, a series of sample surveys
in Dade and Broward counties were conducted. The household estimates on this table
incorporate the results of those surveys.
Source: University of Florida, Bureau of Economic and Business Research, Population Program, *Florida Population Studies*, January 1997, Volume 30, No. 1. Bulletin
No. 116.

University of Florida   **Bureau of Economic and Business Research**

Table 2.10. HOUSE PURCHASE PRICE: COST OF A HOUSE IN THE STATE AND COUNTIES
OF FLORIDA, 1995 AND 1996

(in dollars)

County	1995 A/	1996	Percent-age change	County	1995 A/	1996	Percent-age change
Alachua	83,789	85,360	1.9	Lake	90,181	90,248	0.1
Baker	75,134	76,044	1.2	Lee	96,398	101,528	5.3
Bay	80,301	81,297	1.2	Leon	81,981	83,695	2.1
Bradford	78,232	78,912	0.9	Levy	74,902	75,511	0.8
Brevard	84,371	90,929	7.8	Liberty	68,587	69,220	0.9
Broward	109,360	107,554	-1.7	Madison	68,886	69,650	1.1
Calhoun	68,198	68,092	-0.2	Manatee	90,528	95,289	5.3
Charlotte	91,147	85,413	-6.3	Marion	75,760	76,737	1.3
Citrus	79,140	80,849	2.2	Martin	95,671	105,578	10.4
Clay	86,011	87,147	1.3	Monroe	141,640	145,610	2.8
Collier	120,650	116,658	-3.3	Nassau	85,552	86,992	1.7
Columbia	75,199	74,777	-0.6	Okaloosa	84,075	85,517	1.7
Dade	114,667	117,429	2.4	Okeechobee	85,079	85,155	0.1
De Soto	74,401	74,186	-0.3	Orange	93,559	94,147	0.6
Dixie	72,137	72,729	0.8	Osceola	87,032	88,977	2.2
Duval	87,014	88,053	1.2	Palm Beach	101,612	104,167	2.5
Escambia	77,488	79,000	2.0	Pasco	76,809	79,923	4.1
Flagler	87,346	86,881	-0.5	Pinellas	103,809	105,780	1.9
Franklin	81,770	83,497	2.1	Polk	89,363	89,190	-0.2
Gadsden	72,157	71,891	-0.4	Putnam	80,882	81,221	0.4
Gilchrist	76,405	74,955	-1.9	St. Johns	94,315	91,574	-2.9
Glades	87,624	87,297	-0.4	St. Lucie	80,531	87,020	8.1
Gulf	76,339	75,834	-0.7	Santa Rosa	77,517	81,551	5.2
Hamilton	68,699	69,418	1.0	Sarasota	101,532	101,372	-0.2
Hardee	75,038	74,214	-1.1	Seminole	91,695	87,652	-4.4
Hendry	81,971	80,884	-1.3	Sumter	81,030	81,243	0.3
Hernando	82,543	84,611	2.5	Suwannee	69,223	70,652	2.1
Highlands	73,835	75,318	2.0	Taylor	70,303	70,592	0.4
Hillsborough	101,299	100,951	-0.3	Union	70,661	69,665	-1.4
Holmes	70,667	70,920	0.4	Volusia	85,601	89,593	4.7
Indian River	90,712	94,085	3.7	Wakulla	77,535	78,968	1.8
Jackson	69,807	70,427	0.9	Walton	80,599	85,343	5.9
Jefferson	69,805	70,731	1.3	Washington	70,193	70,495	0.4
Lafayette	69,915	69,252	-0.9				

A/ Prices reflect a decrease in the cost of construction as reported by the Florida Department of Revenue.

Note: Data represent the cost of a house as measured by the Florida Price Level
Index (FPLI) and are based on a sample of records for those single-family residential
properties eligible for homestead exemption and which are between 1,200 and 1,600
square feet. The goal of this method is to provide data on homes that would fit on
an "average" lot, eliminate upper and lower income levels, and guard against weekend
homes and part-time residents. Excludes mobile homes. See discussion of FPLI on
Table 24.80.

Source: State of Florida, Department of Education, Office of Education Budget and
Management, unpublished data.

University of Florida   **Bureau of Economic and Business Research**

Table 2.15. APARTMENTS: AVERAGE RENT AND NUMBER OF UNITS BY AGE OF UNIT
IN THE STATE AND COUNTIES OF FLORIDA, FALL 1996

County	Aver-age rent (dol-lars)	Rank	Total	Age of unit (percentage) 0-20 years	21-40 years	40 or more years
Florida	588	(X)	480,261	68.4	30.2	1.4
Alachua	607	14	14,812	67.4	31.5	1.1
Baker	(NA)	(X)	(NA)	(NA)	(NA)	(NA)
Bay	565	21	3,023	79.7	20.3	0.0
Bradford	404	49	207	100.0	0.0	0.0
Brevard	548	25	12,931	77.0	23.0	0.0
Broward	809	2	50,105	77.4	22.6	0.0
Calhoun	437	43	88	100.0	0.0	0.0
Charlotte	329	57	89	100.0	0.0	0.0
Citrus	345	55	531	81.5	1.9	16.6
Clay	584	17	3,780	70.9	29.1	0.0
Collier	644	8	4,726	91.8	8.2	0.0
Columbia	432	44	288	78.5	21.5	0.0
Dade	764	4	56,231	66.6	33.4	0.0
De Soto	442	39	365	43.0	0.0	57.0
Dixie	360	53	32	100.0	0.0	0.0
Duval	594	16	41,871	50.0	49.8	0.2
Escambia	531	30	7,636	55.3	40.4	4.2
Flagler	339	56	471	26.1	0.0	73.9
Franklin	(NA)	(X)	(NA)	(NA)	(NA)	(NA)
Gadsden	568	19	424	79.2	20.8	0.0
Gilchrist	271	60	158	38.0	0.0	62.0
Glades	556	23	28	100.0	0.0	0.0
Gulf	246	61	62	100.0	0.0	0.0
Hamilton	(NA)	(X)	(NA)	(NA)	(NA)	(NA)
Hardee	425	45	179	50.8	0.0	49.2
Hendry	512	32	487	1.2	25.9	72.9
Hernando	440	40	792	100.0	0.0	0.0
Highlands	357	54	535	100.0	0.0	0.0
Hillsborough	607	13	58,477	66.5	33.5	0.0
Holmes	(NA)	(X)	(NA)	(NA)	(NA)	(NA)
Indian River	440	41	1,257	62.7	37.3	0.0
Jackson	505	33	412	59.2	34.5	6.3
Jefferson	391	51	107	100.0	0.0	0.0
Lafayette	540	28	541	6.7	0.0	93.3

See footnotes at end of table.   Continued . . .

Table 2.15. APARTMENTS: AVERAGE RENT AND NUMBER OF UNITS BY AGE OF UNIT
IN THE STATE AND COUNTIES OF FLORIDA, FALL 1996 (Continued)

County	Aver-age rent (dol-lars)	Rank	Units 1/ Total	Age of unit (percentage) 0-20 years	21-40 years	40 or more years
Lake	438	42	5,879	46.1	4.9	48.9
Lee	641	9	7,823	86.4	13.6	0.0
Leon	567	20	11,557	63.8	36.1	0.1
Levy	424	46	217	56.2	0.0	43.8
Liberty	(NA)	(X)	(NA)	(NA)	(NA)	(NA)
Madison	456	38	186	88.7	0.0	11.3
Manatee	536	29	7,042	81.4	18.5	0.2
Marion	544	26	3,602	63.4	31.4	5.2
Martin	560	22	943	84.9	11.0	4.0
Monroe	888	1	640	78.6	21.4	0.0
Nassau	632	11	1,502	26.6	73.4	0.0
Okaloosa	598	15	2,951	60.0	33.2	6.8
Okeechobee	392	50	125	92.8	0.0	7.2
Orange	637	10	54,383	68.4	31.6	0.0
Osceola	583	18	7,636	86.3	13.7	0.0
Palm Beach	773	3	28,349	88.2	11.8	0.0
Pasco	422	47	3,618	95.1	4.9	0.0
Pinellas	614	12	37,486	51.4	48.6	0.0
Polk	542	27	8,507	75.1	24.7	0.2
Putnam	411	48	992	74.0	26.0	0.0
St. Johns	720	5	1,757	93.6	4.3	2.1
St. Lucie	549	24	1,381	92.2	7.8	0.0
Santa Rosa	469	34	628	97.6	0.0	2.4
Sarasota	714	6	4,757	54.7	30.3	15.1
Seminole	661	7	17,002	78.3	21.7	0.0
Sumter	286	59	106	100.0	0.0	0.0
Suwannee	370	52	188	98.4	0.0	1.6
Taylor	464	35	205	31.7	68.3	0.0
Union	460	36	32	100.0	0.0	0.0
Volusia	517	31	9,855	72.9	27.1	0.0
Wakulla	(NA)	(X)	(NA)	(NA)	(NA)	(NA)
Walton	459	37	255	47.1	18.8	34.1
Washington	325	58	12	0.0	100.0	0.0

(X) Not applicable.
(NA) Not available.
1/ Data are from a BEBR survey of 480,261 apartment complex units conducted in the fall of 1996 and are estimated to represent more than half of all the apartment rental units in the state with leases of 6 months or longer.

Source: University of Florida, Bureau of Economic and Business Research, *Florida Business Briefs*, February 1997.

University of Florida   **Bureau of Economic and Business Research**

Table 2.20. HOMES FOR THE AGING: HOMES, RESIDENTIAL UNITS, AND BEDS FOR HOMES
WHICH ARE MEMBERS OF THE FLORIDA ASSOCIATION OF HOMES FOR THE AGING (FAHA)
IN THE STATE, FAHA DISTRICTS, AND CITIES OF FLORIDA, 1996

District and city	Homes	Resi-dential units	Nursing beds	District and city	Homes	Resi-dential units	Nursing beds
Florida	237	37,343	9,881	District 5 (Cont.)			
				Ft. Myers	2	1,215	280
District 1	49	7,606	1,517	Grove City	1	100	0
Atlantic Beach	1	380	80	Naples	3	803	204
Dowling Park	1	341	161	North Ft. Myers	1	80	0
Ft. Walton Beach	1	95	0	Port Charlotte	2	50	104
Gainesville	1	97	0	Sarasota	8	1,282	328
Jacksonville	26	3,815	809	Sebring	3	505	120
Jacksonville Beach	1	199	0	Venice	2	451	60
Keystone Heights	1	94	0	District 6	29	3,304	1,205
Lake City	1	150	0	Florida City	1	30	0
Marianna	2	124	60	Hialeah	4	285	0
Milton	1	0	120	Miami	16	2,125	664
Ocala	2	161	0	Miami Beach	4	601	60
Palatka	1	76	0	Miami Springs	1	50	269
Panama City	1	216	0	North Miami	1	0	212
Penney Farms	1	291	40	Opa-Locka	1	113	0
Pensacola	2	482	106	Sweetwater	1	100	0
Ponte Vedra Beach	1	258	30	District 7	29	6,571	1,140
St. Augustine	1	0	51	Boca Raton	5	1,400	240
Shalimar	1	379	0	Coral Springs	1	432	0
Tallahassee	3	448	60	Dania	1	60	0
District 2	29	4,555	1,269	Deerfield Beach	2	388	0
Apopka	1	32	0	Delray Beach	3	926	244
Davenport	1	70	60	Ft. Lauderdale	2	363	0
Eustis	1	45	0	Hallandale	1	120	0
Fern Park	1	176	0	Hollywood	1	376	0
Lakeland	1	389	60	Jensen Beach	1	99	0
Leesburg	1	0	120	Juno Beach	1	289	60
Longwood	1	241	60	Lake Worth	2	261	60
Maitland	1	102	39	Palm Beach Gardens	1	337	100
Mount Dora	2	317	120	Palm City	1	168	42
Orlando	13	2,001	629	Pembroke Pines	1	0	120
Sanford	1	158	0	Plantation	1	328	60
Winter Haven	1	68	0	Pompano Beach	3	842	184
Winter Park	4	956	181	Port St. Lucie	1	98	30
District 3	15	2,030	427	West Palm Beach	1	84	0
Pinellas Park	2	195	0	District 8	12	1,580	294
Seminole	1	0	120	Cocoa	1	0	0
St. Petersburg	11	1,655	307	Melbourne	4	150	0
South Pasadena	1	180	0	Merritt Island	1	586	0
District 4	16	2,416	300	Palm Bay	1	158	96
Lakeland	1	183	0	Vero Beach	2	66	0
Lake Wales	1	0	100	Viera	1	620	84
Plant City	1	75	0	West Melbourne	2	0	114
Tampa	12	1,959	200	District 9	19	2,250	710
Winter Haven	1	199	0	Belleair	1	0	0
District 5	26	5,201	1,189	Brooksville	2	0	126
Bradenton	3	543	93	Clearwater	6	88	180
Cape Coral	1	172	0	Dade City	1	614	116

See footnote at end of table.   Continued . . .

Table 2.20. HOMES FOR THE AGING: HOMES, RESIDENTIAL UNITS, AND BEDS FOR HOMES
WHICH ARE MEMBERS OF THE FLORIDA ASSOCIATION OF HOMES FOR THE AGING (FAHA)
IN THE STATE, FAHA DISTRICTS, AND CITIES OF FLORIDA, 1996 (Continued)

District and city	Homes	Resi- dential units	Nursing beds	District and city	Homes	Resi- dential units	Nursing beds
District 9 (Cont.)				District 9 (Cont.)			
Dunedin	1	360	100	Zephyrhills	1	48	48
Hudson	1	70	0	District 11	13	1,830	1,830
Lecanto	1	48	0	Daytona Beach	6	477	477
New Port Richey	1	135	0	DeLand	3	468	468
Palm Harbor	2	590	140	Holly Hill	2	343	343
Port Richey	1	80	0	Orange City	1	470	470
Spring Hill	1	217	0	Port Orange	1	72	72

Note: Includes personal care units, cluster homes, adult congregate living facility units and/or assisted living units. Excludes homes in construction.
Source: Florida Association of Homes for the Aging, *1996 Directory of Members.*

Table 2.21. HOME SALES: SALES AND MEDIAN SALES PRICE OF EXISTING SINGLE-FAMILY
HOMES IN SPECIFIED METROPOLITAN STATISTICAL AREAS (MSAS)
OF FLORIDA, 1995 AND 1996

MSA	Number of homes sold			Median sales price		
	1995	1996	Per- centage change	1995 (dol- lars)	1996 (dol- lars)	Per- centage change
Florida 1/	121,789	128,515	5.5	87,700	91,800	4.7
Daytona Beach	4,551	4,665	2.5	72,300	75,400	4.3
Ft. Lauderdale	12,597	12,494	-0.8	105,900	112,300	6.0
Ft. Myers-Cape Coral 1/	3,511	3,538	0.8	86,800	86,600	-0.2
Ft. Pierce-Port St. Lucie 1/	2,583	2,754	6.6	76,900	80,100	4.2
Ft. Walton Beach 1/	2,185	2,269	3.8	93,100	94,400	1.4
Gainesville	1,890	1,928	2.0	89,900	94,200	4.8
Jacksonville 1/	8,018	8,497	6.0	83,900	90,200	7.5
Lakeland-Winter Haven 1/	1,832	1,975	7.8	68,500	74,000	8.0
Melbourne-Titusville- Palm Bay	3,890	4,289	10.3	78,000	81,000	3.8
Miami 1/	10,172	10,794	6.1	107,100	112,700	5.2
Naples	1,520	1,771	16.5	149,000	172,200	15.6
Ocala	2,206	2,606	18.1	61,200	63,800	4.2
Orlando 1/	14,015	14,695	4.9	86,100	90,300	4.9
Panama City	1,603	1,676	4.6	77,300	81,700	5.7
Pensacola	3,627	4,164	14.8	79,600	84,500	6.2
Punta Gorda	1,701	1,888	11.0	71,000	72,700	2.4
Sarasota-Bradenton 1/	5,615	6,096	8.6	99,100	102,400	3.3
Tallahassee	1,806	2,025	12.1	99,800	109,600	9.8
Tampa-St. Petersburg- Clearwater	24,954	26,143	4.8	78,000	81,100	4.0
West Palm Beach-Boca Raton	9,114	9,376	2.9	122,700	126,900	3.4

1/ Due to periodic unavailability of data, figures are adjusted for comparison
purposes.
Source: Florida Association of Realtors and University of Florida, Real Estate
Research Center, unpublished data.

University of Florida   **Bureau of Economic and Business Research**

Table 2.30. PUBLIC LODGING: LICENSED LODGINGS, APARTMENTS, ROOMING HOUSES, RENTAL CONDOMINIUMS, AND TRANSIENT APARTMENTS IN THE STATE AND COUNTIES OF FLORIDA, FISCAL YEAR 1996-97

County	Total licensed lodgings 1/		Apartment buildings		Rooming houses		Rental condominiums		Transient apartment buildings 2/	
	Number	Units	Number	Units	Number	Units	Number	Units	Number	Units
Florida	30,401	1,231,386	17,451	806,886	637	8,198	5,981	64,449	1,677	17,494
Alachua	405	23,801	343	20,028	7	73	0	0	2	116
Baker	5	166	2	59	0	0	0	0	0	0
Bay	610	18,547	111	4,492	2	14	286	4,820	4	126
Bradford	28	770	12	367	1	2	0	0	1	4
Brevard	555	29,075	343	18,659	8	81	40	1,473	53	676
Broward	3,763	132,247	2,776	98,759	34	313	43	1,461	377	4,241
Calhoun	4	111	2	88	0	0	0	0	0	0
Charlotte	137	3,126	24	798	1	2	63	835	22	228
Citrus	75	1,986	33	814	4	37	2	127	11	89
Clay	55	5,297	40	4,376	4	38	1	30	2	14
Collier	260	15,655	108	6,568	2	35	66	3,633	8	79
Columbia	85	3,122	46	1,076	2	14	0	0	4	72
Dade	6,857	224,791	6,172	173,840	131	1,557	44	2,041	9	90
De Soto	22	424	13	262	3	25	0	0	0	0
Dixie	13	188	1	32	1	9	0	0	1	7
Duval	788	72,311	643	60,966	28	319	5	40	2	27
Escambia	450	16,177	101	9,716	4	9	270	1,076	4	38
Flagler	43	1,041	9	139	4	37	10	173	3	5
Franklin	280	952	5	131	1	9	255	392	1	8
Gadsden	29	825	14	633	2	13	5	25	0	0
Gilchrist	5	95	1	60	2	6	0	0	1	1
Glades	16	238	2	33	0	0	1	8	2	8

See footnotes at end of table.

Continued . . .

Table 2.30. PUBLIC LODGING: LICENSED LODGINGS, APARTMENTS, ROOMING HOUSES, RENTAL CONDOMINIUMS, AND TRANSIENT APARTMENTS IN THE STATE AND COUNTIES OF FLORIDA, FISCAL YEAR 1996-97 (Continued)

County	Total licensed lodgings 1/		Apartment buildings		Rooming houses		Rental condominiums		Transient apartment buildings 2/	
	Number	Units	Number	Units	Number	Units	Number	Units	Number	Units
Gulf	146	594	3	113	1	12	130	357	2	15
Hamilton	17	539	7	148	0	0	0	0	1	20
Hardee	19	346	10	227	1	10	0	0	5	64
Hendry	34	690	19	319	0	0	1	14	0	0
Hernando	39	1,528	21	898	2	24	1	1	1	10
Highlands	135	3,436	67	1,495	6	44	4	212	32	504
Hillsborough	969	92,791	776	77,413	26	337	1	237	24	311
Holmes	10	286	5	93	0	0	0	0	0	0
Indian River	140	4,000	71	1,842	3	32	25	384	5	55
Jackson	34	1,224	22	667	0	0	1	10	0	0
Jefferson	20	425	10	240	5	16	0	0	1	22
Lafayette	4	70	1	36	2	26	0	0	0	0
Lake	228	6,528	112	4,111	16	137	34	143	16	146
Lee	582	25,604	237	12,160	3	18	130	5,525	51	349
Leon	382	24,710	317	18,812	7	991	2	40	2	13
Levy	52	807	11	278	4	38	8	132	6	30
Liberty	1	13	0	0	0	0	0	0	0	0
Madison	14	465	10	322	1	5	0	0	0	0
Manatee	507	14,977	143	9,952	10	67	155	1,286	128	602
Marion	198	7,872	107	4,373	6	46	1	14	11	46
Martin	113	3,529	69	1,835	4	56	9	181	5	211
Monroe	602	13,286	89	1,775	35	364	97	2,080	186	957
Nassau	78	2,882	17	682	9	60	24	1,038	2	6
Okaloosa	318	11,935	104	3,626	1	24	153	3,826	4	177

Continued . . .

See footnotes at end of table.

Table 2.30. PUBLIC LODGING: LICENSED LODGINGS, APARTMENTS, ROOMING HOUSES, RENTAL CONDOMINIUMS, AND TRANSIENT APARTMENTS IN THE STATE AND COUNTIES OF FLORIDA, FISCAL YEAR 1996-97 (Continued)

County	Total licensed lodgings 1/ Number	Units	Apartment buildings Number	Units	Rooming houses Number	Units	Rental condominiums Number	Units	Transient apartment buildings 2/ Number	Units
Okeechobee	23	572	6	136	1	14	0	0	5	60
Orange	1,270	138,578	654	73,922	38	465	333	5,571	42	799
Osceola	2,659	35,518	85	8,245	11	133	2,415	6,038	20	681
Palm Beach	1,385	63,276	993	44,887	56	1,017	20	825	100	1,442
Pasco	190	9,010	104	6,297	3	41	35	771	10	84
Pinellas	2,147	85,560	1,321	59,701	33	485	114	4,960	269	2,253
Polk	1,053	22,773	327	13,169	29	513	513	1,585	64	1,113
Putnam	52	1,380	18	760	8	50	1	23	3	25
St. Johns	210	9,082	52	2,965	29	185	44	1,768	8	47
St. Lucie	143	4,652	62	1,763	2	26	14	494	26	218
Santa Rosa	140	2,297	36	1,233	0	0	93	346	0	0
Sarasota	579	16,593	222	8,140	10	89	166	3,456	94	893
Seminole	173	27,935	137	25,076	4	29	0	0	2	10
Sumter	28	958	14	377	3	9	0	0	3	20
Suwannee	25	588	9	244	1	2	0	0	5	20
Taylor	38	791	7	282	2	2	0	0	4	29
Union	3	84	2	80	1	4	0	0	0	0
Volusia	850	37,484	360	15,909	17	211	108	3,840	31	421
Wakulla	8	165	0	0	0	0	2	25	0	0
Walton	289	4,404	10	345	6	23	256	3,132	2	12
Washington	9	204	3	42	0	0	1	1	0	0

1/ Includes hotels and motels shown separately in Table 19.60.
2/ Apartments which rent for six months or less.

Source: State of Florida, Department of Business and Professional Regulation, Division of Hotels and Restaurants, *Master File Statistics: Public Lodging and Food Service Establishments*, Fiscal Year 1996-97.

Table 2.36. MOBILE HOME AND RECREATIONAL VEHICLE TAGS: NUMBER SOLD IN THE
STATE AND COUNTIES OF FLORIDA, FISCAL YEAR 1995-96

County	Mobile homes 1/	Real proper-ty 2/	Recrea-tional vehicles	County	Mobile homes 1/	Real proper-ty 2/	Recrea-tional vehicles
Florida	506,216	33,325	197,469	Lake	17,878	904	6,527
				Lee	32,544	698	6,960
Alachua	4,003	413	2,073	Leon	6,703	813	2,168
Baker	396	375	500	Levy	905	1,163	837
Bay	4,498	668	2,918	Liberty	181	60	95
Bradford	624	158	581	Madison	1,089	264	253
Brevard	12,322	495	8,496	Manatee	24,222	711	5,119
Broward	19,510	165	7,633	Marion	13,741	1,634	6,395
Calhoun	168	151	135	Martin	5,049	230	2,377
Charlotte	8,884	166	2,919	Monroe	1,631	167	2,579
Citrus	3,796	650	3,368	Nassau	1,501	562	1,043
Clay	1,161	799	2,044	Okaloosa	2,319	409	2,329
Collier	5,901	497	2,927	Okeechobee	1,866	304	2,041
Columbia	1,525	1,016	977	Orange	15,020	290	7,467
Dade	10,960	73	7,173	Osceola	7,098	440	2,646
De Soto	1,716	129	1,240	Palm Beach	16,508	314	6,581
Dixie	144	281	337	Pasco	28,162	1,254	11,550
Duval	15,928	708	7,594	Pinellas	50,120	3,198	11,650
Escambia	4,051	555	4,365	Polk	42,472	2,268	10,771
Flagler	938	182	955	Putnam	1,446	805	1,812
Franklin	107	90	190	St. Johns	2,100	431	1,956
Gadsden	849	417	311	St. Lucie	14,623	167	2,701
Gilchrist	587	383	343	Santa Rosa	1,885	509	2,106
Glades	420	142	231	Sarasota	19,545	427	5,666
Gulf	139	107	254	Seminole	4,171	97	3,160
Hamilton	422	162	141	Sumter	2,356	343	1,772
Hardee	1,161	173	724	Suwannee	2,362	716	683
Hendry	2,422	384	804	Taylor	468	270	410
Hernando	4,896	428	2,558	Union	311	138	151
Highlands	10,428	248	3,167	Volusia	23,848	434	7,182
Hillsborough	32,756	1,234	11,216	Wakulla	411	374	429
Holmes	459	258	220	Walton	645	346	512
Indian River	9,401	45	1,801	Washington	451	262	271
Jackson	1,350	455	677	Office agency	347	94	99
Jefferson	223	138	182	Refunds	0	0	7
Lafayette	93	84	110				

1/ Includes military mobile homes.
2/ Tags sold to mobile home owners who also own the land on which the mobile home
stands. A real property tag is bought only once, not annually.

Source: State of Florida, Department of Highway Safety and Motor Vehicles, *Reve-nue Report, July 1, 1995 through June 30, 1996.*

University of Florida   **Bureau of Economic and Business Research**

VITAL STATISTICS
AND HEALTH

Abortion Rate in Counties Reporting Terminations of Pregnancy in 1996

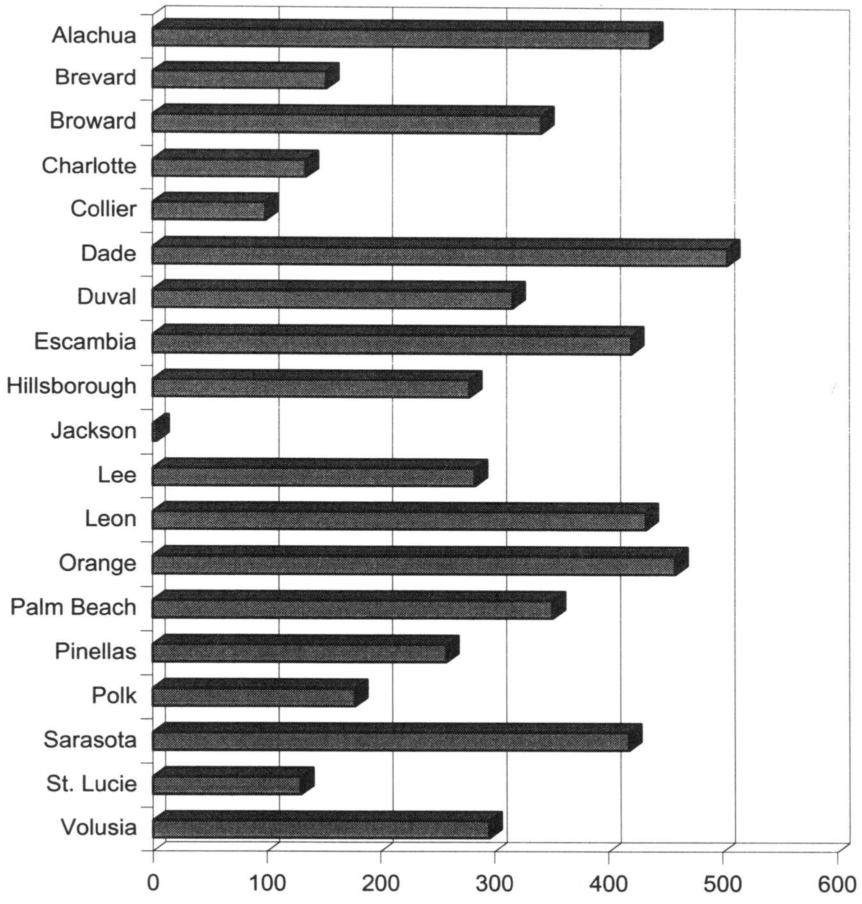

County	
Alachua	
Brevard	
Broward	
Charlotte	
Collier	
Dade	
Duval	
Escambia	
Hillsborough	
Jackson	
Lee	
Leon	
Orange	
Palm Beach	
Pinellas	
Polk	
Sarasota	
St. Lucie	
Volusia	

0   100   200   300   400   500   600

Note: Rate per 10,000 female population aged 15-44.

Source: Table 3.11

SECTION 3.00
VITAL STATISTICS AND HEALTH

TABLES LISTED BY MAJOR HEADINGS

Table 3.01. BIRTH AND DEATH RATES: RESIDENT LIVE BIRTH AND DEATH RATES BY RACE IN FLORIDA AND THE UNITED STATES, 1986 THROUGH 1996

	Birth rates						Death rates					
	Total		White		Nonwhite		Total		White		Nonwhite	
	Flor-		Flor-		Flor-		Flor-		Flor-		Flor-	
Year	ida	U.S.	ida	U.S.	ida	U.S.	ida	U.S.	ida	U.S.	ida	U.S.
1986	14.3	15.6	12.6	14.6	23.9	21.4	10.5	8.8	11.0	9.0	7.6	7.5
1987	14.5	15.7	12.8	14.6	24.3	21.7	10.5	8.8	10.9	9.0	7.9	7.5
1988	14.8	15.9	13.1	14.8	24.9	22.5	10.5	8.8	11.0	9.1	7.8	7.6
1989	15.2	16.3	13.4	15.1	24.9	23.1	10.3	8.7	10.8	8.9	7.6	7.5
1990	15.1	16.7	13.4	15.5	24.3	19.0	10.1	8.6	10.6	8.9	7.2	7.4
1991	14.6	16.3	12.9	15.4	23.9	20.6	10.2	8.6	10.7	8.9	7.3	7.3
1992	14.2	15.9	12.6	15.0	23.2	20.5	10.3	8.5	10.8	8.8	7.3	7.2
1993	14.1	15.5	12.5	14.7	22.6	19.8	10.6	8.8	11.1	9.1	7.6	7.4
1994	13.7	15.2	12.2	14.4	21.6	19.9	10.5	8.8	11.1	9.1	7.5	7.3
1995	13.3	15.0	12.0	(NA)	19.8	(NA)	10.7	8.8	11.3	9.1	7.4	7.2
1996	13.1	(NA)	11.8	(NA)	19.5	(NA)	10.5	(NA)	11.2	(NA)	7.0	(NA)

(NA) Not available.

Note: Rates per 1,000 population based on July 1 population estimates for noncensus years. Some data are revised; some 1995 or 1996 data are preliminary.

Source: U.S., Department of Commerce, Bureau of the Census, *Statistical Abstract of the United States, 1997,* annual editions and State of Florida, Department of Health, Office of Vital Statistics, Public Health Statistics Section, *Florida Vital Statistics Annual Report, 1996,* preliminary final, and previous editions.

Table 3.02. BIRTHS: NUMBER OF RESIDENT LIVE BIRTHS BY AGE OF MOTHER IN FLORIDA 1991 THROUGH 1996

Age of mother	1991	1992	1993	1994	1995	1996 A/
All ages	193,717	191,530	192,453	190,546	188,535	189,338
Less than 13	(NA)	(NA)	(NA)	24	20	25
13	(NA)	(NA)	(NA)	132	128	110
14	(NA)	(NA)	(NA)	594	588	507
15	1,559	1,598	1,635	1,646	1,583	1,542
16	3,125	3,035	3,228	3,341	3,236	3,172
17	5,087	4,910	4,856	5,151	5,166	4,791
18	7,240	6,874	6,833	6,753	6,971	6,694
19	9,255	8,758	8,455	8,524	8,112	8,596
20-24	51,544	50,703	50,420	48,540	46,865	46,331
25-29	56,974	55,097	53,612	51,017	49,649	50,496
30-34	40,442	41,043	42,545	43,423	43,689	43,339
35-39	15,216	16,013	17,166	18,053	19,020	(NA)
35-44	(NA)	(NA)	(NA)	(NA)	(NA)	23,588
40 years and over	2,433	2,684	2,891	3,295	3,472	(NA)
45 years and over	(NA)	(NA)	(NA)	(NA)	(NA)	115
Age not stated	86	74	40	53	36	32
Less than 19 years, number	17,767	17,158	17,324	17,641	17,692	16,841
Percentage of total	9.2	9.0	9.0	9.3	9.4	8.9

(NA) Not available.

A/ Preliminary.

Source: State of Florida, Department of Health, Office of Vital Statistics, Public Health Statistics Section, *Florida Vital Statistics Annual Report, 1996,* preliminary final, and previous editions.

Table 3.05. BIRTHS TO UNWED MOTHERS: RESIDENT LIVE BIRTHS AND BIRTHS
TO UNWED MOTHERS BY AGE AND RACE OF THE MOTHER IN THE STATE
AND COUNTIES OF FLORIDA, 1996

County	Total resi- dent live births	Num- ber 1/	Percent- age of total	Age of mother Under 20	Age of mother 20 and over	Race of mother White 2/	Race of mother Non- white
Florida	189,338	68,082	36.0	20,312	47,759	38,509	29,546
Alachua	2,480	853	34.4	264	589	349	504
Baker	282	105	37.2	33	72	76	29
Bay	1,958	636	32.5	209	427	407	229
Bradford	323	113	35.0	47	66	63	50
Brevard	5,004	1,455	29.1	438	1,017	1,020	434
Broward	19,927	6,624	33.2	1,702	4,921	2,809	3,813
Calhoun	144	45	31.3	15	30	28	17
Charlotte	993	312	31.4	91	221	276	36
Citrus	871	286	32.8	81	205	263	23
Clay	1,644	406	24.7	137	269	328	78
Collier	2,495	902	36.2	259	642	701	201
Columbia	670	269	40.1	97	171	163	106
Dade	31,843	12,973	40.7	3,147	9,824	6,480	6,481
De Soto	371	147	39.6	57	90	88	59
Dixie	150	62	41.3	25	37	51	11
Duval	11,893	4,204	35.3	1,409	2,794	1,675	2,527
Escambia	3,850	1,548	40.2	505	1,043	649	899
Flagler	309	102	33.0	40	62	67	35
Franklin	98	30	30.6	11	19	15	15
Gadsden	655	385	58.8	144	241	73	312
Gilchrist	137	47	34.3	19	28	39	8
Glades	78	30	38.5	12	18	17	13
Gulf	164	65	39.6	24	41	38	27
Hamilton	149	64	43.0	27	37	24	40
Hardee	462	148	32.0	62	86	126	22
Hendry	581	273	47.0	109	164	186	87
Hernando	1,014	363	35.8	123	240	310	53
Highlands	854	351	41.1	113	238	225	126
Hillsborough	13,673	5,116	37.4	1,665	3,450	3,025	2,087
Holmes	203	64	31.5	24	40	57	7
Indian River	979	335	34.2	117	218	207	128
Jackson	547	199	36.4	63	136	99	100
Jefferson	155	77	49.7	28	49	12	65
Lafayette	71	24	33.8	7	17	14	10
Lake	1,949	724	37.1	261	463	513	211

See footnotes at end of table.   Continued . . .

University of Florida   **Bureau of Economic and Business Research**

Table 3.05. BIRTHS TO UNWED MOTHERS: RESIDENT LIVE BIRTHS AND BIRTHS
TO UNWED MOTHERS BY AGE AND RACE OF THE MOTHER IN THE STATE
AND COUNTIES OF FLORIDA, 1996 (Continued)

County	Total resident live births	Births to unwed mothers					
		Number 1/	Percentage of total	Age of mother		Race of mother	
				Under 20	20 and over	White 2/	Non-white
Lee	4,450	1,644	36.9	528	1,116	1,200	444
Leon	2,789	929	33.3	279	650	292	636
Levy	362	135	37.3	62	73	99	36
Liberty	80	27	33.8	7	20	18	9
Madison	210	113	53.8	36	77	28	85
Manatee	2,880	1,128	39.2	392	736	803	325
Marion	2,503	970	38.8	346	624	613	356
Martin	1,132	370	32.7	102	268	248	122
Monroe	871	280	32.1	52	228	232	48
Nassau	698	193	27.7	67	126	148	45
Okaloosa	2,363	574	24.3	170	404	399	175
Okeechobee	435	152	34.9	62	90	126	26
Orange	11,737	4,284	36.5	1,330	2,953	2,395	1,889
Osceola	2,041	701	34.3	231	470	596	105
Palm Beach	12,582	4,220	33.5	1,168	3,050	2,135	2,083
Pasco	3,214	1,076	33.5	343	733	988	88
Pinellas	9,177	3,289	35.8	926	2,362	2,063	1,225
Polk	6,193	2,662	43.0	925	1,737	1,665	997
Putnam	905	383	42.3	145	238	197	186
St. Johns	1,148	322	28.0	104	218	221	101
St. Lucie	2,145	844	39.3	257	587	423	420
Santa Rosa	1,401	349	24.9	138	211	298	51
Sarasota	2,518	741	29.4	215	526	568	173
Seminole	4,367	1,167	26.7	364	803	789	378
Sumter	380	167	43.9	68	99	108	59
Suwannee	380	128	33.7	48	80	88	40
Taylor	228	78	34.2	24	54	39	39
Union	120	38	31.7	16	22	27	11
Volusia	4,202	1,496	35.6	451	1,045	1,032	464
Wakulla	224	71	31.7	21	50	54	17
Walton	376	117	31.1	41	76	90	27
Washington	251	97	38.6	29	68	54	43

1/ Includes data for mothers whose age was not stated.
2/ Persons designating "Hispanic" as a race were counted as white.
Correction: Data for births to unwed nonwhite mothers were erroneously duplicated as births to unwed white mothers in the 1996 *Abstract*. See source for births to unwed white mothers in 1995.
Source: State of Florida, Department of Health, Office of Vital Statistics, Public Health Statistics Section, *Florida Vital Statistics Annual Report, 1996*, preliminary final.

University of Florida   **Bureau of Economic and Business Research**

Table 3.06. BIRTHS TO TEENAGERS: NUMBER, PERCENTAGE, AND RATE BY RACE OF THE MOTHER IN THE STATE AND COUNTIES OF FLORIDA, 1996

| | Births to mothers under age 20 | | | | Teenage birth rate to mothers aged 15-19 | |
| | White | | Nonwhite | | | |
County	Number	As a percentage of all white births	Number	As a percentage of all nonwhite births	White A/	Nonwhite B/
Florida	15,554	10.9	9,875	21.1	48.4	102.2
Alachua	146	8.8	183	22.5	19.4	71.7
Baker	48	19.8	3	7.7	66.3	32.6
Bay	221	13.9	84	22.8	58.2	98.9
Bradford	45	17.2	21	33.9	74.6	152.2
Brevard	396	9.3	157	20.8	36.6	85.4
Broward	828	6.3	1,108	16.5	34.7	103.0
Calhoun	15	12.3	10	45.5	39.4	130.4
Charlotte	106	11.6	12	14.8	40.7	45.5
Citrus	109	13.3	5	9.6	48.4	34.7
Clay	171	11.6	35	20.6	40.4	79.8
Collier	302	13.9	65	20.3	70.5	177.7
Columbia	85	16.3	45	30.2	57.0	102.9
Dade	1,993	9.2	1,848	18.4	45.6	90.7
De Soto	59	20.1	28	36.4	101.0	169.8
Dixie	34	25.4	4	25.0	95.4	173.9
Duval	851	11.2	916	21.5	55.8	114.2
Escambia	296	11.7	330	25.2	42.0	107.7
Flagler	28	10.9	18	36.0	35.0	135.3
Franklin	18	22.8	6	31.6	74.7	111.1
Gadsden	36	14.6	123	30.1	80.8	92.3
Gilchrist	25	19.7	2	20.0	71.0	66.7
Glades	9	15.5	7	35.0	44.8	82.4
Gulf	31	23.8	11	33.3	86.1	114.6
Hamilton	27	29.7	14	24.1	87.0	55.8
Hardee	91	21.2	14	42.4	126.9	259.3
Hendry	101	21.4	35	32.4	121.9	142.9
Hernando	150	16.0	26	32.9	57.6	118.7
Highlands	106	15.5	47	27.3	73.3	117.2
Hillsborough	1,323	12.6	741	23.6	59.7	127.3
Holmes	39	20.5	1	7.7	78.5	32.3
Indian River	97	12.2	51	28.2	47.5	24.5
Jackson	61	15.6	35	22.6	55.5	67.1
Jefferson	6	7.6	27	35.5	22.0	103.2
Lafayette	3	4.9	5	50.0	16.8	27.9
Lake	271	16.5	85	27.6	75.1	120.4

See footnotes at end of table.   Continued . . .

University of Florida   **Bureau of Economic and Business Research**

Table 3.06. BIRTHS TO TEENAGERS: NUMBER, PERCENTAGE, AND RATE BY RACE OF THE MOTHER IN THE STATE AND COUNTIES OF FLORIDA, 1996 (Continued)

| | Births to mothers under age 20 | | | | Teenage birth rate to mothers aged 15-19 | |
| | White | | Nonwhite | | | |
County	Number	As a percentage of all white births	Number	As a percentage of all nonwhite births	White A/	Nonwhite B/
Lee	437	11.4	188	31.0	55.6	153.0
Leon	137	7.8	191	18.5	17.3	41.8
Levy	69	22.0	19	39.6	90.2	127.5
Liberty	14	20.0	0	0.0	72.2	0.0
Madison	14	13.7	27	25.0	44.4	89.7
Manatee	371	15.4	126	27.3	78.7	159.1
Marion	302	15.4	138	25.4	59.5	115.1
Martin	95	10.1	33	17.3	42.7	108.3
Monroe	65	8.3	14	15.9	43.2	88.1
Nassau	100	16.1	15	20.0	63.7	74.6
Okaloosa	216	11.0	60	15.3	50.6	63.5
Okeechobee	84	21.4	15	35.7	84.0	135.1
Orange	936	10.9	637	20.4	47.9	99.8
Osceola	269	14.9	47	19.7	67.8	99.4
Palm Beach	718	7.8	654	19.4	39.3	123.0
Pasco	417	13.7	36	21.8	62.9	92.8
Pinellas	685	9.3	401	22.4	39.4	115.4
Polk	816	16.9	385	28.4	74.5	33.3
Putnam	126	19.2	85	34.1	76.4	134.1
St. Johns	96	9.7	35	22.7	34.7	99.1
St. Lucie	147	9.6	159	26.1	41.4	125.6
Santa Rosa	178	13.9	22	17.9	60.2	88.4
Sarasota	183	8.1	74	29.2	33.3	12.4
Seminole	288	7.8	154	23.4	31.7	104.4
Sumter	54	17.8	30	39.5	58.5	118.4
Suwannee	60	19.1	16	24.2	63.3	84.7
Taylor	28	15.9	10	19.2	57.7	69.4
Union	19	17.9	3	21.4	75.4	65.2
Volusia	389	11.1	167	24.3	41.4	92.0
Wakulla	23	11.9	5	16.7	42.6	48.5
Walton	60	18.0	14	33.3	65.2	135.9
Washington	31	16.5	13	20.6	59.3	78.3

A/ Per 1,000 female white population aged 15-19.
B/ Per 1,000 female nonwhite population aged 15-19.
Note: Resident live births. Persons designating "Hispanic" as a race were counted as white.

Source: State of Florida, Department of Health, Office of Vital Statistics, Public Health Statistics Section, *Florida Vital Statistics Annual Report, 1996*, preliminary final.

Table 3.07. ABORTIONS: REPORTED TERMINATIONS OF PREGNANCY IN FLORIDA 1985 THROUGH 1996

Year	Induced abortions 2/	Resident live births	Total known pregnancies 1/ Number	Total known pregnancies 1/ Rate per 100 women aged 15-44	Abortion rate per 100 pregnancies
1985	53,011	163,732	218,315	9.2	24.3
1986	50,262	167,628	219,491	9.0	22.9
1987	52,697	175,072	229,387	9.0	23.0
1988	65,153	183,998	250,889	9.5	26.0
1989	62,626	192,887	257,315	9.5	24.3
1990	66,073	199,146	267,030	9.7	24.7
1991	71,254	193,717	266,663	9.6	26.7
1992	69,285	191,530	262,313	9.3	26.4
1993	70,069	192,453	263,969	9.3	26.5
1994	73,394	190,546	265,459	9.3	27.6
1995	74,749	188,535	264,815	9.0	28.2
1996	80,040	189,338	270,856	9.3	29.6

1/ Includes induced abortions, total resident births, and total reported resident fetal deaths.
2/ Abortions have been legal in Florida since April 1972.
Note: Some data may be revised.
Source: State of Florida, Department of Health, Office of Vital Statistics, Public Health Statistics Section, *Florida Vital Statistics Annual Report, 1996*, preliminary final, previous editions, and unpublished data.

Table 3.08. INFANT DEATHS: NUMBER AND RATE OF RESIDENT INFANT DEATHS BY RACE IN FLORIDA, 1985 THROUGH 1996

Year	Number of deaths Total 1/	Number of deaths White 2/	Number of deaths Non-white	Mortality rate per 1,000 live births Total 1/	Mortality rate per 1,000 live births White 2/	Mortality rate per 1,000 live births Non-white
1985	1,846	1,128	718	11.3	9.1	17.8
1986	1,837	1,097	739	11.0	8.7	18.0
1987	1,844	1,039	802	10.5	7.9	18.6
1988	1,949	1,167	782	10.6	8.5	17.0
1989	1,899	1,141	756	9.8	7.9	15.8
1990	1,909	1,121	786	9.6	7.5	16.0
1991	1,726	966	758	8.9	6.7	15.6
1992	1,685	987	695	8.8	6.9	14.4
1993	1,654	951	699	8.6	6.6	14.5
1994	1,540	927	611	8.1	6.5	12.9
1995	1,402	840	562	7.4	5.9	12.1
1996	1,405	821	583	7.4	5.8	12.4

1/ Unknown race included in total only.
2/ Persons designating "Hispanic" as a race were counted as white.
Note: Infants are considered to be less than one year. Some data may be revised.
Source: State of Florida, Department of Health, Office of Vital Statistics, Public Health Statistics Section, *Florida Vital Statistics Annual Report, 1996*, preliminary final, previous editions, and unpublished data.

Table 3.09. BIRTHS AND DEATHS: NUMBER OF RESIDENT LIVE BIRTHS AND DEATHS
1995 AND 1996, AND NUMBER BY RACE, 1996, IN THE STATE AND COUNTIES
OF FLORIDA

County	Number of births 1995	Number of births, 1996 Total 1/	White 2/	Non-white	Number of deaths 1995	Number of deaths, 1996 Total 1/	White 2/	Non-white
Florida	188,535	189,338	142,391	46,848	151,619	152,697	135,773	16,858
Alachua	2,444	2,480	1,666	813	1,360	1,406	1,080	326
Baker	308	282	243	39	155	170	152	18
Bay	1,997	1,958	1,585	368	1,248	1,282	1,138	143
Bradford	270	323	261	62	252	279	239	40
Brevard	4,908	5,004	4,247	756	4,274	4,454	4,185	269
Broward	20,059	19,927	13,219	6,696	15,804	15,921	14,244	1,665
Calhoun	137	144	122	22	132	144	129	15
Charlotte	932	993	912	81	1,950	1,900	1,841	59
Citrus	850	871	819	52	1,727	1,713	1,694	19
Clay	1,647	1,644	1,474	170	886	879	835	43
Collier	2,478	2,495	2,175	320	1,780	1,965	1,900	65
Columbia	660	670	521	149	496	535	435	100
Dade	32,089	31,843	21,745	10,062	19,181	18,501	15,020	3,472
De Soto	381	371	294	77	311	297	268	29
Dixie	160	150	134	16	124	117	110	7
Duval	11,541	11,893	7,632	4,257	6,261	6,205	4,520	1,682
Escambia	3,830	3,850	2,540	1,310	2,466	2,600	2,059	540
Flagler	322	309	258	50	455	503	443	60
Franklin	94	98	79	19	136	108	102	6
Gadsden	640	655	246	408	440	438	189	249
Gilchrist	150	137	127	10	115	143	136	7
Glades	63	78	58	20	114	108	92	16
Gulf	125	164	130	33	143	164	138	26
Hamilton	148	149	91	58	120	133	89	44
Hardee	444	462	429	33	202	207	191	16
Hendry	608	581	473	108	255	263	223	40
Hernando	1,028	1,014	935	79	1,718	1,820	1,780	40
Highlands	828	854	682	172	1,266	1,131	1,056	74
Hillsborough	13,499	13,673	10,521	3,136	8,060	8,013	6,932	1,078
Holmes	187	203	190	13	198	240	232	8
Indian River	959	979	798	181	1,281	1,367	1,279	88
Jackson	473	547	392	155	475	489	382	107
Jefferson	158	155	79	76	140	120	68	52
Lafayette	66	71	61	10	47	52	50	2
Lake	2,027	1,949	1,641	308	2,485	2,490	2,334	155
Lee	4,270	4,450	3,841	607	4,480	4,645	4,438	203

See footnotes at end of table.   Continued . . .

Table 3.09. BIRTHS AND DEATHS: NUMBER OF RESIDENT LIVE BIRTHS AND DEATHS 1995 AND 1996, AND NUMBER BY RACE, 1996, IN THE STATE AND COUNTIES OF FLORIDA (Continued)

County	Number of births 1995	Number of births, 1996 Total 1/	White 2/	Non-white	Number of deaths 1995	Number of deaths, 1996 Total 1/	White 2/	Non-white
Leon	2,785	2,789	1,753	1,035	1,312	1,312	952	359
Levy	346	362	314	48	365	372	342	30
Liberty	58	80	70	10	52	52	42	10
Madison	182	210	102	108	184	180	105	75
Manatee	2,834	2,880	2,416	462	3,142	3,069	2,906	162
Marion	2,670	2,503	1,958	544	2,866	3,030	2,762	268
Martin	1,100	1,132	941	191	1,475	1,504	1,451	53
Monroe	830	871	783	88	724	741	697	44
Nassau	696	698	622	75	410	426	382	44
Okaloosa	2,450	2,363	1,970	393	1,165	1,127	1,032	94
Okeechobee	496	435	393	42	346	367	337	30
Orange	11,639	11,737	8,611	3,124	5,599	5,702	4,755	945
Osceola	2,009	2,041	1,801	238	1,191	1,135	1,069	66
Palm Beach	12,281	12,582	9,203	3,373	11,742	11,890	10,805	1,074
Pasco	3,339	3,214	3,048	165	4,814	4,974	4,918	55
Pinellas	9,237	9,177	7,382	1,794	12,381	12,424	11,756	665
Polk	6,145	6,193	4,838	1,354	4,818	4,816	4,266	548
Putnam	941	905	656	249	816	835	718	117
St. Johns	1,158	1,148	994	154	952	1,032	918	113
St. Lucie	2,110	2,145	1,534	610	2,047	1,993	1,694	298
Santa Rosa	1,361	1,401	1,278	123	661	762	729	33
Sarasota	2,505	2,518	2,265	253	4,479	4,528	4,385	142
Seminole	4,374	4,367	3,708	659	2,210	2,213	1,977	235
Sumter	424	380	304	76	506	442	396	46
Suwannee	352	380	314	66	371	398	343	55
Taylor	213	228	176	52	217	202	159	43
Union	129	120	106	14	188	165	123	42
Volusia	4,301	4,202	3,515	687	5,359	5,466	5,092	372
Wakulla	208	224	194	30	156	154	131	23
Walton	358	376	334	42	322	362	335	26
Washington	224	251	188	63	212	222	193	28

1/ Unknown race included in total only.
2/ Persons designating "Hispanic" as a race were counted as white.
Note: Data are for births and deaths occurring to residents of the specified area regardless of place of occurrence.

Source: State of Florida, Department of Health, Office of Vital Statistics, Public Health Statistics Section, *Florida Vital Statistics Annual Report, 1996*, preliminary final, and previous edition.

Table 3.10. BIRTH AND DEATH RATES: RESIDENT LIVE BIRTH AND DEATH RATES BY RACE IN THE STATE AND COUNTIES OF FLORIDA, 1996

County	Birth rate			Death rate		
	Total	White 1/	Non-white	Total	White 1/	Non-white
Florida	13.1	11.8	19.5	10.5	11.2	7.0
Alachua	12.3	10.5	18.7	7.0	6.8	7.5
Baker	13.6	13.8	12.2	8.2	8.7	5.6
Bay	13.8	13.0	17.8	9.0	9.4	6.9
Bradford	13.1	13.8	10.7	11.3	12.6	6.9
Brevard	11.0	10.4	15.8	9.8	10.3	5.6
Broward	14.3	12.0	23.2	11.4	12.9	5.8
Calhoun	11.7	12.2	9.3	11.7	13.0	6.3
Charlotte	7.5	7.3	10.3	14.3	14.8	7.5
Citrus	7.9	7.7	14.2	15.6	16.0	5.2
Clay	13.0	12.8	15.0	6.9	7.2	3.8
Collier	12.6	11.7	25.4	9.9	10.3	5.2
Columbia	12.8	12.3	14.7	10.2	10.3	9.9
Dade	15.6	14.2	20.1	9.1	9.8	6.9
De Soto	13.6	13.5	13.8	10.9	12.3	5.2
Dixie	11.7	11.7	11.6	9.1	9.6	5.1
Duval	16.4	14.7	20.4	8.5	8.7	8.1
Escambia	13.4	11.6	19.1	9.1	9.4	7.9
Flagler	7.7	7.2	11.4	12.5	12.3	13.7
Franklin	9.4	9.2	10.4	10.4	11.9	3.3
Gadsden	14.3	12.7	15.5	9.6	9.7	9.4
Gilchrist	11.0	11.4	7.5	11.5	12.2	5.2
Glades	8.2	7.8	9.9	11.4	12.4	7.9
Gulf	11.9	12.5	9.8	11.9	13.3	7.7
Hamilton	11.0	11.1	10.9	9.8	10.8	8.3
Hardee	20.6	21.7	12.2	9.2	9.7	5.9
Hendry	19.1	19.9	16.1	8.6	9.4	6.0
Hernando	8.2	8.0	12.7	14.7	15.2	6.4
Highlands	10.8	9.8	18.5	14.3	15.1	7.9
Hillsborough	15.0	13.8	21.1	8.8	9.1	7.2
Holmes	11.7	12.1	7.9	13.9	14.8	4.9
Indian River	9.5	8.5	19.1	13.2	13.6	9.3
Jackson	11.4	11.3	11.9	10.2	11.0	8.2
Jefferson	11.3	9.9	13.5	8.8	8.5	9.2
Lafayette	10.1	11.0	6.7	7.4	9.0	1.3
Lake	10.6	9.9	16.4	13.5	14.1	8.3
Lee	11.4	10.7	19.2	11.9	12.4	6.4

See footnotes at end of table.   Continued . . .

University of Florida   **Bureau of Economic and Business Research**

Table 3.10. BIRTH AND DEATH RATES: RESIDENT LIVE BIRTH AND DEATH RATES BY RACE IN THE STATE AND COUNTIES OF FLORIDA, 1996 (Continued)

| | | Birth rate | | | Death rate | |
| | | White | Non- | | | White | Non- |
County	Total	1/	white	Total	1/	white
Leon	12.5	10.7	17.4	5.9	5.8	6.1
Levy	11.7	11.7	12.2	12.1	12.7	7.6
Liberty	10.9	12.5	5.8	7.1	7.5	5.8
Madison	11.3	9.6	13.6	9.7	9.9	9.5
Manatee	12.1	11.2	20.6	12.9	13.4	7.2
Marion	10.7	9.8	16.9	13.0	13.8	8.3
Martin	9.8	8.9	19.1	13.0	13.7	5.3
Monroe	10.4	10.1	13.9	8.8	9.0	7.0
Nassau	13.7	13.5	14.7	8.3	8.3	8.6
Okaloosa	14.2	13.7	17.2	6.8	7.2	4.1
Okeechobee	12.7	12.6	13.6	10.7	10.8	9.7
Orange	14.9	14.0	18.6	7.3	7.7	5.6
Osceola	14.1	13.9	15.9	7.9	8.3	4.4
Palm Beach	12.7	10.9	22.6	12.0	12.8	7.2
Pasco	10.3	10.1	13.9	15.9	16.4	4.6
Pinellas	10.5	9.4	20.5	14.2	14.9	7.6
Polk	13.7	12.5	20.6	10.6	11.0	8.3
Putnam	12.9	11.4	19.7	11.9	12.4	9.3
St. Johns	11.1	10.6	16.7	10.0	9.8	12.3
St. Lucie	12.0	10.3	20.7	11.2	11.4	10.1
Santa Rosa	14.0	13.7	16.5	7.6	7.8	4.4
Sarasota	8.2	7.8	14.2	14.7	15.2	7.9
Seminole	13.1	12.6	16.3	6.6	6.7	5.8
Sumter	9.3	9.5	8.8	10.8	12.3	5.3
Suwannee	12.1	11.5	15.4	12.6	12.6	12.9
Taylor	12.1	11.9	12.8	10.7	10.8	10.6
Union	9.3	11.5	3.8	12.8	13.4	11.3
Volusia	10.2	9.6	15.4	13.3	13.9	8.3
Wakulla	12.2	12.4	11.2	8.4	8.4	8.6
Walton	10.8	10.6	13.1	10.4	10.7	8.1
Washington	12.7	11.7	16.8	11.2	12.0	7.5

1/ Persons designating "Hispanic" as a race were counted as white.
Note: Rates per 1,000 population, July 1, 1996. Data are for births and deaths occurring to residents of the specified area regardless of place of occurrence.

Source: State of Florida, Department of Health, Office of Vital Statistics, Public Health Statistics Section, *Florida Vital Statistics Annual Report, 1996*, preliminary final.

Table 3.11. ABORTIONS: REPORTED TERMINATIONS OF PREGNANCY IN THE STATE
AND COUNTIES OF FLORIDA, 1990 THROUGH 1996

County	1990	1991	1992	1993	1994	1995	1996 Number	Rate 1/
Florida	66,073	71,254	69,285	70,069	73,394	74,749	80,040	274.4
Alachua	3,070	2,943	2,708	2,684	2,473	2,552	2,454	436.9
Bay	28	57	96	82	65	0	0	0.0
Brevard	1,886	1,799	1,325	1,300	1,418	1,467	1,363	152.3
Broward	8,398	7,982	7,452	7,919	8,199	8,668	9,662	341.6
Charlotte	0	1	1	228	174	207	245	134.4
Collier	382	302	152	271	314	306	325	99.1
Dade	10,720	13,934	14,344	18,046	18,180	20,612	22,254	504.3
De Soto	0	0	0	1	0	0	0	0.0
Duval	5,820	6,079	6,012	5,973	5,451	4,671	5,363	316.4
Escambia	2,002	2,080	1,935	2,116	2,664	2,531	2,698	420.3
Hillsborough	5,425	5,225	5,362	5,524	5,541	5,425	5,711	278.1
Jackson	0	2	3	1	1	0	3	3.2
Lee	1,874	2,131	1,937	1,725	1,748	1,674	1,879	283.1
Leon	4,128	3,220	2,858	3,063	3,018	2,886	2,787	433.1
Manatee	0	0	0	0	1	0	0	0.0
Marion	0	0	0	2	0	1	0	0.0
Monroe	2	0	5	1	1	0	0	0.0
Okaloosa	920	805	848	515	0	0	0	0.0
Orange	6,045	7,365	6,690	4,447	7,063	7,226	8,559	459.0
Palm Beach	4,277	4,219	4,587	4,860	5,934	6,086	6,396	351.6
Pinellas	5,769	5,562	5,239	5,026	4,601	4,232	4,181	257.9
Polk	1,513	1,554	1,576	1,466	1,459	1,452	1,540	177.6
St. Lucie	863	973	932	1,069	509	352	421	130.0
Santa Rosa	0	0	0	0	1	0	0	0.0
Sarasota	2,441	2,236	2,067	1,934	2,011	1,896	1,938	418.1
Seminole	320	389	535	579	0	0	0	0.0
Volusia	190	2,396	2,621	1,237	2,568	2,505	2,261	295.5

1/ Rate per 10,000 female population aged 15-44.
Note: Only counties reporting induced terminations of pregnancy are shown.

Source: State of Florida, Department of Health, Office of Vital Statistics, Public Health Statistics Section, unpublished data.

Table 3.15. DEATHS: DEATH RATES BY LEADING CAUSE IN THE STATE, LOCAL HEALTH
COUNCILS DISTRICTS, AND COUNTIES OF FLORIDA, 1991 TO 1995

(rate per 100,000 population)

District and county	All causes 1/	Heart disease	Cancer	Stroke	Lung disease	Pneumonia and influenza	HIV/ AIDS	Diabetes	Motor vehicle crashes
Florida	498.4	133.4	128.6	24.3	19.7	9.6	26.2	11.0	18.4
Northwest--1	538.0	153.8	139.9	30.1	23.0	12.3	10.7	12.9	17.8
Escambia	568.0	151.4	146.9	34.3	23.1	11.5	16.5	15.3	15.4
Okaloosa	504.2	156.4	139.4	21.9	23.8	14.0	4.4	9.8	14.4
Santa Rosa	508.2	151.2	123.8	31.1	24.8	12.4	6.0	11.9	26.8
Walton	544.8	171.2	129.6	25.6	17.9	12.1	8.9	10.6	31.4
Big Bend--2	547.2	143.8	138.6	28.5	26.8	11.0	10.9	15.3	22.4
Bay	539.8	138.8	144.1	23.7	33.7	12.0	11.9	12.0	16.6
Calhoun	659.6	176.7	156.4	29.5	37.5	11.3	1.7	22.5	42.0
Franklin	576.8	150.7	149.0	30.2	28.1	17.7	5.6	24.6	20.1
Gadsden	656.5	170.0	147.8	43.2	22.9	14.7	14.2	28.2	37.2
Gulf	631.7	176.8	152.5	33.7	26.3	11.8	2.1	16.3	28.2
Holmes	620.5	187.4	140.5	21.3	31.3	11.7	6.3	20.1	49.5
Jackson	552.7	163.3	126.5	25.0	22.6	10.7	6.5	16.2	30.6
Jefferson	549.8	135.2	137.0	41.9	20.2	12.6	15.6	15.0	33.4
Leon	485.9	114.1	127.8	30.4	21.4	7.5	12.7	12.4	15.5
Liberty	527.0	139.7	144.3	21.7	25.5	7.7	6.1	12.2	13.0
Madison	587.7	174.8	131.0	40.4	16.1	11.2	8.1	13.2	29.9
Taylor	666.1	176.7	171.7	30.6	35.9	9.5	7.9	28.3	37.5
Wakulla	539.4	133.4	159.9	15.5	29.6	7.5	9.1	18.5	37.5
Washington	593.0	176.2	138.9	22.8	34.2	18.8	9.3	12.0	27.5
North Central--3	517.1	137.5	138.1	28.0	21.7	8.7	15.7	12.1	25.2
Alachua	533.6	117.4	137.6	30.0	20.1	12.5	15.7	17.5	16.4
Bradford	659.8	155.9	173.1	41.6	35.0	15.0	17.9	19.8	26.2
Citrus	471.0	139.1	137.0	22.9	19.1	8.6	6.5	9.2	25.0
Columbia	588.5	166.0	136.9	35.6	39.2	8.4	10.5	15.4	29.0
Dixie	563.6	144.1	157.3	32.7	26.9	11.2	3.7	11.0	35.7
Gilchrist	577.6	143.8	140.4	33.0	32.5	6.9	6.4	18.3	41.0
Hamilton	600.3	165.0	175.9	28.6	21.0	23.4	9.1	12.2	25.5
Hernando	460.8	125.2	132.6	20.2	17.2	7.3	11.4	10.4	24.5
Lafayette	515.6	134.6	113.8	36.1	24.0	6.2	2.8	24.1	28.3
Lake	480.5	131.1	136.2	25.7	19.1	8.2	10.6	10.0	24.3
Levy	551.0	131.7	151.9	27.5	22.5	10.4	6.2	15.5	24.6
Marion	518.5	140.7	138.5	34.8	20.9	6.4	12.9	12.2	29.4
Putnam	602.4	144.6	149.2	25.2	27.7	12.2	10.1	13.3	38.9
Sumter	555.5	176.4	131.8	26.7	24.8	11.7	12.5	10.7	32.5
Suwannee	634.6	166.4	142.2	37.9	41.8	9.7	16.5	18.2	42.1
Union 2/	1,018.6	205.3	227.2	30.3	33.6	15.6	266.7	15.3	24.7
Northeast Central--4	543.2	148.9	141.7	27.0	25.0	12.2	16.3	12.5	17.7
Baker	628.6	166.6	163.1	33.3	48.4	17.2	4.1	12.2	20.6
Clay	527.0	157.7	142.9	24.7	27.8	12.6	7.1	10.3	18.7
Duval	593.0	160.9	149.5	31.0	28.0	14.7	20.1	14.9	15.6
Flagler	457.1	119.5	123.3	16.6	15.3	4.8	15.9	12.1	25.6
Nassau	593.1	166.7	152.6	25.8	29.9	17.0	7.2	15.2	32.6
St. Johns	488.6	116.3	141.4	23.3	20.1	9.4	11.8	6.6	17.7
Volusia	508.5	144.2	134.0	25.4	22.3	10.4	14.8	11.5	19.3

See footnotes at end of table.   Continued . . .

Table 3.15. DEATHS: DEATH RATES BY LEADING CAUSE IN THE STATE, LOCAL HEALTH COUNCILS DISTRICTS, AND COUNTIES OF FLORIDA, 1991 TO 1995 (Continued)

(rate per 100,000 population)

District and county	All causes 1/	Heart disease	Cancer	Stroke	Lung disease	Pneumonia and influenza	HIV/ AIDS	Diabetes	Motor vehicle crashes
Suncoast--5	483.2	129.8	125.9	23.9	19.6	9.2	18.5	9.5	15.4
Pasco	476.8	129.4	126.1	20.0	20.3	9.2	11.0	10.4	21.6
Pinellas	486.2	130.1	125.9	25.4	19.3	9.2	20.7	9.2	13.5
West Central--6	514.1	138.6	130.9	26.0	23.1	9.5	21.0	11.9	22.7
Hardee	524.7	142.7	117.2	24.8	30.4	14.5	4.8	14.2	37.7
Highlands	509.5	124.8	132.8	25.2	26.6	10.3	13.2	13.8	32.2
Hillsborough	550.6	148.3	140.0	28.6	25.8	10.5	23.9	13.4	20.8
Manatee	454.4	120.7	124.4	23.8	19.2	7.5	21.0	7.7	18.9
Polk	510.3	142.3	124.9	24.2	21.1	10.1	16.2	12.5	27.1
East Central--7	469.3	128.7	131.0	22.3	21.8	10.4	17.0	11.3	14.7
Brevard	458.6	123.1	135.1	21.1	22.1	9.5	11.8	10.1	15.6
Orange	493.6	133.7	134.6	24.1	21.2	11.4	23.3	12.0	13.9
Osceola	457.0	136.8	111.6	20.5	24.6	10.1	13.4	12.1	22.7
Seminole	443.3	126.5	126.3	21.7	21.6	9.8	10.7	11.7	12.5
Southwest--8	437.6	111.9	115.8	20.5	16.1	8.8	18.3	8.5	21.9
Charlotte	416.5	113.2	119.3	17.1	13.7	15.6	13.1	10.8	18.2
Collier	393.8	92.7	108.4	15.4	15.5	6.2	16.9	7.1	24.8
De Soto	566.3	136.1	142.9	25.3	25.2	10.5	6.4	10.2	35.6
Glades	495.7	132.8	118.3	24.3	20.1	6.8	13.6	15.8	40.0
Hendry	623.1	182.5	133.0	22.4	16.6	8.6	22.8	24.7	50.0
Lee	452.1	120.9	119.0	19.3	16.9	7.9	22.7	9.0	22.2
Sarasota	422.7	105.5	111.5	24.6	15.8	7.9	16.1	6.7	15.3
Treasure Coast--9	466.9	122.1	124.4	22.1	16.1	7.4	32.2	8.4	19.3
Indian River	439.4	109.9	132.0	27.7	19.5	7.1	12.2	5.3	21.7
Martin	443.1	114.5	130.9	19.8	19.1	6.0	13.5	6.8	20.2
Okeechobee	563.5	154.0	150.3	20.5	28.1	14.5	11.2	11.2	31.6
Palm Beach	460.9	119.5	119.7	21.7	14.8	7.4	36.8	8.8	18.1
St. Lucie	513.0	143.6	136.8	21.7	16.8	7.5	32.0	9.5	22.2
Broward Regional--10	505.2	134.6	129.6	23.2	17.0	7.1	45.7	10.7	15.3
Broward	505.2	134.6	129.6	23.2	17.0	7.1	45.7	10.7	15.3
South--11	534.0	142.7	120.8	24.0	16.4	11.9	49.1	13.0	16.3
Dade	536.9	145.0	120.6	24.1	16.4	12.1	49.2	13.2	16.2
Monroe	470.8	92.0	124.1	21.7	15.2	7.9	48.0	7.3	18.5

HIV/AIDS Human Immunodeficiency Virus/Acquired Immunodeficiency Syndrome.
1/ Includes causes not shown separately.
2/ The Florida Department of Corrections health center is located in Union County, which may account for some larger rates than exhibited in other counties.
Note: Rates are based on Office of the Governor July 1, 1993, population estimates printed in March 1996. Local health councils were established in 1982 by the legislature to serve 11 planning districts throughout the state. These councils are responsible for establishing and maintaining the district health plans.

Source: State of Florida, Agency for Health Care Administration, *Florida 1997 Health Data SourceBook.* Compiled by Local Health Councils of Florida.

Table 3.17. DEATHS: NUMBER OF RESIDENT DEATHS BY CAUSE IN FLORIDA
1994, 1995, AND 1996

Cause of death and international list number	1994	1995	1996
All causes	146,869	151,619	152,697
Intestinal infectious diseases, 001-009	33	49	44
Tuberculosis, 010-018	112	83	90
Meningococcal infection, 036	23	26	12
Septicemia, 038	784	779	793
Human immunodeficiency virus (HIV), 042-044	4,142	4,336	3,093
Herpes zoster and simplex, 053-054	17	9	14
Viral hepatitis, 070	237	270	300
Syphilis, 090-097	6	8	6
Mycoses, 110-118	122	148	146
Late effects--tuberculosis, 137	10	12	10
Other infectious and parasitic diseases, 020-139	293	258	226
Malignant neoplasm (cancer), 140-208	36,145	36,866	37,476
Neoplasm not specified malignant, 210-239	418	475	422
Diabetes mellitus, 250	3,328	3,652	3,797
Nutritional deficiencies, 260-269	144	170	197
Anemias, 280-285	263	290	304
Alcohol psychosis, dependence, abuse, 291, 303, 305.0	415	378	409
Meningitis, 320-322	35	39	44
Parkinson's disease, 332	597	800	911
Motor neurone disease, 335.2	258	288	271
Major cardiovascular diseases, 390-448	61,242	62,829	63,276
Phlebitis and thrombophlebitis, 451	81	94	92
Venous embolism and thrombosis, 452-453	18	25	31
Other circulatory diseases, 454-459	125	141	137
Pneumonia and influenza, 480-487	3,751	3,810	3,785
Chronic obstructive pulmonary disease, 490-496	7,110	7,455	7,679
Pulmonary fibrosis and other alveular pneumopathy, 515-516	560	568	634
Ulcer of stomach and duodenum, 531-533	382	387	359
Hernia and intestinal obstruction, 550-553, 560	309	309	363
Diverticula of intestine, 562	225	209	225
Chronic liver disease and cirrhosis, 571	1,881	1,829	1,821
Cholelithiasis, other gallbladder diseases, 574-575	154	175	163
Diseases of pancreas, 577	201	190	188
Nephritis, nephrosis, renal failure, 580-589	1,006	1,071	1,008
Infections of kidney, 590	58	48	52
Maternal causes, 630-676	17	18	21
Congenital anomalies, 740-759	661	630	643
Perinatal conditions, 760-779	753	653	647
Symptoms, signs, ill-defined condition, 780-799	2,112	2,543	2,574
All other diseases, 240-739	10,424	11,022	11,631
Unintentional injury (accident), E800-E949	4,971	5,259	5,373
Suicide, E950-E959	2,062	2,139	2,144
Homicide and legal intervention, E960-E978	1,307	1,209	1,189
All other external causes, E980-E999	77	70	97

Source: State of Florida, Department of Health, Office of Vital Statistics, Public Health Statistics Section, *Florida Vital Statistics Annual Report, 1996*, preliminary final, and previous editions.

Table 3.18. DEATHS: NUMBER OF RESIDENT DEATHS AND DEATH RATES BY LEADING CAUSE AND BY RACE IN FLORIDA, 1996

Cause	Number of deaths			Death rate 1/		
	Total 2/	White 3/	Non-white	Total 2/	White 3/	Non-white
Heart disease	49,480	45,188	4,281	341.8	374.4	177.9
Malignant neoplasm (cancer)	37,476	34,005	3,462	258.8	281.7	143.8
Cerebrovascular disease (stroke)	9,828	8,704	1,122	67.9	72.1	46.6
Chronic obstructive pulmonary disease (COPD)	7,679	7,258	418	53.0	60.1	17.4
Unintentional injury (accident)	5,373	4,578	792	37.1	37.9	32.9
Diabetes mellitus	3,797	3,110	685	26.2	25.8	28.5
Pneumonia and influenza	3,785	3,397	387	26.1	28.1	16.1
Human Immunodeficiency Virus (HIV)	3,093	1,526	1,567	21.4	12.6	65.1
Suicide	2,144	1,992	152	14.8	16.5	6.3
Chronic liver disease and cirrhosis	1,821	1,667	154	12.6	13.8	6.4
Aortic aneurysm	1,194	1,116	78	8.2	9.2	3.2
Homicide and legal intervention	1,189	659	530	8.2	5.5	22.0

1/ Rate per 100,000 population, July 1, 1996.
2/ Unknown race included in total only.
3/ Persons designating "Hispanic" as a race were counted as white.
Note: Data are for deaths occurring to residents of Florida regardless of the state of occurrence.

Table 3.19. DEATHS: RESIDENT ACCIDENT AND SUICIDE DEATHS AND DEATH RATES BY RACE AND SEX IN FLORIDA, 1992 THROUGH 1996

Year	Number of deaths					Death rate 1/				
	Total 3/	White 2/		Nonwhite		Total 3/	White 2/		Nonwhite	
		Male	Female	Male	Female		Male	Female	Male	Female
	Unintentional injury (accident)									
1992	4,834	2,669	1,424	499	237	35.9	48.3	24.3	50.0	21.8
1993	5,065	2,766	1,494	554	238	36.9	49.2	25.1	54.2	21.4
1994	4,971	2,763	1,408	577	204	35.6	48.4	23.3	55.0	17.9
1995	5,259	2,942	1,520	566	228	37.0	51.1	24.9	50.1	18.0
1996	5,373	2,963	1,615	552	240	37.1	50.5	26.1	47.4	19.3
	Suicide									
1992	2,015	1,481	414	97	22	15.0	26.8	7.1	9.7	2.0
1993	2,107	1,498	474	110	22	15.4	26.7	8.0	10.8	2.0
1994	2,062	1,528	392	109	27	14.8	26.8	6.5	10.4	2.4
1995	2,139	1,589	408	114	27	15.1	27.6	6.7	10.1	2.1
1996	2,144	1,588	404	128	24	14.8	27.0	6.5	11.0	1.9

1/ Rate per 100,000 population, July 1, 1996.
2/ Persons designating "Hispanic" as a race were counted as white.
3/ Unknown race included in total only.

Source for Tables 3.18 and 3.19: State of Florida, Department of Health, Office of Vital Statistics, Public Health Statistics Section, *Florida Vital Statistics Annual Report*, 1996, preliminary final.

Table 3.20. CHILD WELL-BEING: INDICATORS OF CHILD WELL-BEING
IN THE STATE AND COUNTIES OF FLORIDA, 1994

County	Child deaths 2/	Teen violent deaths 1/ Number	Teen violent deaths 1/ Rate 3/	Children affected by disso- lution of marriage	Runaways
Florida	855	538	6.7	57,158	55,149
Alachua	16	7	3.8	792	910
Baker	1	0	0.0	105	3
Bay	8	7	7.8	892	435
Bradford	2	2	12.7	131	24
Brevard	17	10	4.0	1,821	1,536
Broward	82	41	6.2	4,726	4,188
Calhoun	1	2	24.3	23	0
Charlotte	8	1	2.0	347	361
Citrus	4	5	10.4	406	226
Clay	6	4	4.8	588	1
Collier	10	4	4.6	574	684
Columbia	3	3	8.4	287	168
Dade	147	88	7.4	7,812	5,840
De Soto	2	0	0.0	131	58
Dixie	0	0	0.0	59	21
Duval	53	36	8.1	3,812	4,156
Escambia	26	12	6.2	1,314	1,593
Flagler	0	2	10.5	77	1
Franklin	0	1	14.8	51	0
Gadsden	1	4	11.9	124	33
Gilchrist	2	1	11.0	44	0
Glades	1	1	18.1	19	6
Gulf	1	1	11.8	10	0
Hamilton	1	1	9.7	67	0
Hardee	3	0	0.0	130	0
Hendry	6	2	9.5	147	0
Hernando	3	6	9.7	366	424
Highlands	6	4	10.6	253	226
Hillsborough	48	52	9.4	3,946	5,590
Holmes	3	2	15.9	91	0
Indian River	9	2	3.9	327	348
Jackson	3	3	8.3	241	21
Jefferson	0	0	0.0	210	0
Lafayette	1	0	0.0	21	0
Lake	15	5	5.8	761	553
Lee	18	19	10.7	1,466	1,691
Leon	10	6	3.0	763	1,027
Levy	4	4	23.5	151	13

See footnotes at end of table.   Continued . . .

Table 3.20. CHILD WELL-BEING: INDICATORS OF CHILD WELL-BEING
IN THE STATE AND COUNTIES OF FLORIDA, 1994 (Continued)

County	Child deaths 2/	Teen violent deaths 1/ Number	Rate 3/	Children affected by dissolution of marriage	Runaways
Liberty	0	0	0.0	20	0
Madison	0	1	7.8	67	9
Manatee	8	4	3.6	755	1,352
Marion	9	7	6.0	1,126	602
Martin	6	4	8.2	378	290
Monroe	4	2	6.0	255	162
Nassau	6	5	15.3	280	38
Okaloosa	10	2	1.9	910	405
Okeechobee	7	1	4.3	140	129
Orange	42	27	5.5	3,208	3,731
Osceola	12	8	9.2	640	812
Palm Beach	53	30	6.9	3,161	2,758
Pasco	19	10	7.2	1,088	1,424
Pinellas	27	17	4.2	2,922	5,323
Polk	31	24	8.8	2,242	2,253
Putnam	2	8	17.6	349	399
St. Johns	6	2	3.5	319	376
St. Lucie	15	6	6.4	669	690
Santa Rosa	4	5	7.9	483	163
Sarasota	18	6	4.8	1,308	987
Seminole	18	11	5.2	1,358	1,325
Sumter	6	2	9.4	106	104
Suwannee	5	5	22.5	164	74
Taylor	2	1	10.0	118	13
Union	0	0	0.0	53	0
Volusia	22	10	4.6	1,665	1,543
Wakulla	0	2	16.8	81	49
Walton	2	0	0.0	139	0
Washington	0	0	0.0	69	1

1/ Deaths from homicides, suicides, and accidents to teens aged 15-19 years.
2/ Deaths from all causes to children aged 1-14 years.
3/ Per 10,000 population aged 15-19 years.

Source: University of South Florida, Florida Mental Health Institute, and State
of Florida, Center for Children and Youth, *Key Facts About the Children, A Report on
the Status of Florida's Children: Volume VI, The 1996 Florida Kids Count Data Book*,
(copyright).

University of Florida   **Bureau of Economic and Business Research**

Table 3.28. ACQUIRED IMMUNODEFICIENCY SYNDROME (AIDS): ADULT CASES OF AIDS, 1996
AND CUMULATIVE CASES, JANUARY 1, 1980 THROUGH DECEMBER 31, 1996
IN THE STATE AND COUNTIES OF FLORIDA

County	Number of cases Diag-nosed	Re-port-ed 1/	Cumulative cases 1980-96 Number 2/	Rate per 100,000 popula-tion 3/	County	Number of cases Diag-nosed	Re-port-ed 1/	Cumulative cases 1980-96 Number 2/	Rate per 100,000 popula-tion 3/
Florida	5,090	7,187	57,896	497.6	Lake	17	27	155	101.8
					Lee	70	93	1,033	325.0
Alachua	23	47	361	219.8	Leon	17	22	380	210.2
Baker	0	0	13	81.1	Levy	2	3	23	92.5
Bay	15	22	207	185.5	Liberty	0	0	3	48.9
Bradford	0	2	14	68.6	Madison	1	1	19	129.9
Brevard	74	114	901	247.2	Manatee	40	56	485	246.1
Broward	801	1,142	9,047	802.8	Marion	28	47	299	159.3
Calhoun	0	0	4	39.3	Martin	15	30	203	209.5
Charlotte	6	14	136	121.1	Monroe	64	133	908	1,289.5
Citrus	2	4	64	69.1	Nassau	3	5	54	135.5
Clay	6	13	111	115.4	Okaloosa	7	14	135	105.4
Collier	53	62	500	314.1	Okeechobee	2	7	44	167.9
Columbia	9	13	64	157.1	Orange	263	367	3,101	505.3
Dade	1,556	2,044	17,588	1,102.7	Osceola	27	39	266	243.0
De Soto	5	11	42	194.1	Palm Beach	650	789	5,317	658.6
Dixie	0	0	7	68.1	Pasco	20	31	357	135.8
Duval	232	321	2,902	514.8	Pinellas	178	259	2,327	313.5
Escambia	54	96	696	308.3	Polk	59	116	820	226.0
Flagler	3	8	47	141.3	Putnam	2	4	84	150.8
Franklin	1	1	8	92.4	St. Johns	12	21	175	209.4
Gadsden	4	6	69	195.1	St. Lucie	88	173	811	572.3
Gilchrist	0	1	4	40.7	Santa Rosa	7	12	66	85.9
Glades	4	6	16	207.4	Sarasota	40	60	568	214.6
Gulf	2	2	7	62.7	Seminole	29	53	517	198.5
Hamilton	1	1	7	65.0	Sumter	2	4	23	68.3
Hardee	2	3	35	200.9	Suwannee	2	3	34	134.9
Hendry	7	10	80	360.6	Taylor	3	3	19	128.2
Hernando	9	14	101	99.4	Union	1	1	6	55.1
Highlands	7	10	92	138.8	Volusia	40	72	703	208.3
Hillsborough	309	422	3,357	467.5	Wakulla	1	2	19	133.8
Holmes	1	1	10	70.6	Walton	1	1	23	81.4
Indian River	8	24	136	159.0	Washington	2	4	14	88.5
Jackson	5	8	39	97.4					
Jefferson	0	1	17	156.1	Unknown	0	0	6	(X)
Lafayette	0	0	3	51.9	DOC	198	312	2,214	(X)

DOC Department of Corrections.
(X) Not applicable.
1/ Includes diagnosed cases from earlier years not previously reported. See Appendix for further discussion.
2/ Excludes 1,229 diagnosed and reported pediatric (under age 13) cases of AIDS.
3/ Based on April 1, 1996 population estimates for persons aged 15 and over.

Source: State of Florida, Department of Health, State Health Office, *The Florida AIDS, STD, and TB Monthly Surveillance Report,* January 1997.

Table 3.32. MARRIAGES AND DISSOLUTIONS OF MARRIAGE: NUMBER PERFORMED OR GRANTED
IN THE STATE AND COUNTIES OF FLORIDA, 1995 AND 1996

County	Marriages 1/ 1995	Marriages 1/ 1996	Dissolutions of marriage 2/ 1995	Dissolutions of marriage 2/ 1996	County	Marriages 1/ 1995	Marriages 1/ 1996	Dissolutions of marriage 2/ 1995	Dissolutions of marriage 2/ 1996
Florida	145,090	150,599	78,416	77,750	Lafayette	85	79	51	46
					Lake	1,476	1,502	974	1,030
Alachua	1,950	1,906	966	960	Lee	3,328	3,308	1,953	2,035
Baker	281	274	132	139	Leon	2,293	2,296	1,061	965
Bay	2,036	1,971	1,203	1,050	Levy	268	235	162	159
Bradford	324	317	177	165	Liberty	64	73	34	42
Brevard	3,844	3,793	2,266	1,742	Madison	177	183	86	80
Broward	12,660	13,504	5,172	6,810	Manatee	1,842	1,826	977	850
Calhoun	116	136	104	97	Marion	2,137	2,168	1,518	1,233
Charlotte	934	947	570	419	Martin	963	928	518	535
Citrus	852	830	552	450	Monroe	1,948	2,156	499	429
Clay	1,378	1,418	782	822	Nassau	645	651	340	299
Collier	1,893	1,976	930	940	Okaloosa	2,122	2,184	1,286	1,212
Columbia	618	678	339	387	Okeechobee	361	345	201	186
Dade	24,998	27,835	12,034	12,898	Orange	9,300	9,504	4,493	4,355
De Soto	243	257	132	131	Osceola	3,113	3,590	937	863
Dixie	135	131	76	69	Palm Beach	8,060	8,983	4,301	4,589
Duval	7,281	7,362	4,539	4,527	Pasco	2,251	2,221	1,488	1,361
Escambia	3,663	3,203	1,877	1,736	Pinellas	7,879	7,837	4,789	4,011
Flagler	279	332	154	169	Polk	4,141	4,237	2,813	2,877
Franklin	136	133	71	81	Putnam	679	653	417	420
Gadsden	397	338	196	202	St. Johns	1,329	1,437	556	535
Gilchrist	131	129	68	55	St. Lucie	1,282	1,358	964	886
Glades	48	44	13	16	Santa Rosa	886	887	620	537
Gulf	128	153	75	69	Sarasota	2,586	2,562	1,844	1,644
Hamilton	138	132	63	72	Seminole	2,824	2,955	1,700	1,591
Hardee	216	235	125	101	Sumter	305	297	229	230
Hendry	459	391	166	156	Suwannee	294	337	201	183
Hernando	844	865	472	544	Taylor	208	199	124	146
Highlands	642	633	368	385	Union	95	106	61	50
Hillsborough	9,175	9,162	5,613	5,421	Volusia	3,649	3,735	2,254	2,267
Holmes	333	231	139	114	Wakulla	199	198	82	44
Indian River	861	903	558	490	Walton	395	432	210	223
Jackson	473	432	331	278	Washington	249	188	130	66
Jefferson	191	298	280	276					

1/ State total may include a few marriages performed out of state but recorded in
Florida.
2/ Includes divorces and annulments.
Source: State of Florida, Department of Health, Office of Vital Statistics, Public Health Statistics Section, *Florida Vital Statistics Annual Report, 1996*, preliminary final, and previous edition.

EDUCATION

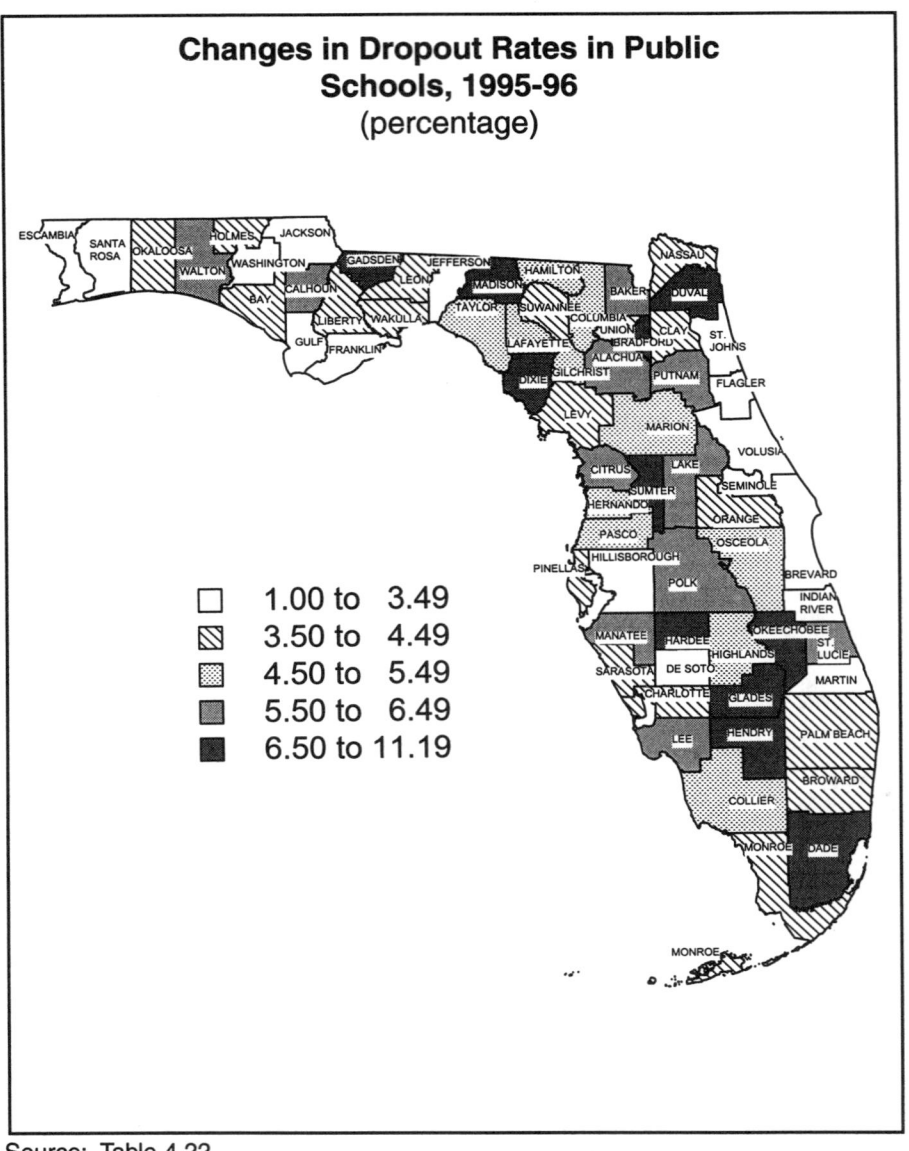

Changes in Dropout Rates in Public Schools, 1995-96
(percentage)

☐ 1.00 to 3.49
▨ 3.50 to 4.49
▦ 4.50 to 5.49
▩ 5.50 to 6.49
■ 6.50 to 11.19

Source: Table 4.22

SECTION 4.00
EDUCATION

TABLES LISTED BY MAJOR HEADINGS

SECTION 4.00
EDUCATION
(Continued)

TABLES LISTED BY MAJOR HEADINGS

Table 4.02. ELEMENTARY AND SECONDARY SCHOOLS: SPECIFIED STUDENT DATA
IN FLORIDA, 1992-93 THROUGH 1995-96

Item	1992-93	1993-94	1994-95	1995-96	Percentage change since 1992-93
Student membership 1/	1,981,731	2,041,714	2,109,052	2,176,930	9.85
Prekindergarten	31,490	35,681	46,433	51,629	63.95
Kindergarten	161,720	167,142	172,004	176,775	9.31
Grade 1	167,609	169,055	175,026	180,172	7.50
Grade 2	169,417	168,310	169,557	175,887	3.82
Grade 3	165,863	170,876	170,567	172,036	3.72
Grade 4	164,432	168,505	173,194	173,189	5.33
Grade 5	160,342	166,156	170,309	175,354	9.36
Grade 6	155,943	163,451	169,018	174,078	11.63
Grade 7	150,821	157,890	165,490	171,383	13.63
Grade 8	142,381	149,034	155,814	163,522	14.85
Grade 9	154,399	164,988	172,850	183,053	18.56
Grade 10	138,850	140,284	147,925	154,067	10.96
Grade 11	117,538	119,696	120,030	126,206	7.37
Grade 12	100,926	100,646	100,835	99,579	-1.33
Graduates (standard diplomas)	89,428	88,032	(NA)	(NA)	(NA)
Exceptional student membership	311,468	329,201	350,658	369,788	18.72
Educable mentally handicapped	19,289	21,041	22,862	24,628	27.68
Trainable mentally handicapped	7,078	7,338	7,524	7,714	8.99
Speech/language and hearing	76,014	78,929	82,199	85,699	12.74
Emotionally handicapped	21,803	23,098	24,020	24,740	13.47
Specific learning disability	102,380	109,557	115,816	122,606	19.76
Gifted	67,847	70,874	78,558	83,576	23.18
Profoundly handicapped	9,074	9,726	10,466	11,267	24.17
Other exceptionalities	7,983	8,638	9,213	9,558	19.73
Disciplinary actions					
Out-of-school suspensions	177,894	184,424	192,841	(NA)	(NA)
In-school suspensions	173,033	200,547	217,170	(NA)	(NA)
Referrals to dropout prevention for disciplinary reasons	56,475	62,828	64,126	(NA)	(NA)
Corporal punishment	20,315	14,731	13,900	(NA)	(NA)
Expulsions	953	740	1,168	(NA)	(NA)
Referrals to court/juvenile authorities	3,386	3,219	3,272	(NA)	(NA)
Nonpromotions	77,640	82,440	85,915	(NA)	(NA)
Dropouts K-12	24,943	28,299	28,355	(NA)	(NA)

(NA) Not available.
1/ Based on fall membership survey.
Note: Data are for public schools only.

Source: State of Florida, Department of Education, Division of Administration,
Profiles of Florida School Districts, 1995-96, Student and Staff Data. EIAS Series
97-21, December 1996.

University of Florida   **Bureau of Economic and Business Research**

Table 4.03. ELEMENTARY AND SECONDARY SCHOOLS: MEMBERSHIP IN EXCEPTIONAL STUDENT
PROGRAMS IN THE STATE AND COUNTIES OF FLORIDA, FALL 1996

| County | Total | Students in specified programs (percentage) | | | | |
		Specific learning disabil- ities	Speech language and hearing	Gifted	Educable mentally handi- capped	Emotion- ally handi- capped
Florida	385,893	33.63	23.02	22.20	6.82	6.55
Alachua	6,735	26.92	14.03	36.04	5.89	10.84
Baker	646	34.67	25.23	11.15	15.48	4.64
Bay	5,416	37.63	18.65	21.71	5.69	7.79
Bradford	858	43.36	15.73	7.23	14.34	15.15
Brevard	14,042	36.13	19.03	30.95	4.38	4.02
Broward	28,914	23.56	38.85	19.42	5.60	3.09
Calhoun	395	31.14	36.71	13.67	8.35	8.10
Charlotte	2,694	47.48	17.74	14.70	4.05	6.57
Citrus	3,347	38.84	26.56	14.70	4.90	6.72
Clay	5,100	36.39	28.08	18.59	3.57	8.71
Collier	5,264	37.04	33.61	12.99	5.41	4.33
Columbia	1,412	30.52	25.71	8.85	12.89	11.12
Dade	48,281	35.56	12.27	31.32	5.55	6.18
De Soto	856	39.95	24.18	14.84	7.59	8.41
Dixie	564	30.32	40.43	0.00	11.52	11.88
Duval	22,876	37.23	21.13	15.66	8.17	8.27
Escambia	8,192	34.39	21.83	20.84	7.82	6.45
Flagler	1,092	54.95	17.77	11.90	3.75	5.40
Franklin	237	27.43	35.44	3.38	16.88	10.55
Gadsden	1,414	39.32	29.14	2.83	16.97	2.33
Gilchrist	419	36.99	28.16	5.49	10.98	10.98
Glades	129	51.94	24.81	0.00	12.40	5.43
Gulf	327	31.80	18.35	24.46	13.15	8.26
Hamilton	343	25.07	35.86	1.75	14.87	4.66
Hardee	773	41.66	18.24	13.45	13.58	7.63
Hendry	1,006	51.39	16.20	6.16	13.92	4.57
Hernando	2,744	34.80	29.63	17.97	4.01	6.67
Highlands	2,310	45.58	14.11	18.05	6.75	8.87
Hillsborough	26,358	25.05	22.22	27.89	7.78	8.15
Holmes	455	41.98	25.49	0.00	20.44	7.47
Indian River	2,824	39.45	21.07	21.07	6.55	4.82
Jackson	1,466	19.44	27.76	10.03	14.73	14.12
Jefferson	393	25.95	37.40	7.63	15.78	11.20
Lafayette	139	24.46	41.01	10.79	14.39	7.91
Lake	4,314	30.69	32.64	10.13	11.91	6.10
Lee	11,570	32.20	17.63	33.26	4.73	6.29

See footnote at end of table.   Continued . . .

University of Florida   **Bureau of Economic and Business Research**

Table 4.03. ELEMENTARY AND SECONDARY SCHOOLS: MEMBERSHIP IN EXCEPTIONAL STUDENT
PROGRAMS IN THE STATE AND COUNTIES OF FLORIDA, FALL 1996 (Continued)

County	Total	Students in specified programs (percentage)				
		Specific learning disabil- ities	Speech language and hearing	Gifted	Educable mentally handi- capped	Emotion- ally handi- capped
Leon	8,067	22.87	35.48	27.48	5.32	2.37
Levy	1,002	32.44	26.85	8.48	10.58	13.17
Liberty	226	27.88	49.12	0.00	11.06	10.18
Madison	767	37.29	23.47	16.17	12.65	4.82
Manatee	6,309	39.99	25.99	11.03	6.15	8.05
Marion	6,382	37.86	21.94	14.74	9.26	6.78
Martin	2,531	37.97	23.03	15.57	5.77	9.56
Monroe	1,688	39.16	21.80	17.06	4.03	11.08
Nassau	1,606	53.67	13.95	10.71	6.23	10.27
Okaloosa	4,688	35.71	22.82	25.87	6.63	3.22
Okeechobee	1,232	40.18	26.95	7.31	12.34	5.60
Orange	20,549	34.41	22.80	18.59	10.97	5.41
Osceola	4,135	35.94	32.50	9.89	7.26	6.19
Palm Beach	24,374	33.00	24.36	26.15	5.75	5.48
Pasco	8,306	36.99	29.62	11.80	5.69	7.80
Pinellas	23,555	37.75	20.47	20.45	4.81	7.76
Polk	12,049	37.73	18.52	22.08	10.22	5.86
Putnam	1,910	40.00	28.90	5.76	14.50	3.35
St. Johns	2,595	37.61	25.28	22.93	6.78	3.28
St. Lucie	4,764	24.92	31.42	20.45	8.82	7.75
Santa Rosa	3,142	35.07	28.61	17.89	6.68	5.25
Sarasota	7,779	32.30	15.43	33.47	3.15	9.05
Seminole	9,018	26.35	27.56	29.65	5.00	5.47
Sumter	1,044	26.25	24.43	15.52	13.79	11.30
Suwannee	844	33.41	29.15	7.11	18.25	7.46
Taylor	671	48.58	21.46	11.18	7.45	5.37
Union	385	36.88	27.79	7.53	7.53	15.32
Volusia	10,262	36.06	22.04	15.75	6.50	10.82
Wakulla	910	33.74	32.97	16.48	6.70	5.27
Walton	765	38.69	33.99	4.31	10.72	7.84
Washington	433	34.87	32.79	7.85	8.08	11.55

Note: Data were obtained from the Fall 1996 Florida DOE Student Information Data
Base, Survey 2, as of December 6, 1996, and are for public schools only.

Source: State of Florida, Department of Education, Division of Administration,
Education Information and Accountability Services, *Statistical Brief: Membership in
Programs for Exceptional Students, Fall 1996.* Series 97-23B.

University of Florida   **Bureau of Economic and Business Research**

Table 4.05. ELEMENTARY AND SECONDARY SCHOOLS: SPECIFIED CHARACTERISTICS
IN FLORIDA, 1981-82 THROUGH 1995-96

School year	Resident population 1/ Total	Aged 5-17	Fall member- ship 2/	High School gradu- ates 3/	Instruc- tional personnel
1981-82	10,375,332	1,998,658	1,485,593	89,199	88,912
1982-83	10,591,701	2,040,338	1,482,270	86,871	89,898
1983-84	10,891,701	1,724,795	1,492,366	85,908	90,348
1984-85	10,930,389	1,752,422	1,520,975	81,140	94,048
1985-86	11,287,932	1,675,790	1,559,507	81,508	97,139
1986-87	11,549,831	1,667,636	1,603,033	83,692	100,498
1987-88	12,043,618	1,688,627	1,664,563	90,792	104,848
1988-89	12,417,608	1,695,383	1,720,927	92,449	109,865
1989-90	13,152,691	1,700,468	1,789,925	90,790	114,501
1990-91	12,937,926	2,016,641	1,861,671	89,494	119,123
1991-92	13,195,952	2,057,688	1,930,719	93,368	121,185
1992-93	13,424,416	2,100,608	1,981,731	91,423	118,713
1993-94	13,608,627	2,135,410	2,041,714	90,034	124,027
1994-95	14,149,317	2,207,525	2,109,052	91,899	129,223
1995-96	14,411,563	2,297,513	2,176,930	(NA)	132,079

	Average teacher salary 4/ (dollars)	Number of schools	Assessed valuation of property ($1,000)	Total expenditure all purposes ($1,000)	Current expense per pupil 5/ (dollars)
1981-82	16,779.52	2,347	193,536,278	4,133,541	2,283
1982-83	18,351.76	2,350	226,683,285	4,521,420	2,463
1983-84	19,449.12	2,284	243,385,858	4,950,393	2,676
1984-85	20,836.47	2,304	266,774,135	5,461,194	2,964
1985-86	22,250.08	2,296	323,579,927	6,103,747	3,205
1986-87	23,733.76	2,400	353,683,447	6,909,814	3,423
1987-88	25,198.00	2,438	378,703,589	7,643,660	3,679
1988-89	26,974.00	2,485	411,786,114	8,793,842	3,964
1989-90	28,803.00	2,591	414,018,411	10,125,835	4,248
1990-91	30,555.00	2,694	449,979,199	11,308,952	4,475
1991-92	31,067.00	2,730	475,960,538	11,745,293	4,439
1992-93	31,174.00	2,784	479,892,429	11,750,331	4,525
1993-94	31,948.00	2,867	488,458,004	12,780,952	4,724
1994-95	32,600.00	2,946	511,789,104	13,801,787	4,879
1995-96	33,330.00	3,003	(NA)	(NA)	(NA)

(NA) Not available.
1/ Population figures for noncensus years are mid-year estimates as of April 1;
1985-86 through 1989-90 population breakdowns are for aged 15-24. Population figures
as of 1992-93 are from the University of Florida, Bureau of Economic and Business Research, Population Program.
2/ Based on fall membership survey.
3/ Regular day school only; excludes state/university schools and adult programs.
Includes standard and special diplomas.
4/ A professional paid on the instructional salary schedule negotiated by a Florida school district.
5/ Based on full-time equivalent student count.
Note: Data are for public schools only.
Source: State of Florida, Department of Education, *Profiles of Florida School
Districts, 1995-96, Student and Staff Data,* and *Profiles of Florida School Districts,
1994-95, Financial Data Statistical Report.*

University of Florida   **Bureau of Economic and Business Research**

Table 4.06. ELEMENTARY AND SECONDARY SCHOOLS: ENROLLMENT IN KINDERGARTEN
THROUGH GRADE TWELVE IN THE STATE AND COUNTIES OF FLORIDA
1987-88 THROUGH 1996-97

School year	Total enrollment	Public schools Enrollment	Percentage of total	Nonpublic schools 1/ Enrollment	Percentage of total
1987-88	1,861,904	1,658,624	89.08	203,380	10.92
1988-89	1,910,310	1,712,613	89.65	197,695	10.35
1989-90	1,973,333	1,775,529	89.98	197,804	10.02
1990-91	2,035,145	1,841,206	90.47	193,939	9.53
1991-92	2,097,761	1,902,563	90.69	195,198	9.31
1992-93	2,150,377	1,950,114	90.69	200,263	9.31
1993-94	2,227,240	2,005,970	90.06	221,270	9.93
1994-95	2,298,752	2,064,884	89.82	233,868	10.17
1995-96	2,370,328	2,125,099	89.65	245,229	10.35
1996-97	2,446,044	2,188,239	89.46	257,805	10.54

1/ Private (nonpublic) elementary and secondary schools in Florida are not li-
censed, approved, accredited, or regulated by the state but they are required to make
their existence known to the Department of Education and respond to an annual survey.
See Glossary under Private school for definition.
Note: Based on DOE survey taken during the school year. Data may differ slightly
from data based on fall surveys as shown in other *Abstract* tables.
Source: State of Florida, Department of Education, Division of Public Schools,
Statistical Brief: Florida's Nonpublic Schools, 1996-97. Series 98-03B.

Table 4.07. ELEMENTARY AND SECONDARY SCHOOLS: CHANGE IN MEMBERSHIP
IN PREKINDERGARTEN THROUGH GRADE TWELVE IN THE STATE AND
COUNTIES OF FLORIDA, FALL 1991 TO FALL 1995

County	Number	Per-cent-age	County	Number	Per-cent-age	County	Number	Per-cent-age
Florida	245,335	12.71	Glades	128	13.14	Nassau	800	9.11
			Gulf	45	2.01	Okaloosa	2,342	8.64
Alachua	1,962	7.21	Hamilton	48	2.08	Okeechobee	548	9.28
Baker	312	7.22	Hardee	907	20.66	Orange	16,401	15.38
Bay	2,562	11.30	Hendry	953	15.59	Osceola	4,925	23.74
Bradford	-67	-1.60	Hernando	1,968	14.66	Palm Beach	21,449	19.36
Brevard	6,747	11.46	Highlands	1,257	13.23	Pasco	6,253	17.60
Broward	38,239	22.48	Hillsborough	15,777	12.38	Pinellas	7,995	8.30
Calhoun	130	6.05	Holmes	325	9.46	Polk	5,963	8.92
Charlotte	2,008	14.78	Indian River	1,627	13.51	Putnam	575	4.65
Citrus	1,787	14.71	Jackson	123	1.56	St. Johns	2,857	22.78
Clay	2,430	10.83	Jefferson	-12	-0.56	St. Lucie	4,288	18.84
Collier	4,521	20.69	Lafayette	-57	-5.14	Santa Rosa	3,499	21.49
Columbia	785	9.40	Lake	2,979	13.64	Sarasota	2,212	7.67
Dade	29,215	9.59	Lee	6,646	15.00	Seminole	3,763	7.40
De Soto	477	11.83	Leon	2,947	10.38	Sumter	480	9.08
Dixie	330	16.98	Levy	822	16.73	Suwannee	209	3.81
Duval	7,946	6.85	Liberty	86	7.44	Taylor	294	8.18
Escambia	1,111	2.52	Madison	170	5.21	Union	252	13.01
Flagler	1,113	26.20	Manatee	4,381	15.98	Volusia	6,688	13.35
Franklin	80	4.92	Marion	5,069	16.64	Wakulla	764	21.79
Gadsden	333	3.99	Martin	2,168	17.77	Walton	613	13.27
Gilchrist	546	27.55	Monroe	1,111	13.23	Washington	130	4.27

Source: State of Florida, Department of Education, Division of Administration,
Statistical Brief: Membership in Florida Public Schools, Fall 1995. Series 96-16B.

University of Florida   **Bureau of Economic and Business Research**

Table 4.20. ELEMENTARY AND SECONDARY SCHOOLS: PUPIL MEMBERSHIP
IN PREKINDERGARTEN THROUGH GRADE TWELVE BY RACE
OR HISPANIC ORIGIN IN THE STATE AND COUNTIES
OF FLORIDA, FALL 1996

			Percentage of membership				
				Race			
County	Total member- ship	Total mi- nority	White	Black	Asian/ Pacific Islander	American Indian/ Alaskan native	His- panic ori- gin 1/
Florida	2,240,283	969,350	56.73	25.35	1.78	0.23	15.90
Alachua	29,648	12,706	57.14	37.19	2.22	0.17	3.28
Baker	4,630	806	82.59	16.80	0.32	0.06	0.22
Bay	25,665	4,864	81.05	15.17	2.11	0.27	1.40
Bradford	4,192	1,000	76.15	22.38	0.72	0.12	0.64
Brevard	66,679	13,508	79.74	14.60	1.77	0.24	3.65
Broward	218,576	115,022	47.38	35.33	2.60	0.26	14.43
Calhoun	2,288	391	82.91	14.95	0.52	0.09	1.53
Charlotte	16,083	2,084	87.04	8.47	1.19	0.16	3.14
Citrus	14,194	1,206	91.50	4.59	1.10	0.27	2.54
Clay	25,915	3,574	86.21	9.01	2.00	0.22	2.57
Collier	28,177	10,509	62.70	11.20	0.48	0.48	25.14
Columbia	9,263	2,551	72.46	24.68	0.58	0.40	1.88
Dade	341,120	294,982	13.53	33.64	1.31	0.08	51.45
De Soto	4,616	1,808	60.83	21.60	0.41	0.13	17.03
Dixie	2,323	246	89.41	9.99	0.04	0.00	0.56
Duval	126,100	58,324	53.75	40.66	2.65	0.15	2.80
Escambia	45,692	18,086	60.42	35.06	2.75	0.57	1.19
Flagler	5,662	1,205	78.72	14.41	1.59	0.25	5.03
Franklin	1,575	303	80.76	17.78	0.51	0.13	0.83
Gadsden	8,546	7,843	8.23	85.03	0.08	0.04	6.62
Gilchrist	2,651	186	92.98	5.70	0.15	0.11	1.06
Glades	1,149	562	51.09	26.72	0.26	1.04	20.89
Gulf	2,346	479	79.58	19.22	0.34	0.21	0.64
Hamilton	2,336	1,277	45.33	50.81	0.13	0.09	3.64
Hardee	4,974	2,435	51.05	9.77	0.26	0.18	38.74
Hendry	7,257	4,085	43.71	20.34	0.50	0.62	34.84
Hernando	15,842	2,136	86.52	7.70	0.78	0.11	4.89
Highlands	11,020	3,965	64.02	21.64	0.69	0.52	13.13
Hillsborough	147,788	65,076	55.97	24.13	1.95	0.32	17.64
Holmes	3,820	170	95.55	3.25	0.45	0.21	0.55
Indian River	13,972	3,559	74.53	17.76	0.77	0.18	6.76
Jackson	8,098	2,780	65.67	32.75	0.23	0.22	1.12
Jefferson	2,127	1,480	30.42	69.06	0.28	0.05	0.19
Lafayette	1,109	179	83.86	11.90	0.00	0.00	4.24
Lake	26,133	6,456	75.30	17.82	0.82	0.22	5.84
Lee	52,302	15,123	71.09	15.87	1.11	0.22	11.72

See footnotes at end of table.   Continued . . .

University of Florida   **Bureau of Economic and Business Research**

Table 4.20. ELEMENTARY AND SECONDARY SCHOOLS: PUPIL MEMBERSHIP
IN PREKINDERGARTEN THROUGH GRADE TWELVE BY RACE
OR HISPANIC ORIGIN IN THE STATE AND COUNTIES
OF FLORIDA, FALL 1996 (Continued)

| | | | Percentage of membership | | | | |
| | | | Race | | | | |
County	Total member- ship	Total mi- nority	White	Black	Asian/ Pacific Islander	American Indian/ Alaskan native	His- panic ori- gin 1/
Leon	31,558	13,192	58.20	38.56	1.54	0.11	1.60
Levy	5,831	1,259	78.41	18.57	0.43	0.15	2.44
Liberty	1,247	199	84.04	13.23	0.16	0.00	2.57
Madison	3,479	2,057	40.87	57.92	0.06	0.14	1.01
Manatee	32,797	9,957	69.64	18.09	0.77	0.13	11.37
Marion	36,244	10,333	71.49	22.10	0.68	0.21	5.52
Martin	14,823	3,427	76.88	12.46	0.90	0.08	9.67
Monroe	9,369	2,556	72.72	9.35	1.11	0.25	16.58
Nassau	10,189	1,324	87.01	11.83	0.34	0.13	0.70
Okaloosa	30,048	5,820	80.63	12.75	3.23	0.41	2.98
Okeechobee	6,597	1,952	70.41	8.63	0.62	1.83	18.51
Orange	128,941	63,535	50.73	28.43	3.36	0.31	17.17
Osceola	27,376	11,253	58.89	9.59	2.78	0.16	28.57
Palm Beach	137,600	63,539	53.82	29.56	1.96	0.38	14.27
Pasco	43,461	4,845	88.85	4.00	1.13	0.23	5.79
Pinellas	107,051	26,694	75.06	18.96	2.67	0.16	3.14
Polk	74,800	24,578	67.14	23.43	0.87	0.17	8.39
Putnam	13,294	4,744	64.31	27.70	0.53	0.21	7.24
St. Johns	16,365	2,362	85.57	11.71	0.75	0.16	1.80
St. Lucie	27,669	11,065	60.01	30.97	0.95	0.25	7.82
Santa Rosa	20,668	1,780	91.39	5.39	1.49	0.51	1.22
Sarasota	31,951	5,340	83.29	10.80	1.25	0.14	4.53
Seminole	55,972	15,787	71.79	14.58	2.78	0.20	10.65
Sumter	5,921	1,849	68.77	27.34	0.30	0.25	3.33
Suwannee	5,851	1,273	78.24	19.36	0.27	0.07	2.05
Taylor	3,840	999	73.98	24.71	0.34	0.47	0.49
Union	2,317	454	80.41	18.17	0.35	0.04	1.04
Volusia	58,004	14,179	75.56	16.32	0.97	0.23	6.93
Wakulla	4,444	621	86.03	13.19	0.23	0.23	0.34
Walton	5,459	715	86.90	10.42	0.82	0.51	1.34
Washington	3,249	696	78.58	19.08	0.98	0.49	0.86

1/ Persons of Hispanic origin may be of any race. However, these data are not distributed by race.

Note: Data were obtained from the Florida DOE Student Information Data Base, Survey 2, as of December 6, 1996, and are for public schools only.

Source: State of Florida, Department of Education, Division of Administration, *PK-12 Student Membership by Racial/Ethnic Category, Fall 1996,* at Internet site http://www.firn.edu/doe/.

University of Florida   **Bureau of Economic and Business Research**

Table 4.22. SECONDARY SCHOOLS: DROPOUT RATES IN THE STATE
AND COUNTIES OF FLORIDA, 1991-92 THROUGH 1995-96

County	1991-92	1992-93	1993-94	1994-95	1995-96	Percent-age change 1991-92 to 1995-96
Florida	4.56	4.86	5.63	5.24	5.02	10.09
Alachua	4.65	5.38	7.16	7.02	6.36	36.77
Baker	3.68	5.43	6.48	6.96	6.10	65.76
Bay	2.96	3.52	4.10	5.43	4.06	37.16
Bradford	5.38	8.12	8.33	7.31	10.88	102.23
Brevard	1.82	2.20	2.48	2.79	2.73	50.00
Broward	3.64	2.91	7.27	3.43	3.83	5.22
Calhoun	3.66	3.58	3.87	2.55	5.80	58.47
Charlotte	5.40	5.02	5.00	3.57	3.58	-33.70
Citrus	3.53	4.52	5.83	6.63	6.39	81.02
Clay	2.91	4.80	3.73	4.07	4.17	43.30
Collier	4.44	4.24	6.78	4.94	5.30	19.37
Columbia	4.77	3.93	6.96	5.55	4.77	0.00
Dade	5.84	7.29	8.12	7.94	7.89	35.10
De Soto	4.37	4.41	4.53	4.48	3.33	-23.80
Dixie	7.06	9.39	8.79	6.64	8.48	20.11
Duval	9.58	5.51	5.14	6.45	8.05	-15.97
Escambia	1.58	1.96	1.76	2.50	3.06	93.67
Flagler	1.69	2.80	1.14	1.61	1.80	6.51
Franklin	4.73	2.65	2.06	1.47	2.38	-49.68
Gadsden	10.24	9.15	7.42	8.41	7.23	-29.39
Gilchrist	6.57	5.16	4.11	5.82	4.52	-31.20
Glades	5.41	6.28	9.76	5.84	11.19	106.84
Gulf	1.05	2.68	1.64	2.24	1.27	20.95
Hamilton	6.22	6.70	7.30	7.58	4.88	-21.54
Hardee	4.72	6.09	8.68	10.15	7.21	52.75
Hendry	11.42	8.06	6.75	7.74	8.42	-26.27
Hernando	3.86	3.28	4.66	5.66	5.00	29.53
Highlands	6.40	3.90	7.19	6.17	4.60	-28.13
Hillsborough	2.74	2.87	2.94	3.58	3.36	22.63
Holmes	2.91	3.85	3.14	3.70	4.16	42.96
Indian River	4.76	7.13	4.15	4.04	3.24	-31.93
Jackson	3.46	4.00	3.67	2.34	2.16	-37.57
Jefferson	5.26	3.33	3.04	2.23	3.15	-40.11
Lafayette	8.65	9.90	6.69	4.20	5.05	-41.62
Lake	5.78	7.17	7.67	5.53	6.32	9.34
Lee	5.65	5.55	5.74	5.72	6.15	8.85

See footnote at end of table.   Continued . . .

Table 4.22. SECONDARY SCHOOLS: DROPOUT RATES IN THE STATE
AND COUNTIES OF FLORIDA, 1991-92 THROUGH 1995-96 (Continued)

County	1991-92	1992-93	1993-94	1994-95	1995-96	Percent-age change 1991-92 to 1995-96
Leon	4.48	4.27	4.10	4.34	4.49	0.22
Levy	6.42	5.77	7.16	5.38	4.40	-31.46
Liberty	0.34	2.47	1.11	2.28	3.54	941.18
Madison	2.75	4.14	8.71	11.28	9.86	258.55
Manatee	4.53	5.35	5.24	5.96	6.20	36.87
Marion	5.46	5.46	5.22	4.49	5.40	-1.10
Martin	2.25	2.49	3.66	3.25	2.57	14.22
Monroe	5.24	8.66	10.75	6.09	3.68	-29.77
Nassau	3.91	4.50	3.69	3.14	4.05	3.58
Okaloosa	2.45	3.28	3.50	3.26	3.70	51.02
Okeechobee	9.45	8.41	8.82	7.86	8.70	-7.94
Orange	4.86	4.44	4.34	4.42	3.70	-23.87
Osceola	3.41	4.58	4.95	6.56	4.61	35.19
Palm Beach	4.15	5.22	6.07	5.78	4.24	2.17
Pasco	4.20	4.58	4.93	4.95	4.70	11.90
Pinellas	3.31	5.05	6.51	4.22	4.16	25.68
Polk	4.09	5.84	6.52	5.03	6.01	46.94
Putnam	8.44	5.23	6.35	7.93	5.81	-31.16
St. Johns	9.20	9.10	8.14	6.24	3.42	-62.83
St. Lucie	8.61	6.41	6.18	6.39	6.39	-25.78
Santa Rosa	2.85	3.21	2.57	2.56	2.86	0.35
Sarasota	2.06	1.78	4.82	6.26	3.78	83.50
Seminole	3.08	3.44	3.29	4.70	2.77	-10.06
Sumter	7.81	5.96	7.33	8.14	10.19	30.47
Suwannee	4.71	3.11	3.67	4.88	3.89	-17.41
Taylor	4.59	7.20	7.67	5.56	5.03	9.59
Union	3.48	3.16	2.13	4.75	4.21	20.98
Volusia	3.38	5.46	4.40	5.55	2.95	-12.72
Wakulla	1.69	2.10	2.94	3.38	3.99	136.09
Walton	2.85	3.95	3.51	4.12	6.07	112.98
Washington	1.83	1.56	3.14	2.08	1.00	-45.36

Note: Data are for public schools only.

Source: State of Florida, Department of Education, Internet site http://www.firn.
edu/doe/.

University of Florida   **Bureau of Economic and Business Research**

Table 4.23. SECONDARY SCHOOLS: DISTRIBUTION OF DROPOUTS BY SPECIFIED
RACE OR HISPANIC ORIGIN IN THE STATE AND COUNTIES OF FLORIDA
1995-96

County	Total	Percentage distribution 1/ Race White	Black	Hispanic origin 2/	County	Total	Percentage distribution 1/ Race White	Black	Hispanic origin 2/
Florida	28,235	45.49	32.06	21.06	Lafayette	16	93.75	6.25	0.00
					Lake	408	72.55	19.61	7.35
Alachua	490	48.37	47.96	2.45	Lee	820	59.39	25.24	14.39
Baker	72	77.78	22.22	0.00	Leon	369	45.53	53.12	0.81
Bay	270	76.67	18.89	1.48	Levy	58	72.41	20.69	5.17
Bradford	117	86.32	11.97	0.85	Liberty	11	100.00	0.00	0.00
Brevard	458	70.09	23.80	4.80	Madison	93	30.11	69.89	0.00
Broward	1,996	35.42	44.69	17.94	Manatee	466	67.81	19.96	11.59
Calhoun	32	78.13	15.63	0.00	Marion	511	67.51	26.42	5.28
Charlotte	166	84.94	9.64	4.82	Martin	97	62.89	22.68	14.43
Citrus	248	89.11	6.85	4.03	Monroe	87	67.82	10.34	19.54
Clay	279	81.00	14.70	1.79	Nassau	97	77.32	19.59	3.09
Collier	339	48.38	11.50	38.05	Okaloosa	308	72.08	19.81	3.57
Columbia	108	63.89	34.26	0.93	Okeechobee	144	70.14	7.64	20.14
Dade	6,809	11.03	34.69	53.31	Orange	1,228	41.94	36.56	19.54
De Soto	35	48.57	17.14	34.29	Osceola	332	51.81	10.24	36.45
Dixie	48	87.50	12.50	0.00	Palm Beach	1,450	41.03	38.21	19.52
Duval	2,329	51.78	43.32	2.58	Pasco	505	87.33	5.35	6.93
Escambia	378	50.00	46.56	0.53	Pinellas	1,183	64.92	28.74	3.63
Flagler	28	85.71	14.29	0.00	Polk	1,098	60.66	27.60	11.02
Franklin	10	70.00	30.00	0.00	Putnam	190	50.53	41.05	8.42
Gadsden	162	14.20	80.25	5.56	St. Johns	131	77.10	19.08	1.53
Gilchrist	31	83.87	16.13	0.00	St. Lucie	406	41.38	48.52	9.11
Glades	31	61.29	22.58	9.68	Santa Rosa	153	83.66	13.07	2.61
Gulf	8	37.50	62.50	0.00	Sarasota	313	72.84	22.68	3.51
Hamilton	33	39.39	60.61	0.00	Seminole	424	58.49	25.24	12.97
Hardee	88	37.50	14.77	47.73	Sumter	142	61.27	35.21	2.82
Hendry	145	39.31	16.55	42.76	Suwannee	64	65.63	29.69	4.69
Hernando	212	79.72	15.09	3.77	Taylor	50	56.00	44.00	0.00
Highlands	130	62.31	19.23	18.46	Union	26	80.77	19.23	0.00
Hillsborough	1,183	51.99	28.66	18.01	Volusia	450	67.11	23.33	9.11
Holmes	46	95.65	4.35	0.00	Wakulla	43	90.70	6.98	0.00
Indian River	117	58.97	40.17	0.85	Walton	86	80.23	16.28	1.16
Jackson	47	59.57	36.17	4.26	Washington	9	77.78	11.11	11.11
Jefferson	18	33.33	66.67	0.00					

1/ Does not include other races. Distribution may not add to 100 percent.
2/ Persons of Hispanic origin may be of any race. However, these data are not distributed by race.
Note: A dropout is a student over the age of compulsory school attendance (16) who
meets one or more of the criteria set forth by the Department of Education. Data are
for public schools only. Some data are revised. See Glossary for definition.

Source: State of Florida, Department of Education, Division of Administration,
Education Information and Accountability Services, unpublished data.

University of Florida   **Bureau of Economic and Business Research**

Table 4.25. HOME EDUCATION: NUMBER OF CHILDREN AND FAMILIES REGISTERED IN
HOME EDUCATION PROGRAMS IN THE STATE AND COUNTIES OF FLORIDA, 1995-96

County	Children	Families	County	Children	Families
Florida	22,285	14,964	Lafayette	187	134
			Lake	463	319
Alachua	637	413	Lee	469	295
Baker	11	10	Leon	512	349
Bay	442	299	Levy	103	71
Bradford	59	40	Liberty	2	2
Brevard	975	653	Madison	34	25
Broward	2,049	1,418	Manatee	167	126
Calhoun	19	13	Marion	336	223
Charlotte	155	103	Martin	93	64
Citrus	267	198	Monroe	185	132
Clay	209	139	Nassau	94	67
Collier	332	207	Okaloosa	373	222
Columbia	590	253	Okeechobee	77	51
Dade	1,163	768	Orange	1,278	846
De Soto	39	23	Osceola	93	56
Dixie	17	13	Palm Beach	471	383
Duval	1,842	1,298	Pasco	360	276
Escambia	885	622	Pinellas	1,067	680
Flagler	43	30	Polk	1,187	831
Franklin	9	6	Putnam	108	75
Gadsden	130	80	St. Johns	192	125
Gilchrist	32	17	St. Lucie	118	88
Glades	24	14	Santa Rosa	373	275
Gulf	9	8	Sarasota	507	326
Hamilton	13	10	Seminole	666	442
Hardee	25	17	Sumter	39	28
Hendry	58	37	Suwannee	46	33
Hernando	297	194	Taylor	40	29
Highlands	189	121	Union	14	7
Hillsborough	1,071	706	Volusia	530	364
Holmes	40	30	Wakulla	25	19
Indian River	101	68	Walton	131	80
Jackson	89	49	Washington	88	48
Jefferson	36	16			

Note: Data are for public schools only.

Source: State of Florida, Department of Education, Division of Public Schools,
Statistical Brief: Florida Home Education Programs, 1995-96. Series 97-09B.

Table 4.26. NONPUBLIC ELEMENTARY AND SECONDARY SCHOOLS: PUPIL MEMBERSHIP
IN THE STATE AND COUNTIES OF FLORIDA, 1996-97

County	Member-ship K-12	Per-centage change 1995-96 to 1996-97	As a percent-age of total K-12 member-ship	County	Member-ship K-12	Per-centage change 1995-96 to 1996-97	As a percent-age of total K-12 member-ship
Florida	257,805	5.13	10.54	Lafayette	0	(X)	0.00
				Lake	1,983	5.82	7.17
Alachua	2,248	4.27	7.31	Lee	5,104	1.31	9.12
Baker	8	(X)	0.18	Leon	4,682	9.01	13.29
Bay	1,491	2.40	5.62	Levy	61	17.31	1.05
Bradford	59	59.46	1.43	Liberty	0	(X)	0.00
Brevard	8,471	6.33	11.47	Madison	292	21.67	8.10
Broward	29,113	4.99	12.00	Manatee	2,867	7.62	8.24
Calhoun	0	(X)	0.00	Marion	5,119	27.56	12.59
Charlotte	710	-0.28	4.34	Martin	1,706	9.99	10.53
Citrus	641	7.55	4.41	Monroe	605	12.04	6.23
Clay	2,601	1.52	9.23	Nassau	260	-21.69	2.52
Collier	2,300	3.00	7.80	Okaloosa	1,673	11.09	5.36
Columbia	369	5.73	3.93	Okeechobee	131	-24.71	2.05
Dade	49,679	-0.16	13.01	Orange	17,443	5.15	12.10
De Soto	43	-20.37	0.95	Osceola	1,758	56.68	6.14
Dixie	0	(X)	0.00	Palm Beach	20,976	6.14	13.49
Duval	18,521	6.67	13.09	Pasco	1,679	2.69	3.82
Escambia	6,304	6.58	12.46	Pinellas	15,691	6.15	12.99
Flagler	114	267.74	2.00	Polk	5,431	8.21	6.90
Franklin	153	3.38	9.24	Putnam	529	-14.68	3.95
Gadsden	714	-1.65	8.28	St. Johns	1,458	8.08	8.28
Gilchrist	318	-12.40	11.22	St. Lucie	2,198	1.15	7.51
Glades	20	(X)	1.82	Santa Rosa	541	73.95	2.62
Gulf	101	-19.20	4.31	Sarasota	4,420	3.25	12.39
Hamilton	10	(X)	0.44	Seminole	7,248	12.01	11.67
Hardee	34	-34.62	0.66	Sumter	26	-54.39	0.45
Hendry	254	-0.78	3.48	Suwannee	362	-7.42	5.96
Hernando	1,230	25.77	7.32	Taylor	0	(X)	0.00
Highlands	521	-2.98	4.63	Union	0	(X)	0.00
Hillsborough	19,889	5.27	12.10	Volusia	5,231	2.91	8.40
Holmes	2	(X)	0.05	Wakulla	58	45.00	1.35
Indian River	1,659	3.24	10.84	Walton	120	64.38	2.20
Jackson	232	8.92	2.91	Washington	6	0.00	0.19
Jefferson	338	-4.52	14.63				

K-12 Kindergarten through grade 12; no prekindergarten.
(X) Not applicable.
Note: See Glossary under Private school for definition of nonpublic schools.
  Source: State of Florida, Department of Education, Division of Public Schools,
Statistical Brief: Florida's Nonpublic Schools, 1996-97. Series 98-03B.

University of Florida   **Bureau of Economic and Business Research**

Table 4.27. ELEMENTARY AND SECONDARY SCHOOLS: NUMBER AND PUPIL MEMBERSHIP
IN THE STATE AND COUNTIES OF FLORIDA, SCHOOL YEAR 1995-96

County	Number of schools	Membership 1/ Total	Membership 1/ Percentage change from 1995-96	County	Number of schools	Membership 1/ Total	Membership 1/ Percentage change from 1995-96
Florida 2/	3,003	2,125,301	3.0	Lake	47	24,444	5.0
				Lee	77	49,627	3.2
Alachua	49	27,965	1.0	Leon	48	30,371	2.8
Baker	8	4,493	0.2	Levy	14	5,602	4.1
Bay	35	24,650	1.7	Liberty	5	1,146	3.2
Bradford	10	3,980	-0.4	Madison	10	3,250	2.9
Brevard	101	64,430	1.4	Manatee	68	30,931	2.5
Broward	198	203,421	4.5	Marion	49	34,500	4.3
Calhoun	7	2,185	0.0	Martin	32	14,071	5.1
Charlotte	22	15,143	3.0	Monroe	18	9,252	1.0
Citrus	20	13,657	2.7	Nassau	18	9,439	2.1
Clay	29	24,532	4.1	Okaloosa	37	29,013	1.2
Collier	39	25,548	5.2	Okeechobee	14	6,125	1.7
Columbia	14	8,896	1.6	Orange	165	121,239	3.8
Dade	353	325,324	3.3	Osceola	32	25,220	5.9
De Soto	14	4,346	2.7	Palm Beach	166	129,582	3.6
Dixie	6	2,160	0.0	Pasco	52	40,603	4.2
Duval	158	120,898	1.9	Pinellas	147	102,548	2.1
Escambia	80	43,776	0.7	Polk	121	71,724	2.3
Flagler	8	5,330	9.0	Putnam	22	12,536	0.5
Franklin	7	1,621	4.3	St. Johns	26	15,173	5.2
Gadsden	23	8,058	0.6	St. Lucie	36	26,377	2.9
Gilchrist	7	2,415	6.5	Santa Rosa	30	19,252	4.0
Glades	8	1,022	0.8	Sarasota	36	30,432	2.2
Gulf	8	2,174	1.5	Seminole	57	53,419	2.1
Hamilton	10	2,260	-0.7	Sumter	12	5,574	2.3
Hardee	11	5,034	13.7	Suwannee	8	5,549	1.9
Hendry	15	6,841	4.4	Taylor	9	3,640	2.7
Hernando	20	15,174	3.8	Union	6	2,164	6.4
Highlands	16	10,515	2.7	Volusia	77	55,853	2.3
Hillsborough	186	140,067	3.3	Wakulla	7	4,087	4.4
Holmes	8	3,659	1.1	Walton	11	5,084	1.9
Indian River	21	13,297	3.2	Washington	10	3,097	1.7
Jackson	19	7,678	-0.8	Deaf/Blind	10	606	-1.0
Jefferson	7	1,961	-1.8	Dozier School	3	259	0.4
Lafayette	5	1,002	1.9				

1/ Based on kindergarten through grade 12 fall membership survey.
2/ Detail may not add to total due to receipt of reports not distributed by county.
Note: Data are for public schools only.

Source: State of Florida, Department of Education, Division of Administration,
Profiles of Florida School Districts, 1995-96, Student and Staff Data. EIAS Series
97-21, December 1996.

University of Florida   **Bureau of Economic and Business Research**

Table 4.28. ELEMENTARY AND SECONDARY SCHOOLS: PUPIL PARTICIPATION
IN THE FREE AND REDUCED LUNCH PROGRAMS IN THE STATE
AND COUNTIES OF FLORIDA, 1996-97

County	Total school membership	Percentage eligible for free/ reduced lunch	Students eligible for free lunch		Students eligible for reduced lunch	
			Number	Percentage	Number	Percentage
Florida	2,242,212	43.15	819,782	36.56	147,631	6.58
Alachua	29,648	45.61	11,815	39.85	1,707	5.76
Baker	4,630	41.92	1,629	35.18	312	6.74
Bay	25,665	45.62	9,084	35.39	2,625	10.23
Bradford	4,192	53.46	1,849	44.11	392	9.35
Brevard	66,663	29.74	16,010	24.02	3,817	5.73
Broward	218,608	36.84	67,149	30.72	13,387	6.12
Calhoun	2,288	47.60	905	39.55	184	8.04
Charlotte	16,088	42.08	4,869	30.26	1,901	11.82
Citrus	14,194	42.29	5,044	35.54	958	6.75
Clay	25,940	22.28	4,242	16.35	1,537	5.93
Collier	28,177	42.61	10,396	36.90	1,609	5.71
Columbia	9,263	47.97	3,808	41.11	635	6.86
Dade	341,117	59.29	182,831	53.60	19,424	5.69
De Soto	4,616	62.50	2,517	54.53	368	7.97
Dixie	2,323	60.44	1,238	53.29	166	7.15
Duval	126,118	46.53	48,085	38.13	10,599	8.40
Escambia	45,744	55.07	20,452	44.71	4,738	10.36
Flagler	5,677	38.21	1,691	29.79	478	8.42
Franklin	1,589	54.50	703	44.24	163	10.26
Gadsden	8,546	83.36	6,424	75.17	700	8.19
Gilchrist	2,651	50.25	1,126	42.47	206	7.77
Glades	1,149	57.62	570	49.61	92	8.01
Gulf	2,345	47.63	914	38.98	203	8.66
Hamilton	2,338	62.06	1,279	54.70	172	7.36
Hardee	5,377	56.87	2,739	50.94	319	5.93
Hendry	7,257	55.08	3,630	50.02	367	5.06
Hernando	15,859	46.06	5,735	36.16	1,569	9.89
Highlands	11,030	52.06	4,880	44.24	862	7.82
Hillsborough	147,826	48.87	62,477	42.26	9,761	6.60
Holmes	3,831	59.31	1,842	48.08	430	11.22
Indian River	13,977	40.50	4,769	34.12	891	6.37
Jackson	8,098	52.78	3,444	42.53	830	10.25
Jefferson	2,126	67.07	1,269	59.69	157	7.38

See footnote at end of table.

Continued . . .

University of Florida   **Bureau of Economic and Business Research**

Table 4.28. ELEMENTARY AND SECONDARY SCHOOLS: PUPIL PARTICIPATION
IN THE FREE AND REDUCED LUNCH PROGRAMS IN THE STATE
AND COUNTIES OF FLORIDA, 1996-97 (Continued)

County	Total school membership	Percentage eligible for free/ reduced lunch	Students eligible for free lunch		Students eligible for reduced lunch	
			Number	Percentage	Number	Percentage
Lafayette	1,109	52.84	511	46.08	75	6.76
Lake	26,131	40.72	8,947	34.24	1,693	6.48
Lee	52,317	44.04	18,268	34.92	4,771	9.12
Leon	31,560	23.37	6,354	20.13	1,022	3.24
Levy	5,918	55.58	2,739	46.28	550	9.29
Liberty	1,247	44.35	474	38.01	79	6.34
Madison	3,479	63.06	1,972	56.68	222	6.38
Manatee	32,794	43.15	11,586	35.33	2,565	7.82
Marion	36,242	50.47	15,398	42.49	2,893	7.98
Martin	14,823	30.67	3,905	26.34	641	4.32
Monroe	9,379	35.17	2,726	29.06	573	6.11
Nassau	10,235	31.34	2,486	24.29	722	7.05
Okaloosa	30,067	30.19	6,364	21.17	2,712	9.02
Okeechobee	6,597	54.07	3,055	46.31	512	7.76
Orange	129,143	38.20	41,815	32.38	7,521	5.82
Osceola	27,376	0.00	0	0.00	0	0.00
Palm Beach	137,585	29.48	36,243	26.34	4,314	3.14
Pasco	43,461	44.21	15,331	35.28	3,881	8.93
Pinellas	107,060	37.93	33,170	30.98	7,441	6.95
Polk	74,808	53.06	33,231	44.42	6,462	8.64
Putnam	13,296	62.11	7,267	54.66	991	7.45
St. Johns	16,374	26.48	3,408	20.81	928	5.67
St. Lucie	27,672	53.21	12,374	44.72	2,349	8.49
Santa Rosa	20,668	30.99	4,883	23.63	1,523	7.37
Sarasota	31,950	33.68	8,103	25.36	2,657	8.32
Seminole	55,972	25.43	11,127	19.88	3,104	5.55
Sumter	5,921	62.88	3,235	54.64	488	8.24
Suwannee	5,851	44.98	2,287	39.09	345	5.90
Taylor	3,840	46.74	1,557	40.55	238	6.20
Union	2,317	42.38	841	36.30	141	6.09
Volusia	58,004	39.84	19,505	33.63	3,606	6.22
Wakulla	4,444	36.16	1,341	30.18	266	5.99
Walton	5,459	50.93	2,308	42.28	472	8.65
Washington	3,249	52.29	1,384	42.60	315	9.70

Note: Data were obtained from the Florida DOE Student Information Data Base,
Survey 2 for Fall 1996, and are for public schools only.

Source: State of Florida, Department of Education, Division of Administration,
Education, Information and Accountability Services, unpublished data.

Table 4.50. HIGHER EDUCATION: ENROLLMENT IN SELECTED COLLEGES AND
UNIVERSITIES IN SPECIFIED CITIES AND COUNTIES OF FLORIDA
ACADEMIC YEAR 1994-95

School 1/	City	County	Enroll-ment 2/
Art Institute of Ft. Lauderdale	Ft. Lauderdale	Broward	1,802
ATI Health Education Center	Miami	Dade	175
Barry University	Miami	Dade	6,850
Barry University/Brevard County branch	Merritt Island	Brevard	279
Bethune Cookman College	Daytona Beach	Volusia	2,210
Brevard Community College	Cocoa	Brevard	14,425
Broward Community College	Ft. Lauderdale	Broward	25,714
Caribbean Center for Advanced Studies/ Miami Institute of Psychology	Miami	Dade	427
Central Florida Community College	Ocala	Marion	5,919
Chipola Junior College	Marianna	Jackson	2,684
Clearwater Christian College	Clearwater	Pinellas	452
Daytona Beach Community College	Daytona Beach	Volusia	11,654
Eckerd College	St. Petersburg	Pinellas	1,391
Edison Community College	Ft. Myers	Lee	9,933
Edward Waters College	Jacksonville	Duval	786
Embry-Riddle Aeronautical University	Daytona Beach	Volusia	11,210
Flagler Career Institute	Jacksonville	Duval	200
Flagler College	St. Augustine	St. Johns	1,389
Florida Agricultural and Mechanical University	Tallahassee	Leon	9,876
Florida Atlantic University	Boca Raton	Palm Beach	15,769
Florida Baptist Theological College	Graceville	Jackson	490
Florida Bible College	Kissimmee	Osceola	104
Florida Christian College Inc.	Kissimmee	Osceola	160
Florida College	Temple Terrace	Hillsborough	404
Florida Community College at Jacksonville	Jacksonville	Duval	21,228
Florida Institute of Technology	Melbourne	Brevard	4,983
Florida Institute of Traditional Chinese Medicine	Pinellas Park	Pinellas	56
Florida International University	Miami	Dade	24,321
Florida Keys Community College	Key West	Monroe	2,120
Florida Memorial College	Miami	Dade	1,579
Florida Southern College	Lakeland	Polk	2,417
Florida State University	Tallahassee	Leon	28,575
Ft. Lauderdale College	Ft. Lauderdale	Broward	454
Gulf Coast Community	Panama City	Bay	5,872
Hillsborough Community College	Tampa	Hillsborough	21,497
Hobe Sound Bible College	Hobe Sound	Martin	166
Indian River Community College	Ft. Pierce	St. Lucie	12,071
International Academy of Merchandising and Design	Tampa	Hillsborough	375
International College	Naples	Collier	514
International College	Ft. Myers	Lee	(NA)

See footnotes at end of table.   Continued . . .

University of Florida   **Bureau of Economic and Business Research**

Table 4.50. HIGHER EDUCATION: ENROLLMENT IN SELECTED COLLEGES AND
UNIVERSITIES IN SPECIFIED CITIES AND COUNTIES OF FLORIDA
ACADEMIC YEAR 1994-95 (Continued)

School 1/	City	County	Enroll-ment 2/
International Fine Arts College	Miami	Dade	647
ITT Technical Institute	Tampa	Hillsborough	689
ITT Technical Institute	Maitland	Orange	634
Jacksonville University	Jacksonville	Duval	2,406
Johnson and Wales University/ Florida campus	North Miami	Dade	(NA)
Jones College Jacksonville	Jacksonville	Duval	674
Jones College/Miami campus	Miami	Dade	(NA)
Keiser College of Technology	Ft. Lauderdale	Broward	872
Keiser College/Melbourne	Melbourne	Brevard	373
Keiser College/Tallahassee	Tallahassee	Leon	(NA)
Lake City Community College	Lake City	Columbia	2,652
Lake-Sumter Community College	Leesburg	Lake	2,658
Lynn University	Boca Raton	Palm Beach	1,333
Manatee Community College	Bradenton	Manatee	8,056
Miami-Dade Community College	Miami	Dade	48,232
National Education Center-Bauder College campus	Ft. Lauderdale	Broward	604
National Education Center-Bauder College campus	Miami	Dade	354
National Education Center-Tampa Technical Institute	Tampa	Hillsborough	1,042
New England Institute of Technology/ Palm Beach	West Palm Beach	Palm Beach	300
New York Institute of Technology/ Florida campus	Boca Raton	Palm Beach	(NA)
North Florida Junior College	Madison	Madison	1,144
Nova Southeastern University	Ft. Lauderdale	Broward	11,049
Okaloosa-Walton Community College	Niceville	Okaloosa	6,162
Orlando College	Orlando	Orange	838
Orlando College South	Orlando	Orange	734
Palm Beach Atlantic College	West Palm Beach	Palm Beach	1,867
Palm Beach Community College	Lake Worth	Palm Beach	18,586
Pasco-Hernando Community College	Dade City	Pasco	5,335
Pensacola Junior College	Pensacola	Escambia	11,788
Phillips Junior College/Daytona Beach	Daytona Beach	Volusia	247
Phillips Junior College/Melbourne	Melbourne	Brevard	277
Polk Community College	Winter Haven	Polk	5,815
Prospect Hall School of Business	Hollywood	Broward	178
Ringling School of Art and Design	Sarasota	Sarasota	771
Rollins College	Winter Park	Orange	3,361
Rollins College/Brevard campus	West Melbourne	Brevard	(NA)
St. John Vianney College Seminary	Miami	Dade	53
St. Johns River Community College	Palatka	Putnam	3,250
St. Leo College	St. Leo	Pasco	7,131
St. Petersburg Junior College	St. Petersburg	Pinellas	22,799

See footnotes at end of table. Continued . . .

University of Florida   **Bureau of Economic and Business Research**

Table 4.50. HIGHER EDUCATION: ENROLLMENT IN SELECTED COLLEGES AND
UNIVERSITIES IN SPECIFIED CITIES AND COUNTIES OF FLORIDA
ACADEMIC YEAR 1994-95 (Continued)

School 1/	City	County	Enroll-ment 2/
St. Thomas University	Miami	Dade	2,792
St. Vincent of De Paul Regional Seminary	Boynton Beach	Palm Beach	90
Santa Fe Community College	Gainesville	Alachua	12,438
Sarasota County Technical Institute	Sarasota	Sarasota	1,980
Seminole Community College	Sanford	Seminole	8,446
South Florida Community College	Avon Park	Highlands	2,582
Southeastern College Assemblies of God	Lakeland	Polk	1,144
Spurgeon Baptist Bible College	Mulberry	Polk	32
Stetson University	DeLand	Volusia	2,955
Tallahassee Community	Tallahassee	Leon	9,390
Talmudic College of Florida	Tampa	Hillsborough	44
Tampa College	Tampa	Hillsborough	1,077
Tampa College/Brandon	Tampa	Hillsborough	940
Tampa College/Lakeland	Lakeland	Polk	700
Tampa College/Pinellas	Clearwater	Pinellas	974
The University of West Florida	Pensacola	Escambia	7,750
Trinity College at Miami	Miami	Dade	338
Trinity College of Florida	New Port Richey	Pasco	189
University of Central Florida	Orlando	Orange	23,692
University of Florida	Gainesville	Alachua	37,324
University of Miami	Coral Gables	Dade	13,842
University of North Florida	Jacksonville	Duval	9,382
University of Sarasota	Sarasota	Sarasota	359
University of South Florida	Tampa	Hillsborough	34,768
University of Tampa	Tampa	Hillsborough	2,377
Valencia Community College	Orlando	Orange	22,593
Ward Stone College	Miami	Dade	(NA)
Warner Southern College	Lake Wales	Polk	531
Webber College	Babson Park	Polk	437

(NA) Not available.
1/ Includes institutions accredited at the college level by an agency recognized
by the U.S. Secretary of Education.
2/ Includes undergraduate, graduate, first-professional, and unclassified students, both full- and part-time.

Source: U.S., Department of Education, National Center for Education Statistics,
Office of Educational Research and Improvement, *1995 Directory of Postsecondary Institutions: Volume I, 4-Year and 2-Year Institutions.*

University of Florida   **Bureau of Economic and Business Research**

Table 4.53. HIGHER EDUCATION: ENROLLMENT IN THE UNIVERSITIES OF THE STATE
UNIVERSITY SYSTEM OF FLORIDA BY LEVEL, SEX, RACE OR HISPANIC ORIGIN
AND STATUS, FALL 1995

Sex and race	Educational and general Under-graduate	Graduate	Health or medical center 1/ Under-graduate	Graduate	IFAS Under-graduate	Graduate
Part-time 2/						
Total	57,590	15,614	297	1,141	435	241
Sex						
Female	32,819	8,794	250	693	212	93
Male	24,762	6,820	47	448	223	148
Not reported	9	0	0	0	0	0
Race						
Asian	2,173	466	16	77	22	10
Black	6,664	1,067	13	53	24	6
American Indian or Alaskan native	190	29	0	10	4	2
White	36,938	11,573	247	900	337	151
Other	742	907	2	23	7	62
Not reported	566	1	1	2	2	1
Hispanic origin 3/	10,317	1,571	18	76	39	9
Full-time 4/						
Total	110,714	15,420	1,772	1,972	2,387	450
Sex						
Female	60,163	7,780	1,363	1,102	1,260	185
Male	50,546	7,640	409	870	1,127	265
Not reported	5	0	0	0	0	0
Race						
Asian	4,660	481	148	164	162	9
Black	17,466	1,343	121	107	162	9
American Indian or Alaskan native	374	66	9	8	12	0
White	70,991	10,131	1,381	1,426	1,783	227
Other	3,020	2,226	6	124	30	189
Not reported	128	16	0	4	3	0
Hispanic origin 3/	14,075	1,157	107	139	235	16

IFAS Institute of Food and Agriculture Science.
1/ Includes veterinary medicine.
2/ Includes undergraduates enrolled for fewer than 12 hours and graduate students enrolled for fewer than 9 hours.
3/ Persons of Hispanic origin may be of any race. However, these data are not distributed by race.
4/ Includes undergraduates enrolled for 12 or more hours and graduate students enrolled for 9 or more hours.
Note: Unclassified students are counted as undergraduates. Data are from the student data course file enrollment report, Fall 1995. Staff and senior citizen waivers are excluded.

Source: State of Florida, State University System, Board of Regents, *Fact Book, 1995-96.*

University of Florida   **Bureau of Economic and Business Research**

Table 4.54. HIGHER EDUCATION: ENROLLMENT IN THE UNIVERSITIES OF THE STATE
UNIVERSITY SYSTEM OF FLORIDA, FALL 1989 THROUGH 1996

University	1989	1990	1991	1992
Total	168,311	175,960	181,889	182,896
Educational and general, total	163,155	170,548	176,077	176,762
University of Florida	31,481	31,569	32,159	31,922
Florida State University	27,582	28,054	28,093	27,810
Florida A & M University	7,182	8,030	8,801	9,049
University of South Florida	30,255	30,691	31,771	32,467
Florida Atlantic University	11,629	13,004	14,264	14,822
University of West Florida	7,631	7,842	7,943	7,386
University of Central Florida	20,084	21,376	21,267	21,682
Florida International University	19,767	22,122	23,275	22,597
University of North Florida	7,544	7,860	8,504	9,027
Special units, total 1/	5,156	5,412	5,812	6,134
University of Florida				
Institute of Food and Agriculture				
Science	1,453	1,620	1,748	1,971
Health and Medical Center	2,747	2,759	2,932	2,961
University of South Florida				
Medical Center	956	1,033	1,132	1,202

	1993	1994	1995	1996
Total	188,928	197,931	203,478	208,033
Educational and general, total	182,579	191,148	196,246	199,338
University of Florida	32,578	32,827	33,394	32,314
Florida State University	27,951	28,794	29,390	29,345
Florida A & M University	9,378	9,650	9,784	10,206
University of South Florida	32,773	33,614	33,829	34,024
Florida Atlantic University	15,760	17,367	17,671	18,350
University of West Florida	7,564	7,716	8,087	7,882
University of Central Florida	23,531	25,363	26,325	27,411
Florida International University	23,832	26,040	27,542	29,098
University of North Florida	9,212	9,777	10,224	10,708
Special units, total 1/	6,349	6,783	7,232	8,695
University of Florida				
Institute of Food and Agriculture				
Science	2,141	2,403	2,772	3,513
Health and Medical Center	2,965	3,087	3,174	3,845
University of South Florida				
Medical Center	1,243	1,293	1,286	1,337

1/ Includes medical professionals.
Note: Data are from the student data course file enrollment reports. Staff and
senior citizen waivers are excluded.

Source: State of Florida, State University System, Board of Regents, *Fact Book,
1995-96.*

University of Florida   **Bureau of Economic and Business Research**

Table 4.60. PUBLIC COMMUNITY COLLEGES: COLLEGE LEVEL HEADCOUNT ENROLLMENT
BY PROGRAM AND INSTITUTION IN FLORIDA, 1995-96

Community college	Total Undupli-cated	Dupli-cated	Advanced and profes-sional	Voca-tional (credit)	Adult general	Community instruc-tional serv-ices 1/	Lifelong learning
Total	783,154	1,009,904	199,152	299,614	161,661	338,921	10,556
Brevard	38,288	50,853	9,619	24,622	3,341	12,739	532
Broward	43,134	62,712	13,903	9,905	10,441	27,004	1,459
Central Florida	17,967	21,070	2,281	7,190	2,624	6,754	2,221
Chipola	6,283	6,241	1,618	3,379	698	546	0
Daytona Beach	35,952	40,163	6,783	13,426	12,922	6,353	679
Edison	21,572	21,692	5,591	7,419	2,343	5,872	467
Florida Community College at Jacksonville	85,208	98,994	7,754	48,225	27,208	15,807	0
Florida Keys	4,442	5,088	750	1,144	362	2,637	195
Gulf Coast	21,221	25,899	4,587	13,586	1,740	5,978	8
Hillsborough	38,080	46,850	14,472	11,463	6,893	14,022	0
Indian River	42,197	56,021	4,385	11,262	13,569	26,805	0
Lake City	8,128	9,801	724	4,944	1,700	2,433	0
Lake-Sumter	5,879	8,951	1,301	2,014	961	4,267	408
Manatee	17,241	20,719	4,481	7,206	1,789	7,243	0
Miami-Dade	101,386	140,740	25,693	27,350	18,978	68,719	0
North Florida	2,912	2,957	752	1,150	704	351	0
Okaloosa-Walton	14,600	20,245	4,023	1,821	3,100	11,301	0
Palm Beach	49,064	54,764	7,483	19,839	4,952	22,072	418
Pasco-Hernando	12,407	14,741	4,937	6,475	1,202	1,084	1,043
Pensacola	25,613	32,518	6,676	5,914	6,491	11,890	1,547
Polk	17,728	28,096	3,194	10,945	1,842	11,756	359
St. Johns River	6,994	7,501	3,667	1,248	2,070	516	0
St. Petersburg	47,396	68,486	15,704	20,193	7,453	25,136	0
Santa Fe	20,207	34,288	11,526	2,274	4,220	16,268	0
Seminole	24,896	37,329	6,476	12,139	7,461	10,736	517
South Florida	10,669	15,399	1,505	4,223	5,271	4,400	0
Tallahassee	16,150	18,681	7,656	1,698	2,481	6,846	0
Valencia	47,540	59,105	21,611	18,560	8,845	9,386	703

1/ Includes students awaiting enrollment in limited access programs, students enrolled in apprenticeship courses, students who are enrolled in courses related to employment, as general freshmen or for other personal objectives.
Note: There may be some duplication between major program areas.

Source: State of Florida, Department of Education, Division of Community Colleges, *The Fact Book: Report for the Florida Community College System,* January 1997.

Table 4.61. PUBLIC COMMUNITY COLLEGES: TRANSFER STUDENTS FROM FLORIDA COMMUNITY
COLLEGES TO FLORIDA UNIVERSITIES BY SEX AND UNIVERSITY, FALL 1993 AND 1994

Institution	1993			1994		
	Total	Male	Female	Total	Male	Female
State University System, total	73,021	32,361	40,660	76,636	33,732	42,897
Florida Agricultural and						
Mechanical University	1,299	596	703	1,341	620	721
Florida Atlantic University	7,369	2,962	4,407	7,826	3,119	4,707
Florida International University	11,223	4,600	6,623	11,677	4,848	6,829
Florida State University	11,386	5,256	6,130	11,716	5,320	6,396
University of Central Florida	14,104	6,575	7,529	14,747	6,784	7,963
University of Florida	6,927	3,808	3,119	7,523	4,106	3,417
University of North Florida	4,471	1,840	2,631	4,674	1,956	2,718
University of South Florida	13,052	5,442	7,610	13,718	5,615	8,096
University of West Florida	3,190	1,282	1,908	3,414	1,364	2,050

Table 4.62. PUBLIC COMMUNITY COLLEGES: TRANSFER STUDENTS FROM FLORIDA COMMUNITY
COLLEGES TO FLORIDA UNIVERSITIES BY RACE OR HISPANIC ORIGIN
AND UNIVERSITY, FALL 1994

Institution	Total	Race					His-panic origin 2/
		White	Black	Amer-ican Indian	Asian	Other 1/	
State University System, total	76,636	55,701	6,243	250	2,484	1,219	10,739
Florida Agricultural and							
Mechanical University	1,341	359	851	1	41	18	71
Florida Atlantic University	7,826	5,813	755	20	305	170	763
Florida International University	11,677	3,188	1,425	13	307	396	6,348
Florida State University	11,716	9,872	841	42	245	50	666
University of Central Florida	14,747	11,778	824	60	605	263	1,217
University of Florida	7,523	6,188	270	32	298	175	560
University of North Florida	4,674	3,971	352	16	181	17	137
University of South Florida	13,718	11,535	714	32	401	121	915
University of West Florida	3,414	2,997	211	34	101	9	62

1/ Includes students classified as nonresident aliens and unclassified students.
2/ Persons of Hispanic origin may be of any race. However, these data are not
distributed by race.

Source for Tables 4.61 and 4.62: State of Florida, Department of Education, State
Board of Community Colleges, *Articulation Report,* March 1996.

University of Florida   **Bureau of Economic and Business Research**

Table 4.76. TESTING: PERCENTAGE OF STUDENTS PASSING THE HIGH SCHOOL
COMPETENCY TEST (HSCT) IN THE STATE AND COUNTIES
OF FLORIDA, OCTOBER 1995 AND 1996

County	Communications 1995	1996	Mathematics 1995	1996	County	Communications 1995	1996	Mathematics 1995	1996
Florida	89	77	77	75	Lafayette	83	86	62	70
					Lake	91	77	78	72
Alachua	94	86	83	80	Lee	87	74	72	70
Baker	85	75	65	64	Leon	93	81	80	76
Bay	92	75	77	71	Levy	93	81	79	77
Bradford	93	77	66	67	Liberty	93	81	79	77
Brevard	94	82	85	80	Madison	91	86	59	64
Broward	86	72	74	71	Manatee	90	80	79	79
Calhoun	94	88	86	82	Marion	89	74	75	70
Charlotte	93	86	84	84	Martin	93	85	81	79
Citrus	95	87	85	85	Monroe	88	79	78	76
Clay	90	80	79	76	Nassau	94	84	76	79
Collier	89	77	81	82	Okaloosa	95	83	84	80
Columbia	93	79	79	71	Okeechobee	94	79	78	72
Dade	80	67	66	66	Orange	91	78	79	76
De Soto	86	78	73	67	Osceola	90	74	70	64
Dixie	98	70	81	67	Palm Beach	89	77	79	76
Duval	89	79	69	72	Pasco	92	89	80	88
Escambia	92	79	76	71	Pinellas	93	82	84	78
Flagler	94	83	81	78	Polk	91	80	78	75
Franklin	95	72	78	58	Putnam	88	70	67	62
Gadsden	77	62	53	52	St. Johns	92	81	81	77
Gilchrist	92	81	67	78	St. Lucie	89	79	70	76
Glades	89	72	69	57	Santa Rosa	91	80	81	77
Gulf	93	85	88	82	Sarasota	91	84	84	84
Hamilton	89	70	73	56	Seminole	92	82	84	83
Hardee	88	65	72	71	Sumter	86	74	66	68
Hendry	85	74	66	65	Suwannee	91	74	76	75
Hernando	96	85	81	78	Taylor	92	80	75	70
Highlands	94	77	80	73	Union	91	75	72	63
Hillsborough	94	84	87	86	Volusia	93	83	79	79
Holmes	89	81	73	79	Wakulla	91	85	80	81
Indian River	92	87	77	85	Walton	92	84	80	72
Jackson	92	69	77	77	Washington	91	75	83	76
Jefferson	85	64	68	72	Developmental 1/	93	76	80	73

1/ Developmental research schools funded through and administered by the State
University System.
   Note: Data are for public school students in grade 11. The High School Competency Test (HSCT) measures the application of basic skills to everyday life situa-
tions. Minimum student performance skills were established in the basic areas of
reading and writing (communications) and mathematics. Passing both the communications section and the mathematics section of the HSCT is a requirement for high
school graduation in Florida.
   Source: State of Florida, Department of Education, Division of Public Schools,
*High School Competency Test (HSCT): State, District, and School Report of Statewide
Assessment Results,* October 1996, and previous edition.

Table 4.77. TESTING: MEDIAN NATIONAL PERCENTILE RANK OF PUBLIC SCHOOL STUDENTS
TAKING THE GRADE TEN ASSESSMENT TEST (GTAT) IN THE STATE
AND COUNTIES OF FLORIDA, APRIL 1995 AND 1996

County	Reading compre- hension 1995	1996	Mathe- matics 1995	1996	County	Reading compre- hension 1995	1996	Mathe- matics 1995	1996
Florida	50	47	51	54	Lafayette	36	42	36	50
					Lake	53	49	54	54
Alachua	61	53	58	57	Lee	53	47	54	54
Baker	42	40	43	38	Leon	56	53	54	61
Bay	56	55	58	57	Levy	50	40	51	45
Bradford	42	37	43	41	Liberty	49	49	67	57
Brevard	58	55	61	61	Madison	37	35	38	30
Broward	45	45	51	50	Manatee	50	49	54	57
Calhoun	53	47	63	50	Marion	50	45	51	50
Charlotte	56	53	58	57	Martin	58	53	58	57
Citrus	53	58	58	57	Monroe	48	53	46	57
Clay	56	55	61	61	Nassau	53	53	54	54
Collier	53	49	61	61	Okaloosa	58	58	61	61
Columbia	45	45	51	45	Okeechobee	42	33	38	38
Dade	35	31	38	38	Orange	42	45	43	45
De Soto	41	40	46	45	Osceola	48	40	51	45
Dixie	45	35	43	41	Palm Beach	53	49	58	57
Duval	50	49	54	54	Pasco	53	53	54	57
Escambia	45	42	51	45	Pinellas	56	53	58	54
Flagler	58	55	58	54	Polk	48	47	54	54
Franklin	49	35	58	38	Putnam	45	40	43	41
Gadsden	20	22	26	23	St. Johns	58	58	61	57
Gilchrist	44	53	46	57	St. Lucie	40	45	46	45
Glades	40	41	49	40	Santa Rosa	58	53	58	57
Gulf	45	51	51	50	Sarasota	61	62	64	65
Hamilton	28	31	34	30	Seminole	58	58	64	65
Hardee	35	40	43	41	Sumter	45	45	46	45
Hendry	35	35	38	38	Suwannee	45	45	51	50
Hernando	58	55	58	57	Taylor	42	45	51	45
Highlands	50	47	54	54	Union	37	40	38	38
Hillsborough	53	49	58	57	Volusia	53	53	54	54
Holmes	48	47	54	54	Wakulla	48	55	54	59
Indian River	53	55	54	54	Walton	48	47	46	50
Jackson	50	45	51	45	Washington	53	49	58	45
Jefferson	28	31	30	26					

Note: The Grade Ten Assessment Test (GTAT), is a standardized, norm-referenced achievement test that measures the performance levels of Florida's public schools tenth grade students in the subject areas of reading comprehension and mathematics. It was established in response to changes in the law by the 1990 Legislature. Scores derived from a national sample of students are norms that permit the test user to compare performance of Florida students with that of the nationally representative group. The national percentile rank (NPR) score indicates the percentage of students in the national norm group whose scores fell below a student's raw score.

Source: State of Florida, Department of Education, Division of Public Schools, *Grade Ten Assessment Test (GTAT) State, District, and School Report: Florida State-wide Assessment Program,* April 1996 and previous edition.

University of Florida   **Bureau of Economic and Business Research**

Table 4.78. TESTING: AVERAGE SCORES FOR STUDENTS TAKING THE FLORIDA
WRITING ASSESSMENT TEST IN THE STATE AND COUNTIES
OF FLORIDA, 1997

County	Grade 4	Grade 8	Grade 10	County	Grade 4	Grade 8	Grade 10
Florida	2.6	3.4	3.6	Leon	2.6	3.3	3.8
				Levy	2.5	3.2	3.5
Alachua	2.7	3.4	3.7	Liberty	2.5	3.4	3.7
Baker	2.3	2.9	2.8	Madison	1.9	2.9	2.9
Bay	2.5	3.4	3.5	Manatee	2.7	3.4	3.6
Bradford	2.6	3.5	3.3	Marion	2.4	3.0	3.4
Brevard	2.8	3.5	3.8	Martin	2.5	3.3	3.8
Broward	2.6	3.4	3.6	Monroe	2.7	3.4	3.6
Calhoun	2.9	3.4	3.3	Nassau	2.4	3.3	3.8
Charlotte	2.8	3.7	4.0	Okaloosa	2.8	3.6	3.9
Citrus	2.3	3.4	3.6	Okeechobee	2.5	2.9	3.5
Clay	2.5	3.1	3.5	Orange	2.5	3.3	3.5
Collier	2.6	3.3	3.5	Osceola	2.5	3.3	3.5
Columbia	2.3	3.0	3.4	Palm Beach	2.5	3.5	3.5
Dade	2.6	3.3	3.6	Pasco	2.6	3.3	3.6
De Soto	2.3	3.1	3.4	Pinellas	2.9	3.5	3.9
Dixie	2.3	3.1	3.0	Polk	2.6	3.3	3.7
Duval	2.6	3.3	3.7	Putnam	2.4	3.0	3.3
Escambia	2.4	2.9	3.2	St. Johns	2.7	3.5	3.6
Flagler	2.3	3.7	3.6	St. Lucie	2.6	3.2	3.7
Franklin	2.4	2.6	3.2	Santa Rosa	2.5	3.5	3.7
Gadsden	1.7	2.8	2.9	Sarasota	2.9	3.5	3.7
Gilchrist	2.4	2.9	3.2	Seminole	2.9	3.5	3.8
Glades	2.1	2.7	3.4	Sumter	2.1	3.1	3.4
Gulf	2.2	3.1	3.2	Suwannee	2.3	3.3	3.5
Hamilton	2.1	2.8	3.1	Taylor	2.2	3.0	3.4
Hardee	2.2	2.8	3.0	Union	2.8	3.6	3.4
Hendry	2.2	3.1	3.5	Volusia	2.5	3.4	3.6
Hernando	2.4	3.0	3.5	Wakulla	2.7	3.5	3.7
Highlands	2.5	3.1	3.1	Walton	2.4	3.2	3.6
Hillsborough	2.9	3.6	3.8	Washington	2.3	3.4	3.5
Holmes	2.4	3.4	3.3	A.D. Henderson	3.3	3.6	(NA)
Indian River	2.4	3.4	3.4	FSU Developmental	2.9	3.5	3.7
Jackson	2.4	3.3	3.4	Florida A & M			
Jefferson	2.0	3.0	3.5	University			
Lafayette	2.3	3.3	3.5	High	2.6	2.9	3.8
Lake	2.6	3.2	3.3	P.K. Yonge			
Lee	2.5	3.2	3.5	Developmental	2.9	3.2	3.9

(NA) Not available.
Note: The Florida Writing Assessment Program is given to public elementary and
secondary students in grades 4, 8, and 10 and is designed to assess higher-order
skills and to measure students' proficiency in writing responses to assigned topics
within a designated tested period. It was established in response to changes in the
law made by the 1990 legislature. Student writings are scored by trained readers con-
sidering four elements: focus, organization, support, and conventions. Scores range
from U (unscorable) to 6.
Source: State of Florida, Department of Education, Division of Public Schools,
unpublished data.

University of Florida   **Bureau of Economic and Business Research**

Table 4.80. HIGH SCHOOL GRADUATES: GRADUATION RATES IN THE STATE
AND COUNTIES OF FLORIDA, 1991-92 THROUGH 1995-96

County	1991-92	1992-93	1993-94	1994-95	1995-96	Percent-age change 1991-92 to 1995-96
Florida	77.86	78.73	75.64	72.94	73.22	-5.96
Alachua	78.22	81.25	79.77	75.16	76.00	-2.84
Baker	84.67	75.24	87.37	72.87	77.89	-8.01
Bay	75.95	74.35	71.01	68.45	67.95	-10.53
Bradford	76.92	79.29	75.56	75.81	50.32	-34.58
Brevard	87.77	81.50	79.00	76.20	73.01	-16.82
Broward	76.58	74.22	64.05	70.61	73.26	-4.34
Calhoun	73.13	80.67	75.32	80.57	73.08	-0.07
Charlotte	92.53	84.21	82.51	76.22	76.48	-17.35
Citrus	85.66	81.11	82.93	77.75	77.26	-9.81
Clay	84.46	90.56	85.07	85.04	81.19	-3.87
Collier	81.11	68.26	93.99	69.93	75.52	-6.89
Columbia	64.99	82.41	75.69	69.40	71.33	9.76
Dade	73.90	74.75	75.01	73.95	74.56	0.89
De Soto	66.54	76.36	75.21	74.42	80.08	20.35
Dixie	64.36	50.35	61.70	52.14	50.26	-21.91
Duval	77.59	84.00	78.16	77.35	71.47	-7.89
Escambia	85.08	68.53	72.39	64.40	63.48	-25.39
Flagler	89.30	84.75	78.19	86.17	83.43	-6.57
Franklin	67.92	70.40	75.47	62.28	61.48	-9.48
Gadsden	60.31	65.99	62.86	50.00	52.01	-13.76
Gilchrist	70.87	73.85	73.68	88.98	77.18	8.90
Glades	70.69	107.84	56.41	58.11	48.65	-31.18
Gulf	91.58	84.18	97.55	80.10	93.42	2.01
Hamilton	69.70	67.02	79.59	73.98	67.89	-2.60
Hardee	77.66	81.06	83.00	65.53	55.59	-28.42
Hendry	66.84	65.14	77.44	73.81	72.95	9.14
Hernando	88.74	77.02	75.25	66.12	73.09	-17.64
Highlands	74.68	78.55	77.57	74.62	71.80	-3.86
Hillsborough	84.23	85.74	78.57	76.23	76.70	-8.94
Holmes	82.63	82.00	82.72	74.72	83.97	1.62
Indian River	83.77	73.39	72.41	66.04	72.85	-13.04
Jackson	77.65	77.97	79.19	83.63	75.25	-3.09
Jefferson	66.86	75.57	80.27	71.86	63.78	-4.61
Lafayette	88.46	88.00	76.60	71.05	90.91	2.77
Lake	84.18	79.48	69.38	61.88	68.46	-18.67
Lee	87.65	91.40	85.50	80.01	82.47	-5.91

See footnote at end of table.   Continued . . .

Table 4.80. HIGH SCHOOL GRADUATES: GRADUATION RATES IN THE STATE
AND COUNTIES OF FLORIDA, 1991-92 THROUGH 1995-96 (Continued)

County	1991-92	1992-93	1993-94	1994-95	1995-96	Percent-age change 1991-92 to 1995-96
Leon	80.56	79.89	70.86	72.59	74.15	-7.96
Levy	61.92	77.51	58.04	58.68	73.01	17.91
Liberty	106.58	89.53	92.98	78.48	85.54	-19.74
Madison	67.06	62.90	64.73	65.22	66.95	-0.16
Manatee	77.43	71.94	71.48	68.60	61.16	-21.01
Marion	74.87	74.85	67.41	65.99	68.74	-8.19
Martin	86.43	74.03	74.80	79.84	70.86	-18.01
Monroe	82.49	71.61	70.77	66.46	77.54	-6.00
Nassau	88.16	75.77	67.27	61.30	72.63	-17.62
Okaloosa	90.98	90.27	89.60	86.98	82.10	-9.76
Okeechobee	75.00	77.96	82.37	67.65	64.24	-14.35
Orange	74.27	93.30	77.78	76.53	78.53	5.74
Osceola	88.99	86.57	85.31	80.86	75.57	-15.08
Palm Beach	72.59	80.03	79.55	66.17	74.86	3.13
Pasco	70.54	77.31	76.51	74.63	69.56	-1.39
Pinellas	75.23	77.96	83.54	75.11	75.08	-0.20
Polk	72.90	72.46	69.62	70.29	64.15	-12.00
Putnam	60.05	68.89	57.22	49.51	51.10	-14.90
St. Johns	76.56	70.20	74.16	75.24	76.07	-0.64
St. Lucie	65.55	68.15	65.14	62.97	60.78	-7.28
Santa Rosa	90.17	87.17	78.01	75.68	73.59	-18.39
Sarasota	76.98	83.89	82.50	75.44	79.90	3.79
Seminole	86.62	80.60	81.02	73.61	78.65	-9.20
Sumter	73.39	68.45	66.49	56.83	67.04	-8.65
Suwannee	81.35	81.38	67.49	72.21	67.16	-17.44
Taylor	78.07	70.76	65.28	57.78	82.63	5.84
Union	76.86	59.84	80.17	64.57	81.40	5.91
Volusia	79.66	79.94	86.45	81.17	82.04	2.99
Wakulla	80.77	90.04	76.30	78.60	80.08	-0.85
Walton	72.12	78.41	76.97	79.78	74.29	3.01
Washington	75.29	82.85	87.01	102.86	89.52	18.90

Note: Data are for public schools only.

Source: State of Florida, Department of Education, Internet site http://www.firn.
edu/doe/.

University of Florida   **Bureau of Economic and Business Research**

Table 4.81. HIGH SCHOOL GRADUATES: NONPUBLIC HIGH SCHOOL GRADUATES, 1997, AND GRADUATES CONTINUING EDUCATION BY TYPE OF POST-SECONDARY INSTITUTION ENTERED, 1997-98, IN THE STATE AND COUNTIES OF FLORIDA

County	Total grad- uates 1997 A/	Graduates continuing education							
			Graduates entering--						
			Florida community colleges		Florida colleges and uni- versities		Out-of- state col- leges and uni- versi- ties	Technical trade and other	
		Total	Pub- lic	Pri- vate	Pub- lic	Pri- vate		In- state	Out- of- state
Florida	10,320	9,648	2,845	286	2,580	1,024	2,789	93	31
Alachua	48	44	14	1	12	2	13	0	2
Baker	0	0	0	0	0	0	0	0	0
Bay	54	31	24	0	4	1	2	0	0
Bradford	3	0	0	0	0	0	0	0	0
Brevard	265	233	67	0	57	52	56	1	0
Broward	1,595	1,256	223	8	412	132	460	21	0
Calhoun	(NA)	0	(NA)	(NA)	(NA)	(NA)	(NA)	(NA)	(NA)
Charlotte	2	2	1	0	1	0	0	0	0
Citrus	9	5	3	0	0	2	0	0	0
Clay	170	71	15	0	21	7	26	0	2
Collier	65	60	11	0	9	5	35	0	0
Columbia	3	8	7	0	0	0	1	0	0
Dade	2,381	2,278	605	12	824	284	535	6	12
De Soto	1	0	0	0	0	0	0	0	0
Dixie	(NA)	0	(NA)	(NA)	(NA)	(NA)	(NA)	(NA)	(NA)
Duval	712	1,219	650	105	177	53	233	1	0
Escambia	200	187	64	3	29	29	62	0	0
Flagler	3	2	2	0	0	0	0	0	0
Franklin	0	1	1	0	0	0	0	0	0
Gadsden	35	28	17	0	1	0	10	0	0
Gilchrist	17	32	7	12	2	8	3	0	0
Glades	4	2	2	0	0	0	0	0	0
Gulf	5	0	0	0	0	0	0	0	0
Hamilton	0	0	0	0	0	0	0	0	0
Hardee	0	0	0	0	0	0	0	0	0
Hendry	4	3	3	0	0	0	0	0	0
Hernando	16	13	2	0	1	4	6	0	0
Highlands	18	20	7	5	0	1	5	2	0
Hillsborough	768	689	97	5	274	81	227	4	1
Holmes	0	0	0	0	0	0	0	0	0
Indian River	67	65	9	0	12	10	34	0	0
Jackson	8	15	9	2	1	2	1	0	0
Jefferson	21	15	11	0	1	2	1	0	0
Lafayette	(NA)	0	(NA)	(NA)	(NA)	(NA)	(NA)	(NA)	(NA)
Lake	67	38	12	4	8	3	11	0	0

See footnotes at end of table.   Continued . . .

University of Florida   **Bureau of Economic and Business Research**

Table 4.81. HIGH SCHOOL GRADUATES: NONPUBLIC HIGH SCHOOL GRADUATES, 1997, AND GRADUATES CONTINUING EDUCATION BY TYPE OF POST-SECONDARY INSTITUTION ENTERED, 1997-98, IN THE STATE AND COUNTIES OF FLORIDA (Continued)

		Graduates continuing education							
			Graduates entering--						
County	Total grad-uates 1997 A/	Total	Florida community colleges		Florida colleges and uni-versities		Out-of-state col-leges and uni-versi-ties	Technical trade and other	
			Pub-lic	Pri-vate	Pub-lic	Pri-vate		In-state	Out-of-state
Lee	259	240	92	0	47	23	76	1	1
Leon	142	127	45	1	32	7	40	1	1
Levy	2	0	0	0	0	0	0	0	0
Liberty	(NA)	0	(NA)	(NA)	(NA)	(NA)	(NA)	(NA)	(NA)
Madison	0	0	0	0	0	0	0	0	0
Manatee	236	120	29	0	12	11	65	3	0
Marion	161	92	42	0	6	7	36	1	0
Martin	18	15	2	0	1	7	5	0	0
Monroe	10	9	3	0	3	1	2	0	0
Nassau	2	2	0	0	0	1	1	0	0
Okaloosa	14	12	7	0	0	3	2	0	0
Okeechobee	1	0	0	0	0	0	0	0	0
Orange	574	607	154	100	119	49	174	10	1
Osceola	19	15	6	0	3	2	2	2	0
Palm Beach	747	676	166	5	161	79	250	14	1
Pasco	22	4	3	0	0	1	0	0	0
Pinellas	575	531	149	1	148	47	180	5	1
Polk	176	157	48	0	22	29	49	4	5
Putnam	16	8	7	0	0	0	1	0	0
St. Johns	76	72	24	4	26	2	5	10	1
St. Lucie	119	109	54	0	38	6	11	0	0
Santa Rosa	33	24	1	2	0	10	11	0	0
Sarasota	173	162	41	2	53	25	34	4	3
Seminole	233	194	59	11	24	17	82	1	0
Sumter	3	1	0	0	1	0	0	0	0
Suwannee	13	5	2	0	1	1	1	0	0
Taylor	0	0	0	0	0	0	0	0	0
Union	(NA)	0	(NA)	(NA)	(NA)	(NA)	(NA)	(NA)	(NA)
Volusia	154	148	48	3	37	18	40	2	0
Wakulla	1	1	0	0	0	0	1	0	0
Walton	0	0	0	0	0	0	0	0	0
Washington	0	0	0	0	0	0	0	0	0

A/ Includes standard and special diploma graduates.
Note: See Glossary under Private school for definition of nonpublic schools. Data are based on a survey and are unaudited.

Source: State of Florida, Department of Education, Division of Public Schools, *Statistical Brief: Florida's Nonpublic Schools, 1996-97.* Series 98-03B.

University of Florida   **Bureau of Economic and Business Research**

Table 4.82. HIGH SCHOOL GRADUATES: GRADUATES, 1996, AND GRADUATES CONTINUING EDUCATION BY TYPE OF POST-SECONDARY INSTITUTION ENTERED, 1996-97 IN THE STATE AND COUNTIES OF FLORIDA

							Florida colleges and uni-versities		Non-Florida college	Technical trade and other	
	Total diploma grad-uates	Total		Florida community colleges						Out-	
County	1996 A/	Num-ber	Per-cent-age	Pub-lic	Pri-vate		Pub-lic	Pri-vate	or uni-versity	In-state	of-state
Florida	91,495	59,462	64.9	27,856	523		16,377	3,027	7,303	3,722	654
Alachua	1,234	982	79.6	535	9		277	36	104	10	11
Baker	190	136	71.6	77	0		21	14	9	15	0
Bay	1,043	667	64.0	334	4		127	13	95	69	25
Bradford	153	89	58.2	81	0		2	2	3	1	0
Brevard	2,916	1,382	47.4	750	21		283	80	170	41	37
Broward	8,375	6,382	76.2	2,474	62		2,218	383	701	456	88
Calhoun	87	47	54.0	39	0		2	1	3	1	1
Charlotte	810	398	49.1	150	4		110	3	83	44	4
Citrus	635	197	31.0	90	0		67	8	22	9	1
Clay	1,156	807	69.8	420	5		195	21	93	70	3
Collier	960	679	70.7	274	6		168	56	114	55	6
Columbia	347	135	38.9	91	1		19	4	16	1	3
Dade	14,057	9,941	70.7	4,582	48		2,844	672	1,023	695	77
De Soto	174	101	58.1	40	0		16	6	2	36	1
Dixie	67	43	64.2	37	0		3	0	0	2	1
Duval	4,409	2,886	65.5	1,210	0		1,006	201	403	66	0
Escambia	2,085	1,468	70.4	664	31		394	26	267	60	26
Flagler	273	155	56.8	68	0		42	9	28	6	2
Franklin	74	37	50.0	24	0		3	0	3	6	1
Gadsden	319	171	53.6	75	5		59	2	10	19	1
Gilchrist	113	60	53.1	49	0		7	0	4	0	0
Glades	35	26	74.3	9	0		4	1	8	4	0
Gulf	136	92	67.7	62	0		5	1	9	14	1
Hamilton	116	91	78.5	47	0		22	1	12	5	4
Hardee	189	121	64.0	73	0		11	10	17	7	3
Hendry	286	168	58.7	105	2		21	6	21	13	0
Hernando	719	517	71.9	274	6		123	29	40	37	8
Highlands	443	338	76.3	215	3		54	18	36	7	5
Hillsborough	5,816	3,978	68.4	1,266	45		1,586	189	518	354	20
Holmes	209	154	73.7	82	0		12	0	27	32	1
Indian River	520	417	80.2	234	2		79	25	49	7	21
Jackson	421	151	35.9	111	0		9	1	12	14	4
Jefferson	95	85	89.5	15	1		30	0	8	23	8
Lafayette	65	52	80.0	33	0		8	1	6	4	0
Lake	1,049	673	64.1	364	0		144	29	63	71	2
Lee	2,229	1,156	51.9	579	8		289	64	135	66	15
Leon	1,337	981	73.4	450	19		362	34	96	13	7
Levy	222	112	50.5	77	0		19	2	13	1	0
Liberty	60	56	93.3	36	5		3	0	4	5	3

See footnotes at end of table. Continued . . .

University of Florida   **Bureau of Economic and Business Research**

Table 4.82. HIGH SCHOOL GRADUATES: GRADUATES, 1996, AND GRADUATES CONTINUING EDUCATION BY TYPE OF POST-SECONDARY INSTITUTION ENTERED, 1996-97 IN THE STATE AND COUNTIES OF FLORIDA (Continued)

		Graduates continuing education								
				Graduates entering--						
	Total diploma grad-uates	Total		Florida community colleges		Florida colleges and uni-versities		Non-Florida college or uni-versity	Technical trade and other	
										Out-
County	1996 A/	Num-ber	cent-age	Pub-lic	Pri-vate	Pub-lic	Pri-vate		In-state	of-state
Madison	144	94	65.3	55	0	12	0	2	21	4
Manatee	1,088	656	60.3	319	47	151	9	74	49	7
Marion	1,459	925	63.4	611	9	164	16	78	34	13
Martin	541	360	66.5	160	0	116	25	52	6	1
Monroe	406	304	74.9	131	1	66	22	58	16	10
Nassau	327	163	49.9	87	1	40	10	9	16	0
Okaloosa	1,565	1,118	71.4	581	4	200	22	269	22	20
Okeechobee	270	137	50.7	84	5	18	1	18	9	2
Orange	5,943	3,287	55.3	1,780	1	716	125	487	175	3
Osceola	1,175	786	66.9	456	7	143	30	71	69	10
Palm Beach	5,545	1,994	36.0	818	10	657	99	238	144	28
Pasco	1,691	843	49.9	452	9	186	51	67	62	16
Pinellas	4,422	3,252	73.5	1,567	2	919	131	410	217	6
Polk	2,760	1,958	70.9	999	13	367	160	190	189	40
Putnam	444	295	66.4	151	3	43	5	34	48	11
St. Johns	656	419	63.9	156	4	143	25	66	22	3
St. Lucie	984	681	69.2	452	1	145	24	45	10	4
Santa Rosa	886	691	78.0	299	14	164	10	159	28	17
Sarasota	1,380	901	65.3	330	2	281	51	172	50	15
Seminole	2,541	1,968	77.5	760	24	727	117	265	63	12
Sumter	188	123	65.4	70	3	28	6	4	10	2
Suwannee	283	196	69.3	119	0	26	2	7	42	0
Taylor	154	105	68.2	72	0	11	1	5	15	1
Union	103	75	72.8	54	0	6	5	6	0	4
Volusia	2,514	1,797	71.5	1,004	8	372	119	242	34	18
Wakulla	181	122	67.4	7	68	7	12	11	17	0
Walton	221	158	71.5	102	0	17	1	20	4	14
Washington	200	123	61.5	84	0	8	0	17	11	3

A/ Includes standard and special diploma graduates.

Note: Data were obtained from the Florida DOE Student Information Data Base, Survey 5, as of December 19, 1996, and are for public schools only. Because some high schools do not have a formal follow-up program for graduates, it was necessary for the principal or guidance counselor to prepare estimates for some of the items included. Figures include twelfth grade graduates from adult centers and exceptional and gifted schools.

Source: State of Florida, Department of Education, Division of Administration, Education Information and Accountability Services, *Statistical Brief: Florida Public High School Graduates, 1995-96 School Year*. Series 97-19B.

Table 4.83. HIGH SCHOOL GRADUATES: GRADUATES RECEIVING STANDARD DIPLOMAS BY SEX AND BY RACE OR HISPANIC ORIGIN IN THE STATE AND COUNTIES OF FLORIDA, 1995-96

County	Total Male	Total Female	White Male	White Female	Black Male	Black Female	Asian or Pacific Islander Male	Asian or Pacific Islander Female	American Indian, Eskimo, or Aleut Male	American Indian, Eskimo, or Aleut Female	Hispanic origin 1/ Male	Hispanic origin 1/ Female
Florida	42,155	47,020	26,373	28,209	8,314	10,459	1,200	1,268	90	91	6,178	6,993
Alachua	581	615	418	412	113	168	25	14	1	3	24	18
Baker	84	95	71	75	11	20	2	0	0	0	0	0
Bay	511	525	432	430	62	75	8	15	1	0	8	5
Bradford	67	73	49	54	16	16	0	1	1	0	1	2
Brevard	1,337	1,514	1,066	1,219	172	178	27	50	2	3	70	64
Broward	3,784	4,417	2,027	2,286	1,095	1,382	143	146	8	10	511	593
Calhoun	43	42	36	36	5	5	0	1	0	0	2	0
Charlotte	407	395	349	328	40	41	5	11	1	1	12	14
Citrus	297	334	277	291	8	23	4	10	0	0	8	10
Clay	550	584	489	500	34	48	18	20	1	0	8	16
Collier	445	490	341	352	40	45	3	3	1	2	60	88
Columbia	162	167	120	119	35	40	3	3	1	1	3	4
Dade	6,421	7,362	1,134	1,089	1,875	2,401	122	137	3	3	3,287	3,732
De Soto	75	95	48	61	18	20	1	2	0	0	8	12
Dixie	33	30	28	27	5	3	0	0	0	0	0	0
Duval	1,784	2,399	1,053	1,378	596	841	91	116	3	2	41	62
Escambia	950	1,047	665	687	227	294	48	54	6	2	4	10
Flagler	139	134	110	103	21	16	4	3	0	0	4	12
Franklin	37	33	31	24	6	9	0	0	0	0	0	0
Gadsden	146	171	13	10	133	156	0	0	0	0	0	5
Gilchrist	56	53	53	50	3	2	0	0	0	0	0	1
Glades	17	16	11	6	5	7	0	0	0	0	1	3
Gulf	55	77	38	57	16	19	0	1	1	0	0	0
Hamilton	47	64	33	37	13	26	0	0	0	0	1	1

Continued . . .

See footnotes at end of table.

Table 4.83. HIGH SCHOOL GRADUATES: GRADUATES RECEIVING STANDARD DIPLOMAS BY SEX AND BY RACE OR HISPANIC ORIGIN IN THE STATE AND COUNTIES OF FLORIDA, 1995-96 (Continued)

| County | Total | | Race | | | | | | | | | |
| | | | White | | Black | | Asian or Pacific Islander | | American Indian, Eskimo, or Aleut | | Hispanic origin 1/ | |
	Male	Female	Male	Female	Male	Female	Male	Female	Male	Female	Male	Female
Hardee	94	89	59	57	12	6	3	0	0	1	20	25
Hendry	152	129	74	62	31	22	3	2	0	0	44	43
Hernando	340	362	295	312	22	22	3	2	0	0	20	26
Highlands	195	219	143	149	34	42	1	4	0	1	17	23
Hillsborough	2,649	3,071	1,744	1,870	414	610	92	101	9	7	390	483
Holmes	92	107	89	102	1	3	1	1	0	0	1	1
Indian River	244	268	187	223	40	34	6	1	0	0	11	11
Jackson	204	210	138	125	65	82	0	0	0	1	1	2
Jefferson	45	45	10	11	35	34	0	0	0	0	0	0
Lafayette	26	37	23	32	3	5	0	0	0	0	0	0
Lake	426	537	357	428	49	72	7	11	2	3	11	23
Lee	1,095	1,073	886	839	114	131	10	14	4	2	81	87
Leon	601	687	416	475	157	190	19	12	0	0	9	10
Levy	98	115	74	95	20	17	1	1	1	0	2	2
Liberty	32	28	27	22	3	5	0	1	1	0	1	1
Madison	71	69	45	33	26	36	0	0	0	0	0	1
Manatee	511	532	410	427	68	68	10	8	0	1	23	28
Marion	686	727	517	540	104	140	9	10	1	1	55	36
Martin	258	276	224	237	22	24	3	4	0	0	9	11
Monroe	178	209	146	161	12	21	4	2	1	0	15	25
Nassau	155	169	130	140	23	26	1	0	0	1	1	2
Okaloosa	753	784	609	657	87	78	38	29	3	2	16	18
Okeechobee	134	125	98	95	18	16	1	2	1	1	16	11
Orange	2,832	2,975	1,573	1,593	569	708	159	151	16	8	515	515
Osceola	528	602	340	383	45	47	14	23	2	1	127	148
Palm Beach	2,551	2,896	1,578	1,732	613	727	80	80	3	8	277	349

See footnotes at end of table.

Continued . . .

Table 4.83. HIGH SCHOOL GRADUATES: GRADUATES RECEIVING STANDARD DIPLOMAS BY SEX AND BY RACE OR HISPANIC ORIGIN IN THE STATE AND COUNTIES OF FLORIDA, 1995-96 (Continued)

	Total		White		Race — Black		Asian or Pacific Islander		American Indian, Eskimo, or Aleut		Hispanic origin 1/	
County	Male	Female	Male	Female	Male	Female	Male	Female	Male	Female	Male	Female
Pasco	780	884	695	808	22	22	23	19	0	3	40	32
Pinellas	2,011	2,300	1,629	1,822	255	365	71	65	2	3	54	45
Polk	1,248	1,393	958	1,004	204	278	21	29	3	5	62	77
Putnam	222	218	149	141	66	68	0	1	0	1	7	7
St. Johns	316	329	274	265	34	49	6	5	0	0	2	10
St. Lucie	477	487	269	309	167	142	8	9	3	1	30	26
Santa Rosa	450	419	412	377	20	26	10	6	0	2	8	8
Sarasota	629	698	552	602	48	53	7	18	1	0	21	25
Seminole	1,217	1,291	916	931	111	161	51	48	2	4	137	147
Sumter	84	99	63	73	18	23	1	0	1	0	1	3
Suwannee	143	131	113	111	27	20	0	0	0	0	3	0
Taylor	75	75	57	50	17	23	0	0	0	1	0	1
Union	52	47	40	38	10	9	2	0	0	0	0	1
Volusia	1,180	1,286	929	1,001	126	179	30	21	2	6	93	79
Wakulla	87	86	78	73	9	12	0	1	2	0	0	0
Walton	110	104	87	92	19	10	0	2	2	0	2	0
Washington	96	100	68	81	25	18	1	0	0	0	2	1

1/ Persons of Hispanic origin may be of any race. However, these data are not distributed by race.
Note: Data were obtained from the Florida DOE Student Information Data Base, Survey 5, as of November 8, 1996, and are for public schools only. Standard diplomas are awarded to students who have mastered eleventh grade minimum student performance standards, passed both sections of the High School Competency Test (HSCT or SSAT II), successfully completed the minimum number of academic credits, and successfully completed any other requirements prescribed by state or the local school board. Also includes differentiated diplomas awarded in lieu of the standard diplomas to those students exceeding the prescribed minimums.

Source: State of Florida, Department of Education, Division of Administration, Education Information and Accountability Services, *Statistical Brief: Florida Public High School Graduates, 1995-96 School Year.* Series 97-19B.

Table 4.84. READINESS FOR COLLEGE: PERCENTAGE OF STUDENTS ENTERING
COLLEGE WHO TESTED COMPETENT IN READING, WRITING, AND MATHEMATICS
SKILLS IN THE STATE AND COUNTIES OF FLORIDA, 1995-96

County	Students taking college entry test 1/	Percentage ready in - - All areas	Reading	Writing	Mathe- matics	Per- centage change from 1994-95 A/
Florida	40,363	54.10	75.80	72.00	68.60	-4.10
Alachua	695	55.40	79.90	69.60	75.70	-20.78
Baker	75	61.30	85.30	81.30	72.00	8.70
Bay	540	53.90	81.90	80.70	65.90	12.37
Bradford	84	47.60	72.60	67.90	64.30	17.50
Brevard	1,394	66.50	85.90	83.90	74.40	2.70
Broward	3,481	58.70	78.10	76.80	69.70	2.35
Calhoun	45	66.70	86.70	77.80	73.30	-3.33
Charlotte	318	55.00	81.40	67.90	74.80	-8.00
Citrus	313	72.50	86.90	85.60	82.10	19.82
Clay	538	58.90	85.70	70.10	75.10	-6.94
Collier	355	59.40	85.60	70.70	77.50	-1.90
Columbia	188	55.30	74.50	76.60	64.40	7.69
Dade	7,179	34.40	53.30	55.00	55.60	-18.65
De Soto	36	63.90	91.70	97.20	63.90	21.74
Dixie	31	48.40	83.90	80.60	58.10	13.33
Duval	1,992	61.30	78.70	80.50	73.50	4.83
Escambia	967	59.50	79.00	84.70	65.50	-12.17
Flagler	75	53.30	86.70	81.30	62.70	-42.50
Franklin	20	20.00	45.00	75.00	50.00	-75.00
Gadsden	87	39.10	52.90	56.30	55.20	-23.53
Gilchrist	57	54.40	82.50	73.70	66.70	16.13
Glades	9	55.60	77.80	66.70	77.80	40.00
Gulf	63	60.30	82.50	82.50	73.00	21.05
Hamilton	30	33.30	56.70	50.00	50.00	-20.00
Hardee	63	49.20	76.20	73.00	55.60	-9.68
Hendry	95	51.60	77.90	73.70	65.30	10.20
Hernando	298	59.10	81.20	74.20	73.80	21.59
Highlands	145	54.50	80.00	77.20	63.40	-35.44
Hillsborough	2,601	56.70	80.10	69.20	74.20	-7.18
Holmes	44	70.50	84.10	81.80	77.30	-12.90
Indian River	216	66.20	86.60	81.50	77.30	-3.50
Jackson	222	56.30	73.90	71.60	72.10	4.80
Jefferson	34	52.90	64.70	64.70	64.70	38.89
Lafayette	15	46.70	73.30	80.00	60.00	-157.14
Lake	361	53.50	72.00	69.30	79.80	1.55
Lee	749	51.80	83.30	63.80	75.70	-22.68

See footnotes at end of table.   Continued . .

Table 4.84. READINESS FOR COLLEGE: PERCENTAGE OF STUDENTS ENTERING COLLEGE WHO TESTED COMPETENT IN READING, WRITING, AND MATHEMATICS SKILLS IN THE STATE AND COUNTIES OF FLORIDA, 1995-96 (Continued)

County	Students taking college entry test 1/	Percentage ready in - - All areas	Reading	Writing	Mathe- matics	Per- centage change from 1994-95 A/
Leon	684	60.20	81.90	71.30	76.90	-6.80
Levy	87	56.30	73.60	77.00	71.30	-6.12
Liberty	21	47.60	57.10	66.70	61.90	80.00
Madison	29	65.50	75.90	82.80	89.70	36.84
Manatee	493	51.70	82.80	63.50	77.70	-24.31
Marion	658	62.00	77.40	78.90	74.30	13.24
Martin	280	68.90	86.80	82.50	78.90	0.52
Monroe	133	46.60	76.70	67.70	56.40	-24.19
Nassau	71	64.80	83.10	84.50	70.40	2.17
Okaloosa	732	76.60	91.70	90.70	82.10	5.88
Okeechobee	72	59.70	83.30	80.60	76.40	0.00
Orange	2,177	50.30	76.70	75.60	58.90	-4.56
Osceola	402	46.50	74.10	72.90	58.00	-8.56
Palm Beach	2,376	64.60	79.70	78.70	75.80	8.33
Pasco	613	49.60	77.50	68.20	64.40	-0.66
Pinellas	2,358	53.80	81.80	73.50	65.30	-13.09
Polk	1,162	51.50	75.70	73.70	63.90	3.85
Putnam	176	63.10	91.50	75.60	79.50	6.31
St. Johns	306	62.10	86.60	75.50	76.50	20.53
St. Lucie	380	53.20	77.10	75.80	64.50	-0.99
Santa Rosa	435	71.30	88.00	90.10	76.80	-4.52
Sarasota	626	60.10	85.90	65.00	85.30	-15.96
Seminole	1,496	59.90	84.30	75.80	75.90	-0.78
Sumter	56	41.10	66.10	60.70	62.50	-13.04
Suwannee	125	60.00	80.80	76.00	70.40	-1.33
Taylor	34	50.00	76.50	67.60	55.90	-70.59
Union	40	67.50	75.00	80.00	77.50	3.70
Volusia	556	61.20	88.10	79.10	75.40	-45.29
Wakulla	63	65.10	81.00	76.20	79.40	12.20
Walton	91	65.90	89.00	86.80	72.50	20.00
Washington	61	60.70	85.20	82.00	77.00	-27.03

A/ Change in overall readiness.
1/ 1994-95 high school graduates who enrolled as degree-seeking students in Florida public community colleges and state universities during the 1995-96 academic year.

Source: State of Florida, Department of Education, Internet site http://www.firn edu/doe/.

University of Florida   **Bureau of Economic and Business Research**

INCOME
AND WEALTH

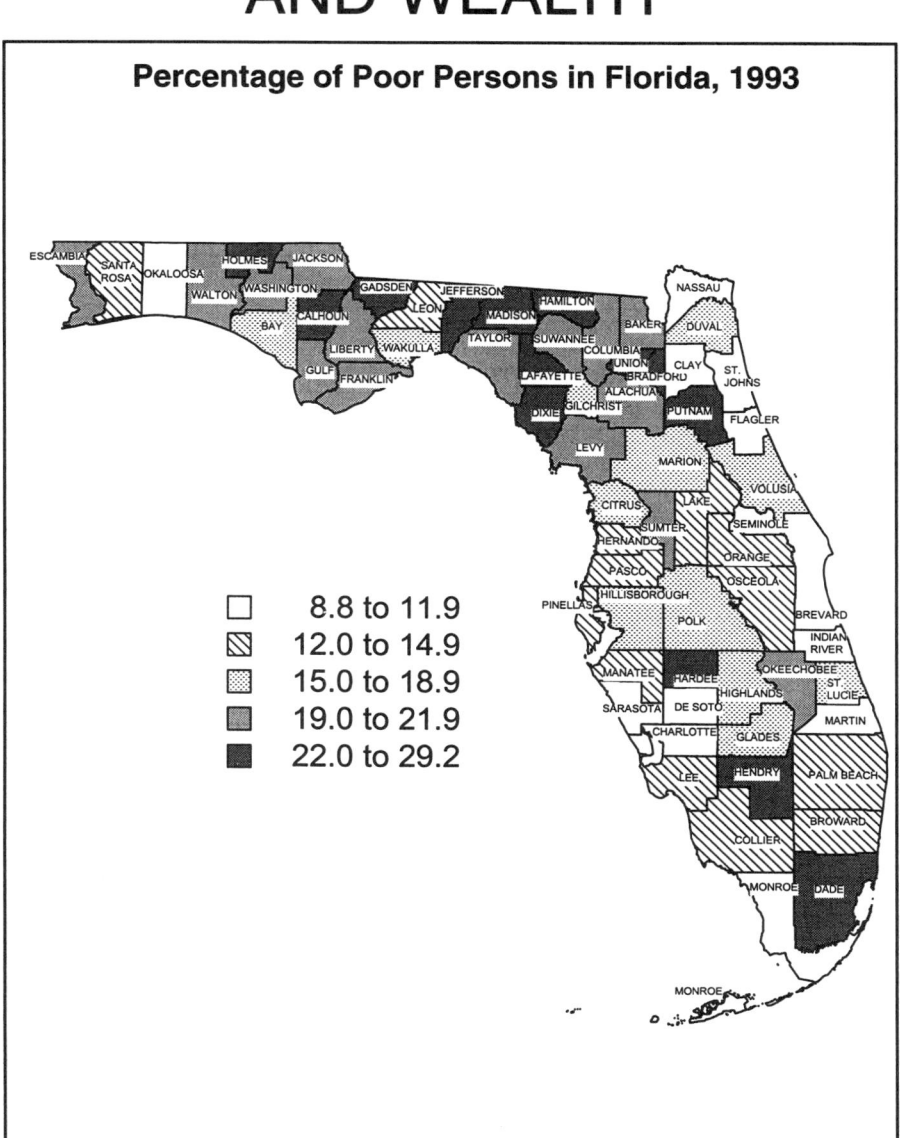

Percentage of Poor Persons in Florida, 1993

Legend:
- 8.8 to 11.9
- 12.0 to 14.9
- 15.0 to 18.9
- 19.0 to 21.9
- 22.0 to 29.2

Source: Table 5.48

SECTION 5.00
INCOME AND WEALTH

TABLES LISTED BY MAJOR HEADINGS

University of Florida   Bureau of Economic and Business Research

SECTION 5.00
INCOME AND WEALTH
(Continued)

TABLES LISTED BY MAJOR HEADINGS

University of Florida   **Bureau of Economic and Business Research**

Table 5.01. INDIVIDUAL INCOME TAX RETURNS: SPECIFIED INCOME, DEDUCTION, AND
TAX ITEMS IN FLORIDA AND THE UNITED STATES, 1995

(amounts in thousands of dollars, except where indicated)

Item	Florida	United States
All returns	6,553,487	118,783,943
Number of exemptions 1/	14,280,823	257,737,035
Adjusted gross income (less deficit)	221,514,573	4,182,770,178
Salaries and wages, number of returns	5,279,952	101,001,283
Amount	148,844,992	105,926
Interest income, number of returns	3,438,200	66,551,439
Amount	12,174,005	155,642,373
Dividends, number of returns	1,527,733	26,234,029
Amount	8,360,286	96,467,992
Net capital gain (less loss), number of returns	1,027,041	15,398,973
Amount	14,162,257	163,846,325
Taxable pensions and annuities, number of returns	1,187,067	18,465,095
Amount	16,078,624	221,023,736
Unemployment compensation, number of returns	292,327	7,981,529
Amount	668,030	19,027,760
Number of sole proprietorship returns	911,902	16,426,765
Number of farm returns (Schedule F) 2/	33,469	1,869,880
Total itemized deductions, number of returns	1,554,874	34,504,922
Amount	23,092,587	541,072,446
Average (whole dollars)	14,852	15,681
Medical and dental expense, number of returns	390,944	5,606,462
Amount	2,567,668	32,601,105
Taxes paid deductions, number of returns	1,466,371	33,958,708
Amount	4,496,075	190,947,194
Interest paid deductions, number of returns	1,340,451	28,870,928
Amount	10,673,423	219,263,856
Contributions, number of returns	1,336,664	30,550,389
Amount	3,758,958	74,824,415
Taxable income, number of returns	5,102,333	94,834,902
Amount	153,137,252	768
Total tax liability, number of returns	5,286,330	97,582,462
Amount	34,967,706	620,971,983
Average (whole dollars)	6,615	6,364
Earned income credit, number of returns	1,237,631	19,653,815
Amount	1,638,174	26,036,328
Excess earned income credit 3/		
Number of returns	971,859	15,374,246
Amount	1,303,362	20,825,606
Overpayment, number of returns	4,481,584	82,899,610
Amount	5,678,390	105,273,347
Tax due at time of filing, number of returns	1,649,823	29,456,584
Amount	4,798,205	71,216,982

1/ Includes exemptions for age and blindness.
2/ Excludes those farm returns which also included a nonfarm sole proprietorship
business schedule(s). These returns are included with the "number of sole proprietorship returns."
3/ Represents the refundable portion of the credit and equals the amount in excess
of total tax liability, including any advance earned income credit payments for those
returns which had such an excess.
Note: Data are estimates based on samples and are preliminary.
Source: U.S., Department of the Treasury, Internal Revenue Service, *Statistics
of Income: SOI Bulletin,* Spring 1997.

Table 5.02. INDIVIDUAL INCOME TAXES: RETURNS, ADJUSTED GROSS INCOME, EXEMPTIONS AND INCOME TAX IN FLORIDA AND THE UNITED STATES, 1985 THROUGH 1995

| | Number (1,000) | | | | Amount ($1,000,000) | | | |
| | Returns | | Exemptions 1/ | | Adjusted gross income 2/ | | Total income tax | |
Year	Florida	United States	Florida	United States	Florida	United States	Florida	United States
1985	5,113	101,660	12,030	244,180	110,593	2,305,951	17,310	325,710
1986	5,301	(NA)	12,413	(NA)	123,771	(NA)	20,901	(NA)
1987	5,533	106,996	12,473	217,495	140,279	2,773,824	20,737	369,203
1988	5,760	109,708	12,559	221,884	159,547	3,083,020	23,849	412,870
1989	5,971	112,136	12,973	223,756	169,688	3,256,358	25,035	432,940
1990	6,141	113,717	13,390	227,549	176,297	3,405,427	25,643	447,127
1991	6,250	114,730	13,721	231,297	177,889	3,464,534	25,504	448,430
1992	6,239	113,605	13,702	230,547	187,754	3,629,130	27,732	476,239
1993	6,282	115,061	13,840	253,489	193,995	3,720,611	29,539	532,213
1994	6,381	116,466	13,945	253,599	203,882	3,898,340	31,427	564,526
1995	6,553	118,784	14,281	257,737	221,515	4,182,770	34,968	620,972

(NA) Not available.
1/ Includes exemptions for age and blindness.
2/ Less deficit. Starting 1987, data are not comparable to earlier years because of major changes in the law.
Note: Includes taxable and nontaxable returns. All figures are estimates based on samples. Some data are revised. 1995 data are preliminary.

Source: U.S., Department of the Treasury, Internal Revenue Service, *Statistics of Income: SOI Bulletin,* Spring 1996, and previous editions.

Table 5.03. HOUSEHOLD INCOME: PERCENTAGE DISTRIBUTION OF ANNUAL INCOME BY INCOME CATEGORY AND HOUSEHOLD SIZE IN FLORIDA, 1996

| Income category | Total house-holds | Household size | | | | | |
		1	2	3	4	5	6 or more
Total	100.00	23.44	33.08	17.95	15.73	6.50	3.30
Less than $10,000	8.22	4.05	1.97	1.21	0.59	0.20	0.21
$10,000 to $19,999	14.65	5.15	4.35	2.40	1.68	0.57	0.51
$20,000 to $29,999	19.56	5.90	6.24	3.05	2.38	1.24	0.76
$30,000 to $39,999	17.05	3.68	5.68	3.32	2.89	1.06	0.41
$40,000 to $49,999	12.16	1.88	4.73	2.26	2.05	0.92	0.33
$50,000 to $59,999	9.10	1.07	3.00	2.05	2.02	0.62	0.35
$60,000 to $79,000	9.24	0.81	3.54	1.69	2.07	0.84	0.31
$80,000 to $99,000	3.92	0.28	1.33	0.96	0.83	0.32	0.20
$100,000 or more	6.10	0.64	2.26	1.01	1.22	0.74	0.23

Note: Distribution of household income is based on telephone surveys with sample size of approximately 1,000 Florida households. The surveys are conducted throughout the year and the monthly results have been pooled to develop the annual frequency distributions. Due to revisions to income categories, these data are not comparable to those found in previous *Abstracts.*
Source: University of Florida, Bureau of Economic and Business Research, Survey Program, unpublished data.

University of Florida   **Bureau of Economic and Business Research**

Table 5.05.   PERSONAL INCOME: TOTAL AND PER CAPITA AMOUNTS IN FLORIDA, OTHER
SUNBELT STATES, OTHER POPULOUS STATES, AND THE UNITED STATES
1994 THROUGH 1996

| | Total personal income ($1,000,000) | | | | Per capita personal income (amounts in dollars) | | | |
| | | | | Per-cent-age change 1995-1996 | | | 1996 | |
State	1994	1995	1996	1996	1994	1995	Amount	Rank among states
			Sunbelt states					
Florida	304,114	326,668	347,092	6.3	21,777	23,030	24,104	20
Alabama	77,018	81,578	85,698	5.1	18,271	19,212	20,055	39
Arizona	79,010	86,420	92,942	7.5	19,310	20,074	20,989	36
Arkansas	42,142	44,958	47,506	5.7	17,167	18,093	18,928	47
California	715,923	760,431	801,532	5.4	22,828	24,091	25,144	12
Georgia	145,420	156,555	166,984	6.7	20,589	21,718	22,709	26
Louisiana	78,050	82,422	86,246	4.6	18,090	19,000	19,824	40
Mississippi	42,458	44,998	47,452	5.5	15,913	16,690	17,471	50
New Mexico	28,338	30,685	32,160	4.8	17,079	18,158	18,770	48
North Carolina	141,017	151,841	161,179	6.2	19,922	21,082	22,010	32
Oklahoma	58,254	60,901	63,872	4.9	17,904	18,596	19,350	44
South Carolina	65,735	69,786	73,067	4.7	18,044	19,031	19,755	41
Tennessee	103,398	110,579	115,778	4.7	19,980	21,076	21,764	33
Texas	370,561	397,067	421,676	6.2	20,102	21,119	22,045	31
Virginia	150,305	158,669	166,385	4.9	22,948	23,985	24,925	14
			Other populous states					
Illinois	281,732	298,413	315,091	5.6	24,010	25,310	26,598	7
Indiana	117,815	124,384	131,063	5.4	20,489	21,457	22,440	29
Massachusetts	159,142	170,185	179,355	5.4	26,339	28,032	29,439	3
Michigan	214,473	228,369	238,032	4.2	22,609	23,943	24,810	16
New Jersey	224,474	237,155	248,052	4.6	28,393	29,833	31,053	2
New York	476,626	501,965	523,403	4.3	26,193	27,595	28,782	4
Ohio	236,614	251,037	262,972	4.8	21,323	22,547	23,537	21
Pennsylvania	269,632	284,386	297,402	4.6	22,361	23,580	24,668	18
United States	5,739,851	6,097,977	6,428,129	5.4	22,045	23,196	24,231	(X)

(X) Not applicable.
Note: Data for 1994 and 1995 are revised; 1996 are preliminary.

Source: U.S., Department of Commerce, Bureau of Economic Analysis, *Survey of Current Business,* May 1997.

University of Florida   **Bureau of Economic and Business Research**

Table 5.08. DISPOSABLE PERSONAL INCOME: TOTAL AND PER CAPITA AMOUNTS IN FLORIDA
OTHER SUNBELT STATES, OTHER POPULOUS STATES, AND THE UNITED STATES
1991 THROUGH 1996

| State | Total disposable personal income ($1,000,000) | | | | | | Per-
cent-
age
change
1995-
1996 |
	1991	1992	1993	1994	1995	1996	1996
	Sunbelt states						
Florida	230,800	239,705	257,811	269,445	288,663	305,059	5.7
Alabama	58,215	62,603	65,350	68,776	72,565	75,999	4.7
Arizona	56,203	60,203	64,327	69,479	75,795	81,068	7.0
Arkansas	31,454	34,119	35,622	37,703	39,969	42,121	5.4
California	566,187	599,359	610,952	626,385	662,435	693,674	4.7
Georgia	104,621	112,873	118,872	127,268	136,465	144,595	6.0
Louisiana	59,554	63,398	66,661	70,567	74,203	77,378	4.3
Mississippi	31,793	34,051	35,874	38,805	41,046	43,216	5.3
New Mexico	20,833	22,246	23,836	25,278	27,348	28,569	4.5
North Carolina	101,555	109,870	116,897	123,288	132,248	139,941	5.8
Oklahoma	44,745	47,847	49,752	51,620	53,717	56,051	4.3
South Carolina	49,905	52,984	55,471	58,535	61,896	64,608	4.4
Tennessee	75,817	82,648	87,123	93,043	99,138	103,419	4.3
Texas	278,206	298,696	315,061	332,371	355,144	375,323	5.7
Virginia	112,075	118,647	124,538	130,223	137,016	143,084	4.4
	Other populous states						
Illinois	210,388	225,864	232,820	243,391	256,739	269,844	5.1
Indiana	86,413	93,398	98,041	102,473	108,514	113,499	4.6
Massachusetts	121,408	126,110	130,021	135,045	143,644	150,603	4.8
Michigan	156,155	164,992	173,503	186,129	197,553	205,088	3.8
New Jersey	170,560	181,016	187,235	192,913	204,095	212,242	4.0
New York	364,002	384,759	388,934	406,562	426,583	443,345	3.9
Ohio	177,927	188,687	195,409	205,903	218,018	227,250	4.2
Pennsylvania	209,020	220,043	228,917	235,681	247,956	258,126	4.1
United States	4,326,807	4,599,171	4,782,261	5,009,339	5,304,700	5,565,400	4.9

See footnotes at end of table.   Continued . . .

Table 5.08. DISPOSABLE PERSONAL INCOME: TOTAL AND PER CAPITA AMOUNTS IN FLORIDA
OTHER SUNBELT STATES, OTHER POPULOUS STATES, AND THE UNITED STATES
1991 THROUGH 1996 (Continued)

State	Per capita disposable personal income (in dollars)						Rank among states
	1991	1992	1993	1994	1995	1996	1996

Sunbelt states

State	1991	1992	1993	1994	1995	1996	1996
Florida	17,366	17,739	18,800	19,295	20,351	21,185	20
Alabama	14,245	15,155	15,627	16,316	17,089	17,785	40
Arizona	14,989	15,673	16,273	16,981	17,606	18,308	37
Arkansas	13,264	14,240	14,679	15,359	16,086	16,783	44
California	18,627	19,407	19,599	19,973	20,986	21,760	11
Georgia	15,792	16,679	17,212	18,019	18,931	19,664	27
Louisiana	14,042	14,834	15,538	16,355	17,105	17,786	39
Mississippi	12,266	13,035	13,595	14,544	15,224	15,911	50
New Mexico	13,454	14,050	14,722	15,235	16,184	16,674	46
North Carolina	15,037	16,062	16,796	17,417	18,362	19,110	34
Oklahoma	14,125	14,919	15,386	15,865	16,403	16,980	43
South Carolina	14,036	14,740	15,288	16,068	16,879	17,467	41
Tennessee	15,319	16,464	17,103	17,979	18,895	19,441	29
Texas	16,019	16,878	17,440	18,031	18,889	19,621	28
Virginia	17,830	18,572	19,235	19,882	20,712	21,434	15

Other populous states

State	1991	1992	1993	1994	1995	1996	1996
Illinois	18,269	19,477	19,951	20,742	21,775	22,778	8
Indiana	15,423	16,525	17,180	17,821	18,719	19,433	30
Massachusetts	20,237	21,026	21,607	22,351	23,660	24,720	3
Michigan	16,672	17,518	18,354	19,621	20,712	21,376	17
New Jersey	21,959	23,174	23,882	24,401	25,674	26,570	2
New York	20,181	21,258	21,405	22,342	23,451	24,380	4
Ohio	16,280	17,153	17,669	18,555	19,581	20,340	21
Pennsylvania	17,497	18,354	19,024	19,545	20,560	21,410	16
United States	17,163	18,035	18,551	19,239	20,178	20,979	(X)

(X) Not applicable.
Note: Disposable personal income is equal to total personal income less personal
tax and nontax payments. Personal taxes are tax payments by persons (except personal
contributions to social insurance) and include income, estate and gift, and personal
property taxes. Nontaxes include passport fees, fines and penalties, donations, and
tuitions and fees paid to government schools and hospitals. 1991 through 1995 data
are revised; 1996 data are preliminary.

Source: U.S., Department of Commerce, Bureau of Economic Analysis, *Survey of Current Business,* May 1997.

University of Florida   **Bureau of Economic and Business Research**

Table 5.09. PERSONAL INCOME: TOTAL AMOUNT ON A PLACE-OF-RESIDENCE BASIS IN THE UNITED STATES AND IN THE STATE AND COUNTIES OF FLORIDA, 1986 THROUGH 1995

(in millions, rounded to hundred thousands of dollars)

County	1986	1987	1988	1989	1990	1991	1992	1993	1994	1995
United States 1/	3,635,655	3,862,977	4,160,730	4,474,014	4,774,005	4,950,802	5,248,613	5,471,129	5,739,851	6,097,977
Florida	176,986.9	191,911.6	209,827.7	232,144.6	248,746.5	259,049.5	269,669.1	290,075.3	304,113.2	326,670.1
Alachua	2,130.0	2,300.6	2,510.8	2,740.2	2,943.8	3,102.3	3,283.0	3,473.5	3,662.9	3,904.8
Baker	170.6	184.1	201.5	213.8	231.5	242.5	257.0	273.8	286.2	308.3
Bay	1,440.8	1,522.4	1,639.5	1,759.0	1,921.2	2,067.0	2,204.3	2,372.5	2,470.8	2,592.1
Bradford	203.5	211.9	227.8	241.6	256.4	268.8	289.3	304.2	320.3	348.3
Brevard	5,187.8	5,613.5	6,161.6	6,869.6	7,325.9	7,741.9	8,210.5	8,564.2	8,938.2	9,341.0
Broward	21,096.1	22,698.2	24,417.6	26,990.8	28,501.6	29,214.7	30,446.7	32,716.0	34,274.0	37,007.7
Calhoun	78.5	86.3	99.0	105.2	119.3	124.2	131.7	137.0	146.1	149.9
Charlotte	1,257.3	1,394.9	1,577.4	1,849.9	1,988.7	2,071.6	2,172.0	2,293.9	2,455.8	2,648.9
Citrus	954.9	1,053.2	1,158.6	1,302.3	1,405.8	1,485.2	1,566.3	1,647.5	1,742.5	1,844.1
Clay	1,303.1	1,432.7	1,564.7	1,687.1	1,827.4	1,907.1	2,015.0	2,145.1	2,288.7	2,501.3
Collier	2,458.6	2,820.9	3,437.5	3,947.2	4,308.1	4,565.2	4,919.2	5,342.9	5,601.5	6,014.6
Columbia	421.1	443.1	485.6	525.7	555.4	584.2	628.2	676.5	729.4	790.9
Dade	26,250.8	28,361.7	30,336.4	32,955.3	34,649.0	35,764.7	34,033.4	39,110.3	40,344.5	43,087.3
De Soto	228.9	254.8	304.1	327.7	338.4	381.8	385.6	406.3	410.5	445.7
Dixie	77.6	85.5	95.6	108.3	115.1	114.4	120.5	122.0	145.1	153.8
Duval	9,137.1	9,849.4	10,523.0	11,398.0	12,259.4	12,705.2	13,391.4	14,111.8	14,724.9	15,748.1
Escambia	3,133.9	3,302.1	3,493.3	3,735.0	3,987.1	4,163.2	4,427.0	4,597.9	4,756.9	4,964.4
Flagler	254.3	300.8	355.4	389.3	431.9	463.4	513.3	571.5	632.0	692.3
Franklin	85.6	88.5	96.8	104.6	113.3	119.6	128.9	139.0	150.7	156.8
Gadsden	362.6	390.1	427.1	458.3	485.1	513.1	551.6	579.6	590.2	618.4
Gilchrist	78.5	81.9	92.6	101.2	111.7	120.9	133.4	142.5	150.4	158.8

See footnotes at end of table.

Continued . . .

Table 5.09. PERSONAL INCOME: TOTAL AMOUNT ON A PLACE-OF-RESIDENCE BASIS IN THE UNITED STATES AND IN THE STATE AND COUNTIES OF FLORIDA, 1986 THROUGH 1995 (Continued)

(in millions, rounded to hundred thousands of dollars)

County	1986	1987	1988	1989	1990	1991	1992	1993	1994	1995
Glades	59.7	63.8	75.9	80.6	87.5	96.8	97.1	108.0	101.8	109.5
Gulf	115.7	118.8	127.2	134.5	142.8	150.3	162.8	176.3	189.7	196.2
Hamilton	87.5	93.9	103.9	114.3	122.0	122.3	129.5	129.2	134.7	146.3
Hardee	209.8	221.6	273.5	283.3	284.7	305.2	303.0	312.7	313.8	338.9
Hendry	285.6	324.7	384.1	383.2	396.8	460.0	461.0	507.7	477.1	526.3
Hernando	949.4	1,072.1	1,277.0	1,439.6	1,555.5	1,643.8	1,746.6	1,856.3	2,013.0	2,169.4
Highlands	779.4	840.3	950.0	1,027.8	1,078.6	1,146.0	1,182.2	1,270.4	1,316.1	1,425.2
Hillsborough	10,405.8	11,378.2	12,389.5	13,513.1	14,406.0	15,080.5	15,956.6	16,818.7	17,790.4	19,066.6
Holmes	132.5	134.4	148.5	161.5	168.1	181.4	193.0	202.7	215.5	223.0
Indian River	1,448.0	1,611.6	1,854.0	2,121.1	2,309.9	2,427.4	2,542.2	2,686.5	2,827.4	3,065.5
Jackson	373.3	405.6	447.5	477.7	513.9	552.9	585.0	603.4	625.1	646.7
Jefferson	104.4	111.9	124.1	134.9	149.2	160.3	168.6	180.9	188.3	207.1
Lafayette	49.7	49.8	52.6	59.3	64.8	66.8	72.0	73.6	76.1	78.7
Lake	1,848.2	1,984.6	2,119.9	2,397.6	2,517.5	2,671.0	2,872.0	3,062.0	3,268.3	3,505.5
Lee	4,417.2	4,892.4	5,435.5	6,271.3	6,704.9	6,951.1	7,321.8	7,784.2	8,259.1	8,879.8
Leon	2,218.2	2,434.1	2,709.1	3,001.2	3,281.6	3,474.7	3,671.2	3,924.1	4,193.9	4,465.0
Levy	230.7	243.7	271.5	291.9	315.0	334.8	360.3	383.3	403.4	434.7
Liberty	44.9	48.1	52.4	59.2	65.1	67.3	70.4	74.2	79.1	83.3
Madison	141.2	147.9	159.6	169.5	182.7	190.6	200.8	206.6	216.2	234.1
Manatee	2,868.0	3,112.2	3,387.0	3,865.7	4,164.9	4,342.6	4,634.2	4,955.0	5,239.5	5,690.4
Marion	2,026.7	2,224.0	2,451.2	2,721.8	2,945.2	3,089.6	3,353.0	3,533.4	3,803.8	4,089.8
Martin	1,760.8	1,962.1	2,256.6	2,630.2	2,943.6	3,067.0	3,188.7	3,406.1	3,521.7	3,815.3
Monroe	1,128.7	1,233.9	1,366.7	1,572.1	1,702.2	1,750.8	1,800.6	1,982.2	2,054.3	2,208.2
Nassau	577.5	609.0	654.1	719.2	781.1	828.2	884.3	954.3	1,003.9	1,089.8

See footnotes at end of table.

Continued . . .

Table 5.09. PERSONAL INCOME: TOTAL AMOUNT ON A PLACE-OF-RESIDENCE BASIS IN THE UNITED STATES AND IN THE STATE AND COUNTIES OF FLORIDA, 1986 THROUGH 1995 (Continued)

(in millions, rounded to hundred thousands of dollars)

County	1986	1987	1988	1989	1990	1991	1992	1993	1994	1995
Okaloosa	1,684.1	1,854.2	2,013.6	2,183.7	2,350.3	2,521.2	2,720.4	2,913.9	3,059.7	3,237.0
Okeechobee	282.4	299.4	336.5	362.4	387.7	409.2	426.4	456.7	461.1	490.8
Orange	8,662.0	9,447.0	10,403.4	11,481.8	12,473.3	12,963.5	13,682.3	14,556.1	15,256.6	16,274.4
Osceola	1,024.2	1,162.8	1,320.1	1,464.5	1,580.1	1,688.5	1,791.3	1,895.8	2,003.3	2,137.9
Palm Beach	16,292.5	18,113.4	20,247.3	22,724.1	25,814.7	27,223.3	28,840.8	30,994.5	32,423.7	35,204.1
Pasco	3,211.6	3,415.3	3,733.1	4,036.8	4,276.5	4,417.6	4,641.2	4,896.2	5,266.3	5,747.4
Pinellas	14,019.7	14,557.2	15,405.8	17,212.1	17,752.7	18,167.9	18,920.3	20,362.8	20,794.2	22,407.2
Polk	4,606.6	4,984.4	5,498.8	5,995.7	6,249.6	6,477.5	6,839.9	7,174.8	7,708.9	8,343.8
Putnam	613.7	642.5	697.0	726.8	770.6	813.3	887.0	949.8	974.7	1,054.5
St. Johns	1,129.2	1,279.3	1,486.6	1,690.9	1,893.1	2,011.2	2,204.6	2,394.8	2,612.6	2,869.3
St. Lucie	1,509.4	1,662.6	1,971.1	2,165.4	2,309.0	2,418.4	2,539.9	2,719.6	2,840.8	3,051.0
Santa Rosa	859.6	936.2	1,022.3	1,118.9	1,250.6	1,366.0	1,501.0	1,631.6	1,727.3	1,853.4
Sarasota	5,137.1	5,604.0	6,112.9	7,143.0	7,548.4	7,771.8	8,141.0	8,533.6	9,135.0	9,866.8
Seminole	3,673.0	4,022.0	4,585.7	5,086.1	5,542.2	5,797.4	6,224.9	6,666.1	7,161.5	7,727.2
Sumter	257.3	299.0	325.5	358.1	375.8	401.9	437.6	464.6	496.2	535.5
Suwannee	257.3	268.3	307.3	342.1	371.9	390.6	418.9	440.6	464.4	497.9
Taylor	185.7	186.9	201.7	212.4	222.8	227.4	243.0	237.6	269.3	282.4
Union	71.9	77.5	83.3	89.0	93.4	98.3	104.8	110.2	114.6	121.4
Volusia	4,394.7	4,759.2	5,192.5	5,652.4	6,004.4	6,222.2	6,498.7	6,845.4	7,235.1	7,772.1
Wakulla	129.4	137.6	157.4	175.0	195.5	208.6	224.6	243.5	265.2	277.2
Walton	247.1	254.8	280.2	304.5	331.3	363.7	393.1	433.4	465.5	487.2
Washington	143.9	152.7	168.0	178.6	192.8	207.4	222.3	233.8	243.7	258.9

1/ United States numbers are rounded to millions of dollars.
Note: Some data are revised.
Source: U.S., Department of Commerce, Bureau of Economic Analysis, Regional Economic Information System, CD-ROM, August 1997.

Table 5.10. PERSONAL INCOME: PER CAPITA AMOUNTS ON A PLACE-OF-RESIDENCE BASIS IN THE UNITED STATES AND IN THE STATE AND COUNTIES OF FLORIDA, 1985 THROUGH 1995

(rounded to dollars)

County	1985	1986	1987	1988	1989	1990	1991	1992	1993	1994	1995
United States	14,406	15,140	15,944	17,017	18,127	19,142	19,638	20,582	21,223	22,044	23,196
Florida	14,356	15,169	15,996	17,050	18,369	19,107	19,491	19,956	21,153	21,777	23,031
Alachua	11,664	12,403	13,182	14,195	15,262	16,155	16,697	17,365	18,193	18,961	19,984
Baker	9,570	10,062	10,685	11,435	11,759	12,462	12,627	13,213	13,858	14,442	15,258
Bay	11,663	12,194	12,539	13,237	13,993	15,091	15,901	16,519	17,295	17,680	18,229
Bradford	8,462	9,099	9,433	10,191	10,735	11,359	11,637	12,399	13,023	13,327	14,565
Brevard	14,436	14,857	15,609	16,584	17,870	18,172	18,645	19,316	19,663	20,161	20,747
Broward	17,173	18,273	19,221	20,206	21,890	22,583	22,662	23,201	24,175	24,736	26,192
Calhoun	7,589	8,135	8,794	9,629	9,613	10,813	11,009	11,631	12,034	12,431	12,622
Charlotte	13,862	14,606	15,204	16,220	17,779	17,638	17,644	18,080	18,636	19,483	20,539
Citrus	11,777	12,072	12,672	13,469	14,534	14,855	15,231	15,650	16,180	16,719	17,189
Clay	13,638	14,268	14,966	15,733	16,354	17,112	17,334	17,695	18,348	19,000	20,132
Collier	18,590	20,267	22,052	25,385	27,262	27,921	28,369	29,638	31,084	31,447	32,878
Columbia	10,085	10,567	11,046	11,956	12,548	12,971	13,419	14,171	14,870	15,591	16,414
Dade	14,010	14,572	15,487	16,237	17,264	17,841	18,144	17,072	19,699	20,056	21,058
De Soto	9,727	10,533	11,418	13,308	13,935	14,127	15,562	15,763	16,391	16,352	17,625
Dixie	8,152	8,472	8,997	9,806	10,570	10,804	10,377	10,721	10,688	12,380	12,707
Duval	13,708	14,369	15,181	15,907	17,283	18,112	18,411	18,921	20,123	20,941	22,337
Escambia	11,579	12,159	12,603	13,528	14,225	15,142	15,690	16,373	17,177	17,370	18,089
Flagler	13,239	13,819	14,740	15,495	15,099	14,648	14,692	15,278	15,934	16,677	17,195
Franklin	9,072	10,040	10,146	10,931	11,704	12,645	12,883	13,769	14,293	15,198	15,431
Gadsden	8,003	8,639	9,235	10,194	11,171	11,762	12,142	13,077	13,575	13,725	14,229
Gilchrist	9,491	9,917	10,083	10,566	11,021	11,465	11,721	12,753	12,700	12,582	12,888
Glades	8,069	8,761	9,136	10,660	10,806	11,512	12,872	13,002	14,430	13,342	14,223

See footnote at end of table.

Continued . .

Table 5.10. PERSONAL INCOME: PER CAPITA AMOUNTS ON A PLACE-OF-RESIDENCE BASIS IN THE UNITED STATES AND IN THE STATE AND COUNTIES OF FLORIDA, 1985 THROUGH 1995 (Continued)

(rounded to dollars)

County	1984	1985	1986	1987	1988	1989	1990	1991	1992	1993	1994
Gulf	9,594	10,287	10,484	11,072	11,660	12,413	13,041	14,060	14,233	14,536	14,753
Hamilton	8,855	9,293	9,715	10,112	10,632	11,115	10,874	11,408	11,379	11,648	12,198
Hardee	10,319	10,639	11,347	14,224	14,515	14,555	15,187	14,972	15,369	15,343	16,647
Hendry	12,199	12,347	13,460	15,341	14,845	15,351	16,945	16,551	17,883	16,336	17,789
Hernando	11,389	12,195	12,807	14,214	15,105	15,145	15,383	15,917	16,350	17,157	18,190
Highlands	12,137	13,126	13,528	14,768	15,494	15,637	16,312	16,589	17,505	17,844	19,124
Hillsborough	12,923	13,381	14,250	15,171	16,332	17,232	17,837	18,634	19,410	20,328	21,509
Holmes	8,177	8,708	8,872	9,643	10,238	10,630	11,380	11,862	12,297	12,708	12,456
Indian River	16,843	18,381	19,854	22,102	24,229	25,418	26,284	27,132	28,524	29,646	31,845
Jackson	8,885	9,215	9,847	10,935	11,579	12,407	13,209	13,598	13,905	14,322	14,604
Jefferson	8,991	9,673	10,346	11,365	12,107	13,134	13,351	13,653	14,460	14,745	15,826
Lafayette	10,200	10,287	9,410	9,703	10,927	11,524	11,801	12,676	13,057	12,941	12,375
Lake	13,225	14,100	14,455	15,020	16,341	16,393	16,912	17,712	18,288	18,840	19,459
Lee	14,812	15,748	16,570	17,714	19,461	19,819	20,009	20,741	21,672	22,450	23,664
Leon	11,808	13,012	13,891	14,991	15,967	16,945	17,470	18,118	18,928	19,781	20,875
Levy	9,276	9,709	10,102	11,096	11,551	12,076	12,605	13,274	13,635	13,976	14,631
Liberty	8,710	9,051	9,338	10,233	10,897	11,659	11,753	12,379	12,876	12,619	12,856
Madison	8,570	9,025	9,407	10,103	10,306	11,016	11,396	11,940	12,196	12,571	13,478
Manatee	14,581	15,431	16,281	17,163	18,861	19,533	20,002	21,143	22,221	23,120	24,758
Marion	11,327	12,123	12,754	13,597	14,512	14,959	15,242	16,165	16,673	17,318	18,130
Martin	19,273	20,575	21,769	24,118	27,009	28,894	29,454	30,332	31,762	32,251	34,529
Monroe	14,161	15,579	16,624	18,026	20,402	21,759	22,136	22,568	24,251	25,219	27,210
Nassau	13,703	14,770	15,040	15,757	16,733	17,655	18,210	18,857	19,736	20,255	21,488
Okaloosa	12,049	12,635	13,514	14,395	15,357	16,269	17,006	17,782	18,491	19,007	19,795
Okeechobee	10,063	10,649	10,934	11,947	12,387	13,015	13,393	13,876	14,650	14,855	15,921

Continued . . .

See footnote at end of table.

Table 5.10. PERSONAL INCOME: PER CAPITA AMOUNTS ON A PLACE-OF-RESIDENCE BASIS IN THE UNITED STATES AND IN THE STATE AND COUNTIES OF FLORIDA, 1985 THROUGH 1995 (Continued)

(rounded to dollars)

County	1984	1985	1986	1987	1988	1989	1990	1991	1992	1993	1994
Orange	14,166	14,855	15,629	16,730	17,651	18,224	18,492	19,212	20,027	20,652	21,868
Osceola	11,769	12,496	13,316	14,158	14,768	14,364	14,570	15,033	15,377	15,822	16,317
Palm Beach	20,438	21,626	23,079	24,843	26,985	29,666	30,569	31,685	33,197	33,862	36,057
Pasco	12,009	12,763	13,096	13,853	14,639	15,176	15,498	16,180	16,760	17,601	18,808
Pinellas	16,011	17,171	17,662	18,571	20,469	20,762	21,073	21,931	23,570	23,984	25,765
Polk	11,834	12,381	13,113	14,130	15,056	15,346	15,695	16,336	16,972	17,930	19,126
Putnam	9,632	10,263	10,350	11,189	11,353	11,794	12,267	13,252	14,008	14,195	15,237
St. Johns	14,957	16,148	17,641	19,479	21,015	22,323	22,963	24,574	25,347	26,557	28,140
St. Lucie	11,573	12,435	13,019	14,701	15,265	15,142	15,380	15,750	16,470	16,781	17,747
Santa Rosa	11,732	12,320	12,847	13,509	14,148	15,221	15,986	16,669	17,246	17,451	17,856
Sarasota	18,753	20,330	21,630	23,025	26,331	27,022	27,355	28,560	29,649	31,259	33,445
Seminole	14,232	15,159	15,891	17,385	18,493	19,041	19,233	20,117	21,049	22,080	23,400
Sumter	9,023	9,492	10,042	10,794	11,555	11,843	12,521	13,504	14,205	14,858	15,364
Suwannee	9,458	10,196	10,517	11,946	12,951	13,824	14,110	14,830	15,210	15,729	16,621
Taylor	10,166	10,828	10,827	11,887	12,428	12,983	13,091	14,048	13,776	15,514	15,722
Union	6,648	6,901	7,404	8,340	8,751	9,089	8,720	9,245	9,360	9,299	9,944
Volusia	12,952	13,653	14,243	14,974	15,763	16,057	16,208	16,622	17,227	17,842	18,951
Wakulla	9,330	10,282	10,806	11,908	12,874	13,599	14,035	14,562	15,101	15,883	15,958
Walton	8,954	9,449	9,498	10,310	11,017	11,913	12,310	12,978	13,896	14,223	14,360
Washington	8,783	9,157	9,494	10,203	10,718	11,364	12,034	12,799	13,109	13,535	13,618

Note: These data were derived by dividing each type of income by the total population of the area, not just the segment of the population receiving that particular type of income. All per capita figures are prepared by the Bureau of Economic Analysis using Bureau of the Census population data and are not comparable to those found in previous Abstracts.

Source: U.S., Department of Commerce, Bureau of Economic Analysis, Regional Economic Information System, CD-ROM, August 1997.

Table 5.11. PERSONAL INCOME: TOTAL AND PER CAPITA AMOUNTS ON A PLACE-OF-RESIDENCE BASIS IN THE STATE AND METROPOLITAN AREAS OF FLORIDA, 1993, 1994, AND 1995

Metropolitan area	Total personal income ($1,000,000)			Per capita personal income (dollars)		
	1993	1994	1995	1993	1994	1995
Florida	290,075	304,113	326,670	21,153	21,777	23,031
Daytona Beach	7,417	7,867	8,464	17,120	17,742	18,794
Flagler County	572	632	692	15,934	16,677	17,195
Volusia County	6,845	7,235	7,772	17,227	17,842	18,951
Ft. Lauderdale	32,716	34,274	37,008	24,175	24,736	26,192
Ft. Myers-Cape Coral	7,784	8,259	8,880	21,672	22,450	23,664
Ft. Pierce-Port St. Lucie	6,126	6,362	6,866	22,491	22,847	24,313
Martin County	3,406	3,522	3,815	31,762	32,251	34,529
St. Lucie County	2,720	2,841	3,051	16,470	16,781	17,747
Ft. Walton Beach	2,914	3,060	3,237	18,491	19,007	19,795
Gainesville	3,473	3,663	3,905	18,193	18,961	19,984
Jacksonville	19,606	20,630	22,209	20,401	21,234	22,617
Clay County	2,145	2,289	2,501	18,348	19,000	20,132
Duval County	14,112	14,725	15,748	20,123	20,941	22,337
Nassau County	954	1,004	1,090	19,736	20,255	21,488
St. Johns County	2,395	2,613	2,869	25,347	26,557	28,140
Lakeland-Winter Haven	7,175	7,709	8,344	16,972	17,930	19,126
Melbourne-Titusville-Palm Bay	8,564	8,938	9,341	19,663	20,161	20,747
Miami	39,110	40,344	43,087	19,699	20,056	21,058
Naples	5,343	5,601	6,015	31,084	31,447	32,878
Ocala	3,533	3,804	4,090	16,673	17,318	18,130
Orlando	26,180	27,690	29,645	19,621	20,313	21,395
Lake County	3,062	3,268	3,506	18,288	18,840	19,459
Orange County	14,556	15,257	16,274	20,027	20,652	21,868
Osceola County	1,896	2,003	2,138	15,377	15,822	16,317
Seminole County	6,666	7,162	7,727	21,049	22,080	23,440
Panama City	2,373	2,471	2,592	17,295	17,680	18,229
Pensacola	6,229	6,484	6,818	17,195	17,391	18,025
Escambia County	4,598	4,757	4,964	17,177	17,370	18,089
Santa Rosa County	1,632	1,727	1,853	17,246	17,451	17,856
Punta Gorda	2,294	2,456	2,649	18,636	19,483	20,539
Sarasota-Bradenton	13,489	14,375	15,557	26,406	27,704	29,641
Manatee County	4,955	5,240	5,690	22,221	23,120	24,758
Sarasota County	8,534	9,135	9,867	29,649	31,259	33,445
Tallahassee	4,504	4,784	5,083	18,014	18,760	19,753
Gadsden County	580	590	618	13,575	13,725	14,229
Leon County	3,924	4,194	4,465	18,928	19,781	20,875
Tampa-St. Petersburg-Clearwater	43,934	45,864	49,391	20,567	21,246	22,646
Hernando County	1,856	2,013	2,169	16,350	17,157	18,190
Hillsborough County	16,819	17,790	19,067	19,410	20,328	21,509
Pasco County	4,896	5,266	5,747	16,760	17,601	18,808
Pinellas County	20,363	20,794	22,407	23,570	23,984	25,765
West Palm Beach-Boca Raton	30,995	32,424	35,204	33,197	33,862	36,057

Note: Data for Metropolitan Statistical Areas (MSAs) and Primary Metropolitan Statistical Areas (PMSAs) based on 1992 MSA designations. See Glossary for definitions and map at the front of the book for area boundaries. Data for 1993 and 1994 are revised. See footnote on per capita computation on Table 5.10.

Source: U.S., Department of Commerce, Bureau of Economic Analysis, Regional Economic Information System, CD-ROM, August 1997.

University of Florida   **Bureau of Economic and Business Research**

Table 5.12. PERSONAL INCOME: PER CAPITA AMOUNTS BY TYPE IN THE UNITED STATES AND IN THE STATE AND COUNTIES OF FLORIDA, 1994 AND 1995

(rounded to dollars)

County	1994 Total per- sonal income	1994 Non- farm per- sonal income	1994 Transfer payments Income main- te- nance 1/	1994 Transfer payments Unem- ploy- ment insur- ance 1/	1994 Transfer payments Re- tire- ment and other	1994 Divi- dends inter- est and rent 2/	1995 Total per- sonal income	1995 Non- farm per- sonal income	1995 Transfer payments Income main- te- nance 1/	1995 Transfer payments Unem- ploy- ment insur- ance 1/	1995 Transfer payments Re- tire- ment and other	1995 Divi- dends inter- est and rent 2/
United States	22,044	21,875	352	93	1,771	3,763	23,196	23,067	368	84	1,853	4,010
Florida	21,777	21,659	298	61	2,104	5,457	23,031	22,897	319	52	2,190	5,865
Alachua	18,961	18,869	338	35	1,408	3,096	19,984	19,899	366	30	1,466	3,349
Baker	14,442	13,828	365	48	1,328	1,289	15,258	14,639	373	41	1,385	1,381
Bay	17,680	17,684	312	71	2,298	2,705	18,229	18,233	339	56	2,410	2,649
Bradford	13,327	13,091	411	32	1,530	1,423	14,565	14,280	451	27	1,634	1,564
Brevard	20,161	20,136	206	70	2,678	3,854	20,747	20,726	217	61	2,778	4,152
Broward	24,736	24,725	212	79	1,953	6,517	26,192	26,179	223	71	2,027	7,011
Calhoun	12,431	11,948	555	47	1,662	1,404	12,622	12,133	580	38	1,744	1,082
Charlotte	19,483	19,421	130	29	3,446	7,175	20,539	20,464	141	24	3,548	7,692
Citrus	16,719	16,713	230	64	3,232	5,015	17,189	17,188	240	54	3,317	5,217
Clay	19,000	18,971	145	37	1,898	2,277	20,132	20,079	148	29	1,948	2,413
Collier	31,447	30,740	182	48	2,563	14,638	32,878	32,202	183	42	2,637	15,274
Columbia	15,591	15,448	475	60	1,730	2,105	16,414	16,281	502	44	1,795	2,234
Dade	20,056	19,988	521	85	1,237	3,851	21,058	20,975	557	75	1,287	4,145
De Soto	16,352	14,778	430	43	1,937	3,557	17,625	15,711	450	37	2,031	3,875
Dixie	12,380	12,265	563	47	1,819	1,780	12,707	12,612	575	52	1,894	1,884
Duval	20,941	20,927	356	47	1,796	2,902	22,322	22,322	378	39	1,885	3,163
Escambia	17,370	17,333	411	33	2,369	2,529	18,089	18,069	447	30	2,463	2,628
Flagler	16,677	16,544	192	35	3,442	3,840	17,195	17,108	193	26	3,434	3,967
Franklin	15,198	15,198	575	27	1,652	2,725	15,431	15,431	606	36	1,696	2,420
Gadsden	13,725	12,977	737	37	1,387	1,581	14,229	13,410	788	29	1,462	1,296
Gilchrist	12,582	11,719	305	25	1,628	1,495	12,888	12,337	312	20	1,697	1,587
Glades	13,342	11,969	340	79	1,077	2,914	14,223	12,728	363	72	1,133	3,153
Gulf	14,536	14,536	458	49	2,151	2,043	14,753	14,753	482	45	2,248	1,822

See footnotes at end of table.

Continued . . .

Table 5.12. PERSONAL INCOME: PER CAPITA AMOUNTS BY TYPE IN THE UNITED STATES AND IN THE STATE AND COUNTIES OF FLORIDA, 1994 AND 1995 (Continued)

(rounded to dollars)

County	1994 Total personal income	1994 Non-farm personal income	1994 Transfer payments Income maintenance 1/	1994 Transfer payments Unemployment insurance	1994 Transfer payments Retirement and other	1994 Dividends interest and rent 2/	1995 Total personal income	1995 Non-farm personal income	1995 Transfer payments Income maintenance 1/	1995 Transfer payments Unemployment insurance	1995 Transfer payments Retirement and other	1995 Dividends interest and rent 2/
Hamilton	11,648	11,061	538	34	1,305	1,157	12,198	11,669	563	23	1,342	1,217
Hardee	15,343	13,575	597	99	1,471	2,244	16,647	14,721	647	95	1,570	2,471
Hendry	16,336	13,696	424	132	1,152	2,496	17,789	14,524	443	122	1,208	2,692
Hernando	17,157	17,122	211	43	3,410	4,362	18,190	18,165	228	34	3,553	4,701
Highlands	17,844	17,309	300	59	3,265	5,256	19,124	18,343	328	53	3,411	5,704
Hillsborough	20,328	20,206	340	60	1,654	3,031	21,509	21,370	360	52	1,729	3,272
Holmes	12,708	11,968	569	30	1,682	1,415	12,456	11,778	607	34	1,696	1,056
Indian River	29,646	29,323	176	80	3,383	14,001	31,845	31,314	185	74	3,542	15,213
Jackson	14,322	13,906	445	39	1,629	1,734	14,604	14,179	489	32	1,719	1,464
Jefferson	14,745	14,092	583	23	1,542	2,279	15,826	15,267	611	22	1,601	2,438
Lafayette	12,941	10,548	341	25	1,406	1,423	12,375	10,482	322	21	1,372	1,440
Lake	18,840	18,621	257	56	3,181	5,118	19,459	19,235	270	48	3,253	5,402
Lee	22,450	22,341	180	36	2,748	7,690	23,664	23,556	192	32	2,843	8,266
Leon	19,781	19,773	260	26	1,248	2,724	20,875	20,869	275	21	1,309	2,752
Levy	13,976	13,554	415	36	2,012	2,479	14,631	14,126	433	31	2,078	2,635
Liberty	12,619	12,557	371	13	1,358	1,061	12,856	12,822	399	8	1,394	649
Madison	12,571	12,249	618	30	1,352	1,628	13,478	13,238	669	25	1,420	1,764
Manatee	23,120	22,810	218	35	2,567	6,941	24,758	24,394	230	32	2,676	7,505
Marion	17,318	17,192	327	44	2,760	3,857	18,130	18,009	344	34	2,862	4,114
Martin	32,251	31,833	170	68	3,063	15,872	34,529	34,000	180	58	3,199	17,214
Monroe	25,219	25,219	204	25	1,736	9,724	27,210	27,210	229	24	1,837	10,679
Nassau	20,255	20,041	223	45	1,734	3,420	21,488	21,289	224	36	1,802	3,656
Okaloosa	19,007	18,988	186	42	2,900	3,500	19,795	19,780	199	35	3,047	3,651
Okeechobee	14,855	13,681	334	67	2,250	2,504	15,921	14,803	351	63	2,407	2,754
Orange	20,652	20,528	285	50	1,602	3,025	21,868	21,719	307	41	1,673	3,284
Osceola	15,822	15,764	250	52	1,609	2,036	16,317	16,264	269	44	1,642	2,151

See footnotes at end of table.   Continued . . .

Table 5.12. PERSONAL INCOME: PER CAPITA AMOUNTS BY TYPE IN THE UNITED STATES AND IN THE STATE AND COUNTIES OF FLORIDA, 1994 AND 1995 (Continued)

(rounded to dollars)

	1994						1995					
			Transfer payments						Transfer payments			
County	Total per-sonal income	Non-farm per-sonal income	Income main-te-nance 1/	Unem-ploy-ment insur-ance	Re-tire-ment and other	Divi-dends inter-est and rent 2/	Total per-sonal income	Non-farm per-sonal income	Income main-te-nance 1/	Unem-ploy-ment insur-ance	Re-tire-ment and other	Divi-dends inter-est and rent 2/
Palm Beach	33,862	33,710	191	89	2,542	14,711	36,057	35,829	195	73	2,640	15,851
Pasco	17,601	17,528	223	44	2,796	3,866	18,808	18,742	238	37	2,889	4,146
Pinellas	23,984	23,978	222	51	2,720	6,422	25,765	25,761	266	43	2,853	7,014
Polk	17,930	17,780	328	68	2,017	3,519	19,126	18,947	352	57	2,110	3,794
Putnam	14,195	14,029	512	48	2,074	2,016	15,237	15,084	549	38	2,176	2,183
St. Johns	26,557	26,421	205	44	2,240	6,800	28,140	28,041	211	31	2,283	7,188
St. Lucie	16,781	16,569	309	118	2,240	3,840	17,747	17,497	319	104	2,338	4,139
Santa Rosa	17,451	17,339	227	33	1,927	2,494	17,856	17,778	237	31	1,956	2,343
Sarasota	31,259	31,234	144	35	3,647	13,647	33,445	33,426	154	29	3,815	14,830
Seminole	22,080	22,041	180	52	1,450	3,255	23,400	23,365	189	41	1,500	3,493
Sumter	14,858	14,498	461	39	3,314	2,405	15,364	15,138	466	32	3,365	2,520
Suwannee	15,729	14,422	425	37	1,983	2,283	16,621	15,309	460	28	2,086	2,466
Taylor	15,514	15,499	542	80	1,914	1,809	15,722	15,718	561	66	1,965	1,909
Union	9,299	9,186	257	15	1,051	972	9,944	9,832	277	17	1,123	1,075
Volusia	17,842	17,736	239	52	2,507	4,727	18,951	18,826	262	41	2,620	5,120
Wakulla	15,883	15,889	348	21	1,436	1,844	15,958	15,971	358	20	1,463	1,245
Walton	14,223	14,110	361	34	2,472	2,132	14,360	14,184	385	30	2,607	1,807
Washington	13,535	13,209	488	58	2,033	1,644	13,618	13,352	516	56	2,050	1,266

1/ Includes supplemental security income payments, payments to families with dependent children (AFDC), general assistance payments, food stamp payments, and other assistance payments, including emergency assistance.

2/ Includes the capital consumption adjustment for rental income of persons.

Note: These data were derived by dividing each type of income by the total population of the area, not just the segment of the population receiving that particular type of income. All per capita figures are prepared by the Bureau of Economic Analysis using Bureau of the census population data and are not comparable to those found in previous Abstracts

Source: U.S., Department of Commerce, Bureau of Economic Analysis, Regional Economic Information System, CD-ROM, August 1997.

Table 5.13.   DERIVATION OF PERSONAL INCOME: DERIVATION ON A PLACE-OF-RESIDENCE
BASIS IN THE STATE AND METROPOLITAN AREAS OF FLORIDA, 1995

(in millions of dollars)

Metropolitan Statistical Area (MSA) 1/	Total earnings by place of work	Less personal contributions for social insurance	Plus residence adjustment	Plus dividends interest and rent	Plus transfer payments	Personal income by place of residence
Florida	326,670	194,536	13,611	740	83,192	61,813
Daytona Beach	3,835	294	524	2,260	2,140	8,464
Flagler County	692	237	20	113	160	203
Volusia County	7,772	3,598	275	412	2,100	1,937
Ft. Lauderdale	19,942	1,421	2,696	9,906	5,885	37,008
Ft. Myers-Cape Coral	4,277	318	-25	3,102	1,844	8,880
Ft. Pierce-Port St. Lucie	2,767	205	288	2,614	1,403	6,866
Martin County	3,815	1,352	102	67	1,902	597
St. Lucie County	3,051	1,415	103	222	712	806
Ft. Walton Beach	2,148	136	-138	597	766	3,237
Gainesville	2,939	158	-225	654	695	3,905
Jacksonville	16,257	1,106	-47	3,448	3,656	22,209
Clay County	2,501	819	58	1,055	300	386
Duval County	15,748	14,055	950	-2,287	2,230	2,700
Nassau County	1,090	461	30	311	185	162
St. Johns County	2,869	922	67	873	733	409
Lakeland-Winter Haven	5,170	370	124	1,655	1,765	8,344
Melbourne-Titusville-Palm Bay	5,784	410	14	1,869	2,084	9,341
Miami	32,590	2,202	-4,011	8,480	8,230	43,087
Naples	2,585	186	28	2,794	793	6,015
Ocala	2,007	153	189	928	1,119	4,090
Orlando	22,263	1,552	-876	4,852	4,958	29,645
Lake County	3,506	1,418	115	234	973	997
Orange County	16,274	16,275	1,115	-3,920	2,444	2,591
Osceola County	2,138	1,151	81	346	282	441
Seminole County	7,727	3,420	240	2,464	1,153	930
Panama City	1,713	112	-19	377	634	2,592
Pensacola	4,378	290	147	964	1,618	6,818
Escambia County	4,964	3,706	245	-482	721	1,264
Santa Rosa County	673	46	629	243	354	1,853
Punta Gorda	914	78	68	992	753	2,649
Sarasota-Bradenton	6,727	525	354	6,100	2,901	15,557
Manatee County	5,690	2,929	219	191	1,725	1,065
Sarasota County	9,867	3,798	306	164	4,375	1,836
Tallahassee	4,135	203	-255	645	762	5,083
Gadsden County	618	340	17	62	56	177
Leon County	4,465	3,795	187	-317	589	585
Tampa-St. Petersburg-Clearwater	30,672	2,231	-211	10,828	10,332	49,391
Hernando County	2,169	679	62	259	561	733
Hillsborough County	19,067	16,194	1,097	-2,183	2,900	3,252
Pasco County	5,747	1,819	162	1,166	1,267	1,658
Pinellas County	22,407	11,980	910	548	6,100	4,689
West Palm Beach-Boca Raton	14,932	1,085	1,103	15,477	4,777	35,204

1/ Based on 1992 MSA designations.
Note: See Table 5.14 for derivation of personal income notes. See Glossary for
MSA definitions and map at the front of the book for area boundaries.
  Source: U.S., Department of Commerce, Bureau of Economic Analysis, Regional Economic Information System, CD-ROM, August 1997.

Table 5.14. DERIVATION OF PERSONAL INCOME: DERIVATION ON A PLACE-OF-RESIDENCE
BASIS IN THE UNITED STATES AND IN THE STATE AND COUNTIES OF FLORIDA
1994 AND 1995

(rounded to millions of dollars)

County	Total earn-ings by place of work 1/	Less personal contri-butions for social insurance	Plus resi-dence adjust-ment 2/	Plus dividends interest and rent 3/	Plus transfer payments	Personal income by place of residence
			1994 A/			
United States	4,081,780	277,574	-832	979,891	956,586	5,739,851
Florida	182,261	12,693	703	76,211	57,632	304,113
Alachua	2,785	149	-215	598	644	3,663
Baker	131	6	76	26	59	286
Bay	1,629	106	-19	378	589	2,471
Bradford	150	8	59	34	85	320
Brevard	5,667	399	3	1,709	1,959	8,938
Broward	18,531	1,315	2,527	9,030	5,501	34,274
Calhoun	71	4	16	16	47	146
Charlotte	858	72	63	904	703	2,456
Citrus	673	59	39	523	566	1,742
Clay	765	54	942	274	362	2,289
Collier	2,395	171	24	2,607	746	5,601
Columbia	420	26	51	98	185	729
Dade	30,881	2,083	-3,785	7,746	7,586	40,344
De Soto	215	11	5	89	112	410
Dixie	70	5	11	21	47	145
Duval	13,075	885	-2,030	2,041	2,524	14,725
Escambia	3,566	233	-461	693	1,192	4,757
Flagler	211	17	103	146	190	632
Franklin	70	5	14	27	45	151
Gadsden	323	16	53	68	163	590
Gilchrist	58	3	35	18	42	150
Glades	37	2	25	22	19	102
Gulf	116	8	-5	27	60	190
Hamilton	124	7	-34	13	38	135
Hardee	178	9	23	46	76	314
Hendry	312	15	15	73	92	477
Hernando	644	57	230	512	684	2,013
Highlands	546	44	-6	388	432	1,316
Hillsborough	15,044	1,018	-1,931	2,653	3,043	17,790
Holmes	87	5	37	24	73	216
Indian River	1,043	81	-9	1,335	539	2,827
Jackson	360	20	28	76	181	625

See footnotes at end of table.   Continued . . .

University of Florida   **Bureau of Economic and Business Research**

Table 5.14. DERIVATION OF PERSONAL INCOME: DERIVATION ON A PLACE-OF-RESIDENCE
BASIS IN THE UNITED STATES AND IN THE STATE AND COUNTIES OF FLORIDA
1994 AND 1995 (Continued)

(rounded to millions of dollars)

County	Total earnings by place of work 1/	Less personal contributions for social insurance	Plus residence adjustment 2/	Plus dividends interest and rent 3/	Plus transfer payments	Personal income by place of residence
			1994 A/ (Continued)			
Jefferson	71	4	46	29	47	188
Lafayette	42	1	10	8	17	76
Lake	1,314	106	246	888	926	3,268
Lee	4,021	297	-22	2,829	1,727	8,259
Leon	3,523	173	-277	578	543	4,194
Levy	162	11	63	72	119	403
Liberty	40	2	12	7	22	79
Madison	114	7	18	28	63	216
Manatee	2,602	193	259	1,573	999	5,240
Marion	1,873	141	186	847	1,039	3,804
Martin	1,241	94	86	1,733	555	3,522
Monroe	998	67	67	792	264	2,054
Nassau	438	28	272	170	153	1,004
Okaloosa	1,997	126	-86	563	711	3,060
Okeechobee	225	15	27	78	145	461
Orange	15,347	1,048	-3,697	2,234	2,420	15,257
Osceola	1,073	76	340	258	408	2,003
Palm Beach	13,819	1,004	1,053	14,086	4,470	32,424
Pasco	1,726	150	985	1,157	1,549	5,266
Pinellas	11,189	844	516	5,568	4,364	20,794
Polk	4,862	348	36	1,513	1,646	7,709
Putnam	484	33	91	138	295	975
St. Johns	839	60	781	669	384	2,613
St. Lucie	1,346	97	190	650	752	2,841
Santa Rosa	645	43	551	247	327	1,727
Sarasota	3,545	281	160	3,988	1,723	9,135
Seminole	3,167	221	2,287	1,056	873	7,162
Sumter	177	13	58	80	194	496
Suwannee	250	16	34	67	129	464
Taylor	188	13	-12	31	75	269
Union	98	4	-18	12	27	115
Volusia	3,376	252	392	1,917	1,802	7,235
Wakulla	86	6	103	31	51	265
Walton	223	15	46	70	142	466
Washington	123	7	14	30	84	244

See footnotes at end of table.   Continued . . .

Table 5.14. DERIVATION OF PERSONAL INCOME: DERIVATION ON A PLACE-OF-RESIDENCE
BASIS IN THE UNITED STATES AND IN THE STATE AND COUNTIES OF FLORIDA
1994 AND 1995 (Continued)

(rounded to millions of dollars)

County	Total earnings by place of work 1/	Less personal contributions for social insurance	Plus residence adjustment 2/	Plus dividends interest and rent 3/	Plus transfer payments	Personal income by place of residence
			1995			
United States	4,315,915	294,013	-873	1,054,107	1,022,841	6,097,977
Florida	194,536	13,611	740	83,192	61,813	326,670
Alachua	2,939	158	-225	654	695	3,905
Baker	138	6	85	28	64	308
Bay	1,713	112	-19	377	634	2,592
Bradford	165	9	61	37	93	348
Brevard	5,784	410	14	1,869	2,084	9,341
Broward	19,942	1,421	2,696	9,906	5,885	37,008
Calhoun	74	5	17	13	51	150
Charlotte	914	78	68	992	753	2,649
Citrus	695	63	47	560	605	1,844
Clay	819	58	1,055	300	386	2,501
Collier	2,585	186	28	2,794	793	6,015
Columbia	456	28	54	108	202	791
Dade	32,590	2,202	-4,011	8,480	8,230	43,087
De Soto	234	12	5	98	120	446
Dixie	72	5	12	23	51	154
Duval	14,055	950	-2,287	2,230	2,700	15,748
Escambia	3,706	245	-482	721	1,264	4,964
Flagler	237	20	113	160	203	692
Franklin	74	5	15	25	48	157
Gadsden	340	17	62	56	177	618
Gilchrist	59	3	38	20	45	159
Glades	40	2	27	24	20	109
Gulf	120	8	-5	24	64	196
Hamilton	137	8	-39	15	41	146
Hardee	190	10	25	50	84	339
Hendry	352	16	14	80	96	526
Hernando	679	62	259	561	733	2,169
Highlands	591	47	-5	425	461	1,425
Hillsborough	16,194	1,097	-2,183	2,900	3,252	19,067
Holmes	90	5	40	19	80	223
Indian River	1,125	87	-11	1,464	573	3,066
Jackson	374	21	32	65	197	647
Jefferson	74	4	55	32	51	207
Lafayette	43	2	10	9	19	79
Lake	1,418	115	234	973	997	3,506
Lee	4,277	318	-25	3,102	1,844	8,880
Leon	3,795	187	-317	589	585	4,465

See footnotes at end of table.   Continued . . .

University of Florida   **Bureau of Economic and Business Research**

Table 5.14. DERIVATION OF PERSONAL INCOME: DERIVATION ON A PLACE-OF-RESIDENCE
BASIS IN THE UNITED STATES AND IN THE STATE AND COUNTIES OF FLORIDA
1994 AND 1995 (Continued)

(rounded to millions of dollars)

County	Total earnings by place of work 1/	Less personal contributions for social insurance	Plus residence adjustment 2/	Plus dividends interest and rent 3/	Plus transfer payments	Personal income by place of residence
			1995 (Continued)			
Levy	176	12	64	78	128	435
Liberty	44	3	13	4	24	83
Madison	125	8	19	31	68	234
Manatee	2,929	219	191	1,725	1,065	5,690
Marion	2,007	153	189	928	1,119	4,090
Martin	1,352	102	67	1,902	597	3,815
Monroe	1,062	72	70	867	281	2,208
Nassau	461	30	311	185	162	1,090
Okaloosa	2,148	136	-138	597	766	3,237
Okeechobee	238	16	29	85	156	491
Orange	16,275	1,115	-3,920	2,444	2,591	16,274
Osceola	1,151	81	346	282	441	2,138
Palm Beach	14,932	1,085	1,103	15,477	4,777	35,204
Pasco	1,819	162	1,166	1,267	1,658	5,747
Pinellas	11,980	910	548	6,100	4,689	22,407
Polk	5,170	370	124	1,655	1,765	8,344
Putnam	531	37	93	151	317	1,055
St. Johns	922	67	873	733	409	2,869
St. Lucie	1,415	103	222	712	806	3,051
Santa Rosa	673	46	629	243	354	1,853
Sarasota	3,798	306	164	4,375	1,836	9,867
Seminole	3,420	240	2,464	1,153	930	7,727
Sumter	196	15	58	88	208	535
Suwannee	266	17	37	74	138	498
Taylor	192	13	-11	34	80	282
Union	102	4	-19	13	29	121
Volusia	3,598	275	412	2,100	1,937	7,772
Wakulla	89	6	117	22	56	277
Walton	237	16	49	61	156	487
Washington	140	8	12	24	91	259

A/ Revised.
1/ Consists of wage and salary disbursements, other labor income, and proprietors'
income.
2/ An estimate of the net gain or loss to an area because of commuting from place
of residence to place of work. Some persons earn income in the area in which they
live; others earn income outside that area. United States includes adjustments for
border workers, U.S. residents commuting outside U.S. borders less income of foreign
residents commuting inside U.S. borders, plus certain Caribbean seasonal workers.
3/ Includes the capital consumption adjustment for rental income of persons.

Source: U.S., Department of Commerce, Bureau of Economic Analysis, Regional Economic Information System, CD-ROM, August 1997.

University of Florida   **Bureau of Economic and Business Research**

Table 5.20. EARNED INCOME: TOTAL EARNINGS ON A PLACE-OF-WORK BASIS AND PERCENTAGE DISTRIBUTION BY TYPE AND MAJOR INDUSTRIAL SOURCE IN FLORIDA, OTHER SUNBELT STATES, OTHER POPULOUS STATES AND THE UNITED STATES, 1995

Item	Florida	Other sunbelt states								North Caro- lina	Okla- homa	South Caro- lina
		Ala- bama	Ari- zona	Ar- kansas	Cali- fornia	Georgia	Loui- siana	Mis- sis- sippi	New Mexico			
Earnings by place of work ($1,000,000)	194,536	57,597	59,565	31,718	541,029	117,962	56,288	30,591	21,437	113,640	41,263	49,772
	Percentage distribution by type of income											
Wage and salary disbursements	81.9	80.0	81.0	75.3	76.7	79.9	78.4	78.5	79.8	79.6	76.7	82.0
Other labor income	9.2	10.1	9.6	10.1	9.7	9.7	9.6	10.1	9.5	9.8	9.9	10.1
Proprietors' income	8.9	9.9	9.4	14.6	13.6	10.3	12.0	11.4	10.7	10.6	13.4	7.9
	Percentage distribution by industrial source of income											
Farm	1.0	1.5	1.1	4.1	1.1	1.6	0.9	1.7	1.3	2.5	0.9	0.7
Agricultural services 1/	1.1	0.6	0.9	0.8	1.1	0.6	0.5	0.7	0.7	0.6	0.6	0.6
Mining	0.2	1.1	1.1	0.5	0.4	0.3	4.5	0.7	3.5	0.1	5.0	0.2
Construction	5.9	5.7	7.4	5.5	5.0	5.4	6.8	5.4	7.2	6.0	4.7	6.4
Manufacturing	9.4	22.8	14.2	24.0	15.6	17.4	14.3	23.8	7.8	25.5	15.8	26.3
Transportation, communications, and public utilities	6.8	6.9	6.1	8.7	6.3	9.5	8.0	6.8	6.0	6.3	8.4	5.8
Wholesale trade	6.6	5.8	6.0	5.3	6.3	8.5	5.6	4.8	4.2	6.2	5.5	4.7
Retail trade	11.7	9.5	11.1	10.8	9.3	9.4	9.5	10.1	11.2	9.7	10.2	11.0
Finance, insurance, and real estate	8.3	4.8	7.6	4.4	7.2	6.7	5.1	4.4	4.6	5.5	5.1	4.9
Services	33.2	22.5	28.2	20.7	32.2	25.1	27.3	22.2	27.9	21.2	24.0	21.1
Government	15.9	18.9	16.2	15.2	15.5	15.6	17.5	19.5	25.7	16.3	19.9	18.3

See footnotes at end of table.

Continued . . .

Table 5.20. EARNED INCOME: TOTAL EARNINGS ON A PLACE-OF-WORK BASIS AND PERCENTAGE DISTRIBUTION BY TYPE AND MAJOR INDUSTRIAL SOURCE IN FLORIDA, OTHER SUNBELT STATES, OTHER POPULOUS STATES AND THE UNITED STATES, 1995 (Continued)

| Item | Other sunbelt states (Continued) | | | Other populous states | | | | | | | | United States |
	Tennessee	Texas	Virginia	Illinois	Indiana	Massachusetts	Michigan	New Jersey	New York	Ohio	Pennsylvania	
Earnings by place of work ($1,000,000)	82,482	298,576	109,398	215,671	90,885	123,970	164,552	156,478	356,642	179,129	192,279	4,315,915
Percentage distribution by type of income												
Wage and salary disbursements	78.5	75.6	83.4	80.6	80.0	80.3	80.8	80.8	80.1	80.9	78.1	79.3
Other labor income	10.1	9.1	9.4	10.2	11.2	9.8	12.2	9.5	9.1	10.2	10.5	9.8
Proprietors' income	11.4	15.3	7.2	9.2	8.8	9.9	7.0	9.7	10.8	8.9	11.5	10.9
Percentage distribution by industrial source of income												
Farm	0.4	0.7	0.4	0.1	0.1	0.1	0.3	0.2	0.1	0.4	0.3	0.8
Agricultural services 1/	0.5	0.6	0.5	0.5	0.4	0.5	0.4	0.4	0.3	0.5	0.5	0.7
Mining	0.3	4.2	0.6	0.4	0.4	0.1	0.3	0.1	0.1	0.4	0.7	0.9
Construction	5.8	5.9	5.8	5.4	6.2	4.5	4.8	4.4	3.6	5.3	5.5	5.5
Manufacturing	23.2	16.3	14.0	20.2	32.7	17.8	33.8	16.4	13.0	28.7	21.3	18.5
Transportation, communications, and public utilities	7.5	8.8	6.5	7.5	6.3	5.3	4.9	8.7	6.2	5.8	7.0	6.9
Wholesale trade	6.5	6.7	5.5	7.6	5.7	6.8	6.1	8.6	6.0	6.4	5.9	6.3
Retail trade	10.5	9.4	8.9	8.4	9.3	8.6	8.4	8.2	6.9	9.4	9.4	9.3
Finance, insurance, and real estate	5.4	6.2	6.2	8.6	5.2	9.3	5.0	8.0	16.3	5.8	7.0	7.5
Services	26.2	26.0	28.2	28.5	21.3	35.3	23.5	30.3	32.4	24.4	29.5	28.1
Government	13.7	15.1	23.4	12.8	12.4	11.8	12.6	14.7	15.1	13.1	13.0	15.6

1/ Includes forestry, fisheries, and other.
Note: Data differ from figures on other income tables because of revisions made after publication of these numbers.

Source: U.S., Department of Commerce, Bureau of Economic Analysis, *Survey of Current Business, October 1996.*

Table 5.21. PERSONAL INCOME: AMOUNTS BY MAJOR SOURCE IN THE METROPOLITAN AND NONMETROPOLITAN AREAS OF FLORIDA, THE SOUTHEAST, AND THE UNITED STATES, 1994 AND 1995

(rounded to millions of dollars)

Item	Florida Total	Florida Metro-politan areas	Florida Non-metro-politan areas	Southeast Total	Southeast Metro-politan areas	Southeast Non-metro-politan areas	United States Total	United States Metro-politan areas	United States Non-metro-politan areas
Income by place of residence, 1994 A/									
Total personal income	304,113	287,059	17,054	1,249,309	956,561	292,749	6,629,458	5,739,851	889,607
Derivation of personal income									
Total earnings by place of work	182,261	174,318	7,943	860,793	679,267	181,526	4,630,458	4,081,780	548,678
Less: Personal contributions for social insurance	12,693	12,159	534	59,023	46,416	12,607	315,234	277,574	37,660
Plus: Adjustment for residence	703	-238	941	6,539	-5,753	12,292	36,685	-832	37,517
Equals: Net earnings by place of residence	170,271	161,921	8,350	808,310	627,099	181,211	4,351,910	3,803,374	548,536
Plus: Dividends, interest, and rent	76,211	71,881	4,329	215,013	172,740	42,273	1,127,413	979,891	147,522
Plus: Transfer payments	57,632	53,257	4,375	225,987	156,722	69,265	1,150,135	956,586	193,549
Earnings by place of work, 1994 A/									
Components of earnings									
Wages and salaries	149,609	143,576	6,033	691,308	553,045	138,264	3,644,781	3,233,236	411,545
Other labor income	16,857	16,160	697	84,058	65,890	18,169	455,869	402,011	53,858
Proprietors' income 1/	15,794	14,582	1,213	85,427	60,333	25,094	529,808	446,533	83,275
Farm	836	519	317	10,507	3,179	7,329	51,663	30,654	21,009
Nonfarm	14,958	14,062	896	74,920	57,155	17,765	478,145	415,879	62,266

See footnotes at end of table.

Continued . . .

Table 5.21. PERSONAL INCOME: AMOUNTS BY MAJOR SOURCE IN THE METROPOLITAN AND NONMETROPOLITAN AREAS OF FLORIDA THE SOUTHEAST, AND THE UNITED STATES, 1994 AND 1995 (Continued)

(rounded to millions of dollars)

Earnings by place of work, 1994 A/ (Continued)

Item	Florida			Southeast			United States		
	Total	Metro-politan areas	Non-metro-politan areas	Total	Metro-politan areas	Non-metro-politan areas	Total	Metro-politan areas	Non-metro-politan areas
Earnings by industry									
Farm	1,645	1,181	463	13,109	4,412	8,698	71,110	43,990	27,120
Nonfarm	180,616	173,136	7,480	847,684	674,856	172,829	4,559,348	4,037,790	521,558
Private	150,904	145,267	5,638	696,000	555,770	140,230	3,804,351	3,386,362	417,989
Agricultural services 2/	1,905	B/ 1,611	B/ 294	3,721	B/ 3,721	(D)	33,194	26,907	6,287
Mining	268	B/ 268	(D)	7,849	B/ 3,629	B/ 4,220	50,230	36,514	13,716
Construction	10,949	10,407	B/ 542	50,713	B/ 40,705	B/ 10,008	259,836	226,432	33,404
Manufacturing	17,806	16,958	847	159,315	107,212	52,103	890,509	760,619	129,890
Nondurable goods	6,139	6,139	(D)	76,826	B/ 50,222	B/ 26,604	354,965	298,976	55,989
Durable goods	11,143	10,819	B/ 324	80,369	B/ 56,786	B/ 23,583	535,545	461,643	73,902
Transportation 3/	12,419	11,952	B/ 467	61,594	B/ 51,763	B/ 9,831	316,623	281,709	34,914
Wholesale trade	11,784 B/	11,543 B/	B/ 241	52,162	B/ 45,709	B/ 6,453	275,693	254,075	21,618
Retail trade	21,511	20,512	998	86,958	B/ 68,973	B/ 17,985	433,683	376,811	56,872
Finance, insurance, and real estate	14,965	14,647	B/ 318	51,660	B/ 46,302	B/ 5,358	323,025	305,108	17,917
Services	59,032	57,246 B/	B/ 1,786	216,377	186,550	B/ 29,827	1,221,558	1,118,187	103,371
Government 4/	29,712	27,870	1,842	151,685	119,086	32,599	754,997	651,428	103,569
Federal, civilian	5,066	4,870	196	31,762	27,704	4,058	145,402	131,277	14,125
Federal, military	2,705	2,628	76	18,335	15,653	2,682	53,984	47,324	6,660
State and local	21,941	20,372	1,569	101,588	75,728	25,860	555,611	472,827	82,784

Continued . . .

See footnotes at end of table.

Table 5.21. PERSONAL INCOME: AMOUNTS BY MAJOR SOURCE IN THE METROPOLITAN AND NONMETROPOLITAN AREAS OF FLORIDA THE SOUTHEAST, AND THE UNITED STATES, 1994 AND 1995 (Continued)

(rounded to millions of dollars)

Item	Florida Total	Florida Metropolitan areas	Florida Non-metropolitan areas	Southeast Total	Southeast Metropolitan areas	Southeast Non-metropolitan areas	United States Total	United States Metropolitan areas	United States Non-metropolitan areas
			Income by place of residence, 1995						
Total personal income	535,557	507,184	28,372	2,318,774	1,791,539	527,235	12,292,264	10,707,032	1,585,232
Derivation of personal income									
Total earnings by place of work	194,536	186,034	8,502	915,810	725,387	190,423	4,884,968	4,315,915	569,053
Less: Personal contributions for social insurance	13,611	13,036	574	62,997	49,625	13,372	333,918	294,013	39,905
Plus: Adjustment for residence	740	-270	1,010	6,599	-6,769	13,368	39,701	-873	40,574
Equals: Net earnings by place of residence	181,665	172,728	8,938	859,412	668,992	190,419	4,590,751	4,021,029	569,722
Plus: Dividends, interest, and rent	83,192	78,542	4,650	231,399	186,164	45,235	1,212,638	1,054,107	158,531
Plus: Transfer payments	61,813	57,114	4,699	242,557	168,141	74,416	1,230,288	1,022,841	207,447
			Earnings by place of work, 1995						
Components of earnings									
Wages and salaries	159,372	152,951	6,421	735,921	590,268	145,653	3,855,982	3,423,330	432,652
Other labor income	17,819	17,075	744	89,189	69,968	19,221	480,628	423,799	56,829
Proprietors' income 1/	17,345	16,009	1,336	90,700	65,150	25,550	548,358	468,786	79,572
Farm	1,047	676	370	9,225	2,907	6,319	31,738	19,529	12,209
Nonfarm	16,298	15,332	966	81,475	62,244	19,231	516,619	449,257	67,362

Continued . . .

See footnotes at end of table.

Table 5.21. PERSONAL INCOME: AMOUNTS BY MAJOR SOURCE IN THE METROPOLITAN AND NONMETROPOLITAN AREAS OF FLORIDA, THE SOUTHEAST, AND THE UNITED STATES, 1994 AND 1995 (Continued)

(rounded to millions of dollars)

Earnings by place of work, 1995 (Continued)

Item	Florida Total	Florida Metropolitan areas	Florida Non-metropolitan areas	Southeast Total	Southeast Metropolitan areas	Southeast Non-metropolitan areas	United States Total	United States Metropolitan areas	United States Non-metropolitan areas
Earnings by industry									
Farm	1,898	1,372	525	11,891	4,190	7,701	52,492	33,882	18,610
Nonfarm	192,638	184,662	7,977	903,919	721,196	182,723	4,832,476	4,282,033	550,443
Private	161,656	155,653	6,002	746,178	597,664	148,514	4,050,627	3,607,964	442,663
Agricultural services 2/	2,020	B/ 1,716	B/ 303	(D)	(D)	(D)	35,616	28,839	6,777
Mining	316	B/ 316	(D)	7,824	B/ 3,823	B/ 4,001	51,594	37,599	13,995
Construction	11,455	B/ 10,871	584	53,267	B/ 42,959	B/ 10,308	269,550	235,315	34,235
Manufacturing	18,288	17,402	B/ 886	166,375	B/ 112,340	B/ 54,034	932,330	796,685	135,645
Nondurable goods	6,301	6,301	(D)	49,869	B/ 49,869	(D)	367,242	309,853	57,389
Durable goods	11,101	11,101	(D)	57,605	B/ 57,605	(D)	565,088	486,832	78,256
Transportation 3/	13,203	12,742	B/ 461	65,302	B/ 54,964	B/ 10,338	334,792	297,621	37,171
Wholesale trade	12,856	B/ 12,610	B/ 246	56,606	B/ 49,601	B/ 7,005	297,087	273,968	23,119
Retail trade	22,666	21,605	1,060	93,094	B/ 73,814	B/ 19,280	460,529	399,957	60,572
Finance, insurance, and real estate	16,059	15,719	B/ 340	55,398	B/ 49,717	B/ 5,681	343,441	324,524	18,917
Services	64,551	62,605	B/ 1,946	237,034	B/ 204,522	B/ 32,512	1,325,686	1,213,456	112,230
Government 4/	30,983	29,009	1,974	157,741	123,532	34,209	781,849	674,069	107,780
Federal, civilian	5,237	5,019	218	32,412	28,171	4,240	147,091	132,706	14,385
Federal, military	2,654	2,582	73	18,217	15,563	2,653	53,599	47,079	6,520
State and local	23,092	21,408	1,684	107,113	79,798	27,315	581,160	494,284	86,876

(D) Data withheld to avoid disclosure of information about individual firms.
A/ Revised. B/ This estimate constitutes the major portion of the true estimate.
1/ Includes the inventory valuation and capital consumption adjustments. 2/ Includes forestry, fisheries, and other. "Other" includes wages and salaries of U.S. residents employed by foreign embassies, consulates, and international organizations in the United States. 3/ Includes communications and public utilities. 4/ Includes government enterprises.
Note: See Table 5.14 for derivation of personal income notes.
Source: U.S., Department of Commerce, Bureau of Economic Analysis, Regional Economic Information System, CD-ROM, August 1997.

Table 5.23. PERSONAL INCOME: AMOUNTS BY MAJOR SOURCE IN FLORIDA, FOURTH QUARTER 1995 THROUGH FOURTH QUARTER 1996

(in millions of dollars)

Item	Fourth quarter 1995	1996 First quarter	1996 Second quarter	1996 Third quarter	1996 Fourth quarter
Total personal income 1/	333,550	340,377	344,040	349,360	352,426
Derivation of total personal income					
Total earnings by place of work	198,583	203,370	205,593	209,343	210,706
Less personal contributions for social insurance	13,854	14,188	14,271	14,511	14,554
Plus adjustment for residence	747	744	761	772	789
Equals net earnings by place of residence	185,476	189,925	192,082	195,604	196,941
Plus dividends, interest, and rent 2/	84,977	86,146	86,816	87,940	88,966
Plus transfer payments	63,097	64,306	65,141	65,816	66,520
State unemployment benefits	737	682	681	731	789
Other transfer payments	62,360	63,624	64,461	65,084	65,730
Components of earnings 1/					
Wages and salaries	162,864	167,496	169,138	172,384	173,541
Other labor income	18,125	18,384	18,424	18,679	18,694
Proprietors' income 3/	17,594	17,489	18,030	18,280	18,471
Farm	1,142	666	944	1,065	1,074
Nonfarm	16,452	16,824	17,086	17,215	17,397
Earnings by industry 1/					
Farm	2,032	1,566	1,856	1,989	2,010
Nonfarm	196,551	201,803	203,737	207,354	208,696
Private	165,975	168,700	172,084	174,695	176,935
Agricultural services, forestry, and fisheries, and other 4/	2,147	2,153	2,278	2,346	2,299
Mining	355	361	347	359	500
Construction	11,510	12,429	12,600	12,811	12,693
Manufacturing	18,487	18,781	19,222	19,244	19,240
Nondurable goods	6,910	6,656	6,947	7,005	7,166
Durable goods	11,577	12,125	12,275	12,238	12,075
Transportation, communications, and public utilities	13,696	13,621	13,976	14,047	14,109
Wholesale trade	13,120	13,779	14,255	14,009	14,327
Retail trade	23,181	23,871	24,001	24,215	24,712
Finance, insurance, and real estate	16,564	16,863	17,515	18,135	18,192
Services	66,915	66,840	67,889	69,529	70,863
Government and government enterprises	30,577	33,103	31,653	32,659	31,761
Federal, civilian	5,301	5,359	5,408	5,388	5,443
Federal, military	2,766	2,864	2,845	2,839	2,885
State and local	22,510	24,880	23,400	24,432	23,433

1/ Income by place of residence; earnings by place of work.
2/ Includes capital consumption adjustment for rental income of persons.
3/ Includes the inventory valuation and capital consumption adjustments.
4/ Includes wages and salaries of U.S. residents employed by foreign embassies, consulates, and international organizations in the United States.
Note: Seasonally adjusted at annual rates. Data reported in April 1997. See Table 5.14 for derivation of personal income notes.
Source: U.S., Department of Commerce, Bureau of Economic Analysis, Regional Economic Information System, CD-ROM, August 1997.

Table 5.26.   EARNED INCOME: TOTAL EARNINGS ON A PLACE-OF-WORK BASIS BY MAJOR TYPE
OF INCOME IN THE UNITED STATES AND IN THE STATE AND
COUNTIES OF FLORIDA, 1994 AND 1995

(in thousands of dollars)

County	Total earnings	Wage and salary dis- bursements	Other labor income	Proprietors' income Total 1/	Farm	Nonfarm
			1994 A/			
United States 2/	4,081,780	3,233,236	402,011	446,533	30,654	415,879
Florida	182,260,792	149,609,464	16,856,908	15,794,420	836,374	14,958,046
Alachua	2,785,467	2,333,301	268,603	183,563	13,475	170,088
Baker	131,055	95,506	11,931	23,618	9,228	14,390
Bay	1,628,653	1,334,230	136,550	157,873	-733	158,606
Bradford	149,921	118,769	13,812	17,340	5,586	11,754
Brevard	5,667,204	4,761,014	578,926	327,264	7,005	320,259
Broward	18,530,859	15,394,569	1,700,629	1,435,661	5,408	1,430,253
Calhoun	70,507	51,106	5,980	13,421	4,682	8,739
Charlotte	857,543	655,128	72,070	130,345	3,973	126,372
Citrus	673,256	526,804	64,542	81,910	540	81,370
Clay	764,879	588,386	66,495	109,998	1,218	108,780
Collier	2,394,514	1,818,695	195,816	380,003	71,083	308,920
Columbia	420,394	336,615	40,364	43,415	6,134	37,281
Dade	30,880,585	25,523,732	2,866,586	2,490,267	67,547	2,422,720
De Soto	214,504	142,020	15,905	56,579	31,441	25,138
Dixie	70,084	49,752	6,024	14,308	1,351	12,957
Duval	13,075,280	10,981,842	1,213,805	879,633	5,386	874,247
Escambia	3,566,160	3,034,834	327,294	204,032	8,908	195,124
Flagler	210,740	177,810	22,164	10,766	4,207	6,559
Franklin	69,890	48,652	5,547	15,691	0	15,691
Gadsden	322,725	259,556	30,629	32,540	14,653	17,887
Gilchrist	58,498	38,757	4,539	15,202	8,135	7,067
Glades	37,469	22,798	2,558	12,113	6,598	5,515
Gulf	115,713	95,133	12,902	7,678	0	7,678
Hamilton	124,494	99,199	14,683	10,612	4,599	6,013
Hardee	177,738	123,562	13,750	40,426	25,811	14,615
Hendry	312,075	222,310	24,522	65,243	40,372	24,871
Hernando	644,358	508,696	58,056	77,606	2,762	74,844
Highlands	546,293	407,662	46,458	92,173	19,128	73,045
Hillsborough	15,043,961	12,622,583	1,424,514	996,864	48,971	947,893
Holmes	87,155	58,138	6,905	22,112	12,235	9,877
Indian River	1,042,752	814,200	87,670	140,882	16,236	124,646
Jackson	360,053	279,016	33,639	47,398	17,041	30,357

See footnotes at end of table.   Continued . . .

Table 5.26.   EARNED INCOME: TOTAL EARNINGS ON A PLACE-OF-WORK BASIS BY MAJOR TYPE
OF INCOME IN THE UNITED STATES AND IN THE STATE AND
COUNTIES OF FLORIDA, 1994 AND 1995 (Continued)

(in thousands of dollars)

County	Total earnings	Wage and salary disbursements	Other labor income	Proprietors' income Total 1/	Farm	Nonfarm
		1994 A/	(Continued)			
Jefferson	70,947	50,999	6,181	13,767	6,017	7,750
Lafayette	42,104	22,106	2,681	17,317	12,863	4,454
Lake	1,313,739	1,035,390	119,946	158,403	14,645	143,758
Lee	4,021,138	3,198,401	356,060	466,677	17,529	449,148
Leon	3,522,948	2,987,732	321,033	214,183	257	213,926
Levy	161,963	115,637	13,430	32,896	7,311	25,585
Liberty	40,200	31,362	4,095	4,743	384	4,359
Madison	114,263	89,739	11,186	13,338	4,526	8,812
Manatee	2,602,126	2,069,238	233,021	299,867	35,344	264,523
Marion	1,872,634	1,484,857	189,096	198,681	11,913	186,768
Martin	1,241,220	976,073	110,524	154,623	32,648	121,975
Monroe	998,463	778,470	76,781	143,212	0	143,212
Nassau	437,694	350,424	39,894	47,376	5,823	41,553
Okaloosa	1,997,367	1,717,245	153,854	126,268	2,622	123,646
Okeechobee	225,203	165,032	17,510	42,661	16,082	26,579
Orange	15,347,480	12,784,492	1,455,873	1,107,115	32,317	1,074,798
Osceola	1,072,820	875,059	94,667	103,094	1,688	101,406
Palm Beach	13,818,518	11,161,197	1,266,925	1,390,396	5,899	1,384,497
Pasco	1,725,841	1,388,038	158,358	179,445	12,501	166,944
Pinellas	11,189,421	9,259,249	1,059,154	871,018	1,589	869,429
Polk	4,862,102	3,886,142	461,488	514,472	25,773	488,699
Putnam	483,557	406,997	49,837	26,723	6,935	19,788
St. Johns	839,497	655,328	77,109	107,060	8,790	98,270
St. Lucie	1,346,258	1,080,016	121,998	144,244	22,727	121,517
Santa Rosa	645,122	500,371	53,598	91,153	10,364	80,789
Sarasota	3,545,013	2,828,859	309,689	406,465	3,769	402,696
Seminole	3,167,443	2,559,903	293,846	313,694	4,979	308,715
Sumter	176,882	129,179	15,953	31,750	9,638	22,112
Suwannee	250,121	153,603	18,278	78,240	33,936	44,304
Taylor	187,904	156,054	20,606	11,244	240	11,004
Union	97,600	81,345	9,728	6,527	1,244	5,283
Volusia	3,376,389	2,783,724	321,521	271,144	14,346	256,798
Wakulla	86,219	62,465	8,490	15,264	-85	15,349
Walton	222,728	164,388	19,412	38,928	3,533	35,395
Washington	123,089	95,975	11,218	15,896	5,247	10,649

See footnotes at end of table.   Continued . . .

Table 5.26.   EARNED INCOME: TOTAL EARNINGS ON A PLACE-OF-WORK BASIS BY MAJOR TYPE
OF INCOME IN THE UNITED STATES AND IN THE STATE AND
COUNTIES OF FLORIDA, 1994 AND 1995 (Continued)

(in thousands of dollars)

County	Total earnings	Wage and salary dis- bursements	Other labor income	Proprietors' income Total 1/	Farm	Nonfarm
			1995			
United States 2/	4,315,915	3,423,330	423,799	468,786	19,529	449,257
Florida	194,535,997	159,371,863	17,819,138	17,344,996	1,046,868	16,298,128
Alachua	2,938,611	2,459,584	284,044	194,983	12,261	182,722
Baker	137,794	100,650	12,423	24,721	9,472	15,249
Bay	1,713,072	1,402,840	142,254	167,978	-831	168,809
Bradford	165,431	130,522	15,300	19,609	6,746	12,863
Brevard	5,783,677	4,848,154	582,021	353,502	5,090	348,412
Broward	19,942,095	16,560,873	1,803,588	1,577,634	7,477	1,570,157
Calhoun	74,014	53,803	6,294	13,917	4,727	9,190
Charlotte	913,711	695,680	76,002	142,029	5,545	136,484
Citrus	695,002	541,453	66,525	87,024	(L)	87,030
Clay	818,684	628,373	70,034	120,277	4,040	116,237
Collier	2,585,195	1,967,683	208,824	408,688	66,333	342,355
Columbia	455,824	365,839	44,623	45,362	5,926	39,436
Dade	32,590,057	26,852,960	3,000,450	2,736,647	93,676	2,642,971
De Soto	233,655	150,227	16,809	66,619	39,650	26,969
Dixie	72,383	51,025	6,430	14,928	1,149	13,779
Duval	14,055,213	11,800,140	1,307,325	947,748	4,672	943,076
Escambia	3,705,677	3,156,710	340,376	208,591	4,542	204,049
Flagler	236,832	201,397	25,597	9,838	2,324	7,514
Franklin	74,195	51,144	5,927	17,124	0	17,124
Gadsden	340,402	272,614	32,049	35,739	17,285	18,454
Gilchrist	59,416	42,460	5,078	11,878	4,265	7,613
Glades	40,427	23,932	2,623	13,872	7,384	6,488
Gulf	120,470	99,007	13,489	7,974	0	7,974
Hamilton	137,243	110,447	16,651	10,145	3,685	6,460
Hardee	190,077	131,482	14,528	44,067	28,259	15,808
Hendry	352,469	243,252	26,377	82,840	56,092	26,748
Hernando	679,104	535,428	61,013	82,663	2,219	80,444
Highlands	591,058	427,184	47,991	115,883	37,215	78,668
Hillsborough	16,194,054	13,585,500	1,512,437	1,096,117	62,237	1,033,880
Holmes	90,312	60,687	7,324	22,301	12,067	10,234
Indian River	1,125,439	859,527	91,819	174,093	35,917	138,176
Jackson	373,937	289,162	35,128	49,647	17,588	32,059
Jefferson	73,601	53,766	6,489	13,346	5,046	8,300
Lafayette	42,713	24,245	2,976	15,492	10,819	4,673

See footnotes at end of table.   Continued . . .

Table 5.26.   EARNED INCOME: TOTAL EARNINGS ON A PLACE-OF-WORK BASIS BY MAJOR TYPE
OF INCOME IN THE UNITED STATES AND IN THE STATE AND
COUNTIES OF FLORIDA, 1994 AND 1995 (Continued)

(in thousands of dollars)

County	Total earnings	Wage and salary dis- bursements	Other labor income	Proprietors' income Total 1/	Farm	Nonfarm
			1995 (Continued)			
Lake	1,417,546	1,119,987	128,107	169,452	15,240	154,212
Lee	4,276,526	3,394,078	374,692	507,756	16,762	490,994
Leon	3,795,017	3,225,087	343,653	226,277	-226	226,503
Levy	176,388	124,801	14,579	37,008	9,251	27,757
Liberty	44,276	34,805	4,593	4,878	225	4,653
Madison	124,741	99,301	12,513	12,927	3,130	9,797
Manatee	2,928,568	2,340,479	253,575	334,514	46,039	288,475
Marion	2,006,935	1,598,397	199,723	208,815	10,567	198,248
Martin	1,352,009	1,055,213	119,420	177,376	42,832	134,544
Monroe	1,061,817	821,878	81,837	158,102	0	158,102
Nassau	461,179	368,919	42,007	50,253	5,342	44,911
Okaloosa	2,148,274	1,852,522	162,917	132,835	1,830	131,005
Okeechobee	237,534	175,436	18,510	43,588	14,972	28,616
Orange	16,274,602	13,517,221	1,530,815	1,226,566	46,016	1,180,550
Osceola	1,150,994	939,007	100,412	111,575	1,108	110,467
Palm Beach	14,932,122	11,964,685	1,342,733	1,624,704	81,615	1,543,089
Pasco	1,819,129	1,462,292	166,117	190,720	10,537	180,183
Pinellas	11,980,037	9,911,626	1,119,277	949,134	1,167	947,967
Polk	5,170,058	4,103,700	491,818	574,540	40,327	534,213
Putnam	530,612	448,295	55,697	26,620	5,676	20,944
St. Johns	921,574	725,594	85,213	110,767	4,875	105,892
St. Lucie	1,414,557	1,127,531	127,155	159,871	29,859	130,012
Santa Rosa	672,579	523,343	58,040	91,196	7,223	83,973
Sarasota	3,798,120	3,027,334	328,271	442,515	1,938	440,577
Seminole	3,420,121	2,767,919	314,865	337,337	3,775	333,562
Sumter	195,945	147,820	18,537	29,588	5,566	24,022
Suwannee	265,727	164,851	19,716	81,160	34,440	46,720
Taylor	192,236	159,319	21,105	11,812	(L)	11,765
Union	101,614	84,621	10,215	6,778	1,132	5,646
Volusia	3,597,807	2,957,986	339,840	299,981	22,710	277,271
Wakulla	89,352	64,878	8,804	15,670	-209	15,879
Walton	236,654	174,396	20,573	41,685	5,732	35,953
Washington	139,503	110,792	12,991	15,720	4,499	11,221

A/ Revised.
1/ Includes the inventory valuation and capital consumption adjustments.
2/ United States numbers are rounded to millions of dollars.

Source: U.S., Department of Commerce, Bureau of Economic Analysis, Regional Economic Information System, CD-ROM, August 1997.

University of Florida   **Bureau of Economic and Business Research**

Table 5.30. EARNED INCOME: TOTAL, FARM, AND NONFARM EARNINGS ON A PLACE-OF-WORK BASIS IN THE UNITED STATES AND IN THE STATE AND COUNTIES OF FLORIDA, 1994 AND 1995

(in thousands of dollars)

1994 A/

County	Total earnings	Farm income	Nonfarm Total	Private 1/	Government and government enterprises Total	Federal Civilian	Military	State and local
United States 2/	4,081,780	43,990	4,037,790	3,386,362	651,428	131,277	47,324	472,827
Florida	182,260,792	1,644,865	180,615,927	150,904,152	29,711,775	5,066,166	2,704,555	21,941,054
Alachua	2,785,467	17,742	2,767,725	1,763,923	1,003,802	137,472	7,924	858,406
Baker	131,055	12,170	118,885	61,900	56,985	2,395	380	54,210
Bay	1,628,653	-559	1,629,212	1,131,841	497,371	126,910	158,344	212,117
Bradford	149,921	5,670	144,251	84,861	59,390	1,413	446	57,531
Brevard	5,667,204	11,312	5,655,892	4,753,672	902,220	282,472	117,940	501,808
Broward	18,530,859	15,470	18,515,389	15,954,792	2,560,597	313,730	35,334	2,211,533
Calhoun	70,507	5,674	64,833	42,509	22,324	1,396	223	20,705
Charlotte	857,543	7,797	849,746	720,955	128,791	9,472	2,496	116,823
Citrus	673,256	575	672,681	577,628	95,053	6,995	1,998	86,060
Clay	764,879	3,474	761,405	641,740	119,665	12,264	2,334	105,067
Collier	2,394,514	125,920	2,268,594	2,031,491	237,103	23,513	3,397	210,193
Columbia	420,394	6,685	413,709	282,131	131,578	40,542	922	90,114
Dade	30,880,585	136,886	30,743,699	26,078,536	4,665,163	874,274	92,216	3,698,673
De Soto	214,504	39,515	174,989	106,038	68,951	1,860	475	66,616
Dixie	70,084	1,351	68,733	45,491	23,242	984	226	22,032
Duval	13,075,280	10,383	13,064,897	10,597,440	2,467,457	644,403	799,161	1,023,893
Escambia	3,566,160	9,992	3,556,168	2,545,962	1,010,206	335,450	288,616	386,140
Flagler	210,740	5,041	205,699	168,296	37,403	3,468	730	33,205
Franklin	69,890	0	69,890	54,301	15,589	1,281	185	14,123
Gadsden	322,725	32,194	290,531	159,409	131,122	4,430	914	125,778
Gilchrist	58,498	10,305	48,193	25,262	22,931	843	223	21,865

Continued . . .

See footnotes at end of table.

Table 5.30. EARNED INCOME: TOTAL, FARM, AND NONFARM EARNINGS ON A PLACE-OF-WORK BASIS IN THE UNITED STATES AND IN THE STATE AND COUNTIES OF FLORIDA, 1994 AND 1995 (Continued)

(in thousands of dollars)

1994 A/ (Continued)

County	Total earnings	Farm income	Total	Private 1/	Nonfarm Government and government enterprises Total	Federal Civilian	Federal Military	State and local
Glades	37,469	10,478	26,991	19,043	7,948	452	145	7,351
Gulf	115,713	0	115,713	90,102	25,611	801	232	24,578
Hamilton	124,494	6,788	117,706	85,659	32,047	1,024	220	30,803
Hardee	177,738	36,162	141,576	100,755	40,821	1,852	386	38,583
Hendry	312,075	77,076	234,999	178,582	56,417	3,927	544	51,946
Hernando	644,358	4,067	640,291	513,390	126,901	9,919	2,255	114,727
Highlands	546,293	39,428	506,865	414,617	92,248	11,056	1,421	79,771
Hillsborough	15,043,961	106,478	14,937,483	12,744,186	2,193,297	474,104	178,711	1,540,482
Holmes	87,155	12,550	74,605	45,402	29,203	1,855	322	27,026
Indian River	1,042,752	30,782	1,011,970	873,454	138,516	14,563	1,836	122,117
Jackson	360,053	18,160	341,893	202,431	139,462	21,221	1,405	116,836
Jefferson	70,947	8,332	62,615	40,839	21,776	1,165	228	20,383
Lafayette	42,104	14,081	28,023	14,366	13,657	536	112	13,009
Lake	1,313,739	37,832	1,275,907	1,084,288	191,619	18,755	5,472	167,392
Lee	4,021,138	39,983	3,981,155	3,351,071	630,084	69,565	7,890	552,629
Leon	3,522,948	1,759	3,521,189	2,095,714	1,425,475	76,007	10,658	1,338,810
Levy	161,963	12,199	149,764	111,423	38,341	2,568	1,024	34,749
Liberty	40,200	384	39,816	23,545	16,271	1,492	116	14,663
Madison	114,263	5,532	108,731	75,214	33,517	1,615	330	31,572
Manatee	2,602,126	70,246	2,531,880	2,237,023	294,857	42,283	4,878	247,696
Marion	1,872,634	27,735	1,844,899	1,526,684	318,215	23,183	4,237	290,795
Martin	1,241,220	45,678	1,195,542	1,058,992	136,550	11,168	2,281	123,101
Monroe	998,463	0	998,463	769,200	229,263	48,931	56,453	123,879

See footnotes at end of table.

Continued . . .

Table 5.30. EARNED INCOME: TOTAL, FARM, AND NONFARM EARNINGS ON A PLACE-OF-WORK BASIS IN THE UNITED STATES AND IN THE STATE AND COUNTIES OF FLORIDA, 1994 AND 1995 (Continued)

(in thousands of dollars)

County	Total earnings	Farm income	Nonfarm Total	Private 1/	Government and government enterprises Total	Federal Civilian	Military	State and local
			1994 A/ (Continued)					
Nassau	437,694	10,589	427,105	322,268	104,837	46,425	951	57,461
Okaloosa	1,997,367	3,061	1,994,306	1,179,885	814,421	196,602	443,829	173,990
Okeechobee	225,203	36,431	188,772	149,936	38,836	2,701	587	35,548
Orange	15,347,480	91,545	15,255,935	13,419,468	1,836,467	348,029	286,002	1,202,436
Osceola	1,072,820	7,295	1,065,525	897,055	168,470	10,250	2,419	155,801
Palm Beach	13,818,518	145,565	13,672,953	12,062,828	1,610,125	193,436	20,556	1,396,133
Pasco	1,725,841	21,778	1,704,063	1,415,885	288,178	23,037	5,749	259,392
Pinellas	11,189,421	4,477	11,184,944	9,855,666	1,329,278	290,117	43,176	995,985
Polk	4,862,102	64,502	4,797,600	4,145,297	652,303	58,005	8,610	585,688
Putnam	483,557	11,392	472,165	358,206	113,959	5,698	1,318	106,943
St. Johns	839,497	13,337	826,160	693,373	132,787	13,467	2,559	116,761
St. Lucie	1,346,258	35,835	1,310,423	1,066,251	244,172	21,643	4,772	217,757
Santa Rosa	645,122	11,082	634,040	454,260	179,780	26,057	62,596	91,127
Sarasota	3,545,013	7,248	3,537,765	3,094,005	443,760	39,412	5,866	398,482
Seminole	3,167,443	12,763	3,154,680	2,765,080	389,600	56,861	6,220	326,519
Sumter	176,882	12,027	164,855	118,439	46,416	3,878	639	41,899
Suwannee	250,121	38,599	211,522	171,869	39,653	3,900	567	35,186
Taylor	187,904	267	187,637	160,980	26,657	1,448	333	24,876
Union	97,600	1,400	96,200	40,384	55,816	723	205	54,888
Volusia	3,376,389	42,887	3,333,502	2,735,834	597,668	53,580	9,257	534,831
Wakulla	86,219	-85	86,304	64,611	21,693	2,373	318	19,002
Walton	222,728	3,681	219,047	174,419	44,628	3,013	2,039	39,576
Washington	123,089	5,862	117,227	73,995	43,232	1,902	347	40,983

See footnotes at end of table.

Continued . . .

Table 5.30. EARNED INCOME: TOTAL, FARM, AND NONFARM EARNINGS ON A PLACE-OF-WORK BASIS IN THE UNITED STATES AND IN THE STATE AND COUNTIES OF FLORIDA, 1994 AND 1995 (Continued)

(in thousands of dollars)

1995

County	Total earnings	Farm income	Nonfarm Total	Nonfarm Private 1/	Government and government enterprises Total	Federal Civilian	Military	State and local
United States 2/	4,315,915	33,882	4,282,033	3,607,964	674,069	132,706	47,079	494,284
Florida	194,535,997	1,897,638	192,638,359	161,655,592	30,982,767	5,236,529	2,654,486	23,091,752
Alachua	2,938,611	16,647	2,921,964	1,881,191	1,040,773	129,581	7,977	903,215
Baker	137,794	12,510	125,284	63,372	61,912	2,523	381	59,008
Bay	1,713,072	-634	1,713,706	1,192,498	521,208	130,851	170,677	219,680
Bradford	165,431	6,826	158,605	96,803	61,802	1,306	457	60,039
Brevard	5,783,677	9,533	5,774,144	4,847,489	926,655	273,291	131,156	522,208
Broward	19,942,095	18,589	19,923,506	17,217,113	2,706,393	332,991	35,468	2,337,934
Calhoun	74,014	5,807	68,207	44,595	23,612	1,351	224	22,037
Charlotte	913,711	9,579	904,132	767,333	136,799	9,859	2,511	124,429
Citrus	695,002	59	694,943	593,858	101,085	7,667	2,027	91,391
Clay	818,684	6,600	812,084	684,457	127,627	13,311	2,380	111,936
Collier	2,585,195	123,664	2,461,531	2,207,867	253,664	24,363	3,451	225,850
Columbia	455,824	6,434	449,390	307,749	141,641	44,094	940	96,607
Dade	32,590,057	169,903	32,420,154	27,544,885	4,875,269	907,000	90,232	3,878,037
De Soto	233,655	48,405	185,250	112,287	72,963	2,028	473	70,462
Dixie	72,383	1,158	71,225	46,342	24,883	840	230	23,813
Duval	14,055,213	10,618	14,044,595	11,462,570	2,582,025	709,294	801,328	1,071,403
Escambia	3,705,677	5,475	3,700,202	2,716,825	983,377	294,348	287,229	401,800
Flagler	236,832	3,508	233,324	192,658	40,666	3,632	767	36,267
Franklin	74,195	0	74,195	57,310	16,885	1,336	194	15,355
Gadsden	340,402	35,578	304,824	166,317	138,507	4,597	820	133,090
Gilchrist	59,416	6,798	52,618	27,952	24,666	866	233	23,567

See footnotes at end of table.

Continued . . .

Table 5.30. EARNED INCOME: TOTAL, FARM, AND NONFARM EARNINGS ON A PLACE-OF-WORK BASIS IN THE UNITED STATES AND IN THE STATE AND COUNTIES OF FLORIDA, 1994 AND 1995 (Continued)

(in thousands of dollars)

County	Total earnings	Farm income	Nonfarm Total	Nonfarm Private 1/	Government and government enterprises Total	Federal Civilian	Federal Military	State and local
			1995 (Continued)					
Glades	40,427	11,507	28,920	20,499	8,421	458	144	7,819
Gulf	120,470	0	120,470	92,629	27,841	834	253	26,754
Hamilton	137,243	6,346	130,897	97,671	33,226	1,041	223	31,962
Hardee	190,077	39,193	150,884	107,511	43,373	2,016	376	40,981
Hendry	352,469	96,620	255,849	194,770	61,079	4,364	531	56,184
Hernando	679,104	2,938	676,166	543,591	132,575	10,530	2,303	119,742
Highlands	591,058	58,248	532,810	436,191	96,619	11,419	1,407	83,793
Hillsborough	16,194,054	123,489	16,070,565	13,771,261	2,299,304	478,280	187,849	1,633,175
Holmes	90,312	12,140	78,172	47,146	31,026	1,976	330	28,720
Indian River	1,125,439	51,179	1,074,260	927,959	146,301	15,356	1,835	129,110
Jackson	373,937	18,846	355,091	208,373	146,718	23,154	1,435	122,129
Jefferson	73,601	7,326	66,275	43,085	23,190	1,194	245	21,751
Lafayette	42,713	12,044	30,669	14,432	16,237	568	114	15,555
Lake	1,417,546	40,357	1,377,189	1,173,254	203,935	19,541	6,266	178,128
Lee	4,276,526	40,604	4,235,922	3,552,626	683,296	78,451	8,004	596,841
Leon	3,795,017	1,381	3,793,636	2,271,702	1,521,934	80,294	10,298	1,431,342
Levy	176,388	15,014	161,374	121,334	40,040	2,560	1,049	36,431
Liberty	44,276	225	44,051	26,061	17,990	1,590	121	16,279
Madison	124,741	4,158	120,583	85,323	35,260	1,679	325	33,256
Manatee	2,928,568	83,751	2,844,817	2,536,242	308,575	45,551	4,900	258,124
Marion	2,006,935	27,222	1,979,713	1,641,567	338,146	24,394	4,284	309,468
Martin	1,352,009	58,409	1,293,600	1,149,077	144,523	11,609	2,261	130,653
Monroe	1,061,817	0	1,061,817	825,417	236,400	52,633	52,965	130,802
Nassau	461,179	10,059	451,120	343,269	107,851	47,603	959	59,289

See footnotes at end of table.

Continued . .

Table 5.30. EARNED INCOME: TOTAL, FARM, AND NONFARM EARNINGS ON A PLACE-OF-WORK BASIS IN THE UNITED STATES AND IN THE STATE AND COUNTIES OF FLORIDA, 1994 AND 1995 (Continued)

(in thousands of dollars)

1995 (Continued)

County	Total earnings	Farm income	Nonfarm Total	Private 1/	Government and government enterprises Total	Federal Civilian	Military	State and local
Okaloosa	2,148,274	2,341	2,145,933	1,273,503	872,430	191,562	497,951	182,917
Okeechobee	237,534	34,469	203,065	161,264	41,801	2,862	571	38,366
Orange	16,274,602	110,521	16,164,081	14,427,709	1,736,372	327,133	155,625	1,253,614
Osceola	1,150,994	6,949	1,144,045	962,095	181,950	10,855	2,469	168,626
Palm Beach	14,932,122	222,660	14,709,462	12,967,331	1,742,131	256,224	20,628	1,465,279
Pasco	1,819,129	20,123	1,799,006	1,496,666	302,340	26,661	5,784	269,895
Pinellas	11,980,037	4,018	11,976,019	10,589,329	1,386,690	290,932	43,899	1,051,859
Polk	5,170,058	78,492	5,091,566	4,395,613	695,953	60,329	8,723	626,901
Putnam	530,612	10,605	520,007	401,909	118,098	5,951	1,312	110,835
St. Johns	921,574	10,114	911,460	767,185	144,275	14,616	2,763	126,896
St. Lucie	1,414,557	43,100	1,371,457	1,109,176	262,281	22,397	4,707	235,177
Santa Rosa	672,579	8,034	664,545	483,418	181,127	27,558	56,917	96,652
Sarasota	3,798,120	5,735	3,792,385	3,353,352	439,033	41,014	5,867	392,152
Seminole	3,420,121	11,636	3,408,485	3,001,217	407,268	59,977	6,249	341,042
Sumter	195,945	7,856	188,089	128,096	59,993	12,020	657	47,316
Suwannee	265,727	39,299	226,428	184,675	41,753	4,193	569	36,991
Taylor	192,236	85	192,151	158,443	33,708	1,345	329	32,034
Union	101,614	1,375	100,239	40,390	59,849	725	235	58,889
Volusia	3,597,807	51,318	3,546,489	2,962,883	583,606	60,336	9,176	514,094
Wakulla	89,352	-209	89,561	65,908	23,653	2,395	323	20,935
Walton	236,654	5,958	230,696	181,952	48,744	3,245	1,749	43,750
Washington	139,503	5,046	134,457	81,017	53,440	1,973	351	51,116

A/ Revised.
1/ See Table 5.34 for private nonfarm income by industrial source.
2/ In millions of dollars.
Source: U.S., Department of Commerce, Bureau of Economic Analysis, Regional Economic Information System, CD-ROM, August 1997.

Table 5.33. EARNED INCOME: PRIVATE NONFARM EARNINGS ON A PLACE-OF-WORK BASIS BY INDUSTRIAL SOURCE IN FLORIDA 1990 THROUGH 1995

(in thousands of dollars)

Item	1990	1991	1992	1993	1994	1995	Percentage change 1/
Agricultural services, forestry, fisheries, and other 2/	1,580,162	1,685,770	1,757,429	1,857,639	2,011,162	2,084,925	31.9
Agricultural services	1,435,569	1,557,729	1,647,087	1,757,612	1,880,331	1,963,467	36.8
Forestry	27,534	27,154	29,343	25,567	25,574	27,044	-1.8
Fisheries	114,791	98,444	78,484	71,624	102,444	91,532	-20.3
Other 2/	2,268	2,443	2,515	2,836	2,813	2,882	27.1
Mining	336,391	331,509	333,526	317,004	309,964	350,843	4.3
Coal mining	(D)	(D)	17,176	(D)	18,199	19,581	(X)
Oil and gas extraction	37,010	48,678	70,378	49,520	49,547	57,138	54.4
Metal mining	(D)	(D)	9,344	(D)	8,573	7,432	(X)
Nonmetallic minerals, except fuels	264,462	249,754	236,628	240,726	233,645	266,692	0.8
Construction	10,372,042	9,209,422	9,248,750	10,125,195	10,983,525	11,470,032	10.6
General building contractors	2,537,898	2,170,203	2,240,990	2,502,684	2,595,551	2,689,219	6.0
Heavy construction contractors	1,329,949	1,194,634	1,223,678	1,210,474	1,368,831	1,444,707	8.6
Special trade contractors	6,504,195	5,844,585	5,784,082	6,412,037	7,019,143	7,336,106	12.8
Manufacturing	16,142,912	16,265,618	16,973,910	17,295,957	17,805,549	18,295,817	13.3
Nondurable goods	5,927,074	6,048,847	6,355,195	6,469,994	6,644,906	6,816,343	15.0
Food and kindred products	1,366,511	1,386,755	1,404,466	1,449,005	1,459,349	1,466,819	7.3
Textile mill products	82,551	103,981	105,218	104,109	104,047	110,541	33.9
Apparel and other textile products	522,352	544,492	581,409	587,577	575,560	548,746	5.1
Paper and allied products	524,767	528,360	589,404	601,445	618,058	641,807	22.3
Printing and publishing	1,866,064	1,898,885	1,965,662	2,027,056	2,116,216	2,191,149	17.4
Chemicals and allied products	910,395	944,959	1,020,237	986,307	1,025,912	1,064,217	16.9
Petroleum and coal products	70,945	68,030	72,745	79,759	78,719	75,374	6.2
Tobacco products	34,326	27,337	28,472	31,510	33,782	50,285	46.5

See footnotes at end of table.

Continued . . .

Table 5.33. EARNED INCOME: PRIVATE NONFARM EARNINGS ON A PLACE-OF-WORK BASIS BY INDUSTRIAL SOURCE IN FLORIDA 1990 THROUGH 1995 (Continued)

(in thousands of dollars)

Item	1990	1991	1992	1993	1994	1995	Percentage change 1/
Manufacturing (Continued)							
Nondurable goods (Continued)							
Rubber and miscellaneous plastics products	507,443	506,180	543,960	560,397	588,172	614,828	21.2
Leather and leather products	41,720	39,868	43,622	42,829	45,091	52,577	26.0
Durable goods	10,215,838	10,216,771	10,618,715	10,825,963	11,160,643	11,479,474	12.4
Lumber and wood products	547,820	486,936	502,609	559,039	602,778	629,080	14.8
Furniture and fixtures	294,829	280,427	293,564	321,030	328,607	350,052	18.7
Primary metal industries	176,808	173,782	177,652	180,105	199,532	221,214	25.1
Fabricated metal products	943,973	910,261	889,185	936,489	983,514	1,011,743	7.2
Industrial machinery and equipment	1,530,622	1,609,458	1,644,443	1,625,448	1,690,040	1,608,348	5.1
Electronic and other electric equipment	2,034,811	2,239,184	2,455,951	2,575,147	2,695,219	2,781,762	32.8
Transportation equipment, excluding motor vehicles	2,379,177	2,320,004	2,310,587	2,151,499	2,053,906	2,139,767	-10.1
Motor vehicles and equipment	193,591	174,333	218,388	250,060	260,565	296,591	53.2
Stone, clay, and glass products	687,424	598,512	604,011	660,675	717,524	766,193	11.5
Instruments and related products	1,151,142	1,208,124	1,302,503	1,311,660	1,360,686	1,407,659	22.3
Miscellaneous manufacturing industries	215,641	215,750	219,822	254,811	268,272	267,065	23.8
Transportation, communications, and public utilities	9,811,001	10,198,085	10,942,886	11,853,390	12,430,198	13,237,410	34.9
Railroad transportation	323,999	354,710	428,870	413,859	422,257	449,207	38.6
Trucking and warehousing	1,900,904	1,939,692	2,068,865	2,292,536	2,475,021	2,697,119	41.9
Water transportation	485,838	556,069	594,526	607,364	648,210	677,312	39.4
Other transportation	2,615,162	2,586,499	2,651,223	2,955,867	3,133,020	3,340,296	27.7
Local and interurban passenger transit	300,956	330,684	384,418	393,295	422,716	429,817	42.8
Transportation by air	1,713,507	1,603,251	1,528,764	1,737,338	1,787,172	1,878,380	9.6
Pipelines, except natural gas	2,531	3,170	3,666	3,986	5,672	5,734	126.6
Transportation services	598,168	649,394	734,375	821,248	917,460	1,026,365	71.6

See footnotes at end of table.

Continued . . .

Table 5.33. EARNED INCOME: PRIVATE NONFARM EARNINGS ON A PLACE-OF-WORK BASIS BY INDUSTRIAL SOURCE IN FLORIDA 1990 THROUGH 1995 (Continued)

(in thousands of dollars)

Item	1990	1991	1992	1993	1994	1995	Per- cent- age change 1/
Transportation, communications, and public utilities (Continued)							
Communications	2,736,052	2,897,835	3,195,890	3,547,456	3,827,267	4,122,905	50.7
Electric, gas, and sanitary services	1,749,046	1,863,280	2,003,512	2,036,308	1,924,423	1,950,571	11.5
Wholesale trade	9,765,255	9,937,976	10,704,835	11,111,129	11,816,692	12,894,946	32.0
Retail trade	18,156,356	18,253,030	19,273,180	20,421,389	21,510,652	22,665,814	24.8
Building materials and garden equipment	890,356	854,864	904,635	1,006,525	1,052,701	1,107,946	24.4
General merchandise stores	1,930,127	1,950,908	2,072,343	2,159,894	2,244,918	2,360,942	22.3
Food stores	2,958,765	3,124,619	3,235,703	3,317,971	3,462,401	3,647,276	23.3
Automotive dealers and service stations	3,011,458	2,987,805	3,168,955	3,522,839	3,794,428	4,027,498	33.7
Apparel and accessory stores	843,686	907,097	958,302	981,427	1,002,588	1,051,220	24.6
Home furniture and furnishings stores	1,292,586	1,176,279	1,175,554	1,250,442	1,346,218	1,438,582	11.3
Eating and drinking places	4,494,031	4,597,875	4,884,088	5,162,794	5,478,132	5,675,943	26.3
Miscellaneous retail	2,735,347	2,653,583	2,873,600	3,019,497	3,129,266	3,356,407	22.7
Finance, insurance, and real estate	10,802,485	11,151,855	13,051,976	14,334,106	14,965,790	16,060,563	48.7
Depository and nondepository credit institutions	3,788,443	3,797,994	4,051,197	4,333,234	4,552,152	4,763,356	25.7
Other finance, insurance, and real estate	7,014,042	7,353,861	9,000,779	10,000,872	10,413,638	11,297,207	61.1
Security and commodity brokers and services	1,185,034	1,296,660	1,674,012	1,942,619	1,859,923	2,047,970	72.8
Insurance carriers	2,189,225	2,359,649	2,541,220	2,685,479	2,876,029	3,006,254	37.3
Insurance agents, brokers, and services	1,608,867	1,635,968	1,715,258	1,860,880	1,984,481	2,156,962	34.1
Real estate	1,625,914	1,530,331	2,420,399	3,096,760	3,264,835	3,588,214	120.7
Holding and other investment companies	405,002	531,253	649,890	415,134	428,370	497,807	22.9

See footnotes at end of table.

Continued . . .

Table 5.33. EARNED INCOME: PRIVATE NONFARM EARNINGS ON A PLACE-OF-WORK BASIS BY INDUSTRIAL SOURCE IN FLORIDA 1990 THROUGH 1995 (Continued)

(in thousands of dollars)

Item	1990	1991	1992	1993	1994	1995	Percentage change 1/
Services	45,167,388	47,445,444	51,502,621	55,203,895	59,070,620	64,595,242	43.0
Hotels and other lodging places	2,361,587	2,356,113	2,528,565	2,721,414	2,743,190	2,902,692	22.9
Personal services	1,564,005	1,574,177	1,669,603	1,867,757	1,930,210	2,010,676	28.6
Private households	585,180	573,339	638,478	678,809	695,492	750,856	28.3
Business services	7,266,284	7,488,502	8,379,358	9,457,532	10,558,841	12,274,168	68.9
Auto repair, services, and parking	1,436,394	1,462,607	1,534,261	1,681,813	1,759,780	1,897,058	32.1
Miscellaneous repair services	770,711	696,803	699,950	789,369	817,832	884,037	14.7
Amusement and recreation services	2,359,013	2,475,284	2,922,092	2,915,712	3,112,707	3,428,386	45.3
Motion pictures	312,042	370,158	390,505	460,168	481,724	546,234	75.1
Health services	15,246,854	16,660,581	18,056,245	19,080,335	20,464,179	22,202,199	45.6
Legal services	3,676,912	3,840,739	4,052,466	4,164,726	4,364,610	4,547,118	23.7
Educational services	1,132,084	1,244,362	1,302,624	1,392,862	1,457,472	1,538,078	35.9
Social services	1,217,022	1,374,012	1,543,270	1,696,338	1,850,701	1,976,568	62.4
Museums, botanical, zoological gardens	35,820	42,356	45,979	50,214	55,989	63,363	76.9
Membership organizations	1,674,266	1,759,733	1,864,906	2,132,671	2,205,903	2,389,212	42.7
Engineering and management services	5,026,089	5,093,849	5,454,729	5,788,284	6,191,857	6,761,047	34.5
Miscellaneous services	503,125	432,829	419,590	325,891	380,133	423,550	-15.8
Government and government enterprises	25,203,752	26,727,995	27,587,642	28,799,600	29,711,775	30,982,767	22.9
Federal, civilian	4,214,369	4,465,578	4,803,652	5,008,026	5,066,166	5,236,529	24.3
Military	2,956,412	3,069,169	3,121,213	2,928,850	2,704,555	2,654,486	-10.2
State and local	18,032,971	19,193,248	19,662,777	20,862,724	21,941,054	23,091,752	28.1

(D) Data withheld to avoid disclosure of information about individual industries.   (X) Not applicable.
1/ Percentage change 1990 to 1995.
2/ Includes wages and salaries of U.S. residents employed by foreign embassies, consulates and international organizations in the United States.
   Note: Some data are revised.
   Source: U.S., Department of Commerce, Bureau of Economic Analysis, Regional Economic Information System, CD-ROM, August 1997.

Table 5.34. EARNED INCOME: PRIVATE NONFARM EARNINGS ON A PLACE-OF-WORK BASIS BY MAJOR INDUSTRIAL SOURCE IN THE UNITED STATES AND IN THE STATE AND COUNTIES OF FLORIDA, 1994 AND 1995

(in thousands of dollars)

1994 A/

County	Total private nonfarm earnings	Agriculture services 1/	Manufacturing	Mining	Construction	Wholesale trade	Retail trade	Finance insurance and real estate	Transportation 2/	Services
United States 3/	3,386,362	26,907	760,619	36,514	226,432	254,075	376,811	305,108	281,709	1,118,187
Florida 3/	150,904	2,011	17,806	310	10,984	11,817	21,511	14,966	12,430	59,071
Alachua	1,763,923	(D)	180,195	(D)	132,862	65,247	292,260	143,140	73,355	855,846
Baker	61,900	391	8,604	0	(D)	2,768	13,153	2,612	12,324	(D)
Bay	1,131,841	11,577	102,551	B/	129,836	72,099	234,195	80,384	92,390	408,772
Bradford	84,861	1,051	9,899	(D)	7,130	(D)	16,657	2,724	7,819	24,420
Brevard	4,753,672	34,630	1,353,037	2,482	314,733	146,976	540,266	194,014	173,473	1,994,061
Broward	15,954,792	131,937	1,641,389	11,398	1,219,930	1,394,908	2,424,109	1,746,116	1,164,856	6,220,149
Calhoun	42,509	2,219	7,559	0	5,339	2,483	8,151	1,325	2,039	13,394
Charlotte	720,955	14,034	22,311	1,165	91,841	17,625	147,245	50,752	37,469	338,513
Citrus	577,628	9,558	27,215	890	71,391	13,617	98,266	31,797	114,327	210,567
Clay	641,740	10,668	43,979	9,711	83,023	24,162	148,990	28,217	61,420	231,570
Collier	2,031,491	96,463	79,248	5,837	266,357	79,321	349,053	243,105	70,420	841,687
Columbia	282,131	2,829	40,554	B/	33,406	27,999	55,463	13,612	20,853	87,382
Dade	26,078,536	163,221	2,362,048	29,445	1,295,603	2,916,785	3,228,693	2,796,301	3,105,237	10,181,203
De Soto	106,038	27,653	2,623	B/	8,913	4,426	20,953	3,836	6,446	31,175
Dixie	45,491	1,981	13,868	(D)	7,647	(D)	7,441	925	2,387	8,000
Duval	10,597,440	(D)	1,146,508	(D)	739,682	935,523	1,215,215	1,846,167	1,264,666	3,370,859
Escambia	2,545,960	16,522	376,192	4,633	246,315	157,263	383,622	135,744	208,995	1,016,676
Flagler	168,296	3,213	37,115	141	12,207	1,902	26,035	24,508	6,871	56,304
Franklin	54,301	5,940	3,795	0	3,733	4,848	9,080	2,874	5,155	18,876
Gadsden	159,409	7,903	33,463	(D)	15,447	(D)	28,871	6,824	9,921	34,616

Continued . .

See footnotes at end of table.

Table 5.34. EARNED INCOME: PRIVATE NONFARM EARNINGS ON A PLACE-OF-WORK BASIS BY MAJOR INDUSTRIAL SOURCE IN THE UNITED STATES AND IN THE STATE AND COUNTIES OF FLORIDA, 1994 AND 1995 (Continued)

(in thousands of dollars)

1994 A/ (Continued)

County	Total private nonfarm earnings	Agriculture services 1/	Manufacturing	Mining	Construction	Wholesale trade	Retail trade	Finance insurance and real estate	Transportation 2/	Services
Gilchrist	25,262	2,239	3,519	0	2,267	1,937	3,403	1,388	2,706	7,803
Glades	19,043	5,478	144	(D)	2,212	293	2,607	(D)	3,483	3,481
Gulf	90,102	1,459	43,297	0	10,196	394	6,870	2,745	12,183	12,958
Hamilton	85,659	663	62,341	0	2,163	329	6,702	455	6,112	6,894
Hardee	100,755	19,632	5,186	(D)	(D)	8,643	16,061	6,363	5,540	25,249
Hendry	178,582	39,282	42,873	(D)	12,282	6,523	23,520	6,660	(D)	35,565
Hernando	513,390	8,112	41,543	9,635	54,706	17,841	103,258	34,669	37,392	206,234
Highlands	414,617	35,066	39,998	878	43,820	14,275	76,046	26,777	23,529	154,228
Hillsborough	12,744,186	101,090	1,240,078	1,454	753,238	1,514,848	1,496,666	1,502,016	1,144,621	4,990,175
Holmes	45,402	447	9,006	B/	3,708	1,502	9,615	1,611	3,334	16,166
Indian River	873,454	77,705	67,645	1,631	84,096	48,450	138,608	78,077	25,335	351,907
Jackson	202,431	3,812	47,930	515	13,001	17,414	40,398	14,735	17,762	46,864
Jefferson	40,839	1,616	5,548	0	4,506	1,383	6,263	3,029	5,020	13,474
Lafayette	14,366	3,460	3,139	0	796	1,217	1,585	(D)	(D)	2,339
Lake	1,084,288	28,014	129,432	7,946	122,203	41,478	180,818	74,265	91,216	408,916
Lee	3,351,071	58,451	177,508	4,834	429,082	183,125	611,886	305,731	240,450	1,340,004
Leon	2,095,714	14,441	109,232	886	159,308	120,333	346,331	174,367	128,157	1,042,659
Levy	111,423	(D)	7,150	(D)	19,691	4,728	22,955	6,319	12,648	26,714
Liberty	23,545	505	7,324	0	3,903	B/	1,945	481	3,708	5,656
Madison	75,214	1,901	29,608	0	1,706	2,963	11,092	2,104	5,119	20,721
Manatee	2,237,023	48,761	393,944	605	127,531	78,843	302,458	103,616	67,101	1,114,164
Marion	1,526,684	29,300	313,401	3,731	139,843	131,098	282,371	94,763	91,737	440,440
Martin	1,058,992	38,572	100,926	555	105,086	47,533	178,394	107,536	74,040	406,350
Monroe	769,200	21,835	14,448	1,115	65,751	24,238	190,907	50,705	52,039	348,162

See footnotes at end of table.

Continued . . .

Table 5.34. EARNED INCOME: PRIVATE NONFARM EARNINGS ON A PLACE-OF-WORK BASIS BY MAJOR INDUSTRIAL SOURCE IN THE UNITED STATES AND IN THE STATE AND COUNTIES OF FLORIDA, 1994 AND 1995 (Continued)

(in thousands of dollars)

1994 A/ (Continued)

County	Total private nonfarm earnings	Agriculture services 1/	Manufacturing	Mining	Construction	Wholesale trade	Retail trade	Finance insurance and real estate	Transportation 2/	Services
Nassau	322,268	14,606	90,126	B/	34,035	10,736	47,522	12,821	20,429	91,971
Okaloosa	1,179,885	10,054	118,193	389	109,842	31,123	240,673	100,095	59,776	509,740
Okeechobee	149,936	10,036	6,116	0	12,401	11,316	31,777	9,902	9,683	58,705
Orange	13,419,468	108,919	1,469,167	7,584	803,917	1,085,025	1,554,647	1,195,509	1,270,926	5,923,774
Osceola	897,055	10,310	80,254	B/	81,459	45,149	189,309	64,709	23,398	402,456
Palm Beach	12,062,828	228,799	1,639,168	13,714	836,817	795,412	1,626,484	1,433,152	747,637	4,741,645
Pasco	1,415,885	27,356	105,348	1,270	148,648	49,668	272,635	87,885	116,311	606,764
Pinellas	9,855,666	76,522	1,570,882	2,011	629,566	666,305	1,443,512	955,163	522,301	3,989,404
Polk	4,145,297	128,241	716,540	133,603	293,712	276,873	721,396	253,547	374,619	1,246,766
Putnam	358,206	3,238	130,997	2,639	36,735	9,322	53,601	13,855	21,151	86,668
St. Johns	693,373	9,275	94,668	299	49,051	46,147	122,930	36,034	34,064	300,905
St. Lucie	1,066,251	79,574	77,369	2,074	104,064	57,606	172,457	70,054	129,787	373,266
Santa Rosa	454,260	7,157	74,401	8,813	64,591	14,139	64,437	17,320	37,686	165,716
Sarasota	3,094,005	34,789	278,933	3,314	276,925	143,299	528,879	326,675	132,729	1,368,462
Seminole	2,765,080	32,703	350,808	312	310,634	228,187	485,861	217,227	204,315	935,033
Sumter	118,439	2,445	17,676	2,134	9,055	8,333	23,592	5,095	23,688	26,421
Suwannee	171,869	(D)	31,179	(D)	29,539	8,367	31,024	7,067	17,017	39,751
Taylor	160,980	3,823	80,626	1,544	(D)	3,982	18,454	6,018	5,077	(D)
Union	40,384	808	10,407	(D)	4,180	(D)	3,512	1,215	9,362	10,305
Volusia	2,735,834	26,156	408,227	82	224,977	145,988	520,873	184,504	134,034	1,090,993
Wakulla	64,611	2,569	21,397	0	8,979	2,960	7,957	2,985	3,848	13,916
Walton	174,419	4,382	27,309	408	25,955	4,083	29,124	8,597	14,426	60,135
Washington	73,995	(D)	18,385	(D)	7,626	2,159	11,519	1,768	13,257	18,350

See footnotes at end of table.

Continued . . .

Table 5.34. EARNED INCOME: PRIVATE NONFARM EARNINGS ON A PLACE-OF-WORK BASIS BY MAJOR INDUSTRIAL SOURCE IN THE UNITED STATES AND IN THE STATE AND COUNTIES OF FLORIDA, 1994 AND 1995 (Continued)

(in thousands of dollars)

County	Total private nonfarm earnings	Agriculture services 1/	Manufacturing	Mining	Construction	Wholesale trade	Retail trade	Finance insurance and real estate	Transportation 2/	Services 2/
1995										
United States 3/	3,607,964	28,839	796,685	37,599	235,315	273,968	399,957	324,524	297,621	1,213,456
Florida 3/	161,656	2,085	18,296	351	11,470	12,895	22,666	16,061	13,237	64,595
Alachua	1,881,191	(D)	179,097	(D)	143,649	72,842	312,062	155,631	80,549	915,082
Baker	63,372	430	8,024	0	(D)	2,570	13,917	2,757	12,304	(D)
Bay	1,192,498	11,718	103,240	B/	131,103	77,143	252,385	83,142	95,515	438,207
Bradford	96,803	1,171	11,878	0	9,885	(D)	19,068	2,805	9,326	(D)
Brevard	4,847,489	35,162	1,298,430	2,257	306,890	165,460	561,290	211,769	179,765	2,086,593
Broward	17,217,113	136,115	1,701,741	10,541	1,261,186	1,516,111	2,535,623	1,854,886	1,279,765	6,921,145
Calhoun	44,595	2,521	7,613	0	5,807	3,158	8,465	1,477	2,278	13,276
Charlotte	767,333	13,994	24,023	1,182	88,482	17,844	153,904	54,297	40,368	373,239
Citrus	593,858	8,608	34,406	803	60,375	12,671	99,775	34,729	112,787	229,704
Clay	684,457	12,012	47,455	9,220	84,641	25,487	158,650	31,008	62,683	253,301
Collier	2,207,867	98,988	84,031	4,733	278,055	89,373	371,454	277,369	77,674	926,190
Columbia	307,749	3,195	46,813	B/	37,222	27,704	62,292	13,966	22,110	94,407
Dade	27,544,885	166,241	2,409,486	33,601	1,349,513	3,147,994	3,355,336	2,939,580	3,295,377	10,847,757
De Soto	112,287	29,916	3,038	B/	8,894	4,608	21,245	4,256	6,026	34,289
Dixie	46,342	1,565	15,012	(D)	7,231	(D)	7,253	1,037	2,563	8,200
Duval	11,462,570	74,434	1,236,727	12,729	809,446	990,717	1,306,608	1,959,146	1,339,672	3,733,091
Escambia	2,716,825	18,428	377,613	4,349	269,506	169,074	401,028	147,074	225,910	1,103,843
Flagler	192,658	(D)	47,222	(D)	12,564	3,330	28,637	23,080	9,248	64,741
Franklin	57,310	(D)	4,149	(D)	4,129	5,511	8,986	3,432	5,506	19,946
Gadsden	166,317	6,966	36,097	(D)	15,374	(D)	30,063	6,945	10,672	37,908
Gilchrist	27,952	2,533	3,684	0	2,107	2,074	3,818	1,624	3,088	9,024
Glades	20,499	5,703	(D)	(D)	2,235	325	2,882	(D)	3,400	3,952

See footnotes at end of table.

Continued . . .

Table 5.34. EARNED INCOME: PRIVATE NONFARM EARNINGS ON A PLACE-OF-WORK BASIS BY MAJOR INDUSTRIAL SOURCE IN THE UNITED STATES AND IN THE STATE AND COUNTIES OF FLORIDA, 1994 AND 1995 (Continued)

(in thousands of dollars)

1995 (Continued)

County	Total private nonfarm earnings	Agri-culture ser-vices 1/	Manufac-turing	Mining	Construc-tion	Wholesale trade	Retail trade	Finance insurance and real estate	Trans-porta-tion 2/	Services
Gulf	92,629	1,159	43,601	0	9,932	307	6,942	3,125	12,638	14,925
Hamilton	97,671	688	69,645	0	2,228	325	7,269	488	6,504	10,524
Hardee	107,511	19,279	5,374	(D)	(D)	9,264	16,515	7,025	5,557	28,790
Hendry	194,770	45,361	48,270	(D)	12,321	7,392	24,350	6,891	(D)	37,506
Hernando	543,591	8,650	43,499	9,623	53,579	19,671	109,430	37,290	38,526	223,323
Highlands	436,191	37,072	43,090	(D)	41,759	15,382	80,674	26,208	(D)	167,702
Hillsborough	13,771,261	101,302	1,249,706	1,649	831,718	1,627,716	1,606,422	1,591,086	1,235,455	5,526,207
Holmes	47,146	490	8,007	B/	3,843	1,709	9,399	1,819	3,720	18,144
Indian River	927,959	79,283	74,755	1,814	86,711	46,464	150,054	78,870	27,338	382,670
Jackson	208,373	(D)	43,512	(D)	11,601	20,861	42,996	15,075	18,899	50,890
Jefferson	43,085	1,703	5,859	0	5,136	1,631	6,282	3,367	4,898	14,209
Lafayette	14,432	3,694	2,313	0	1,030	1,309	1,636	484	1,511	2,455
Lake	1,173,254	27,719	132,436	9,120	129,177	46,966	190,422	86,075	93,181	458,158
Lee	3,552,626	60,810	200,517	4,793	414,900	197,321	655,021	343,066	254,186	1,422,012
Leon	2,271,702	(D)	116,338	(D)	165,544	135,832	366,593	185,387	146,984	1,137,102
Levy	121,334	8,253	8,816	(D)	19,205	(D)	26,918	6,719	13,768	30,644
Liberty	26,061	(D)	(D)	0	5,100	B/	2,033	(D)	4,448	5,924
Madison	85,323	2,348	33,089	0	1,766	2,676	11,909	2,605	5,397	25,533
Manatee	2,536,242	46,370	404,963	608	144,610	88,938	314,318	110,890	67,415	1,358,128
Marion	1,641,567	31,987	324,701	3,678	144,832	140,185	295,969	114,529	104,789	480,897
Martin	1,149,077	38,244	111,896	707	123,611	48,838	185,357	114,523	76,202	449,699
Monroe	825,417	23,670	14,385	1,161	72,905	24,517	199,953	56,896	54,446	377,484
Nassau	343,269	15,420	93,536	B/	34,100	10,868	51,799	14,128	22,113	101,281
Okaloosa	1,273,503	12,035	124,153	556	118,374	36,143	259,964	113,742	64,665	543,871
Okeechobee	161,264	10,718	5,437	0	12,185	11,647	34,478	13,647	9,930	63,222
Orange	14,427,709	115,901	1,524,365	7,590	841,491	1,198,749	1,685,999	1,260,359	1,312,265	6,480,990

See footnotes at end of table.

Continued . . .

Table 5.34. EARNED INCOME: PRIVATE NONFARM EARNINGS ON A PLACE-OF-WORK BASIS BY MAJOR INDUSTRIAL SOURCE IN THE UNITED STATES AND IN THE STATE AND COUNTIES OF FLORIDA, 1994 AND 1995 (Continued)

(in thousands of dollars)

1995 (Continued)

County	Total private nonfarm earnings	Agriculture services 1/	Manufacturing	Mining	Construction	Wholesale trade	Retail trade	Finance insurance and real estate	Transportation 2/	Services
Osceola	962,095	11,564	80,590	B/	79,397	53,049	209,782	64,263	23,831	439,607
Palm Beach	12,967,331	238,359	1,595,968	15,937	905,986	913,571	1,675,440	1,634,545	801,608	5,185,917
Pasco	1,496,666	29,694	105,253	1,280	128,946	55,405	281,490	94,798	125,674	674,126
Pinellas	10,589,329	77,972	1,640,372	2,183	635,200	784,542	1,480,882	1,011,429	556,306	4,400,443
Polk	4,395,613	125,381	776,299	163,374	307,943	263,039	745,435	266,718	408,316	1,339,108
Putnam	401,909	3,952	139,151	2,778	58,063	10,323	57,419	14,747	21,104	94,372
St. Johns	767,185	10,293	104,366	369	52,936	49,897	131,792	45,887	32,575	339,070
St. Lucie	1,109,176	82,039	75,804	1,962	94,099	59,227	180,411	73,800	140,615	401,219
Santa Rosa	483,418	7,640	78,362	9,883	69,021	14,279	65,891	18,749	42,177	177,416
Sarasota	3,353,352	36,334	301,720	3,564	274,542	158,549	556,905	358,673	137,603	1,525,462
Seminole	3,001,217	36,637	362,813	346	335,575	270,466	534,753	236,784	219,988	1,003,855
Sumter	128,096	2,248	19,594	2,095	9,014	10,023	25,550	5,759	26,076	27,737
Suwannee	184,675	(D)	34,793	(D)	29,776	10,087	32,561	7,731	16,811	44,208
Taylor	158,443	4,485	76,364	1,572	16,160	4,412	19,790	6,434	5,172	24,054
Union	40,390	852	8,945	(D)	2,991	(D)	3,683	1,469	10,033	11,710
Volusia	2,962,883	27,911	409,656	85	234,536	161,717	554,303	198,099	140,559	1,236,017
Wakulla	65,908	2,475	20,872	0	9,624	2,425	8,417	3,252	3,910	14,933
Walton	181,952	(D)	25,580	(D)	25,850	4,764	30,316	9,297	16,028	65,275
Washington	81,017	(D)	19,770	(D)	9,065	1,865	13,551	1,988	13,489	20,140

(D) Data withheld to avoid disclosure of information about individual industries.
A/ Revised.
B/ Less than $50,000. Estimates are included in totals.
1/ Includes forestry, fisheries, and other.
2/ Includes communications and public utilities.
3/ United States and Florida numbers are rounded to millions of dollars.
Source: U.S., Department of Commerce, Bureau of Economic Analysis, Regional Economic Information System, CD-ROM, August 1997.

Table 5.38.   TRANSFER PAYMENTS: AMOUNTS BY TYPE IN FLORIDA, 1994 AND 1995

(in thousands of dollars)

Type of transfer payment	1994 A/	1995
Total personal income by place of residence	304,113,177	326,670,110
Total transfer payments	57,631,724	61,813,035
Percentage of personal income	18.95	18.92
Government payments to individuals	55,829,311	59,945,649
Retirement and disability insurance benefit payments	29,386,416	31,061,142
Old age, survivors, and disability insurance	21,553,064	22,801,644
Railroad retirement and disability	407,122	412,179
Federal civilian employee retirement	2,734,093	2,855,694
Military retirement	2,881,329	3,009,489
State and local government employee retirement	1,491,257	1,650,841
Workers' compensation (federal and state)	256,812	268,264
Other government disability insurance and retirement 1/	62,739	63,031
Medical payments 2/	19,551,204	21,620,040
Income maintenance benefit payments	4,165,161	4,519,438
Supplemental Security Income (SSI)	1,178,457	1,319,533
Aid to Families with Dependent Children (AFDC)	851,155	802,985
Food stamps	1,325,369	1,302,027
Other income maintenance 3/	810,180	1,094,893
Unemployment insurance benefit payments	852,399	740,324
State unemployment insurance compensation	819,372	714,129
Unemployment Compensation for Federal Civilian Employees (UCFE)	8,779	7,094
Unemployment Compensation for Railroad Employees	1,120	1,102
Unemployment Compensation for Veterans (UCX)	22,662	16,517
Other unemployment compensation 4/	466	1,482
Veterans' benefit payments	1,489,214	1,549,600
Veterans' pensions and compensation	1,263,603	1,305,642
Educational assistance to veterans, dependents, and survivors 5/	64,327	77,082
Veterans' life insurance benefit	157,802	163,344
Other assistance to veterans 6/	3,482	3,532
Federal education and training assistance payments (excluding veterans) 7/	363,160	428,796
Other payments to individuals 8/	21,757	26,309
Payments to nonprofit institutions	1,065,061	1,127,852
Federal government payments	283,685	302,991
State and local government payments 9/	441,104	481,550
Business payments	340,272	343,311
Business payments to individuals 10/	737,352	739,534

A/ Revised.   1/ Includes temporary disability and black lung payments.   2/ Medicare, medical vendor, and CHAMPUS payments.   3/ Includes general, emergency, refugee, and energy assistance, foster home care payments and earned-income tax credits.
4/ Includes trade readjustment, public service employment benefit, and transitional benefit payments.   5/ Includes veterans' readjustment benefit payments and educational assistance to spouses and children of disabled or deceased veterans.   6/ Includes payments to paraplegics, transportation payments for disabled veterans, and veterans' aid and bonuses.   7/ Includes federal fellowship and Job Corps payments, basic educational opportunity grants, and loan interest subsidies.   8/ Includes Bureau of Indian Affairs and education exchange payments, compensation of survivors of public safety officers, crime victims, Japanese interment, natural disasters, and other special payments. 9/ Foster home care supervised by private agency, educational assistance to nonprofit institutions and other payments to nonprofit institutions.
10/ Personal injury payments to individuals other than employees and other business transfer payments.
Source: U.S., Department of Commerce, Bureau of Economic Analysis, Regional Economic Information System, CD-ROM, August 1997.

Table 5.39. TRANSFER PAYMENTS: TOTAL AMOUNTS IN THE UNITED STATES AND IN THE
STATE AND COUNTIES OF FLORIDA, 1993, 1994, AND 1995

(amounts in thousands of dollars)

County	1993 A/ Amount	As a percentage of total personal income	1994 A/ Amount	As a percentage of total personal income	1995 Amount	As a percentage of total personal income
United States	910,632,000	16.6	956,586,000	16.7	1,022,841,000	16.8
Florida	54,238,193	18.7	57,631,724	19.0	61,813,035	18.9
Alachua	608,612	17.5	643,794	17.6	694,953	17.8
Baker	57,060	20.8	59,243	20.7	63,715	20.7
Bay	546,203	23.0	589,217	23.8	633,569	24.4
Bradford	79,104	26.0	84,903	26.5	93,439	26.8
Brevard	1,815,078	21.2	1,958,781	21.9	2,083,765	22.3
Broward	5,209,266	15.9	5,500,942	16.0	5,885,335	15.9
Calhoun	44,240	32.3	47,420	32.5	50,733	33.9
Charlotte	644,945	28.1	702,762	28.6	752,924	28.4
Citrus	531,431	32.3	566,360	32.5	604,613	32.8
Clay	336,961	15.7	361,704	15.8	385,687	15.4
Collier	681,517	12.8	745,984	13.3	793,084	13.2
Columbia	172,612	25.5	185,333	25.4	201,536	25.5
Dade	7,285,923	18.6	7,586,089	18.8	8,230,047	19.1
De Soto	102,451	25.2	112,412	27.4	120,408	27.0
Dixie	42,897	35.2	47,452	32.7	50,932	33.1
Duval	2,424,302	17.2	2,524,438	17.1	2,699,609	17.1
Escambia	1,126,016	24.5	1,191,631	25.1	1,264,043	25.5
Flagler	168,165	29.4	189,539	30.0	202,552	29.3
Franklin	41,635	30.0	44,629	29.6	48,380	30.9
Gadsden	157,076	27.1	162,597	27.5	176,780	28.6
Gilchrist	38,160	26.8	42,087	28.0	44,993	28.3
Glades	17,882	16.6	18,646	18.3	19,852	18.1
Gulf	53,735	30.5	59,956	31.6	64,279	32.8
Hamilton	35,354	27.4	38,190	28.4	41,469	28.3
Hardee	68,982	22.1	76,173	24.3	83,696	24.7
Hendry	85,396	16.8	91,901	19.3	96,240	18.3
Hernando	618,892	33.3	684,201	34.0	732,907	33.8
Highlands	391,551	30.8	431,771	32.8	461,330	32.4
Hillsborough	2,893,437	17.2	3,043,157	17.1	3,252,328	17.1
Holmes	67,097	33.1	72,525	33.6	79,583	35.7
Indian River	500,698	18.6	538,916	19.1	573,377	18.7
Jackson	170,191	28.2	181,137	29.0	197,087	30.5
Jefferson	42,585	23.5	46,600	24.8	50,678	24.5
Lafayette	17,072	23.2	17,342	22.8	18,518	23.5
Lake	845,174	27.6	925,925	28.3	996,619	28.4

See footnote at end of table.   Continued . . .

Table 5.39. TRANSFER PAYMENTS: TOTAL AMOUNTS IN THE UNITED STATES AND IN THE
STATE AND COUNTIES OF FLORIDA, 1993, 1994, AND 1995 (Continued)

(amounts in thousands of dollars)

County	1993 A/ Amount	As a percentage of total personal income	1994 A/ Amount	As a percentage of total personal income	1995 Amount	As a percentage of total personal income
Lee	1,624,908	20.9	1,727,137	20.9	1,843,573	20.8
Leon	503,332	12.8	543,372	13.0	584,987	13.1
Levy	109,041	28.5	118,642	29.4	128,226	29.5
Liberty	21,158	28.5	22,017	27.9	23,974	28.8
Madison	60,165	29.1	63,364	29.3	68,120	29.1
Manatee	936,365	18.9	998,758	19.1	1,064,949	18.7
Marion	944,117	26.7	1,038,914	27.3	1,118,561	27.4
Martin	520,221	15.3	555,013	15.8	597,015	15.6
Monroe	248,646	12.5	263,816	12.8	281,473	12.7
Nassau	139,889	14.7	152,671	15.2	162,065	14.9
Okaloosa	663,127	22.8	710,964	23.2	765,970	23.7
Okeechobee	136,297	29.8	145,442	31.5	155,547	31.7
Orange	2,281,822	15.7	2,420,159	15.9	2,590,891	15.9
Osceola	374,995	19.8	408,189	20.4	440,750	20.6
Palm Beach	4,174,084	13.5	4,469,877	13.8	4,777,224	13.6
Pasco	1,466,678	30.0	1,548,903	29.4	1,657,603	28.8
Pinellas	4,177,012	20.5	4,364,432	21.0	4,689,486	20.9
Polk	1,531,677	21.3	1,646,305	21.4	1,765,102	21.2
Putnam	280,152	29.5	295,064	30.3	317,198	30.1
St. Johns	350,872	14.7	383,904	14.7	408,679	14.2
St. Lucie	705,168	25.9	752,141	26.5	805,879	26.4
Santa Rosa	339,653	20.8	327,325	19.0	354,146	19.1
Sarasota	1,572,307	18.4	1,723,045	18.9	1,836,069	18.6
Seminole	813,501	12.2	873,083	12.2	929,597	12.0
Sumter	176,192	37.9	194,371	39.2	208,306	38.9
Suwannee	119,454	27.1	128,763	27.7	138,480	27.8
Taylor	69,007	29.0	75,143	27.9	80,383	28.5
Union	25,760	23.4	27,112	23.7	29,080	23.9
Volusia	1,692,002	24.7	1,801,894	24.9	1,937,318	24.9
Wakulla	47,689	19.6	51,404	19.4	55,712	20.1
Walton	130,608	30.1	142,307	30.6	156,306	32.1
Washington	80,594	34.5	84,436	34.6	91,306	35.3

A/ Revised.

Source: U.S., Department of Commerce, Bureau of Economic Analysis, Regional Economic Information System, CD-ROM, August 1997.

University of Florida   **Bureau of Economic and Business Research**

Table 5.41. MILITARY RETIREES: PERSONS RECEIVING MILITARY RETIREMENT INCOME AND AMOUNT OF MONTHLY PAYMENT IN FLORIDA, SEPTEMBER 30, 1995 AND 1996

Branch and type of service	Total 1/ 1995	Total 1/ 1996	Paid by Department of Defense 1995	Paid by Department of Defense 1996	Monthly payment 2/ ($1,000) 1995	Monthly payment 2/ ($1,000) 1996
Total	174,225	176,972	156,171	158,162	239,038	247,141
Army	42,468	43,042	37,854	38,229	55,475	57,064
Navy	55,461	56,664	50,883	51,927	74,003	76,994
Marine Corps	7,394	7,523	6,336	6,432	10,047	10,435
Air Force	65,302	66,017	61,098	61,574	93,969	96,784
Coast Guard	3,600	3,726	A/ 3,429	A/ 3,551	5,544	5,864
Officers	54,221	54,307	52,688	52,706	118,272	121,352
Nondisabled and reserve	49,544	49,791	48,448	48,658	109,934	113,234
Disabled	4,677	4,516	4,240	4,048	8,338	8,118
Enlisted	116,404	118,939	103,483	105,456	115,222	119,924
Nondisabled and reserve	102,570	105,023	96,237	98,356	110,106	114,892
Disabled	13,834	13,916	7,246	7,100	5,116	5,032

A/ Paid by the Department of Transportation.
1/ Includes retirees whose monthly payment is zero or less after survivor benefit deductions and/or other offsets such as Veterans Administration payments, dual compensation, pay cap limitations from civil service employment, and refusal of retired pay.
2/ Monthly payment prior to deductions for withholding taxes and allotments, but after deductions for survivor benefits, waivers to obtain benefits from the Veterans Administration, dual compensation, and other adjustments.

Table 5.42. MILITARY RETIREES: SURVIVING FAMILIES RECEIVING RETIREMENT PAYMENTS AND AMOUNT OF MONTHLY PAYMENT IN FLORIDA, SEPTEMBER 30 1994, 1995, AND 1996

Branch of service	Total 1994	Total 1995	Total 1996	Monthly payment received (dollars) 1994	Monthly payment received (dollars) 1995	Monthly payment received (dollars) 1996
Total	19,874	20,830	21,900	12,474,413	13,373,789	14,335,084
Army	7,197	7,394	7,712	4,652,584	4,871,992	5,168,236
Navy	5,865	6,179	6,477	3,401,022	3,674,082	3,918,257
Marine Corps	600	654	710	392,298	437,784	496,769
Air Force	6,212	6,603	7,001	4,028,509	4,389,931	4,751,822

Note: Data are for families receiving payments under the Retired Servicemen's Family Protection Plan or the Survivor Benefit Plan.

Source for Tables 5.41 and 5.42: U.S., Department of Defense, Office of the Actuary, *DOD Statistical Report on the Military Retirement System, Fiscal Year 1996,* and previous editions.

University of Florida   **Bureau of Economic and Business Research**

Table 5.46. POVERTY THRESHOLDS: AVERAGE POVERTY THRESHOLDS FOR A FAMILY OF FOUR
AND THE ANNUAL CONSUMER PRICE INDEX IN THE UNITED STATES, 1983 THROUGH 1996

Year	Average threshold (dollars)	Consumer Price Index (1982-84=100)	Year	Average threshold (dollars)	Consumer Price Index (1982-84=100)
1983	10,178	99.6	1990	13,359	130.7
1984	10,609	103.9	1991	13,924	136.2
1985	10,989	107.6	1992	14,335	140.3
1986	11,203	109.6	1993	14,763	144.5
1987	11,611	113.6	1994	15,141	148.2
1988	12,092	118.3	1995	15,569	152.4
1989	12,674	124.0	1996 A/	16,029	156.9

A/ Preliminary.
Note: See Glossary under Poverty status for definition of poverty thresholds.

Source: U.S., Department of Commerce, Bureau of the Census, *Statistical Abstract
of the United States, 1995,* previous editions, and Internet site http://www.census.
gov/, U.S., Department of Commerce, Bureau of Economic Analysis, *Survey of Current
Business*, May 1994, and previous editions, and U.S., Department of Commerce, Bureau
of Labor Statistics, Internet site http://stats.bls.gov:80/.

Table 5.47. POVERTY THRESHOLDS: POVERTY LEVEL BASED ON MONEY INCOME BY SIZE OF
FAMILY IN THE UNITED STATES, 1993 THROUGH 1996

(in dollars)

Size of family unit	1993	1994	1995	1996 A/
1 person (unrelated individual)	7,363	7,547	7,763	7,992
Under 65 years	7,518	7,710	7,929	8,163
65 years and over	6,930	7,108	7,309	7,525
2 persons	9,414	9,661	9,933	10,226
Householder under 65 years	9,728	9,976	10,259	10,562
Householder 65 years and over	8,740	8,967	9,219	9,491
3 persons	11,522	11,821	12,158	12,517
4 persons	14,763	15,141	15,569	16,029
5 persons	17,449	17,900	18,408	18,951
6 persons	19,718	20,235	20,804	21,418
7 persons	22,383	22,923	23,552	24,247
8 persons	24,838	25,427	26,237	27,012
9 persons or more	29,529	30,300	31,280	32,203

A/ Preliminary.
Note: See Glossary under Poverty status for definition of poverty thresholds.
Some data may be revised.

Source: U.S., Department of Commerce, Bureau of the Census, *Current Population
Reports: Consumer Income,* and Internet site http://www.census.gov/.

University of Florida   **Bureau of Economic and Business Research**

Table 5.48. INCOME AND POVERTY ESTIMATES: MEDIAN HOUSEHOLD INCOME
POOR PERSONS, AND POOR RELATED CHILDREN AGED 5 TO 17
IN THE STATE AND COUNTIES OF FLORIDA, 1993

County	Median household income (dollars)	Poor persons		Poor related children aged 5 to 17	
		Total	Per-centage	Total	Per-centage
Florida	28,230	2,211,865	15.9	499,148	21.8
Alachua	26,683	37,710	19.6	7,694	24.1
Baker	27,568	3,567	19.6	873	18.4
Bay	26,927	22,849	16.4	5,214	19.2
Bradford	25,207	4,349	22.3	831	19.3
Brevard	33,061	51,045	11.5	10,431	14.4
Broward	31,289	167,490	12.1	35,100	16.9
Calhoun	21,378	2,412	22.6	497	21.2
Charlotte	26,094	12,469	9.9	2,134	14.2
Citrus	21,458	16,102	15.5	2,559	18.1
Clay	38,102	10,632	8.8	2,392	8.8
Collier	33,598	23,004	13.0	4,990	19.0
Columbia	25,343	9,356	20.0	2,416	24.1
Dade	26,743	519,974	25.7	130,803	37.5
De Soto	20,443	5,874	25.3	1,553	35.0
Dixie	17,029	2,921	25.9	643	29.7
Duval	31,892	107,466	15.2	26,286	19.6
Escambia	27,738	54,556	20.2	14,769	28.4
Flagler	28,109	4,148	10.8	764	13.4
Franklin	19,803	1,988	21.3	434	24.7
Gadsden	20,678	11,971	29.2	3,673	36.9
Gilchrist	23,158	1,911	18.1	410	19.1
Glades	22,320	1,366	18.0	296	20.8
Gulf	24,290	2,184	20.0	501	21.2
Hamilton	20,811	2,545	24.5	700	26.8
Hardee	21,105	5,515	27.3	1,572	34.8
Hendry	25,047	6,558	23.1	1,914	28.9
Hernando	23,095	16,312	14.0	3,192	19.2
Highlands	21,514	12,343	16.8	2,455	23.2
Hillsborough	30,296	147,614	16.9	33,556	21.4
Holmes	19,975	3,956	24.7	948	28.6
Indian River	29,518	10,996	11.5	2,082	15.0
Jackson	22,573	8,193	21.0	1,909	23.2
Jefferson	22,903	2,604	23.7	678	24.5
Lafayette	23,111	1,180	23.0	267	23.8
Lake	24,804	24,575	14.1	4,792	18.1
Lee	29,174	45,402	12.3	9,465	17.8

See footnote at end of table.   Continued . . .

Table 5.48. INCOME AND POVERTY ESTIMATES: MEDIAN HOUSEHOLD INCOME
POOR PERSONS, AND POOR RELATED CHILDREN AGED 5 TO 17
IN THE STATE AND COUNTIES OF FLORIDA, 1993 (Continued)

County	Median household income (dollars)	Poor persons Total	Poor persons Per-centage	Poor related children aged 5 to 17 Total	Poor related children aged 5 to 17 Per-centage
Leon	32,005	29,615	14.1	5,766	15.7
Levy	20,559	5,517	19.2	1,369	25.0
Liberty	23,900	994	20.4	208	18.1
Madison	20,564	3,802	23.7	957	26.8
Manatee	27,441	28,758	12.7	6,072	19.1
Marion	23,200	40,828	18.7	9,425	25.6
Martin	32,358	11,682	10.8	2,397	16.7
Monroe	30,720	9,411	11.4	1,587	15.8
Nassau	33,586	5,910	11.9	1,408	13.5
Okaloosa	31,520	17,584	11.1	4,152	13.2
Okeechobee	21,669	6,640	21.8	1,720	28.6
Orange	31,649	105,049	14.4	23,634	18.3
Osceola	27,921	17,954	14.2	3,973	16.7
Palm Beach	33,094	116,869	12.2	24,701	18.1
Pasco	22,071	42,685	14.3	7,764	19.4
Pinellas	29,009	108,741	12.6	21,790	18.8
Polk	26,191	76,200	17.8	16,454	21.1
Putnam	21,684	17,139	25.0	4,161	31.1
St. Johns	32,974	11,564	11.8	2,458	15.1
St. Lucie	26,387	26,704	15.8	6,315	21.9
Santa Rosa	31,938	12,493	12.6	3,052	15.0
Sarasota	30,662	29,286	10.0	4,877	14.0
Seminole	37,495	31,700	9.7	6125	9.7
Sumter	19,982	6,903	21.4	1,661	28.9
Suwannee	21,767	5,701	19.4	1,326	21.1
Taylor	23,304	3,625	20.7	1,001	26.8
Union	25,524	1,548	23.5	369	17.3
Volusia	26,071	61,586	15.4	12,814	21.5
Wakulla	27,567	2,585	15.5	583	15.5
Walton	23,283	5,878	19.0	1,348	22.8
Washington	20,806	3,777	21.1	887	25

Note: Estimates are based on a model which combines population, federal income tax returns, food stamp participation, and the 1990 decennial census.

Source: U.S., Department of Commerce, Bureau of the Census, Internet site http:// www.census.gov/.

University of Florida   **Bureau of Economic and Business Research**

LABOR FORCE, EMPLOYMENT, AND EARNINGS

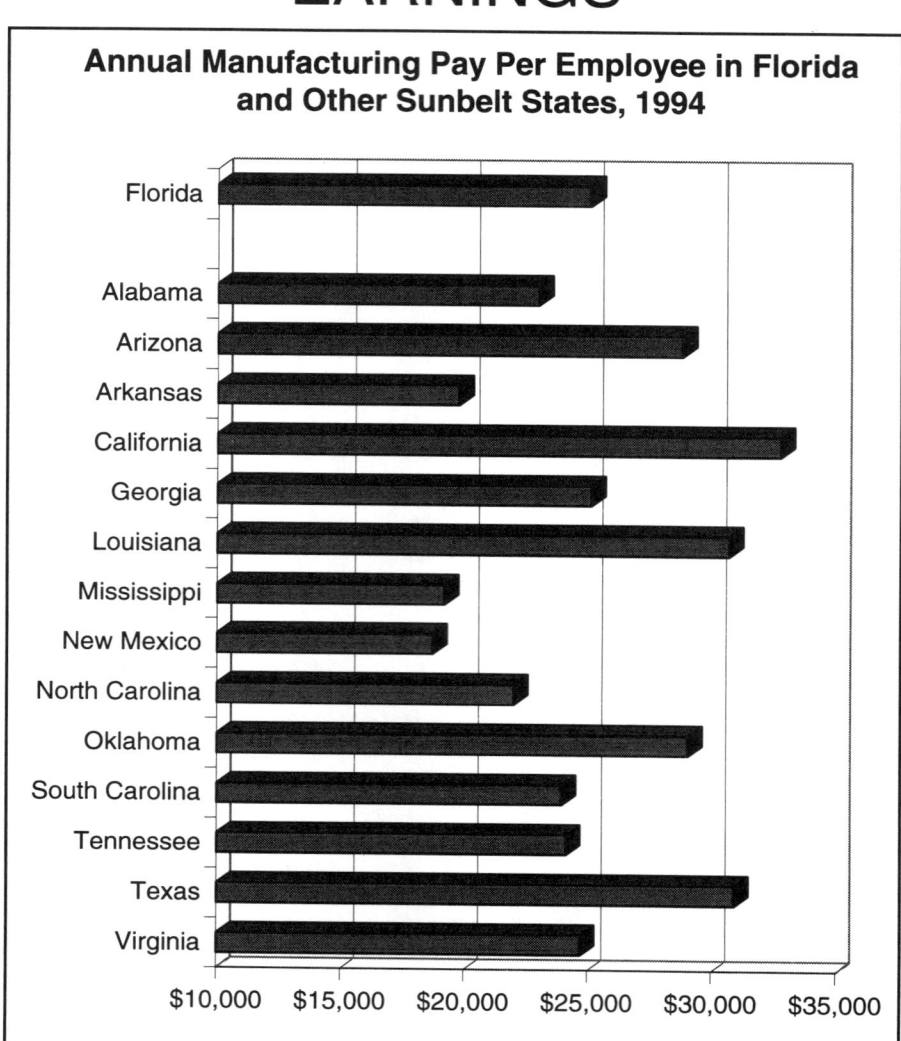

Annual Manufacturing Pay Per Employee in Florida and Other Sunbelt States, 1994

Source: Table 6.55

SECTION 6.00
LABOR FORCE, EMPLOYMENT, AND EARNINGS
(Continued)

TABLES LISTED BY MAJOR HEADINGS

Table 6.01.   NONAGRICULTURAL EMPLOYMENT: EMPLOYMENT BY INDUSTRIAL CLASSIFICATION
IN FLORIDA, 1958 THROUGH 1996

(in thousands)

Year	Total	Min-ing	Con-struc-tion	Manu-factur-ing	Trans-porta-tion and public utili-ties 1/	Whole-sale and retail trade	Fi-nance insur-ance and real estate	Serv-ices	Gov-ern-ment
1958	1,185.6	7.7	127.7	180.3	94.4	313.1	70.0	197.2	195.2
1959	1,273.0	7.8	134.6	199.9	97.6	333.4	76.9	215.2	207.6
1960	1,320.6	8.2	124.7	207.5	100.2	349.7	82.1	227.7	220.5
1961	1,333.9	8.3	112.4	211.8	99.8	350.9	84.6	233.8	232.3
1962	1,387.8	8.2	112.7	223.1	99.4	365.0	87.4	244.6	247.4
1963	1,447.4	8.5	120.2	229.3	100.7	375.1	90.8	260.3	262.5
1964	1,526.5	9.2	130.1	237.9	106.0	395.0	93.7	275.9	278.7
1965	1,619.1	9.6	138.8	252.6	109.9	417.7	97.4	291.9	301.2
1966	1,726.8	9.7	137.1	276.1	116.8	443.1	101.7	316.1	326.2
1967	1,816.4	8.9	131.7	293.8	127.1	466.3	106.2	340.1	342.3
1968	1,932.3	8.4	143.6	311.4	135.1	491.5	112.6	367.9	361.8
1969	2,069.9	7.8	169.2	329.2	145.4	521.3	123.0	396.1	377.9
1970	2,152.1	8.3	175.7	322.5	154.5	545.8	131.3	416.2	397.8
1971	2,276.4	8.9	186.8	322.7	161.7	583.5	143.8	449.9	419.1
1972	2,513.1	8.8	230.1	351.3	173.5	643.5	162.4	505.6	437.9
1973	2,778.6	9.2	290.2	380.6	186.7	703.2	182.6	556.2	469.9
1974	2,863.8	9.9	276.1	375.9	189.8	727.6	192.5	581.5	510.5
1075	2,746.4	9.4	182.5	339.4	182.9	713.6	188.3	584.3	546.0
1976	2,784.3	8.8	166.7	354.0	181.4	730.8	191.3	608.5	542.8
1977	2,933.2	9.1	178.9	380.9	185.1	771.0	202.5	640.0	565.7
1978	3,180.6	9.5	209.5	415.5	194.2	836.9	219.3	693.9	601.8
1979	3,381.2	10.1	241.4	443.6	208.5	889.5	235.0	752.6	600.5
1980	3,576.2	11.0	263.9	456.4	220.8	939.8	254.2	814.6	618.8
1981	3,736.0	11.3	283.1	472.2	229.8	984.2	274.3	861.0	620.1
1982	3,761.9	9.6	256.6	456.7	229.9	995.0	276.6	905.0	632.5
1983	3,905.4	9.6	268.8	464.3	231.4	1,034.5	283.2	974.3	639.3
1984	4,204.2	10.2	318.3	501.9	241.1	1,118.0	299.5	1,065.7	649.5
1985	4,410.0	10.1	334.3	514.4	243.0	1,184.8	319.2	1,129.8	674.4
1986	4,599.4	9.3	339.5	517.2	247.4	1,238.8	339.7	1,205.6	701.9
1987	4,848.1	8.7	341.5	531.0	254.8	1,316.7	359.3	1,304.4	731.8
1988	5,066.6	9.1	346.3	539.6	260.8	1,378.8	365.1	1,393.9	773.0
1989	5,260.9	9.2	340.2	537.9	266.4	1,432.6	370.3	1,504.3	800.1
1990	5,387.4	8.9	323.2	522.1	278.4	1,444.4	370.7	1,593.0	846.7
1991	5,294.3	8.2	276.9	492.8	274.9	1,402.6	358.2	1,621.5	859.3
1992	5,358.7	7.1	266.5	482.9	275.8	1,411.7	351.9	1,692.7	870.1
1993	5,571.4	6.3	285.3	485.2	287.1	1,456.3	360.3	1,809.2	881.6
1994	5,799.4	6.8	296.0	484.0	296.3	1,507.2	375.6	1,922.9	910.6
1995	5,996.1	6.8	308.3	486.5	305.5	1,553.8	378.7	2,038.2	918.4
1996	6,182.5	6.9	323.5	490.4	314.1	1,606.9	393.8	2,117.6	929.2

1/ Includes communications except U.S. Postal Service.
Note: Benchmark 1996, not seasonally adjusted. Data for some years have been re-vised.

Source: U.S., Department of Labor, Bureau of Labor Statistics, *Employment and
Earnings,* May issues, and Internet site http://stats.bls.gov/.

Table 6.02. EMPLOYMENT AND EARNINGS: NUMBER OF JOBS AND PROPRIETORS AND AVERAGE
EARNINGS PER JOB IN THE UNITED STATES AND IN THE STATE AND COUNTIES
OF FLORIDA, 1994 AND 1995

	Total employment 1/			Average earnings per job (dollars)		
County	Wage and salary jobs	Number of proprietors		Total	Wage and salary	Per non-farm pro-prietor
		Non-farm 2/	Farm			
	1994 A/					
United States	121,978,000	22,026,200	2,108,000	27,936	26,507	18,881
Florida	6,258,395	1,069,242	36,232	24,751	23,905	13,989
Alachua	109,300	15,312	1,179	22,144	21,348	11,108
Baker	5,452	905	207	19,966	17,518	15,901
Bay	64,669	11,984	69	21,228	20,632	13,235
Bradford	6,292	998	344	19,639	18,876	11,778
Brevard	179,663	33,176	516	26,562	26,500	9,653
Broward	608,186	106,463	298	25,919	25,312	13,434
Calhoun	3,008	547	145	19,056	16,990	15,976
Charlotte	32,945	10,605	216	19,594	19,886	11,916
Citrus	25,756	7,185	306	20,250	20,454	11,325
Clay	31,015	7,987	223	19,500	18,971	13,620
Collier	83,865	21,965	269	22,569	21,686	14,064
Columbia	16,653	2,447	568	21,375	20,213	15,235
Dade	971,521	137,684	1,637	27,799	26,272	17,596
De Soto	8,897	1,396	892	19,178	15,963	18,007
Dixie	2,712	817	121	19,201	18,345	15,859
Duval	423,723	63,992	378	26,789	25,918	13,662
Escambia	130,260	17,731	488	24,018	23,298	11,005
Flagler	9,192	696	98	21,104	19,344	9,424
Franklin	2,896	1,508	0	15,870	16,800	10,405
Gadsden	14,393	1,638	357	19,693	18,033	10,920
Gilchrist	2,144	566	381	18,925	18,077	12,486
Glades	1,510	351	216	18,040	15,098	15,712
Gulf	4,089	716	0	24,082	23,266	10,723
Hamilton	4,167	434	255	25,637	23,806	13,855
Hardee	7,772	1,281	1,282	17,198	15,898	11,409
Hendry	12,889	1,631	415	20,896	17,248	15,249
Hernando	25,813	7,128	421	19,314	19,707	10,500
Highlands	23,713	5,247	649	18,450	17,191	13,921
Hillsborough	510,196	62,403	2,878	26,142	24,741	15,190
Holmes	3,501	881	582	17,557	16,606	11,211
Indian River	37,371	8,026	425	22,757	21,787	15,530
Jackson	14,984	2,131	924	19,960	18,621	14,245
Jefferson	3,108	626	336	17,432	16,409	12,380

See footnotes at end of table.   Continued . . .

Table 6.02. EMPLOYMENT AND EARNINGS: NUMBER OF JOBS AND PROPRIETORS AND AVERAGE
EARNINGS PER JOB IN THE UNITED STATES AND IN THE STATE AND COUNTIES
OF FLORIDA, 1994 AND 1995 (Continued)

| | Total employment 1/ | | | Average earnings per job (dollars) | | |
| | Wage and salary jobs | Number of proprietors | | | Wage and salary | Per non-farm pro-prietor |
County		Non-farm 2/	Farm	Total		
		1994 A/ (Continued)				
Lafayette	1,304	236	282	23,109	16,952	18,873
Lake	53,105	11,973	1,302	19,791	19,497	12,007
Lee	146,173	35,921	541	22,017	21,881	12,504
Leon	132,168	17,467	273	23,501	22,606	12,247
Levy	6,848	2,011	519	17,271	16,886	12,723
Liberty	1,653	270	79	20,080	18,973	16,144
Madison	5,096	672	537	18,123	17,610	13,113
Manatee	107,458	19,629	738	20,357	19,256	13,476
Marion	73,261	15,923	1,723	20,599	20,268	11,729
Martin	42,905	10,450	275	23,144	22,750	11,672
Monroe	37,078	10,228	0	21,106	20,995	14,002
Nassau	14,886	3,252	298	23,741	23,541	12,778
Okaloosa	81,357	13,086	354	21,070	21,108	9,449
Okeechobee	9,027	2,113	398	19,518	18,282	12,579
Orange	513,699	60,573	911	26,683	24,887	17,744
Osceola	44,938	4,818	537	21,331	19,473	21,047
Palm Beach	422,387	87,004	671	27,092	26,424	15,913
Pasco	69,558	14,255	951	20,361	19,955	11,711
Pinellas	388,551	75,981	95	24,083	23,830	11,443
Polk	173,138	29,364	2,397	23,729	22,445	16,643
Putnam	19,336	1,643	417	22,600	21,049	12,044
St. Johns	32,943	7,019	172	20,917	19,893	14,001
St. Lucie	50,393	11,415	548	21,590	21,432	10,645
Santa Rosa	23,873	6,922	465	20,637	20,960	11,671
Sarasota	130,718	32,838	340	21,630	21,641	12,263
Seminole	110,423	29,266	356	22,617	23,183	10,549
Sumter	7,000	1,702	764	18,686	18,454	12,992
Suwannee	8,994	2,669	1,026	19,712	17,078	16,599
Taylor	6,633	836	134	24,714	23,527	13,163
Union	4,115	350	188	20,976	19,768	15,094
Volusia	139,734	18,630	1,036	21,182	19,922	13,784
Wakulla	3,197	1,195	88	19,245	19,539	12,844
Walton	9,638	2,042	418	18,410	17,056	17,333
Washington	5,153	1,032	324	18,911	18,625	10,319

See footnotes at end of table.   Continued . . .

Table 6.02. EMPLOYMENT AND EARNINGS: NUMBER OF JOBS AND PROPRIETORS AND AVERAGE EARNINGS PER JOB IN THE UNITED STATES AND IN THE STATE AND COUNTIES OF FLORIDA, 1994 AND 1995 (Continued)

County	Total employment 1/			Average earnings per job (dollars)		
	Wage and salary jobs	Number of proprietors			Wage and	Per non- farm pro-
		Non- farm 2/	Farm	Total	salary	prietor
		1995				
United States	124,853,000	22,320,100	2,117,000	28,910	27,419	20,128
Florida	6,447,538	1,082,861	36,236	25,710	24,718	15,051
Alachua	112,471	15,506	1,180	22,752	21,869	11,784
Baker	5,510	924	207	20,749	18,267	16,503
Bay	65,311	12,167	69	22,091	21,479	13,874
Bradford	6,670	1,021	344	20,589	19,569	12,598
Brevard	179,089	33,636	516	27,123	27,071	10,358
Broward	638,371	107,643	298	26,721	25,942	14,587
Calhoun	3,081	560	145	19,549	17,463	16,411
Charlotte	33,472	10,740	216	20,566	20,784	12,708
Citrus	25,582	7,309	306	20,936	21,165	11,907
Clay	31,955	8,117	223	20,317	19,664	14,320
Collier	86,051	22,178	269	23,827	22,866	15,437
Columbia	17,772	2,486	568	21,887	20,585	15,863
Dade	985,238	139,253	1,637	28,940	27,255	18,980
De Soto	9,321	1,423	892	20,080	16,117	18,952
Dixie	2,784	835	121	19,354	18,328	16,502
Duval	438,593	64,859	378	27,897	26,905	14,540
Escambia	132,818	17,998	488	24,492	23,767	11,337
Flagler	9,991	703	98	21,945	20,158	10,688
Franklin	3,002	1,559	0	16,267	17,037	10,984
Gadsden	14,415	1,667	357	20,707	18,912	11,070
Gilchrist	2,277	576	381	18,372	18,647	13,217
Glades	1,544	357	216	19,096	15,500	18,174
Gulf	4,130	731	0	24,783	23,973	10,908
Hamilton	4,444	443	255	26,691	24,853	14,582
Hardee	7,780	1,309	1,283	18,326	16,900	12,076
Hendry	13,488	1,667	415	22,638	18,035	16,046
Hernando	26,396	7,249	421	19,935	20,284	11,097
Highlands	24,059	5,327	649	19,679	17,756	14,768
Hillsborough	528,488	63,214	2,875	27,236	25,706	16,355
Holmes	3,559	897	582	17,926	17,052	11,409
Indian River	38,661	8,119	425	23,842	22,232	17,019
Jackson	15,203	2,167	924	20,440	19,020	14,794
Jefferson	3,102	640	336	18,048	17,333	12,969
Lafayette	1,421	241	282	21,972	17,062	19,390

See footnotes at end of table.   Continued . . .

Table 6.02. EMPLOYMENT AND EARNINGS: NUMBER OF JOBS AND PROPRIETORS AND AVERAGE EARNINGS PER JOB IN THE UNITED STATES AND IN THE STATE AND COUNTIES OF FLORIDA, 1994 AND 1995 (Continued)

County	Wage and salary jobs	Number of proprietors Non-farm 2/	Farm	Total	Wage and salary	Per non-farm pro-prietor
		1995 (Continued)				
Lake	55,976	12,153	1,302	20,417	20,008	12,689
Lee	152,030	36,331	541	22,639	22,325	13,514
Leon	137,146	17,662	273	24,471	23,516	12,824
Levy	7,281	2,053	520	17,900	17,141	13,520
Liberty	1,776	278	79	20,758	19,597	16,737
Madison	5,414	687	537	18,792	18,342	14,261
Manatee	118,327	19,901	739	21,074	19,780	14,496
Marion	75,694	16,182	1,724	21,442	21,117	12,251
Martin	45,177	10,560	275	24,138	23,357	12,741
Monroe	37,760	10,418	0	22,039	21,766	15,176
Nassau	15,315	3,306	298	24,376	24,089	13,585
Okaloosa	83,506	13,271	354	22,117	22,184	9,872
Okeechobee	9,036	2,155	398	20,497	19,415	13,279
Orange	524,608	61,304	911	27,733	25,766	19,257
Osceola	46,938	4,888	537	21,981	20,005	22,600
Palm Beach	432,374	87,834	671	28,667	27,672	17,568
Pasco	71,495	14,481	951	20,927	20,453	12,443
Pinellas	400,334	76,955	95	25,095	24,758	12,318
Polk	176,486	29,805	2,397	24,774	23,252	17,924
Putnam	20,586	1,669	417	23,404	21,777	12,549
St. Johns	34,052	7,106	172	22,298	21,308	14,902
St. Lucie	50,807	11,596	548	22,471	22,192	11,212
Santa Rosa	24,800	7,029	466	20,826	21,103	11,947
Sarasota	139,079	33,191	340	22,004	21,767	13,274
Seminole	114,619	29,614	357	23,654	24,149	11,264
Sumter	7,522	1,734	764	19,555	19,652	13,854
Suwannee	9,421	2,718	1,026	20,184	17,498	17,189
Taylor	6,952	853	134	24,214	22,917	13,792
Union	4,189	358	188	21,460	20,201	15,771
Volusia	143,900	18,898	1,036	21,960	20,556	14,672
Wakulla	3,362	1,220	88	19,133	19,297	13,016
Walton	9,779	2,081	418	19,275	17,834	17,277
Washington	5,748	1,049	324	19,590	19,275	10,697

A/ Revised.
1/ Full- and part-time jobs.
2/ Includes limited partners.

Source: U.S., Department of Commerce, Bureau of Economic Analysis, Regional Economic Information System, CD-ROM, August 1997.

Table 6.03. EMPLOYMENT: AVERAGE MONTHLY PRIVATE EMPLOYMENT COVERED BY UNEMPLOYMENT COMPENSATION LAW BY INDUSTRY IN FLORIDA, 1995 AND 1996

SIC code	Industry	1995	1996
01-99	All industries	5,106,891	5,274,322
01-09	Agriculture, forestry, and fishing	152,914	154,230
01	Agricultural production--crops	61,277	59,631
02	Agricultural production--livestock and animal specialties	6,349	6,393
07	Agricultural services	83,428	86,262
08	Forestry	906	1,197
09	Fishing, hunting, and trapping	954	747
10-14	Mining	6,867	6,894
13	Oil and gas extraction	414	399
14	Nonmetallic minerals, except fuels	6,309	6,336
15-17	Construction	304,463	324,827
15	Building--general contractors and builders	68,885	70,405
16	Heavy construction other than building construction--contractors	40,758	42,641
17	Special trade contractors	194,821	211,781
20-39	Manufacturing	480,388	488,618
20	Food and kindred products	41,624	41,283
21	Tobacco products	1,257	1,537
22	Textile mill products	4,024	4,085
23	Apparel and other finished products made from fabrics and similar materials	27,562	25,944
24	Lumber and wood products, except furniture	21,288	21,566
25	Furniture and fixtures	12,252	12,900
26	Paper and allied products	14,513	14,241
27	Printing, publishing, and allied industries	63,756	63,744
28	Chemicals and allied products	20,835	19,916
29	Petroleum refining and related industries	1,542	1,667
30	Rubber and miscellaneous plastics products	20,607	20,891
31	Leather and leather products	2,899	3,528
32	Stone, clay, glass, and concrete products	21,423	22,092
33	Primary metal industries	5,738	6,138
34	Fabricated metal products, except machinery and transportation equipment	30,030	31,899
35	Industrial and commercial machinery and computer equipment	38,131	37,466
36	Electronic and other electrical equipment and components, except computer equipment	61,015	61,885
37	Transportation equipment	48,715	51,244
38	Measuring, analyzing, and controlling instruments; photographic, medical, and optical goods; watches and clocks	33,972	36,614
39	Miscellaneous manufacturing industries	9,202	9,981
40-49	Transportation, communications, and public utilities	294,613	305,494
41	Passenger transportation	13,105	14,835
42	Motor freight transportation and warehousing	69,899	59,704
44	Water transportation	20,516	20,715
45	Transportation by air	51,406	68,899
46	Pipelines, except natural gas	133	127
47	Transportation services	31,442	33,245
48	Telecommunications	72,989	73,145

See footnotes at end of table.

Continued . . .

University of Florida   **Bureau of Economic and Business Research**

Table 6.03. EMPLOYMENT: AVERAGE MONTHLY PRIVATE EMPLOYMENT COVERED BY UNEMPLOYMENT COMPENSATION LAW BY INDUSTRY IN FLORIDA, 1995 AND 1996 (Continued)

SIC code	Industry	1995	1996
40-49	Transportation, communications, and public utilities (Continued)		
49	Electric, gas, and sanitary services	35,124	34,806
50-51	Wholesale trade	318,176	333,607
50	Wholesale trade--durable goods	184,026	195,496
51	Wholesale trade--nondurable goods	134,150	138,111
52-59	Retail trade	1,229,421	1,275,150
52	Building materials, hardware, garden supply, and mobile home dealers	46,156	49,344
53	General merchandise stores	146,282	150,817
54	Food stores	228,790	237,589
55	Automotive dealers and gasoline service stations	120,179	125,816
56	Apparel and accessory stores	67,700	67,224
57	Furniture and home furnishings stores	59,024	60,738
58	Eating and drinking places	420,906	437,562
59	Miscellaneous retail	140,385	146,062
60-67	Finance, insurance, and real estate	372,171	386,730
60	Depository institutions	94,825	95,077
61	Nondeposit credit institutions	34,869	39,010
62	Security and commodity brokers, dealers, exchanges, and services	23,941	25,693
63	Insurance carriers	65,213	66,696
64	Insurance agents, brokers, and service	43,088	45,633
65	Real estate	100,885	104,667
67	Holding and other investment offices	9,351	9,954
70-89	Services	1,916,467	1,973,897
70	Hotels, rooming houses, camps, and other lodging places	137,217	142,486
72	Personal services	67,513	69,725
73	Business services	516,914	512,254
75	Automotive repair services, and parking	61,069	65,910
76	Miscellaneous repair services	24,193	25,240
78	Motion pictures	17,914	19,660
79	Amusement and recreation services	122,578	131,203
80	Health services	538,208	557,035
81	Legal services	59,075	60,734
82	Educational services	47,768	50,514
83	Social services	109,165	110,817
84	Museums, art galleries, botanical and zoological gardens	3,268	3,506
86	Membership organizations	49,309	50,674
87	Engineering, accounting, research, management and related services	143,410	154,754
88	Private households	17,253	17,006
89	Services, NEC	1,614	2,383
99	Nonclassifiable establishments	31,410	24,877

NEC Not elsewhere classified.
Note: Private employment. Data for 1995 are revised and data for 1996 are preliminary. Detail may not add to totals due to disclosure editing and/or rounding. See Tables 23.70, 23.71, 23.72, 23.73, and 23.74 for public employment data.

Source: State of Florida, Department of Labor and Employment Security, Bureau of Labor Market Information, "Employment and Wages" (ES-202), unpublished data.

Table 6.04. EMPLOYMENT AND PAYROLL: AVERAGE MONTHLY PRIVATE REPORTING UNITS
EMPLOYMENT, AND PAYROLL COVERED BY UNEMPLOYMENT COMPENSATION LAW
FOR ALL INDUSTRIES IN THE STATE AND COUNTIES OF FLORIDA
1995 AND 1996

County	Number of reporting units	Number of employees	Payroll ($1,000)	County	Number of reporting units	Number of employees	Payroll ($1,000)
			All industries, 1995 A/ (SIC codes 01-99)				
Florida	386,421	5,106,891	10,257,365	Lake	3,585	44,653	72,649
				Lee	9,965	119,778	214,280
Alachua	4,756	67,812	116,973	Leon	5,778	77,506	140,304
Baker	255	2,708	3,521	Levy	512	5,135	6,863
Bay	3,702	44,184	70,019	Liberty	82	906	1,380
Bradford	328	3,732	5,625	Madison	319	3,725	5,290
Brevard	9,856	139,826	309,393	Manatee	4,671	73,871	123,909
Broward	43,721	491,152	1,060,748	Marion	4,734	57,942	99,701
Calhoun	223	1,939	2,490	Martin	3,744	36,208	71,199
Charlotte	2,413	26,000	43,688	Monroe	3,323	28,068	45,732
Citrus	1,927	19,976	34,682	Nassau	1,004	11,374	20,560
Clay	2,224	25,143	38,837	Okaloosa	4,118	50,700	78,850
Collier	6,725	72,263	133,476	Okeechobee	687	7,326	11,176
Columbia	992	11,748	18,276	Orange	22,568	438,900	920,029
Dade	65,747	780,109	1,724,150	Osceola	2,590	37,567	58,648
De Soto	503	5,741	7,191	Palm Beach	32,056	348,879	802,852
Dixie	190	1,543	2,202	Pasco	5,130	55,035	91,304
Duval	18,476	333,448	706,771	Pinellas	23,640	331,502	669,536
Escambia	6,127	94,507	172,502	Polk	8,808	140,529	267,897
Flagler	711	7,637	12,741	Putnam	1,083	14,885	26,607
Franklin	284	2,115	2,705	St. Johns	2,575	26,625	48,281
Gadsden	606	8,100	11,668	St. Lucie	3,314	39,018	71,916
Gilchrist	144	1,148	1,538	Santa Rosa	1,612	16,912	30,300
Glades	91	663	1,045	Sarasota	10,005	105,319	219,008
Gulf	221	2,674	5,607	Seminole	8,356	93,820	206,374
Hamilton	169	2,903	6,257	Sumter	478	4,588	7,345
Hardee	530	5,986	7,657	Suwannee	519	7,281	10,371
Hendry	584	11,627	16,591	Taylor	395	5,055	10,102
Hernando	1,894	19,600	31,737	Union	126	1,638	2,296
Highlands	1,699	18,764	26,766	Volusia	9,400	113,813	187,516
Hillsborough	23,706	426,956	884,465	Wakulla	230	2,158	3,325
Holmes	215	2,034	2,454	Walton	577	7,185	9,818
Indian River	3,201	31,390	56,243	Washington	292	3,343	4,731
Jackson	724	8,380	12,118	Multicounty 1/	6,866	120,400	235,329
Jefferson	238	1,939	2,545	Out-of-			
Lafayette	84	679	722	state 2/	22	820	1,894

See footnotes at end of table.

Continued . . .

Table 6.04. EMPLOYMENT AND PAYROLL: AVERAGE MONTHLY PRIVATE REPORTING UNITS
EMPLOYMENT, AND PAYROLL COVERED BY UNEMPLOYMENT COMPENSATION LAW
FOR ALL INDUSTRIES IN THE STATE AND COUNTIES OF FLORIDA
1995 AND 1996 (Continued)

County	Number of reporting units	Number of employees	Payroll ($1,000)	County	Number of reporting units	Number of employees	Payroll ($1,000)
			All industries, 1996 B/	(SIC codes 01-99)			
Florida	396,277	5,274,322	11,010,717	Lake	3,806	47,843	79,653
				Lee	10,503	123,016	229,537
Alachua	4,928	70,605	124,798	Leon	5,978	78,757	150,792
Baker	231	2,603	3,364	Levy	517	5,384	7,609
Bay	3,716	46,231	75,805	Liberty	76	895	1,450
Bradford	328	3,872	6,040	Madison	317	3,826	5,593
Brevard	9,923	141,745	320,046	Manatee	5,178	88,867	150,147
Broward	44,627	514,949	1,148,238	Marion	4,967	61,395	107,982
Calhoun	227	2,115	2,977	Martin	3,884	38,803	77,426
Charlotte	2,486	27,281	47,551	Monroe	3,354	29,015	49,547
Citrus	2,017	20,995	37,084	Nassau	1,053	11,745	21,921
Clay	2,285	26,597	42,695	Okaloosa	4,247	52,735	86,372
Collier	7,168	76,002	146,671	Okeechobee	706	7,907	11,826
Columbia	1,047	12,638	21,283	Orange	23,111	463,467	1,000,326
Dade	65,869	793,692	1,813,797	Osceola	2,705	38,617	62,163
De Soto	506	5,822	7,801	Palm Beach	32,623	367,311	877,607
Dixie	180	1,475	2,353	Pasco	5,377	58,083	98,116
Duval	18,628	344,247	764,513	Pinellas	24,063	344,282	724,657
Escambia	6,399	96,395	182,294	Polk	9,018	144,845	289,733
Flagler	771	8,540	14,914	Putnam	1,110	14,139	25,265
Franklin	283	1,811	2,368	St. Johns	2,662	27,685	48,281
Gadsden	607	8,195	12,058	St. Lucie	3,340	39,526	71,916
Gilchrist	147	1,243	1,716	Santa Rosa	1,703	18,283	30,300
Glades	92	717	1,155	Sarasota	10,509	113,048	219,008
Gulf	222	2,643	5,669	Seminole	8,698	100,071	206,374
Hamilton	170	2,829	6,293	Sumter	484	4,815	7,345
Hardee	522	5,826	7,961	Suwannee	531	7,409	10,371
Hendry	597	11,677	16,950	Taylor	373	5,147	10,555
Hernando	1,980	21,200	35,019	Union	133	1,592	2,416
Highlands	1,672	18,700	27,560	Volusia	9,505	115,107	196,424
Hillsborough	24,278	447,955	962,955	Wakulla	233	2,210	3,612
Holmes	220	2,053	2,609	Walton	586	7,533	10,660
Indian River	3,264	32,967	62,479	Washington	295	3,494	4,926
Jackson	727	8,304	12,211	Multicounty 1/	8,167	82,144	206,374
Jefferson	239	1,978	2,620	Out-of-			
Lafayette	82	711	768	state 2/	33	722	1,819

A/ Revised.
B/ Preliminary.
1/ Reporting units without a fixed location within the state or of unknown county
location.
2/ Employment based in Florida, but working out of the state or country.
Note: Private employment. Detail may not add to totals due to disclosure editing
and/or rounding. See Tables 23.70, 23.71, 23.72, 23.73, and 23.74 for public employment data.

Source: State of Florida, Department of Labor and Employment Security, Bureau of
Labor Market Information, "Employment and Wages" (ES-202), unpublished data.

Table 6.05. EMPLOYMENT: AVERAGE MONTHLY PRIVATE EMPLOYMENT COVERED BY UNEMPLOYMENT COMPENSATION LAW BY MAJOR INDUSTRY GROUP IN THE STATE AND COUNTIES OF FLORIDA, 1995 AND 1996

1995 A/

County	All industries (01-99)	Agriculture forestry and fishing (01-09)	Mining (10-14)	Construction (15-17)	Manufacturing (20-39)	Transportation communications and public utilities (40-49)	Wholesale trade (50-51)	Retail trade (52-59)	Finance insurance and real estate (60-67)	Services (70-89)	Other (99)
Florida	5,106,891	152,914	6,867	304,463	480,388	294,613	318,176	1,229,421	372,171	1,916,467	31,410
Alachua	67,812	1,205	(NA)	3,941	5,423	2,070	2,115	21,160	4,346	27,320	204
Baker	2,708	(NA)	(NA)	153	255	170	70	987	106	627	(NA)
Bay	44,184	227	(NA)	3,459	2,856	2,174	2,193	16,049	2,972	14,091	164
Bradford	3,732	32	(NA)	285	401	164	333	1,375	106	1,020	(NA)
Brevard	139,826	1,716	37	8,474	26,862	4,386	4,516	34,587	5,526	53,123	598
Broward	491,152	5,666	166	32,372	41,538	28,402	34,092	128,216	40,907	175,561	4,232
Calhoun	1,939	131	(NA)	187	291	41	149	550	63	503	(NA)
Charlotte	26,000	582	(NA)	2,042	892	997	537	8,840	1,486	10,506	83
Citrus	19,976	259	34	1,679	1,219	1,826	423	6,226	1,057	7,206	47
Clay	25,143	677	(NA)	2,076	1,516	934	703	10,194	818	7,931	111
Collier	72,263	10,702	34	7,217	2,300	2,001	1,964	18,807	4,473	24,392	372
Columbia	11,748	146	(NA)	968	1,598	497	844	3,901	507	3,253	34
Dade	780,109	11,839	(NA)	35,875	76,665	76,188	72,732	163,736	65,198	271,097	6,403
De Soto	5,741	2,631	(NA)	168	98	155	191	1,249	166	1,075	(NA)
Dixie	1,543	(NA)	(NA)	(NA)	521	63	60	446	47	184	(NA)
Duval	333,448	2,828	(NA)	20,667	28,874	27,716	22,678	69,932	45,665	113,709	1,187
Escambia	94,507	727	(NA)	7,969	8,664	5,234	5,033	24,607	4,608	37,396	185
Flagler	7,637	299	(NA)	431	1,540	224	120	2,053	614	2,303	47
Franklin	2,115	31	(NA)	86	129	118	175	594	142	808	29
Gadsden	8,100	1,878	(NA)	427	1,337	239	458	1,934	244	1,383	(NA)
Gilchrist	1,148	229	(NA)	28	155	34	72	214	56	354	(NA)
Glades	663	237	(NA)	24	(NA)	(NA)	7	174	14	95	(NA)

See footnotes at end of table.

Continued . . .

Table 6.05. EMPLOYMENT: AVERAGE MONTHLY PRIVATE EMPLOYMENT COVERED BY UNEMPLOYMENT COMPENSATION LAW BY MAJOR INDUSTRY GROUP IN THE STATE AND COUNTIES OF FLORIDA, 1995 AND 1996 (Continued)

1995 A/ (Continued)

County	All industries (01-99)	Agriculture forestry and fishing (01-09)	Mining (10-14)	Construction (15-17)	Manufacturing (20-39)	Transportation communications and public utilities (40-49)	Wholesale trade (50-51)	Retail trade (52-59)	Finance insurance and real estate (60-67)	Services (70-89)	Other (99)
Gulf	2,674	35	(NA)	(NA)	(NA)	282	15	451	127	514	(NA)
Hamilton	2,903	(NA)	(NA)	61	(NA)	85	(NA)	406	19	400	(NA)
Hardee	5,986	2,677	(NA)	306	239	117	320	958	232	1,002	(NA)
Hendry	11,627	6,534	(NA)	255	1,113	(NA)	195	1,530	270	1,238	(NA)
Hernando	19,600	294	323	1,372	1,247	906	595	6,761	1,128	6,918	56
Highlands	18,764	3,524	(NA)	1,051	1,358	624	528	5,158	852	5,597	42
Hillsborough	426,956	11,692	(NA)	22,226	35,933	26,461	34,336	84,974	37,969	171,293	2,059
Holmes	2,034	(NA)	(NA)	84	488	60	72	565	56	689	(NA)
Indian River	31,390	3,865	(NA)	2,591	2,113	650	938	8,304	1,656	11,143	122
Jackson	8,380	204	(NA)	402	1,878	296	762	2,730	463	1,587	27
Jefferson	1,939	249	(NA)	130	215	109	61	449	119	592	(NA)
Lafayette	679	239	(NA)	32	(NA)	23	53	104	(NA)	56	(NA)
Lake	44,653	3,184	289	3,244	4,316	2,113	1,420	11,291	2,912	15,634	249
Lee	119,778	4,476	(NA)	10,742	6,087	6,371	4,910	35,509	8,170	42,943	480
Leon	77,506	839	(NA)	4,624	3,506	3,276	3,304	24,943	4,843	31,925	216
Levy	5,135	528	(NA)	543	351	277	184	1,867	267	974	34
Liberty	906	(NA)	(NA)	(NA)	279	100	(NA)	131	(NA)	229	(NA)
Madison	3,725	155	(NA)	45	1,281	116	151	834	81	1,012	(NA)
Manatee	73,871	5,445	(NA)	3,326	11,568	1,502	2,272	17,266	2,872	29,282	331
Marion	57,942	2,073	96	3,784	10,365	2,445	4,329	17,128	3,057	14,492	173
Martin	36,208	2,255	(NA)	3,124	2,561	1,753	1,001	10,151	2,289	12,872	198
Monroe	28,068	409	(NA)	2,069	512	1,664	673	10,345	1,443	10,672	264
Nassau	11,374	623	(NA)	921	1,928	448	263	3,273	388	3,463	(NA)
Okaloosa	50,700	424	(NA)	3,717	4,043	1,853	1,152	16,822	3,794	18,689	204

See footnotes at end of table.

Continued . . .

Table 6.05. EMPLOYMENT: AVERAGE MONTHLY PRIVATE EMPLOYMENT COVERED BY UNEMPLOYMENT COMPENSATION LAW BY MAJOR INDUSTRY GROUP IN THE STATE AND COUNTIES OF FLORIDA, 1995 AND 1996 (Continued)

1995 A/ (Continued)

County	All industries (01-99)	Agriculture forestry and fishing (01-09)	Mining (10-14)	Construction (15-17)	Manufacturing (20-39)	Transportation communications and public utilities (40-49)	Wholesale trade (50-51)	Retail trade (52-59)	Finance insurance and real estate (60-67)	Services (70-89)	Other (99)
Okeechobee	7,326	1,839	(NA)	368	170	196	452	2,118	233	1,914	(NA)
Orange	438,900	8,715	105	22,535	33,727	29,526	27,543	84,605	29,244	200,889	2,010
Osceola	37,567	705	(NA)	2,245	1,768	736	1,530	13,552	2,419	14,468	144
Palm Beach	348,879	17,103	23	23,140	28,990	14,559	17,763	85,585	26,353	132,414	2,950
Pasco	55,035	2,188	(NA)	3,753	3,864	2,501	1,681	17,620	2,898	20,271	220
Pinellas	331,502	2,746	(NA)	16,880	44,843	12,569	18,701	78,624	22,887	132,372	1,856
Polk	140,529	10,076	3,506	7,793	20,310	8,123	7,455	36,930	7,497	38,455	384
Putnam	14,885	737	80	(NA)	3,626	459	383	3,811	526	3,373	(NA)
St. Johns	26,625	914	(NA)	1,358	3,006	522	1,271	8,363	1,160	9,861	157
St. Lucie	39,018	5,513	28	2,477	2,535	2,735	1,718	10,217	2,183	11,434	177
Santa Rosa	16,912	355	153	1,767	2,365	1,044	412	4,444	680	5,614	79
Sarasota	105,319	1,461	(NA)	6,616	8,246	3,572	3,999	29,722	7,666	43,460	531
Seminole	93,820	1,807	(NA)	8,474	9,560	4,796	6,215	28,897	5,791	27,620	656
Sumter	4,588	242	70	192	561	460	293	1,686	202	865	17
Suwannee	7,281	(NA)	44	423	(NA)	346	343	1,845	284	1,611	(NA)
Taylor	5,055	94	(NA)	(NA)	1,827	111	(NA)	1,283	226	807	(NA)
Union	1,638	59	(NA)	(NA)	(NA)	333	(NA)	207	(NA)	429	(NA)
Volusia	113,813	3,894	(NA)	6,862	11,916	3,466	4,865	34,316	5,795	42,246	(NA)
Wakulla	2,158	(NA)	(NA)	186	617	97	36	629	112	422	(NA)
Walton	7,185	168	(NA)	427	1,098	415	174	1,956	337	2,535	(NA)
Washington	3,343	73	(NA)	273	923	264	94	927	67	690	(NA)
Multicounty 1/	120,400	(NA)	(NA)	2,672	933	2,103	15,999	4,156	3,392	86,920	(NA)
Out-of-state 2/	820	(NA)	(NA)	(NA)	(NA)	(NA)	(NA)	(NA)	(NA)	(NA)	(NA)

See footnotes at end of table.

Continued . . .

Table 6.05. EMPLOYMENT: AVERAGE MONTHLY PRIVATE EMPLOYMENT COVERED BY UNEMPLOYMENT COMPENSATION LAW BY MAJOR INDUSTRY GROUP IN THE STATE AND COUNTIES OF FLORIDA, 1995 AND 1996 (Continued)

1996 B/

County	All industries (01-99)	Agriculture forestry and fishing (01-09)	Mining (10-14)	Construction (15-17)	Manufacturing (20-39)	Transportation communications and public utilities (40-49)	Wholesale trade (50-51)	Retail trade (52-59)	Finance insurance and real estate (60-67)	Services (70-89)	Other (99)
Florida	5,274,322	154,230	6,894	324,827	488,618	305,494	333,607	1,275,150	386,730	1,973,897	24,877
Alachua	70,605	1,239	(NA)	4,288	5,521	2,237	2,312	21,819	4,722	28,281	155
Baker	2,603	309	(NA)	168	228	156	55	925	77	685	(NA)
Bay	46,231	277	(NA)	4,037	3,032	2,214	2,294	16,328	3,048	14,943	59
Bradford	3,872	35	(NA)	220	571	166	347	1,349	109	1,073	(NA)
Brevard	141,745	1,760	37	9,295	26,018	4,516	4,888	35,259	5,581	53,959	432
Broward	514,949	5,866	138	33,638	42,783	30,050	35,797	132,247	42,857	187,941	3,634
Calhoun	2,115	131	(NA)	199	271	(NA)	158	551	69	528	(NA)
Charlotte	27,281	619	(NA)	2,292	1,045	943	639	9,302	1,543	10,792	59
Citrus	20,995	286	(NA)	1,767	1,186	1,896	455	6,498	1,073	7,737	66
Clay	26,597	676	176	2,311	1,658	965	748	10,721	885	8,376	80
Collier	76,002	10,305	46	8,143	2,481	2,230	2,057	19,528	4,730	26,056	426
Columbia	12,638	171	(NA)	1,029	1,886	616	868	4,111	532	3,418	8
Dade	793,692	11,825	377	34,762	76,989	79,087	74,532	166,719	65,721	278,576	5,104
De Soto	5,822	2,636	(NA)	182	229	116	195	1,249	182	1,029	(NA)
Dixie	1,475	18	(NA)	94	543	72	59	420	50	165	(NA)
Duval	344,247	2,985	(NA)	22,179	29,589	27,841	24,417	72,906	46,654	116,912	560
Escambia	96,395	762	119	8,448	8,846	5,299	5,377	26,162	4,982	36,218	184
Flagler	8,540	304	(NA)	482	1,655	211	144	2,387	561	2,778	13
Franklin	1,811	25	(NA)	124	131	110	180	576	163	477	17
Gadsden	8,195	1,845	(NA)	497	1,408	256	355	1,890	235	1,501	(NA)
Gilchrist	1,243	240	(NA)	42	179	23	73	222	52	411	(NA)
Glades	717	244	(NA)	48	(NA)	(NA)	16	192	17	96	(NA)
Gulf	2,643	25	(NA)	202	928	280	40	429	137	595	7

See footnotes at end of table.

Continued . . .

Table 6.05. EMPLOYMENT: AVERAGE MONTHLY PRIVATE EMPLOYMENT COVERED BY UNEMPLOYMENT COMPENSATION LAW BY MAJOR INDUSTRY GROUP IN THE STATE AND COUNTIES OF FLORIDA, 1995 AND 1996 (Continued)

1996 B/ (Continued)

County	All industries (01-99)	Agriculture forestry and fishing (01-09)	Mining (10-14)	Construction (15-17)	Manufacturing (20-39)	Transportation communications and public utilities (40-49)	Wholesale trade (50-51)	Retail trade (52-59)	Finance insurance and real estate (60-67)	Services (70-89)	Other (99)
Hamilton	2,829	(NA)	(NA)	59	(NA)	158	22	399	28	368	(NA)
Hardee	5,826	2,464	(NA)	277	249	126	256	992	239	1,063	(NA)
Hendry	11,677	6,418	(NA)	263	1,155	413	224	1,640	274	1,225	17
Hernando	21,200	308	331	1,621	1,318	911	750	7,368	1,166	7,341	87
Highlands	18,700	3,492	(NA)	1,038	1,387	632	538	5,154	957	5,442	26
Hillsborough	447,955	11,017	(NA)	24,111	35,772	27,526	33,724	90,230	40,780	183,037	1,734
Holmes	2,053	(NA)	(NA)	113	445	82	68	541	62	718	(NA)
Indian River	32,967	3,802	(NA)	2,671	2,210	676	996	8,616	1,756	12,142	90
Jackson	8,304	209	(NA)	391	1,729	353	776	2,735	444	1,626	11
Jefferson	1,978	238	(NA)	126	178	102	67	517	123	605	24
Lafayette	711	254	(NA)	28	161	25	77	92	(NA)	55	(NA)
Lake	47,843	3,356	308	3,580	4,673	2,114	1,584	12,250	3,151	16,698	131
Lee	123,016	4,022	(NA)	12,097	6,719	6,482	5,132	36,826	8,169	43,228	245
Leon	78,757	869	(NA)	5,453	3,831	3,410	3,652	23,155	5,130	32,969	255
Levy	5,384	529	(NA)	599	412	330	159	1,921	261	1,040	(NA)
Liberty	895	(NA)	(NA)	(NA)	295	77	(NA)	134	(NA)	231	(NA)
Madison	3,826	182	(NA)	45	1,212	124	142	881	78	1,148	15
Manatee	88,867	6,165	(NA)	4,257	11,245	1,650	2,953	19,210	3,094	40,069	218
Marion	61,395	2,234	109	4,477	10,639	2,610	4,091	18,162	3,234	15,648	194
Martin	38,803	2,231	(NA)	3,195	2,748	1,725	1,211	11,194	2,418	13,931	145
Monroe	29,015	406	(NA)	2,090	552	1,716	672	10,751	1,492	11,105	215
Nassau	1,745	677	(NA)	850	1,964	411	295	3,454	432	3,644	19
Okaloosa	52,735	512	(NA)	4,181	3,941	1,887	1,320	17,546	3,731	19,488	118
Okeechobee	7,907	1,848	(NA)	361	203	230	456	2,323	300	2,171	17
Orange	463,467	8,644	91	25,045	35,347	29,987	29,217	88,079	30,690	214,623	1,745
Osceola	38,617	763	(NA)	2,035	1,466	713	1,684	14,222	2,336	15,239	160

See footnotes at end of table.   Continued . . .

Table 6.05. EMPLOYMENT: AVERAGE MONTHLY PRIVATE EMPLOYMENT COVERED BY UNEMPLOYMENT COMPENSATION LAW BY MAJOR INDUSTRY GROUP IN THE STATE AND COUNTIES OF FLORIDA, 1995 AND 1996 (Continued)

1996 B/ (Continued)

County	All industries (01-99)	Agriculture forestry and fishing (01-09)	Mining (10-14)	Construction (15-17)	Manufacturing (20-39)	Transportation communications and public utilities (40-49)	Wholesale trade (50-51)	Retail trade (52-59)	Finance insurance and real estate (60-67)	Services (70-89)	Other (99)
Palm Beach	367,311	17,841	24	24,122	28,843	15,317	19,118	88,165	27,832	143,764	2,286
Pasco	58,083	2,243	(NA)	4,273	3,974	2,252	1,760	18,299	2,827	22,202	218
Pinellas	344,282	3,165	10	17,885	45,367	13,508	19,839	80,082	23,793	139,222	1,412
Polk	144,845	10,145	3,393	8,470	20,973	8,440	7,976	37,578	7,408	40,236	229
Putnam	14,139	785	81	1,051	3,392	471	436	3,789	564	3,567	(NA)
St. Johns	27,685	972	(NA)	1,446	3,163	603	1,380	8,466	1,189	10,362	88
St. Lucie	39,526	5,217	29	2,703	2,618	2,719	1,719	10,228	2,353	11,810	131
Santa Rosa	18,283	390	144	2,217	2,430	996	443	4,758	742	6,112	52
Sarasota	113,048	1,850	(NA)	7,792	8,999	3,573	4,390	30,827	7,959	47,165	445
Seminole	100,071	1,834	(NA)	9,102	9,788	5,488	6,867	30,933	6,101	29,333	622
Sumter	4,815	277	82	215	596	392	371	1,856	175	835	18
Suwannee	7,409	571	(NA)	427	(NA)	381	371	1,822	302	1,610	(NA)
Taylor	5,147	91	47	581	1,785	110	169	1,287	225	848	(NA)
Union	1,592	69	(NA)	56	239	346	(NA)	210	47	556	(NA)
Volusia	115,107	3,797	(NA)	6,782	12,371	3,340	4,943	34,519	5,869	43,160	327
Wakulla	2,210	44	(NA)	239	589	115	63	580	124	440	(NA)
Walton	7,533	149	(NA)	486	1,072	466	174	2,140	384	2,622	16
Washington	3,494	64	(NA)	381	894	282	77	971	76	719	27
Multicounty 1/	82,144	(NA)	28	3,058	1,117	2,677	17,359	8,439	4,405	41,304	2,591
Out-of-state 2/	722	(NA)	(NA)	(NA)	(NA)	(NA)	(NA)	25	(NA)	(NA)	(NA)

(NA) Not available.
A/ Revised. B/ Preliminary. 1/ Reporting units without a fixed or known location within the state. 2/ Employment based in Florida, but working out of the state or country.
Note: Private employment. Detail may not add to totals due to disclosure editing and/or rounding. See Tables 23.70, 23.71, 23.72, 23.73, and 23.74 for public employment data.
Source: State of Florida, Department of Labor and Employment Security, Bureau of Labor Market Information, "Employment and Wages" (ES-202), unpublished data.

Table 6.06. EMPLOYMENT: AVERAGE MONTHLY EMPLOYMENT COVERED BY UNEMPLOYMENT COMPENSATION LAW IN THE STATE AND METROPOLITAN STATISTICAL AREAS (MSAS) OF FLORIDA, 1996

Metropolitan area	Total 1/	Private	Government Federal	Government State	Government Local
Florida	6,182,521	5,274,322	120,154	200,966	587,079
MSA, total	5,688,457	4,877,104	103,971	172,892	534,490
Daytona Beach	146,163	123,647	1,338	3,155	18,023
Flagler County	10,413	8,540	81	138	1,654
Volusia County	135,750	115,107	1,257	3,017	16,369
Ft. Lauderdale	592,074	514,949	6,876	7,810	62,439
Ft. Myers-Cape Coral	146,164	123,016	1,696	3,284	18,169
Ft. Pierce-Port St. Lucie	91,817	78,329	761	2,114	10,614
Martin County	43,617	38,803	282	860	3,673
St. Lucie County	48,199	39,526	479	1,255	6,941
Gainesville	109,068	70,605	2,879	25,753	9,831
Jacksonville	473,451	410,274	18,144	9,211	35,823
Clay County	31,073	26,597	329	401	3,746
Duval County	394,675	344,247	16,855	7,189	26,384
Nassau County	14,657	11,745	614	266	2,032
St. Johns County	33,046	27,685	345	1,355	3,661
Lakeland-Winter Haven	169,539	144,845	1,403	4,410	18,882
Melbourne-Titusville-Palm Bay	165,918	141,745	5,630	2,199	16,345
Miami	924,672	793,692	17,871	17,079	96,030
Naples	84,279	76,002	549	761	6,968
Ocala	74,411	61,395	640	2,115	10,260
Orlando	729,583	649,998	8,928	13,069	57,588
Lake County	55,334	47,843	484	1,034	5,973
Orange County	515,412	463,467	6,840	10,657	34,448
Osceola County	45,319	38,617	250	492	5,960
Seminole County	113,518	100,071	1,354	886	11,208
Panama City	57,949	46,231	3,354	1,161	7,202
Pensacola	141,318	114,678	7,084	5,325	14,231
Escambia County	118,213	96,395	6,378	4,697	10,743
Santa Rosa County	23,105	18,283	706	629	3,489
Sarasota-Bradenton	224,058	201,915	1,901	2,631	17,611
Manatee County	99,583	88,867	1,058	979	8,680
Sarasota County	124,475	113,048	844	1,652	8,931
Tallahassee	144,459	86,952	1,787	43,187	12,535
Gadsden County	14,006	8,195	121	3,922	1,769
Leon County	130,453	78,757	1,666	39,265	10,766
Tampa-St. Petersburg-Clearwater	994,428	871,520	17,503	21,403	84,002
Hernando County	26,015	21,200	269	598	3,948
Hillsborough County	513,820	447,955	10,839	14,986	40,040
Pasco County	69,302	58,083	620	1,264	9,335
Pinellas County	385,293	344,282	5,776	4,555	30,679
West Palm Beach-Boca Raton	419,109	367,311	5,629	8,228	37,940

1/ Total private and public employment. Private industry data appear in various tables throughout the *Abstract*. See Section 23.00 for additional public employment tables.

Note: Data are preliminary. Detail may not add to totals due to disclosure editing and/or rounding.

Source: State of Florida, Department of Labor and Employment Security, Bureau of Labor Market Information, "Employment and Wages" (ES-202), unpublished data.

Table 6.09. LABOR FORCE PARTICIPATION: LABOR FORCE STATUS OF THE POPULATION
16 YEARS OLD AND OVER BY SEX, RACE AND HISPANIC ORIGIN, IN FLORIDA
AND THE UNITED STATES, ANNUAL AVERAGES 1994

Area and population group	Civilian noninsti- tutional popu- lation (1,000)	Civilian labor force		Employment		Unemployment		
		Number (1,000)	Per- centage of pop- ulation	Number (1,000)	Per- centage of pop- ulation	Number (1,000)	Rate	Error range of rate 1/
Florida								
Total	10,894	6,824	62.6	6,376	58.5	448	6.6	6.3-6.9
Men	5,179	3,660	70.7	3,430	66.2	229	6.3	5.8-6.7
Women	5,715	3,164	55.4	2,945	51.5	219	6.9	6.4-7.4
Both sexes, 16-19 years	671	353	52.7	281	42.0	72	20.4	18.5-22.3
White	9,139	5,667	62.0	5,351	58.6	316	5.6	5.2-5.9
Men	4,381	3,075	70.2	2,912	66.5	163	5.3	4.9-5.7
Women	4,758	2,591	54.5	2,438	51.3	153	5.9	5.4-6.4
Both sexes, 16-19 years	504	283	56.1	235	46.7	47	16.7	14.6-18.8
Black	1,496	998	66.7	881	58.9	117	11.7	10.7-12.8
Men	675	494	73.1	436	64.5	58	11.7	10.2-13.2
Women	821	504	61.5	445	54.2	59	11.8	10.3-13.2
Both sexes, 16-19 years	145	61	42.4	38	26.4	23	37.8	33.3-42.2
Hispanic origin 2	1,622	1,045	64.4	949	58.5	96	9.2	8.2-10.1
Men	799	606	75.8	557	69.7	49	8.1	7.0-9.3
Women	822	439	53.4	392	47.7	47	10.6	9.1-12.1
Both sexes, 16-19 years	137	69	50.4	54	39.4	15	21.8	16.9-26.6
United States								
Total	196,814	131,056	66.6	123,060	62.5	7,996	6.1	6.0-6.2
Men	94,355	70,817	75.1	66,450	70.4	4,367	6.2	6.1-6.3
Women	102,460	60,239	58.8	56,610	55.3	3,629	6.0	5.9-6.1
Both sexes, 16-19 years	14,196	7,481	52.7	6,161	43.4	1,320	17.6	17.1-18.2
White	165,555	111,082	67.1	105,190	63.5	5,892	5.3	5.2-5.4
Men	80,059	60,727	75.9	57,452	71.8	3,275	5.4	5.3-5.5
Women	85,496	50,356	58.9	47,738	55.8	2,617	5.2	5.1-5.3
Both sexes, 16-19 years	11,264	6,357	56.4	5,398	47.9	960	15.1	14.6-15.6
Black	22,879	14,502	63.4	12,835	56.1	1,666	11.5	11.1-11.9
Men	10,258	7,089	69.1	6,241	60.8	848	12.0	11.4-12.5
Women	12,621	7,413	58.7	6,595	52.3	818	11.0	10.5-11.5
Both sexes, 16-19 years	2,211	852	38.5	552	24.9	300	35.2	33.1-37.4
Hispanic origin 2	18,117	11,975	66.1	10,788	59.5	1,187	9.9	9.6-10.3
Men	9,104	7,210	79.2	6,530	71.7	680	9.4	9.0-9.9
Women	9,014	4,765	52.9	4,258	47.2	508	10.7	10.1-11.2
Both sexes, 16-19 years	1,818	807	44.4	609	33.5	198	24.5	22.8-26.2

1/ If repeated samples were drawn from the same population and an error range con-
structed around each sample estimate, in 9 out of 10 cases the true value based on a
complete census of the population would be contained within these error ranges.
    2/ Persons of Hispanic origin may be of any race.
Source: U.S., Department of Labor, Bureau of Labor Statistics, *Geographic Profile
of Employment and Unemployment, 1994.*

Table 6.10. LABOR FORCE PARTICIPATION: FULL- AND PART-TIME STATUS AND UNEMPLOYED PERSONS SEEKING WORK BY SEX, AGE, AND RACE AND HISPANIC ORIGIN IN FLORIDA, ANNUAL AVERAGES 1994

(in thousands)

Population group	Total	Employed 1/									Unemployed	
		Full-time workers				Part-time workers 2/						
		35 hours or more	1 to 34 hours			Total	At work			Seeking full-time work	Seeking part-time work
			Economic reasons	Non-economic reasons	Not at work		Part-time for economic reasons	Part-time for non-economic reasons	Not at work		
Total	5,251	4,576	80	397	198	1,124	184	872	68.0	361	87
Men	3,009	2,660	52	197	100	421	84	312	25.0	196	33
Women	2,242	1,915	28	200	98	703	100	560	43.0	165	54
Both sexes, 16-19 years	82	69	4	8	2	199	20	172	8.0	36	36
White	4,414	3,865	56	326	167	936	133	745	58.0	248	68
Black	722	612	21	62	28	158	46	104	8.0	100	18
Hispanic origin 3/	788	703	13	46	25	162	41	114	6.0	77	19

1/ Employed persons are classified as full- or part-time workers based on their usual weekly hours at all jobs regardless of the number of hours they are at work during the reference week. Persons absent from work are classified according to their usual status.
2/ Includes some persons at work 35 hours or more classified by their reason for working part time.
3/ Persons of Hispanic origin may be of any race.

Source: U.S., Department of Labor, Bureau of Labor Statistics, *Geographic Profile of Employment and Unemployment, 1994.*

Table 6.11. LABOR FORCE: ESTIMATES BY EMPLOYMENT STATUS IN THE UNITED STATES AND IN THE STATE AND COUNTIES OF FLORIDA, 1994, 1995, AND 1996

County	1994 A/				1995 A/				1996 B/			
	Labor force	Employ-ment	Unemployment Number	Rate	Labor force	Employ-ment	Unemployment Number	Rate	Labor force	Employ-ment	Unemployment Number	Rate
United States 1/	131,056	123,060	7,996	6.1	132,304	124,900	7,404	5.6	133,943	126,708	7,236	5.4
Florida	6,824,000	6,376,000	448,000	6.6	6,830,000	6,455,000	375,000	5.5	6,938,000	6,586,000	352,000	5.1
Alachua	100,917	97,139	3,778	3.7	100,035	97,184	2,851	2.9	100,935	98,138	2,797	2.8
Baker	9,449	8,886	563	6.0	8,668	8,206	462	5.3	8,497	8,088	409	4.8
Bay	63,818	58,379	5,439	8.5	62,985	58,803	4,182	6.6	64,572	60,731	3,841	5.9
Bradford	9,354	8,874	480	5.1	9,301	8,951	350	3.8	9,742	9,394	348	3.6
Brevard	207,600	192,769	14,831	7.1	200,861	187,722	13,139	6.5	197,794	187,038	10,756	5.4
Broward	713,544	667,364	46,180	6.5	719,043	678,033	41,010	5.7	733,252	695,512	37,740	5.1
Calhoun	4,565	4,265	300	6.6	4,536	4,326	210	4.6	5,169	4,941	228	4.4
Charlotte	44,701	41,997	2,704	6.0	43,986	41,917	2,069	4.7	44,430	42,575	1,855	4.2
Citrus	34,646	31,896	2,750	7.9	34,136	31,804	2,332	6.8	35,412	33,281	2,131	6.0
Clay	57,869	55,362	2,507	4.3	60,916	59,033	1,883	3.1	63,610	61,721	1,889	3.0
Collier	80,129	73,704	6,425	8.0	81,500	75,839	5,661	6.9	83,140	78,316	4,824	5.8
Columbia	21,741	19,931	1,810	8.3	21,990	20,734	1,256	5.7	23,525	22,397	1,128	4.8
Dade	1,039,186	956,198	82,988	8.0	1,032,583	957,048	75,535	7.3	1,030,090	955,205	74,885	7.3
De Soto	9,512	8,774	738	7.8	9,710	9,057	653	6.7	10,153	9,443	710	7.0
Dixie	3,892	3,579	313	8.0	4,043	3,709	334	8.3	3,946	3,627	319	8.1
Duval	364,928	346,043	18,885	5.2	365,509	351,572	13,937	3.8	368,467	354,629	13,838	3.8
Escambia	124,670	118,312	6,358	5.1	121,039	115,932	5,107	4.2	119,729	114,857	4,872	4.1
Flagler	13,187	12,530	657	5.0	14,143	13,651	492	3.5	14,971	14,464	507	3.4
Franklin	4,739	4,532	207	4.4	4,832	4,627	205	4.2	4,286	3,988	298	7.0
Gadsden	19,085	17,902	1,183	6.2	18,827	18,029	798	4.2	18,806	17,886	920	4.9
Gilchrist	4,165	3,961	204	4.9	4,214	4,061	153	3.6	4,420	4,238	182	4.1
Glades	3,453	3,122	331	9.6	3,426	3,096	330	9.6	3,687	3,338	349	9.5

See footnotes at end of table.

Continued . .

Table 6.11. LABOR FORCE: ESTIMATES BY EMPLOYMENT STATUS IN THE UNITED STATES AND IN THE STATE AND COUNTIES OF FLORIDA, 1994, 1995, AND 1996 (Continued)

County	1994 A/ Labor force	Employ-ment	Unemployment Number	Rate	1995 A/ Labor force	Employ-ment	Unemployment Number	Rate	1996 B/ Labor force	Employ-ment	Unemployment Number	Rate
Gulf	5,439	5,080	359	6.6	5,779	5,458	321	5.6	5,700	5,316	384	6.7
Hamilton	3,379	3,044	335	9.9	3,502	3,261	241	6.9	3,772	3,491	281	7.4
Hardee	9,806	8,388	1,418	14.5	11,159	9,723	1,436	12.9	11,416	9,912	1,504	13.2
Hendry	15,713	13,345	2,368	15.1	15,702	13,309	2,393	15.2	16,279	14,014	2,265	13.9
Hernando	40,184	37,198	2,986	7.4	41,718	39,458	2,260	5.4	42,731	40,790	1,941	4.5
Highlands	26,447	23,853	2,594	9.8	27,669	25,279	2,390	8.6	28,108	25,792	2,316	8.2
Hillsborough	487,826	461,488	26,338	5.4	489,853	468,599	21,254	4.3	494,975	476,009	18,966	3.8
Holmes	6,687	6,199	488	7.3	6,896	6,422	474	6.9	6,686	6,226	460	6.9
Indian River	39,270	35,128	4,142	10.5	41,172	37,151	4,021	9.8	43,208	39,349	3,859	8.9
Jackson	19,485	18,070	1,415	7.3	18,866	17,852	1,014	5.4	18,698	17,864	834	4.5
Jefferson	5,396	5,107	289	5.4	5,238	4,988	250	4.8	5,271	5,024	247	4.7
Lafayette	2,439	2,313	126	5.2	2,635	2,545	90	3.4	2,551	2,477	74	2.9
Lake	71,383	66,638	4,745	6.6	73,711	69,734	3,977	5.4	77,361	73,871	3,490	4.5
Lee	167,034	158,240	8,794	5.3	170,063	162,995	7,068	4.2	170,212	163,834	6,378	3.7
Leon	121,659	116,849	4,810	4.0	123,663	120,240	3,423	2.8	123,283	119,784	3,499	2.8
Levy	11,846	11,147	699	5.9	11,994	11,417	577	4.8	13,007	12,448	559	4.3
Liberty	2,329	2,231	98	4.2	2,408	2,354	54	2.2	2,452	2,386	66	2.7
Madison	6,919	6,525	394	5.7	7,242	6,947	295	4.1	7,476	7,144	332	4.4
Manatee	100,412	95,455	4,957	4.9	99,370	95,377	3,993	4.0	106,639	102,849	3,790	3.6
Marion	89,549	83,053	6,496	7.3	88,351	83,561	4,790	5.4	91,289	86,852	4,437	4.9
Martin	44,916	41,007	3,909	8.7	44,435	40,970	3,465	7.8	46,396	43,067	3,329	7.2
Monroe	42,497	40,877	1,620	3.8	43,369	42,190	1,179	2.7	44,202	43,023	1,179	2.7
Nassau	24,219	22,823	1,396	5.8	25,342	24,311	1,031	4.1	26,216	25,166	1,050	4.0
Okaloosa	72,892	68,898	3,994	5.5	76,357	73,075	3,282	4.3	74,486	71,610	2,876	3.9
Okeechobee	15,046	13,416	1,630	10.8	14,974	13,465	1,509	10.1	16,899	15,269	1,630	9.6

See footnotes at end of table.

Continued . .

Table 6.11. LABOR FORCE: ESTIMATES BY EMPLOYMENT STATUS IN THE UNITED STATES AND IN THE STATE AND COUNTIES OF FLORIDA, 1994, 1995, AND 1996 (Continued)

County	1994 A/ Labor force	1994 A/ Employ-ment	1994 A/ Unemployment Number	1994 A/ Unemployment Rate	1995 A/ Labor force	1995 A/ Employ-ment	1995 A/ Unemployment Number	1995 A/ Unemployment Rate	1996 B/ Labor force	1996 B/ Employ-ment	1996 B/ Unemployment Number	1996 B/ Unemployment Rate
Orange	426,155	401,471	24,684	5.8	422,112	403,167	18,945	4.5	434,114	417,811	16,303	3.8
Osceola	67,004	62,971	4,033	6.0	68,035	64,743	3,292	4.8	71,243	68,510	2,733	3.8
Palm Beach	456,173	418,300	37,873	8.3	451,190	418,765	32,425	7.2	466,565	435,431	31,134	6.7
Pasco	115,151	107,383	7,768	6.7	118,553	112,470	6,083	5.1	121,282	115,367	5,915	4.9
Pinellas	440,258	417,355	22,903	5.2	440,030	422,104	17,926	4.1	441,877	425,581	16,296	3.7
Polk	199,491	183,007	16,484	8.3	196,632	182,519	14,113	7.2	194,994	182,086	12,908	6.6
Putnam	28,628	26,625	2,003	7.0	29,667	28,154	1,513	5.1	28,872	27,346	1,526	5.3
St. Johns	47,484	44,701	2,783	5.9	51,014	49,223	1,791	3.5	53,302	51,750	1,552	2.9
St. Lucie	73,032	63,264	9,768	13.4	72,536	63,435	9,101	12.5	76,044	66,795	9,249	12.2
Santa Rosa	43,060	40,886	2,174	5.0	45,622	43,702	1,920	4.2	46,882	45,212	1,670	3.6
Sarasota	129,481	123,528	5,953	4.6	127,250	122,908	4,342	3.4	135,824	131,613	4,211	3.1
Seminole	186,908	176,813	10,095	5.4	187,294	179,723	7,571	4.0	193,759	186,942	6,817	3.5
Sumter	11,965	11,135	830	6.9	12,280	11,598	682	5.6	13,642	13,023	619	4.5
Suwannee	12,148	11,281	867	7.1	12,839	12,184	655	5.1	13,134	12,555	579	4.4
Taylor	7,385	6,537	848	11.5	7,533	6,806	727	9.7	7,642	6,908	734	9.6
Union	3,857	3,694	163	4.2	4,110	3,932	178	4.3	3,830	3,650	180	4.7
Volusia	176,467	165,452	11,015	6.2	173,277	164,918	8,359	4.8	173,280	165,946	7,334	4.2
Wakulla	8,990	8,567	423	4.7	8,877	8,497	380	4.3	9,778	9,372	406	4.2
Walton	14,424	13,626	798	5.5	14,460	13,824	636	4.4	14,786	14,145	641	4.3
Washington	7,838	7,265	573	7.3	8,687	8,153	534	6.1	8,883	8,361	522	5.9

A/ Benchmark 1995.
B/ Benchmark 1996.
1/ United States numbers are rounded to thousands. Data are from U.S., Department of Labor, Bureau of Labor Statistics.

Note: Civilian labor force. Data are generated for federal fund allocations. Caution is urged when using these data for short-term economic analysis. Detail may not add to totals because of rounding.

Source: State of Florida, Department of Labor and Employment Security, Bureau of Labor Market Information, *Labor Force Summary: 1996 Annual Averages*, and previous editions.

Table 6.12. LABOR FORCE: ESTIMATES BY EMPLOYMENT STATUS IN THE STATE, METROPOLITAN STATISTICAL AREAS (MSAS) AND SELECTED CITIES OF FLORIDA, 1995 AND 1996

MSA or city 1/	1995 Labor force	1995 Employ-ment	1995 Unemployment Number	1995 Unemployment Rate	1996 Labor force	1996 Employ-ment	1996 Unemployment Number	1996 Unemployment Rate
Florida	6,830,000	6,455,000	375,000	5.5	6,938,000	6,586,000	352,000	5.1
Daytona Beach MSA	187,420	178,570	8,850	4.7	188,250	180,410	7,840	4.2
Ft. Lauderdale MSA	719,043	678,033	41,010	5.7	733,252	695,512	37,740	5.1
Ft. Myers-Cape Coral MSA	170,063	162,995	7,068	4.2	170,212	163,834	6,378	3.7
Ft. Pierce-Port St. Lucie MSA	116,971	104,405	12,566	10.7	122,439	109,862	12,577	10.3
Ft. Walton Beach MSA	76,357	73,075	3,282	4.3	74,486	71,610	2,876	3.9
Gainesville MSA	100,035	97,184	2,851	2.9	100,935	98,138	2,797	2.8
Jacksonville MSA	502,782	484,139	18,643	3.7	511,595	493,266	18,329	3.6
Lakeland-Winter Haven MSA	196,632	182,519	14,113	7.2	194,994	182,086	12,908	6.6
Melbourne-Titusville-Palm Bay MSA	200,861	187,722	13,139	6.5	197,794	187,038	10,756	5.4
Miami MSA	1,032,583	957,048	75,535	7.3	1,030,090	955,205	74,885	7.3
Naples MSA	81,500	75,839	5,661	6.9	83,140	78,316	4,824	5.8
Ocala MSA	88,351	83,561	4,790	5.4	91,289	86,852	4,437	4.9
Orlando MSA	751,153	717,367	33,786	4.5	776,475	747,133	29,342	3.8
Panama City MSA	62,985	58,803	4,182	6.6	64,572	60,731	3,841	5.9
Pensacola MSA	166,660	159,634	7,026	4.2	166,610	160,068	6,542	3.9
Punta Gorda MSA	43,986	41,917	2,069	4.7	44,430	42,575	1,855	4.2
Sarasota-Bradenton MSA	226,620	218,285	8,335	3.7	242,463	234,462	8,001	3.3
Tallahassee MSA	142,489	138,268	4,221	3.0	142,089	137,670	4,419	3.1
Tampa-St. Petersburg-Clearwater MSA	1,090,153	1,042,630	47,523	4.4	1,100,864	1,057,747	43,117	3.9
West Palm Beach-Boca Raton MSA	451,190	418,765	32,425	7.2	466,565	435,431	31,134	6.7
Altamonte Springs	26,220	25,198	1,022	3.9	27,130	26,130	920	3.4
Boca Raton	34,439	32,844	1,595	4.6	35,682	34,151	1,531	4.3
Boynton Beach	22,853	21,175	1,678	7.3	23,629	22,018	1,611	6.8
Bradenton	20,624	19,670	954	4.6	22,117	21,211	906	4.1
Cape Carol	38,801	37,223	1,578	4.1	38,838	37,414	1,424	3.7
Clearwater	52,139	49,887	2,252	4.3	52,347	50,299	2,048	3.9
Coconut Creek	13,988	13,059	929	6.6	14,251	13,396	855	6.0
Cooper City	13,191	12,782	409	3.1	13,487	13,111	376	2.8
Coral Gables	22,943	22,063	880	3.8	22,894	22,021	873	3.8
Coral Springs	49,116	47,095	2,021	4.1	50,169	48,309	1,860	3.7

Continued . . .

See footnotes at end of table.

Table 6.12. LABOR FORCE: ESTIMATES BY EMPLOYMENT STATUS IN THE STATE, METROPOLITAN STATISTICAL AREAS (MSAS) AND SELECTED CITIES OF FLORIDA, 1995 AND 1996 (Continued)

MSA or city 1/	1995 Labor force	1995 Employ-ment	1995 Unemployment Number	1995 Rate	1996 Labor force	1996 Employ-ment	1996 Unemployment Number	1996 Rate
Davie	30,853	29,317	1,536	5.0	31,487	30,073	1,414	4.5
Daytona Beach	30,275	28,338	1,937	6.4	30,214	28,514	1,700	5.6
Deerfield Beach	23,428	22,231	1,197	5.1	23,907	22,805	1,102	4.6
Delray Beach	23,504	21,165	2,339	10.0	24,253	22,007	2,246	9.3
Deltona	(NA)	(NA)	(NA)	(NA)	24,133	22,987	1,146	4.7
Dunedin	16,680	16,097	583	3.5	16,759	16,229	530	3.2
Ft. Lauderdale	88,510	82,211	6,299	7.1	90,128	84,331	5,797	6.4
Ft. Myers	24,693	23,256	1,437	5.8	24,672	23,375	1,297	5.3
Ft. Pierce	17,530	13,957	3,573	20.4	18,328	14,697	3,631	19.8
Gainesville	45,418	43,877	1,541	3.4	45,819	44,307	1,512	3.3
Hallandale	12,267	11,313	954	7.8	12,482	11,604	878	7.0
Hialeah	103,134	95,254	7,880	7.6	102,883	95,071	7,812	7.6
Hollywood	68,204	63,797	4,407	6.5	69,498	65,442	4,056	5.8
Homestead	(NA)	(NA)	(NA)	(NA)	12,805	11,923	882	6.9
Jacksonville	342,769	329,442	13,327	3.9	345,540	332,307	13,233	3.8
Jupiter	14,891	14,137	754	5.1	15,424	14,700	724	4.7
Key West	13,963	13,583	380	2.7	14,231	13,851	380	2.7
Kissimmee	21,648	20,429	1,219	5.6	22,630	21,618	1,012	4.5
Lake Worth	15,316	14,114	1,202	7.8	15,830	14,676	1,154	7.3
Lakeland	34,283	32,029	2,254	6.6	34,015	31,953	2,062	6.1
Largo	32,999	31,839	1,160	3.5	33,155	32,101	1,054	3.2
Lauderdale Lakes	13,423	12,353	1,070	8.0	13,656	12,671	985	7.2
Lauderhill	27,721	26,080	1,641	5.9	28,263	26,753	1,510	5.3
Margate	22,889	21,597	1,292	5.6	23,343	22,154	1,189	5.1
Melbourne	30,573	28,286	2,287	7.5	30,055	28,183	1,872	6.2
Miami	179,654	160,719	18,935	10.5	179,182	160,410	18,772	10.5
Miami Beach	43,928	40,186	3,742	8.5	43,818	40,108	3,710	8.5
Miramar	25,453	24,149	1,304	5.1	25,971	24,771	1,200	4.6
North Lauderdale	17,526	16,585	941	5.4	17,879	17,013	866	4.8
North Miami	28,391	26,158	2,233	7.9	28,322	26,108	2,214	7.8
North Miami Beach	18,504	17,392	1,112	6.0	18,460	17,358	1,102	6.0
Oakland Park	18,178	17,285	893	4.9	18,551	17,730	821	4.4

Continued . . .

See footnotes at end of table.

Table 6.12. LABOR FORCE: ESTIMATES BY EMPLOYMENT STATUS IN THE STATE, METROPOLITAN STATISTICAL AREAS (MSAS) AND SELECTED CITIES OF FLORIDA, 1995 AND 1996 (Continued)

MSA or city 1/	1995 Labor force	1995 Employment	1995 Unemployment Number	1995 Unemployment Rate	1996 Labor force	1996 Employment	1996 Unemployment Number	1996 Unemployment Rate
Ocala	20,418	19,244	1,174	5.7	21,089	20,002	1,087	5.2
Orlando	99,166	94,402	4,764	4.8	101,930	97,831	4,099	4.0
Ormond Beach	14,032	13,558	474	3.4	14,058	13,642	416	3.0
Palm Bay	32,767	30,546	2,221	6.8	32,253	30,434	1,819	5.6
Palm Beach Gardens	13,801	13,300	501	3.6	14,310	13,829	481	3.4
Panama City	16,949	15,602	1,347	7.9	17,351	16,113	1,238	7.1
Pembroke Pines	37,954	36,528	1,426	3.8	38,782	37,470	1,312	3.4
Pensacola	27,006	25,760	1,246	4.6	26,709	25,521	1,188	4.4
Pinellas Park	23,071	22,203	868	3.8	23,175	22,386	789	3.4
Plantation	42,811	41,024	1,787	4.2	43,725	42,081	1,644	3.8
Plant City	12,037	11,521	516	4.3	12,164	11,703	461	3.8
Pompano Beach	38,662	36,052	2,610	6.8	39,383	36,981	2,402	6.1
Port Orange	17,671	17,025	646	3.7	17,698	17,131	567	3.2
Port St. Lucie	28,643	25,837	2,806	9.8	30,058	27,206	2,852	9.5
Riviera Beach	14,583	12,768	1,815	12.4	15,019	13,276	1,743	11.6
St. Petersburg	126,989	121,018	5,971	4.7	127,442	122,015	5,427	4.3
Sanford	18,563	17,620	943	5.1	19,177	18,328	849	4.4
Sarasota	26,463	25,346	1,117	4.2	28,226	27,142	1,084	3.8
Sunrise	35,619	33,768	1,851	5.2	36,342	34,639	1,703	4.7
Tallahassee	78,964	76,245	2,719	3.4	78,735	75,956	2,779	3.5
Tamarac	19,680	18,460	1,220	6.2	20,060	18,937	1,123	5.6
Tampa	156,005	147,598	8,407	5.4	157,434	149,932	7,502	4.8
Titusville	19,958	18,659	1,289	6.5	19,647	18,591	1,056	5.4
Wellington	(NA)	(NA)	(NA)	(NA)	11,912	11,472	440	3.7
West Palm Beach	39,786	36,194	3,592	9.0	41,083	37,634	3,449	8.4
Winter Haven	11,416	10,666	750	6.6	11,326	10,640	686	6.1
Winter Springs	14,357	13,862	495	3.4	14,865	14,419	446	3.0

(NA) Not available.
1/ Metropolitan Statistical Areas (MSAs) and Primary Metropolitan Statistical Areas (PMSAs) based on 1992 MSA designations and cities with a population of 25,000 or more in 1996.
  Note: Civilian labor force.
  Source: State of Florida, Department of Labor and Employment Security, Bureau of Labor Market Information, *Labor Force Summary: 1996 Annual Averages*, and previous edition.

Table 6.20. OCCUPATIONS: PRIVATE INDUSTRY EMPLOYMENT, PARTICIPATION RATE, AND OCCUPATIONAL DISTRIBUTION OF WHITE AND MINORITY EMPLOYEES BY SEX AND BY OCCUPATION IN FLORIDA, 1995

Occupation	All Male	All Female	White Male	White Female	Minority 1/ Male	Minority 1/ Female
		Number	employed	(1,000)		
Total	895,563	878,308	623,502	600,252	272,061	278,056
Officials and managers	115,187	61,953	98,412	50,693	16,775	11,260
Professionals	100,988	132,062	83,556	104,887	17,432	27,175
Technicians	54,333	50,947	41,085	36,409	13,248	14,538
Sales workers	134,740	159,239	98,138	115,485	36,602	43,754
Office and clerical workers	52,764	227,827	35,016	159,731	17,748	68,096
Craft workers	103,126	15,394	78,935	10,680	24,191	4,714
Operatives	124,640	49,574	75,531	24,854	49,109	24,720
Laborers	76,451	28,570	38,423	13,720	38,028	14,850
Service workers	133,334	152,742	74,406	83,793	58,928	68,949
		Participation	rate	(percentage)		
Total	50.5	49.5	35.1	33.8	15.3	15.7
Officials and managers	65.0	35.0	55.6	28.6	9.5	6.4
Professionals	43.3	56.7	35.9	45.0	7.5	11.7
Technicians	51.6	48.4	39.0	34.6	12.6	13.8
Sales workers	45.8	54.2	33.4	39.3	12.5	14.9
Office and clerical workers	18.8	81.2	12.5	56.9	6.3	24.3
Craft workers	87.0	13.0	66.6	9.0	20.4	4.0
Operatives	71.5	28.5	43.4	14.3	28.2	14.2
Laborers	72.8	27.2	36.6	13.1	36.2	14.1
Service workers	46.6	53.4	26.0	29.3	20.6	24.1
		Occupational	distribution	(percentage)		
Total	100.0	100.0	100.0	100.0	100.0	100.0
Officials and managers	12.9	7.1	15.8	8.4	6.2	4.0
Professionals	11.3	15.0	13.4	17.5	6.4	9.8
Technicians	6.1	5.8	6.6	6.1	4.9	5.2
Sales workers	15.0	18.1	15.7	19.2	13.5	15.7
Office and clerical workers	5.9	25.9	5.6	26.6	6.5	24.5
Craft workers	11.5	1.8	12.7	1.8	8.9	1.7
Operatives	13.9	5.6	12.1	4.1	18.1	8.9
Laborers	8.5	3.3	6.2	2.3	14.0	5.3
Service workers	14.9	17.4	11.9	14.0	21.7	24.8

1/ Includes Black, Asian or Pacific Islander, American Indian, Eskimo, or Aleut, and persons of Hispanic origin.
Note: Private industry data, based on 1987 standard industrial classification (SIC) codes, from the 1995 Equal Employment Opportunity employer information report (EEO-1). Includes private employers with 100 or more employees, or 50 or more employees and: 1) have a federal contract or first-tier subcontract worth $50,000 or more, or 2) act as depositories of federal funds in any amount, or 3) act as issuing and paying agents for U.S. Savings Bonds and Notes. EEO-1 businesses account for 48.6 percent of all private U.S. employment.
Source: U.S., Equal Employment Opportunity Commission, *Job Patterns for Minorities and Women in Private Industry, 1995.*

University of Florida   **Bureau of Economic and Business Research**

Table 6.21. MINORITY EMPLOYMENT: PRIVATE INDUSTRY EMPLOYMENT OF FEMALE AND MINORITY EMPLOYEES BY INDUSTRY AND BY OCCUPATION IN FLORIDA, 1995

Occupation and minority group 1/	Agriculture forestry and fishing SIC 01-09 (64 units)	Mining SIC 10-14 (21 units)	Construction SIC 10-14 (185 units)	Manufacturing SIC 20-39 (1,047 units)	Transportation communications and public utilities SIC 40-49 (833 units)	Wholesale trade SIC 50-51 (408 units)	Retail trade SIC 52-59 (3,640 units)	Finance insurance and real estate SIC 60-67 (790 units)	Services SIC 70-89 (2,284 units)
Total employment	15,931	3,735	32,917	265,347	190,585	61,093	450,459	129,358	624,446
Female	4,098	447	4,396	91,880	64,955	19,526	230,189	86,565	376,252
Minority	7,051	1,200	8,532	79,238	57,626	18,713	129,775	38,487	209,495
Officials and managers	1,629	502	3,204	30,840	22,013	7,518	39,777	20,483	51,174
Female	185	24	379	5,756	5,994	1,542	13,664	10,487	23,922
Minority	213	73	291	3,772	4,037	1,218	6,566	3,707	8,158
Professionals	425	285	1,827	40,845	19,534	3,726	4,624	23,986	137,798
Female	126	70	330	10,629	5,705	1,140	1,983	15,091	96,988
Minority	33	63	185	6,289	3,115	1,036	872	5,272	27,742
Technicians	329	155	870	17,219	11,039	2,668	4,258	5,843	62,899
Female	118	20	86	3,859	2,082	573	1,215	3,573	39,421
Minority	64	19	126	3,749	2,308	713	1,103	1,709	17,995
Sales workers	130	31	791	12,738	12,375	12,328	227,001	9,078	19,507
Female	35	5	345	4,744	7,189	3,863	127,969	4,213	10,876
Minority	17	3	82	2,691	4,045	2,468	64,204	2,039	5,457
Office and clerical workers	1,000	281	2,904	27,394	41,770	7,518	31,412	59,064	106,148
Female	848	233	2,348	22,053	31,447	1,542	25,310	49,658	87,794
Minority	132	58	448	6,392	14,429	1,218	8,061	20,932	32,380

See footnotes at end of table.

Continued . . .

Table 6.21. MINORITY EMPLOYMENT: PRIVATE INDUSTRY EMPLOYMENT OF FEMALE AND MINORITY EMPLOYEES BY INDUSTRY AND BY OCCUPATION IN FLORIDA, 1995 (Continued)

Occupation and minority group 1/	Agriculture forestry and fishing SIC 01-09 (64 units)	Mining SIC 10-14 (21 units)	Construction SIC 10-14 (185 units)	Manufacturing SIC 20-39 (1,047 units)	Transportation communications and public utilities SIC 40-49 (833 units)	Wholesale trade SIC 50-51 (408 units)	Retail trade SIC 52-59 (3,640 units)	Finance insurance and real estate SIC 60-67 (790 units)	Services SIC 70-89 (2,284 units)
Craft workers	2,602	1,193	11,749	36,932	28,479	3,464	13,470	1,117	19,514
Female	132	25	254	4,544	2,385	375	4,665	98	2,916
Minority	684	348	2,451	8,935	6,796	923	3,013	327	5,428
Operatives	5,212	1,006	5,814	71,913	31,491	12,546	16,240	1,643	28,349
Female	1,089	46	263	30,130	2,671	2,137	3,165	213	9,860
Minority	2,604	484	2,019	32,455	12,134	5,037	5,332	743	13,021
Laborers	4,270	258	5,339	24,402	15,019	6,980	27,863	1,688	19,202
Female	1,412	22	226	9,203	2,081	1,365	8,879	186	5,196
Minority	3,159	138	2,796	14,152	7,480	3,844	10,732	990	9,587
Service workers	334	24	419	3,064	8,865	1,245	85,814	6,456	179,855
Female	153	2	165	962	5,401	395	43,339	3,046	99,279
Minority	145	14	134	1,453	3,282	462	29,892	2,768	89,727

1/ Includes Black, Asian or Pacific Islander, American Indian, Eskimo, or Aleut, and persons of Hispanic origin.
Note: Private industry data, based on 1987 standard industrial classification (SIC) codes, from the 1995 Equal Employment Opportunity employer information report (EEO-1). Includes private employers with 100 or more employees, or 50 or more employees and: 1) have a federal contract or first-tier subcontract worth $50,000 or more, or 2) act as depositories of federal funds in any amount, or 3) act as issuing and paying agents for U.S. Savings Bonds and Notes. EEO-1 businesses account for 48.6 percent of all private U.S. employment.

Source: U.S., Equal Employment Opportunity Commission, *Job Patterns for Minorities and Women in Private Industry,* 1995.

Table 6.25. OCCUPATIONS: EMPLOYMENT ESTIMATES, 1994, PROJECTIONS, 2005, AND AVERAGE ANNUAL JOB OPENINGS FOR MAJOR OCCUPATIONAL CATEGORIES IN THE STATE OF FLORIDA

Occupation	Estimates 1994	Projections 2005	Change Number	Change Percentage	Average annual openings Total	Average annual openings Due to growth	Average annual openings Due to separations
All occupations, total	6,527,347	8,170,109	1,642,762	25.17	294,227	149,337	144,890
Executive, administrative, and managerial	435,711	555,987	120,276	27.60	20,195	10,934	9,261
Professional, paraprofessional, and technical	1,250,851	1,645,525	394,674	31.55	59,940	35,873	24,067
Management support	197,776	249,205	51,429	26.00	8,449	4,673	3,776
Engineers and related occupations	114,957	141,824	26,867	23.37	4,896	2,440	2,456
Computer and mathematical	45,206	69,944	24,738	54.72	3,121	2,247	874
Social scientists, recreation, and religion	79,879	110,469	30,590	38.30	4,363	2,783	1,580
Law and related occupations	56,187	69,982	13,795	24.55	1,967	1,253	714
Teachers, librarians, and counselors	285,334	377,957	92,623	32.46	14,417	8,419	5,998
Health practitioners, and technicians	336,616	450,960	114,344	33.97	16,248	10,394	5,854
Marketing and sales	916,702	1,151,239	234,537	25.58	46,607	21,322	25,285
Administrative support and clerical	1,171,806	1,404,031	232,225	19.82	44,002	21,108	22,894
Secretarial and general office	652,668	784,935	132,267	20.27	24,628	12,023	12,605
Service	1,194,829	1,568,692	373,863	31.29	64,051	33,991	30,060
First line supervisor	54,413	68,191	13,778	25.32	2,710	1,253	1,457
Protective	153,324	213,276	59,952	39.10	9,761	5,450	4,311
Food and beverage	518,746	664,889	146,143	28.17	28,939	13,286	15,653
Health	132,623	194,473	61,850	46.64	7,970	5,623	2,347
Cleaning and building	189,065	234,324	45,259	23.94	7,478	4,116	3,362
Personal service	136,019	179,822	43,803	32.20	6,681	3,983	2,698
Agriculture, forestry, and fishing	261,950	297,807	35,857	13.69	8,227	3,258	4,969
Production, construction, operators, maintenance, and related workers	1,295,498	1,546,828	251,330	19.40	51,205	22,851	28,354
Mechanics, installers, and repairers	255,212	308,556	53,344	20.90	10,712	4,848	5,864
Construction trades and extraction	199,213	230,355	31,142	15.63	6,915	2,830	4,085
Operators, fabricators, and laborers	676,620	816,869	140,249	20.73	27,824	12,754	15,070

Source: State of Florida, Department of Labor and Employment Security, Bureau of Labor Market Information, *Florida Industry and Occupational Employment Projections, 1994-2005, Statewide.*

Table 6.26. OCCUPATIONS: EMPLOYMENT ESTIMATES, 1994, AND PROJECTIONS, 2005, OF THE FASTEST-GROWING OCCUPATIONS IN THE STATE OF FLORIDA

Occupation	Estimates 1994	Projections 2005	Percentage change
Systems analyst	17,911	32,235	79.97
Home health aide	25,846	45,475	75.95
Computer engineer	8,392	14,368	71.21
Physical, corrective therapy assistant	3,936	6,497	65.07
Residential counselor	4,063	6,602	62.49
Physical therapist	5,762	9,335	62.01
Correction officer and jailer	25,400	40,924	61.12
Personal home care aide	3,928	6,296	60.29
Human services worker	5,455	8,742	60.26
Medical assistant	12,424	19,859	59.84
Medical records technician	4,814	7,532	56.46
Data processing equipment repairer	3,920	6,002	53.11
Teacher, special education	19,854	29,214	47.14
Adjustment clerk	19,592	28,801	47.00
Radiologic technologist	7,840	11,415	45.60
Amusement and recreation attendant	14,003	20,237	44.52
Emergency medical technician	6,928	9,970	43.91
Social worker, medical and psychiatric	10,442	14,915	42.84
Sheriff and deputy sheriff	9,833	13,979	42.16
Teacher's aide and educational assistant	15,452	21,898	41.72
Tax preparer	5,607	7,941	41.63
Police patrol officer	15,553	21,951	41.14
Management analyst	16,103	22,508	39.78
Designer, except interior designer	10,231	14,294	39.71
Medicine and health service manager	9,374	13,070	39.43
Food service and lodging manager	35,250	49,050	39.15
Medical secretary	14,811	20,579	38.94
Taxi driver and chauffeur	8,482	11,783	38.92
Flight attendant	5,270	7,320	38.90
Baker, bread and pastry	10,951	15,184	38.65
Paralegal	6,414	8,850	37.98
Dental assistant	10,568	14,554	37.72
Dental hygienist	6,874	9,465	37.69
Teacher, preschool and kindergarten	24,940	34,267	37.40
Social worker, except medical and psychiatric	20,560	28,244	37.37
Guard	60,289	82,777	37.30
Hand packer and packager	58,546	80,309	37.17
Instructor, nonvocational education	8,964	12,267	36.85
Nursery worker	7,841	10,728	36.82
Teacher's aide, paraprofessional	25,010	34,181	36.67
Physician	30,432	41,512	36.41
Lawn maintenance worker	15,661	21,286	35.92
Artist and commercial artist	12,391	16,815	35.70
Receptionist, information clerk	63,915	86,614	35.51
Bill and account collector	16,103	21,783	35.27
Personnel, training, labor relations specialist	19,229	25,874	34.56
Child care worker	50,675	68,172	34.53
Nursing aide and orderly	65,797	88,454	34.43
Waiter and waitress	140,551	188,871	34.38
Instructor and coach, sports	7,876	10,580	34.33
Sales agent, business services	12,877	17,286	34.24
Engineering, math, natural sciences manager	12,611	16,878	33.84
Recreation worker	10,186	13,626	33.77

See footnote at end of table. Continued . . .

University of Florida **Bureau of Economic and Business Research**

Table 6.26. OCCUPATIONS: EMPLOYMENT ESTIMATES, 1994, AND PROJECTIONS, 2005, OF THE FASTEST-GROWING OCCUPATIONS IN THE STATE OF FLORIDA (Continued)

Occupation	Estimates 1994	Projections 2005	Percentage change
Personnel, training, labor relations manager	6,517	8,716	33.74
Fire fighter	12,666	16,935	33.70
Counselor	8,288	11,065	33.51
Teacher, vocational education	10,426	13,917	33.48
Securities, financial service sales	17,646	23,520	33.29
Teacher, secondary school	65,267	86,836	33.05
Computer programmer	15,535	20,643	32.88
Registered nurse	114,244	151,782	32.86
Pharmacy technician	6,341	8,420	32.79
Marketing, advertising, public relations manager	17,323	22,903	32.21
Licensed practical nurse	50,188	66,217	31.94
Bus driver	9,564	12,613	31.88
Clergy	16,240	21,387	31.69
Insurance adjuster, investigator	8,558	11,262	31.60
Food preparation worker	71,071	93,283	31.25
Music director, singer, and related	8,319	10,917	31.23
Musician, instrumental	9,340	12,250	31.16
Welfare eligibility worker	8,492	11,104	30.76
Animal caretaker, except farm	11,923	15,508	30.07
Customer service representative, utilities	9,961	12,936	29.87
Counter and rental clerk	22,266	28,906	29.82
Grader and sorter, agricultural products	10,941	14,159	29.41
First line supervisor, clerical	65,124	84,224	29.33
Cook, restaurant	47,544	61,477	29.31
Graduate assistant, teaching	8,954	11,573	29.25
Financial manager	37,845	48,916	29.25
Administrative service manager	15,839	20,436	29.02
Laundry, drycleaning machine operator	11,103	14,308	28.87
Cashier	181,892	234,302	28.81
Host and hostess, restaurant, lounge	17,218	22,142	28.60
Dispatcher, except police, fire, ambulance	7,859	10,107	28.60
Accountant and auditor	45,118	57,850	28.22
Order clerk, materials, service	13,813	17,704	28.17
Heating, A/C, refrigeration mechanic	18,697	23,875	27.69
Cook, fast food	35,685	45,467	27.41
Vehicle, equipment cleaner	16,344	20,808	27.31
Cook, short order	15,397	19,599	27.29
Pharmacist	10,276	13,070	27.19
Telemarketer, door-to-door sales, street vendor	30,469	38,726	27.10
Bus driver, school	14,943	18,968	26.94
Sales representative, scientific products, except retail	35,495	44,990	26.75
Medical/clinical laboratory technologist	9,059	11,469	26.60
Bus, truck, diesel engine mechanic	10,114	12,797	26.53
Education administrator	16,268	20,568	26.43
Hotel desk clerk	10,741	13,576	26.39
Loan officer and counselor	9,487	11,977	26.25
First line supervisor, sales	140,782	177,305	25.94

Note: Occupations are ranked based on the anticipated rate of growth between 1994 and 2005. Only occupations with a minimum total change of 2,000 jobs are included.

Source: State of Florida, Department of Labor and Employment Security, Bureau of Labor Market Information, *Florida Industry and Occupational Employment Projections, 1994-2005, Statewide.*

University of Florida   **Bureau of Economic and Business Research**

Table 6.30. EMPLOYERS: NAME AND LOCATION OF CORPORATE HEADQUARTERS OF THE 50 LARGEST PRIVATE EMPLOYERS IN FLORIDA, FEBRUARY 2, 1995

Firm and headquarters location	Number of employees	Firm and headquarters location	Number of employees
Barnett Banks, Inc.--Jacksonville, FL	A/	Beverly Enterprises--Fort Smith, AR	C/
Columbia/HCA Healthcare Corp.--Miami Lakes, FL	A/	GTE Florida, Inc.--Tampa, FL	C/
Walt Disney World Co.--Lake Buena Vista, FL	A/	Harris Corporation--Melbourne, FL	C/
Eckerd Corp.--Largo, FL	A/	The Home Depot, Inc.--Atlanta, GA	C/
Kelly Services, Inc.--Troy, MI	A/	Kash-N-Karry Food Stores, Inc.--Tampa, FL	C/
K Mart Corp.--Troy, MI	A/	Martin Marietta Corp.--Bethesda, MD	C/
Olsten Corp.--Westbury, NY	A/	J. C. Penney Co., Inc.-Dallas, TX	C/
Publix Super Markets, Inc.--Lakeland, FL	A/	Sun Bank, N.A.--Orlando, FL	C/
Sears, Roebuck and Co.--Chicago, IL	A/	Walgreen Co.--Deerfield, IL	C/
Southern Bell Telephone and Telegraph Co.--Atlanta, GA	A/	American Express Co.--New York, NY	D/
The Staff Leasing Group--Bradenton, FL	A/	Blue Cross/Blue Shield of Florida, Inc.--Jacksonville, FL	D/
Wal-Mart Stores, Inc.--Bentonville, AR	A/	Brinker International, Inc.--Dallas, TX	D/
Winn Dixie Stores, Inc.--Jacksonville, FL	A/	Delta Air Lines, Inc.--Atlanta, GA	D/
American Telephone & Telegraph Co.--New York, NY	B/	Employee Services, Inc.--Bradenton, FL	D/
Burdine's Inc.--Miami, FL	B/	Food Lion, Inc.--Salisbury, NC	D/
First Union National Bank of Florida--Jacksonville, FL	B/	Morrison Restaurants, Inc.--Mobile, AL	D/
Florida Power & Light Co.-- Juno Beach, FL	B/	Motorola, Inc.--Schaumberg, IL	D/
General Mills Restaurants, Inc.--Orlando, FL	B/	Nationsbank of Florida, N.A.--Tampa, FL	D/
Payroll Transfers, Inc.--Tampa, FL	B/	The Prudential Insurance Co. of America--Newark, NJ	D/
United Parcel Service of America, Inc.--Atlanta, GA	B/	Scotty's, Inc.--Winter Haven, FL	D/
The Vincam Group, Inc.--Coral Gables, FL	B/	Staff Management Systems, Inc.--Tampa, FL	D/
Albertson's, Inc.--Boise, ID	C/	Staffing Concepts International, Inc.--Tampa, FL	D/
America Airlines, Inc.--Dallas/Ft. Worth Airport, TX	C/	Steak & Ale of Florida--Dallas, TX	D/
Anheuser-Busch Companies, Inc.--St. Louis, MO	C/	Target Stores--Minneapolis, MN	
		United Technologies Corp.--Hartford, CT	D/
		United Telephone Company of Florida--Altamonte Springs, FL	D/

A/ 15,001 and over.   B/ 10,001-15,000.   C/ 7,501-10,000.   D/ 5,000-7,500.
Note: Employers are listed alphabetically within employment size ranges. Employment estimates do not include out-of-state employees in cases where the employer also has operations outside of Florida. Employees of franchise operations are not included in corporate totals. Hospitals and universities are excluded. Employment estimates for help supply services employers include the total number of help available for supplying temporary or continuing help.
Source: State of Florida, Department of Commerce, Bureau of Economic Analysis, *Florida Facts: Florida's Fifty Largest Private Employers*, February 2, 1995.

Table 6.40. INDUSTRY GROWTH TRENDS: EMPLOYMENT ESTIMATES, 1994, AND
PROJECTIONS, 2005, OF THE FASTEST-GROWING INDUSTRIES AND
INDUSTRIES GAINING THE MOST NEW GROWTH
IN THE STATE OF FLORIDA

SIC code	Industry	Estimates 1994	Projec- tions 2005	Change Number	Per- centage
	Fastest-growing industries 1/				
83	Social services	121,679	180,777	59,098	48.57
87	Engineering and management services	134,185	193,245	59,060	44.01
73	Business services	452,812	648,519	195,707	43.22
80	Health services	515,030	717,509	202,479	39.31
41	Local and interurban transit	13,677	18,899	5,222	38.18
54	Food stores	219,582	296,888	77,306	35.21
62	Security and commodity brokers	23,254	31,145	7,891	33.93
61	Nondepository institutions	35,214	47,095	11,881	33.74
84	Museum and botanical and zoological gardens	3,087	4,105	1,018	32.98
07	Agricultural services	137,464	182,499	45,035	32.76
79	Amusement and recreation services	116,985	152,944	35,959	30.74
82	Educational services	62,924	81,590	18,666	29.66
58	Eating and drinking places	415,233	536,048	120,815	29.10
93	Local government	592,350	762,882	170,532	28.79
75	Auto repair services and parking	59,923	77,000	17,077	28.50
42	Trucking and warehousing	67,067	85,929	18,862	28.12
57	Furniture and homefurnishings stores	56,437	71,778	15,341	27.18
45	Transportation by air	49,536	62,919	13,383	27.02
86	Membership organizations	105,699	134,002	28,303	26.78
51	Wholesale trade, nondurable goods	131,114	165,536	34,422	26.25
	Industries gaining the most new jobs				
80	Health services	515,030	717,509	202,479	39.31
73	Business services	452,812	648,519	195,707	43.22
93	Local government	592,350	762,882	170,532	28.79
58	Eating and drinking places	415,233	536,048	120,815	29.10
54	Food stores	219,582	296,888	77,306	35.21
83	Social services	121,679	180,777	59,098	48.57
87	Engineering and management services	134,185	193,245	59,060	44.01
92	State government	193,218	242,032	48,814	25.26
07	Agricultural services	137,464	182,499	45,035	32.76
79	Amusement and recreation services	116,985	152,944	35,959	30.74
51	Wholesale trade, nondurable goods	131,114	165,536	34,422	26.25
59	Miscellaneous retail stores	137,837	172,154	34,317	24.90
50	Wholesale trade, durable goods	174,531	208,446	33,915	19.43
70	Hotels and other lodging places	140,253	174,014	33,761	24.07
53	General merchandise stores	142,524	170,930	28,406	19.93
86	Membership organizations	105,699	134,002	28,303	26.78
17	Special trade contractors	188,892	215,385	26,493	14.03
55	Auto dealers and service stations	117,008	137,104	20,096	17.17
42	Trucking and warehousing	67,067	85,929	18,862	28.12
82	Educational services	62,924	81,590	18,666	29.66

1/ Industries with a minimum total change of 1,000 jobs.
Source: State of Florida, Department of Labor and Employment Security, Bureau of
Labor Market Information, *Florida Industry and Occupational Employment Projections,
1994-2005, Statewide.*

University of Florida   **Bureau of Economic and Business Research**

Table 6.55. MANUFACTURING PAY: ANNUAL MANUFACTURING PAY AND MANUFACTURING
JOBS IN FLORIDA, OTHER STATES, AND THE UNITED STATES, 1994

State	Annual manufacturing pay per employee Amount (dollars)	Rank	Manufacturing jobs (percentage)	State	Annual manufacturing pay per employee Amount (dollars)	Rank	Manufacturing jobs (percentage)
Florida	25,083	32	7.2	Montana	23,883	39	4.4
				Nebraska	24,654	35	5.5
Alabama	22,983	42	11.6	Nevada	25,182	30	3.1
Alaska	23,688	41	7.4	New Hampshire	29,450	17	11.8
Arizona	28,789	20	8.5	New Jersey	32,292	7	13.2
Arkansas	19,765	47	9.0	New Mexico	18,710	49	3.2
California	32,750	6	16.9	New York	30,025	15	10.4
Colorado	29,584	16	8.3	North Carolina	21,997	43	18.9
Connecticut	36,414	3	16.3	North Dakota	21,161	46	1.9
Delaware	37,798	2	2.7	Ohio	31,636	8	15.7
Georgia	25,114	31	9.4	Oklahoma	29,043	18	9.7
Hawaii	28,332	22	2.5	Oregon	27,302	25	15.7
Idaho	21,418	44	8.4	Pennsylvania	28,794	19	13.5
Illinois	30,870	11	16.1	Rhode Island	23,732	40	16.2
Indiana	28,625	21	16.1	South Carolina	23,945	38	12.8
Iowa	26,922	26	5.7	South Dakota	21,272	45	3.3
Kansas	32,956	5	12.1	Tennessee	24,123	37	10.5
Kentucky	26,309	27	8.7	Texas	30,914	10	11.6
Louisiana	30,682	12	4.9	Utah	24,185	36	9.8
Maine	25,211	29	7.5	Vermont	24,713	33	8.7
Maryland	30,655	13	4.8	Virginia	24,702	34	4.9
Massachusetts	33,281	4	14.9	Washington	27,497	24	10.4
Michigan	38,199	1	19.8	West Virginia	26,217	28	4.1
Minnesota	31,257	9	12.4	Wisconsin	30,647	14	19.3
Mississippi	19,175	48	10.6	Wyoming	17,134	50	1.3
Missouri	27,846	23	10.1	United States	30,197	(X)	12.5

(X) Not applicable.

Source: University of Florida, Bureau of Economic and Business Research, *Florida Business Briefs,* July 1997. Data from U.S., Department of Commerce, Bureau of the Census, *County Business Patterns 1993-1994.*

Table 6.57. AVERAGE ANNUAL PAY: PAY OF EMPLOYEES COVERED BY STATE AND FEDERAL
UNEMPLOYMENT INSURANCE PROGRAMS IN THE UNITED STATES AND IN THE STATE
AND METROPOLITAN AREAS OF FLORIDA, 1994 AND 1995

Industry or metropolitan area	1994 (dollars)	1995 (dollars)	Percentage change 1994-95	Ranking of MSAs in the U.S. By 1995 level	By percentage change 1994-95
United States	26,939	27,845	3.4	(X)	(X)
Florida	23,918	24,710	3.3	(X)	(X)
Private industry 1/	23,310	24,099	3.4	(X)	(X)
Mining	36,087	37,034	2.6	(X)	(X)
Construction	24,236	25,151	3.8	(X)	(X)
Manufacturing	30,094	31,000	3.0	(X)	(X)
Transportation, communications, and public utilities	31,472	32,420	3.0	(X)	(X)
Wholesale trade	32,683	34,159	4.5	(X)	(X)
Retail trade	14,697	15,117	2.9	(X)	(X)
Finance, insurance, and real estate	31,097	32,956	6.0	(X)	(X)
Services	23,305	24,010	3.0	(X)	(X)
Government	27,260	28,163	3.3	(X)	(X)
MSA					
Daytona Beach	19,895	20,494	3.0	291	168
Ft. Lauderdale	25,830	26,695	3.3	91	132
Ft. Myers-Cape Coral	21,814	22,230	1.9	252	255
Ft. Pierce-Port St. Lucie	22,275	23,065	3.5	217	104
Ft. Walton Beach	19,325	19,789	2.4	302	224
Gainesville	21,302	21,822	2.4	263	224
Jacksonville	24,315	25,255	3.9	128	66
Lakeland-Winter Haven	22,377	23,238	3.9	205	66
Melbourne-Titusville-Palm Bay	26,325	26,853	2.0	86	251
Miami	26,488	27,452	3.6	67	94
Naples	21,568	22,747	5.5	229	9
Ocala	20,273	21,084	4.0	283	59
Orlando	23,630	24,448	3.5	162	104
Panama City	19,858	20,489	3.2	292	141
Pensacola	22,078	22,509	2.0	240	251
Punta Gorda	20,048	21,058	5.0	284	15
Sarasota-Bradenton	21,282	22,279	4.7	248	23
Tallahassee	22,246	23,141	4.0	210	59
Tampa-St. Petersburg-Clearwater	23,767	24,650	3.7	155	83
West Palm Beach-Boca Raton	26,617	27,911	4.9	55	19

(X) Not applicable.
1/ Includes industries not listed separately.
Note: Some 1994 data are revised. 1995 data are preliminary. Data are for Metropolitan Statistical Areas (MSAs) and Primary Metropolitan Statistical Areas (PMSAs) defined as of December 31, 1992, and are not comparable to data in previous *Abstracts* See Glossary for definitions and map at the front of the book for area boundaries.
Source: U.S., Department of Labor, Bureau of Labor Statistics, *News: Average Annual Pay by State and Industry, 1995,* release of September 25, 1996, and *News: Average Annual Pay Levels in Metropolitan Areas, 1995*, release of November 8, 1996.

University of Florida   **Bureau of Economic and Business Research**

SOCIAL INSURANCE
AND WELFARE

Workers' Compensation Costs for Disabling Work Injuries by Accident Type, 1996
(dollar amounts in thousands)

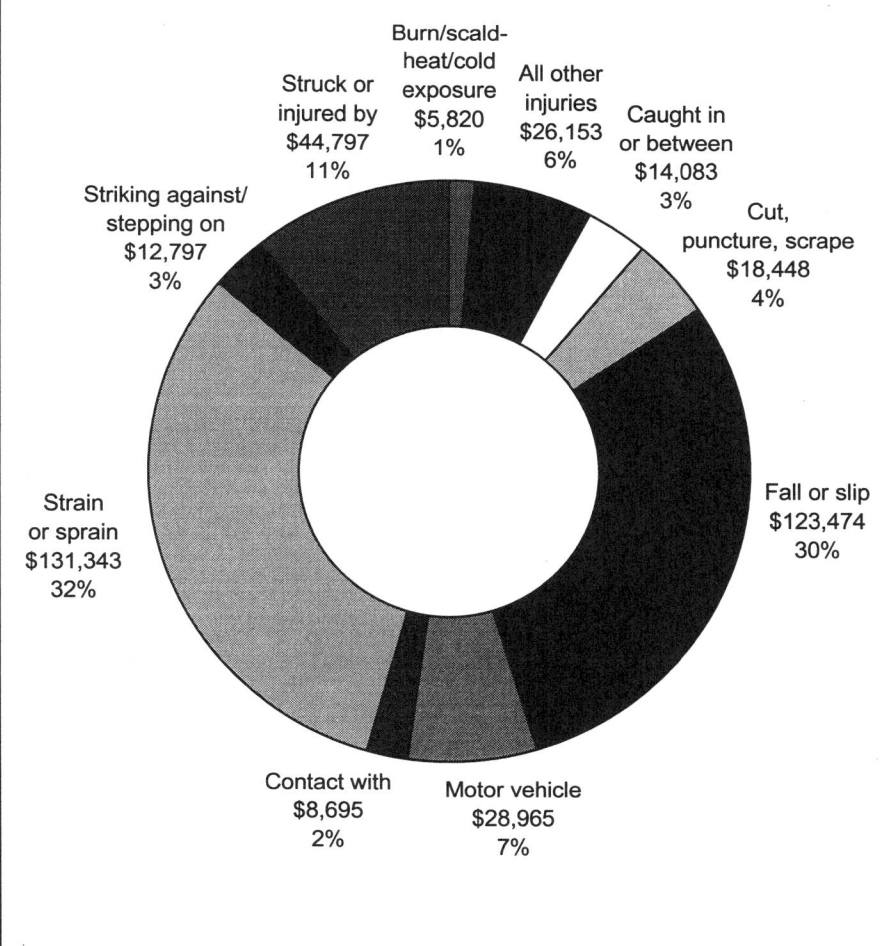

Struck or injured by $44,797 11%

Burn/scald-heat/cold exposure $5,820 1%

All other injuries $26,153 6%

Caught in or between $14,083 3%

Striking against/stepping on $12,797 3%

Cut, puncture, scrape $18,448 4%

Strain or sprain $131,343 32%

Fall or slip $123,474 30%

Contact with $8,695 2%

Motor vehicle $28,965 7%

Source: Table 7.59

SECTION 7.00
SOCIAL INSURANCE AND WELFARE

TABLES LISTED BY MAJOR HEADINGS

Table 7.03. MEDICARE: ENROLLMENT IN HOSPITAL AND/OR MEDICAL INSURANCE
BY METROPOLITAN/NONMETROPOLITAN RESIDENCE IN FLORIDA, 1995 AND 1996

Item	Total enrollment 1995	Total enrollment 1996	Persons aged 65 and over 1995	Persons aged 65 and over 1996	Disability benefi- ciaries 1/ 1995	Disability benefi- ciaries 1/ 1996
Florida, total	2,627,511	2,685,198	2,395,890	2,434,438	231,621	250,760
Metropolitan counties 2/	2,324,246	2,372,888	2,121,535	2,153,580	202,711	219,308
With central city	2,060,192	2,100,354	1,883,343	1,909,315	176,849	191,039
Without central city	264,054	272,534	238,192	244,265	25,862	28,269
Nonmetropolitan counties	301,254	310,630	272,505	279,334	28,749	31,296

1/ Persons under age 65 entitled to cash disability benefits for at least 24
consecutive months and also those eligible solely on the basis of end-stage
renal disease.
2/ Counties included in Metropolitan Statistical Areas (MSAs).

Table 7.04. MEDICARE: ENROLLMENT, JULY 1, AND BENEFIT PAYMENTS OR REIMBURSEMENTS
CALENDAR YEARS, OF PERSONS AGED 65 AND OVER IN FLORIDA, 1983 THROUGH 1996

Year	Hospital and/or medical insurance Enroll- ment (1,000)	Hospital and/or medical insurance Payments 1/ ($1,000)	Hospital insurance Enroll- ment (1,000)	Hospital insurance Payments 1/ ($1,000)	Supplementary medical insurance Enroll- ment (1,000)	Supplementary medical insurance Payments 1/ ($1,000)
1983	1,736	3,411,057	1,704	2,178,642	1,709	1,232,415
1984	1,791	4,296,524	1,757	2,775,313	1,765	1,521,211
1985	1,856	5,040,418	1,820	3,267,584	1,829	1,772,834
1986	1,921	5,394,033	1,881	3,347,974	1,893	2,046,059
1987	2,135	5,720,000	2,092	3,275,000	2,095	2,445,000
1988	2,114	5,517,000	2,070	2,869,000	2,072	2,648,000
1989	2,174	6,470,000	2,165	3,340,000	2,129	3,130,000
1990	2,174	6,960,000	2,165	3,565,000	2,129	3,394,000
1991	2,230	7,440,000	2,221	3,742,000	2,183	3,698,000
1992	2,273	8,247,006	2,265	4,789,953	2,228	3,457,053
1993	2,322	8,812,192	2,313	5,087,368	2,275	3,724,823
1994	2,367	(NA)	2,359	(NA)	2,318	(NA)
1995	2,396	(NA)	2,385	(NA)	2,344	(NA)
1996	2,434	(NA)	2,421	(NA)	2,381	(NA)

(NA) Not available.
1/ Benefit payments were reported prior to 1993. Beginning in 1993 reimbursement
payments derived from reimbursed bills or claims for services were reported. Reimbursement data for the aged are inflated for a 5 percent sample of Medicare beneficiaries. Data prior to 1993 are not comparable with later years.
Note: Geographic classification is based on the address to which the enrollee's
cash benefit check is being mailed or the mailing address recorded in the health insurance master file. Data from 1985 are estimated.

Source for Tables 7.03 and 7.04: U.S., Department of Health and Human Services,
Health Care Financing Administration, unpublished data.

Table 7.12. SOCIAL SECURITY: NUMBER OF BENEFICIARIES AND AMOUNT OF BENEFITS
IN CURRENT-PAYMENT STATUS BY TYPE OF BENEFICIARY IN THE STATE
AND COUNTIES OF FLORIDA, DECEMBER 1995

Residence of beneficiary	Total	Retired workers 1/	Disabled workers	Wives and husbands	Children	Widows and widowers 2/
		Number of beneficiaries				
Florida	2,985,768	2,019,526	230,502	216,338	192,587	326,815
Alachua	25,817	15,265	2,550	1,740	3,160	3,105
Baker	2,815	1,365	475	165	455	355
Bay	24,290	14,360	2,535	2,000	2,125	3,270
Bradford	2,993	1,700	340	205	335	410
Brevard	99,666	67,175	7,980	8,100	5,810	10,605
Broward	283,435	197,810	18,375	17,320	15,370	34,560
Calhoun	2,223	1,165	270	185	250	350
Charlotte	47,275	35,515	2,450	3,730	1,555	4,025
Citrus	39,955	29,155	2,585	3,070	1,695	3,450
Clay	16,216	9,720	1,675	1,250	1,660	1,910
Collier	47,531	33,840	2,155	5,090	1,795	4,650
Columbia	9,662	5,530	1,215	670	1,070	1,175
Dade	297,471	196,385	24,590	21,210	24,085	31,200
De Soto	5,832	3,730	625	415	500	560
Dixie	2,810	1,555	415	225	315	300
Duval	100,868	59,850	10,705	6,450	10,310	13,550
Escambia	46,728	27,030	4,655	4,270	4,310	6,460
Flagler	13,552	10,145	830	980	670	930
Franklin	2,179	1,355	235	160	150	275
Gadsden	8,165	4,405	1,125	410	1,325	900
Gilchrist	2,357	1,325	300	175	255	305
Glades	1,629	1,100	145	110	115	160
Gulf	2,642	1,480	275	260	200	425
Hamilton	2,107	1,065	300	145	290	305
Hardee	4,047	2,375	425	300	480	470
Hendry	4,471	2,580	440	310	590	550
Hernando	45,208	33,075	3,115	3,430	2,120	3,465
Highlands	27,832	20,380	1,565	2,190	1,300	2,400
Hillsborough	146,135	89,345	16,390	9,735	13,495	17,170
Holmes	4,128	2,125	525	345	430	700
Indian River	31,976	23,090	1,555	2,880	1,240	3,210
Jackson	9,045	4,900	985	645	1,175	1,340
Jefferson	2,425	1,420	255	165	250	335
Lafayette	969	550	110	80	90	135
Lake	56,164	40,770	3,575	4,160	2,310	5,350
Lee	105,351	76,005	6,095	8,275	5,195	9,785
Leon	23,248	14,515	1,925	1,520	2,370	2,915
Levy	7,188	4,430	795	555	635	775
Liberty	1,007	505	145	75	135	145
Madison	3,387	1,835	415	240	390	505
Manatee	65,163	46,565	3,895	4,880	2,815	7,005
Marion	68,781	48,085	5,325	5,070	4,180	6,120
Martin	34,291	24,920	1,645	3,030	1,195	3,500
Monroe	13,025	9,045	975	1,055	595	1,355
Nassau	7,993	4,495	935	675	850	1,035
Okaloosa	23,659	14,465	2,080	2,235	1,855	3,025
Okeechobee	6,810	4,135	755	505	640	775

See footnotes at end of table.   Continued . . .

Table 7.12. SOCIAL SECURITY: NUMBER OF BENEFICIARIES AND AMOUNT OF BENEFITS
IN CURRENT-PAYMENT STATUS BY TYPE OF BENEFICIARY IN THE STATE
AND COUNTIES OF FLORIDA, DECEMBER 1995 (Continued)

Residence of beneficiary	Total	Retired workers 1/	Disabled workers	Wives and husbands	Children	Widows and widowers 2/
		Number of beneficiaries (Continued)				
Orange	109,536	66,620	12,250	7,440	10,945	12,280
Osceola	22,941	14,010	2,580	1,515	2,535	2,300
Palm Beach	248,729	181,850	11,815	18,165	10,440	26,460
Pasco	102,289	73,250	7,510	6,950	4,700	9,880
Pinellas	230,946	162,195	16,095	14,800	10,035	27,820
Polk	99,292	65,530	8,890	6,935	7,325	10,610
Putnam	16,835	10,030	1,950	1,275	1,685	1,895
St. Johns	21,124	13,945	1,660	1,785	1,425	2,310
St. Lucie	45,762	31,665	3,830	3,180	3,020	4,065
Santa Rosa	15,098	8,730	1,680	1,460	1,450	1,780
Sarasota	100,327	73,920	4,470	8,405	2,850	10,680
Seminole	46,467	29,115	4,350	3,395	4,250	5,360
Sumter	10,897	7,360	975	720	760	1,085
Suwannee	7,103	4,050	855	535	690	970
Taylor	3,847	2,150	440	275	420	565
Union	1,323	690	165	90	210	170
Volusia	109,374	75,055	8,780	7,640	6,330	11,570
Wakulla	2,646	1,515	290	175	335	330
Walton	6,626	3,940	750	565	585	785
Washington	4,024	2,220	465	335	410	590
Unknown	61	30	0	10	15	5
		Amount of monthly cash benefits ($1,000)				
Florida	1,977,286	1,450,576	158,275	78,543	66,056	223,836
Alachua	16,142	10,706	1,671	634	1,125	2,006
Baker	1,625	893	317	48	160	206
Bay	14,614	9,511	1,681	658	727	2,038
Bradford	1,717	1,080	226	64	109	238
Brevard	65,907	47,957	5,744	2,889	2,071	7,248
Broward	201,298	150,709	12,946	6,530	5,654	25,458
Calhoun	1,207	712	175	52	76	188
Charlotte	32,385	25,723	1,878	1,367	548	2,868
Citrus	26,571	20,590	1,932	1,088	601	2,359
Clay	10,049	6,590	1,196	430	618	1,214
Collier	34,635	26,609	1,589	2,164	651	3,620
Columbia	5,536	3,518	805	205	324	685
Dade	180,394	130,146	15,186	6,999	7,903	20,158
De Soto	3,589	2,540	404	136	148	359
Dixie	1,597	996	272	67	92	170
Duval	63,194	41,441	7,100	2,318	3,621	8,714
Escambia	27,410	17,586	3,088	1,393	1,431	3,913
Flagler	9,464	7,519	674	366	249	656
Franklin	1,272	860	156	53	45	153
Gadsden	4,251	2,626	650	123	369	485
Gilchrist	1,377	847	218	53	82	179
Glades	1,035	750	109	38	38	100
Gulf	1,657	1,032	189	93	70	273
Hamilton	1,137	660	194	39	83	161

See footnotes at end of table.   Continued . . .

Table 7.12. SOCIAL SECURITY: NUMBER OF BENEFICIARIES AND AMOUNT OF BENEFITS
IN CURRENT-PAYMENT STATUS BY TYPE OF BENEFICIARY IN THE STATE
AND COUNTIES OF FLORIDA, DECEMBER 1995 (Continued)

Residence of beneficiary	Total	Retired workers 1/	Disabled workers	Wives and husbands	Children	Widows and widowers 2/
		Amount of monthly cash benefits ($1,000) (Continued)				
Hardee	2,313	1,546	248	95	154	270
Hendry	2,711	1,794	284	104	187	342
Hernando	30,377	23,585	2,445	1,216	732	2,394
Highlands	18,093	14,199	1,085	767	408	1,635
Hillsborough	92,812	62,593	10,908	3,456	4,552	11,301
Holmes	2,118	1,231	337	90	110	350
Indian River	22,406	17,316	1,113	1,147	453	2,378
Jackson	4,869	2,971	625	183	385	705
Jefferson	1,316	865	157	49	75	171
Lafayette	548	350	71	24	28	74
Lake	37,170	28,784	2,493	1,492	769	3,632
Lee	72,455	55,986	4,448	3,113	1,881	7,031
Leon	14,999	10,423	1,236	581	839	1,921
Levy	4,324	2,928	553	174	203	467
Liberty	552	319	90	23	44	74
Madison	1,795	1,114	249	67	101	261
Manatee	44,462	33,961	2,741	1,844	967	4,947
Marion	44,580	33,649	3,757	1,752	1,369	4,055
Martin	24,552	19,091	1,208	1,217	425	2,608
Monroe	8,641	6,401	707	394	231	908
Nassau	5,173	3,239	688	246	317	681
Okaloosa	13,986	9,384	1,371	731	661	1,842
Okeechobee	4,171	2,811	511	161	193	494
Orange	69,531	47,072	8,118	2,627	3,611	8,105
Osceola	14,273	9,689	1,801	478	813	1,490
Palm Beach	185,675	145,285	8,573	7,623	3,765	20,431
Pasco	67,617	51,388	5,486	2,391	1,591	6,761
Pinellas	155,070	115,750	11,072	5,424	3,599	19,226
Polk	64,029	46,053	5,974	2,491	2,423	7,085
Putnam	10,117	6,728	1,305	404	505	1,174
St. Johns	14,171	10,199	1,160	689	520	1,605
St. Lucie	30,572	22,931	2,695	1,152	961	2,835
Santa Rosa	9,140	5,870	1,194	483	519	1,076
Sarasota	70,987	55,390	3,261	3,299	1,087	7,949
Seminole	30,259	20,871	3,034	1,204	1,487	3,663
Sumter	6,831	5,024	662	234	235	678
Suwannee	4,085	2,563	582	160	218	560
Taylor	2,305	1,442	305	88	134	337
Union	726	424	110	26	68	96
Volusia	71,878	52,912	6,231	2,716	2,207	7,815
Wakulla	1,514	972	193	53	106	191
Walton	3,776	2,468	510	173	183	442
Washington	2,209	1,367	298	98	129	318
Unknown	34	21	2	3	4	4

1/ Includes "special age 72" beneficiaries.
2/ Includes nondisabled and disabled widows and widowers, widowed mothers and fa-
thers, and parents.
Note: Detail may not add to totals because of rounding.
Source: U.S., Department of Health and Human Services, Social Security Administration, *OASDI Beneficiaries by State and County, December 1995.*

University of Florida   **Bureau of Economic and Business Research**

Table 7.14. SOCIAL SECURITY: AVERAGE MONTHLY BENEFITS OF BENEFICIARIES AGED
65 AND OVER IN THE STATE AND COUNTIES OF FLORIDA, DECEMBER 1995

(in dollars)

County	All bene-ficiaries	Retired workers	County	All bene-ficiaries	Retired workers
Florida	662.24	718.28	Lafayette	565.53	636.36
			Lake	661.81	706.01
Alachua	625.25	701.34	Lee	687.75	736.61
Baker	577.26	654.21	Leon	645.17	718.08
Bay	601.65	662.33	Levy	601.56	660.95
Bradford	573.67	635.29	Liberty	548.16	631.68
Brevard	661.28	713.91	Madison	529.97	607.08
Broward	710.21	761.89	Manatee	682.32	729.32
Calhoun	542.96	611.16	Marion	648.14	699.78
Charlotte	685.03	724.29	Martin	715.99	766.09
Citrus	665.02	706.23	Monroe	663.42	707.68
Clay	619.70	677.98	Nassau	647.19	720.58
Collier	728.68	786.32	Okaloosa	591.15	648.74
Columbia	572.97	636.17	Okeechobee	612.48	679.81
Dade	606.43	662.71	Orange	634.78	706.57
De Soto	615.40	680.97	Osceola	622.16	691.58
Dixie	568.33	640.51	Palm Beach	746.50	798.93
Duval	626.50	692.41	Pasco	661.04	701.54
Escambia	586.59	650.61	Pinellas	671.46	713.65
Flagler	698.35	741.15	Polk	644.86	702.78
Franklin	583.75	634.69	Putnam	600.95	670.79
Gadsden	520.64	596.14	St. Johns	670.85	731.37
Gilchrist	584.22	639.25	St. Lucie	668.07	724.17
Glades	635.36	681.82	Santa Rosa	605.38	672.39
Gulf	627.18	697.30	Sarasota	707.56	749.32
Hamilton	539.63	619.72	Seminole	651.19	716.85
Hardee	571.53	650.95	Sumter	626.87	682.61
Hendry	606.35	695.35	Suwannee	575.11	632.84
Hernando	671.94	713.08	Taylor	599.17	670.70
Highlands	650.06	696.71	Union	548.75	614.49
Hillsborough	635.11	700.58	Volusia	657.18	704.98
Holmes	513.08	579.29	Wakulla	572.18	641.58
Indian River	700.71	749.94	Walton	569.88	626.40
Jackson	538.31	606.33	Washington	548.96	615.77
Jefferson	542.68	609.15			

Source: U.S., Department of Health and Human Services, Social Security Administration, *OASDI Beneficiaries by State and County, December 1995.*

University of Florida   **Bureau of Economic and Business Research**

Table 7.15. PUBLIC ASSISTANCE: DIRECT ASSISTANCE PAYMENTS, CALENDAR YEARS, 1992
THROUGH 1995, AND MEDICAL ASSISTANCE PAYMENTS, FISCAL YEARS 1992-93
THROUGH 1995-96, BY PROGRAM IN FLORIDA

(rounded to thousands of dollars)

Type of assistance	1992	1993	1994	1995
Direct assistance, total	1,603,925	1,904,745	1,995,811	2,082,385
Basic Supplemental Security Income (SSI)	911,480	1,049,339	1,160,442	1,299,714
Old-Age Assistance (OAA)	236,640	255,228	271,391	288,175
Aid to the Blind (AB)	11,511	12,095	12,437	12,827
Aid to the Disabled (AD)	663,329	782,016	876,614	998,712
SSI State Supplementation 1/	18,836	18,535	18,608	18,836
Aid to Families with Dependent Children (AFDC)	673,609	836,871	816,761	763,835

	1992-93	1993-94	1994-95	1995-96
Medical assistance, total 2/	4,131,306	4,754,229	4,802,304	4,743,272
Aid to the Blind	13,557	15,849	15,945	15,266
Aid to the Disabled	1,339,888	1,615,261	1,785,254	2,067,941
Aid to Families with Dependent Children (AFDC)	1,441,465	1,700,996	1,385,984	1,351,103
Old-Age Assistance	1,263,255	1,429,508	1,551,516	1,249,245

1/ Payments to persons eligible for state benefits but not eligible under federal requirements.
2/ Federal fiscal year ending September 30. Excludes "other."
Source: U.S., Department of Health and Human Services, Social Security Administration, *Social Security Bulletin: Annual Statistical Supplement, 1997,* prepublication release and previous editions, and State of Florida, Agency for Health Care Administration, unpublished data.

Table 7.16. MEDICAL ASSISTANCE: NUMBER OF RECIPIENTS BY AGE OF RECIPIENT
IN FLORIDA, FISCAL YEAR 1995-96

Type of service	Total	Aged 5 and under	Aged 6 to 20	Aged 21 to 64	Aged 65 to 84	Aged 85 and over
Unduplicated total	1,810,203	482,746	546,026	535,730	184,124	61,577
Inpatient hospital	250,882	40,615	36,421	116,785	41,123	15,938
Mental hospital--aged	196	0	0	8	167	21
Intermediate care facilities	49,498	6	223	6,881	20,284	22,103
Skilled nursing facilities	64,157	54	77	6,169	28,683	29,174
Physician	1,478,103	429,620	452,828	442,732	120,298	32,625
Dental	359,991	90,217	204,648	36,310	20,294	8,522
Other practitioners	183,816	22,880	28,240	72,714	41,969	18,013
Outpatient hospital	658,311	171,594	148,149	238,058	79,024	21,486
Clinic	22,700	2,352	2,737	8,783	7,647	1,181
Home health	91,959	23,565	14,891	37,837	11,630	4,036
Family planning	126,812	131	39,164	87,106	334	77
Lab and X-ray	768,732	202,787	188,727	301,919	56,077	19,222
Prescribed drugs	1,066,383	276,779	246,639	338,841	153,176	50,948
Early and periodic screening	220,138	169,036	50,993	109	0	0
Rural health clinic	5,830	27	23	1,853	3,067	860
Other care	603,382	102,995	148,045	212,103	101,358	38,881

Note: Data are for fiscal year ending September 30.
Source: State of Florida, Agency for Health Care Administration, unpublished data.

Table 7.18.　PUBLIC ASSISTANCE:　AVERAGE MONTHLY AID TO FAMILIES WITH DEPENDENT CHILDREN (AFDC) CASES BY TYPE OF RECIPIENT AND AVERAGE MONTHLY PAYMENTS FOR ALL CASES IN THE STATE, DEPARTMENT OF HEALTH DISTRICTS, AND COUNTIES OF FLORIDA, FISCAL YEAR 1995-96

| District and county | Assistance groups (families) | Average monthly cases | | | Average monthly expenditure (dollars) |
		Adults	Children	Persons	
Florida	211,626	165,388	396,262	561,650	54,111,295
District 1	8,537	6,619	15,969	22,588	2,130,160
Escambia	5,576	4,234	10,809	15,043	1,410,969
Okaloosa	1,268	968	2,232	3,200	307,419
Santa Rosa	1,198	1,044	1,996	3,040	292,541
Walton	495	373	932	1,305	119,231
District 2	10,621	8,355	18,898	27,253	2,633,838
Bay	2,121	1,772	3,776	5,548	532,491
Calhoun	295	263	524	787	76,051
Franklin	127	98	221	319	30,721
Gadsden	1,533	1,101	2,848	3,949	375,791
Gulf	243	201	416	617	60,300
Holmes	422	334	728	1,062	101,191
Jackson	742	530	1,282	1,812	177,372
Jefferson	329	252	610	862	82,428
Leon	3,166	2,573	5,586	8,159	791,366
Liberty	104	78	170	248	25,459
Madison	407	263	760	1,023	102,889
Taylor	470	369	823	1,192	115,858
Wakulla	284	230	490	720	69,357
Washington	378	291	664	955	92,564
District 3	9,861	7,927	18,410	26,337	2,530,153
Alachua	3,867	3,156	7,266	10,422	1,007,098
Bradford	698	578	1,265	1,843	175,703
Columbia	1,140	871	2,128	2,999	285,256
Dixie	325	284	581	865	81,971
Gilchrist	201	174	363	537	50,054
Hamilton	353	281	673	954	89,659
Lafayette 1/	0	0	0	0	0
Levy	595	476	1,073	1,549	148,695
Putnam	1,958	1,553	3,741	5,294	511,870
Suwannee	724	554	1,320	1,874	179,847
Union 2/	0	0	0	0	0
District 4	15,781	12,492	29,055	41,547	4,024,350
Baker	405	336	734	1,070	101,496
Clay	846	665	1,500	2,165	209,145
Duval	13,128	10,463	24,431	34,894	3,377,196
Nassau	523	355	870	1,225	120,194
St. Johns	879	673	1,520	2,193	216,319
District 5	13,302	10,527	23,457	33,984	3,350,575
Pasco	3,399	2,838	5,847	8,685	850,139
Pinellas	9,903	7,689	17,610	25,299	2,500,436
District 6	18,414	13,886	35,506	49,392	4,839,331
Hillsborough	15,923	12,184	30,791	42,975	4,202,581
Manatee	2,491	1,702	4,715	6,417	636,750

See footnotes at end of table.　　　　　　　　　　　Continued . . .

Health Districts
Effective July 1, 1993

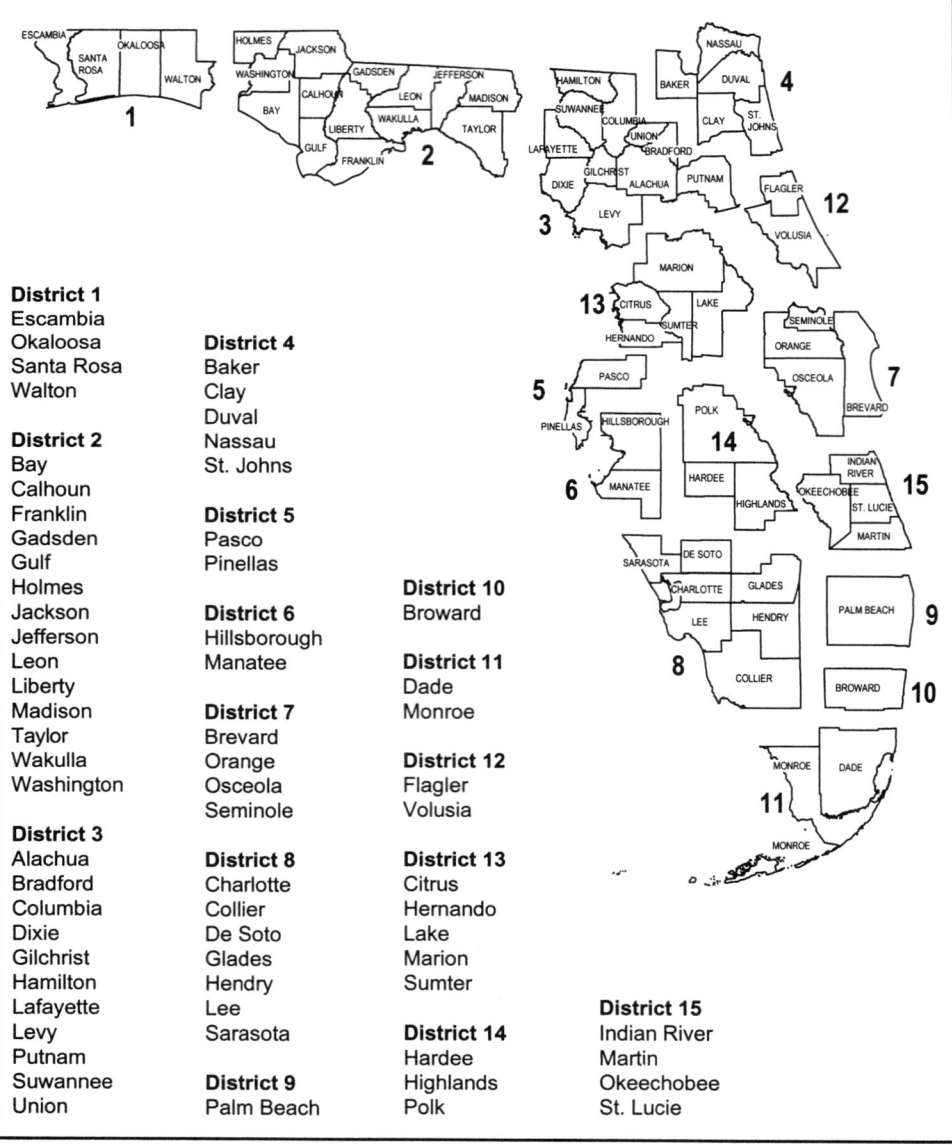

District 1
Escambia
Okaloosa
Santa Rosa
Walton

District 2
Bay
Calhoun
Franklin
Gadsden
Gulf
Holmes
Jackson
Jefferson
Leon
Liberty
Madison
Taylor
Wakulla
Washington

District 3
Alachua
Bradford
Columbia
Dixie
Gilchrist
Hamilton
Lafayette
Levy
Putnam
Suwannee
Union

District 4
Baker
Clay
Duval
Nassau
St. Johns

District 5
Pasco
Pinellas

District 6
Hillsborough
Manatee

District 7
Brevard
Orange
Osceola
Seminole

District 8
Charlotte
Collier
De Soto
Glades
Hendry
Lee
Sarasota

District 9
Palm Beach

District 10
Broward

District 11
Dade
Monroe

District 12
Flagler
Volusia

District 13
Citrus
Hernando
Lake
Marion
Sumter

District 14
Hardee
Highlands
Polk

District 15
Indian River
Martin
Okeechobee
St. Lucie

Table 7.18. PUBLIC ASSISTANCE: AVERAGE MONTHLY AID TO FAMILIES WITH DEPENDENT
CHILDREN (AFDC) CASES BY TYPE OF RECIPIENT AND AVERAGE MONTHLY PAYMENTS FOR
ALL CASES IN THE STATE, DEPARTMENT OF HEALTH DISTRICTS, AND COUNTIES
OF FLORIDA, FISCAL YEAR 1995-96 (Continued)

District and county	Assistance groups (families)	Average monthly cases			Average monthly expend- iture (dollars)
		Adults	Children	Persons	
District 7	21,061	16,074	38,411	54,485	5,331,091
Brevard	4,778	3,565	8,320	11,885	1,184,030
Orange	11,269	8,494	21,177	29,671	2,888,990
Osceola	1,920	1,584	3,400	4,984	478,544
Seminole	3,094	2,431	5,514	7,945	779,527
District 8	8,522	6,233	15,911	22,144	2,147,986
Charlotte	693	532	1,161	1,693	168,757
Collier	1,497	1,098	2,844	3,942	375,981
De Soto	576	444	1,090	1,534	149,480
Glades 3/	0	0	0	0	0
Hendry	837	664	1,662	2,326	224,058
Lee	3,269	2,391	6,234	8,625	827,397
Sarasota	1,650	1,104	2,920	4,024	402,313
District 9	9,170	7,081	18,053	25,134	2,368,993
Palm Beach	9,170	7,081	18,053	25,134	2,368,993
District 10	16,178	12,387	31,091	43,478	4,131,681
Broward	16,178	12,387	31,091	43,478	4,131,681
District 11	50,382	40,143	97,140	137,283	13,054,069
Dade	49,698	39,599	95,951	135,550	12,886,539
Monroe	684	544	1,189	1,733	167,530
District 12	5,558	4,541	9,713	14,254	1,373,670
Flagler	427	354	733	1,087	103,580
Volusia	5,131	4,187	8,980	13,167	1,270,090
District 13	9,698	7,912	17,632	25,544	2,443,250
Citrus	1,197	1,010	2,057	3,067	297,316
Hernando	1,452	1,208	2,517	3,725	359,034
Lake	2,504	2,030	4,570	6,600	633,653
Marion	3,794	3,084	7,060	10,144	962,235
Sumter	751	580	1,428	2,008	191,012
District 14	9,782	7,723	18,092	25,815	2,540,395
Hardee	556	466	1,130	1,596	158,207
Highlands	1,122	856	2,060	2,916	284,443
Polk	8,104	6,401	14,902	21,303	2,097,745
District 15	4,759	3,488	8,924	12,412	1,211,753
Indian River	753	519	1,350	1,869	188,009
Martin	913	691	1,671	2,362	233,453
Okeechobee	434	319	804	1,123	106,591
St. Lucie	2,659	1,959	5,099	7,058	683,700

1/ Payments issued by Suwannee County.
2/ Payments issued by Bradford County.
3/ Payments issued by Hendry County.
Note: Detail may not add to total because of rounding.

Source: State of Florida, Department of Health, unpublished data.

Table 7.19. PUBLIC ASSISTANCE: RECIPIENTS OF SUPPLEMENTAL SECURITY INCOME AND AMOUNT OF PAYMENTS IN THE STATE AND COUNTIES OF FLORIDA DECEMBER 1995 AND DECEMBER 1996

		Beneficiaries						
		Reason for eligibility					Aged	
		Adults			Children		65 and	Payments
County	Total	Aged	Blind	Dis-abled	Blind	Dis-abled	over	($1,000)
			December 1995					
Florida	338,244	99,038	2,944	177,661	311	58,290	133,458	115,203
Alachua	4,511	665	74	2,776	3	993	1,065	1,464
Baker	437	76	5	262	1	93	122	149
Bay	3,239	600	33	2,029	6	571	968	1,071
Bradford	687	127	10	443	0	107	227	221
Brevard	6,675	1,109	42	3,688	7	1,829	1,469	2,307
Broward	22,346	6,220	183	11,750	16	4,177	7,872	7,545
Calhoun	464	118	8	293	0	45	209	147
Charlotte	1,245	281	16	716	2	230	361	395
Citrus	1,346	276	13	831	0	226	385	391
Clay	1,051	180	12	600	2	257	264	342
Collier	1,758	433	20	964	2	339	605	565
Columbia	1,876	330	17	1,212	2	315	536	623
Dade	108,002	53,116	732	46,069	46	8,039	68,423	37,378
De Soto	692	146	7	386	2	151	199	216
Dixie	454	77	4	309	1	63	129	165
Duval	17,356	3,178	164	9,656	15	4,343	4,713	6,048
Escambia	7,965	1,299	91	4,936	20	1,619	2,034	2,767
Flagler	410	89	5	195	0	121	125	137
Franklin	432	123	4	243	1	61	186	147
Gadsden	2,681	558	25	1,514	1	583	879	798
Gilchrist	322	82	5	189	0	46	127	101
Glades	127	31	1	65	2	28	42	39
Gulf	350	84	2	231	1	32	148	127
Hamilton	563	160	5	322	0	76	230	189
Hardee	823	189	6	506	3	119	265	240
Hendry	574	131	6	297	2	138	184	201
Hernando	1,581	262	21	983	4	311	366	550
Highlands	1,827	347	16	985	4	475	488	641
Hillsborough	23,681	4,725	207	13,642	25	5,082	6,770	8,411
Holmes	768	242	10	445	0	71	361	253
Indian River	1,243	213	7	720	4	299	320	376
Jackson	2,085	584	13	1,247	2	239	883	666
Jefferson	655	209	4	347	0	95	298	205
Lafayette	184	39	1	122	0	22	61	64

Continued . . .

Table 7.19.　PUBLIC ASSISTANCE:　RECIPIENTS OF SUPPLEMENTAL SECURITY INCOME AND
AMOUNT OF PAYMENTS IN THE STATE AND COUNTIES OF FLORIDA
DECEMBER 1995 AND DECEMBER 1996 (Continued)

		Beneficiaries						
		Reason for eligibility					Aged	
		Adults			Children		65 and	Payments
County	Total	Aged	Blind	Dis-abled	Blind	Dis-abled	over	($1,000)
		December 1995 (Continued)						
Lake	3,332	593	21	1,881	4	833	848	1,135
Lee	5,136	788	57	3,163	10	1,118	1,137	1,708
Leon	3,610	730	71	2,051	9	749	1,074	1,185
Levy	828	194	5	486	0	143	288	244
Liberty	234	43	4	165	1	21	75	71
Madison	1,110	241	13	638	1	217	375	375
Manatee	3,244	510	31	1,876	4	823	735	1,075
Marion	5,296	908	51	3,074	4	1,259	1,349	1,788
Martin	1,277	232	9	683	2	351	316	410
Monroe	1,058	323	13	626	0	96	437	366
Nassau	694	126	6	439	2	121	196	210
Okaloosa	2,310	387	19	1,498	4	402	637	801
Okeechobee	805	137	11	474	0	183	212	269
Orange	17,657	3,271	146	9,528	17	4,695	4,526	6,255
Osceola	1,738	379	14	934	1	410	521	594
Palm Beach	12,342	3,226	122	6,295	17	2,682	4,177	4,083
Pasco	4,877	763	29	3,177	4	904	1,058	1,656
Pinellas	13,759	2,613	159	8,200	17	2,770	3,632	4,549
Polk	10,899	1,744	79	6,001	6	3,069	2,545	3,727
Putnam	2,443	389	28	1,554	5	467	619	824
St. Johns	1,631	310	25	949	5	342	434	491
St. Lucie	4,005	539	23	2,211	1	1,231	758	1,453
Santa Rosa	1,321	253	18	848	2	200	392	416
Sarasota	2,957	640	30	1,783	3	501	806	927
Seminole	4,054	840	34	2,151	3	1,026	1,149	1,417
Sumter	1,253	226	9	670	0	348	318	416
Suwannee	1,004	277	10	612	1	104	405	273
Taylor	682	140	1	391	1	149	225	262
Union	264	70	2	163	0	29	98	75
Volusia	7,350	1,221	108	4,499	11	1,511	1,785	2,401
Wakulla	408	98	5	231	0	74	142	115
Walton	829	217	10	526	1	75	351	240
Washington	825	194	11	546	1	73	345	258
Unknown	602	117	1	365	0	119	179	194

Continued . . .

University of Florida　　　　　　　　**Bureau of Economic and Business Research**

Table 7.19. PUBLIC ASSISTANCE: RECIPIENTS OF SUPPLEMENTAL SECURITY INCOME AND
AMOUNT OF PAYMENTS IN THE STATE AND COUNTIES OF FLORIDA
DECEMBER 1995 AND DECEMBER 1996 (Continued)

			Beneficiaries					
			Reason for eligibility					
			Adults			Children		Aged
County	Total	Aged	Blind	Dis-abled	Blind	Dis-abled	65 and over	Payments ($1,000)
			December 1996					
Florida	352,770	99,546	2,918	187,160	295	62,851	134,794	120,617
Alachua	4,692	638	65	2,924	3	1,062	1,050	1,581
Baker	470	64	5	293	1	107	115	160
Bay	3,274	555	27	2,114	7	571	905	1,048
Bradford	730	122	8	465	0	135	218	245
Brevard	7,128	1,111	39	3,965	7	2,006	1,476	2,450
Broward	23,841	6,464	190	12,647	19	4,521	8,220	8,162
Calhoun	502	123	8	322	0	49	212	155
Charlotte	1,352	287	17	778	1	269	368	431
Citrus	1,464	269	13	929	0	253	383	433
Clay	1,112	171	16	647	2	276	250	369
Collier	1,830	452	20	998	1	359	624	619
Columbia	2,007	334	15	1,310	2	346	547	680
Dade	110,664	53,917	735	47,150	38	8,824	69,485	38,635
De Soto	709	135	7	397	2	168	179	219
Dixie	484	65	4	335	1	79	120	161
Duval	17,941	3,138	162	10,021	17	4,603	4,686	6,275
Escambia	8,192	1,211	85	5,194	17	1,685	1,955	2,784
Flagler	437	90	4	205	0	138	118	148
Franklin	422	116	3	243	1	59	175	120
Gadsden	2,691	528	23	1,542	1	597	852	820
Gilchrist	332	80	3	198	0	51	130	111
Glades	122	30	2	59	2	29	40	41
Gulf	367	75	3	259	0	30	138	118
Hamilton	572	148	6	340	0	78	217	192
Hardee	803	183	5	471	2	142	268	256
Hendry	596	126	8	320	3	139	183	200
Hernando	1,728	269	23	1,082	6	348	388	574
Highlands	1,895	336	16	1,055	4	484	488	612
Hillsborough	24,701	4,676	210	14,449	23	5,343	6,780	8,786
Holmes	791	226	9	476	0	80	336	229
Indian River	1,337	210	6	781	3	337	326	425
Jackson	2,104	545	17	1,271	2	269	858	621
Jefferson	668	192	4	359	0	113	277	202
Lafayette	147	33	2	94	0	18	54	43

Continued . . .

Table 7.19.   PUBLIC ASSISTANCE: RECIPIENTS OF SUPPLEMENTAL SECURITY INCOME AND
AMOUNT OF PAYMENTS IN THE STATE AND COUNTIES OF FLORIDA
DECEMBER 1995 AND DECEMBER 1996 (Continued)

County	Total	Adults Aged	Adults Blind	Adults Dis-abled	Children Blind	Children Dis-abled	Aged 65 and over	Payments ($1,000)
				December 1996 (Continued)				
Lake	3,554	603	19	2,026	4	902	873	1,201
Lee	5,423	804	60	3,341	8	1,210	1,156	1,761
Leon	3,684	695	67	2,086	7	829	1,045	1,157
Levy	911	189	4	545	0	173	278	313
Liberty	253	38	3	185	1	26	69	64
Madison	1,117	233	11	623	0	250	362	355
Manatee	3,349	494	25	1,951	6	873	737	1,065
Marion	5,662	945	49	3,322	5	1,341	1,411	1,901
Martin	1,289	232	11	720	2	324	321	422
Monroe	1,118	327	15	661	0	115	447	385
Nassau	751	113	7	484	0	147	192	250
Okaloosa	2,375	368	19	1,563	4	421	604	818
Okeechobee	894	147	12	528	0	207	224	300
Orange	18,908	3,359	144	10,244	17	5,144	4,695	6,563
Osceola	1,957	401	12	1,085	0	459	557	722
Palm Beach	12,899	3,302	134	6,596	17	2,850	4,296	4,351
Pasco	5,360	753	31	3,573	5	998	1,075	1,869
Pinellas	14,506	2,559	151	8,766	15	3,015	3,590	4,837
Polk	11,504	1,682	83	6,464	7	3,268	2,505	4,043
Putnam	2,578	388	28	1,661	3	498	639	903
St. Johns	1,761	303	21	1,054	3	380	432	549
St. Lucie	4,290	520	21	2,451	1	1,297	765	1,654
Santa Rosa	1,375	232	17	903	2	221	373	433
Sarasota	3,091	645	29	1,864	4	549	813	952
Seminole	4,252	831	38	2,277	4	1,102	1,160	1,394
Sumter	1,299	221	9	707	0	362	310	437
Suwannee	1,043	263	10	650	1	119	393	294
Taylor	700	143	1	402	1	153	223	232
Union	275	60	3	180	0	32	90	87
Volusia	7,707	1,203	97	4,759	9	1,639	1,787	2,499
Wakulla	427	88	6	254	1	78	136	142
Walton	868	189	9	582	2	86	325	284
Washington	843	181	11	569	1	81	318	249
Unknown	642	116	1	391	0	134	172	226

Source: U.S., Department of Health and Human Services, Social Security Administration, *SSI Recipients by State and County*, December 1996, and previous edition.

University of Florida   **Bureau of Economic and Business Research**

Table 7.20. MEDICAID: RECIPIENTS AND EXPENDITURE IN THE STATE AND COUNTIES
OF FLORIDA, FISCAL YEAR 1995-96

County	Recipients	Expenditure (dollars)	County	Recipients	Expenditure (dollars)
Florida	A/ 1,972,784	5,406,733,541	Lafayette	942	2,185,683
Other states 1/	6	8,922	Lake	23,909	55,709,256
Alachua	28,598	115,981,658	Lee	39,096	125,023,551
Baker	3,606	7,418,342	Leon	23,289	61,442,982
Bay	22,265	59,019,745	Levy	5,524	13,320,622
Bradford	4,507	14,210,091	Liberty	1,041	5,607,170
Brevard	46,151	115,822,977	Madison	3,927	11,336,478
Broward	145,213	389,300,911	Manatee	26,694	61,672,648
Calhoun	2,732	7,806,127	Marion	35,906	73,850,825
Charlotte	10,587	33,914,449	Martin	10,283	30,770,762
Citrus	13,148	35,572,613	Monroe	6,967	21,869,704
Clay	9,136	14,593,944	Nassau	5,310	12,341,155
Collier	20,821	39,629,993	Okaloosa	14,137	42,624,736
Columbia	10,172	27,976,897	Okeechobee	5,798	14,449,556
Dade	434,090	1,334,390,945	Orange	106,587	274,055,866
De Soto	5,780	14,988,811	Osceola	20,402	45,231,077
Dixie	2,856	5,505,364	Palm Beach	94,606	271,266,752
Duval	105,345	288,135,783	Pasco	37,810	94,179,868
Escambia	47,305	116,508,359	Pinellas	95,440	340,654,483
Flagler	3,798	7,400,079	Polk	74,875	155,991,992
Franklin	1,747	7,613,837	Putnam	15,810	34,006,538
Gadsden	11,788	30,215,790	St. Johns	10,060	32,964,810
Gilchrist	2,043	6,619,392	St. Lucie	26,202	63,936,670
Glades	146	512,026	Santa Rosa	11,079	24,516,114
Gulf	2,471	6,849,342	Sarasota	21,594	75,624,879
Hamilton	2,736	5,906,022	Seminole	29,660	68,691,140
Hardee	6,857	13,380,467	Sumter	7,052	14,289,074
Hendry	8,187	16,607,497	Suwannee	5,581	18,539,918
Hernando	14,341	33,851,582	Taylor	4,027	10,099,997
Highlands	11,481	30,154,452	Union	1,555	2,523,937
Hillsborough	142,988	316,804,846	Volusia	50,218	138,921,910
Holmes	4,530	11,480,604	Wakulla	2,592	7,482,079
Indian River	8,669	19,955,355	Walton	5,533	13,958,078
Jackson	8,004	40,092,836	Washington	4,358	11,584,122
Jefferson	2,816	7,779,348			

A/ Unduplicated total.
1/ Florida residents receiving treatment in Alabama or Georgia.
Note: A person may receive aid and be counted as a recipient in more than one
county, therefore detail will not add to the state total.

Source: State of Florida, Agency for Health Care Administration, unpublished data.

University of Florida   **Bureau of Economic and Business Research**

Table 7.21. MEDICAID: PERSONS ELIGIBLE FOR MEDICAID, ALL AGES AND AGED
65 AND OVER, IN THE STATE, LOCAL HEALTH COUNCILS DISTRICTS
AND COUNTIES OF FLORIDA, 1996

District and county	Total	Aged 65 and over Number	Aged 65 and over Percentage	District and county	Total	Aged 65 and over Number	Aged 65 and over Percentage
Florida	1,538,013	246,120	16.0	Northeast Central--4 (Continued)			
Northwest--1	62,070	7,791	12.6				
Escambia	38,068	33,796	88.8	Duval	80,578	10,352	12.8
Okaloosa	11,135	1,660	14.9	Flagler	2,822	296	10.5
Santa Rosa	8,545	1,047	12.3	Nassau	3,709	417	11.2
Walton	4,322	812	18.8	St. Johns	7,404	1,222	16.5
Big Bend--2	78,287	12,498	16.0	Volusia	37,792	5,110	13.5
Bay	17,433	2,394	13.7	Suncoast--5	101,656	16,228	16.0
Calhoun	2,275	492	21.6	Pasco	28,225	3,681	13.0
Franklin	1,336	356	26.6	Pinellas	73,431	12,547	17.1
Gadsden	10,037	1,470	14.6	West Central--6	200,260	23,988	12.0
Gulf	1,997	365	18.3	Hardee	5,129	501	9.8
Holmes	3,685	762	20.7	Highlands	8,515	1,219	14.3
Jackson	6,917	1,572	22.7	Hillsborough	110,179	13,456	12.2
Jefferson	2,302	516	22.4	Manatee	19,475	2,273	11.7
Leon	19,139	2,128	11.1	Polk	56,962	6,539	11.5
Liberty	900	144	16.0	East Central--7	152,572	18,171	11.9
Madison	3,397	694	20.4	Brevard	35,911	4,149	11.6
Taylor	3,341	550	16.5	Orange	80,590	9,551	11.9
Wakulla	2,039	346	17.0	Osceola	14,473	1,804	12.5
Washington	3,489	709	20.3	Seminole	21,598	2,667	12.3
North Central--3	141,294	18,596	13.2	Southwest--8	77,352	10,967	14.2
Alachua	24,111	2,223	9.2	Charlotte	7,570	1,513	20.0
Bradford	3,620	539	14.9	Collier	14,651	1,536	10.5
Citrus	10,201	1,694	16.6	De Soto	4,207	474	11.3
Columbia	8,227	1,175	14.3	Glades	129	40	31.0
Dixie	2,388	284	11.9	Hendry	5,778	519	9.0
Gilchrist	1,635	278	17.0	Lee	28,928	3,641	12.6
Hamilton	2,362	402	17.0	Sarasota	16,089	3,244	20.2
Hernando	10,983	1,315	12.0	Treasure Coast--9	107,673	14,306	13.3
Lafayette	787	98	12.5				
Lake	19,072	2,680	14.1	Indian River	6,617	974	14.7
Levy	4,447	741	16.7	Martin	7,598	1,041	13.7
Marion	28,879	3,773	13.1	Okeechobee	3,908	538	13.8
Putnam	12,997	1,567	12.1	Palm Beach	69,319	9,682	14.0
Sumter	5,728	741	12.9	St. Lucie	20,231	2,071	10.2
Suwannee	4,568	935	20.5	Broward Regional--10	110,619	14,295	12.9
Union	1,289	151	11.7				
Northeast Central--4	141,332	18,133	12.8	Broward	110,619	14,295	12.9
				South--11	364,892	91,145	25.0
Baker	2,618	205	7.8	Dade	359,366	90,166	25.1
Clay	6,409	531	8.3	Monroe	5,526	979	17.7

Note: Local health councils were established in 1982 by the legislature to serve
11 planning districts throughout the state. These councils are responsible for establishing and maintaining the district health plans.

Source: State of Florida, Agency for Health Care Administration, *Florida 1997
Health Data SourceBook*. Compiled by Local Health Councils of Florida.

Table 7.22. FOOD STAMPS: RECIPIENTS AND BENEFITS IN THE STATE AND COUNTIES
OF FLORIDA, DECEMBER 1996

County	Recipients Total	Recipients Receiving public assistance	Benefits in food stamps ($1,000)	County	Recipients Total	Recipients Receiving public assistance	Benefits in food stamps ($1,000)
Florida	1,295,006	434,169	98,586	Lafayette	724	180	47
				Lake	15,520	5,108	1,107
Alachua	20,740	8,520	1,579	Lee	21,280	6,250	1,536
Baker	2,436	785	175	Leon	17,598	6,861	1,375
Bay	15,383	4,401	1,113	Levy	4,075	1,203	283
Bradford	3,399	1,164	252	Liberty	726	248	50
Brevard	30,492	8,997	2,302	Madison	2,453	817	163
Broward	89,542	33,183	7,151	Manatee	15,733	4,654	1,211
Calhoun	1,877	525	124	Marion	25,305	7,917	1,797
Charlotte	5,387	1,299	386	Martin	6,004	1,878	463
Citrus	9,308	2,303	658	Monroe	4,166	1,198	330
Clay	4,548	1,628	353	Nassau	2,511	709	172
Collier	11,005	2,573	832	Okaloosa	8,790	2,311	623
Columbia	7,627	2,520	561	Okeechobee	2,867	845	198
Dade	327,520	103,441	25,599	Orange	65,680	22,702	4,926
De Soto	3,811	1,052	279	Osceola	14,358	4,306	1,099
Dixie	2,091	607	147	Palm Beach	55,687	18,732	4,295
Duval	61,619	25,977	4,779	Pasco	23,111	6,989	1,726
Escambia	31,988	10,998	2,256	Pinellas	57,028	19,869	4,379
Flagler	2,559	934	187	Polk	50,113	17,921	3,856
Franklin	803	226	56	Putnam	11,695	4,116	837
Gadsden	9,160	2,974	622	St. Johns	5,354	1,526	392
Gilchrist	1,153	324	77	St. Lucie	17,008	5,865	1,276
Glades 1/	(X)	(X)	(X)	Santa Rosa	6,721	2,067	479
Gulf	1,777	498	127	Sarasota	10,869	2,464	799
Hamilton	1,761	751	126	Seminole	17,385	6,310	1,326
Hardee	4,846	1,236	376	Sumter	5,784	1,861	390
Hendry 1/	5,578	1,817	412	Suwannee	3,726	1,185	264
Hernando	9,445	2,865	694	Taylor	2,980	928	204
Highlands	6,758	2,123	494	Union	1,204	384	87
Hillsborough	89,233	35,177	7,030	Volusia	32,604	11,382	2,488
Holmes	3,415	723	220	Wakulla	1,614	496	115
Indian River	5,392	1,520	407	Walton	3,610	922	242
Jackson	4,876	1,376	323	Washington	3,111	732	208
Jefferson	2,083	716	142				

(X) Not applicable.
1/ No food stamp issuance office located in Glades County. Food stamp activities
are handled in Hendry County.
Note: Figures represent regular participation. Issuance includes duplicate mail
issuance.

Source: State of Florida, Department of Health and Rehabilitative Services, Office of Economic Services, *Florida Food Stamp Program Participation Statistics for
State Fiscal Year 1996-1997.*

Table 7.56. AVERAGE WEEKLY WAGES: AMOUNT RECEIVED BY PERSONS COVERED BY
UNEMPLOYMENT COMPENSATION LAW IN FLORIDA, 1958 THROUGH 1996

(in dollars)

Year	Average weekly wages 1/	Year	Average weekly wages 1/	Year	Average weekly wages 1/
1958	74.43	1971	131.97	1984	306.55
1959	78.28	1972	138.02	1985	314.88
1960	80.89	1973	143.30	1986	329.60
1961	82.64	1974	155.82	1987	344.32
1962	85.50	1975	167.02	1988	362.41
1963	88.23	1976	175.27	1989	382.00
1964	92.54	1977	185.69	1990	392.18
1965	96.34	1978	195.01	1991	408.82
1966	100.25	1979	210.73	1992	424.66
1967	104.80	1980	227.97	1993	443.95
1968	111.71	1981	252.92	1994	453.38
1969	122.57	1982	271.25	1995	465.23
1970	129.33	1983	288.34	1996	479.30

1/ Data prior to 1972 do not include state, local, or federal government figures.
Beginning in 1972 state data were included, and beginning in 1974 local data were included. Does not include federal data after 1974. Data are for fiscal years from
1971 to date; data are for calendar years prior to 1971.
Note: In 1972 and 1978 changes were made extending coverage of workers.

Table 7.57. UNEMPLOYMENT INSURANCE: CONTRIBUTIONS AND DISBURSEMENTS FOR
UNEMPLOYMENT INSURANCE IN FLORIDA, 1958 THROUGH 1996

(rounded to thousands of dollars)

Year	Contributions deposits 1/	Total disbursements 2/	Year	Contributions deposits 1/	Total disbursements 2/	Year	Contributions deposits 1/	Total disbursements 2/
1958	20,118	28,559	1971	57,425	49,704	1984	526,691	279,457
1959	36,721	22,484	1972	71,799	45,441	1985	514,281	277,463
1960	34,766	31,925	1973	85,861	44,962	1986	478,859	315,337
1961	41,970	43,830	1974	99,304	117,453	1987	469,296	285,736
1962	52,392	33,201	1975	263,243	496,688	1988	468,348	304,930
1963	45,079	29,652	1976	342,166	407,060	1989	480,211	355,749
1964	45,956	24,492	1977	360,650	271,917	1990	461,103	488,961
1965	45,160	20,273	1978	424,988	136,723	1991	560,898	897,263
1966	40,720	17,410	1979	389,370	135,457	1992	1,275,490	1,512,423
1967	37,029	20,639	1980	321,578	197,981	1993	1,259,207	1,199,657
1968	34,094	22,343	1981	305,028	206,012	1994	927,283	801,120
1969	42,145	20,875	1982	326,706	379,067	1995	694,134	632,215
1970	48,594	37,306	1983	451,459	406,075	1996	647,922	635,512

1/ Includes interest, reimbursable interstate and state and local government benefits.
2/ Includes payable interstate benefits.
Source for Tables 7.56 and 7.57: State of Florida, Department of Labor and Employment Security, Division of Employment Security, *Historical Series of Unemployment
Insurance Statistical Data, 1937-1979,* and State of Florida, Department of Labor and
Employment Security, Division of Unemployment Compensation, unpublished data.

Table 7.58. UNEMPLOYMENT INSURANCE: SPECIFIED DATA FOR FLORIDA
1992, 1993, and 1994

Item	1992	1993	1994
Covered employment			
Average monthly number of workers (1,000)	5,243	5,463	5,695
Total payroll ($1,000,000)	119,900	127,151	135,051
Insured unemployment as percentage			
of covered employment	2.4	2.2	1.7
Number of first payments	339,288	276,244	285,055
Average weekly benefit for total unemployment			
Amount (dollars)	158.01	167.16	168.65
Percentage of average weekly wages	36.4	37.3	37.0
Average weekly insured unemployment	126,952	122,519	99,478
Average actual duration (weeks)	16.3	15.2	14.9
Claimants exhausting benefits			
Number (1,000)	191	148	138,150
Percentage of first payments	54.0	51.0	47.2
Contributions collected ($1,000,000)	468.7	618.3	700.0
Benefits paid ($1,000,000)	860.7	697.0	714.0
Average employer contribution rate 1/	1.5	1.8	1.9

1/ As a percentage of taxable payroll. The standard contribution rate for most states is 2.7 percent.

Source: U.S., Department of Health and Human Services, Social Security Administration, *Social Security Bulletin: Annual Statistical Supplement, 1996,* and previous editions.

Table 7.59. WORKERS' COMPENSATION: DISABLING WORK INJURIES AND COST
BY ACCIDENT TYPE IN FLORIDA, 1996.

Cause of injury	Number	Costs ($1,000)			
		Total	Medical	Indemnity	Settlement
Total	71,376	414,575	239,123	137,170	38,282
Burn/scald-heat/cold exposure	1,321	5,820	3,677	1,437	706
Caught in or between	2,149	14,083	7,995	3,722	2,366
Cut, puncture, scrape	3,783	18,448	12,313	5,190	945
Fall or slip	18,531	123,474	72,505	39,944	11,025
Motor vehicle	3,565	28,965	18,544	8,454	1,967
Strain or sprain	25,819	131,343	70,405	48,744	12,196
Striking against/stepping on	2,629	12,797	7,381	4,373	1,043
Struck or injured by	7,499	44,797	26,691	14,009	4,097
Contact with	1,152	8,695	5,513	2,248	934
All other injuries	4,928	26,153	14,103	9,048	3,003

Source: State of Florida, Department of Labor and Employment Security, Division of Workers' Compensation, Workers' Compensation Research and Educational Unit, *1996 Report on Occupational Injuries.*

University of Florida   **Bureau of Economic and Business Research**

Table 7.60. WORKERS' COMPENSATION: NUMBER OF INJURIES AND PAYMENTS IN THE STATE
AND COUNTIES OF FLORIDA, 1996

County	Work injuries	Payments (dollars) Total	Medical	Indemnity	Settlement
Florida	71,376	414,574,745	239,122,784	137,170,202	38,281,759
Alachua	833	4,918,120	3,107,365	1,657,617	153,138
Baker	118	615,662	428,484	181,928	5,250
Bay	710	3,905,203	2,350,236	1,366,667	188,300
Bradford	80	467,194	278,242	161,590	27,362
Brevard	2,163	11,800,172	6,197,544	4,331,425	1,271,203
Broward	5,796	38,553,496	21,749,602	12,053,588	4,750,307
Calhoun	45	263,557	172,056	91,501	0
Charlotte	511	2,675,328	1,762,205	878,373	34,750
Citrus	398	2,792,580	1,826,953	731,977	233,650
Clay	410	1,870,501	1,053,757	704,094	112,650
Collier	1,203	7,754,910	4,608,325	2,392,874	753,711
Columbia	190	1,008,278	604,368	382,069	21,841
Dade	8,704	47,594,172	27,791,906	16,325,557	3,476,709
De Soto	204	983,592	591,747	330,452	61,393
Dixie	48	316,877	215,935	99,442	1,500
Duval	3,969	21,700,504	12,396,250	7,548,758	1,755,497
Escambia	1,177	6,493,887	3,656,915	2,199,503	637,469
Flagler	166	879,071	489,995	321,008	68,068
Franklin	52	200,265	111,896	76,992	11,376
Gadsden	252	1,126,791	634,661	405,230	86,900
Gilchrist	38	164,933	86,901	78,032	0
Glades	54	1,096,211	836,792	181,418	78,000
Gulf	58	694,733	465,965	224,268	4,500
Hamilton	44	270,313	153,232	117,081	0
Hardee	163	1,061,858	678,830	283,028	100,000
Hendry	288	1,516,866	974,032	439,204	103,630
Hernando	463	2,263,531	1,449,385	663,612	150,534
Highlands	318	1,707,647	1,153,431	419,915	134,300
Hillsborough	4,650	26,009,478	15,326,092	8,762,575	1,920,810
Holmes	38	136,190	76,850	52,590	6,750
Indian River	547	3,854,680	2,235,557	1,268,697	350,426
Jackson	185	908,965	585,212	323,753	0
Jefferson	36	149,957	84,084	65,873	0
Lafayette	29	157,372	111,879	45,493	0
Lake	818	4,276,133	2,473,997	1,354,385	447,750
Lee	1,886	12,302,993	7,446,352	3,664,406	1,192,235

See footnote at end of table.   Continued . . .

University of Florida   **Bureau of Economic and Business Research**

Table 7.60. WORKERS' COMPENSATION: NUMBER OF INJURIES AND PAYMENTS IN THE STATE
AND COUNTIES OF FLORIDA, 1996 (Continued)

County	Work injuries	Payments (dollars) Total	Medical	Indemnity	Settlement
Leon	800	3,924,708	2,363,251	1,233,091	328,366
Levy	100	444,489	303,079	113,160	28,250
Liberty	22	193,685	124,610	57,075	12,000
Madison	62	386,181	261,668	122,013	2,500
Manatee	992	5,151,213	3,179,232	1,570,509	401,471
Marion	1,154	6,359,486	3,605,403	2,209,020	545,064
Martin	619	4,262,047	2,444,928	1,426,445	390,674
Monroe	428	2,997,672	1,792,687	995,235	209,750
Nassau	228	1,342,701	783,949	482,683	76,070
Okaloosa	701	4,023,000	2,627,055	1,236,770	159,175
Okeechobee	175	939,203	645,206	236,247	57,750
Orange	5,694	31,874,012	18,005,799	10,172,729	3,695,484
Osceola	636	3,381,901	1,932,108	1,045,528	404,265
Palm Beach	4,667	30,733,478	17,579,844	10,504,500	2,649,134
Pasco	1,006	6,942,036	3,388,602	1,773,763	1,779,671
Pinellas	3,486	18,459,913	10,746,764	6,418,020	1,295,129
Polk	1,849	9,337,987	5,301,495	3,210,995	825,497
Putnam	253	1,983,943	1,300,649	587,445	95,850
St. Johns	445	2,718,291	1,519,870	967,160	231,260
St. Lucie	915	6,402,366	3,947,875	1,952,289	502,203
Santa Rosa	326	1,661,971	977,098	610,673	74,200
Sarasota	1,505	7,123,097	4,033,390	2,471,457	618,250
Seminole	1,154	7,033,290	3,883,749	2,049,697	1,099,845
Sumter	130	746,124	427,156	218,298	100,670
Suwannee	120	498,184	271,825	166,934	59,425
Taylor	82	320,655	199,311	96,344	25,000
Union	65	349,970	192,657	118,285	39,028
Volusia	1,543	8,741,978	4,532,105	2,956,578	1,253,295
Wakulla	43	166,768	80,367	76,801	9,600
Walton	164	910,391	632,582	277,809	0
Washington	97	661,689	468,477	181,712	11,500
Out-of-state	664	5,190,799	2,721,687	2,104,762	364,350
Unknown	4,607	26,819,495	14,681,273	9,341,197	2,797,024

Note: Injuries are reported on a place-of-occurrence basis.

Source: State of Florida, Department of Labor and Employment Security, Division of Workers' Compensation, Workers' Compensation Research and Education Unit, *1996 Report on Occupational Injuries.*

University of Florida   **Bureau of Economic and Business Research**

Table 7.61. WORKERS' COMPENSATION: NUMBER OF WORK INJURIES BY ACCIDENT TYPE AND BY INDUSTRY IN FLORIDA, 1996

Industry 1/	Total	Struck by or caught in	Slips/ falls	Cut	Motor Vehi- cle	Strain/ sprain	Strik- ing against	Other 2/
Total	71,376	9,648	18,531	3,783	3,565	25,819	2,629	7,401
Agriculture, forestry, and fishing	3,267	541	834	270	221	890	128	383
Mining	117	12	35	4	17	28	6	15
Construction	8,862	1,366	2,419	694	346	2,890	362	785
Building construction, general contractors	1,512	217	467	161	34	455	63	115
Construction, special trade contractors	6,177	885	1,726	472	226	2,062	243	563
Manufacturing	6,751	1,186	1,273	588	210	2,467	234	793
Food and kindred products	860	131	205	55	35	328	28	78
Transportation, communications, and public utilities	5,121	690	1,071	131	401	2,203	220	405
Motor freight transportation and warehousing	2,242	307	439	54	178	1,046	90	128
Wholesale and retail trade	14,550	1,903	4,192	949	500	5,102	475	1,429
Wholesale trade	3,055	497	635	153	146	1,196	108	320
Food stores	2,909	416	767	207	23	1,137	84	275
Eating and drinking places	3,729	269	1,603	383	75	799	105	495
Finance, insurance, and real estate	2,178	182	581	55	113	847	65	335
Real estate	958	103	297	38	34	354	32	100
Services	17,596	2,107	4,773	711	881	6,751	605	1,768
Business services	5,787	826	1,635	358	329	1,864	205	570
Health services	4,219	379	986	50	206	2,114	120	364
Government	1,801	264	501	34	134	578	83	207
Establishments, NEC	4,057	580	1,065	172	136	1,503	143	458

NEC Not elsewhere classified.
1/ Major industry group totals include data for industries not shown separately.
2/ Includes burn or scald and contact with injuries and injuries reported with no accident type given.

Source: State of Florida, Department of Labor and Employment Security, Division of Workers' Compensation, Workers' Compensation Research and Education Unit, *1996 Report on Occupational Injuries*.

PHYSICAL GEOGRAPHY AND ENVIRONMENT

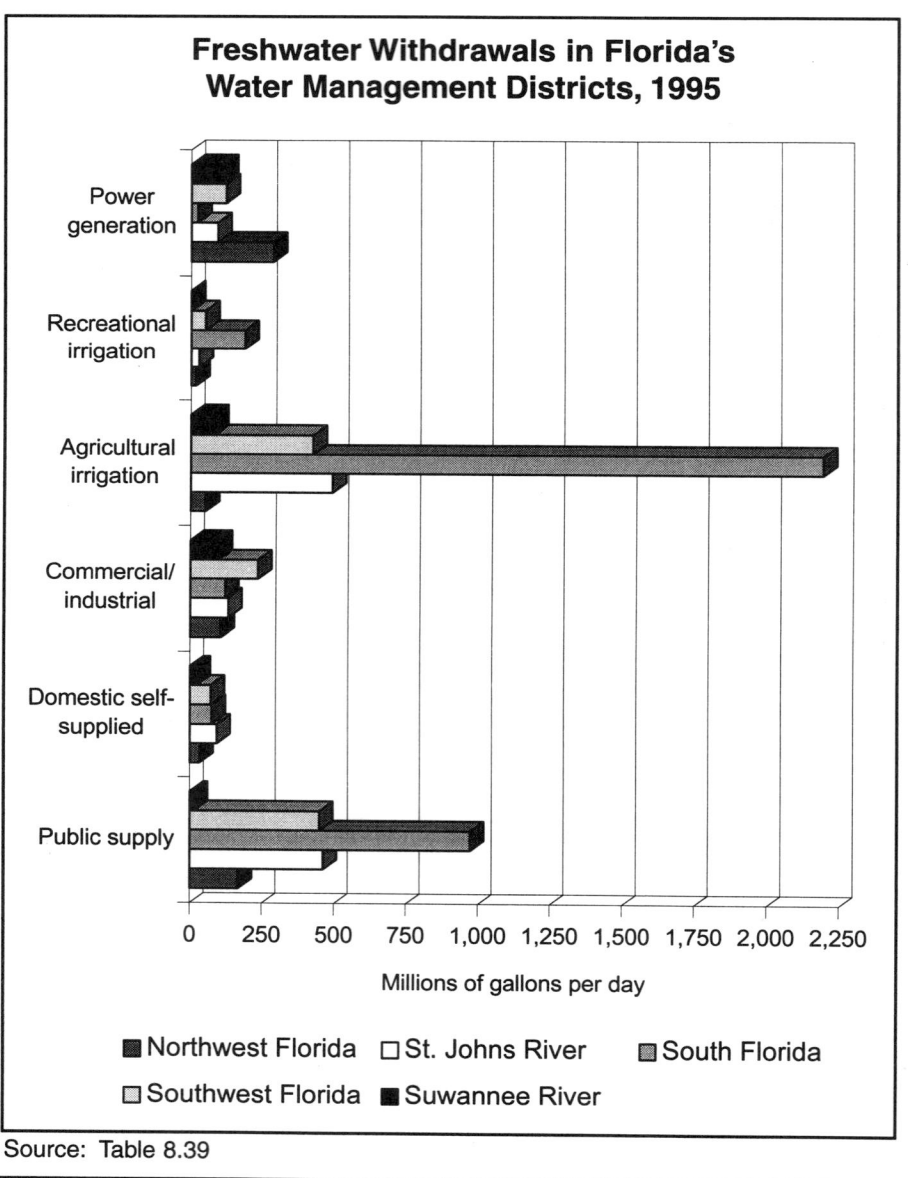

Freshwater Withdrawals in Florida's Water Management Districts, 1995

Power generation

Recreational irrigation

Agricultural irrigation

Commercial/ industrial

Domestic self-supplied

Public supply

0   250   500   750   1,000   1,250   1,500   1,750   2,000   2,250

Millions of gallons per day

■ Northwest Florida   □ St. Johns River   ▨ South Florida

▨ Southwest Florida   ■ Suwannee River

Source: Table 8.39

SECTION 8.00
PHYSICAL GEOGRAPHY AND ENVIRONMENT

TABLES LISTED BY MAJOR HEADINGS

University of Florida   Bureau of Economic and Business Research

Table 8.01. GEOGRAPHY: LAND AND WATER AREAS, COASTLINE, AND ELEVATIONS OF FLORIDA OTHER SUNBELT STATES, OTHER POPULOUS STATES, AND THE UNITED STATES, 1990

	Area (square miles)			Coastline (statute miles)		Elevation (feet)		
State	Total	Land 1/	Water 2/	General coast-line 3/	Tidal shore-line 4/	High-est	Low-est	Ap-prox-imate mean
			Sunbelt states					
Florida	59,928	53,937	5,991	1,350	8,426	345	A/	100
Alabama	52,237	50,750	1,486	53	607	2,405	A/	500
Arizona	114,006	113,642	364	0	0	12,633	70	4,100
Arkansas	53,182	52,075	1,107	0	0	2,753	55	650
California	158,869	155,973	2,895	840	3,427	14,494	-282	2,900
Georgia	58,977	57,919	1,058	100	2,344	4,784	A/	600
Louisiana	49,651	43,566	6,085	397	7,721	535	-8	100
Mississippi	48,286	46,914	1,372	44	359	806	A/	300
New Mexico	121,598	121,364	234	0	0	13,161	2,842	5,700
North Carolina	52,672	48,718	3,954	301	3,375	6,684	A/	700
Oklahoma	69,903	68,679	1,224	0	0	4,973	289	1,300
South Carolina	31,189	30,111	1,078	187	2,876	3,560	A/	350
Tennessee	42,146	41,219	926	0	0	6,643	178	900
Texas	267,277	261,914	5,363	367	3,359	8,749	A/	1,700
Virginia	42,326	39,598	2,729	112	3,315	5,729	A/	950
			Other populous states					
Illinois	57,918	55,593	2,325	0	0	1,235	279	600
Indiana	36,420	35,870	550	0	0	1,257	320	700
Massachusetts	9,241	7,838	1,403	192	1,519	3,487	A/	500
Michigan	96,705	56,809	39,895	0	0	1,979	571	900
New Jersey	8,215	7,419	796	130	1,792	1,803	A/	250
New York	53,989	47,224	6,766	127	1,850	5,344	A/	1,000
Ohio	44,828	40,953	3,875	0	0	1,549	455	850
Pennsylvania	46,058	44,820	1,239	0	89	3,213	A/	1,100
United States	3,717,796	3,536,278	181,518	12,383	88,633	20,320	-282	2,500

A/ Sea level.
1/ Dry land and land temporarily or partially covered by water, as marshland and swamps.
2/ Includes inland and coastal waters. In 1990, inland water was defined as lakes, reservoirs, ponds and rivers, canals, estuaries, and bays from the point downstream at which they are narrower than one nautical mile to the point upstream where they appear as a single line feature on the Census Bureau's TIGER File. Coastal water is within embayments separated from territorial waters by 1 to 24 nautical miles. Excludes territorial waters (waters between the 3-mile limit and the shoreline).
3/ Figures are lengths of general outline of seacoast. Unit of measure is 30 minutes of latitude on charts at approximate scale of 1:1,200,000.
4/ Figures are lengths of shoreline of outer coast, offshore islands, sounds, bays, rivers, and creeks to the head of tidewater, and were obtained in 1961.
Note: Some data are revised.

Source: U.S., Department of Commerce, Bureau of the Census, *Statistical Abstract of the United States, 1997,* U.S., Department of Commerce, Geography Division, unpublished data, and U.S., Department of Commerce, National Oceanic and Atmospheric Administration, unpublished data.

University of Florida   **Bureau of Economic and Business Research**

Table 8.03. LAND AND WATER AREA: AREA OF THE STATE AND COUNTIES
OF FLORIDA, APRIL 1, 1990

(square miles)

County	Total 1/	Land area	Water area 1/			
			Total	Inland	Coastal	Terri- torial
Florida	65,758.1	53,937.0	11,821.1	4,682.9	1,308.1	5,830.0
Alachua	969.2	874.3	94.9	94.9	0.0	0.0
Baker	588.9	585.3	3.7	3.7	0.0	0.0
Bay	1,033.4	763.7	269.6	118.9	0.0	150.7
Bradford	300.1	293.2	6.9	6.9	0.0	0.0
Brevard	1,557.3	1,018.5	538.8	276.0	0.0	262.8
Broward	1,319.7	1,208.9	110.9	12.7	0.0	98.2
Calhoun	574.4	567.4	7.0	7.0	0.0	0.0
Charlotte	859.3	693.7	165.6	122.4	0.0	43.2
Citrus	773.2	583.6	189.6	79.8	0.0	109.8
Clay	643.7	601.1	42.6	42.6	0.0	0.0
Collier	2,305.1	2,025.5	279.6	91.0	0.0	188.7
Columbia	801.1	797.2	4.0	4.0	0.0	0.0
Dade	2,429.6	1,944.5	485.1	76.8	199.8	208.5
De Soto	639.6	637.3	2.2	2.2	0.0	0.0
Dixie	863.7	704.1	159.7	20.4	0.0	139.2
Duval	918.3	773.9	144.4	75.7	0.0	68.8
Escambia	893.9	663.6	230.3	88.1	0.0	142.2
Flagler	570.8	485.0	85.8	22.6	0.0	63.1
Franklin	1,026.5	534.0	492.5	32.1	198.9	261.5
Gadsden	528.5	516.2	12.4	12.4	0.0	0.0
Gilchrist	355.5	348.9	6.6	6.6	0.0	0.0
Glades	986.2	773.5	212.7	212.7	0.0	0.0
Gulf	755.8	565.1	190.7	17.9	65.3	107.6
Hamilton	519.4	514.9	4.5	4.5	0.0	0.0
Hardee	638.4	637.4	1.0	1.0	0.0	0.0
Hendry	1,189.9	1,152.7	37.2	37.2	0.0	0.0
Hernando	589.1	478.3	110.8	23.7	0.0	87.1
Highlands	1,106.4	1,028.5	77.9	77.9	0.0	0.0
Hillsborough	1,266.4	1,051.0	215.3	39.7	155.9	19.8
Holmes	488.8	482.6	6.2	6.2	0.0	0.0
Indian River	617.0	503.3	113.7	36.8	0.0	76.9
Jackson	954.7	915.8	38.9	38.9	0.0	0.0
Jefferson	636.7	597.8	38.9	15.4	0.0	23.5
Lafayette	548.0	542.8	5.1	5.1	0.0	0.0
Lake	1,156.5	953.1	203.4	203.4	0.0	0.0
Lee	1,212.0	803.6	408.4	236.5	6.1	165.9

See footnote at end of table.   Continued . . .

Table 8.03.   LAND AND WATER AREA: AREA OF THE STATE AND COUNTIES
OF FLORIDA, APRIL 1, 1990 (Continued)

(square miles)

County	Total 1/	Land area	Water area 1/ Total	Inland	Coastal	Terri- torial
Leon	701.8	666.8	35.0	35.0	0.0	0.0
Levy	1,412.4	1,118.4	294.0	46.9	0.0	247.1
Liberty	843.2	835.9	7.3	7.3	0.0	0.0
Madison	715.9	692.0	23.9	23.9	0.0	0.0
Manatee	892.8	741.2	151.6	55.2	46.7	49.8
Marion	1,663.1	1,579.0	84.1	84.1	0.0	0.0
Martin	752.9	555.7	197.2	121.4	0.0	75.8
Monroe	3,737.4	997.3	2,740.2	406.8	540.6	1,792.8
Nassau	725.9	651.6	74.3	18.5	0.0	55.7
Okaloosa	1,082.1	935.8	146.3	59.8	0.0	86.5
Okeechobee	892.0	774.3	117.7	117.7	0.0	0.0
Orange	1,004.3	907.6	96.7	96.7	0.0	0.0
Osceola	1,506.5	1,322.0	184.5	184.5	0.0	0.0
Palm Beach	2,386.5	1,974.2	412.3	256.3	0.0	156.0
Pasco	868.0	745.0	123.0	23.1	0.0	99.9
Pinellas	607.8	280.2	327.6	65.4	94.9	167.3
Polk	2,010.2	1,874.9	135.3	135.3	0.0	0.0
Putnam	827.2	722.2	105.1	105.1	0.0	0.0
St. Johns	821.5	609.0	212.4	64.0	0.0	148.4
St. Lucie	688.1	572.5	115.6	43.3	0.0	72.3
Santa Rosa	1,155.3	1,015.8	139.5	128.7	0.0	10.8
Sarasota	725.3	571.8	153.5	34.2	0.0	119.3
Seminole	344.9	308.2	36.7	36.7	0.0	0.0
Sumter	580.4	545.7	34.7	34.7	0.0	0.0
Suwannee	691.9	687.7	4.3	4.3	0.0	0.0
Taylor	1,232.1	1,042.0	190.1	13.5	0.0	176.6
Union	249.7	240.3	9.4	9.4	0.0	0.0
Volusia	1,432.5	1,105.9	326.6	159.0	0.0	167.7
Wakulla	735.8	606.7	129.1	32.9	0.0	96.2
Walton	1,238.1	1,057.7	180.5	90.1	0.0	90.3
Washington	615.8	579.9	36.0	36.0	0.0	0.0

1/ Water area measurement figures in the 1990 census data reflect all water, including inland, coastal, territorial, new reservoirs, and other man-made lakes. Measurement figures reported in previous censuses were only for inland water; the total
water area of the state has increased substantially. See note on Table 8.01 for definitions of inland, coastal, and territorial waters.

Source: U.S., Department of Commerce, Bureau of the Census, Geography Division,
unpublished data.

University of Florida   **Bureau of Economic and Business Research**

Table 8.15. SOLID WASTE: TONNAGE BY DISPOSAL PROCESS AND PER CÁPITA AMOUNT
IN THE STATE AND COUNTIES OF FLORIDA, 1995 AND 1996

| County | Disposal process 1/ | | | | | | Per capita tons 2/ | |
| | Recycled | | Landfilled | | Combusted | | | |
	1995	1996	1995	1996	1995	1996	1995	1996
Florida	9,714.7	8,564.6	9,214.5	9,096.3	5,382.6	5,346.2	1.72	1.60
Alachua	119.8	113.6	135.7	149.4	0.0	0.0	1.29	1.30
Baker	3.7	7.9	15.4	12.4	0.0	0.0	0.94	0.98
Bay	41.9	74.5	17.2	37.3	146.5	141.7	1.48	1.78
Bradford	4.9	6.1	14.4	13.8	0.0	0.0	0.79	0.80
Brevard	290.7	351.5	317.2	302.9	0.0	0.0	1.37	1.45
Broward	1,260.3	651.3	652.6	454.1	1,016.5	1,004.6	2.15	1.52
Calhoun	1.7	2.3	0.2	0.2	4.8	5.3	0.55	0.62
Charlotte	80.0	82.1	89.5	91.0	0.0	0.0	1.33	1.34
Citrus	65.6	59.5	141.5	136.0	0.0	0.0	1.96	1.81
Clay	32.8	25.7	77.9	82.8	0.0	0.0	0.92	0.86
Collier	123.5	150.9	160.5	152.4	0.0	0.0	1.52	1.57
Columbia	3.4	12.4	43.9	44.0	0.0	0.0	0.94	1.07
Dade	1,207.8	1,063.4	1,116.9	1,091.0	1,342.4	1,299.7	1.82	1.69
De Soto	3.5	1.6	15.7	14.4	0.6	1.0	0.74	0.64
Dixie	0.5	0.4	7.9	8.2	0.0	0.0	0.67	0.68
Duval	810.9	606.3	843.4	793.7	0.0	0.0	2.30	1.92
Escambia	94.7	105.2	299.9	352.8	0.0	0.0	1.40	1.60
Flagler	8.2	9.7	26.2	31.9	0.0	0.0	0.93	1.07
Franklin	0.8	9.5	1.6	2.0	8.4	7.8	1.05	1.86
Gadsden	13.5	3.8	31.4	24.0	0.0	5.3	1.00	0.72
Gilchrist	0.4	0.8	4.3	4.2	0.0	0.0	0.39	0.41
Glades	1.5	0.9	7.6	6.1	0.0	0.0	1.07	0.74
Gulf	3.7	3.8	10.1	10.1	6.5	6.5	1.53	1.51
Hamilton	1.7	0.7	6.8	6.5	0.0	0.0	0.68	0.54
Hardee	3.4	5.0	18.6	12.3	0.0	0.0	0.96	0.77
Hendry	2.3	1.3	10.3	12.9	22.3	21.3	1.18	1.18
Hernando	38.0	24.5	30.3	39.1	50.4	47.4	1.01	0.93
Highlands	39.1	30.2	69.5	64.9	0.0	0.0	1.41	1.22
Hillsborough	501.9	570.4	63.5	95.5	752.5	727.1	1.48	1.53
Holmes	0.4	0.6	7.6	7.8	0.0	0.0	0.46	0.48
Indian River	46.1	57.0	124.7	126.2	0.9	1.3	1.71	1.81
Jackson	1.2	3.9	26.8	25.3	0.0	0.0	0.60	0.60
Jefferson	1.2	1.2	8.3	8.2	0.0	0.0	0.70	0.69
Lafayette	0.4	0.2	1.8	1.7	0.0	0.0	0.35	0.27
Lake	36.2	39.7	22.6	12.4	128.6	135.3	1.06	1.03
Lee	191.0	231.0	77.9	113.0	190.2	223.7	1.22	1.48

See footnotes at end of table.   Continued . . .

University of Florida   **Bureau of Economic and Business Research**

Table 8.15. SOLID WASTE: TONNAGE BY DISPOSAL PROCESS AND PER CAPITA AMOUNT
IN THE STATE AND COUNTIES OF FLORIDA, 1995 AND 1996 (Continued)

County	Recycled 1995	Recycled 1996	Landfilled 1995	Landfilled 1996	Combusted 1995	Combusted 1996	Per capita tons 2/ 1995	Per capita tons 2/ 1996
Leon	142.4	146.8	238.1	230.7	0.0	0.0	1.75	1.70
Levy	4.1	5.9	14.7	15.1	0.0	0.0	0.63	0.68
Liberty	1.1	0.4	3.1	2.9	0.0	0.0	0.61	0.45
Madison	2.4	1.2	14.1	13.7	0.0	0.0	0.90	0.80
Manatee	141.7	158.3	298.1	360.8	0.0	0.0	1.89	2.19
Marion	153.3	77.3	173.2	197.0	0.0	0.0	1.45	1.20
Martin	65.1	55.3	138.0	137.2	0.0	0.0	1.81	1.68
Monroe	39.4	67.6	68.0	66.9	33.2	34.9	1.69	2.02
Nassau	7.5	18.8	36.6	39.0	0.0	0.0	0.90	1.13
Okaloosa	62.6	73.4	128.2	160.4	0.0	0.0	1.17	1.41
Okeechobee	10.9	10.4	37.6	33.9	0.0	0.0	1.48	1.32
Orange	450.7	571.8	1,125.3	1,073.6	0.0	0.0	2.08	2.12
Osceola	60.3	48.9	124.4	86.2	0.0	0.0	1.35	0.97
Palm Beach	1,261.1	948.9	341.2	417.0	542.3	546.3	2.23	1.95
Pasco	127.7	109.0	17.1	17.4	240.3	241.5	1.26	1.19
Pinellas	812.3	856.0	78.1	75.0	818.0	818.8	1.95	1.99
Polk	386.3	227.9	396.4	405.7	46.8	43.2	1.87	1.50
Putnam	25.4	26.4	54.0	53.6	0.0	0.0	1.14	1.14
St. Johns	28.1	45.9	103.7	104.8	0.0	0.0	1.34	1.48
St. Lucie	161.7	95.7	156.4	169.6	0.0	0.0	1.86	1.51
Santa Rosa	12.3	11.4	68.0	60.4	1.1	1.2	0.85	0.74
Sarasota	311.3	317.1	246.0	237.4	0.0	0.0	1.85	1.81
Seminole	161.0	112.4	316.6	272.1	0.0	0.0	1.47	1.17
Sumter	14.4	19.9	21.1	21.3	19.4	19.3	1.50	1.49
Suwannee	5.7	10.4	26.1	25.8	0.3	0.3	1.05	1.16
Taylor	1.9	5.0	12.1	14.1	0.0	0.8	0.77	1.05
Union	2.1	4.7	6.1	8.1	0.0	0.0	0.65	0.98
Volusia	217.1	222.7	442.3	424.7	0.1	0.8	1.64	1.59
Wakulla	4.2	1.7	2.9	4.2	6.8	7.1	0.82	0.72
Walton	3.0	3.1	21.2	21.1	0.0	0.0	0.72	0.70
Washington	1.0	1.3	6.3	6.1	3.7	4.0	0.58	0.58

1/ In thousand tons, rounded to hundreds.
2/ Based on April 1, 1995 and 1996 population estimates prepared by the Bureau of
Economic and Business Research, University of Florida.
Note: Data are for fiscal year 1995 and calendar year 1996 and are not comparable.
Detail may not add to totals because of rounding.

Source: State of Florida, Department of Environmental Protection, Division of
Waste Management, Bureau of Solid and Hazardous Waste, *Solid Waste Management in
Florida*, June 1997.

University of Florida   **Bureau of Economic and Business Research**

Table 8.36. WATER USE: WITHDRAWALS BY CATEGORY OF USE AND
BY SOURCE IN FLORIDA, 1995

Category	Freshwater			Saline		
	Total	Ground	Surface	Total	Ground	Saline
Total	7,216	4,336	2,880	10,966	5	10,961
Public supply	2,066	1,856	210	0	0	0
Domestic self-supplied	297	297	0	0	0	0
Commercial/industrial	692	438	254	6	0	6
Agricultural irrigation	3,245	1,528	1,717	0	0	0
Recreational irrigation	280	196	84	0	0	0
Power generation	636	21	615	10,960	5	10,955

See footnotes at bottom of page.

Table 8.39. WATER USE: FRESHWATER WITHDRAWALS BY CATEGORY OF USE AND BY WATER
MANAGEMENT DISTRICT IN FLORIDA, 1995

Category	Northwest Florida	St. Johns River	South Florida	Southwest Florida	Suwannee River
Total	660	1,298	3,571	1,351	334
Public supply	168	462	973	449	14
Domestic self-supplied	33	93	75	72	23
Commercial/industrial	106	132	121	235	98
Agricultural irrigation	52	492	2,193	424	83
Recreational irrigation	16	27	187	50	1
Power generation	285	92	22	121	115

Note: In millions of gallons per day. Values may not be identical to the data
reported by the water management districts due to differences in data collection or
revisions. Detail may not add to totals because of rounding. See additional notes
at bottom of page.

Source for Table 8.36 and 8.39: U.S., Department of the Interior, Geological Survey, Water Resource Division, unpublished water-use data, Tallahassee, FL, August
1997.

Table 8.40. WATER USE: FRESHWATER WITHDRAWALS BY CATEGORY OF USE IN FLORIDA
1970, 1975, 1980, 1985, 1990 AND 1995

Disposition	1970	1975	1980	1985	1990	1995
Total	1,970	1,975	1,980	1,985	1,990	1,995
Public supply	883	1,124	1,406	1,685	1,925	2,065
Domestic self-supplied	209	228	243	259	299	297
Commercial/industrial	900	883	700	709	770	692
Agricultural irrigation 1/	2,100	2,930	3,026	2,798	3,495	3,244
Recreational irrigation 2/	(NA)	(NA)	(NA)	182	310	280
Power generation	1,520	1,608	1,326	680	784	637

(NA) Not available.
1/ Withdrawals for crops, livestock, and fish farming.   2/ Withdrawals for turf
grass and landscaping. Included under agricultural irrigation prior to 1985.
Note: In millions of gallons per day. Detail may not add to totals due to rounding.

Source: U.S., Department of the Interior, Geological Survey, Water Resource Division, unpublished water-use data, Tallahassee, FL, August 1997, and U.S. Geological
Survey Open-File Report 94-521, *Water-use Data by Category, County, and Water Management District in Florida, 1950-1990.*

University of Florida   **Bureau of Economic and Business Research**

Water Management Districts

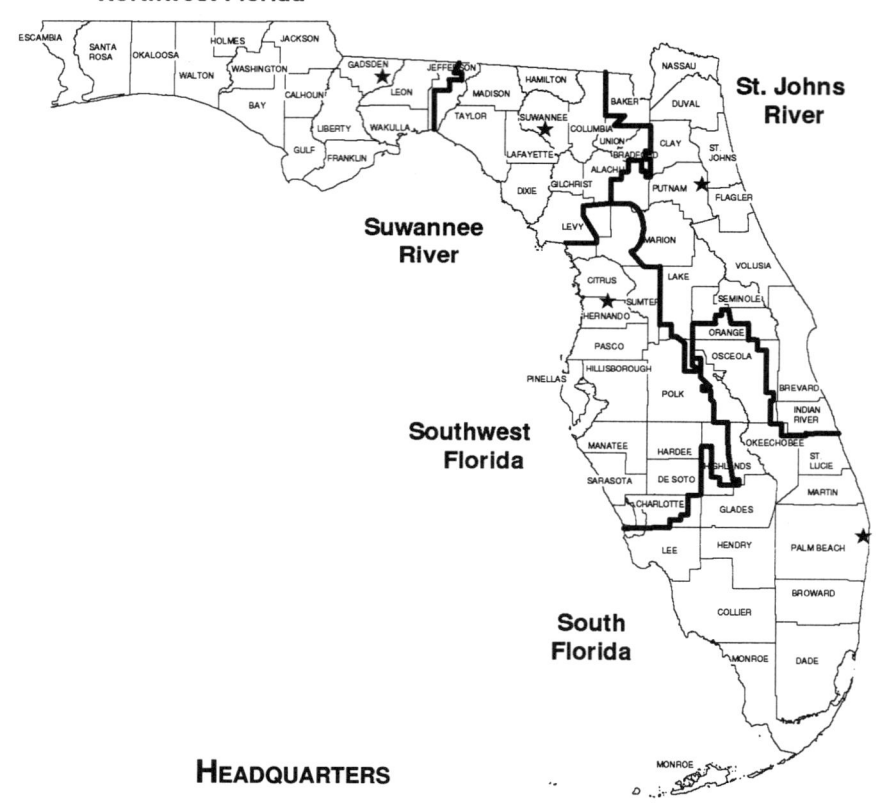

Northwest Florida

St. Johns River

Suwannee River

Southwest Florida

South Florida

HEADQUARTERS

District	City	County
Northwest Florida	Havana	Gadsden
Suwannee River	Live Oak	Suwannee
St. Johns River	Palatka	Putnam
Southwest Florida	Brooksville	Hernando
South Florida	West Palm Beach	Palm Beach

Table 8.41. WATER USE: WATER WITHDRAWALS BY SOURCE IN THE STATE AND COUNTIES
OF FLORIDA, 1995

(in millions of gallons per day)

County	Total	Ground Total	Ground Fresh	Ground Saline	Surface Total	Surface Fresh	Surface Saline
Florida	18,180.63	4,340.21	4,335.58	4.63	13,840.42	2,879.36	10,961.06
Alachua	48.31	47.56	47.56	0.00	0.75	0.75	0.00
Baker	5.37	4.74	4.74	0.00	0.63	0.63	0.00
Bay	318.51	14.26	14.26	0.00	304.25	44.60	259.65
Bradford	7.51	7.46	7.46	0.00	0.05	0.05	0.00
Brevard	1,332.84	113.03	113.03	0.00	1,219.81	22.50	1,197.31
Broward	1,515.60	267.58	267.58	0.00	1,248.02	19.75	1,228.27
Calhoun	4.19	3.38	3.38	0.00	0.81	0.81	0.00
Charlotte	49.88	36.17	36.17	0.00	13.71	13.71	0.00
Citrus	1,685.32	28.28	28.28	0.00	1,657.04	1.73	1,655.31
Clay	21.52	21.28	21.28	0.00	0.24	0.24	0.00
Collier	208.20	186.98	186.98	0.00	21.22	21.22	0.00
Columbia	16.74	16.15	16.15	0.00	0.59	0.59	0.00
Dade	651.75	554.73	550.42	4.31	97.02	18.83	78.19
De Soto	70.94	58.59	58.59	0.00	12.35	12.35	0.00
Dixie	3.41	3.41	3.41	0.00	0.00	0.00	0.00
Duval	720.18	144.61	144.61	0.00	575.57	0.48	575.09
Escambia	269.55	86.83	86.83	0.00	182.72	182.72	0.00
Flagler	14.15	13.30	13.30	0.00	0.85	0.85	0.00
Franklin	2.89	2.89	2.89	0.00	0.00	0.00	0.00
Gadsden	16.38	7.71	7.71	0.00	8.67	8.67	0.00
Gilchrist	9.36	9.26	9.26	0.00	0.10	0.10	0.00
Glades	99.59	20.95	20.95	0.00	78.64	78.64	0.00
Gulf	36.85	3.11	3.11	0.00	33.74	27.98	5.76
Hamilton	46.18	46.18	46.18	0.00	0.00	0.00	0.00
Hardee	51.00	50.49	50.49	0.00	0.51	0.51	0.00
Hendry	557.01	156.35	156.35	0.00	400.66	400.66	0.00
Hernando	41.62	39.58	39.58	0.00	2.04	2.04	0.00
Highlands	119.47	112.83	112.83	0.00	6.64	6.64	0.00
Hillsborough	2,628.16	169.22	169.22	0.00	2,458.94	77.12	2,381.82
Holmes	7.24	6.53	6.53	0.00	0.71	0.71	0.00
Indian River	266.46	76.58	76.58	0.00	189.88	136.29	53.59
Jackson	81.05	28.22	28.22	0.00	52.83	52.83	0.00
Jefferson	11.61	11.09	11.09	0.00	0.52	0.52	0.00
Lafayette	7.45	7.11	7.11	0.00	0.34	0.34	0.00
Lake	83.11	75.43	75.43	0.00	7.68	7.68	0.00
Lee	499.26	112.56	112.56	0.00	386.70	21.45	365.25

See footnote at end of table.   Continued . . .

University of Florida   **Bureau of Economic and Business Research**

Table 8.41. WATER USE: WATER WITHDRAWALS BY SOURCE IN THE STATE AND COUNTIES
OF FLORIDA, 1995 (Continued)

(in millions of gallons per day)

County	Total	Ground Total	Ground Fresh	Ground Saline	Surface Total	Surface Fresh	Surface Saline
Leon	39.30	38.55	38.55	0.00	0.75	0.75	0.00
Levy	23.42	20.93	20.93	0.00	2.49	2.49	0.00
Liberty	1.63	1.56	1.56	0.00	0.07	0.07	0.00
Madison	9.33	8.78	8.78	0.00	0.55	0.55	0.00
Manatee	122.72	90.70	90.70	0.00	32.02	32.02	0.00
Marion	52.07	51.03	51.03	0.00	1.04	1.04	0.00
Martin	170.03	49.80	49.80	0.00	120.23	120.23	0.00
Monroe	2.10	2.10	1.78	0.32	0.00	0.00	0.00
Nassau	44.65	44.54	44.54	0.00	0.11	0.11	0.00
Okaloosa	29.94	29.71	29.71	0.00	0.23	0.23	0.00
Okeechobee	41.22	35.75	35.75	0.00	5.47	5.47	0.00
Orange	259.56	228.56	228.56	0.00	31.00	31.00	0.00
Osceola	81.48	68.27	68.27	0.00	13.21	13.21	0.00
Palm Beach	1,432.60	219.80	219.80	0.00	1,212.80	740.04	472.76
Pasco	1,169.25	129.63	129.63	0.00	1,039.62	12.19	1,027.43
Pinellas	529.91	42.73	42.73	0.00	487.18	2.02	485.16
Polk	391.85	242.98	242.98	0.00	148.87	148.87	0.00
Putnam	88.43	38.11	38.11	0.00	50.32	50.32	0.00
St. Johns	46.37	45.73	45.73	0.00	0.64	0.64	0.00
St. Lucie	1,485.34	80.76	80.76	0.00	1,404.58	229.11	1,175.47
Santa Rosa	23.25	23.03	23.03	0.00	0.22	0.22	0.00
Sarasota	47.86	38.84	38.84	0.00	9.02	9.02	0.00
Seminole	69.78	68.90	68.90	0.00	0.88	0.88	0.00
Sumter	66.14	12.55	12.55	0.00	53.59	53.59	0.00
Suwannee	142.48	29.10	29.10	0.00	113.38	113.38	0.00
Taylor	53.08	51.10	51.10	0.00	1.98	1.98	0.00
Union	2.70	2.57	2.57	0.00	0.13	0.13	0.00
Volusia	156.60	81.16	81.16	0.00	75.44	75.44	0.00
Wakulla	72.52	3.60	3.60	0.00	68.92	68.92	0.00
Walton	11.77	10.59	10.59	0.00	1.18	1.18	0.00
Washington	4.59	4.32	4.32	0.00	0.27	0.27	0.00

Note: Values may not be identical to the data reported or published by the water
management districts due to differences in data collection procedures and categories
used or revisions in reported values.

Source: U.S., Department of the Interior, Geological Survey, Water Resource Division, unpublished water-use data, Tallahassee, FL, August 1997.

University of Florida   **Bureau of Economic and Business Research**

Table 8.42.   WATER USE: PUBLIC SUPPLY WATER DELIVERIES AND WATER USE BY TYPE
OF USE IN THE STATE AND COUNTIES OF FLORIDA, 1995

(in millions of gallons per day)

				Water use			
				Commer-		Public	
			Resi-	cial/		uses and	
	Population		dential/	insti-	Indus-	losses	Other
County	served	Total	domestic	tutional	trial	1/	2/
Florida	12,213,389	2,065.27	1,260.29	385.83	103.34	284.75	31.06
Alachua	153,809	24.09	13.32	6.51	0.67	3.23	0.36
Baker	4,130	0.68	0.29	0.26	0.04	0.09	0.00
Bay	109,645	49.32	12.37	4.23	25.37	6.61	0.74
Bradford	8,502	1.33	0.69	0.39	0.06	0.18	0.01
Brevard	403,819	51.09	30.32	10.34	2.81	6.85	0.77
Broward	1,351,085	222.30	144.08	38.56	6.54	29.79	3.33
Calhoun	4,170	0.68	0.38	0.16	0.05	0.09	0.00
Charlotte	102,919	14.05	9.65	2.11	0.21	1.88	0.20
Citrus	56,740	10.08	6.71	1.63	0.24	1.35	0.15
Clay	93,055	12.04	8.13	1.78	0.34	1.61	0.18
Collier	163,396	39.30	27.22	5.62	0.60	5.27	0.59
Columbia	19,570	2.87	1.26	1.04	0.15	0.38	0.04
Dade	1,947,265	372.53	244.41	60.68	11.93	49.92	5.59
De Soto	7,762	4.79	0.83	0.27	0.02	3.65	0.02
Dixie	4,212	0.64	0.42	0.09	0.04	0.09	0.00
Duval	641,774	99.62	54.54	22.22	8.02	13.35	1.49
Escambia	259,387	37.73	23.77	6.67	1.66	5.06	0.57
Flagler	26,213	4.51	3.12	0.54	0.18	0.60	0.07
Franklin	8,352	1.75	1.29	0.19	0.02	0.23	0.02
Gadsden	27,673	3.86	2.34	0.79	0.15	0.52	0.06
Gilchrist	1,765	0.22	0.10	0.08	0.01	0.03	0.00
Glades	3,456	0.38	0.29	0.04	0.00	0.05	0.00
Gulf	10,108	1.28	0.92	0.17	0.01	0.17	0.01
Hamilton	6,342	0.87	0.46	0.25	0.04	0.12	0.00
Hardee	8,565	1.61	1.06	0.30	0.01	0.22	0.02
Hendry	20,826	4.02	1.61	0.37	1.44	0.54	0.06
Hernando	102,490	17.07	12.79	1.48	0.25	2.29	0.26
Highlands	55,760	8.33	5.52	1.40	0.17	1.12	0.12
Hillsborough	760,450	118.77	64.08	29.95	7.04	15.92	1.78
Holmes	5,360	1.18	0.67	0.26	0.07	0.16	0.02
Indian River	61,886	11.16	6.98	2.19	0.32	1.50	0.17
Jackson	16,270	2.31	1.02	0.69	0.26	0.31	0.03
Jefferson	4,852	0.71	0.46	0.12	0.03	0.10	0.00
Lafayette	1,225	0.18	0.10	0.04	0.02	0.02	0.00
Lake	160,089	26.46	18.90	3.08	0.53	3.55	0.40
Lee	317,708	40.73	21.67	9.78	1.18	7.49	0.61

See footnotes at end of table.   Continued . . .

Table 8.42. WATER USE: PUBLIC SUPPLY WATER WITHDRAWALS AND WATER USE BY TYPE
OF USE IN THE STATE AND COUNTIES OF FLORIDA, 1995 (Continued)

(in millions of gallons per day)

County	Population served	Total	Resi-dential/domestic	Commer-cial/insti-tutional	Indus-trial	Public uses and losses 1/	Other 2/
				Water use			
Leon	186,440	28.74	15.66	8.17	0.63	3.85	0.43
Levy	9,700	1.85	1.16	0.33	0.08	0.25	0.03
Liberty	2,679	0.32	0.22	0.05	0.01	0.04	0.00
Madison	7,341	1.58	0.64	0.28	0.43	0.21	0.02
Manatee	205,300	33.10	22.19	5.00	0.97	4.44	0.50
Marion	107,610	20.27	12.00	4.00	1.25	2.72	0.30
Martin	72,577	14.00	8.65	2.82	0.44	1.88	0.21
Monroe	80,500	14.07	7.92	3.20	0.15	2.59	0.21
Nassau	26,499	4.96	2.92	1.16	0.15	0.66	0.07
Okaloosa	149,665	21.20	13.41	4.01	0.62	2.84	0.32
Okeechobee	21,200	1.95	1.20	0.44	0.05	0.26	0.00
Orange	695,162	141.05	78.36	35.82	5.85	18.90	2.12
Osceola	100,855	19.15	11.93	4.05	0.31	2.57	0.29
Palm Beach	881,737	186.88	124.85	28.88	5.12	25.04	2.99
Pasco	223,605	26.14	17.33	4.45	0.47	3.50	0.39
Pinellas	867,440	113.35	65.60	24.28	6.58	15.19	1.70
Polk	386,054	58.42	37.29	9.35	3.07	7.83	0.88
Putnam	21,118	3.59	2.06	0.83	0.17	0.48	0.05
St. Johns	76,651	10.30	5.84	2.59	0.34	1.38	0.15
St. Lucie	107,162	15.31	9.27	2.82	0.40	2.05	0.77
Santa Rosa	91,030	12.08	8.84	1.19	0.25	1.62	0.18
Sarasota	247,250	36.18	19.06	8.34	1.54	7.06	0.18
Seminole	277,249	50.73	34.51	6.84	1.82	6.80	0.76
Sumter	16,609	2.45	1.56	0.41	0.13	0.33	0.02
Suwannee	9,276	1.42	0.79	0.36	0.07	0.19	0.01
Taylor	10,127	1.93	1.03	0.37	0.25	0.26	0.02
Union	4,000	0.38	0.20	0.09	0.04	0.05	0.00
Volusia	352,682	48.78	29.80	10.23	1.47	6.55	0.73
Wakulla	8,563	1.06	0.71	0.17	0.03	0.14	0.01
Walton	29,138	4.35	2.89	0.79	0.05	0.58	0.04
Washington	7,540	1.14	0.63	0.23	0.12	0.15	0.01

1/ Water used for fire fighting system flushing or maintenance and water lost to
leakage or processing.
    2/ Includes water used for power generation, heating and cooling systems, and ur-
ban irrigation.
    Note: Public supply refers to municipal or other private water utilities which
serve the public.

    Source: U.S., Department of the Interior, Geological Survey, Water Resource Divi-
sion, unpublished water-use data, Tallahassee, FL, August 1997.

University of Florida   **Bureau of Economic and Business Research**

Table 8.43. WATER USE: WATER DISCHARGED FROM WASTEWATER TREATMENT FACILITIES
BY TYPE OF FACILITY IN THE STATE AND COUNTIES OF FLORIDA, 1995

(in millions of gallons per day)

County	Total	Domes-tic	Indus-trial	County	Total	Domes-tic	Indus-trial
Florida	1,836.74	1,544.39	292.35	Lafayette	0.24	0.24	0.00
				Lake	10.01	8.93	1.08
Alachua	17.24	16.53	0.71	Lee	34.76	34.76	0.00
Baker	0.96	0.96	0.00	Leon	17.46	17.46	0.00
Bay	37.76	37.76	0.00	Levy	0.65	0.65	0.00
Bradford	9.89	2.28	7.61	Liberty	0.11	0.11	0.00
Brevard	40.21	40.21	0.00	Madison	0.92	0.92	0.00
Broward	191.19	191.19	0.00	Manatee	28.93	25.81	3.12
Calhoun	0.69	0.69	0.00	Marion	7.41	7.41	0.00
Charlotte	7.15	7.15	0.00	Martin	5.63	5.28	0.35
Citrus	2.57	2.57	0.00	Monroe	9.05	9.05	0.00
Clay	16.58	8.78	7.80	Nassau	39.21	3.36	35.85
Collier	20.77	20.77	0.00	Okaloosa	17.41	17.41	0.00
Columbia	1.90	1.90	0.00	Okeechobee	0.57	0.57	0.00
Dade	323.91	323.91	0.00	Orange	94.67	94.67	0.00
De Soto	1.31	1.31	0.00	Osceola	14.36	14.36	0.00
Dixie	0.30	0.30	0.00	Palm Beach	107.80	107.70	0.10
Duval	100.76	81.41	19.35	Pasco	26.37	16.27	10.10
Escambia	69.56	20.29	49.27	Pinellas	121.73	121.73	0.00
Flagler	3.15	3.15	0.00	Polk	41.30	28.47	12.83
Franklin	1.10	1.10	0.00	Putnam	31.80	3.22	28.58
Gadsden	2.07	2.07	0.00	St. Johns	7.82	7.82	0.00
Gilchrist	0.16	0.16	0.00	St. Lucie	10.55	10.55	0.00
Glades	0.00	0.00	0.00	Santa Rosa	5.39	2.91	2.48
Gulf	36.99	28.65	8.34	Sarasota	27.93	22.79	5.14
Hamilton	18.74	0.81	17.93	Seminole	35.73	35.73	0.00
Hardee	1.59	1.59	0.00	Sumter	0.79	0.79	0.00
Hendry	4.23	1.77	2.46	Suwannee	2.30	0.96	1.34
Hernando	3.98	3.98	0.00	Taylor	50.02	1.00	49.02
Highlands	2.15	2.15	0.00	Union	0.40	0.40	0.00
Hillsborough	112.06	86.33	25.73	Volusia	40.02	40.02	0.00
Holmes	0.70	0.70	0.00	Wakulla	1.53	0.13	1.40
Indian River	6.46	5.63	0.83	Walton	3.35	2.42	0.93
Jackson	2.87	2.87	0.00	Washington	0.98	0.98	0.00
Jefferson	0.54	0.54	0.00				

Note: Discharge is to both surface and ground. Domestic facilities include those
operated by public or private utilities. Industrial facilities exclude discharge
from power plants or mining operations.

Source: U.S., Department of the Interior, Geological Survey, Water Resource Division, unpublished water-use data, Tallahassee, FL, August 1997.

University of Florida   **Bureau of Economic and Business Research**

National Weather Station Offices

Office

City	County
Apalachicola	Franklin
Daytona Beach	Volusia
Ft. Myers	Lee
Jacksonville	Duval
Key West	Monroe
Melbourne	Brevard
Miami	Dade
Orlando	Orange
Pensacola	Escambia
Tallahassee	Leon
Tampa	Hillsborough
West Palm Beach	Palm Beach

Table 8.70. CLIMATE: TEMPERATURE CHARACTERISTICS AND TOTAL PRECIPITATION AT NATIONAL WEATHER STATION OFFICES IN FLORIDA BY MONTH, 1996

(temperature in degrees Fahrenheit)

Station and characteristics	January	February	March	April	May	June	July	August	September	October	November	December
Apalachicola												
Temperature												
Average maximum	63.5	65.7	65.6	74.1	86.4	89.3	89.8	88.2	86.5	79.3	72.9	67.9
Average minimum	40.4	43.2	47.8	55.0	66.1	70.6	74.7	73.4	71.2	59.6	48.7	45.9
Heating degree days	399	320	264	82	3	0	0	0	0	7	153	256
Cooling degree days	3	22	15	74	362	455	541	499	424	151	35	12
Days with maximum 90 degrees or more	0	0	0	0	8	12	24	6	5	0	0	0
Days with minimum 32 degrees or less	6	8	3	0	0	0	0	0	0	0	0	4
Precipitation (inches)	2.4	3.9	10.6	4.3	0.6	2.0	10.5	11.2	6.5	20.5	1.1	5.5
Pensacola												
Temperature												
Average maximum	60.4	63.7	65.7	73.5	86.5	88.9	91.1	89.6	87.6	78.5	70.1	65.2
Average minimum	38.6	43.9	45.4	55.6	66.5	71.0	74.4	73.0	70.7	59.7	50.2	46.2
Heating degree days	474	339	302	79	2	0	0	0	0	26	187	311
Cooling degree days	0	24	18	74	367	453	560	513	433	161	47	28
Days with maximum 90 degrees or more	0	0	0	0	10	13	22	17	9	0	0	0
Days with minimum 32 degrees or less	8	8	5	0	0	0	0	0	0	0	0	5
Precipitation (inches)	4.2	6.2	8.6	8.0	1.9	6.3	7.8	9.1	5.3	2.8	2.1	5.3
Tallahassee												
Temperature												
Average maximum	64.5	67.5	68.5	76.6	89.5	90.5	92.2	89.7	87.4	79.5	71.8	66.7
Average minimum	36.9	41.2	43.4	48.3	62.7	68.3	72.2	70.6	67.0	54.4	46.1	41.0
Heating degree days	440	327	301	136						50	206	342
Cooling degree days	3	25	26	66	358	442	540	480	372	120	31	0
Days with maximum 90 degrees or more	0	0	0	0	16	20	24	19	12	0	0	0
Days with minimum 32 degrees or less	13	11	8	2	0	0	0	0	0	0	1	6
Precipitation (inches)	2.9	3.6	8.4	3.7	1.9	4.7	3.4	8.2	4.0	8.7	1.1	6.1

See footnotes at end of table.

Continued . . .

Table 8.70. CLIMATE: TEMPERATURE CHARACTERISTICS AND TOTAL PRECIPITATION AT NATIONAL WEATHER STATION OFFICES IN FLORIDA BY MONTH, 1996 (Continued)

(temperature in degrees Fahrenheit)

Station and characteristics	January	February	March	April	May	June	July	August	September	October	November	December
Jacksonville												
Temperature												
Average maximum	65.2	69.3	69.0	78.5	86.9	88.2	91.2	87.4	86.9	79.3	70.8	66.5
Average minimum	39.8	43.7	45.7	52.5	64.4	69.0	73.7	70.9	67.9	60.4	48.5	44.2
Heating degree days	393	271	267	79	6	0	0	0	0	19	186	302
Cooling degree days	12	32	38	101	344	416	549	445	381	179	32	11
Days with maximum 90 degrees or more	0	0	0	0	12	12	22	8	5	0	0	0
Days with minimum 32 degrees or less	8	7	3	0	0	0	0	0	0	0	0	4
Precipitation (inches)	1.1	1.1	6.8	2.9	0.7	11.4	4.2	7.8	8.5	11.5	1.4	3.2
Daytona Beach												
Temperature												
Average maximum	68.2	70.9	70.5	77.2	84.6	86.2	89.8	87.6	87.4	80.5	75.4	70.8
Average minimum	45.4	47.5	50.8	56.1	66.6	70.2	72.5	71.4	70.4	65.2	57.0	50.7
Heating degree days	272	212	197	55	0	0	0	0	0	11	62	155
Cooling degree days	24	50	72	114	338	402	505	459	427	262	106	29
Days with maximum 90 degrees or more	0	0	0	0	3	0	18	6	0	0	0	0
Days with minimum 32 degrees or less	2	4	1	0	0	0	0	0	0	0	0	1
Precipitation (inches)	5.5	1.3	12.2	2.2	2.3	11.4	1.9	5.7	3.9	11.2	1.0	2.0
Orlando												
Temperature												
Average maximum	70.6	72.9	73.9	82.8	90.4	91.1	92.3	90.3	89.3	82.6	78.0	73.3
Average minimum	47.5	49.7	51.9	60.3	69.9	72.4	73.5	72.9	71.9	64.9	57.0	51.3
Heating degree days	208	173	149	12	0	0	0	0	0	6	38	122
Cooling degree days	33	72	93	217	477	512	561	524	478	283	124	46
Days with maximum 90 degrees or more	2	2	0	5	23	19	26	20	14	0	0	0
Days with minimum 32 degrees or less	2	2	0	0	0	0	0	0	0	0	0	0
Precipitation (inches)	5.4	1.5	9.9	0.7	5.1	6.5	4.1	11.3	6.0	3.3	0.7	2.1

Continued . . .

See footnotes at end of table.

Table 8.70. CLIMATE: TEMPERATURE CHARACTERISTICS AND TOTAL PRECIPITATION AT NATIONAL WEATHER STATION OFFICES IN FLORIDA BY MONTH, 1996 (Continued)

(temperature in degrees Fahrenheit)

Station and characteristics	January	February	March	April	May	June	July	August	September	October	November	December
Melbourne												
Temperature												
Average maximum	71.8	73.2	74.7	79.1	85.7	87.7	90.7	89.8	89.4	83.0	78.1	73.7
Average minimum	48.9	47.6	52.5	58.7	68.5	70.5	72.9	72.0	71.8	66.4	60.4	52.0
Heating degree days	190	183	141	31	0	0	0	0	0	3	30	109
Cooling degree days	53	58	103	159	384	430	528	501	478	309	166	50
Days with maximum 90 degrees or more	0	0	0	1	4	7	20	17	15	0	0	0
Days with minimum 32 degrees or less	2	4	0	0	0	0	0	0	0	0	0	0
Precipitation (inches)	3.6	0.8	11.6	1.0	2.4	9.0	3.2	5.6	3.6	5.1	2.0	1.8
Tampa												
Temperature												
Average maximum	69.2	69.3	71.7	79.7	87.4	88.7	90.7	90.7	89.7	83.5	77.7	72.8
Average minimum	49.2	50.8	53.0	61.0	71.1	73.0	76.7	75.6	74.2	68.1	58.4	54.2
Heating degree days	198	188	152	16	0	0	0	0	0	3	36	101
Cooling degree days	27	50	76	182	450	482	589	570	516	348	135	63
Days with maximum 90 degrees or more	0	0	0	1	4	12	22	23	20	1	0	0
Days with minimum 32 degrees or less	1	2	0	0	0	0	0	0	0	0	0	0
Precipitation (inches)	5.4	3.0	4.7	4.2	1.5	9.0	2.7	7.4	5.4	3.1	0.9	2.1
Miami												
Temperature												
Average maximum	76.3	76.8	77.5	82.7	87.6	89.4	90.5	89.7	89.8	84.0	80.4	78.0
Average minimum	59.8	56.6	61.9	69.2	74.8	75.5	78.5	76.5	76.5	72.8	68.1	62.4
Heating degree days	65	77	41	0	0	0	0	0	0	0	0	26
Cooling degree days	168	134	193	335	512	532	609	566	555	421	284	195
Days with maximum 90 degrees or more	0	0	0	1	7	15	25	19	13	0	0	0
Days with minimum 32 degrees or less	0	0	0	0	0	0	0	0	0	0	0	0
Precipitation (inches)	2.3	0.8	1.4	3.4	8.3	11.7	5.3	5.6	7.2	10.1	0.7	1.0

Continued . . .

See footnotes at end of table.

Table 8.70. CLIMATE: TEMPERATURE CHARACTERISTICS AND TOTAL PRECIPITATION AT NATIONAL WEATHER STATION OFFICES IN FLORIDA BY MONTH, 1996 (Continued)

(temperature in degrees Fahrenheit)

Station and characteristics	Janu-ary	Febru-ary	March	April	May	June	July	August	Sep-tember	Octo-ber	Novem-ber	Decem-ber
West Palm Beach												
Temperature												
Average maximum	74.4	75.6	76.9	80.9	85.6	87.7	90.4	89.1	89.3	83.9	79.9	77.4
Average minimum	57.1	53.1	58.6	65.7	72.9	73.7	76.5	74.9	74.8	71.7	65.9	59.6
Heating degree days	105	105	62	6	0	0	0	0	0	0	1	35
Cooling degree days	136	93	155	263	451	478	579	534	519	405	246	153
Days with maximum 90 degrees or more	0	0	0	0	3	5	22	16	14	0	0	0
Days with minimum 32 degrees or less	0	0	0	0	0	0	0	0	0	0	0	0
Precipitation (inches)	1.5	0.7	5.1	0.8	6.5	7.6	2.8	4.2	7.5	6.5	2.1	1.6
Key West												
Temperature												
Average maximum	74.4	74.9	75.2	80.5	85.3	87.6	89.4	88.9	88.6	83.4	79.9	77.6
Average minimum	62.8	59.9	64.6	71.1	76.0	77.5	80.1	78.5	78.4	74.5	71.3	67.4
Heating degree days	37	61	29	0	0	0	0	0	0	0	0	12
Cooling degree days	158	137	188	333	490	533	621	586	562	439	323	249
Days with maximum 90 degrees or more	0	0	0	0	0	4	17	9	10	0	0	0
Days with minimum 32 degrees or less	0	0	0	0	0	0	0	0	0	0	0	0
Precipitation (inches)	0.9	0.2	1.9	2.8	2.6	3.2	3.2	6.5	6.6	11.9	0.1	1.4

Note: Degree day totals are the sums of the negative (heating) or positive (cooling) departures of average daily temperatures from 65 degrees Fahrenheit. Data for the Ft. Myers weather station were not available.
Source: U.S., Department of Commerce, National Oceanic and Atmospheric Administration, National Environmental Satellite, Data and Information Service, Climatological Data: Florida, 1996 monthly reports.

Table 8.74. CLIMATE: CHARACTERISTICS FOR JACKSONVILLE, MIAMI, LOS ANGELES, ATLANTA CHICAGO, AND NEW YORK, SPECIFIED DATES THROUGH 1995

Characteristic	Jackson-ville Florida	Miami Florida	Los Angeles Cali-fornia	Atlanta Georgia	Chicago Illinois	New York New York 1/
Normal temperature 2/						
January average	52.4	67.2	56.8	41.0	21.0	31.5
July average	81.6	82.6	69.1	78.8	73.2	76.8
Annual average	68.0	75.9	63.0	61.3	49.0	54.7
January normal high	64.2	75.2	65.7	50.4	29.0	37.6
July normal high	91.4	89.0	75.3	88.0	83.7	85.2
Annual average high	78.9	82.8	70.4	71.2	58.6	62.3
January normal low	40.5	59.2	47.8	31.5	12.9	25.3
July normal low	71.9	76.2	62.8	69.5	62.6	68.4
Annual average low	57.1	69.0	55.5	51.3	39.5	47.1
Extreme temperatures 3/						
Highest temperature of record	105	98	110	105	104	106
Lowest temperature of record	7	30	23	-8	-27	-15
Length of record (years)	54	53	60	47	37	127
Normal annual precipitation 2/						
(inches)	51.32	55.91	12.01	50.77	35.82	47.25
Average number of days precipi-						
tation 0.01 or more 3/	116	130	35	115	126	121
Length of record (years)	54	53	60	61	37	126
Average total snow and						
ice pellets 3/ (inches)	T	0.0	T	2.0	38.2	28.3
Length of record (years)	54	53	60	61	37	127
Average annual percentage of						
possible sunshine 3/ 4/	61	68	72	59	52	64
Length of record (years)	46	45	59	60	36	42
Average annual wind speed 3/						
(MPH)	7.9	9.3	7.5	9.1	10.4	9.4
Length of record (years)	45	45	46	56	36	58
Heating and cooling degree						
days 2/ 5/						
Heating degree days	1,434	200	1,458	2,991	6,536	4,805
Cooling degree days	2,551	4,198	727	1,667	752	1,096
Average relative humidity 3/						
Length of record	58	30	35	34	36	61
Annual (percentage)						
Morning	88	84	79	82	80	72
Afternoon	56	61	64	56	60	56

T Trace.   MPH Miles per hour.
1/ City office data.
2/ Based on 1961-90 period of record.
3/ Record through 1995.
4/ Percentage of days that are either clear or partly cloudy.
5/ Degree day normals are used to determine relative estimates of heating requirements for buildings. Each day that the average temperature for a day is below 65 degrees F. produces one heating degree day and each day it is above 65 degrees F. produces one cooling degree day.
Note: All temperatures are in degrees Fahrenheit.

Source: U.S., Department of Commerce, Bureau of the Census, *Statistical Abstract
of the United States, 1997*. Data from U.S. National Oceanic and Atmospheric Administration.

University of Florida   **Bureau of Economic and Business Research**

Table 8.76. HURRICANES: AREA OF LANDFALL, NAME, YEAR, FORCE CATEGORY, AND RANK OF
THE FIFTEEN DEADLIEST HURRICANES IN THE UNITED STATES, 1900 THROUGH 1996

Area of landfall/name	Year	Force cate-gory 1/	Deaths Number	Rank
Galveston, Texas/(NA)	1900	4	6,000	1
Lake Okeechobee, Florida/(NA)	1928	4	1,836	2
Florida Keys; S. Texas/(NA)	1919	4	600	3
New England/(NA)	1938	3	600	4
Florida Keys/(NA)	1935	5	408	5
S.W. Louisiana; N. Texas/Audrey	1957	4	390	6
N.E. United States/(NA)	1944	3	390	7
Grand Isle, Louisiana/(NA)	1909	4	350	8
New Orleans, Louisiana/(NA)	1915	4	275	9
Galveston, Texas/(NA)	1915	4	275	10
Mississippi; Louisiana/Camille	1969	5	256	11
Miami, Florida/(NA)	1926	4	243	12
N.E. United States/Diane	1955	1	184	13
S.E. Florida/(NA)	1906	2	164	14
Mississippi; Alabama; Pensacola, Florida/(NA)	1906	3	134	15

(NA) Not available.
1/ Assigned based on the Saffir/Simpson scale. Ratings are 1-5 and a "5" indicate
central pressure less than 920 millibars or winds greater than 155 mph or storm surge
higher than 18 feet and damage classified as catastrophic.

Table 8.77. HURRICANES: AREA OF LANDFALL, NAME, YEAR, FORCE CATEGORY, AND RANK OF
THE TEN COSTLIEST HURRICANES IN THE UNITED STATES, 1900 THROUGH 1996

Area of landfall/name	Year	Force cate-gory 1/	Value of damage 2/ Amount ($1,000)	Rank
Florida; Louisiana/Andrew	1992	4	25,000,000	1
South Carolina/Hugo	1989	4	7,155,120	2
Florida; Louisiana/Betsy	1965	3	6,461,303	3
N.E. United States/Agnes	1972	1	6,418,143	4
Mississippi; Alabama/Camille	1969	5	5,242,380	5
N.E. United States/Diane	1955	1	4,199,645	6
New England/(NA)	1938	3	3,593,853	7
Alabama; Mississippi/Frederic	1979	3	3,502,942	8
North Carolina/Fran	1996	3	A/ 3,200,000	9
Florida/Opal	1995	4	A/ 3,000,000	10

(NA) Not available.
A/ Preliminary estimate.
1/ Assigned based on the Saffir/Simpson scale. Ratings are 1-5 and a "5" indicates central pressure less than 920 millibars or winds greater than 155 mph or storm
surge higher than 18 feet and damage classified as catastrophic.
2/ Adjusted to 1990 dollars on basis of U.S. Department of Commerce composite construction cost indexes.

Source for Tables 8.76 and 8.77: U.S., Department of Commerce, National Oceanic
and Atmospheric Administration, *The Deadliest, Costliest, and Most Intense United
States Hurricanes of this Century.* NOAA Technical Memorandum NWS NHC-31, and National Climatic Data Center, *1996 Atlantic Tropical Storms,* Technical Report 97-02.

Table 8.80. AIR POLLUTION: PARTICULATE MATTER (PM) CONCENTRATIONS
IN SPECIFIED CITIES OF FLORIDA, 1996

County and area 1/	Site Address	2nd highest 24-hour value 2/	Annual arith-metic mean 3/
		PM10 concentration (UG/M^3)	
Alachua			
Gainesville	721 NW 6th Street	42	19
Bay			
Panama City	Cherry Street & Henderson Avenue S.T.P.	50	23
Brevard			
Merritt Island	2575 N Courtenay Parkway	40	18
Titusville	611 Singleton Avenue	44	18
Broward			
Davie	U of F AG RSCH, 3205 SW 70th Avenue	46	17
Ft. Lauderdale	N.W. Corner of Lincoln Park	46	20
Hollywood	12701 Plunkett Street	47	17
Pembroke Pines	11251 Taft Street	48	16
Plantation	Mirror Lake Elementary School, 1200 NW 72	46	15
Pompano Beach	Pompano Beach Water Plant, 301 North	45	17
Tamarac	7601 N University Drive	21	16
Collier			
Naples	E Naples Fire Dept, SR 858	45	16
Dade			
Homestead	Fire Station 325 NW 2nd Street	60	27
Miami	FS, NW 12th Avenue & 20th Street	62	28
Duval			
Jacksonville	Roselle & Copeland adjacent to I-10	53	26
Escambia			
Cantonment	St. Regis Golf Course	35	21
Pensacola	Ellyson Industrial Park	37	21
Gulf			
Port St. Joe	Water Plant on Kenny's Mill Road	47	20
Hamilton			
White Springs	County Road 137	62	26
Hernando			
Brooksville	17045 Ft. Dade Avenue (Lykes site)	40	16
Ridge Manor	6223 Kettering Road	39	16
Spring Hill	Forest Oaks Boulevard	40	16
Hillsborough			
Brandon	2829 S. Kingsway Avenue	44	22
County	Gardinier Park, HWY 41 N	46	23
Gibsonton	ICWU Building, Highway 41 North Gibsonton	81	35
Tampa	4702 Central Avenue (Seminole Adult SC)	54	29
Lee			
Ft. Myers	Ft. Myers Water Treatment Plant	38	17
Manatee			
Bradenton	End of Piney Point Road	48	20
County	Holland House 100 yards east of US 41	41	21
Palmetto	Police Station, 1115 10th Street W	42	22
Marion			
Ocala	16XX NW 20th Court	34	21
Martin			
Indiantown	16550 SW Warfield Blvd.	42	19

See footnotes at end of table.   Continued . . .

Table 8.80. AIR POLLUTION: PARTICULATE MATTER (PM) CONCENTRATIONS
IN SPECIFIED CITIES OF FLORIDA, 1996 (Continued)

County and area 1/	Site Address	PM10 concentration (UG/M³) 2nd highest 24-hour value 2/	PM10 concentration (UG/M³) Annual arith-metic mean 3/
Nassau			
Fernandina Beach	WWTP 5th St. N of Lime Avenue	54	25
Orange			
Orlando	2401 W 33rd Street	56	26
Winter Park	Lake Isle Estates	67	22
Zellwood	Zellwood Elementary School	42	17
Palm Beach			
Belle Glade	38745 SR 80.	54	23
Delray Beach	345 S Congress	55	19
Palm Beach Gardens	3188 PGA Boulevard	48	18
West Palm Beach	3730 Belvedere Road	56	19
Pinellas			
Largo	1301 Ulmerton Road	49	24
St. Petersburg	1313 19th Street North	50	24
Tarpon Springs	Brooker Creek Park	43	22
Polk			
Auburndale	300 E. Bridgers Avenue	34	20
County	Anderson & Pine Crest Road	45	22
Lakeland	1501 W. Bella Vista St.	26	17
Mulberry	Mulberry High School, NE 4th Circle	28	21
Putnam			
Palatka	100 feet west of Comfort intersection	45	22
St. Johns			
St. Augustine	30 Pellicer Lane, City Warehouse	51	25
St. Lucie			
Ft. Pierce	6120 SW Glades Cutoff Road	37	19
Sarasota			
Sarasota	1642 12th Street (Reverse Osmosis Plant)	42	21
Venice	448 East Venice Avenue	37	25
Seminole			
Altamonte Springs	2150 Sand Lake Road	47	19
Sanford	City Hall 2nd Story N Park Avenue	49	18
Volusia			
Daytona Beach	Williamson Blvd. and US Hwy 92	49	21
Holly Hill	1200 Center Avenue	50	20

UG/M³ Micrograms per cubic meter.
1/ Source includes more sites than could be reported here. Major cities in each
county are reported. If more than one site was available, the one with the highest
annual arithmetic mean is reported.   2/ Florida standard is 150 UG/M³, not to be ex-
ceeded more than once per year.   3/ Florida standard is 50 UG/M³.
     Note: Particulate describes airborne solid or liquid particles of about 0.1 to 50
microns in diameter (1 micron = 0.0001 centimeter). PM consists of sulfate, nitrate,
and acidic particles formed by oxidation of the pollutant gases sulfur dioxide and
nitrogen dioxide; of soot and organic particles released in forest fires and other
low-temperature combustion processes; of lead-containing particles emitted from motor
vehicles; of products of industrial processes and high temperature fuel combustion;
of local soil; and of airborne sea salt. PM10 is a subset of particulate matter and
refers to airborne particles that are 10 microns or less in size.
     Source: State of Florida, Department of Environmental Protection, Division of Air
Resources Management, *Comparison of Air Quality Data with the National Ambient Air
Quality Standards, 1996.*

AGRICULTURE

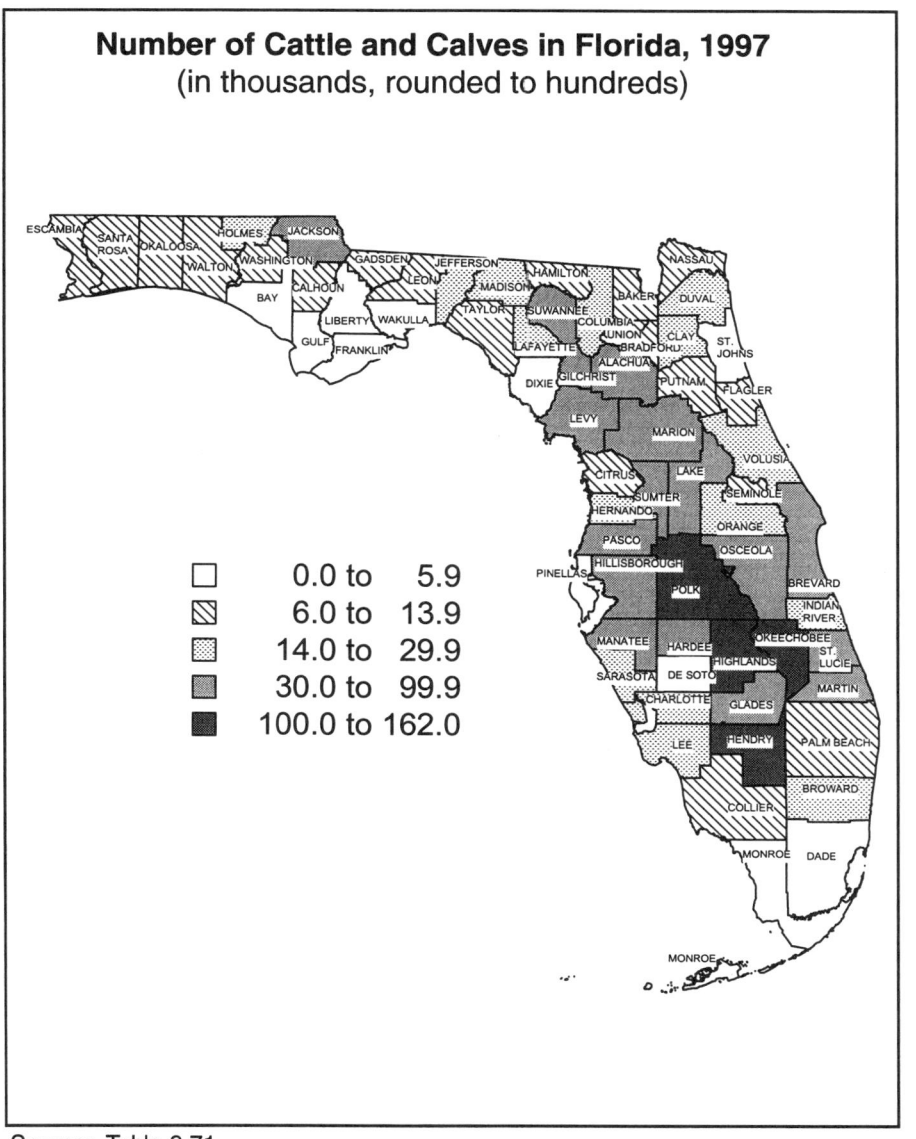

Number of Cattle and Calves in Florida, 1997
(in thousands, rounded to hundreds)

☐	0.0 to 5.9
▨	6.0 to 13.9
▦	14.0 to 29.9
▨	30.0 to 99.9
■	100.0 to 162.0

Source: Table 9.71

SECTION 9.00
AGRICULTURE

TABLES LISTED BY MAJOR HEADINGS

TABLES LISTED BY MAJOR HEADINGS

SECTION 9.00
AGRICULTURE
(Continued)

TABLES LISTED BY MAJOR HEADINGS

Table 9.04. VETERINARIANS: LICENSED DOCTORS OF VETERINARY MEDICINE IN THE STATE
AND COUNTIES OF FLORIDA, JULY 6, 1997

Location of licensee	Doctors of veterinary medicine	Location of licensee	Doctors of veterinary medicine
Total 1/	5,047	Jefferson	7
NonFlorida	1,867	Lafayette	1
Unknown	0	Lake	36
Alachua	190	Lee	95
Baker	1	Leon	58
Bay	27	Levy	12
Bradford	8	Liberty	0
Brevard	82	Madison	4
Broward	326	Manatee	32
Calhoun	1	Marion	120
Charlotte	25	Martin	37
Citrus	14	Monroe	30
Clay	33	Nassau	10
Collier	36	Okaloosa	40
Columbia	9	Okeechobee	8
Dade	319	Orange	143
De Soto	7	Osceola	21
Dixie	2	Palm Beach	259
Duval	139	Pasco	50
Escambia	64	Pinellas	195
Flagler	5	Polk	74
Franklin	2	Putnam	16
Gadsden	7	St. Johns	27
Gilchrist	2	St. Lucie	28
Glades	0	Santa Rosa	20
Gulf	1	Sarasota	87
Hamilton	1	Seminole	82
Hardee	4	Sumter	10
Hendry	5	Suwannee	14
Hernando	19	Taylor	3
Highlands	11	Union	0
Hillsborough	200	Volusia	74
Holmes	0	Wakulla	2
Indian River	29	Walton	7
Jackson	4	Washington	5

1/ Total includes all active, involuntary inactive, and voluntary inactive licensed persons.

Source: State of Florida, Department of Business and Professional Regulation, unpublished data.

University of Florida   **Bureau of Economic and Business Research**

Table 9.10. EMPLOYMENT: ESTIMATES OF AVERAGE MONTHLY EMPLOYMENT OF FARM
PROPRIETORS AND WAGE AND SALARY WORKERS IN THE UNITED STATES AND
IN THE STATE AND COUNTIES OF FLORIDA, 1994 AND 1995

	1994 A/			1995		
		Farm wage and salary employees			Farm wage and salary employees	
County	Farm proprie- tors	Number	As a per- centage of all wage and salary employees	Farm proprie- tors	Number	As a per- centage of all wage and salary employees
United States	2,108,000	842,000	0.69	2,117,000	867,000	0.69
Florida	36,232	59,858	0.96	36,236	52,878	0.82
Alachua	1,179	352	0.32	1,180	308	0.27
Baker	207	278	5.10	207	245	4.45
Bay	69	15	0.02	69	13	0.02
Bradford	344	5	0.08	344	5	0.07
Brevard	516	288	0.16	516	248	0.14
Broward	298	658	0.11	298	622	0.10
Calhoun	145	106	3.52	145	70	2.27
Charlotte	216	198	0.60	216	182	0.54
Citrus	306	4	0.02	306	6	0.02
Clay	223	170	0.55	223	158	0.49
Collier	269	6,423	7.66	269	5,649	6.56
Columbia	568	44	0.26	568	41	0.23
Dade	1,637	5,069	0.52	1,637	4,646	0.47
De Soto	892	559	6.28	892	522	5.60
Dixie	121	0	0.00	121	1	0.04
Duval	378	321	0.08	378	311	0.07
Escambia	488	153	0.12	488	107	0.08
Flagler	98	69	0.75	98	82	0.82
Franklin	0	0	0.00	0	0	0.00
Gadsden	357	1,409	9.79	357	1,272	8.82
Gilchrist	381	154	7.18	381	143	6.28
Glades	216	206	13.64	216	176	11.40
Gulf	0	0	0.00	0	0	0.00
Hamilton	255	244	5.86	255	273	6.14
Hardee	1,282	867	11.16	1,283	743	9.55
Hendry	415	2,415	18.74	415	2,076	15.39
Hernando	421	93	0.36	421	48	0.18
Highlands	649	1,259	5.31	649	1,106	4.60
Hillsborough	2,878	5,965	1.17	2,875	5,389	1.02
Holmes	582	31	0.89	582	5	0.14
Indian River	425	838	2.24	425	723	1.87
Jackson	924	131	0.87	924	108	0.71
Jefferson	336	188	6.05	336	160	5.16
Lafayette	282	128	9.82	282	119	8.37

See footnote at end of table.   Continued . . .

Table 9.10. EMPLOYMENT: ESTIMATES OF AVERAGE MONTHLY EMPLOYMENT OF FARM PROPRIETORS AND WAGE AND SALARY WORKERS IN THE UNITED STATES AND IN THE STATE AND COUNTIES OF FLORIDA, 1994 AND 1995 (Continued)

| | 1994 A/ | | | 1995 | | |
| | Farm wage and salary employees | | | Farm wage and salary employees | | |
County	Farm proprie- tors	Number	As a per- centage of all wage and salary employees	Farm proprie- tors	Number	As a per- centage of all wage and salary employees
Lake	1,302	1,556	2.93	1,302	1,435	2.56
Lee	541	2,098	1.44	541	1,826	1.20
Leon	273	119	0.09	273	106	0.08
Levy	519	300	4.38	520	286	3.93
Liberty	79	0	0.00	79	0	0.00
Madison	537	97	1.90	537	85	1.57
Manatee	738	2,764	2.57	739	2,838	2.40
Marion	1,723	1,021	1.39	1,724	918	1.21
Martin	275	845	1.97	275	843	1.87
Monroe	0	0	0.00	0	0	0.00
Nassau	298	194	1.30	298	205	1.34
Okaloosa	354	34	0.04	354	32	0.04
Okeechobee	398	1,092	12.10	398	913	10.10
Orange	911	3,701	0.72	911	3,292	0.63
Osceola	537	327	0.73	537	298	0.63
Palm Beach	671	8,084	1.91	671	6,571	1.52
Pasco	951	717	1.03	951	635	0.89
Pinellas	95	161	0.04	95	131	0.03
Polk	2,397	2,537	1.47	2,397	2,084	1.18
Putnam	417	468	2.42	417	425	2.06
St. Johns	172	327	0.99	172	295	0.87
St. Lucie	548	746	1.48	548	647	1.27
Santa Rosa	465	64	0.27	466	58	0.23
Sarasota	340	237	0.18	340	212	0.15
Seminole	356	392	0.35	357	308	0.27
Sumter	764	180	2.57	764	143	1.90
Suwannee	1,026	442	4.91	1,026	403	4.28
Taylor	134	3	0.05	134	5	0.07
Union	188	16	0.39	188	20	0.48
Volusia	1,036	2,637	1.89	1,036	2,257	1.57
Wakulla	88	0	0.00	88	0	0.00
Walton	418	11	0.11	418	14	0.14
Washington	324	48	0.93	324	36	0.63

A/ Revised.

Source: U.S., Department of Commerce, Bureau of Economic Analysis, Regional Economic Information System, CD-ROM, August 1997.

Table 9.15. PRODUCTION AND SERVICES: AVERAGE MONTHLY PRIVATE REPORTING UNITS
EMPLOYMENT, AND PAYROLL COVERED BY UNEMPLOYMENT COMPENSATION LAW
IN THE STATE AND COUNTIES OF FLORIDA, 1996

County	Number of reporting units	Number of employees	Payroll ($1,000)	County	Number of reporting units	Number of employees	Payroll ($1,000)
Agriculture production--crops (SIC code 01)								

County	Number of reporting units	Number of employees	Payroll ($1,000)	County	Number of reporting units	Number of employees	Payroll ($1,000)
Florida	2,473	59,631	77,774	Lake	91	1,632	2,311
				Lee	39	1,645	1,883
Alachua	26	320	356	Leon	10	112	143
Bay	4	289	270	Levy	11	57	92
Baker	4	21	26	Madison	9	68	52
Brevard	20	175	207	Manatee	70	3,593	3,736
Broward	60	679	1,002	Marion	24	221	251
Calhoun	5	91	115	Martin	33	921	1,392
Charlotte	14	192	363	Okeechobee	18	473	930
Collier	74	7,269	6,171	Orange	184	4,074	6,778
Dade	316	5,979	8,127	Osceola	30	301	449
De Soto	44	639	871	Palm Beach	263	8,274	13,894
Duval	14	355	546	Pasco	36	368	365
Flagler	10	115	132	Pinellas	14	201	311
Gadsden	20	1,569	1,904	Polk	162	2,359	3,431
Gilchrist	3	14	18	Putnam	32	489	416
Glades	8	125	253	St. Johns	47	357	486
Hardee	61	715	808	St. Lucie	34	594	1,008
Hendry	54	2,306	4,019	Santa Rosa	11	76	84
Hernando	5	16	18	Sarasota	22	276	389
Highlands	79	1,065	1,871	Seminole	26	392	807
Hillsborough	231	6,155	5,512	Sumter	8	140	180
Indian River	40	805	1,428	Suwannee	15	320	306
Jackson	8	123	100	Taylor	3	9	6
Jefferson	11	156	180	Union	4	31	32
Lafayette	3	13	6	Volusia	135	2,676	2,675

County	Number of reporting units	Number of employees	Payroll ($1,000)	County	Number of reporting units	Number of employees	Payroll ($1,000)
Agriculture production--livestock (SIC code 02)								

County	Number of reporting units	Number of employees	Payroll ($1,000)	County	Number of reporting units	Number of employees	Payroll ($1,000)
Florida	615	6,393	9,512	Highlands	21	290	417
				Hillsborough	40	478	699
Alachua	18	111	165	Indian River	6	59	102
Brevard	8	126	220	Jackson	7	25	23
Broward	9	60	102	Jefferson	5	32	31
Clay	6	167	230	Lafayette	17	128	124
Collier	6	27	42	Lake	15	225	367
Columbia	4	40	32	Lee	3	3	8
Dade	16	74	105	Leon	5	20	22
De Soto	11	93	148	Levy	13	291	524
Duval	8	88	136	Madison	5	46	68
Escambia	3	35	36	Manatee	15	124	145
Gilchrist	5	182	269	Marion	100	991	1,332
Glades	5	100	166	Martin	8	60	85
Hardee	25	196	298	Monroe	4	58	129
Hendry	6	28	43	Nassau	6	40	61
Hernando	7	29	38	Okeechobee	42	786	1,276

See footnote at end of table.   Continued . . .

Table 9.15. PRODUCTION AND SERVICES: AVERAGE MONTHLY PRIVATE REPORTING UNITS EMPLOYMENT, AND PAYROLL COVERED BY UNEMPLOYMENT COMPENSATION LAW IN THE STATE AND COUNTIES OF FLORIDA, 1996 (Continued)

County	Number of reporting units	Number of employees	Payroll ($1,000)	County	Number of reporting units	Number of employees	Payroll ($1,000)
			Agriculture production--livestock (SIC code 02) (Continued)				
Orange	8	64	112	Sarasota	9	60	77
Osceola	14	106	174	Seminole	3	19	66
Palm Beach	16	87	118	Sumter	8	48	61
Pasco	26	355	565	Suwannee	18	163	182
Polk	26	222	326	Volusia	10	109	157
St. Lucie	6	31	78				
			Agriculture services (SIC code 07)				
Florida	9,063	86,262	110,265	Leon	107	701	909
				Levy	20	151	187
Alachua	103	764	999	Madison	5	37	16
Baker	4	9	6	Manatee	192	2,446	2,853
Bay	44	245	312	Marion	162	1,010	1,378
Bradford	9	31	36	Martin	137	1,249	1,657
Brevard	242	1,434	1,916	Monroe	61	236	327
Broward	826	5,084	7,752	Nassau	21	142	184
Charlotte	63	395	527	Okaloosa	86	445	541
Citrus	47	246	295	Okeechobee	29	571	565
Clay	69	446	592	Orange	507	4,473	7,004
Collier	302	2,995	3,457	Osceola	63	357	532
Columbia	19	110	147	Palm Beach	941	9,416	13,223
Dade	683	5,767	7,911	Pasco	174	1,487	1,761
De Soto	74	1,896	1,971	Pinellas	478	2,885	3,937
Duval	361	2,414	3,473	Polk	408	7,546	8,640
Escambia	99	608	797	Putnam	30	206	195
Flagler	30	189	195	St. Johns	54	611	540
Gadsden	17	240	240	St. Lucie	192	4,585	5,674
Hardee	100	1,539	1,272	Santa Rosa	51	289	392
Hendry	71	4,084	3,733	Sarasota	277	1,507	2,089
Hernando	64	250	332	Seminole	227	1,420	2,084
Highlands	140	2,124	2,083	Sumter	13	89	70
Hillsborough	490	4,291	5,151	Suwannee	16	79	91
Indian River	195	2,938	4,195	Taylor	8	20	32
Jackson	15	48	65	Union	5	30	33
Jefferson	8	30	31	Volusia	225	975	1,145
Lake	147	1,495	1,720	Wakulla	5	40	45
Lee	298	2,153	2,806	Walton	13	137	202
				Washington	4	16	20

Note: Private employment. Three-digit classifications of these two-digit groups are listed in Table 9.27. Data are preliminary. Only counties for which data are disclosed are shown. Detail may not add to totals due to disclosure editing and/or rounding. See Tables in 23.70, 23.71, 23.72, 23.73, and 23.74 for public employment data.

Source: State of Florida, Department of Labor and Employment Security, Bureau of Labor Market Information, "Employment and Wages" (ES-202), unpublished data.

University of Florida   **Bureau of Economic and Business Research**

Table 9.21. LABOR AND PROPRIETORS' INCOME: FARM LABOR AND EXPENSE IN FLORIDA
1992 THROUGH 1995

(in thousands of dollars)

Item	1992	1993	1994	1995
Cash receipts from marketing	6,221,286	6,171,500	6,068,474	5,913,775
Total livestock and products	1,248,907	1,303,257	1,276,401	1,194,183
Total crops	4,972,379	4,868,243	4,792,073	4,719,592
Other income	232,669	321,964	254,242	260,341
Government payments	53,085	110,680	58,588	55,716
Imputed income and rent received 1/	179,584	211,284	195,654	204,625
Production expenses	3,916,705	4,261,007	4,340,094	4,679,979
Feed purchased	280,267	305,857	294,940	303,245
Livestock purchased	131,497	154,518	139,972	117,102
Seed purchased	184,386	193,443	193,734	206,326
Fertilizer and lime purchased	577,709	636,157	623,920	680,525
Petroleum products purchased	111,557	112,297	104,121	125,424
Hired farm labor 2/	1,064,620	1,173,449	1,198,270	1,375,057
All other production expenses 3/	1,566,669	1,685,286	1,785,137	1,872,300
Value of inventory change	11,112	23,888	28,868	-29,243
Livestock	2,886	30,929	25,276	-19,002
Crops	8,226	-7,041	3,592	-10,241
Derivation of farm labor and proprietors' income:				
Total cash receipts and other income	6,453,955	6,493,464	6,322,716	6,174,116
Less: Total production expenses	3,916,705	4,261,007	4,340,094	4,679,979
Realized net income	2,537,250	2,232,457	1,982,622	1,494,137
Plus: Value of inventory change	11,112	23,888	28,868	-29,243
Total net income including corporate farms	2,548,362	2,256,345	2,011,490	1,464,894
Less: Corporate farms	966,322	341,075	1,175,114	418,021
Plus: Statistical Adjustment	A/	A/	A/	A/
Total net farm proprietors' income	1,582,046	1,915,263	836,374	1,046,868
Plus: Farm wages and perquisites	675,486	760,594	743,590	789,629
Plus: Farm other labor income	55,884	68,617	64,901	61,141
Total farm labor and proprietors' income	2,313,416	2,744,474	1,644,865	1,897,638

A/ Less than $50,000. Estimates are included in totals.
1/ Includes imputed income such as gross rental value of dwellings and value
of home consumption and other farm-related income components such as machine hire
and custom work income, rental income, and income from forest products.
2/ Consists of hired workers' cash wages, social security, perquisites, and contract labor, machine hire and custom work expenses.
3/ Includes repair and operation of machinery; depreciation, interest, rent and
taxes; and other miscellaneous expenses, including agricultural chemicals.
Note: Data for 1992 through 1994 may be revised.

Source: U.S., Department of Commerce, Bureau of Economic Analysis, Regional Economic Information System, CD-ROM, August 1997.

University of Florida   **Bureau of Economic and Business Research**

Table 9.22. LABOR AND PROPRIETORS' INCOME: DERIVATION OF FARM LABOR AND PROPRIETORS' INCOME IN THE UNITED STATES AND IN THE STATE AND COUNTIES OF FLORIDA, 1994 AND 1995

(in thousands of dollars)

1994 A/

County	Cash receipts from marketings	Plus other income 1/	Less production expenses	Plus value of inventory change	Total net farm income	Less corporate farm income	Total net farm proprietors' income 2/	Plus farm wages	Plus other farm labor income	Total farm labor and proprietors' income
United States 3/	187,195	24,178	184,132	11,107	38,348	7,694	30,654	12,318	1,018	43,990
Florida	6,068,474	254,242	4,340,094	28,868	2,011,490	1,175,114	836,374	743,590	64,901	1,644,865
Alachua	46,198	5,562	36,571	817	16,006	2,531	13,475	3,903	364	17,742
Baker	30,410	1,048	20,428	95	11,125	1,897	9,228	2,674	268	12,170
Bay	953	223	1,939	B/	-748	B/	-733	159	B/	-559
Bradford	19,598	1,003	13,914	209	6,896	1,310	5,586	77	B/	5,670
Brevard	39,640	2,224	31,913	452	10,403	3,398	7,005	3,971	336	11,312
Broward	39,571	2,510	30,243	257	12,095	6,687	5,408	9,294	768	15,470
Calhoun	18,224	1,626	14,079	64	5,835	1,153	4,682	895	97	5,674
Charlotte	43,535	2,606	35,152	400	11,389	7,416	3,973	3,557	267	7,797
Citrus	6,975	1,207	7,481	158	859	319	540	B/	B/	575
Clay	37,453	1,340	30,775	198	8,216	6,998	1,218	2,074	182	3,474
Collier	319,751	3,154	202,352	208	120,761	49,678	71,083	49,230	5,607	125,920
Columbia	23,095	3,529	20,084	299	6,839	705	6,134	504	B/	6,685
Dade	428,533	26,330	266,063	158	188,958	121,411	67,547	63,801	5,538	136,886
De Soto	148,958	5,308	100,412	1,083	54,937	23,496	31,441	7,443	631	39,515
Dixie	3,415	297	2,420	70	1,362	B/	1,351	0	0	1,351
Duval	25,360	1,605	19,905	202	7,262	1,876	5,386	4,622	375	10,383
Escambia	18,779	2,597	12,406	56	9,026	118	8,908	959	125	9,992
Flagler	11,864	858	8,603	125	4,244	B/	4,207	764	70	5,041
Franklin	0	0	0	0	0	0	0	0	0	0
Gadsden	81,445	1,861	56,118	119	27,307	12,654	14,653	16,081	1,460	32,194
Gilchrist	31,978	1,401	24,664	452	9,167	1,032	8,135	1,999	171	10,305

See footnotes at end of table.

Continued . . .

Table 9.22. LABOR AND PROPRIETORS' INCOME: DERIVATION OF FARM LABOR AND PROPRIETORS' INCOME IN THE UNITED STATES AND IN THE STATE AND COUNTIES OF FLORIDA, 1994 AND 1995 (Continued)

(in thousands of dollars)

1994 A/ (Continued)

County	Cash receipts from marketings	Plus other income 1/	Less production expenses	Plus value of inventory change	Total net farm income	Less corporate farm income	Total net farm proprietors' income 2/	Plus farm wages	Plus other farm labor income	Total plus farm labor and proprietors' income
Glades	66,031	1,884	45,579	926	23,262	16,664	6,598	3,609	271	10,478
Gulf	0	0	0	0	0	0	0	0	0	0
Hamilton	16,600	1,887	13,410	206	5,283	684	4,599	1,972	217	6,788
Hardee	144,926	7,745	108,567	1,260	45,364	19,553	25,811	9,462	889	36,162
Hendry	309,849	7,251	208,915	1,338	109,523	69,151	40,372	33,927	2,777	77,076
Hernando	21,426	1,156	18,240	419	4,761	1,999	2,762	1,201	104	4,067
Highlands	208,580	8,866	140,192	1,523	78,777	59,649	19,128	18,797	1,503	39,428
Hillsborough	307,553	9,610	218,465	1,129	99,827	50,856	48,971	52,009	5,498	106,478
Holmes	34,837	3,806	26,706	298	12,235	0	12,235	286	B/	12,550
Indian River	164,446	5,572	111,739	303	58,582	42,346	16,236	13,502	1,044	30,782
Jackson	62,729	6,143	44,251	566	25,187	8,146	17,041	1,004	115	18,160
Jefferson	25,372	2,351	20,324	266	7,665	1,648	6,017	2,121	194	8,332
Lafayette	48,469	1,910	36,805	403	13,977	1,114	12,863	1,102	116	14,081
Lake	101,967	9,251	82,641	477	29,054	14,409	14,645	21,391	1,796	37,832
Lee	96,517	2,621	70,330	197	29,005	11,476	17,529	20,433	2,021	39,983
Leon	4,476	2,203	6,323	154	510	253	257	1,377	125	1,759
Levy	49,955	2,870	36,733	644	16,736	9,425	7,311	4,528	360	12,199
Liberty	1,146	183	971	B/	388	B/	384	0	0	384
Madison	22,671	2,119	20,242	358	4,906	380	4,526	878	128	5,532
Manatee	248,553	4,998	164,744	961	89,768	54,424	35,344	32,013	2,889	70,246
Marion	86,127	7,368	73,825	1,013	20,683	8,770	11,913	14,626	1,196	27,735
Martin	177,664	3,814	117,010	476	64,944	32,296	32,648	12,045	985	45,678
Monroe	0	0	0	0	0	0	0	0	0	0

See footnotes at end of table.

Continued . . .

Table 9.22. LABOR AND PROPRIETORS' INCOME: DERIVATION OF FARM LABOR AND PROPRIETORS' INCOME IN THE UNITED STATES AND IN THE STATE AND COUNTIES OF FLORIDA, 1994 AND 1995 (Continued)

(in thousands of dollars)

1994 A/ (Continued)

County	Cash receipts from marketings	Plus other income 1/	Less production expenses	Plus value of inventory change	Total net farm income	Less corporate farm income	Total net farm proprietors' income 2/	Plus farm wages	Plus farm other labor income	Total farm labor and proprietors' income
Nassau	30,638	799	24,857	234	6,814	991	5,823	4,467	299	10,589
Okaloosa	8,587	1,291	7,313	101	2,666	B/	2,622	403	B/	3,061
Okeechobee	150,058	3,917	111,380	2,326	44,921	28,839	16,082	18,930	1,419	36,431
Orange	238,403	7,849	164,593	220	81,879	49,562	32,317	54,839	4,389	91,545
Osceola	61,670	4,500	57,776	1,350	9,744	8,056	1,688	5,202	405	7,295
Palm Beach	1,002,643	16,413	691,833	156	327,379	321,478	5,899	129,667	9,999	145,565
Pasco	69,500	4,919	56,866	774	18,327	5,826	12,501	8,513	764	21,778
Pinellas	12,683	205	11,191	B/	1,700	111	1,589	2,683	205	4,477
Polk	231,490	12,664	182,367	1,474	63,261	37,488	25,773	35,786	2,943	64,502
Putnam	36,908	1,740	29,112	211	9,747	2,812	6,935	4,028	429	11,392
St. Johns	49,254	1,276	38,620	354	12,264	3,474	8,790	4,187	360	13,337
St. Lucie	234,395	7,023	182,191	410	59,637	36,910	22,727	12,170	938	35,835
Santa Rosa	31,881	4,002	24,344	-142	11,397	1,033	10,364	655	63	11,082
Sarasota	23,003	2,041	19,719	375	5,700	1,931	3,769	3,209	270	7,248
Seminole	23,309	1,917	18,822	133	6,537	1,558	4,979	7,254	530	12,763
Sumter	43,781	3,374	34,845	795	13,105	3,467	9,638	2,194	195	12,027
Suwannee	103,033	5,192	72,205	764	36,784	2,848	33,936	4,239	424	38,599
Taylor	2,947	589	3,269	99	366	126	240	B/	B/	267
Union	9,166	1,577	9,673	215	1,285	B/	1,244	141	B/	1,400
Volusia	88,714	5,637	72,116	233	32,468	18,122	14,346	25,985	2,556	42,887
Wakulla	1,762	346	2,198	B/	-85	0	-85			-85
Walton	25,390	2,385	21,090	176	6,861	3,328	3,533	129	B/	3,681
Washington	13,630	4,689	12,180	218	6,357	1,110	5,247	565	50	5,862

See footnotes at end of table.

Continued . . .

Table 9.22. LABOR AND PROPRIETORS' INCOME: DERIVATION OF FARM LABOR AND PROPRIETORS' INCOME IN THE UNITED STATES AND IN THE STATE AND COUNTIES OF FLORIDA, 1994 AND 1995 (Continued)

(in thousands of dollars)

1995

County	Cash receipts from marketings	Plus other income 1/	Less production expenses	Plus value of inventory change	Total net farm income	Less corporate farm income	Total net farm proprietors' income 2/	Plus farm wages	Plus farm other labor income	Plus Total farm labor and proprietors' income
United States 3/	198,081	23,812	192,417	-7,540	21,936	2,407	19,529	13,299	1,054	33,882
Florida	5,913,775	260,341	4,679,979	-29,243	1,464,894	418,021	1,046,868	789,629	61,141	1,897,638
Alachua	43,118	10,008	39,000	-822	13,304	1,043	12,261	4,051	335	16,647
Baker	30,332	1,285	21,180	-90	10,347	875	9,472	2,790	248	12,510
Bay	947	271	2,051	B/	-864	B/	-831	183	B/	-634
Bradford	20,261	1,769	14,294	-288	7,448	702	6,746	73	B/	6,826
Brevard	37,939	2,175	33,734	-308	6,072	982	5,090	4,131	312	9,533
Broward	38,432	4,098	32,063	-166	10,301	2,824	7,477	10,344	768	18,589
Calhoun	18,951	1,783	15,044	-450	5,240	513	4,727	1,000	80	5,807
Charlotte	43,644	3,144	38,342	-262	8,184	2,639	5,545	3,774	260	9,579
Citrus	6,809	1,184	7,818	-186	B/	B/	B/	58	B/	59
Clay	36,524	1,288	30,627	-193	6,992	2,952	4,040	2,376	184	6,600
Collier	294,651	2,586	224,224	-135	72,878	6,545	66,333	52,154	5,177	123,664
Columbia	22,700	4,936	21,007	-383	6,246	320	5,926	466	B/	6,434
Dade	407,698	18,831	288,953	-155	137,421	43,745	93,676	70,792	5,435	169,903
De Soto	152,561	5,255	110,382	-767	46,667	7,017	39,650	8,134	621	48,405
Dixie	3,129	628	2,533	-70	1,154	B/	1,149	B/	B/	1,158
Duval	24,363	1,779	20,586	-199	5,357	685	4,672	5,550	396	10,618
Escambia	16,638	1,853	13,133	-786	4,572	B/	4,542	840	93	5,475
Flagler	10,748	992	9,344	-62	2,334	B/	2,324	1,095	89	3,508
Franklin	0			0	0	0	0	0	0	0
Gadsden	79,377	2,093	60,706	-220	20,544	3,259	17,285	16,915	1,378	35,578
Gilchrist	28,374	2,129	25,604	-383	4,516	251	4,265	2,359	174	6,798
Glades	62,405	1,424	49,388	-617	13,824	6,440	7,384	3,866	257	11,507

Continued . . .

See footnotes at end of table.

Table 9.22. LABOR AND PROPRIETORS' INCOME: DERIVATION OF FARM LABOR AND PROPRIETORS' INCOME IN THE UNITED STATES AND IN THE STATE AND COUNTIES OF FLORIDA, 1994 AND 1995 (Continued)

(in thousands of dollars)

1995 (Continued)

County	Cash receipts from marketings	Plus other income 1/	Less production expenses	Plus value of inventory change	Total net farm income	Less corporate farm income	Total net farm proprietors' income 2/	Plus farm wages	Plus other farm labor income	Total farm labor and proprietors' income
Gulf	0	0	0	0	0	0	0	0	0	0
Hamilton	16,692	2,075	14,428	-401	3,938	253	3,685	2,416	245	6,346
Hardee	144,369	8,253	118,030	-928	33,664	5,405	28,259	10,109	825	39,193
Hendry	311,963	8,033	231,190	-914	87,892	31,800	56,092	37,859	2,669	96,620
Hernando	20,988	1,124	18,768	-542	2,802	583	2,219	663	56	2,938
Highlands	213,017	9,420	154,555	-1,106	66,776	29,561	37,215	19,626	1,407	58,248
Hillsborough	305,975	9,313	233,724	-1,262	80,302	18,065	62,237	56,037	5,215	123,489
Holmes	34,940	5,225	27,634	-464	12,067	0	12,067	67	B/	12,140
Indian River	172,883	5,815	122,475	-248	55,975	20,058	35,917	14,281	981	51,179
Jackson	61,453	6,220	47,187	-1,725	10,761	1,173	17,588	1,152	106	18,846
Jefferson	24,573	2,714	21,252	-387	5,648	602	5,046	2,106	174	7,326
Lafayette	46,808	2,272	37,458	-358	11,264	445	10,819	1,115	110	12,044
Lake	101,669	7,465	88,438	-493	20,203	4,963	15,240	23,359	1,758	40,357
Lee	92,212	2,354	75,904	-152	18,510	1,748	16,762	21,957	1,885	40,604
Leon	3,767	2,476	6,520	-180	-457	-231	-226	1,488	119	1,381
Levy	45,629	4,405	38,273	-719	11,042	1,791	9,251	5,386	377	15,014
Liberty	1,102	181	1,028	B/	226	125	225	0	0	225
Madison	22,371	2,356	20,929	-543	3,255	125	3,130	909	119	4,158
Manatee	235,303	4,657	178,057	-709	61,194	15,155	46,039	34,754	2,958	83,751
Marion	84,240	7,525	77,219	-1,170	13,376	2,809	10,567	15,514	1,141	27,222
Martin	181,228	3,517	128,478	-380	55,887	13,055	42,832	14,523	1,054	58,409
Monroe	0	0	0	0	0	0	0	0	0	0
Nassau	30,437	743	25,184	-239	5,757	415	5,342	4,425	292	10,059
Okaloosa	8,400	1,148	7,491	-212	1,845	B/	1,830	474	B/	2,341
Okeechobee	135,893	3,516	115,645	-1,821	21,943	6,971	14,972	18,249	1,248	34,469
Orange	232,258	6,973	175,812	-171	63,248	17,232	46,016	60,252	4,253	110,521

Continued . . . .

See footnotes at end of table.

Table 9.22. LABOR AND PROPRIETORS' INCOME: DERIVATION OF FARM LABOR AND PROPRIETORS' INCOME IN THE UNITED STATES AND IN THE STATE AND COUNTIES OF FLORIDA, 1994 AND 1995 (Continued)

(in thousands of dollars)

1995 (Continued)

County	Cash receipts from marketings	Plus other income 1/	Less production expenses	Plus value of inventory change	Total net farm income	Less corporate farm income	Total net farm proprietors' income 2/	Plus farm wages	Plus other farm labor income	Total farm labor and proprietors' income
Osceola	60,298	3,934	61,383	-1,000	1,849	741	1,108	5,455	386	6,949
Palm Beach	938,420	17,218	754,694	-97	200,847	119,227	81,615	132,090	8,955	222,660
Pasco	68,414	4,731	59,524	-1,114	12,507	1,970	10,537	8,874	712	20,123
Pinellas	12,845	193	11,826	B/	1,206	B/	1,167	2,669	182	4,018
Polk	237,588	12,695	199,560	-1,190	49,533	9,206	40,327	35,564	2,601	78,492
Putnam	35,967	1,971	31,159	-157	6,622	946	5,676	4,514	415	10,605
St. Johns	46,283	1,203	41,724	-94	5,668	793	4,875	4,878	361	10,114
St. Lucie	244,888	6,665	200,604	-283	50,666	20,807	29,859	12,378	863	43,100
Santa Rosa	30,144	2,651	24,886	-325	7,584	361	7,223	748	63	8,034
Sarasota	21,518	1,971	20,876	-286	2,327	389	1,938	3,535	262	5,735
Seminole	22,559	1,695	19,898	-75	4,281	506	3,775	7,389	472	11,636
Sumter	40,475	3,149	36,525	-695	6,404	838	5,566	2,124	166	7,856
Suwannee	104,300	7,185	74,696	-974	35,815	1,375	34,440	4,457	402	39,299
Taylor	2,823	660	3,348	-79	56	B/	B/	B/	B/	85
Union	9,391	2,196	10,178	-258	1,151	B/	1,132	223	B/	1,375
Volusia	89,209	6,138	66,667	-209	28,471	5,761	22,710	26,310	2,298	51,318
Wakulla	1,721	393	2,308	B/	-209	0	-209	0	0	-209
Walton	26,768	2,823	21,749	-295	7,547	1,815	5,732	201	B/	5,958
Washington	12,393	5,579	12,682	-365	4,925	426	4,499	507	B/	5,046

A/ Revised.
B/ Less than $50,000. Estimates are included in totals.
1/ Includes government payments, imputed income, and rent received.
2/ Includes statistical adjustment.
3/ United States numbers are rounded to millions of dollars.
Note: See also tables in Section 5.00.
   Source: U.S., Department of Commerce, Bureau of Economic Analysis, Regional Economic Information System, CD-ROM, August 1997.

Table 9.25. INCOME: ESTIMATED CASH RECEIPTS FROM FARM MARKETINGS BY SPECIFIED
COMMODITY IN THE UNITED STATES AND LEADING STATES IN RANK ORDER, 1995

(in millions of dollars)

Commodity and state	Cash receipts	Commodity and state	Cash receipts	Commodity and state	Cash receipts
All commodities		All livestock 1/		All crops	
United States	185,750,021	United States	86,843,791	United States	98,906,230
California	22,261,109	Texas	8,453,836	California	16,712,582
Texas	13,287,680	California	5,548,527	Illinois	6,176,908
Iowa	10,958,874	Nebraska	5,187,294	Iowa	5,891,122
Nebraska	8,690,446	Iowa	5,067,752	Texas	4,833,844
Illinois	7,887,034	Kansas	4,692,784	Florida	4,719,097
Kansas	7,521,311	Wisconsin	3,926,012	Washington	3,563,581
Minnesota	7,001,667	North Carolina	3,735,338	Minnesota	3,550,943
North Carolina	6,986,814	Minnesota	3,450,724	Nebraska	3,503,152
Florida	5,848,907	Arkansas	3,023,223	North Carolina	3,251,476
Wisconsin	5,582,296	Georgia	2,789,184	Indiana	3,240,106
Greenhouse 2/ (6)		Tobacco (13)		Potatoes (14)	
United States	10,407,898	United States	2,594,363	United States	2,557,604
California	2,171,904	North Carolina	1,048,523	Idaho	702,088
Florida	1,092,639	Kentucky	636,485	Washington	440,228
North Carolina	857,818	Tennessee	233,376	California	177,328
Texas	792,000	Virginia	190,832	Wisconsin	148,381
Ohio	490,699	South Carolina	188,896	Oregon	135,134
Michigan	424,632	Georgia	148,505	Colorado	124,578
Oregon	398,674	Ohio	31,740	North Dakota	114,314
Pennsylvania	314,321	Florida	30,907	Maine	98,611
Oklahoma	263,932	Indiana	22,334	Minnesota	93,817
New York	257,063	Maryland	20,869	Michigan	91,446
Lettuce (16)		Tomatoes (19)		Peanuts (23)	
United States	1,915,213	United States	1,577,065	United States	1,013,822
California	1,385,397	California	865,360	Georgia	417,390
Arizona	482,612	Florida	387,916	Texas	154,980
New Jersey	11,278	Georgia	56,823	Alabama	139,208
Florida	9,561	Virginia	43,586	North Carolina	103,418
New Mexico	8,493	Ohio	36,530	Virginia	62,078
Colorado	6,564	South Carolina	31,122	Oklahoma	60,160
Washington	4,586	New Jersey	26,730	Florida	52,463
Ohio	4,029	Michigan	20,072	New Mexico	14,448
New York	2,093	Indiana	18,641	South Carolina	9,178
Hawaii	600	Tennessee	17,199	Arizona	499
Oranges (17)		Sugarcane (24)			
United States	1,605,227	United States	886,828		
Florida	1,165,832	Florida	458,254		
California	423,078	Louisiana	257,394		
Texas	8,832	Hawaii	129,200		
Arizona	7,485	Texas	41,980		

(D) Data withheld to avoid disclosure of information about individual producers.
1/ Includes poultry and products.   2/ Includes nursery.
Note: Commodities listed are among 25 leading commodities ranked by value of farm
marketings. The number after the commodity name indicates rank order in cash receipts in the United States. Receipts include commodity credit corporation loans.
Source: U.S., Department of Agriculture, Economic Research Service, Internet
site http://www.econ.ag.gov/.

Table 9.26. INCOME: CASH RECEIPTS BY COMMODITY AND COMMODITY GROUP IN FLORIDA
1993 THROUGH 1995

	1993 A/		1994 A/		1995 B/	
Commodity	Cash receipts ($1,000)	Per-cent-age of total	Cash receipts ($1,000)	Per-cent-age of total	Cash receipts ($1,000)	Per-cent-age of total
Cash receipts 1/	6,078,004	100.00	5,984,249	100.00	5,848,907	100.00
Crops	4,866,873	80.07	4,792,116	80.08	4,719,097	80.68
Citrus	1,350,182	22.21	1,414,204	23.63	1,484,703	25.38
Grapefruit	239,353	3.94	231,631	3.87	206,706	3.53
K-early citrus fruit	939	0.02	526	0.01	526	0.01
Lemons	2,879	0.05	2,675	0.04	2,079	0.04
Limes	3,171	0.05	3,687	0.06	2,900	0.05
Oranges	1,021,367	16.80	1,114,201	18.62	1,151,782	19.69
Tangelos	20,361	0.33	12,021	0.20	16,381	0.28
Tangerines	49,654	0.82	36,776	0.61	90,279	1.54
Temples	12,458	0.20	12,687	0.21	14,050	0.24
Other fruits and nuts	137,631	2.26	141,535	2.37	167,552	2.86
Avocados	3,608	0.06	12,320	0.21	11,324	0.19
Mangos	950	0.02	1,500	0.03	1,725	0.03
Pecans	3,460	0.06	1,600	0.03	945	0.02
Strawberries	121,313	2.00	101,425	1.69	118,608	2.03
Blueberries	1,300	0.02	5,690	0.10	5,050	0.09
Other	7,000	0.12	19,000	0.32	29,900	0.51
Vegetables and melons	1,688,676	27.78	1,448,817	24.21	1,267,464	21.67
Cabbage	42,585	0.70	29,689	0.50	18,135	0.31
Carrots	25,551	0.42	11,252	0.19	15,361	0.26
Celery	58,670	0.97	21,571	0.36	0	0.00
Cucumbers	80,010	1.32	58,200	0.97	51,081	0.87
Eggplant	13,075	0.22	15,606	0.26	14,005	0.24
Escarole	7,611	0.13	8,969	0.15	8,900	0.15
Green peppers	215,939	3.55	197,465	3.30	172,125	2.94
Lettuce	26,770	0.44	16,884	0.28	9,561	0.16
Potatoes	128,194	2.11	118,655	1.98	84,010	1.44
Radishes	36,961	0.61	25,888	0.43	23,873	0.41
Snap beans	71,086	1.17	60,645	1.01	55,446	0.95
Squash	38,170	0.63	43,216	0.72	41,686	0.71
Sweet corn	102,588	1.69	105,232	1.76	107,553	1.84
Tomatoes	607,704	10.00	465,663	7.78	387,916	6.63
Watermelons	66,600	1.10	57,868	0.97	61,793	1.06
Other	167,162	2.75	212,014	3.54	216,019	3.69
Field crops	631,116	10.38	663,109	11.08	661,390	11.31
Corn	12,094	0.20	11,045	0.18	11,502	0.20
Cotton	23,393	0.38	37,916	0.63	43,498	0.74
Hay	10,801	0.18	14,025	0.23	12,203	0.21
Peanuts	57,684	0.95	58,302	0.97	52,463	0.90
Soybeans	8,091	0.13	7,490	0.13	5,582	0.10
Sugarcane	442,738	7.28	459,911	7.69	458,254	7.83
Tobacco	30,638	0.50	27,248	0.46	30,907	0.53
Wheat	2,268	0.04	1,717	0.03	1,202	0.02
Other	43,409	0.71	45,455	0.76	45,779	0.78
Foliage and floriculture	542,655	8.93	600,986	10.04	612,639	10.47
Other crops and products	516,613	8.50	523,465	8.75	525,349	8.98
Livestock and products	1,211,131	19.93	1,192,133	19.92	1,129,810	19.32
Milk	385,503	6.34	408,408	6.82	363,528	6.22
Cattle and calves	362,495	5.96	335,837	5.61	289,802	4.95

See footnotes at end of table.   Continued . . .

Table 9.26. INCOME: CASH RECEIPTS BY COMMODITY AND COMMODITY GROUP IN FLORIDA 1993 THROUGH 1995 (Continued)

Commodity	1993 A/ Cash receipts ($1,000)	1993 A/ Per- cent- age of total	1994 A/ Cash receipts ($1,000)	1994 A/ Per- cent- age of total	1995 B/ Cash receipts ($1,000)	1995 B/ Per- cent- age of total
Livestock and products (Cont.)						
Poultry and eggs	298,831	4.9	291,605	4.9	315,237	5.4
Broilers	187,714	3.1	191,151	3.2	218,361	3.7
Eggs	106,838	1.8	98,348	1.6	95,158	1.6
Other	4,279	0.1	2,106	0.0	1,718	0.0
Catfish	364	0.0	280	0.0	280	0.0
Hogs	15,106	0.2	12,399	0.2	11,581	0.2
Honey	11,300	0.2	9,080	0.2	12,461	0.2
Sheep and lambs, wool	82	0.0	104	0.0	144	0.0
Other	137,450	2.3	134,420	2.2	136,777	2.3

A/ Revised.   B/ Preliminary.
1/ Farm marketings. Includes additional receipts not published.
Source: State of Florida, Department of Agriculture and Consumer Services, Florida Agricultural Statistics Service, *Florida Agriculture: Farm Cash Receipts and Expenditures, 1995*.

Table 9.27. PRODUCTION AND SERVICES: AVERAGE MONTHLY PRIVATE REPORTING UNITS EMPLOYMENT, AND PAYROLL COVERED BY UNEMPLOYMENT COMPENSATION LAW BY INDUSTRY IN FLORIDA, 1996

SIC code	Industry	Number of reporting units	Number of em- ployees	Payroll ($1,000)
01	Agricultural production--crops	2,473	59,631	77,774
011	Cash grains	30	322	509
013	Field crops, except cash grains	215	4,293	9,582
016	Vegetables and melons	367	18,120	17,292
017	Fruits and tree nuts	655	11,242	15,929
018	Horticultural specialties	1,185	25,192	33,628
019	General farms, primarily crop	21	463	834
02	Agricultural production--livestock	615	6,393	9,512
021	Livestock, except dairy, and poultry	220	1,333	2,022
024	Dairy farms	160	2,539	3,934
025	Poultry and eggs	31	846	1,236
027	Animal specialties	191	1,599	2,218
029	General farms, primarily animal	14	77	102
07	Agricultural services	9,063	86,262	110,265
071	Soil preparation services	39	223	388
072	Crop services	343	10,443	13,608
074	Veterinary services	1,416	11,462	18,543
075	Animal services, except veterinary	577	1,994	2,401
076	Farm labor and management services	867	27,345	25,469
078	Landscape and horticultural services	5,822	34,795	49,856

Note: Private employment. Detail may not add to totals due to disclosure editing and/or rounding. See Tables 23.70, 23.71, 23.72, 23.73, and 23.74 for public employment data.
Source: State of Florida, Department of Labor and Employment Security, Bureau of Labor Market Information, "Employment and Wages" (ES-202), unpublished data.

University of Florida   **Bureau of Economic and Business Research**

Table 9.28.   INCOME AND EXPENDITURE: FARM INCOME AND EXPENDITURE BY INDICATOR
IN FLORIDA, 1991 THROUGH 1995

(in millions of dollars, except where indicated)

Item	1991	1992	1993	1994	1995
Net farm income	2,650.1	2,722.4	2,416.4	2,219.1	1,704.9
Gross farm income	6,440.7	6,417.7	6,459.4	6,306.4	6,143.1
Gross cash income	6,284.4	6,292.1	6,308.6	6,133.0	6,028.8
Farm marketings	6,144.4	6,139.1	6,078.0	5,984.2	5,848.9
Government payments	40.8	53.1	110.7	58.6	55.7
Farm-related income	99.2	99.9	119.9	90.1	124.2
Noncash income	121.2	114.9	125.8	144.4	142.9
Value of home consumption	4.9	4.6	3.5	3.3	2.8
Rental value of dwellings	116.3	110.4	122.3	141.0	140.1
Value of inventory adjustment	35.1	10.7	25.0	29.1	-28.6
Production expenditure	3,790.6	3,695.4	4,043.1	4,087.2	4,438.2
Intermediate product expenditure	2,076.7	2,008.8	2,245.6	2,254.3	2,453.3
Farm origin	537.0	513.1	561.7	544.4	562.3
Manufactured inputs	729.6	689.3	748.5	728.0	805.9
Other	810.1	806.4	935.4	981.9	1,085.1
Interest from real estate and nonreal estate	305.3	278.3	285.9	331.5	343.0
Contract and hired labor expenditure	908.0	886.9	1,028.6	1,006.5	1,132.0
Net rent to nonoperator landlords	33.6	37.8	42.1	41.6	45.8
Capital consumption	268.7	262.8	262.0	265.9	273.0
Property taxes	198.2	220.9	178.8	187.3	191.1
Gross receipts of farms	6,343.1	6,330.6	6,348.6	6,176.4	6,023.8
Returns to operators	2,615.2	2,700.7	2,374.8	2,166.6	1,665.5
Farm production expenditure	3,727.9	3,629.9	3,973.9	4,009.9	4,358.3
Nonfactor payments	2,652.7	2,615.9	2,822.7	2,862.2	3,155.5
Intermediate product expenditure	2,062.0	1,997.5	2,234.3	2,239.2	2,439.8
Capital consumption	238.6	228.7	228.3	230.1	234.7
Property taxes	188.0	209.4	168.6	175.7	178.3
Contract labor	164.1	180.3	191.5	217.2	302.7
Factor payments	1,075.2	1,014.0	1,151.2	1,147.7	1,202.9
Interest	297.6	269.6	272.0	316.7	327.7
Hired labor expenditure	744.0	706.6	837.1	789.4	829.4
Net rent to nonoperator landlords	33.6	37.8	42.1	41.6	45.8
Gross cash income	6,284.4	6,292.1	6,308.6	6,133.0	6,028.8
Net cash income	2,807.2	2,907.6	2,568.2	2,357.8	1,919.3
Cash expenditure	3,477.3	3,384.5	3,740.4	3,775.2	4,109.5
Cash expenditure, excluding net rent	3,436.9	3,340.2	3,691.9	3,727.1	4,057.0
Intermediate product expenditure	2,062.0	1,997.5	2,234.3	2,239.2	2,439.8
Interest	297.6	269.6	272.0	316.7	327.7
Cash labor expenditure	889.3	863.7	1,017.1	995.5	1,111.2
Property taxes	188.0	209.4	168.6	175.7	178.3
Net rent to nonoperator landlords	40.3	44.3	48.5	48.1	52.5
Number of farms	40,000	39,000	39,000	39,000	39,000

Source: State of Florida, Department of Agriculture and Consumer Services, Florida Agricultural Statistics Service, *Florida Agriculture: Farm Cash Receipts and Expenditures, 1995*.

University of Florida   **Bureau of Economic and Business Research**

Table 9.34. FARMS: SPECIFIED CHARACTERISTICS OF FARMS IN FLORIDA
1987 AND 1992

Item	All farms 1987	All farms 1992	Percentage change	Farms with sales of $10,000 or more 1987	Farms with sales of $10,000 or more 1992	Percentage change
Number of farms	36,556	35,204	-3.7	14,667	14,945	1.9
By size						
1 to 9 acres	7,300	7,664	5.0	1,968	2,185	11.0
10 to 49 acres	13,346	12,692	-4.9	3,919	4,074	4.0
50 to 179 acres	8,379	7,738	-7.7	3,274	3,309	1.1
180 to 499 acres	4,255	4,011	-5.7	2,706	2,683	-0.8
500 to 999 acres	1,598	1,451	-9.2	1,279	1,195	-6.6
1,000 to 1,999 acres	789	776	-1.6	708	689	-2.7
2,000 acres or more	889	872	-1.9	813	810	-0.4
With irrigated land	11,981	13,500	12.7	7,788	8,265	6.1
By SIC code						
Cash grains (011)	635	449	-29.3	236	166	-29.7
Field crops, except cash grains (013)	2,218	2,106	-5.0	1,203	1,257	4.5
Vegetables and melons (016)	1,511	1,483	-1.9	1,057	1,110	5.0
Fruits and tree nuts (017)	8,388	8,853	5.5	4,007	3,838	-4.2
Horticultural specialties (018)	4,096	4,942	20.7	2,849	3,483	22.3
General farms, primarily crop (019)	434	394	-9.2	219	206	-5.9
Livestock, except dairy, poultry, and animal specialties (021)	14,738	12,811	-13.1	3,296	3,295	0.0
Dairy farms (024)	358	372	3.9	358	337	-5.9
Poultry and eggs (025)	746	618	-17.2	629	502	-20.2
Animal specialties (27)	3,170	2,807	-11.5	798	731	-8.4
General farms, primarily livestock (29)	234	369	57.7	15	20	33.3
Selected farm production expenses 1/ ($1,000)						
Livestock and poultry purchased	148,405	131,497	-11.4	(NA)	123,668	(X)
Feed for livestock and poultry	336,690	382,945	13.7	322,471	369,869	14.7
Commercial fertilizer	209,617	283,424	35.2	198,090	268,075	35.3
Petroleum products	104,591	128,168	22.5	96,529	120,122	24.4
Hired farm labor	721,540	937,571	29.9	716,905	932,283	30.0
Interest expense	191,913	219,234	14.2	(NA)	207,581	(X)
Agricultural chemicals 2/	227,063	320,675	41.2	218,474	311,910	42.8
Livestock and poultry inventory						
Cattle and calves						
Farms	17,321	15,522	-10.4	5,403	5,474	1.3
Number	1,879,124	1,783,968	-5.1	1,609,538	1,553,165	-3.5

See footnotes at end of table.   Continued . . .

Table 9.34. FARMS: SPECIFIED CHARACTERISTICS OF FARMS IN FLORIDA 1987 AND 1992 (Continued)

Item	All farms 1987	All farms 1992	Percentage change	Farms with sales of $10,000 or more 1987	1992	Percentage change
Livestock/poultry inventory (Continued)						
Cattle and calves (Continued)						
Beef cows						
Farms	14,672	13,423	-8.5	4,653	4,785	2.8
Number	995,250	962,527	-3.3	835,048	827,655	-0.9
Milk cows						
Farms	1,073	877	-18.3	503	487	-3.2
Number	176,993	171,675	-3.0	175,647	170,852	-2.7
Chickens 3/						
Farms	2,275	1,454	-36.1	(NA)	(NA)	(X)
Number	12,964,760	10,802,573	-16.7	(NA)	(NA)	(X)
Crops harvested 4/						
Corn						
Farms	2,088	1,548	-25.9	1,079	905	-16.1
Acres	95,874	86,407	-9.9	82,973	76,488	-7.8
Soybeans						
Farms	708	415	-41.4	575	351	-39.0
Acres	89,938	49,072	45.4	86,038	47,215	-45.1
Sugarcane						
Farms	138	139	0.7	(NA)	(NA)	(X)
Acres	403,014	431,677	7.1	(NA)	(NA)	(X)
Hay						
Farms	5,643	4,892	-13.3	2,589	2,527	-2.4
Acres	280,639	270,404	-3.6	219,396	218,675	-0.3
Vegetables						
Farms	2,053	1,988	-3.2	1,456	1,532	5.2
Acres	311,659	299,867	-3.8	308,960	297,934	-3.6
Orchards						
Farms	9,965	10,258	2.9	4,669	4,539	-2.8
Acres	762,068	914,642	20.0	693,903	834,170	20.2

SIC Standard Industrial Classification. See Glossary.
(NA) Not available.
(X) Not applicable.
1/ Data are based on a sample of farms. In current dollars and unadjusted.
2/ Excludes the cost of lime.
3/ Three months old or older.
4/ Corn for grain or seed; soybeans for beans; sugarcane for sugar; hay includes alfalfa, and other tame, small grain, wild, grass silage, green chop, etc.; vegetables harvested for sale; vegetable acreage is counted only once even when it is replanted.
   Note: Livestock and poultry inventories are as of December 31. Crop and livestock production, sales, and expense data are for the calendar year, except for a few crops for which the production and calendar years overlap. The agriculture census is on a 5-year cycle collecting data for years ending in 2 or 7.
   Source: U.S., Department of Commerce, Bureau of the Census, *1992 Census of Agriculture: State and County Data, Florida.* AC92-A-9.

Table 9.35. FARMS: NUMBER, LAND IN FARMS, AND VALUE OF LAND AND BUILDINGS
IN THE STATE AND COUNTIES OF FLORIDA, 1987 AND 1992

County	Number of farms 1987	Number of farms 1992	Land in farms (acres) Total 1987	Land in farms (acres) Total 1992	Average size of farm 1987	Average size of farm 1992	Average estimated market value of land and buildings per farm 1/ (dollars) 1987	Average estimated market value of land and buildings per farm 1/ (dollars) 1992
Florida	36,556	35,204	11,194,090	10,766,077	306	306	543,830	619,265
Alachua	1,161	1,089	192,255	191,140	166	176	284,184	275,767
Baker	220	193	27,937	24,489	127	127	177,109	227,722
Bay	85	63	11,448	9,135	135	145	161,306	220,367
Bradford	349	315	41,178	36,230	118	115	190,212	202,625
Brevard	495	496	165,082	199,724	333	403	423,756	562,655
Broward	448	393	35,909	23,735	80	60	395,098	315,376
Calhoun	159	132	48,166	43,314	303	328	298,088	355,378
Charlotte	197	214	214,364	227,202	1,088	1,062	1,143,893	1,310,837
Citrus	331	288	74,264	70,672	224	245	280,141	449,229
Clay	244	210	83,994	86,026	344	410	580,689	884,620
Collier	224	254	332,177	301,977	1,483	1,189	1,755,839	2,305,229
Columbia	535	523	98,620	96,968	184	185	209,752	234,203
Dade	1,623	1,891	83,061	83,681	51	44	342,513	389,694
De Soto	654	804	351,402	334,623	537	416	721,087	848,575
Dixie	114	106	56,416	31,693	495	299	388,298	227,346
Duval	434	378	41,766	40,039	96	106	248,028	307,468
Escambia	502	454	65,426	57,179	130	126	194,191	166,769
Flagler	104	93	83,332	52,259	801	562	712,875	797,013
Franklin	6	6	(D)	(D)	(D)	(D)	(D)	49,979
Gadsden	348	333	62,114	57,853	178	174	243,289	322,888
Gilchrist	336	329	87,500	70,987	260	216	414,080	317,870
Glades	194	206	222,232	369,965	1,146	1,796	1,054,114	1,243,443
Gulf	35	27	33,644	14,203	961	526	564,314	733,567
Hamilton	256	224	73,603	69,405	288	310	244,828	251,658
Hardee	1,130	1,169	303,892	327,611	269	280	493,415	569,627
Hendry	396	389	545,111	529,835	1,377	1,362	2,215,972	2,539,049
Hernando	431	411	66,167	61,019	154	148	296,826	339,864
Highlands	735	652	413,381	483,835	562	742	871,313	1,532,899
Hillsborough	2,754	2,760	287,951	265,443	105	96	325,425	364,794
Holmes	572	523	86,701	86,706	152	166	118,550	141,788
Indian River	539	447	195,671	174,673	363	391	1,189,302	1,400,034
Jackson	910	808	269,663	244,185	296	302	256,502	247,068
Jefferson	296	297	130,376	118,352	440	398	433,835	575,501
Lafayette	273	252	94,847	95,833	347	380	255,901	373,438

See footnotes at end of table.   Continued . . .

University of Florida   **Bureau of Economic and Business Research**

Table 9.35. FARMS: NUMBER, LAND IN FARMS, AND VALUE OF LAND AND BUILDINGS
IN THE STATE AND COUNTIES OF FLORIDA, 1987 AND 1992 (Continued)

County	Number of farms 1987	Number of farms 1992	Land in farms (acres) Total 1987	Land in farms (acres) Total 1992	Average size of farm 1987	Average size of farm 1992	Average estimated market value of land and buildings per farm 1/ (dollars) 1987	Average estimated market value of land and buildings per farm 1/ (dollars) 1992
Lake	1,285	1,320	232,657	199,098	181	151	447,166	480,005
Lee	415	517	132,665	106,721	320	206	633,500	606,292
Leon	302	263	101,885	100,764	337	383	452,103	666,946
Levy	540	473	179,608	190,553	333	403	383,861	374,647
Liberty	80	71	17,507	11,738	219	165	121,675	186,451
Madison	482	481	132,173	132,208	274	275	208,608	212,290
Manatee	766	728	329,388	299,699	430	412	759,265	796,187
Marion	1,707	1,654	311,074	296,242	182	179	475,794	448,675
Martin	316	305	231,522	190,788	733	626	1,882,291	1,863,414
Monroe	16	15	27	32	2	2	(D)	173,818
Nassau	317	277	48,999	44,962	155	162	245,448	250,847
Okaloosa	322	315	62,662	56,704	195	180	274,201	232,732
Okeechobee	400	418	384,169	351,885	960	842	1,003,723	1,264,286
Orange	1,125	990	161,900	138,418	144	140	489,619	541,725
Osceola	503	499	787,046	716,542	1,565	1,436	1,639,801	1,492,793
Palm Beach	975	924	659,438	637,934	676	690	2,202,349	2,417,525
Pasco	1,011	922	218,953	221,232	217	240	478,293	506,609
Pinellas	166	124	8,549	4,123	52	33	220,491	227,337
Polk	2,638	2,294	602,461	611,336	228	266	569,292	676,596
Putnam	421	400	106,993	105,621	254	264	347,653	352,198
St. Johns	172	166	49,414	48,839	287	294	486,269	558,362
St. Lucie	522	539	297,433	300,622	570	558	1,597,356	1,667,942
Santa Rosa	435	430	81,667	79,270	188	184	223,359	202,461
Sarasota	352	328	166,766	151,242	474	461	624,344	878,490
Seminole	390	352	59,933	59,642	154	169	360,221	476,796
Sumter	705	720	253,897	253,330	360	352	347,387	489,501
Suwannee	985	932	182,409	161,936	185	174	221,691	232,428
Taylor	158	125	77,346	(D)	490	(D)	255,975	353,773
Union	205	175	67,317	48,280	328	276	386,156	355,457
Volusia	920	978	192,768	138,208	210	141	346,207	382,517
Wakulla	87	83	(D)	8,679	(D)	105	(D)	149,612
Walton	430	383	104,239	96,730	242	253	154,098	228,124
Washington	318	274	61,647	45,214	194	165	124,191	143,811

(D) Data withheld to avoid disclosure of information about individual farms.
1/ Data are based on a sample of farms.
Note: The agriculture census is on a 5-year cycle collecting data for years ending in 2 and 7.

Source: U.S., Department of Commerce, Bureau of the Census, *1992 Census of Agriculture: State and County Data, Florida.* AC92-A-9.

University of Florida   **Bureau of Economic and Business Research**

Table 9.36. FARMS: LAND IN FARMS BY USE IN THE STATE AND COUNTIES
OF FLORIDA, 1992

(in acres)

County	Total land in farms	Land according to use		Wood-land 1/	Pasture-land 2/	Other 3/	Irri-gated land
		Cropland					
		Total	Har-vested				
Florida	10,766,077	3,841,505	2,400,704	1,922,035	4,456,686	545,851	1,782,680
Alachua	191,140	79,607	29,566	40,604	63,430	7,499	7,371
Baker	24,489	8,820	3,002	12,246	1,969	1,454	456
Bay	9,135	2,829	634	5,342	(D)	(D)	309
Bradford	36,230	14,185	4,447	9,815	10,473	1,757	553
Brevard	199,724	35,435	21,081	38,164	117,465	8,660	24,958
Broward	23,735	(D)	4,398	(D)	12,803	1,858	3,388
Calhoun	43,314	30,422	20,725	9,285	2,709	898	1,148
Charlotte	227,202	35,622	21,927	24,646	160,603	6,331	17,882
Citrus	70,672	15,057	4,904	14,377	30,517	10,721	658
Clay	86,026	6,818	3,042	59,604	17,108	2,496	1,293
Collier	301,977	87,628	65,021	72,485	114,537	27,327	64,611
Columbia	96,968	49,628	14,402	31,903	11,456	3,981	2,597
Dade	83,681	68,795	61,342	1,892	9,619	3,375	52,363
De Soto	334,623	89,670	62,250	21,213	210,951	12,789	58,806
Dixie	31,693	8,412	1,805	4,709	17,733	839	990
Duval	40,039	13,056	5,474	17,628	5,270	4,085	1,203
Escambia	57,179	38,720	29,986	12,718	2,529	3,212	641
Flagler	52,259	8,818	5,277	31,745	10,791	905	4,744
Franklin	(D)	(D)	0	(D)	0	(D)	0
Gadsden	57,853	22,244	9,387	28,477	2,997	4,135	3,378
Gilchrist	70,987	43,487	19,366	14,463	11,378	1,659	6,440
Glades	369,965	43,236	27,856	28,477	287,709	10,543	60,239
Gulf	14,203	6,382	1,875	2,074	3,672	2,075	(D)
Hamilton	69,405	32,639	11,805	20,888	12,257	3,621	3,591
Hardee	327,611	99,729	61,233	28,176	186,603	13,103	53,777
Hendry	529,835	195,139	178,124	63,679	222,952	48,065	178,504
Hernando	61,019	22,726	6,730	10,994	25,939	1,360	521
Highlands	483,835	118,077	80,883	72,729	285,005	8,024	83,301
Hillsborough	265,443	104,125	60,092	41,765	102,220	17,333	45,709
Holmes	86,706	40,690	17,202	26,921	12,949	6,146	421
Indian River	174,673	86,343	76,610	24,031	56,776	7,523	77,493
Jackson	244,185	151,053	80,035	60,704	21,657	10,771	13,365
Jefferson	118,352	37,031	16,669	59,579	11,414	10,328	4,257
Lafayette	95,833	25,383	7,917	21,359	47,014	2,077	3,198
Lake	199,098	95,428	39,843	24,481	56,037	23,152	24,373
Lee	106,721	29,990	19,673	12,477	58,212	6,042	17,114

See footnotes at end of table.   Continued . . .

University of Florida   **Bureau of Economic and Business Research**

Table 9.36. FARMS: LAND IN FARMS BY USE IN THE STATE AND COUNTIES
OF FLORIDA, 1992 (Continued)

(in acres)

County	Total land in farms	Land according to use					Irri-gated land
		Cropland		Wood-land 1/	Pasture-land 2/	Other 3/	
		Total	Har-vested				
Leon	100,764	19,769	7,881	63,363	11,378	6,254	2,781
Levy	190,553	70,593	24,494	49,460	63,629	6,871	9,895
Liberty	11,738	2,014	638	7,480	1,754	490	(D)
Madison	132,208	58,083	25,666	51,156	13,607	9,362	2,686
Manatee	299,699	109,143	61,950	61,002	113,797	15,757	54,568
Marion	296,242	114,134	40,290	74,302	90,059	17,747	5,217
Martin	190,788	79,264	66,727	16,228	77,902	17,394	58,742
Monroe	32	(D)	17	0	(D)	(D)	10
Nassau	44,962	13,490	4,541	22,808	6,708	1,956	33
Okaloosa	56,704	21,978	9,731	18,444	14,303	1,979	1,778
Okeechobee	351,885	72,717	30,509	14,192	247,552	17,424	27,662
Orange	138,418	50,507	33,697	51,898	26,043	9,970	25,249
Osceola	716,542	63,060	26,074	38,486	596,209	18,787	14,474
Palm Beach	637,934	578,699	510,263	12,475	16,373	30,387	422,966
Pasco	221,232	65,105	27,267	43,381	96,886	15,860	11,024
Pinellas	4,123	1,888	706	610	1,374	251	288
Polk	611,336	201,621	125,944	65,830	322,637	21,248	116,734
Putnam	105,621	23,655	13,337	54,709	22,258	4,999	9,560
St. Johns	48,839	28,658	25,190	9,583	8,715	1,883	24,208
St. Lucie	300,622	136,715	122,471	20,477	130,746	12,684	138,133
Santa Rosa	79,270	57,747	42,462	15,819	2,999	2,705	337
Sarasota	151,242	25,290	7,832	11,743	110,626	3,583	5,207
Seminole	59,642	9,542	4,499	12,867	29,512	7,721	3,155
Sumter	253,330	62,382	27,905	50,523	131,057	9,368	3,974
Suwannee	161,936	96,048	40,934	40,342	17,784	7,762	12,869
Taylor	(D)	(D)	1,237	49,039	20,488	1,657	433
Union	48,280	13,076	3,626	28,280	5,668	1,256	470
Volusia	138,208	25,068	13,583	43,719	59,443	9,978	8,460
Wakulla	8,679	3,623	1,103	3,896	655	505	(D)
Walton	96,730	51,080	12,310	27,369	6,663	11,618	989
Washington	45,214	24,704	13,237	12,263	4,543	3,704	179

(D) Data withheld to avoid disclosure of information about individual farms.
1/ Includes woodland pasture.
2/ Pastureland and rangeland other than cropland and woodland pasture.
3/ Land in house lots, ponds, roads, wasteland, etc.
Note: Because data for selected items are collected from a sample of operators,
the results are subject to sampling variability. The agriculture census is on a 5-
year cycle collecting data for years ending in 2 or 7.

Source: U.S., Department of Commerce, Bureau of the Census, *1992 Census of Agriculture: State and County Data, Florida.* AC92-A-9.

Table 9.37. INCOME: CASH RECEIPTS BY COMMODITY GROUP AND SPECIFIED
COMMODITY IN FLORIDA, 1991 THROUGH 1995

(in thousands of dollars)

Commodity 1/	1991	1992	1993	1994	1995
All commodities	6,144,436	6,139,086	6,078,004	5,984,249	5,848,907
Livestock and products	1,171,626	1,165,874	1,211,131	1,192,133	1,129,810
Meat animals	380,784	362,616	377,674	348,328	301,509
Cattle and calves	363,351	349,447	362,495	335,837	289,802
Hogs	17,304	13,126	15,106	12,399	11,581
Dairy products, wholesale milk	372,947	401,700	385,503	408,408	363,528
Poultry and eggs	277,068	259,678	298,831	291,605	315,237
Broilers	151,704	164,356	187,714	191,151	218,361
Farm chickens	3,764	3,028	3,569	1,406	1,018
Chicken eggs	120,930	91,104	106,838	98,348	95,158
Crops	4,972,810	4,973,212	4,866,873	4,792,116	4,719,097
Food grains, wheat	1,837	2,349	2,268	1,717	1,202
Feed crops, corn	9,645	11,117	12,094	11,045	11,502
Hay	9,929	13,389	10,801	14,025	12,203
Cotton	18,718	20,502	23,393	37,916	43,498
Tobacco	26,392	31,729	30,638	27,248	30,907
Oil crops, peanuts	73,551	57,886	57,684	58,302	52,463
Soybeans	6,949	7,375	8,091	7,490	5,582
Vegetables	1,558,416	1,756,993	1,688,676	1,448,817	1,267,464
Potatoes	164,515	92,359	128,194	118,655	84,010
Carrots	22,563	20,228	25,551	11,252	15,361
Corn, sweet	91,674	73,149	102,588	105,232	107,553
Cucumbers, fresh	78,489	78,747	72,072	47,488	37,795
Eggplant, all	12,974	17,410	13,075	15,606	14,005
Escarole	10,633	7,000	7,611	8,969	8,900
Lettuce	18,913	18,128	26,770	16,884	9,561
Peppers, green	173,628	209,630	215,939	197,465	172,125
Tomatoes, fresh	570,801	821,805	607,464	465,663	387,916
Radishes	35,269	21,578	36,961	25,888	23,873
Squash	50,221	45,850	38,170	43,216	41,686
Watermelons	80,767	66,150	66,600	57,868	61,793
Fruits and nuts	1,711,873	1,496,193	1,487,813	1,555,739	1,652,255
Grapefruit	346,755	309,484	239,353	231,631	206,706
Lemons	5,072	2,637	2,879	2,675	2,079
Limes	26,901	11,213	3,171	3,687	2,900
Oranges	1,135,547	966,764	1,033,825	1,126,888	1,165,832
Tangelos	24,088	14,994	20,361	12,021	16,381
Tangerines, processed	4,108	3,434	3,143	4,228	4,893
Avocados	13,455	7,701	3,608	12,320	11,324
Mangos	6,150	4,280	950	1,500	1,725
Strawberries	84,876	108,864	121,313	101,425	118,608
Blueberries	2,719	3,752	1,300	5,690	5,050
Pecans	3,325	3,770	3,460	1,600	945

1/ Totals include data for "other" categories not shown separately.
Note: Data are estimates. Value of sales for some individual commodities may
be understated; balance is included in "other."
Source: U.S., Department of Agriculture, Economic Research Service, Internet
site http://www.econ.ag.gov/.

Table 9.38. INCOME: MARKET VALUE OF AGRICULTURAL PRODUCTS SOLD
IN THE STATE AND COUNTIES OF FLORIDA, 1992

(in thousands of dollars, except where indicated)

County	Total	Average per farm (dollars)	Crops 1/	Livestock poultry and their products
Florida	5,266,033	149,586	4,197,420	1,068,613
Alachua	39,680	36,437	24,219	15,461
Baker	27,816	144,127	11,760	16,056
Bay	831	13,197	716	115
Bradford	16,900	53,652	1,914	14,986
Brevard	35,136	70,838	20,834	14,302
Broward	34,742	88,403	26,982	7,760
Calhoun	15,159	114,843	13,534	1,625
Charlotte	37,903	177,117	31,928	5,975
Citrus	5,561	19,308	2,504	3,056
Clay	33,967	161,747	1,932	32,035
Collier	260,740	1,026,536	254,916	5,825
Columbia	20,636	39,457	8,728	11,908
Dade	356,967	188,772	352,988	3,979
De Soto	128,656	160,020	113,091	15,565
Dixie	2,678	25,263	1,299	1,379
Duval	22,443	59,373	6,868	15,575
Escambia	15,653	34,479	8,812	6,841
Flagler	10,129	108,911	8,809	1,320
Franklin	79	13,161	0	79
Gadsden	71,048	213,357	66,088	4,960
Gilchrist	28,218	85,770	6,943	21,276
Glades	56,706	275,270	32,584	24,121
Gulf	(D)	(D)	(D)	152
Hamilton	14,445	64,488	9,078	5,368
Hardee	127,720	109,255	95,257	32,462
Hendry	273,308	702,590	254,368	18,939
Hernando	18,675	45,439	2,210	16,465
Highlands	185,929	285,168	152,296	33,633
Hillsborough	259,221	93,921	188,542	70,680
Holmes	31,327	59,898	5,646	25,680
Indian River	145,065	324,530	139,807	5,258
Jackson	52,626	65,132	34,299	18,327
Jefferson	21,046	70,861	10,202	10,844
Lafayette	43,709	173,449	4,214	39,495

See footnotes at end of table.   Continued . . .

University of Florida   **Bureau of Economic and Business Research**

Table 9.38. INCOME: MARKET VALUE OF AGRICULTURAL PRODUCTS SOLD
IN THE STATE AND COUNTIES OF FLORIDA, 1992 (Continued)

(in thousands of dollars, except where indicated)

County	All products Total	Average per farm (dollars)	Crops 1/	Livestock poultry and their products
Lake	90,258	68,378	72,082	18,177
Lee	81,553	157,742	78,932	2,620
Leon	3,843	14,613	1,663	2,180
Levy	42,558	89,975	10,384	32,175
Liberty	647	9,114	(D)	(D)
Madison	19,888	41,348	6,584	13,304
Manatee	209,865	288,277	187,741	22,124
Marion	64,074	38,739	17,688	46,387
Martin	155,038	508,320	136,964	18,073
Monroe	(D)	(D)	286	(D)
Nassau	27,816	100,418	770	27,046
Okaloosa	6,213	19,725	2,758	3,456
Okeechobee	133,235	313,743	23,706	109,528
Orange	207,782	209,881	204,286	3,496
Osceola	53,197	105,607	30,647	22,550
Palm Beach	891,196	964,497	884,066	7,130
Pasco	62,193	67,455	21,511	40,683
Pinellas	11,460	92,423	11,228	233
Polk	203,350	88,644	169,614	33,737
Putnam	33,318	83,296	27,916	5,402
St. Johns	45,831	276,089	44,285	1,546
St. Lucie	207,123	384,273	194,784	12,339
Santa Rosa	21,460	49,907	19,291	2,169
Sarasota	18,903	57,631	13,026	5,877
Seminole	20,399	57,951	18,199	2,200
Sumter	36,892	51,239	15,270	21,622
Suwannee	93,048	99,837	27,044	66,004
Taylor	2,630	21,042	699	1,931
Union	8,144	46,536	2,708	5,436
Volusia	78,882	80,656	71,537	7,345
Wakulla	1,516	18,261	426	1,090
Walton	22,256	58,108	3,275	18,981
Washington	10,994	40,123	3,464	7,529

(D) Data withheld to avoid disclosure of information about individual farms.
1/ Includes nursery and greenhouse products.
Note: The agriculture census is on a 5-year cycle collecting data for years ending in 2 and 7.

Source: U.S., Department of Commerce, Bureau of the Census, *1992 Census of Agriculture: State and County Data, Florida*. AC92-A-9.

Table 9.39. FARM OPERATORS: NUMBER OF OPERATORS BY PRINCIPAL OCCUPATION
AGE, AND RACE AND HISPANIC ORIGIN AND NUMBER OF FARMS AND ACRES
OPERATED BY FEMALES IN THE STATE AND COUNTIES
OF FLORIDA, 1992

County	Total	Principal occupation Farming	Other	Average age (years)	Non-white	His-panic ori-gin 1/	Female operators Number of farms	Land in farms (acres)
Florida	35,204	16,557	18,647	55.3	1,126	928	4,851	748,592
Alachua	1,089	482	607	54.0	77	13	178	11,736
Baker	193	80	113	54.8	6	0	11	702
Bay	63	15	48	55.2	0	0	8	264
Bradford	315	112	203	56.2	5	6	43	2,651
Brevard	496	173	323	56.7	14	10	73	5,442
Broward	393	202	191	52.6	19	26	80	1,213
Calhoun	132	71	61	56.5	4	0	9	1,997
Charlotte	214	93	121	57.3	0	0	23	11,865
Citrus	288	121	167	57.3	3	4	47	4,719
Clay	210	86	124	56.9	3	3	27	1,459
Collier	254	143	111	50.2	7	7	23	(D)
Columbia	523	214	309	55.6	28	5	69	8,912
Dade	1,891	943	948	53.2	179	403	205	2,294
De Soto	804	345	459	57.1	10	8	107	9,096
Dixie	106	34	72	57.7	0	0	11	2,197
Duval	378	168	210	57.2	7	5	50	7,335
Escambia	454	185	269	55.2	16	0	33	2,778
Flagler	93	41	52	50.9	0	0	7	123
Franklin	6	1	5	52.7	0	0	0	0
Gadsden	333	127	206	57.1	23	4	31	4,343
Gilchrist	329	171	158	54.0	3	3	47	8,817
Glades	206	113	93	56.3	6	5	19	13,077
Gulf	27	7	20	55.6	0	0	0	0
Hamilton	224	109	115	53.3	19	0	19	6,148
Hardee	1,169	537	632	57.1	7	15	165	29,262
Hendry	389	221	168	55.3	9	17	38	26,347
Hernando	411	166	245	55.1	15	14	69	3,723
Highlands	652	320	332	54.4	9	6	92	58,986
Hillsborough	2,760	1,268	1,492	56.6	80	94	443	17,144
Holmes	523	248	275	54.5	6	0	45	6,041
Indian River	447	244	203	55.9	5	6	65	2,676
Jackson	808	443	365	55.2	79	4	47	9,463
Jefferson	297	119	178	56.6	28	0	28	16,565
Lafayette	252	128	124	52.8	0	0	26	3,389
Lake	1,320	601	719	55.3	23	13	183	20,099
Lee	517	230	287	53.0	4	6	71	4,547

See footnotes at end of table.   Continued . . .

Table 9.39. FARM OPERATORS: NUMBER OF OPERATORS BY PRINCIPAL OCCUPATION
AGE, AND RACE AND HISPANIC ORIGIN AND NUMBER OF FARMS AND ACRES
OPERATED BY FEMALES IN THE STATE AND COUNTIES
OF FLORIDA, 1992 (Continued)

		Principal occupation		Average age	Non-	His- panic ori-	Female operators Number of	Land in farms
County	Total	Farming	Other	(years)	white	gin 1/	farms	(acres)
Leon	263	84	179	56.3	30	0	34	22,955
Levy	473	228	245	54.8	10	5	75	9,974
Liberty	71	23	48	57.4	0	0	7	3,720
Madison	481	224	257	56.8	24	0	67	13,238
Manatee	728	362	366	55.3	7	7	109	21,561
Marion	1,654	817	837	55.2	82	43	328	31,708
Martin	305	147	158	55.0	7	7	35	17,111
Monroe	15	6	9	54.7	0	0	7	9
Nassau	277	116	161	55.1	0	0	28	3,744
Okaloosa	315	138	177	56.4	3	3	26	2,301
Okeechobee	418	192	226	52.8	4	14	50	21,630
Orange	990	510	480	55.1	48	9	172	16,853
Osceola	499	240	259	55.6	8	0	80	49,098
Palm Beach	924	555	369	51.4	34	54	139	8,502
Pasco	922	405	517	56.6	10	24	144	22,443
Pinellas	124	51	73	54.1	0	0	38	715
Polk	2,294	959	1,335	56.8	35	18	358	36,862
Putnam	400	188	212	54.8	12	3	64	11,348
St. Johns	166	107	59	52.7	4	3	17	5,051
St. Lucie	539	285	254	53.6	3	4	53	8,290
Santa Rosa	430	220	210	55.0	0	0	27	1,344
Sarasota	328	133	195	54.1	0	4	57	22,654
Seminole	352	186	166	55.3	21	6	62	7,250
Sumter	720	347	373	56.1	22	11	130	23,786
Suwannee	932	509	423	55.7	25	10	100	17,722
Taylor	125	50	75	58.2	0	0	8	(D)
Union	175	78	97	57.1	0	0	18	1,098
Volusia	978	495	483	53.8	13	9	160	8,798
Wakulla	83	30	53	54.5	4	0	13	283
Walton	383	178	205	56.0	11	0	39	30,653
Washington	274	133	141	57.3	3	0	14	1,061
Other	0	0	0	0.0	12	17	0	0

(D) Data withheld to avoid disclosure of information about individual farms.
1/ Persons of Hispanic origin may be of any race.
Note: The agriculture census is on a 5-year cycle collecting data for years ending in 2 and 7.

Source: U.S., Department of Commerce, Bureau of the Census, *1992 Census of Agriculture: State and County Data, Florida.* AC92-A-9.

Table 9.42. INCOME: CASH RECEIPTS FROM FARMING IN FLORIDA
OTHER AGRICULTURAL STATES, AND THE UNITED STATES, 1995

(amounts in thousands of dollars)

State	Total	Rank among states	Per-centage change from previous year	Crops	Livestock and products	Govern-ment payments
Florida	5,848,907	9	2.3	4,719,097	1,129,810	55,716
California	22,261,109	1	-4.4	16,712,582	5,548,527	237,760
Texas	13,287,680	2	-2.7	4,833,844	8,453,836	642,878
Iowa	10,958,874	3	-8.8	5,891,122	5,067,752	784,639
Nebraska	8,690,446	4	-1.9	3,503,152	5,187,294	507,347
Illinois	7,887,034	5	0.7	6,176,908	1,710,126	543,735
Kansas	7,521,311	6	1.4	2,828,527	4,692,784	423,021
Minnesota	7,001,667	7	-8.5	3,550,943	3,450,724	467,901
North Carolina	6,986,814	8	-7.8	3,251,476	3,735,338	40,159
Wisconsin	5,582,296	10	-3.6	1,656,284	3,926,012	183,840
Georgia	5,166,101	11	-9.2	2,376,917	2,789,184	66,466
Washington	5,157,957	12	-7.5	3,563,581	1,594,376	115,927
Arkansas	5,065,456	13	6.5	2,042,233	3,023,223	383,265
Indiana	4,981,458	14	-6.4	3,240,106	1,741,352	246,066
Ohio	4,576,009	15	-3.0	2,986,816	1,589,193	167,307
United States	185,750,021	(X)	-2.7	98,906,230	86,843,791	7,252,270

(X) Not applicable.

Source: U.S., Department of Agriculture, *Agricultural Statistics, 1997.*

Table 9.43. TAXES: AMOUNT LEVIED ON FARM REAL ESTATE IN FLORIDA AND THE UNITED
STATES, 1992, 1993, AND 1994

Item	Florida 1992	1993	1994	United States 1/ 1992	1993	1994
Total taxes levied ($1,000,000)	143.8	140.7	130.8	4,869.2	5,023.3	4,908.6
Taxes per acre Amount (dollars)	14.75	14.71	13.68	5.80	5.98	5.86
Taxes per $100 of full value (dollars)	0.72	0.71	0.62	0.84	0.85	0.75

1/ Excludes Alaska.

Source: U.S., Department of Agriculture, *Agricultural Statistics, 1997*, and previous edition.

University of Florida   **Bureau of Economic and Business Research**

Table 9.45.   LAND: TOTAL FARM ACREAGE, 1990, AND ACREAGE OWNED BY NONRESIDENT
ALIENS, 1995, IN THE STATE AND COUNTIES OF FLORIDA

County	Estimated total farmland acreage 1/	Reported value 3/ ($1,000)	Amount	As a percentage of total farmland	County total as a percentage of state total
			Acreage foreign-owned 2/		
Florida	24,300,104	1,194,287	620,654	2.55	100.00
Alachua	519,000	6,822	11,904	2.29	1.92
Baker	301,528	0	0	0.00	0.00
Bay	410,490	0	0	0.00	0.00
Bradford	173,000	0	0	0.00	0.00
Brevard	478,050	12,621	5,900	1.23	0.95
Broward	28,670	20,423	1,932	6.74	0.31
Calhoun	343,710	2,239	2,397	0.70	0.39
Charlotte	268,170	15,860	7,250	2.70	1.17
Citrus	178,310	1,010	973	0.55	0.16
Clay	368,000	10,500	7,088	1.93	1.14
Collier	576,400	24,748	11,764	2.04	1.90
Columbia	534,065	1,986	4,505	0.84	0.73
Dade	85,306	197,290	17,928	21.02	2.89
De Soto	354,000	10,473	4,964	1.40	0.80
Dixie	278,725	157	157	0.06	0.03
Duval	301,900	0	0	0.00	0.00
Escambia	308,207	401	249	0.08	0.04
Flagler	310,100	0	0	0.00	0.00
Franklin	310,000	17,107	37,026	11.94	5.97
Gadsden	261,800	2,608	5,699	2.18	0.92
Gilchrist	216,560	2,614	10,031	4.63	1.62
Glades	443,500	6,931	5,907	1.33	0.95
Gulf	363,000	256	311	0.09	0.05
Hamilton	333,219	386	1,154	0.35	0.19
Hardee	326,302	10,906	4,659	1.43	0.75
Hendry	734,000	23,599	12,356	1.68	1.99
Hernando	216,299	0	0	0.00	0.00
Highlands	600,549	10,699	4,893	0.81	0.79
Hillsborough	530,000	20,047	12,057	2.27	1.94
Holmes	343,300	0	0	0.00	0.00
Indian River	210,161	61,003	26,507	12.61	4.27
Jackson	576,000	5,224	6,167	1.07	0.99
Jefferson	346,072	1,293	3,408	0.98	0.55
Lafayette	337,868	0	0	0.00	0.00
Lake	515,245	32,293	13,635	2.65	2.20
Lee	244,484	37,581	7,599	3.11	1.22
Leon	304,350	0	0	0.00	0.00
Levy	646,185	2,561	9,981	1.54	1.61
Liberty	268,375	393	850	0.32	0.14
Madison	417,961	16	80	0.02	0.01

See footnotes at end of table.   Continued . . .

University of Florida   **Bureau of Economic and Business Research**

Table 9.45. LAND: TOTAL FARM ACREAGE, 1990, AND ACREAGE OWNED BY NONRESIDENT
ALIENS, 1995, IN THE STATE AND COUNTIES OF FLORIDA (Continued)

County	Estimated total farmland acreage 1/	Reported value 3/ ($1,000)	Amount	As a percentage of total farmland	County total as a percentage of state total
			Acreage foreign-owned 2/		
Manatee	329,388	31,542	9,555	2.90	1.54
Marion	575,000	53,306	18,453	3.21	2.97
Martin	278,000	70,552	33,252	11.96	5.36
Monroe	0	0	0	(X)	0.00
Nassau	351,800	1,009	315	0.09	0.05
Okaloosa	208,069	24,075	21,818	10.49	3.52
Okeechobee	465,500	20,935	17,822	3.83	2.87
Orange	323,984	151,304	27,085	8.36	4.36
Osceola	802,100	69,776	17,552	2.19	2.83
Palm Beach	569,135	110,683	139,755	24.56	22.52
Pasco	324,755	7,742	2,491	0.77	0.40
Pinellas	47,000	900	55	0.12	0.01
Polk	851,600	45,016	27,598	3.24	4.45
Putnam	330,670	849	1,829	0.55	0.29
St. Johns	340,000	1,488	1,156	0.34	0.19
St. Lucie	294,158	21,571	13,768	4.68	2.22
Santa Rosa	550,080	1,089	1,263	0.23	0.20
Sarasota	166,766	1,077	513	0.31	0.08
Seminole	116,200	16,965	2,087	1.80	0.34
Sumter	595,000	5,862	4,252	0.71	0.69
Suwannee	441,600	4,668	4,582	1.04	0.74
Taylor	296,800	3	20	0.01	A/
Union	149,932	0	0	0.00	0.00
Volusia	529,360	11,942	8,321	1.57	1.34
Wakulla	160,472	56	61	0.04	0.01
Walton	505,222	1,820	27,720	5.49	4.47
Washington	334,652	0	0	0.00	0.00

(X) Not applicable.
A/ Less than 0.005 percent.
1/ Land currently used for agricultural, forestry, or timber production or, if
idle, land used for such purposes within the last five years.
2/ A foreign investor is defined as any nonresident alien, any corporation incorporated outside the U.S., or any U.S. corporation with 5 percent or more foreign interest. A foreign investor holding more than 5 percent or more interest in any agricultural lands must disclose such holdings.
3/ Reported value is purchase price or nonpurchase price (estimated value) at time
of acquisition.
Note: Data were compiled by the U.S. Department of Agriculture, Agricultural Stabilization and Conservation Service from disclosure forms filed under the Agriculture
Foreign Investment Disclosure Act of 1978. Detail may not add to total because of
rounding.

Source: U.S., Department of Agriculture, Agricultural Stabilization and Conservation Service, *Foreign Ownership of U.S. Agricultural Land Through December 31, 1995.*

University of Florida   **Bureau of Economic and Business Research**

Table 9.50. IRRIGATION: AGRICULTURAL ACREAGE UNDER IRRIGATION AND WATER USE BY TYPE OF PRODUCT AND SOURCE IN FLORIDA, 1995

Product	Acreage irrigated	Irrigated water use (millions of gallons per day) Total 1/	Ground	Surface	Reclaimed
Total 2/	2,096,085	3,444.54	1,657.14	1,787.40	217.86
Agricultural irrigation	1,974,693	3,125.56	1,425.13	1,700.43	70.84
Vegetable crops	268,772	374.07	288.34	85.73	0.00
Cabbage	8,683	14.00	13.84	0.16	0.00
Carrots	7,425	8.61	1.15	7.46	0.00
Cucumbers	15,725	29.79	22.60	7.19	0.00
Peppers	21,460	44.22	34.00	10.22	0.00
Potatoes	36,860	51.62	51.09	0.53	0.00
Tomatoes	48,560	92.78	82.45	10.33	0.00
Sweet corn	32,265	29.73	9.27	20.46	0.00
Other	97,794	103.32	73.94	29.38	0.00
Fruit crops	879,882	1,420.47	759.31	661.16	35.90
Blueberries	2,037	1.97	1.90	0.07	0.00
Citrus 3/	817,835	1,350.09	691.48	658.61	35.90
Grapes	513	0.44	0.39	0.05	0.00
Peaches	138	0.17	0.17	0.00	0.00
Pecans	3,355	3.90	3.85	0.05	0.00
Strawberries	6,204	6.35	6.05	0.30	0.00
Watermelons	38,332	34.17	32.11	2.06	0.00
Other	11,468	23.38	23.36	0.02	0.00
Field crops	566,118	928.65	96.08	832.57	14.13
Cotton	14,081	11.10	10.04	1.06	0.00
Field corn	26,315	27.67	24.38	3.29	0.00
Peanuts	29,193	23.04	21.50	1.54	0.00
Rice	18,414	10.97	0.16	10.81	0.00
Sorghum	6,818	3.46	3.38	0.08	0.00
Soybeans	3,388	2.85	2.75	0.10	0.00
Sugarcane	444,000	832.80	17.80	815.00	0.00
Tobacco	6,382	6.67	6.33	0.34	0.00
Wheat	2,000	1.27	1.18	0.09	0.00
Other	15,527	8.82	8.56	0.26	14.13
Ornamentals/grasses 4/	259,921	402.37	281.40	120.97	20.81
Nonagricultural irrigation	0	53.24	47.82	5.42	8.23
Recreation/landscape	121,392	265.74	184.19	81.55	138.79

1/ Reclaimed water use values are not included in the totals.
2/ Includes crops not shown separately.
3/ Includes oranges, grapefruit, limes, lemons, and all other citrus.
4/ Includes ferns, ornamentals (field and container grown), improved pasture, and sod.
5/ Includes livestock, fish farming, and other nonirrigation uses.

Source: U.S., Department of the Interior, Geological Survey, Water Resource Division, unpublished water-use data, Tallahassee, FL, August 1997, and State of Florida, Department of Agriculture and Consumer Services, Florida Agricultural Statistics Service.

University of Florida   **Bureau of Economic and Business Research**

Table 9.51. CITRUS: ESTIMATED PRODUCTION AND VALUE OF CITRUS BY TYPE IN FLORIDA
CROP YEARS 1991-92 THROUGH 1995-96

Type of citrus	1991-92	1992-93	1993-94	1994-95	1995-96 A/
Production (1,000 boxes)					
All citrus	191,815	251,540	235,760	271,020	265,275
Oranges	139,800	186,600	174,400	205,500	203,200
Early and midseason	83,400	114,300	107,300	119,700	121,200
Late (Valencia)	56,400	72,300	67,100	85,800	82,000
Grapefruit	42,400	55,150	51,050	55,700	52,350
Seedy	1,200	1,750	1,050	1,300	1,050
White seedless	19,100	25,700	24,500	25,700	23,200
Colored seedless	22,100	27,700	25,500	28,700	28,100
Other citrus	9,615	9,790	10,310	9,820	9,725
Temples	2,350	2,500	2,250	2,550	2,150
Tangelos	2,600	3,050	3,350	3,150	2,450
Tangerines 1/	1,330	1,400	2,370	2,350	2,900
Honey tangerines	1,270	1,400	1,730	1,200	1,600
K-early citrus	165	185	210	120	160
Limes	1,600	B/ 1,000	200	230	300
Lemons 2/	300	255	200	220	165
Value of production ($1,000)					
All citrus	1,208,944	855,812	939,854	904,977	1,230,738
Oranges	828,749	649,713	713,312	732,222	940,319
Early and midseason	453,501	369,438	403,802	367,401	428,885
Late (Valencia)	375,248	280,275	309,510	364,821	511,434
Grapefruit	280,629	146,432	167,211	112,049	102,639
Seedy	5,484	3,290	1,869	2,379	1,712
White seedless	123,337	56,973	79,254	57,430	52,908
Colored seedless	151,808	86,169	86,088	52,240	48,019
Other citrus	99,566	59,667	59,331	60,706	77,780
Temples	15,289	7,475	6,136	7,361	8,821
Tangelos	18,618	10,092	7,976	6,882	9,042
Tangerines 1/	24,453	20,070	23,172	18,837	30,522
Honey tangerines	22,344	18,433	17,131	23,703	25,608
K-early citrus	489	1,015	377	257	420
Limes	14,589	B/ 1,017	2,541	1,989	2,006
Lemons 2/	3,784	1,565	1,998	1,677	1,361

A/ Preliminary.
B/ Hurricane Andrew August 1992.
1/ Excludes honey tangerines. Fallglo tangerines not included prior to 1993-94.
2/ Florida lemons bloom and harvest during the calendar year; data are for the
years 1991 through 1995.
Note: Some data may be revised.

Source: State of Florida, Department of Agriculture and Consumer Services,
Florida Agricultural Statistics Service, *Florida Agricultural Statistics: Citrus
Summary, 1995-96.*

University of Florida   **Bureau of Economic and Business Research**

Table 9.52. ORANGES AND GRAPEFRUIT: BEARING ACREAGE, PRODUCTION, AND YIELD PER
ACRE IN FLORIDA, OTHER CITRUS STATES, AND THE UNITED STATES, CROP YEARS
1989-90 THROUGH 1995-96

State and year	Oranges Bearing acreage (1,000 acres)	Produc- tion (1,000 tons)	Yield per acre (tons)	Grapefruit Bearing acreage (1,000 acres)	Produc- tion (1,000 tons)	Yield per acre (tons)
Florida						
1989-90	399.5	4,959	12.4	103.0	1,517	14.7
1990-91	420.9	6,822	16.2	104.2	1,916	18.4
1991-92	444.4	6,291	14.2	104.7	1,802	17.2
1992-93	489.2	8,397	17.2	111.9	2,344	20.9
1993-94	510.8	7,849	15.4	118.3	2,170	18.3
1994-95	562.8	9,248	16.4	127.3	2,367	18.6
1995-96 A/	594.8	9,144	15.4	132.8	2,225	16.8
Arizona						
1989-90	10.2	59	5.8	6.4	71	11.1
1990-91	9.9	66	6.7	6.2	77	12.4
1991-92	10.4	89	8.6	5.9	89	15.1
1992-93	10.6	69	6.5	5.9	69	11.7
1993-94	10.6	71	6.7	5.9	B/ 59	10.0
1994-95	10.4	39	3.8	5.7	47	8.2
1995-96 A/	9.6	63	6.6	5.3	40	7.5
California						
1989-90	175.1	2,676	15.3	19.2	310	16.1
1990-91	178.4	960	5.4	18.3	263	14.4
1991-92	181.8	2,528	13.9	18.5	330	17.8
1992-93	184.0	2,505	13.6	17.8	303	17.0
1993-94	185.0	2,385	12.9	18.0	B/ 312	17.3
1994-95	191.0	2,101	11.0	18.4	312	17.0
1994-95 A/	196.0	2,477	12.6	18.8	271	14.4
Texas						
1989-90	13.0	51	3.9	18.7	80	4.3
1990-91	3.5	0	0.0	4.5	0	0.0
1991-92	3.5	1	0.3	7.5	3	0.4
1992-93	4.4	21	4.8	10.1	75	7.4
1993-94	5.5	24	4.4	12.8	120	9.4
1994-95	7.0	44	6.3	15.0	186	12.4
1995-96 A/	7.9	39	4.9	17.7	182	10.3
United States						
1989-90	597.8	7,745	13.0	147.3	1,978	13.4
1990-91	612.7	7,848	12.8	133.2	2,256	16.9
1991-92	640.1	8,909	13.9	136.6	2,224	16.3
1992-93	688.2	10,992	16.0	145.7	2,791	19.2
1993-94	711.9	10,329	14.5	155.0	2,661	17.2
1994-95	771.2	11,432	14.8	166.4	2,912	17.5
1995-96 A/	808.3	11,723	14.5	174.6	2,718	15.6

A/ Preliminary.
B/ Box weight for California Desert and Arizona grapefruit changed in 1993-94.
Note: Some data may be revised.
Source: State of Florida, Department of Agriculture and Consumer Services,
Florida Agricultural Statistics Service, *Florida Agricultural Statistics: Citrus
Summary, 1995-96.*

University of Florida   **Bureau of Economic and Business Research**

Table 9.53.   ORANGES AND GRAPEFRUIT: SEASON AVERAGE ON-TREE PRICES PER BOX AND
VALUE OF PRODUCTION IN FLORIDA AND THE UNITED STATES, CROP YEARS
1988-89 THROUGH 1995-96

	Season average price (in dollars per box)			Value of production (in thousands of dollars)		
Crop year	Total	Fresh use	Process-ing	Total	Fresh use	Process-ing
Oranges 1/						
Florida						
1988-89	7.41	7.61	7.40	1,086,319	64,628	1,021,691
1989-90	6.21	10.31	5.98	684,226	61,053	623,173
1990-91	5.89	8.46	5.66	892,675	105,289	787,386
1991-92	5.93	8.52	5.69	828,749	98,404	730,345
1992-93	3.48	3.81	3.46	649,713	40,877	608,836
1993-94	4.09	5.98	3.98	713,312	59,162	654,150
1994-95	3.56	4.82	3.50	732,222	50,347	681,875
1995-96 A/	4.63	6.11	4.55	940,319	60,877	879,442
United States						
1988-89	7.08	8.21	6.76	1,470,582	426,433	1,044,149
1989-90	6.13	8.49	5.25	1,128,626	463,303	665,323
1990-91	6.78	14.84	5.29	1,239,979	462,185	777,794
1991-92	5.52	8.06	4.72	1,146,430	439,856	706,574
1992-93	3.88	6.92	3.03	1,005,498	433,663	571,835
1993-94	4.40	7.67	3.48	1,067,256	448,199	619,057
1994-95	4.09	7.79	3.21	1,098,650	444,638	654,012
1995-96 A/	4.93	8.19	4.08	1,350,465	511,762	838,703
Grapefruit						
Florida						
1988-89	4.45	6.03	3.24	243,874	144,068	99,806
1989-90	5.65	10.00	3.06	201,756	133,413	68,343
1990-91	5.66	8.83	2.08	255,328	211,244	44,084
1991-92	6.62	8.69	4.20	280,629	198,391	82,238
1992-93	2.66	4.86	1.06	146,432	112,476	33,956
1993-94	3.28	5.52	1.51	167,211	124,167	43,044
1994-95	2.01	4.53	0.34	112,049	100,635	11,414
1995-96 A/	1.96	4.90	-0.32	102,639	112,035	-9,396
United States						
1988-89	4.41	6.05	2.84	305,644	210,151	95,493
1989-90	5.86	10.00	2.53	291,150	227,152	63,998
1990-91	5.55	8.74	1.65	306,652	268,479	38,173
1991-92	6.20	8.34	3.44	336,939	258,803	78,136
1992-93	2.75	5.10	0.77	188,014	162,415	25,599
1993-94	3.33	5.61	1.21	217,055	179,341	37,714
1994-95	2.24	4.78	0.15	162,458	158,494	3,964
1995-96 A/	2.37	5.38	-0.42	161,253	176,538	-15,285

A/ Preliminary.
1/ Includes early, midseason, and late type (Valencia) oranges.
Note: Charges for picking, hauling, and packing are deducted from the weighted
average of prices obtained from all segments of the citrus industry to arrive at the
final on-tree price received by producers. United States data include Arizona, California, Florida, and Texas. Some data may be revised.
Source: State of Florida, Department of Agriculture and Consumer Services, Florida Agricultural Statistics Service, *Florida Agricultural Statistics: Citrus Summary,
1995-96.*

University of Florida   **Bureau of Economic and Business Research**

Table 9.54. CITRUS: ESTIMATED PRODUCTION OF PRINCIPAL TYPES OF CITRUS IN THE
STATE AND COUNTIES OF FLORIDA, CROP YEAR 1995-96

(in 1,000 boxes)

Area and county	Total 1/	Oranges All oranges	Oranges Early and mid-season	Valen-cias	All grape-fruit	Spe-cialty fruit 2/
Florida	264,810	203,200	121,200	82,000	52,350	9,260
District						
Indian River	52,345	18,000	9,800	8,200	32,800	1,545
Northern	11,405	9,612	7,874	1,738	364	1,429
Central	66,769	57,561	30,384	27,177	6,369	2,839
Western	61,760	58,011	39,607	18,404	2,268	1,481
Southern	72,531	60,016	33,535	26,481	10,549	1,966
County						
Brevard	2,196	1,461	899	562	670	65
Charlotte	5,252	4,150	2,128	2,022	962	140
Collier	10,855	9,203	5,154	4,049	1,405	247
De Soto	23,435	22,452	12,831	9,621	518	465
Glades	3,034	2,835	1,974	861	149	50
Hardee	19,630	18,719	14,296	4,423	411	500
Hendry	31,663	26,064	14,334	11,730	4,766	833
Highlands	26,627	23,653	9,830	13,823	1,829	1,145
Hillsborough	9,704	9,022	7,207	1,815	398	284
Indian River	18,475	5,707	3,374	2,333	12,296	472
Lake	5,008	3,818	3,164	654	240	950
Lee	3,433	2,933	1,562	1,371	453	47
Manatee	8,170	7,239	4,964	2,275	740	191
Martin	13,601	10,933	5,070	5,863	2,383	285
Okeechobee	3,303	2,658	1,883	775	590	55
Orange	2,360	2,040	1,460	580	43	277
Osceola	5,923	5,016	3,526	1,490	657	250
Palm Beach	4,002	2,392	1,674	718	1,271	339
Pasco	3,083	2,922	2,488	434	63	98
Polk	34,655	29,229	17,319	11,910	3,946	1,480
St. Lucie	28,429	9,216	4,911	4,305	18,276	937
Sarasota	760	540	288	252	184	36
Seminole	284	244	193	51	1	39
Volusia	303	232	190	42	61	10
Other 3/	625	522	481	41	38	65

1/ Does not include lemon and lime production.
2/ Includes tangelos, temples, tangerines, and K-early citrus.
3/ Includes Broward, Citrus, Flagler, Hernando, Marion, Pinellas, Putnam, and Sumter counties.
Note: Citrus districts are based on citrus marketings/production areas. Several counties are in more than one district.

Source: State of Florida, Department of Agriculture and Consumer Services, Florida Agricultural Statistics Service, *Florida Agricultural Statistics: Citrus Summary, 1995-96.*

University of Florida   **Bureau of Economic and Business Research**

Table 9.55. CITRUS: ACREAGE BY TYPE OF FRUIT IN THE STATE AND SPECIFIED
COUNTIES OF FLORIDA, JANUARY 1, 1996

County	Total	All oranges 1/	Oranges Early and mid-season	Valencias	All grape-fruit 1/	Specialty fruit 2/
Florida	857,861	656,598	338,501	307,878	144,416	56,847
Brevard	11,569	8,605	5,088	3,106	2,175	789
Broward	108	85	45	40	18	5
Charlotte	21,183	16,256	6,588	9,390	3,498	1,429
Citrus	242	194	175	14	26	22
Collier	36,583	31,172	14,219	16,853	4,086	1,325
Dade 3/	2,792	0	0	0	0	2,792
De Soto	66,182	62,082	30,262	31,363	1,792	2,308
Glades	9,402	8,631	5,186	3,347	390	381
Hardee	52,578	48,976	34,455	14,066	1,018	2,584
Hendry	99,770	84,464	35,570	48,051	10,148	5,158
Hernando	1,114	996	946	22	25	93
Highlands	76,586	66,903	24,730	41,859	4,456	5,227
Hillsborough	28,236	25,690	19,355	5,754	1,006	1,540
Indian River	66,561	28,216	14,616	13,158	35,923	2,422
Lake	21,468	15,767	12,857	2,302	1,240	4,461
Lee	12,155	10,017	4,252	5,440	1,238	900
Manatee	24,200	21,094	13,218	7,778	1,984	1,122
Marion	1,147	894	838	28	52	201
Martin	47,090	39,838	14,402	24,365	5,746	1,506
Okeechobee	12,206	9,971	5,919	4,039	1,699	536
Orange	10,029	8,295	5,631	2,530	282	1,452
Osceola	15,404	12,927	8,745	4,038	1,528	949
Palm Beach	12,746	7,820	4,622	2,919	2,637	2,289
Pasco	11,567	10,684	8,694	1,682	295	588
Pinellas	211	125	66	59	59	27
Polk	103,884	84,690	44,953	37,889	9,157	10,037
Putnam	123	90	78	12	1	32
St. Lucie	107,224	48,077	20,362	26,407	53,239	5,908
Sarasota	2,414	1,695	802	893	480	239
Seminole	1,412	1,107	890	200	29	276
Volusia.	1,502	1,203	903	274	189	110
Other 4/	173	34	34	0	0	139

1/ Includes unidentified variety acreage.
2/ Includes limes and lemons.
3/ Surveyed as of October 1996. Reflected in the state total.
4/ Includes Flagler and Sumter counties.

Source: State of Florida, Department of Agriculture and Consumer Services, Florida Agricultural Statistics Service, *Florida Agricultural Statistics: Citrus Summary,
1995-96.*

University of Florida   **Bureau of Economic and Business Research**

Table 9.56. ORANGE JUICE SALES: GALLONS SOLD AND CONSUMER RETAIL DOLLARS SPENT
IN UNITED STATES FOOD STORES, SEASONS 1982-1983 THROUGH 1995-1996

Season 1/	Amount	Total Percentage change from previous year	Chilled orange juice 2/	Canned single strength	Frozen concentrated orange juice
		Reconstituted gallons (rounded to millions)			
1982-83	863.0	7.3	346.0	23.1	494.0
1983-84	856.0	-0.8	378.0	20.3	457.0
1984-85	817.0	-4.6	373.0	18.0	426.0
1985-86	884.0	8.2	437.0	17.3	430.0
1986-87 A/	700.6	(X)	357.5	9.2	333.8
1987-88	666.6	-4.9	355.6	8.8	301.7
1988-89	690.2	3.5	391.8	8.5	289.4
1989-90	628.2	-9.0	363.4	8.3	256.0
1990-91	700.7	11.5	412.2	8.3	279.7
1991-92	688.9	-1.7	417.0	8.3	263.1
1992-93	747.8	8.5	479.6	8.4	259.8
1993-94	741.8	-0.8	494.8	7.9	239.0
1994-95	746.9	0.7	519.1	7.5	220.2
1995-96	726.0	-2.8	521.1	7.2	197.7
		Consumer retail dollars (rounded to millions)			
1982-83	2,628.0	5.2	1,156.0	90.7	1,381.0
1983-84	2,993.0	13.9	1,418.0	91.0	1,483.0
1984-85	3,102.0	3.6	1,512.0	87.8	1,502.0
1985-86	2,871.0	-7.4	1,550.0	77.0	1,244.0
1986-87 A/	2,081.1	(X)	1,145.3	41.2	894.5
1987-88	2,394.2	15.0	1,386.4	42.2	962.9
1988-89	2,568.4	7.3	1,589.2	41.8	934.6
1989-90	2,683.6	4.5	1,694.9	42.3	943.6
1990-91	2,570.0	-4.2	1,693.1	39.6	835.0
1991-92	2,644.5	2.9	1,790.1	39.8	812.2
1992-93	2,504.7	-5.3	1,773.1	37.4	694.1
1993-94	2,508.3	0.1	1,826.8	34.9	646.6
1994-95	2,573.0	2.6	1,943.6	31.9	597.5
1995-96	2,683.2	4.3	2,067.1	31.8	584.3

(X) Not applicable.
A/ Data not comparable to previous years due to changes in data collection method.
1/ December of the previous year through November of the present year.
2/ Includes glass and plastic containers and cartons.
Note: Data for 1982-83 through 1985-86 come from an audit of 1,300 food stores
throughout the United States and relate to the retail market only. Data for 1986-87
through 1995-96 come from scanner supermarkets doing over $4 million in retail sales
annually. Sales from these stores are estimated to represent 73 percent of total retail sales. Some data may be revised.

Source: State of Florida, Department of Citrus, *Market Research Report: A.C.
Nielsen Retail Food Index, Annual Summary, 1986,* and previous editions and *Market Research Report: Nielsen Scantrack, Annual Summary, 1993,* previous editions, and unpublished data.

University of Florida   **Bureau of Economic and Business Research**

Table 9.61. FIELD CROPS: ACREAGE HARVESTED, PRODUCTION, YIELD, AND VALUE
OF PRODUCTION IN FLORIDA, CROP YEARS 1994 AND 1995

| | Harvested acres (1,000) | | | Production | | | | | |
| | | | | Total (1,000) | | Yield per acre | | Value ($1,000) | |
Crop	1994	1995	Unit	1994	1995	1994	1995	1994	1995
Corn 1/	80	60	Bu.	6,800	5,400	85	90	16,320	17,280
Cotton	68	109	2/	104	107	735	472	36,077	41,165
Cottonseed	(X)	(X)	Tons	33	38	(X)	(X)	2,640	(D)
Hay, all	240	230	Tons	744	575	3	3	70,680	45,425
Peanuts 3/	84	81	Lbs.	207,480	193,590	2,470	2,390	58,302	52,463
Potatoes	46	43	Cwt.	9,992	9,003	215	210	119,329	84,490
Soybeans 4/	42	28	Bu.	1,302	728	31	26	7,031	4,732
Sugarcane 5/	444	437	Tons	14,937	15,122	34	35	457,072	462,733
Tobacco, flue- cured 14	7	7	Lbs.	16,575	17,676	2,550	2,455	27,349	31,127
Wheat	15	12	Bu.	630	384	42	32	1,764	1,210

(X) Not applicable.
(D) Data withheld to avoid disclosure of information about individual farms.
1/ Harvested for grain.
2/ Production in 480 net weight bales. Yield in pounds.
3/ Harvested for dry nuts.
4/ Harvested for beans.
5/ For sugar and seed.
Note: Data for 1994 may be revised. All 1995 estimates are preliminary.

Table 9.62. CORN: ACREAGE HARVESTED FOR GRAIN AND BUSHELS PRODUCED IN THE STATE
CROP-REPORTING DISTRICTS, AND SPECIFIED COUNTIES OF FLORIDA, 1995

District and county	Acres harvested	Production (1,000 bushels)	District and county	Acres harvested	Production (1,000 bushels)
Florida	60,000	5,400	District 1--West (Cont.)		
			Other counties	500	39
District 1--West	32,600	2,810	District 3--North	16,100	1,391
Calhoun	1,200	104	Columbia	2,200	172
Escambia	5,000	534	Hamilton	5,700	518
Gadsden	1,100	83	Madison	3,600	274
Holmes	1,600	118	Suwannee	3,500	346
Jackson	13,500	1,148	Other counties	1,100	81
Jefferson	2,800	226	District 5--Central	7,800	688
Leon	900	69	Alachua	2,500	219
Okaloosa	900	71	Gilchrist	500	40
Santa Rosa	900	77	Levy	2,800	251
Walton	1,800	152	Other counties	2,000	178
Washington	2,400	189	District 8--South	3,500	511

Note: See accompanying map for counties in crop-reporting districts. Data are
preliminary.
Source for Tables 9.61 and 9.62: State of Florida, Department of Agriculture and
Consumer Services, Florida Agricultural Statistics Service, *Florida Agricultural
Statistics: Field Crops Summary, 1995.*

Crop-reporting Districts

District 1 - West
Bay
Calhoun
Escambia
Franklin
Gadsden
Gulf
Holmes
Jackson
Jefferson
Leon
Liberty
Okaloosa
Santa Rosa
Wakulla
Walton
Washington

District 3 - North
Baker
Columbia
Dixie
Duval
Hamilton
Lafayette
Madison
Nassau
Suwannee
Taylor

District 5 - Central
Alachua
Bradford
Citrus
Clay
Flagler
Gilchrist
Hernando
Hillsborough
Lake
Levy
Marion
Orange
Osceola
Pasco
Pinellas
Polk
Putnam
St. Johns
Seminole
Sumter
Union
Volusia

District 8 - South
Brevard
Broward
Charlotte
Collier
Dade
De Soto
Glades
Hardee
Hendry
Highlands
Indian River
Lee
Manatee
Martin
Monroe
Okeechobee
Palm Beach
St. Lucie
Sarasota

Table 9.63. POTATOES: ACREAGE HARVESTED IN THE STATE AND SPECIFIED COUNTIES
OF FLORIDA, 1990 THROUGH 1995

(in acres)

County or season	1990	1991	1992	1993	1994	1995
Florida	44,700	43,000	40,100	41,900	46,400	42,900
Winter	7,700	7,600	8,100	8,400	7,800	6,900
Spring	37,000	35,400	32,000	33,500	38,600	36,000
Dade	4,800	4,800	4,900	4,700	4,300	3,100
Flagler	3,100	2,500	1,975	2,500	2,600	2,000
Putnam	4,900	4,200	4,800	4,900	5,400	5,000
St. Johns	20,700	20,300	18,225	18,600	21,000	20,000
Other counties	11,200	11,200	10,200	11,200	13,100	12,800

Note: 1995 data are preliminary.

Table 9.64. PEANUTS: ACREAGE HARVESTED AND PRODUCTION IN THE STATE
CROP-REPORTING DISTRICTS, AND SPECIFIED COUNTIES OF FLORIDA, 1995

District and county	Acres har- vested	Production (1,000 pounds)	District and county	Acres har- vested	Production (1,000 pounds)
Florida	81,000	193,590	District 3--North	6,900	19,342
			Columbia	1,500	3,677
District 1--West	64,400	145,624	Madison	800	2,172
Calhoun	3,500	7,816	Suwannee	4,300	12,630
Gadsden	700	1,395	Other counties	300	863
Holmes	5,300	9,090			
Jackson	33,100	68,655	District 5--Central	9,700	28,624
Jefferson	900	2,491	Alachua	1,400	4,146
Leon	400	1,020	Gilchrist	400	1,006
Okaloosa	800	2,140	Levy	5,500	16,920
Santa Rosa	11,900	35,139	Marion	2,300	6,382
Walton	5,300	11,964	Other counties	100	170
Washington	2,100	5,207			
Other counties	400	707			

Note: See accompanying map for counties in crop-reporting districts.

Table 9.65. SOYBEANS: ACREAGE HARVESTED FOR BEANS AND BUSHELS PRODUCED IN
THE STATE AND SPECIFIED COUNTIES OF FLORIDA, 1995

County	Acres har- vested	Production (1,000 bushels)	County	Acres har- vested	Production (1,000 bushels)
Florida	28,000	728	Jefferson	1,000	19
Calhoun	4,300	125	Okaloosa	400	10
Escambia	3,300	131	Santa Rosa	1,300	38
Gadsden	500	17	Walton	1,000	16
Holmes	1,500	36	Washington	1,100	33
Jackson	6,900	183	Other counties	6,700	120

Source for Tables 9.63, 9.64 and 9.65: State of Florida, Department of Agriculture
and Consumer Services, Florida Agricultural Statistics Service, *Florida Agricultural
Statistics: Field Crops Summary, 1995.*

University of Florida   **Bureau of Economic and Business Research**

Table 9.66. COTTON: ACREAGE HARVESTED AND PRODUCTION IN THE STATE, CROP
REPORTING DISTRICTS, AND SPECIFIED COUNTIES OF FLORIDA, 1995

District and county	Acres har- vested	Produc- tion (bales)	District and county	Acres har- vested	Produc- tion (bales)
Florida	109,000	107,200	District 1 (Cont.)		
			Santa Rosa	26,800	30,600
District 1	99,400	95,100	Walton	5,000	4,600
Calhoun	6,200	6,800	Other counties	1,300	1,600
Escambia	17,100	14,100			
Gadsden	2,000	1,700	Districts 3 and 5	9,600	12,100
Holmes	3,100	2,700	Columbia	1,200	1,200
Jackson	30,500	25,200	Hamilton	2,100	3,400
Jefferson	2,700	3,300	Suwannee	2,300	3,400
Okaloosa	4,700	4,500	Other counties	4,000	4,100

Note: Data are preliminary. See accompanying map for counties in crop-reporting
districts.

Table 9.67. SUGARCANE: ACREAGE HARVESTED AND PRODUCTION IN THE
STATE AND SPECIFIED COUNTIES OF FLORIDA, 1995

County	Acres har- vested	Produc- tion (tons)	County	Acres har- vested	Produc- tion (tons)
Florida	417,000	14,445,000	Hendry	70,000	2,478,000
			Martin	12,000	401,000
Glades	19,000	619,000	Palm Beach	316,000	10,947,000

Note: Data are preliminary.

Table 9.68. TOBACCO: ACREAGE HARVESTED AND PRODUCTION OF FLUE-CURED TOBACCO IN THE
STATE, CROP-REPORTING DISTRICTS, AND SPECIFIED COUNTIES OF FLORIDA, 1995

District and county	Acres har- vested	Produc- tion (pounds)	District and county	Acres har- vested	Produc- tion (pounds)
Florida	7,200	17,676,000	District 3 (Cont.)		
			Madison	910	1,907,000
District 1--West	370	741,000	Suwannee	1,820	4,576,000
Gadsden	120	210,000	Taylor	100	223,000
Jefferson	140	344,000	Other counties	70	221,000
Other counties	110	187,000	District 5--Central	1,410	3,438,000
District 3--North	5,420	13,497,000	Alachua	890	2,135,000
Baker	110	287,000	Bradford	100	252,000
Columbia	740	2,021,000	Gilchrist	140	372,000
Hamilton	1,100	2,660,000	Union	200	520,000
Lafayette	570	1,602,000	Other counties	80	159,000

Note: Data are preliminary. See accompanying map for counties in crop-reporting
districts.
   Source for Tables 9.66, 9.67, and 9.68: State of Florida, Department of Agriculture and Consumer Services, Florida Agricultural Statistics Service, *Florida Agricultural Statistics: Field Crops Summary, 1995.*

University of Florida   **Bureau of Economic and Business Research**

Table 9.69. CROPS: ACREAGE PLANTED AND HARVESTED, PRODUCTION, AND
VALUE OF CROPS IN FLORIDA, CROP YEAR 1995-96

Crop	Acreage planted	Acreage harvested	Production (1,000 CWT)	Total value ($1,000)
All crops, total	369,200	350,800	65,754	1,484,897
Vegetables, total	194,500	184,200	34,507	944,915
Snap beans	28,500	25,300	1,396	73,178
Cabbage	9,400	9,000	2,655	29,691
Carrots 1/	7,100	5,600	840	12,768
Sweet corn	42,000	41,900	5,248	91,284
Cucumbers	10,900	10,200	2,931	48,369
Eggplant	2,100	2,100	408	10,926
Escarole	2,600	2,300	295	5,590
Bell peppers	21,000	20,300	5,326	185,672
Radishes	13,700	12,400	725	20,021
Squash	10,800	9,600	847	27,297
Tomatoes	46,400	45,500	13,836	440,119
Other 2/	81,900	81,000	12,960	246,240
Watermelons	40,000	34,000	7,140	49,980
Potatoes	46,800	44,300	9,564	A/ 126,165
Strawberries	6,000	6,000	1,560	112,632
Blueberries	0	1,300	23	4,965

CWT Hundred weight.
A/ Production sold.
1/ Fresh and processing.
2/ Fresh and processing vegetables and cantaloupes.

Source: State of Florida, Department of Agriculture and Consumer Services, Florida Agricultural Statistics Service, *Florida Agricultural Statistics: Vegetable Summary, 1995-96.*

Table 9.70. LIVESTOCK: CASH RECEIPTS FROM MARKETINGS IN FLORIDA
1990 THROUGH 1996

(in thousands of dollars, except where indicated)

Year	Total livestock and products Amount	Percentage of total farm cash receipts	Cattle and calves	Hogs	Milk	Chickens and eggs	Honey
1990	1,258,961	22	383,791	20,558	421,007	288,108	10,032
1991	1,171,626	19	363,351	17,304	372,947	276,371	9,898
1992	1,165,874	19	349,447	13,126	401,700	258,988	12,126
1993	1,211,131	20	362,495	15,106	385,503	298,121	11,300
1994	1,191,133	20	335,836	12,399	408,408	290,905	9,080
1995	1,129,810	19	289,802	11,581	363,528	314,990	12,659
1996	1,149,961	18	217,008	14,441	431,280	353,811	22932

Note: Data are for calendar year, except for hogs, chickens and eggs, and honey which report for a marketing year of December through November. Value of eggs is for total production including consumption on farms where produced. Data do not include government payments. Some data are revised.
Source: State of Florida, Department of Agriculture and Consumer Services, Florida Agricultural Statistics Service, *Florida Agricultural Statistics: Livestock, Poultry, Dairy Summary, 1996.*

University of Florida   **Bureau of Economic and Business Research**

Table 9.71. CATTLE AND CALVES: NUMBER AND RANK OF CATTLE AND CALVES AND BEEF COWS IN THE STATE AND COUNTIES OF FLORIDA, JANUARY 1, 1997

(number in thousands, rounded to hundreds)

County	Cattle and calves 1/ Number	Rank	Beef cows 2/ Number	Rank	County	Cattle and calves 1/ Number	Rank	Beef cows 2/ Number	Rank
Florida	1,970.0	(X)	1,072.0	(X)	Lafayette	25.0	26	5.0	42
					Lake	31.0	21	16.5	20
Alachua	52.0	13	28.0	13	Lee	15.0	34	9.5	30
Baker	6.0	55	2.0	57	Leon	7.5	49	4.0	51
Bay	1.0	62	0.5	63	Levy	43.0	15	23.0	15
Bradford	11.5	41	6.0	37	Liberty	2.0	61	1.0	61
Brevard	33.0	19	15.0	23	Madison	17.0	29	10.0	27
Broward	21.0	28	8.0	33	Manatee	75.0	8	44.0	9
Calhoun	6.0	55	3.0	55	Marion	54.0	12	31.0	12
Charlotte	28.0	23	20.0	17	Martin	36.0	17	21.0	16
Citrus	9.5	43	5.0	42	Nassau	12.0	40	4.5	48
Clay	14.5	37	1.5	59	Okaloosa	7.0	52	3.5	53
Collier	13.0	38	7.0	34	Okeechobee	162.0	1	60.0	5
Columbia	16.5	30	10.0	27	Orange	16.5	30	11.5	26
Dade	5.5	58	2.0	57	Osceola	99.0	5	67.0	3
De Soto	84.0	7	50.0	7	Palm Beach	9.0	45	4.5	48
Dixie	3.0	60	1.5	59	Pasco	44.0	14	26.0	14
Duval	16.0	32	5.0	42	Polk	104.0	4	66.0	4
Escambia	8.0	48	2.5	56	Putnam	9.0	45	6.0	37
Flagler	7.0	52	5.0	42	St. Johns	5.0	59	3.5	53
Gadsden	6.0	55	4.5	48	St. Lucie	31.0	21	18.0	18
Gilchrist	32.0	20	7.0	34	Santa Rosa	7.0	52	4.0	51
Glades	75.0	8	46.0	8	Sarasota	27.0	24	16.0	21
Hamilton	9.0	45	6.0	37	Seminole	7.5	49	5.5	41
Hardee	91.5	6	52.0	6	Sumter	56.0	11	34.0	11
Hendry	110.0	3	69.0	2	Suwannee	38.0	16	17.0	19
Hernando	25.0	26	14.0	24	Taylor	7.5	49	6.0	37
Highlands	121.0	2	72.0	1	Union	12.5	39	9.5	30
Hillsborough	75.0	8	36.0	10	Volusia	15.0	34	10.0	27
Holmes	15.0	34	7.0	34	Walton	11.0	42	5.0	42
Indian River	26.0	25	13.0	25	Washington	9.5	43	5.0	42
Jackson	36.0	17	16.0	21					
Jefferson	16.0	32	9.0	32	Other 3/	2.0	(X)	1.0	(X)

(X) Not applicable.
1/ All classes, beef and dairy.
2/ Beef production brood cows only, which have calved at least once.
3/ Includes Franklin, Gulf, Monroe, Pinellas, and Wakulla counties.

Source: State of Florida, Department of Agriculture and Consumer Services, Florida Agricultural Statistics Service, *Florida Agricultural Statistics: Livestock, Poultry, Dairy Summary, 1996.*

University of Florida   **Bureau of Economic and Business Research**

Table 9.72. CATTLE AND CALVES: MARKETINGS, PRICE, AND CASH RECEIPTS IN FLORIDA AND THE UNITED STATES, 1992 THROUGH 1996

	Florida				United States			
Year	Market-ings 1/ (1,000 lbs.)	Price per 100 lbs. (dollars) Cattle	Calves	Cash re-ceipts 2/ ($1,000)	Market-ings 1/ (1,000 lbs.)	Price per 100 lbs. (dollars) Cattle	Calves	Cash re-ceipts 2/ ($1,000)
1992	457,950	56.60	89.70	349,447	52,273,573	71.30	89.00	37,272,292
1993	454,450	58.80	94.20	362,495	53,030,343	72.60	91.20	39,361,709
1994	468,900	53.20	84.60	335,836	54,092,555	66.70	87.20	36,394,806
1995	488,900	44.30	70.00	289,802	56,296,036	61.80	73.10	34,004,481
1996	476,000	33.40	54.60	217,008	56,246,986	58.70	58.40	31,138,043

1/ Excludes custom slaughter for use on farms where produced and interfarm sales within states.
2/ Receipts from marketings and sales of farm slaughter.

Table 9.73. LIVESTOCK INVENTORY: NUMBER ON FARMS IN FLORIDA, LEADING STATE AND THE UNITED STATES, 1996 OR 1997

(numbers in thousands)

Type of livestock	Florida Rank among states	Number	Leading state Name	Number	United States
Cattle and calves 1/	15	1,970	Texas	14,100	101,209
Beef cows 1/	10	1,072	Texas	5,460	34,280
Hogs 2/	32	65	Iowa	12,200	56,171

1/ January 1, 1997.
2/ December 1, 1996.

Table 9.74. HONEY: PRODUCTION AND VALUE IN FLORIDA AND THE UNITED STATES 1993 THROUGH 1996

	Florida			United States		
Year	Number of colonies (1,000)	Production (1,000 pounds)	Value ($1,000)	Number of colonies (1,000)	Production (1,000 pounds)	Value ($1,000)
1993	200	22,600	11,300	2,876	230,655	124,323
1994	230	19,320	9,080	2,770	217,168	114,665
1995	230	19,780	12,659	2,648	210,516	144,203
1996	240	25,200	22,932	2,566	198,095	177,097

Note: Some data may be revised.

Source for Tables 9.72, 9.73, and 9.74: State of Florida, Department of Agriculture and Consumer Services, Florida Agricultural Statistics Service, *Florida Agricultural Statistics: Livestock, Poultry, Dairy Summary, 1996*.

Table 9.86. DAIRY PRODUCTION: NUMBER OF MILK COWS AND ANNUAL MILK PRODUCTION
IN FLORIDA, OTHER LEADING PRODUCTION STATES, AND THE UNITED STATES, 1996

State	Milk cows 2/ (1,000)	Total milk (1,000,000 pounds)	Rank among states	Per milk cow (pounds)
Florida	156	2,401	15	15,391
California	1,264	25,859	1	20,458
Wisconsin	1,449	22,376	2	15,442
New York	702	11,529	3	16,423
Pennsylvania	644	10,640	4	16,522
Minnesota	598	9,440	5	15,786
Texas	398	6,120	6	15,377
Michigan	320	5,430	7	16,969
Washington	264	5,279	8	19,996
Idaho	256	4,735	9	18,496
Ohio	285	4,370	10	15,333
Iowa	250	3,826	11	15,304
Vermont	156	2,590	12	16,603
Arizona	120	2,473	13	20,608
Missouri	179	2,440	14	13,631
United States	9,351	154,331	(X)	16,505

(X) Not applicable.
1/ Excludes milk sucked by calves.
2/ Average number on farms during year, excluding heifers not yet fresh.

Table 9.87. CHICKEN AND EGGS: CASH RECEIPTS IN FLORIDA, MARKETING YEARS 1989
THROUGH 1996

(in thousands of collars)

Year	Total	Broilers	Eggs 1/	Other chickens 2/
1989	308,032	181,636	123,078	3,318
1990	288,108	152,012	133,610	2,486
1991	276,371	151,704	120,903	3,764
1992	258,988	164,856	91,104	3,028
1993	298,121	187,714	106,838	3,569
1994	290,905	191,151	98,348	1,406
1995	314,990	218,361	95,519	1,110
1996	353,811	230,607	122,064	1,140

1/ Total production, including consumption on farms where produced.
2/ Value of sales.
Note: Data are for marketing years beginning December 1 and ending November 30.
Some data may be revised.

Source for Tables 9.86 and 9.87: State of Florida, Department of Agriculture and
Consumer Services, Florida Agricultural Statistics Service, *Florida Agricultural Statistics: Livestock, Poultry, Dairy Summary, 1996.*

University of Florida   **Bureau of Economic and Business Research**

FORESTRY, FISHERIES, AND MINERALS

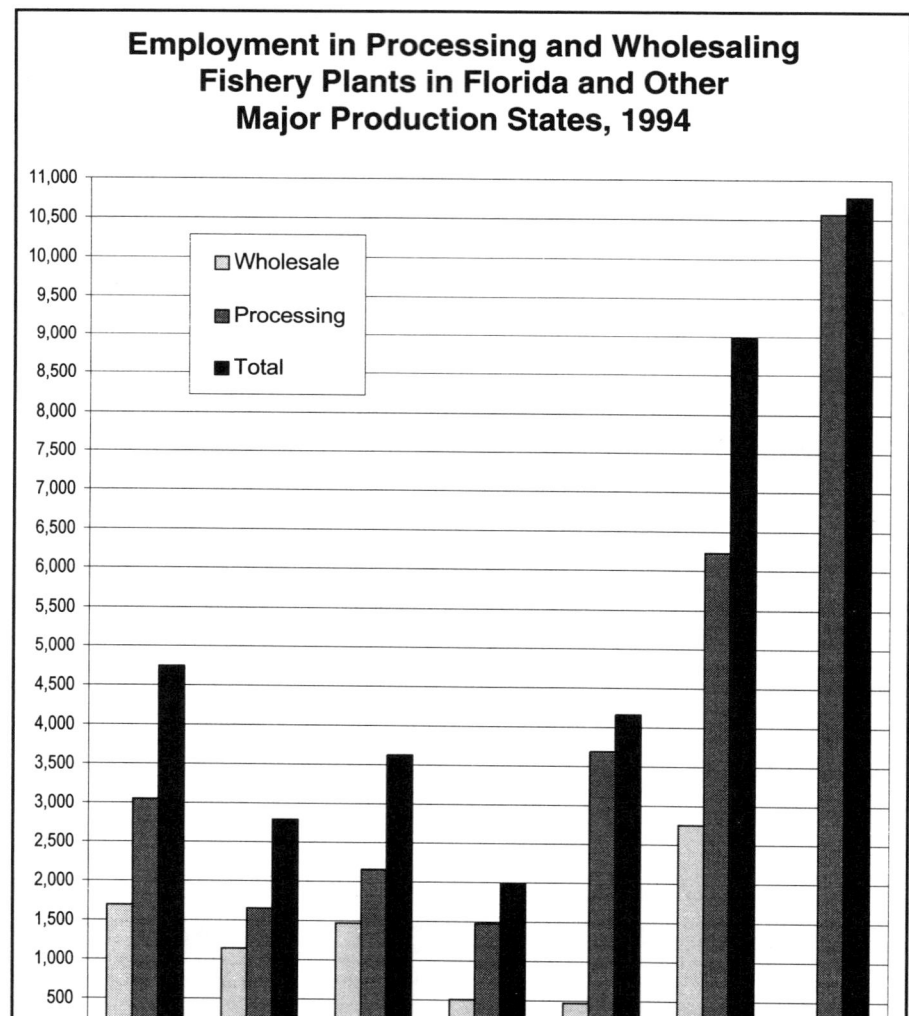

Employment in Processing and Wholesaling Fishery Plants in Florida and Other Major Production States, 1994

Source: Table 10.36

TABLES LISTED BY MAJOR HEADINGS

Table 10.07.   FOREST PRODUCTS: HARVEST BY PRODUCT AND BY SPECIES GROUP IN THE STATE AND COUNTIES OF FLORIDA, 1995

	Softwood				Hardwood			
County	Saw logs (MBF)	Veneer logs (MBF)	Pulp- wood 1/ (Cords)	Other pro- ducts 2/ (MCF)	Saw logs (MBF)	Veneer logs (MBF)	Pulp- wood 3/ (Cords)	Other pro- ducts 2/ (MCF)
Florida	769,017	141,626	3,957,034	23,697	36,260	11,274	534,851	3,243
Alachua	23,714	11,352	124,934	1,280	355	0	10,816	56
Baker	28,170	5,676	76,792	477	0	120	3,494	0
Bay	17,687	0	171,620	120	1,484	0	1,625	0
Bradford	39,409	5,676	79,309	267	5	0	25,989	0
Brevard	877	0	7,810	0	0	0	594	0
Broward	0	0	2,491	0	0	0	0	0
Calhoun	19,295	5,441	164,201	208	9,110	105	19,255	0
Charlotte	124	0	4,876	132	165	0	0	0
Citrus	1,585	0	19,311	0	0	150	5,081	0
Clay	20,850	5,676	45,174	396	0	0	5,869	0
Collier	26	0	436	0	0	0	47	0
Columbia	38,282	5,676	131,526	131	5	777	12,606	512
Dade	0	0	22	0	0	0	0	0
De Soto	324	0	1,546	0	0	0	0	0
Dixie	30,457	5,676	136,020	1,089	2,265	777	60,270	0
Duval	18,095	5,676	73,269	282	28	0	778	0
Escambia	25,366	2,908	86,243	250	1	191	8,799	0
Flagler	24,552	5,676	61,823	401	0	0	9,492	0
Franklin	7,661	0	70,307	56	0	0	28	0
Gadsden	5,361	6,801	118,838	133	2,937	1,036	21,233	18
Gilchrist	12,063	5,676	51,424	163	0	518	4,495	56
Glades	198	0	30,939	63	261	0	0	0
Gulf	6,588	0	66,534	123	1,939	105	1,338	0
Hamilton	14,120	0	57,464	860	0	0	10,486	0
Hardee	173	0	2,456	0	228	0	0	0
Hendry	0	0	10,189	0	0	0	0	0
Hernando	1,884	0	17,669	89	350	0	2,826	0
Highlands	0	0	0	547	0	0	0	0
Hillsborough	710	0	5,779	25	0	930	64	0
Holmes	17,051	0	53,022	154	1,216	396	16,721	0
Indian River	0	0	801	0	0	0	0	0
Jackson	26,768	4,761	132,698	272	4,094	396	17,308	0
Jefferson	12,775	5,441	44,512	3	875	0	28,992	994
Lafayette	13,897	5,676	33,589	278	0	260	10,343	0
Lake	3,954	0	12,829	614	0	300	1,142	0
Lee	0	0	2,276	132	0	0	0	0

See footnotes at end of table.   Continued . . .

Table 10.07. FOREST PRODUCTS: HARVEST BY PRODUCT AND BY SPECIES GROUP
IN THE STATE AND COUNTIES OF FLORIDA, 1995 (Continued)

	Softwood				Hardwood			
County	Saw logs (MBF)	Veneer logs (MBF)	Pulp- wood 1/ (Cords)	Other pro- ducts 2/ (MCF)	Saw logs (MBF)	Veneer logs (MBF)	Pulp- wood 3/ (Cords)	Other pro- ducts 2/ (MCF)
Leon	10,902	0	39,262	95	830	210	14,929	73
Levy	30,092	5,676	78,564	3,053	2,224	1,036	21,011	28
Liberty	6,273	3,400	95,546	140	2,157	0	6,904	0
Madison	17,688	0	62,596	704	0	571	31,648	994
Manatee	85	0	1,811	0	0	0	0	0
Marion	23,029	5,676	83,280	771	2,566	150	17,649	0
Martin	0	0	63	0	0	0	0	0
Monroe	0	0	10	0	0	0	0	0
Nassau	58,813	0	128,891	1,882	19	0	14,972	0
Okaloosa	7,883	4,017	116,446	190	0	205	5,552	0
Okeechobee	0	0	847	0	0	0	0	0
Orange	1,023	0	8,423	289	0	0	0	0
Osceola	7,838	0	8,626	2,364	0	180	12	0
Palm Beach	0	0	71	0	0	0	0	0
Pasco	5,727	0	13,122	515	0	630	2,610	0
Pinellas	0	0	62	0	0	0	0	0
Polk	13,350	0	9,246	692	0	0	0	0
Putnam	18,371	5,676	76,703	305	166	150	10,231	0
St. Johns	7,337	5,676	110,578	168	18	0	11,525	0
St. Lucie	0	0	2,487	0	0	0	0	0
Santa Rosa	11,349	4,017	136,432	1,400	0	0	4,616	0
Sarasota	399	0	6,067	0	0	0	0	0
Seminole	565	0	15,079	275	0	0	0	0
Sumter	4,065	0	19,575	194	0	90	4,711	0
Suwannee	12,088	5,676	73,078	52	0	518	9,388	0
Taylor	37,612	0	564,241	304	1,340	777	39,000	512
Union	20,743	5,676	66,919	238	5	0	5,588	0
Volusia	19,713	0	97,757	536	0	300	6,282	0
Wakulla	12,473	3,400	25,505	165	0	0	4,993	0
Walton	13,313	2,908	133,062	158	0	0	13,145	0
Washington	16,270	2,040	83,956	162	1,617	396	30,394	0

MBF Thousand board feet.
MCF Thousand cubic feet.
1/ Includes 82,548 roundwood that was delivered to nonpulp mills, chipped and then sold to pulp mills as residues.
2/ Includes composite board, poles/piling, post and other industrial.
3/ Includes 2,213 roundwood that was delivered to nonpulp mills, chipped and then sold to pulp mills as residues.

Source: State of Florida, Department of Agriculture and Consumer Services, Division of Forestry, unpublished data.

Table 10.25. NATIONAL FOREST LAND: GROSS AND NET AREA OF NATIONAL FOREST
AND OTHER LAND ADMINISTERED BY THE NATIONAL FOREST SYSTEM IN FLORIDA
AND THE UNITED STATES AS OF SEPTEMBER 30, 1996

(in acres)

Unit name and area	Gross area within unit boundaries	National forest sy-stem lands	Other lands within unit boundaries
Florida	1,409,654	1,261,954	147,700
Apalachicola National Forest	632,890	565,465	67,425
National wilderness areas			
Bradwell Bay 1/	24,602	24,602	0
Mud Swamp/New River	8,090	8,090	0
Choctawhatchee National Forest	1,152	1,152	0
Ocala National Forest	430,446	383,224	47,222
National wilderness areas			
Alexander Springs	7,941	7,941	0
Billies Bay	3,092	3,092	0
Juniper Prairie	14,281	14,277	4
Little Lake George	2,833	2,833	0
National game refuge, Ocala	79,735	79,735	0
Osceola National Forest	190,932	157,883	33,049
National wilderness area, Big Gum Swamp	13,660	13,660	0
United States	231,744,246	191,644,936	40,099,310

1/ Protected under the Clean Air Act, without visibility protection.

Table 10.26. NATIONAL FOREST LAND: NET AREA OF LAND ADMINISTERED BY THE
NATIONAL FOREST SYSTEM IN THE STATE AND COUNTIES OF FLORIDA
AND THE UNITED STATES AS OF SEPTEMBER 30, 1996

County	National forest area	Acres
Florida	(X)	1,146,668
Baker	Nekoosa Purchase Units	13
	Osceola National Forest	79,409
	Pinhook Purchase Units	23,203
Columbia	Nekoosa Purchase Units	78
	Osceola National Forest	78,474
	Pinhook Purchase Units	11,597
Franklin	Apalachicola National Forest	21,816
	Tates Hell-New River Purchase Units	976
Lake	Ocala National Forest	84,110
Leon	Apalachicola National Forest	104,490
Liberty	Apalachicola National Forest	267,298
	Tates Hell-New River Purchase Units	3,077
Marion	Ocala National Forest	275,502
Okaloosa	Choctawhatchee National Forest	523
Putnam	Ocala National Forest	23,612
Santa Rosa	Choctawhatchee National Forest	108
Wakulla	Apalachicola National Forest	171,861
Walton	Choctawhatchee National Forest	521
United States	(X)	191,644,936

(X) Not applicable.
  Source for Tables 10.25 and 10.26: U.S., Department of Agriculture, Forest Service, *Land Areas of the National Forest System as of September 30, 1996.*

University of Florida   **Bureau of Economic and Business Research**

Table 10.34. FORESTRY: AVERAGE MONTHLY PRIVATE REPORTING UNITS, EMPLOYMENT
AND PAYROLL COVERED BY UNEMPLOYMENT CCMPENSATION LAW IN THE STATE
AND COUNTIES OF FLORIDA, 1996

County	Number of reporting units	Number of employees	Payroll ($1,000)	County	Number of reporting units	Number of employees	Payroll ($1,000)
				Forestry (SIC code 08)			
Florida	144	1,197	2,648	Leon	7	36	51
Alachua	4	44	104	Levy	5	18	40
Broward	5	32	37	Marion	4	11	17
Calhoun	6	26	50	Nassau	8	280	822
Clay	5	40	102	Orange	4	32	64
Duval	6	54	153	Palm Beach	4	51	79
Gadsden	6	33	53	Taylor	5	59	168
Jackson	4	13	30	Washington	3	16	20

Note: Private employment. For a list of three-digit code industries included see
Table 10.35. Data are preliminary. Only counties for which data are disclosed are
shown. Detail may not add to totals due to disclosure editing and/or rounding. See
Tables 23.70, 23.71, 23.72, 23.73, and 23.74 for public employment data.

Table 10.35. FORESTRY AND FISHING INDUSTRIES: AVERAGE MONTHLY PRIVATE REPORTING
UNITS, EMPLOYMENT, AND PAYROLL COVERED BY UNEMPLOYMENT COMPENSATION LAW
BY INDUSTRY IN FLORIDA, 1996

SIC code	Industry	Number of reporting units	Number of employees	Payroll ($1,000)
08	Forestry	144	1,197	2,648
081	Timber tracts	71	490	1,025
083	Forest products	16	180	256
085	Forestry services	58	527	1,368
09	Fishing, hunting, and trapping	233	747	1,376
091	Commercial fishing	213	665	1,270
092	Fish hatcheries and preserves	10	27	35
097	Hunting and trapping, and game propagation	11	55	70

Note: Private employment. Data are preliminary. Detail may not add to totals
due to disclosure editing and/or rounding. See Tables 23.70, 23.71, 23.72, 23.73,
and 23.74 for public employment data.

Source for Tables 10.34 and 10.35: State of Florida, Department of Labor and Employment Security, Bureau of Labor Market Information, "Employment and Wages"
(ES-202), unpublished data.

University of Florida   **Bureau of Economic and Business Research**

Table 10.36. FISHERIES: NUMBER OF PROCESSING AND WHOLESALING PLANTS AND AVERAGE ANNUAL EMPLOYMENT IN FLORIDA, GEOGRAPHIC AREAS, OTHER MAJOR PRODUCTION STATES AND THE UNITED STATES, 1994

	Number of plants			Average annual employment		
Area	Total	Pro- cessing	Whole- sale	Total	Pro- cessing	Whole- sale
Area						
South Atlantic	584	132	452	5,829	3,760	2,069
New England	820	206	614	8,265	4,794	3,471
Mid-Atlantic	461	144	317	8,092	5,036	3,056
Gulf	1,136	426	710	11,758	9,211	2,547
Pacific	1,162	514	648	25,428	21,896	3,532
Inland States	84	49	35	1,413	1,126	287
State						
Florida	451	144	307	4,743	3,048	1,695
Maine	359	67	292	2,792	1,653	1,139
Massachusetts	311	98	213	3,627	2,156	1,471
North Carolina	219	79	140	1,988	1,479	509
Washington	237	115	122	4,164	3,691	473
California	517	161	356	8,982	6,229	2,753
Alaska	321	191	130	10,778	10,564	214
United States 1/	4,349	1,504	2,845	71,248	55,744	15,504

1/ Includes American Samoa, Hawaii, and Puerto Rico, and Northern Marianas.
Source: U.S., Department of Commerce, National Oceanic and Atmospheric Adminis-tration, National Marine Fisheries Service, *Fisheries of the United States, 1995*.

Table 10.37. FISHING, HUNTING, AND TRAPPING: AVERAGE MONTHLY PRIVATE REPORTING UNITS, EMPLOYMENT, AND PAYROLL COVERED BY UNEMPLOYMENT COMPENSATION LAW IN THE STATE AND COUNTIES OF FLORIDA, 1996

County	Number of re- porting units	Number of em- ployees	Payroll ($1,000)	County	Number of re- porting units	Number of em- ployees	Payroll ($1,000)
Fishing, hunting, and trapping (SIC code 09)							
Florida	233	747	1,376	Lee	44	180	328
				Monroe	31	101	153
Bay	4	3	5	Nassau	10	25	54
Brevard	8	23	36	Okaloosa	8	20	41
Broward	8	11	19	Pasco	7	17	39
Citrus	4	10	13	Pinellas	19	66	189
Duval	27	74	114	Polk	3	11	15
Escambia	5	16	13	St. Lucie	4	7	12
Franklin	9	14	23	Volusia	7	12	7
Hillsborough	13	72	195				

Note: Private employment. For a list of three-digit code industries included see Table 10.35. Data are preliminary. Only counties for which data are disclosed are shown. Detail may not add to totals due to disclosure editing and/or rounding. See Tables 23.70, 23.71, 23.72, 23.73, and 23.74 for public employment data.
Source: State of Florida, Department of Labor and Employment Security, Bureau of Labor Market Information, "Employment and Wages" (ES-202), unpublished data.

University of Florida   **Bureau of Economic and Business Research**

Table 10.40. FISH AND SHELLFISH: QUANTITY OF LANDINGS BY TYPE OF SPECIES AND TRIPS IN THE STATE AND SPECIFIED COUNTIES OF FLORIDA, 1996

Area and county	Landings 1/ (pounds)			Trips 3/
	Total	Fish	Shellfish 2/	
Florida	144,737,705	53,099,165	91,638,540	362,860
East coast	50,487,075	16,163,529	34,323,546	150,081
West coast	93,951,686	36,709,949	57,241,737	212,362
Inland/out of state 4/	298,944	225,687	73,257	417
Bay	4,084,115	2,929,252	1,154,863	7,938
Brevard	22,661,879	2,838,348	19,823,531	76,707
Broward	1,476,864	1,046,394	430,470	4,103
Charlotte	2,441,250	685,891	1,755,359	10,562
Citrus	4,097,429	1,006,749	3,090,680	12,994
Clay	29,012	495	28,517	113
Collier	3,733,897	1,671,950	2,061,947	9,649
Dade	1,957,071	700,240	1,256,831	11,596
Dixie	1,300,200	74,527	1,225,673	3,907
Duval	4,036,398	1,387,402	2,648,996	8,716
Escambia	1,510,917	818,075	692,842	3,097
Flagler	24,697	11,644	13,053	76
Franklin	6,771,603	1,286,350	5,485,253	16,939
Gulf	3,656,391	2,787,264	869,127	1,091
Hernando	947,208	25,436	921,772	3,711
Hillsborough	3,519,712	466,457	3,053,255	3,596
Indian River	1,321,726	1,236,473	85,253	9,138
Lee	11,724,483	1,804,028	9,920,455	26,490
Levy	2,171,265	158,152	2,013,113	6,523
Manatee	3,208,876	2,769,732	439,144	3,401
Martin	2,106,876	2,082,667	24,209	4,548
Monroe	23,827,659	7,120,798	16,706,861	67,693
Nassau	1,437,555	82,990	1,354,565	2,976
Okaloosa	2,588,039	2,418,517	169,522	3,877
Palm Beach	1,823,569	1,673,501	150,068	10,546
Pasco	1,365,961	326,127	1,039,834	3,916
Pinellas	12,618,599	8,881,083	3,737,516	16,899
Putnam	141,774	8,460	133,314	756
St. Johns	2,107,061	222,249	1,884,812	4,686
St. Lucie	8,289,156	2,724,315	5,564,841	6,066
Santa Rosa	349,606	191,030	158,576	1,541
Sarasota	307,996	140,620	167,376	999
Taylor	901,640	549,771	351,869	2,196
Volusia	3,073,437	2,148,351	925,086	10,054
Wakulla	2,701,691	583,171	2,118,520	4,885
Walton	123,149	14,969	108,180	458

1/ Based on whole weight of species with some exceptions, e.g., stone crabs, sponges.

2/ Includes clams, conch, crabs, lobster, octopus, oysters, scallops, shrimp, sponges, and squid.

3/ Only successful trips of fishermen.

4/ Landings from seafood dealers residing in inland counties or out-of-state who bought Florida produced seafood.

Note: Landings are recorded in county where products first crossed the shore. Data are preliminary.

Source: State of Florida, Department of Natural Resources, Marine Fisheries Information System, unpublished data.

Table 10.60. MINERAL INDUSTRIES: ESTABLISHMENTS, EMPLOYMENT, PAYROLL
VALUE ADDED BY MINING, AND CAPITAL EXPENDITURE IN FLORIDA
CENSUS YEARS 1972 THROUGH 1992

Year	Number of establishments Total	With 20 employees or more	All employees Number (1,000)	Payroll (million dollars)	Value added by mining (million dollars)	Capital expenditure 1/ (million dollars)
1972	277	72	9.0	81.1	297.5	107.8
1977	321	69	9.9	132.4	1,038.9	100.3
1982	361	(NA)	10.5	216.0	1,860.4	321.9
1987	343	78	9.6	231.9	1,027.4	166.5
1992	293	61	8.3	260.5	979.9	130.8

(NA) Not available.
1/ New and used capital expenditure.
Note: The minerals industries census is on a 5-year cycle collecting data for years ending in 2 and 7.

Table 10.61. MINERAL INDUSTRIES: CHARACTERISTICS OF MINERAL INDUSTRIES
IN FLORIDA, 1992

(in millions of dollars, except where indicated)

Item	1992
Establishments during year (number)	293
0-4 employees	147
5-9 employees	52
10-19 employees	33
20-49 employees	31
50-99 employees	11
100-249 employees	14
250-499 employees	2
500-999 employees	2
1,000-2,499 employees	1
All employees	
Average for the year (1,000)	8.3
Production, development, and exploration workers (1,000)	6.3
Payroll	260.5
Supplemental labor costs not included in payroll	67.0
Value added by mining	979.9
Inventories, beginning of year	288.4
Inventories, end of year	315.4
Cost of supplies	699.4
Cost of purchased communications services	2.4
Value of shipments and receipts	1,548.6
Capital expenditure during year (except land and mineral rights)	130.8
New	82.0
Used	46.3
Rental payments during year	8.7
Expensed mineral exploration, development, land, and rights 1/	57.4

1/ Excludes mining services industries and natural gas liquids industries and data for mineral land and rights for the crude petroleum and natural gas industries.
Note: The minerals industries census is on a 5-year cycle collecting data for years ending in 2 and 7.
Source for Tables 10.60 and 10.61: U.S., Department of Commerce, Bureau of the Census, *1992 Census of Mineral Industries: South Atlantic States.* Geographic Area Series MIC92-A-10.

Table 10.71. NONFUEL MINERAL PRODUCTION: QUANTITY AND VALUE IN FLORIDA
1994 THROUGH 1996

(quantity in thousand metric tons; value in millions of dollars)

	1994		1995		1996	
Mineral	Quan-tity	Value	Quan-tity	Value	Quan-tity	Value
Total	(X)	1,400	(X)	1,540	(X)	1,540
Cement: Masonry	400	35	383	35	418	38
Portland	3,370	228	3,170	233	3,210	236
Clays 1/	430	55	421	54	433	56
Gemstones	(NA)	(D)	(NA)	(D)	(NA)	0
Peat	206	3	294	5	288	6
Sand and gravel: Construction	16,600	61	19,300	69	20,500	77
Industrial	540	6	547	6	535	7
Stone (crushed) 2/	66,300	343	68,000	350	70,000	368
Combined value 3/	(X)	669	(X)	783	(X)	749

(X) Not applicable.
(NA) Not available.
(D) Data withheld to avoid disclosure of information about individual companies.
1/ Excludes certain clays; included with "Combined value."
2/ Excludes certain stones in 1994; included with "Combined value."
3/ Includes minerals not listed separately and values indicated by symbol (D).
Note: Production as measured by mine shipments, sales, or marketable production
(including consumption by producers). Some data are estimated. 1996 data are preliminary.
Source: U.S., Department of the Interior, U.S. Geological Survey, *The Minerals
Yearbook, Volume II: Area Reports, Domestic*, 1996.

Table 10.72. MINING: AVERAGE MONTHLY PRIVATE REPORTING UNITS, EMPLOYMENT
AND PAYROLL COVERED BY UNEMPLOYMENT COMPENSATION LAW
BY INDUSTRY IN FLORIDA, 1996

SIC code	Industry	Number of re-porting units	Number of em-ployees	Payroll ($1,000)
	Mining	52	399	3,874
13	Oil and gas extraction	11	141	707
131	Crude petroleum and natural gas	41	251	3,151
138	Oil and gas fields services	141	6,336	19,607
14	Nonmetallic minerals, except fuels	5	44	84
141	Dimension stone	40	1,587	4,470
142	Crushed and broken stone, including riprap	42	763	1,891
144	Sand and gravel	4	205	659
145	Clay, ceramic, and refractory minerals	13	3,298	11,489
147	Chemical and fertilizer mineral mining	6	40	92
148	Nonmetallic minerals services, except fuels	32	399	922
149	Miscellaneous nonmetallic minerals, except fuels	32	399	922

Note: Private employment. Data are preliminary. Detail may not add to totals
due to disclosure editing and/or rounding. See Tables 23.70, 23.71, 23.72, 23.73,
and 23.74 for public employment data.
Source: State of Florida, Department of Labor and Employment Security, Bureau of
Labor Market Information, "Employment and Wages" (ES-202), unpublished data.

Table 10.84. PHOSPHATE ROCK PRODUCTION: SALES OR USE BY PRODUCERS BY TYPE OF
USE AND BY REGION IN THE UNITED STATES, CROP YEARS 1994-95 AND 1995-96

(in thousand metric tons)

| | Year ending June 30, 1995 | | | | Year ending June 30, 1996 | | | |
| | Domestic 1/ | | | Ex- | Domestic 1/ | | | Ex- |
Region	Total	Agri-cultural	Indus-trial	port 2/	Total	Agri-cultural	Indus-trial	port 2/
Florida and								
North Carolina								
Rock	38,100	35,200	131	2,760	A/ 17,600	36,500	A/ 36	A/ 955
P205 content	11,400	10,450	42	875	A/ 5,290	10,830	A/ 12	A/ 302
Idaho, Montana,								
and Utah								
Rock	5,620	4,070	1,543	0	5,460	3,090	2,380	0
P205 content	1,600	1,184	418	0	1,620	965	655	0

A/ Only six months of data provided to avoid disclosure of information about individual companies.
1/ Includes rock converted to products and exported.
2/ Exports reported to U.S. Geological Survey by companies.

Table 10.85. PHOSPHATE ROCK PRODUCTION: PRODUCTION AND SALES BY REGION IN THE
UNITED STATES, CROP YEARS 1994-95 AND 1995-96

	Year ending June 30, 1995				Year ending June 30, 1996			
	Thousand metric tons		Value 1/		Thousand metric tons		Value 1/	
			Total (mil-	Aver-age per			Total (mil-	Aver-age per
		P205 con-	lion dol-	ton (dol-		P205 con-	lion dol-	ton (dol-
Item	Rock	tent	lars)	lars)	Rock	tent	lars)	lars)
Mine production	165,000	25,300	(X)	(X)	179,000	23,800	(X)	(X)
Florida and								
North Carolina	157,600	23,200	(X)	(X)	169,700	21,640	(X)	(X)
Idaho, Montana,								
and Utah	9,310	2,180	(X)	(X)	8,840	2,127	(X)	(X)
Marketable production	43,500	12,800	947	21.77	45,400	13,300	1,060	23.35
Florida and								
North Carolina	38,000	11,200	840	22.11	39,200	11,570	928	23.67
Idaho, Montana,								
and Utah	5,490	1,632	106	19.27	6,220	1,730	135	21.74
Sold or used by								
producers	43,720	13,000	950	21.73	43,500	12,900	1,020	23.45
Florida and								
North Carolina	38,100	11,400	842	22.10	38,100	11,300	902	23.67
Idaho, Montana,								
and Utah	5,620	1,600	108	19.22	5,460	1,620	116	21.25

(X) Not applicable.
Note: Detail may not add to totals because of rounding or revisions made to totals
only. Data for Montana were reported in 1994-95 only.
    Source for Tables 10.84 and 10.85: U. S., Department of the Interior, U.S. Geolog-
ical Survey, *The Minerals Yearbook, Volume I: Minerals and Metals, 1996,* and previous edition.

University of Florida   **Bureau of Economic and Business Research**

CONSTRUCTION

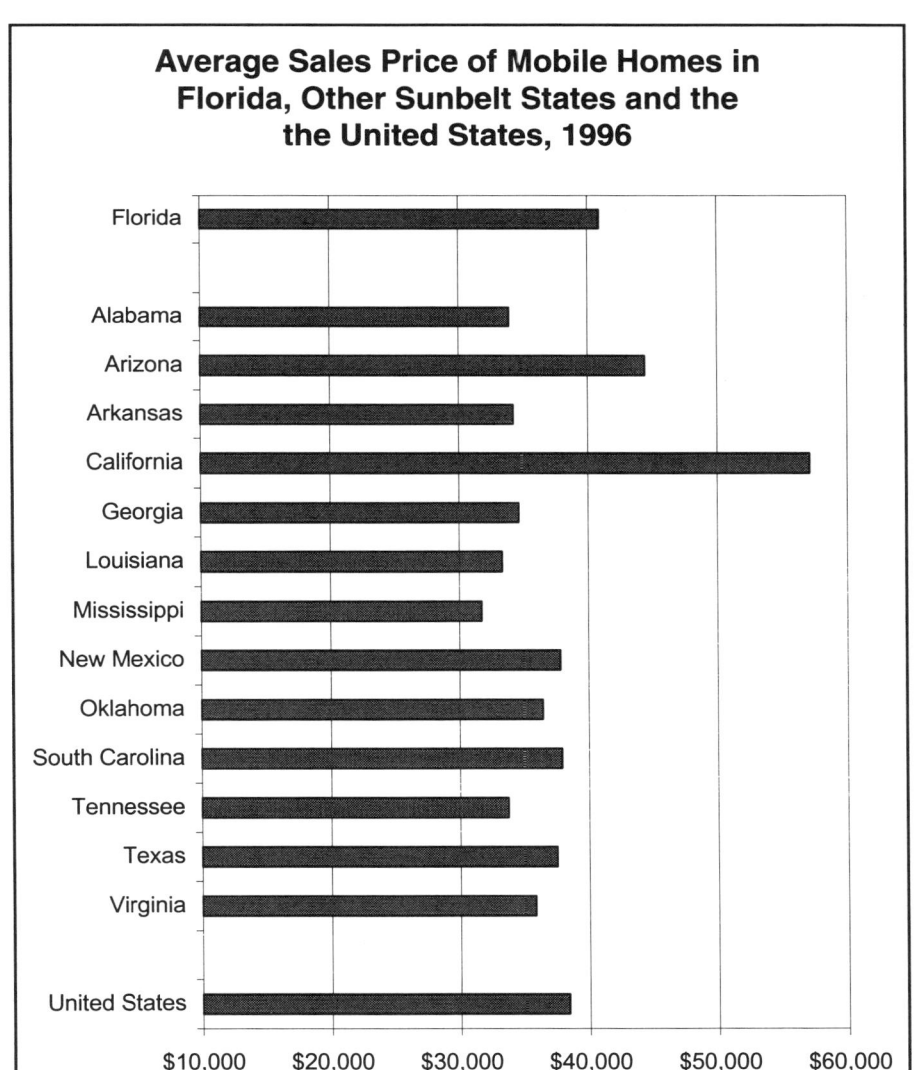

Average Sales Price of Mobile Homes in Florida, Other Sunbelt States and the the United States, 1996

Florida
Alabama
Arizona
Arkansas
California
Georgia
Louisiana
Mississippi
New Mexico
Oklahoma
South Carolina
Tennessee
Texas
Virginia
United States

$10,000 $20,000 $30,000 $40,000 $50,000 $60,000

Source: Table 11.25

TABLES LISTED BY MAJOR HEADINGS

Table 11.04. BUILDING PERMIT ACTIVITY: NUMBER OF PRIVATE RESIDENTIAL HOUSING
UNITS AUTHORIZED BY BUILDING PERMITS IN FLORIDA, OTHER SUNBELT STATES
OTHER POPULOUS STATES, AND THE UNITED STATES, 1992 THROUGH 1996

State	1992	1993	1994	1995	1996
Florida	102,022	115,103	128,602	122,903	125,020
Other sunbelt states					
Alabama 1/	13,905	16,105	19,136	20,114	19,868
Arizona	31,793	38,656	51,832	52,714	53,715
Arkansas 1/	7,934	9,962	12,374	11,707	11,144
California	97,781	84,341	96,982	83,864	92,060
Georgia 1/	44,566	53,874	64,860	72,225	74,874
Louisiana 1/	9,750	11,226	14,782	14,723	17,998
Mississippi 1/	6,321	8,116	10,933	10,753	10,367
New Mexico	7,240	8,874	11,545	11,009	10,180
North Carolina 1/	48,158	53,281	62,859	60,923	66,997
Oklahoma 1/	7,678	8,673	9,507	10,066	10,640
South Carolina	20,221	21,060	24,586	23,959	29,403
Tennessee 1/	23,319	26,984	31,874	35,096	40,522
Texas 1/	64,235	77,754	102,580	105,102	118,823
Virginia	40,205	44,963	46,830	43,129	45,919
Other populous states					
Illinois	40,430	44,742	49,290	47,467	49,592
Indiana	28,739	30,803	34,432	35,715	37,219
Massachusetts	16,411	17,460	18,115	16,428	17,261
Michigan	37,026	39,755	46,475	47,226	52,355
New Jersey	19,072	25,188	25,388	21,521	24,173
New York	29,851	28,604	31,135	28,060	34,895
Ohio 1/	42,610	44,235	47,152	44,812	49,280
Pennsylvania	38,282	40,126	40,210	36,250	37,895
United States	1,094,933	1,199,063	1,371,637	1,332,549	1,425,616

1/ Percentage of population in permit-issuing places is less than 90.
Note: Data are from a national sample of 17,000 permit-issuing places in 1992
and 1993 and 19,000 in 1994 through 1996, a universe which accounts for approximately
92 percent of new residential construction. Some data may be revised. See also
Table 24.20.

Source: U.S., Department of Commerce, Bureau of the Census, Internet site http://
www.census.gov/.

University of Florida   **Bureau of Economic and Business Research**

Table 11.05. CONSTRUCTION ACTIVITY: SINGLE- AND MULTIFAMILY HOUSING UNITS PERMITTED AND CONSTRUCTION STARTS IN THE STATE AND COUNTIES OF FLORIDA, 1994, 1995, AND 1996

| | Single-family housing units | | | | | | Multifamily housing units | | | | | |
| | Permitted | | | Construction starts | | | Permitted | | | Construction starts | | |
County	1994	1995 A/	1996 B/	1994	1995 A/	1996 B/	1994	1995 A/	1996 B/	1994	1995 A/	1996 B/
Florida	96,283	84,298	90,333	94,397	86,355	91,329	32,354	38,554	33,737	30,272	33,393	32,581
Alachua	1,062	924	1,073	1,038	953	1,097	520	1,047	1,172	526	668	1,248
Baker	93	82	83	86	80	79	0	0	0	0	0	0
Bay	984	810	937	990	846	929	35	234	46	98	206	69
Bradford	75	66	52	69	66	45	0	0	0	0	0	0
Brevard	3,622	2,521	3,003	3,554	2,664	3,039	385	243	435	364	192	366
Broward	10,667	8,188	9,556	10,310	8,771	9,584	5,061	4,682	5,371	4,978	4,111	5,095
Calhoun	30	49	48	30	41	44	0	0	0	0	0	0
Charlotte	1,331	941	941	1,315	1,001	956	255	32	124	203	79	88
Citrus	1,219	1,052	968	1,177	1,100	999	8	9	0	27	9	0
Clay	1,341	1,195	1,479	1,317	1,223	1,492	0	203	0	9	72	209
Collier	1,964	1,957	2,370	1,897	1,980	2,385	2,358	2,300	3,124	2,075	2,221	2,771
Columbia	252	266	305	242	255	304	9	0	18	6	1	16
Dade	6,080	7,344	3,826	5,979	6,728	4,366	5,231	7,372	2,669	4,373	6,606	3,129
De Soto	74	76	78	73	71	74	4	46	46	11	40	26
Dixie	43	29	46	46	24	40	0	0	0	0	0	0
Duval	3,991	3,499	3,640	3,911	3,610	3,694	1,182	836	3,426	1,227	762	2,548
Escambia	1,407	1,376	1,898	1,394	1,367	1,901	100	408	1,163	74	289	900
Flagler	855	821	961	838	839	956	61	19	16	38	29	14
Franklin	99	124	115	96	117	110	0	0	0	0	0	0
Gadsden	150	126	111	145	122	109	6	2	0	13	3	0
Gilchrist	61	55	53	53	53	50	0	0	0	0	0	0

See footnotes at end of table.

Continued . . .

Table 11.05. CONSTRUCTION ACTIVITY: SINGLE- AND MULTIFAMILY HOUSING UNITS PERMITTED AND CONSTRUCTION STARTS IN THE STATE AND COUNTIES OF FLORIDA, 1994, 1995, AND 1996 (Continued)

County	Single-family housing units						Multifamily housing units					
	Permitted			Construction starts			Permitted			Construction starts		
	1994	1995 A/	1996 B/	1994	1995 A/	1996 B/	1994	1995 A/	1996 B/	1994	1995 A/	1996 B/
Glades	23	30	23	24	25	22	0	0	0	0	0	0
Gulf	80	92	74	81	82	66	0	0	0	0	0	0
Hamilton	45	27	38	27	44	32	0	0	0	4	0	0
Hardee	39	30	41	39	28	35	0	0	0	0	0	0
Hendry	153	88	99	150	85	94	8	0	2	9	1	2
Hernando	1,192	935	992	1,227	971	984	60	16	42	66	14	33
Highlands	679	537	548	658	556	545	105	92	36	109	77	46
Hillsborough	5,208	4,664	4,774	5,073	4,824	4,829	2,340	2,466	3,407	1,749	2,368	3,013
Holmes	61	53	59	58	49	53	0	8	0	0	4	1
Indian River	1,041	782	911	999	823	915	158	331	193	148	275	160
Jackson	130	119	109	125	116	100	27	40	41	25	25	29
Jefferson	62	43	46	59	39	43	0	0	0	0	0	0
Lafayette	20	20	23	22	18	20	0	0	0	0	0	0
Lake	2,157	2,103	2,593	2,219	2,180	2,594	307	150	67	204	260	74
Lee	3,736	3,028	3,536	3,693	3,171	3,567	1,580	1,974	1,946	1,524	1,664	1,880
Leon	1,615	1,596	1,411	1,610	1,604	1,449	482	1,157	390	457	756	503
Levy	143	139	115	144	135	111	36	14	2	34	9	0
Liberty	22	15	21	20	13	17	0	0	0	0	0	0
Madison	53	45	49	51	40	44	0	0	0	0	0	0
Manatee	1,917	1,604	1,942	1,873	1,661	1,955	272	767	425	222	558	542
Marion	2,290	1,932	2,271	2,258	2,016	2,267	26	179	169	63	75	179
Martin	825	850	965	775	905	947	373	272	341	376	294	298
Monroe	286	406	323	286	377	312	69	135	40	98	119	55
Nassau	456	464	536	444	454	533	9	232	116	24	100	191

See footnotes at end of table.

Continued . .

Table 11.05. CONSTRUCTION ACTIVITY: SINGLE- AND MULTIFAMILY HOUSING UNITS PERMITTED AND CONSTRUCTION STARTS IN THE STATE AND COUNTIES OF FLORIDA, 1994, 1995, AND 1996 (Continued)

| | Single-family housing units | | | | | | Multifamily housing units | | | | | |
| | Permitted | | | Construction starts | | | Permitted | | | Construction starts | | |
County	1994	1995 A/	1996 B/	1994	1995 A/	1996 B/	1994	1995 A/	1996 B/	1994	1995 A/	1996 B/
Okaloosa	1,637	1,036	1,475	1,627	1,084	1,445	708	586	332	531	662	366
Okeechobee	111	79	137	109	72	132	5	4	4	7	1	2
Orange	6,121	5,253	5,782	6,044	5,458	5,833	3,055	4,431	2,881	3,664	3,875	2,951
Osceola	1,670	1,559	1,950	1,657	1,609	1,956	238	159	31	463	139	42
Palm Beach	8,587	7,399	8,114	8,289	7,631	8,251	3,060	2,872	1,708	2,221	2,808	1,682
Pasco	2,177	1,786	2,124	2,131	1,845	2,131	239	267	160	211	230	152
Pinellas	2,420	2,137	1,978	2,393	2,200	2,000	1,123	1,467	521	1,188	1,167	646
Polk	2,573	2,186	2,502	2,588	2,256	2,517	111	179	114	111	148	91
Putnam	159	141	149	162	128	140	86	0	20	54	31	19
St. Johns	1,389	1,414	1,612	1,333	1,445	1,639	193	569	213	161	288	459
St. Lucie	1,486	1,228	1,513	1,426	1,301	1,525	566	441	486	492	389	465
Santa Rosa	1,715	998	1,393	1,690	1,040	1,398	51	62	84	31	62	62
Sarasota	2,238	2,083	2,205	2,216	2,167	2,218	729	557	1,053	628	552	814
Seminole	2,406	2,067	2,088	2,375	2,118	2,125	700	292	612	850	125	623
Sumter	703	858	863	683	859	859	0	0	4	0	0	2
Suwannee	147	144	130	140	139	127	18	0	5	16	0	5
Taylor	46	25	43	45	22	36	0	0	0	0	0	0
Union	43	52	34	41	47	30	0	0	0	0	0	0
Volusia	2,189	1,957	2,299	2,153	2,015	2,298	304	803	142	398	571	203
Wakulla	140	151	181	137	136	179	0	0	2	0	0	2
Walton	600	552	620	593	574	609	75	599	529	82	454	499
Washington	93	90	99	90	82	94	26	0	9	30	4	11

A/ Revised.
B/ Preliminary.
Note: Permit data compiled by BEBR based on data from the U.S. Bureau of the Census.

Source: University of Florida, Bureau of Economic and Business Research, unpublished data.

Table 11.15. BUILDING PERMIT ACTIVITY: VALUE REPORTED ON BUILDING PERMITS AND NEW HOUSING UNITS AUTHORIZED BY BUILDING PERMITS IN THE STATE, COUNTIES, MUNICIPALITIES, AND UNINCORPORATED AREAS OF FLORIDA, 1996

Area 1/	Number of months reported	Total residential value ($1,000)	Number of housekeeping units 2/ Single-family	Multi-family
Florida	(X)	11,471,660	91,040	33,980
Alachua	(X)	125,957	1,040	813
Alachua	12	7,782	107	0
Archer	11	112	2	0
Gainesville	12	18,435	209	60
Hawthorne	12	260	5	0
High Springs	12	1,188	18	0
Micanopy	12	108	2	0
Newberry	12	1,986	33	0
Waldo	12	35	1	0
County office	12	96,052	663	753
Baker	(X)	4,756	77	0
Macclenny	12	642	17	0
County office	12	4,115	65	0
Bay	(X)	67,952	948	50
Lynn Haven	12	17,327	156	4
Panama City Beach	12	19,358	215	0
County office	12	31,268	577	46
Bradford	(X)	3,089	49	0
Hampton	12	3,089	49	0
Brevard	(X)	347,259	2,910	391
Cape Canaveral	12	17,383	9	166
Cocoa	12	9,718	22	46
Cocoa Beach	12	1,530	22	9
Indialantic	12	664	8	0
Indian Harbour Beach	12	9,434	33	2
Malabar	12	3,553	26	0
Melbourne	12	41,267	411	56
Brevard (Continued)				
Melbourne Beach	12	1,657	14	3
Melbourne Village	12	516	4	0
Palm Bay	12	54,465	584	0
Palm Shores	12	712	11	0
Rockledge	12	10,547	87	16
Satellite Beach	12	2,297	18	4
Titusville	11	4,345	46	0
West Melbourne	12	11,072	139	0
County office	12	178,101	1,498	89
Broward	(X)	1,385,709	9,584	4,835
Coconut Creek	12	70,278	586	278
Cooper City	12	7,954	78	0
Coral Springs	12	112,303	983	22
Dania	12	10,069	19	235
Davie	12	75,940	546	213
Deerfield Beach	12	17,313	231	68
Ft. Lauderdale	12	72,662	67	297
Hallandale	12	1,401	14	8
Hillsboro Beach	12	331	1	0
Hollywood	12	46,608	486	10
Lauderdale-by-the-sea	2	1,200	4	0
Lauderhill	12	4,627	23	58
Lighthouse Point	12	2,032	10	0
Margate	12	22,145	210	86
Miramar	12	135,429	1,188	133
North Lauderdale	12	16,575	0	376
Oakland Park	11	502	5	2
Parkland	12	41,552	190	24

Continued . . .

See footnotes at end of table.

Table 11.15. BUILDING PERMIT ACTIVITY: VALUE REPORTED ON BUILDING PERMITS AND NEW HOUSING UNITS AUTHORIZED BY BUILDING PERMITS IN THE STATE, COUNTIES, MUNICIPALITIES, AND UNINCORPORATED AREAS OF FLORIDA, 1996 (Continued)

Area 1/	Number of months reported	Total residential value ($1,000)	Number of housekeeping units 2/ Single-family	Multi-family
Broward (Continued)				
Pembroke Pines	12	308,901	1,978	1,614
Plantation	12	60,985	383	272
Pompano Beach	12	23,885	89	189
Sunrise	12	33,323	235	216
Tamarac	12	24,492	226	226
County office	12	295,202	2,032	508
Calhoun	(X)	2,998	49	0
Blountstown	1	309	7	0
County office	12	2,689	42	0
Charlotte	(X)	103,123	941	124
Punta Gorda	12	23,226	192	26
County office	12	79,897	749	98
Citrus	(X)	59,241	967	0
Crystal River	12	807	5	0
Inverness	12	960	16	0
County office	11	57,474	946	0
Clay	(X)	141,112	1,481	0
Green Cove Springs	12	4,606	40	0
Orange Park	12	1,854	15	0
Penney Farms	12	426	6	0
County office	12	134,226	1,420	0
Collier	(X)	533,219	2,383	3,066
Everglades	12	180	2	0
Naples	12	85,530	67	94
County office	12	447,509	2,314	2,972
Columbia	(X)	16,303	315	18
Lake City	11	1,479	27	16
County office	12	14,824	288	2

Area 1/	Number of months reported	Total residential value ($1,000)	Number of housekeeping units 2/ Single-family	Multi-family
Dade	(X)	540,183	3,802	2,749
Bal Harbour	12	1,674	5	0
Bay Harbor Islands	12	545	1	0
Coral Gables	6	35,300	41	135
Florida City	12	930	19	0
Golden Beach	12	2,556	5	0
Hialeah	12	15,325	53	230
Hialeah Gardens	12	10,412	213	24
Homestead	12	4,057	12	0
Indian Creek Village	12	850	1	0
Miami	11	31,874	46	690
Miami Beach	12	38,765	9	195
Miami Springs	12	180	2	0
North Miami	12	1,003	1	20
North Miami Beach	11	665	3	0
Opa-Locka	12	85	2	0
South Miami	12	1,315	12	0
Surfside	0	365	4	0
Sweetwater	11	354	1	4
Virginia Gardens	4	298	2	0
County office	12	393,632	3,370	1,451
De Soto	(X)	7,250	78	46
County office	12	7,250	78	46
Dixie	(X)	2,390	46	0
Horseshoe Beach	12	60	1	0
County office	12	2,330	45	0
Duval	(X)	523,556	3,833	3,504
Atlantic Beach	12	7,094	59	22
Baldwin	12	346	6	0

See footnotes at end of table.

Continued . . .

Table 11.15. BUILDING PERMIT ACTIVITY: VALUE REPORTED ON BUILDING PERMITS AND NEW HOUSING UNITS AUTHORIZED BY BUILDING PERMITS IN THE STATE, COUNTIES, MUNICIPALITIES, AND UNINCORPORATED AREAS OF FLORIDA, 1996 (Continued)

Area 1/	Number of months reported	Total residential value ($1,000)	Number of housekeeping units 2/ Single-family	Multi-family
Duval (Continued)				
Jacksonville 3/	12	491,433	3,634	3,300
Jacksonville Beach	12	23,254	123	182
Neptune Beach	12	1,428	11	0
Escambia	(X)	181,849	1,914	1,174
Pensacola	12	16,197	139	45
County office	12	165,652	1,775	1,129
Flagler	(X)	63,733	960	16
Bunnell	12	198	3	2
Flagler Beach	12	3,633	33	0
County office	12	59,902	924	14
Franklin	(X)	14,910	98	2
Apalachicola	12	663	7	2
County office	12	14,247	91	0
Gadsden	(X)	12,162	120	0
Quincy	12	1,177	12	0
County office	12	10,985	108	0
Gilchrist	(X)	4,360	52	0
County office	12	4,360	52	0
Glades	(X)	1,980	27	0
Moore Haven	12	361	8	0
County office	12	1,618	19	0
Gulf	(X)	6,714	73	0
County office	12	6,714	73	0
Hamilton	(X)	3,220	39	0
County office	12	3,220	39	0

Area 1/	Number of months reported	Total residential value ($1,000)	Number of housekeeping units 2/ Single-family	Multi-family
Hardee	(X)	4,351	45	0
Wauchula	12	595	8	0
County office	12	3,757	37	0
Hendry	(X)	5,559	73	2
Clewiston	12	401	3	2
La Belle	12	792	13	0
County office	9	4,366	57	0
Hernando	(X)	85,649	1,005	42
Brooksville	12	552	9	0
County office	12	85,097	996	42
Highlands	(X)	37,863	551	36
Avon Park	11	683	10	2
Sebring	12	912	14	4
County office	12	36,268	527	30
Hillsborough	(X)	639,290	4,915	3,945
Plant City	12	22,705	174	278
Tampa	12	160,960	625	1,280
Temple Terrace	12	2,242	10	0
County office	12	453,383	4,106	2,387
Holmes	(X)	4,454	63	0
County office	12	4,454	63	0
Indian River	(X)	148,451	902	99
Fellsmere	12	1,171	19	0
Indian River Shores	12	22,989	50	0
Orchid	12	3,207	8	0
Sebastian	12	18,899	237	8

Continued . . .

See footnotes at end of table.

Table 11.15. BUILDING PERMIT ACTIVITY: VALUE REPORTED ON BUILDING PERMITS AND NEW HOUSING UNITS AUTHORIZED BY BUILDING PERMITS IN THE STATE, COUNTIES, MUNICIPALITIES, AND UNINCORPORATED AREAS OF FLORIDA, 1996 (Continued)

Area 1/	Number of months reported	Total residential value ($1,000)	Number of housekeeping units 2/ Single-family	Multi-family
Indian River (Continued)				
Vero Beach	12	11,160	79	0
County office	12	91,025	509	91
Jackson	(X)	7,422	86	25
County office	11	7,422	86	25
Jefferson	(X)	4,834	46	0
County office	11	4,834	46	0
Lafayette	(X)	1,571	23	0
County office	12	1,571	23	0
Lake	(X)	252,411	2,591	44
Eustis	12	10,581	117	0
Fruitland Park	12	639	9	0
Lady Lake	12	1,560	19	4
Leesburg	12	3,796	41	0
Mascotte	12	1,024	24	0
Mount Dora	12	10,702	94	20
Tavares	12	6,299	81	4
Umatilla	12	402	9	0
County office	12	217,408	2,197	16
Lee	(X)	618,802	3,677	2,033
Cape Coral	12	57,706	1,041	46
Ft. Myers	12	3,575	43	7
Sanibel	12	17,239	54	12
County office	12	540,283	2,539	1,968
Leon	(X)	166,693	1,428	378
Tallahassee	12	82,262	687	340
County office	12	84,432	741	38
Levy	(X)	8,996	112	2
Cedar Key	12	1,590	15	0
Chiefland	12	343	9	2
Fanning Springs	12	146	3	0
Williston	11	358	6	0
County office	12	6,559	79	0
Liberty	(X)	1,727	21	0
County office	12	1,727	21	0
Madison	(X)	2,984	44	0
Madison	0	313	9	0
County office	6	2,672	35	0
Manatee	(X)	196,425	1,877	570
Anna Maria	12	1,050	9	0
Bradenton	12	5,762	99	0
Bradenton Beach	12	1,394	6	8
Holmes Beach	12	1,196	8	2
Palmetto	12	8,108	31	79
County office	12	178,916	1,724	481
Marion	(X)	158,024	2,246	188
Belleview	12	203	4	0
McIntosh	12	105	2	0
Ocala	12	13,370	128	95
County office	12	144,346	2,112	93
Martin	(X)	227,874	965	341
Jupiter Island	12	7,952	7	0
Sewall's Point	12	3,405	12	0
Stuart	12	896	7	0
County office	12	215,621	939	341

See footnotes at end of table.

Continued . . .

Table 11.15. BUILDING PERMIT ACTIVITY: VALUE REPORTED ON BUILDING PERMITS AND NEW HOUSING UNITS AUTHORIZED BY BUILDING PERMITS IN THE STATE, COUNTIES, MUNICIPALITIES, AND UNINCORPORATED AREAS OF FLORIDA, 1996 (Continued)

Area 1/	Number of months reported	Total residential value ($1,000)	Number of housekeeping units 2/ Single-family	Number of housekeeping units 2/ Multi-family
Monroe	(X)	38,383	416	4
Key Colony Beach	12	2,055	9	2
Key West	12	19,115	201	2
Layton	12	80	1	0
County office	12	17,132	205	0
Nassau	(X)	69,508	531	116
Fernandina Beach	12	13,232	121	10
Hilliard	12	536	11	0
County office	12	55,740	399	106
Okaloosa	(X)	141,226	1,535	308
Crestview	12	15,450	252	5
Destin	12	31,563	195	195
Ft. Walton Beach	12	2,822	45	0
Mary Esther	12	530	7	0
Niceville	12	6,515	74	0
Valparaiso	12	1,030	15	0
County office	12	83,316	947	108
Okeechobee	(X)	10,104	139	4
Okeechobee	11	815	14	0
County office	12	9,289	125	4
Orange	(X)	702,477	5,788	2,891
Apopka	12	19,775	328	19
Eatonville	11	254	4	0
Edgewood	12	5,239	25	0
Maitland	12	12,038	47	10
Oakland	12	1,143	11	0
Ocoee	12	39,338	418	0
Orange (Continued)				
Orlando	12	100,707	410	1,138
Winter Garden	12	15,960	143	0
Winter Park	12	6,372	28	97
County office	12	501,651	4,374	1,627
Osceola	(X)	185,630	1,904	142
Kissimmee	12	32,828	366	3
St. Cloud	12	13,098	172	0
County office	12	139,704	1,366	139
Palm Beach	(X)	1,086,165	8,328	1,643
Belle Glade	12	1,369	20	2
Boca Raton	12	61,998	378	17
Boynton Beach	12	42,700	420	115
Delray Beach	12	47,365	229	422
Golf Village	12	495	1	0
Greenacres	12	25,983	154	268
Highland Beach	10	17,204	41	168
Hypoluxo	12	3,149	0	53
Jupiter	12	49,186	169	72
Jupiter Inlet Colony	12	647	3	0
Lake Clarke Shores	12	132	1	0
Lake Worth	12	536	8	0
Lantana	12	2,590	10	2
North Palm Beach	12	2,769	15	0
Ocean Ridge	12	3,914	7	0
Pahokee	12	1,489	26	0
Palm Beach	12	35,532	28	6

See footnotes at end of table.

Continued . . .

Table 11.15. BUILDING PERMIT ACTIVITY: VALUE REPORTED ON BUILDING PERMITS AND NEW HOUSING UNITS AUTHORIZED BY BUILDING PERMITS IN THE STATE, COUNTIES, MUNICIPALITIES, AND UNINCORPORATED AREAS OF FLORIDA, 1996 (Continued)

Area 1/	Number of months reported	Total residential value ($1,000)	Number of housekeeping units 2/ Single-family	Multi-family	Area 1/	Number of months reported	Total residential value ($1,000)	Number of housekeeping units 2/ Single-family	Multi-family
Palm Beach (Continued)					Pinellas (Continued)				
Palm Beach Gardens	12	92,951	382	14	Pinellas Park	11	4,793	44	5
Palm Beach Shores	12	197	2	0	Redington Beach	12	970	5	0
Riviera Beach	12	14,935	185	24	Safety Harbor	12	6,383	48	0
Royal Palm Beach	12	17,132	182	2	St. Petersburg	12	20,805	130	42
South Bay	12	306	5	0	St. Pete Beach	12	4,175	13	25
Tequesta	12	2,007	11	0	South Pasadena	12	211	1	0
West Palm Beach	12	46,512	397	58	Tarpon Springs	8	9,712	104	0
County office	12	615,068	5,654	420	Treasure Island	12	660	2	0
Pasco	(X)	163,278	2,123	160	County office	12	248,410	1,297	221
Dade City	12	570	11	0	Polk	(X)	187,822	2,504	122
New Port Richey	12	682	11	0	Auburndale	12	3,209	42	2
Port Richey	12	1,601	10	0	Bartow	12	1,821	28	0
San Antonio	12	893	11	2	Davenport	10	64	1	0
Zephyrhills	12	4,595	72	8	Dundee	12	2,094	30	0
County office	12	154,937	2,008	150	Eagle Lake	12	125	2	0
Pinellas	(X)	363,284	1,963	527	Ft. Meade	12	721	10	0
Belleair	12	5,356	14	0	Frostproof	0	121	2	0
Belleair Beach	12	637	4	0	Haines City	12	7,359	96	6
Clearwater	12	26,355	65	117	Lake Alfred	12	567	7	0
Dunedin	12	8,300	38	24	Lake Hamilton	12	230	2	2
Gulfport	11	6,371	18	0	Lake Wales	12	2,355	40	0
Indian Rocks Beach	12	3,905	33	14	Lakeland	12	16,574	144	42
Indian Shores	12	450	1	2	Mulberry	11	101	2	0
Largo	12	3,363	42	0	Polk City	9	194	3	0
North Redington Beach	12	864	4	0	Winter Haven	12	8,966	81	42
Oldsmar	12	11,565	100	75	County office	12	143,321	2,014	28

See footnotes at end of table.

Continued . . .

Table 11.15. BUILDING PERMIT ACTIVITY: VALUE REPORTED ON BUILDING PERMITS AND NEW HOUSING UNITS AUTHORIZED BY BUILDING PERMITS IN THE STATE, COUNTIES, MUNICIPALITIES, AND UNINCORPORATED AREAS OF FLORIDA, 1996 (Continued)

Area 1/	Number of months reported	Total residential value ($1,000)	Number of housekeeping units 2/ Single-family	Multi-family
Putnam	(X)	9,035	127	0
Palatka	12	692	12	0
County office	12	8,343	115	0
St. Johns	(X)	261,938	1,614	211
St. Augustine	1	3,346	40	0
St. Augustine Beach	12	5,290	38	0
County office	12	253,301	1,536	211
St. Lucie	(X)	159,456	1,474	480
Ft. Pierce	12	2,268	21	8
Port St. Lucie	12	106,037	1,039	209
St. Lucie Village	12	88	1	0
County office	12	51,063	413	263
Santa Rosa	(X)	136,866	1,393	84
County office 4/	12	136,066	1,393	84
Sarasota	(X)	417,887	2,230	1,515
Longboat Key	11	21,817	43	25
North Port Charlotte	11	46,143	403	0
Sarasota	12	33,211	62	291
Venice	12	8,856	85	7
County office	12	307,860	1,637	1192
Seminole	(X)	328,597	2,112	612
Altamonte Springs	12	12,513	38	307
Casselberry	12	1,898	21	0
Lake Mary	12	32,749	279	0
Longwood	12	1,696	16	2
Oviedo	12	70,529	437	0
Sanford	12	8,478	128	11
Seminole (Continued)				
Winter Springs	12	50,982	336	16
County office	12	149,753	857	276
Sumter	(X)	85,173	881	4
Bushnell	12	656	12	4
Wildwood	12	1,068	19	0
County office	12	83,450	850	0
Suwannee	(X)	9,492	129	5
Live Oak	12	522	12	5
County office	2	8,970	117	5
Taylor	(X)	3,894	52	0
Perry	12	1,573	16	0
County office	12	2,321	36	0
Union	(X)	2,197	34	0
County office	12	2,197	34	0
Volusia	(X)	230,050	2,351	128
Daytona Beach	12	7,282	61	4
Daytona Beach Shores	12	620	6	0
DeLand	12	6,781	79	2
Edgewater	12	6,865	75	2
Holly Hill	12	765	11	0
Lake Helen	12	1,259	17	0
New Smyrna Beach	12	8,879	83	22
Oak Hill	12	558	8	0
Orange City	12	2,718	28	0
Ormond Beach	12	26,876	197	0
Pierson	12	35	1	0

Continued . . .

See footnotes at end of table.

Table 11.15. BUILDING PERMIT ACTIVITY: VALUE REPORTED ON BUILDING PERMITS AND NEW HOUSING UNITS AUTHORIZED BY BUILDING PERMITS IN THE STATE, COUNTIES, MUNICIPALITIES, AND UNINCORPORATED AREAS OF FLORIDA, 1996 (Continued)

Area 1/	Number of months reported	Total residential value ($1,000)	Number of housekeeping units 2/ Single-family	Multi-family
Volusia (Continued)				
Ponce Inlet	12	3,108	21	0
Port Orange	12	45,107	413	3
South Daytona	12	2,642	31	0
County office	12	116,557	1,320	95
Wakulla	(X)	14,901	201	2
County office	12	14,901	201	2

Area 1/	Number of months reported	Total residential value ($1,000)	Number of housekeeping units 2/ Single-family	Multi-family
Walton	(X)	132,129	620	529
DeFuniak Springs	12	900	11	0
County office	12	131,229	609	529
Washington	(X)	5,761	135	0
County office	12	5,761	135	0

(X) Not applicable.
1/ County office data includes permitting for unincorporated areas and occasionally may include incorporated areas in the same county not shown separately. The definition is more service-based than geographical.
2/ Excludes mobile homes.
3/ Includes unincorporated Duval County.
4/ Includes unincorporated Navarre Beach located entirely in Escambia County.
Note: Data are based on voluntary reports from local building officials processed by the Bureau of the Census by the 12th working day of the month. Data may also include estimates for nonreports. Value figures are estimated on a cost-per-foot basis by each jurisdiction and may not be comparable to other locations.

Source: University of Florida, Bureau of Economic and Business Research, *Building Permit Activity in Florida, Calendar Year 1996, Revised.*

Table 11.20. EMPLOYMENT: AVERAGE MONTHLY PRIVATE REPORTING UNITS, EMPLOYMENT
AND PAYROLL COVERED BY UNEMPLOYMENT COMPENSATION LAW
BY CONSTRUCTION INDUSTRY IN FLORIDA, 1996

SIC code	Industry	Number of reporting units	Number of employees	Payroll ($1,000)
	Construction	36,703	324,827	708,793
15	Building--general contractors and operative builders	9,682	70,405	175,347
152	General building contractors--residential	7,887	43,308	101,374
153	Operative builders	121	1,541	4,596
154	General building contractors--nonresidential	1,674	25,556	69,377
16	Heavy construction other than building--contractors	1,891	42,641	105,185
161	Highway and street, except elevated highways	359	12,619	30,576
162	Heavy construction, except highway and street	1,532	30,022	74,609
17	Special trade contractors	25,131	211,781	428,261
171	Plumbing, heating, and air-conditioning	4,752	47,096	101,883
172	Painting and paper hanging	2,200	11,094	19,422
173	Electrical work	4,200	45,590	98,922
174	Masonry, stonework, tile setting, and plastering	3,383	28,058	53,556
175	Carpentry and floor work	2,478	12,855	23,022
176	Roofing, siding, and sheet metal work	1,977	17,833	31,480
177	Concrete work	1,843	17,678	32,362
178	Water well drilling	238	1,281	2,563
179	Miscellaneous special trade contractors	4,062	30,297	65,051

Note: Private employment. Detail may not add to totals due to disclosure editing
and/or rounding. See Tables 23.70, 23.71, 23.72, 23.73, and 23.74 for public employment data.

Source: State of Florida, Department of Labor and Employment Security, Bureau of
Labor Market Information, "Employment and Wages" (ES-202), unpublished data.

University of Florida   **Bureau of Economic and Business Research**

Table 11.21. EMPLOYMENT: AVERAGE MONTHLY PRIVATE REPORTING UNITS, EMPLOYMENT
AND PAYROLL COVERED BY UNEMPLOYMENT COMPENSATION LAW IN THE STATE
AND COUNTIES OF FLORIDA, 1996

County	Number of reporting units	Number of employees	Payroll ($1,000)	County	Number of reporting units	Number of employees	Payroll ($1,000)
				Construction (SIC codes 15-17)			
Florida	36,703	324,827	708,793	Lafayette	7	28	38
				Lake	448	3,580	7,066
Alachua	451	4,288	8,437	Lee	1,459	12,097	25,596
Baker	27	168	235	Leon	623	5,453	10,766
Bay	432	4,037	7,517	Levy	53	599	1,187
Bradford	28	220	354	Madison	18	45	57
Brevard	1,099	9,295	19,406	Manatee	526	4,257	9,250
Broward	3,822	33,638	79,656	Marion	557	4,477	7,648
Calhoun	28	199	352	Martin	448	3,195	7,010
Charlotte	374	2,292	4,199	Monroe	340	2,090	4,244
Citrus	273	1,767	2,737	Nassau	136	850	1,607
Clay	309	2,311	4,387	Okaloosa	539	4,187	7,604
Collier	906	8,143	18,377	Okeechobee	75	361	567
Columbia	129	1,029	2,100	Orange	2,019	25,045	57,939
Dade	3,852	34,762	79,689	Osceola	234	2,035	4,242
De Soto	45	182	297	Palm Beach	2,977	24,122	55,900
Dixie	15	94	158	Pasco	709	4,273	7,324
Duval	1,768	22,179	51,500	Pinellas	1,986	17,885	38,225
Escambia	722	8,448	17,328	Polk	885	8,470	18,046
Flagler	123	482	847	Putnam	130	1,051	1,724
Franklin	27	124	173	St. Johns	246	1,446	2,639
Gadsden	63	497	796	St. Lucie	437	2,703	5,044
Gilchrist	21	42	47	Santa Rosa	287	2,217	3,751
Glades	11	48	94	Sarasota	1,215	7,792	16,540
Gulf	26	202	546	Seminole	917	9,102	21,216
Hamilton	19	59	67	Sumter	52	215	337
Hardee	31	277	563	Suwannee	56	427	885
Hendry	49	263	465	Taylor	25	581	1,241
Hernando	328	1,621	2,773	Union	11	56	74
Highlands	205	1,038	1,663	Volusia	1,029	6,782	13,214
Hillsborough	1,965	24,111	57,174	Wakulla	43	239	325
Holmes	16	113	172	Walton	77	486	708
Indian River	397	2,671	5,043	Washington	38	381	579
Jackson	62	391	479				
Jefferson	22	126	227	Multicounty 1/	451	3,058	7,962

1/ Reporting units without a fixed location within the state or of unknown county
location.

Note: Construction includes general contractors and operative builders (SIC code
15), heavy construction contractors (SIC code 16), and special trade contractors (SIC
code 17). Private employment. Data are preliminary. Only counties for which data
are disclosed are shown. Detail may not add to totals due to disclosure editing
and/or rounding. See Tables 23.70, 23.71, 23.72, 23.73, and 23.74 for public employment data.

Source: State of Florida, Department of Labor and Employment Security, Bureau of
Labor Market Information, "Employment and Wages" (ES-202), unpublished data.

University of Florida   **Bureau of Economic and Business Research**

Table 11.22. BUILDING MATERIALS, HARDWARE, GARDEN SUPPLY, AND MOBILE HOME DEALERS
AVERAGE MONTHLY PRIVATE REPORTING UNITS, EMPLOYMENT, AND PAYROLL COVERED
BY UNEMPLOYMENT COMPENSATION LAW IN THE STATE AND COUNTIES
OF FLORIDA, 1996

County	Number of reporting units	Number of employees	Payroll ($1,000)	County	Number of reporting units	Number of employees	Payroll ($1,000)
			Building materials, hardware, garden supply, and mobile home dealers (SIC code 52)				
Florida	3,618	49,344	86,470	Lake	68	821	1,234
				Lee	109	1,900	3,491
Alachua	44	754	1,122	Leon	61	1,063	1,902
Baker	7	37	36	Levy	17	104	147
Bay	54	836	1,211	Madison	7	33	33
Bradford	7	47	65	Manatee	55	670	1,060
Brevard	117	1,443	2,162	Marion	94	1,139	1,848
Broward	294	4,243	8,330	Martin	38	667	1,078
Calhoun	4	37	61	Monroe	40	436	796
Charlotte	34	442	785	Nassau	17	149	217
Citrus	40	355	473	Okaloosa	65	894	1,291
Clay	30	498	912	Okeechobee	9	113	152
Collier	63	924	1,745	Orange	191	2,752	5,104
Columbia	26	308	526	Osceola	23	439	722
Dade	388	5,209	9,451	Palm Beach	213	2,987	5,833
De Soto	7	52	84	Pasco	71	783	1,237
Dixie	5	34	40	Pinellas	198	2,864	4,578
Duval	169	2,718	4,995	Polk	116	2,006	3,674
Escambia	89	1,421	2,281	Putnam	27	242	337
Flagler	11	76	112	St. Johns	33	301	490
Franklin	4	31	49	St. Lucie	39	349	639
Gadsden	7	72	75	Santa Rosa	33	188	239
Gilchrist	4	33	43	Sarasota	103	1,364	2,385
Gulf	8	50	61	Seminole	80	1,475	2,789
Hardee	5	54	74	Sumter	9	39	36
Hendry	14	128	223	Suwannee	11	128	214
Hernando	24	356	509	Taylor	7	50	69
Highlands	21	173	204	Union	3	12	18
Hillsborough	187	2,747	5,425	Volusia	111	1,511	2,221
Holmes	3	15	17	Wakulla	6	19	18
Indian River	38	289	529	Walton	15	145	177
Jackson	17	96	147	Washington	6	41	58
Jefferson	5	24	28	Multicounty 1/	19	115	538

1/ Reporting units without a fixed location within the state or of unknown county
location.
Note: Private employment. For a list of three-digit code industries included see
Table 11.20. Data are preliminary. Only counties for which data are disclosed are
shown. Detail may not add to totals due to disclosure editing and/or rounding. See
Tables in 23.70, 23.71, 23.72, 23.73, and 23.74 for public employment data.

Source: State of Florida, Department of Labor and Employment Security, Bureau of
Labor Market Information, "Employment and Wages" (ES-202), unpublished data.

University of Florida   **Bureau of Economic and Business Research**

Table 11.25. MOBILE HOMES: PLACEMENTS OF NEW MOBILE HOMES AND AVERAGE
SALES PRICES IN FLORIDA, SELECTED STATES AND THE UNITED STATES, 1996

	Placements (1,000)			Average sales price (dollars)		
State 1/	Total 2/	Single-wide	Double-wide	Total	Single-wide	Double-wide
Florida	15.1	3.9	10.4	40,900	26,300	44,500
Alabama	15.5	9.2	6.1	33,900	26,000	45,400
Arizona	7.0	2.2	4.7	44,400	30,000	50,300
Arkansas	6.8	4.4	2.4	34,200	27,800	45,400
California	3.7	(D)	(D)	57,100	(D)	(D)
Colorado	4.5	1.9	2.5	46,200	33,800	54,500
Georgia	19.4	8.0	11.0	34,600	24,600	40,900
Idaho	2.2	(D)	1.6	48,200	(D)	53,200
Illinois	4.3	1.8	2.5	42,600	29,600	50,200
Indiana	8.0	3.7	4.3	38,600	28,100	47,500
Iowa	2.5	1.3	1.2	42,300	33,300	51,200
Kansas	3.4	2.2	1.2	36,100	29,800	47,300
Kentucky	10.4	6.4	4.0	31,400	25,000	41,400
Louisiana	8.2	6.2	1.9	33,300	27,900	49,200
Maine	2.0	1.2	0.7	36,800	30,700	47,700
Michigan	12.1	3.9	8.2	40,700	30,000	46,000
Minnesota	3.1	1.9	1.3	41,200	34,800	49,600
Mississippi	10.4	7.3	3.1	31,700	26,300	44,500
Missouri	7.6	4.3	3.3	38,900	34,300	44,700
Nevada	2.7	(D)	2.3	52,300	(D)	53,700
New Mexico	6.3	3.5	2.8	37,800	29,600	48,100
New York	5.4	2.5	2.9	39,800	29,500	49,000
North Carolina	33.2	16.3	16.7	38,500	27,500	49,000
Ohio	8.2	4.3	3.8	37,000	27,400	47,500
Oklahoma	5.5	3.1	2.4	36,400	27,400	47,800
Oregon	6.3	(D)	5.1	50,700	(D)	49,500
Pennsylvania	6.3	3.1	3.2	40,400	28,900	51,900
South Carolina	19.8	8.7	10.8	37,900	27,300	45,800
Tennessee	15.4	8.8	6.4	33,700	26,100	43,400
Texas	32.2	19.3	12.6	37,500	29,900	48,500
Virginia	5.5	2.8	2.7	35,800	26,100	45,800
Washington	5.4	(D)	4.3	51,400	(D)	49,600
West Virginia	5.3	2.9	2.4	34,400	25,100	45,700
Wisconsin	3.8	2.0	1.7	39,700	32,400	47,600
United States	319.7	154.1	160.3	38,400	28,200	47,300

(D) Data withheld to avoid disclosure of information about individual firms.
1/ States with 1996 placements of 2,000 or more are listed.
2/ Includes mobile homes with more than two sections.

Source: U.S., Department of Commerce, Bureau of the Census, *Current Construction Reports: Housing Starts,* May 1997.

University of Florida   **Bureau of Economic and Business Research**

Table 11.42. PRODUCER PRICES: INDEX OF PRODUCER PRICES OF MATERIALS USED IN CONSTRUCTION BY SPECIFIED GROUP AND COMMODITY IN THE UNITED STATES, ANNUAL AVERAGES 1992 THROUGH 1995

(1982 = 100, except where indicated)

Group and commodity	1992	1993	1994	1995	Percentage change annual 1994 to 1995
All construction materials	122.5	128.6	133.8	138.9	3.8
Softwood lumber	148.6	193.0	198.1	178.9	-9.7
Hardwood lumber	140.7	163.3	168.3	167.0	-0.8
General millwork	146.3	158.5	163.6	165.5	1.2
Prefabricated structural members	132.7	159.7	169.3	163.5	-3.4
Softwood plywood	147.2	169.7	176.7	188.2	6.5
Hardwood plywood	106.9	115.4	122.3	122.1	-0.2
Particleboard, platen-type 1/	121.1	139.3	155.8	155.7	-0.1
Fabricated hardboard products 2/	100.7	107.1	109.6	112.6	2.7
Prefabricated wood buildings and components 3/	122.8	132.5	141.6	147.8	4.4
Mobile homes	121.7	127.8	137.0	145.9	6.5
Construction machinery and equipment	128.7	132.0	133.7	136.6	2.2
Prepared paint	131.6	133.2	135.3	142.1	5.0
Builders hardware	141.4	144.9	148.0	153.2	3.5
Plastic construction products					
Group index 4/	112.7	116.6	122.9	134.2	9.2
Plumbing products	94.0	101.8	111.1	120.7	8.6
Plastic pipe and fittings 1/	90.1	98.2	108.9	119.7	9.9
Lighting fixtures					
Residential	136.4	137.8	139.5	143.2	2.7
Commercial and industrial	131.8	132.4	133.7	138.9	3.9
Welded wire for concrete reinforcement	101.3	104.5	108.7	108.1	-0.6
Concrete reinforcing bars 5/	100.1	104.4	115.0	116.1	1.0
Roofing steel	106.3	107.0	109.6	119.1	8.7
Building wire and cable 1/	145.6	131.2	148.9	165.5	11.1
Metal door sash and trim	135.0	136.6	142.0	156.4	10.1
Metal molding, trim, and storefronts 6/	163.9	169.0	(NA)	(NA)	(NA)
Steel fencing and fence gates 5/	117.0	116.3	110.6	123.9	12.0
Cast iron pressure and soil pipe and fittings	138.2	141.4	137.7	156.7	13.8
Steel for buildings	115.5	118.4	122.3	127.2	4.0
Steel for bridges	108.7	101.3	94.4	68.9	-27.0
Architectural and ornamental metalwork 7/	117.7	119.5	113.0	127.9	13.2
Prefab metal buildings 8/	112.3	117.0	113.1	130.4	15.3
Heating equipment					
Group index 4/	137.3	140.4	142.5	147.5	3.5
Steam and hot water	138.0	138.9	138.6	141.6	2.2
Warm air furnaces and attachments	134.8	137.3	138.0	141.3	2.4
Water heaters, domestic	127.9	133.4	137.9	146.1	5.9
Heating stoves, domestic	118.4	118.2	120.2	124.2	3.3
Unitary air conditioners including heat pumps	115.9	115.0	115.5	118.9	2.9

See footnotes at end of table.   Continued . . .

Table 11.42. PRODUCER PRICES: INDEX OF PRODUCER PRICES OF MATERIALS USED
IN CONSTRUCTION BY SPECIFIED GROUP AND COMMODITY IN THE UNITED
STATES, ANNUAL AVERAGES 1992 THROUGH 1995 (Continued)

(1982 = 100, except where indicated)

Group and commodity	1992	1993	1994	1995	Per- centage change annual 1994 to 1995
Plumbing fixtures and brass fittings					
Group index	153.1	155.9	159.6	166.0	4.0
Vitreous china fixtures	127.6	127.0	128.9	131.9	2.3
Brass fittings	167.7	172.3	177.3	185.1	4.4
Metal fixtures 9/	120.7	121.4	123.4	128.2	3.9
Hard-surfaced floor coverings	142.0	145.2	147.5	153.2	3.9
Soft-surfaced floor coverings	117.4	116.7	118.1	119.5	1.2
Concrete ingredients					
Group index 4/	119.4	123.4	128.7	134.6	4.6
Sand, gravel, and crushed stone	130.6	134.0	137.9	142.3	3.2
Portland cement	106.3	111.7	119.5	128.0	7.1
Concrete products					
Group index 4/	117.2	120.2	124.6	129.5	3.9
Building block	130.7	132.8	136.0	141.0	3.7
Concrete pipe	114.3	114.9	117.2	121.9	4.0
Ready mixed concrete	115.3	118.8	123.8	129.1	4.3
Precast concrete	128.6	130.1	133.2	136.4	2.4
Prestressed concrete	100.4	102.6	108.9	112.2	3.0
Structural clay products					
Group index 4/	132.0	135.1	138.3	141.4	2.2
Brick and structural clay tile 3/	118.0	122.0	125.6	128.9	2.6
Ceramic floor and wall tile	132.6	133.5	135.5	138.0	1.8
Gypsum products					
Group index 4/	99.9	108.3	136.1	154.5	13.5
Wallboard 1/2 inch	87.3	97.0	112.4	(NA)	(NA)
Type X wallboard	94.8	103.1	131.4	(NA)	(NA)
Cut stone and stone products 3/	128.1	129.6	130.7	133.0	1.8
Prepared asphalt roofing	94.3	94.9	92.9	97.8	5.3
Sheet, plate, and float glass	94.1	96.6	106.9	115.1	7.7
Insulation materials	102.3	105.8	112.0	118.8	6.1
Paving mixtures and blocks	100.2	102.0	103.3	105.9	2.5

(NA) Not available.
1/ December 1982 = 100.
2/ June 1984 = 100.
3/ December 1984 = 100.
4/ Includes items not shown separately.
5/ June 1982 = 100.
6/ June 1983 = 100.
7/ December 1983 = 100.
8/ December 1987 = 100.
9/ January 1987 = 100.
Note: Some data may be revised.

Source: U.S., Department of Commerce, International Trade Administration, *Con-struction Review,* Fall and Winter 1995-96.

University of Florida   **Bureau of Economic and Business Research**

MANUFACTURING

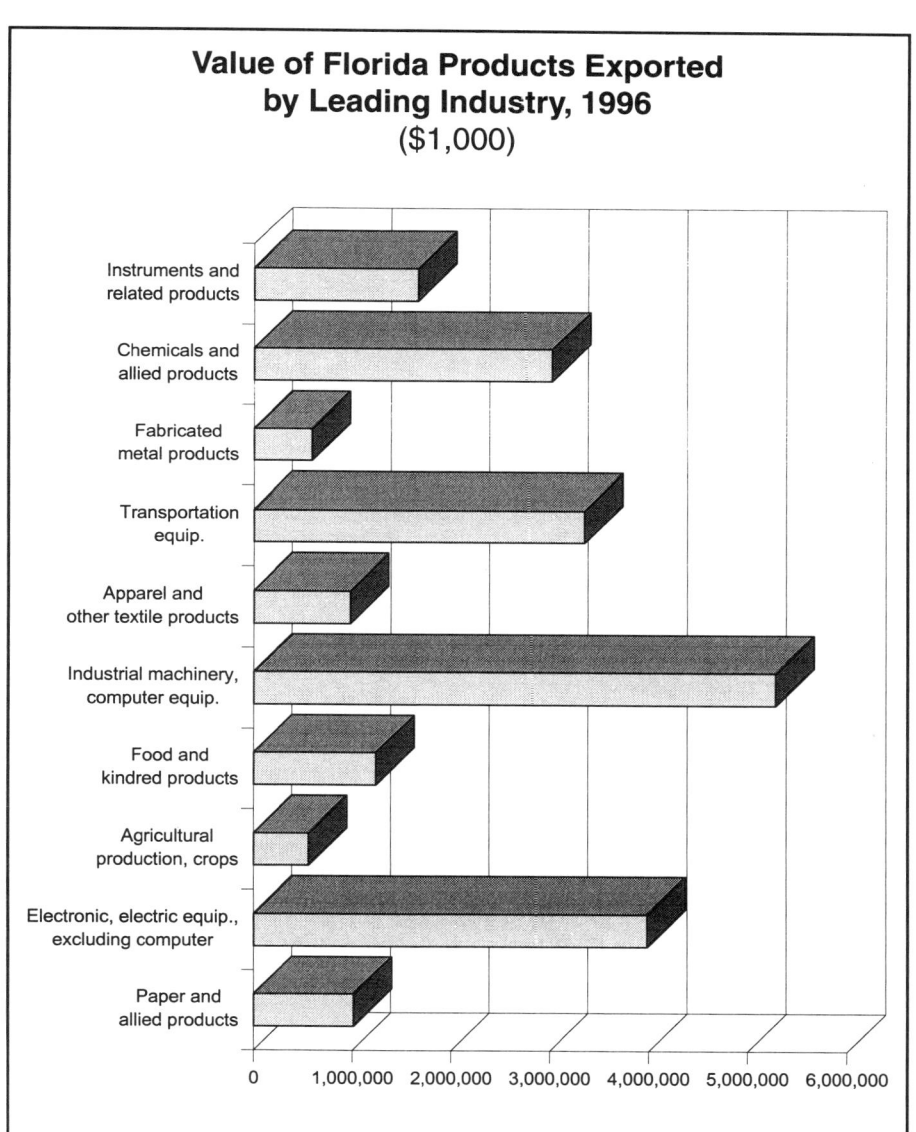

Value of Florida Products Exported
by Leading Industry, 1996
($1,000)

Source: Table 12.86

TABLES LISTED BY MAJOR HEADINGS

SECTION 12.00
MANUFACTURING
(Continued)

TABLES LISTED BY MAJOR HEADINGS

Table 12.01. MANUFACTURING: CHARACTERISTICS IN THE STATE AND SELECTED CONSOLIDATED
METROPOLITAN STATISTICAL AREAS (CMSAS), PRIMARY METROPOLITAN STATISTICAL
AREAS (PMSAS), AND METROPOLITAN STATISTICAL AREAS (MSAS) OF FLORIDA
SPECIFIED YEARS 1987 THROUGH 1995

Year and source 2/	Number of establishments 1/ Total	With 20 employ- ees or more	All employees Number (1,000)	Payroll (million dollars)	Per- centage of U.S. total	Value added by manu- facture (million dollars)	New capital expendi- ture (million dollars)
Florida							
1987--census	15,603	4,046	499.3	10,954.0	2.63	27,574.2	1,910.7
1989--ASM	(NA)	(NA)	496.6	11,880.9	2.61	28,844.4	1,887.3
1990--ASM	(NA)	(NA)	497.9	12,381.5	2.64	29,792.7	1,866.9
1991--ASM	(NA)	(NA)	473.1	12,201.3	2.62	29,054.7	1,791.9
1992--census	16,382	3,758	472.4	12,991.0	2.59	32,634.4	2,111.5
1993--ASM	(NA)	(NA)	479.9	13,845.0	2.56	37,933.6	2,361.1
1994--ASM	(NA)	(NA)	472.0	13,257.5	2.58	35,100.6	2,040.9
1995--ASM	(NA)	(NA)	479.9	13,257.9	2.63	33,615.2	1,772.3
Miami-Ft. Lauderdale CMSA 3/							
1987--census	5,185	1,338	132.6	2,504.3	0.70	5,700.2	254.0
1992--census	5,215	1,185	122.1	3,047.6	0.67	7,130.4	337.2
Ft. Lauderdale PMSA							
1987--census 4/	1,790	397	43.3	936.0	0.23	2,138.3	122.0
1992--census	1,879	370	41.8	1,236.3	0.23	2,888.4	133.9
Miami PMSA							
1987--census 5/	3,395	941	89.3	1,568.4	0.47	3,561.9	132.0
1992--census	3,336	815	80.3	1,811.3	0.44	4,242.0	203.3
Orlando MSA							
1987--census	1,249	358	51.9	1,302.9	0.27	3,197.8	203.4
1992--census	1,574	390	53.3	1,661.5	0.29	3,754.2	195.2
Tampa-St. Petersburg- Clearwater MSA							
1987--census	2,546	681	84.5	1,834.5	0.45	4,139.8	279.1
1992--census	2,583	639	83.7	2,330.5	0.46	5,164.9	315.5

(NA) Not available.
1/ Includes establishments with payroll at any time during the year.
2/ Data for the years 1987 and 1992 are from the Census of Manufactures. Data for
Annual Survey of Manufactures (ASM) years are estimates based on a representative
sample of establishments canvassed annually and may differ from results of a complete
canvas of all establishments.
3/ Consists of Dade and Broward counties.
4/ Ft. Lauderdale-Hollywood-Pompano Beach PMSA.
5/ Miami-Hialeah PMSA.
Note: Data are reported for metropolitan areas with 40,000 manufacturing employees or more in 1992. The manufactures census is on a 5-year cycle collecting data
for years ending in 2 and 7. See Glossary for definitions of metropolitan areas and
maps at the front of the book for area boundaries.

Source: U.S., Department of Commerce, Bureau of the Census, *1992 Census of Manufactures: Florida.* Geographic Area Series M92-A-10, and *1995 Annual Survey of Manufactures.* Geographic Area Series M95(AS)-1.

Table 12.06. MANUFACTURING: ESTABLISHMENTS, EMPLOYMENT, VALUE ADDED
BY MANUFACTURE, VALUE OF SHIPMENTS, AND NEW CAPITAL
EXPENDITURE IN THE STATE AND COUNTIES
OF FLORIDA, 1992

(in millions of dollars, except where indicated)

County	Estab-lish-ments 1/ (number)	All employees 1/ Number (1,000)	All employees 1/ Payroll	Value added by manu-facture	Value of ship-ments 2/	New capital expen-diture
Florida	16,382	472.4	12,991.0	32,634.4	64,274.7	2,111.5
Alachua	174	5.3	132.2	323.9	691.1	33.7
Baker	15	0.3	6.1	19.2	73.1	0.6
Bay	132	3.3	87.0	235.9	565.7	26.5
Bradford	23	0.5	8.4	20.9	35.4	1.8
Brevard	425	22.3	853.5	1,789.5	2,792.4	65.1
Broward	1,879	41.8	1,236.3	2,888.4	4,822.6	133.9
Calhoun	29	0.2	3.6	9.6	22.4	0.5
Charlotte	72	0.6	11.1	19.4	39.9	0.8
Citrus	58	0.9	15.6	37.1	68.4	2.5
Clay	82	1.4	33.0	79.5	211.0	14.7
Collier	177	2.2	52.2	107.4	188.0	9.4
Columbia	49	1.2	25.5	50.7	133.0	2.3
Dade	3,336	80.3	1,811.3	4,242.0	7,650.5	203.3
De Soto	8	0.2	3.6	15.6	20.3	0.1
Dixie	25	0.4	8.0	16.1	46.4	0.6
Duval	755	27.8	780.0	2,595.5	5,236.4	290.9
Escambia	244	8.7	287.3	866.8	1,893.8	71.2
Flagler	35	1.1	22.3	59.0	133.8	2.1
Franklin	11	0.1	1.5	2.7	6.6	0.3
Gadsden	46	1.5	28.0	84.8	156.7	3.7
Gilchrist	8	0.1	0.9	2.0	4.9	0.1
Glades	5	A/	0.4	0.8	1.6	A/
Gulf	16	(D)	(D)	(D)	(D)	(D)
Hamilton	7	(D)	(D)	(D)	(D)	(D)
Hardee	13	0.2	3.4	6.4	27.0	0.4
Hendry	21	0.9	27.2	128.2	429.9	15.1
Hernando	77	1.1	21.8	80.5	146.4	2.3
Highlands	58	1.1	24.4	61.1	161.8	4.7
Hillsborough	1,002	36.5	951.1	2,178.0	4,983.5	152.3
Holmes	28	0.4	5.7	13.7	21.4	0.6
Indian River	113	1.5	38.1	87.8	173.4	2.9
Jackson	33	1.9	32.5	60.9	171.4	5.5
Jefferson	14	0.2	3.5	6.3	11.1	0.5
Lafayette	7	0.1	1.2	2.6	5.3	0.3
Lake	161	3.8	83.3	196.0	686.6	8.0
Lee	352	5.6	119.1	298.8	535.6	13.1

See footnotes at end of table.   Continued . . .

Table 12.06. MANUFACTURING: ESTABLISHMENTS, EMPLOYMENT, VALUE ADDED
BY MANUFACTURE, VALUE OF SHIPMENTS, AND NEW CAPITAL
EXPENDITURE IN THE STATE AND COUNTIES
OF FLORIDA, 1992 (Continued)

(in millions of dollars, except where indicated)

County	Estab-lish-ments 1/ (number)	All employees 1/ Number (1,000)	Payroll	Value added by manu-facture	Value of ship-ments 2/	New capital expen-diture
Leon	130	2.8	60.2	131.4	222.5	7.5
Levy	33	0.3	6.5	14.8	33.5	1.1
Liberty	21	0.2	3.1	7.7	24.5	0.6
Madison	38	1.2	21.9	81.1	296.3	9.2
Manatee	219	8.1	211.1	749.7	1,761.4	23.1
Marion	234	8.6	194.9	651.3	1,579.5	16.1
Martin	158	3.0	79.8	173.9	368.6	5.2
Monroe	84	0.4	8.2	19.8	37.0	1.0
Nassau	66	2.2	74.1	274.7	802.0	(D)
Okaloosa	136	4.2	80.9	201.4	365.5	7.0
Okeechobee	23	0.3	5.0	13.6	59.6	0.4
Orange	920	36.9	1,228.9	2,818.5	5,007.4	153.9
Osceola	75	2.0	75.6	125.1	240.3	6.1
Palm Beach	1,003	30.5	1,056.5	3,320.5	5,524.1	133.2
Pasco	170	3.5	77.0	168.1	570.2	17.7
Pinellas	1,334	42.6	1,280.6	2,738.3	4,447.4	143.1
Polk	508	20.0	522.5	1,481.1	4,340.4	247.7
Putnam	66	3.0	83.0	230.9	578.7	8.3
St. Johns	72	1.8	37.4	85.9	169.2	(D)
St. Lucie	121	2.2	45.2	137.0	388.9	15.9
Santa Rosa	63	2.1	41.6	109.8	254.9	8.4
Sarasota	423	10.2	252.1	582.5	963.1	28.2
Seminole	418	10.5	273.7	614.6	1,269.8	27.2
Sumter	29	0.7	15.7	34.2	148.4	1.8
Suwannee	29	1.3	21.7	12.7	117.5	(D)
Taylor	35	2.0	59.5	242.1	450.7	(D)
Union	11	0.6	8.6	23.2	44.4	0.8
Volusia	413	12.1	304.2	691.1	1,265.3	33.6
Wakulla	11	(D)	(D)	(D)	(D)	(D)
Walton	23	1.2	18.2	28.5	105.9	1.2
Washington	26	0.9	13.9	37.6	83.4	4.8

(D) Data withheld to avoid disclosure of information about individual companies.
A/ Less than 500 employees or $500,000.
1/ Includes establishments with payroll at anytime during the year.
2/ The total value of shipments may include extensive duplication arising from
shipments between establishments in the same industry classification.
Note: The manufactures census is on a 5-year cycle collecting data for years ending in 2 and 7.
Source: U.S., Department of Commerce, Bureau of the Census, *1992 Census of Manufactures: Florida.* Geographic Area Series M92-A-10.

University of Florida   **Bureau of Economic and Business Research**

Table 12.50. EMPLOYMENT: AVERAGE MONTHLY PRIVATE REPORTING UNITS, EMPLOYMENT AND PAYROLL COVERED BY UNEMPLOYMENT COMPENSATION LAW BY MANUFACTURING INDUSTRY IN FLORIDA, 1995 and 1996

SIC code	Industry	Number of reporting units	Number of employees	Payroll ($1,000)
		1995 A/		
	Manufacturing	15,285	480,388	1,240,572
20	Food and kindred products	659	41,624	103,191
201	Meat products	71	6,071	10,472
202	Dairy products	32	1,981	5,092
203	Canned, frozen, and preserved fruits, vegetables, and food specialties	109	11,343	28,236
204	Grain mill products	56	778	2,097
205	Bakery products	98	5,726	13,179
206	Sugar and confectionery products	32	2,979	10,040
207	Fats and oils	7	205	476
208	Beverages	63	6,920	22,162
209	Miscellaneous food preparations and kindred products	193	5,620	11,439
21	Tobacco products	21	1,257	3,214
212	Cigars	19	1,236	3,120
22	Textile mill products	195	4,024	7,941
221	Broadwoven fabric mills, cotton	17	181	271
224	Narrow fabrics and other smallwares mills-- cotton, wool, silk, and manmade fiber	13	332	886
225	Knitting mills	32	1,227	2,261
226	Dyeing and finishing textiles, except wool fabrics and knit goods	77	1,315	2,223
227	Carpets and rugs	10	45	93
228	Yarn and thread mills	10	115	135
229	Miscellaneous textile goods	29	673	1,725
23	Apparel and other fabricated textile products	1,138	27,562	38,562
232	Men's and boys' furnishings, work clothing, and allied garments	97	5,492	8,817
233	Women's, misses', and juniors' outerwear	355	8,133	10,045
234	Women's, misses', children's, and infants' undergarments	16	1,468	1,633
235	Hats, caps, and millinery	15	476	622
236	Girls', children's, and infants' outerwear	41	1,534	2,126
238	Miscellaneous apparel and accessories	44	1,412	1,812
239	Miscellaneous fabricated textile products	564	8,701	13,091
24	Lumber and wood products, except furniture	1,071	21,288	40,592
241	Logging	334	2,715	5,377
242	Sawmills and planing mills	83	2,759	5,531
243	Millwork, veneer, plywood, and structural wood members	450	9,582	18,025
244	Wood containers	51	1,096	1,760

See footnotes at end of table.

Continued . . .

Table 12.50. EMPLOYMENT: AVERAGE MONTHLY PRIVATE REPORTING UNITS, EMPLOYMENT
AND PAYROLL COVERED BY UNEMPLOYMENT COMPENSATION LAW BY MANUFACTURING
INDUSTRY IN FLORIDA, 1995 and 1996 (Continued)

SIC code	Industry	Number of reporting units	Number of employees	Payroll ($1,000)
	1995 A/ (Continued)			
24	Lumber and wood products, except furniture (Continued)			
245	Wood buildings and mobile homes	25	3,149	6,348
249	Miscellaneous wood products	128	1,987	3,551
25	Furniture and fixtures	538	12,252	21,866
251	Household furniture	276	6,461	10,814
252	Office furniture	35	588	1,009
253	Public building and related furniture	16	539	1,039
254	Partitions, shelving, lockers, and office and store fixtures	83	2,031	4,022
259	Miscellaneous furniture and fixtures	129	2,633	4,983
26	Paper and allied products	208	14,513	45,404
262	Paper mills	10	1,933	7,867
263	Paperboard mills	13	2,158	8,008
265	Paperboard containers and boxes	81	4,478	11,916
267	Converted paper and paperboard products, except containers and boxes	97	5,101	14,054
27	Printing, publishing, and allied industries	3,445	63,756	150,218
271	Newspapers: publishing, or publishing and printing	315	26,185	60,643
272	Periodicals: publishing, or publishing and printing	425	6,829	17,609
273	Books	154	2,746	7,663
274	Miscellaneous publishing	306	5,175	14,484
275	Commercial printing	2,013	18,661	39,956
276	Manifold business forms	24	971	2,466
278	Blankbooks, looseleaf binders, and bookbinding and related work	51	1,281	2,482
279	Service industries for the printing trade	154	1,860	4,793
28	Chemicals and allied products	519	20,835	71,975
281	Industrial inorganic chemicals	42	1,070	6,186
283	Drugs	62	3,247	11,422
284	Soap, detergents, and cleaning preparations; perfumes, cosmetics, and other toilet preparations	129	2,606	6,278
285	Paints, varnishes, lacquers, enamels, and allied products	75	1,422	3,685
286	Industrial organic chemicals	27	2,011	7,587
287	Agricultural chemicals	82	6,365	21,244
289	Miscellaneous chemical products	62	1,505	4,512
29	Petroleum refining and related industries	60	1,542	4,224
291	Petroleum refining	5	14	34

See footnotes at end of table.   Continued . . .

Table 12.50. EMPLOYMENT: AVERAGE MONTHLY PRIVATE REPORTING UNITS, EMPLOYMENT
AND PAYROLL COVERED BY UNEMPLOYMENT COMPENSATION LAW BY MANUFACTURING
INDUSTRY IN FLORIDA, 1995 and 1996 (Continued)

SIC code	Industry	Number of reporting units	Number of employees	Payroll ($1,000)
	1995 A/ (Continued)			
28	Petroleum refining and related industries (Continued)			
295	Asphalt paving and roofing materials	47	1,269	3,573
299	Miscellaneous products of petroleum and coal	9	259	617
30	Rubber and miscellaneous plastics products	706	20,607	44,208
302	Rubber and plastics footwear	5	1,129	1,490
305	Gaskets, packing, and sealing devices and rubber and plastics hose and belting	15	1,090	2,403
306	Fabricated rubber products, NEC	60	1,967	4,360
308	Miscellaneous plastics products	625	16,377	35,863
31	Leather and leather products	66	2,899	3,747
313	Boot and shoe cut stock and findings	3	19	50
314	Footwear, except rubber	17	538	764
316	Luggage	11	363	502
317	Handbags and other personal leather goods	26	846	1,050
32	Stone, clay, glass, and concrete products	745	21,423	52,576
321	Flat glass	15	158	341
322	Glass and glassware, pressed or blown	13	1,056	3,256
323	Glass products, made of purchased glass	84	1,953	3,577
324	Cement, hydraulic	14	710	2,307
325	Structural clay products	16	745	1,844
326	Pottery and related products	34	230	346
327	Concrete, gypsum, and plaster products	464	14,789	35,896
328	Cut stone and stone products	40	537	1,063
329	Abrasive, asbestos, and miscellaneous nonmetallic mineral products	67	1,247	3,946
33	Primary metal industries	135	5,738	15,074
331	Steel works, blast furnaces and rolling and finishing mills	35	1,852	6,191
332	Iron and steel foundries	12	610	1,677
335	Rolling, drawing, and extruding of nonferrous metals	44	2,542	5,477
336	Nonferrous foundries (castings)	26	472	1,066
339	Miscellaneous primary metal products	11	158	387
34	Fabricated metal products, except machinery and transportation equipment	1,222	30,030	68,289
341	Metal cans and shipping containers	16	1,085	4,226
342	Cutlery, handtools, and general hardware	73	1,847	4,129
343	Heating equipment, except electric and warm air; and plumbing fixtures	27	260	543
344	Fabricated structural metal products	615	15,069	31,261

See footnotes at end of table.   Continued . . .

Table 12.50. EMPLOYMENT: AVERAGE MONTHLY PRIVATE REPORTING UNITS, EMPLOYMENT AND PAYROLL COVERED BY UNEMPLOYMENT COMPENSATION LAW BY MANUFACTURING INDUSTRY IN FLORIDA, 1995 and 1996 (Continued)

SIC code	Industry	Number of reporting units	Number of employees	Payroll ($1,000)
	1995 A/ (Continued)			
34	Fabricated metal products, except machinery and transportation equipment (Continued)			
345	Screw machine products, and bolts, nuts, screws, rivets, and washers	48	1,111	2,674
346	Metal forgings and stampings	77	2,688	6,290
347	Coating, engraving, and allied services	160	1,783	4,024
348	Ordnance and accessories, except vehicles and guided missiles	28	694	2,041
349	Miscellaneous fabricated metal products	180	5,493	13,100
35	Industrial and commercial machinery and computer equipment	1,540	38,131	112,136
351	Engines and turbines	27	2,415	10,737
352	Farm and garden machinery and equipment	41	1,111	2,437
353	Construction, mining, and materials handling machinery and equipment	112	2,833	7,111
354	Metalworking machinery and equipment	277	4,692	11,895
355	Special industry machinery, except metal-working machinery	109	2,748	7,869
356	General industrial machinery and equipment	162	4,476	12,157
357	Computer and office equipment	87	8,769	35,128
358	Refrigeration and service industry machinery	142	5,721	13,196
359	Miscellaneous industrial and commercial machinery and equipment	584	5,366	11,605
36	Electronic and other electrical equipment and components, except computer equipment	724	61,015	187,346
361	Electric transmission and distribution equipment	35	2,114	5,120
362	Electrical industrial apparatus	58	2,446	7,142
363	Household appliances	15	443	1,524
364	Electric lighting and wiring equipment	107	3,579	6,660
365	Household audio and video equipment, and audio recordings	42	2,035	4,134
366	Communications equipment	130	21,215	76,410
367	Electronic components and accessories	252	21,867	66,872
369	Miscellaneous electrical machinery, equipment, and supplies	85	7,317	19,485
37	Transportation equipment	1,034	48,715	153,652
371	Motor vehicles and motor vehicle equipment	189	7,293	15,247
372	Aircraft and parts	145	14,330	53,207
373	Ship and boat building and repairing	593	13,835	30,459
375	Motorcycles, bicycles, and parts	13	100	143
376	Guided missiles and space vehicles and parts	37	11,984	52,312
379	Miscellaneous transportation equipment	51	815	1,472

See footnotes at end of table.

Continued . . .

Table 12.50. EMPLOYMENT: AVERAGE MONTHLY PRIVATE REPORTING UNITS, EMPLOYMENT AND PAYROLL COVERED BY UNEMPLOYMENT COMPENSATION LAW BY MANUFACTURING INDUSTRY IN FLORIDA, 1995 and 1996 (Continued)

SIC code	Industry	Number of reporting units	Number of employees	Payroll ($1,000)
	1995 A/ (Continued)			
38	Measuring, analyzing, and controlling instruments; photographic, medical, and optical goods; watches and clocks	514	33,972	98,158
381	Search, detection, navigation, guidance, aeronautical, and nautical systems, instruments, and equipment	44	8,667	31,006
382	Laboratory apparatus and analytical, optical, measuring, and controlling instruments	155	5,070	12,734
384	Surgical, medical, and dental instruments and supplies	224	13,931	38,519
385	Ophthalmic goods	63	5,948	15,097
386	Photographic equipment and supplies	21	288	663
387	Watches, clocks, clockwork operated devices, and parts	7	69	137
39	Miscellaneous manufacturing industries	748	9,202	18,197
391	Jewelry, silverware, and plated ware	111	1,099	2,169
393	Musical instruments	10	210	367
394	Dolls, toys, games, and sporting and athletic goods	181	2,190	4,017
395	Pens, pencils, and other artists' materials	40	1,075	2,559
396	Costume jewelry, costume novelties, buttons, and miscellaneous notions, except precious metal	23	630	1,249
399	Miscellaneous manufacturing industries	383	3,998	7,836

See footnotes at end of table.   Continued . . .

Table 12.50. EMPLOYMENT: AVERAGE MONTHLY PRIVATE REPORTING UNITS, EMPLOYMENT
AND PAYROLL COVERED BY UNEMPLOYMENT COMPENSATION LAW BY MANUFACTURING
INDUSTRY IN FLORIDA, 1995 and 1996 (Continued)

SIC code	Industry	Number of re-porting units	Number of em-ployees	Payroll ($1,000)
		1996 B/		
	Manufacturing	15,729	488,618	1,299,532
20	Food and kindred products	694	41,283	105,247
201	Meat products	77	5,852	10,146
202	Dairy products	38	1,852	4,932
203	Canned, frozen, and preserved fruits, vegetables, and food specialties	114	10,965	29,788
204	Grain mill products	53	787	2,157
205	Bakery products	103	5,755	13,508
206	Sugar and confectionery products	31	3,002	10,125
207	Fats and oils	8	208	511
208	Beverages	65	6,629	21,624
209	Miscellaneous food preparations and kindred products	206	6,235	12,457
21	Tobacco products	21	1,537	3,947
212	Cigars	18	1,506	3,859
22	Textile mill products	188	4,085	8,623
221	Broadwoven fabric mills, cotton	17	220	392
222	Broadwoven fabric mills, manmade fiber and silk	10	167	401
224	Narrow fabrics and other smallwares mills-- cotton, wool, silk, and manmade fiber	14	338	985
225	Knitting mills	29	1,203	2,577
226	Dyeing and finishing textiles, except wool fabrics and knit goods	68	1,328	2,277
227	Carpets and rugs	14	102	219
228	Yarn and thread mills	6	91	108
229	Miscellaneous textile goods	32	635	1,664
23	Apparel and other fabricated textile products	1,090	25,944	38,071
231	Men's and boys' suits, coats, and overcoats	9	148	213
232	Men's and boys' furnishings, work clothing, and allied garments	87	5,013	8,189
233	Women's, misses', and juniors' outerwear	294	7,224	9,406
234	Women's, misses', children's, and infants' undergarments	17	1,186	1,278
235	Hats, caps, and millinery	18	566	821
236	Girls', children's, and infants' outerwear	36	1,419	1,966
238	Miscellaneous apparel and accessories	53	1,454	2,007
239	Miscellaneous fabricated textile products	577	8,935	14,191
24	Lumber and wood products, except furniture	1,127	21,566	43,212
241	Logging	340	2,653	5,264
242	Sawmills and planing mills	81	2,643	5,858

See footnotes at end of table.   Continued . . .

Table 12.50. EMPLOYMENT: AVERAGE MONTHLY PRIVATE REPORTING UNITS, EMPLOYMENT AND PAYROLL COVERED BY UNEMPLOYMENT COMPENSATION LAW BY MANUFACTURING INDUSTRY IN FLORIDA, 1995 and 1996 (Continued)

SIC code	Industry	Number of reporting units	Number of employees	Payroll ($1,000)
	1996 B/ (Continued)			
24	Lumber and wood products, except furniture (Continued)			
243	Millwork, veneer, plywood, and structural wood members	486	9,947	19,303
244	Wood containers	57	1,142	1,956
245	Wood buildings and mobile homes	23	3,235	7,213
249	Miscellaneous wood products	140	1,947	3,618
25	Furniture and fixtures	559	12,900	24,335
251	Household furniture	279	6,646	11,733
252	Office furniture	39	663	1,216
253	Public building and related furniture	15	554	1,103
254	Partitions, shelving, lockers, and office and store fixtures	88	2,135	4,590
259	Miscellaneous furniture and fixtures	139	2,903	5,693
26	Paper and allied products	215	14,241	45,917
262	Paper mills	12	1,876	7,937
263	Paperboard mills	13	1,962	7,672
265	Paperboard containers and boxes	87	4,518	12,529
267	Converted paper and paperboard products, except containers and boxes	98	5,045	14,298
27	Printing, publishing, and allied industries	3,480	63,744	155,592
271	Newspapers: publishing, or publishing and printing	312	25,205	60,835
272	Periodicals: publishing, or publishing and printing	447	7,182	18,652
273	Books	158	2,797	8,529
274	Miscellaneous publishing	315	5,107	14,787
275	Commercial printing	2,036	19,414	42,989
276	Manifold business forms	20	929	2,371
277	Greeting cards	4	14	50
278	Blankbooks, looseleaf binders, and bookbinding and related work	48	1,204	2,452
279	Service industries for the printing trade	142	1,894	4,927
28	Chemicals and allied products	534	19,916	69,397
281	Industrial inorganic chemicals	37	564	2,005
282	Plastics materials and synthetic resins, synthetic rubber, cellulosic and other manmade fibers, except glass	43	2,784	12,007
283	Drugs	66	2,277	8,660
284	Soap, detergents, and cleaning preparations; perfumes, cosmetics, and other toilet preparations	130	2,666	7,014

See footnotes at end of table.   Continued . . .

Table 12.50. EMPLOYMENT: AVERAGE MONTHLY PRIVATE REPORTING UNITS, EMPLOYMENT
AND PAYROLL COVERED BY UNEMPLOYMENT COMPENSATION LAW BY MANUFACTURING
INDUSTRY IN FLORIDA, 1995 and 1996 (Continued)

SIC code	Industry	Number of reporting units	Number of employees	Payroll ($1,000)
	1996 B/ (Continued)			
28	Chemicals and allied products (Continued)			
285	Paints, varnishes, lacquers, enamels, and allied products	70	1,396	3,790
286	Industrial organic chemicals	29	2,014	8,062
287	Agricultural chemicals	88	6,623	22,800
289	Miscellaneous chemical products	71	1,592	5,059
29	Petroleum refining and related industries	63	1,667	4,659
291	Petroleum refining	5	15	27
295	Asphalt paving and roofing materials	49	1,369	3,955
299	Miscellaneous products of petroleum and coal	10	284	677
30	Rubber and miscellaneous plastics products	713	20,891	47,101
302	Rubber and plastics footwear	4	927	1,193
305	Gaskets, packing, and sealing devices and rubber and plastics hose and belting	16	1,002	2,448
306	Fabricated rubber products, NEC	60	2,291	5,143
308	Miscellaneous plastics products	632	16,619	38,216
31	Leather and leather products	68	3,528	4,876
311	Leather tanning and finishing	7	47	86
314	Footwear, except rubber	15	522	754
316	Luggage	12	426	646
317	Handbags and other personal leather goods	24	1,014	1,245
319	Leather goods, NEC	7	1,502	2,098
32	Stone, clay, glass, and concrete products	763	22,092	58,322
321	Flat glass	14	168	365
322	Glass and glassware, pressed or blown	18	1,065	3,205
323	Glass products, made of purchased glass	81	1,711	3,221
324	Cement, hydraulic	13	621	2,071
325	Structural clay products	21	707	2,003
326	Pottery and related products	30	175	275
327	Concrete, gypsum, and plaster products	474	15,558	39,408
328	Cut stone and stone products	47	611	1,267
329	Abrasive, asbestos, and miscellaneous nonmetallic mineral products	67	1,475	6,508
33	Primary metal industries	170	6,138	16,485
331	Steel works, blast furnaces and rolling and finishing mills	38	1,827	6,194
332	Iron and steel foundries	14	667	1,842
334	Secondary smelting and refining of nonferrous metals	6	121	321
335	Rolling, drawing, and extruding of nonferrous metals	67	2,831	6,519

See footnotes at end of table.   Continued . . .

Table 12.50. EMPLOYMENT: AVERAGE MONTHLY PRIVATE REPORTING UNITS, EMPLOYMENT AND PAYROLL COVERED BY UNEMPLOYMENT COMPENSATION LAW BY MANUFACTURING INDUSTRY IN FLORIDA, 1995 and 1996 (Continued)

SIC code	Industry	Number of reporting units	Number of employees	Payroll ($1,000)
	1996 B/ (Continued)			
33	Primary metal industries (Continued)			
336	Nonferrous foundries (castings)	31	530	1,189
339	Miscellaneous primary metal products	12	156	413
34	Fabricated metal products, except machinery and transportation equipment	1,272	31,899	73,338
341	Metal cans and shipping containers	17	1,120	4,490
342	Cutlery, handtools, and general hardware	71	1,946	4,394
343	Heating equipment, except electric and warm air; and plumbing fixtures	43	484	1,008
344	Fabricated structural metal products	638	16,083	33,767
345	Screw machine products, and bolts, nuts, screws, rivets, and washers	49	1,233	3,018
346	Metal forgings and stampings	78	2,683	6,473
347	Coating, engraving, and allied services	161	1,885	4,320
348	Ordnance and accessories, except vehicles and guided missiles	24	660	1,781
349	Miscellaneous fabricated metal products	191	5,805	14,086
35	Industrial and commercial machinery and computer equipment	1,618	37,466	110,813
351	Engines and turbines	28	2,428	11,081
352	Farm and garden machinery and equipment	52	1,114	2,445
353	Construction, mining, and materials handling machinery and equipment	123	2,937	7,707
354	Metalworking machinery and equipment	297	4,813	12,659
355	Special industry machinery, except metalworking machinery	116	2,737	8,440
356	General industrial machinery and equipment	166	4,789	13,474
357	Computer and office equipment	97	7,061	27,929
358	Refrigeration and service industry machinery	157	5,986	14,300
359	Miscellaneous industrial and commercial machinery and equipment	581	5,602	12,778
36	Electronic and other electrical equipment and components, except computer equipment	750	61,885	195,157
361	Electric transmission and distribution equipment	35	2,163	5,400
362	Electrical industrial apparatus	62	2,605	7,865
363	Household appliances	18	514	1,904
364	Electric lighting and wiring equipment	111	3,609	7,104
365	Household audio and video equipment, and audio recordings	43	2,411	5,405
366	Communications equipment	140	21,341	77,518
367	Electronic components and accessories	254	22,288	71,163
369	Miscellaneous electrical machinery, equipment, and supplies	87	6,956	18,799

See footnotes at end of table.   Continued . . .

Table 12.50. EMPLOYMENT: AVERAGE MONTHLY PRIVATE REPORTING UNITS, EMPLOYMENT
AND PAYROLL COVERED BY UNEMPLOYMENT COMPENSATION LAW BY MANUFACTURING
INDUSTRY IN FLORIDA, 1995 and 1996 (Continued)

SIC code	Industry	Number of reporting units	Number of employees	Payroll ($1,000)
	1996 B/ (Continued)			
37	Transportation equipment	1,072	51,244	162,695
371	Motor vehicles and motor vehicle equipment	187	8,135	18,131
372	Aircraft and parts	171	15,657	59,593
373	Ship and boat building and repairing	599	14,836	33,168
374	Railroad equipment	7	338	748
375	Motorcycles, bicycles, and parts	13	96	151
376	Guided missiles and space vehicles and parts	33	11,091	48,822
379	Miscellaneous transportation equipment	63	1,091	2,081
38	Measuring, analyzing, and controlling instruments; photographic, medical, and optical goods; watches and clocks	539	36,614	111,266
381	Search, detection, navigation, guidance, aeronautical, and nautical systems, instruments, and equipment	47	8,752	32,076
382	Laboratory apparatus and analytical, optical, measuring, and controlling instruments	171	6,205	17,317
384	Surgical, medical, and dental instruments and supplies	230	15,256	44,737
385	Ophthalmic goods	66	6,049	16,305
386	Photographic equipment and supplies	18	241	623
387	Watches, clocks, clockwork operated devices, and parts	7	111	207
39	Miscellaneous manufacturing industries	796	9,981	20,476
391	Jewelry, silverware, and plated ware	108	1,144	2,203
393	Musical instruments	13	195	373
394	Dolls, toys, games, and sporting and athletic goods	187	2,226	4,269
395	Pens, pencils, and other artists' materials	45	1,187	3,052
396	Costume jewelry, costume novelties, buttons, and miscellaneous notions, except precious metal	21	536	1,163
399	Miscellaneous manufacturing industries	423	4,694	9,416

NEC Not elsewhere classified.
A/ Revised.
B/ Preliminary.
Note: Private employment. Detail may not add to totals due to disclosure editing
and/or rounding. See Tables 23.70, 23.71, 23.72, 23.73, and 23.74 for public employ-
ment data.

Source: State of Florida, Department of Labor and Employment Security, Bureau of
Labor Market Information, "Employment and Wages" (ES-202), unpublished data.

Table 12.51. EMPLOYMENT: AVERAGE MONTHLY PRIVATE REPORTING UNITS, EMPLOYMENT AND PAYROLL COVERED BY UNEMPLOYMENT COMPENSATION LAW IN THE STATE AND COUNTIES OF FLORIDA, 1995 AND 1996

County	Number of re- porting units	Number of em- ployees	Payroll ($1,000)	County	Number of re- porting units	Number of em- ployees	Payroll ($1,000)
			Manufacturing industry, 1995 A/ (SIC codes 20-39)				
Florida	15,285	480,388	1,240,572	Lake	150	4,316	8,725
				Lee	340	6,087	13,663
Alachua	153	5,423	12,294	Leon	129	3,506	7,840
Baker	12	255	541	Levy	35	351	592
Bay	134	2,856	6,815	Liberty	17	279	508
Bradford	25	401	785	Madison	23	1,281	2,213
Brevard	445	26,862	88,162	Manatee	230	11,568	27,784
Broward	1,774	41,538	117,693	Marion	212	10,365	21,745
Calhoun	31	291	450	Martin	139	2,561	7,889
Charlotte	67	892	1,586	Monroe	82	512	900
Citrus	47	1,219	2,199	Nassau	60	1,928	6,348
Clay	81	1,516	3,041	Okaloosa	136	4,043	8,360
Collier	168	2,300	5,660	Okeechobee	19	170	367
Columbia	51	1,598	3,203	Orange	855	33,727	103,073
Dade	2,903	76,665	166,065	Osceola	81	1,768	5,627
De Soto	17	98	198	Palm Beach	886	28,990	107,584
Dixie	22	521	895	Pasco	161	3,864	7,135
Duval	735	28,874	78,007	Pinellas	1,255	44,843	113,387
Escambia	235	8,664	25,773	Polk	473	20,310	49,146
Flagler	40	1,540	3,205	Putnam	70	3,626	9,824
Franklin	14	129	229	St. Johns	73	3,006	6,618
Gadsden	42	1,337	2,485	St. Lucie	118	2,535	5,176
Gilchrist	8	155	242	Santa Rosa	57	2,365	5,269
Hardee	13	239	353	Sarasota	351	8,246	20,459
Hendry	18	1,113	3,369	Seminole	374	9,560	24,675
Hernando	62	1,247	2,943	Sumter	31	561	1,280
Highlands	50	1,358	2,727	Taylor	36	1,827	5,329
Hillsborough	925	35,933	84,697	Volusia	368	11,916	28,179
Holmes	26	488	560	Wakulla	18	617	1,398
Indian River	113	2,113	4,958	Walton	17	1,098	1,761
Jackson	25	1,878	3,071	Washington	28	923	1,398
Jefferson	17	215	361	Multicounty 1/	137	933	2,804

See footnotes at end of table.   Continued . . .

Table 12.51. EMPLOYMENT: AVERAGE MONTHLY PRIVATE REPORTING UNITS, EMPLOYMENT
AND PAYROLL COVERED BY UNEMPLOYMENT COMPENSATION LAW IN THE STATE
AND COUNTIES OF FLORIDA, 1995 AND 1996 (Continued)

County	Number of reporting units	Number of employees	Payroll ($1,000)	County	Number of reporting units	Number of employees	Payroll ($1,000)
			Manufacturing industry, 1996 B/ (SIC codes 20-39)				
Florida	15,729	488,618	1,299,532	Lake	164	4,673	9,713
				Lee	393	6,719	15,560
Alachua	164	5,521	12,887	Leon	138	3,831	8,548
Baker	10	228	463	Levy	38	412	726
Bay	140	3,032	7,390	Liberty	16	295	520
Bradford	26	571	1,033	Madison	23	1,212	2,160
Brevard	461	26,018	87,147	Manatee	265	11,245	28,516
Broward	1,748	42,783	123,790	Marion	226	10,639	23,934
Calhoun	32	271	445	Martin	154	2,748	8,167
Charlotte	81	1,045	1,913	Monroe	85	552	1,028
Citrus	53	1,186	2,101	Nassau	64	1,964	6,651
Clay	78	1,658	3,662	Okaloosa	133	3,941	8,818
Collier	199	2,481	6,295	Okeechobee	20	203	425
Columbia	52	1,886	4,127	Orange	861	35,347	109,610
Dade	2,815	76,989	176,074	Osceola	80	1,466	5,187
De Soto	20	229	474	Palm Beach	914	28,843	106,291
Dixie	23	543	1,018	Pasco	177	3,974	7,576
Duval	756	29,589	82,012	Pinellas	1,267	45,367	117,410
Escambia	231	8,846	27,904	Polk	495	20,973	54,664
Flagler	38	1,655	3,831	Putnam	71	3,392	9,560
Franklin	14	131	216	St. Johns	81	3,163	7,501
Gadsden	44	1,408	2,660	St. Lucie	124	2,618	5,489
Gilchrist	10	179	283	Santa Rosa	60	2,430	5,441
Gulf	15	928	2,958	Sarasota	403	8,999	22,405
Hardee	15	249	382	Seminole	392	9,788	26,302
Hendry	19	1,155	3,596	Sumter	31	596	1,377
Hernando	67	1,318	3,160	Taylor	38	1,785	5,271
Highlands	52	1,387	2,970	Union	15	239	482
Hillsborough	959	35,772	86,491	Volusia	401	12,371	30,038
Holmes	27	445	528	Wakulla	18	589	1,381
Indian River	111	2,210	5,506	Walton	24	1,072	1,609
Jackson	28	1,729	2,846	Washington	26	894	1,378
Jefferson	17	178	361				
Lafayette	5	161	158	Multicounty 1/	190	1,117	3,772

A/ Revised.
B/ Preliminary.
1/ Reporting units without a fixed location within the state or of unknown county location.
Note: See Table 12.50 for a list of industries. Private employment. Only counties for which data are disclosed are shown. Detail may not add to totals due to disclosure editing and/or rounding. See Tables 23.70, 23.71, 23.72, 23.73, and 23.74 for public employment data.

Source: State of Florida, Department of Labor and Employment Security, Bureau of Labor Market Information, "Employment and Wages" (ES-202), unpublished data.

University of Florida   **Bureau of Economic and Business Research**

Table 12.52. FOOD PRODUCTS: AVERAGE MONTHLY PRIVATE REPORTING UNITS, EMPLOYMENT
AND PAYROLL COVERED BY UNEMPLOYMENT COMPENSATION LAW IN THE STATE
AND COUNTIES OF FLORIDA, 1996

County	Number of reporting units	Number of employees	Payroll ($1,000)	County	Number of reporting units	Number of employees	Payroll ($1,000)
			Food and kindred products (SIC code 20)				
Florida	694	41,283	105,247	Martin	5	197	478
				Monroe	6	46	54
Alachua	4	58	50	Okaloosa	4	9	16
Bay	6	61	83	Okeechobee	5	84	208
Brevard	7	87	117	Orange	32	2,791	7,710
Broward	41	1,881	4,396	Osceola	5	160	496
Clay	7	241	470	Palm Beach	40	3,064	9,796
Collier	3	30	41	Pinellas	32	992	2,361
Columbia	3	53	88	Polk	42	4,477	12,301
Dade	153	5,280	13,293	Putnam	4	66	104
Duval	31	4,004	12,035	St. Johns	5	95	54
Escambia	6	83	142	St. Lucie	9	522	1,089
Franklin	5	77	106	Sarasota	6	77	131
Hendry	8	1,044	3,396	Seminole	13	294	844
Hillsborough	64	4,287	10,810	Volusia	16	411	762
Lake	15	1,405	3,351	Wakulla	5	150	93
Lee	19	535	1,192				
Marion	11	225	492	Multicounty 1/	11	41	126
			Meat products (SIC code 201)				
Florida	77	5,852	10,146	Dade	21	655	1,170
Broward	4	77	143	Hillsborough	5	645	2,149
			Canned, frozen, and preserved fruits, vegetables, and food specialties (SIC code 203)				
Florida	114	10,965	29,788	Lake	8	1,260	3,131
				Orange	6	281	906
Dade	18	393	719	Pinellas	5	306	921
Hendry	3	416	1,037	Polk	19	2,379	7,364
Hillsborough	10	285	670	St. Lucie	5	477	989
			Bakery products (SIC code 205)				
Florida	103	5,755	13,508	Orange	7	666	1,730
				Palm Beach	5	322	831
Broward	8	150	264	Pinellas	4	31	29
Dade	35	1,652	4,289	Polk	4	1,182	2,845
Duval	6	545	1,360	Sarasota	3	74	129
Hillsborough	13	486	788				

1/ Reporting units without a fixed location within the state or of unknown county
location.
Note: Private employment. For a list of three-digit code industries included see
Table 12.50. Data are preliminary. Only counties for which data are disclosed are
shown. Detail may not add to totals due to disclosure editing and/or rounding. See
Tables 23.70, 23.71, 23.72, 23.73, and 23.74 for public employment data.
Source: State of Florida, Department of Labor and Employment Security, Bureau of
Labor Market Information, "Employment and Wages" (ES-202), unpublished data.

Table 12.53. TOBACCO, TEXTILE, AND APPAREL PRODUCTS: AVERAGE MONTHLY PRIVATE REPORTING UNITS, EMPLOYMENT, AND PAYROLL COVERED BY UNEMPLOYMENT COMPENSATION LAW IN THE STATE AND COUNTIES OF FLORIDA, 1996

County	Number of reporting units	Number of employees	Payroll ($1,000)	County	Number of reporting units	Number of employees	Payroll ($1,000)
			Tobacco products (SIC code 21)				
Florida	21	1,537	3,947	Hillsborough	6	629	1,403
Dade	13	156	314				
			Textile mill products (SIC code 22)				
Florida	188	4,085	8,623	Hillsborough	7	15	27
				Lee	3	6	8
Alachua	3	37	49	Orange	8	63	100
Broward	25	367	1,067	Palm Beach	8	20	114
Dade	73	2,612	5,133	Pinellas	8	94	118
Duval	5	35	67	Sarasota	5	56	87
Escambia	4	236	536				
			Apparel and other textile products (SIC code 23)				
Florida	1,090	25,944	38,071	Manatee	17	604	1,078
				Marion	7	64	96
Brevard	23	123	188	Martin	17	93	166
Broward	128	1,341	2,308	Monroe	6	34	61
Charlotte	5	17	28	Okaloosa	15	633	786
Collier	9	63	106	Orange	28	240	352
Dade	490	13,361	18,243	Palm Beach	43	464	1,132
Duval	22	277	420	Pasco	9	120	141
Gadsden	6	115	155	Pinellas	64	1,176	1,973
Hillsborough	30	2,350	4,265	Polk	15	402	587
Holmes	3	281	249	Sarasota	21	111	166
Indian River	8	69	86	Seminole	18	301	523
Lake	7	41	48	Volusia	17	116	200
Lee	31	252	439				
Leon	5	182	265	Multicounty 1/	5	10	30

1/ Reporting units without a fixed location within the state or of unknown county location.

Note: Private employment. For a list of three-digit code industries included see Table 12.50. Data are preliminary. Only counties for which data are disclosed are shown. Detail may not add to totals due to disclosure editing and/or rounding. See Tables 23.70, 23.71, 23.72, 23.73, and 23.74 for public employment data.

Source: State of Florida, Department of Labor and Employment Security, Bureau of Labor Market Information, "Employment and Wages" (ES-202), unpublished data.

University of Florida   **Bureau of Economic and Business Research**

Table 12.57. LUMBER AND WOOD PRODUCTS, EXCEPT FURNITURE: AVERAGE MONTHLY PRIVATE REPORTING UNITS, EMPLOYMENT, AND PAYROLL COVERED BY UNEMPLOYMENT COMPENSATION LAW IN THE STATE AND COUNTIES OF FLORIDA, 1996

County	Number of reporting units	Number of employees	Payroll ($1,000)	County	Number of reporting units	Number of employees	Payroll ($1,000)

Lumber and wood products, except furniture (SIC code 24)

County	Number of reporting units	Number of employees	Payroll ($1,000)	County	Number of reporting units	Number of employees	Payroll ($1,000)
Florida	1,127	21,566	43,212	Lake	22	687	1,251
				Lee	25	261	492
Alachua	11	316	613	Leon	7	84	183
Baker	4	16	22	Levy	22	239	353
Bay	22	314	611	Liberty	15	288	514
Bradford	8	98	222	Madison	17	308	610
Brevard	17	458	755	Manatee	11	207	393
Broward	59	767	1,679	Marion	34	1,490	3,075
Calhoun	26	190	352	Martin	4	31	54
Charlotte	8	98	130	Monroe	4	19	32
Clay	14	71	136	Nassau	30	210	430
Collier	16	116	252	Okaloosa	15	142	286
Columbia	22	780	1,580	Orange	32	832	1,720
Dade	94	1,703	3,098	Osceola	6	112	178
DeSoto	5	29	80	Palm Beach	47	807	2,049
Dixie	20	517	990	Pasco	17	242	373
Duval	40	912	2,265	Pinellas	50	1,125	2,463
Escambia	25	194	319	Polk	36	2,072	4,397
Flagler	6	154	290	Putnam	26	623	1,603
Franklin	4	33	72	St. Lucie	7	233	415
Gilchrist	5	69	106	Santa Rosa	11	108	195
Gulf	4	31	71	Sarasota	15	196	381
Hardee	7	77	128	Seminole	18	242	459
Hernando	7	132	221	Sumter	8	78	107
Hillsborough	66	1,440	2,658	Taylor	16	336	791
Holmes	16	68	111	Union	12	223	457
Indian River	7	58	89	Volusia	38	474	803
Jackson	10	250	476	Washington	16	137	203
Jefferson	8	112	269				

Note: Private employment. For a list of three-digit code industries included see Table 12.50. Data are preliminary. Only counties for which data are disclosed are shown. Detail may not add to totals due to disclosure editing and/or rounding. See Tables 23.70, 23.71, 23.72, 23.73, and 23.74 for public employment data.

Source: State of Florida, Department of Labor and Employment Security, Bureau of Labor Market Information, "Employment and Wages" (ES-202), unpublished data.

Table 12.63. FURNITURE AND FIXTURES AND PAPER AND ALLIED PRODUCTS: AVERAGE
MONTHLY PRIVATE REPORTING UNITS, EMPLOYMENT, AND PAYROLL COVERED
BY UNEMPLOYMENT COMPENSATION LAW IN THE STATE AND COUNTIES
OF FLORIDA, 1996

County	Number of reporting units	Number of employees	Payroll ($1,000)	County	Number of reporting units	Number of employees	Payroll ($1,000)
			Furniture and fixtures (SIC code 25)				
Florida	559	12,900	24,335	Lee	11	94	158
				Manatee	11	323	623
Alachua	3	5	3	Marion	14	378	593
Bay	7	51	74	Martin	6	45	100
Brevard	10	129	227	Orange	27	865	1,765
Broward	80	2,040	4,760	Palm Beach	34	386	856
Charlotte	4	16	13	Pasco	6	88	153
Collier	8	130	205	Pinellas	35	736	1,324
Dade	174	3,419	6,009	Polk	12	412	639
Duval	26	626	1,238	Sarasota	14	208	406
Escambia	3	221	313	Seminole	16	528	1,076
Hillsborough	22	784	1,551	Volusia	8	54	73
Lake	3	26	44				
			Household furniture (SIC code 251)				
Florida	279	6,646	11,733	Manatee	7	314	609
				Marion	5	299	483
Broward	42	480	1,179	Orange	16	534	1,090
Collier	4	15	25	Palm Beach	18	287	638
Dade	100	1,761	2,680	Pasco	3	15	15
Duval	12	221	543	Pinellas	10	304	500
Escambia	3	221	313	Polk	8	387	599
Hillsborough	6	180	426	Sarasota	9	117	218
Lee	4	51	85	Seminole	6	129	220
			Paper and allied products (SIC code 26)				
Florida	215	14,241	45,917	Marion	5	146	295
				Nassau	3	1,032	3,876
Broward	16	420	1,168	Orange	16	557	1,628
Dade	42	1,865	4,083	Palm Beach	5	31	86
Duval	36	2,532	7,795	Pasco	3	76	184
Escambia	4	1,540	6,438	Pinellas	9	302	592
Hillsborough	22	1,028	2,832	Polk	9	570	1,669
Lee	3	22	405	Sarasota	3	44	94

Note: Private employment. For a list of three-digit code industries included see
Table 12.50. Data are preliminary. Only counties for which data are disclosed are
shown. Detail may not add to totals due to disclosure editing and/or rounding. See
Tables 23.70, 23.71, 23.72, 23.73, and 23.74 for public employment data.

Source: State of Florida, Department of Labor and Employment Security, Bureau of
Labor Market Information, "Employment and Wages" (ES-202), unpublished data.

Table 12.64. PRINTING, PUBLISHING, AND ALLIED INDUSTRIES: AVERAGE MONTHLY PRIVATE REPORTING UNITS, EMPLOYMENT, AND PAYROLL COVERED BY UNEMPLOYMENT COMPENSATION LAW IN THE STATE AND COUNTIES OF FLORIDA, 1996

County	Number of reporting units	Number of employees	Payroll ($1,000)	County	Number of reporting units	Number of employees	Payroll ($1,000)
\multicolumn{8}{c}{Printing, publishing, and allied industries (SIC code 27)}						
Florida	3,480	63,744	155,592	Marion	29	676	1,190
				Martin	33	574	1,278
Alachua	45	856	1,746	Monroe	21	177	336
Bay	18	374	713	Nassau	10	66	127
Brevard	76	1,335	3,196	Okaloosa	27	357	574
Broward	411	5,859	16,873	Okeechobee	4	44	70
Charlotte	19	332	590	Orange	242	5,881	16,531
Citrus	12	207	294	Osceola	19	170	320
Clay	19	212	379	Palm Beach	246	3,869	11,040
Collier	51	754	1,863	Pasco	35	341	622
Columbia	6	61	136	Pinellas	241	6,738	15,101
Dade	627	10,748	31,853	Polk	75	1,119	2,466
Duval	176	3,280	7,526	Putnam	4	111	247
Escambia	57	955	1,813	St. Johns	22	358	616
Flagler	4	28	56	St. Lucie	29	377	660
Hernando	16	206	469	Santa Rosa	11	124	209
Highlands	8	117	175	Sarasota	108	1,441	3,427
Hillsborough	224	8,431	17,204	Seminole	94	702	1,434
Indian River	28	369	923	Sumter	3	16	22
Lake	32	377	631	Taylor	4	23	28
Lee	102	1,334	2,842	Volusia	81	1,533	3,317
Leon	69	1,447	3,177				
Manatee	38	577	1,481	Multicounty 1/	56	467	926

1/ Reporting units without a fixed location within the state or of unknown county location.

Note: Private employment. For a list of three-digit code industries included see Table 12.50. Data are preliminary. Only counties for which data are disclosed are shown. Detail may not add to totals due to disclosure editing and/or rounding. See Tables 23.70, 23.71, 23.72, 23.73, and 23.74 for public employment data.

Source: State of Florida, Department of Labor and Employment Security, Bureau of Labor Market Information, "Employment and Wages" (ES-202), unpublished data.

Table 12.67. CHEMICALS AND ALLIED PRODUCTS: AVERAGE MONTHLY PRIVATE REPORTING
UNITS, EMPLOYMENT, AND PAYROLL COVERED BY UNEMPLOYMENT COMPENSATION
LAW IN THE STATE AND COUNTIES OF FLORIDA, 1996

County	Number of re- porting units	Number of em- ployees	Payroll ($1,000)	County	Number of re- porting units	Number of em- ployees	Payroll ($1,000)
			Chemicals and allied products (SIC code 28)				
Florida	534	19,916	69,397	Marion	4	90	290
				Martin	4	70	164
Alachua	7	311	887	Orange	30	576	1,870
Brevard	18	285	866	Osceola	3	12	11
Broward	41	550	1,399	Palm Beach	23	323	963
Collier	4	15	34	Pinellas	36	1,132	3,549
Dade	88	2,334	7,660	Polk	42	3,774	13,090
Duval	41	1,744	6,455	Putnam	4	28	76
Highlands	3	10	18	Santa Rosa	5	640	2,929
Hillsborough	58	1,995	6,804	Sarasota	12	105	418
Lake	7	123	247	Seminole	13	155	343
Lee	11	179	471	Volusia	12	568	1,399
Manatee	10	186	582	Multicounty 1/	17	237	1,457
			Drugs (SIC code 283)				
Florida	66	2,277	8,660	Hillsborough	5	41	177
				Orange	3	36	74
Broward	8	75	186	Pinellas	8	737	2,630
Dade	17	1,042	3,885				
			Soap, detergents, and cleaning preparations; perfumes, cosmetics, and other toilet preparations (SIC code 284)				
Florida	130	2,666	7,014	Hillsborough	13	275	660
				Orange	7	51	159
Brevard	6	70	113	Palm Beach	8	52	88
Broward	12	199	472	Pinellas	12	129	265
Dade	37	577	1,540	Polk	5	161	471
Duval	8	698	2,153	Seminole	4	23	33
			Agricultural chemicals (SIC code 287)				
Florida	88	6,623	22,800	Manatee	3	74	184
				Orange	5	156	542
Dade	3	54	125	Palm Beach	3	15	41
Hillsborough	13	1,387	5,082	Polk	23	3,134	10,889
Lake	3	85	172	Putnam	3	18	23
Lee	4	49	112				

1/ Reporting units without a fixed location within the state or of unknown county
location.
     Note: Private employment. For a list of three-digit code industries included see
Table 12.50. Data are preliminary. Only counties for which data are disclosed are
shown. Detail may not add to totals due to disclosure editing and/or rounding. See
Tables 23.70, 23.71, 23.72, 23.73, and 23.74 for public employment data.

     Source: State of Florida, Department of Labor and Employment Security, Bureau of
Labor Market Information, "Employment and Wages" (ES-202), unpublished data.

Table 12.70. PETROLEUM, RUBBER, PLASTICS, AND LEATHER PRODUCTS: AVERAGE MONTHLY PRIVATE REPORTING UNITS, EMPLOYMENT, AND PAYROLL COVERED BY UNEMPLOYMENT COMPENSATION LAW IN THE STATE AND COUNTIES OF FLORIDA, 1996

County	Number of reporting units	Number of employees	Payroll ($1,000)	County	Number of reporting units	Number of employees	Payroll ($1,000)
Petroleum refining and related industries (SIC code 29)							
Florida	63	1,667	4,659	Hillsborough	8	401	1,297
				Orange	4	82	155
Broward	7	373	1,124	Pinellas	4	47	130
Duval	6	213	620	Polk	5	47	107
Rubber and miscellaneous plastics products (SIC code 30)							
Florida	713	20,891	47,101	Marion	18	912	2,216
				Martin	6	59	359
Alachua	8	222	450	Okaloosa	6	114	196
Bay	5	113	152	Orange	44	1,966	5,106
Brevard	34	514	903	Osceola	9	367	2,610
Broward	86	1,994	4,212	Palm Beach	28	700	1,109
Collier	12	166	384	Pasco	4	76	110
Dade	97	3,737	7,567	Pinellas	64	2,253	5,045
Duval	35	1,034	2,593	Polk	40	1,078	2,018
Escambia	12	130	314	St. Johns	5	40	76
Hillsborough	47	1,098	2,548	St. Lucie	8	275	553
Indian River	7	113	196	Sarasota	22	1,638	3,778
Lake	7	217	469	Seminole	17	417	997
Lee	11	207	420	Volusia	28	583	1,141
Manatee	12	112	188				
Leather and leather products (SIC code 31)							
Florida	68	3,528	4,876	Highlands	3	18	21
				Palm Beach	8	63	105
Dade	5	11	29	Pinellas	6	538	692

Note: Private employment. For a list of three-digit code industries included see Table 12.50. Data are preliminary. Only counties for which data are disclosed are shown. Detail may not add to totals due to disclosure editing and/or rounding. See Tables 23.70, 23.71, 23.72, 23.73, and 23.74 for public employment data.

Source: State of Florida, Department of Labor and Employment Security, Bureau of Labor Market Information, "Employment and Wages" (ES-202), unpublished data.

Table 12.71. STONE, CLAY, GLASS, AND CONCRETE PRODUCTS: AVERAGE MONTHLY PRIVATE REPORTING UNITS, EMPLOYMENT, AND PAYROLL COVERED BY UNEMPLOYMENT COMPENSATION LAW IN THE STATE AND COUNTIES OF FLORIDA, 1996

County	Number of reporting units	Number of employees	Payroll ($1,000)	County	Number of reporting units	Number of employees	Payroll ($1,000)
Stone, clay, glass, and concrete products (SIC code 32)							
Florida	763	22,092	58,322	Leon	5	97	186
				Manatee	18	664	1,674
Alachua	12	208	440	Marion	17	319	690
Bay	5	127	315	Martin	10	232	583
Brevard	23	361	806	Monroe	6	84	185
Broward	78	1,842	4,598	Okaloosa	4	54	113
Charlotte	6	107	250	Orange	43	1,427	3,478
Citrus	10	131	259	Osceola	8	77	180
Collier	19	436	1,114	Palm Beach	52	1,761	7,535
Columbia	3	49	119	Pasco	18	337	694
Dade	94	2,982	7,232	Pinellas	31	582	1,541
Duval	33	2,450	5,983	Polk	24	1,152	3,320
Escambia	14	761	2,333	St. Johns	4	28	52
Flagler	3	46	95	St. Lucie	10	200	477
Gadsden	6	68	141	Santa Rosa	4	50	102
Hernando	8	297	1,028	Sarasota	32	592	1,380
Hillsborough	44	1,650	4,895	Seminole	18	300	670
Indian River	9	96	246	Sumter	5	34	68
Lake	11	713	1,522	Volusia	16	388	863
Lee	32	905	2,061				
Concrete, gypsum, and plaster products (SIC code 327)							
Florida	474	15,558	39,408	Manatee	11	152	330
				Marion	12	184	405
Alachua	10	181	390	Martin	7	143	391
Brevard	14	261	636	Monroe	5	81	183
Broward	38	1,492	3,809	Okaloosa	4	54	113
Charlotte	5	105	249	Orange	30	1,247	3,121
Citrus	7	119	244	Osceola	5	67	163
Collier	10	348	930	Palm Beach	27	1,002	3,048
Dade	53	1,958	4,665	Pasco	13	277	620
Duval	23	1,335	3,524	Pinellas	18	510	1,389
Escambia	10	362	767	Polk	16	463	1,041
Flagler	3	46	95	St. Johns	4	28	52
Hernando	7	243	885	St. Lucie	8	150	374
Hillsborough	24	1,364	4,146	Santa Rosa	3	46	95
Indian River	4	60	177	Sarasota	20	525	1,279
Lake	9	683	1,454	Seminole	9	164	400
Lee	18	825	1,935	Sumter	4	30	65
Leon	5	96	186	Volusia	10	323	754

Note: Private employment. For a list of three-digit code industries included see Table 12.50. Data are preliminary. Only counties for which data are disclosed are shown. Detail may not add to totals due to disclosure editing and/or rounding. See Tables 23.70, 23.71, 23.72, 23.73, and 23.74 for public employment data.

Source: State of Florida, Department of Labor and Employment Security, Bureau of Labor Market Information, "Employment and Wages" (ES-202), unpublished data.

University of Florida   **Bureau of Economic and Business Research**

Table 12.72. FABRICATED METAL PRODUCTS, EXCEPT MACHINERY AND TRANSPORTATION
EQUIPMENT: AVERAGE MONTHLY PRIVATE REPORTING UNITS, EMPLOYMENT, AND
PAYROLL COVERED BY UNEMPLOYMENT COMPENSATION LAW IN THE STATE
AND COUNTIES OF FLORIDA, 1996

County	Number of reporting units	Number of employees	Payroll ($1,000)	County	Number of reporting units	Number of employees	Payroll ($1,000)
			Fabricated metal products, except machinery and transportation equipment (SIC code 34)				
Florida	1,272	31,899	73,338	Manatee	31	1,015	2,421
				Marion	17	1,137	2,048
Alachua	8	520	1,582	Martin	10	63	116
Bay	12	375	855	Monroe	5	32	98
Brevard	46	913	2,138	Okaloosa	10	99	160
Broward	147	2,699	7,006	Orange	80	1,885	4,732
Charlotte	7	28	67	Osceola	6	75	147
Citrus	4	35	45	Palm Beach	70	960	2,241
Clay	7	204	511	Pasco	10	166	323
Collier	18	273	874	Pinellas	114	3,810	8,073
Dade	176	4,231	8,228	Polk	47	1,002	2,111
Duval	73	2,893	7,233	Putnam	6	162	368
Escambia	26	827	1,624	St. Lucie	11	169	427
Hernando	7	89	167	Santa Rosa	3	58	131
Highlands	9	37	59	Sarasota	36	1,332	3,311
Hillsborough	103	2,975	8,078	Seminole	43	832	1,867
Indian River	12	105	226	Taylor	6	217	354
Lake	7	215	496	Volusia	28	543	1,298
Lee	32	535	1,084				
Leon	13	437	989	Multicounty 1/	15	46	133
			Fabricated structural metal products (SIC code 344)				
Florida	638	16,083	33,767	Leon	5	71	134
				Manatee	16	314	715
Alachua	6	154	314	Marion	9	192	346
Bay	6	68	114	Martin	7	29	56
Brevard	16	258	628	Monroe	3	29	96
Broward	64	1,453	3,599	Okaloosa	5	20	40
Charlotte	4	17	47	Orange	36	823	1,984
Collier	11	58	91	Palm Beach	37	636	1,362
Dade	94	2,541	4,619	Pasco	5	48	108
Duval	48	1,936	4,100	Pinellas	48	1,910	3,394
Escambia	11	395	903	Polk	25	696	1,510
Hernando	5	48	103	Putnam	5	159	364
Hillsborough	57	1,442	3,554	Sarasota	16	442	845
Indian River	8	70	143	Seminole	24	567	1,137
Lake	3	137	330	Volusia	9	81	151
Lee	18	425	844	Multicounty 1/	6	22	88

1/ Reporting units without a fixed location within the state or of unknown county
location.
Note: Private employment. For a list of three-digit code industries included see
Table 12.50. Data are preliminary. Only counties for which data are disclosed are
shown. Detail may not add to totals due to disclosure editing and/or rounding. See
Tables 23.70, 23.71, 23.72, 23.73, and 23.74 for public employment data.
Source: State of Florida, Department of Labor and Employment Security, Bureau of
Labor Market Information, "Employment and Wages" (ES-202), unpublished data.

Table 12.74. INDUSTRIAL AND COMMERCIAL MACHINERY AND COMPUTER EQUIPMENT: AVERAGE
MONTHLY PRIVATE REPORTING UNITS, EMPLOYMENT, AND PAYROLL COVERED
BY UNEMPLOYMENT COMPENSATION LAW IN THE STATE AND COUNTIES
OF FLORIDA, 1996

County	Number of reporting units	Number of employees	Payroll ($1,000)	County	Number of reporting units	Number of employees	Payroll ($1,000)
				Industrial and commercial machinery and computer equipment (SIC code 35)			
Florida	1,618	37,466	110,813	Levy	3	5	6
				Manatee	42	1,040	2,810
Alachua	13	387	1,072	Marion	25	680	1,715
Bay	11	172	444	Martin	13	186	1,021
Brevard	49	1,740	3,874	Nassau	4	41	61
Broward	198	4,418	14,289	Okaloosa	13	154	345
Charlotte	12	203	437	Okeechobee	3	10	17
Citrus	4	28	38	Orange	92	4,361	16,033
Clay	10	196	421	Osceola	9	58	151
Collier	17	186	523	Palm Beach	89	2,497	11,136
Columbia	7	81	224	Pasco	25	403	952
Dade	194	3,336	7,447	Pinellas	224	5,197	16,867
Duval	81	2,043	5,425	Polk	75	2,061	5,210
Escambia	24	241	501	Putnam	4	34	55
Flagler	9	177	552	St. Johns	9	83	221
Hendry	6	23	48	St. Lucie	18	265	660
Hernando	5	24	84	Sarasota	46	618	1,870
Hillsborough	89	1,558	3,858	Seminole	35	1,059	2,856
Indian River	10	388	1,017	Volusia	53	1,272	3,022
Lake	16	204	428				
Lee	29	685	2,476	Multicounty 1/	15	47	139
				Computer and office equipment (SIC code 357)			
Florida	97	7,061	27,929	Orange	8	600	1,899
				Palm Beach	12	1,200	6,752
Brevard	8	1,228	2,677	Pinellas	15	1,916	7,873
Broward	17	1,175	5,820	Seminole	5	40	115
Dade	9	169	499				

1/ Reporting units without a fixed location within the state or of unknown county
location.
Note: Private employment. For a list of three-digit code industries included see
Table 12.50. Data are preliminary. Only counties for which data are disclosed are
shown. Detail may not add to totals due to disclosure editing and/or rounding. See
Tables 23.70, 23.71, 23.72, 23.73, and 23.74 for public employment data.

Source: State of Florida, Department of Labor and Employment Security, Bureau of
Labor Market Information, "Employment and Wages" (ES-202), unpublished data.

Table 12.77. ELECTRONIC AND OTHER ELECTRICAL EQUIPMENT AND COMPONENTS, EXCEPT
COMPUTER EQUIPMENT: AVERAGE MONTHLY PRIVATE REPORTING UNITS, EMPLOYMENT
AND PAYROLL COVERED BY UNEMPLOYMENT COMPENSATION LAW IN THE STATE
AND COUNTIES OF FLORIDA, 1996

County	Number of reporting units	Number of employees	Payroll ($1,000)	County	Number of reporting units	Number of employees	Payroll ($1,000)
	Electronic and other electrical equipment and components, except computer equipment (SIC code 36)						
Florida	750	61,885	195,157	Leon	8	951	2,563
				Manatee	12	1,366	3,295
Bay	5	45	120	Marion	11	297	622
Brevard	43	9,575	35,959	Martin	8	164	559
Broward	114	10,842	38,791	Okaloosa	7	518	1,251
Citrus	4	46	49	Orange	54	5,323	16,653
Collier	7	48	133	Palm Beach	56	6,474	25,625
Dade	80	2,079	3,840	Pasco	4	21	33
Duval	24	750	1,707	Pinellas	93	7,897	21,630
Flagler	3	399	929	Polk	9	385	821
Hernando	5	313	824	St. Lucie	5	51	106
Hillsborough	39	3,477	8,992	Sarasota	20	1,465	4,072
Indian River	3	20	86	Seminole	47	3,548	10,330
Lake	8	103	144	Volusia	20	2,361	6,922
Lee	15	663	1,427	Multicounty 1/	12	28	132
	Communications equipment (SIC code 366)						
Florida	140	21,341	77,518	Lee	3	23	32
				Leon	5	836	2,363
Brevard	13	893	2,625	Manatee	3	364	1,193
Broward	19	8,272	31,184	Orange	6	311	810
Dade	13	83	293	Palm Beach	11	4,386	19,015
Hillsborough	10	1,518	3,647	Sarasota	6	339	1,273
	Electronic components and accessories (SIC code 367)						
Florida	254	22,288	71,163	Okaloosa	7	517	1,242
				Orange	17	2,578	9,835
Broward	50	1,275	3,636	Palm Beach	26	1,860	6,087
Dade	11	413	768	Pinellas	43	3,390	8,563
Hillsborough	11	932	2,034	Seminole	16	633	1,490
Lee	6	471	977	Volusia	9	424	763

1/ Reporting units without a fixed location within the state or of unknown county
location.

Note: Private employment. For a list of three-digit code industries included see
Table 12.50. Data are preliminary. Only counties for which data are disclosed are
shown. Detail may not add to totals due to disclosure editing and/or rounding. See
Tables 23.70, 23.71, 23.72, 23.73, and 23.74 for public employment data.

Source: State of Florida, Department of Labor and Employment Security, Bureau of
Labor Market Information, "Employment and Wages" (ES-202), unpublished data.

Table 12.83. SHIP AND BOAT BUILDING: AVERAGE MONTHLY PRIVATE REPORTING UNITS EMPLOYMENT, AND PAYROLL COVERED BY UNEMPLOYMENT COMPENSATION LAW IN THE STATE AND COUNTIES OF FLORIDA, 1996

County	Number of reporting units	Number of em- ployees	Payroll ($1,000)	County	Number of reporting units	Number of em- ployees	Payroll ($1,000)
Ship and boat building and repairing (SIC code 373)							
Florida	599	14,836	33,168	Lee	24	249	511
				Martin	18	197	474
Alachua	8	661	1,274	Monroe	23	94	173
Bay	23	353	652	Okaloosa	7	22	37
Brevard	19	1,282	3,291	Orange	11	806	1,777
Broward	95	1,704	4,238	Pinellas	58	813	1,543
Charlotte	5	60	118	Polk	9	30	42
Collier	11	48	100	Putnam	4	57	104
Dade	84	1,399	2,975	St. Lucie	7	232	515
Duval	24	1,363	3,661	Seminole	4	48	101
Escambia	11	152	289	Walton	3	82	146
Hillsborough	20	681	1,800				

Note: See Note on Table 12.84.

Table 12.84. INSTRUMENTS AND RELATED PRODUCTS: AVERAGE MONTHLY PRIVATE REPORTING UNITS, EMPLOYMENT, AND PAYROLL COVERED BY UNEMPLOYMENT COMPENSATION LAW IN THE STATE AND COUNTIES OF FLORIDA, 1996

County	Number of reporting units	Number of em- ployees	Payroll ($1,000)	County	Number of reporting units	Number of em- ployees	Payroll ($1,000)
Instruments and related products (SIC code 38)							
Florida	539	36,614	111,266	Marion	7	1,122	3,555
				Martin	9	93	299
Alachua	15	223	497	Okaloosa	9	540	1,761
Bay	5	14	39	Orange	38	1,267	3,662
Brevard	25	3,088	11,445	Palm Beach	42	758	2,659
Broward	55	2,222	6,403	Pasco	5	61	95
Citrus	5	25	47	Pinellas	82	9,040	27,264
Collier	4	27	83	Polk	9	812	1,808
Dade	75	9,727	30,697	St. Lucie	5	134	259
Duval	21	2,138	7,820	Santa Rosa	6	59	132
Hillsborough	18	483	1,470	Sarasota	14	288	822
Lake	4	281	524	Seminole	16	364	784
Lee	11	567	1,199	Volusia	15	1,913	4,671
Leon	3	21	55				
Manatee	7	625	1,278	Multicounty 1/	9	34	152

1/ Reporting units without a fixed location within the state or of unknown county location.

Note: Private employment. For a list of three-digit code industries included see Table 12.50. Data are preliminary. Only counties for which data are disclosed are shown. Detail may not add to totals due to disclosure editing and/or rounding. See Tables 23.70, 23.71, 23.72, 23.73, and 23.74 for public employment data.

Source for Tables 12.83 and 12.84: State of Florida, Department of Labor and Employment Security, Bureau of Labor Market Information, "Employment and Wages" (ES-202), unpublished data.

University of Florida   **Bureau of Economic and Business Research**

Table 12.86. TRADE: VALUE OF FLORIDA PRODUCTS EXPORTED BY INDUSTRY IN FLORIDA 1994, 1995, AND 1996

Industry	Value ($1,000)			Percentage change	
				1994 to 1995	1995 to 1996
	1994	1995	1996		
Total	20,513,534	23,671,149	24,989,247	15.4	5.6
Industrial machinery, computer equipment	4,012,624	4,657,411	5,279,199	16.1	13.4
Electronic, electric equipment, excluding computer	3,173,170	3,599,897	3,984,891	13.4	10.7
Transportation equipment	2,836,382	2,858,726	3,351,812	0.8	17.2
Chemicals and allied products	2,600,922	3,354,043	3,023,756	29.0	-9.8
Instruments and related products	1,332,465	1,563,177	1,663,882	17.3	6.4
Food and kindred products	1,005,541	1,218,393	1,238,466	21.2	1.6
Paper and allied products	667,912	1,040,422	1,012,274	55.8	-2.7
Apparel and other textile products	1,023,109	973,212	976,619	-4.9	0.4
Fabricated metal products	521,324	553,211	587,962	6.1	6.3
Agricultural production, crops	543,937	606,573	558,295	11.5	-6.0
Rubber and miscellaneous plastics products	419,663	492,894	522,550	17.4	6.0
Primary metal industries	373,758	464,330	468,656	24.2	0.9
Miscellaneous manufacturing industries	367,425	450,428	407,189	22.6	-9.8
Textile mill products	284,136	281,568	277,691	-0.9	-1.4
Printing and publishing	196,348	185,701	201,376	-5.4	8.4
Stone, clay, and glass products	157,643	169,069	189,575	7.2	12.1
Lumber and wood products	157,689	169,226	174,981	7.3	3.4
Scrap and waste	92,143	250,952	170,380	172.3	-32.1
Furniture and fixtures	145,946	161,648	160,330	10.8	-0.8
Special classification provisions, NEC	86,391	83,751	133,545	-3.1	59.5
Used or second-hand merchandise	121,222	100,948	130,437	-16.7	29.2
Leather and leather products	67,290	92,419	127,586	37.3	38.1
Fishing, hunting, and trapping	72,663	95,958	86,565	32.1	-9.8
Petroleum and coal products	80,797	59,829	79,698	-26.0	33.2
Canadian, nonCanadian goods returned to Canada	50,297	44,620	53,793	-11.3	20.8
Forestry	37,203	32,624	39,464	-12.3	21.0
Agricultural production, livestock	37,403	42,834	39,439	14.5	-7.9
Tobacco manufactures	32,027	34,346	28,460	7.2	-17.1
Nonmetallic minerals, except fuels	13,909	27,961	15,454	101.0	-44.7
Metal mining	1,392	3,270	3,169	135.0	-3.1
Oil and gas extraction	800	1,590	1,666	98.7	4.8
Bituminous coal and lignite mining	3	121	87	3,679.1	-28.7

NEC Not elsewhere classified.

Source: Enterprise Florida, Department of Research, unpublished trade data prepared by the University of Massachusetts Institute for Social and Economic Research (MISER).

University of Florida   **Bureau of Economic and Business Research**

Table 12.87. TRADE: VALUE OF FLORIDA PRODUCTS EXPORTED
BY SELECTED DESTINATIONS, 1994, 1995, AND 1996

	Value ($1,000)			Percentage change	
				1994 to	1995 to
Location 1/	1994	1995	1996	1995	1996
Total	20,513,534	23,671,149	24,989,247	15.4	5.6
Brazil	1,412,017	2,027,351	2,623,377	43.6	29.4
Canada	1,568,673	1,710,089	1,791,246	9.0	4.7
Colombia	1,259,752	1,477,825	1,454,554	17.3	-1.5
Dominican Republic	996,689	1,058,666	1,102,327	6.2	4.1
Venezuela	882,020	1,064,976	1,096,087	20.7	2.9
Argentina	1,058,326	866,881	1,017,915	-18.1	17.4
Japan	748,471	951,402	889,246	27.1	-6.5
Mexico	844,148	569,707	750,447	-32.5	31.7
United Kingdom	549,410	617,174	686,244	12.3	11.2
Paraguay	593,543	730,304	684,162	23.0	-6.3
Chile	568,751	588,042	624,955	3.4	6.3
China (Mainland)	694,174	1,059,799	611,597	52.7	-42.3
France	351,679	442,108	562,478	25.7	27.2
Australia	346,704	407,309	509,546	17.5	25.1
Germany	380,589	478,999	487,096	25.9	1.7
Peru	432,257	477,438	486,481	10.5	1.9
Guatemala	480,626	515,603	478,742	7.3	-7.1
Netherlands	302,338	396,302	417,914	31.1	5.5
Honduras	386,128	376,921	415,081	-2.4	10.1
Panama	464,860	442,445	414,159	-4.8	-6.4
Bahamas	407,553	389,785	396,140	-4.4	1.6
Costa Rica	405,926	382,410	385,718	-5.8	0.9
Italy	175,722	237,317	373,845	35.1	57.5
Jamaica	285,093	378,930	373,068	32.9	-1.5
Ecuador	441,813	432,032	353,420	-2.2	-18.2
Singapore	196,480	267,605	284,610	36.2	6.4
Spain	153,414	297,820	277,819	94.1	-6.7
Saudi Arabia	111,843	123,355	255,293	10.3	107.0
El Salvador	240,220	259,014	254,186	7.8	-1.9
Korea, Republic of	177,082	280,726	248,266	58.5	-11.6
Belgium	148,738	230,807	245,327	55.2	6.3
Haiti	84,595	246,423	241,950	191.3	-1.8
Netherlands Antilles	196,427	200,560	225,473	2.1	12.4
Hong Kong	169,290	250,092	212,372	47.7	-15.1
Uruguay	95,018	124,300	178,565	30.8	43.7
Israel	119,454	127,585	174,238	6.8	36.6
China (Taiwan)	171,204	130,100	157,976	-24.0	21.4
Finland	41,593	55,797	151,321	34.1	171.2
Cayman Islands	107,356	113,173	133,970	5.4	18.4
Switzerland	80,161	115,206	133,147	43.7	15.6
Trinidad and Tobago	83,149	120,381	132,493	44.8	10.1
Pakistan	77,098	56,996	125,921	-26.1	120.9
Russia	46,724	117,917	124,978	152.4	6.0
Kuwait	23,683	61,635	124,148	160.2	101.4
India	129,885	253,310	115,818	95.0	-54.3
Republic of South Africa	74,187	115,823	110,390	56.1	-4.7
Nicaragua	74,907	89,761	108,172	19.8	20.5
Other locations	1,873,762	1,952,944	1,986,965	4.2	1.7

1/ Countries, areas, and agencies receiving an annual value of shipments in 1996
of $100,000,000 or more are shown separately.
Source: Enterprise Florida, Department of Research, unpublished trade data prepared by the University of Massachusetts Institute for Social and Economic Research
(MISER).

TRANSPORTATION

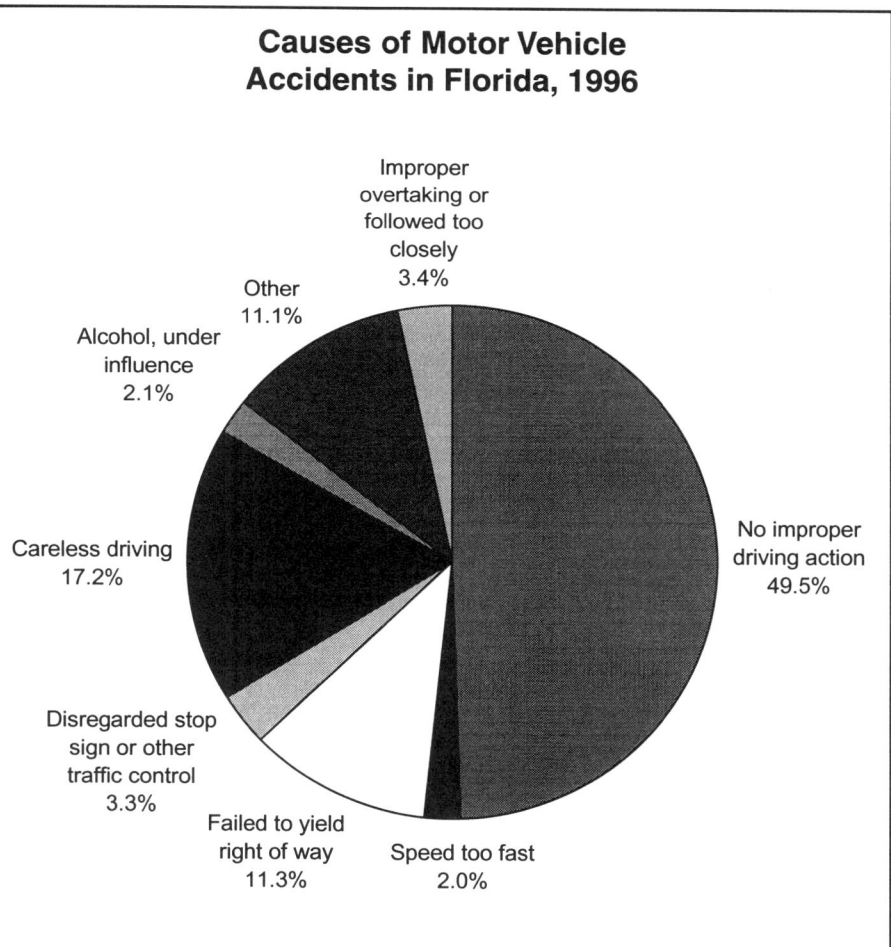

**Causes of Motor Vehicle
Accidents in Florida, 1996**

Improper
overtaking or
followed too
closely
3.4%

Other
11.1%

Alcohol, under
influence
2.1%

Careless driving
17.2%

No improper
driving action
49.5%

Disregarded stop
sign or other
traffic control
3.3%

Failed to yield
right of way
11.3%

Speed too fast
2.0%

Source: Table 13.46

SECTION 13.00
TRANSPORTATION

TABLES LISTED BY MAJOR HEADINGS

University of Florida   Bureau of Economic and Business Research

SECTION 13.00
TRANSPORTATION
(Continued)

TABLES LISTED BY MAJOR HEADINGS

Table 13.01. TRANSPORTATION, COMMUNICATIONS, AND PUBLIC UTILITIES
ESTABLISHMENTS, REVENUE, AND ANNUAL PAYROLL BY KIND
OF BUSINESS IN FLORIDA, 1992

SIC code	Kind of business	Number of establish- ments	Revenue ($1,000)	Annual payroll ($1,000)
41	Passenger transportation	720	474,152	165,895
411	Local and suburban	353	266,790	101,973
412	Taxicabs	123	57,192	15,353
413	Intercity and rural bus service	30	42,597	18,018
414	Charter bus service	75	81,268	22,378
415	School buses	139	26,305	8,173
417	Bus terminal and service facilities	0	0	0
42	Motor freight transportation and warehousing	4,247	5,927,195	1,540,605
421	Trucking and courier services, except air	3,579	5,550,333	1,461,909
422	Public warehousing and storage	663	(D)	(D)
423	Trucking terminal facilities	5	(D)	(D)
44	Water transportation	980	4,013,806	535,141
441, 2	Deep sea foreign and domestic freight	52	1,071,455	77,612
443, 4	Other water transportation of freight	14	31,094	5,769
448	Water transportation of passengers	200	2,215,908	198,858
449	Services incidental to water transportation	714	695,349	252,902
45 pt.	Air transportation 1/	782	2,576,518	552,906
451 pt.	Scheduled and air courier services 1/	317	1,503,994	272,129
452	Nonscheduled	144	348,528	59,106
458	Airport terminal services	321	723,996	221,671
46	Pipelines, except natural gas	13	27,382	3,856
47	Transportation services	3,953	1,657,528	523,497
472	Arrangement of passenger transportation	2,732	953,208	287,656
473	Freight shipping services	1,069	574,929	190,297
474	Rental of railroad cars	0	0	0
478	Miscellaneous services incidental to transportation	155	129,391	45,544
48	Communications	1,979	12,585,982	2,390,833
481	Telephone	1,216	10,014,974	1,858,007
482	Telegraph	29	24,545	3,690
483	Radio and television broadcasting	448	1,098,434	323,659
484	Cable and other pay television	204	1,365,139	189,399
489	Communication services, NEC	82	82,890	16,078
49	Electric, gas, and sanitary services	718	11,325,998	1,615,058
491	Electric services	178	9,730,288	1,323,847
492	Gas production and distribution	57	402,366	58,818
493	Combination utility services	29	172,307	31,766
494	Water supply	141	134,997	31,948
495	Sanitary services	303	881,254	167,800
496, 7	Miscellaneous utility services	10	4,786	879

NEC Not elsewhere classified.
(D) Data withheld to avoid disclosure of information about individual firms.
1/ Excludes large, certificated passenger carrier reporting to the Office of Airline Statistics.

Source: U.S., Department of Commerce, Bureau of the Census, *1992 Census of Transportation, Communications, and Public Utilities.* Geographic Area Series UC92-A-1
Summary.

University of Florida   **Bureau of Economic and Business Research**

Table 13.16. ROADS AND HIGHWAYS: EXISTING MILEAGE OF PUBLIC ROADS AND HIGHWAYS BY JURISDICTION IN FLORIDA, DECEMBER 1992 THROUGH 1995

Jurisdiction	1992	1993	1994	1995
Total	110,640	112,808	113,478	113,778
Rural mileage	62,003	63,630	65,084	65,440
Under state control 1/	7,592	7,509	6,995	6,976
Under local control	54,305	54,815	56,780	57,155
County roads	54,115	54,616	56,587	56,969
Other jurisdictions 2/	190	199	193	186
Under federal control 3/	106	1,306	1,309	1,309
Urban mileage	48,637	49,178	48,394	48,338
Under state control 1/	4,278	4,423	4,926	4,945
Under local control	44,359	44,755	43,468	43,393
County roads	1,403	1,861	2,914	2,992
Other jurisdictions 2/	42,956	42,894	40,554	40,401

1/ Includes state highway agency, state park, state toll, and other state agency roadways.

2/ Includes mileage not identified by ownership. Contains mainly municipal mileage for urban summaries.

3/ Includes mileage in federal parks, forests, and reservations that are not part of the state and local highway system.

Table 13.17. ROADS AND HIGHWAYS: EXISTING MILEAGE OF PUBLIC ROADS AND HIGHWAYS BY FUNCTIONAL SYSTEM OF HIGHWAY AND BY PAVEMENT CONDITION IN FLORIDA DECEMBER 31, 1995

Function	Total existing mileage	Pavement conditions				
		Poor	Medi- ocre	Fair	Good	Very good
Total	113,778	(NA)	(NA)	(NA)	(NA)	(NA)
Rural	65,440	(NA)	(NA)	(NA)	(NA)	(NA)
Interstate	946	1	3	640	268	34
Other principal arterial	3,443	47	228	2,193	884	91
Minor arterial	2,838	3	244	1,810	720	61
Major collector	4,483	0	627	1,766	952	1,138
Minor collector	4,816	(NA)	(NA)	(NA)	(NA)	(NA)
Local	48,914	(NA)	(NA)	(NA)	(NA)	(NA)
Urban	48,338	(NA)	(NA)	(NA)	(NA)	(NA)
Interstate	526	0	10	383	121	12
Other freeways and expressways	389	6	7	318	55	3
Other principal arterial	2,655	94	234	1,722	545	60
Minor arterial	2,997	122	338	1,040	826	671
Collector	6,045	529	821	2,667	1,253	775
Local	35,726	(NA)	(NA)	(NA)	(NA)	(NA)

(NA) Not available.

Source for Tables 13.16 and 13.17: U.S., Department of Transportation, Federal Highway Administration, *Highway Statistics, 1995,* and previous editions.

University of Florida   **Bureau of Economic and Business Research**

Table 13.20. ROADS AND HIGHWAYS: RECEIPTS AND DISBURSEMENTS FOR ROADS
AND HIGHWAYS BY ALL UNITS OF GOVERNMENT IN FLORIDA
FISCAL YEARS 1991-92 THROUGH 1993-94

(in thousands of dollars)

Item	1991-92	1992-93	1993-94
Total receipts	3,739,425	4,325,929	4,321,218
Bond proceeds, par value 1/	327,072	524,099	188,025
Total current income	3,412,353	3,801,830	4,133,193
Highway-user tax revenue 2/	2,150,937	2,389,815	2,608,216
Federal agencies	476,513	610,710	777,828
State agencies	1,284,409	1,369,634	1,359,705
Local	390,015	409,471	470,683
Road and crossing tolls	271,632	297,509	338,745
Appropriations from general fund	211,418	330,176	341,405
Property taxes	154,848	82,603	94,025
Other imposts	349,595	430,791	479,324
Miscellaneous receipts 3/	273,923	270,936	271,478
Total disbursements 4/	3,858,336	4,346,445	4,404,934
Bond retirement, par value 1/	153,681	374,748	196,938
Total direct expenditure	3,704,655	3,971,697	4,207,996
Capital outlay	2,122,527	2,320,608	2,527,825
State-administered highways	1,440,203	1,675,637	1,800,280
Locally administered roads	681,642	642,870	723,850
Federal roads and unclassified	682	2,101	3,695
Maintenance	649,505	694,500	756,663
State-administered highways	282,812	311,412	375,355
Locally administered roads	366,381	382,882	381,108
Federal roads and unclassified	312	206	200
Administration and miscellaneous	428,351	376,608	394,313
Highway law enforcement and safety	271,756	309,105	310,212
Interest	232,516	270,876	218,983

1/ Excludes short-term notes and refunding bond issues.
2/ Excludes amounts allocated for collection expenses and nonhighway purposes.
3/ Includes interest earned on Highway Trust Fund reserves.
4/ Disbursements are classified by system on which expended, rather than by ex-
pending agencies; capital outlay on county and other local rural roads includes expenditures from federal, state, and local funds.
Note: This table presents combined summaries of the highway finances of all government agencies in net amounts; duplications that would otherwise have resulted from
interfund or intergovernmental transfers have been removed. Data may include estimates.

Source: U.S., Department of Transportation, Federal Highway Administration, *Highway Statistics, 1995,* and previous editions.

Table 13.21. ROAD AND HIGHWAY BRIDGES: NUMBER BY FUNCTIONAL SYSTEM
OF HIGHWAY IN FLORIDA AND THE UNITED STATES, 1994 AND 1995

Functional system	Florida		United States	
	1994	1995	1994	1995
Total	10,836	10,852	577,481	578,770
Rural	5,973	5,773	456,806	456,251
Interstate	830	821	28,768	28,757
Other principal arterial	1,312	1,250	35,102	34,404
Minor arterial	739	741	37,514	38,350
Major collector	683	621	98,306	97,441
Minor collector	665	648	49,392	47,955
Local	1,744	1,692	207,724	209,344
Urban	4,863	5,079	120,675	122,519
Interstate	949	955	25,682	26,122
Other freeways and expressways	713	854	13,649	14,197
Other principal arterial	1,021	973	23,371	23,451
Minor arterial	648	727	19,782	20,202
Collector	456	475	14,644	14,574
Local	1,076	1,095	23,547	23,973

Note: Highway bridges greater than or equal to 20 feet. Because functional system has been estimated or assigned in some cases, data may not be precise.
Source: U.S., Department of Transportation, Federal Highway Administration, *Highway Statistics, 1995,* and previous edition.

Table 13.22. ROADS AND HIGHWAYS: PERCENTAGE DISTRIBUTION OF ANNUAL VEHICLE
DISTANCE TRAVELED BY FUNCTIONAL SYSTEM OF HIGHWAY AND
BY VEHICLE TYPE IN FLORIDA, 1995

Type of vehicle	Rural			Urban			
	Inter-state	Other major arte-rial	Minor arte-rial	Inter-state	Other freeways and express-ways	Other prin-cipal arte-rial	Minor arte-rial
All motor vehicles	100.0	100.0	100.0	100.0	100.0	100.0	100.0
Passenger cars and other 2-axle, 4-tire vehicles	80.4	87.4	90.5	91.0	94.6	93.9	94.3
Passenger cars	69.3	72.4	74.9	80.5	83.9	83.5	84.2
Motorcycles	0.3	0.4	0.4	0.4	0.3	0.7	0.6
Buses	0.6	0.5	0.5	0.5	0.4	0.5	0.5
Other 2-axle, 4-tire vehicles 1/	11.1	15.0	15.6	10.4	10.7	10.4	10.2
Single unit 2-axle, 6-tire or more and combination trucks	18.6	11.6	8.6	8.1	4.8	5.0	4.6
Single unit 2-axle, 6-tire or more trucks	3.5	4.3	3.2	3.1	2.8	2.4	2.3
Combination trucks							
Single trailer	14.4	7.0	5.1	4.7	1.8	2.4	2.1
Multiple trailer	0.8	0.3	0.2	0.3	0.2	0.2	0.2

1/ Excludes passenger cars. Includes vans, pickup trucks, and sport/utility vehicles.
Source: U.S., Department of Transportation, Federal Highway Administration, *Highway Statistics, 1995.*

University of Florida   **Bureau of Economic and Business Research**

Table 13.29. ROADS AND HIGHWAYS: ESTIMATED ANNUAL VEHICLE MILES OF TRAVEL
BY FUNCTIONAL SYSTEM OF HIGHWAY IN FLORIDA, 1994 AND 1995

(in millions of miles)

Functional system of highway	Total 1994 A/	Total 1995	Rural 1994 A/	Rural 1995	Urban 1994 A/	Urban 1995
Total	121,989	127,801	31,727	32,403	90,262	95,398
Interstate	24,001	24,923	9,502	9,685	14,499	15,238
Other freeways and expressways	5,978	6,227	0	0	5,978	6,227
Other principal arterial	37,237	38,294	10,518	10,978	26,719	27,316
Minor arterial	18,512	20,092	4,311	4,385	14,201	15,707
Collector	13,375	15,386	3,860	3,784	9,515	11,602
Local	22,886	22,879	3,536	3,571	19,350	19,308

A/ Revised.
Note: Data are estimated highway travel based on traffic counts taken at selected
highway locations.

Table 13.30. MOTOR VEHICLE REGISTRATIONS: NUMBER BY TYPE OF VEHICLE IN FLORIDA
1978 THROUGH 1995

(rounded to hundreds, except where indicated)

Year	All motor vehicles 1/	Percentage change from previous year	Automobiles 2/	Buses	Trucks 2/	Motorcycles
1978	7,068.9	9.7	5,738.0	26.1	1,151.8	152.9
1979	7,519.4	6.4	6,011.0	28.2	1,259.7	220.5
1980	7,833.0	4.2	6,196.6	29.3	1,387.6	219.5
1981	8,194.1	4.6	6,484.6	30.4	1,459.1	220.0
1982	8,561.0	4.5	6,753.6	32.2	1,548.8	226.4
1983	9,041.0	5.6	7,113.9	33.3	1,661.3	232.5
1984	9,635.1	6.6	7,552.4	34.4	1,807.4	240.9
1985	10,096.8	4.8	7,849.1	35.8	1,979.9	232.0
1986	10,591.2	4.9	8,263.3	34.2	2,064.0	229.7
1987	10,903.1	2.9	8,521.6	34.8	2,127.1	219.5
1988	11,183.1	2.6	8,713.2	35.5	2,234.9	199.5
1989	11,410.8	2.0	8,972.7	36.2	2,197.9	203.9
1990	11,155.6	-2.2	8,694.9	36.8	2,218.1	205.8
1991	10,176.1	-8.8	7,910.3	37.5	2,032.3	196.0
1992	10,426.1	2.5	8,131.4	38.1	2,062.8	193.7
1993	10,358.4	-0.6	8,072.5	38.8	2,058.3	188.8
1994	10,429.2	0.7	7,519.2	39.6	2,693.0	177.4
1995	10,559.5	1.2	7,594.9	40.3	2,734.3	190.1

1/ Includes motorcycles.
2/ Beginning in 1994, personal passenger vans, passenger minivans, and utility-
type vehicles were classified by the source as trucks rather than automobiles.
Therefore, caution should be used when making comparisons to earlier years.
Note: Excludes vehicles owned by the military service.
Source for Tables 13.29 and 13.30: U.S., Department of Transportation, Federal
Highway Administration, *Highway Statistics, 1995,* and previous editions.

Table 13.32. MOTOR VEHICLE TAGS: TOTAL TAGS AND PASSENGER CAR TAGS SOLD AND
REVENUE COLLECTED IN THE STATE AND COUNTIES OF FLORIDA
FISCAL YEAR 1995-96

County	Total tags Number	Per-centage change from 1994-95	Passenger car tags Number	Per-centage change from 1994-95	Total revenue ($1,000)
Florida 1/	17,671,987	4.1	7,537,147	2.2	412,798
Alachua	227,891	3.2	110,447	2.5	4,401
Baker	25,474	6.2	9,827	5.7	566
Bay	170,250	3.6	83,059	1.9	3,662
Bradford	31,705	-0.6	11,259	1.6	634
Brevard	544,495	2.1	264,947	-0.5	10,856
Broward	1,368,241	0.0	747,301	2.4	30,319
Calhoun	11,492	5.9	4,425	0.1	249
Charlotte	162,510	3.2	81,153	0.1	3,445
Citrus	136,378	2.9	60,258	2.1	2,828
Clay	154,525	3.0	71,111	2.6	3,163
Collier	245,419	3.6	132,351	3.6	5,978
Columbia	66,223	11.1	23,653	5.8	1,305
Dade	2,426,683	10.1	1,286,815	10.5	57,164
De Soto	35,692	2.3	11,296	0.9	786
Dixie	13,036	2.8	4,271	1.2	327
Duval	878,118	4.8	399,663	4.0	18,158
Escambia	295,953	5.0	157,869	4.4	6,605
Flagler	51,073	5.2	27,025	4.5	1,107
Franklin	10,645	12.2	4,410	5.3	237
Gadsden	36,616	3.8	16,975	4.2	820
Gilchrist	14,407	7.1	4,995	9.5	339
Glades	6,520	3.2	2,157	0.5	170
Gulf	14,131	3.3	6,322	2.9	337
Hamilton	10,573	7.4	4,195	3.7	235
Hardee	29,795	-1.4	9,361	-0.3	691
Hendry	42,205	4.7	14,629	2.1	1,162
Hernando	127,819	0.5	66,065	1.1	2,707
Highlands	111,323	5.1	43,885	1.5	2,284
Hillsborough	1,110,028	5.9	491,011	5.3	25,221
Holmes	17,228	1.6	6,879	1.3	400
Indian River	137,380	3.2	65,807	1.8	2,827
Jackson	53,272	2.9	20,733	0.8	1,056
Jefferson	12,456	1.2	4,974	-1.2	301
Lafayette	6,242	4.1	2,181	6.8	142
Lake	250,027	2.7	99,582	3.6	5,164
Lee	507,420	5.7	237,679	6.5	10,750
Leon	258,302	1.5	124,606	1.1	5,068
Levy	40,033	6.5	14,216	5.2	1,001

See footnotes at end of table.   Continued . . .

Table 13.32. MOTOR VEHICLE TAGS: TOTAL TAGS AND PASSENGER CAR TAGS SOLD AND
REVENUE COLLECTED IN THE STATE AND COUNTIES OF FLORIDA
FISCAL YEAR 1995-96 (Continued)

County	Total tags Number	Per-centage change from 1994-95	Passenger car tags Number	Per-centage change from 1994-95	Total revenue ($1,000)
Liberty	6,855	5.5	2,209	2.9	187
Madison	17,678	2.8	6,965	2.2	403
Manatee	572,811	10.0	275,277	6.5	14,360
Marion	309,378	3.0	127,393	1.3	6,626
Martin	161,657	0.6	83,551	2.9	3,654
Monroe	104,178	4.6	46,769	1.6	2,246
Nassau	58,114	5.0	25,429	4.9	1,289
Okaloosa	213,865	0.0	103,686	-0.4	4,171
Okeechobee	45,221	-0.1	14,513	0.0	1,101
Orange	1,011,850	2.8	481,869	1.5	23,168
Osceola	176,639	3.0	79,472	3.3	3,344
Palm Beach	959,198	1.6	585,484	1.3	24,522
Pasco	419,247	3.0	185,810	1.4	8,423
Pinellas	1,045,377	3.4	518,992	3.6	20,395
Polk	573,172	2.5	232,397	0.9	13,005
Putnam	78,005	-1.7	30,528	0.1	1,653
St. Johns	126,825	5.2	65,310	4.7	2,783
St. Lucie	213,283	3.8	96,795	3.1	4,368
Santa Rosa	120,443	8.8	54,271	5.2	2,434
Sarasota	404,060	5.4	210,626	3.2	8,507
Seminole	431,875	2.6	211,178	1.8	8,512
Sumter	42,916	3.0	16,214	2.9	986
Suwannee	40,026	0.1	13,116	0.9	841
Taylor	22,541	0.5	7,801	1.4	490
Union	11,173	3.1	3,796	8.3	297
Volusia	506,065	4.0	234,967	3.0	10,005
Wakulla	19,056	6.7	7,079	7.3	448
Walton	29,976	6.9	12,868	6.6	659
Washington	18,526	7.6	7,420	4.3	417
Office agency	31,330	-11.0	7,199	-31.0	1,106
DHSMV 2/	181,361	-11.2	0	0.0	194
Motor carrier service	60,872	6.8	0	0.0	29,808

1/ Details may not add to totals due to reporting practices involving tags outside
the computer system and refunds.
2/ Sales made by the Department of Highway Safety and Motor Vehicles district offices.
Note: See Table 2.36 for mobile home and recreational vehicle tag sales.

Source: State of Florida, Department of Highway Safety and Motor Vehicles, *Revenue Report, July 1, 1995 through June 30, 1996.*

University of Florida   **Bureau of Economic and Business Research**

Table 13.33. DRIVER LICENSES: NUMBER ISSUED BY TYPE AND BY AGE OF DRIVER
IN FLORIDA, JANUARY 1, 1997

Age	Re-strict-ed	Oper-ator	Chauf-feur	Com-mer-cial	Age	Re-strict-ed	Oper-ator	Chauf-feur	Com-mer-cial
Total	295,867	10,631,574	978,159	437,998	45	1,879	181,668	25,431	12,043
					46	1,836	175,084	24,068	11,223
15	49,283	135	0	0	47	1,675	173,630	23,399	10,982
16	46,825	59,678	11	0	48	1,577	174,674	23,179	10,738
17	28,576	101,969	77	0	49	1,411	182,108	23,615	10,972
18	16,588	129,989	370	66	50	1,444	165,644	21,423	10,087
19	12,558	150,394	1,129	255	51	1,236	139,078	18,179	8,594
20	10,872	156,889	1,833	621	52	1,212	140,321	18,057	8,696
21	10,300	168,811	2,930	1,359	53	1,130	145,839	18,305	8,921
22	10,098	182,731	4,055	2,579	54	1,159	142,236	17,685	8,154
23	7,426	184,315	5,467	3,734	55	967	125,763	15,618	7,468
24	6,312	198,942	7,361	5,407	56	964	122,050	15,191	6,974
25	5,826	223,444	10,330	7,144	57	898	117,414	14,482	6,473
26	5,181	232,503	13,088	8,397	58	838	118,527	14,130	6,432
27	4,598	222,575	14,606	8,893	59	770	114,362	13,364	5,817
28	4,416	215,374	16,643	9,850	60	701	113,002	12,935	5,499
29	4,178	215,222	18,172	10,406	61	630	112,263	12,270	4,940
30	4,106	218,527	20,716	11,516	62	588	111,660	12,084	4,463
31	4,138	225,445	22,916	12,498	63	508	109,748	11,339	3,820
32	4,008	238,263	25,990	13,692	64	482	116,769	11,616	3,642
33	3,884	239,167	27,384	14,275	65	470	116,531	10,930	3,125
34	3,647	237,892	28,586	14,505	66	486	123,856	11,438	2,799
35	3,195	236,287	29,253	15,076	67	420	121,458	10,501	2,205
36	3,161	233,258	29,851	15,039	68	397	125,993	10,427	1,763
37	3,039	225,813	29,914	14,580	69	387	125,903	10,138	1,455
38	2,883	221,756	29,644	14,375	70	317	123,640	9,194	1,119
39	2,659	219,827	29,762	14,700	71	308	121,771	8,429	874
40	2,538	212,984	29,283	14,614	72	274	122,706	7,770	627
41	2,445	205,366	28,601	13,897	73	244	116,036	6,507	529
42	2,353	200,751	28,622	13,454	74	228	111,918	6,033	399
43	2,172	193,045	27,286	12,765	75	167	110,474	5,422	330
44	1,992	188,761	26,607	12,380	76+	1,007	789,335	24,513	758

Note: Data are essentially an inventory of current licenses as of January 1,
1997, according to the records of the Florida Department of Highway Safety and Motor
Vehicles. Figures do not include temporary permits.

Source: State of Florida, Department of Highway Safety and Motor Vehicles, Division of Driver Licenses, unpublished data.

University of Florida   **Bureau of Economic and Business Research**

Table 13.34. DRIVER LICENSES: NUMBER ISSUED BY COUNTY OF DRIVER'S MAILING ADDRESS AND BY SEX OF LICENSE HOLDER IN THE STATE AND COUNTIES OF FLORIDA JANUARY 1, 1997

County of driver's mailing address	Male	Female	County of driver's mailing address	Male	Female
Florida	6,322,595	6,021,003	Lake	80,739	80,849
			Lee	174,480	169,443
Alachua	80,939	79,884	Leon	84,258	85,929
Baker	7,094	7,044	Levy	11,827	11,481
Bay	64,846	63,063	Liberty	1,980	1,911
Bradford	8,228	8,154	Madison	5,910	5,874
Brevard	203,668	194,673	Manatee	97,472	97,166
Broward	634,609	598,097	Marion	101,066	101,612
Calhoun	3,913	3,931	Martin	54,286	51,877
Charlotte	57,825	58,065	Monroe	49,047	36,786
Citrus	49,166	48,114	Nassau	23,452	22,255
Clay	53,682	52,371	Okaloosa	73,490	70,930
Collier	94,619	85,722	Okeechobee	15,849	13,481
Columbia	17,763	17,994	Orange	352,372	330,458
Dade	877,140	756,979	Osceola	66,502	60,995
De Soto	10,177	8,991	Palm Beach	455,301	438,062
Dixie	4,606	4,331	Pasco	137,220	136,468
Duval	280,916	286,306	Pinellas	376,391	383,619
Escambia	116,224	114,912	Polk	178,365	174,675
Flagler	18,273	18,006	Putnam	25,455	24,521
Franklin	3,812	3,676	St. Johns	46,084	45,676
Gadsden	14,526	14,460	St. Lucie	74,856	71,752
Gilchrist	4,136	4,011	Santa Rosa	44,410	43,401
Glades	2,288	1,947	Sarasota	141,010	145,086
Gulf	5,103	5,006	Seminole	137,167	135,360
Hamilton	3,957	3,971	Sumter	14,202	14,016
Hardee	9,977	8,006	Suwannee	12,368	12,128
Hendry	13,982	10,707	Taylor	6,872	6,895
Hernando	53,125	53,301	Union	3,109	3,086
Highlands	34,810	33,583	Volusia	184,539	178,287
Hillsborough	375,331	363,964	Wakulla	6,835	6,678
Holmes	6,576	6,351	Walton	12,285	11,832
Indian River	49,087	48,616	Washington	7,530	7,445
Jackson	16,276	16,532	Unknown county 1/	20,475	18,145
Jefferson	4,359	4,320	Out-of-state 2/	62,667	36,139
Lafayette	1,691	1,597			

1/ Licenses mailed to addresses which do not permit specification of county. Also includes licenses with incorrect or unknown zip codes.

2/ Licenses mailed to out-of-state addresses.

Note: Data are essentially an inventory of current licenses as of January 1, 1997, according to the records of the Florida Department of Highway Safety and Motor Vehicles. Figures include restricted, operator, chauffeur, and commercial licenses. Figures do not include temporary permits.

Source: State of Florida, Department of Highway Safety and Motor Vehicles, Division of Driver Licenses, unpublished data.

Table 13.35. EMPLOYMENT: AVERAGE MONTHLY PRIVATE REPORTING UNITS, EMPLOYMENT
AND PAYROLL COVERED BY UNEMPLOYMENT COMPENSATION LAW
BY TRANSPORTATION INDUSTRY IN FLORIDA, 1996

SIC code	Industry	Number of reporting units	Number of employees	Payroll ($1,000)
41	Passenger transportation	858	14,835	24,281
411	Local and suburban passenger transportation	496	9,243	16,210
412	Taxicabs	118	1,437	2,347
413	Intercity and rural bus transportation	34	820	1,449
414	Bus charter service	82	2,079	3,193
415	School buses	117	1,221	1,028
417	Terminal and service facilities for motor vehicle passenger transportation	12	35	55
42	Motor freight transportation and warehousing	5,024	59,704	134,102
421	Trucking and courier services, except air	4,300	53,480	122,051
422	Public warehousing and storage	710	6,141	11,850
423	Terminal and joint terminal maintenance facilities for motor freight transportation	15	84	202
44	Water transportation	1,106	20,715	51,418
441	Deep sea foreign transportation of freight	28	1,199	4,384
442	Deep sea domestic transportation of freight	19	1,437	5,189
444	Water transportation of freight, NEC	18	637	1,779
448	Water transportation of passengers	117	5,883	15,172
449	Services incidental to water transportation	924	11,560	24,895
45	Air transportation	1,205	68,899	173,974
451	Air transportation, scheduled, and air courier services	488	50,165	137,567
452	Air transportation, nonscheduled	224	5,221	12,942
458	Airports, flying fields, and airport terminal services	494	13,513	23,465
47	Transportation services	4,563	33,245	68,738
472	Arrangement of passenger transportation	2,674	18,691	34,949
473	Arrangement of transportation of freight and cargo	1,672	11,447	29,338
474	Rental of railroad cars	5	79	191
478	Miscellaneous services incidental to transportation	212	3,029	4,260

NEC Not elsewhere classified.
Note: Private employment. Data are preliminary. Detail may not add to totals due
to disclosure editing and/or rounding. See Tables 23.70, 23.71, 23.72, 23.73, and
23.74 for public employment data.

Source: State of Florida, Department of Labor and Employment Security, Bureau of
Labor Market Information, "Employment and Wages" (ES-202), unpublished data.

University of Florida   **Bureau of Economic and Business Research**

Table 13.36. TRANSPORTATION AND PUBLIC UTILITIES: AVERAGE MONTHLY PRIVATE
REPORTING UNITS, EMPLOYMENT, AND PAYROLL COVERED BY UNEMPLOYMENT
COMPENSATION LAW IN THE STATE AND COUNTIES OF FLORIDA, 1996

County	Number of reporting units	Number of employees	Payroll ($1,000)	County	Number of reporting units	Number of employees	Payroll ($1,000)

Transportation and public utilities (SIC codes 40-49)

County	Number of reporting units	Number of employees	Payroll ($1,000)	County	Number of reporting units	Number of employees	Payroll ($1,000)
Florida	15,569	305,494	838,694	Lake	133	2,114	5,545
				Lee	386	6,482	14,653
Alachua	129	2,237	5,553	Leon	163	3,410	9,400
Baker	21	156	400	Levy	23	330	632
Bay	160	2,214	5,215	Liberty	14	77	134
Bradford	18	166	454	Madison	19	124	288
Brevard	320	4,516	11,427	Manatee	154	1,650	3,998
Broward	1,608	30,050	81,372	Marion	208	2,610	6,673
Charlotte	72	943	2,247	Martin	141	1,725	4,879
Citrus	97	1,896	7,464	Monroe	159	1,716	3,564
Clay	75	965	2,614	Nassau	65	411	996
Collier	226	2,230	5,238	Okaloosa	146	1,887	4,593
Columbia	48	616	1,614	Okeechobee	30	230	525
Dade	3,464	79,087	227,997	Orange	1,030	29,987	79,565
De Soto	23	116	176	Osceola	99	713	1,359
Dixie	19	72	107	Palm Beach	942	15,317	47,665
Duval	944	27,841	71,230	Pasco	197	2,252	5,249
Escambia	293	5,299	14,553	Pinellas	679	13,508	37,037
Flagler	27	211	507	Polk	449	8,440	20,295
Franklin	20	110	221	Putnam	44	471	1,269
Gadsden	26	256	601	St. Johns	85	603	1,279
Gilchrist	6	23	68	St. Lucie	121	2,719	9,328
Gulf	14	280	658	Santa Rosa	72	996	2,461
Hamilton	11	158	343	Sarasota	284	3,573	9,271
Hardee	16	126	293	Seminole	260	5,488	16,240
Hendry	26	413	548	Sumter	31	392	1,160
Hernando	72	911	1,955	Suwannee	37	381	870
Highlands	63	632	1,482	Taylor	18	110	274
Hillsborough	934	27,526	83,361	Union	17	346	617
Holmes	15	82	181	Volusia	290	3,340	8,111
Indian River	83	676	1,341	Wakulla	15	115	255
Jackson	36	353	827	Walton	32	466	997
Jefferson	8	102	283	Washington	15	282	812
Lafayette	5	25	48	Multicounty 1/	322	2,677	7,684

1/ Reporting units without a fixed location within the state or of unknown county
location.

Note: See Table 13.35 for a list of industries. Private employment. Only counties for which data are disclosed are shown. Detail may not add to totals due to disclosure editing and/or rounding. See Tables 23.70, 23.71, 23.72, 23.73, and 23.74 for public employment data.

Source: State of Florida, Department of Labor and Employment Security, Bureau of Labor Market Information, "Employment and Wages" (ES-202), unpublished data.

University of Florida   **Bureau of Economic and Business Research**

Table 13.37. PASSENGER TRANSPORTATION AND MOTOR FREIGHT TRANSPORTATION AND WAREHOUSING: AVERAGE MONTHLY PRIVATE REPORTING UNITS, EMPLOYMENT AND PAYROLL COVERED BY UNEMPLOYMENT COMPENSATION LAW IN THE STATE AND COUNTIES OF FLORIDA, 1996

County	Number of reporting units	Number of employees	Payroll ($1,000)	County	Number of reporting units	Number of employees	Payroll ($1,000)
			Passenger transportation (SIC code 41)				
Florida	858	14,835	24,281	Marion	13	68	96
				Martin	3	24	31
Alachua	10	60	83	Monroe	16	183	299
Brevard	21	292	465	Okaloosa	4	9	7
Broward	78	1,694	2,707	Orange	74	2,602	4,662
Charlotte	6	76	123	Palm Beach	59	847	1,645
Citrus	4	19	20	Pasco	11	137	164
Collier	9	76	83	Pinellas	45	1,200	1,975
Dade	141	2,481	4,759	Polk	15	172	197
Duval	137	2,270	3,059	Putnam	3	53	81
Escambia	14	247	338	St. John	6	42	42
Hernando	7	16	13	St. Lucie	11	110	136
Hillsborough	25	435	709	Sarasota	18	96	109
Lake	5	123	254	Seminole	12	111	165
Lee	23	204	261	Suwanee	3	17	19
Leon	10	161	246	Volusia	16	441	771
Manatee	7	50	79	Multicounty 1/	9	67	86
			Motor freight transportation and warehousing (SIC code 42)				
Florida	5,024	59,704	134,102	Highlands	23	154	242
				Hillsborough	345	5,177	12,138
Alachua	48	661	1,391	Holmes	9	30	35
Baker	12	54	87	Indian River	28	144	287
Bay	58	486	881	Jackson	19	53	82
Bradford	13	124	271	Lafayette	4	18	23
Brevard	102	971	1,946	Lake	58	480	959
Broward	438	3,560	7,926	Lee	121	921	1,906
Charlotte	16	77	109	Leon	58	742	1,490
Citrus	46	188	258	Levy	13	162	215
Clay	34	160	280	Liberty	11	38	51
Collier	66	238	435	Madison	8	18	22
Columbia	32	200	399	Manatee	55	550	1,055
Dade	786	8,451	19,904	Marion	113	1,434	3,479
De Soto	13	49	63	Martin	39	723	1,886
Dixie	7	23	52	Monroe	20	194	401
Duval	396	9,380	24,916	Nassau	31	103	222
Escambia	143	1,154	2,066	Okaloosa	37	423	778
Flagler	8	29	51	Okeechobee	17	103	223
Franklin	4	7	8	Orange	347	5,750	12,596
Gadsden	12	72	111	Osceola	28	88	117
Gilchrist	3	5	5	Palm Beach	287	3,206	6,684
Gulf	4	18	24	Pasco	84	932	1,855
Hamilton	5	75	171	Pinellas	168	1,643	3,237
Hardee	9	18	27	Polk	253	5,788	13,108
Hendry	13	164	162	Putnam	19	137	203
Hernando	28	313	592	St. Johns	20	138	179

See footnotes at end of table.   Continued . . .

Table 13.37. PASSENGER TRANSPORTATION AND MOTOR FREIGHT TRANSPORTATION AND
WAREHOUSING: AVERAGE MONTHLY PRIVATE REPORTING UNITS, EMPLOYMENT
AND PAYROLL COVERED BY UNEMPLOYMENT COMPENSATION LAW IN THE
STATE AND COUNTIES OF FLORIDA, 1996 (Continued)

County	Number of reporting units	Number of employees	Payroll ($1,000)	County	Number of reporting units	Number of employees	Payroll ($1,000)

Motor freight transportation and warehousing (SIC code 42) (Continued)

County	Number of reporting units	Number of employees	Payroll ($1,000)	County	Number of reporting units	Number of employees	Payroll ($1,000)
St. Lucie	46	241	491	Taylor	5	10	15
Santa Rosa	24	98	119	Union	14	326	589
Sarasota	73	578	1,118	Volusia	108	670	1,254
Seminole	78	428	796	Wakulla	5	37	73
Sumter	20	115	246	Walton	11	41	74
Suwannee	20	109	163	Washington	5	18	33
				Multicounty 1/	99	1,222	3,136

1/ Reporting units without a fixed location within the state or of unknown county
location.
   Note: Private employment. For a list of three-digit code industries included see
Table 13.35. Data are preliminary. Only counties for which data are disclosed are
shown. Detail may not add to totals due to disclosure editing and/or rounding. See
Tables 23.70, 23.71, 23.72, 23.73, and 23.74 for public employment data.

Table 13.38. WATER AND AIR TRANSPORTATION AND TRANSPORTATION SERVICES: AVERAGE
MONTHLY PRIVATE REPORTING UNITS, EMPLOYMENT, AND PAYROLL COVERED
BY COMPENSATION LAW IN THE STATE AND COUNTIES
OF FLORIDA, 1996

County	Number of reporting units	Number of employees	Payroll ($1,000)	County	Number of reporting units	Number of employees	Payroll ($1,000)

Water transportation (SIC code 44)

County	Number of reporting units	Number of employees	Payroll ($1,000)	County	Number of reporting units	Number of employees	Payroll ($1,000)
Florida	1,106	20,715	51,418	Lee	45	282	470
				Manatee	25	163	363
Bay	27	295	554	Martin	33	147	246
Brevard	32	529	976	Monroe	61	523	872
Broward	174	2,847	7,124	Okaloosa	23	99	134
Charlotte	6	49	69	Orange	5	16	28
Citrus	7	46	61	Palm Beach	79	394	898
Collier	32	295	577	Pasco	8	27	44
Dade	163	8,163	21,305	Pinellas	69	559	954
Dixie	4	16	14	Putnam	4	16	44
Duval	89	3,536	9,876	St. Johns	11	49	114
Escambia	25	335	579	St. Lucie	7	63	95
Flagler	5	21	26	Sarasota	17	126	220
Franklin	6	36	48	Seminole	8	92	159
Hendry	3	42	47	Volusia	21	117	168
Hillsborough	59	1,292	4,397	Wakulla	5	49	54
Lake	4	25	35	Multicounty 1/	16	32	87

See footnotes at end of table.   Continued . . .

Table 13.38. WATER AND AIR TRANSPORTATION AND TRANSPORTATION SERVICES: AVERAGE MONTHLY PRIVATE REPORTING UNITS, EMPLOYMENT, AND PAYROLL COVERED BY COMPENSATION LAW IN THE STATE AND COUNTIES OF FLORIDA, 1996 (Continued)

County	Number of re- porting units	Number of em- ployees	Payroll ($1,000)	County	Number of re- porting units	Number of em- ployees	Payroll ($1,000)
			Air transportation (SIC code 45)				
Florida	1,205	68,899	173,974	Manatee	7	128	281
				Marion	7	180	399
Alachua	8	283	766	Martin	10	96	214
Bay	12	226	453	Monroe	14	197	388
Brevard	23	688	1,596	Okaloosa	15	388	1,044
Broward	152	7,825	18,545	Orange	92	7,674	18,682
Charlotte	6	127	308	Osceola	6	44	65
Collier	15	287	675	Palm Beach	70	1,637	3,879
Dade	390	29,388	84,632	Pasco	7	120	223
Duval	47	4,606	8,611	Pinellas	37	1,418	2,948
Escambia	20	748	2,160	Polk	20	467	1,042
Highlands	9	62	133	St. Lucie	12	443	890
Hillsborough	53	6,550	15,410	Santa Rosa	6	310	866
Indian River	10	88	181	Sarasota	19	527	1,186
Lake	6	206	517	Seminole	14	760	1,540
Lee	23	1,653	2,376	Volusia	21	447	958
Leon	14	452	995	Multicounty 1/	31	393	799
			Transportation services (SIC code 47)				
Florida	4,563	33,245	68,738	Manatee	34	123	159
				Marion	23	77	137
Alachua	28	140	229	Martin	33	123	222
Bay	23	102	169	Monroe	22	100	136
Brevard	79	363	623	Nassau	10	41	84
Broward	507	4,155	8,978	Okaloosa	29	134	180
Charlotte	18	77	102	Okeechobee	5	15	14
Citrus	16	50	65	Orange	322	3,318	6,130
Clay	12	70	176	Osceola	41	320	496
Collier	58	234	391	Palm Beach	298	1,923	4,803
Dade	1,644	12,946	30,210	Pasco	45	149	210
Duval	153	1,382	3,169	Pinellas	225	2,081	3,014
Escambia	31	120	177	Polk	74	441	959
Flagler	5	20	27	Putnam	6	16	21
Hernando	21	82	96	St. Johns	23	62	125
Highlands	10	19	47	St. Lucie	23	116	167
Hillsborough	238	1,863	3,305	Santa Rosa	12	47	52
Indian River	22	76	108	Sarasota	86	453	890
Lake	29	131	207	Seminole	88	703	931
Lee	89	286	396	Volusia	68	307	432
Leon	24	151	254	Multicounty 1/	66	156	465

1/ Reporting units without a fixed location within the state or of unknown county location.

Note: Private employment. For a list of three-digit code industries included see Table 13.35. Data are preliminary. Only counties for which data are disclosed are shown. Detail may not add to totals due to disclosure editing and/or rounding. See Tables 23.70, 23.71, 23.72, 23.73, and 23.74 for public employment data.

Source for Tables 13.37 and 13.38: State of Florida, Department of Labor and Employment Security, Bureau of Labor Market Information, "Employment and Wages" (ES-202), unpublished data.

University of Florida					**Bureau of Economic and Business Research**

Table 13.40. MOTOR VEHICLE REGISTRATIONS: NUMBER OF OUT-OF-STATE VEHICLES
REGISTERED IN FLORIDA BY STATE OF PREVIOUS REGISTRATION
1992 THROUGH 1996

State in 1996 rank order	1992	1993	1994	1995	1996 Number	1996 Percentage of total
Total	359,198	382,452	403,095	479,275	478,842	100.0
New York	37,940	40,188	44,185	51,013	49,153	10.3
Georgia	31,727	33,314	35,120	45,040	46,924	9.8
New Jersey	23,020	23,357	24,982	27,896	27,332	5.7
Alabama	17,778	18,969	20,695	25,948	26,687	5.2
Ohio	17,418	19,217	19,929	24,341	24,811	5.2
Pennsylvania	16,269	17,836	18,714	23,032	23,049	4.8
Michigan	16,920	18,498	18,825	21,945	22,547	4.7
North Carolina	14,459	15,891	16,896	20,837	20,563	4.3
Virginia	14,747	15,030	16,331	19,998	19,906	3.5
Illinois	13,399	15,107	15,929	18,475	17,891	3.7
Texas	14,088	14,388	15,412	17,505	16,779	4.2
California	14,395	15,782	15,525	17,816	16,202	3.4
Tennessee	11,401	11,536	10,896	14,221	16,047	3.4
Massachusetts	13,777	14,095	13,686	15,232	13,745	2.9
South Carolina	9,254	9,978	10,772	12,677	12,518	2.6
Maryland	9,055	9,211	9,985	11,740	11,519	2.4
Indiana	7,908	9,064	9,471	11,211	10,879	2.3
Connecticut	9,210	9,516	9,545	10,995	10,397	2.2
Louisiana	4,568	5,169	5,220	6,217	6,894	1.3
Kentucky	4,529	4,967	5,239	6,358	6,324	1.4
Missouri	4,333	4,451	4,852	5,608	5,623	1.2
Wisconsin	3,915	4,345	4,567	5,379	5,571	1.2
Mississippi	3,224	3,323	3,897	4,562	5,005	1.0
Colorado	3,212	3,466	3,991	4,941	4,818	1.0
New Hampshire	3,693	4,048	3,983	4,684	4,490	0.9
Minnesota	2,547	2,983	3,046	3,667	3,842	0.7
Arizona	2,506	2,560	2,753	3,494	3,826	0.8
Maine	2,720	2,948	3,083	3,837	3,461	0.6
Oklahoma	2,075	2,414	3,391	3,090	3,097	0.6
West Virginia	2,366	2,373	2,559	2,872	2,976	0.8
Washington	1,753	1,962	2,121	2,523	2,859	0.6
Rhode Island	2,433	2,617	2,581	2,971	2,718	0.5
Arkansas	1,763	1,927	2,054	2,315	2,636	0.5
Iowa	1,764	1,986	1,955	2,573	2,393	0.6
Kansas	1,643	2,001	2,042	2,192	2,290	0.6
Other states	11,793	12,430	12,639	14,559	16,051	3.4
Other areas 1/	5,233	5,134	5,987	7,225	6,762	1.4
Special affidavit	363	371	237	286	257	0.1

1/ Includes Canada, Puerto Rico, other Caribbean islands, and other foreign countries.

Source: State of Florida, Department of Highway Safety and Motor Vehicles, Division of Motor Vehicles, unpublished data.

Table 13.41. MOTOR VEHICLE REGISTRATIONS: NUMBER OF OUT-OF-STATE VEHICLES
REGISTERED BY COUNTY OF REGISTRATION IN THE STATE AND COUNTIES
OF FLORIDA, 1995 AND 1996

County	1995	1996 Number	1996 Per-centage of total	County	1995	1996 Number	1996 Per-centage of total
Florida	479,275	478,842	100.0	Lafayette	109	167	A/
				Lake	7,024	7,051	1.5
Alachua	6,103	5,947	1.2	Lee	16,364	15,641	3.3
Baker	381	495	0.1	Leon	7,920	7,646	1.6
Bay	9,627	9,229	1.9	Levy	798	748	0.2
Bradford	602	542	0.1	Liberty	179	156	A/
Brevard	16,271	15,969	3.3	Madison	611	676	0.1
Broward	27,351	24,176	5.0	Manatee	11,473	10,857	2.3
Calhoun	252	260	0.1	Marion	9,669	9,806	2.0
Charlotte	5,849	5,922	1.2	Martin	4,874	4,478	0.9
Citrus	4,371	4,352	0.9	Monroe	4,655	4,233	0.9
Clay	5,061	5,277	1.1	Nassau	2,153	2,281	0.5
Collier	9,718	9,736	2.0	Okaloosa	11,814	11,810	2.5
Columbia	1,527	1,620	0.3	Okeechobee	1,148	1,152	0.2
Dade	41,911	42,854	8.9	Orange	27,357	29,848	6.2
De Soto	859	1,142	0.2	Osceola	5,851	6,156	1.3
Dixie	284	300	0.1	Palm Beach	27,934	27,775	5.8
Duval	25,004	27,185	5.7	Pasco	11,907	11,533	2.4
Escambia	17,200	18,273	3.8	Pinellas	27,603	26,189	5.5
Flagler	2,624	2,450	0.5	Polk	13,943	14,079	2.9
Franklin	393	388	0.1	Putnam	1,927	1,703	0.4
Gadsden	1,089	1,039	0.2	St. Johns	4,698	5,025	1.0
Gilchrist	294	296	0.1	St. Lucie	6,433	6,342	1.3
Glades	191	140	A/	Santa Rosa	5,986	6,481	1.4
Gulf	486	461	0.1	Sarasota	12,643	12,848	2.7
Hamilton	387	432	0.1	Seminole	12,143	11,760	2.5
Hardee	696	691	0.1	Sumter	1,346	1,608	0.3
Hendry	1,051	1,041	0.2	Suwannee	978	1,031	0.2
Hernando	4,109	3,875	0.8	Taylor	526	518	0.1
Highlands	2,933	3,018	0.6	Union	213	221	A/
Hillsborough	26,213	24,995	5.2	Volusia	16,041	15,894	3.3
Holmes	980	1,006	0.2	Wakulla	480	490	0.1
Indian River	3,868	4,185	0.9	Walton	1,416	1,397	0.3
Jackson	2,295	2,753	0.6	Washington	656	719	0.2
Jefferson	423	474	0.1				

A/ Less than 0.05 percent.

Source: State of Florida, Department of Highway Safety and Motor Vehicles, Division of Motor Vehicles, unpublished data.

Table 13.45. TRAFFIC STATISTICS: DRIVERS, VEHICLES, MILEAGE, ACCIDENTS, INJURIES
AND DEATHS IN FLORIDA, 1986 THROUGH 1996

Year	Licensed drivers	Registered vehicles	Vehicle miles (millions)	Acci- dents 1/	Nonfatal injuries	Deaths	Mileage death rate 2/
1986	9,924,110	11,651,253	87,325	242,381	219,352	2,874	3.3
1987	10,241,063	11,738,273	92,865	240,429	215,886	2,891	3.1
1988	10,648,019	11,997,948	105,030	256,543	230,738	3,152	3.0
1989	11,109,288	12,276,272	108,876	252,439	230,060	3,033	2.8
1990	11,612,402	12,465,790	109,997	216,245	214,208	2,951	2.7
1991	12,170,821 A/	11,184,146	113,484	195,312	195,122	2,523	2.2
1992	A/ 11,550,126	11,205,298	114,000	196,176	205,432	2,480	2.2
1993	11,767,409	11,159,938	119,768	199,039	212,454	2,719	2.3
1994	11,992,578	11,393,982	120,929	206,183	223,458	2,722	2.3
1995	12,019,156	12,062,731	127,800	228,589	233,900	2,847	2.2
1996	12,343,598	12,003,929	129,637	241,377	243,320	2,806	2.2

A/ Decrease reflects changes in accounting method.
1/ Statutory revisions in 1989 reduced the number of non-injury accidents required
be reported.
2/ The number of deaths per 100 million vehicle miles traveled.
Note: Some data may be revised. See Note on Table 13.47.

Table 13.46. MOTOR VEHICLE ACCIDENTS: NUMBER OF DRIVERS AND PEDESTRIANS ASSIGNED
A CONTRIBUTING CAUSE BY TYPE OF CIRCUMSTANCE IN FLORIDA, 1996

Cause of accident	All accidents		Fatal accidents		Injury accidents	
	Number	Percentage of total	Number	Percentage of total	Number	Percentage of total
Total	413,890	100.0	5,322	100.0	302,941	100.0
No improper driving action	204,952	49.5	1,905	35.8	144,708	47.8
Speed too fast	8,357	2.0	438	8.2	6,282	2.1
Failed to yield right of way	46,797	11.3	663	12.5	36,440	12.0
Disregarded stop sign	3,921	0.9	77	1.4	3,100	1.0
Disregarded other traffic control	9,762	2.4	121	2.3	7,833	2.6
Drove left of center	1,937	0.5	146	2.7	1,413	0.5
Improper overtaking	6,959	1.7	103	1.9	5,077	1.7
Followed too closely	7,266	1.8	10	0.2	5,528	1.8
Alcohol, under influence	8,850	2.1	236	4.4	4,903	1.6
Careless driving	71,183	17.2	749	14.1	54,755	18.1
Mechanical defect	2,469	0.6	40	0.8	1,790	0.6
Other	41,437	10.0	834	15.7	31,112	10.3

Note: See Note on Table 13.47.

Source for Tables 13.45 and 13.46: State of Florida, Department of Highway Safety
and Motor Vehicles, Office of Management and Planning Services, *Florida Traffic Crash
Facts, 1996.*

University of Florida   **Bureau of Economic and Business Research**

Table 13.47. MOTOR VEHICLE ACCIDENTS: NUMBER OF ACCIDENTS AND PERSONS INVOLVED
BY TYPE OF ACCIDENT IN FLORIDA, 1996

	Number of accidents			
Type of accident	Total	Fatal	Nonfatal injury	Property damage
Total	241,377	2,550	149,565	89,282
Motor vehicle in transport	167,725	1,139	110,891	55,695
Fixed object	26,366	420	12,842	13,104
Other object	650	1	274	375
Parked motor vehicle	11,698	14	1,193	10,491
Pedestrian	7,508	526	6,781	201
Bicyclist	5,304	88	4,852	364
Moped	79	7	62	10
Overturning	4,141	134	3,200	807
Noncollison	6,626	132	4,065	2,429
Motor vehicle on other roadway	517	7	342	188
Animal	479	3	297	179
Railway train	57	7	23	27
Other and not stated	10,227	72	4,743	5,412

	Number of persons			
		Injured		
	Total killed	Incapac- itating injury	Non- incapac- itating or possible injury	No in- jury 1/
Total	2,806	31,870	211,450	369,970
Motor vehicle in transport	1,296	21,733	171,753	308,245
Fixed object	468	3,626	13,883	16,292
Other object	1	30	339	931
Parked motor vehicle	16	194	1,333	9,109
Pedestrian	534	2,007	5,357	8,765
Bicyclist	88	899	4,201	6,485
Moped	7	15	60	111
Overturning	149	1,140	3,587	1,813
Noncollison	147	1,176	4,342	4,686
Motor vehicle on other roadway	9	48	572	907
Animal	4	63	323	360
Railway train	11	7	21	112
Other and not stated	76	932	5,679	12,154

1/ Drivers only.
Note: Legally reportable accidents are those involving death, bodily injury, or
one or more of the following circumstances: (1) driver leaves the accident scene
where death, injury, or property damage has occurred; (2) driver is under the influence of alcohol or drugs; and, (3) a wrecker is required to remove an inoperative vehicle.

Source: State of Florida, Department of Highway Safety and Motor Vehicles, Office
of Management and Planning Services, *Florida Traffic Crash Facts, 1996.*

Table 13.48. MOTOR VEHICLE ACCIDENTS: DRIVERS AND MOTOR VEHICLES INVOLVED
IN ACCIDENTS BY AGE, SEX, AND RESIDENCE OF DRIVER AND BY TYPE
OF MOTOR VEHICLE IN FLORIDA, 1996

Item	All accidents	Fatal accidents	Injury accidents
Drivers involved in accidents, total 1/	384,652	1,553	158,595
Age and sex			
15 and under	3,443	34	2,616
16	7,906	26	3,233
17	9,954	27	4,067
18	11,217	39	4,594
19	11,088	29	4,690
20	10,065	32	4,227
21-24	39,235	133	16,145
25-34	92,944	300	37,699
35-44	77,325	264	31,587
45-54	48,322	179	19,857
55-64	28,555	121	11,612
65-74	22,519	152	9,129
75 and over	16,993	203	7,169
Not stated	5,086	14	1,970
Male	233,078	1,163	85,551
Female	150,967	389	73,013
Not stated	607	1	31
Residence			
County of crash	320,475	1,158	133,386
Resident elsewhere in state	46,363	312	19,119
Nonresident of state	14,176	73	5,082
Foreign	2,725	4	778
Not stated	913	6	230
Vehicles involved in accidents, total	475,202	4,278	299,204
Passenger vehicle	339,538	2,795	224,695
Recreational	335	9	175
Light truck (pickup)	61,339	664	39,700
Medium truck	5,329	101	3,421
Truck (heavy)	2,924	56	1,835
Truck-tractor (all combination)	4,755	157	2,905
Motorcycle	4,819	158	4,264
All terrain vehicle	304	11	243
Moped	411	10	354
Bicycle	7,138	114	6,512
Law enforcement vehicle	2,774	17	1,600
Emergency vehicle	434	6	259
Taxi cab	2,645	21	1,709
School bus	1,019	13	592
Bus	1,252	14	847
Government/military equipment	1,622	10	985
Other	38,564	122	9,108

1/ Includes bicycle drivers.
Note: Legally reportable accidents are those involving death, bodily injury, or
one or more of the following circumstances: (1) driver leaves the accident scene
where death, injury, or property damage has occurred; (2) driver is under the influence of alcohol or drugs; and, (3) a wrecker is required to remove an inoperative vehicle.

Source: State of Florida, Department of Highway Safety and Motor Vehicles, Office
of Management and Planning Services, *Florida Traffic Crash Facts, 1996.*

Table 13.49. MOTOR VEHICLE ACCIDENTS: PERSONS KILLED OR INJURED AND TOTAL ACCIDENTS IN THE STATE AND COUNTIES OF FLORIDA, 1996

County	Total	Fatal Number	Fatal Per-centage	Injury Number	Injury Per-centage	Persons killed	Persons injured
Florida 1/	241,377	2,550	1.06	148,585	61.96	2,806	243,320
Alachua	3,671	38	1.04	2,208	60.15	45	3,304
Baker	255	4	1.57	173	67.84	8	296
Bay	2,238	26	1.16	1,391	62.15	32	2,253
Bradford	324	4	1.23	191	56.95	4	297
Brevard	4,917	65	1.32	3,441	69.98	74	5,710
Broward	27,508	200	0.73	16,811	61.11	210	26,720
Calhoun	119	8	8.72	88	73.95	9	173
Charlotte	1,497	21	1.40	929	82.06	26	1,675
Citrus	1,121	20	1.78	784	89.94	22	1,460
Clay	1,113	18	1.62	739	66.40	20	1,222
Collier	2,500	39	1.56	1,519	80.78	44	2,511
Columbia	710	27	3.80	551	77.61	27	968
Dade	48,634	307	0.63	26,131	53.73	326	43,285
De Soto	313	7	2.24	233	74.44	9	436
Dixie	148	5	3.38	102	68.92	5	181
Duval	13,005	112	0.86	7,645	58.79	122	11,676
Escambia	4,195	36	0.86	2,912	69.42	40	4,721
Flagler	385	9	2.34	291	75.58	10	488
Franklin	126	1	0.79	81	64.29	1	130
Gadsden	727	14	1.93	420	57.77	17	698
Gilchrist	115	3	2.61	85	73.91	3	142
Glades	95	9	9.47	67	70.53	14	126
Gulf	82	3	3.58	82	75.61	3	104
Hamilton	144	5	3.47	112	77.78	5	213
Hardee	276	9	3.25	185	67.03	11	306
Hendry	340	12	3.53	207	60.88	15	349
Hernando	1,121	34	3.03	828	73.86	39	1,436
Highlands	680	19	2.79	500	73.53	20	947
Hillsborough	21,445	170	0.79	12,918	60.24	188	20,630
Holmes	150	5	3.33	111	74.00	5	172
Indian River	1,215	19	1.56	806	66.34	24	1,342
Jackson	535	15	2.80	420	76.50	17	756
Jefferson	175	12	6.88	121	69.14	14	204
Lafayette	60	4	6.67	41	68.33	5	73
Lake	1,828	35	1.91	1,285	70.46	39	2,107
Lee	4,810	70	1.46	3,020	62.79	78	4,946

See footnotes at end of table.   Continued . . .

Table 13.49. MOTOR VEHICLE ACCIDENTS: PERSONS KILLED OR INJURED AND TOTAL
ACCIDENTS IN THE STATE AND COUNTIES OF FLORIDA, 1996 (Continued)

| | | Reported accidents | | | | | |
| | | Fatal | | Injury | | | |
County	Total	Number	Per-centage	Number	Per-centage	Persons killed	Persons injured
Leon	5,013	30	0.60	2,594	51.75	31	4,008
Levy	370	9	2.43	243	65.68	9	441
Liberty	64	1	1.56	45	70.31	1	70
Madison	221	5	2.26	160	72.40	5	267
Manatee	3,362	49	1.45	1,975	58.74	55	3,127
Marion	2,842	46	1.62	2,145	75.48	49	3,735
Martin	1,511	20	1.32	948	62.74	20	1,468
Monroe	1,185	21	1.77	802	67.68	21	1,290
Nassau	443	12	2.71	285	64.33	13	471
Okaloosa	1,793	27	1.51	1,281	71.44	29	2,092
Okeechobee	427	10	2.34	274	84.17	12	463
Orange	14,398	134	0.93	9,820	68.20	140	15,739
Osceola	2,027	36	1.78	1,377	67.93	43	2,382
Palm Beach	14,756	175	1.19	9,493	64.33	199	15,160
Pasco	4,088	53	1.30	2,996	73.29	60	5,116
Pinellas	12,359	123	1.00	8,580	69.42	128	13,980
Polk	7,357	92	1.25	4,632	62.96	103	7,924
Putnam	949	17	1.79	594	62.59	17	974
St. Johns	1,448	20	1.38	911	82.91	22	1,542
St. Lucie	2,251	33	1.47	1,440	63.97	43	2,454
Santa Rosa	1,134	16	1.41	829	73.10	18	1,473
Sarasota	4,670	45	0.96	2,855	61.13	49	4,550
Seminole	3,616	26	0.72	2,376	65.71	30	3,701
Sumter	429	20	4.66	319	74.36	24	567
Suwannee	380	15	3.95	259	68.16	15	475
Taylor	263	4	1.52	148	56.27	4	247
Union	91	1	1.10	69	75.82	1	120
Volusia	6,171	104	1.69	3,892	63.07	112	6,048
Wakulla	219	6	2.74	154	70.32	6	273
Walton	478	8	1.67	362	75.73	8	630
Washington	202	5	2.97	144	71.29	7	263

1/ Includes data not distributed by county.
Note: Legally reportable accidents are those involving death, bodily injury, or
one or more of the following circumstances: (1) driver leaves the accident scene
where death, injury, or property damage has occurred; (2) driver is under the influence of alcohol or drugs; and, (3) a wrecker is required to remove an inoperative vehicle.

Source: State of Florida, Department of Highway Safety and Motor Vehicles, Office
of Management and Planning Services, *Florida Traffic Crash Facts, 1996.*

Table 13.50. ALCOHOL-RELATED MOTOR VEHICLE ACCIDENTS AND FATALITIES: NUMBER
PERCENTAGE OF TOTAL, AND ACCIDENTS PER 100,000 POPULATION IN THE
STATE AND COUNTIES OF FLORIDA, 1996

County	Total	Alcohol-related accidents As a percentage of all accidents	Per 100,000 population	Total	Alcohol-related fatalities As a percentage of all fatalities
Florida 1/	24,875	10.31	172.6	944	33.64
Alachua	368	10.02	182.1	16	35.56
Baker	44	17.25	212.5	0	0.00
Bay	382	17.07	268.7	12	37.50
Bradford	52	16.05	208.1	3	75.00
Brevard	803	16.33	178.4	34	45.95
Broward	2,243	8.15	161.1	54	25.71
Calhoun	29	24.37	231.9	7	77.78
Charlotte	183	12.22	141.3	8	30.77
Citrus	166	14.81	153.9	8	36.36
Clay	169	15.18	134.7	8	40.00
Collier	374	14.96	193.7	24	54.55
Columbia	127	17.89	241.6	14	51.85
Dade	2,661	5.47	130.2	56	17.18
De Soto	64	20.45	239.6	7	77.78
Dixie	28	18.92	222.2	3	60.00
Duval	1,291	9.93	177.2	40	32.79
Escambia	664	15.83	231.9	14	35.00
Flagler	60	15.58	153.6	4	40.00
Franklin	35	27.78	337.3	1	100.00
Gadsden	121	16.64	261.2	11	64.71
Gilchrist	21	18.26	172.8	1	33.33
Glades	19	20.00	201.8	6	42.86
Gulf	18	21.95	132.9	2	66.67
Hamilton	18	12.50	134.0	0	0.00
Hardee	33	11.96	146.5	3	27.27
Hendry	65	19.12	215.5	4	26.67
Hernando	174	15.52	145.1	14	35.90
Highlands	90	13.24	115.4	4	20.00
Hillsborough	2,068	9.64	227.0	64	34.04
Holmes	22	14.67	126.3	1	20.00
Indian River	153	12.59	149.7	8	33.33
Jackson	84	15.70	172.7	8	35.29
Jefferson	34	19.43	247.9	8	57.14
Lafayette	12	20.00	171.1	1	20.00
Lake	231	12.64	126.7	14	35.90

See footnotes at end of table.   Continued . . .

University of Florida   **Bureau of Economic and Business Research**

Table 13.50. ALCOHOL-RELATED MOTOR VEHICLE ACCIDENTS AND FATALITIES: NUMBER PERCENTAGE OF TOTAL, AND ACCIDENTS PER 100,000 POPULATION IN THE STATE AND COUNTIES OF FLORIDA, 1996 (Continued)

County	Total	Alcohol-related accidents As a percentage of all accidents	Per 100,000 population	Total	Alcohol-related fatalities As a percentage of all fatalities
Lee	649	13.49	169.1	40	51.28
Leon	446	8.90	201.2	13	41.94
Levy	68	18.38	221.6	4	44.44
Liberty	15	23.44	201.6	1	100.00
Madison	15	6.79	80.0	0	0.00
Manatee	487	14.49	205.7	21	38.18
Marion	319	11.22	139.1	19	38.78
Martin	237	15.68	207.1	3	15.00
Monroe	224	18.90	267.3	9	42.86
Nassau	85	19.19	166.4	7	53.85
Okaloosa	380	21.19	229.9	14	48.28
Okeechobee	71	16.63	211.0	5	41.67
Orange	1,421	9.87	182.8	57	40.71
Osceola	241	11.89	172.5	16	37.21
Palm Beach	1,557	10.55	158.6	48	24.12
Pasco	493	12.06	159.1	23	38.33
Pinellas	1,420	11.49	161.1	31	24.22
Polk	800	10.87	176.7	39	37.86
Putnam	152	16.02	216.3	7	41.18
St. Johns	229	15.81	225.1	8	36.36
St. Lucie	293	13.02	167.0	19	44.19
Santa Rosa	202	17.81	205.1	6	33.33
Sarasota	587	12.57	191.9	19	38.78
Seminole	394	10.90	119.7	10	33.33
Sumter	64	14.92	157.7	5	20.83
Suwannee	66	17.37	210.0	8	40.00
Taylor	51	19.39	268.1	1	25.00
Union	15	16.48	115.2	1	100.00
Volusia	772	12.51	189.6	43	38.39
Wakulla	57	26.03	316.3	2	33.33
Walton	108	22.59	314.6	3	37.50
Washington	23	11.39	116.4	4	57.14

1/ Includes data not distributed by county.
Note: Legally reportable accidents are those involving death, bodily injury, or one or more of the following circumstances: (1) driver leaves the accident scene where death, injury, or property damage has occurred; (2) driver is under the influence of alcohol or drugs; and, (3) a wrecker is required to remove an inoperative vehicle.

Source: State of Florida, Department of Highway Safety and Motor Vehicles, Office of Management and Planning Services, *Florida Traffic Crash Facts, 1996.*

Table 13.60. RAILROADS: MILES OF TRACK AND PERCENTAGE OF STATE SYSTEM
BY RAILROAD COMPANY IN FLORIDA, 1996

Company	Tracks (in miles)	Percentage of state system	Company	Tracks (in miles)	Percentage of state system
Total	2,888	100.0	Florida West Coast	14	0.5
Apalachicola Northern	96	3.4	Georgia and Florida	48	1.7
Bay Line	63	2.2	Norfolk Southern	96	3.4
Burlington Northern	44	1.6	Seminole Gulf	119	4.2
CSX Transportation 1/	A/ 1,621	57.7	South Central Florida	101	3.6
Florida Central	66	2.4	South Florida Rail		
Florida East Coast	442	15.8	Corridor 2/	81	2.8
Florida Midland	40	1.4	Terminal Companies	30	1.1
Florida Northern	27	1.0			

A/ Includes the Southeast Florida Rail Corridor owned by the State of Florida between West Palm Beach and Miami.
1/ Amtrak operates in Florida but owns no trackage in the state other than yard and terminal tracks. It operates mainly over CSXT main tracks. It also operates over trackage owned by the State of Florida between West Palm Beach and Miami (81 miles).
2/ Not an operating carrier.
Source: State of Florida, Department of Transportation, Office of Planning, *1996 Florida Rail System Plan.*

Table 13.70. PORT ACTIVITY: TONNAGE HANDLED IN SPECIFIED PORTS IN FLORIDA
FISCAL YEAR 1995-96 OR CALENDAR YEAR 1996

Port and type of cargo	Short tons	Port and type of cargo	Short tons
Canaveral (fiscal year 1995-96),		Manatee (Cont.)	
total	3,656,703	Imports	3,233,751
Exports	1,154,292	Miami (fiscal year	
Imports	2,502,411	1995-96), total	5,859,538
Everglades (fiscal year 1995-96),		Exports	2,899,486
total	20,880,536	Imports	2,945,052
Exports	2,620,691	Palm Beach 2/ (fiscal year	
Imports	6,834,243	1995-96), total	3,718,524
Domestic	10,543,129	Panama City (calendar	
Bunker	882,473	year 1995), total	659,521
Ft. Pierce (calendar year 1996),		Exports	330,244
total	123,648	Imports	153,392
Exports	21,824	Domestic	175,885
Imports	101,824	Pensacola (fiscal year	
Jacksonville 1/ (fiscal year		1995-96), total	715,659
1995-96), total JPA terminals	5,706,854	Exports	383,769
General cargo exports	3,058,223	Imports	331,891
General cargo imports	2,648,631	Tampa (fiscal year	
Containerized cargo	3,649,439	1995-96), total	51,858,583
Bulk cargo and other	1,860,705	Exports	12,581,431
Manatee (fiscal year 1995-96), total	4,228,181	Imports	5,809,049
Exports	994,430	Domestic	8,269,014

1/ Tonnage passing through facilities owned by the Jacksonville Port Authority only; therefore they differ from movements into and out of the Port of Jacksonville.
2/ Only general cargo tonnage were reported in previous *Abstracts*. Export and import data are not available.
Source: Data are reported in annual or cumulative monthly reports of each port authority.

University of Florida   **Bureau of Economic and Business Research**

Table 13.73. EXPORTS AND IMPORTS: VALUE OF SHIPMENTS HANDLED BY CUSTOMS
DISTRICTS IN FLORIDA, 1995 AND 1996

(amounts in thousands of dollars)

Customs district and port	Total merchandise trade		Per-centage change	Value of exports	Value of imports
	1995	1996			
Tampa customs district 18	15,228,090	15,307,957	0.5	6,930,126	8,377,830
Tampa	2,952,436	2,685,278	-9.0	1,882,976	802,302
Jacksonville	965,909	9,671,501	0.1	339,948	6,272,023
Fernandina	417,144	355,603	-14.8	323,871	31,732
Boca Grande	2,911	110	-96.2	110	0
Orlando	83,516	843,222	1.0	469,857	373,365
St. Petersburg	1,238	10,914	781.3	1,560	9,355
Port Canaveral	616,999	967,288	56.8	441,725	525,563
Panama City	285,523	253,408	-11.2	198,059	55,349
Pensacola	126,222	73,627	-41.7	70,487	3,139
Port Manatee	329,247	366,352	11.3	81,694	284,658
S. W. Florida International	1,320	4,723	257.8	2,185	254
Sanford Regional	140	71,948	51,280.6	5,466	17,291
Sarasota/Bradenton	100	68	-31.7	0	68
Daytona International	293	720	145.7	663	56
Melbourne Regional	265	3,195	1,105.7	2,805	390
Miami customs district 52	37,219,877	41,130,634	10.5	2,447,863	16,652,009
Port of Miami	12,280,294	128,263	4.4	7,195,793	5,630,514
Key West	7,444	12,583	69.0	11,618	965
Port Everglades	7,365,031	7,987,478	8.5	3,922,599	4,064,879
West Palm Beach	1,264,141	1,239,407	-2.0	711,193	528,215
Ft. Pierce	26,446	23,673	-10.5	19,040	4,633
Miami International Airport	1,627,652	19,041,186	17.0	12,618,383	6,422,803

Note: Data do not reflect shipments to or from Puerto Rico, Virgin Islands, or
U.S. Territories. Data from the Foreign Trade Division of the U.S. Bureau of the
Census.

Source: Enterprise Florida, Department of Research, unpublished data.

University of Florida   **Bureau of Economic and Business Research**

Table 13.74. EXPORTS AND IMPORTS: LEADING MERCHANDISE TRADING PARTNERS
FLORIDA, 1996

(in dollars)

Country in 1996 rank order	Total trade	Value of exports	Value of imports
Brazil	6,179,451,601	4,852,647,525	1,326,804,076
Japan	4,206,107,873	366,674,606	3,839,433,267
Colombia	3,664,061,240	2,350,187,126	1,313,874,114
Venezuela	3,384,359,836	2,372,867,410	1,011,492,426
Dominican Republic	3,310,790,584	1,673,569,822	1,637,220,762
Argentina	2,275,870,816	1,971,812,906	304,057,910
Honduras	2,131,189,882	937,113,575	1,194,076,307
Germany	2,080,593,336	649,318,026	1,431,275,310
Costa Rica	1,958,723,347	897,237,000	1,061,486,257
Chile	1,783,219,400	1,458,326,578	324,892,822

Table 13.75. EXPORTS AND IMPORTS: LEADING TYPES AND VALUE OF MERCHANDISE EXPORTED
AND IMPORTED THROUGH FLORIDA CUSTOMS DISTRICTS, 1996

(in dollars)

Commodity exported	Value	Commodity imported	Value
Total	5,632,186,633	Total	5,632,186,633
Office machines parts/ accessories	1,705,570,868	Passenger vehicles	4,611,523,509
Fertilizers	1,515,031,252	Trousers, overalls, shorts	940,036,372
Passenger vehicles	1,034,492,254	Special trans- actions	787,814,709
Data processing units	761,732,960	T-shirts, singlets and similar apparel	538,372,744
Telecommunication parts/ accessories	615,359,299	Frozen crustaceans	472,652,838

Source for Tables 13.74 and 13.75: Enterprise Florida, Department of Research,
unpublished data.

University of Florida   **Bureau of Economic and Business Research**

Table 13.90. AIRPORT ACTIVITY: OPERATIONS AT AIRPORTS WITH FEDERAL AVIATION
ADMINISTRATION (FAA)-OPERATED AND CONTRACTED TRAFFIC CONTROL
TOWERS IN FLORIDA, FISCAL YEAR 1996-97

Location and type of operation	Total operations 1/	Air carrier 2/	Air taxi 3/	General aviation 4/	Military
Florida	4,387,937	809,623	559,712	2,904,192	114,410
Itinerant	3,205,607	809,623	559,712	1,760,339	75,933
Local	1,182,330	0	0	1,143,853	38,477
Craig Field Jacksonville	102,311	0	5,812	82,147	14,352
Itinerant	72,132	0	5,812	54,277	12,043
Local	30,179	0	0	27,870	2,309
Daytona Beach	213,891	6,310	908	205,974	699
Itinerant	176,038	6,310	908	168,215	605
Local	37,853	0	0	37,759	94
Ft. Lauderdale	210,015	94,265	46,102	69,078	570
Itinerant	208,890	94,265	46,102	67,953	570
Local	1,125	0	0	1,125	0
Ft. Lauderdale Executive	177,529	0	5,794	171,659	76
Itinerant	140,643	0	5,794	134,773	76
Local	36,886	0	0	36,886	0
Ft. Myers Page Field	67,028	0	2,509	64,309	210
Itinerant	40,891	0	2,509	38,218	164
Local	26,137	0	0	26,091	46
Ft. Myers Regional	53,482	31,317	11,679	9,616	870
Itinerant	52,296	31,317	11,679	8,825	475
Local	1,186	0	0	791	395
Ft. Pierce	110,898	4	1,060	109,631	203
Itinerant	56,803	4	1,060	55,536	203
Local	54,095	0	0	54,095	0
Gainesville	63,520	2,335	9,485	47,382	4,318
Itinerant	46,724	2,335	9,485	33,209	1,695
Local	16,796	0	0	14,173	2,623
Hollywood	89,378	0	0	89,360	18
Itinerant	30,863	0	0	30,845	18
Local	58,515	0	0	58,515	0
Jacksonville International	113,115	36,766	32,819	35,113	8,417
Itinerant	103,137	36,766	32,819	29,059	4,493
Local	9,978	0	0	6,054	3,924
Key West	96,522	4	29,548	54,874	12,096
Itinerant	73,747	4	29,548	35,731	8,464
Local	22,775	0	0	19,143	3,632
Kissimmee	11,217	0	77	11,130	10
Itinerant	6,279	0	77	6,196	6
Local	4,938	0	0	4,934	4

See footnotes at end of table.   Continued . . .

Table 13.90. AIRPORT ACTIVITY: OPERATIONS AT AIRPORTS WITH FEDERAL AVIATION
ADMINISTRATION (FAA)-OPERATED AND CONTRACTED TRAFFIC CONTROL
TOWERS IN FLORIDA, FISCAL YEAR 1996-97 (Continued)

Location and type of operation	Total operations 1/	Air carrier 2/	Air taxi 3/	General aviation 4/	Military
Lakeland	160,752	0	597	157,801	2,354
Itinerant	83,576	0	597	82,063	916
Local	77,176	0	0	75,738	1,438
Melbourne	98,630	4,758	1,210	92,076	586
Itinerant	57,719	4,758	1,210	51,165	586
Local	40,911	0	0	40,911	0
Miami International	444,132	256,604	128,365	55,166	3,997
Itinerant	444,132	256,604	128,365	55,166	3,997
Local	0	0	0	0	0
Naples	89,106	0	11,687	77,190	229
Itinerant	66,614	0	11,687	54,862	65
Local	22,492	0	0	22,328	164
Opa-Locka	90,651	11	2,889	80,474	7,277
Itinerant	48,906	11	2,889	41,606	4,400
Local	41,745	0	0	38,868	2,877
Orlando Executive	128,499	0	9,071	118,654	774
Itinerant	89,568	0	9,071	79,888	609
Local	38,931	0	0	38,766	165
Orlando International	298,947	193,075	74,450	26,442	4,980
Itinerant	298,883	193,075	74,450	26,378	4,980
Local	64	0	0	64	0
Panama City-Bay County	75,758	2,629	14,439	54,299	4,391
Itinerant	43,453	2,629	14,439	24,444	1,941
Local	32,305	0	0	29,855	2,450
Pensacola	91,169	9,668	19,220	43,074	19,207
Itinerant	67,813	9,668	19,220	25,098	13,827
Local	23,356	0	0	17,976	5,380
Pompano Beach Airpark	77,874	0	0	77,874	0
Itinerant	22,579	0	0	22,579	0
Local	55,295	0	0	55,295	0
Sanford	253,543	2,835	83	250,335	290
Itinerant	93,998	2,835	83	91,009	71
Local	159,545	0	0	159,326	219
Sarasota-Bradenton	126,087	12,923	10,039	101,619	1,506
Itinerant	100,673	12,923	10,039	76,487	1,224
Local	25,414	0	0	25,132	282
St. Petersburg-Clearwater	135,000	6,117	3,481	109,473	15,929
Itinerant	78,939	6,117	3,481	63,408	5,933
Local	56,061	0	0	46,065	9,996

See footnotes at end of table.   Continued . . .

University of Florida   **Bureau of Economic and Business Research**

Table 13.90. AIRPORT ACTIVITY: OPERATIONS AT AIRPORTS WITH FEDERAL AVIATION
ADMINISTRATION (FAA)-OPERATED AND CONTRACTED TRAFFIC CONTROL
TOWERS IN FLORIDA, FISCAL YEAR 1996-97 (Continued)

Location and type of operation	Total operations 1/	Air carrier 2/	Air taxi 3/	General aviation 4/	Military
St. Petersburg Whitt	65,971	0	2,081	63,562	328
Itinerant	31,519	0	2,081	29,324	114
Local	34,452	0	0	34,238	214
Stuart/Witham Field	77,074	0	1,010	75,579	485
Itinerant	41,349	0	1,010	39,894	445
Local	35,725	0	0	35,685	40
Tallahassee	92,301	4,006	33,847	48,402	6,046
Itinerant	72,763	4,006	33,847	31,000	3,910
Local	19,538	0	0	17,402	2,136
Tamiami	126,760	0	170	126,548	42
Itinerant	56,099	0	170	55,899	30
Local	70,661	0	0	70,649	12
Tampa International	211,535	99,729	75,168	33,849	2,789
Itinerant	211,247	99,729	75,168	33,561	2,789
Local	288	0	0	288	0
Titusville-Cocoa	89,429	2	4	89,197	226
Itinerant	43,575	2	4	43,361	208
Local	45,854	0	0	45,836	18
Vero Beach	173,554	3	1,357	172,069	125
Itinerant	89,401	3	1,357	87,964	77
Local	84,153	0	0	84,105	48
West Palm Beach	172,259	46,262	24,751	100,236	1,010
Itinerant	154,358	46,262	24,751	82,346	999
Local	17,901	0	0	17,890	11

1/ An aircraft arrival at or departure from an airport with FAA traffic control.
2/ Air carrier authorized by the Department of Transportation to provide scheduled
service over specified routes with limited nonscheduled operations.
3/ Performs at least five round trips per week between two or more points and publishes flight schedules or transports mail.
4/ All operations not classified as an air carrier, air taxi, or military.
Note: Itinerant includes all aircraft arrivals and departures other than local.
Local includes aircraft operations which operate in the local traffic pattern or
within sight of the tower.

Source: U.S., Department of Transportation, Federal Aviation Administration,
Internet site http://www.apo.data.faa.gov/.

Table 13.92. AIRPORT ACTIVITY: ENPLANED REVENUE PASSENGERS AND ENPLANED REVENUE TONS OF FREIGHT AND MAIL CARGO OF CERTIFICATED ROUTE AIR CARRIERS BY COMMUNITY SERVED AND AIRPORT IN FLORIDA, 1994

Community served	Airport 2/	Enplaned passengers 3/	Enplaned cargo tons 1/ Total	Freight	Mail
Daytona Beach	Daytona Beach Regional	385,469	333	329	4
Destin	Ft. Walton Beach	0	345	345	0
Ft. Myers	Page Field	0	22	22	0
Ft. Myers	Southwest	1,812,528	6,173	3,246	2,926
Ft. Pierce	Ft. Pierce	0	158	158	0
Gainesville	Gainesville Municipal	134,346	255	251	3
Jacksonville	Craig Municipal	0	110	110	0
Jacksonville	Jacksonville International	1,746,759	16,393	6,490	9,903
Key West	Key West International	8,476	163	162	1
Marathon	Marathon Flight Strip	282	84	84	0
Melbourne	Cape Kennedy Regional	283,066	394	325	69
Miami/Ft. Lauderdale	Dade-Collier	0	2	2	0
Miami/Ft. Lauderdale	Ft. Lauderdale-Hollywood International	4,612,512	60,977	53,461	7,517
Miami/Ft. Lauderdale	Miami International	10,831,532	460,308	432,221	28,087
Orlando	Orlando International	9,166,580	65,173	50,882	14,291
Panama City	Panama City-Bay County	113,946	1,276	502	774
Pensacola	Pensacola Regional	422,365	1,784	733	1,051
Sarasota/Bradenton	Sarasota-Bradenton	778,330	773	584	189
Tallahassee	Tallahassee Municipal	379,674	2,943	2,070	872
Tampa and St. Petersburg/Clearwater	St. Petersburg/Clearwater International	174,367	79	79	0
Tampa and St. Petersburg/Clearwater	Tampa International	5,439,230	48,573	27,554	21,018
Valparaiso	Eglin Air Force Base	149,715	124	124	0
West Palm Beach/Palm Beach	Palm Beach International	2,621,125	9,589	3,827	5,762

1/ Includes originating and transfer tons.
2/ Data are included for only those airports at which aircraft departures were performed in scheduled service in 1994.
3/ Includes all revenue passengers boarding aircraft.
Note: Data are for all services operations of large air carriers (seating capacity of 60 seats or a maximum payload capacity of more than 18,000 pounds) holding a Certificate of Public Convenience and Necessity issued by the U.S. Department of Transportation. Excluded are data for charter only, commuter, intrastate, and foreign-flag air carriers.

Source: U.S., Department of Transportation, Federal Aviation Administration, *Airport Activity Statistics of Certificated Route Air Carriers, Calendar Year 1993*, and unpublished data.

University of Florida   **Bureau of Economic and Business Research**

Table 13.93. AIRCRAFT PILOTS: ACTIVE AIRCRAFT PILOTS BY TYPE OF CERTIFICATE
AND FLIGHT INSTRUCTORS IN THE STATE AND COUNTIES OF FLORIDA
DECEMBER 31, 1995

County	Total	Student 2/	Private	Commercial	Airline transport 3/	Miscellaneous 4/	Flight instructors
Florida	45,637	6,536	16,223	10,550	11,541	787	5,969
Alachua	495	100	216	107	55	17	51
Baker	15	0	10	3	2	0	0
Bay	570	79	184	174	123	10	76
Bradford	18	5	8	3	2	0	3
Brevard	2,052	299	825	487	411	30	284
Broward	5,015	603	1,432	1,098	1,808	74	804
Calhoun	20	1	7	9	2	1	2
Charlotte	393	44	155	80	106	8	55
Citrus	243	24	126	55	37	1	26
Clay	584	71	152	144	210	7	59
Collier	915	92	375	168	274	6	109
Columbia	96	19	52	15	10	0	6
Dade	5,254	693	1,302	1,346	1,828	85	629
De Soto	47	4	22	17	4	0	6
Dixie	10	0	4	3	2	1	2
Duval	1,712	285	583	409	392	43	209
Escambia	1,147	130	282	317	385	33	94
Flagler	120	16	41	33	28	2	25
Franklin	28	6	12	4	6	0	2
Gadsden	47	6	27	7	5	2	6
Gilchrist	10	1	5	2	2	0	1
Glades	16	2	6	7	1	0	0
Gulf	18	3	5	7	3	0	0
Hamilton	5	1	2	1	1	0	1
Hardee	43	2	25	11	4	1	1
Hendry	84	24	28	19	12	1	10
Hernando	190	31	93	35	29	2	20
Highlands	200	21	107	45	24	3	26
Hillsborough	2,160	380	875	409	449	47	228
Holmes	13	2	7	3	1	0	1
Indian River	876	117	301	306	146	6	172
Jackson	73	11	33	20	7	2	6
Jefferson	12	4	4	3	1	0	0
Lafayette	6	0	4	0	1	1	0
Lake	523	77	245	112	80	9	60
Lee	1,237	191	524	254	259	9	112

See footnotes at end of table.   Continued . . .

Table 13.93. AIRCRAFT PILOTS: ACTIVE AIRCRAFT PILOTS BY TYPE OF CERTIFICATE
AND FLIGHT INSTRUCTORS IN THE STATE AND COUNTIES OF FLORIDA
DECEMBER 31, 1995 (Continued)

| | | | Pilots | | | | |
| | | | Airplane pilots 1/ | | | | |
County	Total	Stu-dent 2/	Private	Commer-cial	Airline trans-port 3/	Miscel-lane-ous 4/	Flight instruc-tors
Leon	524	118	210	103	82	11	55
Levy	63	11	30	16	6	0	6
Liberty	5	1	1	1	1	1	0
Madison	20	4	11	3	2	0	3
Manatee	517	68	200	113	128	8	68
Marion	596	80	273	125	112	6	74
Martin	494	59	200	101	130	4	73
Monroe	723	78	249	134	259	3	72
Nassau	242	33	83	61	61	4	31
Okaloosa	937	122	259	255	283	18	112
Okeechobee	97	10	57	19	9	2	5
Orange	2,269	346	820	502	541	60	338
Osceola	318	70	108	67	63	10	58
Palm Beach	3,603	449	1,369	705	1,022	58	456
Pasco	500	80	216	117	70	17	50
Pinellas	2,804	458	1,171	530	599	46	301
Polk	1,026	166	456	235	153	16	152
Putnam	125	25	54	25	17	4	15
St. Johns	677	74	115	224	239	25	55
St. Lucie	1,031	131	470	236	181	13	123
Santa Rosa	1,155	198	423	286	223	25	187
Sarasota	387	53	156	84	88	6	50
Seminole	423	59	198	101	63	2	55
Sumter	43	11	28	2	2	0	3
Suwannee	81	16	36	19	9	1	10
Taylor	18	3	9	5	1	0	2
Union	4	1	2	1	0	0	0
Volusia	2,584	449	892	742	465	36	518
Wakulla	30	6	11	7	6	0	5
Walton	49	6	20	12	10	1	3
Washington	25	3	14	4	3	1	2
Unknown	20	4	3	2	3	8	1

1/ Includes pilots with airplane only certificates and with airplane and helicopter and/or glider certificates.
2/ Category of certificate unknown.
3/ Includes airline transport airplane only and airline transport airplane and helicopter certificates.
4/ Includes helicopter, gyroplane, glider and recreational certificates.

Source: U.S., Department of Transportation, Federal Aviation Administration, Office of Aviation Policy and Plans, *U.S. Civil Airmen Statistics, Calendar Year 1994,* and unpublished data.

University of Florida   **Bureau of Economic and Business Research**

COMMUNICATIONS

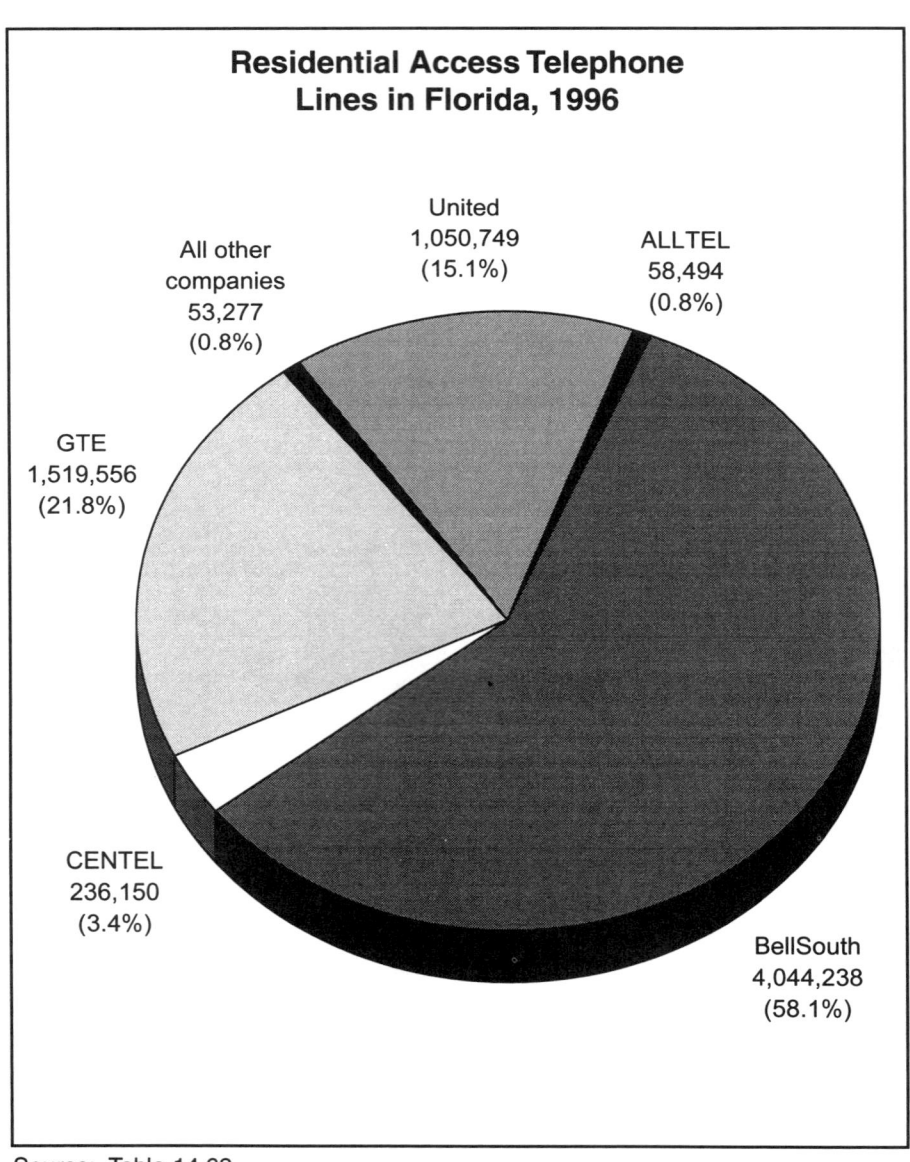

**Residential Access Telephone
Lines in Florida, 1996**

United
1,050,749
(15.1%)

ALLTEL
58,494
(0.8%)

All other
companies
53,277
(0.8%)

GTE
1,519,556
(21.8%)

CENTEL
236,150
(3.4%)

BellSouth
4,044,238
(58.1%)

Source: Table 14.62

SECTION 14.00
COMMUNICATONS

TABLES LISTED BY MAJOR HEADINGS

University of Florida   **Bureau of Economic and Business Research**

Table 14.33. POST OFFICES: ZIP CODES AND NET POSTAL REVENUE IN THE STATE AND
SPECIFIED CITIES OF FLORIDA, FISCAL YEAR 1995-96

First class post office	ZIP code	Net revenue (dollars)	Percentage change from prior year	First class post office	ZIP code	Net revenue (dollars)	Percentage change from prior year
Florida	(X)	2,580,315,536	6.0	Crestview	32536	1,685,525	3.1
				Cross City	32628	348,789	13.3
Alachua	32615	630,486	2.8	Crystal River	34429	1,891,941	3.2
Altamonte				Dade City	33525	2,509,191	5.2
Springs	32714	8,944,854	-0.1	Dania	33004	2,148,213	-3.4
Apalachicola	32320	394,777	4.6	Davenport	33837	519,873	10.5
Apopka	32703	15,561,399	6.2	Daytona Beach	32114	39,478,686	-2.1
Arcadia	33821	1,333,884	4.7	DeBary	32713	780,861	3.8
Auburndale	33823	1,595,554	8.6	Deerfield Beach	33441	10,080,801	14.1
Avon Park	33825	1,569,935	7.9	DeFuniak			
Bartow	33830	2,791,324	-4.2	Springs	32433	1,081,633	4.1
Bay Pines	33504	863,239	11.9	DeLand	32720	6,884,196	28.8
Belle Glade	33430	1,122,456	5.0	De Leon Springs	32130	413,230	4.9
Belleview	34420	1,237,619	3.1	Delray Beach	33444	10,114,704	4.7
Blountstown	32424	557,379	15.4	Destin	32541	3,152,844	14.0
Boca Grande	33921	354,719	9.0	Dundee	33838	415,001	-0.4
Boca Raton	33431	39,397,559	9.4	Dunedin	34698	3,678,793	-4.8
Bonifay	32425	636,101	5.9	Dunnellon	34432	1,113,654	5.1
Bonita Springs	33923	3,246,255	8.8	Eagle Lake	33839	346,694	0.5
Boynton Beach	33436	7,383,667	9.5	Eaton Park	33840	1,110,213	7.1
Bradenton	34205	14,118,991	-4.7	Edgewater	32132	1,421,778	-1.0
Bradenton Beach	34217	349,937	-32.2	Eglin Air Force			
Brandon	33511	7,884,217	4.9	Base	32542	932,218	-2.2
Bronson	32621	309,635	(X)	Elfers	34259	1,468,891	6.5
Brooksville	34601	9,621,914	6.7	Ellenton	34222	877,922	2.0
Bunnell	32110	602,364	-2.5	Englewood	34223	3,081,467	4.3
Bushnell	33513	619,381	5.0	Estero	33928	992,247	-4.7
Callahan	32011	512,438	5.6	Eustis	32726	1,660,229	5.7
Cantonment	32533	677,129	9.1	Fernandina Beach	32834	2,194,950	-14.7
Cape Canaveral	32920	1,226,632	2.5	Flagler Beach	32136	23,576,092	14.3
Captiva	33924	320,015	-2.1	Floral City	34436	386,721	13.7
Casselberry	32707	6,789,866	5.7	Ft. Lauderdale	33310	229,876,118	23.9
Chattahoochee	32324	372,466	1.5	Ft. Meade	33841	345,228	7.8
Chiefland	32626	815,329	2.8	Ft. Myers	33906	40,457,532	2.0
Chipley	32428	812,676	7.9	Ft. Myers Beach	33931	1,677,164	2.7
Christmas	32709	312,166	6.0	Ft. Pierce	34981	12,216,964	6.8
Clearwater	34625	49,717,215	3.2	Ft. Walton Beach	32548	5,974,495	4.2
Clermont	34711	1,594,809	7.8	Frostproof	33843	488,161	0.2
Clewiston	33440	972,045	3.6	Fruitland Park	34731	664,490	7.0
Cocoa	32922	4,268,436	-2.8	Gainesville	32601	23,917,842	-1.1
Cocoa Beach	32931	1,616,555	-1.1	Goldenrod	32733	1,603,060	9.8
Crawfordville	32327	550,055	10.7	Gonzalez	32560	562,144	19.5
Crescent City	32112	947,682	-0.7	Gotha	34734	503,176	4.1

See footnotes at end of table.   Continued . . .

Table 14.33. POST OFFICES: ZIP CODES AND NET POSTAL REVENUE IN THE STATE AND SPECIFIED CITIES OF FLORIDA, FISCAL YEAR 1995-96 (Continued)

First class post office	ZIP code	Net revenue (dollars)	Per- cent- age change from prior year	First class post office	ZIP code	Net revenue (dollars)	Per- cent- age change from prior year
Graceville	32440	480,174	-7.5	Land O' Lakes	34639	1,133,954	17.1
Green Cove				Largo	34640	17,506,694	-1.9
Springs	32043	1,156,336	9.2	Lecanto	34465	1,353,791	7.3
Groveland	34736	374,506	10.8	Leesburg	34748	4,595,669	9.8
Gulf Breeze	32561	2,627,887	3.9	Lehigh Acres	33936	1,665,514	4.7
Haines City	33844	1,584,320	-0.8	Live Oak	32060	1,853,241	6.3
Hallandale	33809	5,076,551	10.0	Longboat Key	34228	1,354,401	4.5
Havana	32333	473,765	4.7	Longwood	32779	7,734,182	-6.9
Hernando	34442	748,084	2.5	Loxahatchee	33470	973,499	-17.6
Hialeah	33010	23,612,277	-5.3	Lutz	33549	1,616,804	8.8
Highland City	33846	452,844	-4.7	Lynn Haven	32444	1,297,851	6.4
High Springs	32643	484,448	7.3	Macclenny	32063	696,013	7.8
Hobe Sound	33455	1,381,308	3.7	Madison	32348	788,645	2.8
Hollywood	33022	24,497,069	0.5	Maitland	32751	16,936,157	-8.2
Homestead	33030	3,664,026	5.0	Malabar	32950	484,271	12.3
Homosassa				Mango	34262	12,256,130	25.9
Springs	34447	1,191,570	7.3	Marathon	33050	1,725,102	4.5
Immokalee	33934	900,109	5.8	Marco	33937	2,492,994	3.9
Indian Rocks				Marianna	32446	1,717,699	0.7
Beach	34635	1,193,124	4.9	Mary Esther	32569	1,565,737	1.0
Indiantown	34956	494,898	-3.1	Melbourne	32901	23,773,053	6.7
Interlachen	32148	294,735	-0.4	Merritt Island	32952	3,332,707	5.3
Inverness	32650	2,758,002	2.5	Miami	33152	292,008,551	4.2
Islamorada	33036	651,298	3.1	Middleburg	32068	983,630	4.8
Jacksonville	32203	233,109,608	2.0	Milton	32570	2,891,794	4.0
Jasper	32052	348,879	-1.2	Mims	32754	413,038	7.1
Jensen Beach	34957	2,068,441	5.9	Minneola	34755	331,088	6.4
Jupiter	33458	6,884,830	5.0	Monticello	32344	635,302	7.5
Kathleen	33849	519,635	2.7	Moore Haven	33471	301,220	(X)
Key Largo	33037	1,716,932	3.9	Mount Dora	32757	2,053,048	-4.0
Keystone Heights	32656	1,142,763	4.6	Mulberry	33860	2,362,816	2.1
Key West	33040	5,191,883	2.9	Naples	33940	21,913,675	7.8
Kissimmee	34744	9,527,429	2.8	New Port Richey	34652	4,873,038	6.3
La Belle	33935	916,453	2.2	New Smyrna Beach	32169	3,107,758	11.3
Lady Lake	32159	1,882,010	9.4	Niceville	32578	1,965,948	5.3
Lake Alfred	33858	462,424	3.6	Nokomis	34275	1,521,544	8.8
Lake Butler	32054	388,360	5.6	Ocala	34478	16,675,953	-1.9
Lake City	32055	3,874,416	-19.2	Ocklawaha	32179	332,362	-5.4
Lakeland	33802	20,133,632	3.6	Ocoee	34761	1,374,370	15.4
Lake Mary	32746	10,330,802	69.9	Odessa	33556	567,053	23.5
Lake Monroe	32747	407,664	15.1	Okeechobee	34972	1,989,669	7.4
Lake Placid	33852	1,352,017	6.8	Oldsmar	34677	3,316,900	75.8
Lake Wales	33853	2,370,706	-1.8	Oneco	34264	915,179	12.6
Lake Worth	33461	10,894,813	0.0	Opa-locka	33054	3,655,089	19.0

See footnotes at end of table.   Continued . . .

University of Florida   **Bureau of Economic and Business Research**

Table 14.33. POST OFFICES: ZIP CODES AND NET POSTAL REVENUE IN THE STATE AND
SPECIFIED CITIES OF FLORIDA, FISCAL YEAR 1995-96 (Continued)

First class post office	ZIP code	Net revenue (dollars)	Per-cent-age change from prior year	First class post office	ZIP code	Net revenue (dollars)	Per-cent-age change from prior year
Orange City	32763	4,422,005	23.0	Sarasota	34230	30,015,112	2.5
Orange Park	32073	5,158,247	5.7	Sebastian	32958	1,531,795	4.4
Orlando	32862	174,377,242	6.9	Sebring	33870	3,381,387	1.6
Ormond Beach	32174	5,927,944	3.4	Seffner	33584	1,028,076	2.5
Osprey	34229	1,358,965	3.3	Shalimar	32579	1,268,263	5.5
Oviedo	32765	2,538,399	7.6	Sharpes	32959	558,759	-0.9
Pahokee	33476	319,624	0.0	Silver Springs	34488	1,146,549	6.9
Palatka	32177	2,145,140	0.6	Sorento	32776	308,562	(X)
Palm Beach	33480	3,240,583	2.7	Starke	32091	910,917	3.7
Palm City	34990	1,958,622	10.6	Stuart	34994	10,366,171	4.3
Palmetto	34221	1,862,877	5.6	Summerfield	34491	387,194	21.7
Palm Harbor	34683	7,642,923	3.9	Summerland Key	33042	1,032,831	6.0
Panama City	32401	12,516,247	6.9	Sumterville	34267	429,041	8.1
Pembroke Pines	33082	58,411,038	16.7	Tallahassee	32301	61,652,551	3.5
Pensacola	32501	30,047,974	0.8	Tallevast	34270	1,768,464	4.7
Perry	32347	1,134,279	3.3	Tampa	33630	301,965,281	6.5
Pinellas Park	34665	4,765,210	-51.6	Tampa	33622	6,910,784	22.4
Placida	33946	458,175	12.4	Tarpon Springs	34689	4,881,339	14.9
Plant City	33566	3,145,928	5.0	Tavares	32778	1,772,122	0.7
Plymouth	32768	316,559	10.8	Tavernier	33070	924,187	-27.3
Polk City	33868	293,236	(X)	Thonotosassa	33592	460,832	7.7
Pompano Beach	33060	37,291,671	12.6	Titusville	32780	4,833,800	0.1
				Trenton	32693	405,433	7.8
Ponte Vedra Beach	32082	2,643,064	13.7	Umatilla	32784	586,292	-0.3
Port Richey	34668	5,849,627	8.1	Valpariso	32580	699,189	4.7
Port St. Joe	32456	673,618	6.8	Valrico	33594	1,594,441	11.3
Port Salerno	34992	958,144	9.2	Venice	34285	8,456,749	6.4
Punta Gorda	33950	9,819,172	4.0	Vero Beach	32960	11,451,640	1.7
Quincy	32351	2,400,745	-22.2	Wabasso	32970	2,110,748	13.8
Riverview	33569	1,307,973	19.0	Wauchula	33873	1,077,142	6.8
Rockledge	32955	2,001,727	13.1	Weirsdale	32195	955,789	-0.6
Roseland	32957	473,669	11.1	West Palm Beach	33406	56,116,840	4.6
Ruskin	33570	2,709,022	6.1	White Springs	32096	485,051	9.1
Safety Harbor	34695	1,423,856	-14.6	Wildwood	34785	600,203	3.9
St. Augustine	32084	6,473,835	4.8	Williston	32696	594,484	6.5
St. Cloud	34769	2,055,163	10.3	Windermere	34786	1,327,268	29.8
St. James City	33956	314,115	5.6	Winter Garden	32787	1,266,394	1.7
St. Petersburg	33730	93,708,326	-3.7	Winter Haven	33880	9,892,723	4.0
Sanford	32771	4,440,006	10.6	Winter Park	32789	12,200,257	-0.6
Sanibel	33957	1,598,198	3.7	Yulee	32097	1,199,576	259.2
Santa Rosa Beach	32459	676,592	18.1	Zephyrhills	33540	3,156,755	6.5

(X) Not applicable.
Note: Data are for first class post offices. Florida totals include revenue from
all post offices.
Source: U.S., Postal Service Headquarters, unpublished data.

University of Florida   **Bureau of Economic and Business Research**

Table 14.35. EMPLOYMENT: AVERAGE MONTHLY PRIVATE REPORTING UNITS, EMPLOYMENT
AND PAYROLL COVERED BY UNEMPLOYMENT COMPENSATION LAW
BY INDUSTRY IN FLORIDA, 1996

SIC code	Industry	Number of reporting units	Number of employees	Payroll ($1,000)
27	Printing, publishing, and allied industries	3,480	63,744	155,592
48	Telecommunications	1,983	73,145	253,314
481	Telephone communications	1,210	49,271	179,867
482	Telegraph and other message communications	26	260	1,375
483	Radio and television broadcasting stations	419	12,379	42,212
484	Cable and other pay television services	272	10,731	28,252
489	Communication services, NEC	56	505	1,608

NEC Not elsewhere classified.

Table 14.36. TELECOMMUNICATIONS: AVERAGE MONTHLY PRIVATE REPORTING UNITS
EMPLOYMENT, AND PAYROLL COVERED BY UNEMPLOYMENT COMPENSATION LAW
IN THE STATE AND COUNTIES OF FLORIDA, 1996

County	Number of reporting units	Number of employees	Payroll ($1,000)	County	Number of reporting units	Number of employees	Payroll ($1,000)
			Telecommunications (SIC code 48)				
Florida	1,983	73,145	253,314	Manatee	17	278	913
Alachua	25	903	2,586	Marion	27	537	1,571
Baker	4	74	210	Martin	8	214	688
Bay	27	750	1,844	Monroe	15	271	746
Brevard	53	1,115	3,765	Nassau	5	49	143
Broward	207	7,529	27,437	Okaloosa	24	513	1,592
Charlotte	10	260	692	Okeechobee	4	80	203
Citrus	14	213	541	Orange	154	9,363	33,466
Clay	7	125	298	Palm Beach	128	4,555	15,782
Collier	24	617	1,722	Pasco	16	312	930
Columbia	5	184	482	Pinellas	103	3,912	13,554
Dade	291	12,246	45,173	Polk	46	790	2,536
De Soto	4	36	67	Putnam	7	81	223
Dixie	3	10	22	St. Johns	12	162	402
Duval	88	6,086	20,031	St. Lucie	16	800	2,257
Escambia	42	1,564	4,789	Santa Rosa	8	286	827
Flagler	4	29	57	Sarasota	43	984	3,004
Gadsden	8	59	156	Seminole	41	2,768	10,526
Hendry	4	50	125	Sumter	6	31	83
Hernando	5	131	372	Suwannee	5	85	246
Highlands	119	5,891	23,538	Taylor	4	54	119
Indian River	13	232	637	Volusia	39	584	1,679
Jackson	6	66	168	Washington	5	172	466
Lee	59	2,175	6,256	Multicounty 1/	82	573	2,403
Leon	49	1,680	5,776				

1/ Units without a fixed or known location within the state.
Note for Tables 14.35 and 14.36: Private employment. Data are preliminary. De-
tail may not add to totals due to disclosure editing and/or rounding. See Tables in
Section 23.00 for public employment data. See Appendix for an explanation of selec-
tion of industries included.
Source for Tables 14.35 and 14.36: State of Florida, Department of Labor and Em-
ployment Security, Bureau of Labor Market Information, "Employment and Wages"
(ES-202), unpublished data.

University of Florida   **Bureau of Economic and Business Research**

Table 14.37. NEWSPAPER PRINTING AND PUBLISHING, TELEPHONE COMMUNICATIONS, AND
RADIO AND TELEVISION BROADCASTING STATIONS: AVERAGE MONTHLY PRIVATE
REPORTING UNITS, EMPLOYMENT, AND PAYROLL COVERED BY UNEMPLOYMENT
COMPENSATION LAW IN THE STATE AND COUNTIES OF FLORIDA, 1996

County	Number of reporting units	Number of employees	Payroll ($1,000)	County	Number of reporting units	Number of employees	Payroll ($1,000)
Newspaper printing and publishing (SIC code 271)							
Florida	312	25,205	60,835	Okaloosa	3	227	382
Alachua	6	381	701	Osceola	4	99	191
Broward	27	2,000	6,524	Palm Beach	20	1,741	5,280
Dade	38	2,967	11,141	Pasco	3	179	297
Highlands	3	101	155	Polk	8	561	1,203
Lake	10	290	481	Santa Rosa	3	58	77
Lee	9	854	1,703	Sarasota	6	681	1,647
Manatee	4	339	845	Seminole	6	79	138
Monroe	3	91	168	Volusia	10	892	2,080
Telephone communications (SIC code 481)							
Florida	1,210	49,271	179,867	Leon	22	1,079	3,783
Bay	9	354	1,038	Martin	5	99	421
Brevard	27	542	2,447	Orange	106	6,806	25,169
Broward	148	5,479	20,800	Palm Beach	72	2,973	10,159
Dade	188	7,661	27,773	Pasco	11	146	599
Duval	64	4,240	15,216	Pinellas	67	2,395	8,155
Escambia	24	1,125	3,768	Putnam	4	50	177
Hernando	4	119	358	Saint Lucie	7	589	1,813
Hillsborough	116	6,024	24,317	Seminole	31	2,511	9,726
Indian River	6	90	335	Volusia	13	161	480
Lee	36	1,487	4,478	Multicounty 1/	50	245	1,408
Radio and television broadcasting stations (SIC code 483)							
Florida	419	12,379	42,212	Manatee	3	5	17
Alachua	9	237	482	Marion	7	103	213
Bay	13	281	541	Monroe	10	78	141
Brevard	15	169	293	Okaloosa	11	119	204
Broward	26	714	3,285	Orange	21	1,130	4,064
Collier	6	124	340	Palm Beach	29	898	3,227
Dade	48	2,963	12,130	Pasco	3	41	66
Duval	21	1,069	2,917	Pinellas	19	839	3,611
Escambia	13	225	478	Polk	9	94	210
Hillsborough	18	1,055	3,915	St. Johns	4	32	32
Indian River	4	22	55	St. Lucie	7	112	321
Lee	19	534	1,460	Sarasota	9	187	435
Leon	21	456	1,664	Volusia	14	144	335

1/ Reporting units without a fixed location within the state or of unknown county
location.
Note: Private employment. Data are preliminary. Only counties for which data
are disclosed are shown. Detail may not add to totals due to disclosure editing
and/or rounding. See Tables 23.70, 23.71, 23.72, 23.73, and 23.74 for public employment data.

Source: State of Florida, Department of Labor and Employment Security, Bureau of
Labor Market Information, "Employment and Wages" (ES-202), unpublished data.

Table 14.60. TELEPHONE COMPANIES: SPECIFIED CHARACTERISTICS OF COMPANIES
IN FLORIDA, DECEMBER 1996

| | | Florida access lines 1/ | | |
| | Number of ex-changes | Total number | Percent-age of state total | Annual growth rate (per-centage) |
Companies and headquarters				
Florida	282	9,973,132	100.00	7.74
ALLTEL Florida, Inc.				
Live Oak	27	73,139	0.73	6.56
BellSouth Telecommunications Company				
Miami	101	5,882,901	58.99	9.25
Central Telephone Company of Florida				
Tallahassee	35	378,965	3.80	6.17
Florala Telephone Company				
Florala, Alabama	2	2,237	0.02	7.60
Frontier Communications of the South				
Atmore, Alabama	2	3,932	0.04	4.55
GTE Florida, Inc.				
Tampa	24	2,124,835	21.31	5.35
Gulf Telephone Company				
Perry	2	9,030	0.09	4.34
Indiantown Telephone System, Inc.				
Indiantown	1	3,325	0.03	1.84
Northeast Florida Telephone Company				
Macclenny	2	7,539	0.08	5.53
Quincy Telephone Company				
Quincy	3	12,756	0.13	2.34
St. Joseph Telephone and Telegraph Company				
Port St. Joe	13	29,994	0.30	10.99
United Telephone Company of Florida				
Altamonte Springs	69	1,432,595	14.36	5.85
Vista-United Telecommunications				
Lake Buena Vista	1	11,884	0.12	0.32

1/ An access line is the line going to a home or building for the main telephone located there.
    Note: Telephone companies listed above have headquarters in Florida, except as specified. Detail may not add to totals due to rounding.

    Source: State of Florida, Public Service Commission, *1996 Annual Report.*

University of Florida   **Bureau of Economic and Business Research**

Table 14.61. TELEPHONE COMPANIES: NUMBER OF CALLS AND BILLED ACCESS MINUTES BY TELEPHONE COMPANY IN FLORIDA, 1995

(rounded to thousands)

Company	Local calls	IntraLATA toll calls completed (originating)	InterLATA toll calls completed (originating)			InterLATA billed access minutes (originating and terminating)		
			Total	Interstate	Intrastate	Total	Interstate	Intrastate
Florida	31,373,098	906,477	4,719,168	3,299,091	1,420,077	38,512,022	27,897,856	10,614,165
ALLTEL	(NA)	6,797	10,666	4,356	6,310	263,464	153,286	110,179
CENTEL	1,040,158	27,449	173,417	102,132	71,285	1,547,754	991,114	556,640
Florala 1/	4,401	316	348	243	105	6,741	5,359	1,381
Frontier 1/	(NA)	530	4,915	3,812	1,103	9,750	7,727	2,023
GTE	5,567,700	76,986	1,428,719	970,059	458,660	7,954,980	5,820,313	2,134,667
Gulf	41,081	2,942	5,318	2,440	2,878	30,617	15,759	14,858
Indiantown	2,650	1,088	1,426	767	659	10,981	6,728	4,253
Northeast	16,969	619	695	409	286	19,407	12,360	7,047
Quincy 1/	(NA)	8	4,832	3,170	1,662	36,447	23,563	12,884
St. Joseph	33,981	5,587	4,778	2,217	2,561	(NA)	(NA)	(NA)
Southern Bell	21,826,509	663,660	2,398,154	1,817,766	580,388	22,603,236	16,801,889	5,801,347
United	2,719,501	119,312	668,298	377,235	291,063	5,892,041	3,944,803	1,947,238
Vista-United	120,147	1,182	17,602	14,484	3,118	136,604	114,956	21,649

LATA Local Access Transport Area.
(NA) Not available.
1/ Florida only.
Note: See Table 14.60 for a complete list of company names and headquarters.

Source: State of Florida, Public Service Commission, Division of Research and Regulatory Review, *Statistics of the Florida Local Exchange Companies, 1995.*

Table 14.62. TELEPHONE COMPANIES: LOCAL EXCHANGE COMPANIES (LEC) ACCESS LINES IN SERVICE BY TYPE IN FLORIDA, DECEMBER 31, 1996

Company	Total	Residential access lines		Business access lines		Inter-exchange access lines	LEC pay-phones	CPE coin access lines
		Number	Per-centage all lines	Number	Per-centage all lines			
Florida	9,996,892	6,961,464	69.6	2,893,782	28.9	24,800	63,088	53,758
ALLTEL	74,970	58,494	78.0	13,714	18.3	1,831	379	552
BellSouth	5,900,112	4,044,238	68.5	1,765,113	29.9	17,722	39,919	33,120
CENTEL	379,133	235,150	62.0	139,248	36.7	168	1,988	2,579
Florala	2,237	2,039	91.1	188	8.4	0	6	4
Frontier	3,932	3,594	91.4	318	8.1	0	14	6
GTE	2,126,555	1,519,556	71.5	584,066	27.5	1,720	12,652	8,561
Gulf	8,503	6,213	73.1	2,126	25.0	2	50	112
Indiantown	3,325	2,285	68.7	921	27.7	0	47	72
Northeast	7,539	6,054	80.3	1,387	18.4	0	38	60
Quincy	12,756	9,633	75.5	2,873	22.5	0	59	191
St. Joseph	29,994	22,626	75.4	6,894	23.0	0	149	325
United	1,433,512	1,050,749	73.3	367,279	25.6	917	7,538	7,029
Vista-United	14,324	833	5.8	9,655	67.4	2,440	249	1,147

CPE Customer Premises Exchange.
Note: See Table 14.60 for a complete list of company names and headquarters.

Source: State of Florida, Public Service Commission, Division of Research and Regulatory Review, *Statistics of Florida Telecommunications Companies, 1996.*

POWER
AND ENERGY

Gallons of Gasoline Sold Per Person, 1995

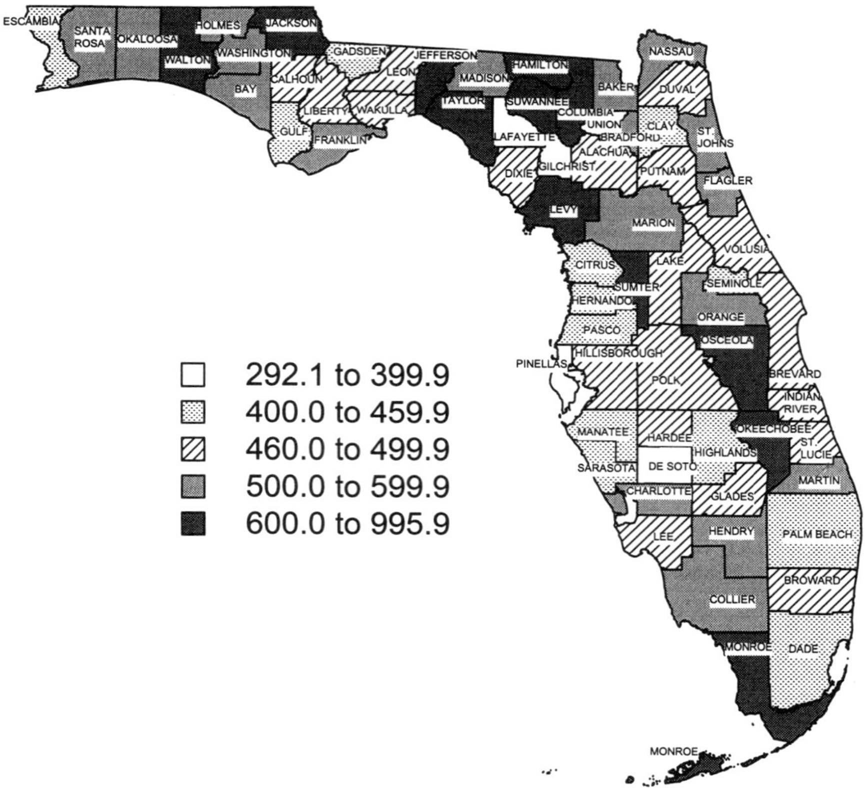

☐	292.1 to 399.9
▦	400.0 to 459.9
▨	460.0 to 499.9
▓	500.0 to 599.9
■	600.0 to 995.9

Source: Table 15.67

SECTION 15.00
POWER AND ENERGY

TABLES LISTED BY MAJOR HEADINGS

University of Florida   **Bureau of Economic and Business Research**

Table 15.06. ENERGY CONSUMPTION ESTIMATES: AMOUNT CONSUMED BY TYPE OF FUEL
IN FLORIDA 1985 THROUGH 1994

(in trillions of British thermal units)

Year	Total	Petro- leum 1/	Natural gas	Coal	Nuclear	Electric inter- state 2/	Hydro- elec- tric
1985	2,610.5	1,325.5	305.1	472.4	253.7	251.4	2.5
1986	2,693.9	1,509.3	298.9	459.4	238.0	186.1	2.2
1987	2,793.1	1,469.1	313.6	586.6	202.3	219.2	2.3
1988	2,954.4	1,583.7	305.8	611.5	281.4	169.8	2.2
1989	3,026.1	1,585.9	337.2	630.2	224.3	246.0	2.4
1990	3,155.4	1,573.8	342.0	624.3	232.6	285.7	1.8
1991	3,110.9	1,548.1	361.0	642.8	220.3	239.8	2.7
1992	3,163.9	1,573.1	370.3	652.7	268.2	196.2	2.4
1993	3,228.6	1,632.1	353.4	652.2	276.5	206.9	2.2
1994	3,382.1	1,686.1	392.5	641.7	284.9	265.8	2.8

1/ Includes asphalt, aviation gasoline, jet fuel, distillates, kerosene, lubri-
cants, motor gasoline, residual fuel, and liquefied petroleum gas.
2/ Combines electric sales and energy losses associated with interstate sales.
Losses estimated to be 7,088 of the 10,400 British thermal units per kilowatt-hour
purchased.
Note: Totals from 1990 include expanded coverage of nonelectric utility use of
renewable energy and are not comparable to previous years.

Table 15.07.   ENERGY CONSUMPTION ESTIMATES: PER CAPITA ENERGY CONSUMPTION
BY TYPE OF FUEL IN FLORIDA, 1985 THROUGH 1994

(in millions of British thermal units)

Year	Total	Petro- leum 1/	Natural gas	Coal	Nuclear	Electric inter- state 2/	Hydro- elec- tric
1985	231.3	117.4	27.0	41.9	22.5	22.3	0.2
1986	231.1	129.5	25.6	39.4	20.4	16.0	0.2
1987	231.9	122.0	26.0	48.7	16.8	18.2	0.2
1988	237.9	127.5	24.6	49.2	22.7	13.7	0.2
1989	236.5	123.9	26.3	49.2	17.5	19.2	0.2
1990	236.5	121.6	26.4	48.3	18.0	22.1	0.1
1991	228.7	117.6	27.4	48.7	16.7	18.1	0.2
1992	228.4	117.5	27.6	48.6	20.0	14.6	0.2
1993	229.9	120.2	26.1	47.9	20.3	15.2	0.2
1994	234.7	117.0	27.2	44.5	19.8	18.4	0.2

1/ Includes asphalt, aviation gasoline, jet fuel, distillates, kerosene, lubri-
cants, motor gasoline, residual fuel, and liquefied petroleum gas.
2/ Combines electric sales and energy losses associated with interstate sales.
Losses estimated to be 7,088 of the 10,400 British thermal units per kilowatt-hour
purchased.
Note: Totals from 1990 include expanded coverage of nonelectric utility use of
renewable energy and are not comparable to previous years. Per capita is computed
using Bureau of the Census data for 1990 and *Florida Estimates of Population* for all
other years.
Source for Tables 15.06 and 15.07: U.S., Department of Energy, Energy Information
Administration, *State Energy Data Report, 1994: Consumption Estimates,* October 1996.
Compiled by State of Florida, Department of Community Affairs.

University of Florida   **Bureau of Economic and Business Research**

Table 15.08. ENERGY CONSUMPTION: CONSUMPTION OF RENEWABLE ENERGY BY TYPE
IN FLORIDA, 1989 THROUGH 1994

(in trillions of British thermal units)

Type of energy	1989	1990	1991	1992	1993	1994
Total	167.7	168.7	171.1	180.8	177.2	176.7
Direct solar	4.4	4.8	5.1	5.6	6.0	6.3
Biomass energy, total	160.9	162.1	163.3	172.8	169.1	167.6
Wood	115.9	113.3	109.9	114.1	109.5	111.1
Pulp and paper industry	98.9	95.9	90.7	94.8	89.8	91.7
Residential	15.6	16.0	16.3	16.5	16.8	16.5
Electric utility	1.4	1.4	2.9	2.9	2.9	2.9
Crop residues	14.0	16.5	16.8	16.0	16.5	16.2
Alcohol fuels	0.6	0.7	0.8	0.5	0.6	0.2
Municipal solid waste	28.0	29.8	33.1	39.8	42.6	40.0
Hydroelectric energy	2.4	1.8	2.7	2.4	2.2	2.8

Note: Consumption of renewable energy in Florida from wind systems and animal
waste is negligible (greater than 0 but less than 0.05 trillion British thermal
units) and consumption of geothermal energy is significant, but impossible to measure. Therefore, these data are not included in this table. Detail may not add to
totals because of rounding.

Source: State of Florida, Department of Community Affairs, *Florida Energy Data Report, 1970-1992*, and unpublished data.

Table 15.09. CRUDE OIL AND NATURAL GAS: AMOUNT PRODUCED BY FIELD IN FLORIDA
1994 THROUGH 1996

Field	Crude oil (barrels)			Natural gas (1,000 cubic feet)		
	1994	1995	1996	1994	1995	1996
Total	6,095,150	5,681,618	6,291,954	8,514,155	7,171,557	6,742,302
South Florida	1,502,617	1,545,308	2,105,874	281,703	198,105	220,165
Bear Island	123,877	90,125	95,331	24,453	23,099	9,178
Corkscrew	61,667	47,136	48,474	0	0	0
Lake Trafford	2,590	0	1,423	0	0	0
Lehigh Park	50,153	43,271	52,941	66,851	6,318	6,045
Mid-Felda	17,074	10,299	18,850	0	0	0
Raccoon Point	891,456	991,719	1,536,131	162,299	(NA)	169,686
Sunniland	0	0	0	0	0	0
Sunoco Felda	0	0	0	0	0	0
Townsend Canal	2,590	4,816	3,832	0	0	0
West Felda	353,210	357,942	348,892	28,100	(NA)	35,256
Northwest Florida	4,592,533	4,136,310	4,186,080	8,232,452	6,973,452	6,522,137
Blackjack Creek	354,722	301,964	272,750	814,154	738,079	657,651
Bluff Springs	0	0	0	0	0	0
Coldwater Creek	32,699	3,404	0	0	0	0
Jay	4,159,336	3,810,967	3,895,660	7,410,410	6,230,813	5,859,793
McLellan	24,842	17,238	17,594	7,888	4,560	4,693
Mt. Carmel	20,934	2,737	76	0	0	0

(NA) Not available.
Note: Data from Florida Geological Survey.
Source: State of Florida, Department of Community Affairs, unpublished data.

University of Florida   **Bureau of Economic and Business Research**

Table 15.14. ELECTRIC UTILITY INDUSTRY: SALES, CUSTOMERS, AND COUNTIES SERVED
BY PRIVATELY AND PUBLICLY OWNED UTILITIES AND BY RURAL
ELECTRIC COOPERATIVES IN FLORIDA, 1995

Utility	Electricity sales to ultimate customers (MWH)	Number of ultimate customers December 1/	Counties served
Investor-owned systems			
Florida Power 2/	29,499,476	1,271,766	Alachua, Bay, Brevard, Citrus, Columbia, Dixie, Flagler, Franklin, Gadsden, Gilchrist, Gulf, Hamilton, Hardee, Hernando, Highlands, Jefferson, Lafayette, Lake, Leon, Levy, Liberty, Madison, Marion, Orange, Osceola, Pasco, Pinellas, Polk, Seminole, Sumter, Suwannee, Taylor, Volusia, Wakulla
Florida Power and Light	76,246,930	3,488,779	Alachua, Baker, Bradford, Brevard, Broward, Charlotte, Clay, Collier, Columbia, Dade, De Soto, Duval, Flagler, Glades, Hardee, Hendry, Highlands, Indian River, Lee, Manatee, Martin, Monroe, Nassau, Okeechobee, Palm Beach, Putnam, St. Johns, St. Lucie, Sarasota, Seminole, Suwannee, Union, Volusia
Florida Public Utilities	596,834	22,613	Calhoun, Jackson, Liberty, Nassau
Gulf Power	8,534,484	325,110	Bay, Escambia, Holmes, Jackson, Okaloosa, Santa Rosa, Walton, Washington
Tampa Electric	14,599,955	495,194	Hillsborough, Pasco, Pinellas, Polk
Generating municipal systems			
Ft. Pierce	521,731	23,963	St. Lucie
Gainesville	1,449,119	71,697	Alachua
Homestead	(NA)	(NA)	Dade
Jacksonville	9,659,431	316,284	Clay, Duval, St. Johns
Key West	583,038	25,884	Monroe
Kissimmee	857,503	40,568	Osceola
Lake Worth	334,995	24,539	Palm Beach
Lakeland	2,277,296	101,983	Polk
New Smyrna Beach	299,311	20,167	Volusia
Orlando	3,935,058	170,969	Orange
Reedy Creek	895,168	1,147	Orange
St. Cloud	254,441	15,094	Orange, Osceola
Starke	61,124	2,557	Bradford
Tallahassee	2,147,368	86,335	Leon
Vero Beach	553,710	26,806	Indian River
Wauchula	52,394	2,583	Hardee
Florida Keys	550,015	28,579	Monroe

See footnotes at end of table.   Continued . . .

University of Florida   **Bureau of Economic and Business Research**

Table 15.14. ELECTRIC UTILITY INDUSTRY: SALES, CUSTOMERS, AND COUNTIES SERVED BY PRIVATELY AND PUBLICLY OWNED UTILITIES AND BY RURAL ELECTRIC COOPERATIVES IN FLORIDA, 1995 (Continued)

Utility	Electricity sales to ultimate customers (MWH)	Number of ultimate customers December 1/	Counties served
Nongenerating municipal systems			
Alachua	54,484	2,360	Alachua
Bartow	224,784	9,967	Polk
Blountstown	33,555	1,409	Calhoun
Bushnell	17,990	885	Sumter
Chattahoochee	50,432	1,330	Gadsden
Clewiston	98,000	3,698	Hendry
Ft. Meade	37,456	2,566	Polk
Green Cove Springs	106,017	2,691	Clay
Havana	20,848	1,331	Gadsden
Jacksonville Beach	550,768	26,750	Duval
Leesburg	390,174	17,335	Lake
Moore Haven	14,961	1,100	Glades
Mount Dora	74,625	4,550	Lake
Newberry	27,948	888	Alachua
Ocala	1,046,058	41,535	Marion
Quincy	139,435	4,482	Gadsden
Williston	24,101	1,202	Levy
Nongenerating rural electric cooperatives			
Central Florida	294,189	23,704	Alachua, Dixie, Gilchrist, Levy
Choctawhatchee	405,307	26,233	Holmes, Okaloosa, Santa Rosa, Walton
Clay	1,936,194	113,430	Alachua, Baker, Bradford, Clay, Columbia, Duval, Lake, Levy, Marion, Putnam, Union, Volusia
Escambia River	124,684	8,046	Escambia, Santa Rosa
Glades	231,606	13,109	Collier, Glades, Hendry, Highlands, Okeechobee
Gulf Coast	194,554	14,096	Bay, Calhoun, Gulf, Jackson, Walton, Washington
Lee County	2,195,372	132,165	Charlotte, Collier, Hendry, Lee
Okefenokee 4/	112,026	6,802	Baker, Duval, Nassau, Okeechobee
Peace River	276,368	20,263	Brevard, De Soto, Hardee, Highlands, Hillsborough, Indian River, Manatee, Osceola, Polk, Sarasota, Sumter
Sumter	1,108,483	82,404	Citrus, Hernando, Lake, Levy, Marion, Pasco, Sumter
Suwannee Valley	238,572	17,104	Columbia, Hamilton, Lafayette, Suwannee
Talquin	687,248	41,308	Gadsden, Leon, Liberty, Wakulla
Tri-county	162,268	13,210	Dixie, Jefferson, Madison, Taylor
West Florida	284,237	22,557	Calhoun, Holmes, Jackson, Washington

See footnotes at end of table.   Continued . . .

Table 15.14. ELECTRIC UTILITY INDUSTRY: SALES, CUSTOMERS, AND COUNTIES SERVED
BY PRIVATELY AND PUBLICLY OWNED UTILITIES AND BY RURAL
ELECTRIC COOPERATIVES IN FLORIDA, 1995 (Continued)

Utility	Electricity sales to ultimate customers (MWH)	Number of ultimate customers Decem- ber 1/	Counties served
Nongenerating rural elec- tric cooperatives (Continued)			
Withlacoochee River	2,238,438	138,457	Citrus, Hernando, Pasco, Polk, Sumter

MWH Megawatt-hours (1,000 kilowatt-hours).
(NA) Not available.
(X) Not applicable.
1/ Year-end monthly average.
2/ Includes the Sebring municipal system.
3/ Florida customers only.

Source: State of Florida, Public Service Commission, Division of Research and
Regulatory Review, *Statistics of the Florida Electric Utility Industry, 1995.*

Table 15.15. ELECTRIC, GAS, AND SANITARY SERVICES: AVERAGE MONTHLY PRIVATE
REPORTING UNITS, EMPLOYMENT, AND PAYROLL COVERED BY UNEMPLOYMENT
COMPENSATION LAW BY INDUSTRY IN FLORIDA, 1996

SIC code	Industry	Number of re- porting units	Number of em- ployees	Payroll ($1,000)
49	Electric, gas, and sanitary services	815	34,806	132,445
491	Electric services	169	23,287	102,322
492	Gas production and distribution	54	2,053	6,253
493	Combination electric and gas, and other utility services	39	172	348
494	Water supply	157	1,541	3,450
495	Sanitary services	368	7,621	19,841
497	Irrigation systems	26	110	164

Note: Private employment. Data are preliminary. Detail may not add to totals
due to disclosure editing and/or rounding. See Tables 23.70, 23.71, 23.72, 23.73,
and 23.74 for public employment data.

Source: State of Florida, Department of Labor and Employment Security, Bureau of
Labor Market Information, "Employment and Wages" (ES-202), unpublished data.

Table 15.16. ELECTRIC, GAS, AND SANITARY SERVICES: AVERAGE MONTHLY PRIVATE REPORTING UNITS, EMPLOYMENT, AND PAYROLL COVERED BY UNEMPLOYMENT COMPENSATION LAW IN THE STATE AND COUNTIES OF FLORIDA, 1996

County	Number of reporting units	Number of employees	Payroll ($1,000)	County	Number of reporting units	Number of employees	Payroll ($1,000)
Electric, gas, and sanitary services (SIC code 49)							
Florida	815	34,806	132,445	Leon	8	224	640
				Liberty	3	38	82
Alachua	10	179	478	Madison	6	76	199
Bay	11	349	1,306	Manatee	10	359	1,148
Bradford	3	30	138	Marion	26	314	991
Brevard	12	558	2,055	Martin	14	398	1,593
Broward	51	2,418	8,571	Monroe	10	197	620
Charlotte	11	276	843	Nassau	7	87	243
Clay	12	393	1,309	Okaloosa	13	321	858
Collier	21	477	1,331	Orange	37	1,252	3,942
Columbia	5	127	454	Osceola	7	48	142
Dade	47	5,409	22,003	Pasco	26	576	1,825
Duval	33	571	1,546	Polk	39	776	2,441
Flagler	5	112	344	Putnam	5	169	697
Gulf	5	98	264	St. Johns	10	68	213
Hendry	3	23	55	Santa Rosa	18	218	553
Hernando	5	230	577	Sarasota	29	808	2,746
Highlands	9	110	350	Seminole	21	627	2,123
Hillsborough	52	4,367	16,584	Sumter	3	235	804
Holmes	3	37	94	Taylor	6	39	133
Indian River	3	15	24	Volusia	17	776	2,849
Jackson	5	172	504	Walton	12	184	416
Lake	14	323	1,033	Washington	3	37	166
Lee	26	962	2,989	Multicounty 1/	19	235	708
Sanitary services (SIC code 495)							
Florida	368	7,621	19,841	Marion	7	22	30
				Martin	5	25	58
Alachua	6	105	229	Monroe	9	69	185
Bay	5	53	138	Okaloosa	5	86	162
Brevard	7	70	96	Orange	21	271	523
Broward	37	1,184	3,547	Osceola	3	11	21
Charlotte	3	116	290	Pasco	8	41	72
Clay	7	80	216	Polk	19	318	676
Collier	10	204	484	St. Johns	6	25	68
Dade	33	1,261	3,624	Sarasota	16	240	575
Duval	22	446	1,187	Seminole	8	160	388
Hillsborough	21	920	2,446	Volusia	6	163	304
Lake	5	201	641	Walton	6	76	122
Lee	10	222	521				

Note: Private employment. For a list of three-digit industries included see Table 15.15. Data are preliminary. Only counties for which data are disclosed are shown. Detail may not add to totals due to disclosure editing and/or rounding. See Tables 23.70, 23.71, 23.72, 23.73, and 23.74 for public employment data.

Source: State of Florida, Department of Labor and Employment Security, Bureau of Labor Market Information, "Employment and Wages" (ES-202), unpublished data.

Table 15.25. ELECTRIC RATES: RESIDENTIAL ELECTRIC RATES CHARGED
BY MUNICIPAL, COOPERATIVE, AND INVESTOR-OWNED UTILITIES
IN FLORIDA, DECEMBER 31, 1995

(in dollars)

Utility	Minimum bill or customer charge	500 KWH	750 KWH	1,000 KWH	1,500 KWH
Municipal					
Alachua	8.00	49.40	70.10	90.80	132.20
Bartow	5.50	41.61	59.66	77.71	113.82
Blountstown	3.50	44.00	64.25	84.50	125.00
Bushnell	6.75	46.04	65.68	85.32	124.61
Chattahoochee	4.50	40.73	58.84	76.95	113.18
Clewiston	6.50	41.25	58.63	76.00	110.75
Ft. Meade	8.67	50.84	71.93	93.01	135.18
Ft. Pierce	5.35	39.88	57.15	74.41	108.94
Gainesville	4.90	38.65	55.53	73.45	109.30
Green Cove Springs	6.00	42.69	61.03	79.38	116.07
Havana	6.00	49.99	71.98	93.97	137.96
Homestead	5.50	47.26	68.15	89.03	130.79
Jacksonville	5.50	37.33	53.24	69.15	100.98
Jacksonville Beach	4.50	41.00	59.25	77.50	114.00
Key West	4.76	44.36	64.16	83.96	123.56
Kissimmee	4.00	39.86	57.78	75.71	111.57
Lake Worth	3.94	38.52	55.81	73.10	107.68
Lakeland	2.78	40.83	59.85	78.87	116.92
Leesburg	5.00	41.10	59.15	77.20	113.30
Moore Haven	8.50	44.70	62.80	80.90	117.10
Mount Dora	4.94	43.19	62.32	81.44	119.69
New Smyrna Beach	5.00	41.88	60.32	78.76	115.64
Newberry	4.75	48.98	71.10	93.21	137.44
Ocala	7.00	40.92	57.88	74.84	108.76
Orlando	6.00	41.74	59.60	77.47	113.21
Quincy	2.40	42.38	62.37	82.36	122.34
Reedy Creek	2.85	37.11	54.23	71.36	105.62
St. Cloud	6.45	39.70	56.33	72.95	117.20
Starke	7.39	46.13	67.56	88.99	131.85
Tallahassee	4.94	46.89	67.87	88.84	130.79
Vero Beach	7.00	48.04	68.55	89.07	130.11
Wauchula	8.62	45.09	63.33	81.56	118.03
Williston	6.00	52.06	75.09	98.12	144.18

See footnotes at end of table.   Continued . . .

Table 15.25. ELECTRIC RATES: RESIDENTIAL ELECTRIC RATES CHARGED
BY MUNICIPAL, COOPERATIVE, AND INVESTOR-OWNED UTILITIES
IN FLORIDA, DECEMBER 31, 1995 (Continued)

(in dollars)

Utility	Minimum bill or customer charge	500 KWH	750 KWH	1,000 KWH	1,500 KWH
Cooperative					
Central Florida	8.50	59.25	84.63	110.00	160.75
Choctawhatchee	12.32	43.50	59.10	74.69	105.87
Clay	9.00	56.35	80.03	103.70	156.25
Escambia River	7.00	42.40	60.10	77.80	113.20
Florida Keys	6.40	38.26	54.18	70.11	101.97
Glades	10.50	53.00	74.25	95.50	138.00
Gulf Coast	7.00	43.05	61.08	79.10	115.15
Lee County	5.00	44.80	64.70	84.60	124.40
Okefenokee	10.00	47.97	66.96	85.94	123.91
Peace River	10.50	52.75	73.88	95.00	137.25
Sumter	8.37	56.26	80.21	104.15	152.04
Suwannee Valley	8.73	28.32	38.11	47.90	67.49
Talquin	8.00	44.50	62.75	81.00	117.50
Tri-county	8.00	49.39	70.08	90.77	132.16
West Florida	8.00	44.51	62.77	81.02	117.53
Withlacoochee River	9.75	44.87	62.42	79.98	115.10
Investor-owned					
Florida Power	8.85	44.92	62.96	80.99	117.06
Florida Power and Light	5.65	39.01	55.69	74.87	113.23
Florida Public Utilities					
Fernandina Beach					
division	7.00	39.30	55.45	71.60	103.90
Marianna division	8.30	38.83	54.10	69.36	99.89
Gulf Power 1/	8.07	38.58	53.84	69.09	99.60
Tampa Electric	8.50	44.31	62.22	80.12	115.93

1/ Summer/winter rates in effect. Winter rates are shown.
Note: Cost excludes local taxes. December 1995 fuel costs are included for municipal and cooperative utilities. October 1995 through March 1996 fuel costs are included for investor-owned utilities.

Source: State of Florida, Public Service Commission, Division of Research and
Regulatory Review, *Statistics of the Florida Electric Utility Industry, 1995.*

Table 15.26. ELECTRIC RATES: COMMERCIAL AND INDUSTRIAL ELECTRIC RATES
CHARGED BY MUNICIPAL, COOPERATIVE, AND INVESTOR-OWNED UTILITIES
IN FLORIDA, DECEMBER 31, 1995

(in dollars)

Utility	15,000 KWH	45,000 KWH	150,000 KWH	400,000 KWH	800,000 KWH
Municipal					
Alachua	1,378	3,642	12,088	30,213	60,403
Bartow	1,434	3,695	12,273	30,163	60,307
Blountstown	1,353	4,046	13,471	35,911	71,815
Bushnell	1,452	3,806	12,637	31,397	62,773
Chattahoochee	1,208	3,694	12,313	31,160	62,320
Clewiston	1,273	3,478	11,510	29,435	58,835
Ft. Meade	1,308	4,011	13,161	32,226	64,362
Ft. Pierce	1,216	3,144	10,411	25,746	51,462
Gainesville	1,169	3,109	10,326	22,641	45,221
Green Cove Springs	1,336	3,432	11,382	23,777	47,428
Havana	1,326	3,965	13,202	35,194	70,382
Homestead	1,466	4,000	13,414	33,747	67,528
Jacksonville	1,101	2,771	9,120	21,260	42,320
Jacksonville Beach	1,584	4,081	13,566	33,316	66,616
Key West	1,611	4,305	14,340	35,935	71,865
Kissimmee	1,247	3,027	10,509	23,986	47,930
Lake Worth	1,070	2,813	10,406	24,706	49,036
Lakeland	1,450	3,823	12,713	31,646	63,280
Leesburg	1,351	3,418	11,352	27,577	55,137
Moore Haven	1,416	3,761	12,483	31,283	62,543
Mount Dora	1,069	2,808	9,325	23,195	46,375
New Smyrna Beach	1,421	3,484	11,579	27,519	55,023
Newberry	1,600	4,299	14,253	36,018	72,002
Ocala	1,063	2,701	8,956	21,863	43,705
Orlando	1,122	2,811	9,337	22,539	45,063
Quincy	1,109	2,927	9,616	24,308	47,508
Reedy Creek	1,092	2,937	9,755	24,615	49,215
St. Cloud	1,337	3,991	13,284	35,409	70,809
Starke	1,472	4,044	13,423	32,473	68,605
Tallahassee	1,302	3,283	10,805	26,330	52,620
Vero Beach	1,348	3,695	12,109	30,978	61,887
Wauchula	1,136	3,628	11,941	29,911	59,757
Williston	1,536	4,198	13,742	34,562	71,017

See footnotes at end of table.   Continued . . .

University of Florida   **Bureau of Economic and Business Research**

Table 15.26. ELECTRIC RATES: COMMERCIAL AND INDUSTRIAL ELECTRIC RATES
CHARGED BY MUNICIPAL, COOPERATIVE, AND INVESTOR-OWNED UTILITIES
IN FLORIDA, DECEMBER 31, 1995 (Continued)

(in dollars)

Utility	15,000 KWH	45,000 KWH	150,000 KWH	400,000 KWH	800,000 KWH
Cooperative					
Central Florida	1,738	4,565	15,100	37,350	74,650
Choctawhatchee	1,045	2,741	9,450	21,199	41,898
Clay	1,568	4,312	14,245	36,645	67,810
Escambia River	1,233	3,205	10,590	26,340	52,640
Florida Keys	1,154	3,360	11,323	29,366	58,784
Glades	1,616	4,508	14,425	35,175	70,175
Gulf Coast	1,026	2,754	9,152	23,052	46,092
Lee County	1,194	3,177	11,130	27,055	54,095
Okefenokee	1,277	3,157	10,291	25,176	50,252
Peace River	1,198	3,050	10,050	24,750	49,450
Sumter	1,581	4,166	13,772	34,018	67,986
Suwannee Valley	851	2,008	6,597	15,469	30,897
Talquin	1,111	2,968	10,080	22,280	44,260
Tri-county	1,321	3,237	10,556	24,658	49,217
West Florida	1,081	2,692	8,855	21,530	43,010
Withlacoochee River	1,140	2,909	9,639	23,609	47,193
Investor-owned					
Florida Power	956	2,559	8,501	21,384	42,756
Florida Power and Light	1,028	3,021	9,834	23,211	46,378
Florida Public Utilities					
Fernandina Beach division	930	2,581	8,513	22,048	44,058
Marianna division	860	2,311	7,602	19,400	38,756
Gulf Power 1/	956	2,447	8,958	20,653	41,079
Tampa Electric	1,197	2,963	9,778	23,713	47,171

KWH Kilowatt-hour.
1/ Summer/winter rates in effect. Winter rates are shown.
Note: Cost excludes local taxes. December 1995 fuel costs are included for municipal and cooperative utilities. October 1995 through March 1996 fuel costs are included for investor-owned utilities.

Source: State of Florida, Public Service Commission, Division of Research and
Regulatory Review, *Statistics of the Florida Electric Utility Industry, 1995*.

University of Florida   **Bureau of Economic and Business Research**

Table 15.27. ELECTRIC UTILITY INDUSTRY: CAPACITY, NET GENERATION, FUEL
CONSUMPTION, SALES, PER CAPITA CONSUMPTION, AND REVENUE
IN FLORIDA, 1991 THROUGH 1995

Item	1991	1992	1993	1994	1995
Nameplate capacity, total (MW)	36,979	36,988	38,039	39,084	38,954
Conventional steam	26,968	26,784	27,316	27,263	27,107
Internal combustion and gas turbine	5,138	5,217	5,925	6,234	6,261
Combined cycle	728	842	652	1,442	1,442
Hydroelectric	21	21	21	21	20
Steam, nuclear	4,124	4,124	4,124	4,124	4,124
Net generation, total (GWH)	134,443	140,060	149,388	152,779	159,156
By prime mover					
Conventional steam	109,226	110,126	119,286	115,196	117,474
Internal combustion and					
gas turbine	1,223	1,070	2,267	8,537	10,348
Combined cycle	2,836	2,361	0	0	0
Hydroelectric	27	247	225	295	250
Steam, nuclear	21,121	26,256	27,610	28,750	31,084
By fuel type					
Natural gas	17,472	17,744	18,064	20,420	33,483
Coal	66,037	58,836	61,000	62,511	65,714
Residual	31,207	28,588	33,985	33,286	22,521
Distillate	637	10,145	10,885	10,267	9,665
Hydroelectric	28	54	51	80	47
Nuclear	19,062	24,693	25,403	26,216	27,726
By type of ownership					
Investor-owned	101,821	104,776	112,251	117,134	121,496
Municipal	32,622	35,284	37,137	35,645	37,660
Fuel consumed for generation					
Natural gas (billion cubic feet)	203	137	174	181	322
Coal (1,000 short tons)	27,955	31,260	28,954	30,239	30,912
Residual (1,000 barrels)	46,611	43,577	54,347	52,233	33,662
Distillate (1,000 barrels)	1,798	1,472	1,426	1,195	1,283
U-235 (trillion BTU)	205	268	301	286	301
Sales to ultimate consumers,					
total (GWH)	146,105	149,238	152,219	159,570	167,311
Residential	72,694	73,293	76,843	80,405	85,536
Commercial	46,810	45,879	48,598	51,519	51,446
Industrial	21,672	24,960	22,022	22,057	24,973
Other public utilities	4,929	5,107	4,755	5,589	5,356
Per capita consumption 1/ (KWH)					
Sales per capita, total	11,293	11,309	11,339	11,725	12,055
Residential sales per capita	5,619	5,554	5,724	5,908	6,163
Kilowatt-hours per capita 2/	10,391	10,614	11,128	11,226	11,467

See footnotes at end of table.   Continued . . .

University of Florida   **Bureau of Economic and Business Research**

Table 15.27. ELECTRIC UTILITY INDUSTRY: CAPACITY, NET GENERATION, FUEL
CONSUMPTION, SALES, PER CAPITA CONSUMPTION, AND REVENUE
IN FLORIDA, 1991 THROUGH 1995 (Continued)

Item	1991	1992	1993	1994	1995
Revenues per GWH by class of					
service ($1,000)	71.5	69.0	72.1	69.5	70.4
Residential	78.9	77.5	79.9	77.8	77.6
Commercial	68.8	64.1	64.3	63.3	64.2
Industrial	52.9	53.6	61.8	55.6	54.2
Other	69.5	65.9	73.7	64.3	90.6

MW Megawatt (1,000 kilowatts).
GWH Gigawatt-hours (million kilowatt-hours).
BTU British thermal units.
KWH Kilowatt-hours.
1/ Total sales divided by population.
2/ Net generation divided by population.
Note: Detail may not add to totals because of rounding. Some data are revised.

Source: State of Florida, Public Service Commission, Division of Research and
Regulatory Review, *Statistics of the Florida Electric Utility Industry, 1995*.

Table 15.41. NATURAL GAS: TYPICAL NATURAL GAS BILLS FOR RESIDENTIAL SERVICE
OF COMPANIES IN FLORIDA, DECEMBER 31, 1996

(amounts in dollars)

Company	Mini-mum bill	20 therms	30 therms	40 therms	50 therms	100 therms
Chesapeake Utilities Company	6.50	22.89	31.08	39.28	47.47	88.44
City Gas Company of Florida	7.00	25.35	34.53	43.71	52.88	98.77
Florida Public Utilities Company	8.00	22.41	29.61	36.81	44.02	80.03
Indiantown Gas Company	5.00	13.29	17.44	21.58	25.73	46.46
Peoples Gas System, Inc.	7.00	23.64	31.96	40.27	48.59	90.18
Sebring Gas System, Inc.	7.00	21.22	28.33	35.44	42.55	78.11
St. Joe Natural Gas Company	3.00	10.41	14.12	17.83	21.53	40.06
South Florida Natural Gas Company	7.00	24.85	33.77	42.70	51.62	96.24
West Florida Natural Gas Company	7.00	22.45	30.18	37.91	45.63	84.27

1 Therm = 100,000 British thermal units.

Source: State of Florida, Public Service Commission, *1996 Annual Report*.

Table 15.42. NATURAL GAS: PRODUCTION, MOVEMENT, AND CONSUMPTION IN FLORIDA
AND THE UNITED STATES, 1994 AND 1995

(quantity in millions of cubic feet)

Item	Florida 1994	Florida 1995	United States 1994	United States 1995
Marketed production 1/	7,486	6,463	19,709,525	19,506,474
Net interstate movements	359,143	523,687	0	0
Net movements across U.S. borders	0	0	2,477,361	2,686,929
Net storage changes 2/	0	0	285,916	-414,768
Extraction loss	1,789	1,630	888,500	907,795
Supplemental gas supplies	0	0	110,826	110,290
Balancing item 3/	2,713	-12,921	-415,579	-230,002
Consumption, total	367,552	515,598	20,707,717	21,580,665
Delivered to consumers	361,428	507,329	18,898,635	19,660,161
Lease fuel	653	620	699,842	792,315
Plant fuel	167	145	423,878	427,853
Pipeline fuel	5,304	7,504	685,362	700,335

1/ Gross withdrawals from gas and oil wells less gas used for repressuring, non-
hydrocarbon gases removed, and quantities vented and flared.
2/ Positive numbers indicate an increase in storage, thus a decrease in supply.
3/ Represents an imbalance between available supplies and consumption.
Note: Some data may be revised.

Source: U.S., Department of Energy, Energy Information Administration, *Historical
Natural Gas Annual, 1930 Through 1995,* Internet site http://www.eia.doe.gov/.

Table 15.43. NATURAL GAS: VOLUME CONSUMED, CONSUMERS, AND PRICE OF NATURAL
GAS DELIVERED TO CONSUMERS IN FLORIDA AND THE UNITED STATES, 1995

Item	Resi-dential	Com-mercial	Indus-trial	Vehi-cle fuel	Electric util-ities
Florida					
Volume consumed (MCF)	14,540	40,383	133,477	75	318,854
Consumers	512,365	46,459	515	(NA)	(NA)
Average price (dollars per thousand cubic feet)	9.85	5.33	3.28	3.86	2.70
United States					
Volume consumed (MCF)	4,850,318	3,031,077	8,579,585	2,674	3,196,507
Consumers	54,322,179	4,636,500	209,398	(NA)	(NA)
Average price (dollars per thousand cubic feet)	6.06	5.05	2.71	3.98	2.04

MCF Million cubic feet.
(NA) Not available.

Source: U.S., Department of Energy, Energy Information Administration, *Historical
Natural Gas Annual, 1930 Through 1995.*

University of Florida   **Bureau of Economic and Business Research**

Table 15.50. NUCLEAR POWER PLANTS: NUMBER OF UNITS, NET GENERATION, AND NET
SUMMER CAPABILITY IN FLORIDA, OTHER LEADING GENERATING STATES,
AND THE UNITED STATES, 1994

Leading State	Number of units	Net generation Total (million KWH)	Net generation Percent-age of total	Net summer capability Total (million KWH)	Net summer capability Percent-age of total
Florida	5	26,682	18.8	3,822	10.8
Illinois	13	72,654	52.7	12,609	38.3
Pennsylvania	9	67,207	39.8	8,788	26.2
South Carolina	7	44,466	59.9	6,364	38.1
California	4	33,752	26.6	4,310	10.0
North Carolina	5	32,346	35.4	4,639	23.2
New York	6	29,231	28.2	4,831	14.7
Georgia	4	28,927	29.3	3,840	17.4
Texas	4	28,745	11.3	4,782	7.5
Virginia	4	25,429	48.2	3,349	24.0
United States	109	640,440	22.0	99,148	14.1

KWH Kilo-watt hour.
Source: U.S., Department of Commerce, Bureau of the Census, *Statistical Abstract
of the United States, 1996.*

Table 15.51. ENERGY CONSUMPTION ESTIMATES: AMOUNT CONSUMED BY SECTOR IN FLORIDA
1980 THROUGH 1994

(in trillions of British thermal units)

Year	Total	Resi-dential	Commer-cial 1/	Indus-trial 2/	Transpor-tation 3/
1980	2,444.3	568.0	384.1	541.7	950.6
1981	2,428.9	576.9	422.7	474.7	954.5
1982	2,322.5	558.0	426.4	401.2	937.0
1983	2,388.7	586.0	460.7	403.8	938.2
1984	2,459.1	611.2	487.7	432.9	927.2
1985	2,610.5	664.2	559.6	435.4	951.2
1986	2,693.9	694.4	589.4	404.1	1,006.0
1987	2,793.1	721.3	612.5	398.8	1,060.5
1988	2,954.4	752.4	640.7	434.9	1,126.4
1989	3,026.0	790.7	667.1	426.6	1,141.7
1990	3,060.0	807.2	690.8	426.3	1,135.6
1991	3,018.1	823.7	699.6	420.7	1,074.1
1992	3,066.4	820.7	695.3	438.0	1,112.4
1993	3,128.2	853.3	701.0	467.8	1,106.1
1994	3,382.0	919.6	719.6	554.2	1,188.6

1/ Includes establishments under SIC codes 15-17, 48-49 (except 491 and part of
493), 50-59, 70-89, and 91-93.
2/ Includes establishments under SIC codes 1-14 and 20-39.
3/ Includes establishments under SIC codes 40-47.

Source: U.S., Department of Energy, Energy Information Administration, *State
Energy Data Report, 1994: Consumption Estimates,* October, 1996. Compiled by State
of Florida, Department of Community Affairs.

Table 15.60. MOTOR FUELS: CONSUMPTION BY USE IN FLORIDA, 1959 THROUGH 1995

(in thousands of gallons)

Year	Total quantity consumed 1/	Nonhighway use 2/	Highway use
1959	1,933,950	276,033	1,641,576
1960	1,950,650	167,431	1,765,819
1961	1,980,408	160,451	1,800,927
1962	2,071,490	133,801	1,917,987
1963	2,169,084	124,988	2,022,714
1964	2,286,002	112,073	2,160,479
1965	2,409,617	104,646	2,291,031
1966	2,562,586	120,505	2,428,962
1967	2,711,163	135,851	2,561,698
1968	2,959,259	138,496	2,803,754
1969	3,215,457	129,949	3,069,173
1970	3,484,439	153,969	3,312,830
1971	3,771,337	146,210	3,585,727
1972	4,215,995	124,098	4,045,322
1973	4,695,983	126,054	4,494,951
1974	4,510,456	123,058	4,342,185
1975	4,639,217	135,547	4,456,610
1976	4,827,840	136,774	4,650,302
1977	5,023,007	131,635	4,846,201
1978	5,337,604	139,114	5,152,263
1979	5,374,535	142,358	5,171,693
1980	5,293,548	164,430	5,116,312
1981	5,390,545	137,165	5,240,229
1982	5,469,775	139,779	5,317,892
1983	5,723,316	163,810	5,548,590
1984	5,934,391	181,767	5,740,587
1985	6,110,435	254,402	5,843,396
1986	6,394,295	263,337	6,116,961
1987	6,700,629	275,337	6,387,472
1988	6,863,376	281,739	6,530,151
1989	7,034,489	292,036	6,680,708
1990	7,043,054	306,520	6,674,542
1991	6,930,325	319,863	6,549,254
1992	7,163,374	264,516	6,827,210
1993	7,431,207	169,860	7,187,669
1994	7,487,188	178,304	7,308,884
1995	7,680,638	206,176	7,474,462

1/ Includes losses allowed for evaporation and handling.
2/ Gasoline. Includes gasohol.
Note: Includes gasoline and all other fuels (except under nonhighway use) under state motor fuel laws. Data for prior years may not be comparable due to revised estimation procedures.

Source: U.S., Department of Transportation, Federal Highway Administration, *Highway Statistics, 1995,* and previous editions.

University of Florida   **Bureau of Economic and Business Research**

Table 15.66. GASOLINE: AVERAGE PRICES IN SELECTED CITIES IN FLORIDA, DECEMBER 1996
AND ANNUALLY IN FLORIDA AND THE UNITED STATES, 1992 THROUGH 1994

(prices in dollars per gallon)

| | Average pump price | | | | | |
| | Full service unleaded | | | Self-service unleaded | | |
City	Regular	Mid-grade	Premium	Regular	Mid-grade	Premium
Bradenton	1.595	1.647	1.749	1.292	1.398	1.487
Brandon	(NA)	(NA)	(NA)	1.264	1.356	1.440
Cocoa/Melbourne	1.649	1.751	1.851	1.264	1.367	1.467
Daytona Beach	1.497	1.619	1.712	1.281	1.390	1.487
Delray Beach	0.000	0.000	0.000	1.374	1.492	1.564
Ft. Lauderdale	1.641	1.779	1.789	1.316	1.426	1.498
Ft. Myers	1.639	1.713	1.793	1.340	1.406	1.486
Ft. Pierce	1.583	1.673	1.761	1.285	1.391	1.475
Gainesville	1.462	1.562	1.662	1.343	1.413	1.511
Jacksonville	1.652	1.729	1.819	1.286	1.391	1.489
Lakeland	1.409	1.499	1.587	1.274	1.368	1.456
Leesburg	1.555	1.639	1.725	1.278	1.327	1.476
Miami	1.642	1.752	1.804	1.342	1.458	1.507
Naples	1.526	1.655	1.716	1.347	1.440	1.507
Ocala	1.551	1.651	1.755	1.259	1.361	1.457
Orlando	1.622	1.721	1.787	1.293	1.417	1.487
Palm Beach	1.708	1.809	1.896	1.364	1.475	1.554
Pensacola	1.579	1.662	1.762	1.234	1.340	1.446
Pompano Beach	1.548	1.641	1.726	1.301	1.422	1.497
Port Charlotte	1.483	1.529	1.645	1.253	1.369	1.472
Port Richey	(NA)	(NA)	(NA)	1.241	1.325	1.403
St. Petersburg	1.577	1.659	1.751	1.271	1.368	1.451
Sarasota	1.767	1.876	1.981	1.274	1.400	1.490
Stuart	(NA)	(NA)	(NA)	1.294	1.423	1.484
Tallahassee	1.559	1.662	1.762	1.252	1.364	1.465
Tampa	1.682	1.782	1.882	1.269	1.373	1.458
Venice	(NA)	(NA)	(NA)	1.267	1.377	1.468

	Average sales price to end users 1/			
			Constant price	
		Implicit price	(1987 dollars)	
	Nominal	deflator 2/		Percentage
	price	(1987 = 1.000)	Amount	change
Florida				
1992	78.7	1.235	63.7	-7.0
1993	76.5	1.266	60.4	-5.2
1994	72.7	1.293	56.2	-7.0
United States				
1992	78.7	1.235	63.7	-5.9
1993	75.3	1.266	59.5	-6.7
1994	72.9	1.293	56.4	-5.2

(NA) Not available.
1/ Prices are in cents per gallon and exclude all federal, state, and county taxes.
2/ For personal consumption expenditures. Data from U.S. Department of Commerce,
Bureau of Economic Analysis.
  Note: City data are from AAA Clubs of Florida Survey. Some data may be revised.
  Source: State of Florida, Department of Community Affairs, unpublished data, and
U.S., Department of Energy, Energy Information Administration, *Petroleum Marketing
Annual 1995*, and previous editions.

University of Florida   **Bureau of Economic and Business Research**

Table 15.67. GASOLINE: TOTAL AND PER CAPITA GALLONS SOLD IN THE STATE AND
COUNTIES OF FLORIDA, 1994 AND 1995

County	Total sales (1,000 gallons)			Per capita sales (gallons)		
	1994	1995	Per-centage change 1994-95	1994	1995	Per-centage change 1994-95
Florida	6,493,727	6,616,985	1.9	467.9	467.7	0.0
Alachua	90,212	93,945	4.1	465.3	473.8	1.8
Baker	11,684	11,846	1.4	593.1	584.3	-1.5
Bay	75,565	76,170	0.8	554.4	547.3	-1.3
Bradford	13,484	13,883	3.0	557.0	570.5	2.4
Brevard	208,627	212,342	1.8	478.1	477.2	-0.2
Broward	638,842	648,436	1.5	476.7	475.3	-0.3
Calhoun	5,983	5,915	-1.1	517.3	493.4	-4.6
Charlotte	62,308	67,238	7.9	498.9	526.8	5.6
Citrus	43,341	43,920	1.3	421.4	416.4	-1.2
Clay	54,038	55,042	1.9	458.8	455.3	-0.8
Collier	92,606	93,432	0.9	512.9	501.0	-2.3
Columbia	37,837	39,897	5.4	773.8	791.8	2.3
Dade	804,736	806,822	0.3	404.3	400.6	-0.9
De Soto	10,314	10,165	-1.4	392.8	381.6	-2.9
Dixie	6,986	6,009	-14.0	575.0	484.0	-15.8
Duval	335,471	343,434	2.4	472.1	478.1	1.3
Escambia	128,883	128,225	-0.5	465.2	453.5	-2.5
Flagler	18,242	19,428	6.5	516.9	525.1	1.6
Franklin	3,972	5,569	40.2	397.4	544.1	36.9
Gadsden	19,471	19,827	1.8	434.1	443.2	2.1
Gilchrist	3,414	3,473	1.7	296.2	292.1	-1.4
Glades	3,959	4,245	7.2	473.2	496.4	4.9
Gulf	5,535	5,398	-2.5	417.3	406.8	-2.5
Hamilton	10,414	11,393	9.4	873.8	912.4	4.4
Hardee	10,886	10,985	0.9	484.8	480.0	-1.0
Hendry	16,536	16,911	2.3	576.4	573.3	-0.5
Hernando	49,695	51,238	3.1	432.6	434.6	0.5
Highlands	35,874	35,532	-1.0	472.9	459.8	-2.8
Hillsborough	412,836	416,885	1.0	469.6	466.9	-0.6
Holmes	8,756	9,209	5.2	517.3	529.7	2.4
Indian River	46,519	47,138	1.3	477.5	470.2	-1.5
Jackson	29,554	31,463	6.5	650.7	675.5	3.8
Jefferson	9,960	8,777	-11.9	761.2	649.7	-14.6
Lafayette	2,361	2,227	-5.7	405.3	341.8	-15.7
Lake	78,976	83,053	5.2	461.4	469.4	1.7
Lee	181,609	183,646	1.1	494.3	487.5	-1.4

See footnotes at end of table.

Continued . . .

University of Florida   **Bureau of Economic and Business Research**

Table 15.67. GASOLINE: TOTAL AND PER CAPITA GALLONS SOLD IN THE STATE AND
COUNTIES OF FLORIDA, 1994 AND 1995 (Continued)

	Total sales (1,000 gallons)			Per capita sales (gallons)		
County	1994	1995	Per-centage change 1994-95	1994	1995	Per-centage change 1994-95
Leon	105,082	104,423	-0.6	495.4	480.0	-3.1
Levy	17,560	18,563	5.7	603.2	622.0	3.1
Liberty	3,120	3,434	10.1	477.2	499.6	4.7
Madison	9,851	10,112	2.6	554.4	551.2	-0.6
Manatee	97,647	100,080	2.5	427.7	429.2	0.3
Marion	126,329	124,657	-1.3	579.9	555.0	-4.3
Martin	55,807	56,924	2.0	506.3	508.1	0.4
Monroe	50,054	50,469	0.8	608.5	605.1	-0.6
Nassau	25,487	25,427	-0.2	538.0	517.6	-3.8
Okaloosa	84,360	86,552	2.6	532.9	532.0	-0.2
Okeechobee	21,317	22,363	4.9	659.5	680.7	3.2
Orange	397,091	404,969	2.0	536.5	533.6	-0.5
Osceola	81,486	85,190	4.5	621.5	623.5	0.3
Palm Beach	417,002	422,151	1.2	444.9	438.5	-1.5
Pasco	119,170	124,609	4.6	398.8	407.8	2.3
Pinellas	341,021	347,490	1.9	391.7	396.6	1.3
Polk	212,750	216,857	1.9	486.6	489.4	0.6
Putnam	32,034	32,232	0.6	464.4	463.7	-0.2
St. Johns	55,049	57,037	3.6	580.9	580.9	0.0
St. Lucie	80,744	83,906	3.9	484.1	490.2	1.3
Santa Rosa	47,504	51,366	8.1	506.4	534.6	5.6
Sarasota	126,101	125,769	-0.3	426.0	417.1	-2.1
Seminole	131,972	137,689	4.3	416.9	424.8	1.9
Sumter	31,534	36,308	15.1	896.1	995.9	11.1
Suwannee	17,999	20,109	11.7	614.3	658.6	7.2
Taylor	12,799	12,410	-3.0	733.0	677.3	-7.6
Union	3,919	4,005	2.2	312.7	316.7	1.3
Volusia	179,925	187,148	4.0	453.6	464.4	2.4
Wakulla	7,526	8,418	11.9	457.8	495.0	8.1
Walton	22,353	23,185	3.7	701.6	693.9	-1.1
Washington	9,643	10,018	3.9	532.3	527.0	-1.0

Note: Includes gasohol. Per capita is computed using Bureau of Economic and
Business Research *Florida Estimates of Population*. Some data are revised.
    Correction: Due to processing error, total sales data shown for Leon through Wash-
ington counties as 1993 data in the previous *Abstract* were actually 1992 figures.

    Source: State of Florida, Department of Community Affairs, *1995 Florida Motor
Gasoline and Diesel Fuel Report,* April 1996, and unpublished data. Data from State
of Florida, Department of Revenue.

WHOLESALE AND RETAIL TRADE

Automotive Dealers and Gasoline Service Stations Employment by Industry in Florida, 1996

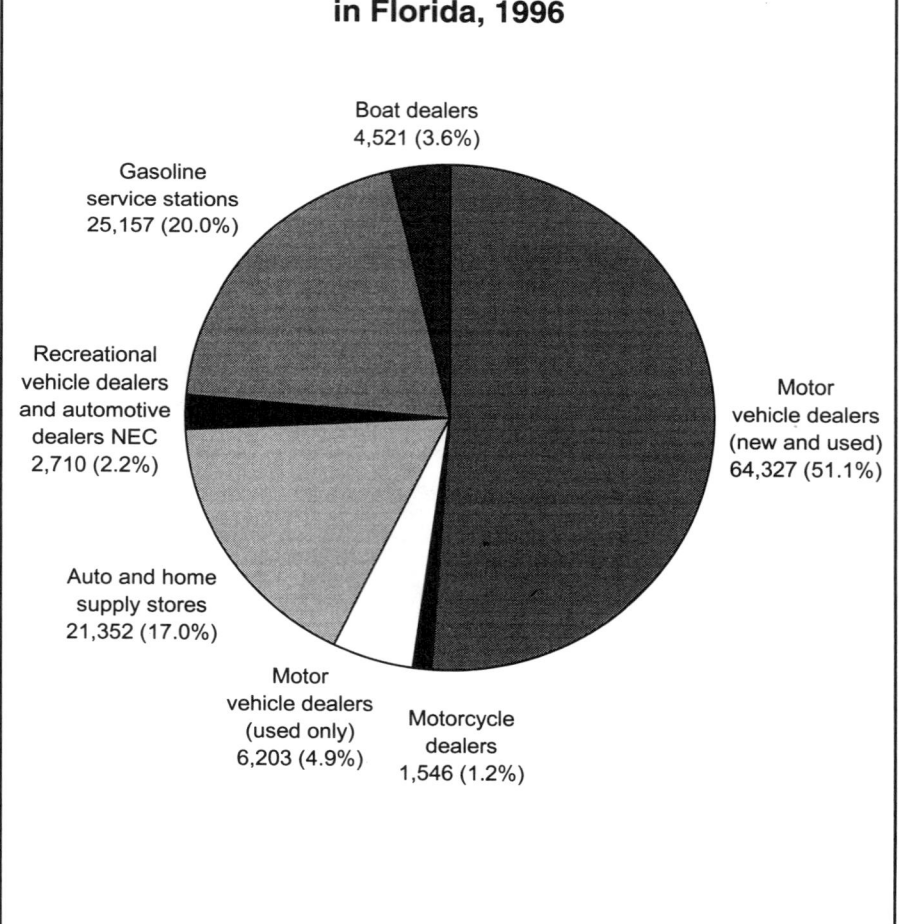

Boat dealers
4,521 (3.6%)

Gasoline
service stations
25,157 (20.0%)

Recreational
vehicle dealers
and automotive
dealers NEC
2,710 (2.2%)

Motor
vehicle dealers
(new and used)
64,327 (51.1%)

Auto and home
supply stores
21,352 (17.0%)

Motor
vehicle dealers
(used only)
6,203 (4.9%)

Motorcycle
dealers
1,546 (1.2%)

Source: Table 16.43

SECTION 16.00
WHOLESALE AND RETAIL TRADE

TABLES LISTED BY MAJOR HEADINGS

University of Florida   **Bureau of Economic and Business Research**

SECTION 16.00
WHOLESALE AND RETAIL TRADE
(Continued)

TABLES LISTED BY MAJOR HEADINGS

Table 16.01. WHOLESALE TRADE: ESTABLISHMENTS, SALES, AND SALES PER ESTABLISHMENT
IN FLORIDA, CENSUS YEARS 1967 THROUGH 1992

Census year	Establishments Number	Establishments Per-centage change	Sales Amount ($1,000)	Sales Per-centage change	Sales per establishment Amount (dollars)	Sales per establishment Per-centage change
1967	9,650	8.5	10,302,824	37.6	1,067,650	26.9
1972	13,450	39.4	19,983,912	94.0	1,485,793	39.2
1977	15,409	14.6	34,380,491	72.0	2,231,195	50.2
1982	19,537	26.8	65,614,610	90.8	3,358,479	50.5
1987	25,636	31.2	97,360,044	48.4	3,797,786	13.1
1992	30,137	17.6	132,562,218	36.2	4,398,653	15.8

Note: The wholesale trade census is on a 5-year cycle collecting data for years
ending in 2 and 7.

Table 16.02. WHOLESALE TRADE: ESTABLISHMENTS, SALES, AND SALES PER ESTABLISHMENT
BY KIND OF BUSINESS IN FLORIDA, 1992

SIC code	Kind of business	Number of es-tablish-ments	Sales ($1,000)	Sales per estab-lishment (dollars)
	Total	30,137	132,562,218	4,398,653
50	Durable goods	19,725	68,135,799	3,454,286
501	Motor vehicles and automotive parts and supplies	2,902	21,011,402	7,240,318
502	Furniture and home furnishings	1,268	2,263,815	1,785,343
503	Lumber and other construction materials	1,325	4,504,328	3,399,493
504	Sporting, recreational, photographic, and hobby goods, toys, and supplies	3,212	9,993,446	3,111,285
505	Metals and minerals, except petroleum	482	2,244,623	4,656,894
506	Electrical goods	2,672	11,309,423	4,232,568
507	Hardware and plumbing and heating equipment and supplies	1,560	3,226,598	2,068,332
508	Machinery, equipment, and supplies	3,938	8,573,734	2,177,180
509	Miscellaneous durable goods	2,366	5,008,430	2,116,834
51	Nondurable goods	10,412	64,426,419	6,187,708
511	Paper and paper products	1,112	3,887,952	3,496,360
512	Drugs, drug proprietaries, and druggists' sundries	542	5,531,365	10,205,470
513	Apparel, piece goods, and notions	1,217	2,389,730	1,963,624
514	Groceries and related products	2,956	26,713,857	9,037,164
515	Farm-product raw materials	141	1,731,637	12,281,113
516	Chemicals and allied products	782	2,569,769	3,286,150
517	Petroleum and petroleum products	587	8,940,891	15,231,501
518	Beer, wine, and distilled alcoholic beverages	179	3,984,416	22,259,307
519	Miscellaneous nondurable goods	2,896	8,676,802	2,996,133

Note: The wholesale trade census is on a 5-year cycle collecting data for years
ending in 2 and 7.
Source for tables 16.01 and 16.02: U.S., Department of Commerce, Bureau of the
Census, *1992 Census of Wholesale Trade: Florida,* and previous editions.

University of Florida   **Bureau of Economic and Business Research**

Table 16.06. WHOLESALE AND RETAIL TRADE: SALES IN THE STATE AND COUNTIES
OF FLORIDA, 1992

(in thousands of dollars)

County	Wholesale trade	Retail trade	County	Wholesale trade	Retail trade
Florida	132,562,218	118,741,770	Lafayette	11,076	8,179
			Lake	742,333	1,085,771
Alachua	493,922	1,525,129	Lee	1,203,415	3,393,129
Baker	20,597	73,257	Leon	805,067	1,721,972
Bay	437,901	1,224,342	Levy	33,793	141,320
Bradford	22,642	114,224	Liberty	2,288	12,677
Brevard	1,161,850	3,915,909	Madison	60,679	64,687
Broward	17,740,357	14,539,331	Manatee	1,115,600	1,580,441
Calhoun	32,676	41,730	Marion	1,309,987	1,552,749
Charlotte	106,716	816,794	Martin	249,237	1,036,012
Citrus	77,310	619,974	Monroe	154,886	821,142
Clay	199,149	811,838	Nassau	75,847	292,388
Collier	545,847	1,783,047	Okaloosa	248,735	1,283,036
Columbia	303,760	388,240	Okeechobee	149,866	199,974
Dade	30,878,059	17,642,481	Orange	18,607,483	7,397,885
De Soto	66,063	125,956	Osceola	799,070	1,133,792
Dixie	5,443	37,284	Palm Beach	6,491,016	9,084,460
Duval	11,327,784	6,015,387	Pasco	315,471	1,762,857
Escambia	1,298,888	2,272,972	Pinellas	4,509,687	8,451,895
Flagler	34,378	147,856	Polk	3,450,660	3,047,387
Franklin	40,591	39,422	Putnam	78,485	340,567
Gadsden	398,886	163,923	St. Johns	343,453	649,153
Gilchrist	8,850	18,746	St. Lucie	656,637	1,132,724
Glades	6,044	13,300	Santa Rosa	89,906	405,117
Gulf	17,567	35,059	Sarasota	854,195	2,921,187
Hamilton	7,396	47,529	Seminole	2,756,110	2,725,323
Hardee	81,901	112,876	Sumter	52,969	162,223
Hendry	55,542	149,486	Suwannee	66,149	158,275
Hernando	96,608	585,906	Taylor	34,230	100,169
Highlands	166,907	646,525	Union	4,691	18,371
Hillsborough	18,935,505	7,686,678	Volusia	988,130	3,048,473
Holmes	9,759	40,405	Wakulla	63,596	42,385
Indian River	1,374,614	781,201	Walton	69,381	169,587
Jackson	162,417	282,640	Washington	30,621	54,907
Jefferson	21,540	42,109			

Source: U.S., Department of Commerce, Bureau of the Census, *1992 Census of Whole-sale Trade: Florida,* and *1992 Census of Retail Trade: Florida.*

University of Florida   **Bureau of Economic and Business Research**

Table 16.11. RETAIL TRADE: ESTABLISHMENTS, SALES, AND SALES PER ESTABLISHMENT IN FLORIDA, CENSUS YEARS 1948 THROUGH 1992

Census year	Establishments Number	Percentage change	Retail sales Amount ($1,000)	Percentage change	Sales per establishment Amount (dollars)	Percentage change
1948	32,513	13.6	2,326,682	278.7	71,562	233.2
1954	41,303	27.0	4,014,417	72.5	97,194	35.8
1958	49,547	20.0	5,839,600	45.5	117,860	21.3
1963	53,293	7.6	7,609,717	30.3	142,790	21.2
1967	58,727	10.2	10,280,334	35.1	175,053	22.6
1972	70,898	20.7	19,430,163	89.0	274,058	56.6
1977	83,013	17.1	31,300,103	61.1	377,051	37.6
1982	88,733	6.9	55,468,945	77.2	625,122	65.8
1987 A/	83,808	(X)	87,925,609	(X)	1,049,131	(X)
1992 A/	87,653	4.6	118,741,770	35.0	1,354,680	29.1

(X) Not applicable.

A/ Establishments with payroll only.

Note: Prior to 1987, establishments represented the number of businesses at the end of the year. Subsequent counts include establishments in business at any time during the year. Therefore caution should be used in comparing these data. The retail trade census is now on a 5-year cycle collecting data for years ending in 2 and 7.

Table 16.12. RETAIL TRADE: ESTABLISHMENTS, SALES, AND ANNUAL PAYROLL BY KIND OF BUSINESS IN FLORIDA, 1992

SIC code	Kind of business	Number of estab- lishments	Sales ($1,000)	Annual payroll Total ($1,000)	Per em- ployee 1/ (dollars)
	Total	87,653	118,741,770	13,275,960	12,044
52	Building materials and garden supplies stores	3,792	5,523,991	613,331	15,190
53	General merchandise stores	1,631	14,096,715	1,441,509	12,497
54	Food stores	9,734	21,195,238	2,159,126	11,476
55	Automotive dealers and gasoline service stations	11,556	37,492,434	2,471,751	(NA)
56	Apparel and accessory stores	9,626	6,506,119	742,788	10,384
57	Furniture and home furnishings stores	7,604	6,148,396	740,917	16,921
58	Eating and drinking places	22,664	12,110,554	3,195,546	8,107
59	Drug, proprietary and miscellaneous retail	21,046	15,668,323	1,910,992	(NA)

(NA) Not available.

1/ Based on number of employees for pay period ending March 12.

Note: The retail trade census is on a 5-year cycle collecting data for years ending in 2 and 7.

Source for Tables 16.11 and 16.12: U.S., Department of Commerce, Bureau of the Census, *1992 Census of Retail Trade: Florida,* and previous editions.

Table 16.43. EMPLOYMENT: AVERAGE MONTHLY PRIVATE REPORTING UNITS, EMPLOYMENT
AND PAYROLL COVERED BY UNEMPLOYMENT COMPENSATION LAW BY WHOLESALE AND
RETAIL TRADE INDUSTRY IN FLORIDA, 1995 AND 1996

SIC code	Industry	Number of reporting units	Number of employees	Payroll ($1,000)
		1995 A/		
	Wholesale trade	36,408	318,176	906,608
50	Wholesale trade--durable goods	23,516	184,026	543,063
501	Motor vehicles and motor vehicle parts and supplies	2,665	26,007	59,543
502	Furniture and homefurnishings	1,220	6,780	17,774
503	Lumber and other construction materials	1,591	12,547	32,844
504	Professional and commercial equipment and supplies	5,189	44,830	160,971
505	Metals and minerals, except petroleum	422	3,598	11,154
506	Electrical goods	3,241	26,018	81,767
507	Hardware, plumbing and heating equipment and supplies	1,809	14,742	41,516
508	Machinery, equipment, and supplies	4,513	33,048	96,775
509	Miscellaneous durable goods	2,868	16,457	40,720
51	Wholesale trade--nondurable goods	12,892	134,150	363,545
511	Paper and paper products	1,293	15,983	41,773
512	Drugs, drug proprietaries, and druggists' sundries	1,114	12,153	43,360
513	Apparel, piece goods, and notions	1,477	9,192	20,476
514	Groceries and related products	3,532	47,310	120,871
515	Farm-product raw materials	115	920	1,554
516	Chemicals and allied products	1,032	6,990	25,798
517	Petroleum and petroleum products	491	6,336	17,011
518	Beer, wine, and distilled alcoholic beverages	264	9,422	31,428
519	Miscellaneous nondurable goods	3,574	25,844	61,275
	Retail trade	77,754	1,229,421	1,548,259
52	Building materials, hardware, garden supply, and mobile home dealers	3,516	46,156	77,982
521	Lumber and other building materials dealers	1,014	30,442	53,213
523	Paint, glass, and wallpaper stores	693	3,644	7,227
525	Hardware stores	742	5,615	7,743
526	Retail nurseries, lawn and garden supply stores	732	4,418	5,873
527	Mobile home dealers	335	2,037	3,926
53	General merchandise stores	1,678	146,282	174,134
531	Department stores	847	129,405	156,634
533	Variety stores	397	5,625	5,508
539	Miscellaneous general merchandise stores	434	11,252	11,992
54	Food stores	8,919	228,790	257,767
541	Grocery stores	6,314	210,378	237,118
542	Meat and fish markets and freezer provisioners	478	3,192	4,099
543	Fruit and vegetable markets	293	2,087	2,658
544	Candy, nut, and confectionery stores	175	1,085	962

See footnotes at end of table.   Continued . . .

Table 16.43. EMPLOYMENT: AVERAGE MONTHLY PRIVATE REPORTING UNITS, EMPLOYMENT AND PAYROLL COVERED BY UNEMPLOYMENT COMPENSATION LAW BY WHOLESALE AND RETAIL TRADE INDUSTRY IN FLORIDA, 1995 AND 1996 (Continued)

SIC code	Industry	Number of reporting units	Number of employees	Payroll ($1,000)
	1995 <u>A</u>/ (Continued)			
	Retail trade (Continued)			
54	Food stores (Continued)			
546	Retail bakeries	963	8,344	8,347
549	Miscellaneous food stores	626	3,436	4,378
55	Automotive dealers and gasoline service stations	9,499	120,209	282,027
551	Motor vehicle dealers (new and used)	1,143	61,695	186,253
552	Motor vehicle dealers (used only)	1,404	5,973	12,233
553	Auto and home supply stores	2,502	20,506	36,838
554	Gasoline service stations	3,434	23,991	29,575
555	Boat dealers	600	4,193	8,339
556	Recreational vehicle dealers	159	1,980	4,805
557	Motorcycle dealers	183	1,462	3,056
559	Automotive dealers, NEC	75	409	927
56	Apparel and accessory stores	7,599	67,637	73,835
561	Men's and boys' clothing and accessory stores	536	3,322	4,779
562	Women's clothing stores	2,320	20,429	19,899
563	Women's accessory and specialty stores	452	3,021	3,127
564	Children's and infants' wear stores	236	1,997	1,855
565	Family clothing stores	946	18,346	19,509
566	Shoe stores	1,825	11,739	13,344
569	Miscellaneous apparel and accessory stores	1,284	8,784	11,322
57	Furniture and home furnishings stores	7,764	58,999	103,505
571	Home furniture and furnishings store	4,784	34,190	59,429
572	Household appliance stores	524	3,173	5,838
573	Radio, television, and computer stores	2,457	21,636	38,238
58	Eating and drinking places	20,802	420,144	366,734
59	Miscellaneous retail	17,176	140,467	211,792
591	Drug stores and proprietary stores	1,154	36,919	61,148
592	Liquor stores	732	4,265	4,538
593	Used merchandise stores	1,391	5,306	6,526
594	Miscellaneous shopping goods stores	6,899	46,212	57,152
596	Nonstore retailers	982	14,686	32,058
598	Fuel dealers	346	3,122	5,986
599	Retail stores, NEC	5,674	29,957	44,386

See footnotes at end of table.   Continued . . .

University of Florida   **Bureau of Economic and Business Research**

Table 16.43. EMPLOYMENT: AVERAGE MONTHLY PRIVATE REPORTING UNITS, EMPLOYMENT AND PAYROLL COVERED BY UNEMPLOYMENT COMPENSATION LAW BY WHOLESALE AND RETAIL TRADE INDUSTRY IN FLORIDA, 1995 AND 1996 (Continued)

SIC code	Industry	Number of reporting units	Number of employees	Payroll ($1,000)
	1996 B/			
	Wholesale trade	38,884	333,607	997,226
50	Wholesale trade--durable goods	25,030	195,496	598,923
501	Motor vehicles and motor vehicle parts and supplies	2,710	26,668	63,273
502	Furniture and homefurnishings	1,177	7,159	19,578
503	Lumber and other construction materials	1,650	13,849	37,082
504	Professional and commercial equipment and supplies	5,179	46,230	171,482
505	Metals and minerals, except petroleum	467	4,271	13,019
506	Electrical goods	3,396	28,570	97,704
507	Hardware, plumbing and heating equipment and supplies	1,771	15,223	44,526
508	Machinery, equipment, and supplies	4,565	34,812	105,367
509	Miscellaneous durable goods	4,115	18,715	46,891
51	Wholesale trade--nondurable goods	13,854	138,111	398,303
511	Paper and paper products	1,278	16,814	57,601
512	Drugs, drug proprietaries, and druggists' sundries	1,092	12,409	46,356
513	Apparel, piece goods, and notions	1,464	9,472	21,584
514	Groceries and related products	3,416	47,324	124,669
515	Farm-product raw materials	122	926	1,715
516	Chemicals and allied products	1,036	7,136	25,432
517	Petroleum and petroleum products	489	6,246	17,957
518	Beer, wine, and distilled alcoholic beverages	263	9,721	34,215
519	Miscellaneous nondurable goods	4,696	28,064	68,773
52	Retail trade	78,868	1,275,150	1,661,382
	Building materials, hardware, garden supply, and mobile home dealers	3,618	49,344	86,470
521	Lumber and other building materials dealers	1,108	32,911	59,484
523	Paint, glass, and wallpaper stores	717	3,845	8,037
525	Hardware stores	752	5,907	8,368
526	Retail nurseries, lawn and garden supply stores	710	4,572	6,335
527	Mobile home dealers	331	2,108	4,245
53	General merchandise stores	1,775	150,817	181,608
531	Department stores	902	134,330	163,582
533	Variety stores	397	4,840	4,794
539	Miscellaneous general merchandise stores	476	11,646	13,232
54	Food stores	9,098	237,589	275,742
541	Grocery stores	6,330	216,755	251,795
542	Meat and fish markets and freezer provisioners	487	3,311	4,387
543	Fruit and vegetable markets	317	2,243	3,022
544	Candy, nut, and confectionery stores	161	1,101	1,013
545	Dairy products stores	64	342	262

See footnotes at end of table.   Continued . . .

Table 16.43. EMPLOYMENT: AVERAGE MONTHLY PRIVATE REPORTING UNITS, EMPLOYMENT AND PAYROLL COVERED BY UNEMPLOYMENT COMPENSATION LAW BY WHOLESALE AND RETAIL TRADE INDUSTRY IN FLORIDA, 1995 AND 1996 (Continued)

SIC code	Industry	Number of reporting units	Number of employees	Payroll ($1,000)
	1996 B/ (Continued)			
	Retail trade (Continued)			
54	Food stores (Continued)			
546	Retail bakeries	1,023	9,562	9,892
549	Miscellaneous food stores	718	4,274	5,370
55	Automotive dealers and gasoline service stations	9,710	125,816	301,706
551	Motor vehicle dealers (new and used)	1,252	64,327	198,099
552	Motor vehicle dealers (used only)	1,399	6,203	13,474
553	Auto and home supply stores	2,526	21,352	39,637
554	Gasoline service stations	3,475	25,157	30,974
555	Boat dealers	625	4,521	9,277
556	Recreational vehicle dealers	172	2,210	5,760
557	Motorcycle dealers	183	1,546	3,365
559	Automotive dealers, NEC	80	500	1,119
56	Apparel and accessory stores	7,422	67,224	77,025
561	Men's and boys' clothing and accessory stores	502	3,258	4,936
562	Women's clothing stores	2,206	18,986	19,806
563	Women's accessory and specialty stores	414	3,016	3,346
564	Children's and infants' wear stores	248	1,783	1,789
565	Family clothing stores	918	18,881	20,685
566	Shoe stores	1,802	11,546	13,652
569	Miscellaneous apparel and accessory stores	1,333	9,756	12,812
57	Furniture and home furnishings stores	8,067	60,738	112,696
571	Home furniture and furnishings store	4,853	34,891	63,890
572	Household appliance stores	540	3,119	6,056
573	Radio, television, and computer stores	2,674	22,728	42,750
58	Eating and drinking places	21,599	437,562	396,779
59	Miscellaneous retail	17,581	146,062	229,356
591	Drug stores and proprietary stores	1,085	37,664	64,519
592	Liquor stores	721	4,150	4,616
593	Used merchandise stores	1,442	5,878	7,462
594	Miscellaneous shopping goods stores	6,919	47,146	60,559
596	Nonstore retailers	1,002	15,588	36,544
598	Fuel dealers	377	3,124	6,292
599	Retail stores, NEC	6,036	32,513	49,365

NEC Not elsewhere classified.
A/ Revised.
B/ Preliminary.
Note: Private employment. Detail may not add to totals due to disclosure editing and/or rounding. See Tables 23.70, 23.71, 23.72, 23.73, and 23.74 for public employment data.

Source: State of Florida, Department of Labor and Employment Security, Bureau of Labor Market Information, "Employment and Wages" (ES-202), unpublished data.

Table 16.44. WHOLESALE TRADE: AVERAGE MONTHLY PRIVATE REPORTING UNITS, EMPLOYMENT
AND PAYROLL COVERED BY UNEMPLOYMENT COMPENSATION LAW IN THE STATE
AND COUNTIES OF FLORIDA, 1996

County	Number of reporting units	Number of employees	Payroll ($1,000)	County	Number of reporting units	Number of employees	Payroll ($1,000)
			Wholesale trade (SIC codes 50-51)				
Florida	38,884	333,607	997,226	Jefferson	15	67	113
				Lafayette	7	77	105
Alachua	291	2,312	5,549	Lake	245	1,584	3,663
Baker	11	55	103	Lee	694	5,132	12,644
Bay	238	2,294	5,433	Leon	336	3,652	9,635
Bradford	23	347	1,130	Levy	27	159	207
Brevard	687	4,888	11,789	Madison	19	142	204
Broward	4,580	35,797	110,397	Manatee	320	2,953	7,929
Calhoun	19	158	221	Marion	355	4,091	8,968
Charlotte	129	639	1,320	Martin	231	1,211	3,546
Citrus	87	455	772	Monroe	165	672	1,786
Clay	152	748	1,723	Nassau	54	295	773
Collier	396	2,057	5,765	Okaloosa	207	1,320	2,728
Columbia	79	868	2,000	Okeechobee	40	456	818
Dade	9,338	74,532	213,107	Orange	2,484	29,217	89,529
De Soto	22	195	299	Osceola	151	1,684	3,731
Dixie	8	59	163	Palm Beach	2,511	19,118	76,447
Duval	1,696	24,417	74,126	Pasco	310	1,760	3,895
Escambia	520	5,377	12,219	Pinellas	2,102	19,839	57,250
Flagler	45	144	294	Polk	770	7,976	19,170
Franklin	27	180	288	Putnam	66	436	833
Gadsden	28	355	794	St. Johns	191	1,380	3,730
Gilchrist	15	73	107	St. Lucie	235	1,719	3,663
Glades	4	16	50	Santa Rosa	113	443	898
Gulf	7	40	55	Sarasota	702	4,390	11,008
Hamilton	6	22	24	Seminole	1,067	6,867	19,883
Hardee	37	256	533	Sumter	35	371	736
Hendry	36	224	533	Suwannee	51	371	640
Hernando	122	750	1,600	Taylor	22	169	258
Highlands	81	538	1,082	Volusia	583	4,943	10,348
Hillsborough	2,805	33,724	106,753	Wakulla	19	63	185
Holmes	13	68	93	Walton	31	174	307
Indian River	179	996	4,269	Washington	15	77	87
Jackson	57	776	1,368	Multicounty 1/	2,970	17,359	77,386

1/ Reporting units without a fixed location within the state or of unknown county
location.
  Note: Private employment. For a list of three-digit code industries included see
Table 16.43. Data are preliminary. Only counties for which data are disclosed are
shown. Detail may not add to totals due to disclosure editing and/or rounding. See
Tables 23.70, 23.71, 23.72, 23.73, and 23.74 for public employment data.

  Source: State of Florida, Department of Labor and Employment Security, Bureau of
Labor Market Information, "Employment and Wages" (ES-202), unpublished data.

Table 16.45. RETAIL TRADE: AVERAGE MONTHLY PRIVATE REPORTING UNITS, EMPLOYMENT
AND PAYROLL COVERED BY UNEMPLOYMENT COMPENSATION LAW IN THE STATE
AND COUNTIES OF FLORIDA, 1995 AND 1996

County	Number of reporting units	Number of employees	Payroll ($1,000)	County	Number of reporting units	Number of employees	Payroll ($1,000)
			Retail trade, 1995 A/ (SIC codes 52-59)				
Florida	77,754	1,229,421	1,548,259	Lafayette	20	104	86
				Lake	800	11,291	12,654
Alachua	1,106	21,160	20,676	Lee	2,142	35,509	43,728
Baker	83	987	860	Leon	1,140	24,943	25,030
Bay	970	16,049	16,818	Levy	138	1,867	1,644
Bradford	86	1,375	1,225	Liberty	15	131	122
Brevard	2,251	34,587	38,255	Madison	87	834	781
Broward	8,186	128,216	177,558	Manatee	1,051	17,266	20,485
Calhoun	60	550	521	Marion	1,115	17,128	19,723
Charlotte	567	8,840	10,298	Martin	748	10,151	12,801
Citrus	510	6,226	6,689	Monroe	914	10,345	12,550
Clay	571	10,194	10,793	Nassau	264	3,273	3,254
Collier	1,399	18,807	24,952	Okaloosa	1,116	16,822	17,794
Columbia	264	3,901	4,133	Okeechobee	181	2,118	2,195
Dade	11,859	163,736	229,507	Orange	4,322	84,605	113,606
De Soto	103	1,249	1,308	Osceola	704	13,552	14,557
Dixie	52	446	377	Palm Beach	5,727	85,585	116,045
Duval	3,808	69,932	86,161	Pasco	1,172	17,620	19,205
Escambia	1,541	24,607	27,348	Pinellas	4,758	78,624	100,632
Flagler	157	2,053	2,035	Polk	1,953	36,930	51,509
Franklin	79	594	541	Putnam	263	3,811	4,016
Gadsden	156	1,934	2,005	St. Johns	679	8,363	8,603
Gilchrist	36	214	200	St. Lucie	727	10,217	12,139
Glades	21	174	146	Santa Rosa	376	4,444	4,237
Gulf	69	451	410	Sarasota	2,075	29,722	37,714
Hamilton	62	406	359	Seminole	1,570	28,897	35,195
Hardee	95	958	1,026	Sumter	143	1,686	1,561
Hendry	124	1,530	1,481	Suwannee	133	1,845	2,026
Hernando	446	6,761	7,375	Taylor	118	1,283	1,262
Highlands	380	5,158	5,310	Union	24	207	192
Hillsborough	4,298	84,974	107,647	Volusia	2,269	34,316	37,964
Holmes	64	565	499	Wakulla	52	629	475
Indian River	664	8,304	10,108	Walton	190	1,956	1,822
Jackson	227	2,730	2,792	Washington	74	927	854
Jefferson	55	449	362	Multicounty 1/	346	4,156	11,747

See footnotes at end of table.   Continued . . .

Table 16.45. RETAIL TRADE: AVERAGE MONTHLY PRIVATE REPORTING UNITS, EMPLOYMENT
AND PAYROLL COVERED BY UNEMPLOYMENT COMPENSATION LAW IN THE STATE
AND COUNTIES OF FLORIDA, 1995 AND 1996 (Continued)

County	Number of re- porting units	Number of em- ployees	Payroll ($1,000)	County	Number of re- porting units	Number of em- ployees	Payroll ($1,000)
			Retail trade, 1996 B/	(SIC codes 52-59)			
Florida	78,868	1,275,150	1,661,382	Lake	844	12,250	13,919
				Lee	2,232	36,826	48,192
Alachua	1,130	21,819	21,875	Leon	1,201	23,155	24,250
Baker	71	925	839	Levy	144	1,921	1,814
Bay	965	16,328	17,399	Liberty	16	134	129
Bradford	85	1,349	1,242	Madison	90	881	844
Brevard	2,240	35,259	40,169	Manatee	1,165	19,210	23,696
Broward	8,235	132,247	188,641	Marion	1,138	18,162	21,278
Calhoun	58	551	566	Martin	785	11,194	14,290
Charlotte	586	9,302	10,975	Monroe	921	10,751	13,497
Citrus	522	6,498	7,122	Nassau	276	3,454	3,521
Clay	589	10,721	11,858	Okaloosa	1,134	17,546	19,457
Collier	1,464	19,528	27,024	Okeechobee	189	2,323	2,405
Columbia	288	4,111	4,599	Orange	4,406	88,079	122,405
Dade	11,759	166,719	238,355	Osceola	724	14,222	15,713
De Soto	100	1,249	1,485	Palm Beach	5,766	88,165	124,902
Dixie	53	420	390	Pasco	1,197	18,299	20,527
Duval	3,855	72,906	93,778	Pinellas	4,805	80,082	107,450
Escambia	1,552	26,162	30,309	Polk	1,962	37,578	54,400
Flagler	168	2,387	2,376	Putnam	271	3,789	4,082
Franklin	86	576	543	St. Johns	681	8,466	9,052
Gadsden	155	1,890	1,980	St. Lucie	730	10,228	12,606
Gilchrist	36	222	210	Santa Rosa	390	4,758	4,655
Glades	22	192	150	Sarasota	2,121	30,827	40,710
Gulf	65	429	399	Seminole	1,657	30,933	39,254
Hamilton	61	399	341	Sumter	140	1,856	1,807
Hardee	88	992	1,046	Suwannee	136	1,822	2,090
Hendry	130	1,640	1,648	Taylor	111	1,287	1,273
Hernando	448	7,368	8,171	Union	28	210	215
Highlands	376	5,154	5,513	Volusia	2,244	34,519	39,347
Hillsborough	4,311	90,230	118,963	Wakulla	54	580	472
Holmes	63	541	513	Walton	199	2,140	2,158
Indian River	671	8,616	10,951	Washington	75	971	924
Jackson	230	2,735	2,941				
Jefferson	58	517	402	Multicounty 1/	499	8,439	17,105
Lafayette	17	92	78	Out-of-state	12	25	92

A/ Revised.
B/ Preliminary.
1/ Reporting units without a fixed location within the state or of unknown county location.
Note: For a list of three-digit code industries included see Table 16.43. Private employment. Only counties for which data are disclosed are shown. Detail may not add to totals due to disclosure editing and/or rounding. See Tables 23.70, 23.71, 23.72, 23.73, and 23.74 for public employment data.

Source: State of Florida, Department of Labor and Employment Security, Bureau of Labor Market Information, "Employment and Wages" (ES-202), unpublished data.

Table 16.46. GENERAL MERCHANDISE STORES: AVERAGE MONTHLY PRIVATE REPORTING
UNITS, EMPLOYMENT, AND PAYROLL COVERED BY UNEMPLOYMENT COMPENSATION
LAW IN THE STATE AND COUNTIES OF FLORIDA, 1996

County	Number of reporting units	Number of employees	Payroll ($1,000)	County	Number of reporting units	Number of employees	Payroll ($1,000)
			General merchandise stores (SIC code 53)				
Florida	1,775	150,817	181,608	Lake	23	1,664	1,786
				Lee	51	4,332	5,344
Alachua	32	3,441	3,372	Leon	27	2,908	3,324
Bay	21	2,144	2,340	Madison	3	23	19
Brevard	50	4,785	5,133	Manatee	28	2,056	2,316
Broward	150	14,143	16,723	Marion	29	2,958	3,487
Calhoun	5	19	19	Martin	20	1,544	1,721
Charlotte	20	1,707	1,879	Monroe	16	714	769
Citrus	12	828	828	Nassau	5	282	269
Clay	18	1,566	1,750	Okaloosa	19	2,267	2,421
Collier	23	2,135	2,555	Okeechobee	6	262	286
Columbia	7	638	722	Orange	96	8,543	10,914
Dade	248	18,490	24,658	Osceola	14	1,256	1,327
Duval	94	10,018	11,713	Palm Beach	101	9,988	12,738
Escambia	39	3,555	4,324	Pasco	28	2,453	2,739
Flagler	3	391	377	Pinellas	100	8,626	10,524
Franklin	3	11	8	Polk	53	5,503	6,480
Gadsden	10	173	155	Putnam	9	426	438
Gulf	5	20	19	St. Johns	8	557	604
Hernando	10	979	1,569	St. Lucie	20	1,330	1,433
Highlands	11	668	690	Santa Rosa	8	488	465
Hillsborough	103	10,718	12,659	Sarasota	39	3,260	3,732
Holmes	4	10	11	Seminole	51	4,612	5,572
Indian River	15	1,097	1,290	Volusia	45	3,894	4,411
Jackson	10	324	313	Multicounty 1/	27	876	3,271

1/ Reporting units without a fixed location within the state or of unknown county
location.
Note: Private employment. For a list of three-digit code industries included see
Table 16.43. Data are preliminary. Only counties for which data are disclosed are
shown. Detail may not add to totals due to disclosure editing and/or rounding. See
Tables 23.70, 23.71, 23.72, 23.73, and 23.74 for public employment data.

Source: State of Florida, Department of Labor and Employment Security, Bureau of
Labor Market Information, "Employment and Wages" (ES-202), unpublished data.

Table 16.47. FOOD STORES: AVERAGE MONTHLY PRIVATE REPORTING UNITS
EMPLOYMENT, AND PAYROLL COVERED BY UNEMPLOYMENT COMPENSATION
LAW IN THE STATE AND COUNTIES OF FLORIDA, 1996

County	Number of reporting units	Number of employees	Payroll ($1,000)	County	Number of reporting units	Number of employees	Payroll ($1,000)
			Food stores	(SIC code 54)			
Florida	9,098	237,589	275,742	Lafayette	5	44	41
				Lake	118	3,055	2,874
Alachua	131	3,782	3,655	Lee	217	6,282	6,960
Baker	12	238	210	Leon	116	3,733	3,501
Bay	96	2,638	2,504	Levy	23	564	466
Bradford	13	330	279	Liberty	6	38	43
Brevard	243	6,492	6,664	Madison	13	193	155
Broward	838	24,654	30,819	Manatee	130	3,409	3,548
Calhoun	9	178	168	Marion	159	3,608	3,730
Charlotte	54	1,952	1,960	Martin	84	2,150	2,435
Citrus	72	1,603	1,573	Monroe	71	1,875	2,221
Clay	77	2,126	2,233	Nassau	42	863	788
Collier	146	3,926	4,526	Okaloosa	122	2,517	2,625
Columbia	59	840	850	Okeechobee	30	577	553
Dade	1,386	28,338	34,580	Orange	508	14,527	18,425
De Soto	17	311	301	Osceola	98	2,775	2,850
Dixie	8	109	92	Palm Beach	591	15,168	18,459
Duval	528	14,056	18,718	Pasco	148	4,513	4,333
Escambia	176	3,474	3,625	Pinellas	513	13,543	14,307
Flagler	24	700	669	Polk	251	10,373	17,232
Franklin	15	185	171	Putnam	36	1,206	1,262
Gadsden	33	519	497	St. Johns	78	1,720	1,777
Gilchrist	6	87	65	St. Lucie	95	2,308	2,545
Glades	10	89	74	Santa Rosa	62	1,078	933
Gulf	16	189	168	Sarasota	178	6,229	7,581
Hamilton	13	91	72	Seminole	176	5,759	6,364
Hardee	19	355	298	Sumter	29	484	460
Hendry	24	577	492	Suwannee	27	442	421
Hernando	72	2,166	2,041	Taylor	15	290	254
Highlands	51	1,316	1,234	Union	6	94	82
Hillsborough	561	16,120	18,206	Volusia	222	6,824	6,844
Holmes	13	133	115	Walton	27	359	323
Indian River	74	1,726	2,157	Washington	17	193	168
Jackson	29	365	326				
Jefferson	13	200	149	Multicounty 1/	48	755	1,549

1/ Reporting units without a fixed location within the state or of unknown county
location.
   Note: Private employment. For a list of three-digit code industries included see
Table 16.43. Data are preliminary. Only counties for which data are disclosed are
shown. Detail may not add to totals due to disclosure editing and/or rounding. See
Tables 23.70, 23.71, 23.72, 23.73, and 23.74 for public employment data.

   Source: State of Florida, Department of Labor and Employment Security, Bureau of
Labor Market Information, "Employment and Wages" (ES-202), unpublished data.

Table 16.48. AUTOMOTIVE DEALERS AND GASOLINE SERVICE STATIONS: AVERAGE
MONTHLY PRIVATE REPORTING UNITS, EMPLOYMENT, AND PAYROLL COVERED
BY UNEMPLOYMENT COMPENSATION LAW IN THE STATE AND COUNTIES
OF FLORIDA, 1996

County	Number of re- porting units	Number of em- ployees	Payroll ($1,000)	County	Number of re- porting units	Number of em- ployees	Payroll ($1,000)
			Automotive dealers and gasoline service stations (SIC code 55)				
Florida	9,710	125,816	301,706	Lafayette	3	8	6
				Lake	126	1,362	3,032
Alachua	125	1,792	3,739	Lee	257	3,487	8,524
Baker	14	114	122	Leon	149	1,909	4,215
Bay	123	1,453	3,101	Levy	22	167	267
Bradford	18	165	300	Madison	28	246	310
Brevard	299	3,500	8,198	Manatee	157	1,733	3,955
Broward	976	14,029	39,352	Marion	173	2,100	4,364
Calhoun	16	95	135	Martin	107	1,227	2,943
Charlotte	79	1,087	2,375	Monroe	69	572	1,124
Citrus	79	793	1,705	Nassau	40	418	629
Clay	71	925	2,139	Okaloosa	132	1,699	3,487
Collier	114	1,595	4,383	Okeechobee	32	256	457
Columbia	47	488	961	Orange	564	7,523	18,738
Dade	1,362	15,561	37,699	Osceola	73	1,003	2,217
De Soto	18	228	507	Palm Beach	594	8,596	22,489
Dixie	13	67	83	Pasco	163	1,838	4,033
Duval	501	9,241	20,806	Pinellas	521	7,854	19,842
Escambia	209	2,846	6,188	Polk	310	4,180	9,999
Flagler	19	181	373	Putnam	44	374	731
Franklin	8	33	44	St. Johns	76	766	1,424
Gadsden	28	219	368	St. Lucie	105	1,365	3,208
Gilchrist	6	15	18	Santa Rosa	53	639	1,171
Gulf	8	25	38	Sarasota	220	3,062	7,946
Hamilton	20	135	107	Seminole	182	2,319	5,947
Hardee	20	141	281	Sumter	22	386	504
Hendry	22	175	352	Suwannee	31	268	436
Hernando	57	601	1,353	Taylor	21	180	293
Highlands	74	751	1,469	Union	7	27	41
Hillsborough	560	8,243	20,889	Volusia	316	3,437	7,803
Holmes	12	108	116	Wakulla	11	66	70
Indian River	57	875	1,975	Walton	28	197	244
Jackson	44	653	1,061	Washington	15	53	56
Jefferson	13	101	82	Multicounty 1/	44	228	818

1/ Reporting units without a fixed location within the state or of unknown county
location.
Note: Private employment. For a list of three-digit code industries included see
Table 16.43. Data are preliminary. Only counties for which data are disclosed are
shown. Detail may not add to totals due to disclosure editing and/or rounding. See
Tables 23.70, 23.71, 23.72, 23.73, and 23.74 for public employment data.

Source: State of Florida, Department of Labor and Employment Security, Bureau of
Labor Market Information, "Employment and Wages" (ES-202), unpublished data.

Table 16.49. AUTO AND HOME SUPPLY STORES: AVERAGE MONTHLY PRIVATE REPORTING
UNITS, EMPLOYMENT, AND PAYROLL COVERED BY UNEMPLOYMENT COMPENSATION
LAW IN THE STATE AND COUNTIES OF FLORIDA, 1996

County	Number of reporting units	Number of employees	Payroll ($1,000)	County	Number of reporting units	Number of employees	Payroll ($1,000)
			Auto and home supply stores (SIC code 553)				
Florida	2,526	21,352	39,637	Lee	61	521	1,012
				Leon	41	345	622
Alachua	34	345	639	Levy	8	32	42
Baker	6	21	38	Madison	4	22	28
Bay	34	267	443	Manatee	34	284	466
Bradford	4	16	18	Marion	48	435	707
Brevard	77	635	1,093	Martin	25	169	304
Broward	254	1,936	3,868	Monroe	11	82	126
Calhoun	6	37	43	Nassau	10	39	56
Charlotte	22	179	290	Okaloosa	32	259	403
Citrus	21	136	196	Okeechobee	9	60	107
Clay	23	171	339	Orange	143	1,428	2,933
Collier	29	222	419	Osceola	14	208	376
Columbia	10	94	166	Palm Beach	159	1,589	3,487
Dade	387	2,687	4,589	Pasco	38	285	456
De Soto	7	40	55	Pinellas	112	1,035	2,036
Duval	140	1,499	2,880	Polk	77	1,214	2,503
Escambia	58	658	1,043	Putnam	11	93	141
Flagler	7	52	73	St. Johns	13	57	96
Gadsden	10	49	67	St. Lucie	26	264	489
Gilchrist	3	10	12	Santa Rosa	18	111	162
Gulf	6	20	29	Sarasota	47	364	652
Hamilton	3	6	9	Seminole	51	383	746
Hardee	4	27	44	Sumter	5	32	45
Hendry	6	35	62	Suwannee	7	43	53
Hernando	18	140	214	Taylor	4	27	55
Highlands	19	128	213	Union	3	19	34
Hillsborough	137	1,184	2,186	Volusia	80	705	1,243
Holmes	7	32	41	Walton	4	16	19
Indian River	12	92	175	Walton	7	48	73
Jackson	13	92	123	Washington	7	28	31
Lake	36	248	402	Multicounty 1/	21	74	314

1/ Reporting units without a fixed location within the state or of unknown county
location.
Note: Private employment. Data are preliminary. Only counties for which data
are disclosed are shown. Detail may not add to totals due to disclosure editing
and/or rounding. See Tables 23.70, 23.71, 23.72, 23.73, and 23.74 for public employment data.

Source: State of Florida, Department of Labor and Employment Security, Bureau of
Labor Market Information, "Employment and Wages" (ES-202), unpublished data.

Table 16.50. GASOLINE SERVICE STATIONS: AVERAGE MONTHLY PRIVATE REPORTING
UNITS, EMPLOYMENT, AND PAYROLL COVERED BY UNEMPLOYMENT COMPENSATION
LAW IN THE STATE AND COUNTIES OF FLORIDA, 1996

County	Number of reporting units	Number of employees	Payroll ($1,000)	County	Number of reporting units	Number of employees	Payroll ($1,000)
			Gasoline service stations (SIC code 554)				
Florida	3,475	25,157	30,974	Lee	68	548	654
				Leon	52	413	463
Alachua	46	370	390	Levy	11	65	63
Baker	5	77	57	Madison	21	214	268
Bay	32	357	413	Manatee	45	296	335
Bradford	8	41	37	Marion	50	519	539
Brevard	103	576	654	Martin	29	158	182
Broward	351	2,184	2,740	Monroe	28	184	262
Calhoun	4	10	9	Nassau	22	232	222
Charlotte	24	261	253	Okaloosa	44	387	382
Citrus	21	104	105	Okeechobee	10	77	77
Clay	22	163	148	Orange	196	1,179	1,356
Collier	39	308	402	Osceola	27	181	195
Columbia	19	111	102	Palm Beach	240	1,755	2,293
Dade	542	3,252	5,213	Pasco	53	257	269
De Soto	5	34	37	Pinellas	199	1,263	1,603
Dixie	6	25	19	Polk	109	703	742
Duval	158	2,562	3,129	Putnam	11	47	50
Escambia	58	406	427	St. Johns	36	269	279
Flagler	6	53	68	St. Lucie	32	213	226
Franklin	4	16	20	Santa Rosa	20	198	152
Gadsden	12	90	88	Sarasota	81	557	633
Gilchrist	3	6	6	Seminole	51	350	478
Hamilton	16	121	86	Sumter	13	297	299
Hardee	10	32	38	Suwannee	13	83	92
Hendry	10	44	50	Taylor	10	74	69
Hernando	18	87	72	Union	4	9	7
Highlands	19	107	131	Volusia	104	563	622
Hillsborough	225	1,444	1,899	Wakulla	4	39	28
Indian River	23	252	300	Walton	16	104	87
Jackson	22	324	360	Washington	5	16	16
Jefferson	11	96	77				
Lake	31	177	165	Multicounty 1/	11	122	429

1/ Reporting units without a fixed location within the state or of unknown county
location.
Note: Private employment. Data are preliminary. Only counties for which data
are disclosed are shown. Detail may not add to totals due to disclosure editing
and/or rounding. See Tables 23.70, 23.71, 23.72, 23.73, and 23.74 for public employment data.

Source: State of Florida, Department of Labor and Employment Security, Bureau of
Labor Market Information, "Employment and Wages" (ES-202), unpublished data.

Table 16.51. APPAREL AND ACCESSORY STORES: AVERAGE MONTHLY PRIVATE REPORTING UNITS, EMPLOYMENT, AND PAYROLL COVERED BY UNEMPLOYMENT COMPENSATION LAW IN THE STATE AND COUNTIES OF FLORIDA, 1996

County	Number of reporting units	Number of employees	Payroll ($1,000)	County	Number of reporting units	Number of employees	Payroll ($1,000)
				Apparel and accessory stores (SIC code 56)			
Florida	7,422	67,224	77,025	Leon	108	1,444	1,241
				Levy	6	30	18
Alachua	106	867	804	Madison	5	20	16
Bay	105	872	734	Manatee	117	1,848	2,546
Bradford	6	36	25	Marion	73	642	572
Brevard	135	1,185	1,231	Martin	69	462	419
Broward	826	8,170	10,244	Monroe	110	511	595
Charlotte	58	437	374	Nassau	23	105	90
Citrus	29	219	166	Okaloosa	127	1,052	1,070
Clay	57	467	396	Okeechobee	11	99	85
Collier	186	1,436	1,770	Orange	414	4,637	5,104
Columbia	14	88	74	Osceola	60	663	713
Dade	1,514	13,652	17,245	Palm Beach	611	5,844	7,908
De Soto	4	22	19	Pasco	72	543	458
Duval	308	2,851	3,302	Pinellas	405	3,390	3,402
Escambia	124	985	957	Polk	149	1,084	980
Franklin	4	10	5	Putnam	13	59	42
Gadsden	8	23	17	St. Johns	66	462	432
Hardee	4	32	30	St. Lucie	53	362	318
Hendry	5	29	25	Santa Rosa	16	67	50
Hernando	19	145	117	Sarasota	211	1,538	1,611
Highlands	22	161	128	Seminole	158	1,524	1,429
Hillsborough	350	3,424	3,271	Sumter	4	13	13
Indian River	79	455	451	Suwannee	8	27	23
Jackson	19	140	130	Taylor	9	43	37
Jefferson	2	9	5	Volusia	155	1,345	1,149
Lake	41	282	243	Walton	15	126	151
Lee	249	1,967	2,341	Multicounty 1/	69	1,236	2,387

1/ Reporting units without a fixed location within the state or of unknown county location.

Note: Private employment. For a list of three-digit code industries included see Table 16.43. Data are preliminary. Only counties for which data are disclosed are shown. Detail may not add to totals due to disclosure editing and/or rounding. See Tables 23.70, 23.71, 23.72, 23.73, and 23.74 for public employment data.

Source: State of Florida, Department of Labor and Employment Security, Bureau of Labor Market Information, "Employment and Wages" (ES-202), unpublished data.

University of Florida   **Bureau of Economic and Business Research**

Table 16.52. HOME FURNITURE, FURNISHINGS, AND EQUIPMENT STORES: AVERAGE MONTHLY
PRIVATE REPORTING UNITS, EMPLOYMENT, AND PAYROLL COVERED BY UNEMPLOYMENT
COMPENSATION LAW IN THE STATE AND COUNTIES OF FLORIDA, 1996

County	Number of re- porting units	Number of em- ployees	Payroll ($1,000)	County	Number of re- porting units	Number of em- ployees	Payroll ($1,000)
Home furniture, furnishings, and equipment stores (SIC code 57)							
Florida	8,067	60,738	112,696	Lake	82	461	734
				Lee	250	2,385	4,834
Alachua	115	820	1,115	Leon	127	983	1,452
Baker	3	22	30	Levy	9	25	22
Bay	80	482	735	Madison	6	33	36
Bradford	7	25	45	Manatee	111	763	1,169
Brevard	248	1,582	2,369	Marion	114	723	1,145
Broward	953	7,746	15,840	Martin	96	496	824
Calhoun	4	17	21	Monroe	52	216	358
Charlotte	68	431	662	Nassau	14	40	47
Citrus	45	276	354	Okaloosa	104	761	1,217
Clay	50	380	558	Okeechobee	11	47	64
Collier	217	1,210	2,276	Orange	384	3,540	6,609
Columbia	23	144	220	Osceola	48	249	401
Dade	1,156	9,604	17,901	Palm Beach	673	4,405	9,713
De Soto	9	64	98	Pasco	128	841	1,271
Duval	383	2,817	4,938	Pinellas	477	3,312	6,505
Escambia	155	1,308	2,067	Polk	190	2,608	5,430
Flagler	13	52	71	Putnam	23	128	188
Franklin	4	3	5	St. Johns	54	316	462
Gadsden	12	275	388	St. Lucie	90	464	739
Gilchrist	4	12	13	Santa Rosa	36	164	233
Gulf	4	16	18	Sarasota	255	1,634	2,986
Hamilton	4	11	14	Seminole	202	1,622	2,722
Hardee	8	19	25	Sumter	13	107	124
Hendry	5	17	21	Taylor	7	46	105
Hernando	47	200	279	Volusia	212	1,490	2,421
Highlands	37	177	236	Walton	13	49	62
Hillsborough	433	4,088	8,415	Washington	6	43	49
Indian River	96	474	779				
Jackson	16	55	60	Multicounty 1/	66	252	838

1/ Reporting units without a fixed location within the state or of unknown county
location.
Note: Private employment. For a list of three-digit code industries included see
Table 16.43. Data are preliminary. Only counties for which data are disclosed are
shown. Detail may not add to totals due to disclosure editing and/or rounding. See
Tables 23.70, 23.71, 23.72, 23.73, and 23.74 for public employment data.

Source: State of Florida, Department of Labor and Employment Security, Bureau of
Labor Market Information, "Employment and Wages" (ES-202), unpublished data.

Table 16.81. GROSS AND TAXABLE SALES: SALES REPORTED TO THE DEPARTMENT OF REVENUE BY KIND OF BUSINESS IN FLORIDA 1995 AND 1996

(rounded to thousands of dollars)

Code	Kind of business Description	Gross sales 1995	Gross sales 1996	Taxable sales 1995	Taxable sales 1996
	Total	423,309,074	451,962,591	171,551,705	182,140,969
	Food and beverage group	45,688,423	48,972,778	24,529,053	26,183,216
01	Grocery stores	25,563,710	27,841,758	8,072,901	8,653,707
02	Meat markets, poultry	398,402	371,461	12,719	13,716
03	Seafood dealers	194,716	223,662	17,376	20,923
04	Vegetable and fruit markets	281,177	441,657	34,297	46,853
05	Bakeries	280,136	317,387	70,745	83,392
06	Delicatessens	315,502	303,018	132,148	128,731
07	Candy and confectionery	1,180,500	1,298,827	390,375	420,432
08	Restaurants and lunchrooms	15,509,171	16,111,719	13,998,378	14,923,566
09	Taverns, nightclubs, liquor stores	1,965,109	2,063,291	1,800,113	1,891,896
	Apparel group	6,772,977	6,913,505	5,759,994	5,889,526
10	Clothing stores, alterations	5,716,401	5,868,943	4,827,536	4,950,533
11	Shoe stores	986,194	973,251	880,012	891,253
12	Hat shops	70,382	71,310	52,447	47,740
	General merchandise group	42,251,984	44,151,082	26,913,363	27,136,936
13	Department stores	10,916,233	10,528,185	9,536,653	9,274,754
14	Variety stores	10,725,361	12,013,263	7,873,654	8,586,448
15	Drug stores	6,702,069	7,052,801	2,066,091	2,004,481
16	Jewelry, leather, sporting goods	3,815,587	3,881,104	2,324,668	2,482,238
17	Feed, seed, and fertilizer stores	510,701	524,685	105,131	106,015
18	Hardware, paints, machinery	3,584,861	3,948,596	1,825,058	1,963,181
19	Farm implements and supplies	792,874	903,214	379,424	388,564
20	General merchandise stores	4,153,231	4,156,933	2,191,200	1,660,369
21	Second-hand stores	591,745	659,189	347,748	385,678
22	Dry good stores	459,321	483,112	263,737	285,209

See footnotes at end of table.

Continued . . .

Table 16.81. GROSS AND TAXABLE SALES: SALES REPORTED TO THE DEPARTMENT OF REVENUE BY KIND OF BUSINESS IN FLORIDA 1995 AND 1996 (Continued)

(rounded to thousands of dollars)

Code	Kind of business Description	Gross sales 1995	Gross sales 1996	Taxable sales 1995	Taxable sales 1996
	Automotive group	67,961,325	73,741,846	32,226,988	34,167,141
23	Motor vehicle dealers	48,045,351	51,692,070	25,011,870	26,602,288
24	Auto accessories, tires, parts	4,875,794	5,010,427	2,350,761	2,412,470
25	Filling and service stations	6,201,050	6,473,264	1,002,354	1,006,426
26	Garages, auto paint and body shops	3,498,552	3,803,810	2,310,250	2,418,828
27	Aircraft dealers	2,520,098	3,555,585	202,153	240,663
28	Motorboat and yacht dealers	2,820,480	3,206,689	1,349,599	1,486,466
	Furniture and appliances group	23,782,750	26,483,438	11,056,609	12,130,325
29	Furniture stores, new and used	5,071,183	5,651,887	3,563,256	3,909,003
30	Household appliances, dinnerware, etc.	2,064,757	1,895,577	1,271,351	1,295,002
31	Store and office equipment	4,278,108	4,512,333	1,999,713	2,118,750
32	Music stores, radios, televisions	12,368,703	14,423,640	4,222,289	4,807,569
	Lumber, builders, contractors group	16,673,680	18,257,496	9,356,248	10,368,322
33	Building contractors	1,820,163	1,988,028	331,567	403,573
34	Heating and air conditioning	1,643,818	1,721,252	495,523	538,703
35	Electrical and plumbing	2,461,326	2,628,859	1,166,353	1,218,667
36	Decorating, painting, papering	999,734	1,083,676	587,139	631,374
37	Roofing and sheet metal	380,028	412,098	172,881	176,909
38	Lumber and building materials	9,368,611	10,423,583	6,602,785	7,399,096
	General classification group	220,177,935	233,442,447	61,709,451	66,265,502
39	Hotels, apartment houses, etc. 1/	8,598,639	9,138,106	7,768,974	8,432,189
40	Auctioneers and commission dealers	2,059,855	2,372,889	449,796	526,815
41	Barber and beauty shops	1,308,147	1,462,469	574,837	610,371
42	Book stores	918,957	969,158	616,166	666,317
43	Cigar stands and tobacco shops	78,434	136,766	35,335	52,738
44	Florists	504,874	568,292	284,528	299,347
45	Fuel and L.P. gas dealers	4,171,534	4,389,459	406,605	416,914

See footnotes at end of table.

Continued . . .

Table 16.81. GROSS AND TAXABLE SALES: SALES REPORTED TO THE DEPARTMENT OF REVENUE BY KIND OF BUSINESS IN FLORIDA 1995 AND 1996 (Continued)

(rounded to thousands of dollars)

Code	Kind of business — Description	Gross sales 1995	Gross sales 1996	Taxable sales 1995	Taxable sales 1996
	General classification group (Continued)				
46	Funeral directors and monuments	326,828	305,330	102,530	60,667
47	Scrap metal, junk yards	452,181	461,361	40,017	43,762
48	Itinerant vendors	617,520	626,361	259,008	275,007
49	Laundry and cleaning services	568,681	612,012	196,063	199,003
50	Machine shops and foundries	711,175	778,457	192,335	209,154
51	Horse, cattle, pet dealers	2,829,273	2,967,312	1,087,759	1,102,390
52	Photographers, photo and art supplies	1,557,457	1,562,588	873,112	901,775
53	Shoe repair shops	19,708	18,989	16,120	16,981
54	Storage and warehousing	252,215	244,798	120,266	124,620
55	Gift, card, novelty shops	2,382,535	2,532,051	1,690,776	1,818,278
56	Newsstands	186,379	188,525	56,139	59,208
57	Social clubs and associations	536,830	581,485	425,869	455,084
58	Industrial machinery equipment	6,179,096	7,507,871	2,046,732	2,256,659
59	Admissions	3,671,096	4,066,870	3,423,705	3,705,327
60	Holiday season vendors	13,460	14,168	10,228	9,650
61	Rental of tangible property	4,976,807	5,797,114	2,984,691	3,219,221
62	Fabrication, sales of cabinets, etc.	1,880,509	2,040,983	687,956	755,551
63	Manufacturing and mining	34,015,614	36,089,293	3,820,471	4,441,194
64	Bottlers, soft drinks, etc.	939,164	871,824	70,561	80,757
65	Pawn shops	117,614	126,945	92,101	97,822
66	Communications	12,039,981	13,022,313	6,726,352	7,233,820
67	Transportation	448,788	503,300	85,103	94,424
68	Graphic arts and printing	4,357,887	4,611,763	1,535,742	1,609,042
69	Insurance, banking, etc.	789,323	599,025	311,348	210,091
70	Sanitary and industrial supplies	3,222,326	3,068,401	479,696	481,091
71	Packaging materials and paper boxes	1,354,495	1,268,424	126,555	134,341
72	Repair of tangible personal property	3,212,637	3,118,056	999,207	1,006,267
73	Advertising	1,673,448	1,779,307	280,485	295,008

Continued . . .

See footnotes at end of table.

Table 16.81. GROSS AND TAXABLE SALES: SALES REPORTED TO THE DEPARTMENT OF REVENUE BY KIND OF BUSINESS IN FLORIDA 1995 AND 1996 (Continued)

(rounded to thousands of dollars)

Code	Kind of business Description	Gross sales 1995	Gross sales 1996	Taxable sales 1995	Taxable sales 1996
	General classification group (Continued)				
74	Top soil, clay, sand, fill dirt	1,043,218	1,087,789	265,105	277,271
75	Trade stamp redemption centers	641	893	220	326
76	Nurseries and landscaping	1,439,661	1,550,812	405,491	454,773
77	Vending machines	677,874	694,342	342,598	363,409
78	Importing and exporting	13,970,731	15,650,962	175,233	196,450
79	Medical, dental, surgical, optical	5,328,192	6,106,357	518,466	580,108
80	Wholesale dealers	54,047,626	54,213,636	4,493,883	4,554,143
81	Schools and colleges	111,062	111,266	57,339	59,920
82	Office space and commercial rentals	12,578,980	13,882,191	9,902,851	10,534,302
83	Parking lots, boat docking, storage	389,662	397,935	284,545	296,922
84	Utilities, electricity or gas	12,746,460	13,484,854	3,596,336	3,729,294
86	Dual uses of special fuels	210,026	262,167	16,448	16,768
88	Public works, governmental contractor	127,781	223,366	31,857	64,657
90	Flea markets	199,738	212,679	128,841	138,740
91	Fairs, concessions, carnivals	12,156	15,932	7,008	7,381
92	Other professional services	810,205	707,556	24,192	32,471
93	Other personal services	3,292,756	3,039,496	1,190,652	1,286,554
94	Other industrial services	585,063	679,783	80,937	100,398
98	Commercial fisherman	15,834	19,416	2,127	2,172
99	Miscellaneous	5,616,802	6,698,944	1,308,151	1,668,559

1/ Includes sales reported under categories 85 and 89 which are for hotels, rooming houses and apartments.
Note: Data are audited sales reported to the Florida Department of Revenue for the 6 percent regular sales tax, 6 percent use tax, and 3 percent vehicle and farm equipment sales tax. Sales occurred, for the most part, from December 1, 1994, through November 30, 1996. Data are not comparable with retail sales reported by the U.S. Bureau of the Census.

Source: State of Florida, Department of Revenue, unpublished data prepared by the University of Florida, Bureau of Economic and Business Research.

Table 16.82. GROSS AND TAXABLE SALES: SALES REPORTED TO THE DEPARTMENT OF REVENUE
IN THE STATE AND COUNTIES OF FLORIDA, 1995 AND 1996

(rounded to thousands of dollars)

County	Gross sales		Taxable sales	
	1995	1996	1995	1996
Florida	423,309,074	451,962,591	171,551,705	182,140,969
Alachua	3,570,618	3,770,002	2,032,398	2,135,698
Baker	160,024	164,487	70,826	75,867
Bay	3,068,450	3,029,127	1,760,979	1,754,305
Bradford	277,775	305,173	130,997	137,819
Brevard	9,167,169	9,606,615	3,852,810	3,947,671
Broward	41,699,646	45,107,867	17,894,729	18,809,713
Calhoun	124,465	128,930	50,934	57,079
Charlotte	1,848,271	1,915,432	1,131,357	1,157,120
Citrus	1,238,547	1,268,529	692,760	715,976
Clay	1,908,161	1,951,456	983,206	1,016,228
Collier	4,806,919	5,334,647	2,987,310	3,238,538
Columbia	1,044,140	1,112,725	466,331	494,130
Dade	67,940,140	70,217,213	22,119,253	22,964,213
De Soto	278,253	327,317	146,249	164,260
Dixie	108,989	109,590	36,853	37,029
Duval	22,729,671	23,569,815	8,842,822	9,351,142
Escambia	6,002,629	6,239,860	2,795,338	2,940,700
Flagler	651,699	573,168	250,774	210,052
Franklin	181,385	117,489	60,946	64,799
Gadsden	569,851	596,200	171,740	170,393
Gilchrist	64,924	78,202	27,605	30,129
Glades	42,196	76,433	15,302	17,272
Gulf	162,238	141,214	43,831	50,332
Hamilton	158,752	147,688	41,650	40,599
Hardee	262,078	252,512	118,752	108,885
Hendry	749,718	888,632	183,790	193,790
Hernando	3,224,631	1,703,456	658,016	709,399
Highlands	1,090,522	1,185,495	589,547	588,706
Hillsborough	30,544,630	32,852,245	11,733,238	12,474,490
Holmes	110,449	116,223	53,620	54,352
Indian River	1,759,393	1,892,122	965,110	1,035,254
Jackson	598,444	612,933	289,906	295,837
Jefferson	81,905	89,882	37,696	39,133
Lafayette	43,467	46,776	10,658	11,420
Lake	2,751,042	2,990,134	1,363,801	1,437,204
Lee	7,842,774	8,384,822	4,746,429	5,035,343
Leon	4,349,475	4,505,797	2,415,857	2,523,994
Levy	289,968	324,538	157,413	173,095

See footnotes at end of table.   Continued . . .

University of Florida   **Bureau of Economic and Business Research**

Table 16.82. GROSS AND TAXABLE SALES: SALES REPORTED TO THE DEPARTMENT OF REVENUE
IN THE STATE AND COUNTIES OF FLORIDA, 1995 AND 1996 (Continued)

(rounded to thousands of dollars)

County	Gross sales 1995	Gross sales 1996	Taxable sales 1995	Taxable sales 1996
Liberty	63,558	54,071	11,940	12,235
Madison	130,211	137,299	56,873	61,081
Manatee	4,780,536	5,270,974	2,194,532	2,272,094
Marion	4,864,338	5,013,276	2,099,762	2,189,883
Martin	2,767,024	2,910,580	1,443,503	1,505,779
Monroe	2,115,676	2,305,027	1,459,206	1,585,140
Nassau	1,152,528	1,124,768	352,513	384,350
Okaloosa	3,087,901	3,358,049	1,733,666	1,870,318
Okeechobee	457,095	502,186	236,061	243,325
Orange	32,766,347	37,501,871	16,028,827	17,618,276
Osceola	3,690,286	4,151,447	1,740,890	1,897,717
Palm Beach	23,900,981	25,880,983	12,436,455	13,283,399
Pasco	3,823,385	4,014,768	1,993,578	2,063,459
Pinellas	20,545,423	21,420,423	8,953,300	9,278,742
Polk	9,760,546	10,344,105	4,039,131	4,135,667
Putnam	1,456,894	1,415,960	374,511	369,271
St. Johns	1,721,917	1,805,709	972,844	1,030,939
St. Lucie	2,618,665	2,653,600	1,350,074	1,336,976
Santa Rosa	1,228,344	1,185,251	470,890	487,635
Sarasota	6,430,642	6,909,491	3,531,154	3,771,565
Seminole	7,243,584	8,250,319	3,563,657	3,966,479
Sumter	428,986	479,088	152,701	160,831
Suwannee	363,289	403,552	179,156	183,699
Taylor	325,743	349,371	129,989	124,378
Union	156,366	157,451	28,699	30,697
Volusia	7,275,384	7,675,756	3,750,998	3,865,442
Wakulla	132,186	168,793	50,418	59,048
Walton	520,785	659,126	366,776	412,620
Washington	163,163	165,066	77,520	76,091
Out of state	55,290,564	61,869,112	11,482,068	13,320,961
In/out state 1/	2,543,318	2,090,367	359,182	280,903

1/ Reports that have not yet been allocated to counties.
Note: Data are audited sales reported to the Florida Department of Revenue for
the 6 percent regular sales tax, 6 percent use tax, and 3 percent vehicle and farm
equipment sales tax. Sales occurred, for the most part, December 1, 1994, through
November 30, 1996. Kind of business data for counties are available from the Bureau
of Economic and Business Research, University of Florida. Data are not comparable
with retail sales reported by the U.S. Bureau of the Census.

Source: State of Florida, Department of Revenue, unpublished data prepared by the
University of Florida, Bureau of Economic and Business Research.

University of Florida   **Bureau of Economic and Business Research**

FINANCE, INSURANCE, AND REAL ESTATE

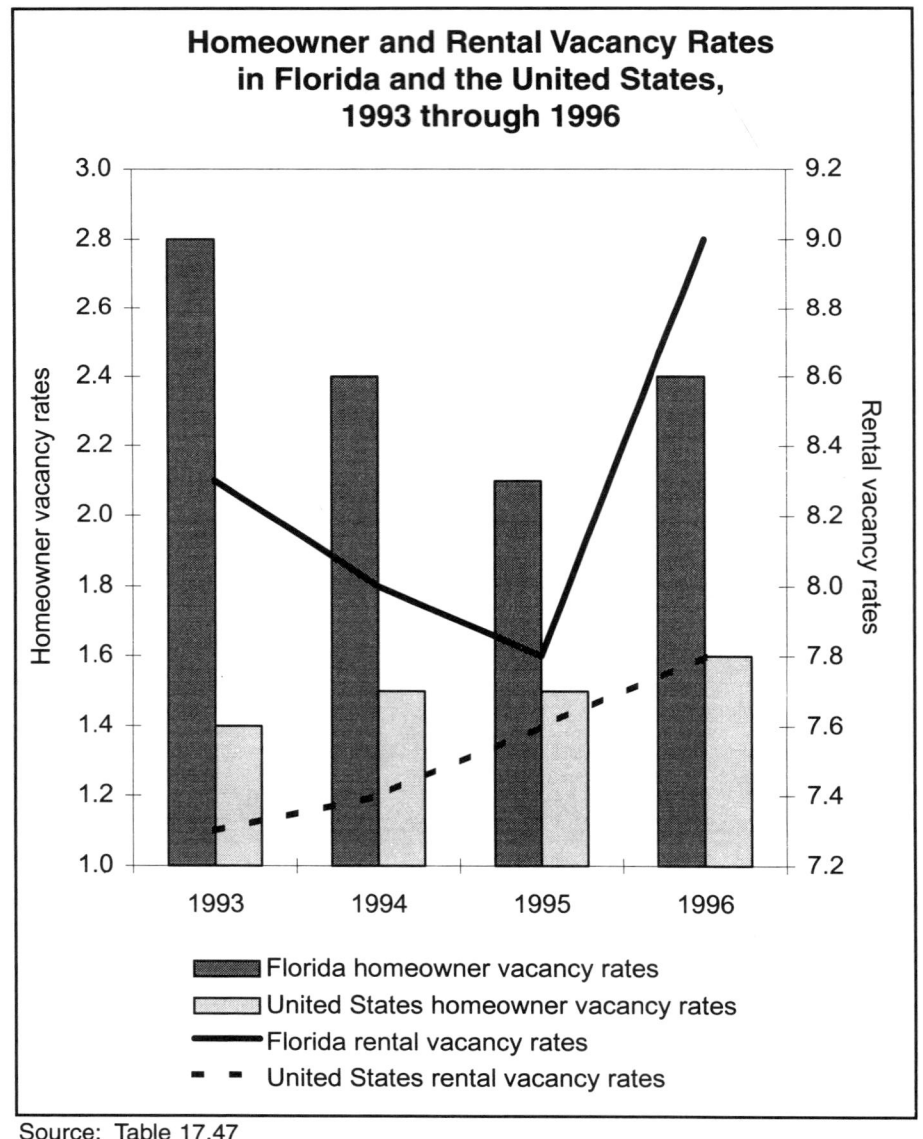

**Homeowner and Rental Vacancy Rates
in Florida and the United States,
1993 through 1996**

- Florida homeowner vacancy rates
- United States homeowner vacancy rates
- Florida rental vacancy rates
- United States rental vacancy rates

Source: Table 17.47

SECTION 17.00
FINANCE, INSURANCE, AND REAL ESTATE

TABLES LISTED BY MAJOR HEADINGS

University of Florida   Bureau of Economic and Business Research

SECTION 17.00
FINANCE, INSURANCE, AND REAL ESTATE
(Continued)

TABLES LISTED BY MAJOR HEADINGS

Table 17.07. BANKING OFFICES: NUMBER OF FDIC-INSURED COMMERCIAL BANKS AND TRUST
COMPANIES BY CHARTER CLASS AND OFFICE TYPE IN FLORIDA
DECEMBER 31, 1995 AND 1996

| | | Banks | | | |
Charter class	All offices	Total	Unit banks	Banks oper- ating branches	Branches
Total by charter class	3,561	289	61	228	3,272
National	2,458	95	14	81	2,363
State	1,103	194	47	147	909
Member of Federal Reserve System	441	52	12	40	389
Nonmember of Federal Reserve System	662	142	35	107	520
Total in operation					
December 31, 1995	4,246	403	(NA)	(NA)	3,843
December 31, 1996	4,215	346	(NA)	(NA)	3,869
Net change during 1996	-31	-57	(NA)	(NA)	26
Beginning operation in 1996	(NA)	8	(NA)	(NA)	(NA)
Ceasing operation in 1996	(NA)	67	(NA)	(NA)	(NA)
Failed banks	(NA)	0	(NA)	(NA)	(X)
Mergers, absorptions, and consolidations	(NA)	67	(NA)	(NA)	(X)

(NA) Not available.
(X) Not applicable.

Table 17.08. BANKING ACTIVITY: NUMBER OF FDIC-INSURED COMMERCIAL BANKS AND TRUST
COMPANIES AND AMOUNT OF ASSETS AND DEPOSITS BY ASSET SIZE
IN FLORIDA, DECEMBER 31, 1996

(amounts in millions of dollars)

Size of assets	Number of banks	Assets	Deposits
All banks	289	160,708	130,468
Less than $25 million	17	304	239
$25 to $50 million	53	2,031	1,752
$50 to $100 million	90	6,457	5,534
$100 to $300 million	82	13,819	11,959
$300 to $500 million	12	4,701	3,740
$500 million to $1 billion	16	12,207	9,282
$1 to $3 billion	13	20,810	16,840
$3 to $10 billion	4	21,910	15,940
$10 billion or more	2	78,468	65,182

Note: Asset size of bank determined from domestic and foreign consolidated assets.

Source for Tables 17.07 and 17.08: Federal Deposit Insurance Corporation, Division of Research and Statistics, *Statistics on Banking, 1996.*

University of Florida   **Bureau of Economic and Business Research**

Table 17.09. BANKING ACTIVITY: NUMBER OF FDIC-INSURED COMMERCIAL AND SAVINGS
BANKS AND BANKING OFFICES AND AMOUNT OF DEPOSITS IN THE STATE
AND COUNTIES OF FLORIDA, JUNE 30, 1996

County	Number of banks 1/	Number of banking offices 2/	Deposits ($1,000)	County	Number of banks 1/	Number of banking offices 2/	Deposits ($1,000)
Florida	644	3,543	149,571	Lafayette	1	1	23
				Lake	12	51	1,786
Alachua	11	47	1,480	Lee	18	138	4,892
Baker	3	4	104	Leon	12	61	1,882
Bay	8	30	714	Levy	4	14	200
Bradford	3	6	154	Liberty	1	1	30
Brevard	12	97	2,995	Madison	2	4	85
Broward	35	296	16,312	Manatee	13	68	2,368
Calhoun	3	3	84	Marion	13	64	2,330
Charlotte	11	36	1,442	Martin	8	40	1,341
Citrus	10	30	1,153	Monroe	8	42	999
Clay	9	26	507	Nassau	6	14	303
Collier	18	87	3,234	Okaloosa	14	57	1,505
Columbia	5	11	309	Okeechobee	3	7	217
Dade	60	416	27,641	Orange	20	160	6,797
De Soto	4	5	180	Osceola	12	25	813
Dixie	2	3	39	Palm Beach	32	248	10,502
Duval	13	138	6,750	Pasco	13	84	3,322
Escambia	15	68	2,198	Pinellas	25	260	11,719
Flagler	5	9	454	Polk	12	108	3,499
Franklin	2	8	70	Putnam	5	12	298
Gadsden	4	9	198	St. Johns	9	26	909
Gilchrist	2	4	59	St. Lucie	7	33	1,325
Glades	2	2	19	Santa Rosa	9	24	640
Gulf	2	4	50	Sarasota	21	121	5,337
Hamilton	1	1	18	Seminole	18	72	2,101
Hardee	3	5	240	Sumter	4	7	163
Hendry	4	9	201	Suwannee	4	6	176
Hernando	8	33	1,539	Taylor	2	4	65
Highlands	8	25	897	Union	1	1	31
Hillsborough	27	188	7,741	Volusia	13	115	4,614
Holmes	3	3	96	Wakulla	2	6	94
Indian River	11	36	1,625	Walton	5	11	216
Jackson	6	14	327	Washington	3	3	82
Jefferson	2	2	78				

1/ Number of banks in each county includes each bank operating at least one office
within the county, regardless of the location of its main office; therefore, a bank
operating a branch in a second county would be counted as a bank in each county, but
only once in the state total.

2/ Includes each location at which deposit business is transacted.

Source: Federal Deposit Insurance Corporation, Division of Supervision, *Data
Book: Operating Banks and Branches, June 30, 1996.*

University of Florida   **Bureau of Economic and Business Research**

Table 17.20. STATE-CHARTERED BANKS AND TRUST COMPANIES: NUMBER, ASSETS
CAPITAL ACCOUNTS, LOANS, AND DEPOSITS IN FLORIDA
SPECIFIED YEARS 1895 THROUGH 1996

(amounts in thousands of dollars)

Year	Number	Assets	Capital accounts	Loans	Deposits
1895	21	1,692	666	943	974
1900	22	4,510	1,006	2,637	3,408
1905	41	14,338	3,222	9,332	10,291
1910	113	27,599	5,607	17,711	20,884
1915	192	42,656	9,811	26,280	30,527
1920	212	114,374	13,272	71,347	95,349
1925	271	539,101	33,427	309,492	501,553
1930	151	92,928	16,422	38,534	70,235
1935	102	64,276	9,768	13,662	53,552
1940	114	116,169	14,233	31,285	101,545
1945	112	450,838	20,135	36,851	430,256
1950	130	619,824	37,603	128,517	580,607
1955	146	1,138,114	67,726	329,340	1,064,763
1960	181	1,781,837	139,368	711,387	1,620,185
1965	243	2,571,685	216,444	1,139,398	2,541,195
1970	282	5,603,445	425,945	2,668,971	4,996,082
1975	449	11,757,147	989,185	5,860,781	10,346,695
1980	358	22,416,088	1,679,111	10,380,658	17,942,643
1981	321	21,303,799	1,609,024	10,423,906	17,991,930
1982	297	20,912,278	1,570,467	9,978,160	18,175,117
1983	274	22,940,431	1,678,551	11,152,310	20,212,039
1984	256	23,186,313	1,636,747	12,568,673	20,319,366
1985	251	24,160,155	1,627,920	13,372,532	21,321,726
1986	241	28,055,385	1,896,402	16,174,559	24,948,817
1987	246	30,362,358	2,136,083	18,647,857	26,683,250
1988	251	31,658,397	2,264,319	19,950,857	27,831,065
1989	258	32,801,720	2,402,253	21,338,510	29,128,762
1990	261	37,247,099	2,587,920	23,793,358	33,324,544
1991	260	39,051,128	2,852,114	24,076,458	35,021,312
1992	256	41,551,323	3,196,327	25,095,945	37,137,219
1993	248	51,271,342	4,265,301	32,194,235	44,490,477
1994	238	58,803,093	4,783,598	38,780,991	50,081,893
1995	224	58,344,123	5,143,296	38,320,163	49,393,436
1996	194	40,904,042	3,693,747	26,214,925	33,128,637

Note: Data for 1986 through 1996 excludes nondeposit trust companies and industrial savings banks.

Source: State of Florida, Office of the Comptroller, *Annual Report of the Division of Banking, 1995,* and unpublished data.

University of Florida   **Bureau of Economic and Business Research**

Table 17.21.   STATE-CHARTERED BANKS AND TRUST COMPANIES: NUMBER
ASSETS, AND DEPOSITS IN THE STATE AND COUNTIES
OF FLORIDA, DECEMBER 31, 1996

(amounts in thousands of dollars)

County	Num-ber	Assets	Deposits	County	Num-ber	Assets	Deposits
Florida	194	40,904,042	33,128,637	Lafayette	1	27,797	23,861
				Lake	4	379,700	334,700
Alachua	4	362,067	322,567	Lee	4	1,493,865	1,212,576
Baker	0	0	0	Leon	4	1,105,694	950,645
Bay	2	156,567	136,546	Levy	3	251,044	223,968
Bradford	1	38,402	32,946	Liberty	1	36,188	32,152
Brevard	3	133,511	111,637	Madison	0	0	0
Broward	9	840,848	739,825	Manatee	2	225,220	191,257
Calhoun	1	50,978	46,947	Marion	4	957,502	791,290
Charlotte	4	255,885	227,121	Martin	1	26,452	24,003
Citrus	3	382,750	342,270	Monroe	3	475,515	410,841
Clay	1	24,722	22,210	Nassau	1	65,205	50,226
Collier	4	378,621	336,005	Okaloosa	5	464,370	409,749
Columbia	1	47,985	42,700	Okeechobee	0	0	0
Dade	24	7,223,506	5,760,442	Orange	6	898,010	767,454
De Soto	1	107,704	90,866	Osceola	1	47,057	42,519
Dixie	0	0	0	Palm Beach	10	1,698,528	1,478,587
Duval	3	1,223,091	1,007,064	Pasco	0	0	0
Escambia	7	1,453,194	1,220,676	Pinellas	14	1,887,495	1,678,934
Flagler	0	0	0	Polk	4	510,938	457,123
Franklin	2	82,336	74,376	Putnam	1	48,815	43,025
Gadsden	2	127,617	104,659	St. Johns	1	86,136	77,746
Gilchrist	2	72,560	64,778	St. Lucie	0	0	0
Glades	0	0	0	Santa Rosa	0	0	0
Gulf	1	30,017	26,383	Sarasota	7	2,236,756	1,840,261
Hamilton	0	0	0	Seminole	1	82,244	69,876
Hardee	1	234,458	200,611	Sumter	0	0	0
Hendry	2	185,257	166,596	Suwannee	1	34,025	30,030
Hernando	2	1,349,540	1,114,805	Taylor	1	41,593	36,979
Highlands	1	59,088	51,834	Union	0	0	0
Hillsborough	17	10,656,472	7,650,213	Volusia	5	1,357,085	1,196,135
Holmes	1	58,659	51,727	Wakulla	2	138,630	127,309
Indian River	1	39,267	34,616	Walton	1	28,199	23,071
Jackson	5	623,299	533,572	Washington	0	0	0
Jefferson	1	101,578	90,328				

Source: State of Florida, Office of the Comptroller, unpublished data.

University of Florida   **Bureau of Economic and Business Research**

Table 17.23. STATE-CHARTERED BANKS AND TRUST COMPANIES: ASSETS, DEPOSITS
CAPITAL, NET INCOME, AND NUMBER OF BANKS BY ASSET SIZE
IN FLORIDA, DECEMBER 31, 1996

(in thousands of dollars, except where indicated)

Item	All banks	Less than 50 million	50-500 million	Over 500 million
Assets	40,904,042	2,560,600	15,055,714	23,287,728
Deposits	33,128,637	2,222,949	13,035,615	17,870,073
Capital	3,693,747	290,915	1,389,187	2,013,645
Net income 1/	436,752	24,139	143,714	268,899
Number of institutions	194	69	110	15

1/ After taxes and extraordinary items.
Note: Nondeposit trust companies and industrial savings banks are excluded.

Source: State of Florida, Office of the Comptroller, unpublished data.

Table 17.24. INTERNATIONAL BANKS: NUMBER AND ASSETS OF AGENCIES BY NATION
OF ORIGIN IN FLORIDA, DECEMBER 31, 1994, 1995, AND 1996

Nation of origin	1994 Number	1994 Assets ($1,000)	1995 Number	1995 Assets ($1,000)	1996 Number	1996 Assets ($1,000)
Total	47	11,423,666	46	13,539,796	43	16,189,262
Argentina	1	111,876	1	77,417	1	89,025
Bolivia	2	51,014	2	74,519	2	89,164
Brazil	4	563,158	4	433,372	4	302,393
Canada	1	531,406	1	546,567	1	554,843
Cayman Islands	1	41,799	1	46,976	1	45,024
Chile	1	23,514	1	68,783	1	131,818
Colombia	1	227,625	1	211,418	1	221,556
Ecuador	2	133,875	2	179,840	2	190,993
England	3	3,479,933	3	3,593,300	3	5,817,957
France	3	626,994	3	665,498	3	746,301
Germany	1	1,142,170	1	2,203,179	1	2,246,776
Israel	3	735,184	3	813,745	3	834,356
Jamaica	1	47,540	1	43,104	1	31,394
Japan	3	300,826	3	300,504	1	342,156
Korea	1	73,332	1	110,635	1	168,227
Netherlands	1	630,787	1	857,984	1	853,193
Panama	1	303,181	1	304,148	1	297,223
Peru	1	254,589	1	263,828	1	326,323
Portugal	1	103,294	1	84,254	1	67,443
Spain	8	1,063,730	7	1,470,353	7	1,649,698
Switzerland	2	589,093	2	829,163	2	774,907
United States	1	38,109	1	38,356	1	47,314
Venezuela	4	350,637	4	322,853	3	361,178

Source: State of Florida, Office of the Comptroller, *Annual Report of the Division of Banking, 1995*, and unpublished data.

University of Florida   **Bureau of Economic and Business Research**

Table 17.30. CREDIT UNIONS: FINANCIAL CONDITION OF STATE-CHARTERED CREDIT UNIONS
IN FLORIDA, DECEMBER 31, 1995

(in thousands of dollars, except where indicated)

Item	Amount	Item	Amount
Number of institutions 1/	115	Gross income, total	316,275
Net loans	2,400,817	Operating expense, total	160,697
Assets, total	3,728,429	Cost of funds	113,490
Shares and deposits, total	3,336,160	Net income	39,001
Liabilities and equity,		Ratio of expense to $100	
total	3,728,429	gross income (dollars)	50.8

1/ Does not include credit unions in liquidation.

Table 17.31. CREDIT UNIONS: ASSETS AND DEPOSITS OF STATE-CHARTERED CREDIT UNIONS
IN THE STATE AND COUNTIES OF FLORIDA, DECEMBER 31, 1996

(amounts in thousands of dollars)

County	Number of institu- tions	Assets	Deposits	County	Number of institu- tions	Assets	Deposits
Florida	114	3,886,243	3,451,035	Lee	2	2,679	2,269
				Leon	7	256,860	231,463
Alachua	5	118,207	104,108	Madison	1	1,561	1,201
Bay	1	39,882	34,258	Marion	3	36,109	31,961
Bradford	1	3,131	2,753	Martin	1	7,108	5,920
Brevard	2	691,967	637,577	Nassau	2	12,044	10,100
Broward	8	332,215	301,222	Orange	3	46,660	40,361
Calhoun	1	15,607	13,693	Palm Beach	7	121,131	107,400
Clay	1	6,102	5,363	Pinellas	5	269,885	234,948
Columbia	1	12,056	10,418	Polk	6	41,240	36,179
Dade	10	187,123	161,818	Putnam	1	15,145	13,181
Duval	14	915,901	809,059	St. Johns	1	6,963	6,181
Escambia	5	298,827	260,197	St. Lucie	1	4,074	3,754
Gadsden	1	38,755	33,387	Santa Rosa	2	17,673	15,020
Hillsborough	7	168,578	145,843	Sarasota	3	108,395	97,559
Holmes	1	7,831	6,624	Taylor	1	7,058	6,466
Jackson	2	14,255	11,405	Volusia	3	9,566	8,096
Jefferson	1	3,960	3,567	Washington	1	15,668	13,099
Lake	3	52,027	44,584				

Source for Tables 17.30 and 17.31: State of Florida, Office of the Comptroller,
Annual Report of the Division of Banking, 1995, prepublication release.

Table 17.33.   MORTGAGE ACTIVITY: NUMBER AND VALUE OF NEW AND EXISTING RESIDENTIAL
PURCHASE LOANS IN SPECIFIED COUNTIES OF FLORIDA, 1994, 1995, and 1996

County	Number of loans			Value ($1,000,000)		
	1994	1995	1996	1994	1995	1996
Total	240,123	230,672	259,297	20,924	20,251	23,699
Alachua	2,592	2,564	2,875	197	189	215
Brevard	7,461	6,744	7,767	565	506	603
Broward	32,325	29,958	33,571	3,138	2,946	3,378
Charlotte	2,199	1,999	2,382	154	141	164
Citrus	1,376	1,431	1,462	71	75	85
Clay	2,424	2,405	2,825	201	212	267
Collier	5,212	5,148	5,717	597	610	682
Dade	32,142	30,696	33,777	2,929	2,836	3,278
De Soto	226	295	335	10	13	18
Duval	10,895	10,816	11,979	897	887	1,043
Escambia	3,731	3,631	4,798	264	263	370
Flagler	796	710	755	60	55	60
Hernando	1,585	1,613	1,810	93	94	108
Highlands	905	857	925	48	46	51
Hillsborough	14,068	14,343	15,751	1,231	1,247	1,415
Indian River	1,504	1,345	1,676	140	118	157
Lake	2,761	2,933	3,378	185	202	239
Lee	8,405	7,555	8,627	751	677	794
Leon	3,762	3,860	4,234	304	309	368
Manatee	4,186	3,961	4,729	325	319	394
Marion	2,481	2,607	3,044	154	160	200
Martin	2,039	1,976	2,193	203	183	227
Monroe	1,679	1,537	1,827	207	202	250
Nassau	735	790	967	69	72	95
Okaloosa	3,256	2,969	3,489	270	265	333
Orange	13,920	13,329	15,080	1,256	1,188	1,418
Osceola	2,638	2,710	2,923	192	193	227
Palm Beach	20,775	19,440	21,788	2,157	2,026	2,325
Pasco	4,752	4,912	5,393	288	303	347
Pinellas	16,235	15,324	16,397	1,281	1,237	1,366
Polk	5,472	5,091	5,624	357	332	389
Putnam	398	453	483	22	26	28
St. Johns	2,242	2,235	2,776	235	244	320
St. Lucie	2,630	2,627	3,079	174	176	218
Santa Rosa	2,168	2,048	2,383	176	170	206
Sarasota	6,047	5,756	6,697	564	568	693
Seminole	6,476	6,168	7,117	615	587	700
Sumter	423	538	650	24	34	44
Volusia	6,227	6,348	6,864	420	433	488
Walton	975	950	1,150	99	108	136

Note: Only counties for which data are collected are shown.
Source: Experian, Anaheim, CA, unpublished data,(copyright).

University of Florida   **Bureau of Economic and Business Research**

Table 17.36. SAVINGS AND LOAN ASSOCIATIONS: NUMBER OF ASSOCIATIONS AND OFFICES
AND AMOUNT OF DEPOSITS IN THE STATE AND COUNTIES OF FLORIDA, JUNE 30, 1996

County	Number of associations	Number of association offices	Deposits 1/ ($1,000)	County	Number of associations	Number of association offices	Deposits 1/ ($1,000)
Florida	177	644	28,952,593	Lafayette	1	1	9,024
				Lake	2	12	387,683
Alachua	0	0	0	Lee	3	10	173,354
Baker	0	0	0	Leon	2	3	66,151
Bay	3	13	473,738	Levy	1	3	39,341
Bradford	0	0	0	Liberty	0	0	0
Brevard	4	18	514,743	Madison	1	1	32,897
Broward	17	93	5,660,385	Manatee	8	19	491,242
Calhoun	0	0	0	Marion	0	0	0
Charlotte	2	7	303,345	Martin	8	19	522,493
Citrus	3	6	265,266	Monroe	0	0	0
Clay	0	0	0	Nassau	0	0	0
Collier	5	7	85,062	Okaloosa	1	2	65,435
Columbia	1	2	40,009	Okeechobee	2	2	55,522
Dade	17	109	7,021,604	Orange	6	17	816,324
De Soto	1	1	23,145	Osceola	2	6	141,373
Dixie	1	1	9,721	Palm Beach	26	149	6,541,227
Duval	3	4	58,793	Pasco	8	10	530,978
Escambia	1	1	46,114	Pinellas	6	31	1,014,445
Flagler	1	1	2,275	Polk	1	6	278,767
Franklin	1	1	10,164	Putnam	1	4	144,136
Gadsden	0	0	0	St. Johns	1	1	16,850
Gilchrist	1	1	7,281	St. Lucie	3	12	427,666
Glades	0	0	0	Santa Rosa	0	0	0
Gulf	1	1	43,411	Sarasota	6	18	513,925
Hamilton	1	2	18,325	Seminole	4	11	494,764
Hardee	0	0	0	Sumter	1	1	33,821
Hendry	1	2	51,664	Suwannee	1	2	74,468
Hernando	5	6	300,396	Taylor	1	1	49,399
Highlands	1	3	156,934	Union	0	0	0
Hillsborough	4	9	231,917	Volusia	2	6	422,954
Holmes	0	0	0	Wakulla	0	0	0
Indian River	4	8	272,731	Walton	0	0	0
Jackson	1	1	11,331	Washington	0	0	0
Jefferson	0	0	0				

1/ Includes savings, NOW accounts, and noninterest bearing deposits.
   Note: Data are for all SAIF-insured (Savings Associations Insurance Fund) OTS
regulated associations and are the result of a survey. Figures indicate the activity
of an association within specific counties whether the county offices are home or
branch offices, although some institutions with centralized accounting do not have
precise data on deposits by office. Detail may not add to totals due to rounding.

   Source: U.S., Office of Thrift Supervision, *Summary of Deposits in SAIF-Insured
OTS Regulated Associations, Regional Data Book, Southeast Region, June 30, 1996.*

Table 17.38. EMPLOYMENT: AVERAGE MONTHLY PRIVATE REPORTING UNITS, EMPLOYMENT, AND
PAYROLL COVERED BY UNEMPLOYMENT COMPENSATION LAW BY FINANCE, INSURANCE
AND REAL ESTATE INDUSTRY IN FLORIDA, 1995 AND 1996

SIC code	Industry	Number of reporting units	Number of employees	Payroll ($1,000)
	1995 A/			
	Finance, insurance, and real estate	34,857	372,171	1,022,552
60	Depository institutions	2,792	94,825	233,876
601	Central reserve depository institutions	3	632	1,682
602	Commercial banks	1,554	66,845	162,425
603	Savings institutions	576	13,590	34,395
606	Credit unions	348	8,170	15,133
608	Foreign banking and branches and agencies of foreign banks	70	2,295	10,645
609	Functions related to depository banking	242	3,293	9,596
61	Nondepository credit institutions	2,699	34,869	101,189
614	Personal credit institutions	899	10,568	30,337
615	Business credit institutions	189	8,879	24,117
616	Mortgage bankers and brokers	1,582	14,175	44,172
62	Security and commodity brokers, dealers, exchanges, and services	1,923	23,941	138,412
621	Security brokers, dealers, flotation companies	1,088	20,858	116,616
622	Commodity contracts brokers and dealers	52	328	6,627
628	Services allied with the exchange of securities or commodities	778	2,748	15,150
63	Insurance carriers	2,327	65,213	194,482
631	Life insurance	583	20,233	57,169
632	Accident and health insurance and medical service plans	234	13,852	41,204
633	Fire, marine, and casualty insurance	754	24,359	78,262
635	Surety insurance	69	513	1,992
636	Title insurance	605	5,703	13,483
637	Pension, health, and welfare funds	63	469	2,029
639	Insurance carriers, NEC	20	83	344
64	Insurance agents, brokers, and service	7,101	43,088	118,476
65	Real estate	16,799	100,885	195,253
651	Real estate operators (except developers) and lessors	5,985	35,034	54,636
653	Real estate agents and managers	9,303	49,454	101,029
654	Title abstract offices	224	1,268	2,733
655	Land subdividers and developers	1,288	15,130	36,856
67	Holding and other investment offices	1,216	9,351	40,863
671	Holding offices	435	5,789	27,789
672	Investment offices	94	354	1,758
673	Trusts	150	987	2,620
679	Miscellaneous investing	537	2,221	8,697

See footnotes at end of table.   Continued . . .

Table 17.38. EMPLOYMENT: AVERAGE MONTHLY PRIVATE REPORTING UNITS, EMPLOYMENT, AND PAYROLL COVERED BY UNEMPLOYMENT COMPENSATION LAW BY FINANCE, INSURANCE AND REAL ESTATE INDUSTRY IN FLORIDA, 1995 AND 1996 (Continued)

SIC code	Industry	Number of reporting units	Number of employees	Payroll ($1,000)
	1996 B/			
	Finance, insurance, and real estate	36,460	386,730	1,124,285
60	Depository institutions	3,284	95,077	250,563
601	Central reserve depository institutions	4	613	1,658
602	Commercial banks	2,014	67,060	173,646
603	Savings institutions	577	12,329	34,589
606	Credit unions	376	8,706	16,685
608	Foreign banking and branches and agencies of foreign banks	70	2,417	11,681
609	Functions related to depository banking	244	3,954	12,304
61	Nondepository credit institutions	3,034	39,010	116,653
611	Federal and federally-sponsored credit agencies	30	1,279	2,739
614	Personal credit institutions	1,013	11,366	34,009
615	Business credit institutions	208	10,394	28,074
616	Mortgage bankers and brokers	1,783	15,973	51,832
62	Security and commodity brokers, dealers, exchanges, and services	2,150	25,693	161,154
621	Security brokers, dealers, flotation companies	1,158	21,904	137,798
622	Commodity contracts brokers and dealers	54	407	4,053
623	Security and commodity exchanges	6	15	48
628	Services allied with the exchange of securities or commodities	932	3,367	19,256
63	Insurance carriers	2,315	66,696	208,574
631	Life insurance	537	20,396	60,480
632	Accident and health insurance and medical service plans	252	15,036	46,878
633	Fire, marine, and casualty insurance	758	23,972	81,580
635	Surety insurance	79	637	2,548
636	Title insurance	611	6,017	14,553
637	Pension, health, and welfare funds	59	521	1,996
639	Insurance carriers, NEC	20	118	539
64	Insurance agents, brokers, and service	7,487	45,633	131,043
65	Real estate	16,976	104,667	211,167
651	Real estate operators (except developers) and lessors	5,631	34,296	56,329
653	Real estate agents and managers	9,727	53,356	112,265
654	Title abstract offices	279	1,572	3,371
655	Land subdividers and developers	1,340	15,442	39,203
67	Holding and other investment offices	1,214	9,954	45,130
671	Holding offices	451	6,236	30,095
672	Investment offices	87	357	1,888
673	Trusts	163	1,032	3,489
679	Miscellaneous investing	514	2,329	9,658

NEC Not elsewhere classified. A/ Revised. B/ Preliminary.

Note: Private employment. Detail may not add to totals due to disclosure editing and/or rounding. See Tables 23.70, 23.71, 23.72, 23.73, and 23.74 for public employment data.

Source: State of Florida, Department of Labor and Employment Security, Bureau of Labor Market Information, "Employment and Wages" (ES-202), unpublished data.

Table 17.39. EMPLOYMENT: AVERAGE MONTHLY PRIVATE REPORTING UNITS, EMPLOYMENT
AND PAYROLL COVERED BY UNEMPLOYMENT COMPENSATION LAW IN THE STATE
AND COUNTIES OF FLORIDA, 1995 AND 1996

County	Number of re-porting units	Number of em-ployees	Payroll ($1,000)	County	Number of re-porting units	Number of em-ployees	Payroll ($1,000)

Finance, insurance, and real estate, 1995 A/ (SIC codes 60-67)

County	Number of re-porting units	Number of em-ployees	Payroll ($1,000)	County	Number of re-porting units	Number of em-ployees	Payroll ($1,000)
Florida	34,857	372,171	1,022,552	Jefferson	17	119	219
				Lake	297	2,912	5,451
Alachua	440	4,346	9,884	Lee	1,039	8,170	20,305
Baker	14	106	175	Leon	583	4,843	12,134
Bay	313	2,972	5,354	Levy	40	267	430
Bradford	25	106	185	Madison	17	81	163
Brevard	808	5,526	12,656	Manatee	439	2,872	6,283
Broward	3,812	40,907	119,001	Marion	406	3,057	7,194
Calhoun	9	63	93	Martin	348	2,289	6,775
Charlotte	230	1,486	3,027	Monroe	249	1,443	3,290
Citrus	181	1,057	2,076	Nassau	71	388	863
Clay	157	818	1,827	Okaloosa	382	3,794	7,089
Collier	724	4,473	14,860	Okeechobee	44	233	871
Columbia	71	507	878	Orange	2,157	29,244	79,900
Dade	5,719	65,198	190,120	Osceola	260	2,419	4,095
De Soto	30	166	267	Palm Beach	3,142	26,353	95,204
Dixie	12	47	57	Pasco	445	2,898	5,999
Duval	1,810	45,665	128,459	Pinellas	2,280	22,887	63,351
Escambia	503	4,608	9,560	Polk	730	7,497	17,084
Flagler	63	614	1,530	Putnam	85	526	985
Franklin	21	142	216	St. Johns	200	1,160	2,738
Gadsden	39	244	440	St. Lucie	269	2,183	4,726
Gilchrist	8	56	104	Santa Rosa	125	680	1,055
Glades	4	14	24	Sarasota	986	7,666	21,719
Gulf	18	127	199	Seminole	755	5,791	14,514
Hamilton	6	19	32	Sumter	27	202	336
Hardee	22	232	461	Suwannee	38	284	472
Hendry	40	270	451	Taylor	21	226	424
Hernando	146	1,128	2,268	Volusia	802	5,795	12,628
Highlands	128	852	1,621	Wakulla	15	112	205
Hillsborough	2,410	37,969	103,913	Walton	53	337	576
Holmes	9	56	103	Washington	18	67	116
Indian River	280	1,656	4,373				
Jackson	56	463	986	Multicounty 1/	407	3,392	10,007

See footnotes at end of table.   Continued . . .

University of Florida   **Bureau of Economic and Business Research**

Table 17.39. EMPLOYMENT: AVERAGE MONTHLY PRIVATE REPORTING UNITS, EMPLOYMENT
AND PAYROLL COVERED BY UNEMPLOYMENT COMPENSATION LAW IN THE STATE
AND COUNTIES OF FLORIDA, 1995 AND 1996 (Continued)

County	Number of reporting units	Number of employees	Payroll ($1,000)	County	Number of reporting units	Number of employees	Payroll ($1,000)
			Finance, insurance, and real estate, 1996 B/ (SIC codes 60-67)				
Florida	36,460	386,730	1,124,285	Jefferson	18	123	236
				Lake	317	3,151	6,098
Alachua	455	4,722	10,934	Lee	1,112	8,169	20,303
Baker	14	77	132	Leon	578	5,130	13,748
Bay	323	3,048	5,775	Levy	41	261	454
Bradford	22	109	196	Madison	18	78	177
Brevard	827	5,581	13,298	Manatee	482	3,094	7,108
Broward	4,022	42,857	136,801	Marion	438	3,234	7,172
Calhoun	11	69	102	Martin	352	2,418	8,087
Charlotte	237	1,543	3,399	Monroe	260	1,492	3,532
Citrus	180	1,073	2,228	Nassau	74	432	1,071
Clay	161	885	2,052	Okaloosa	398	3,731	7,340
Collier	779	4,730	15,077	Okeechobee	47	300	568
Columbia	72	532	961	Orange	2,253	30,690	87,289
Dade	5,957	65,721	203,047	Osceola	282	2,336	4,539
De Soto	28	182	332	Palm Beach	3,261	27,832	104,444
Dixie	12	50	61	Pasco	462	2,827	6,174
Duval	1,848	46,654	138,605	Pinellas	2,339	23,793	69,699
Escambia	538	4,982	10,732	Polk	760	7,408	18,815
Flagler	76	561	1,457	Putnam	92	564	1,119
Franklin	22	163	245	St. Johns	215	1,189	3,143
Gadsden	38	235	433	St. Lucie	274	2,353	5,506
Gilchrist	8	52	98	Santa Rosa	134	742	1,223
Glades	5	17	31	Sarasota	1,040	7,959	23,785
Gulf	18	137	215	Seminole	801	6,101	17,613
Hamilton	7	28	44	Sumter	26	175	344
Hardee	25	239	440	Suwannee	41	302	516
Hendry	39	274	463	Taylor	21	225	585
Hernando	153	1,166	2,489	Union	8	47	74
Highlands	122	957	1,571	Volusia	822	5,869	12,968
Hillsborough	2,513	40,780	118,654	Wakulla	16	124	237
Holmes	10	62	111	Walton	52	384	696
Indian River	287	1,756	5,178	Washington	20	76	137
Jackson	57	444	986	Multicounty 1/	544	4,405	13,271

A/ Revised.
B/ Preliminary.
1/ Reporting units without a fixed location within the state or of unknown county
location.
Note: Private employment. Only counties for which data are disclosed are shown.
Detail may not add to totals due to disclosure editing and/or rounding. See Tables
23.70, 23.71, 23.72, 23.73, and 23.74 for public employment data.

Source: State of Florida, Department of Labor and Employment Security, Bureau of
Labor Market Information, "Employment and Wages" (ES-202), unpublished data.

Table 17.40. DEPOSITORY INSTITUTIONS: AVERAGE MONTHLY PRIVATE REPORTING UNITS
EMPLOYMENT, AND PAYROLL COVERED BY UNEMPLOYMENT COMPENSATION LAW
IN THE STATE AND COUNTIES OF FLORIDA, 1996

County	Number of reporting units	Number of employees	Payroll ($1,000)	County	Number of reporting units	Number of employees	Payroll ($1,000)
			Depository institutions (SIC code 60)				
Florida	3,284	95,077	250,563	Lake	34	1,060	2,154
	0	0	0	Lee	114	2,362	5,834
Alachua	26	1,003	1,974	Leon	55	1,478	3,332
Bay	25	1,117	2,137	Levy	10	171	314
Bradford	5	67	124	Madison	3	36	122
Brevard	73	1,600	3,073	Manatee	75	953	2,038
Broward	293	8,657	30,157	Marion	48	1,145	2,556
Calhoun	4	56	83	Martin	34	679	1,926
Charlotte	30	510	1,086	Monroe	29	634	1,610
Citrus	29	428	940	Nassau	14	168	381
Clay	12	188	337	Okaloosa	49	1,165	2,418
Collier	54	1,271	3,265	Okeechobee	6	151	317
Columbia	9	224	469	Orange	177	5,451	13,306
Dade	505	19,228	57,870	Osceola	23	442	869
De Soto	5	97	184	Palm Beach	244	6,516	20,215
Dixie	3	18	25	Pasco	67	995	2,065
Duval	165	9,440	25,087	Pinellas	228	5,467	12,517
Escambia	60	1,580	3,283	Polk	70	1,941	4,095
Flagler	11	93	166	Putnam	15	263	485
Franklin	5	78	124	St. Johns	15	330	865
Gadsden	8	125	257	St. Lucie	22	1,106	2,602
Gilchrist	3	37	78	Santa Rosa	16	264	473
Gulf	4	96	161	Sarasota	122	2,086	5,079
Hardee	4	165	344	Seminole	49	1,266	2,810
Hendry	5	185	345	Suwannee	7	140	296
Hernando	27	546	1,232	Taylor	5	181	517
Highlands	17	303	618	Volusia	68	1,811	3,877
Hillsborough	214	8,305	20,880	Wakulla	3	98	181
Holmes	4	42	84	Walton	9	86	148
Indian River	26	535	1,341	Washington	4	33	52
Jackson	12	236	478	Multicounty 1/	21	114	368

1/ Reporting units without a fixed location within the state or of unknown county
location.
   Note: Private employment. For a list of three-digit code industries included see
Table 17.38. Data are preliminary. Only counties for which data are disclosed are
shown. Detail may not add to totals due to disclosure editing and/or rounding. See
Tables 23.70, 23.71, 23.72, 23.73, and 23.74 for public employment data.

   Source: State of Florida, Department of Labor and Employment Security, Bureau of
Labor Market Information, "Employment and Wages" (ES-202), unpublished data.

University of Florida   **Bureau of Economic and Business Research**

Table 17.41. NONDEPOSITORY CREDIT INSTITUTIONS AND SECURITY AND COMMODITY BROKERS AVERAGE MONTHLY PRIVATE REPORTING UNITS, EMPLOYMENT, AND PAYROLL COVERED BY UNEMPLOYMENT COMPENSATION LAW IN THE STATE AND COUNTIES OF FLORIDA, 1996

County	Number of reporting units	Number of employees	Payroll ($1,000)	County	Number of reporting units	Number of employees	Payroll ($1,000)
				Nondepository credit institutions (SIC code 61)			
Florida	3,034	39,010	116,653	Lee	77	346	859
				Leon	41	356	1,133
Alachua	36	234	646	Manatee	27	139	373
Bay	22	79	208	Marion	35	202	353
Brevard	68	234	714	Martin	15	153	432
Broward	362	9,105	26,360	Monroe	11	19	49
Charlotte	20	82	207	Okaloosa	29	136	305
Citrus	8	36	86	Orange	194	2,412	7,575
Clay	17	84	189	Osceola	19	81	185
Collier	40	131	381	Palm Beach	221	1,587	6,569
Columbia	7	25	48	Pasco	34	101	240
Dade	520	4,592	14,826	Pinellas	188	1,643	4,909
Duval	183	8,709	25,679	Polk	58	259	657
Escambia	55	599	1,376	Putnam	7	25	56
Flagler	7	29	58	St. Johns	15	42	127
Hernando	8	33	90	St. Lucie	21	215	572
Highlands	7	16	31	Santa Rosa	7	18	33
Hillsborough	280	5,091	14,703	Sarasota	61	378	1,167
Indian River	12	29	49	Seminole	113	758	2,241
Jackson	7	46	118	Volusia	63	283	602
Lake	16	76	110	Multicounty 1/	103	539	2,055
			Security and commodity brokers, dealers, exchanges, and services (SIC code 62)				
Florida	2,150	25,693	161,154	Manatee	18	122	858
				Marion	14	139	721
Alachua	11	71	350	Martin	35	283	2,837
Bay	16	105	414	Monroe	12	24	160
Brevard	45	373	2,184	Nassau	5	7	28
Broward	213	3,126	20,785	Okaloosa	11	73	457
Charlotte	19	82	428	Orange	122	1,388	8,205
Citrus	4	25	130	Osceola	4	15	41
Collier	57	420	3,382	Palm Beach	354	4,366	30,952
Dad	362	3,349	26,246	Pasco	22	182	950
Duval	75	1,753	8,108	Pinellas	156	4,260	20,047
Escambia	24	210	1,099	Polk	32	204	1,109
Hernando	8	39	233	St. Johns	16	91	763
Hillsborough	160	2,430	14,504	St. Lucie	10	31	122
Indian River	29	178	1,448	Sarasota	85	916	5,963
Lake	9	61	367	Seminole	38	228	1,433
Lee	36	393	2,082	Volusia	29	310	1,250
Leon	24	138	1,056	Multicounty 1/	80	242	2,123

1/ Reporting units without a fixed location within the state or of unknown county location.

Note: Private employment. For a list of three-digit code industries included see Table 17.38. Data are preliminary. Only counties for which data are disclosed are shown. Detail may not add to totals due to disclosure editing and/or rounding. See Tables 23.70, 23.71, 23.72, 23.73, and 23.74 for public employment data.

Source: State of Florida, Department of Labor and Employment Security, Bureau of Labor Market Information, "Employment and Wages" (ES-202), unpublished data.

Table 17.43. INSURANCE CARRIERS: AVERAGE MONTHLY PRIVATE REPORTING UNITS EMPLOYMENT, AND PAYROLL COVERED BY UNEMPLOYMENT COMPENSATION LAW IN THE STATE AND COUNTIES OF FLORIDA, 1996

County	Number of reporting units	Number of employees	Payroll ($1,000)	County	Number of reporting units	Number of employees	Payroll ($1,000)
				Insurance carriers (SIC code 63)			
Florida	2,315	66,696	208,574	Levy	3	9	12
				Manatee	20	161	654
Alachua	36	1,531	4,327	Marion	27	284	894
Bay	27	307	791	Martin	12	83	288
Bradford	4	13	28	Monroe	5	17	45
Brevard	64	510	1,804	Nassau	6	36	102
Broward	253	5,305	16,998	Okaloosa	21	277	756
Charlotte	17	109	357	Okeechobee	2	23	33
Citrus	10	84	208	Orange	190	5,954	17,843
Clay	10	138	524	Osceola	13	71	189
Collier	30	207	597	Palm Beach	162	2,527	9,717
Columbia	9	153	262	Pasco	25	238	777
Dade	293	9,890	33,759	Pinellas	130	3,265	10,625
Duval	174	15,781	46,823	Polk	53	1,989	7,253
Escambia	46	513	1,665	Putnam	7	37	62
Hernando	9	78	224	St. Johns	15	58	139
Highlands	8	70	190	St. Lucie	17	210	703
Hillsborough	239	11,790	34,043	Santa Rosa	5	11	51
Indian River	10	43	188	Sarasota	60	1,035	3,391
Jackson	5	60	160	Seminole	38	599	1,698
Lake	12	98	298	Volusia	48	562	1,885
Lee	69	717	2,369	Walton	3	14	33
Leon	54	725	2,431	Multicounty 1/	48	1,006	3,159

1/ Reporting units without a fixed location within the state or of unknown county location.

Note: Private employment. For a list of three-digit code industries included see Table 17.38. Data are preliminary. Only counties for which data are disclosed are shown. Detail may not add to totals due to disclosure editing and/or rounding. See Tables 23.70, 23.71, 23.72, 23.73, and 23.74 for public employment data.

Source: State of Florida, Department of Labor and Employment Security, Bureau of Labor Market Information, "Employment and Wages" (ES-202), unpublished data.

University of Florida   **Bureau of Economic and Business Research**

Table 17.44. INSURANCE AGENTS, BROKERS, AND SERVICE: AVERAGE MONTHLY PRIVATE
REPORTING UNITS, EMPLOYMENT, AND PAYROLL COVERED BY UNEMPLOYMENT
COMPENSATION LAW IN THE STATE AND COUNTIES OF FLORIDA, 1996

County	Number of reporting units	Number of employees	Payroll ($1,000)	County	Number of reporting units	Number of employees	Payroll ($1,000)
			Insurance agents, brokers, and service (SIC code 64)				
Florida	7,487	45,633	131,043	Leon	135	1,069	3,201
				Levy	10	40	73
Alachua	95	503	1,381	Madison	5	16	25
Baker	3	9	15	Manatee	77	347	873
Bay	66	232	600	Marion	109	413	809
Brevard	164	777	2,110	Martin	72	336	901
Broward	942	5,603	15,407	Monroe	26	158	472
Calhoun	5	12	17	Nassau	11	53	107
Charlotte	36	145	296	Okaloosa	72	290	609
Citrus	31	146	285	Okeechobee	11	69	145
Clay	33	80	147	Orange	496	3,681	10,647
Collier	93	473	1,544	Osceola	38	178	392
Columbia	15	40	67	Palm Beach	616	3,397	11,832
Dade	1,149	7,623	22,386	Pasco	101	465	856
De Soto	9	32	48	Pinellas	475	2,972	8,403
Duval	424	3,002	9,050	Polk	179	1,067	2,684
Escambia	127	532	1,170	Putnam	26	157	441
Flagler	8	37	65	St. Johns	26	82	226
Franklin	3	15	28	St. Lucie	71	194	379
Gadsden	10	47	86	Santa Rosa	20	61	111
Gulf	4	12	27	Sarasota	195	1,454	4,505
Hardee	9	20	23	Seminole	198	1,582	6,087
Hendry	9	28	42	Sumter	6	24	47
Hernando	35	175	334	Suwannee	13	67	104
Highlands	25	310	282	Taylor	5	10	11
Hillsborough	551	5,048	14,601	Union	3	4	2
Holmes	4	13	17	Volusia	165	742	1,984
Indian River	62	272	913	Wakulla	3	4	5
Jackson	14	50	64	Walton	5	14	38
Jefferson	6	25	41	Washington	4	15	24
Lake	64	240	484				
Lee	214	822	2,181	Multicounty 1/	99	331	1,300

1/ Reporting units without a fixed location within the state or of unknown county
location.
Note: Private employment. For a list of three-digit code industries included see
Table 17.38. Data are preliminary. Only counties for which data are disclosed are
shown. Detail may not add to totals due to disclosure editing and/or rounding. See
Tables 23.70, 23.71, 23.72, 23.73, and 23.74 for public employment data.

Source: State of Florida, Department of Labor and Employment Security, Bureau of
Labor Market Information, "Employment and Wages" (ES-202), unpublished data.

Table 17.45. REAL ESTATE: AVERAGE MONTHLY PRIVATE REPORTING UNITS, EMPLOYMENT
AND PAYROLL COVERED BY UNEMPLOYMENT COMPENSATION LAW IN THE STATE
AND COUNTIES OF FLORIDA, 1996

County	Number of reporting units	Number of employees	Payroll ($1,000)	County	Number of reporting units	Number of employees	Payroll ($1,000)
			Real estate	(SIC code 65)			
Florida	16,976	104,667	211,167	Lee	576	3,480	6,847
				Leon	254	1,158	1,821
Alachua	239	1,256	1,999	Levy	17	42	55
Baker	5	10	7	Madison	8	23	26
Bay	164	1,200	1,609	Manatee	252	1,239	1,940
Bradford	9	16	18	Marion	194	982	1,526
Brevard	399	2,045	3,274	Martin	170	864	1,606
Broward	1,813	9,864	21,796	Monroe	163	606	1,111
Charlotte	115	615	1,023	Nassau	34	140	314
Citrus	95	351	556	Okaloosa	209	1,717	2,596
Clay	86	386	816	Okeechobee	24	47	56
Collier	484	2,116	5,457	Orange	1,008	11,169	26,923
Columbia	29	85	108	Osceola	184	1,548	2,854
Dade	2,892	20,144	42,365	Palm Beach	1,497	8,780	20,663
De Soto	11	25	27	Pasco	211	840	1,278
Dixie	6	22	21	Pinellas	1,080	5,290	9,247
Duval	749	5,087	11,105	Polk	347	1,911	2,919
Escambia	220	1,523	2,035	Putnam	37	79	69
Flagler	48	383	1,116	St. Johns	121	579	995
Franklin	11	58	74	St. Lucie	130	570	962
Gadsden	13	46	50	Santa Rosa	82	368	467
Gulf	9	29	26	Sarasota	479	1,891	3,234
Hardee	11	45	57	Seminole	341	1,572	2,895
Hendry	22	54	61	Sumter	16	98	80
Hernando	65	293	364	Suwannee	14	58	39
Highlands	62	239	329	Taylor	7	25	42
Hillsborough	1,002	7,128	15,554	Volusia	434	2,058	2,982
Indian River	135	683	1,177	Wakulla	7	11	11
Jackson	19	52	166	Walton	31	260	436
Jefferson	5	14	17	Washington	8	21	48
Lake	173	1,602	2,661	Multicounty 1/	144	1,856	3,228

1/ Reporting units without a fixed location within the state or of unknown county
location.
Note: Private employment. For a list of three-digit code industries included see
Table 17.38. Data are preliminary. Only counties for which data are disclosed are
shown. Detail may not add to totals due to disclosure editing and/or rounding. See
Tables 23.70, 23.71, 23.72, 23.73, and 23.74 for public employment data.

Source: State of Florida, Department of Labor and Employment Security, Bureau of
Labor Market Information, "Employment and Wages" (ES-202), unpublished data.

University of Florida   **Bureau of Economic and Business Research**

Table 17.47. REAL ESTATE: HOMEOWNER AND RENTAL VACANCY RATES IN FLORIDA
OTHER SUNBELT STATES, OTHER POPULOUS STATES, AND THE UNITED
STATES, SPECIFIED YEARS 1990 THROUGH 1996

State	Homeowner vacancy rates					Rental vacancy rates				
	1990	1993	1994	1995	1996	1990	1993	1994	1995	1996
					Sunbelt states					
Florida	2.7	2.8	2.4	2.1	2.4	9.0	8.3	8.0	7.8	9.0
Alabama	1.5	1.4	1.4	1.5	1.8	8.1	6.8	7.2	8.5	8.7
Arizona	2.5	1.3	1.5	1.9	1.7	10.7	7.4	8.8	7.2	10.2
Arkansas	2.5	0.9	1.2	1.5	1.4	7.9	7.2	6.8	7.4	7.2
California	1.8	1.7	2.0	2.1	2.0	6.0	8.2	7.9	8.5	7.2
Georgia	1.8	1.2	1.8	1.2	2.0	9.4	7.3	9.1	11.3	11.6
Louisiana	1.7	0.9	1.5	0.8	1.1	13.1	7.2	9.4	9.6	7.8
Mississippi	1.6	0.9	0.8	0.9	1.0	8.7	8.0	7.9	13.2	13.2
New Mexico	2.4	0.9	1.1	1.1	1.3	13.7	3.5	5.1	4.8	7.1
North Carolina	1.6	1.3	1.1	1.2	1.4	7.2	5.6	6.1	8.2	8.0
Oklahoma	3.1	1.5	1.7	1.5	1.6	14.6	11.5	8.9	10.3	11.0
South Carolina	1.0	1.1	2.4	2.6	1.7	8.4	10.6	12.3	9.3	14.1
Tennessee	2.4	1.0	1.4	1.5	1.6	9.5	4.6	4.6	5.4	5.4
Texas	2.5	1.9	1.8	1.9	1.4	9.7	8.9	7.9	8.2	8.0
Virginia	1.7	1.7	1.5	1.6	2.2	5.8	7.7	8.9	7.6	7.4
					Other populous states					
Illinois	1.3	1.1	1.2	1.1	1.4	6.1	6.3	6.8	7.4	7.9
Indiana	1.5	0.9	0.7	1.2	1.1	5.3	7.2	5.0	5.2	6.9
Massachusetts	1.4	1.2	1.4	1.2	1.1	6.9	7.8	7.1	6.2	5.8
Michigan	1.1	1.1	0.9	1.3	1.4	7.3	7.9	8.9	8.8	10.2
New Jersey	1.8	1.3	1.2	1.5	1.6	5.9	8.2	7.1	6.6	7.7
New York	1.8	1.7	1.9	1.6	1.7	4.9	5.5	5.9	6.3	6.9
Ohio	1.2	1.0	0.9	1.2	1.1	5.5	7.1	6.8	7.4	8.1
Pennsylvania	1.1	1.0	1.1	1.4	1.6	7.2	7.5	8.0	8.0	8.7
United States	1.7	1.4	1.5	1.5	1.6	7.2	7.3	7.4	7.6	7.8

Note: Data are based on a monthly sample survey conducted by the Bureau of the
Census. See Glossary for definitions.

Source: U.S., Department of Commerce, Bureau of the Census, *Housing Vacancy Survey: Annual Statistics, 1996.* Data from Internet site http://www.census.gov/.

University of Florida   **Bureau of Economic and Business Research**

Table 17.48.   REAL ESTATE: LICENSED BROKERS AND SALESPERSONS IN THE STATE
AND COUNTIES OF FLORIDA, JULY 7, 1997

Location of licensee	Brokers	Sales-persons	Location of licensee	Brokers	Sales-persons
Total 1/	66,995	180,422	Jefferson	30	61
NonFlorida	2,867	8,107	Lafayette	4	5
Unknown	65	446	Lake	812	2,017
Alachua	722	1,381	Lee	2,502	7,024
Baker	19	49	Leon	906	1,991
Bay	529	1,315	Levy	113	252
Bradford	51	92	Liberty	3	8
Brevard	1,881	5,221	Madison	21	53
Broward	6,535	21,143	Manatee	906	2,369
Calhoun	16	37	Marion	893	2,182
Charlotte	565	1,729	Martin	859	1,949
Citrus	480	1,227	Monroe	585	1,426
Clay	419	1,188	Nassau	170	418
Collier	1,702	4,927	Okaloosa	840	1,824
Columbia	124	285	Okeechobee	98	197
Dade	7,815	22,070	Orange	3,801	11,310
De Soto	83	173	Osceola	476	1,964
Dixie	25	48	Palm Beach	6,168	16,946
Duval	2,410	5,446	Pasco	868	2,675
Escambia	754	1,912	Pinellas	4,707	11,132
Flagler	230	777	Polk	1,302	2,700
Franklin	55	121	Putnam	169	343
Gadsden	58	125	St. Johns	659	1,532
Gilchrist	29	64	St. Lucie	712	1,739
Glades	12	25	Santa Rosa	362	1,113
Gulf	34	82	Sarasota	2,364	5,817
Hamilton	12	11	Seminole	1,829	4,936
Hardee	53	96	Sumter	80	210
Hendry	67	157	Suwannee	80	156
Hernando	402	1,357	Taylor	35	49
Highlands	298	645	Union	9	25
Hillsborough	3,450	8,497	Volusia	1,842	4,987
Holmes	29	58	Wakulla	61	175
Indian River	669	1,493	Walton	158	307
Jackson	66	142	Washington	45	84

1/ Total includes all active, involuntary inactive, and voluntary inactive licensed persons.

Source: State of Florida, Department of Business and Professional Regulation, unpublished data.

Table 17.60. LIFE INSURANCE: NUMBER OF COMPANIES, POLICIES IN FORCE, PURCHASES
AND AMOUNT OF LIFE INSURANCE, BENEFIT PAYMENTS, PREMIUM RECEIPTS
MORTGAGES, AND REAL ESTATE OWNED BY U.S. LIFE INSURANCE
COMPANIES IN FLORIDA AND THE UNITED STATES, 1995

Item	Florida	United States
Number of U.S. life insurance companies	30	1,736
Purchases of ordinary life insurance ($1,000,000)	61,608	1,101,032
Insurance in force		
Total		
Policies (1,000)	14,438	247,984
Amount ($1,000,000)	607,190	12,576,677
Ordinary		
Policies (1,000)	7,836	151,026
Amount ($1,000,000)	401,390	7,547,537
Group		
Master policies (1,000)	55	989
Amount ($1,000,000)	191,597	4,777,912
Industrial		
Policies (1,000)	1,657	30,462
Amount ($1,000,000)	1,117	19,977
Credit		
Policies 1/ (1,000)	4,890	65,507
Amount ($1,000,000)	13,087	231,251
Average amount in force 2/ (dollars)	102,700	124,100
Insurance and annuity benefit payments ($1,000)	8,389,254	165,672,816
Death payments	1,796,249	33,458,818
Matured endowments	30,597	536,746
Annuity payments	2,150,517	43,153,018
Disability payments	44,222	760,898
Surrender values	3,615,260	70,297,945
Policy and contract dividends	752,409	17,465,391
Payments to beneficiaries ($1,000), total	1,796,249	33,458,818
Ordinary	1,214,703	19,592,737
Group	483,699	12,449,521
Industrial	23,361	442,854
Credit	74,486	973,706
Premium receipts of companies ($1,000,000)	16,962	318,207
Life	4,773	91,004
Annuity	2,307	45,520
Health	5,536	73,728
Deposit-type funds	4,346	107,954
Mortgages owned by companies ($1,000), total	12,709,982	207,467,862
Farm	1,228,303	9,662,293
Nonfarm	11,481,679	197,845,569
Real estate owned by companies ($1,000), total	4,083,109	51,431,244
Farm	249,614	2,547,866
Nonfarm	3,833,495	48,883,378

1/ Includes group credit certificates.
2/ Average amounts per household. See Glossary for a definition of "household."

Source: American Council of Life Insurance, *1996 Life Insurance Fact Book.*

Table 17.61. LIFE INSURANCE: DIRECT WRITINGS, DIRECT LOSSES, AND LIFE INSURANCE IN FORCE IN FLORIDA, 1987 THROUGH 1994

(amounts rounded to thousands of dollars)

Year	Life insurance in force at end of year	Direct writings	Direct losses paid	Losses as a percentage of writings
All life insurance companies				
1987	322,472,329	5,246,052	2,805,237	53.5
1988	312,711,163	5,633,515	1,290,565	22.9
1989	344,548,493	5,675,962	1,328,876	23.4
1990	355,761,910	7,139,533	4,547,212	63.7
1991	378,564,234	5,561,421	4,939,376	88.8
1992	409,360,123	6,130,141	5,321,483	86.8
1993	445,360,646	6,108,608	3,202,293	52.4
1994	498,573,171	6,744,535	3,726,052	55.2
Florida life insurance companies only				
1987	18,051,822	349,383	86,154	24.7
1988	19,746,098	379,699	96,467	25.4
1989	18,548,502	386,459	97,020	25.1
1990	18,548,502	386,459	97,020	25.1
1991	15,232,004	241,948	116,200	48.0
1992	15,839,284	214,372	159,425	74.4
1993	17,893,604	208,847	91,460	43.8
1994	20,478,864	239,026	92,493	38.7

Note: Includes ordinary, group, industrial, and credit insurance and annuities.

Table 17.62. FRATERNAL INSURANCE SOCIETIES: DIRECT PREMIUMS WRITTEN, BENEFITS PAID, AND INSURANCE IN FORCE IN FLORIDA, 1987 THROUGH 1994

(rounded to thousands of dollars)

Year	Life insurance in force at end of year	Direct premiums written		Direct losses paid	
		Life	Accident and health	Life	Accident and health
1987	3,201,595	63,798	3,887	13,166	3,314
1988	3,552,068	659,886	4,105	14,940	3,693
1989	3,907,921	634,901	4,980	18,414	4,744
1990	4,227,258	77,899	5,950	21,432	3,999
1991	4,580,593	112,686	6,650	30,978	5,546
1992	4,951,219	148,764	7,842	29,627	6,559
1993	5,315,106	141,262	7,536	45,781	5,885
1994	5,638,132	135,716	7,215	59,808	7,189

Source for Tables 17.61 and 17.62:   State of Florida, Department of Insurance, *Florida Department of Insurance 1995 Annual Report*, and previous editions.

University of Florida   **Bureau of Economic and Business Research**

Table 17.72. PROPERTY AND CASUALTY INSURANCE: PREMIUMS WRITTEN AND LOSSES PAID BY PROPERTY AND CASUALTY, TITLE, AND LIFE INSURANCE COMPANIES IN FLORIDA, 1994

(rounded to thousands of dollars)

Line of business	All companies		Florida companies	
	Direct premiums written	Direct losses paid	Direct premiums written	Direct losses paid
Total	19,480,175	12,744,931	4,361,109	2,646,542
Fire	152,302	143,807	24,941	9,968
Allied lines	301,062	124,404	80,248	6,362
Multiple peril crop	10,574	4,630	0	0
Farmowners' multiple peril	7,946	4,392	337	48
Homeowners' multiple peril	1,504,144	825,868	91,672	45,310
Commercial multiple peril	1,052,294	572,868	114,068	34,422
Mortgage guaranty	91,405	25,503	71	0
Ocean marine	104,625	54,041	7,978	2,866
Inland marine	344,272	185,166	56,915	12,051
Financial guaranty	48,423	-3,155	170	1,012
Medical malpractice	313,895	136,158	86,815	29,448
Earthquake	2,739	1,915	9	0
Accident and health, total	5,917,272	4,501,429	1,739,359	1,358,532
Group	3,495,019	2,741,846	714,215	556,950
Federal employees	566,806	545,645	465,346	433,122
Credit	114,312	35,252	33,584	10,059
Collectively renewable	228,156	171,453	178,657	136,524
Noncancellable	218,803	185,391	1,413	469
Guaranteed renewable	888,826	525,231	166,548	105,527
Nonrenewable for stated reasons only	113,971	97,777	0	0
Other accident only	12,283	4,999	109	13
All other	279,096	193,834	179,488	115,869
Workers' compensation	959,908	1,036,508	764,262	452,236
Other liability	793,643	484,587	60,168	34,109
Products liability	49,514	23,877	1,006	40
Private passenger automobile no-fault, PIP	936,458	704,032	217,906	154,690
Other private passenger automobile liability	3,156,042	2,011,660	443,449	259,585
Commercial automobile no-fault, PIP	22,365	13,951	4,387	3,480
Other commercial automobile liability	714,803	433,953	113,662	46,784
Private passenger automobile physical damage	1,717,989	1,134,467	292,137	169,481
Commercial automobile physical damage	162,224	90,964	22,726	10,805
Aircraft (all perils)	57,574	31,500	0	0
Fidelity	34,662	24,933	1,528	1,074
Surety	149,530	36,525	27,658	3,079
Glass	2,448	288	29	8
Burglary and theft	6,006	830	1,090	158
Boiler and machinery	28,107	11,873	101	8
Credit	17,696	5,658	2,394	1,685
Title	540,489	26,048	176,151	4,193
All other lines	279,764	96,255	29,874	5,110

PIP Personal injury protection.

Source: State of Florida, Department of Insurance, *Florida Department of Insurance 1995 Annual Report.*

University of Florida   **Bureau of Economic and Business Research**

PERSONAL AND BUSINESS SERVICES

Business Services Employment by Industry in Florida, 1996

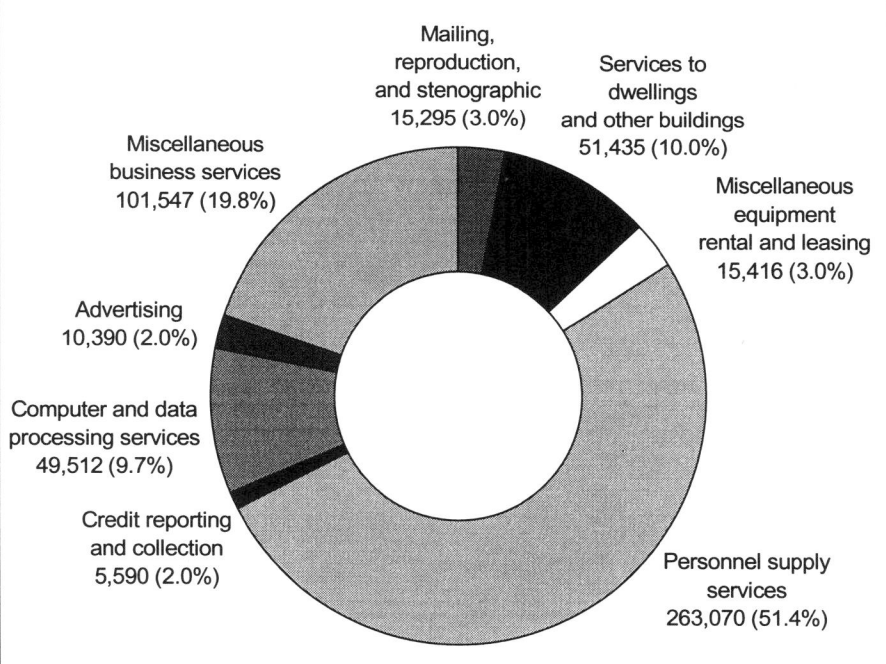

Mailing, reproduction, and stenographic
15,295 (3.0%)

Services to dwellings and other buildings
51,435 (10.0%)

Miscellaneous business services
101,547 (19.8%)

Miscellaneous equipment rental and leasing
15,416 (3.0%)

Advertising
10,390 (2.0%)

Computer and data processing services
49,512 (9.7%)

Credit reporting and collection
5,590 (2.0%)

Personnel supply services
263,070 (51.4%)

Source: Table 18.21

SECTION 18.00
PERSONAL AND BUSINESS SERVICES

TABLES LISTED BY MAJOR HEADINGS

Table 18.01. AUTOMOTIVE, BUSINESS, AND PROFESSIONAL SERVICES: ESTABLISHMENTS AND RECEIPTS, 1987 AND 1992, AND PAYROLL, 1992, IN FLORIDA

(amounts in thousands of dollars)

SIC code	Kind of business	Number of establishments 1987	Number of establishments 1992	Receipts 1987	Receipts 1992	Percentage change	Annual payroll 1992
72	Personal services	10,680	11,893	1,596,527	2,339,691	46.5	792,820
73	Business services	16,132	21,521	7,636,598	13,765,193	80.3	5,577,252
75	Automotive repair, services and parking	7,930	9,552	3,230,507	4,473,536	38.5	886,249
76	Miscellaneous repair services	4,398	5,106	1,248,086	1,944,734	55.8	601,332
81	Legal services	8,965	10,871	3,697,540	5,394,019	45.9	2,647,841
871	Engineering, architectural, and surveying services	3,877	4,372	2,251,146	3,126,227	38.9	1,259,478
872	Accounting, auditing and bookkeeping services	4,377	5,661	1,175,297	1,572,668	33.8	682,637
873	Research, development, and testing services (except 8733 noncommercial research organizations	631	663	379,951	736,964	94.0	291,036
874	Management and public relations services	3,678	5,023	2,198,584	3,638,981	65.5	1,636,869

Note: Data are for firms subject to federal income tax. The service industries census is on a 5-year cycle collecting data for years ending in 2 and 7.

Source: U.S., Department of Commerce, Bureau of the Census, *1992 Census of Service Industries: Florida.* SC92-A-10.

University of Florida   **Bureau of Economic and Business Research**

Table 18.20. PERSONAL AND HOUSEHOLD SERVICES: AVERAGE MONTHLY PRIVATE REPORTING
UNITS, EMPLOYMENT, AND PAYROLL COVERED BY UNEMPLOYMENT COMPENSATION LAW
BY INDUSTRY IN FLORIDA, 1996

SIC code	Industry	Number of reporting units	Number of em- ployees	Payroll ($1,000)
72	Personal services	11,226	69,725	84,895
721	Laundry, cleaning, and garment services	3,254	23,590	30,368
722	Photographic studios, portrait	632	3,428	4,081
723	Beauty shops	5,326	27,613	30,078
724	Barber shops	136	444	489
725	Shoe repair shops and shoeshine parlors	132	278	292
726	Funeral service and crematories	425	4,774	8,968
729	Miscellaneous personal services	1,323	9,598	10,619
88	Private households 1/	12,039	17,006	20,959

1/ Private households which employ workers in domestic services such as cooks,
maids, sitters, butlers, personal secretaries, gardeners and caretakers, and man-
agers of personal affairs.
Note: Private employment. Data are preliminary. Detail may not add to totals
due to disclosure editing and/or rounding. See Tables 23.70, 23.71, 23.72, 23.73,
and 23.74 for public employment data.

Table 18.21. BUSINESS AND MISCELLANEOUS SERVICES: AVERAGE MONTHLY PRIVATE
REPORTING UNITS EMPLOYMENT, AND PAYROLL COVERED BY UNEMPLOYMENT
COMPENSATION LAW BY INDUSTRY IN FLORIDA, 1995 AND 1996

SIC code	Industry	Number of reporting units	Number of em- ployees	Payroll ($1,000)
	1995 A/			
73	Business services	23,424	516,914	774,393
731	Advertising	1,450	10,255	26,482
732	Credit reporting and collection	455	5,446	10,991
733	Mailing, reproduction, and stenographic	2,005	13,147	25,376
734	Services to dwellings and other buildings	4,401	48,596	51,668
735	Miscellaneous equipment rental and leasing	1,868	14,548	33,845
736	Personnel supply services	2,066	296,666	340,409
737	Computer and data processing services	3,776	42,214	151,799
738	Miscellaneous business services	7,404	86,043	133,825
	1996 B/			
73	Business services	26,614	512,254	823,443
731	Advertising	1,511	10,390	29,598
732	Credit reporting and collection	440	5,590	11,941
733	Mailing, reproduction, and stenographic	2,095	15,295	29,528
734	Services to dwellings and other buildings	4,760	51,435	57,418
735	Miscellaneous equipment rental and leasing	1,937	15,416	37,691
736	Personnel supply services	2,462	263,070	308,662
737	Computer and data processing services	4,127	49,512	181,710
738	Miscellaneous business services	9,283	101,547	166,895

A/ Revised.   B/ Preliminary.
Note: Private employment. Detail may not add to totals due to disclosure editing
and/or rounding. See Tables 23.70, 23.71, 23.72, 23.73, and 23.74 for public employment data.
Source for Tables 18.20 and 18.21: State of Florida, Department of Labor and Employment Security, Bureau of Labor Market Information, "Employment and Wages" (ES-202
unpublished data.

University of Florida   **Bureau of Economic and Business Research**

Table 18.22. AUTOMOTIVE AND MISCELLANEOUS REPAIR SERVICES: AVERAGE MONTHLY PRIVATE REPORTING UNITS, EMPLOYMENT, AND PAYROLL COVERED BY UNEMPLOYMENT COMPENSATION LAW BY INDUSTRY IN FLORIDA, 1996

SIC code	Industry	Number of reporting units	Number of em- ployees	Payroll ($1,000)
75	Automotive repair, services, and parking	9,733	65,910	116,615
751	Automotive rental, no driver	749	19,274	39,141
752	Automobile parking	68	2,137	2,260
753	Automotive repair shops	7,356	32,752	60,576
754	Automotive services, except repair	1,561	11,747	14,638
76	Miscellaneous repair services	4,943	25,240	53,001
762	Electrical repair shops	1,739	9,891	22,000
763	Watch, clock, and jewelry repair	127	363	457
764	Reupholstery and furniture repair	467	1,350	1,865
769	Miscellaneous repair shops and related services	2,611	13,636	28,678

Note: Private employment. Data are preliminary. Detail may not add to totals due to disclosure editing and/or rounding. See Tables 23.70, 23.71, 23.72, 23.73, and 23.74 for public employment data.

Table 18.23. ENGINEERING AND MANAGEMENT SERVICES: AVERAGE MONTHLY PRIVATE REPORTING UNITS, EMPLOYMENT, AND PAYROLL COVERED BY UNEMPLOYMENT COMPENSATION LAW BY INDUSTRY IN FLORIDA, 1996

SIC code	Industry	Number of re- porting units	Number of em- ployees	Payroll ($1,000)
87	Engineering, accounting, research, management, and related services	20,912	154,754	485,180
871	Engineering, architectural, and surveying services	4,127	41,680	136,486
872	Accounting, auditing, and bookkeeping services	6,197	34,216	92,459
873	Research, development, and testing services	1,101	14,554	35,282
874	Management and public relations services	9,486	64,303	220,952
89	Miscellaneous services	468	2,383	7,295

Note: Private employment. Data are preliminary. Detail may not add to totals due to disclosure editing and/or rounding. See Tables 23.70, 23.71, 23.72, 23.73, and 23.74 for public employment data.

Source for Tables 18.22 and 18.23: State of Florida, Department of Labor and Employment Security, Bureau of Labor Market Information, "Employment and Wages" (ES-202), unpublished data.

University of Florida   **Bureau of Economic and Business Research**

Table 18.28. SERVICES: AVERAGE MONTHLY PRIVATE REPORTING UNITS, EMPLOYMENT
AND PAYROLL COVERED BY UNEMPLOYMENT COMPENSATION LAW IN THE STATE
AND COUNTIES OF FLORIDA, 1995 AND 1996

County	Number of reporting units	Number of employees	Payroll ($1,000)	County	Number of reporting units	Number of employees	Payroll ($1,000)
			Services, 1995 A/	(SIC codes 70-89)			
Florida	145,429	1,916,467	3,835,235	Lafayette	16	56	57
				Lake	1,260	15,634	26,006
Alachua	2,052	27,320	54,872	Lee	3,477	42,943	81,686
Baker	68	627	776	Leon	2,659	31,925	67,552
Bay	1,369	14,091	24,087	Levy	135	974	1,266
Bradford	106	1,020	1,382	Liberty	18	229	249
Brevard	3,754	53,123	129,060	Madison	102	1,012	1,420
Broward	17,408	175,561	380,637	Manatee	1,715	29,282	46,654
Calhoun	54	503	649	Marion	1,633	14,492	26,112
Charlotte	863	10,506	20,612	Martin	1,467	12,872	25,528
Citrus	690	7,206	12,896	Monroe	1,207	10,672	19,102
Clay	781	7,931	13,742	Nassau	304	3,463	5,223
Collier	2,465	24,392	52,082	Okaloosa	1,493	18,689	32,224
Columbia	329	3,253	5,031	Okeechobee	199	1,914	3,236
Dade	24,785	271,097	615,068	Orange	8,431	200,889	400,058
De Soto	133	1,075	1,728	Osceola	892	14,468	23,963
Dixie	41	184	313	Palm Beach	13,597	132,414	297,614
Duval	6,991	113,709	226,322	Pasco	1,877	20,271	39,563
Escambia	2,241	37,396	67,707	Pinellas	9,558	132,372	264,505
Flagler	220	2,303	4,074	Polk	2,867	38,455	73,140
Franklin	67	808	1,024	Putnam	356	3,373	5,393
Gadsden	204	1,383	1,823	St. Johns	945	9,861	18,957
Gilchrist	34	354	453	St. Lucie	1,112	11,434	22,489
Glades	25	95	103	Santa Rosa	522	5,614	9,072
Gulf	61	514	714	Sarasota	4,006	43,460	81,613
Hamilton	46	400	534	Seminole	2,947	27,620	56,783
Hardee	127	1,002	1,545	Sumter	133	865	1,066
Hendry	154	1,238	1,744	Suwannee	126	1,611	2,006
Hernando	656	6,918	12,497	Taylor	116	807	1,196
Highlands	536	5,597	8,826	Union	35	429	598
Hillsborough	9,031	171,293	337,455	Volusia	3,556	42,246	73,664
Holmes	70	689	910	Wakulla	60	422	603
Indian River	1,177	11,143	21,892	Walton	146	2,535	3,550
Jackson	217	1,587	2,387	Washington	84	690	846
Jefferson	70	592	690	Multicounty 1/	1,562	86,920	117,073

See footnotes at end of table.   Continued . . .

Table 18.28. SERVICES: AVERAGE MONTHLY PRIVATE REPORTING UNITS, EMPLOYMENT
AND PAYROLL COVERED BY UNEMPLOYMENT COMPENSATION LAW IN THE STATE
AND COUNTIES OF FLORIDA, 1995 AND 1996 (Continued)

County	Number of re- porting units	Number of em- ployees	Payroll ($1,000)	County	Number of re- porting units	Number of em- ployees	Payroll ($1,000)
			Services, 1996 B/	(SIC codes 70-89)			
Florida	152,693	1,973,897	4,107,588	Lafayette	16	55	53
				Lake	1,353	16,698	28,376
Alachua	2,115	28,281	57,597	Lee	3,716	43,228	86,850
Baker	68	685	904	Leon	2,749	32,969	72,828
Bay	1,379	14,943	26,617	Levy	136	1,040	1,458
Bradford	113	1,073	1,581	Liberty	18	231	253
Brevard	3,849	53,959	133,568	Madison	103	1,148	1,649
Broward	18,360	187,941	411,965	Manatee	1,902	40,069	62,577
Calhoun	55	528	685	Marion	1,693	15,648	28,825
Charlotte	895	10,792	22,356	Martin	1,538	13,931	28,104
Citrus	727	7,737	14,188	Monroe	1,246	11,105	20,897
Clay	810	8,376	14,668	Nassau	327	3,644	5,648
Collier	2,671	26,056	58,317	Okaloosa	1,561	19,488	34,985
Columbia	345	3,418	5,661	Okeechobee	208	2,171	3,702
Dade	25,625	278,576	648,963	Orange	8,848	214,623	436,292
De Soto	135	1,029	1,726	Osceola	962	15,239	26,045
Dixie	44	165	305	Palm Beach	14,178	143,764	327,712
Duval	7,167	116,912	247,071	Pasco	2,001	22,202	44,194
Escambia	2,384	36,218	67,735	Pinellas	9,918	139,222	290,570
Flagler	241	2,778	5,244	Polk	2,990	40,236	79,826
Franklin	70	477	615	Putnam	366	3,567	5,633
Gadsden	204	1,501	1,979	St. Johns	1,024	10,362	19,774
Gilchrist	39	411	549	St. Lucie	1,133	11,810	23,235
Glades	25	96	114	Santa Rosa	555	6,112	10,658
Gulf	68	595	805	Sarasota	4,257	47,165	91,826
Hamilton	44	368	521	Seminole	3,143	29,333	61,908
Hardee	122	1,063	1,693	Sumter	130	835	1,066
Hendry	159	1,225	1,758	Suwannee	130	1,610	2,134
Hernando	690	7,341	13,631	Taylor	114	848	1,318
Highlands	518	5,442	8,792	Union	34	556	801
Hillsborough	9,535	183,037	376,720	Volusia	3,648	43,160	77,734
Holmes	70	718	995	Wakulla	59	440	686
Indian River	1,260	12,142	24,290	Walton	148	2,622	3,911
Jackson	218	1,626	2,500	Washington	86	719	892
Jefferson	71	605	702	Multicounty 1/	2,330	41,304	68,785

A/ Revised.
B/ Preliminary.
1/ Reporting units without a fixed location within the state or of unknown county
location.
   Note: Private employment. Only counties for which data are disclosed are shown.
Detail may not add to totals due to disclosure editing and/or rounding. See Tables
23.70, 23.71, 23.72, 23.73, and 23.74 for public employment data.

   Source: State of Florida, Department of Labor and Employment Security, Bureau of
Labor Market Information, "Employment and Wages" (ES-202), unpublished data.

Table 18.30. PERSONAL SERVICES: AVERAGE MONTHLY PRIVATE REPORTING UNITS
EMPLOYMENT, AND PAYROLL COVERED BY UNEMPLOYMENT COMPENSATION LAW
IN THE STATE AND COUNTIES OF FLORIDA, 1996

County	Number of re- porting units	Number of em- ployees	Payroll ($1,000)	County	Number of re- porting units	Number of em- ployees	Payroll ($1,000)
			Personal services (SIC code 72)				
Florida	11,226	69,725	84,895	Lafayette	3	5	6
				Lake	106	615	734
Alachua	136	922	947	Lee	290	1,767	2,214
Baker	6	22	18	Leon	171	1,633	2,085
Bay	95	514	579	Levy	10	52	65
Bradford	9	91	114	Madison	9	52	65
Brevard	323	1,879	1,992	Manatee	174	744	815
Broward	1,383	7,988	9,781	Marion	158	907	1,004
Calhoun	8	53	26	Martin	120	612	797
Charlotte	81	396	468	Monroe	68	216	264
Citrus	75	286	328	Nassau	36	126	146
Clay	87	418	423	Okaloosa	121	653	642
Collier	210	1,075	1,437	Okeechobee	15	61	71
Columbia	23	123	106	Orange	598	4,654	6,102
Dade	1,708	10,864	13,544	Osceola	89	418	458
De Soto	14	63	54	Palm Beach	922	5,841	7,688
Duval	579	4,177	5,164	Pasco	207	1,091	1,031
Escambia	184	1,348	1,489	Pinellas	773	5,000	6,349
Flagler	24	105	101	Polk	257	1,661	2,051
Franklin	4	6	5	Putnam	30	146	142
Gadsden	15	65	63	St. Johns	63	318	388
Glades	11	18	11	St. Lucie	92	619	622
Gulf	5	19	17	Santa Rosa	44	207	184
Hardee	5	24	31	Sarasota	314	1,775	2,299
Hendry	8	20	21	Seminole	288	1,811	2,081
Hernando	77	358	352	Sumter	7	35	28
Highlands	48	215	191	Suwannee	11	42	53
Hillsborough	610	4,550	5,318	Taylor	13	46	40
Holmes	3	21	36	Volusia	312	1,767	1,842
Indian River	111	447	541	Walton	4	13	9
Jackson	11	68	77	Washington	7	19	15
Jefferson	5	24	40	Multicounty 1/	52	630	1,287

1/ Reporting units without a fixed location within the state or of unknown county
location.
    Note: Private employment. For a list of three-digit code industries included see
Table 18.20. Data are preliminary. Only counties for which data are disclosed are
shown. Detail may not add to totals due to disclosure editing and/or rounding. See
Tables 23.70, 23.71, 23.72, 23.73, and 23.74 for public employment data.

    Source: State of Florida, Department of Labor and Employment Security, Bureau of
Labor Market Information, "Employment and Wages" (ES-202), unpublished data.

University of Florida   **Bureau of Economic and Business Research**

Table 18.35. BUSINESS SERVICES: AVERAGE MONTHLY PRIVATE REPORTING UNITS
EMPLOYMENT, AND PAYROLL COVERED BY UNEMPLOYMENT COMPENSATION LAW
IN THE STATE AND COUNTIES OF FLORIDA, 1995 AND 1996

County	Number of re- porting units	Number of em- ployees	Payroll ($1,000)	County	Number of re- porting units	Number of em- ployees	Payroll ($1,000)
			Business services, 1995 A/ (SIC code 73)				
Florida	23,424	516,914	774,393	Madison	9	51	114
				Manatee	226	13,906	16,714
Alachua	228	3,372	4,208	Marion	216	2,246	2,841
Baker	4	9	17	Martin	207	1,991	2,482
Bay	179	1,696	2,327	Monroe	134	549	844
Bradford	7	28	41	Nassau	37	134	189
Brevard	613	8,501	17,539	Okaloosa	235	5,189	6,648
Broward	3,118	42,045	75,099	Okeechobee	23	106	157
Citrus	86	799	1,214	Orange	1,651	42,925	66,816
Clay	115	887	1,402	Osceola	121	1,170	1,599
Collier	377	3,706	6,246	Palm Beach	2,052	24,554	43,219
Columbia	32	170	260	Pasco	236	2,174	2,774
Dade	3,840	65,378	105,183	Pinellas	1,622	35,202	62,221
De Soto	8	49	74	Polk	350	7,197	10,491
Duval	1,202	40,757	57,943	Putnam	38	407	586
Escambia	320	10,936	13,638	St. Johns	127	727	1,212
Gadsden	13	24	29	St. Lucie	143	974	1,261
Gilchrist	11	59	83	Santa Rosa	83	866	1,035
Hendry	93	752	1,018	Sarasota	595	10,385	13,279
Hernando	64	637	608	Seminole	654	6,302	12,745
Hillsborough	1,774	75,585	114,437	Sumter	13	37	41
Holmes	7	14	19	Suwannee	24	161	163
Indian River	145	1,212	2,237	Taylor	17	59	70
Jackson	16	93	115	Volusia	501	5,638	7,782
Lake	159	3,416	3,293	Wakulla	8	25	45
Lee	541	9,287	9,818	Walton	22	126	158
Leon	398	5,896	9,260	Washington	10	46	68

See footnotes at end of table.   Continued . . .

University of Florida   **Bureau of Economic and Business Research**

Table 18.35. BUSINESS SERVICES: AVERAGE MONTHLY PRIVATE REPORTING UNITS EMPLOYMENT, AND PAYROLL COVERED BY UNEMPLOYMENT COMPENSATION LAW IN THE STATE AND COUNTIES OF FLORIDA, 1995 AND 1996 (Continued)

County	Number of reporting units	Number of employees	Payroll ($1,000)	County	Number of reporting units	Number of employees	Payroll ($1,000)
				Business services, 1996 B/ (SIC code 73)			
Florida	26,614	512,254	823,443	Lee	650	9,029	11,708
				Leon	427	6,464	10,636
Alachua	243	3,609	4,807	Levy	10	52	99
Baker	5	11	13	Madison	9	105	162
Bay	197	1,998	2,899	Manatee	282	23,461	29,279
Bradford	7	30	42	Marion	241	2,696	3,386
Brevard	680	8,940	18,333	Martin	230	2,089	2,907
Broward	3,539	49,086	89,128	Monroe	154	570	941
Calhoun	5	20	16	Nassau	44	163	267
Charlotte	129	1,457	1,515	Okaloosa	265	5,657	7,906
Citrus	93	699	1,239	Okeechobee	23	103	150
Clay	126	1,023	1,767	Orange	1,816	47,380	76,797
Collier	466	3,797	7,114	Osceola	133	1,492	2,155
Columbia	38	203	316	Palm Beach	2,305	30,245	52,527
Dade	4,256	64,622	106,307	Pasco	270	2,669	3,261
De Soto	12	70	117	Pinellas	1,772	38,829	75,707
Duval	1,291	41,255	65,204	Polk	407	7,601	12,076
Escambia	373	8,408	10,119	Putnam	40	478	661
Flagler	34	718	939	St. Johns	154	1,006	1,738
Franklin	10	60	62	St. Lucie	161	1,210	1,514
Gadsden	19	89	104	Santa Rosa	101	845	1,163
Gilchrist	6	20	33	Sarasota	727	9,731	11,237
Gulf	5	29	33	Seminole	734	7,652	15,874
Hardee	6	12	14	Sumter	11	33	42
Hendry	12	65	89	Suwannee	20	144	164
Hernando	106	891	1,302	Taylor	18	51	74
Highlands	64	591	637	Volusia	531	6,253	8,796
Hillsborough	2,035	85,608	140,492	Wakulla	10	35	58
Holmes	7	14	21	Walton	26	136	194
Indian River	168	1,600	2,958	Washington	9	41	74
Jackson	24	130	180				
Lake	185	3,840	3,835	Multicounty 1/	886	26,833	31,951

A/ Revised.
B/ Preliminary.
1/ Reporting units without a fixed location within the state or of unknown county location.

Note: Private employment. For a list of three-digit code industries included see Table 18.21. Data are preliminary. Only counties for which data are disclosed are shown. Detail may not add to totals due to disclosure editing and/or rounding. See Tables 23.70, 23.71, 23.72, 23.73, and 23.74 for public employment data.

Source: State of Florida, Department of Labor and Employment Security, Bureau of Labor Market Information, "Employment and Wages" (ES-202), unpublished data.

Table 18.40. AUTOMOTIVE REPAIR, SERVICES, AND PARKING: AVERAGE MONTHLY PRIVATE REPORTING UNITS, EMPLOYMENT, AND PAYROLL COVERED BY UNEMPLOYMENT COMPENSATION LAW IN THE STATE AND COUNTIES OF FLORIDA, 1996

County	Number of reporting units	Number of employees	Payroll ($1,000)	County	Number of reporting units	Number of employees	Payroll ($1,000)
			Automotive repair, services, and parking (SIC code 75)				
Florida	9,733	65,910	116,615	Lee	281	2,000	3,444
				Leon	177	1,484	2,320
Alachua	138	920	1,447	Levy	9	39	48
Baker	6	19	26	Madison	11	44	58
Bay	86	497	672	Manatee	128	686	1,287
Bradford	8	21	29	Marion	148	701	1,143
Brevard	300	1,453	2,410	Martin	82	295	527
Broward	1,191	8,790	16,511	Monroe	58	250	394
Charlotte	65	206	348	Nassau	28	120	203
Citrus	62	202	305	Okaloosa	129	785	1,113
Clay	69	448	678	Okeechobee	19	85	115
Collier	135	640	1,157	Orange	524	7,222	12,656
Columbia	38	118	182	Osceola	83	426	658
Dade	1,410	10,805	21,186	Palm Beach	711	4,244	7,667
De Soto	15	48	64	Pasco	181	852	1,360
Duval	528	4,508	8,298	Pinellas	634	3,339	5,795
Escambia	194	1,388	2,054	Polk	245	1,313	2,259
Flagler	14	61	90	Putnam	33	97	139
Gadsden	15	59	82	St. Johns	52	228	350
Gulf	5	19	20	St. Lucie	122	458	727
Hamilton	4	7	9	Santa Rosa	46	253	469
Hardee	9	30	46	Sarasota	245	1,259	1,956
Hendry	19	40	57	Seminole	181	1,075	1,777
Hernando	70	225	358	Sumter	16	71	100
Highlands	38	120	148	Suwannee	10	24	37
Hillsborough	605	5,241	9,412	Taylor	8	31	48
Holmes	7	33	54	Volusia	271	1,394	1,984
Indian River	74	314	499	Wakulla	7	24	29
Jackson	20	76	119	Walton	9	36	56
Jefferson	3	10	14				
Lake	115	460	677	Multicounty 1/	31	280	882

1/ Reporting units without a fixed location within the state or of unknown county location.

Note: Private employment. For a list of three-digit code industries included see Table 18.22. Data are preliminary. Only counties for which data are disclosed are shown. Detail may not add to totals due to disclosure editing and/or rounding. See Tables 23.70, 23.71, 23.72, 23.73, and 23.74 for public employment data.

Source: State of Florida, Department of Labor and Employment Security, Bureau of Labor Market Information, "Employment and Wages" (ES-202), unpublished data.

University of Florida   **Bureau of Economic and Business Research**

Table 18.51. ENGINEERING, ACCOUNTING, RESEARCH, MANAGEMENT, AND RELATED SERVICES
AVERAGE MONTHLY PRIVATE REPORTING UNITS, EMPLOYMENT, AND PAYROLL COVERED
BY UNEMPLOYMENT COMPENSATION LAW IN THE STATE AND COUNTIES
OF FLORIDA, 1996

County	Number of reporting units	Number of employees	Payroll ($1,000)	County	Number of reporting units	Number of employees	Payroll ($1,000)
				Engineering, accounting, research, management, and related services (SIC code 87)			
Florida	20,912	154,754	485,180	Lee	494	3,054	8,622
				Leon	404	3,130	10,348
Alachua	314	2,546	7,127	Levy	15	37	57
Bay	154	1,762	4,455	Madison	9	41	57
Bradford	13	85	200	Manatee	228	895	3,204
Brevard	539	14,797	52,249	Marion	149	569	1,373
Broward	2,560	14,922	49,946	Martin	198	723	2,273
Calhoun	5	11	16	Monroe	140	693	1,888
Charlotte	90	635	1,637	Nassau	42	176	371
Citrus	68	528	1,300	Okaloosa	214	2,938	9,316
Clay	103	576	1,680	Okeechobee	14	69	166
Collier	377	1,359	4,701	Orange	1,428	14,582	46,170
Columbia	28	136	292	Osceola	90	359	770
Dade	3,474	20,847	72,512	Palm Beach	2,044	10,073	37,017
De Soto	9	20	43	Pasco	185	840	1,536
Dixie	4	17	60	Pinellas	1,328	9,196	25,103
Duval	981	10,028	28,963	Polk	341	1,989	6,663
Escambia	281	2,646	7,233	Putnam	35	89	152
Flagler	23	106	348	St. Johns	151	405	1,407
Franklin	8	29	39	St. Lucie	110	701	1,994
Gilchrist	4	18	27	Santa Rosa	67	930	2,334
Gulf	9	53	109	Sarasota	550	3,229	8,568
Hardee	14	56	180	Seminole	554	2,382	7,168
Hendry	16	61	127	Sumter	14	36	65
Hernando	65	223	460	Suwannee	9	29	71
Highlands	38	194	384	Taylor	7	43	69
Hillsborough	1,429	13,506	44,865	Volusia	391	1,618	3,908
Holmes	8	34	54	Wakulla	11	82	146
Indian River	152	649	1,951	Walton	14	67	185
Jackson	13	83	178	Washington	13	50	69
Jefferson	10	34	70				
Lake	146	785	2,096	Multicounty 1/	701	8,001	18,668

1/ Reporting units without a fixed location within the state or of unknown county
location.
   Note: Private employment. For a list of three-digit code industries included see
Table 18.23. Data are preliminary. Only counties for which data are disclosed are
shown. Detail may not add to totals due to disclosure editing and/or rounding. See
Tables 23.70, 23.71, 23.72, 23.73, and 23.74 for public employment data.

   Source: State of Florida, Department of Labor and Employment Security, Bureau of
Labor Market Information, "Employment and Wages" (ES-202), unpublished data.

University of Florida   **Bureau of Economic and Business Research**

Table 18.56. ACCOUNTANTS, ARCHITECTS, AND PROFESSIONAL ENGINEERS: NUMBER
LICENSED IN THE STATE AND COUNTIES OF FLORIDA, JULY 7, 1997

Location of licensee	Accountants	Architects	Professional engineers	Location of licensee	Accountants	Architects	Professional engineers
Total 1/	25,067	8,078	25,152	Jefferson	10	4	10
NonFlorida	4,157	3,696	10,853	Lafayette	2	0	3
Unknown	5	0	0	Lake	136	32	91
Alachua	301	100	476	Lee	404	107	352
Baker	7	0	10	Leon	798	157	624
Bay	115	16	127	Levy	14	1	17
Bradford	14	1	6	Liberty	5	0	2
Brevard	399	54	595	Madison	6	0	4
Broward	2,842	367	1,112	Manatee	207	43	128
Calhoun	6	0	1	Marion	128	22	99
Charlotte	60	13	60	Martin	138	37	194
Citrus	36	9	66	Monroe	66	29	41
Clay	133	19	114	Nassau	22	14	25
Collier	263	83	150	Okaloosa	102	29	107
Columbia	41	1	65	Okeechobee	10	0	7
Dade	3,460	1,099	1,566	Orange	1,594	366	1,207
De Soto	8	0	6	Osceola	61	16	66
Dixie	1	0	0	Palm Beach	1,932	377	1,326
Duval	1,327	226	921	Pasco	140	5	119
Escambia	272	84	248	Pinellas	1,488	240	829
Flagler	19	4	15	Polk	370	49	410
Franklin	6	4	5	Putnam	16	9	36
Gadsden	27	6	16	St. Johns	158	35	118
Gilchrist	2	0	4	St. Lucie	96	13	90
Glades	1	0	0	Santa Rosa	81	9	86
Gulf	5	2	2	Sarasota	442	145	282
Hamilton	3	0	2	Seminole	540	137	543
Hardee	8	1	3	Sumter	6	0	6
Hendry	18	1	10	Suwannee	16	2	11
Hernando	47	7	60	Taylor	11	1	11
Highlands	38	6	20	Union	1	0	2
Hillsborough	1,897	294	1,362	Volusia	367	52	265
Holmes	4	1	6	Wakulla	22	1	16
Indian River	125	40	86	Walton	5	8	9
Jackson	19	2	17	Washington	7	2	32

1/ Total includes all active, involuntary inactive, and voluntary inactive licensed persons.

Source: State of Florida, Department of Business and Professional Regulation, unpublished data.

University of Florida   **Bureau of Economic and Business Research**

TOURISM AND RECREATION

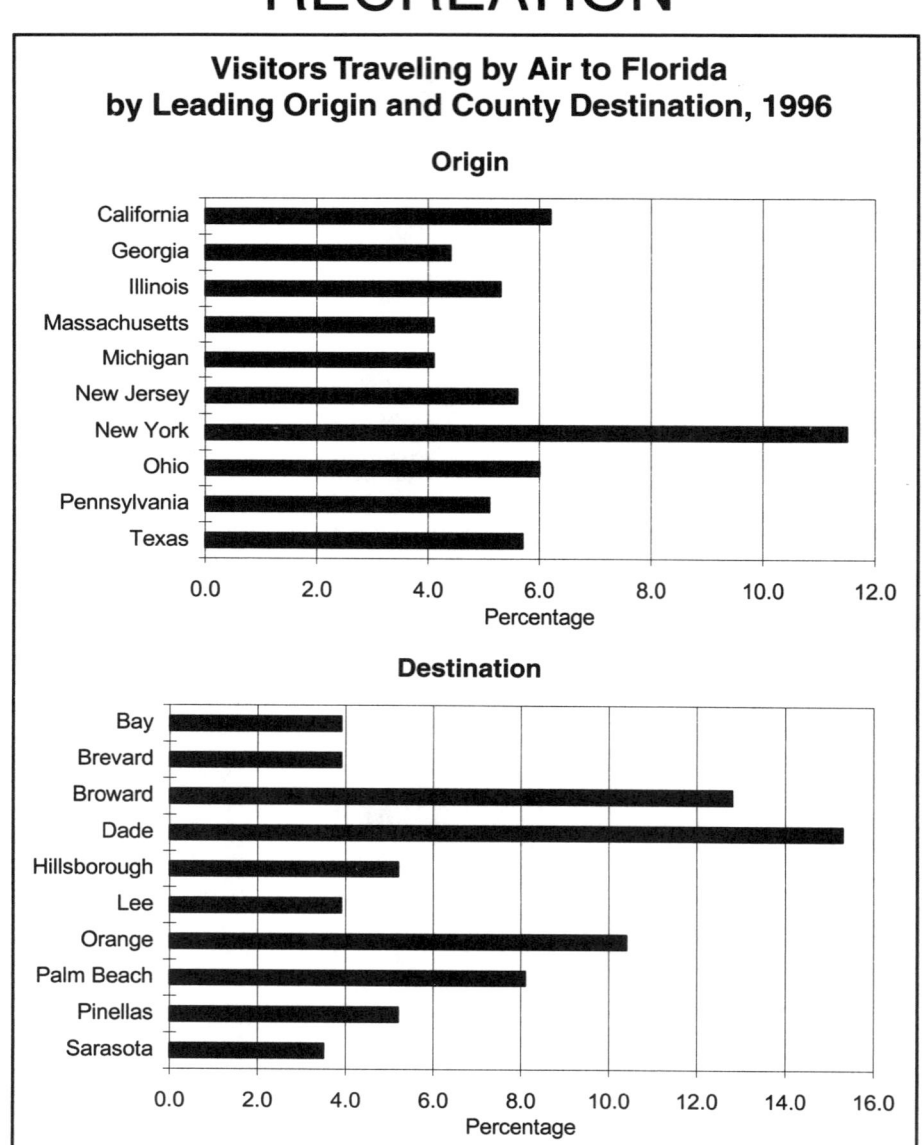

Visitors Traveling by Air to Florida by Leading Origin and County Destination, 1996

Origin

(Percentage)

Origin	
California	
Georgia	
Illinois	
Massachusetts	
Michigan	
New Jersey	
New York	
Ohio	
Pennsylvania	
Texas	

Destination

(Percentage)

Destination	
Bay	
Brevard	
Broward	
Dade	
Hillsborough	
Lee	
Orange	
Palm Beach	
Pinellas	
Sarasota	

Source: Table 19.24

SECTION 19.00
TOURISM AND RECREATION

TABLES LISTED BY MAJOR HEADINGS

University of Florida   **Bureau of Economic and Business Research**

Table 19.24. TOURISTS: PERCENTAGE DISTRIBUTION OF VISITORS TRAVELING BY AIR AND AUTOMOBILE TO FLORIDA BY ORIGIN AND COUNTY DESTINATION, 1996

Origin	Air Percentage	Rank	Automobile Percentage	Rank	County of destination	Air Percentage	Rank	Automobile Percentage	Rank
New York	11.5	1	(NA)	(NA)	Dade	15.3	1	(NA)	(NA)
California	6.2	2	(NA)	(NA)	Broward	12.8	2	3.0	9
Ohio	6.0	3	6.0	2	Orange	10.4	3	16.2	1
Texas	5.7	3	(NA)	(NA)	Palm Beach	8.1	4	2.9	10
New Jersey	5.6	6	(NA)	(NA)	Hillsborough	5.2	6	(NA)	(NA)
Illinois	5.3	6	4.3	7	Pinellas	5.2	6	3.6	7
Pennsylvania	5.1	7	3.8	10	Lee	3.9	9	(NA)	(NA)
Georgia	4.4	8	17.6	1	Brevard	3.9	9	4.8	6
Massachusetts	4.1	9	(NA)	(NA)	Bay	3.9	9	13.1	2
Michigan	4.1	10	4.6	5	Sarasota	3.5	10	(NA)	(NA)
Tennessee	(NA)	(NA)	5.5	3	Volusia	(NA)	(NA)	10.6	3
North Carolina	(NA)	(NA)	5.1	4	Duval	(NA)	(NA)	5.4	4
South Carolina	(NA)	(NA)	4.3	7	Okaloosa	(NA)	(NA)	4.8	6
Alabama	(NA)	(NA)	4.2	9	Osceola	(NA)	(NA)	3.0	9
Ontario	(NA)	(NA)	4.2	9					

(NA) Not available.
Note: Data based on approximately 9,500 person-to-person interviews conducted annually with nonresident visitors to Florida staying longer than one night and less than 180 as they are leaving the state.

Table 19.25. TOURISTS: INTERNATIONAL TRAVELERS TO FLORIDA AND THE UNITED STATES BY SPECIFIED COUNTRY OR REGION OF ORIGIN, 1994 AND 1995

Country or region 2/	Florida 1/			United States		
	1994	1995	Percentage change	1994	1995	Percentage change
Overseas, total	4,099,384	4,161,526	1.5	20,107,799	21,709,735	8.0
Western Europe	1,757,799	1,866,169	6.2	7,864,892	8,492,347	8.0
Germany	300,698	357,393	18.9	1,622,835	1,847,973	13.9
United Kingdom	894,917	924,106	3.3	2,772,345	2,888,195	4.2
South America	1,128,318	1,225,101	8.6	2,111,985	2,449,181	16.0
Argentina	181,126	161,685	-10.7	388,291	381,904	-1.6
Brazil	332,889	405,683	21.9	652,412	838,365	28.5
Columbia	128,993	125,133	-3.0	225,555	233,012	3.3
Venezuela	259,417	305,502	17.8	415,610	511,327	23.0
Central America	228,635	206,139	-9.8	513,054	508,695	-0.9
Other countries/regions						
Asia	138,951	160,680	15.6	5,550,847	6,616,203	19.2
Japan	100,310	118,464	18.1	3,804,551	4,598,354	20.9
Caribbean	499,858	466,408	-6.7	1,030,855	1,043,719	1.3
Mexico	235,416	118,677	-49.6	1,649,853	1,070,769	-35.1

1/ Data are for those travelers whose first intended address was Florida. Excludes those who first visited or stayed in another state.
2/ 150,000 or more travelers to Florida in 1995. Exlcudes Canada.
Source for Tables 19.24 and 19.25: State of Florida, Department of Commerce, Office of Tourism Research, *1996 Florida Visitor Study,* prepublication release, and previous edition.

University of Florida   **Bureau of Economic and Business Research**

Table 19.26. TRAFFIC COUNTS: AVERAGE DAILY TRAFFIC ENTERING AND LEAVING FLORIDA
AND PASSING OTHER SPECIFIC POINTS, MONTHS OF 1995

Location and direction		January	February	March	April	May	June
I-95 Georgia	N	17,612	19,568	24,325	27,280	21,783	21,937
	S	19,820	20,512	20,889	21,734	18,754	20,926
U.S. 1 Georgia	N	4,048	4,252	4,625	5,073	4,743	4,750
	S	4,053	4,203	4,463	4,855	4,626	4,727
I-75 Georgia	N	12,034	12,932	16,865	18,319	14,309	16,008
	S	12,901	13,481	15,590	14,175	12,694	15,466
U.S. 27 Georgia	N	3,171	3,314	3,458	3,588	3,403	3,541
	S	3,234	3,358	3,450	3,591	3,434	3,583
U.S. 231 Alabama	N	4,349	4,672	6,300	6,924	6,370	6,967
	S	4,810	5,041	6,504	6,512	6,660	7,502
I-275 Tampa	N	26,364	29,461	29,830	30,009	28,229	28,229
	S	26,594	28,698	29,263	28,957	27,656	27,713
I-4 Orlando	E	54,593	58,469	60,421	60,643	56,501	59,917
	W	54,777	58,093	59,591	59,742	56,842	60,123
Turnpike Wildwood	N	13,567	16,573	18,061	19,437	15,987	15,724
	S	14,760	15,920	16,056	15,231	13,733	14,527

		July	August	September	October	November	December
I-95 Georgia	N	23,039	21,217	17,711	18,295	19,983	20,406
	S	22,801	21,696	18,734	21,366	22,516	23,583
U.S. 1 Georgia	N	4,838	4,564	4,329	4,477	4,677	4,602
	S	4,842	4,569	4,357	4,532	4,762	4,641
I-75 Georgia	N	16,893	14,547	11,832	12,755	13,930	14,478
	S	16,516	14,531	12,448	14,371	15,911	17,293
U.S. 27 Georgia	N	3,469	(NA)	(NA)	(NA)	(NA)	(NA)
	S	3,537	(NA)	(NA)	(NA)	(NA)	(NA)
U.S. 231 Alabama	N	7,776	6,367	5,679	4,839	4,958	4,808
	S	7,929	6,530	5,990	5,434	5,557	5,616
I-275 Tampa	N	27,793	27,700	27,585	27,649	28,719	29,544
	S	27,581	28,673	26,322	26,649	28,654	29,938
I-4 Orlando	E	62,911	61,098	56,283	58,131	57,390	58,174
	W	62,792	60,866	56,126	58,529	57,665	58,870
Turnpike Wildwood	N	16,017	14,986	13,453	13,315	16,121	17,388
	S	15,525	14,926	13,978	15,248	17,071	17,379

(NA) Not available.

Source: State of Florida, Department of Transportation, Transportation Statistics Office, unpublished data.

University of Florida   **Bureau of Economic and Business Research**

Table 19.45. BOATS: NUMBER REGISTERED BY TYPE IN THE STATE AND COUNTIES
OF FLORIDA, FISCAL YEAR 1995-96

County	Total	Pleasure boats	Commer-cial boats	County	Total	Pleasure boats	Commer-cial boats
Florida	771,459	731,991	33,705	Lafayette	560	551	7
				Lake	16,866	16,533	252
Alachua	9,037	8,755	227	Lee	34,415	32,447	1,731
Baker	1,566	1,565	1	Leon	11,184	11,009	150
Bay	16,519	14,949	1,505	Levy	2,875	2,519	351
Bradford	1,700	1,667	33	Liberty	959	942	15
Brevard	29,902	27,595	1,837	Madison	856	850	4
Broward	43,545	40,906	1,901	Manatee	15,630	14,775	614
Calhoun	1,171	1,159	9	Marion	15,372	15,012	318
Charlotte	16,896	15,952	768	Martin	14,172	13,299	574
Citrus	12,824	11,845	913	Monroe	22,387	18,106	4,194
Clay	8,563	8,365	167	Nassau	3,541	3,341	192
Collier	16,684	15,368	1,209	Okaloosa	16,169	15,227	852
Columbia	3,966	3,941	18	Okeechobee	4,843	4,544	282
Dade	51,772	49,252	2,113	Orange	28,999	28,496	277
De Soto	1,687	1,648	37	Osceola	6,610	6,363	211
Dixie	1,974	1,645	324	Palm Beach	33,216	31,947	992
Duval	29,317	28,473	726	Pasco	17,410	16,736	584
Escambia	16,777	16,195	461	Pinellas	46,417	44,028	1,850
Flagler	2,995	2,884	89	Polk	25,170	24,594	436
Franklin	2,507	1,603	897	Putnam	7,647	7,230	394
Gadsden	2,336	2,269	64	St. Johns	7,390	7,008	345
Gilchrist	1,119	1,088	29	St. Lucie	10,097	9,556	466
Glades	1,191	1,025	159	Santa Rosa	9,073	8,737	312
Gulf	2,379	2,101	270	Sarasota	17,597	16,812	608
Hamilton	658	656	1	Seminole	16,338	15,925	327
Hardee	1,461	1,448	9	Sumter	2,780	2,671	106
Hendry	2,906	2,650	246	Suwannee	2,139	2,111	21
Hernando	5,899	5,678	205	Taylor	2,918	2,720	188
Highlands	8,151	8,009	122	Union	525	523	2
Hillsborough	37,143	36,062	899	Volusia	21,221	20,349	728
Holmes	1,631	1,623	6	Wakulla	3,935	3,523	406
Indian River	8,941	8,382	502	Walton	2,734	2,645	82
Jackson	3,883	3,834	43	Washington	1,600	1,577	23
Jefferson	709	688	21				

Source: State of Florida, Department of Highway Safety and Motor Vehicles,
Bureau of Vessel Titles and Registrations, *Vessels Registered in Florida,
Fiscal Year 1995-96*.

Table 19.46. RECREATIONAL BOATING ACCIDENTS: TOTAL AND NUMBER OF FATAL BOATING
ACCIDENTS AND PERSONAL WATERCRAFT ACCIDENTS BY LOCATION, TYPE, OPERATION
AND OPERATOR IN FLORIDA, 1996

Item	Boats 1/ Number	Fatal	Personal water- craft 2/
Location			
Bay/sound	282	5	132
Canal/cut	106	3	25
Creek	37	0	11
Inlet	62	4	17
Lake/pond	168	15	79
Ocean/gulf	265	3	125
Port/harbor	52	12	5
River	177	9	45
Other	111	1	25
Accidents, total	1,260	52	464
Type 3/			
Capsizing	49	10	6
Collision with fixed object	211	8	48
Collision with floating object	22	0	4
Collision with vessel	480	5	272
Fallen skier	37	2	6
Falls in boat	88	3	45
Falls overboard	61	16	29
Fire or explosion, fuel related	28	2	4
Fire or explosion, nonfuel	22	0	1
Flooding	68	6	1
Grounding	73	0	8
Hit by boat	34	0	26
Hit by prop	12	4	0
Sinking	26	0	1
Other	49	3	4
Operation at time of accident 4/			
At anchor	70	2	4
Being towed	12	0	3
Commercial fishing	7	0	0
Cruising	931	23	473
Docking	37	1	2
Drifting	116	7	59
Fishing	54	7	2
Hunting	0	0	0
Maneuvering	497	3	277
Racing	15	1	9
SCUBA diving	6	0	0
Skiing	62	1	11
Skin diving	1	0	0
Swimming	9	2	3
Tied to dock	148	1	1
Towing	27	2	8
Other commercial	22	1	6
Other	81	5	39

See footnotes at end of table.   Continued . . .

University of Florida   **Bureau of Economic and Business Research**

Table 19.46. RECREATIONAL BOATING ACCIDENTS: TOTAL AND NUMBER OF FATAL BOATING
ACCIDENTS AND PERSONAL WATERCRAFT ACCIDENTS BY, LOCATION, TYPE, OPERATION
AND OPERATOR IN FLORIDA, 1996 (Continued)

Item	Boats 1/		Personal water- craft 2/
	Number	Fatal	
Operators, total	1,662	58	746
Age (years)			
0-16	136	1	107
17-21	208	3	174
22-35	549	10	312
36-50	407	15	103
51 and over	362	29	50
Experience (hours)			
Less than 20	399	6	333
20-100	291	4	185
101-500	274	13	100
500 or more	546	16	85
Data unavailable	152	19	43
With no instruction by age (years)			
All ages	1,057	28	605
1-16	120	1	97
17-21	174	2	152
22-35	402	6	253
36-50	234	8	76
51 and over	127	11	27

1/ Registered recreational vessels.
2/ Accidents involving a small vessel designed to be operated by a person sitting,
standing, or kneeling on, or being towed behind the vessel, rather than in the con-
ventional manner of sitting or standing inside the vessel.
3/ Based on first harmful event.
4/ Each accident may contain multiple entries.
Note: A reportable boat accident is any boating accident that results in death,
disappearance of any person, injury requiring medical treatment beyond first aid,
and/or property damage totaling more than $500.

Source: State of Florida, Department of Environmental Protection, Division of Law
Enforcement, Office of Waterway Management, *1996 Florida Recreational Boating
Accident Report.*

Table 19.48. RECREATIONAL BOATING ACCIDENTS: NUMBER OF VESSELS REGISTERED, REPORTED
ACCIDENTS, PERSONS KILLED OR INJURED, AND PROPERTY DAMAGES RESULTING
FROM RECREATIONAL BOATING AND PERSONAL WATERCRAFT ACCIDENTS
IN THE STATE AND COUNTIES OF FLORIDA, 1996

		Reported accidents 1/					Damages (dollars)	
	Recreational	Boating			Personal watercraft			
	boats		Fatal-	Inju-		Inju-		Personal
County	registered	Number	ities	ries	Number	ries	Boating	watercraft
Florida	731,986	1,260	59	804	465	389	5,559,051	467,921
Alachua	8,755	3	0	3	1	1	10,000	3,500
Baker	1,565	1	0	1	0	0	1,750	0
Bay	14,949	52	3	31	31	21	94,693	18,993
Bradford	1,667	1	0	0	0	0	2,000	0
Brevard	27,595	31	4	22	10	10	236,850	4,600
Broward	40,906	94	0	59	32	27	621,820	36,300
Calhoun	1,159	4	0	1	0	0	7,814	0
Charlotte	15,952	20	1	7	6	4	24,200	2,700
Citrus	11,845	17	2	12	2	1	14,360	810
Clay	8,365	12	2	7	6	4	22,050	4,550
Collier	15,368	42	0	27	12	10	341,438	6,000
Columbia	3,941	1	0	1	0	0	0	0
Dade	49,252	74	4	41	36	28	231,290	49,550
De Soto	1,648	3	0	3	0	0	3,000	0
Dixie	1,645	0	0	0	0	0	0	0
Duval	28,473	23	5	7	3	2	125,300	1,500
Escambia	16,195	31	2	21	23	13	44,810	18,310
Flagler	2,884	4	0	1	1	0	20,800	1,000
Franklin	1,603	7	1	2	0	0	29,300	0
Gadsden	2,269	4	2	2	1	1	1,200	650
Gilchrist	1,088	5	0	7	1	1	6,900	200
Glades	1,025	7	0	8	0	0	22,075	0
Gulf	2,101	5	0	4	3	3	3,400	400
Hamilton	656	0	0	0	0	0	0	0
Hardee	1,448	0	0	0	0	0	0	0
Hendry	2,650	3	0	3	1	0	10,650	0
Hernando	5,678	6	0	2	1	1	6,150	1,500
Highlands	8,009	6	0	6	3	4	5,700	3,700
Hillsborough	36,062	20	2	16	7	7	71,550	15,200
Holmes	1,623	0	0	0	0	0	0	0
Indian River	8,382	17	0	7	5	4	11,984	1,250
Jackson	3,834	1	1	0	0	0	50	0
Jefferson	688	0	0	0	0	0	0	0
Lafayette	551	2	0	2	1	1	0	0
Lake	16,533	14	4	9	3	3	4,500	1,050
Lee	32,447	62	0	47	21	22	545,364	17,139

See footnote at end of table.   Continued . . .

University of Florida   **Bureau of Economic and Business Research**

Table 19.48. RECREATIONAL BOATING ACCIDENTS: NUMBER OF VESSELS REGISTERED, REPORTED ACCIDENTS, PERSONS KILLED OR INJURED, AND PROPERTY DAMAGES RESULTING FROM RECREATIONAL BOATING AND PERSONAL WATERCRAFT ACCIDENTS IN THE STATE AND COUNTIES OF FLORIDA, 1996 (Continued)

| | | Reported accidents 1/ | | | | | Damages (dollars) | |
| | Recreational boats registered | Boating | | | Personal watercraft | | | Personal watercraft |
County		Number	Fatal-ities	Inju-ries	Number	Inju-ries	Boating	
Leon	11,009	2	1	0	0	0	2,533	0
Levy	2,519	3	1	1	0	0	500	0
Liberty	942	1	1	0	0	0	0	0
Madison	850	0	0	0	0	0	0	0
Manatee	14,775	23	0	14	11	6	106,315	13,580
Marion	15,012	14	1	9	7	7	16,591	4,300
Martin	13,299	35	0	22	9	6	439,142	9,642
Monroe	18,106	174	3	88	52	47	543,494	54,945
Nassau	3,341	4	0	2	0	0	351,500	0
Okaloosa	15,227	55	1	50	28	25	335,311	23,250
Okeechobee	4,544	10	2	8	2	1	24,352	4,500
Orange	28,496	37	1	30	18	17	34,626	18,001
Osceola	6,363	11	1	7	1	1	57,800	2,350
Palm Beach	31,947	79	6	39	16	15	409,983	14,049
Pasco	16,736	15	2	11	6	9	46,350	10,600
Pinellas	44,028	84	0	71	50	43	194,588	65,959
Polk	24,594	16	0	12	12	8	14,100	13,600
Putnam	7,230	9	0	4	1	1	27,550	0
St. Johns	7,008	8	0	3	1	1	62,960	60
St. Lucie	9,556	15	0	15	3	4	165,700	6,200
Santa Rosa	8,737	12	1	7	7	6	11,158	6,158
Sarasota	16,812	16	0	13	6	3	17,500	4,700
Seminole	15,925	8	0	6	3	3	6,525	1,725
Sumter	2,671	2	1	2	0	0	4,000	0
Suwannee	2,111	3	0	1	1	0	9,000	2,500
Taylor	2,720	2	0	2	1	1	12,200	11,000
Union	523	0	0	0	0	0	0	0
Volusia	20,349	35	4	19	13	10	94,725	11,050
Wakulla	3,523	1	0	0	0	0	10,000	0
Walton	2,645	11	0	7	6	6	38,450	850
Washington	1,577	3	0	2	1	1	1,100	0

1/ A reportable boat accident is any boating accident that results in death, disappearance of any person, injury requiring medical treatment beyond first aid, and/or property damage totaling more than $500.

Source: State of Florida, Department of Environmental Protection, Division of Law Enforcement, Office of Waterway Management, *1996 Florida Recreational Boating Accident Report*.

University of Florida   **Bureau of Economic and Business Research**

Table 19.52. STATE PARKS AND AREAS: ATTENDANCE AT PARKS IN THE STATE AND SPECIFIED
COUNTIES OF FLORIDA, FISCAL YEARS 1994-95 AND 1995-96

Property designation	County	1994-95	1995-96
Total	(X)	11,790,366	12,490,799
Addison Blockhouse	Volusia	0	0
Alfred B. Maclay Gardens	Leon	54,010	54,280
Amelia Island	Nassau	58,078	65,310
Anastasia	St. Johns	277,835	371,530
Anclote Key	Pasco, Pinellas	108,379	164,125
Avalon	St. Lucie	0	51,084
Bahia Honda	Monroe	367,990	363,801
Barnacle, The	Dade	11,252	18,664
Big Lagoon	Escambia	87,266	93,704
Big Talbot Island	Duval	47,998	53,134
Blackwater River	Santa Rosa	23,910	30,327
Blue Spring	Volusia	288,143	297,233
Bulow Creek	Flagler, Volusia	42,698	44,426
Bulow Plantation Ruins	Flagler	30,836	27,845
Caladesi Island	Pinellas	106,060	125,003
Cape Florida	Dade	372,230	464,626
Cayo Costa	Lee	50,510	47,674
Cedar Key	Levy	21,610	23,861
Collier-Seminole	Collier	62,207	67,826
Constitution Convention	Gulf	1,052	872
Coral Reef	Monroe	950,843	1,003,368
Crystal River	Citrus	21,126	21,855
Curry Hammock	Monroe	16,587	25,940
Dade Battlefield	Sumter	31,754	31,476
De Leon Springs	Volusia	208,885	206,767
Dead Lakes	Gulf	13,809	12,318
Delnor-Wiggins Pass	Collier	444,263	515,225
Devil's Millhopper	Alachua	45,604	45,834
Don Pedro Island	Charlotte	8,454	15,766
Eden	Walton	53,185	49,360
Egmont Key	Hillsborough	75,425	73,907
Fakahatchee Strand	Collier	63,696	83,509
Falling Waters	Washington	28,238	28,270
Faver-Dykes	St. Johns	22,529	25,151
Flagler Beach	Flagler	77,556	77,439
Florida Caverns	Jackson	105,951	113,081
Forest Capital	Taylor	26,748	24,949
Ft. Clinch	Nassau	159,969	158,415
Ft. Cooper	Citrus	24,890	25,723
Ft. George Island	Duval	26,251	26,035
Ft. Pierce Inlet	St. Lucie	121,650	132,859
Ft. Zachary Taylor	Monroe	229,999	215,380
Gamble Plantation	Manatee	25,948	29,094
Gasparilla Island	Hillsborough	362,469	330,470
Gold Head Branch	Clay	58,572	55,775
Grayton Beach	Walton	81,768	67,765
Green Mound	Volusia	0	0
Guana River	St. Johns	160,182	153,752
Henderson Beach	Okaloosa	73,096	97,247
Highlands Hammock	Hardee	172,194	190,854

See footnotes at end of table.   Continued . . .

University of Florida   **Bureau of Economic and Business Research**

Table 19.52. STATE PARKS AND AREAS: ATTENDANCE AT PARKS IN THE STATE AND SPECIFIED
COUNTIES OF FLORIDA, FISCAL YEARS 1994-95 AND 1995-96 (Continued)

Property designation	County	1994-95	1995-96
Hillsborough River	Hillsborough	106,797	116,286
Homosassa Springs	Citrus	207,784	207,493
Honeymoon Island	Pinellas	432,794	428,581
Hontoon Island	Volusia, Lake	30,407	30,092
Hugh Taylor Birch	Broward	263,898	233,265
Ichetucknee Springs	Columbia, Suwannee	155,860	189,025
Indian Key	Monroe	6,659	3,390
John Gorrie	Franklin	6,058	5,419
Jonathan Dickinson	Martin	134,930	144,598
Key Largo Hammock	Monroe	5,418	11,255
Koreshan	Lee	42,863	43,989
Lake Griffin	Lake	27,376	36,545
Lake Jackson Mounds	Leon	23,048	53,701
Lake Kissimmee	Polk	44,347	42,482
Lake Louisa	Lake	26,939	17,670
Lake Manatee	Manatee	44,334	46,853
Lake Talquin	Gadsden, Leon, Liberty	11,224	16,189
Lignumvitae Key	Monroe	3,202	3,322
Little Manatee River	Hillsborough	19,462	21,818
Little Talbot Island	Duval	123,714	118,033
Lloyd Beach	Broward	570,307	550,358
Long Key	Monroe	72,973	71,338
Lovers Key	Lee	58,594	59,800
Lower Wekiva River	Lake, Seminole	2,742	1,822
MacArthur Beach	Palm Beach	90,907	86,840
Madira Bickel Mound	Manatee	2,988	3,121
Manatee Springs	Levy	127,729	126,456
Marjorie Kinnan Rawlings	Alachua	21,883	23,009
Myakka River	Manatee, Sarasota	242,904	239,759
Natural Bridge Battlefield	Leon	23,526	20,282
North Peninsula	Volusia	24,508	24,167
North Shore	Dade	7,656	0
O'Leno	Alachua, Columbia	60,030	61,635
Ochlockonee River	Wakulla	35,640	39,030
Oleta River	Dade	123,852	130,342
Olustee Battlefield	Baker	43,085	34,338
Oscar Scherer	Sarasota	99,435	90,679
Paynes Creek	Hardee	31,701	36,447
Paynes Prairie	Alachua	99,234	105,961
Peacock Springs	Suwannee	8,948	8,464
Perdido Key	Escambia	25,153	27,108
Ponce De Leon Springs	Holmes, Walton	16,161	16,102
Rainbow Springs	Marion	67,899	91,907
Ravine	Putnam	135,460	109,092
Rock Springs Run	Orange	5,744	3,233
Rocky Bayou	Okaloosa	24,651	27,300
St. Andrews	Bay	513,363	512,041
St. George Island	Franklin	172,624	89,221
St. Joseph Peninsula	Gulf	93,711	90,540
St. Lucie Inlet	Martin	24,560	23,717
San Felasco Hammock	Alachua	13,588	24,278
San Marcos de Apalache	Wakulla	19,063	15,125
San Pedro	Monroe	1,289	1,097

See footnotes at end of table.   Continued . . .

Table 19.52. STATE PARKS AND AREAS: ATTENDANCE AT PARKS IN THE STATE AND SPECIFIED COUNTIES OF FLORIDA, FISCAL YEARS 1994-95 AND 1995-96 (Continued)

Property designation	County	1994-95	1995-96
Seabranch	Martin	0	5,776
Sebastian Inlet	Brevard, Indian River	524,642	520,681
Silver River	Marion	11,388	42,865
Spruce Creek	Volusia	0	0
Stephen Foster	Hamilton	57,753	67,711
Sunshine Skyway Fishing Piers	Hillsborough, Pinellas	26,970	80,816
Suwannee River	Hamilton, Madison, Suwannee	45,877	48,909
Tallahassee/St. Marks	Leon	184,947	223,901
Three Rivers	Jackson	19,374	19,870
Tomoka	Volusia	50,863	53,852
Torreya	Liberty	18,326	17,809
Tosohatchee	Orange	13,749	12,714
Van Fleet	Lake, Polk, Sumter	7,536	13,291
Waccasassa Bay	Levy	29,585	27,210
Wakulla Springs	Wakulla	168,699	194,377
Washington Oaks	Flagler	52,250	54,179
Wekiwa Springs	Orange, Seminole	195,572	194,030
Windley Key Fossil Reef	Monroe	954	1,181
Withlacoochee	Citrus, Pasco, Hernando	55,280	142,875
Ybor City	Hillsborough	15,255	15,468
Yulee Sugar Mill Ruins	Citrus	36,275	35,760

(X) Not applicable.
Note: Data include areas reporting actual visitor counts from full-time entrance stations and areas reporting estimates of attendance from sample counts. Some parks may have been closed for repairs. Totals may include data from parks that are closed or no longer under the state system.
Source: State of Florida, Department of Environmental Protection, Recreation and Parks Management Information System, unpublished data.

Table 19.53. NATIONAL PARK SYSTEMS: RECREATIONAL VISITS TO NATIONAL PARK SERVICE AREAS IN FLORIDA, 1994 THROUGH 1996

Park, monument, or memorial	County	1994	1995	1996
Florida	(X)	8,082.6	8,055.5	6,633.6
Big Cypress Preserve	Broward, Hendry	294.3	365.5	424.9
Biscayne Park 1/	Dade	25.1	584.5	338.6
Canaveral Seashore	Brevard, Volusia	1,432.9	1,380.4	1,497.0
Castillo de San Marcos Monument	St. Johns	675.0	643.3	668.2
De Soto Memorial	Dade	250.4	211.5	206.1
Everglades Park 1/	Dade	886.5	820.5	890.2
Ft. Caroline Memorial	Duval	162.0	124.4	122.6
Ft. Matanzas Monument	St. Johns	487.2	451.5	455.4
Gulf Islands Seashore 1/ 2/	Escambia, Okaloosa, Santa Rosa	5,069.5	4,520.4	2,581.0
Jefferson National Expansion Memorial 1/	Monroe	2,553.7	3,235.0	3,649.3

(X) Not applicable.
1/ Due to changes in counting procedures, closings, or special events, data may not be comparable to earlier years.
2/ Part located in Mississippi; excluded from total.
Note: Data are in thousands, rounded to hundreds.
Source: U.S., Department of the Interior, National Park Service, *National Park Service 1996 Statistical Abstract,* and previous editions.

University of Florida   **Bureau of Economic and Business Research**

Table 19.54. TOURIST DEVELOPMENT TAXES: LOCAL OPTION TAX COLLECTIONS IN THE
STATE AND COUNTIES OF FLORIDA, FISCAL YEARS 1994-95 AND 1995-96

(amounts rounded to thousands of dollars)

County	1994-95	1995-96 Amount	1995-96 Percentage change	County	1994-95	1995-96 Amount	1995-96 Percentage change
Florida	182,268	212,202	16.4				
				Manatee	1,988	2,045	2.9
Alachua	950	992	4.4	Monroe	8,146	8,669	6.4
Bay	2,541	2,534	-0.3	Nassau	844	892	5.7
Bradford	39	40	1.4	Okaloosa	1,718	1,627	-5.3
Brevard	3,511	3,698	5.3	Okeechobee	77	84	9.4
Broward	10,942	11,843	8.2	Orange	58,412	73,044	25.0
Charlotte	955	1,005	5.2	Osceola	12,227	14,361	17.5
Citrus	176	208	18.3	Palm Beach	12,399	13,262	7.0
Clay	146	158	7.9	Pasco	570	529	-7.2
Collier	4,259	5,864	37.7	Pinellas	8,700	11,156	28.2
Columbia	257	247	-3.8	Polk	2,220	2,460	10.8
Dade	15,560	16,939	8.9	Putnam	73	78	6.7
Duval	3,602	4,841	34.4	St. Johns	2,366	2,614	10.5
Escambia	2,080	2,165	4.1	St. Lucie	847	847	0.0
Flagler	177	178	0.5	Santa Rosa	68	79	16.0
Hernando	126	129	2.8	Sarasota	2,904	3,024	4.1
Hillsborough	7,269	9,298	27.9	Seminole	1,018	1,167	14.6
Indian River	650	817	25.7	Suwannee	41	39	-5.4
Lake	353	385	9.0	Volusia	3,487	4,155	19.2
Lee	7,709	7,723	0.2	Wakulla	2	13	542.3
Leon	1,311	1,374	4.8	Walton	1,548	1,620	4.6

Note: Data reflect both state- and locally-administered tourist development tax
collections.

Source: State of Florida, Department of Revenue, Internet site http://fcn.state.
fl.us/dor/.

Table 19.60. TOURIST FACILITIES: HOTELS AND MOTELS BY NUMBER OF UNITS AND FOOD
SERVICE ESTABLISHMENTS BY SEATING CAPACITY IN THE STATE AND COUNTIES
OF FLORIDA, FISCAL YEAR 1996-97

	Licensed hotels		Licensed motels		Food service establishments	
County	Number	Units	Number	Units	Number of licenses	Seating capacity
Florida	803	132,992	3,852	201,367	35,261	2,928,768
Alachua	5	779	48	2,805	416	34,015
Baker	0	0	3	107	24	1,359
Bay	2	354	205	8,741	506	43,245
Bradford	1	29	13	368	32	1,831
Brevard	13	1,909	98	6,277	975	82,417
Broward	98	14,584	435	12,889	3,519	283,521
Calhoun	0	0	2	23	20	1,460
Charlotte	1	183	26	1,080	291	26,041
Citrus	2	111	23	808	236	16,561
Clay	1	15	7	824	199	16,340
Collier	16	3,152	60	2,188	685	64,943
Columbia	0	0	33	1,960	93	7,548
Dade	278	33,643	223	13,620	5,403	342,569
De Soto	1	10	5	127	38	3,048
Dixie	0	0	10	140	20	1,208
Duval	24	4,105	86	6,854	1,635	125,222
Escambia	8	900	63	4,438	539	45,931
Flagler	2	232	15	455	111	8,080
Franklin	1	31	17	381	46	3,204
Gadsden	0	0	8	154	44	3,257
Gilchrist	0	0	1	28	14	700
Glades	0	0	11	189	21	1,049
Gulf	1	14	9	83	20	1,269
Hamilton	0	0	9	371	16	762
Hardee	0	0	3	45	29	1,371
Hendry	1	59	13	298	53	4,123
Hernando	0	0	14	595	230	16,139
Highlands	5	494	21	687	161	14,173
Hillsborough	31	7,194	111	7,299	1,968	163,497
Holmes	0	0	5	193	15	1,142
Indian River	1	208	35	1,479	243	20,456
Jackson	0	0	11	547	64	3,817
Jefferson	0	0	4	147	27	1,717
Lafayette	0	0	1	8	6	297
Lake	2	135	48	1,856	365	28,639
Lee	18	2,414	143	5,138	1,088	93,948

See footnote at end of table.   Continued . . .

University of Florida   **Bureau of Economic and Business Research**

Table 19.60. TOURIST FACILITIES: HOTELS AND MOTELS BY NUMBER OF UNITS AND FOOD
SERVICE ESTABLISHMENTS BY SEATING CAPACITY IN THE STATE AND COUNTIES
OF FLORIDA, FISCAL YEAR 1996-97 (Continued)

| | Licensed hotels | | Licensed motels | | Food service establishments | |
County	Number	Units	Number	Units	Number of licenses	Seating capacity
Leon	10	1,356	45	3,498	499	44,516
Levy	0	0	23	329	71	4,180
Liberty	0	0	1	13	4	338
Madison	0	0	3	138	26	1,584
Manatee	2	299	69	2,771	536	46,099
Marion	6	687	67	2,706	450	33,559
Martin	4	336	22	910	334	27,250
Monroe	25	2,066	170	6,044	590	43,726
Nassau	2	461	24	635	120	9,779
Okaloosa	1	44	55	4,238	432	37,984
Okeechobee	0	0	11	362	77	5,379
Orange	78	32,731	125	25,090	2,462	306,397
Osceola	19	4,376	109	16,045	471	52,321
Palm Beach	57	8,904	159	6,201	2,572	233,873
Pasco	0	0	38	1,817	547	42,741
Pinellas	31	4,550	379	13,611	2,188	195,952
Polk	9	673	111	5,720	830	68,983
Putnam	0	0	22	522	116	6,954
St. Johns	6	935	71	3,182	338	23,946
St. Lucie	5	963	34	1,188	356	24,517
Santa Rosa	1	8	10	710	135	8,626
Sarasota	7	719	80	3,296	769	68,269
Seminole	5	651	25	2,169	664	55,870
Sumter	0	0	8	552	93	3,473
Suwannee	0	0	10	322	36	2,237
Taylor	0	0	25	478	36	2,773
Union	0	0	0	0	4	322
Volusia	21	2,250	313	14,853	1,163	98,676
Wakulla	1	28	5	112	38	2,695
Walton	1	400	14	492	123	9,386
Washington	0	0	5	161	29	1,464

Note: Apartment buildings, rooming houses, rental condominiums, transient apartments, and total public lodgings are shown in Table 2.30.

Source: State of Florida, Department of Business and Professional Regulation,
Division of Hotels and Restaurants, *Master File Statistics: Public Lodging and Food
Service Establishments,* Fiscal Year 1996-97.

Table 19.70. TOURIST- AND RECREATION-RELATED BUSINESSES: GROSS AND TAXABLE SALES
AND SALES AND USE TAX COLLECTIONS BY KIND OF BUSINESS IN FLORIDA
1995 AND 1996

(rounded to thousands of dollars)

Kind of business	Gross sales	Taxable sales	Sales and use tax collections
1995			
Candy, sundries, and concessions	1,180,500	390,375	24,934
Restaurants and lunchrooms	15,509,171	13,998,378	856,570
Bars, nightclubs, and liquor stores	1,965,109	1,800,113	111,242
Sporting goods, pro shops, jewelry, and leather	3,815,587	2,324,668	141,160
Motorboats, yachts, and marine parts	2,820,480	1,349,599	82,531
Music, electronics, and record shops	12,368,703	4,222,289	261,942
Hotels, rooming houses, and trailer parks	8,598,639	7,768,974	475,943
Bookstores	918,957	616,166	37,564
Tobacco shops	78,434	35,335	2,141
Photo and art supplies, photographers, and art galleries	1,557,457	873,112	53,317
Gift, novelty, hobby, and toy stores	2,382,535	1,690,776	103,088
Newsstands	186,379	56,139	3,614
Admissions	3,671,096	3,423,705	228,127
Holiday season vendors	13,460	10,228	627
Rental of amusement machines, houseboats, and horses	4,976,807	2,984,691	184,104
Fairs, concessions, and carnivals	12,156	7,008	423
1996			
Candy, sundries, and concessions	1,298,827	420,432	26,627
Restaurants and lunchrooms	16,111,719	14,923,566	908,930
Bars, nightclubs, and liquor stores	2,063,291	1,891,896	115,662
Sporting goods, pro shops, jewelry, and leather	3,881,104	2,482,238	150,401
Motorboats, yachts, and marine parts	3,206,689	1,486,466	90,718
Music, electronics, and record shops	14,423,640	4,807,569	296,769
Hotels, rooming houses, and trailer parks	9,138,106	8,432,189	513,998
Bookstores	969,158	666,317	40,774
Tobacco shops	136,766	52,738	3,203
Photo and art supplies, photographers, and art galleries	1,562,588	901,775	54,775
Gift, novelty, hobby, and toy stores	2,532,051	1,818,278	110,120
Newsstands	188,525	59,208	3,741
Admissions	4,066,870	3,705,327	240,598
Holiday season vendors	14,168	9,650	600
Rental of amusement machines, houseboats, and horses	5,797,114	3,219,221	198,354
Fairs, concessions, and carnivals	15,932	7,381	448

Note: Audited sales reported for the 6 percent regular sales tax, 6 percent use
tax, and 3 percent vehicle and farm equipment sales tax. Sales occurred, for the
most part, from December 1, 1994, through November 30, 1996. Kind of business data
for counties are available from the Bureau of Economic and Business Research, University of Florida. Data includes all sales in the category. See Table 16.81 for taxable sales for all businesses; see Table 23.43 for tax collections.

Source: State of Florida, Department of Revenue, unpublished data prepared by the
University of Florida, Bureau of Economic and Business Research.

University of Florida   **Bureau of Economic and Business Research**

Table 19.73. EATING AND DRINKING PLACES: AVERAGE MONTHLY PRIVATE REPORTING UNITS EMPLOYMENT, AND PAYROLL COVERED BY UNEMPLOYMENT COMPENSATION LAW IN THE STATE AND COUNTIES OF FLORIDA, 1995 AND 1996

County	Number of reporting units	Number of employees	Payroll ($1,000)	County	Number of reporting units	Number of employees	Payroll ($1,000)
				Eating and drinking places, 1995 A/ (SIC code 58)			
Florida	21,067	420,906	367,034	Lafayette	5	23	12
				Lake	203	3,330	2,511
Alachua	305	7,807	5,260	Lee	562	12,089	9,998
Baker	18	300	195	Leon	340	10,959	7,948
Bay	296	6,586	5,031	Levy	42	553	331
Bradford	18	495	259	Madison	16	207	119
Brevard	680	12,246	9,222	Manatee	286	5,417	4,558
Broward	2,343	42,841	39,795	Marion	262	4,934	3,639
Calhoun	10	153	88	Martin	184	2,834	2,397
Charlotte	147	2,436	1,790	Monroe	312	4,637	4,834
Citrus	137	1,742	1,150	Nassau	74	1,313	1,066
Clay	147	3,500	2,443	Okaloosa	302	6,471	4,756
Collier	361	6,234	6,328	Okeechobee	40	590	402
Columbia	51	1,244	797	Orange	1,221	33,808	37,208
Dade	2,897	51,563	54,543	Osceola	245	6,839	5,852
De Soto	26	372	237	Palm Beach	1,588	29,776	27,893
Dixie	19	168	100	Pasco	330	5,432	3,851
Duval	1,063	23,250	18,216	Pinellas	1,421	26,124	21,031
Escambia	403	9,127	6,742	Polk	483	9,138	6,665
Flagler	55	668	451	Putnam	64	1,021	659
Franklin	30	235	165	St. Johns	203	3,396	2,626
Gadsden	22	374	215	St. Lucie	182	3,201	2,340
Gilchrist	9	41	20	Santa Rosa	86	1,501	867
Gulf	13	97	68	Sarasota	528	9,721	8,371
Hardee	21	218	138	Seminole	415	9,761	7,753
Hendry	38	452	304	Sumter	36	647	423
Hernando	127	2,014	1,322	Suwannee	27	535	335
Highlands	83	1,438	954	Taylor	26	468	316
Hillsborough	1,165	31,826	26,376	Volusia	718	12,899	9,878
Holmes	12	225	162	Wakulla	17	252	172
Indian River	151	2,393	1,949	Walton	55	733	556
Jackson	48	747	469	Washington	11	219	154
Jefferson	9	102	49	Multicounty 1/	66	987	2,550

See footnotes at end of table.   Continued . . .

University of Florida   **Bureau of Economic and Business Research**

Table 19.73.   EATING AND DRINKING PLACES: AVERAGE MONTHLY PRIVATE REPORTING UNITS
EMPLOYMENT, AND PAYROLL COVERED BY UNEMPLOYMENT COMPENSATION LAW
IN THE STATE AND COUNTIES OF FLORIDA, 1995 AND 1996 (Continued)

County	Number of re- porting units	Number of em- ployees	Payroll ($1,000)	County	Number of re- porting units	Number of em- ployees	Payroll ($1,000)
			Eating and drinking places, 1996 B/ (SIC code 58)				
Florida	21,599	437,562	396,779	Jefferson	9	111	57
				Lafayette	4	9	5
Alachua	317	8,172	5,603	Lake	219	3,632	2,787
Baker	16	262	179	Lee	619	12,770	11,333
Bay	302	6,653	5,222	Leon	353	8,697	5,778
Bradford	17	554	302	Levy	44	589	379
Brevard	677	12,819	10,023	Madison	15	253	164
Broward	2,341	42,863	40,459	Manatee	339	6,559	5,847
Calhoun	10	156	92	Marion	274	5,365	4,046
Charlotte	149	2,483	1,891	Martin	193	3,269	2,821
Citrus	138	1,862	1,271	Monroe	311	4,868	5,329
Clay	157	3,750	2,701	Nassau	82	1,340	1,178
Collier	390	6,305	6,647	Okaloosa	308	6,698	5,270
Columbia	61	1,358	912	Okeechobee	55	794	589
Dade	2,888	52,154	57,733	Orange	1,261	36,014	40,705
De Soto	26	358	239	Osceola	253	6,894	6,252
Dixie	18	152	105	Palm Beach	1,608	30,527	30,179
Duval	1,106	24,235	19,750	Pasco	332	5,648	4,110
Escambia	414	9,922	7,666	Pinellas	1,467	26,995	22,584
Flagler	61	772	508	Polk	491	9,083	6,999
Franklin	31	230	161	Putnam	67	1,062	691
Gadsden	23	451	254	St. Johns	204	3,471	2,875
Gilchrist	10	43	23	St. Lucie	180	3,038	2,379
Glades	7	81	51	Santa Rosa	93	1,654	1,001
Gulf	11	99	64	Sarasota	566	10,200	9,185
Hamilton	9	91	56	Seminole	434	10,152	8,602
Hardee	17	216	131	Sumter	36	604	400
Hendry	40	504	333	Suwannee	27	510	346
Hernando	133	2,218	1,453	Taylor	27	454	303
Highlands	82	1,417	975	Volusia	699	12,679	10,108
Hillsborough	1,181	33,949	29,526	Wakulla	19	244	161
Holmes	12	209	165	Walton	58	777	647
Indian River	151	2,727	2,332	Washington	14	272	190
Jackson	44	728	452	Multicounty 1/	98	4,448	6,104

A/ Revised.
B/ Preliminary.
1/ Reporting units without a fixed location within the state or of unknown county
location.
    Note: Private employment. Only counties for which data are disclosed are shown.
Detail may not add to totals due to disclosure editing and/or rounding. See Tables
23.70, 23.71, 23.72, 23.73, and 23.74 for public employment data.

    Source: State of Florida, Department of Labor and Employment Security, Bureau of
Labor Market Information, "Employment and Wages" (ES-202), unpublished data.

Table 19.75. TOURIST- AND RECREATION-RELATED BUSINESSES: AVERAGE MONTHLY PRIVATE
REPORTING UNITS, EMPLOYMENT, AND PAYROLL COVERED BY UNEMPLOYMENT
COMPENSATION LAW BY INDUSTRY IN FLORIDA, 1996

SIC code	Industry	Number of reporting units	Number of employees	Payroll ($1,000)
413	Intercity and rural bus transportation	34	820	1,449
414	Bus charter service	82	2,079	3,193
448	Water transportation of passengers	117	5,883	15,172
451	Air transportation, scheduled, and air courier services	488	50,165	137,567
452	Air transportation, nonscheduled	224	5,221	12,942
472	Arrangement of passenger transportation	2,674	18,691	34,949
544	Candy, nut, and confectionery stores	161	1,101	1,013
555	Boat dealers	625	4,521	9,277
556	Recreational vehicle dealers	172	2,210	5,760
573	Radio, television, consumer electronics, and music stores	2,674	22,728	42,750
581	Eating and drinking places	21,599	437,562	396,779
592	Liquor stores	721	4,150	4,616
594	Miscellaneous shopping goods stores	6,919	47,146	60,559
701	Hotels and motels	2,973	137,485	182,821
703	Camps and recreational vehicle parks	418	3,112	3,671
751	Automotive rental and leasing, without drivers	749	19,274	39,141
783	Motion picture theaters	282	6,766	4,515
784	Video tape rental	770	8,289	11,321
79	Amusement and recreation services	5,640	131,203	228,847
791	Dance studios, schools, and halls	314	1,384	1,335
792	Theatrical producers, orchestras, entertainers	648	6,486	13,147
793	Bowling centers	156	3,250	2,980
794	Commercial sports	542	12,253	48,820
799	Miscellaneous services 1/	3,980	107,829	162,566
841	Museums and art galleries	115	2,019	2,959
842	Arboreta, botanical and zoological gardens	48	1,487	2,245

1/ Includes physical fitness and membership recreation facilities, public golf and
driving ranges, coin-operated amusement devices, amusement parks, carnivals, fairs,
animal shows, commercial museums and rental of bicycles, motorcycles, pleasure boats,
etc.

Note: Private employment. Data are preliminary. Detail may not add to totals
due to disclosure editing and/or rounding. See Tables 23.70, 23.71, 23.72, 23.73,
and 23.74 for public employment data.

Source: State of Florida, Department of Labor and Employment Security, Bureau of
Labor Market Information, "Employment and Wages" (ES-202), unpublished data.

Table 19.76. HOTELS, ROOMING HOUSES, CAMPS, AND LODGING PLACES: AVERAGE MONTHLY PRIVATE REPORTING UNITS, EMPLOYMENT, AND PAYROLL COVERED BY UNEMPLOYMENT COMPENSATION LAW IN THE STATE AND COUNTIES OF FLORIDA, 1996

County	Number of reporting units	Number of employees	Payroll ($1,000)	County	Number of reporting units	Number of employees	Payroll ($1,000)
Hotels, rooming houses, camps, and lodging places (SIC code 70)							
Florida	3,549	142,486	189,234	Lake	45	917	947
				Lee	132	4,263	6,354
Alachua	65	1,094	982	Leon	58	1,269	1,100
Baker	3	33	18	Levy	13	66	43
Bay	114	2,371	2,659	Manatee	53	677	720
Bradford	65	2,009	2,073	Marion	55	899	796
Brevard	249	7,684	10,319	Martin	19	763	1,023
Broward	93	2,663	3,637	Monroe	184	4,842	7,465
Charlotte	27	385	376	Nassau	20	1,548	2,268
Citrus	12	369	351	Okaloosa	44	1,127	1,138
Clay	50	3,078	4,739	Okeechobee	13	145	150
Collier	35	1,320	1,989	Orange	202	35,953	49,636
Columbia	310	14,096	19,724	Osceola	124	5,102	6,450
Dade	106	4,843	7,111	Palm Beach	146	8,708	14,409
De Soto	4	17	15	Pasco	41	426	434
Duval	95	2,760	2,903	Pinellas	254	7,106	9,048
Escambia	48	930	774	Polk	108	2,405	3,094
Flagler	10	259	282	Putnam	13	175	132
Franklin	13	122	112	St. Johns	83	2,321	2,945
Gadsden	8	36	19	St. Lucie	25	702	640
Glades	7	26	22	Santa Rosa	11	355	334
Hamilton	5	47	25	Sarasota	77	2,740	3,642
Hardee	5	21	19	Seminole	27	706	734
Hendry	11	174	165	Sumter	17	110	74
Hernando	10	197	160	Suwannee	9	48	32
Highlands	23	174	170	Taylor	11	79	50
Hillsborough	112	6,826	8,427	Volusia	207	4,298	4,107
Holmes	4	22	11	Walton	11	1,294	1,927
Indian River	25	741	791	Washington	4	20	12
Jackson	7	113	86				

Note: Private employment. Data are preliminary. Only counties for which data are disclosed are shown. Detail may not add to totals due to disclosure editing and/or rounding. See Tables 23.70, 23.71, 23.72, 23.73, and 23.74 for public employment data.

Source: State of Florida, Department of Labor and Employment Security, Bureau of Labor Market Information, "Employment and Wages" (ES-202), unpublished data.

University of Florida   **Bureau of Economic and Business Research**

Table 19.78. AMUSEMENT AND RECREATION SERVICES: AVERAGE MONTHLY PRIVATE REPORTING
UNITS, EMPLOYMENT, AND PAYROLL COVERED BY UNEMPLOYMENT COMPENSATION LAW
IN THE STATE AND COUNTIES OF FLORIDA, 1996

County	Number of reporting units	Number of employees	Payroll ($1,000)	County	Number of reporting units	Number of employees	Payroll ($1,000)
				Amusement and recreation services (SIC code 79)			
Florida	5,640	131,203	228,847	Lee	164	2,441	2,995
				Leon	74	690	667
Alachua	62	1,205	1,619	Levy	10	47	45
Bay	107	1,083	1,077	Madison	6	52	86
Brevard	134	1,779	1,849	Manatee	81	1,394	1,880
Broward	704	10,996	20,267	Marion	64	985	1,103
Calhoun	3	12	6	Martin	86	1,737	2,601
Charlotte	39	528	569	Monroe	166	916	2,117
Citrus	41	419	430	Nassau	13	60	43
Clay	34	833	969	Okaloosa	102	780	861
Collier	111	3,050	4,893	Okeechobee	9	70	71
Columbia	15	150	125	Orange	335	44,036	82,436
Dade	649	11,296	26,011	Osceola	64	1,122	1,425
De Soto	7	102	128	Palm Beach	555	11,419	18,979
Duval	185	2,851	7,587	Pasco	77	747	900
Escambia	90	1,029	960	Pinellas	301	4,710	6,116
Flagler	9	121	130	Polk	109	2,103	2,631
Gadsden	5	16	10	Putnam	9	42	23
Hardee	7	30	30	St. Johns	45	1,096	3,242
Hendry	6	16	18	St. Lucie	37	538	626
Hernando	29	503	504	Santa Rosa	33	280	243
Highlands	17	295	374	Sarasota	180	3,794	5,622
Hillsborough	304	8,462	15,281	Seminole	123	1,737	2,249
Holmes	4	21	23	Suwannee	5	28	16
Indian River	48	1,507	2,291	Taylor	4	12	13
Jackson	8	49	28	Volusia	185	2,580	3,847
Lake	54	492	528	Multicounty 1/	107	545	1,902

1/ Reporting units without a fixed location within the state or of unknown county
location.
    Note: Private employment. For a list of three-digit code industries included see
Table 19.75. Data are preliminary. Only counties for which data are disclosed are
shown. Detail may not add to totals due to disclosure editing and/or rounding. See
Tables 23.70, 23.71, 23.72, 23.73, and 23.74 for public employment data.

    Source: State of Florida, Department of Labor and Employment Security, Bureau of
Labor Market Information, "Employment and Wages" (ES-202), unpublished data.

University of Florida   **Bureau of Economic and Business Research**

HEALTH, EDUCATION, AND CULTURAL SERVICES

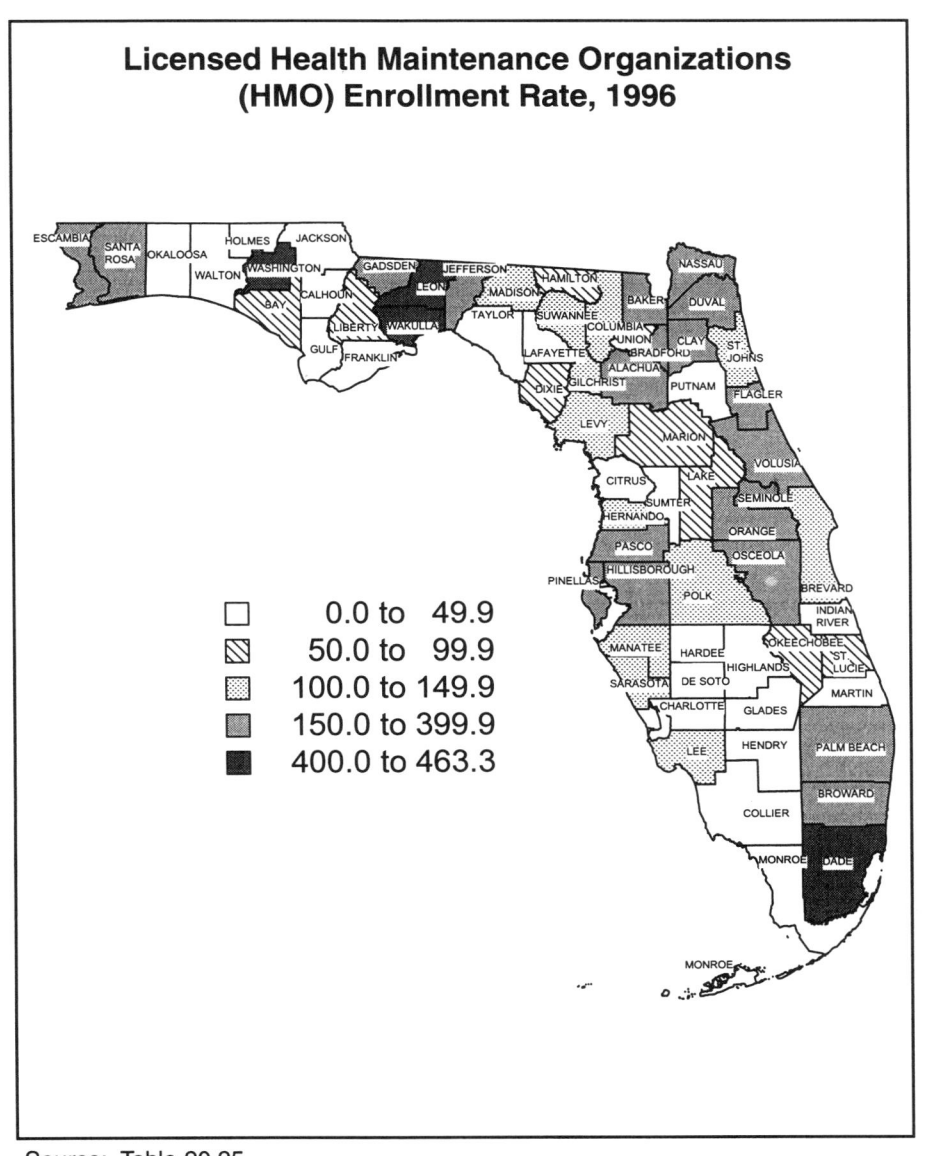

Licensed Health Maintenance Organizations (HMO) Enrollment Rate, 1996

Legend:
- ☐ 0.0 to 49.9
- ▨ 50.0 to 99.9
- ▦ 100.0 to 149.9
- ▨ 150.0 to 399.9
- ■ 400.0 to 463.3

Source: Table 20.25

TABLES LISTED BY MAJOR HEADINGS

TABLES LISTED BY MAJOR HEADINGS

University of Florida   **Bureau of Economic and Business Research**

Table 20.01. HEALTH, EDUCATIONAL, AND SOCIAL SERVICES: ESTABLISHMENTS AND
RECEIPTS, 1987 AND 1992, AND PAYROLL, 1992, IN FLORIDA

(amounts in thousands of dollars)

SIC code	Kind of business	Number of establishments 1987	1992	Receipts 1987	1992	Per-cent-age change	Annual payroll 1992
80	Health services	24,048	29,601	12,901,041	23,306,589	80.7	9,632,590
801	Offices and clinics of doctors of medicine	12,533	14,487	6,002,814	10,360,884	72.6	4,942,036
802	Offices and clinics of dentists	4,674	5,374	1,212,130	1,893,179	56.2	735,558
803	Offices and clinics of doctors of osteo-pathy	610	762	189,828	325,522	71.5	147,644
804	Offices and clinics of other health prac-titioners	3,243	4,909	608,044	1,239,318	103.8	438,625
805	Nursing and personal care facilities	543	722	932,501	1,906,975	104.5	816,684
806	Hospitals	142	160	2,836,850	4,795,458	69.0	1,564,118
807	Medical and dental labs labs	971	1,294	392,044	874,743	123.1	253,152
808	Home health care ser-vices	465	852	284,363	1,141,072	301.3	485,872
809	Miscellaneous health and allied ser-vices, NEC	867	1,041	442,467	769,438	73.9	248,901
823, 4, 9	Selected educational services	623	955	324,286	423,789	30.7	132,236
823	Libraries	7	9	905	1,206	33.3	520
824	Vocational schools	219	304	207,430	234,636	13.1	74,185
829	Schools and educational services, NEC	397	642	115,951	187,947	62.1	57,531
83	Social services	2,832	3,797	458,635	824,710	79.8	326,313
835	Child day care services	1,910	2,409	232,856	378,299	62.5	167,498
832, 3, 6, 9	Other social services	922	1,388	225,779	446,411	97.7	158,815
832	Individual and family social services	(NA)	477	(NA)	96,298	(X)	38,019
833	Job training and vo-cational rehabili-tation services	(NA)	128	(NA)	58,756	(X)	25,941
836	Residential care	(NA)	691	(NA)	275,792	(X)	90,559
839	Social services, NEC	(NA)	92	(NA)	15,565	(X)	4,296

NEC Not elsewhere classified.
(NA) Not available.
(X) Not applicable.
Note: Data are for firms subject to federal income tax. The service industries census is on a 5-year cycle collecting data for years ending in 2 and 7.
Source: U.S., Department of Commerce, Bureau of the Census, *1992 Census of Service Industries: Florida.* SC92-A-10.

Table 20.05. EMPLOYMENT: AVERAGE MONTHLY PRIVATE REPORTING UNITS, EMPLOYMENT
AND PAYROLL COVERED BY UNEMPLOYMENT COMPENSATION LAW BY INDUSTRY
IN FLORIDA, 1995 AND 1996

SIC code	Industry	Units	Em-ployees	Payroll ($1,000)
1995 A/				
80	Health services	29,345	538,208	1,399,004
801	Offices and clinics of doctors of medicine	13,687	108,000	483,297
802	Offices and clinics of dentists	5,352	31,456	77,751
803	Offices and clinics of doctors of osteopathy	652	3,942	13,674
804	Offices of other health practitioners	5,410	28,136	68,687
805	Nursing and personal care facilities	737	77,979	114,022
806	Hospitals	385	209,895	490,420
807	Medical and dental laboratories	1,363	12,678	30,969
808	Home health care services	971	45,107	77,397
809	Miscellaneous health and allied services, NEC	788	21,016	42,788
82	Educational services	1,777	47,768	89,102
821	Elementary and secondary schools	535	17,589	29,067
822	Colleges and universities	129	19,295	42,105
823	Libraries	23	232	307
824	Vocational schools	303	3,512	6,544
829	School and education services, NEC	788	7,140	11,078
83	Social services	5,994	109,165	135,404
832	Individual and family social services	1,309	22,549	31,840
833	Job training and related services	386	11,031	14,521
835	Child day care services	2,408	29,275	26,902
836	Residential care	1,322	38,027	48,045
839	Social services, NEC	570	8,283	14,097
84	Museums, botanical and zoological gardens 1/	152	3,268	4,771
1996 B/				
80	Health services	29,809	557,035	1,476,559
801	Offices and clinics of doctors of medicine	13,710	112,580	504,281
802	Offices and clinics of dentists	5,488	32,871	84,599
803	Offices and clinics of doctors of osteopathy	611	3,804	13,224
804	Offices of other health practitioners	5,373	29,101	71,914
805	Nursing and personal care facilities	828	81,847	125,304
806	Hospitals	422	214,879	515,078
807	Medical and dental laboratories	1,356	12,990	32,856
808	Home health care services	1,063	44,909	78,657
809	Miscellaneous health and allied services, NEC	959	24,056	50,648
82	Educational services	1,921	50,514	98,243
821	Elementary and secondary schools	549	18,571	31,935
822	Colleges and universities	148	19,591	44,774
823	Libraries	28	244	331
824	Vocational schools	313	4,007	7,983
829	School and education services, NEC	884	8,103	13,219
83	Social services	6,220	110,817	143,595
832	Individual and family social services	1,410	23,263	34,194
833	Job training and related services	380	10,422	15,508
835	Child day care services	2,479	30,079	28,718
836	Residential care	1,340	38,807	50,845
839	Social services, NEC	611	8,246	14,330
84	Museums, botanical and zoological gardens 1/	163	3,506	5,204

NEC Not elsewhere classified.
A/ Revised.   B/ Preliminary.   1/ See Table 19.75 for detail.
Note: Private employment. Detail may not add to totals due to disclosure editing
and/or rounding. See Tables in Section 23.00 for public employment data.
Source: State of Florida, Department of Labor and Employment Security, Bureau of
Labor Market Information, "Employment and Wages" (ES-202), unpublished data.

University of Florida   **Bureau of Economic and Business Research**

Table 20.06. OFFICES AND CLINICS OF DOCTORS OF MEDICINE: AVERAGE MONTHLY
PRIVATE REPORTING UNITS, EMPLOYMENT, AND PAYROLL COVERED
BY UNEMPLOYMENT COMPENSATION LAW IN THE STATE AND
AND COUNTIES OF FLORIDA, 1996

County	Number of reporting units	Number of employees	Payroll ($1,000)	County	Number of reporting units	Number of employees	Payroll ($1,000)
Offices and clinics of doctors of medicine (SIC code 801)							
Florida	13,710	112,580	504,281	Lee	251	3,100	17,122
				Leon	176	2,278	9,499
Alachua	229	2,306	9,379	Levy	6	25	30
Baker	6	27	64	Manatee	187	1,594	6,832
Bay	127	1,062	4,816	Marion	188	1,427	6,722
Bradford	6	59	112	Martin	116	889	3,860
Brevard	356	2,981	15,900	Monroe	64	275	1,240
Broward	1,551	11,224	51,385	Nassau	12	48	188
Charlotte	105	991	5,837	Okaloosa	110	930	3,295
Citrus	79	576	2,262	Okeechobee	27	138	451
Clay	71	463	1,686	Orange	667	7,701	35,872
Collier	173	1,160	6,587	Osceola	100	824	3,279
Columbia	34	208	793	Palm Beach	1,184	8,211	43,553
Dade	2,969	18,712	75,164	Pasco	321	2,483	11,150
De Soto	14	63	241	Pinellas	888	7,324	35,740
Duval	623	7,434	35,805	Polk	200	3,436	11,752
Escambia	176	2,819	11,765	Putnam	39	298	917
Flagler	17	125	346	St. Johns	96	428	1,942
Franklin	5	17	50	St. Lucie	132	946	3,607
Gadsden	6	21	38	Santa Rosa	40	309	1,084
Hamilton	4	12	32	Sarasota	376	2,814	13,448
Hardee	10	61	175	Seminole	220	1,816	7,566
Hendry	7	24	47	Suwannee	7	33	59
Hernando	86	466	2,638	Taylor	8	63	162
Highlands	70	318	1,105	Union	4	29	47
Hillsborough	927	7,916	34,992	Volusia	272	2,764	11,830
Holmes	7	36	90	Walton	7	38	105
Indian River	121	1,127	4,646	Washington	7	29	79
Jackson	19	163	459				
Lake	155	1,217	4,686	Multicounty 1/	34	357	953

1/ Reporting units without a fixed location within the state or of unknown county location.

Note: Private employment. Data are preliminary. Only counties for which data are disclosed are shown. Detail may not add to totals due to disclosure editing and/or rounding. See Tables 23.70, 23.71, 23.72, 23.73, and 23.74 for public employment data.

Source: State of Florida, Department of Labor and Employment Security, Bureau of Labor Market Information, "Employment and Wages" (ES-202), unpublished data.

University of Florida   **Bureau of Economic and Business Research**

Table 20.07. OFFICES AND CLINICS OF DENTISTS: AVERAGE MONTHLY PRIVATE REPORTING
UNITS, EMPLOYMENT, AND PAYROLL COVERED BY UNEMPLOYMENT COMPENSATION LAW
IN THE STATE AND COUNTIES OF FLORIDA, 1996

County	Number of reporting units	Number of employees	Payroll ($1,000)	County	Number of reporting units	Number of employees	Payroll ($1,000)
			Offices and clinics of dentists (SIC code 802)				
Florida	5,488	32,871	84,599	Lake	59	380	857
				Lee	130	816	2,354
Alachua	80	542	1,237	Leon	73	581	1,566
Bay	43	326	853	Levy	4	33	46
Bradford	6	34	86	Manatee	91	558	1,453
Brevard	155	1,167	3,040	Marion	68	487	1,038
Broward	646	3,597	9,663	Martin	50	266	819
Calhoun	3	14	30	Monroe	24	142	343
Charlotte	39	254	668	Nassau	11	74	165
Citrus	19	159	390	Okaloosa	65	402	794
Clay	43	300	703	Okeechobee	6	41	74
Collier	91	457	1,267	Orange	313	1,954	5,477
Columbia	12	78	156	Osceola	32	229	600
Dade	894	4,615	11,190	Palm Beach	534	2,847	8,030
De Soto	3	16	21	Pasco	71	451	1,137
Dixie	3	18	35	Pinellas	397	2,499	6,786
Duval	269	1,734	4,382	Polk	110	741	1,978
Escambia	101	647	1,595	Putnam	10	84	171
Flagler	7	61	176	St. Johns	31	191	451
Gadsden	6	34	60	St. Lucie	46	278	711
Gulf	3	13	22	Santa Rosa	23	159	332
Hendry	6	41	63	Sarasota	183	959	2,512
Hernando	30	285	704	Seminole	118	824	1,977
Highlands	22	93	201	Suwannee	4	39	84
Hillsborough	335	2,085	5,502	Volusia	137	798	1,824
Indian River	45	273	633	Walton	6	27	35
Jackson	8	49	79	Washington	4	13	17

Note: Private employment. Data are preliminary. Only counties for which data
are disclosed are shown. Detail may not add to totals due to disclosure editing
and/or rounding. See Tables 23.70, 23.71, 23.72, 23.73, and 23.74 for public employment data.

Source: State of Florida, Department of Labor and Employment Security, Bureau of
Labor Market Information, "Employment and Wages" (ES-202), unpublished data.

University of Florida   **Bureau of Economic and Business Research**

Table 20.11. NURSING AND PERSONAL CARE FACILITIES AND HOSPITALS: AVERAGE MONTHLY PRIVATE REPORTING UNITS, EMPLOYMENT, AND PAYROLL COVERED BY UNEMPLOYMENT COMPENSATION LAW IN THE STATE AND COUNTIES OF FLORIDA, 1996

County	Number of reporting units	Number of employees	Payroll ($1,000)	County	Number of reporting units	Number of employees	Payroll ($1,000)
			Nursing and personal care facilities (SIC code 805)				
Florida	828	81,847	125,304	Manatee	17	1,787	2,317
				Marion	10	918	1,286
Alachua	10	912	1,250	Martin	6	718	997
Bay	7	718	1,058	Monroe	3	290	420
Brevard	23	2,469	3,705	Nassau	4	391	576
Broward	52	5,397	8,435	Okaloosa	11	803	1,031
Charlotte	8	1,075	1,499	Okeechobee	3	366	512
Citrus	10	1,163	1,590	Orange	36	4,095	6,020
Clay	10	784	1,153	Osceola	9	1,222	1,796
Collier	8	1,044	1,607	Palm Beach	61	6,885	11,686
Columbia	3	282	362	Pasco	19	1,772	2,555
Dade	90	7,683	12,680	Pinellas	101	9,561	14,782
Duval	38	3,424	4,986	Polk	21	2,454	3,502
Escambia	11	1,408	1,876	Putnam	4	330	444
Hernando	4	619	809	St. Johns	9	527	794
Highlands	5	603	738	St. Lucie	6	824	1,259
Hillsborough	35	3,412	5,279	Santa Rosa	4	338	381
Indian River	5	692	908	Sarasota	41	3,345	6,060
Jackson	3	228	262	Seminole	14	1,233	1,849
Lake	11	1,139	1,492	Suwannee	3	587	709
Lee	17	1,540	2,339	Volusia	34	3,339	4,527
Leon	12	977	1,411				
Madison	4	195	255	Multicounty 1/	12	1,220	4,164
			Hospitals (SIC code 806)				
Florida	422	214,879	515,078	Leon	8	4,420	9,237
				Manatee	7	3,264	6,909
Alachua	8	7,104	17,499	Monroe	4	925	2,150
Brevard	13	5,666	13,060	Okaloosa	5	1,649	3,468
Broward	30	11,646	27,165	Orange	25	17,124	42,839
Charlotte	5	2,620	5,618	Osceola	5	1,402	3,265
Citrus	12	1,413	3,057	Palm Beach	29	15,194	38,296
Dade	60	36,457	97,570	Pasco	14	5,314	11,725
Duval	17	14,683	33,755	Pinellas	29	16,864	38,137
Escambia	5	6,084	13,056	Polk	8	6,434	15,576
Hernando	6	1,922	3,949	St. Lucie	8	2,443	5,768
Highlands	3	1,297	2,689	Santa Rosa	7	1,124	2,242
Hillsborough	25	13,412	31,402	Sarasota	8	6,353	15,781
Indian River	3	1,932	4,347	Seminole	7	2,837	6,524
Lake	5	2,997	6,273	Volusia	11	5,776	13,147
Lee	9	4,085	9,688				

1/ Reporting units without a fixed location within the state or of unknown county location.

Note: Private employment. Data are preliminary. Only counties for which data are disclosed are shown. Detail may not add to totals due to disclosure editing and/or rounding. See Tables 23.70, 23.71, 23.72, 23.73, and 23.74 for public employment data.

Source: State of Florida, Department of Labor and Employment Security, Bureau of Labor Market Information, "Employment and Wages" (ES-202), unpublished data.

Table 20.14. VETERANS ADMINISTRATION MEDICAL CENTERS (VAMC): INPATIENT AND
OUTPATIENT MEDICAL AND DENTAL CARE BY VAMC IN FLORIDA
FISCAL YEAR 1995

Item	Bay Pines	Gaines- ville	Lake City	Miami	Tampa	West Palm Beach
Inpatient medical care						
Hospitals						
Average operating beds 1/ 2/	533	348	267	603	513	132
Medical 3/	263	125	179	332	271	72
Surgical	122	133	42	85	128	32
Psychiatric	148	98	46	186	114	28
Patients treated 2/ 4/	10,864	8,924	5,782	10,718	12,550	715
Medical 3/	6,227	3,684	3,735	6,469	6,439	345
Surgical	2,654	3,868	1,246	2,177	4,042	167
Psychiatric	1,983	1,372	801	2,072	2,069	203
Average daily census 5/	377	255	202	407	380	17
Nursing homes						
Patients treated in VAMC facility	497	164	285	404	486	63
Patients treated in community						
home 6/	481	152	50	167	443	67
State home	0	202	0	0	0	0
Domiciliaries						
Patients treated in VAMC facility	596	0	0	0	0	0
State home	0	0	241	0	0	0
Outpatient medical care						
Visits to VAMC staff	284,490	249,499	96,761	342,861	422,169	116,803
Fee basis care	55,429	321	733	0	681	114
Inpatient dental care						
Patients treated in VAMC facility	3,777	513	19,137	3,665	1,319	227
Outpatient dental care						
Visits to VAMC staff	8,765	3,528	2,770	9,578	8,337	6,034
Fee based cases completed	1,125	0	1	0	0	0

1/ Based on the number of operating beds at the end of each month for 13 consecutive months (September 1994 through September 1995).

2/ Beds are classified according to their intended use; patients are classified
according to the classification of the beds they occupy, rather than on a diagnostic
basis.

3/ Medical bed section includes medicine, neurology, intermediate care, spinal
cord injury, rehabilitation medicine, and blind rehabilitation.

4/ The number of discharges and deaths during the fiscal year plus the patients
remaining on September 30, 1995, plus the number of interhospital transfers.

5/ Number of patient days during the fiscal year divided by the number of days in
the fiscal year.

6/ Authorized and paid for by Veterans Administration.

Source: U.S., Department of Veterans Affairs, *Annual Report of the Secretary of
Veterans Affairs, Fiscal Year 1995.*

University of Florida   **Bureau of Economic and Business Research**

Community Health Purchasing Alliance (CHPA) Regions

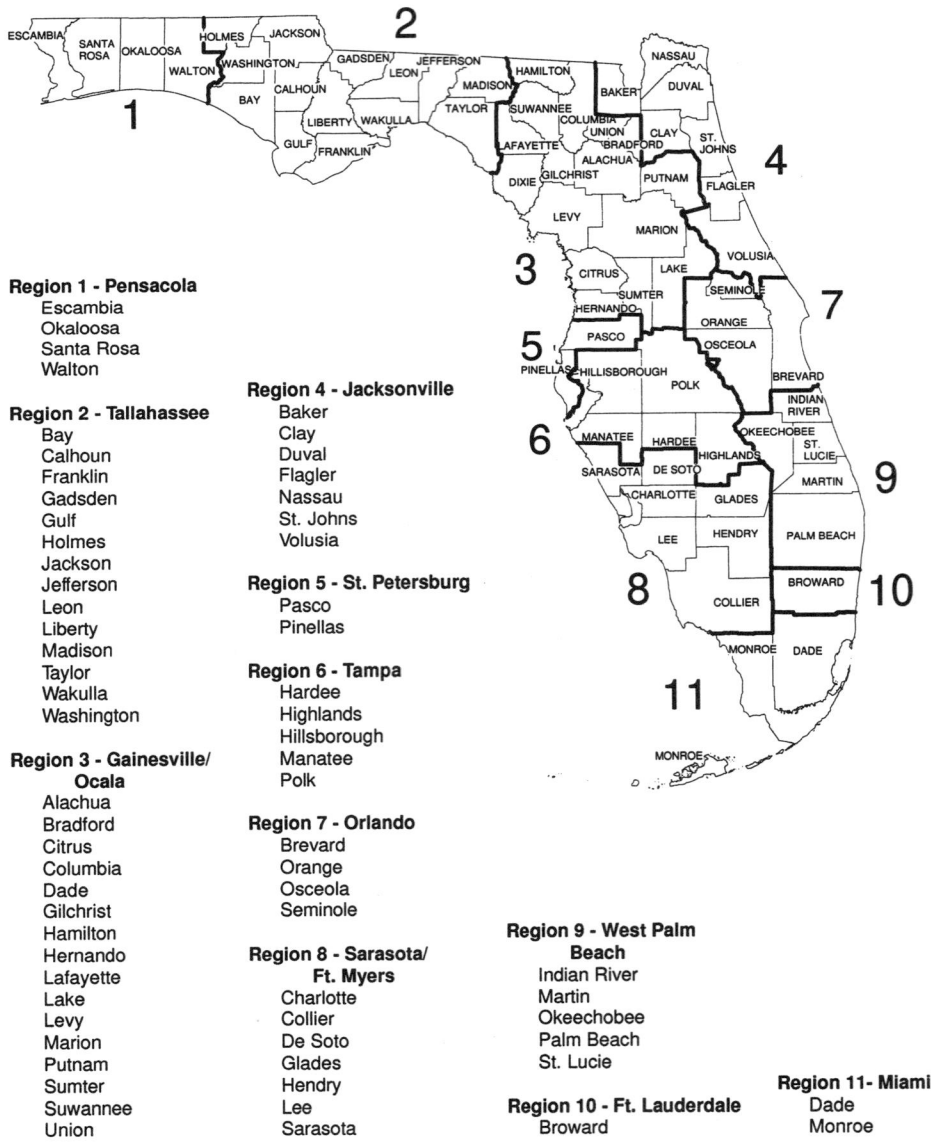

Region 1 - Pensacola
Escambia
Okaloosa
Santa Rosa
Walton

Region 2 - Tallahassee
Bay
Calhoun
Franklin
Gadsden
Gulf
Holmes
Jackson
Jefferson
Leon
Liberty
Madison
Taylor
Wakulla
Washington

Region 3 - Gainesville/ Ocala
Alachua
Bradford
Citrus
Columbia
Dade
Gilchrist
Hamilton
Hernando
Lafayette
Lake
Levy
Marion
Putnam
Sumter
Suwannee
Union

Region 4 - Jacksonville
Baker
Clay
Duval
Flagler
Nassau
St. Johns
Volusia

Region 5 - St. Petersburg
Pasco
Pinellas

Region 6 - Tampa
Hardee
Highlands
Hillsborough
Manatee
Polk

Region 7 - Orlando
Brevard
Orange
Osceola
Seminole

Region 8 - Sarasota/ Ft. Myers
Charlotte
Collier
De Soto
Glades
Hendry
Lee
Sarasota

Region 9 - West Palm Beach
Indian River
Martin
Okeechobee
Palm Beach
St. Lucie

Region 10 - Ft. Lauderdale
Broward

Region 11- Miami
Dade
Monroe

Table 20.15. HOSPITALS: NUMBER OF GENERAL, SHORT-TERM ACUTE CARE HOSPITALS AND
NUMBER OF LICENSED AND ACUTE CARE BEDS IN THE STATE, COMMUNITY HEALTH
PURCHASING ALLIANCE (CHPA) REGIONS, AND COUNTIES OF FLORIDA, 1994

CHPA and county 1/	Number of hospitals	Licensed beds Total	Acute care	CHPA and county 1/	Number of hospitals	Licensed beds Total	Acute care
Florida	202	55,668	48,680	CHPA 4 (Cont.)			
				Volusia	7	1,452	1,268
CHPA 1	10	2,189	1,774	Nassau	1	54	54
Escambia	3	1,463	1,116	St. Johns	1	230	222
Okaloosa	3	432	374	CHPA 5	22	5,647	5,001
Santa Rosa	3	244	234	Pasco	5	1,032	916
Walton	1	50	50	Pinellas	17	4,615	4,085
CHPA 2	14	2,002	1,758	CHPA 6	20	6,543	5,672
Bay	2	529	507	Highlands	2	277	260
Calhoun	1	36	36	Hillsborough	10	3,454	3,052
Franklin	1	29	29	Manatee	2	895	795
Gadsden	1	51	51	Polk	6	1,917	1,565
Gulf	1	45	45	CHPA 7	13	5,194	4,567
Holmes	1	34	34	Brevard	4	1,191	1,146
Jackson	2	157	157	Orange	6	3,402	2,900
Leon	2	950	728	Osceola	1	169	169
Madison	1	42	42	Seminole	2	432	352
Taylor	1	48	48	CHPA 8	15	4,349	3,735
Washington	1	81	81	Charlotte	3	669	582
CHPA 3	21	3,672	3,373	Collier	1	434	381
Alachua	3	1,349	1,165	De Soto	1	82	82
Bradford	1	54	54	Hendry	1	66	66
Citrus	2	299	283	Lee	5	1,536	1,423
Columbia	2	203	178	Sarasota	4	1,562	1,201
Hamilton	1	42	42	CHPA 9	21	4,908	4,419
Hernando	3	370	370	Indian River	2	480	410
Lake	3	544	500	Martin	1	336	331
Levy	1	40	40	Okeechobee	1	101	101
Marion	2	553	553	Palm Beach	15	3,478	3,167
Putnam	1	161	131	St. Lucie	2	513	410
Suwannee	1	30	30	CHPA 10	18	5,889	5,257
Union	1	27	27	Broward	18	5,889	5,257
CHPA 4	19	4,874	4,279	CHPA 11	29	10,401	8,845
Clay	1	224	196	Dade	26	10,132	8,621
Duval	8	2,833	2,458	Monroe	3	269	224
Flagler	1	81	81				

1/ CHPA regions are state-chartered, not-for-profit, private purchasing organizations with exclusive territories that were authorized by the 1993 Legislature to assist their members in securing the highest quality health care at the lowest possible
price. CHPA membership is voluntary and available primarily to businesses that have
50 or fewer employees. See accompanying map for counties in CHPA regions.
Note: Based on reports from 202 hospitals statewide. Reports include some teaching and specialty hospitals. For the most part, data are for general, short-term
acute care hospitals offering more intensive services than those required for room,
board, personal services, and general nursing care. See Glossary for definitions.

Source: State of Florida, Agency for Health Care Administration, *1996 Guide to
Hospitals in Florida.*

Table 20.16. HOSPITALS: DISCHARGES OF PATIENTS OF GENERAL, SHORT-TERM ACUTE CARE HOSPITALS BY SERVICE LINE IN THE STATE, COMMUNITY HEALTH PURCHASING ALLIANCE (CHPA) REGIONS, AND COUNTIES OF FLORIDA, 1994

CHPA and county 1/	Total	Cardiology 2/	Gastroenterology	General surgery	Gynecology 3/	Neonatology	Neurology 4/	Oncology	Orthopedics	Other medicine 5/
Florida	1,484,242	291,899	111,460	149,298	224,991	47,686	86,083	48,150	129,702	394,973
CHPA 1	58,143	10,167	4,400	5,756	9,949	2,050	2,895	2,145	5,354	15,427
Escambia	40,081	7,237	2,649	4,260	7,085	1,658	2,051	1,832	3,452	9,857
Okaloosa	11,365	1,806	942	970	2,044	331	517	216	1,234	3,305
Santa Rosa	5,940	948	692	470	769	61	271	97	668	1,964
Walton	757	176	117	56	51	0	56	0	0	301
CHPA 2	52,685	8,792	4,164	4,561	10,128	1,508	3,082	881	4,364	15,205
Bay	17,070	3,113	1,465	1,741	2,578	380	1,032	358	1,608	4,795
Calhoun	396	100	46	0	0	0	37	0	0	213
Franklin	547	97	89	0	0	0	0	0	44	317
Gadsden	588	53	89	0	31	0	31	0	0	384
Gulf	326	86	71	0	0	0	0	0	0	169
Holmes	882	167	96	40	0	0	47	0	0	532
Jackson	3,758	504	374	228	921	54	179	0	304	1,194
Leon	27,126	4,272	1,713	2,445	6,566	1,074	1,645	523	2,408	6,480
Madison	221	46	0	0	0	0	0	0	0	175
Taylor	641	87	110	63	32	0	30	0	0	319
Washington	1,130	267	111	44	0	0	81	0	0	627
CHPA 3	118,058	23,089	9,645	12,495	16,892	2,445	7,061	3,401	10,160	32,870
Alachua	42,378	6,046	2,896	4,488	7,481	1,642	2,374	1,693	4,278	11,480
Bradford	689	168	105	0	0	0	63	0	0	353
Citrus	11,563	2,321	1,147	1,304	1,269	86	727	317	920	3,472
Columbia	4,577	1,007	533	250	487	71	244	32	120	1,833
Hamilton	346	64	49	0	0	0	0	0	0	233
Hernando	13,257	3,247	1,304	1,507	1,120	104	885	255	965	3,870
Lake	17,375	3,265	1,476	1,998	3,025	276	1,131	435	1,390	4,379
Levy	694	244	97	0	0	0	62	0	0	291
Marion	21,260	5,397	1,526	2,621	2,879	193	1,248	594	2,074	4,728

See footnotes at end of table.

Continued . . .

Table 20.16. HOSPITALS: DISCHARGES OF PATIENTS OF GENERAL, SHORT-TERM ACUTE CARE HOSPITALS BY SERVICE LINE IN THE STATE, COMMUNITY HEALTH PURCHASING ALLIANCE (CHPA) REGIONS, AND COUNTIES OF FLORIDA, 1994 (Continued)

CHPA and county 1/	Total	Cardiology 2/	Gastroenterology	General surgery	Gynecology 3/	Neonatology	Neurology 4/	Oncology	Orthopedics	Other medicine 5/
CHPA 3 (Continued)										
Putnam	5,384	1,263	427	327	631	73	327	75	326	1,935
Suwannee	179	0	36	0	0	0	0	0	0	143
Union	356	67	49	0	0	0	0	0	87	153
CHPA 4	125,775	25,531	9,900	14,402	10,972	4,013	8,077	3,753	11,597	37,530
Clay	7,809	1,275	599	717	1,803	196	391	122	664	2,042
Duval	74,591	15,049	5,205	8,534	6,359	3,015	4,593	2,427	6,645	22,764
Flagler	1,074	262	133	88	0	0	105	0	123	363
Nassau	1,022	194	106	138	88	57	47	0	65	327
St. Johns	5,935	1,015	805	745	324	90	439	110	358	2,049
Volusia	35,344	7,736	3,052	4,180	2,398	655	2,502	1,094	3,742	9,985
CHPA 5	144,848	31,395	12,150	16,063	15,721	2,996	9,619	3,838	14,837	38,229
Pasco	32,160	9,495	3,210	3,584	657	329	2,211	741	2,815	9,118
Pinellas	112,688	21,900	8,940	12,479	15,064	2,667	7,408	3,097	12,022	29,111
CHPA 6	171,931	28,244	12,186	16,219	32,318	6,434	9,471	6,868	15,524	44,667
Highlands	10,775	1,931	1,091	975	1,194	199	690	285	643	3,767
Hillsborough	92,969	12,568	5,773	8,976	19,904	3,935	5,193	4,030	8,765	23,825
Manatee	21,979	4,671	1,773	2,376	3,283	493	1,333	728	2,260	5,062
Polk	46,208	9,074	3,549	3,892	7,937	1,807	2,255	1,825	3,856	12,013
CHPA 7	170,563	34,194	11,633	16,098	33,994	5,642	8,428	5,265	13,079	42,230
Brevard	44,814	9,645	3,630	4,214	6,772	1,171	2,637	1,336	3,794	11,615
Orange	108,020	21,667	6,727	10,110	22,845	3,916	4,962	3,456	8,169	26,168
Osceola	7,331	1,022	395	650	2,367	275	298	144	374	1,806
Seminole	10,398	1,860	881	1,124	2,010	280	531	329	742	2,641
CHPA 8	113,230	25,416	9,591	12,867	9,095	2,412	7,220	4,301	13,964	28,364
Charlotte	17,082	3,945	1,273	1,797	2,198	321	1,007	573	1,489	4,479

See footnotes at end of table.

Continued . . .

Table 20.16. HOSPITALS: DISCHARGES OF PATIENTS OF GENERAL, SHORT-TERM ACUTE CARE HOSPITALS BY SERVICE LINE IN THE STATE, COMMUNITY HEALTH PURCHASING ALLIANCE (CHPA) REGIONS, AND COUNTIES OF FLORIDA, 1994 (Continued)

CHPA and county 1/	Total	Cardiology 2/	Gastroenterology	General surgery	Gynecology 3/	Neonatology	Neurology 4/	Oncology	Orthopedics	Other medicine 5/
CHPA 8 (Continued)										
Collier	15,059	2,550	1,586	1,626	649	347	1,248	637	2,137	4,279
De Soto	2,407	438	214	191	556	94	131	0	0	783
Hendry	941	189	123	90	0	0	81	0	0	458
Lee	40,136	9,425	3,405	4,718	1,363	1,197	2,516	1,380	5,816	10,316
Sarasota	37,605	8,869	2,990	4,445	4,329	453	2,237	1,711	4,522	8,049
CHPA 9	151,722	30,718	11,315	15,052	23,087	4,904	9,403	5,539	13,697	38,007
Indian River	11,764	2,125	1,055	1,363	1,319	271	872	546	1,271	2,942
Martin	10,885	2,109	976	1,413	423	315	812	677	1,177	2,983
Okeechobee	3,201	790	360	275	58	0	236	44	88	1,350
Palm Beach	110,383	22,844	7,778	10,456	18,832	3,753	6,418	3,833	9,800	26,669
St. Lucie	15,489	2,850	1,146	1,545	2,455	565	1,065	439	1,361	4,063
CHPA 10	142,556	30,699	10,086	13,400	24,129	5,013	7,717	4,472	10,848	36,192
Broward	142,556	30,699	10,086	13,400	24,129	5,013	7,717	4,472	10,848	36,192
CHPA 11	234,731	43,654	16,390	22,385	38,706	10,269	13,110	7,687	16,278	66,252
Dade	228,939	42,860	15,935	21,702	37,752	10,190	12,846	7,534	15,639	64,481
Monroe	5,792	794	455	683	954	79	264	153	639	1,771

1/ CHPA regions are state-chartered, not-for-profit, private purchasing organizations with exclusive territories that were authorized by the 1993 Legislature to assist their members in securing the highest quality health care at the lowest possible price. See accompanying map for counties in CHPA regions.
2/ Includes cardiac surgery.
3/ Includes obstetrics.
4/ Includes neurosurgery.
5/ Includes pediatrics, pulmonary medicine, and urology.
Note: Based on reports from 202 hospitals statewide. Reports include some teaching and specialty hospitals. For the most part, data are for general, short-term acute care hospitals which offer more intensive services than those required for room, board, personal services, and general nursing care. See Glossary for definitions.

Source: State of Florida, Agency for Health Care Administration, *1996 Guide to Hospitals in Florida.*

Table 20.17. HOSPITALS: PEDIATRIC DISCHARGES FROM GENERAL, SHORT-TERM ACUTE
CARE HOSPITALS AND AVERAGE CHARGES FOR SERVICES TO PATIENTS AGED
28 DAYS TO 17 YEARS IN THE STATE, COMMUNITY HEALTH PURCHASING
ALLIANCE (CHPA) REGIONS, AND COUNTIES OF FLORIDA, 1994

CHPA and county 1/	Pediatric discharges	Average charges (dollars)	CHPA and county 1/	Pediatric discharges	Average charges (dollars)
Florida	90,795	(X)	CHPA 5	6,082	(X)
			Pasco	538	A/ 12,500
CHPA 1	3,718	(X)	Pinellas	5,544	A/ 38,800
Escambia	2,828	A/ 16,700	CHPA 6	10,558	(X)
Okaloosa	565	A/ 11,300	Highlands	793	9,800
Santa Rosa	293	A/ 5,400	Hillsborough	6,829	A/ 55,000
Walton	32	(NA)	Manatee	699	A/ 5,500
CHPA 2	3,323	(X)	Polk	2,237	A/ 22,500
Bay	984	11,600	CHPA 7	11,478	(X)
Franklin	33	(NA)	Brevard	2,454	17,200
Gadsden	138	3,500	Orange	8,340	27,000
Holmes	54	(NA)	Osceola	396	4,900
Jackson	247	7,500	Seminole	288	A/ 4,500
Leon	1,758	A/ 5,700	CHPA 8	4,615	(X)
Taylor	62	(NA)	Charlotte	1,069	12,500
Washington	47	(NA)	Collier	915	4,900
CHPA 3	7,544	(X)	De Soto	167	4,500
Alachua	4,711	21,800	Hendry	47	(NA)
Citrus	194	A/ 6,300	Lee	1,845	A/ 17,500
Columbia	404	A/ 3,500	Sarasota	572	A/ 4,300
Hamilton	46	(NA)	CHPA 9	7,916	(X)
Hernando	472	A/ 8,500	Indian River	215	7,200
Lake	651	A/ 9,100	Martin	512	4,300
Marion	544	A/ 4,500	Okeechobee	210	5,500
Putnam	464	A/ 6,600	Palm Beach	6,045	A/ 52,300
Union	58	(NA)	St. Lucie	934	10,900
CHPA 4	7,805	(X)	CHPA 10	8,471	(X)
Clay	224	5,400	Broward	8,471	A/ 56,800
Duval	5,848	A/ 31,500	CHPA 11	19,285	(X)
St. Johns	256	3,900	Dade	18,891	A/ 83,600
Volusia	1,477	A/ 13,900	Monroe	394	A/ 3,000

(X) Not applicable.
(NA) Not available.
A/ Excludes hospitals treating fewer than 100 pediatric cases.
1/ CHPA regions are state-chartered, not-for-profit, private purchasing organizations with exclusive territories that were authorized by the 1993 Legislature to assist their members in securing the highest quality health care at the lowest possible
price. CHPA membership is voluntary and available primarily to businesses that have
50 or fewer employees. See accompanying map for counties in CHPA regions.
     Note: Based on reports from 202 hospitals statewide. Reports include some teach-
ing and specialty hospitals. For the most part, data are for general, short-term
acute care hospitals offering more intensive services than those required for room,
board, personal services, and general nursing care. See Glossary for definitions.

     Source: State of Florida, Agency for Health Care Administration, *1996 Guide to
Hospitals in Florida.*

Table 20.25. MANAGED HEALTH CARE: LICENSED HEALTH MAINTENANCE ORGANIZATIONS (HMOS)
ENROLLMENT AND RATES BY TYPE OF PLAN IN THE STATE, LOCAL HEALTH COUNCIL
DISTRICTS, AND COUNTIES OF FLORIDA, 1996

District and county	All plans Number	Rate	Commercial Number	Rate	Medicaid and prepaid health plans Number	Rate 1/	Medicare Number	Rate
Florida	3,858,916	266.7	2,848,188	272.2	488,929	317.9	521,799	211.8
Northwest--1	86,514	147.4	79,417	173.0	7,097	114.3	0	0.0
Escambia	62,309	217.2	55,856	259.0	6,453	169.5	0	0.0
Okaloosa	7,962	48.0	7,962	57.6	0	0.0	0	0.0
Santa Rosa	15,307	153.6	14,663	181.2	644	75.4	0	0.0
Walton	936	27.4	936	38.4	0	0.0	0	0.0
Big Bend--2	147,263	243.7	134,494	289.2	10,210	130.4	2,559	42.0
Bay	7,830	55.2	6,157	57.2	1,673	96.0	0	0.0
Calhoun	4	0.3	4	0.5	0	0.0	0	0.0
Franklin	8	0.8	8	1.1	0	0.0	0	0.0
Gadsden	16,699	367.5	13,653	428.4	2,708	269.8	338	95.5
Gulf	3	0.2	3	0.3	0	0.0	0	0.0
Holmes	0	0.0	0	0.0	0	0.0	0	0.0
Jackson	0	0.0	0	0.0	0	0.0	0	0.0
Jefferson	5,157	379.0	4,356	439.3	728	316.2	73	52.5
Leon	96,715	436.4	90,457	489.2	4,328	226.1	1,930	110.0
Liberty	599	86.0	599	112.0	0	0.0	0	0.0
Madison	2,325	126.0	1,855	141.1	470	138.4	0	0.0
Taylor	879	47.6	879	67.2	0	0.0	0	0.0
Wakulla	8,191	463.3	7,670	559.5	303	148.6	218	112.7
Washington	8,853	455.9	8,853	671.3	0	0.0	0	0.0
North Central--3	118,737	103.1	68,109	88.0	32,434	229.5	18,194	77.1
Alachua	40,047	199.0	28,720	179.5	8,104	336.1	3,223	188.1
Bradford	4,437	180.1	2,927	158.5	1,003	277.1	507	198.5
Citrus	4,479	41.1	2,001	31.4	748	73.3	1,730	49.3
Columbia	5,249	102.1	3,235	87.0	1,340	162.9	674	112.2
Dixie	980	76.7	294	34.5	365	152.8	321	170.7
Gilchrist	1,848	149.7	1,298	142.5	213	130.3	337	211.0
Hamilton	687	53.4	687	72.9	0	0.0	0	0.0
Hernando	17,691	143.5	7,417	102.6	4,936	449.4	5,338	133.5
Lafayette	5	0.8	5	1.0	0	0.0	0	0.0
Lake	14,883	81.7	10,426	90.9	4,457	233.7	0	0.0
Levy	4,580	149.6	2,858	139.0	799	179.7	923	164.9
Marion	15,929	68.7	3,878	25.4	7,834	271.3	4,217	83.4
Putnam	2,468	34.8	295	6.5	2,173	167.2	0	0.0
Sumter	31	0.8	31	1.3	0	0.0	0	0.0
Suwannee	4,321	139.7	3,160	145.0	237	51.9	924	201.6
Union	1,102	85.3	877	81.2	225	174.6	0	0.0
Northeast Central--4	466,055	315.0	360,230	319.3	41,498	293.6	64,327	306.2
Baker	6,783	328.5	5,905	360.2	442	168.8	436	265.9
Clay	35,599	284.9	31,034	289.9	1,593	248.6	2,972	258.1
Duval	279,092	382.6	226,343	393.3	30,824	382.5	21,925	299.1
Flagler	6,901	176.9	2,871	116.1	579	205.2	3,451	301.4
Nassau	15,533	310.7	13,000	320.1	555	149.6	1,938	349.4
St. Johns	13,513	133.3	10,260	133.2	1,657	223.8	1,596	94.2
Volusia	108,634	262.3	70,777	246.9	5,848	154.7	32,009	356.9

See footnotes at end of table.   Continued . . .

Table 20.25. MANAGED HEALTH CARE: LICENSED HEALTH MAINTENANCE ORGANIZATIONS (HMOS) ENROLLMENT AND RATES BY TYPE OF PLAN IN THE STATE, LOCAL HEALTH COUNCIL DISTRICTS, AND COUNTIES OF FLORIDA, 1996 (Continued)

District and county	All plans		Commercial		Medicaid and prepaid health plans		Medicare	
	Number	Rate	Number	Rate	Number	Rate 1/	Number	Rate
Suncoast--5	348,919	291.2	243,288	308.3	36,462	358.7	69,169	224.9
Pasco	83,057	265.2	50,900	269.0	7,740	274.2	24,417	254.9
Pinellas	265,862	300.4	192,388	320.7	28,722	391.1	44,752	211.3
West Central--6	431,785	253.4	324,142	266.1	72,009	359.6	35,634	124.9
Hardee	551	23.9	551	36.7	0	0.0	0	0.0
Highlands	3,242	40.8	1,704	37.8	1,537	180.5	1	0.0
Hillsborough	335,387	368.8	258,902	374.0	43,976	399.1	32,509	303.4
Manatee	27,464	114.8	19,512	124.8	4,839	248.5	3,113	49.1
Polk	65,141	143.9	43,473	140.4	21,657	380.2	11	0.1
East Central--7	450,296	262.5	369,677	273.0	40,997	268.7	39,622	189.9
Brevard	50,827	111.0	42,303	123.8	8,524	237.4	0	0.0
Orange	250,542	322.0	205,091	329.8	21,861	271.3	23,590	311.9
Osceola	47,211	328.7	36,339	329.9	4,486	310.0	6,386	336.0
Seminole	101,716	303.2	85,944	306.8	6,126	283.6	9,646	285.4
Southwest--8	89,015	81.6	72,935	101.1	11,899	153.8	4,181	14.3
Charlotte	5,977	45.0	5,038	64.1	733	96.8	206	4.4
Collier	1,271	6.5	1,251	9.2	0	0.0	20	0.4
De Soto	15	0.5	15	0.8	0	0.0	0	0.0
Glades	0	0.0	0	0.0	0	0.0	0	0.0
Hendry	488	16.1	379	17.6	0	0.0	109	37.4
Lee	47,654	122.6	38,283	144.0	7,946	274.7	1,425	15.2
Sarasota	33,610	109.1	27,969	144.0	3,220	200.1	2,421	24.7
Treasure Coast--9	333,338	235.0	227,976	231.9	28,542	265.1	76,820	234.7
Indian River	1,673	16.3	828	12.2	0	0.0	845	30.1
Martin	4,587	39.7	2,680	35.0	1,142	150.3	765	24.3
Okeechobee	1,876	55.1	1,328	53.5	548	140.2	0	0.0
Palm Beach	312,813	316.4	215,161	310.1	24,637	355.4	73,015	323.8
St. Lucie	12,389	69.9	7,979	66.6	2,215	109.5	2,195	59.3
Broward Regional--10	516,300	371.9	335,062	328.5	75,964	686.7	105,274	408.5
Broward	516,300	371.9	335,062	328.5	75,964	686.7	105,274	408.5
South--11	870,694	408.9	632,858	407.5	131,817	361.2	106,019	501.8
Dade	868,119	424.6	630,773	423.7	131,817	366.8	105,529	537.0
Monroe	2,575	30.4	2,085	32.4	0	0.0	490	33.2

1/ Based on the total population under age 65 and who are Medicaid eligible (see Table 7.21). Only persons eligible for Medicaid based upon being an Aid to Families with Dependent Children (AFDC) recipient are eligible for the prepaid plans.

Note: Rates are per 1,000 population and are based on Office of the Governor, July 1, 1993, population estimates. Local health councils were established in 1982 by the legislature to serve 11 planning districts throughout the state. These councils are responsible for establishing and maintaining the district health plans.

Source: State of Florida, Agency for Health Care Administration, *Florida 1997 Health Data SourceBook.* Compiled by Local Health Councils of Florida.

University of Florida   **Bureau of Economic and Business Research**

Table 20.27. EDUCATIONAL SERVICES: AVERAGE MONTHLY PRIVATE REPORTING UNITS
EMPLOYMENT, AND PAYROLL COVERED BY UNEMPLOYMENT COMPENSATION LAW
IN THE STATE AND COUNTIES OF FLORIDA, 1995 and 1996

County	Number of reporting units	Number of employees	Payroll ($1,000)	County	Number of reporting units	Number of employees	Payroll ($1,000)

Educational services, 1995 A/ (SIC code 82)

County	Number of reporting units	Number of employees	Payroll ($1,000)	County	Number of reporting units	Number of employees	Payroll ($1,000)
Florida	1,777	47,768	89,102	Manatee	18	204	294
				Marion	11	200	233
Alachua	35	620	824	Martin	11	137	212
Bay	13	142	180	Monroe	10	186	270
Brevard	49	1,467	2,804	Okaloosa	10	87	99
Broward	193	5,751	10,794	Orange	129	3,099	5,930
Charlotte	10	99	144	Osceola	16	187	261
Clay	13	227	355	Palm Beach	142	3,160	5,686
Collier	19	484	873	Pinellas	16	454	758
Dade	311	12,986	27,750	Pinellas	138	2,562	5,030
Duval	99	2,808	4,312	Polk	37	1,540	2,413
Escambia	37	1,345	2,094	St. Lucie	7	161	214
Hillsborough	130	2,987	5,474	Santa Rosa	5	12	18
Indian River	11	359	588	Sarasota	39	667	1,216
Lake	14	296	468	Seminole	54	957	1,610
Lee	36	651	919	Volusia	42	2,533	5,299
Leon	42	458	629	Multicounty 1/	25	80	193

Vocational schools, 1995 A/ (SIC code 824)

County	Number of reporting units	Number of employees	Payroll ($1,000)	County	Number of reporting units	Number of employees	Payroll ($1,000)
Florida	303	3,512	6,544	Duval	17	193	285
				Hillsborough	21	152	341
Bay	4	9	11	Orange	27	371	914
Brevard	7	31	42	Palm Beach	29	178	288
Broward	31	536	1,018	Pinellas	24	190	443
Dade	59	957	1,567	Volusia	11	114	198

See footnotes at end of table.   Continued . . .

Table 20.27. EDUCATIONAL SERVICES: AVERAGE MONTHLY PRIVATE REPORTING UNITS EMPLOYMENT, AND PAYROLL COVERED BY UNEMPLOYMENT COMPENSATION LAW IN THE STATE AND COUNTIES OF FLORIDA, 1995 and 1996 (Continued)

County	Number of re- porting units	Number of em- ployees	Payroll ($1,000)	·County	Number of re- porting units	Number of em- ployees	Payroll ($1,000)
			Educational services, 1996 B/ (SIC code 82)				
Florida	1,921	50,514	98,243	Manatee	25	278	388
				Marion	12	202	244
Alachua	42	701	921	Martin	13	150	247
Bay	13	148	200	Monroe	10	195	305
Brevard	56	1,528	2,915	Nassau	6	14	17
Broward	202	6,341	13,093	Okaloosa	8	89	99
Charlotte	10	82	121	Orange	142	3,361	6,610
Citrus	3	38	59	Osceola	18	195	268
Clay	12	279	500	Palm Beach	146	3,452	6,602
Collier	20	516	986	Pasco	21	471	831
Columbia	5	49	45	Pinellas	147	2,699	5,400
Dade	326	13,131	29,177	Polk	40	1,642	2,518
Duval	112	2,909	4,748	Putnam	3	17	17
Escambia	40	1,491	2,445	St. Johns	13	324	615
Hernando	4	109	116	St. Lucie	8	165	231
Hillsborough	137	3,168	6,036	Santa Rosa	6	19	34
Indian River	14	394	663	Sarasota	46	741	1,427
Lake	15	301	487	Seminole	56	1,002	1,837
Lee	36	646	963	Volusia	44	2,607	5,600
Leon	45	527	750	Multicounty 1/	37	165	304
			Vocational schools, 1996 B/ (SIC code 824)				
Florida	313	4,007	7,983	Hillsborough	20	153	378
				Lee	6	18	16
Alachua	8	154	193	Leon	8	39	52
Bay	3	9	11	Orange	28	399	1,044
Brevard	7	35	83	Palm Beach	28	345	675
Broward	30	534	1,039	Pinellas	26	258	615
Dade	62	1,059	1,838	Polk	4	68	142
Duval	19	217	394	Seminole	12	308	700
Escambia	7	57	215	Volusia	10	116	214

A/ Revised.
B/ Preliminary.
1/ Reporting units without a fixed location within the state or of unknown county location.
Note: Private employment. See Table 20.05 for a list of educational services in- cluded. Only counties for which data are disclosed are shown. Detail may not add to totals due to disclosure editing and/or rounding. See tables 23.70, 23.71, 23.72, 23.73, and 23.74 for public employment data.

Source: State of Florida, Department of Labor and Employment Security, Bureau of Labor Market Information, "Employment and Wages" (ES-202), unpublished data.

Table 20.28. SOCIAL SERVICES: AVERAGE MONTHLY PRIVATE EMPLOYMENT COVERED
BY UNEMPLOYMENT COMPENSATION LAW BY TYPE OF SOCIAL SERVICE
IN THE STATE AND COUNTIES OF FLORIDA, 1996

County	Total (SIC 83)	Individual and family (SIC 832)	Job training and vocational reha- bilitation (SIC 833)	Child day care (SIC 835)	Resi- dential care 1/ (SIC 836)	Social services NEC 2/ (SIC 839)
Florida	110,817	23,263	10,422	30,079	38,807	8,246
Alachua	2,012	288	(NA)	680	658	238
Baker	128	(NA)	(NA)	42	(NA)	(NA)
Bay	1,234	323	84	365	437	25
Bradford	127	18	41	49	(NA)	(NA)
Brevard	2,567	478	475	1,065	489	60
Broward	10,135	1,794	600	3,683	3,331	729
Calhoun	71	(NA)	(NA)	(NA)	13	(NA)
Charlotte	558	91	29	207	225	(NA)
Citrus	495	16	(NA)	152	234	(NA)
Clay	882	101	(NA)	259	409	(NA)
Collier	1,500	282	60	383	639	136
Columbia	288	8	(NA)	170	14	(NA)
Dade	13,738	3,317	1,620	3,052	4,248	1,501
De Soto	108	36	(NA)	63	7	(NA)
Dixie	21	11	(NA)	(NA)	(NA)	(NA)
Duval	6,250	1,985	418	1,908	1,641	299
Escambia	3,433	694	(NA)	632	1,654	305
Flagler	147	79	(NA)	12	51	(NA)
Franklin	22	(NA)	(NA)	(NA)	(NA)	(NA)
Gadsden	179	(NA)	(NA)	76	32	61
Gilchrist	9	(NA)	(NA)	(NA)	(NA)	(NA)
Glades	32	(NA)	(NA)	(NA)	(NA)	(NA)
Gulf	69	(NA)	(NA)	(NA)	(NA)	(NA)
Hamilton	24	(NA)	(NA)	(NA)	(NA)	(NA)
Hardee	205	(NA)	(NA)	87	80	(NA)
Hendry	211	(NA)	15	122	53	(NA)
Hernando	513	(NA)	(NA)	65	233	(NA)
Highlands	635	(NA)	(NA)	144	258	(NA)
Hillsborough	8,452	2,290	523	2,394	2,702	543
Holmes	140	(NA)	(NA)	44	(NA)	(NA)
Indian River	830	236	(NA)	254	242	(NA)
Jackson	279	109	(NA)	76	(NA)	(NA)
Jefferson	43	(NA)	(NA)	(NA)	15	(NA)
Lafayette	(NA)	(NA)	(NA)	(NA)	(NA)	(NA)
Lake	1,411	31	60	298	930	(NA)
Lee	3,976	357	308	726	2,354	232
Leon	2,703	793	184	655	764	307
Levy	242	36	(NA)	54	(NA)	(NA)
Liberty	24	(NA)	(NA)	(NA)	(NA)	(NA)
Madison	148	(NA)	(NA)	24	(NA)	(NA)

See footnotes at end of table.   Continued . . .

Table 20.28. SOCIAL SERVICES: AVERAGE MONTHLY PRIVATE EMPLOYMENT COVERED
BY UNEMPLOYMENT COMPENSATION LAW BY TYPE OF SOCIAL SERVICE
IN THE STATE AND COUNTIES OF FLORIDA, 1996 (Continued)

County	Total (SIC 83)	Individual and family (SIC 832)	Job training and vocational reha- bilitation (SIC 833)	Child day care (SIC 835)	Resi- dential care 1/ (SIC 836)	Social services NEC 2/ (SIC 839)
Manatee	1,827	532	(NA)	323	790	(NA)
Marion	1,414	284	268	499	354	(NA)
Martin	832	166	(NA)	185	323	15
Monroe	316	120	(NA)	125	(NA)	9
Nassau	385	203	(NA)	50	(NA)	(NA)
Okaloosa	1,078	188	(NA)	478	343	12
Okeechobee	404	34	(NA)	107	(NA)	(NA)
Orange	6,634	1,348	651	1,856	2,144	636
Osceola	831	175	(NA)	205	36	(NA)
Palm Beach	7,708	1,282	1,010	2,197	2,143	1,076
Pasco	1,493	492	131	428	421	20
Pinellas	9,788	1,662	1,416	1,975	4,304	431
Polk	2,732	419	349	918	992	54
Putnam	488	48	(NA)	101	168	164
St. Johns	1,021	180	(NA)	296	520	17
St. Lucie	1,088	386	32	449	132	90
Santa Rosa	436	115	(NA)	176	137	(NA)
Sarasota	2,405	422	49	350	1,483	102
Seminole	1,851	261	197	812	553	28
Sumter	137	(NA)	(NA)	19	(NA)	(NA)
Suwannee	287	(NA)	(NA)	30	(NA)	(NA)
Taylor	54	(NA)	(NA)	23	(NA)	(NA)
Union	106	(NA)	(NA)	(NA)	(NA)	(NA)
Volusia	3,107	698	129	609	1,402	270
Wakulla	62	(NA)	(NA)	(NA)	13	(NA)
Walton	227	(NA)	(NA)	(NA)	(NA)	(NA)
Washington	149	(NA)	(NA)	34	(NA)	47
Multicounty 3/	100	(NA)	(NA)	(NA)	(NA)	(NA)

NEC Not elsewhere classified.
(NA) Not available.
1/ Residential social and personal care for children, the aged, and other persons
with limits on ability for self-care, but where medical care is not a major concern.
2/ Includes establishments primarily engaged in community improvement and social
change, such as advocacy groups, fundraising organizations (except contract or fee
basis), health and welfare councils, united fund councils, community action agencies,
etc.
3/ Reporting units without a fixed location within the state or of unknown county
location.
Note: Private employment. Data are preliminary. Detail may not add to totals
due to disclosure editing and/or rounding. See Tables 23.70, 23.71, 23.72, 23.73,
and 23.74 for public employment data.

Source: State of Florida, Department of Labor and Employment Security, Bureau of
Labor Market Information, "Employment and Wages" (ES-202), unpublished data.

Table 20.29. MUSEUMS, ART GALLERIES, BOTANICAL AND ZOOLOGICAL GARDENS: AVERAGE
MONTHLY PRIVATE REPORTING UNITS, EMPLOYMENT, AND PAYROLL COVERED
BY UNEMPLOYMENT COMPENSATION LAW IN THE STATE
AND COUNTIES OF FLORIDA, 1996

County	Number of re- porting units	Number of em- ployees	Payroll ($1,000)	County	Number of re- porting units	Number of em- ployees	Payroll ($1,000)
Museums, art galleries, botanical and zoological gardens (SIC code 84)							
Florida	163	3,506	5,204	Monroe	9	126	198
				Okaloosa	5	49	53
Bay	5	111	112	Orange	13	450	656
Broward	18	303	453	Palm Beach	18	321	565
Collier	5	50	81	Pinellas	10	165	269
Dade	16	308	558	Polk	3	83	121
Duval	5	239	355	St. Johns	13	259	279
Hillsborough	8	487	796	Sarasota	6	111	145
Lee	4	29	34				

Note: Private employment. For a list of three-digit industries included see
Table 20.05. Data are preliminary. Detail may not add to totals due to disclosure
editing and/or rounding. See Tables 23.70, 23.71, 23.72, 23.73, and 23.74 for public
employment data.

Table 20.30. MEMBERSHIP ORGANIZATIONS: AVERAGE MONTHLY PRIVATE REPORTING UNITS
EMPLOYMENT, AND PAYROLL COVERED BY UNEMPLOYMENT COMPENSATION LAW
BY INDUSTRY IN FLORIDA, 1996

SIC code	Industry	Number of re- porting units	Number of em- ployees	Payroll ($1,000)
86	Membership organizations	6,031	50,674	75,672
861	Business associations	634	3,826	9,862
862	Professional membership organizations	213	1,846	5,252
863	Labor unions and similar labor organizations	525	3,232	4,799
864	Civic, social, and fraternal organizations	3,732	30,598	36,749
865	Political organizations	56	228	428
866	Religious organizations	573	5,630	7,441
869	Membership organizations, NEC	298	5,313	11,139

NEC Not elsewhere classified.
Note: Private employment. Data are preliminary. Detail may not add to totals
due to disclosure editing and/or rounding. See Tables 23.70, 23.71, 23.72, 23.73,
and 23.74 for public employment data.

Source for Tables 20.29 and 20.30: State of Florida, Department of Labor and Employment Security, Bureau of Labor Market Information, "Employment and Wages"
(ES-202), unpublished data.

Table 20.33. PHYSICIANS: LICENSED DOCTORS OF MEDICINE AND OSTEOPATHY IN THE STATE
AND COUNTIES OF FLORIDA, JULY 7, 1997

Location of licensee	Doctors of-- Medicine	Osteopathy	Location of licensee	Doctors of-- Medicine	Osteopathy
Total 1/	47,141	4,308	Jefferson	4	0
NonFlorida	12,554	1,880	Lafayette	5	0
Unknown	1	1	Lake	266	22
Alachua	1,437	16	Lee	722	108
Baker	15	1	Leon	581	16
Bay	248	9	Levy	18	2
Bradford	14	0	Liberty	1	0
Brevard	841	43	Madison	10	2
Broward	3,424	356	Manatee	440	16
Calhoun	11	0	Marion	344	22
Charlotte	266	25	Martin	280	26
Citrus	168	22	Monroe	173	28
Clay	213	27	Nassau	42	4
Collier	374	21	Okaloosa	264	17
Columbia	90	8	Okeechobee	42	1
Dade	6,986	247	Orange	1,918	140
De Soto	33	0	Osceola	180	15
Dixie	3	3	Palm Beach	2,687	254
Duval	2,055	76	Pasco	478	53
Escambia	718	25	Pinellas	2,252	375
Flagler	39	8	Polk	742	14
Franklin	8	4	Putnam	69	6
Gadsden	39	1	St. Johns	226	13
Gilchrist	3		St. Lucie	255	15
Glades	2	1	Santa Rosa	125	7
Gulf	15	2	Sarasota	838	49
Hamilton	5	1	Seminole	556	54
Hardee	10	1	Sumter	13	2
Hendry	19	3	Suwannee	12	0
Hernando	153	11	Taylor	13	3
Highlands	131	6	Union	14	0
Hillsborough	2,605	144	Volusia	712	87
Holmes	9	0	Wakulla	10	1
Indian River	279	11	Walton	15	0
Jackson	51	2	Washington	15	1

1/ Total includes all active, involuntary inactive, and voluntary inactive licensed persons.

Source: State of Florida, Department of Business and Professional Regulation, unpublished data.

University of Florida   **Bureau of Economic and Business Research**

Table 20.35. DENTISTS AND DENTAL HYGIENISTS: NUMBER LICENSED IN THE STATE AND
COUNTIES OF FLORIDA, JULY 7, 1997

Location of licensee	Dentists	Dental hygienists	Location of licensee	Dentists	Dental hygienists
Total 1/	10,678	8,288	Jefferson	3	6
NonFlorida	2,355	1,489	Lafayette	3	2
Unknown	1	0	Lake	81	69
Alachua	214	169	Lee	198	185
Baker	5	11	Leon	120	146
Bay	61	71	Levy	4	10
Bradford	8	12	Liberty	1	1
Brevard	247	242	Madison	5	2
Broward	939	780	Manatee	112	95
Calhoun	6	4	Marion	93	130
Charlotte	57	45	Martin	82	84
Citrus	39	40	Monroe	37	38
Clay	69	96	Nassau	16	24
Collier	138	85	Okaloosa	88	93
Columbia	16	22	Okeechobee	8	10
Dade	1,455	600	Orange	431	365
De Soto	5	4	Osceola	43	33
Dixie	3	7	Palm Beach	822	624
Duval	401	369	Pasco	82	88
Escambia	145	166	Pinellas	621	529
Flagler	17	9	Polk	143	146
Franklin	2	3	Putnam	16	20
Gadsden	14	18	St. Johns	50	54
Gilchrist	1	2	St. Lucie	64	70
Glades	0	4	Santa Rosa	39	78
Gulf	5	7	Sarasota	249	171
Hamilton	3	3	Seminole	178	202
Hardee	3	0	Sumter	3	4
Hendry	7	6	Suwannee	5	7
Hernando	38	39	Taylor	3	4
Highlands	36	27	Union	1	5
Hillsborough	487	367	Volusia	194	191
Holmes	2	1	Wakulla	1	6
Indian River	70	63	Walton	10	9
Jackson	16	19	Washington	7	7

1/ Total includes all active, involuntary inactive, and voluntary inactive licensed persons.

Source: State of Florida, Department of Business and Professional Regulation, unpublished data.

University of Florida   **Bureau of Economic and Business Research**

Table 20.36. HEALTH PRACTITIONERS: NUMBER LICENSED IN THE STATE AND COUNTIES
OF FLORIDA, JULY 7, 1997

Location of licensee	Chiro- practors	Optome- trists	Podia- trists	Therapists Occupa- tional	Therapists Phys- ical	Nursing home adminis- trators	Psy- chol- ogists
Total 1/	4,728	2,127	1,757	5,529	12,121	1,905	3,203
NonFlorida	1,401	532	724	999	2,356	265	493
Unknown	0	0	1	0	0	0	0
Alachua	42	19	11	156	229	14	148
Baker	1	1	0	1	0	1	1
Bay	25	18	7	46	106	13	13
Bradford	2	2	0	3	1	4	1
Brevard	109	43	23	156	288	36	85
Broward	520	213	185	470	1,255	138	408
Calhoun	2	1	0	0	5	3	1
Charlotte	23	12	11	50	112	10	11
Citrus	17	11	4	29	55	13	2
Clay	20	16	4	35	61	16	10
Collier	55	24	14	71	140	20	19
Columbia	5	7	0	11	32	4	2
Dade	317	209	179	407	1,056	138	553
De Soto	2	2	0	3	3	3	2
Dixie	0	0	0	0	1	0	1
Duval	92	83	37	187	410	77	96
Escambia	48	27	11	56	183	21	56
Flagler	4	2	2	12	21	4	1
Franklin	1	0	1	0	2	6	0
Gadsden	3	3	2	2	5	5	15
Gilchrist	0	0	0	2	1	1	1
Glades	0	0	0	0	1	0	0
Gulf	2	1	0	3	3	1	0
Hamilton	1	1	0	0	2	2	0
Hardee	2	2	0	2	5	0	2
Hendry	4	2	0	4	4	4	1
Hernando	21	8	7	30	60	10	6
Highlands	13	6	2	18	55	13	2
Hillsborough	184	88	47	307	548	85	250
Holmes	1	0	0	1	5	2	0
Indian River	26	9	5	38	86	12	12
Jackson	3	6	0	6	10	6	4
Jefferson	0	1	0	2	0	4	0

See footnote at end of table.   Continued . . .

Table 20.36. HEALTH PRACTITIONERS: NUMBER LICENSED IN THE STATE AND COUNTIES
OF FLORIDA, JULY 7, 1997 (Continued)

Location of licensee	Chiro- practors	Optome- trists	Podia- trists	Therapists Occupa- tional	Phys- ical	Nursing home adminis- trators	Psy- chol- ogists
Lafayette	0	0	0	1	0	1	0
Lake	34	20	6	39	82	22	15
Lee	114	52	31	120	275	40	37
Leon	38	29	5	83	153	21	132
Levy	7	3	0	4	8	1	0
Liberty	0	0	0	0	0	0	0
Madison	1	4	0	3	5	2	0
Manatee	44	24	14	104	162	39	21
Marion	46	17	10	66	176	16	19
Martin	50	20	10	40	81	14	23
Monroe	21	9	0	13	41	7	11
Nassau	9	4	1	6	22	4	2
Okaloosa	26	22	5	41	73	17	20
Okeechobee	4	2	1	2	7	3	1
Orange	155	88	41	231	484	91	91
Osceola	25	12	1	32	56	14	6
Palm Beach	362	141	145	445	825	141	251
Pasco	65	28	15	86	165	37	12
Pinellas	300	108	81	414	1,031	238	146
Polk	73	40	18	98	206	50	29
Putnam	7	4	0	14	23	2	5
St. Johns	22	10	4	37	93	14	17
St. Lucie	33	10	9	50	94	15	10
Santa Rosa	8	4	0	29	69	11	10
Sarasota	140	44	35	209	358	70	65
Seminole	66	40	26	100	246	26	39
Sumter	5	2	0	4	3	2	1
Suwannee	6	1	1	4	10	5	1
Taylor	2	1	1	1	7	1	0
Union	0	0	0	0	3	0	2
Volusia	109	38	20	133	248	66	36
Wakulla	4	0	0	1	3	1	3
Walton	4	1	0	9	8	1	2
Washington	2	0	0	3	3	2	0

1/ Total includes all active, involuntary inactive, and voluntary inactive licensed persons.

Source: State of Florida, Department of Business and Professional Regulation, unpublished data.

Table 20.37.   NURSES: LICENSED REGISTERED AND PRACTICAL NURSES IN THE STATE AND
COUNTIES OF FLORIDA, JULY 7, 1997

Location of licensee	Total registered and practical nurses 1/	Registered nurses	Practical nurses	Location of licensee	Total registered and practical nurses 1/	Registered nurses	Practical nurses
Total	238,816	161,774	77,042	Jefferson	143	69	74
NonFlorida	32,033	23,021	9,012	Lafayette	45	22	23
Unknown	16	10	6	Lake	2,692	1,536	1,156
Alachua	4,495	3,537	958	Lee	6,120	4,156	1,964
Baker	229	160	69	Leon	3,092	2,213	879
Bay	2,293	1,406	887	Levy	385	216	169
Bradford	234	142	92	Liberty	51	17	34
Brevard	6,095	4,422	1,673	Madison	199	84	115
Broward	23,005	15,691	7,314	Manatee	3,695	2,328	1,367
Calhoun	155	69	86	Marion	3,053	2,104	949
Charlotte	2,328	1,433	895	Martin	1,731	1,308	423
Citrus	1,544	936	608	Monroe	1,037	848	189
Clay	2,057	1,492	565	Nassau	554	413	141
Collier	2,711	1,699	1,012	Okaloosa	2,157	1,369	788
Columbia	814	543	271	Okeechobee	386	191	195
Dade	19,628	13,613	6,015	Orange	10,215	6,855	3,360
De Soto	401	178	223	Osceola	1,526	912	614
Dixie	106	53	53	Palm Beach	13,585	9,941	3,644
Duval	9,494	7,038	2,456	Pasco	4,858	2,981	1,877
Escambia	4,533	2,729	1,804	Pinellas	17,384	11,476	5,908
Flagler	602	437	165	Polk	5,750	3,542	2,208
Franklin	125	63	62	Putnam	825	433	392
Gadsden	492	269	223	St. Johns	1,546	1,053	493
Gilchrist	144	86	58	St. Lucie	2,534	1,669	865
Glades	42	24	18	Santa Rosa	1,916	1,277	639
Gulf	172	81	91	Sarasota	6,318	4,004	2,314
Hamilton	98	44	54	Seminole	5,110	3,668	1,442
Hardee	186	81	105	Sumter	307	142	165
Hendry	258	135	123	Suwannee	525	266	259
Hernando	2,050	1,250	800	Taylor	157	62	95
Highlands	1,217	726	491	Union	136	81	55
Hillsborough	13,110	8,813	4,297	Volusia	6,647	4,334	2,313
Holmes	205	93	112	Wakulla	209	102	107
Indian River	1,602	1,114	488	Walton	346	156	190
Jackson	824	442	382	Washington	284	116	168

1/ Includes active, involuntary inactive, and voluntary inactive licensed registered and practical nurses.
Source: State of Florida, Department of Business and Professional Regulation, unpublished data.

University of Florida   **Bureau of Economic and Business Research**

Table 20.38. HEALTH-RELATED RETAILERS: LICENSED DISPENSING OPTICIANS AND
PHARMACISTS IN THE STATE AND COUNTIES OF FLORIDA, JULY 7, 1997

Location of licensee	Dispensing opticians	Phar-macists	Location of licensee	Dispensing opticians	Phar-macists
Total 1/	3,479	20,481	Jefferson	0	11
NonFlorida	241	7,490	Lafayette	0	1
Unknown	0	0	Lake	43	116
Alachua	43	379	Lee	98	334
Baker	0	7	Leon	41	268
Bay	26	126	Levy	5	14
Bradford	3	16	Liberty	0	6
Brevard	99	320	Madison	1	18
Broward	393	1,558	Manatee	46	138
Calhoun	0	14	Marion	56	158
Charlotte	22	86	Martin	21	105
Citrus	22	63	Monroe	13	63
Clay	23	74	Nassau	5	29
Collier	36	148	Okaloosa	17	100
Columbia	6	43	Okeechobee	4	13
Dade	536	1,663	Orange	131	732
De Soto	2	14	Osceola	11	61
Dixie	1	5	Palm Beach	255	984
Duval	106	600	Pasco	81	176
Escambia	37	223	Pinellas	250	1,074
Flagler	5	22	Polk	80	291
Franklin	0	9	Putnam	9	32
Gadsden	7	30	St. Johns	22	89
Gilchrist	3	4	St. Lucie	45	104
Glades	0	0	Santa Rosa	18	109
Gulf	1	7	Sarasota	94	333
Hamilton	0	4	Seminole	51	368
Hardee	1	7	Sumter	1	3
Hendry	3	12	Suwannee	1	18
Hernando	23	91	Taylor	3	7
Highlands	17	56	Union	1	6
Hillsborough	305	1,140	Volusia	84	346
Holmes	0	12	Wakulla	1	6
Indian River	22	78	Walton	6	17
Jackson	2	36	Washington	0	14

1/ Total includes all active, involuntary inactive, and voluntary inactive licensed persons.

Source: State of Florida, Department of Business and Professional Regulation, unpublished data.

University of Florida   **Bureau of Economic and Business Research**

Table 20.39. CLINICAL LAB PERSONNEL: LICENSED LAB DIRECTORS, SUPERVISORS
TECHNOLOGISTS, AND TECHNICIANS IN THE STATE AND COUNTIES OF FLORIDA
MAY 19, 1997

Location of licensee	Total	Di-rec-tors	Su-per-vi-sors	Tech-nolo-gists	Tech-ni-cians	Location of licensee	Total	Di-rec-tors	Su-per-vi-sors	Tech-nolo-gists	Tech-ni-cians
Total 1/	14,388	198	3,846	7,659	2,685	Lafayette	0	0	0	0	0
NonFlorida	874	16	192	561	105	Lake	85	1	34	40	10
Alachua	393	5	112	229	47	Lee	273	1	84	140	48
Baker	8	0	1	6	1	Leon	176	2	44	110	20
Bay	80	1	21	46	12	Levy	21	0	8	12	1
Bradford	11	0	2	6	3	Liberty	1	0	0	1	0
Brevard	499	3	145	282	69	Madison	4	0	3	1	0
Broward	1,528	19	400	717	392	Manatee	138	2	49	58	29
Calhoun	5	0	4	1	0	Marion	123	1	30	65	27
Charlotte	91	1	26	50	14	Martin	85	0	27	45	13
Citrus	95	3	27	53	12	Monroe	53	0	18	24	11
Clay	115	1	36	60	18	Nassau	28	0	5	22	1
Collier	143	4	41	72	26	Okaloosa	107	0	37	53	17
Columbia	62	0	4	47	11	Okeechobee	29	0	6	18	5
Dade	2,588	48	532	1,442	566	Orange	622	8	181	339	94
De Soto	14	0	2	9	3	Osceola	75	0	16	43	16
Dixie	4	0	0	2	2	Palm Beach	798	9	234	435	120
Duval	796	15	196	443	142	Pasco	265	2	82	117	64
Escambia	245	1	66	145	33	Pinellas	950	13	320	466	151
Flagler	21	0	7	12	2	Polk	288	4	91	146	47
Franklin	3	0	0	2	1	Putnam	33	1	9	18	5
Gadsden	19	1	5	10	3	St. Johns	89	2	27	43	17
Gilchrist	2	0	2	0	0	St. Lucie	166	1	34	107	24
Glades	2	0	0	2	0	Santa Rosa	90	0	31	45	14
Gulf	4	0	2	1	1	Sarasota	261	1	101	112	47
Hamilton	6	0	0	5	1	Seminole	216	3	69	110	34
Hardee	9	0	1	2	6	Sumter	9	0	4	3	2
Hendry	12	0	1	8	3	Suwannee	19	0	4	7	8
Hernando	81	1	18	40	22	Taylor	12	0	2	9	1
Highlands	46	0	15	22	9	Union	4	0	1	2	1
Hillsboroug	1,128	20	290	532	286	Volusia	337	5	118	167	47
Holmes	9	0	3	4	2	Wakulla	7	0	4	3	0
Indian Rive	90	2	14	63	11	Walton	11	0	2	7	2
Jackson	24	1	5	14	4	Washington	5	0	1	2	2
Jefferson	1	0	0	1	0						

1/ Total includes all licensed persons regardless of current status.
  Source: State of Florida, Department of Business and Professional Regulation,
Board of Clinical Laboratory Personnel, unpublished data.

Table 20.40. PUBLIC LIBRARIES: OPERATING EXPENDITURE AND NUMBER OF VOLUMES
IN REGIONS AND COUNTIES OF FLORIDA, FISCAL YEAR 1994-95

Area and library	Total operating expenditure (dollars)	Number of volumes 1/	Area and library	Total operating expenditure (dollars)	Number of volumes 1/
Regional and			De Soto		
multi-county			De Soto County	125,305	29,558
systems			Flagler		
Central Florida			Flagler County	259,947	52,091
Regional 2/	1,712,940	187,929	Franklin		
Charlotte-Glades	1,414,764	330,856	Apalachicola	14,069	(NA)
Jacksonville			Gadsden		
Public 3/	14,477,041	3,398,571	Gadsden County	503,962	61,336
Northwest Region-			Hardee		
al 4/	1,595,391	347,364	Hardee County	124,501	29,425
Panhandle Pub-			Hendry		
lic 5/	780,457	109,431	Hendry County	244,960	64,963
Suwannee River			Hernando		
Regional 6/	1,345,931	180,287	Hernando County	1,648,166	184,614
West Florida			Highlands		
Regional 7/	2,476,046	301,165	Highlands		
Wilderness Coast			County	573,207	99,649
Public 8/	677,474	59,873	Hillsborough		
			Bruton Memorial	483,038	77,922
County			Tampa-		
Alachua			Hillsborough	13,644,820	1,910,389
Alachua County	5,375,932	700,793	Temple Terrace	462,221	73,247
Baker			Indian River		
Emily Taber			Indian River	2,417,130	370,167
Public	60,590	41,802	Lake		
Bradford			Eustis Memorial	425,443	88,203
Bradford County	279,091	(NA)	Fruitland Park	67,224	19,710
Brevard			Lake County	1,328,667	145,028
Brevard County	10,277,152	1,126,717	Leesburg	719,200	138,372
Broward			Lee		
Broward County	29,592,610	5,071,496	Ft. Myers Beach	425,777	54,233
Oakland Park	371,899	44,998	Lee County	8,600,136	826,286
Wilton Manors	222,183	21,624	Sanibel	438,600	40,292
Lighthouse Point	228,503	42,725	Leon		
Citrus			Leon County	4,019,192	394,638
Citrus County	1,581,680	115,225	Manatee		
Clay			Manatee County	3,009,766	530,148
Clay County	1,180,017	269,661	Martin		
Collier			Martin County	2,053,076	220,297
Collier County	2,889,245	305,772	Monroe		
Columbia			Monroe County	1,515,505	204,477
Columbia County	575,944	102,800	Okaloosa		
Dade			Destin	73,453	61,720
Brockway Memo-			Ft. Walton Beach	231,154	43,000
rial	213,668	58,978	Mary Esther	90,550	13,459
Miami-Dade	30,806,419	3,863,700	Niceville	153,790	26,630
North Miami	801,597	148,753	Robert L. F.		
North Miami			Sikes	117,996	43,280
Beach	744,338	92,662	Valparaiso	96,490	21,000

See footnotes at end of table.   Continued . . .

Table 20.40. PUBLIC LIBRARIES: OPERATING EXPENDITURE AND NUMBER OF VOLUMES
IN REGIONS AND COUNTIES OF FLORIDA, FISCAL YEAR 1994-95 (Continued)

Area and library	Total operating expenditure (dollars)	Number of volumes 1/	Area and library	Total operating expenditure (dollars)	Number of volumes 1/
Okeechobee			Polk (Continued)		
Okeechobee County	169,492	35,805	Lakeland	1,342,964	292,682
Orange			Latt Maxcy Memorial	109,315	27,770
Maitland	336,543	74,068	Polk City		
Orange County	15,388,500	1,716,834	Municipal	108,035	(NA)
Winter Park	1,081,305	187,565	Winter Haven	407,649	52,739
Osceola			Putnam		
Osceola County	3,376,148	277,063	Putnam County	586,135	75,576
Palm Beach			St. Johns		
Boynton Beach	1,028,309	204,475	St. Johns County	1,683,696	176,227
Delray Beach	610,678	(NA)	St. Lucie		
Highland Beach	89,844	10,200	St. Lucie County	2,606,217	546,951
Lake Park	164,631	46,418	Sarasota		
Lake Worth	307,720	75,912	Sarasota County	4,856,796	595,949
North Palm Beach	397,440	44,228	Seminole		
Palm Beach County	15,137,412	853,764	Altamonte Springs	196,778	46,808
Palm Springs	310,061	60,446	Seminole County	4,075,951	557,515
West Palm Beach	825,078	173,588	Taylor		
Pasco			Taylor County	186,180	66,632
New Port Richey	458,782	63,773	Union		
Pasco County	3,750,079	425,242	Union County	107,085	15,740
Zephyrhills	110,030	31,963	Volusia		
Pinellas			Volusia County	6,569,329	1,047,120
Pinellas	13,957,587	1,810,061	Walton		
Polk			Walton/DeFuniak	185,083	51,699
Fort Meade	108,035	(NA)			
Haines City	114,597	37,153			
Lake Wales	219,620	37,512			

(NA) Not available.
1/ Includes volumes of books and bound periodicals.
2/ Serves Levy and Marion counties.
3/ Serves Duval and Nassau counties.
4/ Serves Bay, Gulf, and Liberty counties.
5/ Serves Calhoun, Holmes, Jackson, and Washington counties.
6/ Serves Hamilton, Madison, and Suwannee counties.
7/ Serves Escambia and Santa Rosa counties.
8/ Serves Franklin, Jefferson, and Wakulla counties.
Note: Libraries are omitted if they failed to report to the Division of Library Services or if they failed to meet or are not part of a system which met all of the following criteria: at least 10 hours of public service per week, a book collection of at least 2,000 volumes, at least 200 volumes purchased a year, and expenditure of at least $1,000 per year.

Source: State of Florida, Department of State, Division of Library and Information Services, *1996 Florida Library Directory with Statistics.*

Table 20.56. ELEMENTARY AND SECONDARY SCHOOLS: TOTAL ADMINISTRATIVE AND
INSTRUCTIONAL STAFF AND DISTRIBUTION OF ADMINISTRATIVE STAFF IN THE
STATE AND COUNTIES OF FLORIDA, FALL 1996

| County | Total staff 1/ | Administrative staff | | | | | | |
		Total	Offi-cials admin-istra-tors mana-gers	Consul-tants/ super-visors of in-struc-tion	Prin-cipals	Assist-ant prin-cipals	Commun-ity educa-tion coordi-nators	Deans/ curri-culum coordi-nators
Florida	144,038	8,594	1,953	568	2,525	3,112	102	334
Alachua	2,023	129	42	15	41	30	1	0
Baker	285	25	12	0	5	6	0	2
Bay	1,743	94	20	10	33	31	0	0
Bradford	291	23	8	0	8	6	0	1
Brevard	4,351	226	32	1	72	38	0	83
Broward	12,097	629	66	3	193	366	0	1
Calhoun	167	9	4	0	5	0	0	0
Charlotte	1,022	70	25	2	20	23	0	0
Citrus	1,025	58	18	4	18	18	0	0
Clay	1,530	108	34	4	26	44	0	0
Collier	1,918	118	30	16	32	24	5	11
Columbia	604	35	14	1	10	10	0	0
Dade	20,364	1,302	319	53	322	569	39	0
De Soto	316	23	9	0	5	6	0	3
Dixie	173	18	10	0	4	4	0	0
Duval	7,434	367	115	14	146	57	34	1
Escambia	2,928	159	36	20	63	40	0	0
Flagler	443	40	26	1	6	7	0	0
Franklin	123	12	8	0	4	0	0	0
Gadsden	605	63	26	8	15	6	0	8
Gilchrist	182	19	10	2	5	2	0	0
Glades	76	8	4	1	2	1	0	0
Gulf	169	15	5	1	7	2	0	0
Hamilton	191	20	10	1	6	1	1	1
Hardee	345	25	12	0	5	8	0	0
Hendry	451	39	16	1	11	11	0	0
Hernando	1,002	58	12	2	15	28	1	0
Highlands	718	48	15	3	15	15	0	0
Hillsborough	10,330	630	88	103	161	172	0	106
Holmes	270	17	5	0	7	5	0	0
Indian River	877	62	26	1	19	12	0	4
Jackson	631	41	14	1	16	10	0	0
Jefferson	160	18	8	2	4	2	1	1
Lafayette	82	8	3	2	2	0	0	1
Lake	1,671	101	13	5	38	29	0	16

See footnotes at end of table.   Continued . . .

Table 20.56. ELEMENTARY AND SECONDARY SCHOOLS: TOTAL ADMINISTRATIVE AND INSTRUCTIONAL STAFF AND DISTRIBUTION OF ADMINISTRATIVE STAFF IN THE STATE AND COUNTIES OF FLORIDA, FALL 1996 (Continued)

County	Total staff 1/	Administrative staff						
		Total	Offi-cials admin-istra-tors mana-gers	Consul-tants/ super-visors of in-struc-tion	Prin-cipals	Assist-ant prin-cipals	Commun-ity educa-tion coordi-nators	Deans/ curri-culum coordi-nators
Lee	3,455	227	67	20	70	55	0	15
Leon	2,279	143	32	8	45	58	0	0
Levy	410	36	16	1	12	6	1	0
Liberty	89	10	6	0	3	1	0	0
Madison	224	25	6	5	7	1	0	6
Manatee	2,122	123	27	7	37	51	1	0
Marion	2,391	147	29	13	43	40	6	16
Martin	1,035	73	19	3	20	23	5	3
Monroe	672	56	16	10	12	18	0	0
Nassau	603	43	15	0	16	7	1	4
Okaloosa	1,866	93	19	12	35	22	0	5
Okeechobee	421	32	12	0	8	10	0	2
Orange	8,650	432	62	60	135	172	0	3
Osceola	1,676	84	21	2	26	35	0	0
Palm Beach	8,787	444	56	14	133	241	0	0
Pasco	3,060	229	87	21	47	67	0	7
Pinellas	7,584	464	75	48	134	190	6	11
Polk	4,980	315	54	16	107	138	0	0
Putnam	876	61	22	4	17	18	0	0
St. Johns	1,235	95	26	11	24	29	0	5
St. Lucie	2,185	98	23	4	33	38	0	0
Santa Rosa	1,335	72	14	5	27	26	0	0
Sarasota	2,139	112	34	4	32	42	0	0
Seminole	3,320	166	20	1	49	88	0	8
Sumter	389	28	10	4	10	4	0	0
Suwannee	356	27	13	0	6	7	0	1
Taylor	281	28	11	2	8	1	0	6
Union	150	13	5	2	3	3	0	0
Volusia	3,974	223	28	7	66	122	0	0
Wakulla	287	23	11	1	5	3	0	3
Walton	363	30	10	4	8	8	0	0
Washington	247	25	12	2	6	5	0	0

1/ Administrative and instructional staff only. Excludes noninstructional, non-administrative professional staff, aides, technicians, clerical/secretarial, service workers, skilled crafts workers, and unskilled laborers.
Note: Data are for public schools only. Excludes special schools.

Source: State of Florida, Department of Education, Division of Administration, Education Information and Accountability Services, *Statistical Brief: Staff in Florida's Public Schools, Fall 1996.*

University of Florida   **Bureau of Economic and Business Research**

Table 20.57. ELEMENTARY AND SECONDARY SCHOOLS: DISTRIBUTION OF INSTRUCTIONAL
STAFF IN THE STATE AND COUNTIES OF FLORIDA, FALL 1996

County	Teachers Elementary 1/	Secondary 2/	Exceptional student education	Other	Guidance counselors	School social workers	School psychologists	Librarians/audiovisual workers	Other 3/
Florida	52,660	44,880	19,802	5,026	4,839	704	931	2,550	4,052
Alachua	672	681	295	14	68	0	14	50	100
Baker	98	110	27	2	9	0	2	6	6
Bay	567	563	297	40	67	4	12	39	60
Bradford	102	98	40	5	8	0	1	9	5
Brevard	1,776	1,264	671	88	135	7	20	87	77
Broward	4,683	3,628	1,304	910	418	99	90	202	134
Calhoun	58	57	23	3	6	0	0	5	6
Charlotte	309	380	140	13	32	4	9	17	48
Citrus	351	343	152	30	33	3	6	19	30
Clay	582	494	231	10	47	3	0	26	29
Collier	743	569	284	24	82	3	18	34	43
Columbia	235	211	77	1	18	1	2	12	12
Dade	7,986	5,545	2,576	1,155	868	101	167	327	337
De Soto	112	108	32	14	8	2	0	5	12
Dixie	66	50	25	1	3	0	0	4	6
Duval	2,988	2,204	1,112	97	199	40	36	145	246
Escambia	1,081	1,032	402	13	92	14	12	62	61
Flagler	129	152	58	27	12	0	2	6	17
Franklin	49	42	14	0	3	0	0	3	0
Gadsden	216	194	62	26	16	3	5	14	6
Gilchrist	60	65	22	3	5	1	1	4	2
Glades	32	27	5	0	2	0	0	2	0
Gulf	59	60	17	4	5	1	2	3	3
Hamilton	62	60	22	4	8	1	1	4	9
Hardee	125	116	34	16	10	0	2	7	10
Hendry	179	127	58	16	14	0	1	10	7
Hernando	353	374	101	6	43	7	7	16	37
Highlands	246	211	116	21	24	4	6	17	25
Hillsborough	4,055	2,994	1,480	212	351	100	78	195	235
Holmes	107	103	25	1	8	0	0	8	1
Indian River	326	280	115	6	20	6	6	19	37
Jackson	207	220	82	22	24	0	2	12	21
Jefferson	54	48	23	4	4	1	0	3	5
Lafayette	32	27	7	2	2	0	0	2	2
Lake	583	510	223	77	66	6	12	36	57
Lee	1,132	1,160	589	47	124	23	28	71	54

See footnotes at end of table.   Continued . . .

University of Florida   **Bureau of Economic and Business Research**

Table 20.57. ELEMENTARY AND SECONDARY SCHOOLS: DISTRIBUTION OF INSTRUCTIONAL
STAFF IN THE STATE AND COUNTIES OF FLORIDA, FALL 1996 (Continued)

County	Teachers Elementary 1/	Secondary 2/	Exceptional student education	Other	Guidance counselors	School social workers	School psychologists	Librarians/ audiovisual workers	Other 3/
Leon	744	704	350	69	81	13	16	42	117
Levy	159	129	50	4	12	2	0	10	8
Liberty	30	30	11	5	1	0	0	2	0
Madison	69	81	35	1	5	0	0	3	5
Manatee	819	645	339	23	67	14	15	39	38
Marion	918	772	306	64	69	14	15	41	45
Martin	320	348	162	45	31	3	6	20	27
Monroe	222	221	96	33	14	4	5	6	15
Nassau	213	203	92	3	22	3	3	15	6
Okaloosa	741	699	165	14	61	2	9	40	42
Okeechobee	161	128	52	12	15	0	2	8	11
Orange	2,893	2,744	1,130	436	271	46	50	112	536
Osceola	536	564	192	77	64	3	12	25	119
Palm Beach	3,056	2,889	1,440	154	252	2	56	123	371
Pasco	1,060	901	519	63	82	21	21	63	101
Pinellas	2,414	2,400	1,264	290	225	67	55	128	277
Polk	1,910	1,550	581	198	175	7	40	112	92
Putnam	340	265	97	22	33	1	6	20	31
St. Johns	419	472	129	9	46	2	6	21	36
St. Lucie	587	608	195	482	72	8	11	33	91
Santa Rosa	499	482	154	4	49	2	7	27	39
Sarasota	802	686	377	9	39	10	10	14	80
Seminole	1,211	1,221	412	42	107	19	15	54	73
Sumter	139	129	45	7	14	0	0	9	18
Suwannee	133	128	31	6	13	0	0	6	12
Taylor	103	74	39	16	6	2	1	4	8
Union	50	60	17	2	6	0	0	2	0
Volusia	1,398	1,301	674	16	145	25	26	70	96
Wakulla	97	100	42	2	8	0	0	7	8
Walton	130	139	41	0	9	0	1	8	5
Washington	72	100	24	4	11	0	1	5	5

1/ Prekindergarten and Kindergarten through grade 5 or 6.
2/ Grades 6 through 12.
3/ Nonadministrative/instructional professional staff.
Note: Data are for public schools only. Excludes special schools.

Source: State of Florida, Department of Education, Division of Administration,
Education Information and Accountability Services, *Statistical Brief: Staff in Florida's Public Schools, Fall 1996*. Series 97-26B.

Table 20.59. ELEMENTARY AND SECONDARY SCHOOLS: NUMBER AND AVERAGE SALARY OF SPECIFIED DISTRICT STAFF PERSONNEL IN THE STATE AND COUNTIES OF FLORIDA, 1996-97

(salaries in dollars)

County	Superin-tendent salary	Principals High school Num-ber	Salary	Junior high/ middle school Num-ber	Salary	Elementary Num-ber	Salary	Board members Num-ber	Salary
Florida	89,506	332	66,601	434	62,620	1,501	60,674	333	21,593
Alachua	107,000	5	66,998	8	61,985	23	55,605	5	24,590
Baker	89,797	1	59,914	1	54,366	3	56,331	5	17,875
Bay	84,480	3	63,237	7	57,685	19	55,559	5	23,135
Bradford	68,482	1	56,863	1	52,598	5	46,811	4	18,126
Brevard	110,250	10	63,183	14	55,369	48	53,431	5	27,280
Broward	167,948	23	79,790	25	76,059	119	71,895	7	28,722
Calhoun	70,635	1	57,300	1	52,300	1	53,400	5	17,027
Charlotte	96,000	3	71,590	4	63,173	9	64,781	5	22,851
Citrus	81,864	3	60,895	4	58,415	9	56,562	5	22,305
Clay	81,098	4	54,419	5	55,372	18	54,779	5	21,389
Collier	103,502	4	81,311	6	67,561	18	62,711	5	24,301
Columbia	85,379 ⁻	1	56,300	2	54,245	7	54,747	5	18,527
Dade	169,681	33	79,689	49	73,508	200	73,549	7	29,450
De Soto	64,036	1	59,386	1	54,294	3	53,239	5	16,936
Dixie	108,233	1	55,500	1	47,795	2	50,495	5	16,438
Duval	139,830	16	62,524	22	56,982	99	53,328	7	26,841
Escambia	108,756	8	59,047	12	55,460	39	52,054	5	25,652
Flagler	80,696	1	59,847	1	53,715	3	49,245	5	18,905
Franklin	69,437	1	53,061	0	0	2	52,685	5	17,257
Gadsden	79,993	5	54,552	2	51,659	7	51,872	5	19,382
Gilchrist	71,519	2	53,830	1	54,602	2	48,722	5	17,359
Glades	66,795	1	46,500	0	0	1	45,414	5	16,899
Gulf	81,479	2	53,079	1	52,592	3	50,969	5	17,444
Hamilton	71,223	1	55,445	1	52,945	3	48,308	5	17,396
Hardee	70,168	1	53,975	0	0	4	49,287	5	18,046
Hendry	70,690	2	57,670	2	56,510	5	55,370	5	16,688
Hernando	83,000	3	59,737	3	56,595	9	55,928	5	21,579
Highlands	86,424	3	69,971	4	62,483	8	59,649	5	21,050
Hillsborough	89,415	14	74,225	30	66,261	103	62,388	7	29,121
Holmes	66,864	2	48,783	1	47,946	2	47,729	5	17,698
Indian River	102,600	2	70,269	3	65,612	12	62,338	5	22,177
Jackson	76,359	2	54,100	1	48,400	5	53,560	5	19,541
Jefferson	66,218	1	55,549	1	54,205	1	47,912	5	14,287
Lafayette	66,333	0	0	0	0	1	42,416	4	16,385
Lake	87,409	6	57,757	8	55,446	19	55,724	5	24,065
Lee	93,554	9	66,626	12	66,936	36	59,407	5	26,806

See footnote at end of table.   Continued . . .

Table 20.59. ELEMENTARY AND SECONDARY SCHOOLS: NUMBER AND AVERAGE SALARY
OF SPECIFIED DISTRICT STAFF PERSONNEL IN THE STATE AND COUNTIES
OF FLORIDA, 1996-97 (Continued)

(salaries in dollars)

County	Superintendent salary	Principals High school Number	Principals High school Salary	Principals Junior high/middle school Number	Principals Junior high/middle school Salary	Elementary Number	Elementary Salary	Board members Number	Board members Salary
Leon	98,543	4	59,342	9	57,010	23	55,695	4	24,848
Levy	65,839	2	48,758	1	50,950	4	46,420	5	17,426
Liberty	64,417	1	49,606	0	0	1	42,885	5	16,473
Madison	67,087	1	48,963	4	46,453	2	48,492	5	17,757
Manatee	112,455	4	66,678	6	63,642	25	59,998	5	25,041
Marion	88,585	6	67,403	7	64,548	26	60,295	4	24,936
Martin	82,374	2	65,252	4	61,627	11	60,177	5	22,467
Monroe	85,100	4	45,461	1	56,960	7	54,305	5	20,147
Nassau	78,708	3	56,341	3	53,480	9	52,917	5	19,652
Okaloosa	86,306	4	64,274	6	60,583	21	58,117	5	23,715
Okeechobee	89,450	1	60,981	2	60,722	5	55,614	5	18,650
Orange	148,340	13	67,731	23	57,283	88	56,432	7	28,570
Osceola	92,140	4	64,502	6	60,560	13	59,254	5	21,699
Palm Beach	135,000	20	67,936	24	63,362	81	59,013	0	0
Pasco	102,373	8	64,672	8	55,739	27	52,292	0	0
Pinellas	130,126	17	66,483	22	65,968	78	62,337	7	29,052
Polk	99,181	14	64,334	20	61,268	64	54,778	5	27,273
Putnam	75,763	3	61,956	4	55,812	8	54,995	5	20,667
St. Johns	80,000	2	60,987	5	55,342	13	52,716	5	22,612
St. Lucie	0	6	62,978	7	60,450	19	59,198	5	23,923
Santa Rosa	80,712	6	63,504	5	58,720	14	57,065	5	21,978
Sarasota	115,000	4	72,183	5	64,716	20	66,353	5	25,883
Seminole	115,791	6	73,870	10	65,636	31	61,322	5	26,161
Sumter	83,391	2	60,188	2	56,231	5	53,799	5	18,872
Suwannee	73,157	1	60,026	1	57,771	2	57,771	5	18,507
Taylor	67,082	2	51,069	1	50,805	3	49,702	5	17,755
Union	69,707	0	0	1	49,960	1	49,960	5	17,406
Volusia	92,750	9	71,640	9	61,605	44	60,693	5	27,108
Wakulla	73,042	1	63,515	1	59,620	3	54,163	5	17,674
Walton	70,595	2	59,781	2	58,867	3	55,982	5	18,685
Washington	67,242	2	59,730	1	53,313	2	52,819	5	17,798

Note: Data are for public schools only. The number of months worked varies from
district to district. Salaries have not been adjusted for a full 12-month calendar
year. Does not include special schools such as university laboratory schools.

Source: State of Florida, Department of Education, Division of Administration,
Education Information and Accountability Services, *Statistical Brief: Florida District Staff Salaries of Selected Positions, 1996-97.* Series 97-25B.

Table 20.60. ELEMENTARY AND SECONDARY SCHOOLS: NUMBER AND AVERAGE SALARY
OF TEACHERS BY DEGREE ATTAINMENT IN THE STATE AND COUNTIES
OF FLORIDA, 1995-96

(salaries in dollars)

County	Total		Bachelor's		Master's		Specialist		Doctorate	
	Num-ber	Aver-age salary	Num-ber	Aver-age salary	Num-ber	Aver-age salary	Num-ber	Aver-age salary	Num-ber	Aver-age salary
Florida	129,206	33,330	78,519	30,496	45,995	37,018	3,361	45,235	1,331	42,993
Alachua	1,826	28,702	735	25,731	936	30,123	111	33,118	44	36,967
Baker	258	29,098	166	27,258	90	32,337	2	36,039	0	0
Bay	1,511	31,235	1,025	29,902	447	33,761	30	37,190	9	37,663
Bradford	270	28,400	179	26,435	84	32,188	5	29,724	2	41,770
Brevard	4,015	31,323	2,447	28,798	1,494	35,128	44	38,924	30	36,599
Broward	10,809	36,908	6,326	34,306	4,110	40,189	247	45,651	126	43,397
Calhoun	155	31,047	96	29,795	57	33,083	0	0	2	33,150
Charlotte	928	30,778	496	27,680	409	34,074	14	38,836	9	39,188
Citrus	920	30,448	510	27,492	384	34,002	16	36,934	10	34,383
Clay	1,366	28,301	904	26,635	453	31,535	5	34,714	4	30,607
Collier	1,629	38,049	825	34,282	756	41,658	31	46,359	17	45,230
Columbia	540	30,336	337	27,934	189	34,158	10	35,733	4	38,688
Dade	18,467	40,193	9,527	35,261	6,904	43,962	1,652	50,461	384	50,587
De Soto	275	29,761	200	28,156	68	33,957	3	37,794	4	32,653
Dixie	155	28,006	105	25,929	46	32,178	2	30,567	2	38,490
Duval	6,732	32,444	4,334	30,287	2,303	36,170	60	40,616	35	40,272
Escambia	2,859	29,014	1,592	27,311	1,214	31,103	29	32,390	24	32,254
Flagler	313	29,733	209	28,352	103	32,410	1	42,478	0	0
Franklin	112	28,114	74	25,981	37	32,125	0	0	1	37,474
Gadsden	505	27,987	333	26,894	168	30,099	3	31,961	1	25,579
Gilchrist	144	30,043	92	28,643	48	32,545	3	32,415	1	31,576
Glades	71	28,188	48	26,150	23	32,441	0	0	0	0
Gulf	150	29,193	101	27,885	48	31,806	0	0	1	35,879
Hamilton	166	27,735	123	26,628	36	30,384	7	33,599	0	0
Hardee	307	29,725	233	28,519	69	33,508	3	33,197	2	34,523
Hendry	380	30,479	359	29,985	15	39,241	0	0	6	38,100
Hernando	935	28,285	587	25,831	330	32,347	12	33,639	6	34,319
Highlands	641	31,857	446	29,866	189	36,485	2	38,834	4	31,676
Hillsborough	9,532	31,684	6,013	29,084	3,330	35,890	117	40,462	72	40,004
Holmes	224	29,986	136	27,588	86	33,640	1	35,494	1	36,363
Indian River	788	32,046	512	30,371	241	34,951	30	36,507	5	36,881
Jackson	573	28,558	287	25,821	266	31,041	17	35,118	3	33,201
Jefferson	138	29,245	87	28,065	47	31,284	3	31,781	1	28,354
Lafayette	71	26,126	52	24,923	18	29,658	1	25,070	0	0

See footnote at end of table.   Continued . . .

Table 20.60. ELEMENTARY AND SECONDARY SCHOOLS: NUMBER AND AVERAGE SALARY
OF TEACHERS BY DEGREE ATTAINMENT IN THE STATE AND COUNTIES
OF FLORIDA, 1995-96 (Continued)

(salaries in dollars)

County	Total Num-ber	Total Average salary	Bachelor's Num-ber	Bachelor's Average salary	Master's Num-ber	Master's Average salary	Specialist Num-ber	Specialist Average salary	Doctorate Num-ber	Doctorate Average salary
Lake	1,494	30,826	1,008	28,650	453	35,131	7	36,925	26	38,509
Lee	3,036	32,490	1,852	29,937	1,112	36,260	46	39,471	26	40,818
Leon	1,960	31,981	977	29,758	897	33,874	54	37,216	32	37,933
Levy	346	29,371	216	27,962	124	31,706	5	32,214	1	29,949
Liberty	75	30,930	50	29,498	25	33,794	0	0	0	0
Madison	206	28,501	138	26,657	65	32,358	3	29,728	0	0
Manatee	1,800	32,563	1,085	29,658	662	36,511	40	42,950	13	41,987
Marion	2,150	28,894	1,447	27,246	656	32,005	33	36,743	14	34,975
Martin	898	30,490	562	28,146	309	33,857	19	40,462	8	41,432
Monroe	578	34,472	362	33,049	212	36,911	1	37,981	3	32,560
Nassau	529	32,365	336	30,493	189	35,620	3	37,770	1	30,137
Okaloosa	1,730	32,383	1,029	30,198	659	35,353	27	37,707	15	42,260
Okeechobee	377	31,996	268	29,948	101	36,964	8	37,869	0	0
Orange	7,597	30,984	4,670	28,569	2,781	34,647	84	38,352	62	38,539
Osceola	1,456	28,418	962	26,650	472	31,696	12	35,619	10	35,141
Palm Beach	8,122	36,870	5,049	34,476	2,841	40,473	132	45,644	100	43,736
Pasco	2,672	28,156	1,779	26,554	873	31,297	6	27,708	14	35,942
Pinellas	6,980	32,846	4,351	30,803	2,469	36,013	100	39,368	60	39,789
Polk	4,289	28,977	3,505	27,537	755	35,335	22	37,851	7	36,303
Putnam	748	29,277	490	27,569	248	32,524	7	32,888	3	31,396
St. Johns	1,030	30,290	641	28,407	385	33,336	0	0	4	38,981
St. Lucie	1,561	32,242	1,039	29,872	481	36,700	29	40,315	12	39,163
Santa Rosa	1,203	29,791	770	27,676	413	33,448	14	34,395	6	38,729
Sarasota	1,863	36,962	916	32,435	864	40,684	57	48,902	26	46,581
Seminole	3,023	34,081	1,983	31,686	932	38,079	76	43,440	32	43,857
Sumter	344	30,403	249	28,688	90	34,771	5	37,153	0	0
Suwannee	321	32,657	203	30,857	115	35,740	3	36,295	0	0
Taylor	231	29,306	146	26,497	77	33,745	4	37,313	4	38,379
Union	132	26,558	97	25,549	35	29,356	0	0	0	0
Volusia	3,752	30,015	2,277	27,546	1,352	33,512	87	37,275	36	37,299
Wakulla	240	28,970	140	27,428	96	30,926	3	36,476	1	34,530
Walton	308	28,102	222	26,942	84	31,011	1	33,526	1	35,784
Washington	204	29,372	113	27,210	88	32,025	2	31,614	1	35,690

Note: Average salary paid to a professional on the instructional salary schedule
negotiated by a Florida school district. Data are for public schools only.
   Source: State of Florida, Department of Education, Division of Administration,
Education Information and Accountability Services, *Statistical Brief: Teacher Salary*, Experience, and Degree Level, 1995-1996, Series 97-05B.

University of Florida   **Bureau of Economic and Business Research**

Table 20.62. ELEMENTARY AND SECONDARY SCHOOLS: STUDENT-TEACHER RATIOS AND
SPECIFIED PERSONNEL PERCENTAGES AND RATIOS IN THE STATE AND
COUNTIES OF FLORIDA, 1995-96

| County | FTE students per FTE teacher | | Percentage of full-time staff who are-- | | Ratio of-- | |
	Elementary 1/	Secondary	Teachers 2/	Administrators	Teacher aides to teachers 2/	Administrators to teachers 2/
Florida	23.83	20.58	49.27	3.66	1:4.51	1:13.45
Alachua	23.89	17.65	43.14	3.55	1:4.06	1:12.14
Baker	26.68	17.80	46.81	4.78	1:4.05	1:9.79
Bay	25.15	19.02	49.61	3.09	1:3.66	1:16.07
Bradford	22.99	16.54	48.16	5.05	1:3.54	1:9.53
Brevard	21.72	21.87	52.77	3.21	1:7.00	1:16.42
Broward	26.73	24.07	52.37	3.61	1:6.17	1:14.50
Calhoun	22.00	15.41	53.21	3.40	1:7.42	1:15.66
Charlotte	25.63	19.23	46.32	3.88	1:4.01	1:11.94
Citrus	21.68	18.55	47.91	3.38	1:5.26	1:14.18
Clay	22.71	22.67	53.29	4.53	1:10.52	1:11.75
Collier	22.37	19.02	46.69	3.59	1:3.17	1:13.00
Columbia	23.75	17.82	46.14	3.13	1:3.43	1:14.76
Dade	23.56	24.98	52.02	3.83	1:4.84	1:13.59
De Soto	23.04	16.92	45.30	4.01	1:2.98	1:11.30
Dixie	18.86	19.46	43.12	5.50	1:3.27	1:7.83
Duval	24.89	22.54	54.42	4.27	1:4.79	1:12.75
Escambia	22.58	17.59	49.12	4.09	1:4.75	1:12.00
Flagler	24.12	18.60	42.10	3.92	1:3.91	1:10.74
Franklin	17.59	19.05	51.98	5.45	1:5.83	1:9.54
Gadsden	20.54	19.28	45.47	5.08	1:3.00	1:8.94
Gilchrist	24.30	18.38	47.92	5.90	1:4.18	1:8.11
Glades	19.67	14.90	50.00	5.38	1:5.00	1:9.28
Gulf	20.14	17.05	49.64	5.36	1:6.61	1:9.26
Hamilton	19.79	16.66	39.63	5.32	1:2.86	1:7.45
Hardee	24.68	17.59	40.89	4.16	1:2.24	1:9.82
Hendry	23.56	21.95	41.18	4.32	1:2.56	1:9.52
Hernando	23.35	18.32	43.16	2.80	1:3.50	1:15.42
Highlands	25.42	22.10	43.27	3.65	1:3.16	1:11.85
Hillsborough	20.45	20.52	48.70	3.52	1:4.38	1:13.82
Holmes	19.98	16.98	50.91	4.34	1:5.18	1:11.73
Indian River	21.81	21.86	49.97	4.78	1:4.91	1:10.44
Jackson	20.37	16.00	46.23	3.55	1:3.56	1:13.02
Jefferson	22.89	16.70	40.76	5.73	1:2.97	1:7.11
Lafayette	16.42	18.26	56.20	6.61	1:5.23	1:8.50
Lake	25.55	21.10	48.22	3.56	1:4.91	1:13.55
Lee	26.03	19.04	51.62	4.15	1:7.66	1:12.44

See footnotes at end of table.   Continued . . .

Table 20.62. ELEMENTARY AND SECONDARY SCHOOLS: STUDENT-TEACHER RATIOS AND
SPECIFIED PERSONNEL PERCENTAGES AND RATIOS IN THE STATE AND
COUNTIES OF FLORIDA, 1995-96 (Continued)

| County | FTE students per FTE teacher | | Percentage of full-time staff who are-- | | Ratio of-- | |
	Elementary 1/	Secondary	Teachers 2/	Administrators	Teacher aides to teachers 2/	Administrators to teachers 2/
Leon	24.23	19.89	44.52	3.61	1:3.49	1:12.32
Levy	23.32	18.17	44.57	4.81	1:3.64	1:9.25
Liberty	21.33	16.32	51.37	6.85	1:7.50	1:7.50
Madison	24.82	17.63	46.57	5.39	1:3.87	1:8.63
Manatee	23.96	20.00	46.36	3.29	1:3.57	1:14.09
Marion	22.33	20.08	45.31	3.39	1:3.25	1:13.37
Martin	26.60	17.89	46.58	4.03	1:4.83	1:11.55
Monroe	23.04	18.28	43.67	4.06	1:3.90	1:10.75
Nassau	27.13	20.30	44.89	4.00	1:3.86	1:11.23
Okaloosa	21.62	18.55	50.20	2.84	1:4.54	1:17.64
Okeechobee	21.36	21.66	43.16	4.02	1:2.29	1:10.75
Orange	25.45	20.22	45.95	2.83	1:4.30	1:16.22
Osceola	28.31	20.62	44.42	3.71	1:3.31	1:11.98
Palm Beach	25.07	18.94	51.24	3.24	1:4.70	1:15.80
Pasco	24.74	18.88	48.47	4.12	1:5.10	1:11.76
Pinellas	24.00	18.73	49.48	3.65	1:3.88	1:13.56
Polk	21.76	19.98	48.05	3.80	1:4.15	1:12.64
Putnam	22.69	20.84	41.55	4.50	1:3.33	1:9.23
St. Johns	23.34	14.26	50.87	5.25	1:5.91	1:9.69
St. Lucie	26.92	18.28	49.17	3.08	1:4.17	1:15.97
Santa Rosa	22.26	18.38	55.04	3.48	1:5.51	1:15.82
Sarasota	24.50	20.92	46.90	3.10	1:4.99	1:15.10
Seminole	25.13	20.20	54.26	3.14	1:5.01	1:17.30
Sumter	23.60	18.55	42.82	3.76	1:2.98	1:11.39
Suwannee	22.23	20.77	46.13	4.27	1:4.70	1:10.81
Taylor	20.06	21.00	43.71	5.61	1:2.69	1:7.79
Union	24.00	16.62	45.39	5.17	1:6.47	1:8.78
Volusia	22.24	17.63	47.21	3.15	1:4.06	1:14.98
Wakulla	24.76	18.98	46.11	5.12	1:4.16	1:9.00
Walton	23.30	15.73	43.23	4.18	1:2.80	1:10.34
Washington	25.35	13.59	45.07	5.87	1:3.49	1:7.68

FTE Full-time equivalent.
1/ Kindergarten through grade 6.
2/ Teachers in grades prekindergarten through grade 12 and exceptional education,
primary education specialists, and others including postsecondary vocational instructors and adult education instructors.
Note: Data are for public schools only.

Source: State of Florida, Department of Education, Division of Administration,
Profiles of Florida School Districts, 1995-96, Student and Staff Data. EIAS
Series 97-21, December 1996.

Table 20.63. ELEMENTARY AND SECONDARY SCHOOLS: ALL FUNDS REVENUE BY MAJOR
SOURCE IN THE STATE AND COUNTIES OF FLORIDA, 1994-95

(in thousands of dollars, except where indicated)

County	Total all revenue receipts	Revenue per FTE (dollars)	Federal sources	State sources	Local sources
Florida 1/	13,014,989	5,696	971,277	6,519,123	5,524,590
Alachua	167,443	5,815	16,817	96,434	54,192
Baker	24,558	5,269	1,782	19,334	3,443
Bay	139,801	5,471	10,866	85,265	43,671
Bradford	22,451	5,289	1,939	16,321	4,191
Brevard	340,713	5,189	22,071	182,448	136,195
Broward	1,322,747	5,634	81,040	661,138	580,569
Calhoun	11,709	5,103	1,125	8,957	1,627
Charlotte	93,559	5,969	5,161	27,113	61,285
Citrus	77,670	5,485	5,275	33,410	38,985
Clay	115,279	4,778	6,515	79,180	29,583
Collier	192,675	7,047	14,689	31,042	146,944
Columbia	46,081	5,095	4,521	32,848	8,712
Dade	2,145,053	5,637	187,230	1,159,149	798,673
De Soto	26,045	5,521	2,872	17,031	6,143
Dixie	13,796	6,238	1,434	10,302	2,060
Duval	662,370	5,449	51,530	377,064	233,776
Escambia	250,505	5,351	24,676	163,740	62,090
Flagler	38,884	6,325	1,591	13,343	23,951
Franklin	9,542	5,734	960	5,268	3,315
Gadsden	48,561	5,743	8,278	34,154	6,130
Gilchrist	13,496	5,782	954	10,551	1,992
Glades	7,200	6,886	918	3,390	2,891
Gulf	13,934	6,089	942	7,648	5,345
Hamilton	16,481	7,082	1,716	9,173	5,593
Hardee	30,204	5,748	4,085	18,664	7,456
Hendry	40,440	5,833	4,546	23,928	11,966
Hernando	84,220	5,587	5,258	40,667	38,295
Highlands	64,171	5,862	5,351	35,670	23,150
Hillsborough	876,828	5,860	82,846	496,803	297,179
Holmes	18,941	5,162	1,951	14,147	2,842
Indian River	87,484	6,602	4,563	23,683	59,239
Jackson	46,900	5,210	4,764	36,069	6,067
Jefferson	12,425	5,580	1,396	9,003	2,026
Lafayette	6,004	5,814	619	4,373	1,012
Lake	126,174	5,133	9,789	69,480	46,905

See footnotes at end of table.   Continued . . .

Table 20.63. ELEMENTARY AND SECONDARY SCHOOLS: ALL FUNDS REVENUE BY MAJOR
SOURCE IN THE STATE AND COUNTIES OF FLORIDA, 1994-95 (Continued)

(in thousands of dollars, except where indicated)

County	Total all revenue receipts	Revenue per FTE (dollars)	Revenue receipts from--		
			Federal sources	State sources	Local sources
Lee	316,231	6,078	20,143	96,895	199,193
Leon	189,700	5,694	12,950	109,524	67,227
Levy	31,379	5,711	2,544	21,589	7,246
Liberty	7,148	5,748	541	5,717	890
Madison	17,943	5,502	2,350	13,185	2,408
Manatee	199,116	6,196	13,459	83,750	101,907
Marion	186,195	5,284	16,216	112,607	57,372
Martin	96,762	6,290	4,767	17,584	74,411
Monroe	62,338	6,451	5,061	12,388	44,889
Nassau	48,932	5,170	2,843	28,500	17,589
Okaloosa	145,526	4,919	12,557	91,372	41,597
Okeechobee	46,635	7,543	4,036	35,334	7,266
Orange	721,340	5,418	50,046	318,107	353,186
Osceola	139,972	5,484	6,975	73,451	59,545
Palm Beach	896,522	6,517	54,697	268,358	573,467
Pasco	237,407	5,744	17,750	138,701	80,956
Pinellas	645,272	5,823	41,196	301,215	302,860
Polk	374,762	5,005	34,569	225,015	115,179
Putnam	69,510	5,512	6,869	42,024	20,618
St. Johns	98,477	5,732	4,677	44,545	49,255
St. Lucie	160,197	6,179	13,010	73,044	74,143
Santa Rosa	97,563	5,036	7,712	64,278	25,574
Sarasota	245,625	7,203	9,653	50,994	184,978
Seminole	280,895	5,231	11,598	148,641	120,656
Sumter	30,139	5,398	2,903	21,174	6,061
Suwannee	38,491	6,580	2,634	30,194	5,662
Taylor	21,967	5,614	3,217	12,983	5,766
Union	11,540	5,431	855	9,297	1,389
Volusia	318,210	5,644	18,795	155,753	143,662
Wakulla	30,492	7,413	1,400	25,335	3,757
Walton	30,848	6,075	2,548	13,379	14,921
Washington	23,509	5,852	2,640	17,399	3,470
Eckerd Youth					

FTE Full-time equivalent.
1/ Includes special schools.
Note: Data are for public schools only.

Source: State of Florida, Department of Education, Division of Public Schools,
Profiles of Florida School Districts, 1994-95, Financial Data Statistical Report.
EIAS Series 96-23, May 1996.

University of Florida   **Bureau of Economic and Business Research**

Table 20.65. ELEMENTARY AND SECONDARY SCHOOLS: ALL FUNDS EXPENDITURE BY MAJOR
TYPE IN THE STATE AND COUNTIES OF FLORIDA, 1994-95

(in thousands of dollars, except where indicated)

County	Total expenditure all funds	Total current expenditure	Current expenditure per FTE (dollars)	Capital outlay	Debt service
Florida 1/	13,801,787	11,147,381	4,879	2,065,156	589,250
Alachua	184,042	143,007	4,966	27,106	13,928
Baker	24,332	21,748	4,666	2,351	233
Bay	143,192	124,076	4,856	16,170	2,945
Bradford	21,410	19,746	4,652	1,315	349
Brevard	378,727	301,810	4,597	66,986	9,932
Broward	1,371,332	1,075,198	4,580	227,238	68,897
Calhoun	12,431	10,825	4,718	1,606	0
Charlotte	94,114	79,765	5,089	10,295	4,053
Citrus	76,497	67,334	4,755	6,602	561
Clay	114,477	100,015	4,145	12,845	1,617
Collier	236,111	153,740	5,624	72,297	10,074
Columbia	49,474	41,807	4,623	4,655	3,012
Dade	2,395,940	1,946,941	5,116	373,798	75,201
De Soto	27,501	24,155	5,121	2,456	889
Dixie	14,039	11,880	5,372	1,977	182
Duval	644,908	568,277	4,675	53,698	22,933
Escambia	267,131	224,860	4,803	34,384	7,888
Flagler	47,847	30,090	4,895	13,810	3,947
Franklin	9,571	8,522	5,121	709	340
Gadsden	55,645	44,188	5,226	9,416	2,040
Gilchrist	12,864	12,051	5,163	673	140
Glades	7,331	6,144	5,878	1,114	73
Gulf	13,942	12,217	5,338	1,491	234
Hamilton	16,869	14,843	6,378	2,025	0
Hardee	31,236	27,272	5,191	3,655	309
Hendry	39,862	35,256	5,085	3,022	1,584
Hernando	89,860	69,211	4,591	11,678	8,971
Highlands	61,849	55,745	5,092	4,342	1,762
Hillsborough	942,467	782,382	5,229	133,451	26,635
Holmes	19,487	17,652	4,810	1,593	243
Indian River	106,567	68,021	5,134	30,894	7,652
Jackson	47,401	40,030	4,447	6,759	612
Jefferson	12,514	11,510	5,169	922	81
Lafayette	6,153	5,254	5,088	557	342
Lake	127,568	108,146	4,400	15,678	3,745
Lee	368,185	272,447	5,236	71,188	24,549

See footnotes at end of table.   Continued . . .

Table 20.65. ELEMENTARY AND SECONDARY SCHOOLS: ALL FUNDS EXPENDITURE BY MAJOR
TYPE IN THE STATE AND COUNTIES OF FLORIDA, 1994-95 (Continued)

(in thousands of dollars, except where indicated)

County	Total expenditure all funds	Total current expenditure	Current expenditure per FTE (dollars)	Capital outlay	Debt service
Leon	202,991	161,309	4,842	30,442	11,241
Levy	31,416	27,127	4,937	1,893	2,393
Liberty	7,337	5,911	4,753	1,305	121
Madison	18,671	16,913	5,187	1,480	278
Manatee	180,182	153,841	4,787	24,275	2,066
Marion	198,458	163,536	4,651	25,398	9,524
Martin	96,247	80,850	5,256	13,156	2,241
Monroe	66,715	55,440	5,737	5,333	5,942
Nassau	52,737	41,043	4,337	11,282	412
Okaloosa	144,632	127,878	4,323	12,462	4,292
Okeechobee	39,546	31,619	5,115	7,495	432
Orange	756,588	616,695	4,632	64,846	75,048
Osceola	142,736	111,057	4,352	23,588	8,092
Palm Beach	978,043	734,293	5,337	206,613	37,137
Pasco	259,551	198,854	4,811	37,359	23,337
Pinellas	651,262	549,869	4,962	97,285	4,107
Polk	402,249	341,670	4,563	51,838	8,742
Putnam	66,995	59,246	4,697	5,107	2,641
St. Johns	102,406	78,407	4,564	16,957	7,041
St. Lucie	171,681	133,362	5,144	27,379	10,940
Santa Rosa	99,873	86,222	4,451	11,290	2,360
Sarasota	228,153	186,584	5,472	29,914	11,655
Seminole	322,364	228,558	4,257	67,907	25,900
Sumter	30,625	26,749	4,791	3,268	607
Suwannee	32,940	27,999	4,787	4,777	164
Taylor	21,666	19,356	4,947	2,074	235
Union	11,904	10,525	4,953	1,101	278
Volusia	331,542	270,925	4,806	36,451	24,166
Wakulla	27,082	18,484	4,494	7,917	681
Walton	29,642	25,082	4,939	3,419	1,141
Washington	22,681	21,808	4,989	791	82

FTE Full-time equivalent.
1/ Includes special schools.
Note: Data are for public schools only.

Source: State of Florida, Department of Education, Division of Public Schools,
Profiles of Florida School Districts, 1994-95, Financial Data Statistical Report.
EIAS Series 95-23, May 1996.

Table 20.66. ELEMENTARY AND SECONDARY SCHOOLS: EXPENDITURE FOR INSTRUCTION
PUPIL PERSONNEL SERVICES, AND INSTRUCTIONAL SUPPORT SERVICES
IN THE STATE AND COUNTIES OF FLORIDA, 1994-95

County	Instruc- tion	Pupil per- sonnel services	Instruc- tional support services	County	Instruc- tion	Pupil per- sonnel services	Instruc- tional support services
Florida	6,397,873	493,124	1,106,108	Lafayette	2,649	237	475
				Lake	60,746	5,296	11,764
Alachua	73,770	6,765	17,035	Lee	144,062	12,861	29,464
Baker	11,156	1,338	2,186	Leon	91,277	6,882	19,279
Bay	76,711	5,196	11,817	Levy	14,972	1,117	2,584
Bradford	11,047	668	1,719	Liberty	3,242	161	496
Brevard	181,025	9,670	25,954	Madison	9,528	599	1,879
Broward	605,678	43,423	120,935	Manatee	89,833	7,350	14,672
Calhoun	6,459	365	1,018	Marion	94,255	9,150	17,983
Charlotte	44,985	4,845	8,791	Martin	45,111	3,828	7,976
Citrus	36,923	3,382	7,916	Monroe	31,115	2,060	4,577
Clay	56,333	5,610	10,412	Nassau	23,017	1,653	2,957
Collier	92,603	7,404	16,248	Okaloosa	75,694	4,950	13,050
Columbia	24,817	1,941	3,510	Okeechobee	18,030	1,722	3,403
Dade	1,164,271	87,205	170,319	Orange	327,335	24,214	70,030
De Soto	13,248	1,078	2,231	Osceola	60,349	5,665	13,835
Dixie	6,064	538	1,212	Palm Beach	458,160	23,205	53,941
Duval	320,032	23,636	49,133	Pasco	107,722	10,883	24,709
Escambia	124,736	10,017	25,125	Pinellas	330,178	24,411	54,609
Flagler	15,995	2,171	3,065	Polk	194,071	17,730	32,494
Franklin	4,969	279	466	Putnam	32,155	2,758	7,115
Gadsden	23,476	2,185	4,923	St. Johns	44,213	5,423	9,146
Gilchrist	6,446	563	1,161	St. Lucie	73,437	6,437	15,258
Glades	3,386	252	529	Santa Rosa	50,161	3,793	8,458
Gulf	6,931	632	1,028	Sarasota	103,515	6,978	16,601
Hamilton	7,509	1,362	2,417	Seminole	135,457	11,207	21,023
Hardee	15,451	1,617	3,048	Sumter	14,823	794	2,439
Hendry	19,284	1,904	3,426	Suwannee	15,693	1,215	2,008
Hernando	37,182	3,546	6,045	Taylor	10,920	1,029	1,895
Highlands	29,559	2,949	5,821	Union	5,403	543	956
Hillsborough	442,566	37,589	86,933	Volusia	153,585	12,382	28,028
Holmes	10,332	514	1,119	Wakulla	9,728	1,043	1,787
Indian River	37,025	3,811	7,595	Walton	14,267	620	2,119
Jackson	23,511	1,406	3,485	Washington	13,490	745	1,423
Jefferson	6,195	322	1,052				

Note: Data are for public schools only.

Source: State of Florida, Department of Education, Division of Public Schools,
Profiles of Florida School Districts, 1994-95, Financial Data Statistical Report.
EIAS Series 96-23, May 1996.

Table 20.67. ELEMENTARY AND SECONDARY SCHOOLS: OPERATING TAX MILLAGE, OPERATING
TAX YIELD, ASSESSED VALUE OF NONEXEMPT PROPERTY AND ASSESSED VALUATION PER
FTE STUDENT IN THE STATE AND COUNTIES OF FLORIDA, 1994-95

County	Operating tax millage	Operating tax yield ($1,000)	Assessed value of nonexempt property Amount ($1,000)	Valuation per FTE student (dollars)
Florida	(X)	3,596,415	511,789,104	181,670
Alachua	7.621	28,300	3,908,905	109,503
Baker	7.536	1,827	255,223	4,492
Bay	7.273	27,932	4,042,661	121,903
Bradford	7.704	2,517	343,890	65,541
Brevard	7.289	94,234	13,608,738	169,584
Broward	7.411	360,102	51,147,590	180,378
Calhoun	6.807	1,051	162,549	58,288
Charlotte	7.375	42,493	6,065,081	309,951
Citrus	7.416	27,974	3,970,717	227,738
Clay	7.025	18,620	2,790,013	95,297
Collier	6.566	99,692	15,982,194	462,006
Columbia	7.641	5,604	772,032	69,892
Dade	7.503	507,152	71,150,811	156,743
De Soto	7.266	4,035	584,573	99,497
Dixie	7.339	1,256	180,209	64,707
Duval	7.414	144,292	20,486,351	135,458
Escambia	7.814	41,208	5,551,208	92,639
Flagler	7.292	14,803	2,136,948	283,308
Franklin	7.254	2,793	405,330	193,302
Gadsden	7.281	3,632	525,029	50,857
Gilchrist	7.752	1,260	171,156	57,534
Glades	7.191	2,127	311,376	247,834
Gulf	7.303	3,822	550,871	195,242
Hamilton	7.480	2,833	398,734	136,343
Hardee	7.269	4,961	718,425	112,627
Hendry	7.258	7,072	1,025,686	121,712
Hernando	7.297	23,290	3,359,636	187,990
Highlands	7.312	15,550	2,238,544	160,418
Hillsborough	7.401	179,208	25,488,456	133,838
Holmes	7.037	1,314	196,575	45,493
Indian River	7.144	37,087	5,464,326	324,587
Jackson	7.317	4,200	604,183	54,203
Jefferson	7.414	1,462	207,594	74,324
Lafayette	7.030	618	92,488	72,495
Lake	6.835	31,612	4,868,491	163,502
Lee	7.372	139,480	19,915,983	301,728

See footnotes at end of table.

Continued . . .

University of Florida   **Bureau of Economic and Business Research**

Table 20.67. ELEMENTARY AND SECONDARY SCHOOLS: OPERATING TAX MILLAGE, OPERATING
TAX YIELD, ASSESSED VALUE OF NONEXEMPT PROPERTY AND ASSESSED VALUATION PER
FTE STUDENT IN THE STATE AND COUNTIES OF FLORIDA, 1994-95 (Continued)

County	Operating tax millage	Operating tax yield ($1,000)	Assessed value of nonexempt property Amount ($1,000)	Valuation per FTE student (dollars)
Leon	7.028	36,945	5,533,545	125,684
Levy	7.504	4,759	667,591	95,644
Liberty	0.769	669	90,580	60,286
Madison	7.305	1,801	259,500	64,778
Manatee	7.420	61,661	8,747,462	214,105
Marion	7.630	38,341	5,289,537	121,629
Martin	7.058	51,427	7,669,865	410,192
Monroe	5.605	36,935	6,936,423	580,300
Nassau	7.063	11,982	1,785,774	157,989
Okaloosa	7.647	31,334	4,313,264	123,082
Okeechobee	7.275	5,600	810,271	102,388
Orange	7.324	236,268	33,957,320	218,852
Osceola	7.460	36,531	5,154,676	166,389
Palm Beach	7.566	378,314	52,633,481	300,948
Pasco	0.782	49,162	7,106,493	135,803
Pinellas	7.359	212,901	30,453,422	214,725
Polk	7.566	82,066	11,417,508	12,602
Putnam	7.271	14,155	2,049,251	133,180
St. Johns	7.399	30,438	4,330,284	211,189
St. Lucie	7.572	51,048	7,096,517	214,390
Santa Rosa	7.284	17,126	2,474,960	107,233
Sarasota	8.462	130,721	16,261,064	358,362
Seminole	7.275	73,823	10,681,576	165,665
Sumter	7.504	3,943	553,138	80,569
Suwannee	7.083	3,424	508,886	72,370
Taylor	7.268	4,022	582,515	123,143
Union	7.654	697	95,903	35,806
Volusia	7.585	89,520	12,423,454	174,764
Wakulla	7.441	1,938	274,227	54,040
Walton	7.191	11,291	1,652,805	272,836
Washington	7.682	2,155	295,236	61,703

FTE Full-time equivalent.
(X) Not applicable.
Note: Data are for public schools only.

Source: State of Florida, Department of Education, Division of Public Schools,
Profiles of Florida School Districts, 1994-95, Financial Data Statistical Report.
EIAS Series 96-23, May 1996.

University of Florida   **Bureau of Economic and Business Research**

Table 20.69. ELEMENTARY AND SECONDARY SCHOOLS: EXPENDITURE FOR LUNCH AND
PUPIL TRANSPORTATION SERVICES IN THE STATE AND COUNTIES
OF FLORIDA, SCHOOL YEAR 1994-95

(in dollars)

County	Lunch services	Trans-portation services	County	Lunch services	Trans-portation services
Florida	537,868,809	461,044,689	Lafayette	298,070	304,232
			Lake	5,611,699	4,480,519
Alachua	7,692,856	5,855,691	Lee	14,242,856	15,176,911
Baker	1,189,879	1,142,144	Leon	6,518,489	6,230,961
Bay	6,975,589	4,424,869	Levy	1,576,818	1,702,607
Bradford	1,037,630	875,672	Liberty	338,054	296,313
Brevard	13,787,896	13,275,706	Madison	1,140,659	870,820
Broward	44,539,194	37,097,903	Manatee	8,149,783	5,939,290
Calhoun	604,970	465,863	Marion	9,048,516	9,582,931
Charlotte	4,414,166	3,440,761	Martin	3,669,726	3,437,326
Citrus	2,925,773	4,276,823	Monroe	2,511,915	2,632,664
Clay	4,500,158	5,100,169	Nassau	2,466,484	2,124,719
Collier	7,951,642	6,679,249	Okaloosa	6,162,833	4,626,204
Columbia	2,233,437	2,225,595	Okeechobee	1,919,981	1,735,334
Dade	89,956,161	64,730,225	Orange	31,334,601	28,369,040
De Soto	1,252,031	1,101,156	Osceola	5,886,891	3,862,900
Dixie	824,023	594,220	Palm Beach	30,442,282	19,482,888
Duval	28,606,670	29,585,533	Pasco	11,104,162	9,329,990
Escambia	12,757,828	10,216,747	Pinellas	20,966,550	18,914,178
Flagler	1,250,516	1,429,877	Polk	21,039,187	11,789,529
Franklin	497,782	291,097	Putnam	4,078,838	2,838,074
Gadsden	3,538,690	1,890,504	St. Johns	2,887,467	2,937,586
Gilchrist	652,163	581,426	St. Lucie	6,831,722	8,497,267
Glades	293,940	230,578	Santa Rosa	4,003,072	4,474,867
Gulf	591,719	646,592	Sarasota	6,984,188	10,654,270
Hamilton	847,817	598,840	Seminole	10,018,584	11,698,242
Hardee	1,673,943	1,586,564	Sumter	1,691,479	1,417,471
Hendry	2,305,736	1,785,035	Suwannee	1,547,486	1,732,809
Hernando	3,330,582	4,158,425	Taylor	1,083,794	1,128,404
Highlands	3,192,425	2,909,009	Union	550,588	480,467
Hillsborough	40,533,266	37,515,488	Volusia	12,456,285	8,743,062
Holmes	1,173,888	1,088,530	Wakulla	933,787	1,227,841
Indian River	3,536,620	3,435,133	Walton	1,408,028	1,428,270
Jackson	2,673,868	1,834,892	Washington	969,405	993,134
Jefferson	651,642	833,219			

Note: Data are for public schools only. Detail may not add to total due to round-ing.
   Source: State of Florida, Department of Education, Division of Public Schools,
Profiles of Florida School Districts, 1994-95, Financial Data Statistical Report.
EIAS Series 96-23, May 1996.

University of Florida   **Bureau of Economic and Business Research**

Table 20.74. FEDERAL AID: SPECIFIED FEDERAL HEALTH AND EDUCATION PROGRAM
EXPENDITURES IN FLORIDA, OTHER SUNBELT STATES, AND THE
UNITED STATES, 1996

(in millions of dollars, except where indicated)

State	Per capita (dollars)	Total 1/	Compensatory education for the disadvantaged	Medicaid	ETA employment/ training
Florida	8,442	586	286	3,382	288
Alabama	3,325	778	125	1,455	88
Arizona	3,095	699	97	1,174	97
Arkansas	2,131	849	71	956	53
California	26,416	829	824	9,021	1,084
Georgia	5,359	729	168	2,276	124
Louisiana	4,735	1,088	186	2,588	99
Mississippi	2,754	1,014	119	1,264	60
New Mexico	1,942	1,133	59	709	41
North Carolina	5,227	714	131	2,591	121
Oklahoma	2,435	738	85	882	72
South Carolina	3,033	820	99	1,482	79
Tennessee	4,477	842	120	2,202	81
Texas	13,299	695	509	6,031	386
Virginia	3,404	510	95	1,137	116
United States	227,572	858	6,379	91,844	6,358

ETA Employment and Training Administration.
1/ Includes other amounts not shown separately.
Source: U.S., Department of Commerce, Bureau of the Census, *Statistical Abstract of the United States, 1997.*

Table 20.75. CULTURE AND THE ARTS: STATE GRANTS TO GROUPS AND INDIVIDUALS
IN THE STATE AND SPECIFIED COUNTIES OF FLORIDA, 1996-97

(in dollars)

County	Amount	County	Amount	County	Amount
Florida	22,179,209	Highlands	8,551	Orange	2,488,595
		Hillsborough	1,245,769	Osceola	23,629
Alachua	367,354	Holmes	1,000	Palm Beach	3,552,547
Bay	78,529	Indian River	589,504	Pasco	11,647
Brevard	240,588	Jackson	10,533	Pinellas	1,481,786
Broward	907,904	Jefferson	19,110	Polk	1,583,876
Calhoun	21,133	Lafayette	887	Putnam	20,755
Charlotte	22,636	Lake	21,028	Santa Rosa	650
Collier	131,014	Lee	141,038	Sarasota	1,758,026
Columbia	20,000	Leon	441,989	Seminole	37,587
Dade	3,763,597	Madison	1,667	St. Johns	12,259
De Soto	1,600	Manatee	26,347	St. Lucie	6,316
Duval	1,002,708	Marion	44,186	Sumter	2,964
Escambia	595,574	Martin	31,688	Suwannee	15,800
Flagler	25,266	Monroe	49,880	Volusia	802,203
Franklin	3,661	Nassau	3,610	Wakulla	1,090
Gilchrist	800	Okaloosa	30,985	Walton	19,810
Hardee	1,000	Okeechobee	508,533		

Source: State of Florida, Department of State, Division of Cultural Affairs,
1996-97 Florida Funding for Culture and the Arts.

University of Florida   **Bureau of Economic and Business Research**

GOVERNMENT AND ELECTIONS

Voter Turnout in Florida, November 5, 1996
(percentage)

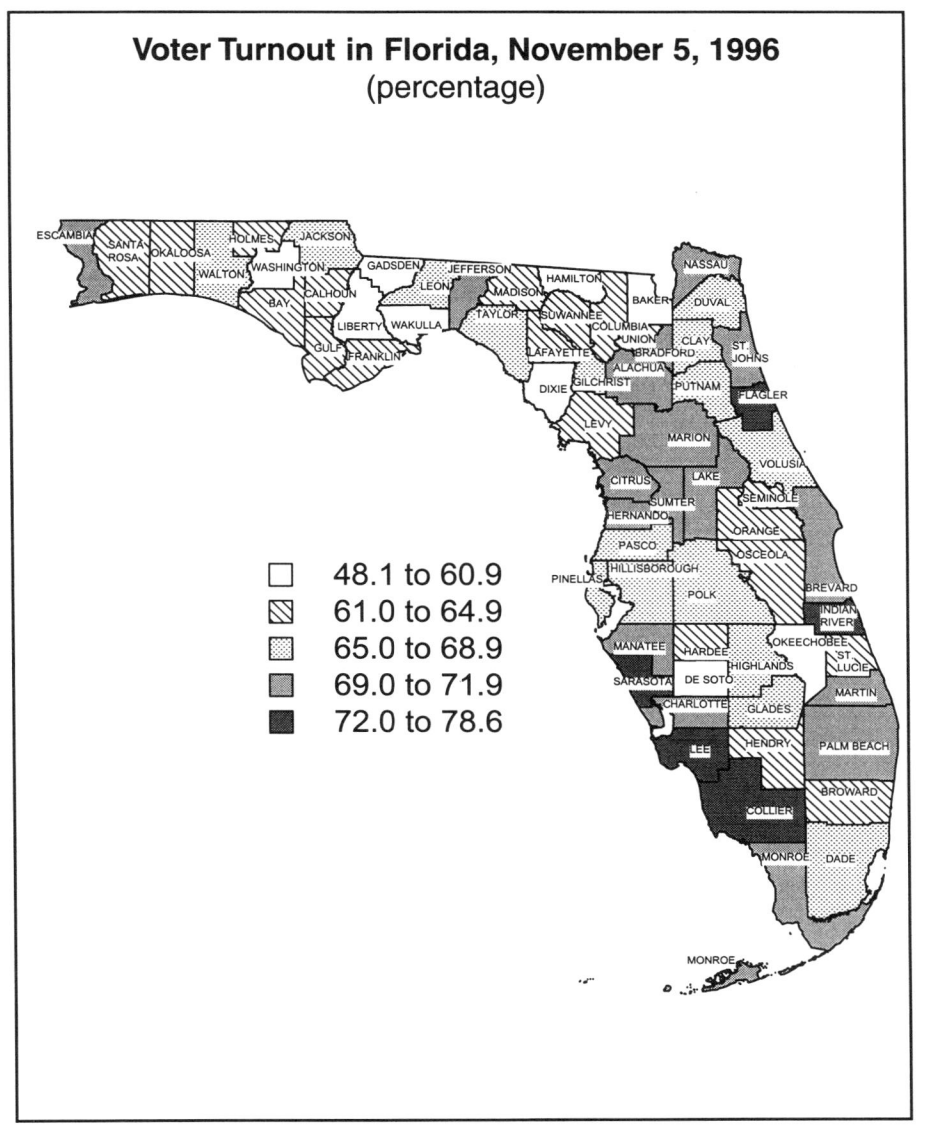

Source: Table 21.31

SECTION 21.00
GOVERNMENT AND ELECTIONS

TABLES LISTED BY MAJOR HEADINGS

HEADING   PAGE

University of Florida   Bureau of Economic and Business Research

Table 21.01. GOVERNMENTAL UNITS: NUMBER BY TYPE IN FLORIDA AND
THE UNITED STATES, 1992

Type of unit	Florida	United States
All units	1,014	85,006
Federal government	0	1
State government	1	50
Local government	1,013	84,955
County 1/	66	3,043
Municipal	390	19,279
School districts	95	14,422
Special districts	462	31,555
With property taxing power	224	14,951
Without property taxing power	238	16,604
Single-function	429	29,036
Education services	7	1,800
Education 2/	4	757
Libraries	3	1,043
Social services	45	1,321
Hospitals	29	737
Health	16	584
Transportation	17	1,306
Highways	3	636
Airports	6	435
Other 3/	8	235
Fire protection	53	5,260
Environment and housing	256	12,959
Natural resources 4/	135	6,228
Drainage and flood control	62	2,709
Irrigation	5	792
Soil and water conservation	63	2,428
Other	5	299
Parks and recreation	13	1,156
Housing and community development	105	3,470
Sewerage	3	1,710
Solid waste management	0	395
Utilities	29	3,763
Water supply	17	3,302
Other 5/	12	461
Cemeteries	0	1,628
Industrial development and mortgage credit	5	155
Other single-function districts	17	844
Multiple-function	33	2,519
Natural resources and water supply	3	131
Sewerage and water supply	5	1,344
Other	25	1,044

1/ In 1968, Duval County and the City of Jacksonville consolidated to form one
government, designated the City of Jacksonville. Jacksonville is counted as a municipal government, rather than as a county government, in census reporting.
2/ Primarily school building authorities.
3/ Includes parking facilities and water transport and terminals.
4/ Functions within the "natural resources" category overlap.
5/ Includes electric power, gas supply, and transit.
Note: The governments census is on a 5-year cycle collecting data for years ending in 2 and 7.
Source: U.S., Department of Commerce, Bureau of the Census, *1992 Census of Governments, Volume I, No. 1: Governmental Organization.*

Table 21.07. LOCAL GOVERNMENTS AND PUBLIC SCHOOL SYSTEMS: NUMBER OF POLITICAL UNITS AND ELECTED OFFICIALS BY TYPE OF GOVERNMENT IN THE STATE AND COUNTIES OF FLORIDA, 1992

County	Political units			Elected officials			
	Munici-palities	School dis-tricts	Special dis-tricts	County	Munici-palities	School dis-tricts	Special dis-tricts
Florida	390	95	462	842	2,238	396	1,178
Alachua	9	2	4	15	48	5	5
Baker	2	1	3	11	10	6	5
Bay	8	2	6	14	40	6	8
Bradford	4	1	1	10	24	6	0
Brevard	15	2	15	10	84	5	28
Broward	28	2	33	11	158	7	98
Calhoun	2	1	0	12	11	6	0
Charlotte	1	1	5	14	5	5	11
Citrus	2	1	2	10	12	6	6
Clay	4	1	4	19	20	6	7
Collier	2	1	14	7	13	5	40
Columbia	2	2	3	11	10	6	5
Dade	26	2	6	36	145	7	12
De Soto	1	1	4	12	6	6	8
Dixie	2	1	1	11	12	5	5
Duval 1/	5	2	2	(X)	50	7	5
Escambia	2	2	5	12	16	6	10
Flagler	4	1	4	10	23	6	13
Franklin	2	1	7	11	10	6	13
Gadsden	6	1	2	11	36	6	5
Gilchrist	3	1	3	11	18	6	11
Glades	1	1	3	12	7	6	11
Gulf	2	1	2	12	10	6	5
Hamilton	3	1	2	11	16	6	5
Hardee	3	1	2	10	20	6	5
Hendry	2	1	18	10	11	6	43
Hernando	2	1	6	12	8	6	10
Highlands	3	2	6	11	19	6	21
Hillsborough	3	2	12	12	19	7	34
Holmes	5	1	3	12	29	6	0
Indian River	5	1	11	12	26	5	37
Jackson	11	2	5	13	60	6	13
Jefferson	1	1	1	10	9	6	5
Lafayette	1	1	1	13	6	6	5
Lake	14	2	4	10	76	6	3
Lee	3	2	32	10	19	5	132

See footnotes at end of table.   Continued . . .

University of Florida   **Bureau of Economic and Business Research**

Table 21.07. LOCAL GOVERNMENTS AND PUBLIC SCHOOL SYSTEMS: NUMBER OF POLITICAL
UNITS AND ELECTED OFFICIALS BY TYPE OF GOVERNMENT IN THE STATE AND
COUNTIES OF FLORIDA, 1992 (Continued)

| County | Political units | | | Elected officials | | | |
	Munici-palities	School dis-tricts	Special dis-tricts	County	Munici-palities	School dis-tricts	Special dis-tricts
Leon	1	2	5	12	5	6	5
Levy	7	1	3	12	39	6	10
Liberty	1	1	0	12	8	6	0
Madison	3	2	2	11	16	6	5
Manatee	6	2	18	21	40	5	36
Marion	5	2	6	10	28	6	5
Martin	4	1	6	9	22	6	15
Monroe	3	2	6	10	16	6	10
Nassau	3	1	4	12	19	6	12
Okaloosa	9	2	12	10	58	6	32
Okeechobee	1	1	3	11	6	5	11
Orange	13	2	15	11	73	7	21
Osceola	2	1	2	10	10	6	5
Palm Beach	37	2	39	14	204	7	104
Pasco	6	2	4	11	31	6	13
Pinellas	24	2	15	66	132	8	19
Polk	17	2	11	10	91	6	17
Putnam	5	2	4	10	28	6	5
St. Johns	3	1	9	14	17	6	38
St. Lucie	3	2	9	10	17	5	26
Santa Rosa	3	1	10	14	21	5	38
Sarasota	3	1	13	10	17	5	59
Seminole	7	2	3	11	37	5	5
Sumter	5	1	1	11	28	6	5
Suwannee	2	1	4	10	14	6	5
Taylor	1	1	1	10	5	6	0
Union	3	1	2	10	17	6	5
Volusia	14	2	13	19	75	5	15
Wakulla	2	1	1	12	10	6	5
Walton	3	1	6	10	20	6	23
Washington	5	1	3	11	48	6	5

(X) Not applicable.
1/ County-type area without any county government.
Note: School districts include community college districts. The governments census is on a 5-year cycle collecting data for years ending in 2 and 7.

Source: U.S., Department of Commerce, Bureau of the Census, *1992 Census of Governments, Volume I, No. 2: Popularly Elected Officials.*

University of Florida   **Bureau of Economic and Business Research**

Table 21.24. VOTING-AGE POPULATION: ESTIMATES BY AGE IN FLORIDA, OTHER SUNBELT STATES, OTHER POPULOUS STATES, AND THE UNITED STATES, JULY 1, 1996

	Population		Percentage of persons who are--			
State	Total (1,000)	Aged 18 and over (1,000)	Aged 18 to 24	Aged 25 to 44	Aged 45 to 64	Aged 65 and over
Sunbelt states						
Florida	14,400	10,977	10.6	38.3	26.9	24.2
Alabama	4,273	3,197	13.6	40.7	28.3	17.4
Arizona	4,428	3,278	13.1	42.1	26.9	17.9
Arkansas	2,510	1,850	13.4	38.4	28.6	19.6
California	31,878	23,012	13.1	46.3	25.3	15.3
Georgia	7,353	5,401	13.6	45.7	27.2	13.5
Louisiana	4,351	3,117	14.7	41.5	27.9	15.9
Mississippi	2,716	1,960	15.3	40.4	27.3	17.0
New Mexico	1,713	1,212	14.1	41.9	28.4	15.6
North Carolina	7,323	5,489	12.8	42.6	27.9	16.7
Oklahoma	3,301	2,420	13.6	39.3	28.7	18.4
South Carolina	3,699	2,761	13.7	42.1	28.0	16.2
Tennessee	5,320	3,997	12.8	41.7	28.9	16.7
Texas	19,128	13,676	14.4	44.3	27.0	14.3
Virginia	6,675	5,044	12.9	44.7	27.6	14.8
Other populous states						
Illinois	11,847	8,691	12.6	43.0	27.3	17.1
Indiana	5,841	4,342	13.2	42.0	27.9	16.9
Massachusetts	6,092	4,670	11.0	44.2	26.4	18.4
Michigan	9,594	7,057	12.8	42.6	27.6	16.9
New Jersey	7,988	6,001	11.1	42.4	28.1	18.3
New York	18,185	13,644	11.8	42.5	27.9	17.8
Ohio	11,173	8,325	12.6	41.5	27.9	18.0
Pennsylvania	12,056	9,161	11.4	40.0	27.7	20.9
United States	265,284	196,235	12.7	42.7	27.4	17.3

Note: Includes Armed Forces residing in each state.

Source: U.S., Department of Commerce, Bureau of the Census, Population Division, Internet site http://www.census.gov/.

University of Florida   **Bureau of Economic and Business Research**

Table 21.25. VOTING-AGE POPULATION: CENSUS COUNTS, APRIL 1,1990, AND ESTIMATES
APRIL 1, 1996, BY SEX AND RACE OF PERSONS AGED 18 AND OVER IN THE
STATE AND COUNTIES OF FLORIDA

		Estimates, 1996				
			Percentage of total			
	Census		Sex		Race	
County	1990	Total	Male	Female	White	Black
Florida	10,054,095	11,160,865	47.77	52.23	86.65	11.76
Alachua	141,760	157,770	49.01	50.99	80.88	16.05
Baker	12,810	14,944	54.38	45.62	84.35	14.89
Bay	94,532	106,063	48.60	51.40	88.44	9.13
Bradford	17,087	19,422	57.39	42.61	78.03	21.01
Brevard	311,152	349,906	48.56	51.44	91.73	6.55
Broward	997,360	1,086,127	47.13	52.87	83.68	14.46
Calhoun	8,127	9,658	53.73	46.27	82.67	15.86
Charlotte	93,590	108,869	47.38	52.62	95.50	3.63
Citrus	76,980	89,567	46.75	53.25	97.55	1.82
Clay	75,330	90,293	48.81	51.19	93.28	4.63
Collier	121,474	153,765	48.49	51.51	95.67	3.67
Columbia	30,642	38,349	50.66	49.34	81.49	17.34
Dade	1,465,595	1,520,403	47.25	52.75	78.91	19.21
De Soto	18,143	20,648	54.70	45.30	82.11	16.97
Dixie	7,979	9,803	53.09	46.91	88.77	10.54
Duval	497,830	538,081	48.21	51.79	75.65	21.89
Escambia	196,088	214,896	48.33	51.67	79.58	17.42
Flagler	23,187	32,109	47.18	52.82	91.66	7.11
Franklin	6,807	8,291	49.46	50.54	88.05	11.06
Gadsden	28,845	33,275	48.86	51.14	44.59	54.56
Gilchrist	7,235	9,244	53.09	46.91	91.31	8.12
Glades	5,724	7,324	50.26	49.74	84.31	10.53
Gulf	8,655	10,591	55.29	44.71	77.41	21.41
Hamilton	7,757	10,054	55.34	44.66	63.07	36.25
Hardee	13,759	16,440	53.56	46.44	89.60	9.26
Hendry	17,614	20,803	51.85	48.15	82.41	14.91
Hernando	82,412	98,063	46.95	53.05	96.47	2.93
Highlands	55,510	64,037	46.25	53.75	92.45	6.75
Hillsborough	630,690	686,440	48.03	51.97	86.84	11.36
Holmes	11,836	13,434	52.49	47.51	91.05	7.36
Indian River	72,602	82,584	47.32	52.68	93.59	5.83
Jackson	31,022	38,008	53.99	46.01	71.35	27.57
Jefferson	8,013	10,290	42.97	57.03	60.27	39.03
Lafayette	4,191	5,502	60.36	39.64	83.01	16.36
Lake	121,614	147,070	46.90	53.10	92.82	6.60
Lee	269,118	307,039	47.41	52.59	94.28	4.95

Continued . . .

Table 21.25. VOTING-AGE POPULATION: CENSUS COUNTS, APRIL 1,1990, AND ESTIMATES
APRIL 1, 1996, BY SEX AND RACE OF PERSONS AGED 18 AND OVER IN THE
STATE AND COUNTIES OF FLORIDA (Continued)

		Estimates, 1996				
	Census		Percentage of total			
			Sex		Race	
County	1990	Total	Male	Female	White	Black
Leon	149,007	172,514	47.34	52.66	75.32	22.71
Levy	19,602	23,714	47.07	52.93	90.01	9.07
Liberty	4,214	5,837	60.70	39.30	79.08	20.08
Madison	11,978	13,841	52.24	47.76	61.56	37.80
Manatee	170,868	190,537	46.50	53.50	93.19	6.00
Marion	151,424	179,968	47.03	52.97	89.17	9.96
Martin	83,024	93,798	48.19	51.81	94.38	4.89
Monroe	64,389	68,471	50.97	49.03	94.56	4.38
Nassau	31,983	37,603	48.83	51.17	91.18	8.15
Okaloosa	106,323	121,812	49.82	50.18	88.53	8.22
Okeechobee	21,521	24,783	50.01	49.99	92.97	5.88
Orange	514,989	587,531	49.21	50.79	83.81	13.60
Osceola	80,433	104,373	48.35	51.65	93.21	4.80
Palm Beach	692,775	779,878	47.12	52.88	88.76	10.02
Pasco	230,665	254,496	46.38	53.62	97.62	1.60
Pinellas	699,455	718,178	46.20	53.80	92.24	6.43
Polk	306,940	346,637	47.45	52.55	88.32	10.72
Putnam	48,414	52,857	47.76	52.24	84.24	14.97
St. Johns	65,007	80,149	47.95	52.05	93.07	6.18
St. Lucie	115,265	135,850	47.86	52.14	86.44	12.60
Santa Rosa	59,385	72,802	49.36	50.64	93.90	3.89
Sarasota	233,828	257,476	46.02	53.98	96.15	3.22
Seminole	214,314	247,487	48.41	51.59	90.75	7.25
Sumter	24,512	32,211	51.88	48.12	84.48	14.76
Suwannee	19,645	23,722	47.50	52.50	87.66	11.69
Taylor	12,272	14,003	50.45	49.55	82.16	16.57
Union	7,616	10,430	68.55	31.45	72.81	25.81
Volusia	297,236	325,580	47.64	52.36	91.47	7.48
Wakulla	10,176	13,325	49.22	50.78	88.26	10.84
Walton	21,139	26,921	50.28	49.72	91.08	6.68
Washington	12,626	14,919	49.90	50.10	82.83	14.56

Source: University of Florida, Bureau of Economic and Business Research, Population Program, *Florida Population Studies,* July 1997, Volume 30, No. 3. Bulletin
No. 118.

University of Florida   **Bureau of Economic and Business Research**

Table 21.26. VOTING-AGE POPULATION: PROJECTIONS, APRIL 1, 2000 AND 2010, OF PERSONS AGED 18 AND OVER BY SEX AND RACE IN THE STATE AND COUNTIES OF FLORIDA

County	2000 Sex		2000 Race		2010 Sex		2010 Race	
	Male	Female	White	Black	Male	Female	White	Black
Florida	5,740,598	6,235,703	10,347,752	1,422,629	6,811,697	7,341,693	12,171,024	1,698,504
Alachua	82,912	85,290	135,447	27,236	95,515	97,342	153,602	31,970
Baker	8,901	7,368	13,816	2,325	10,199	8,650	16,464	2,233
Bay	55,123	58,165	100,295	10,152	64,731	68,339	117,899	11,596
Bradford	11,783	8,673	16,089	4,161	12,885	9,734	18,248	4,127
Brevard	184,157	195,946	348,652	24,754	222,956	237,884	422,717	29,563
Broward	543,150	604,948	945,100	178,477	634,790	695,085	1,056,619	235,915
Calhoun	5,506	4,761	8,510	1,604	6,123	5,361	9,558	1,731
Charlotte	57,896	64,088	116,168	4,669	74,056	81,436	147,403	6,416
Citrus	46,504	52,964	97,049	1,789	58,586	66,198	121,814	2,173
Clay	49,276	51,650	94,021	4,694	62,904	66,183	119,764	6,212
Collier	85,412	90,591	167,868	6,846	111,095	119,465	220,258	8,491
Columbia	21,251	20,735	34,413	7,035	25,779	25,576	42,806	7,780
Dade	751,502	830,114	1,229,626	318,281	850,938	925,695	1,338,728	388,400
De Soto	12,927	10,257	18,762	4,180	14,378	12,089	21,877	4,282
Dixie	5,874	5,216	9,873	1,138	7,135	6,598	12,367	1,255
Duval	272,469	291,825	426,308	122,928	308,944	328,355	478,996	138,219
Escambia	112,254	116,441	181,187	40,160	124,392	128,521	198,855	44,784
Flagler	18,101	20,314	35,215	2,709	25,801	29,113	50,455	3,715
Franklin	4,320	4,676	8,100	824	5,132	5,631	9,800	874
Gadsden	17,475	17,665	15,512	19,249	19,377	19,459	17,446	20,761
Gilchrist	5,610	4,952	9,646	851	7,052	6,463	12,464	958
Glades	4,299	3,736	6,510	1,019	4,934	4,494	7,720	1,140

Continued . . .

Table 21.26. VOTING-AGE POPULATION: PROJECTIONS, APRIL 1, 2000 AND 2010, OF PERSONS AGED 18 AND OVER BY SEX AND RACE IN THE STATE AND COUNTIES OF FLORIDA (Continued)

County	2000 Sex Male	2000 Sex Female	2000 Race White	2000 Race Black	2010 Sex Male	2010 Sex Female	2010 Race White	2010 Race Black
Gulf	7,207	4,942	9,017	2,949	7,697	5,435	9,985	2,895
Hamilton	6,836	4,954	7,299	4,392	7,951	6,109	8,859	5,033
Hardee	9,079	7,903	15,205	1,579	9,562	8,480	16,207	1,631
Hendry	11,676	10,811	18,659	3,233	13,755	13,041	22,723	3,406
Hernando	52,299	59,207	107,636	3,191	69,148	77,677	141,898	3,988
Highlands	32,239	37,626	64,876	4,425	39,084	45,274	78,984	4,680
Hillsborough	350,772	377,531	631,301	83,080	408,577	437,190	729,510	97,846
Holmes	7,433	6,617	12,722	1,092	8,039	7,223	13,770	1,206
Indian River	42,566	47,546	84,853	4,739	51,866	57,707	104,374	4,591
Jackson	21,729	18,538	28,824	10,963	24,179	20,830	32,571	11,798
Jefferson	4,790	6,327	6,843	4,181	5,511	7,117	8,270	4,216
Lafayette	3,814	2,415	5,090	1,099	4,405	3,077	6,244	1,187
Lake	76,669	86,713	152,450	9,961	96,704	108,819	193,414	10,809
Lee	159,947	177,175	317,765	16,612	198,647	218,247	392,879	20,239
Leon	88,677	97,882	140,609	41,940	105,510	115,185	166,280	48,636
Levy	12,238	13,721	23,533	2,175	15,125	16,885	29,380	2,309
Liberty	3,886	2,525	5,134	1,219	4,481	3,141	6,319	1,232
Madison	7,614	6,892	9,023	5,365	8,481	7,668	10,297	5,671
Manatee	96,137	109,597	191,839	12,160	116,002	129,622	229,131	14,166
Marion	93,892	105,701	178,555	19,158	117,951	132,176	224,855	22,543
Martin	49,672	53,351	97,418	4,826	60,824	65,364	119,935	5,265
Monroe	36,133	35,728	68,056	3,044	40,062	41,024	76,970	3,255
Nassau	20,100	21,016	37,806	3,028	24,586	25,703	46,893	3,042
Okaloosa	64,918	66,054	115,440	11,020	77,145	79,549	136,808	13,884

Continued . . .

Table 21.26. VOTING-AGE POPULATION: PROJECTIONS, APRIL 1, 2000 AND 2010, OF PERSONS AGED 18 AND OVER BY SEX AND RACE IN THE STATE AND COUNTIES OF FLORIDA (Continued)

| | 2000 | | | | 2010 | | | |
| | Sex | | Race | | Sex | | Race | |
County	Male	Female	White	Black	Male	Female	White	Black
Okeechobee	14,050	13,480	25,192	1,944	16,506	16,395	30,353	2,077
Orange	313,806	326,203	533,744	88,560	385,341	401,699	649,150	112,825
Osceola	58,388	62,174	112,208	5,830	79,177	84,079	151,436	8,105
Palm Beach	399,279	446,521	750,631	84,227	487,844	537,993	909,484	101,194
Pasco	127,035	146,455	266,743	4,477	151,549	171,456	314,589	5,502
Pinellas	343,504	394,309	678,790	48,526	378,118	422,060	731,685	55,403
Polk	176,421	195,155	328,941	38,802	207,221	228,198	386,677	43,499
Putnam	26,874	29,420	47,418	8,364	31,037	33,964	54,897	9,332
St. Johns	43,312	46,767	84,507	4,920	55,708	59,878	109,772	5,037
St. Lucie	72,672	79,366	132,024	18,451	92,724	101,136	169,637	21,914
Santa Rosa	41,325	41,347	77,015	3,649	52,222	52,968	98,258	4,451
Sarasota	127,067	148,102	264,720	8,645	150,303	171,748	310,163	9,678
Seminole	133,076	140,755	248,666	19,529	167,324	175,932	311,968	23,865
Sumter	20,367	16,791	30,607	6,227	24,215	21,354	38,667	6,483
Suwannee	12,388	13,563	22,933	2,845	14,976	16,363	28,196	2,938
Taylor	7,575	6,937	11,796	2,516	8,054	7,428	12,886	2,383
Union	7,600	3,754	8,521	2,682	8,570	4,819	10,579	2,633
Volusia	167,167	183,220	321,059	25,464	199,829	216,898	383,456	28,296
Wakulla	8,401	7,729	13,935	2,012	10,548	10,010	18,244	2,072
Walton	15,073	14,776	27,233	1,942	18,264	18,359	33,873	1,992
Washington	8,193	7,732	12,949	2,505	9,173	8,742	14,638	2,702

Source: University of Florida, Bureau of Economic and Business Research, Population Program, *Florida Population Studies*, July 1997, Volume 30, No. 3. Bulletin No. 118.

Table 21.30. REGISTERED VOTERS: VOTERS BY PARTY AND BY RACE IN THE STATE AND COUNTIES OF FLORIDA, NOVEMBER 6, 1996

County	Total	Democrat Total	Democrat Black	Republican Total	Republican Black	Other 1/	Number of precincts
Florida	7,704,375	3,728,513	731,525	3,309,105	48,275	666,757	0
Alachua	100,528	62,412	13,623	32,587	726	5,529	50
Baker	11,931	10,641	1,232	1,124	12	166	8
Bay	73,978	43,867	5,634	27,920	453	2,191	47
Bradford	11,615	9,430	1,509	1,990	38	195	19
Brevard	254,300	113,035	13,971	135,252	1,194	6,013	159
Broward	737,776	422,553	79,364	268,123	5,906	47,100	618
Calhoun	6,583	6,048	718	481	8	54	13
Charlotte	84,029	32,918	1,829	48,283	220	2,828	63
Citrus	65,798	33,806	1,004	30,279	61	1,713	30
Clay	65,402	22,355	2,284	40,329	505	2,718	47
Collier	91,626	24,638	1,233	61,171	119	5,817	94
Columbia	26,287	18,612	3,381	6,913	135	762	30
Dade	1,089,631	404,927	150,109	332,454	7,736	352,250	578
De Soto	13,345	9,525	1,411	3,356	57	464	15
Dixie	9,741	8,715	470	787	6	239	11
Duval	365,479	210,832	82,320	139,834	4,406	14,813	257
Escambia	149,156	80,470	22,260	62,943	1,417	5,743	101
Flagler	24,726	11,506	1,862	11,885	141	1,335	25
Franklin	7,247	6,469	711	745	17	33	8
Gadsden	24,360	21,703	12,695	2,161	293	496	16
Gilchrist	7,361	5,934	188	1,306	4	121	10
Glades	5,633	4,181	441	1,080	9	372	13
Gulf	9,481	8,186	1,278	1,272	30	23	14
Hamilton	6,945	6,406	2,199	488	42	51	8
Hardee	11,564	8,359	792	1,845	44	1,360	12
Hendry	15,223	9,964	1,758	3,985	121	1,274	22
Hernando	78,882	36,706	2,038	39,539	179	2,637	51
Highlands	47,828	22,882	2,926	22,631	195	2,315	24
Hillsborough	424,335	218,910	44,860	174,183	3,039	31,242	315
Holmes	10,652	9,688	204	854	4	110	16
Indian River	57,498	20,420	2,637	35,673	284	1,405	38
Jackson	23,083	19,253	4,795	3,393	188	437	26
Jefferson	7,092	6,099	2,580	974	40	19	13
Lafayette	3,809	3,607	231	196	3	6	5
Lake	97,548	40,407	4,827	55,496	845	1,645	77
Lee	204,093	78,027	6,676	118,574	687	7,492	150

See footnotes at end of table.   Continued . . .

Table 21.30. REGISTERED VOTERS: VOTERS BY PARTY AND BY RACE IN THE
STATE AND COUNTIES OF FLORIDA, NOVEMBER 6, 1996 (Continued)

County	Total	Democrat Total	Democrat Black	Republican Total	Republican Black	Other 1/	Number of precincts
Leon	130,530	86,484	28,352	38,110	1,016	5,936	94
Levy	18,281	12,937	1,319	3,983	62	1,361	21
Liberty	3,729	3,598	382	131	1	0	8
Madison	9,678	8,334	3,123	1,105	115	239	11
Manatee	128,077	52,789	6,272	72,244	463	3,044	126
Marion	41,592	20,797	1,360	18,674	138	2,121	33
Martin	121,849	60,766	9,405	58,164	700	2,919	89
Monroe	67,670	21,375	1,879	45,667	400	628	35
Nassau	31,693	17,541	1,931	11,448	89	2,704	17
Okaloosa	92,774	32,034	4,223	56,675	1,466	4,065	47
Okeechobee	17,509	12,343	1,002	4,384	57	782	18
Orange	356,835	150,382	36,400	161,396	2,818	45,057	218
Osceola	79,501	33,951	2,610	30,704	308	14,846	62
Palm Beach	520,647	271,254	39,163	227,944	2,976	21,449	479
Pasco	177,958	86,310	2,074	85,924	185	5,724	128
Pinellas	510,456	229,425	31,738	266,822	2,703	14,209	343
Polk	218,141	117,249	22,280	92,829	1,242	8,063	152
Putnam	39,247	27,570	4,675	10,149	308	1,528	51
St. Johns	61,966	26,547	3,307	33,984	193	1,435	57
St. Lucie	106,095	53,445	12,927	50,023	642	2,627	77
Santa Rosa	62,314	29,387	1,637	31,126	177	1,801	34
Sarasota	184,860	64,862	4,336	117,882	580	2,116	138
Seminole	176,254	64,992	9,947	98,065	1,261	13,197	133
Sumter	20,596	12,548	1,829	7,513	85	535	23
Suwannee	19,410	15,185	2,113	3,823	78	402	16
Taylor	11,812	10,297	1,756	1,297	31	218	14
Union	5,581	5,123	719	417	8	41	11
Volusia	218,804	112,678	15,150	98,283	869	7,843	174
Wakulla	11,735	9,774	1,157	1,861	15	100	12
Walton	21,872	14,712	1,112	6,640	72	520	33
Washington	12,344	10,333	1,297	1,732	53	279	15

1/ Includes registered American, Conservative, F I Socialist Workers, Green, Inde-
pendence, Independent, Libertarian, Natural Law, Reform, Reform Silly, United States
Taxpayers, and those with no party affiliation.
Note: See Table 21.25 for voting-age population.

Source: State of Florida, Department of State, Division of Elections, *1996 Offi-
cial General Election Returns, November 5, 1996.*

University of Florida   **Bureau of Economic and Business Research**

Table 21.31. VOTER TURNOUT: NUMBER REPORTED REGISTERED AND VOTED IN THE
STATE AND COUNTIES OF FLORIDA, NOVEMBER 5, 1996

County	Regis-tered voters	Voter turnout Number	Voter turnout Per-cent-age	County	Regis-tered voters	Voter turnout Number	Voter turnout Per-cent-age
Florida	8,077,877	5,444,245	67.4	Lafayette	3,849	2,399	62.3
				Lake	107,847	76,335	70.8
Alachua	109,835	76,327	69.5	Lee	229,330	170,431	74.3
Baker	12,002	7,123	59.3	Leon	141,100	92,413	65.5
Bay	81,518	52,334	64.2	Levy	18,067	11,493	63.6
Bradford	12,173	8,611	70.7	Liberty	3,766	2,200	58.4
Brevard	282,998	200,828	71.0	Madison	9,702	6,026	62.1
Broward	801,087	519,583	64.9	Manatee	143,258	99,757	69.6
Calhoun	6,644	4,213	63.4	Marion	134,765	93,181	69.1
Charlotte	92,568	64,033	69.2	Martin	76,749	55,157	71.9
Citrus	74,228	51,837	69.8	Monroe	47,176	32,761	69.4
Clay	72,135	48,292	66.9	Nassau	31,220	21,957	70.3
Collier	98,226	77,206	78.6	Okaloosa	100,458	64,484	64.2
Columbia	27,419	17,470	63.7	Okeechobee	17,877	10,376	58.0
Dade	851,919	570,586	67.0	Orange	363,129	234,654	64.6
De Soto	13,700	8,144	59.4	Osceola	77,297	47,438	61.4
Dixie	9,741	4,690	48.1	Palm Beach	591,413	411,798	69.6
Duval	393,787	261,640	66.4	Pasco	200,530	136,779	68.2
Escambia	158,352	109,932	69.4	Pinellas	586,916	384,146	65.5
Flagler	27,313	20,750	76.0	Polk	233,048	153,954	66.1
Franklin	7,478	4,778	63.9	Putnam	41,099	27,935	68.0
Gadsden	24,690	15,031	60.9	St. Johns	68,849	48,978	71.1
Gilchrist	7,641	5,083	66.5	St. Lucie	121,580	74,667	61.4
Glades	5,547	3,690	66.5	Santa Rosa	66,831	43,088	64.5
Gulf	9,716	6,211	63.9	Sarasota	208,659	151,655	72.7
Hamilton	7,069	3,798	53.7	Seminole	187,922	115,745	61.6
Hardee	10,628	6,513	61.3	Sumter	22,002	15,802	71.8
Hendry	15,068	9,240	61.3	Suwannee	20,124	12,818	63.7
Hernando	87,340	60,723	69.5	Taylor	11,852	8,145	68.7
Highlands	50,492	34,621	68.6	Union	5,657	3,584	63.4
Hillsborough	459,249	314,014	68.4	Volusia	242,977	162,874	67.0
Holmes	10,821	6,889	63.7	Wakulla	12,215	7,375	60.4
Indian River	62,509	45,495	72.8	Walton	23,256	15,838	68.1
Jackson	23,527	16,157	68.7	Washington	12,567	6,929	55.1
Jefferson	7,370	5,231	71.0				

Source: State of Florida, Department of State, Division of Elections, *1996 Offi-cial General Election Returns, November 5, 1996.*

Table 21.32. ELECTION RESULTS: VOTES CAST FOR PRESIDENT AND VICE PRESIDENT
IN THE GENERAL ELECTION BY PARTY IN THE STATE AND COUNTIES
OF FLORIDA, NOVEMBER 5, 1996

County	Clinton and Gore (Demo-crat)	Dole and Kemp (Repub-lican)	Perot and Choate (Reform)	County	Clinton and Gore (Demo-crat)	Dole and Kemp (Repub-lican)	Perot and Choate (Reform)
Florida	2,546,870	2,244,536	483,870	Lafayette	829	1,166	316
				Lake	29,750	35,089	8,813
Alachua	40,144	25,303	8,072	Lee	65,692	80,882	18,389
Baker	2,273	3,684	667	Leon	50,058	33,914	6,672
Bay	17,020	28,290	5,922	Levy	4,938	4,299	1,774
Bradford	3,356	4,038	819	Liberty	868	913	376
Brevard	80,416	87,980	25,249	Madison	2,791	2,195	578
Broward	320,736	142,834	38,964	Manatee	41,835	44,059	10,360
Calhoun	1,794	1,717	630	Marion	37,033	41,397	11,340
Charlotte	27,121	27,836	7,783	Martin	20,851	28,516	5,005
Citrus	22,042	20,114	7,244	Monroe	15,219	12,021	4,817
Clay	13,246	30,332	3,281	Nassau	7,276	12,134	1,657
Collier	23,182	42,590	6,320	Okaloosa	16,434	40,631	5,432
Columbia	6,691	7,588	1,970	Okeechobee	4,824	3,415	1,666
Dade	317,378	209,634	24,722	Orange	105,513	106,026	18,191
De Soto	3,219	3,272	965	Osceola	21,870	18,335	6,091
Dixie	1,731	1,398	652	Palm Beach	230,621	133,762	30,739
Duval	112,258	126,857	13,844	Pasco	66,472	48,346	18,011
Escambia	37,768	60,839	8,587	Pinellas	184,728	152,125	36,990
Flagler	9,583	8,232	2,185	Polk	66,735	67,943	14,991
Franklin	2,095	1,563	878	Putnam	12,008	9,781	3,272
Gadsden	9,405	3,813	938	St. Johns	16,713	27,311	4,205
Gilchrist	1,985	1,939	841	St. Lucie	36,168	28,892	8,482
Glades	1,530	1,361	521	Santa Rosa	10,923	26,244	4,957
Gulf	2,480	2,424	1,054	Sarasota	63,648	69,198	14,939
Hamilton	1,734	1,518	406	Seminole	45,051	59,778	9,357
Hardee	2,417	2,926	851	Sumter	7,014	5,960	2,375
Hendry	3,882	3,855	1,135	Suwannee	4,479	5,742	1,874
Hernando	28,520	22,039	7,272	Taylor	3,583	3,188	1,140
Highlands	14,244	15,608	3,739	Union	1,388	1,636	425
Hillsborough	144,223	136,621	25,154	Volusia	78,905	63,067	17,319
Holmes	2,310	3,248	1,208	Wakulla	3,054	2,931	1,091
Indian River	16,373	22,709	4,635	Walton	5,341	7,706	2,342
Jackson	6,665	7,187	1,602	Washington	2,992	3,522	1,287
Jefferson	2,543	1,851	393	Absentees 1/	902	1,212	94

1/ Absentees counted per: Division of Elections Rule 1S-2.013. These votes are
included in state totals but not in county detail.
Note: Excludes other candidates.

Source: State of Florida, Department of State, Division of Elections, *1996 Offi-cial General Election Returns, November 5, 1996.*

Table 21.33. ELECTION RESULTS: VOTES CAST FOR UNITED STATES SENATOR, NOVEMBER 3
1992 AND NOVEMBER 8, 1994, AND FOR GOVERNOR AND LIEUTENANT GOVERNOR
NOVEMBER 8, 1994, IN THE STATE AND COUNTIES OF FLORIDA

| | United States Senator 1/ | | | | Governor/Lieutenant Governor--1994 C/ | |
| | 1992 A/ | | 1994 B/ | | Lawton Chiles/ | Jeb Bush/ |
County	Bob Graham (D)	Bill Grant (R)	Connie Mack (R)	Hugh E. Rodham (D)	Buddy MacKay (D)	Tom Feeney (R)
Florida	3,245,565	1,716,505	2,895,200	1,210,577	2,135,008	2,071,068
Alachua	54,950	20,013	35,723	19,740	35,030	21,624
Baker	4,686	2,647	4,010	1,185	1,654	3,600
Bay	21,912	18,390	29,885	7,951	17,816	23,498
Bradford	5,790	2,400	5,124	1,905	2,642	4,470
Brevard	110,461	82,132	121,019	37,177	72,393	82,878
Broward	339,396	107,396	219,370	170,539	261,368	138,333
Calhoun	2,890	1,263	2,515	926	1,811	1,775
Charlotte	36,374	24,664	38,693	12,980	24,159	27,965
Citrus	27,675	17,697	29,884	10,528	20,094	20,633
Clay	23,700	21,165	28,614	5,561	9,986	24,290
Collier	36,387	33,823	47,974	10,688	22,860	36,370
Columbia	9,474	5,564	9,223	3,303	5,288	7,408
Dade	410,593	111,366	245,803	143,047	215,276	198,371
De Soto	5,021	2,655	4,547	1,667	2,856	3,407
Dixie	3,346	1,385	2,080	1,178	2,003	1,981
Duval	136,447	79,864	134,072	50,415	80,945	108,900
Escambia	57,036	43,668	60,370	17,175	33,210	45,261
Flagler	10,081	5,784	9,946	4,891	7,954	7,160
Franklin	2,444	1,408	2,709	1,107	2,636	1,324
Gadsden	10,479	2,328	5,598	5,311	7,751	3,422
Gilchrist	2,990	1,315	2,629	970	1,701	1,922
Glades	2,350	1,057	1,882	819	1,387	1,310
Gulf	3,490	2,231	3,826	1,449	3,060	2,339
Hamilton	2,669	1,040	1,825	976	1,453	1,429
Hardee	4,128	2,208	3,974	1,292	2,695	2,649
Hendry	5,498	2,369	4,325	1,563	2,623	3,308
Hernando	35,310	19,628	34,727	14,653	25,331	24,532
Highlands	18,809	13,074	19,688	6,396	12,323	14,617
Hillsborough	187,254	117,606	168,720	67,109	117,974	124,561
Holmes	3,740	2,494	3,800	1,069	2,134	2,942
Indian River	23,306	20,121	28,263	7,969	16,410	20,630
Jackson	9,582	5,133	8,659	3,756	5,907	6,698
Jefferson	3,631	1,082	2,493	1,566	2,575	1,625
Lafayette	1,749	797	1,599	406	936	1,105
Lake	42,939	25,830	46,359	13,181	29,797	30,394
Lee	88,273	62,413	103,187	30,201	58,785	75,365
Leon	73,399	22,512	47,243	26,194	47,323	27,265
Levy	7,259	3,643	6,304	2,524	4,588	4,322
Liberty	1,703	695	1,352	513	947	985
Madison	4,386	1,626	3,102	1,573	2,564	2,161

See footnotes at end of table.   Continued . . .

University of Florida   **Bureau of Economic and Business Research**

Table 21.33. ELECTION RESULTS: VOTES CAST FOR UNITED STATES SENATOR, NOVEMBER 3
1992 AND NOVEMBER 8, 1994, AND FOR GOVERNOR AND LIEUTENANT GOVERNOR
NOVEMBER 8, 1994, IN THE STATE AND COUNTIES OF FLORIDA
(Continued)

County	United States Senator 1/				Governor/Lieutenant Governor--1994 C/	
	1992 A/		1994 B/		Lawton Chiles/ Buddy MacKay	Jeb Bush/ Tom Feeney
	Bob Graham	Bill Grant	Connie Mack	Hugh E. Rodham		
	(D)	(R)	(R)	(D)	(D)	(R)
Manatee	58,568	39,896	60,863	20,263	40,473	41,915
Marion	18,196	10,015	15,518	7,607	13,232	10,086
Martin	52,864	32,390	51,032	17,073	31,345	38,784
Monroe	28,342	22,037	34,986	9,603	20,706	25,239
Nassau	10,934	7,022	11,594	3,512	5,331	9,968
Okaloosa	29,759	30,050	40,330	7,390	16,459	31,459
Okeechobee	6,158	3,141	4,790	2,118	3,492	3,545
Orange	143,024	89,915	128,915	46,223	85,098	92,096
Osceola	26,394	15,923	24,112	8,516	15,292	18,437
Palm Beach	249,191	105,937	195,964	117,166	198,638	125,208
Pasco	78,506	44,296	76,901	30,624	57,597	52,418
Pinellas	243,038	133,047	233,140	83,762	166,858	160,115
Polk	90,339	55,474	91,915	31,248	58,364	65,415
Putnam	18,221	7,009	13,420	6,461	9,658	10,505
St. Johns	19,389	15,966	26,912	4,975	11,726	20,345
St. Lucie	70,688	52,946	96,345	29,277	60,770	67,531
Santa Rosa	65,917	48,229	68,643	19,280	39,324	49,387
Sarasota	22,066	17,065	27,043	7,291	12,791	22,036
Seminole	40,085	22,565	37,992	15,928	27,956	27,436
Sumter	7,337	2,987	7,817	2,785	5,603	5,360
Suwannee	7,414	3,934	7,016	1,907	3,935	5,064
Taylor	4,896	2,162	4,271	1,513	2,979	3,024
Union	2,622	980	2,083	679	791	2,009
Volusia	101,346	49,850	84,804	38,268	66,614	58,632
Wakulla	4,933	1,771	4,417	1,678	3,696	2,492
Walton	7,717	5,207	8,727	2,439	5,067	6,493
Washington	4,748	2,856	4,534	1,538	2,968	3,240
Overseas military absentees	1,266	1,349	0	0	(X)	(X)

(D) Democrat.
(R) Republican.
(X) Not applicable.
A/ Does not include 220 write-in votes.
B/ Does not include 1,039 write-in votes.
C/ Does not include 583 write-in votes.
1/ Absentee ballots counted per: Division of Elections Rule 1S-2.013. These votes
are included in state but not in county detail in 1992.

Source: State of Florida, Department of State, Division of Elections, *1994 Elections: Official General Election Returns, November 8, 1994,* and previous edition.

University of Florida   **Bureau of Economic and Business Research**

Table 21.35. FEMALE OFFICIALS: WOMEN IN STATE LEGISLATURES IN FLORIDA
AND THE UNITED STATES, 1997

Area	Total legislators	Women legislators			
		Number	Percentage of total	Senate	House
Florida	160	37	23.1	6	31
United States	7,424	1,596	21.5	365	1,231

Source: Center for the American Woman and Politics (CAWP), National Information
Bank on Women in Public Office, Eagleton Institute of Politics, Rutgers University,
(copyright). Internet site http://www.rci.rutgers.edu/~cawp/.

Table 21.36. BLACK OFFICIALS: BLACK ELECTED OFFICIALS BY OFFICE IN FLORIDA, THE
SOUTH, AND THE UNITED STATES, JANUARY 1992 AND 1993

Office	Florida		South 1/		United States	
	1992	1993	1992	1993	1992	1993
Total	183	200	5,110	5,492	7,517	7,984
U.S. and state legislatures 2/	14	22	280	328	499	561
City and county offices 3/	126	133	3,432	3,675	4,557	4,819
Law enforcement 4/	24	28	474	518	847	922
Education 5/	19	17	924	971	1,614	1,682

1/ Includes Alabama, Arkansas, Delaware, District of Columbia, Florida, Georgia,
Kentucky, Louisiana, Maryland, Mississippi, North Carolina, Oklahoma, South Carolina,
Tennessee, Texas, Virginia, and West Virginia.
2/ Includes elected state administrators.
3/ County commissioners, councilmen, mayors, vice mayors, aldermen, regional officers, and others.
4/ Judges, magistrates, constables, marshals, sheriffs, justices of the peace, and
others.
5/ Members of state education agencies, college boards, school boards, and others.
Source: Joint Center for Political and Economic Studies, Washington, DC, *Black
Elected Officials: A National Roster,* annual, (copyright).

Table 21.37. HISPANIC OFFICIALS: HISPANIC ELECTED OFFICIALS BY OFFICE IN FLORIDA
THE SOUTH, AND THE UNITED STATES, SEPTEMBER 1994

Office	Florida	South	United States
Total	64	2,298	5,459
State executives and legislators, including U.S. representatives	16	61	199
County and municipal officials	33	1,059	2,197
Judicial and law enforcement	12	410	651
Education and school boards	3	768	2,412

Source: U.S., Department of Commerce, Bureau of the Census, *Statistical Abstract
of the United States, 1997.*

University of Florida   **Bureau of Economic and Business Research**

Table 21.42. COMPOSITION OF CONGRESS AND STATE LEGISLATURES: NUMBER OF UNITED STATES REPRESENTATIVES AND SENATORS AND STATE LEGISLATORS BY PARTY AFFILIATION, SPECIFIED YEARS 1989 THROUGH 1996

	Florida				United States			
Year 1/	Demo-crats	Repub-licans	Demo-crats	Repub-licans	Demo-crats	Repub-licans	Demo-crats	Repub-licans
	U.S. represent-atives		U.S. senators		U.S. represent-atives		U.S. senators	
1989	10	9	1	1	259	174	55	45
1991	9	10	1	1	267	167	56	44
1993	10	13	1	1	258	176	57	43
1994	10	13	1	1	257	176	56	44
1995	8	15	1	1	204	230	47	53
1996	8	15	1	1	197	236	46	53
	State represent-atives		State senators		State represent-atives		State senators	
1990	74	46	22	18	3,242	2,202	1,186	757
1992	71	49	20	20	3,186	2,223	1,132	799
1994 A/	63	57	19	21	2,817	2,603	1,021	905
1996 A/	59	61	17	23	2,886	2,539	998	931

A/ Status as of December 7, 1994.
1/ U.S. representative and senator data refer to the beginning of the first session. State legislative data refer to election years.
Note: Excludes vacancies and persons classified as Independents.
Source: U.S., Department of Commerce, Bureau of the Census, *Statistical Abstract of the United States, 1997*. Copyright 1996. The Council of State Governments. Reprinted with permission from *State Elective Officials and the Legislatures,* and 1992, 1994, and 1996 National Conference of State Legislatures, Denver, CO, unpublished data, (copyright).

Table 21.43. APPORTIONMENT: MEMBERSHIP IN THE UNITED STATES HOUSE OF REPRESENTATIVES FOR FLORIDA AND THE UNITED STATES 1840 THROUGH 1990

Census of--	Florida	United States	Census of--	Florida	United States
1840	A/ 1	232	1930	5	435
1850	1	237	1940	6	435
1860	1	243	1950	8	437
1870	2	293	1960	12	435
1880	2	332	1970	15	435
1890	2	357	1980	19	435
1900	3	391	1990	23	435
1910	4	435			

A/ Assigned after apportionment.
Note: Total membership includes representatives assigned to newly admitted states after the apportionment acts. Population figures used for apportionment purposes are those determined for states by each decennial census.
Source: U.S., Department of Commerce, Bureau of the Census, *1990 Census Profile: Population Trends and Congressional Apportionment,* No. 1, March 1991.

COURTS AND LAW ENFORCEMENT

Percentage Change in Violent Youth Offenders
1991-92 to 1995-96

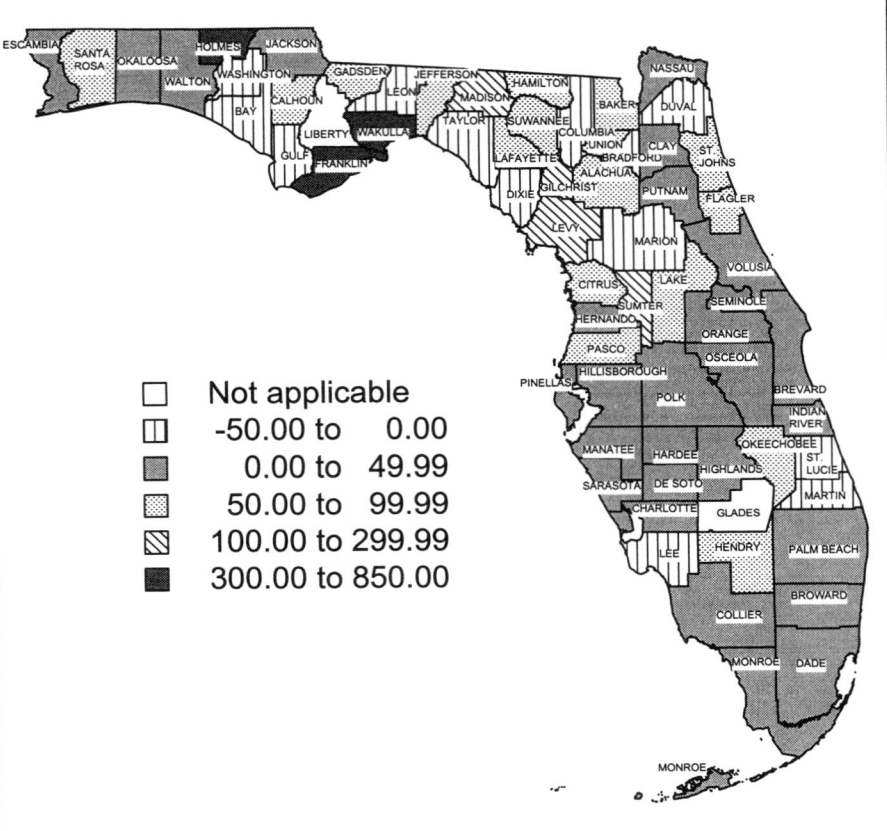

Not applicable
-50.00 to   0.00
  0.00 to 49.99
 50.00 to 99.99
100.00 to 299.99
300.00 to 850.00

SECTION 22.00
COURTS AND LAW ENFORCEMENT

TABLES LISTED BY MAJOR HEADINGS

University of Florida   **Bureau of Economic and Business Research**

613

SECTION 22.00
COURTS AND LAW ENFORCEMENT
(Continued)

TABLES LISTED BY MAJOR HEADINGS

Table 22.01. CRIMINAL OFFENSES AND RATES: CRIME INDEX OFFENSES BY TYPE OF OFFENSE
IN FLORIDA, 1992 THROUGH 1996

Item	Total index of-fenses 1/	Violent crime				Nonviolent crime		
		Mur-der	Forc-ible sex	Rob-bery	Aggra-vated as-sault	Bur-glary	Larceny	Motor ve-hicle theft
Number of index offenses 2/								
1992	1,112,746	1,191	13,429	48,957	97,560	252,003	594,053	105,553
1993	1,116,567	1,187	13,752	47,742	99,108	245,353	594,793	114,632
1994	1,130,875	1,152	13,413	45,263	98,007	233,006	617,195	122,839
1995	1,078,619	1,030	12,259	42,142	94,777	213,050	605,751	109,610
1996	1,079,623	1,077	12,942	41,643	95,688	219,056	605,448	103,769
Percentage change from previous year								
1992	-1.5	-6.7	8.4	-7.8	6.7	-4.8	-1.6	2.6
1993	0.3	-0.3	2.4	-2.5	1.6	-2.6	0.1	8.6
1994	1.3	-2.9	-2.5	-5.2	-1.1	-5.0	3.8	7.2
1995	-4.6	-10.6	-8.6	-6.9	-3.3	-8.6	-1.9	-10.8
1996	0.1	4.6	5.6	-1.2	1.0	2.8	-0.1	-5.3
Rate per 100,000 population								
1992	8,289.0	8.9	100.0	364.7	726.7	1,877.2	4,425.2	786.3
1993	8,204.8	8.7	101.1	350.8	728.3	1,802.9	4,370.7	842.3
1994	8,148.2	8.3	96.6	326.1	706.2	1,678.9	4,447.0	885.1
1995	7,623.1	7.3	86.6	297.8	669.8	1,505.7	4,281.1	774.7
1996	7,491.3	7.5	89.8	289.0	664.0	1,520.0	4,201.1	720.0
Percentage change from previous year								
1992	-3.2	-8.2	6.5	-9.3	4.9	-6.4	-3.3	0.9
1993	-1.0	-1.7	1.0	-3.8	0.2	-4.0	-1.2	7.1
1994	-0.7	-4.8	-4.4	-7.0	-3.0	-6.9	1.7	5.1
1995	-6.4	-12.3	-10.4	-8.7	-5.1	-10.3	-3.7	-12.5
1996	-1.7	2.7	3.7	-3.0	-0.9	0.9	-1.9	-7.1
Percentage cleared								
1992	21.3	67.8	55.6	24.7	59.8	14.5	17.7	15.4
1993	20.7	67.7	55.2	23.8	57.4	14.8	17.6	14.4
1994	21.2	68.8	54.6	24.3	57.8	14.8	18.2	13.8
1995	21.5	63.5	56.1	23.9	59.1	14.4	18.7	13.6
1996	(NA)	(NA)	(NA)	(NA)	(NA)	(NA)	(NA)	(NA)

(NA) Not available.
1/ The crimes selected for use in the index are chosen based on their serious nature, their frequency of occurrence, and the reliability of reporting from citizens
to law enforcement agencies. The Crime Index is used as a basic measure of crime.
2/ Actual offenses known to law enforcement officers, not the number of persons
who committed them or number of injuries they caused.
Note: Rates may not add to totals due to rounding. Percentage changes calculated
by the Bureau of Economic and Business Research.

Source: State of Florida, Department of Law Enforcement, *Crime in Florida: 1996
Annual Report,* previous editions, and unpublished data.

Table 22.02. CRIMINAL OFFENSES AND RATES: CRIME INDEX OFFENSES, CRIME RATES, AND OFFENSES CLEARED IN THE STATE AND COUNTIES OF FLORIDA, 1996

| County | Crime index offenses | | | Crime rate per 100,000 population | Percentage change 1995 to | Offenses cleared 4/ |
	Total 1/	Vio-lent 2/	Nonvio-lent 3/	1996	1996	(percentage)
Florida	1,079,623	151,350	928,273	7,491.3	-1.7	21.5
Alachua	19,325	2,610	16,715	9,560.2	-1.2	23.3
Baker	897	129	768	4,331.5	47.1	30.9
Bay	9,490	930	8,560	6,675.6	5.5	39.5
Bradford	1,389	144	1,245	5,559.8	17.9	25.4
Brevard	25,792	3,221	22,571	5,729.5	2.5	20.9
Broward	117,606	12,213	105,393	8,447.2	1.5	21.3
Calhoun	299	54	245	2,391.2	303.7	47.8
Charlotte	4,041	309	3,732	3,121.2	-3.1	26.0
Citrus	2,990	342	2,648	2,771.4	-3.4	31.4
Clay	4,641	754	3,887	3,700.0	-5.2	48.2
Collier	11,770	1,332	10,438	6,097.3	12.0	20.0
Columbia	3,695	549	3,146	7,029.4	6.9	22.7
Dade	225,293	36,821	188,472	11,025.9	-11.7	18.0
De Soto	1,711	426	1,285	6,404.4	-5.7	34.1
Dixie	731	75	656	5,800.7	26.1	18.3
Duval	62,411	10,085	52,326	8,567.8	-2.8	21.7
Escambia	17,743	3,130	14,613	6,197.3	-1.4	29.2
Flagler	1,454	157	1,297	3,723.2	21.0	29.3
Franklin	272	39	233	2,620.9	-8.4	13.6
Gadsden	2,234	428	1,806	4,822.8	14.9	26.6
Gilchrist	348	102	246	2,864.2	174.6	35.3
Glades	515	38	477	5,471.2	5.6	5.2
Gulf	334	66	268	2,465.9	8.7	43.7
Hamilton	409	53	356	3,045.2	476.2	17.1
Hardee	1,327	158	1,169	5,892.8	0.8	27.9
Hendry	1,645	218	1,427	5,454.8	39.2	19.3
Hernando	5,127	650	4,477	4,275.0	6.3	24.2
Highlands	4,499	580	3,919	5,768.2	1.1	32.3
Hillsborough	85,801	13,523	72,278	9,419.8	3.0	21.0
Holmes	48	20	28	275.7	-83.7	97.9
Indian River	5,404	634	4,770	5,287.1	-5.5	26.4
Jackson	1,404	294	1,110	2,887.2	3.5	34.3
Jefferson	810	235	575	5,906.8	104.6	50.0
Lafayette	41	18	23	584.7	0.0	100.0
Lake	7,820	1,192	6,628	4,289.4	7.6	33.8
Lee	20,051	2,658	17,393	5,225.6	-3.5	31.0

See footnotes at end of table.   Continued . . .

Table 22.02. CRIMINAL OFFENSES AND RATES: CRIME INDEX OFFENSES, CRIME RATES, AND
OFFENSES CLEARED IN THE STATE AND COUNTIES OF FLORIDA, 1996 (Continued)

County	Crime index offenses Total 1/	Crime index offenses Vio- lent 2/	Crime index offenses Nonvio- lent 3/	Crime rate per 100,000 population 1996	Per- centage change 1995 to 1996	Offenses clear- ed 4/ (per- centage)
Leon	18,559	2,212	16,347	8,374.2	-13.3	25.4
Levy	1,627	294	1,333	5,301.4	48.3	30.9
Liberty	100	10	90	1,344.3	156.6	41.0
Madison	513	54	459	2,736.7	15.7	24.0
Manatee	17,658	2,778	14,880	7,336.6	0.4	22.2
Marion	12,522	2,110	10,412	5,461.9	-13.3	36.1
Martin	5,758	540	5,218	5,030.4	-4.5	25.2
Monroe	6,633	613	6,020	7,916.3	-6.4	16.6
Nassau	2,043	259	1,784	3,998.3	-1.3	22.0
Okaloosa	5,058	797	4,261	3,059.5	-10.6	28.4
Okeechobee	1,829	320	1,509	5,436.5	18.6	28.8
Orange	75,500	11,096	64,404	9,709.9	14.1	22.3
Osceola	9,966	1,132	8,834	7,132.6	0.6	29.0
Palm Beach	79,436	8,954	70,482	8,090.9	-6.1	16.1
Pasco	14,340	1,516	12,824	4,626.8	14.2	23.9
Pinellas	58,581	9,354	49,227	6,646.5	2.2	25.5
Polk	33,838	3,719	30,119	7,474.6	1.7	17.9
Putnam	4,904	864	4,040	6,977.1	-17.0	52.5
St. Johns	4,665	657	4,008	4,585.7	14.6	31.3
St. Lucie	10,922	1,662	9,260	6,224.9	6.1	23.5
Santa Rosa	3,601	425	3,176	3,656.2	-14.7	18.1
Sarasota	16,549	1,692	14,857	5,480.9	-4.1	27.5
Seminole	15,938	1,974	13,964	4,843.9	4.1	23.1
Sumter	1,270	194	1,076	3,128.6	-15.1	30.6
Suwannee	622	85	537	1,979.4	-13.3	13.8
Taylor	1,205	211	994	6,334.8	28.0	30.8
Union	65	26	39	499.1	5.2	67.7
Volusia	24,492	3,331	21,161	6,014.8	11.2	24.7
Wakulla	829	159	670	4,599.9	52.8	44.6
Walton	1,016	99	917	2,959.7	63.7	33.8
Washington	217	26	191	1,098.7	-49.1	26.3

1/ Actual offenses known to law enforcement officers, not the number of persons
who committed them or number of injuries they caused.
    2/ Includes murder, forcible sex, robbery, and aggravated assault.
    3/ Includes breaking and entering (burglary), larceny, and auto theft.
    4/ Clearance of an offense occurs when an offender is identified, charged, and
taken into custody, or occasionally when some element beyond law enforcement control
precludes formal charges against the offender.
    Note: Data are aggregates of offenses reported to municipal, county, and state
law enforcement agencies and campus police departments. Percentage changes calculated by Bureau of Economic and Business Research.
    Source: State of Florida, Department of Law Enforcement, unpublished data.

University of Florida   **Bureau of Economic and Business Research**

Table 22.03. CRIMINAL OFFENSES AND RATES: CRIME INDEX OFFENSES AND CRIME RATES
IN THE STATE, COUNTIES, CITIES, AND SPECIFIED AREAS
OF FLORIDA, 1996

Area	Number of index offenses 1/	Crime rate per 100,000 population	Area	Number of index offenses 1/	Crime rate per 100,000 population
Florida	1,079,623	7,491.3	Broward	117,606	8,447.2
			Sheriff's office	21,140	6,888.3
Alachua	19,325	9,560.2	Coconut Creek	1,259	3,646.3
Sheriff's office	7,268	7,735.9	Cooper City	735	2,654.8
Alachua	545	9,265.6	Coral Springs	4,815	4,885.7
Gainesville	9,917	10,151.2	Davie	4,536	7,637.3
High Springs	158	4,424.5	Ft. Lauderdale	25,484	16,972.4
Waldo	30	2,879.1	Hallandale	2,971	9,444.3
Santa Fe Community			Hillsboro Beach	5	285.2
College	91	(X)	Hollywood	12,535	9,973.0
University of Florida	1,315	(X)	Lauderhill	3,632	7,261.1
State agencies	1	(X)	Lighthouse Point	289	2,760.3
			Margate	2,295	4,764.6
Baker	897	4,331.5	Miramar	3,325	7,152.1
Sheriff's office	896	4,326.6	North Lauderdale	1,768	6,463.4
State agencies	1	(X)	Oakland Park	4,322	15,356.7
			Parkland	133	1,281.6
Bay	9,490	6,675.6	Pembroke Pines	4,738	5,021.5
Sheriff's office	3,741	5,233.4	Plantation	6,084	7,981.8
Cedar Grove	54	2,569.0	Pompano Beach	9,496	12,785.6
Lynn Haven	329	2,897.9	Sea Ranch Lakes	22	3,554.1
Panama City	3,309	8,886.6	Sunrise	6,322	8,455.7
Panama City Beach	1,477	32,433.0	Wilton Manors	1,194	10,045.4
Parker	151	3,034.6	Seminole Indian		
Springfield	426	4,492.7	Reservation	420	(X)
State agencies	3	(X)	State agencies	86	(X)
Bradford	1,389	5,559.8	Calhoun	299	2,391.2
Sheriff's office	719	3,627.7	Sheriff's office	195	1,964.1
Starke	670	12,977.0	Blountstown	99	3,985.5
			State agencies	5	(X)
Brevard	25,792	5,729.5			
Sheriff's office	7,883	4,266.3	Charlotte	4,041	3,121.2
Cocoa	1,315	7,357.1	Sheriff's office	3,610	3,081.3
Cocoa Beach	1,008	7,878.7	Punta Gorda	429	3,485.5
Indialantic	154	5,241.7	State agencies	2	(X)
Indian Harbour Beach	209	2,757.6			
Melbourne	6,171	9,214.6	Citrus	2,990	2,771.4
Melbourne Beach	61	1,907.4	Sheriff's office	2,215	2,281.7
Melbourne Village	78	12,745.1	Crystal River	540	13,261.3
Palm Bay	4,125	5,544.7	Inverness	235	3,486.1
Rockledge	1,127	6,113.7			
Satellite Beach	400	3,958.0	Clay	4,641	3,700.0
Titusville	2,767	6,696.4	Sheriff's office	3,854	3,474.1
West Melbourne	486	5,299.3	Green Cove Springs	359	7,197.3
Melbourne Airport	5	(X)	Orange Park	427	4,491.0
State agencies	3	(X)	State agencies	1	(X)

See footnotes at end of table.   Continued . . .

Table 22.03. CRIMINAL OFFENSES AND RATES: CRIME INDEX OFFENSES AND CRIME RATES
IN THE STATE, COUNTIES, CITIES, AND SPECIFIED AREAS
OF FLORIDA, 1996 (Continued)

Area	Number of index offenses 1/	Crime rate per 100,000 popu- lation	Area	Number of index offenses 1/	Crime rate per 100,000 popu- lation
Collier	11,770	6,097.3	Duval	62,411	8,567.8
Sheriff's office	10,326	6,006.7	Atlantic Beach	580	4,422.1
Naples	1,441	6,820.7	Jacksonville	59,530	(X)
State agencies	3	(X)	Jacksonville Beach	1,745	8,687.6
			Neptune Beach	380	5,064.6
Columbia	3,695	7,029.4	Jacksonville Airport	35	(X)
Sheriff's office	2,178	5,122.8	University of North		
Lake City	1,514	15,066.2	Florida	125	(X)
State agencies	3	(X)	State agencies	16	(X)
Dade	225,293	11,025.9	Escambia	17,743	6,197.3
Metro-Dade	125,898	11,440.8	Sheriff's office	13,509	5,986.9
Bal Harbour	161	5,165.2	Pensacola	4,136	6,818.6
Bay Harbor Islands	163	3,495.6	University of West		
Biscayne Park	131	4,323.4	Florida	98	(X)
Coral Gables	4,836	11,736.4			
El Portal	178	7,163.0	Flagler	1,454	3,723.2
Florida City	1,019	18,229.0	Sheriff's office	1,139	3,474.8
Golden Beach	13	1,556.9	Bunnell	195	9,521.5
Hialeah Gardens	904	7,405.0	Flagler Beach	120	2,840.2
Homestead	3,890	15,324.0			
Indian Creek Village	12	24,000.0	Franklin	272	2,620.9
Key Biscayne	421	4,737.8	Sheriff's office	272	3,588.4
Medley	228	25,791.9			
Miami	52,918	14,493.0	Gadsden	2,234	4,822.8
Miami Beach	16,841	18,335.7	Sheriff's office	1,158	3,507.2
Miami Shores	1,002	9,860.3	Chattahoochee	47	1,145.2
Miami Springs	1,349	10,098.8	Havana	219	11,748.9
North Bay Village	361	6,124.9	Quincy	808	11,014.2
North Miami	6,275	12,362.8	State agencies	2	(X)
North Miami Beach	3,217	8,453.1			
Opa-Locka	2,899	18,359.7	Gilchrist	348	2,864.2
South Miami	826	7,839.0	Sheriff's office	299	2,767.5
Surfside	358	8,209.1	Trenton	49	3,640.4
Sweetwater	137	974.4			
Virginia Gardens	95	4,190.6	Glades	515	5,471.2
West Miami	305	5,229.8	Sheriff's office	515	5,471.2
Florida International					
University	570	(X)	Gulf	334	2,465.9
State agencies	286	(X)	Sheriff's office	228	2,421.2
			Port St. Joe	106	2,567.8
De Soto	1,711	6,404.4			
Sheriff's office	854	4,245.4	Hamilton	409	3,045.2
Arcadia	856	12,969.7	Sheriff's office	406	4,161.5
State agencies	1	(X)	State agencies	3	(X)
Dixie	731	5,800.7	Hardee	1,327	5,892.8
Sheriff's office	591	5,611.5	Sheriff's office	898	5,675.3
Cross City	140	6,763.3	Bowling Green	81	4,317.7

See footnotes at end of table.   Continued . . .

Table 22.03. CRIMINAL OFFENSES AND RATES: CRIME INDEX OFFENSES AND CRIME RATES
IN THE STATE, COUNTIES, CITIES, AND SPECIFIED AREAS
OF FLORIDA, 1996 (Continued)

Area	Number of index offenses 1/	Crime rate per 100,000 popu- lation	Area	Number of index offenses 1/	Crime rate per 100,000 popu- lation
Hardee (Continued)			Jackson (Continued)		
Wauchula	348	9,739.7	State agencies	3	(X)
Hendry	1,645	5,454.8	Jefferson	810	5,906.8
Sheriff's office	903	3,792.8	Sheriff's office	323	2,982.7
Clewiston	740	11,655.4	Monticello	487	16,886.3
State agencies	2	(X)			
			Lafayette	41	584.7
Hernando	5,127	4,275.0	Sheriff's office	41	584.7
Sheriff's office	4,366	3,893.5			
Brooksville	760	9,751.1	Lake	7,820	4,289.4
State agencies	1	(X)	Sheriff's office	3,751	3,562.0
			Clermont	434	5,952.5
Highlands	4,499	5,768.2	Eustis	509	3,562.9
Sheriff's office	2,393	3,927.4	Fruitland Park	130	4,361.0
Avon Park	894	11,023.4	Groveland	156	6,272.6
Sebring	1,212	13,534.3	Howey-in-the-Hills	7	879.4
			Lady Lake	226	1,839.3
Hillsborough	85,801	9,419.8	Leesburg	1,349	8,787.1
Sheriff's office	38,356	6,655.6	Mascotte	88	3,703.7
Plant City	2,691	10,317.9	Mount Dora	739	8,711.5
Tampa	42,871	14,817.0	Tavares	311	3,777.5
Temple Terrace	689	3,600.2	Umatilla	118	4,852.0
Tampa International Airport	363	(X)	State agencies	2	(X)
University of South Florida	805	(X)	Lee	20,051	5,225.6
State agencies	26	(X)	Sheriff's office	8,868	3,635.8
			Cape Coral	3,690	4,210.8
			Ft. Myers	7,074	15,269.4
Holmes	48	275.7	Sanibel	254	4,350.8
Sheriff's office	0	0.0	Lee County Airport	146	(X)
Bonifay	46	1,667.3	State agencies	19	(X)
State agencies	2	(X)			
			Leon	18,559	8,374.2
Indian River	5,404	5,287.1	Sheriff's office	3,170	3,830.5
Sheriff's office	3,060	4,672.1	Tallahassee	14,018	10,094.8
Fellsmere	90	3,731.3	Capitol Police	57	(X)
Indian River Shores	73	2,765.2	Florida A & M University	449	(X)
Sebastian	699	5,004.7	Florida State University	847	(X)
Vero Beach	1,476	8,340.4	State agencies	18	(X)
State agencies	6	(X)			
			Levy	1,627	5,301.4
Jackson	1,404	2,887.2	Sheriff's office	947	3,582.8
Sheriff's office	1,193	3,198.5	Chiefland	303	15,233.8
Marianna	136	2,077.6			
Sneads	72	3,435.1			

See footnotes at end of table.   Continued . . .

University of Florida   **Bureau of Economic and Business Research**

Table 22.03. CRIMINAL OFFENSES AND RATES: CRIME INDEX OFFENSES AND CRIME RATES
IN THE STATE, COUNTIES, CITIES, AND SPECIFIED AREAS
OF FLORIDA, 1996 (Continued)

Area	Number of index offenses 1/	Crime rate per 100,000 population	Area	Number of index offenses 1/	Crime rate per 100,000 population
Levy (Continued)			Okaloosa (Continued)		
Williston	375	16,527.1	Ft. Walton Beach	1,186	5,381.9
State agencies	2	(X)	Niceville	299	2,554.5
			Valparaiso	58	874.2
Liberty	100	1,344.3	State agencies	1	(X)
Sheriff's office	98	1,317.4			
State agencies	2	(X)	Okeechobee	1,829	5,436.5
			Sheriff's office	1,456	5,095.5
Madison	513	2,736.7	Okeechobee	372	7,338.7
Sheriff's office	496	3,313.7	State agencies	1	(X)
Lee	14	4,458.6			
State agencies	3	(X)	Orange	75,500	9,709.9
			Sheriff's office	43,078	8,407.5
Manatee	17,658	7,336.6	Apopka	3,064	15,912.8
Sheriff's office	12,111	7,144.6	Edgewood	124	8,384.0
Bradenton	3,753	7,813.7	Maitland	512	5,186.9
Bradenton Beach	137	8,145.1	Oakland	36	4,812.8
Holmes Beach	302	5,988.5	Ocoee	1,499	7,782.6
Longboat Key	124	1,891.4	Orlando	24,055	13,894.8
Palmetto	1,216	12,332.7	Windermere	21	1,182.4
State agencies	15	(X)	Winter Garden	882	7,105.5
			Winter Park	1,893	7,648.5
Marion	12,522	5,461.9	University of		
Sheriff's office	6,406	3,542.4	Central Florida	317	(X)
Dunnellon	72	4,033.6	State agencies	19	(X)
Ocala	6,043	13,945.8			
State agencies	1	(X)	Osceola	9,966	7,132.6
			Sheriff's office	5,012	5,900.1
Martin	5,758	5,030.4	Kissimmee	3,908	10,237.1
Sheriff's office	4,499	4,573.4	St. Cloud	1,044	6,288.8
Jupiter Island	27	4,647.2	State agencies	2	(X)
Sewalls Point	36	2,073.7			
Stuart	1,187	8,618.3	Palm Beach	79,436	8,090.9
State agencies	9	(X)	Sheriff's office	32,454	6,870.6
			Atlantis	59	3,482.9
Monroe	6,633	7,916.3	Boca Raton	2,889	4,264.0
Sheriff's office	3,881	6,835.2	Boynton Beach	5,889	11,560.7
Key West	2,748	10,174.4	Delray Beach	6,388	12,275.4
State agencies	4	(X)	Greenacres City	1,472	6,202.3
			Gulf Stream	16	2,263.1
Nassau	2,043	3,998.3	Highland Beach	74	2,267.2
Sheriff's office	1,365	3,320.4	Juno Beach	44	1,654.8
Fernandina Beach	677	6,778.1	Jupiter	1,577	5,153.8
State agencies	1	(X)	Jupiter Inlet Colony	2	475.1
			Lake Clarke Shores	105	2,884.6
Okaloosa	5,058	3,059.5	Lake Park	1,045	15,173.5
Sheriff's office	2,877	2,557.0	Lake Worth	4,552	15,252.7
Crestview	637	5,125.1	Lantana	1,013	10,286.4

See footnotes at end of table.   Continued . . .

University of Florida   **Bureau of Economic and Business Research**

Table 22.03. CRIMINAL OFFENSES AND RATES: CRIME INDEX OFFENSES AND CRIME RATES
IN THE STATE, COUNTIES, CITIES, AND SPECIFIED AREAS
OF FLORIDA, 1996 (Continued)

Area	Number of index offenses 1/	Crime rate per 100,000 population	Area	Number of index offenses 1/	Crime rate per 100,000 population
Palm Beach (Continued)			Polk	33,838	7,474.6
Manalapan	16	4,848.5	Sheriff's office	16,617	5,901.4
Mangonia Park	460	33,046.0	Auburndale	1,223	13,118.1
Ocean Ridge	57	2,803.7	Bartow	1,530	10,183.0
Pahokee	488	7,036.8	Davenport	31	1,564.9
Palm Beach	412	4,208.4	Dundee	166	6,454.1
Palm Beach Gardens	2,658	8,329.9	Eagle Lake	60	3,152.9
Palm Beach Shores	137	13,326.9	Ft. Meade	455	8,341.0
Riviera Beach	1,787	6,432.2	Frostproof	147	5,062.0
Royal Palm Beach	1,083	6,129.7	Haines City	958	7,420.0
South Bay	329	9,882.9	Lake Alfred	193	5,118.0
South Palm Beach	22	1,468.6	Lake Hamilton	106	9,322.8
Tequesta	152	3,252.7	Lakeland	9,483	12,573.3
West Palm Beach	12,301	15,696.1	Mulberry	190	5,733.3
Florida Atlantic			Winter Haven	2,661	10,441.4
University	283	(X)	State agencies	18	(X)
Palm Beach County					
School Board	1,623	(X)	Putnam	4,904	6,977.1
State agencies	49	(X)	Sheriff's office	3,116	5,395.2
			Crescent City	148	8,013.0
Pasco	14,340	4,626.8	Palatka	1,638	15,329.9
Sheriff's office	11,370	4,091.1	State agencies	2	(X)
Dade City	777	13,030.4			
New Port Richey	1,212	8,327.0	St. Johns	4,665	4,585.7
Port Richey	241	9,167.0	Sheriff's office	2,937	3,436.5
Zephyrhills	724	8,165.1	St. Augustine	1,453	11,959.8
State agencies	16	(X)	St. Augustine Beach	247	6,001.0
			Florida School Deaf		
Pinellas	58,581	6,646.5	and Blind	24	(X)
Sheriff's office	16,733	4,642.0	State agencies	4	(X)
Belleair	63	1,544.1			
Belleair Beach	43	2,011.2	St. Lucie	10,922	6,224.9
Clearwater	7,582	7,443.0	Sheriff's office	2,559	4,043.2
Gulfport	1,103	9,291.6	Ft. Pierce	5,588	14,992.1
Indian Shores	146	3,759.0	Port St. Lucie	2,768	3,695.9
Kenneth City	164	3,784.0	State agencies	7	(X)
Largo	3,536	5,215.5			
Pinellas Park	3,056	6,871.7	Santa Rosa	3,601	3,656.2
Redington Beach 2/	49	1,780.5	Sheriff's office	3,441	4,048.3
St. Petersburg	24,165	10,015.5	Gulf Breeze	157	2,634.7
St. Petersburg			State agencies	3	(X)
Beach	630	6,570.0			
Tarpon Springs	982	5,034.1	Sarasota	16,549	5,480.9
Treasure Island	261	3,552.5	Sheriff's office	9,745	4,509.4
Pinellas County			North Port	380	2,389.2
Campus Police	13	(X)	Sarasota	5,774	11,253.0
University of South			Venice	583	3,131.2
Florida	34	(X)	University of South		
State agencies	21	(X)	Florida	56	(X)

See footnotes at end of table.   Continued . . .

Table 22.03. CRIMINAL OFFENSES AND RATES: CRIME INDEX OFFENSES AND CRIME RATES
IN THE STATE, COUNTIES, CITIES, AND SPECIFIED AREAS
OF FLORIDA, 1996 (Continued)

Area	Number of index offenses 1/	Crime rate per 100,000 population	Area	Number of index offenses 1/	Crime rate per 100,000 population
Sarasota (Continued)			Volusia	24,492	6,014.8
State agencies	11	(X)	Sheriff's office	7,230	4,075.6
			Daytona Beach	7,685	12,046.2
Seminole	15,938	4,843.9	Daytona Beach Shores	360	12,543.6
Sheriff's office	5,209	3,169.1	DeLand	2,449	13,605.6
Altamonte Springs	3,126	8,183.3	Edgewater	686	3,862.4
Casselberry	1,527	6,260.0	Holly Hill	1,286	11,310.5
Lake Mary	233	3,119.1	New Smyrna Beach	952	5,219.6
Longwood	398	2,926.9	Oak Hill	60	5,540.2
Oviedo	720	3,740.8	Orange City	700	11,406.2
Sanford	3,823	10,836.5	Ormond Beach	1,376	4,243.5
Winter Springs	898	3,392.0	Ponce Inlet	50	2,240.1
State agencies	4	(X)	Port Orange	926	2,284.0
			South Daytona	455	3,524.4
Sumter	1,270	3,128.6	Daytona Beach		
Sheriff's office	849	2,671.2	Regional	7	(X)
Bushnell	131	5,555.6	Volusia County Beach		
Center Hill	44	5,774.3	Patrol	264	(X)
Coleman	5	590.3	State agencies	6	(X)
Webster	20	2,341.9			
Wildwood	221	5,540.2	Wakulla	829	4,599.9
			Sheriff's office	829	4,599.9
Suwannee	622	1,979.4			
Sheriff's office	393	1,574.6	Walton	1,016	2,959.7
Live Oak	227	3,511.2	Sheriff's office	749	2,599.2
State agencies	2	(X)	DeFuniak Springs	265	4,808.5
			State agencies	2	(X)
Taylor	1,205	6,334.8			
Sheriff's office	380	3,218.7	Washington	217	1,098.7
Perry	825	11,432.9	Sheriff's office	214	1,368.2
			State agencies	3	(X)
Union	65	499.1			
Sheriff's office	64	491.4			
State agencies	1	(X)			

(X) Not applicable.
1/ Actual offenses known to enforcement officers. Index offenses include murder,
forcible sex, robbery, aggravated assault, burglary, larceny, and auto theft.
2/ Includes North Redington Beach.
Note: The data reflected in this table is by geographic jurisdiction and is not
intended to depict an individual law enforcement agency's activity. Sheriff's office
totals include the activity occurring within those incorporated jurisdictions who do
not report directly to the Uniform Crime Reporting (UCR) program. County totals reflect all UCR activity occurring within that county. State agencies are listed only
for counties with state agency activity.
Source: State of Florida, Department of Law Enforcement, unpublished data.

Table 22.04.   CRIMINAL OFFENSES: ADULT ARRESTS BY SEX AND RACE
AND BY OFFENSE IN FLORIDA, 1996

Offense	Total	Sex		Race		
		Male	Female	White	Black	Other
Total	468,892	374,361	94,531	303,842	164,373	677
Murder	985	884	101	555	430	0
Manslaughter	201	168	33	173	27	1
Forcible rape	2,434	2,402	32	1,538	896	0
Robbery	6,832	6,191	641	2,806	4,019	7
Aggravated assault	37,282	29,829	7,453	20,960	16,258	64
Other assaults	49,626	39,969	9,657	34,986	14,570	70
Burglary	16,551	15,075	1,476	10,716	5,807	28
Larceny theft	53,227	37,645	15,582	33,953	19,165	109
Motor vehicle theft	6,348	5,569	776	3,550	2,791	4
Arson	372	290	82	259	111	2
Forgery/counterfeiting	4,067	2,704	1,363	2,576	1,484	7
Fraud	20,859	12,038	8,821	14,440	6,388	31
Embezzlement	10	6	4	10	0	0
Stolen property	3,062	2,656	406	2,011	1,045	6
Vandalism	2,410	2,008	402	1,748	647	15
Weapons violations	8,073	7,387	686	4,480	3,582	11
Prostitution/commercialized						
vice	4,934	2,219	2,715	3,738	1,194	2
Sex offenses	2,991	2,682	309	2,350	629	12
Drug sale	17,233	14,425	2,808	7,354	9,868	11
Opium/cocaine	12,884	10,818	2,066	4,685	8,191	8
Marijuana	2,677	2,264	413	1,644	1,030	3
Synthetic narcotics	2	2	0	2	0	0
Other dangerous drugs	1,670	1,341	329	1,023	647	0
Drug possession	52,567	43,224	9,343	29,509	22,999	59
Opium/cocaine	25,196	20,262	4,934	11,032	14,141	23
Marijuana	19,426	17,003	2,423	13,626	5,769	31
Synthetic narcotics	3	3	0	3	0	0
Other dangerous drugs	7,942	5,956	1,986	4,848	3,089	5
Bookmaking	46	42	4	27	19	0
Number/lottery	44	33	11	23	21	0
All other gambling	281	265	16	72	206	3
Offense against family	3,333	2,446	887	2,174	1,152	7
Driving under influence	44,143	36,357	7,786	40,860	3,214	69
Liquor laws	179	129	50	149	27	3
Drunkenness	3,831	3,160	671	3,268	558	5
Disorderly conduct	7,668	6,244	1,424	5,051	2,602	15
Vagrancy	0	0	0	0	0	0
All other offenses	117,168	96,378	20,790	73,198	43,837	133
Suspicion	0	0	0	0	0	0
Curfew/loitering	2,135	1,936	199	1,308	824	3

Note: A person is counted each time he/she is arrested or summoned; therefore, arrest counts do not reflect the specific number of persons arrested since one individual may be arrested several times for the same or different crimes. Arrest data are useful for measuring law enforcement activity and involvement in criminal acts by the age, sex, and race of perpetrators.

Source: State of Florida, Department of Law Enforcement, unpublished data.

Table 22.05. CRIMINAL OFFENSES: JUVENILE ARRESTS BY SEX, RACE, AND
OFFENSE IN FLORIDA, 1995 AND 1996

Sex, race, and offense	1995	1996	Percentage Change
Arrests, total	148,492	151,033	1.7
Male	(NA)	114,921	(X)
Female	(NA)	36,033	(X)
Unknown sex	(NA)	79	(X)
White	(NA)	87,584	(X)
Black	(NA)	61,761	(X)
Asian or Pacific Islander	(NA)	735	(X)
American Indian, Eskimo, or Aleut	(NA)	106	(X)
Unknown race	(NA)	847	(X)
Felony arrests	60,595	60,113	-0.8
Murder	132	89	-32.5
Attempted murder	220	195	-11.4
Sexual offenses	1,516	1,559	2.8
Robbery, including armed	3,914	3,551	-9.3
Aggravated assault/battery	8,491	8,753	3.0
Arson	658	573	-12.9
Burglary	19,430	19,483	0.3
Auto theft	6,018	5,490	-8.8
Grand larceny	4,429	4,207	-5.0
Dealing in stolen property	432	450	4.2
Concealed firearm	970	789	-18.7
Forgery	489	452	-7.6
Nonmarijuana felony drug	4,097	4,504	9.9
Felony marijuana	1,130	1,262	11.7
Escape	1,387	1,077	-22.5
Resisting arrest with violence	575	539	0.2
Shoot/throw deadly missile	1,111	1,094	-1.5
Felony traffic offenses	77	77	0.0
Other felony	5,519	5,906	7.0
Misdemeanor arrests	87,897	90,920	3.4
Assault/battery	18,723	20,604	10.0
Prostitution and other sex offenses	241	202	-16.2
Petit theft	6,597	5,868	-11.1
Shoplifting	27,084	27,460	1.4
Dealing in stolen property	106	107	0.9
Concealed weapon	808	831	2.8
Disorderly conduct	2,804	2,783	-0.7
Vandalism	4,751	4,532	-4.6
Trespass	8,086	7,800	-3.5
Loitering	2,662	2,575	0.0
Nonmarijuana misdemeanor drug	2,027	2,264	11.7
Misdemeanor marijuana	4,335	5,030	16.0
Alcohol-related offenses	2,299	2,514	9.4
Violation of game laws	199	150	-24.6
Resist without violence	2,248	2,676	19.0
Unauthorized use of car	44	51	15.9
Other misdemeanor	4,883	5,473	12.1

(NA) Not available.
(X) Not applicable.
Note: A person is counted each time he/she is arrested or summoned. See Note on
Table 22.04.

Source: State of Florida, Department of Law Enforcement, *Crime in Florida, 1996*,
and unpublished data.

Table 22.06. DOMESTIC VIOLENCE OFFENSES: NUMBER AND RELATIONSHIP OF THE VICTIM TO THE OFFENDER IN FLORIDA, 1996

Primary offense	Total	Per-centage change from 1995	Per-centage of all of-fenses 1/	Relationship of victim to offender	
				Spouse	Parent
Total	132,704	1.2	A/	42,358	9,511
Murder	192	-1.5	17.8	67	22
Manslaughter	17	21.4	8.5	2	0
Forcible sex offenses	2,855	-8.8	22.1	233	129
Forcible rape	1,426	-2.6	19.0	197	61
Forcible sodomy	408	-22.4	27.0	17	14
Forcible fondling	1,021	-10.2	26.0	19	54
Aggravated assault	25,680	-0.5	26.8	6,469	1,945
Aggravated stalking	255	0.0	(NA)	141	3
Simple assault	99,116	0.4	(NA)	33,529	7,066
Threat/intimidation	4,022	22.8	(NA)	1,683	338
Simple stalking	567	0.0	(NA)	234	8

	Relationship of victim to offender				
	Child	Sibling	Other family	Cohab-itant	Other
Total	9,774	8,594	7,247	42,976	12,244
Murder	25	5	9	48	16
Manslaughter	6	2	4	3	0
Forcible sex offenses	859	268	658	301	407
Forcible rape	352	102	273	191	250
Forcible sodomy	113	60	122	38	44
Forcible fondling	394	106	263	72	113
Aggravated assault	2,420	2,178	1,905	7,775	2,988
Aggravated stalking	5	2	5	50	49
Simple assault	6,283	5,977	4,401	33,769	8,091
Threat/intimidation	168	156	256	931	490
Simple stalking	8	6	9	99	203

(NA) Not available.

A/ Total number of crimes as represented by the source includes index and manda-tory offenses and excludes optional offenses such as intimidation, weapons viola-tions, destruction/damage/vandalism, etc. for which no report to FDLE is required; therefore a comparison of the totals is not valid.

1/ As a percentage of all similarly committed crimes or arrests.

Source: State of Florida, Department of Law Enforcement, *Crime in Florida: 1996 Annual Report.*

Table 22.08. CRIME RATES: PROPERTY AND VIOLENT CRIME RATES IN FLORIDA
AND THE UNITED STATES, 1986 THROUGH 1995

(rates per 100,000 population)

	Florida			United States		
Year	All crime	Property crime 1/	Violent crime 2/	All crime	Property crime 1/	Violent crime 2/
1985	7,574.2	6,633.1	941.1	5,206.7	4,650.5	556.2
1986	8,228.4	7,191.9	1,036.5	5,480.4	4,862.6	617.7
1987	8,503.2	7,478.7	1,024.4	5,550.0	4,940.3	609.7
1988 A/	8,937.6	7,819.9	1,117.7	5,664.2	5,027.1	637.2
1989	8,804.5	7,695.1	1,109.4	5,741.0	5,077.9	663.1
1990	8,810.8	7,566.5	1,244.3	5,820.3	5,088.5	731.8
1991	8,547.2	7,362.9	1,184.3	5,897.8	5,139.7	758.1
1992	8,358.2	7,151.0	1,207.2	5,660.2	4,902.7	757.5
1993	8,351.0	7,145.0	1,206.0	5,484.4	4,737.6	746.8
1994	8,250.0	7,103.2	1,146.8	5,373.5	4,660.0	713.6
1995	7,701.5	6,630.6	1,071.0	5,277.6	4,593.0	684.6

A/ Data for Florida were unavailable and are estimates.
1/ Includes burglary, larceny-theft, and motor vehicle theft.
2/ Includes murder, forcible rape, robbery, and aggravated assault.
Note: Some data may be revised.
Source: U.S., Department of Justice, Federal Bureau of Investigation, *Crime in the United States, 1995,* Internet site http://www.fbi.gov/, and previous editions.

Table 22.09. CAPITAL PUNISHMENT: PRISONERS UNDER SENTENCE OF DEATH
BY RACE, SEX, AND HISPANIC ORIGIN IN FLORIDA, THE SOUTH
AND THE UNITED STATES, DECEMBER 31, 1994 AND 1995

	Florida		South 1/		
Item	Number	Percentage of United States	Number	Percentage of United States	United States
Prisoners under sentence of death on 12-31-94 A/	353	12.2	1,621	55.8	2,905
Changes during 1995					
Received under death sentence	31	10.0	184	59.4	310
Removed from death row 2/	19	18.1	71	67.6	105
Executed	3	5.4	41	73.2	56
Prisoners under sentence of death on 12-31-95	362	11.9	1,693	55.4	3,054
White	228	13.2	971	56.1	1,730
Black	134	10.5	700	54.9	1,275
Women	6	12.5	20	41.7	48
Hispanic origin 3/	35	14.8	48	20.3	237

A/ Revised.
1/ Includes Alabama, Arkansas, Delaware, Florida, Georgia, Kentucky, Louisiana, Maryland, Mississippi, North Carolina, Oklahoma, South Carolina, Tennessee, Texas, and Virginia.
2/ Excludes executions. Includes suicide, murder, and death by natural causes.
3/ Persons of Hispanic origin may be of any race.

Source: U.S., Department of Justice, Bureau of Justice Statistics, *Bureau of Justice Statistics Bulletin: Capital Punishment, 1995.*

University of Florida   **Bureau of Economic and Business Research**

Table 22.10. PRISONERS: NUMBER UNDER JURISDICTION OF STATE OR FEDERAL CORRECTIONAL AUTHORITIES IN FLORIDA AND THE UNITED STATES DECEMBER 31, 1993 THROUGH 1996

Item	1993	1994 A/	1995 A/	1996 B/
Florida				
Total prisoners	53,048	57,168	63,879	63,763
Percentage change from previous year	9.8	7.8	11.7	-0.2
Prisoners sentenced to more than a year	52,883	57,157	63,866	63,746
Per 100,000 resident population	385	406	447	439
United States				
Total prisoners	970,444	1,055,073	1,126,293	1,182,169
Percentage change from previous year	9.8	8.7	6.8	5.0
Prisoners sentenced to more than a year	932,266	1,017,059	1,085,369	1,138,187
Per 100,000 resident population	351	387	409	427

A/ Revised.
B/ Preliminary.
Source: U.S., Department of Justice, Bureau of Justice Statistics, *Bureau of Justice Statistics Bulletin: Prisoners in 1996,* and previous edition.

Table 22.11. POPULATION UNDER CRIMINAL SENTENCE: INCARCERATED INMATES AND OFFENDERS UNDER COMMUNITY SUPERVISION OF THE FLORIDA DEPARTMENT OF CORRECTIONS, JUNE 30, 1992 THROUGH 1996

Item	1992	1993	1994	1995	1996
Under supervision, total	158,098	180,543	189,718	198,048	201,944
Incarcerated offenders	47,012	50,603	56,052	61,992	64,333
Male	44,508	47,965	53,163	58,497	60,782
White	17,460	18,654	21,117	23,658	25,437
Black	25,901	28,069	30,818	33,586	34,123
Other	A/ 1,147	A/ 1,242	1,228	1,253	1,222
Female	2,504	2,638	2,889	3,495	3,551
White	966	983	1,175	1,494	1,551
Black	1,439	1,536	1,714	1,998	1,977
Other	A/ 99	A/ 119	0	3	23
Offenders under community supervision	111,086	129,940	133,666	136,056	137,611
Probation	82,966	91,070	91,236	93,723	98,420
Felony	81,889	88,782	88,717	90,879	95,183
Misdemeanor	1,077	1,191	1,212	1,362	1,674
Administrative	(NA)	1,097	1,307	1,482	1,563
Drug offender probation	(NA)	3,587	4,808	6,332	7,857
Community control	(NA)	14,892	14,926	14,692	14,465
Pretrial intervention	4,917	5,441	6,455	7,793	7,813
Post-prison release	(NA)	(NA)	(NA)	(NA)	9,056
Parole	2,596	2,907	2,965	2,838	2,747
Other 1/	20,607	12,043	13,276	10,667	6,309

(NA) Not available. A/ Includes data not distributed by race. 1/ Includes conditional, control, supervised community, conditional medical, and other post-prison releases.
Source: State of Florida, Department of Corrections, *1995-96 Annual Report: The Guidebook to Corrections in Florida,* and previous editions.

University of Florida   **Bureau of Economic and Business Research**

Table 22.12. POPULATION UNDER CRIMINAL SENTENCE: INCARCERATED OFFENDERS AND OFFENDERS UNDER COMMUNITY SUPERVISION OF THE FLORIDA DEPARTMENT OF CORRECTIONS BY PRIMARY OFFENSE, JUNE 30, 1996

	Incarcerated offenders		Community supervision				
Primary offense	Total	Admitted 1995-96	Total 1/	Proba- tion 2/	Commu- nity control	Control release	Parole
Total	64,333	20,934	137,611	106,277	14,465	3,210	2,747
Murder, manslaughter	9,432	1,169	2,294	1,404	222	22	554
First degree murder	4,280	407	352	147	40	2	147
Second degree murder	3,964	446	683	305	47	0	294
Third degree murder	100	21	73	55	6	0	10
Other homicide	40	4	84	47	8	0	29
Manslaughter	726	182	774	585	72	14	71
DUI manslaughter	322	109	328	265	49	6	3
Sexual offenses	6,459	1,488	8,415	6,965	998	0	188
Capital sexual battery	2,214	349	929	816	76	0	11
Life sexual battery	1,151	106	276	213	23	0	23
First degree sexual battery	1,290	320	1,792	1,469	192	0	70
Other sexual battery	139	1	182	111	13	0	55
Lewd, lascivious be- havior	1,665	712	5,236	4,356	694	0	29
Robbery	9,488	2,232	4,879	2,842	661	210	429
Robbery with weapon	6,415	1,361	2,275	1,278	310	77	324
Robbery without weapon	3,038	845	2,589	1,557	344	133	104
Home invasion, robbery	35	26	15	7	7	0	1
Violent personal offenses	7,240	3,003	20,401	16,326	2,435	159	166
Home invasion, other	6	3	3	2	1	0	0
Carjacking	141	90	33	19	14	0	0
Aggravated assault	722	401	4,629	3,818	511	17	41
Aggravated battery	2,480	1,071	5,677	4,431	763	71	40
Assault and battery on law enforcement officers	1,236	497	2,920	2,264	340	0	8
Other assault and battery	68	36	394	336	32	1	5
Aggravated stalking	37	34	405	336	53	0	2
Resisting arrest with violence	391	229	1,810	1,442	187	15	2
Kidnapping	1,359	245	741	555	77	11	40
Arson	370	131	790	632	89	21	12
Abuse of children	127	73	840	676	109	3	7
Leaving accident scene	101	75	533	459	56	1	7
DUI, injury	101	74	982	820	104	14	0
Other violent offenses	101	44	644	536	99	5	2
Burglary	11,120	4,032	15,071	11,049	2,055	699	274
Burglary of structure	2,821	1,234	8,000	6,068	964	277	131
Burglary of dwelling	5,036	1,873	4,484	3,123	711	330	91
Armed burglary	1,833	484	761	487	157	62	13
Burglary with assault	1,349	392	829	585	146	19	19
Other burglary offenses	81	49	997	786	77	11	20

See footnotes at end of table.   Continued . . .

Table 22.12. POPULATION UNDER CRIMINAL SENTENCE: INCARCERATED OFFENDERS AND OFFENDERS UNDER COMMUNITY SUPERVISION OF THE FLORIDA DEPARTMENT OF CORRECTIONS BY PRIMARY OFFENSE, JUNE 30, 1996 (Continued)

Primary offense	Incarcerated offenders Total	Incarcerated offenders Admitted 1995-96	Total 1/	Proba- tion 2/	Commu- nity control	Control release	Parole
Theft, forgery, fraud	5,745	2,621	35,442	28,033	3,029	706	265
Grand theft	1,382	682	14,661	11,702	1,115	189	100
Grand theft, automobile	1,221	574	2,773	2,108	315	127	33
Stolen property	1,723	730	3,584	2,737	516	176	39
Forgery, uttering and counterfeiting	626	285	4,599	3,525	455	112	47
Worthless checks	195	91	3,075	2,519	201	26	11
Fraudulent practices	334	159	5,511	4,427	302	41	24
Other theft, property damage	264	100	1,239	1,015	125	35	11
Drugs	10,928	4,800	36,781	27,646	3,875	1,234	686
Sale/purchase/manufac- turing	6,328	2,766	15,351	11,444	1,796	687	232
Trafficking	2,068	724	1,990	1,455	217	136	155
Other possession	2,532	1,310	19,440	14,747	1,862	411	299
Weapons	1,714	813	4,536	3,525	505	99	34
Weapons, discharging	328	184	918	737	126	8	9
Weapons, possession	1,384	627	3,547	2,725	376	91	24
Other weapons offenses	2	2	71	63	3	0	1
Other offenses	2,143	776	8,752	7,637	604	81	86
Escape	1,382	394	770	535	115	32	22
DUI, no injury	237	204	1,120	930	154	16	16
Traffic, other	8	6	417	369	44	1	2
Racketeering	113	39	285	236	31	15	2
Pollution/hazardous materials	6	3	207	151	10	1	0
Other offenses	397	130	5,953	5,416	250	16	44
Data unavailable	64	0	1,040	850	81	0	65

DUI Driving under the influence.
1/ Includes pretrial intervention and post-prison releases not shown separately.
2/ Includes drug offender probation.

Source: State of Florida, Department of Corrections, *1995-96 Annual Report: The Guidebook to Corrections in Florida.*

Table 22.13.   PRISONERS: LENGTH OF SENTENCE, CLASS OF FELONY, AGE, MEDICAL
CLASSIFICATION, EDUCATIONAL LEVEL, LITERACY SKILLS LEVEL, AND
PRIOR COMMITMENTS BY RACE AND SEX OF OFFENDER IN
FLORIDA, JUNE 30, 1996

Item	Total	White Male	White Female	Black Male	Black Female	Other Male	Other Female
Length of sentence (years)							
Total	64,333	25,437	1,551	34,123	1,977	1,222	23
Average 1/	16.4	17.1	10.7	16.5	8.7	18.3	6.3
Median 1/	9.0	9.5	5.0	9.0	5.0	10.0	2.5
1 year or less	19	6	0	11	2	0	0
1 to 5	21,208	8,541	819	10,413	1,079	339	17
6 to 10	15,645	5,606	334	8,923	495	284	3
11 to 15	8,212	3,225	155	4,478	182	171	1
16 to 24	5,813	2,254	75	3,260	83	140	1
25 to 30	3,358	1,334	25	1,890	40	69	0
31 to 50	2,179	894	31	1,202	21	31	0
51 years or more	1,204	478	10	680	11	25	0
Life/death	6,534	3,043	102	3,162	64	162	1
Data unavailable	161	56	0	104	0	1	0
Class of felony 2/							
Capital	2,927	1,573	58	1,169	42	85	0
Life felony	5,081	1,875	73	2,896	81	155	1
First degree, life	2,229	806	40	1,307	29	47	0
First degree	15,523	6,264	330	8,157	414	353	5
Second degree	25,127	9,529	527	13,827	830	403	11
Third degree	12,240	4,923	513	6,058	572	168	6
Misdemeanor	12	4	0	7	1	0	0
Data unavailable	1,194	463	10	702	8	11	0
Current age (years)							
Average age	33	35	34	32	33	34	33
Median age	32	33	33	31	33	33	33
16 and under	220	56	4	142	16	2	0
17	488	159	9	302	8	10	0
18	950	318	15	588	18	11	0
19	1,551	555	12	930	33	21	0
20	1,900	708	30	1,106	32	23	1
21	2,053	679	38	1,252	45	39	0
22 to 24	6,825	2,468	126	3,949	135	144	3
25 to 29	12,128	4,513	298	6,681	411	220	5
30 to 34	12,879	4,807	369	6,956	520	223	4
35 to 39	10,888	4,228	302	5,700	427	224	7
40 to 44	6,906	2,852	171	3,550	195	136	2
45 to 49	3,766	1,792	85	1,722	74	92	1
50 to 54	1,756	1,018	50	627	32	29	0
55 to 64	1,495	939	36	459	23	38	0
65 to 69	258	174	3	69	6	6	0
70 and over	206	144	3	53	2	4	0
Data unavailable	64	27	0	37	0	0	0
Medical grade class-							
ification 3/							
Unrestricted	35,926	13,611	957	19,420	1,224	701	13
Minimum	21,742	8,914	504	11,317	612	386	9
Moderate	5,400	2,303	61	2,809	111	116	0
Severe	842	431	7	382	8	14	0
Data unavailable	423	178	22	195	22	5	1

See footnotes at end of table.   Continued . . .

Table 22.13. PRISONERS: LENGTH OF SENTENCE, CLASS OF FELONY, AGE, MEDICAL
CLASSIFICATION, EDUCATIONAL LEVEL, LITERACY SKILLS LEVEL, AND
PRIOR COMMITMENTS BY RACE AND SEX OF OFFENDER IN
FLORIDA, JUNE 30, 1996 (Continued)

Item	Total	White		Black		Other	
		Male	Female	Male	Female	Male	Female
Tested education grade level 4/							
Median grade level	8	9	9	7	6	7	8
1	1,164	251	3	817	32	61	0
2	3,777	720	26	2,760	159	111	1
3	4,196	835	50	3,036	185	90	0
4	3,955	870	42	2,750	212	78	3
5	5,214	1,325	76	3,491	254	67	1
6	5,103	1,530	90	3,197	223	63	0
7	6,251	2,027	143	3,759	221	97	4
8	7,224	2,899	199	3,824	203	96	3
9	5,441	2,562	146	2,539	122	69	3
10	6,708	3,729	231	2,553	109	84	2
11	1,220	742	61	378	24	15	0
12	6,031	4,238	337	1,278	100	76	2
Data unavailable	8,049	3,709	147	3,741	133	315	4
Tested literacy skill levels 4/							
Median skill level	8	9	9	7	6	7	8
Less than basic literacy (1.0-3.9)	9,137	1,806	79	6,613	376	262	1
Basic literacy skills (4.0-8.9)	27,747	8,651	550	17,021	1,113	401	11
Functional literacy skills (9.0-12.9)	19,400	11,271	775	6,748	355	244	7
Data unavailable	8,049	3,709	147	3,741	133	315	4
Prior DOC commitments							
None	28,416	13,586	1,005	12,151	954	704	16
One	14,505	5,583	301	7,883	442	290	6
Two	9,820	3,151	153	6,060	316	140	0
Three	5,989	1,723	63	3,988	159	55	1
Four	3,171	796	26	2,262	66	21	0
Five	1,447	347	2	1,064	28	6	0
Six	554	128	1	413	8	4	0
Seven	247	70	0	171	4	2	0
Eight	83	19	0	64	0	0	0
Nine or more	36	7	0	29	0	0	0
Data unavailable	65	27	0	38	0	0	0

DOC Department of Corrections.
1/ Sentence lengths of 50 years or longer, life, and death were calculated as 50
years.
2/ Primary offense.
3/ Medical grades are assigned to inmates by health care professionals based primarily on general physical stamina, mental health, and functional capacity.
4/ Most recent Tests of Adult Basic Education (TABE) scores.

Source: State of Florida, Department of Corrections, *1995-96 Annual Report: The
Guidebook to Corrections in Florida*.

Table 22.14. POPULATION UNDER CRIMINAL SENTENCE: INCARCERATED OFFENDERS AND OFFENDERS UNDER COMMUNITY SUPERVISION OF THE FLORIDA DEPARTMENT OF CORRECTIONS BY COUNTY OF COMMITMENT OR SUPERVISION AND BY RACE IN THE STATE AND COUNTIES OF FLORIDA JUNE 30, 1996

County	Incarcerated offenders				Community supervision 1/			
	Total	White	Black	Other races	Total 2/	White	Black	Other races
Florida	64,333	26,988	36,100	1,245	191,314	123,937	64,477	2,856
Alachua	819	220	596	3	2,518	1,169	1,340	9
Baker	123	65	55	3	211	139	71	1
Bay	1,122	620	495	7	3,581	2,665	879	34
Bradford	262	119	138	5	326	198	126	2
Brevard	1,583	788	778	17	4,930	3,527	1,368	35
Broward	6,918	2,580	4,298	40	20,316	12,056	8,033	225
Calhoun	113	45	66	2	140	104	36	0
Charlotte	320	221	95	4	968	845	113	10
Citrus	163	138	25	0	1,008	901	99	8
Clay	285	160	121	4	814	657	152	5
Collier	501	333	161	7	2,613	2,268	310	34
Columbia	446	193	252	1	1,262	778	481	3
Dade	8,434	2,941	5,207	286	20,453	10,763	9,015	672
De Soto	207	83	118	6	508	349	154	5
Dixie	128	74	54	0	287	225	62	0
Duval	3,739	1,081	2,633	25	6,773	3,698	3,008	63
Escambia	1,839	707	1,121	11	7,071	4,069	2,961	39
Flagler	69	33	36	0	421	325	93	3
Franklin	68	39	29	0	173	125	48	0
Gadsden	378	45	332	1	1,044	219	798	26
Gilchrist	27	21	6	0	100	88	9	3
Glades	29	15	13	1	64	41	21	2
Gulf	49	18	30	1	207	131	76	0
Hamilton	77	25	48	4	261	104	155	2
Hardee	138	68	53	17	398	318	70	10
Hendry	118	45	65	8	349	227	107	15
Hernando	358	242	115	1	1,323	1,147	170	6
Highlands	365	169	183	13	836	551	277	8
Hillsborough	6,508	2,616	3,666	226	19,302	12,272	6,700	323
Holmes	80	63	16	1	253	228	24	1
Indian River	432	170	258	4	1,104	792	303	9
Jackson	384	153	222	9	626	354	271	1
Jefferson	93	11	82	0	184	70	113	1
Lafayette	40	17	22	1	67	57	10	0
Lake	595	261	325	9	2,096	1,510	557	28
Lee	1,033	491	497	45	2,694	2,034	616	43

See footnotes at end of table.   Continued . . .

Table 22.14. POPULATION UNDER CRIMINAL SENTENCE: INCARCERATED OFFENDERS AND
OFFENDERS UNDER COMMUNITY SUPERVISION OF THE FLORIDA DEPARTMENT
OF CORRECTIONS BY COUNTY OF COMMITMENT OR SUPERVISION AND
BY RACE IN THE STATE AND COUNTIES OF FLORIDA
JUNE 30, 1996 (Continued)

County	Incarcerated offenders				Community supervision 1/			
	Total	White	Black	Other races	Total 2/	White	Black	Other races
Leon	1,132	243	883	6	5,488	2,499	2,955	32
Levy	76	34	42	0	516	369	143	4
Liberty	35	10	23	2	93	66	24	2
Madison	120	20	99	1	432	155	276	1
Manatee	883	434	425	24	2,853	2,011	752	89
Marion	926	449	472	5	3,810	2,580	1,182	46
Martin	418	159	242	17	1,179	891	280	7
Monroe	641	392	236	13	2,939	2,452	444	43
Nassau	144	68	75	1	318	250	66	2
Okaloosa	515	247	260	8	2,106	1,578	517	11
Okeechobee	160	88	59	13	586	478	104	4
Orange	3,689	1,430	2,119	140	11,681	6,924	4,493	258
Osceola	511	280	207	24	1,949	1,538	337	73
Palm Beach	2,334	820	1,486	28	7,678	4,832	2,494	352
Pasco	1,087	871	199	17	3,406	3,174	213	19
Pinellas	4,312	1,989	2,270	53	13,902	10,099	3,732	71
Polk	3,092	1,544	1,502	46	6,421	4,360	2,017	44
Putnam	468	187	276	5	1,007	603	394	10
St. Johns	383	203	175	5	1,008	715	285	8
St. Lucie	964	292	661	11	2,266	1,279	972	14
Santa Rosa	234	188	43	3	839	742	95	2
Sarasota	761	398	355	8	2,602	2,073	501	28
Seminole	791	395	380	16	3,422	2,478	901	41
Sumter	163	58	105	0	542	342	196	4
Suwannee	181	75	99	7	622	435	184	3
Taylor	199	78	120	1	465	283	182	0
Union	182	73	105	4	70	35	34	1
Volusia	1,598	792	796	10	6,249	4,441	1,749	58
Wakulla	71	47	24	0	295	224	71	0
Walton	121	72	48	1	648	539	108	1
Washington	99	62	34	3	311	230	79	2
Interstate	133	92	30	11	0	0	0	0
Data unavailable	67	28	39	0	330	258	71	0

1/ Felony and misdemeanor probation, community control, pretrial intervention,
control release, parole, and other supervision.
2/ Includes data not distributed by race.

Source: State of Florida, Department of Corrections, *1995-96 Annual Report: The
Guidebook to Corrections in Florida,* and unpublished data.

Table 22.15. COUNTY DETENTION FACILITIES: AVERAGE DAILY INMATE POPULATION
AND INCARCERATION RATES IN THE STATE AND COUNTIES OF FLORIDA
1994 THROUGH 1996

County	Average daily population 1/			Percentage change		Incarceration rate 2/		
	1994	1995	1996	1994-1996	1995-1996	1994	1995	1996
Florida	37,485	42,760	43,268	15.4	1.2	2.7	3.1	3.0
Alachua 3/	509	651	668	31.2	2.6	2.6	3.4	3.4
Baker	73	59	61	-16.4	3.4	3.7	3.0	3.0
Bay	533	512	599	12.4	17.0	3.9	3.8	4.3
Bradford	41	42	101	146.3	140.5	1.7	1.7	4.1
Brevard	736	790	870	18.2	10.1	1.7	1.8	1.9
Broward	3,331	3,546	3,430	3.0	-3.3	2.5	2.6	2.5
Calhoun	15	19	25	66.7	31.6	1.3	1.7	2.1
Charlotte	153	165	189	23.5	14.5	1.2	1.3	1.5
Citrus	163	158	234	43.6	48.1	1.6	1.5	2.2
Clay	127	142	130	2.4	-8.5	1.1	1.2	1.1
Collier	472	513	567	20.1	10.5	2.6	2.8	3.0
Columbia	189	197	256	35.4	29.9	3.9	4.0	5.1
Dade 3/	6,439	6,787	6,962	8.1	2.6	3.2	3.4	3.5
De Soto	80	89	93	16.3	4.5	3.0	3.4	3.5
Dixie	36	54	55	52.8	1.9	3.0	4.4	4.4
Duval	2,496	2,518	2,416	-3.2	-4.1	3.5	3.5	3.4
Escambia	1,123	1,222	1,275	13.5	4.3	4.1	4.4	4.6
Flagler	50	58	62	24.0	6.9	1.4	1.7	1.7
Franklin	39	70	75	92.3	7.1	3.9	7.0	7.4
Gadsden	134	139	130	-3.0	-6.5	3.0	3.1	2.9
Gilchrist	30	27	21	-30.0	-22.2	2.6	2.3	1.8
Glades	28	26	28	0.0	7.7	3.4	3.1	3.3
Gulf	33	30	37	12.1	23.3	2.5	2.3	2.7
Hamilton	58	80	70	20.7	-12.5	4.8	6.7	5.7
Hardee	96	103	95	-1.0	-7.8	4.3	4.6	4.2
Hendry	105	120	129	22.9	7.5	3.7	4.2	4.4
Hernando	230	257	296	28.7	15.2	2.0	2.2	2.5
Highlands	173	198	218	26.0	10.1	2.3	2.6	2.8
Hillsborough	2,150	2,520	2,766	28.7	9.8	2.4	2.9	3.1
Holmes	22	19	19	-13.6	0.0	1.3	1.1	1.1
Indian River	277	288	311	12.3	8.0	2.8	3.0	3.1
Jackson	149	178	241	61.7	35.4	3.3	3.9	5.2
Jefferson 4/	(X)	12	24	(X)	100.0	(X)	0.9	1.8
Lafayette	9	13	11	22.2	-15.4	1.5	2.2	1.7
Lake	432	469	538	24.5	14.7	2.5	2.7	3.1
Lee	791	887	941	19.0	6.1	2.2	2.4	2.5
Leon	588	732	920	56.5	25.7	2.8	3.5	4.3
Levy	79	81	92	16.5	13.6	2.7	2.8	3.1

See footnotes at end of table.   Continued . . .

University of Florida   **Bureau of Economic and Business Research**

Table 22.15. COUNTY DETENTION FACILITIES: AVERAGE DAILY INMATE POPULATION
AND INCARCERATION RATES IN THE STATE AND COUNTIES OF FLORIDA
1994 THROUGH 1996 (Continued)

County	Average daily population 1/			Percentage change		Incarceration rate 2/		
	1994	1995	1996	1994-1996	1995-1996	1994	1995	1996
Liberty	8	8	10	25.0	25.0	1.2	1.2	1.5
Madison	66	75	81	22.7	8.0	3.7	4.2	4.5
Manatee	732	759	897	22.5	18.2	3.2	3.3	3.8
Marion	883	962	1,102	24.8	14.6	4.1	4.4	4.9
Martin	344	348	376	9.3	8.0	3.1	3.2	3.3
Monroe	385	465	546	41.8	17.4	4.7	5.7	6.5
Nassau	92	105	124	34.8	18.1	1.9	2.2	2.6
Okaloosa	347	371	336	-3.2	-9.4	2.2	2.3	2.1
Okeechobee	132	164	160	21.2	-2.4	4.1	5.1	4.8
Orange	3,170	3,198	3,180	0.3	-0.6	4.3	4.3	4.2
Osceola	392	522	564	43.9	8.0	3.0	4.0	4.1
Palm Beach 3/	1,745	2,097	2,067	18.5	-1.4	1.9	2.2	2.2
Pasco	426	480	582	36.6	21.3	1.4	1.6	1.9
Pinellas 3/	1,521	1,806	2,214	45.6	22.6	1.7	2.1	2.5
Polk	1,277	1,337	1,500	17.5	12.2	2.9	3.1	3.4
Putnam	167	188	189	13.2	0.5	2.4	2.7	2.7
St. Johns	209	239	252	20.6	5.4	2.2	2.5	2.6
St. Lucie	652	702	735	12.7	4.7	3.9	4.2	4.3
Santa Rosa	149	149	208	39.6	39.6	1.6	1.6	2.2
Sarasota	562	616	626	11.4	1.6	1.9	2.1	2.1
Seminole	601	667	718	19.5	7.6	1.9	2.1	1.1
Sumter	107	96	116	8.4	20.8	3.1	2.7	3.2
Suwannee	43	59	78	81.4	32.2	1.5	2.0	2.6
Taylor	85	126	71	-16.5	-43.7	4.9	7.2	3.9
Union	11	12	9	-18.2	-25.0	0.9	0.9	0.7
Volusia	1,177	1,199	1,310	11.3	9.3	3.0	3.0	3.2
Wakulla	128	119	114	-10.9	-4.2	7.8	7.2	6.7
Walton	56	86	96	71.4	11.6	1.8	2.7	2.9
Washington	35	40	52	48.6	30.0	2.0	2.2	2.7

(X) Not applicable.

1/ Average annual figures based on monthly data.

2/ Per 1,000 population based upon self-reports of county total population as well as county inmate population.

3/ Data for some months in 1996 were not available, and therefore not included in the annual averages.

4/ Facility closed October 1993 and reopened June 1995.

Note: Data are collected monthly from the 67 county jail systems statewide from January 1, 1994 through December 31, 1996. The high increase in inmate population and incarceration rates in some of the counties is the result of holding a large portion of the inmate population for the U.S. Marshal and the contracting of bedspace.

Source: State of Florida, Department of Corrections, Bureau of Planning, Research, and Statistics, *Florida County Detention Facilities: 1996 Annual Report,* and previous editions.

Table 22.20. JUVENILE DELINQUENCY: CASES AND YOUTHS REFERRED FOR DELINQUENCY BY MOST SERIOUS OFFENSE IN FLORIDA, 1994-95 AND 1995-96

Offense	Cases received			Youths referred		
	1994-95	1995-96	Per-centage change	1994-95	1995-96	Per-centage change
Felonies	63,273	60,026	-5	44,076	43,586	-1
Murder/manslaughter	157	105	-33	157	104	-34
Attempted murder	234	205	-12	224	197	-12
Sex offense	1,495	1,509	1	1,386	1,406	1
Armed robbery	1,662	1,305	-21	1,497	1,193	-20
Other robbery	2,498	2,400	-4	2,195	2,169	-1
Arson	635	603	-5	588	568	-3
Burglary	20,626	19,658	-5	15,348	15,172	-1
Auto theft	7,010	5,655	-19	3,890	3,396	-13
Grand larceny	4,364	4,373	0	2,912	3,011	3
Receiving stolen property	507	425	-16	296	272	-8
Concealed firearm	1,152	883	-23	830	661	-20
Aggravated assault/battery	8,570	8,438	-2	6,296	6,388	1
Forgery	478	451	-6	330	317	-4
Felony nonmarijuana drug	4,201	4,163	-1	2,494	2,704	8
Marijuana felony	1,146	1,220	6	774	886	14
Escape	1,549	1,259	-19	475	445	-6
Resisting arrest with violence	519	569	10	320	372	16
Shooting/throwing missile	1,079	1,127	4	744	808	9
Other felony	5,391	5,678	5	3,320	3,517	6
Misdemeanors	86,085	88,827	3	54,002	56,999	6
Assault/battery	17,884	19,462	9	11,615	12,922	11
Prostitution	79	74	-6	51	43	-16
Sex offense	176	143	-19	116	93	-20
Petty larceny	7,124	6,195	-13	4,423	3,769	-15
Shoplifting	26,405	26,925	2	20,108	20,830	4
Receiving stolen property	108	113	5	45	45	0
Concealed weapon	858	830	-3	504	482	-4
Disorderly conduct	2,739	2,834	3	1,416	1,606	13
Vandalism	4,770	4,564	-4	2,705	2,665	-1
Trespassing	7,868	7,960	1	3,443	3,712	8
Loitering and prowling	2,814	2,555	-9	1,106	1,113	1
Misdemeanor nonmarijuana drug	1,852	2,173	17	1,161	1,405	21
Marijuana misdemeanor	4,111	4,719	15	2,342	2,768	18
Alcohol-related offenses	2,355	2,331	-1	1,654	1,643	-1
Violation of game laws	209	184	-12	175	152	-13
Resisting arrest without violence	2,241	2,492	11	801	962	20
Other misdemeanor	4,492	5,273	17	2,337	2,789	19
Other delinquency	20,060	22,248	11	4,161	4,785	15
Contempt	1,200	1,990	66	325	424	30
Violation of ordinance	21	31	48	9	21	133
Traffic	190	166	-13	84	85	1
Interstate compact	292	283	-3	222	216	-3
Nonlaw violation of community control	7,253	7,952	10	1,260	1,395	11
Nonlaw violation of furlough	6	7	17	2	1	-50
Case reopened	4,640	4,915	6	1,177	1,312	11
Prosecution previously deferred	4,544	5,054	11	896	1,089	22
Transfer from other county	1,914	1,850	-3	186	242	30

Note: 1994-95 data are revised. Percentage change from 1994-95.

Source: State of Florida, Department of Juvenile Justice, Bureau of Data and Research, *Profile of Delinquency Cases and Youths Referred at Each Stage of the Juvenile Justice System, 1991-92 Through 1995-96.*

University of Florida   **Bureau of Economic and Business Research**

Table 22.21. JUVENILE DELINQUENCY: CASES AT VARIOUS STAGES OF THE JUVENILE JUSTICE SYSTEM BY AGE, RACE, AND SEX IN FLORIDA, 1995-96

Item	Received	De- tained 1/	Disposition Non- judicial	Judicial
Total	171,101	30,925	87,247	91,098
0-9	2,138	102	1,601	493
10	1,991	165	1,254	673
11	3,847	387	2,444	1,534
12	8,557	1,152	5,006	3,895
13	17,199	2,912	9,424	8,703
14	26,229	4,723	13,419	14,100
15	33,701	6,732	16,586	18,972
16	37,334	7,493	18,298	20,619
17	36,362	6,552	17,906	19,699
18+	3,743	707	1,309	2,410
White male	74,565	12,140	38,481	39,646
Black male	53,818	12,999	24,667	32,257
Other male	1,367	239	629	705
White female	23,619	2,859	13,944	9,913
Black female	17,180	2,621	9,198	8,360
Other female	450	55	281	156
Unknown	102	12	47	61

Item	Referred to JASP	Disposition (Continued) Placed on community control	Commit- ments 2/	Trans- ferred to adult court
Total	23,284	35,079	10,129	7,100
0-9	574	162	7	2
10	469	262	26	2
11	899	662	61	0
12	1,706	1,773	253	4
13	2,834	3,734	797	34
14	3,761	5,878	1,634	274
15	4,306	7,562	2,590	628
16	4,459	7,567	2,592	2,362
17	4,073	6,807	1,874	3,471
18+	203	672	295	323
White male	10,680	16,572	4,262	2,932
Black male	5,491	10,967	4,419	3,615
Other male	204	263	69	45
White female	4,094	4,002	696	250
Black female	2,716	3,195	673	246
Other female	90	57	10	6
Unknown	9	23	0	6

JASP Juvenile Alternative Services Program.

1/ Placement in detention during the interim between arrest and case disposition.

2/ Placement in commitment programs ranging from day-treatment programs for less serious offenders to secure training schools and boot camps for more serious offenders.

Note: Since not all charges are always disposed in the same way, some duplication may exist.

Source: State of Florida, Department of Juvenile Justice, Bureau of Data and Research, *Profile of Delinquency Cases and Youths Referred at Each Stage of the Juvenile Justice System, 1991-92 Through 1995-96*.

University of Florida   **Bureau of Economic and Business Research**

Table 22.22. JUVENILE DELINQUENCY: YOUTHS REFERRED FOR DELINQUENCY TO THE
JUVENILE JUSTICE SYSTEM BY AGE IN THE STATE AND
COUNTIES OF FLORIDA, 1995-96

County	0-9	10	11	12	13	14	15	16	17	18 and over
Florida	1,833	1,516	2,839	5,873	10,702	15,529	19,328	22,151	23,225	2,374
Alachua	46	30	51	84	142	210	246	262	329	25
Baker	3	3	2	3	9	15	21	45	39	1
Bay	27	38	42	63	107	167	169	240	235	15
Bradford	3	2	4	10	24	25	42	46	62	5
Brevard	46	32	83	137	308	443	606	625	681	60
Broward	144	109	231	471	944	1,375	1,656	1,789	1,891	153
Calhoun	0	2	1	4	5	7	14	22	22	0
Charlotte	7	8	12	29	47	89	109	137	129	15
Citrus	11	6	19	46	53	82	110	136	124	4
Clay	22	17	35	50	111	134	167	198	200	16
Collier	18	18	24	61	114	179	217	254	234	16
Columbia	9	5	19	14	42	59	60	92	73	8
Dade	141	116	258	620	1,277	1,924	2,429	2,779	3,247	421
De Soto	8	6	11	9	14	31	35	37	38	3
Dixie	1	0	0	4	2	10	14	8	9	1
Duval	70	73	148	389	617	952	1,093	1,279	1,197	73
Escambia	36	33	63	118	225	352	427	419	457	55
Flagler	5	4	9	22	32	49	53	59	50	7
Franklin	6	5	2	6	12	16	26	20	26	4
Gadsden	5	4	13	15	45	54	95	87	103	5
Gilchrist	3	2	4	6	12	11	21	24	24	0
Glades	1	0	1	1	5	6	10	9	14	0
Gulf	4	3	5	6	10	20	23	19	17	0
Hamilton	0	2	5	0	4	10	37	29	37	1
Hardee	1	5	7	15	27	37	35	41	46	7
Hendry	3	3	12	20	48	73	68	77	74	7
Hernando	8	2	12	18	53	84	81	98	104	10
Highlands	23	9	22	39	58	89	92	111	108	11
Hillsborough	140	115	225	478	912	1,255	1,515	1,696	1,735	287
Holmes	0	0	0	5	11	13	21	18	27	0
Indian River	11	13	15	49	83	100	115	126	135	11
Jackson	7	7	4	17	19	42	48	70	59	3
Jefferson	0	5	5	3	14	9	21	21	30	0
Lafayette	0	2	1	0	2	3	3	3	2	1
Lake	30	23	49	84	144	173	243	296	282	29
Lee	29	26	52	120	196	337	475	554	588	53
Leon	25	22	47	109	172	242	282	351	350	23

See footnote at end of table.   Continued . . .

Table 22.22. JUVENILE DELINQUENCY: YOUTHS REFERRED FOR DELINQUENCY TO THE
JUVENILE JUSTICE SYSTEM BY AGE IN THE STATE AND
COUNTIES OF FLORIDA, 1995-96 (Continued)

County	0-9	10	11	12	13	14	15	16	17	18 and over
Levy	7	1	4	7	17	34	29	36	37	3
Liberty	0	0	0	1	1	9	5	6	5	1
Madison	3	3	3	13	14	21	13	30	30	5
Manatee	67	41	62	114	202	318	356	407	388	40
Marion	53	34	60	120	174	218	300	300	241	34
Martin	19	20	27	47	75	95	141	148	169	5
Monroe	7	7	16	29	33	68	68	85	126	13
Nassau	8	6	14	19	40	42	68	60	62	6
Okaloosa	8	10	28	61	94	151	226	259	293	36
Okeechobee	1	1	10	11	24	55	66	62	57	5
Orange	133	86	188	383	725	982	1,201	1,440	1,439	129
Osceola	22	26	29	76	129	182	219	242	266	34
Palm Beach	122	102	176	305	593	816	1,067	1,238	1,315	181
Pasco	23	22	56	123	209	291	363	357	352	31
Pinellas	166	107	192	441	704	958	1,099	1,237	1,254	122
Polk	109	100	135	295	442	613	728	868	840	108
Putnam	19	12	26	36	60	97	121	145	146	9
St. Johns	8	7	14	33	45	80	122	143	161	9
St. Lucie	22	25	43	77	137	173	190	267	282	17
Santa Rosa	7	8	11	16	47	81	121	129	145	12
Sarasota	23	22	33	88	162	253	308	348	332	32
Seminole	21	40	58	113	238	311	448	552	590	51
Sumter	8	5	12	24	21	51	59	63	52	5
Suwannee	1	2	4	17	16	36	43	43	35	1
Taylor	3	3	6	12	12	15	41	25	36	1
Union	1	0	2	1	4	5	12	4	5	0
Volusia	61	53	99	210	396	553	689	789	801	93
Wakulla	3	3	5	9	18	26	33	35	39	2
Walton	1	4	0	6	10	21	28	41	48	5
Washington	1	0	3	6	7	16	14	27	20	2
Unknown	0	0	0	1	4	1	9	6	9	10
Out-of-state	13	16	30	54	149	280	462	682	872	42

Note: The number of youths referred is determined by counting only the most serious offense for which a youth is charged during the fiscal year. This differs from
the number of cases received in that the most serious offense on any given date is
counted as one case. Therefore, the same youth may be referred for additional offenses on different dates throughout the year, resulting in more than one case received.

Source: State of Florida, Department of Juvenile Justice, Bureau of Data and Research, *Profile of Delinquency Cases and Youths Referred at Each Stage of the Juvenile Justice System, 1991-92 Through 1995-96,* and unpublished data.

University of Florida   **Bureau of Economic and Business Research**

Table 22.23. JUVENILE DELINQUENCY: YOUTHS REFERRED FOR DELINQUENCY TO THE
JUVENILE JUSTICE SYSTEM BY SEX AND RACE IN THE STATE AND
COUNTIES OF FLORIDA, 1995-96

County	Total	Male			Female			Unknown
		White	Black	Other	White	Black	Other	
Florida	105,370	46,463	28,536	894	17,459	11,602	344	72
Alachua	1,425	440	566	3	175	240	1	0
Baker	141	81	29	0	20	11	0	0
Bay	1,103	579	201	16	201	101	5	0
Bradford	223	115	29	2	55	22	0	0
Brevard	3,021	1,569	531	21	644	240	16	0
Broward	8,763	3,137	3,366	101	1,019	1,101	28	11
Calhoun	77	33	22	1	7	14	0	0
Charlotte	582	345	55	0	163	18	1	0
Citrus	591	396	36	1	149	7	2	0
Clay	950	561	102	13	224	43	7	0
Collier	1,135	677	101	14	279	59	5	0
Columbia	381	180	100	0	61	39	1	0
Dade	13,212	4,931	4,953	55	1,482	1,769	20	2
De Soto	192	96	56	0	23	17	0	0
Dixie	49	33	7	0	8	1	0	0
Duval	5,891	1,908	2,131	93	814	905	37	3
Escambia	2,185	736	807	40	278	308	16	0
Flagler	290	154	47	7	59	22	1	0
Franklin	123	66	26	0	24	7	0	0
Gadsden	426	38	286	2	11	89	0	0
Gilchrist	107	60	9	0	34	4	0	0
Glades	47	19	11	6	8	2	1	0
Gulf	107	43	28	0	28	8	0	0
Hamilton	125	31	61	3	6	24	0	0
Hardee	221	150	20	3	33	15	0	0
Hendry	385	191	69	8	68	44	5	0
Hernando	470	296	51	0	100	21	1	1
Highlands	562	299	114	1	94	53	1	0
Hillsborough	8,358	3,449	2,369	95	1,336	1,058	35	16
Holmes	95	73	9	0	13	0	0	0
Indian River	658	331	125	3	147	52	0	0
Jackson	276	128	80	0	39	29	0	0
Jefferson	108	17	56	0	13	22	0	0
Lafayette	17	8	3	0	1	5	0	0
Lake	1,353	688	272	0	259	132	0	2
Lee	2,430	1,283	399	9	497	236	6	0
Leon	1,623	525	599	7	204	287	1	0

See footnote at end of table.   Continued . . .

Table 22.23. JUVENILE DELINQUENCY: YOUTHS REFERRED FOR DELINQUENCY TO THE
JUVENILE JUSTICE SYSTEM BY SEX AND RACE IN THE STATE AND
COUNTIES OF FLORIDA, 1995-96 (Continued)

County	Total	Male White	Male Black	Male Other	Female White	Female Black	Female Other	Unknown
Levy	175	89	42	0	28	16	0	0
Liberty	28	17	10	0	1	0	0	0
Madison	135	27	69	0	12	27	0	0
Manatee	1,995	928	439	18	382	206	16	6
Marion	1,534	803	324	17	260	128	2	0
Martin	746	405	118	3	171	46	3	0
Monroe	452	289	58	2	92	10	1	0
Nassau	325	175	64	1	63	22	0	0
Okaloosa	1,166	628	196	10	263	62	7	0
Okeechobee	292	180	39	2	55	16	0	0
Orange	6,706	2,629	2,094	47	1,047	856	22	11
Osceola	1,225	712	170	16	263	60	4	0
Palm Beach	5,915	2,276	1,942	56	851	767	20	3
Pasco	1,827	1,215	114	4	452	41	0	1
Pinellas	6,280	2,954	1,346	140	1,128	661	48	3
Polk	4,238	1,948	1,059	5	735	488	2	1
Putnam	671	263	204	4	95	103	2	0
St. Johns	622	310	133	0	126	52	1	0
St. Lucie	1,233	502	415	1	162	153	0	0
Santa Rosa	577	382	44	9	124	14	4	0
Sarasota	1,601	890	267	5	335	100	4	0
Seminole	2,422	1,295	430	6	501	189	1	0
Sumter	300	142	82	0	36	40	0	0
Suwannee	198	97	46	1	40	14	0	0
Taylor	154	59	63	0	19	12	1	0
Union	34	10	17	0	4	3	0	0
Volusia	3,744	1,983	702	16	708	332	2	1
Wakulla	173	115	11	0	41	6	0	0
Walton	164	86	32	0	32	14	0	0
Washington	96	56	20	0	14	6	0	0
Unknown	40	20	2	0	8	0	0	10
Out-of-state	2,600	1,312	258	27	835	153	14	1

Note: The number of youths referred is determined by counting only the most serious offense for which a youth is charged during the fiscal year. This differs from
the number of cases received in that the most serious offense on any given date is
counted as one case. Therefore, the same youth may be referred for additional offenses on different dates throughout the year, resulting in more than one case received.

Source: State of Florida, Department of Juvenile Justice, Bureau of Data and Research, *Profile of Delinquency Cases and Youths Referred at Each Stage of the Juvenile Justice System, 1991-92 Through 1995-96,* and unpublished data.

Table 22.24. JUVENILE DELINQUENCY: YOUTHS COMMITTING VIOLENT FELONY
OFFENSES AND NUMBER OF VIOLENT OFFENSE CASES RECEIVED IN THE STATE
DEPARTMENT OF JUVENILE JUSTICE SERVICE DISTRICTS
AND COUNTIES OF FLORIDA, 1995-96

District and county	Violent youth offenders 1/			Cases received 1/		
	1991-92	1995-96	Per-centage change	1991-92	1995-96	Per-centage change
Florida	10,963	12,637	15.3	14,568	15,658	7.5
District 1	334	403	20.7	416	456	9.6
Escambia	233	273	17.2	294	303	3.1
Okaloosa	67	76	13.4	81	91	12.3
Santa Rosa	25	45	80.0	30	51	70.0
Walton	9	9	0.0	11	11	0.0
District 2	407	485	19.2	556	605	8.8
Bay	75	68	-9.3	95	80	-15.8
Calhoun	6	9	50.0	6	9	50.0
Franklin	2	9	350.0	2	13	550.0
Gadsden	60	92	53.3	93	112	20.4
Gulf	14	11	-21.4	19	13	-31.6
Holmes	2	11	450.0	3	13	333.3
Jackson	28	39	39.3	36	46	27.8
Jefferson	11	18	63.6	23	27	17.4
Leon	172	158	-8.1	231	200	-13.4
Liberty	0	1	(X)	0	1	(X)
Madison	8	28	250.0	11	41	272.7
Taylor	19	18	-5.3	23	23	0.0
Wakulla	2	19	850.0	5	22	340.0
Washington	8	4	-50.0	9	5	-44.4
District 3	302	412	36.4	389	495	27.2
Alachua	108	173	60.2	140	217	55.0
Bradford	27	26	-3.7	37	33	-10.8
Columbia	42	31	-26.2	51	38	-25.5
Dixie	10	6	-40.0	11	7	-36.4
Gilchrist	5	11	120.0	7	12	71.4
Hamilton	10	19	90.0	11	22	100.0
Lafayette	2	3	50.0	3	3	0.0
Levy	9	29	222.2	14	33	135.7
Putnam	71	85	19.7	94	96	2.1
Suwannee	16	26	62.5	17	31	82.4
Union	2	3	50.0	4	3	-25.0
District 4	914	828	-9.4	1,158	973	-16.0
Baker	11	17	54.5	12	20	66.7
Clay	67	73	9.0	87	83	-4.6
Duval	754	617	-18.2	962	719	-25.3
Nassau	28	38	35.7	31	44	41.9
St. Johns	54	83	53.7	66	107	62.1
District 5	821	1,025	24.8	1,140	1,246	9.3
Pasco	107	193	80.4	133	239	79.7
Pinellas	714	832	16.5	1,007	1,007	0.0
District 6	1,041	1,266	21.6	1,401	1,633	16.6
Hillsborough	851	1,014	19.2	1,147	1,303	13.6
Manatee	190	252	32.6	254	330	29.9

See footnotes at end of table.

University of Florida   **Bureau of Economic and Business Research**

Table 22.24. JUVENILE DELINQUENCY: YOUTHS COMMITTING VIOLENT FELONY
OFFENSES AND NUMBER OF VIOLENT OFFENSE CASES RECEIVED IN THE STATE
DEPARTMENT OF JUVENILE JUSTICE SERVICE DISTRICTS
AND COUNTIES OF FLORIDA, 1995-96 (Continued)

District and county	Violent youth offenders 1/			Cases received 1/		
	1991-92	1995-96	Per-centage change	1991-92	1995-96	Per-centage change
District 7	1,164	1,412	21.3	1,511	1,791	18.5
Brevard	206	294	42.7	274	391	42.7
Orange	678	749	10.5	888	932	5.0
Osceola	89	105	18.0	107	133	24.3
Seminole	191	264	38.2	242	335	38.4
District 8	497	560	12.7	644	712	10.6
Charlotte	26	32	23.1	32	42	31.3
Collier	88	97	10.2	106	117	10.4
De Soto	29	29	0.0	36	31	-13.9
Glades	0	5	(X)	0	6	(X)
Hendry	19	32	68.4	31	39	25.8
Lee	195	185	-5.1	267	247	-7.5
Sarasota	140	180	28.6	172	230	33.7
District 9	705	798	13.2	977	989	1.2
Palm Beach	705	798	13.2	977	989	1.2
District 10	924	1,160	25.5	1,234	1,410	14.3
Broward	924	1,160	25.5	1,234	1,410	14.3
District 11	2,290	2,513	9.7	3,114	3,162	1.5
Dade	2,263	2,477	9.5	3,078	3,119	1.3
Monroe	27	36	33.3	36	43	19.4
District 12	344	383	11.3	449	467	4.0
Flagler	16	28	75.0	22	35	59.1
Volusia	328	355	8.2	427	432	1.2
District 13	417	506	21.3	517	624	20.7
Citrus	29	49	69.0	33	62	87.9
Hernando	50	51	2.0	61	58	-4.9
Lake	114	179	57.0	143	211	47.6
Marion	200	175	-12.5	250	228	-8.8
Sumter	24	52	116.7	30	65	116.7
District 14	427	499	16.9	589	628	6.6
Hardee	13	16	23.1	19	21	10.5
Highlands	41	48	17.1	52	60	15.4
Polk	373	435	16.6	518	547	5.6
District 15	277	291	5.1	364	355	-2.5
Indian River	47	57	21.3	55	66	20.0
Martin	67	66	-1.5	84	84	0.0
Okeechobee	28	48	71.4	41	58	41.5
St. Lucie	135	120	-11.1	184	147	-20.1

(X) Not applicable.

1/ The number of youths referred is determined by counting only the most serious
offense for which a youth is charged during the fiscal year. This differs from the
number of cases received in that the most serious offense on any given date is counted as one case. Therefore, the same youth may be referred for additional offenses on
different dates throughout the year, resulting in more than one case received.

Note: Violent felony offenses are defined as murder, attempted murder, manslaugh-
ter, felony sex offenses, robbery, aggravated assault, shooting or throwing a deadly
object, and resisting arrest with violence.

Source: State of Florida, Department of Juvenile Justice, Bureau of Data and Research, *District and County Delinquency Recaps*, January 1997.

University of Florida   **Bureau of Economic and Business Research**

Table 22.30. VICTIM SERVICES: CRIMES COMPENSATION TRUST FUNDS RECEIPTS
IN THE STATE, JUDICIAL CIRCUITS, AND COUNTIES OF FLORIDA
FISCAL YEAR 1995-96

(rounded to thousands of dollars)

Judicial circuit and county	Total	Court cost 1/	Other 2/	Judicial circuit and county	Total	Court cost 1/	Other 2/
Florida	19,056	16,076	2,980	Circuit 8 (Cont.)			
				Levy	21	16	6
Circuit 1	721	572	149	Union	3	1	1
Escambia	432	366	66	Circuit 9	1,731	1,518	213
Okaloosa	141	84	57	Orange	1,581	1,379	201
Santa Rosa	109	91	18	Osceola	151	139	11
Walton	39	32	7	Circuit 10	904	785	119
Circuit 2	471	398	73	Hardee	69	59	10
Franklin	20	16	4	Highlands	89	75	14
Gadsden	92	86	6	Polk	746	651	95
Jefferson	31	29	2	Circuit 11	1,090	903	187
Leon	291	236	55	Dade	1,090	903	187
Liberty	4	4	1	Circuit 12	737	614	123
Wakulla	34	28	6	De Soto	46	31	15
Circuit 3	225	177	48	Manatee	278	238	40
Columbia	72	55	17	Sarasota	413	345	68
Dixie	12	8	4	Circuit 13	1,252	1,037	215
Hamilton	31	30	1	Hillsborough	1,252	1,037	215
Lafayette	6	5	1	Circuit 14	585	491	94
Madison	21	16	5	Bay	376	321	55
Suwannee	36	29	8	Calhoun	14	9	5
Taylor	47	36	11	Gulf	60	54	6
Circuit 4	1,691	1,483	208	Holmes	34	29	5
Clay	198	179	19	Jackson	66	49	18
Duval	1,372	1,193	178	Washington	35	29	5
Nassau	121	111	11	Circuit 15	899	794	105
Circuit 5	907	737	171	Palm Beach	899	794	105
Citrus	132	101	30	Circuit 16	294	247	46
Hernando	125	96	29	Monroe	294	247	46
Lake	214	182	32	Circuit 17	1,180	1,021	158
Marion	402	330	72	Broward	1,180	1,021	158
Sumter	36	28	8	Circuit 18	1,129	913	217
Circuit 6	1,990	1,660	330	Brevard	682	516	165
Pasco	417	364	52	Seminole	448	396	51
Pinellas	1,573	1,295	278	Circuit 19	666	563	103
Circuit 7	976	856	120	Indian River	159	132	27
Flagler	50	40	9	Martin	205	171	34
Putnam	92	79	13	Okeechobee	64	58	6
St. Johns	35	14	21	St. Lucie	239	202	36
Volusia	799	723	76	Circuit 20	1,230	1,007	223
Circuit 8	378	300	78	Charlotte	158	145	12
Alachua	261	223	39	Collier	307	244	63
Baker	50	24	26	Glades	22	19	2
Bradford	30	26	3	Hendry	95	78	17
Gilchrist	14	11	3	Lee	648	520	128

1/ Mandatory court cost is $50 per conviction of which the court clerk retains $1.
However, the average court cost collected per conviction is $28.89.
2/ Includes surcharges, offense, interest, restitution, subrogation, refunds, and
other receipts.
Source: State of Florida, Office of the Attorney General, Division of Victim Services, *Annual Report, 1995-1996.*

Table 22.31.   VICTIM SERVICES: VICTIM COMPENSATION AWARDS AND AMOUNT OF BENEFITS
PAID IN THE STATE, JUDICIAL CIRCUITS, AND COUNTIES OF
FLORIDA, FISCAL YEAR 1995-96

Judicial circuit and county	Number of awards	Benefits awarded (dollars)	Judicial circuit and county	Number of awards	Benefits awarded (dollars)
Florida	5,709	15,320,479	Circuit 8 (Continued)		
			Levy	19	54,323
Circuit 1	207	588,508	Union	5	11,532
Escambia	123	344,201	Circuit 9	241	629,022
Okaloosa	42	148,280	Orange	212	560,006
Santa Rosa	34	76,305	Osceola	29	69,016
Walton	8	19,722	Circuit 10	146	349,239
Circuit 2	205	376,189	Hardee	11	24,281
Franklin	12	30,570	Highlands	17	37,813
Gadsden	38	68,554	Polk	118	287,145
Jefferson	4	2,341	Circuit 11	628	2,330,422
Leon	141	258,460	Dade	628	2,330,422
Liberty	3	1,496	Circuit 12	249	591,440
Wakulla	7	14,768	De Soto	14	54,728
Circuit 3	70	155,297	Manatee	131	241,444
Columbia	27	57,379	Sarasota	104	295,268
Dixie	5	17,482	Circuit 13	547	1,432,004
Hamilton	2	11,475	Hillsborough	547	1,432,004
Lafayette	2	1,457	Circuit 14	161	378,712
Madison	2	2,912	Bay	98	267,501
Suwannee	10	20,413	Calhoun	4	11,897
Taylor	22	44,179	Gulf	5	4,353
Circuit 4	759	1,800,571	Holmes	6	4,272
Clay	30	59,239	Jackson	41	66,678
Duval	717	1,691,084	Washington	7	24,011
Nassau	12	50,248	Circuit 15	266	772,331
Circuit 5	159	352,098	Palm Beach	266	772,331
Citrus	23	50,035	Circuit 16	30	108,313
Hernando	16	56,965	Monroe	30	108,313
Lake	19	53,402	Circuit 17	281	865,476
Marion	93	180,103	Broward	281	865,476
Sumter	8	11,593	Circuit 18	324	710,310
Circuit 6	641	1,944,810	Brevard	243	546,896
Pasco	83	235,979	Seminole	81	163,414
Pinellas	558	1,708,831	Circuit 19	145	363,868
Circuit 7	233	607,844	Indian River	52	119,231
Flagler	15	39,593	Martin	29	68,936
Putnam	41	126,087	Okeechobee	9	37,525
St. Johns	65	147,619	St. Lucie	55	138,176
Volusia	112	294,545	Circuit 20	268	666,837
Circuit 8	149	297,188	Charlotte	16	45,591
Alachua	106	186,035	Collier	68	170,323
Baker	7	17,705	Glades	2	7,342
Bradford	9	18,663	Hendry	17	24,326
Gilchrist	3	8,930	Lee	165	419,255

Note: Victim compensation claims are processed for financial assistance to crime
victims for lost income (lost wages, disability, and loss of support), funeral expenses, and reimbursement of other out-of-pocket and treatment expenses directly related to a crime injury.
    Source: State of Florida, Office of the Attorney General, Division of Victim Ser-
vices, *Annual Report, 1995-1996.*

Table 22.50. HATE CRIMES: HATE-MOTIVATED CRIMES BY TYPE OF OFFENSE AND BY MOTIVATION IN FLORIDA, 1990 THROUGH 1995

Offense and motivation	1990	1991	1992	1993	1994	1995
Offenses, total	306.0	309.0	395.0	313.0	283.0	183.0
Crimes against persons	174.0	217.0	297.0	238.0	206.0	119.0
Percentage of total	56.9	70.2	75.2	76.0	72.8	65.0
Assaults	129.0	165.0	222.0	175.0	153.0	91.0
Percentage of total	42.2	53.4	56.2	55.9	54.1	49.7
Motivation						
Race/color	220.0	221.0	245.0	227.0	198.0	128.0
Percentage of total	71.9	71.5	62.0	72.5	70.0	69.9
Religion	58.0	46.0	48.0	31.0	29.0	23.0
Percentage of total	19.0	14.9	12.2	9.9	10.2	12.6
Ethnicity	28.0	32.0	44.0	29.0	28.0	17.0
Percentage of total	9.1	10.4	11.1	9.3	9.9	9.3
Sexual orientation	(NA)	A/ 10.0	58.0	26.0	28.0	15.0
Percentage of total	(NA)	A/ 3.2	14.7	8.3	9.9	8.2

(NA) Not available.
A/ Collection of data on sexual orientation began on October 1, 1991.
Note: A hate crime is an act committed or attempted by one person or group a-
gainst another person or group, or their property, that in any way constitutes an ex-
pression of hatred toward the victim based on his or her personal characteristics.
It is a crime in which the perpetrator intentionally selects the victim based on one
of the following characteristics: race, color, religion, ethnicity, ancestry, national origin, or sexual orientation.

Source: State of Florida, Office of the Attorney General, *Hate Crimes in Florida,
January 1, 1995 through December 31, 1995,* Internet site http://legal.firn.edu/
justice/.

Table 22.51. LAWYERS: NUMBER AND MEMBERS IN GOOD STANDING OF THE FLORIDA BAR BY SECTION IN FLORIDA, JULY 1, 1997

Section	Number of members	Section	Number of members
Members in good standing, total	56,441	Members in sections (Cont.)	
Florida	45,629	Environmental and land use	1,955
Out-of-state	10,690	Administrative	988
Foreign	122	Practice, management, and	
		technology	882
Members in sections, total	25,915	Labor and employment	1,599
Tax	1,847	International	906
Real property, probate	7,578	Entertainment, arts, and	
Trial	6,366	sports	854
Business	4,000	Health	1,207
General	1,578	Public interest	397
Family	3,209	Governmental	733
Local government	1,182	Elder	1,241
Workers' compensation	1,478	Out-of-state	1,420
Criminal	2,398	Appellate practice	967

Source: The Florida Bar, release from the Records Department, July 1,1997.

Table 22.52. LAWYERS: MEMBERS IN GOOD STANDING OF THE FLORIDA BAR IN THE STATE
AND COUNTIES OF FLORIDA, JULY 1, 1997

County	Number of members	County	Number of members
Total	56,441	Jefferson	17
Out-of-state	10,690	Lafayette	3
Foreign	122	Lake	209
Alachua	711	Lee	776
Baker	6	Leon	2,503
Bay	213	Levy	27
Bradford	16	Liberty	0
Brevard	739	Madison	12
Broward	5,734	Manatee	377
Calhoun	5	Marion	364
Charlotte	131	Martin	335
Citrus	85	Monroe	232
Clay	104	Nassau	30
Collier	594	Okaloosa	222
Columbia	77	Okeechobee	25
Dade	10,792	Orange	3,333
De Soto	22	Osceola	100
Dixie	4	Palm Beach	4,221
Duval	2,209	Pasco	270
Escambia	603	Pinellas	2,533
Flagler	40	Polk	679
Franklin	16	Putnam	59
Gadsden	45	St. Johns	160
Gilchrist	6	St. Lucie	242
Glades	3	Santa Rosa	65
Gulf	11	Sarasota	984
Hamilton	9	Seminole	514
Hardee	12	Sumter	24
Hendry	18	Suwannee	35
Hernando	99	Taylor	17
Highlands	73	Union	4
Hillsborough	3,740	Volusia	820
Holmes	11	Wakulla	26
Indian River	224	Walton	23
Jackson	25	Washington	11

Source: The Florida Bar, release from the Records Department, July 1, 1997.

Table 22.55. LEGAL SERVICES: AVERAGE MONTHLY PRIVATE REPORTING UNITS
EMPLOYMENT, AND PAYROLL COVERED BY UNEMPLOYMENT COMPENSATION LAW
IN THE STATE AND COUNTIES OF FLORIDA, 1996

County	Number of reporting units	Number of employees	Payroll ($1,000)	County	Number of reporting units	Number of employees	Payroll ($1,000)
			Legal services (SIC code 81)				
Florida	11,588	60,734	268,641	Lake	79	333	1,097
				Lee	227	1,228	4,349
Alachua	156	825	2,260	Leon	273	2,207	10,452
Baker	4	11	16	Levy	5	15	31
Bay	65	309	1,042	Madison	4	15	37
Bradford	9	18	34	Manatee	113	508	1,550
Brevard	225	881	3,266	Marion	114	543	1,940
Broward	1,529	6,735	28,271	Martin	90	487	1,738
Calhoun	3	19	33	Monroe	65	206	649
Charlotte	39	238	868	Nassau	13	43	150
Citrus	27	133	335	Okaloosa	97	326	934
Clay	34	137	353	Okeechobee	9	38	71
Collier	177	811	3,773	Orange	754	5,702	26,462
Columbia	22	86	304	Osceola	34	94	189
Dade	2,804	14,217	73,397	Palm Beach	1,144	5,687	26,128
De Soto	5	21	50	Pasco	100	441	1,167
Dixie	3	5	7	Pinellas	688	3,163	11,469
Duval	479	3,296	17,049	Polk	181	1,058	4,460
Escambia	163	1,005	3,890	Putnam	21	75	144
Flagler	11	33	165	St. Johns	38	135	347
Franklin	3	9	13	St. Lucie	72	330	1,346
Gadsden	12	33	51	Santa Rosa	15	84	262
Gilchrist	3	8	12	Sarasota	289	1,456	5,744
Gulf	5	17	38	Seminole	140	479	1,305
Hardee	5	17	30	Sumter	8	21	34
Hendry	9	30	56	Suwannee	11	23	33
Hernando	30	97	207	Taylor	5	22	48
Highlands	31	127	347	Union	3	4	5
Hillsborough	781	5,414	25,926	Volusia	250	1,083	3,343
Holmes	4	10	10	Wakulla	3	9	18
Indian River	64	298	1,186	Walton	9	24	26
Jackson	9	27	38				
Jefferson	6	10	21	Multicounty 1/	15	17	58

1/ Reporting units without a fixed location within the state or of unknown county
location.
   Note: Private employment. These data include establishments which are engaged in
offering legal advice or services and which are headed by a member of the Bar. Data
are preliminary. Only counties for which data are disclosed are shown. Detail may
not add to totals due to disclosure editing and/or rounding. See Tables 23.70,
23.71, 23.72, 23.73, and 23.74 for public employment data.

   Source: State of Florida, Department of Labor and Employment Security, Bureau of
Labor Market Information, "Employment and Wages" (ES-202), unpublished data.

GOVERNMENT FINANCE AND EMPLOYMENT

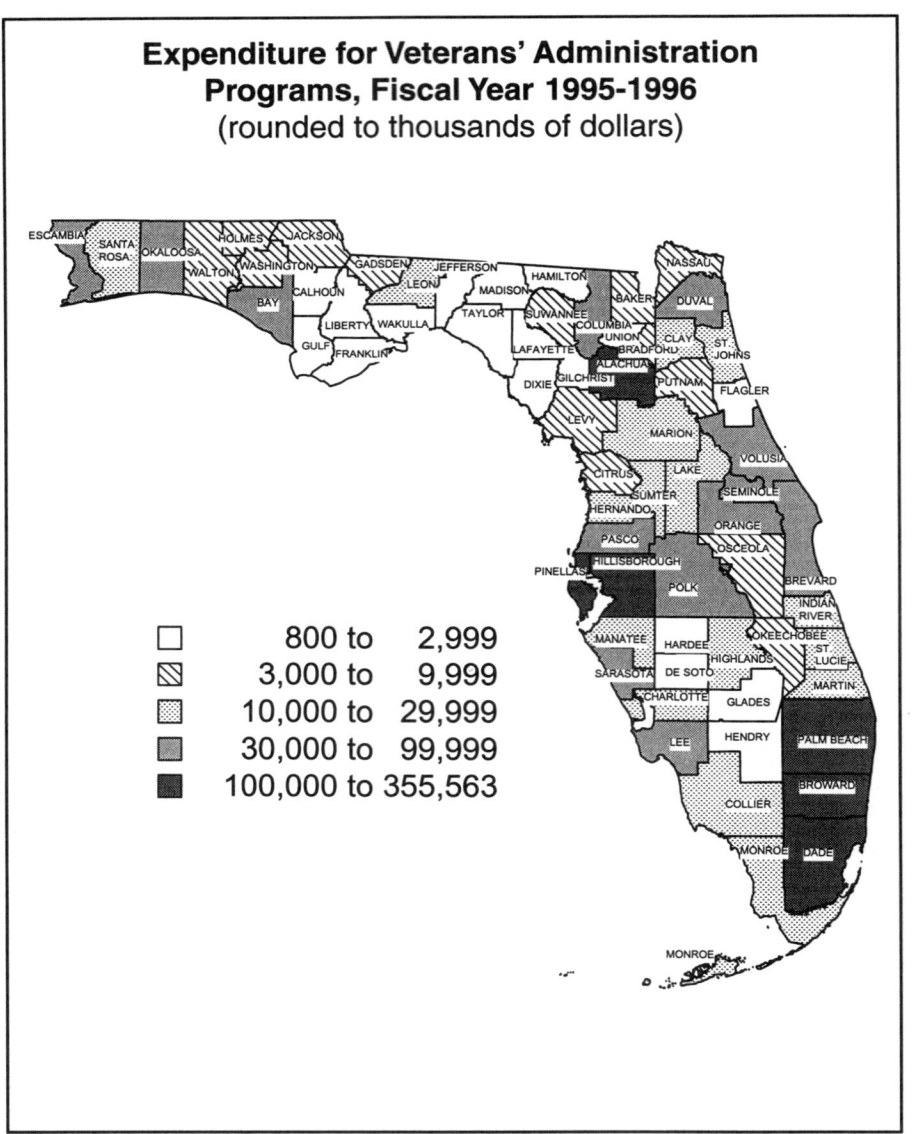

Expenditure for Veterans' Administration Programs, Fiscal Year 1995-1996
(rounded to thousands of dollars)

☐	800 to 2,999
▨	3,000 to 9,999
▦	10,000 to 29,999
▩	30,000 to 99,999
■	100,000 to 355,563

SECTION 23.00
GOVERNMENT FINANCE AND EMPLOYMENT

TABLES LISTED BY MAJOR HEADINGS

University of Florida   Bureau of Economic and Business Research

SECTION 23.00
GOVERNMENT FINANCE AND EMPLOYMENT
(Continued)

TABLES LISTED BY MAJOR HEADINGS

SECTION 23.00
GOVERNMENT FINANCE AND EMPLOYMENT
(Continued)

TABLES LISTED BY MAJOR HEADINGS

Table 23.07. FEDERAL GOVERNMENT FINANCE: EXPENDITURE BY AGENCY AND BY SPECIFIED PROGRAM IN FLORIDA AND THE UNITED STATES, FISCAL YEAR 1995-96

(in thousands of dollars)

Item	Florida	United States
Total (14)	79,166	1,394,057
Grants and other payments to state and		
local governments (46)		
Total	8,441,502	227,541,627
Department of Agriculture	727,798	16,724,910
Agricultural Marketing Service	10,385	322,568
Funds for strengthening markets	10,385	321,368
Cooperative projects in marketing	0	1,200
Cooperative State Research Service--agriculture		
experiment stations	8,194	401,471
Extension Service--extension activities	11,100	443,642
Rural Programs	5,454	468,150
Food and Consumer Service	687,831	14,646,902
Child nutrition programs	403,295	7,614,974
Food stamp program	99,347	3,004,765
Special supplemental food program (WIC)	171,895	3,661,951
Needy family program	8,448	200,179
Commodity assistance program	4,846	165,033
Food Safety and Inspection Service--meat and poultry	1,454	38,012
Forest Service	3,037	338,091
Natural Resources Conservation Service	343	66,074
Department of Commerce	38,660	767,598
Economic Development Administration--development		
assistance programs	20,252	405,703
National Oceanic and Atmospheric Administration	17,746	318,683
National Telecommunications and Information		
Administration--planning and construction	662	43,212
Corporation for Public Broadcasting--public		
broadcasting fund	2,726	142,221
Department of Defense 1/	2,041	247,408
Department of Education	670,655	15,298,720
Bilingual education and minority language affairs	4,053	156,894
Educational research and improvement-libraries	5,983	142,191
Office of Elementary and Secondary Education	353,707	8,610,132
Office of Postsecondary Education	1,261	76,925
Office of Special Education and Rehabilitative Services	253,565	4,977,471
Office of Vocational and Adult Education	51,902	1,328,021
Department of Energy	1,986	209,820
Environmental Protection Agency	77,613	3,204,357
Construction of wastewater treatment works	64,814	2,570,597
Abatement, control, and compliance	10,797	411,932
Hazardous substance response trust fund	2,002	221,828
Equal Employment Opportunity Commission	951	23,279
Federal Emergency Management Agency	137,820	1,516,103
Funds Appropriated to the President--		
Appalachian regional development programs	0	59,298
Department of Health and Human Services	4,765,354	127,636,120
Administration for Children and Families	1,206,924	31,779,906
Family support payments (AFDC)	574,545	16,408,863
Social services block grant	143,360	2,504,729

See footnotes at end of table.   Continued . . .

Table 23.07. FEDERAL GOVERNMENT FINANCE: EXPENDITURE BY AGENCY AND BY SPECIFIED
PROGRAM IN FLORIDA AND THE UNITED STATES, FISCAL YEAR 1995-96 (Continued)

(in thousands of dollars)

Item	Florida	United States
Grants to state and local governments (Continued)		
Department of Health and Human Services (Continued)		
Administration for Children and Families (Continued)		
Children and family services	271,693	6,425,182
Foster care and adoption assistance	106,215	3,704,531
Low-income home energy assistance	15,395	1,185,591
Community services block grant	9,564	176,784
Refugee assistance	68,445	361,117
Job opportunities and basic skills	16,597	906,757
Other	1,110	106,352
Health Care Financing Administration--medical		
assistance (Medicaid)	3,382,113	91,990,238
Public Health Service	114,775	2,370,220
Health Resources and Services Administration	86,264	1,740,940
Centers for Disease Control	28,511	629,280
Substance Abuse, and Mental Health Administration	61,542	1,495,756
Department of Housing and Urban Development	748,903	22,611,706
Community development	193,063	4,552,025
Emergency shelters and homeless assistance	6,605	241,996
Low rent housing--operating assistance	75,427	2,740,728
Lower income housing assistance	362,537	12,483,411
Institute of Museum Services	275	9,191
Department of Interior	14,313	1,826,961
National Park Service	1,991	59,992
Department of Justice	117,971	1,945,852
Department of Labor	288,756	6,614,464
Employment and Training Administration	287,569	6,512,549
Job Training Partnership Act	168,327	3,230,777
State unemployment insurance and employment		
service operations	119,188	3,180,636
Community service employment for older		
Americans	54	101,136
National Foundation on the Arts and the Humanities--		
National Endowment for the Arts	897	38,007
Tennessee Valley Authority-payments in lieu of taxes	0	255,678
Department of Transportation	835,953	26,845,231
Federal Aviation Administration--airport and		
airway trust fund	71,861	1,654,552
Federal Highway Administration	614,447	20,087,226
Federal Transit Administration	139,880	4,884,945
Department of the Treasury-Customs Bureau and IRS rebates	6,361	340,310
Department of Veterans Affairs	1,711	258,046
District of Columbia payment and Metro subsidy	0	938,024
Expenditure for salaries and wages (32)	7,660,372	169,731,101
Department of Defense 1/	3,685,000	72,955,074
Military	2,529,704	43,138,019
Active	2,379,839	38,685,092
Inactive	149,865	4,452,927
Civilian	1,155,296	29,817,055
Army	222,747	22,330,888
Navy	1,942,346	25,379,883

See footnotes at end of table.   Continued . . .

Table 23.07. FEDERAL GOVERNMENT FINANCE: EXPENDITURE BY AGENCY AND BY SPECIFIED
PROGRAM IN FLORIDA AND THE UNITED STATES, FISCAL YEAR 1995-96 (Continued)

(in thousands of dollars)

Item	Florida	United States
Expenditure for salaries and wages (Continued)		
Department of Defense (Continued)		
Air Force	1,407,714	20,257,833
Other defense, civilian	112,193	4,986,470
Nondefense agencies 2/	3,975,372	96,776,027
Agriculture	67,701	4,109,097
Commerce	33,164	1,647,087
Education	226	254,358
Energy	1,821	1,128,749
Environmental Protection Agency	3,974	946,478
Federal Deposit Insurance Corporation 3/	4,612	732,306
Federal Emergency Management Agency	5,364	221,951
General Services Administration	4,727	729,902
Health and Human Services 4/	10,106	2,909,363
Housing and Urban Development	12,947	587,639
Interior	44,101	2,867,767
Justice 5/	282,387	5,246,810
Labor	15,418	798,370
Postal Service	2,202,063	42,675,500
Small Business Administration	4,137	225,115
Transportation	325,790	5,009,483
Treasury	249,435	6,709,786
Veterans Affairs	47,283	9,212,402
Other nondefense	234,916	10,763,864
Direct payments to individuals (1)	53,348,971	749,273,054
Social Security	24,017,140	345,079,555
Retirement insurance payments	17,412,711	231,262,789
Survivors insurance payments	4,138,187	69,107,641
Disability insurance payments	2,466,242	44,709,125
Medicare	15,864,358	194,393,318
Hospital insurance payments	9,442,700	125,011,091
Supplementary medical insurance payments	6,421,658	69,382,227
Federal retirement and disability payments	5,778,144	68,589,676
Civilian 6/	2,796,189	40,666,779
Military	2,981,955	27,922,897
Federal payments for unemployment compensation	841,265	25,302,217
Veterans compensation for service connected disability	958,592	12,252,243
Veterans pensions for nonservice connected disability	112,984	2,371,426
Veterans compensation for service connected death	255,451	3,022,638
Pensions to veterans' surviving spouses and children	33,802	821,984
Veterans educational assistance	62,825	914,021
Other veterans benefit programs	31,230	580,394
Supplemental security income payments	1,357,144	24,342,709
Food stamps	1,295,526	22,490,213
Social insurance payments for railroad workers	419,418	8,144,684
Housing assistance 7/	408,194	7,265,497
Pell grant program	244,951	4,835,108
Excess earned income tax credits	1,303,362	20,805,563
National guaranteed student loan interest subsidies	33,822	2,409,190
Federal workers compensation	128,297	1,864,557
Black lung payments	25,570	1,166,730

See footnotes at end of table.   Continued . . .

Table 23.07. FEDERAL GOVERNMENT FINANCE: EXPENDITURE BY AGENCY AND BY SPECIFIED
PROGRAM IN FLORIDA AND THE UNITED STATES, FISCAL YEAR 1995-96 (Continued)

(in thousands of dollars)

Item	Florida	United States
Procurement contracts 8/ (23)	8,125,596	200,543,115
Department of Defense	5,880,491	128,628,822
Army	1,162,117	26,729,413
Navy	1,384,280	36,353,430
Air Force	3,093,554	38,537,841
Other defense	240,540	27,008,138
Nondefense agencies	2,245,105	71,914,293
Agriculture	25,287	2,316,116
Commerce	2,523	772,309
Education	136	426,124
Energy	62,241	16,148,737
Environmental Protection Agency	10,139	999,655
Federal Emergency Management Agency	1,270	189,286
General Services Administration	121,101	5,457,886
Justice	72,336	2,029,541
Health and Human Services	16,497	2,398,497
Housing and Urban Development	0	232,608
Interior	5,537	800,848
Labor	15,273	827,105
National Aeronautics and Space Administration	1,094,210	11,115,198
Postal Service	538,551	10,436,999
State Department	4,455	416,829
Transportation	153,837	3,041,777
Treasury	19,511	1,694,664
Veterans	87,810	2,394,765
Other nondefense	14,391	10,215,349
Expenditure for other programs (50)	1,589,308	46,967,765
Grants	511,738	21,446,137
Department of Health and Human Services-- research programs	139,331	9,532,741
National Science Foundation	54,260	2,515,139
Direct payments--other than for individuals	1,077,570	25,521,628
Department of Agriculture	50,128	8,147,397
Federal employees life and health insurance programs	443,107	10,952,121
Postal Service	96,183	1,863,998
Legal Services Corporation grants	12,370	269,104
National flood insurance claim payments	391,805	885,055

1/ Includes salaries, wages, and compensation, such as housing allowances; distribution based on duty station.   2/ Estimates based on place of employment.   3/ Includes Resolution Trust Corporation.   4/ Excludes Social Security Administration
salaries, which are now included with "other nondefense" salaries figures.   5/ Includes FBI salaries.   6/ Includes retirement and disability payments to former postal employees.   7/ Includes Section 8 payments to nongovernment agencies and FEMA
individual assistance payments under the Disaster Assistance Program.   8/ Value of
annual contract actions; actual outlays for U.S. Postal Service only. Multiple year
obligations of less than 3 years duration may be included.
Note: The number (after major expenditure categories) indicates Florida's rank
among the states in per capita distribution of federal funds. Expenditures classified as "other" may not be specified in the table and are contained in the totals for
major expenditure categories.

Source: U.S., Department of Commerce, Bureau of the Census, *Federal Expenditures
by State for Fiscal Year 1996.*

University of Florida   **Bureau of Economic and Business Research**

Table 23.08. FEDERAL GOVERNMENT FINANCE: EXPENDITURE BY TYPE IN THE UNITED STATES
AND IN THE STATE AND COUNTIES OF FLORIDA, FISCAL YEAR 1995-96

(in thousands of dollars, except where indicated)

County	Direct expenditure Total	Depart-ment of Defense	Grants	Wages and salaries	Direct payment to individuals Total	Retire-ment and dis-ability
United States 1/	1,398,228	232,050	241,474	169,731	760,958	468,439
Florida	79,614,086	12,663,558	9,055,445	7,660,372	53,695,103	33,198,339
Alachua	925,886	66,679	219,657	132,614	508,894	326,609
Baker	69,355	3,319	18,771	2,147	47,833	31,829
Bay	1,159,141	500,656	71,319	331,719	516,976	379,776
Bradford	89,795	9,927	14,904	6,241	67,714	43,859
Brevard	4,430,970	1,396,521	144,871	401,534	1,819,174	1,339,905
Broward	6,021,447	129,744	512,940	331,799	5,016,878	2,919,370
Calhoun	44,067	1,889	8,374	1,181	33,631	20,955
Charlotte	715,903	34,314	41,961	11,370	657,723	447,972
Citrus	575,327	16,065	34,367	9,863	528,375	360,079
Clay	395,953	112,047	19,967	14,593	355,194	284,266
Collier	779,918	7,298	59,127	24,846	681,905	477,084
Columbia	238,898	13,235	36,458	38,631	160,808	110,626
Dade	8,835,836	248,575	1,523,719	882,467	6,152,072	2,965,030
De Soto	111,347	468	15,857	2,659	92,074	54,205
Dixie	66,780	14,717	11,591	769	54,060	40,942
Duval	4,564,648	1,819,824	423,695	1,510,449	2,094,550	1,364,245
Escambia	2,030,967	801,336	198,370	504,561	1,047,183	772,528
Flagler	210,512	8,979	15,147	4,474	184,012	140,540
Franklin	49,458	2,559	7,871	1,245	37,747	22,628
Gadsden	170,756	5,845	42,149	5,024	121,326	74,802
Gilchrist	40,779	1,577	6,624	1,013	32,818	22,889
Glades	27,853	10,238	1,255	434	25,191	19,934
Gulf	68,424	3,845	13,800	739	49,512	30,987
Hamilton	41,568	1,174	7,892	1,184	31,544	21,052
Hardee	76,238	1,885	13,779	2,435	59,121	36,736
Hendry	97,068	5,090	23,913	3,694	65,742	39,416
Hernando	731,645	17,304	41,520	13,458	672,888	451,158
Highlands	466,146	18,866	36,783	12,589	412,479	276,223
Hillsborough	4,030,579	597,503	568,900	651,065	2,575,373	1,703,771
Holmes	78,575	5,049	13,176	2,473	61,457	39,428
Indian River	590,822	26,217	32,544	16,168	533,114	356,892
Jackson	217,887	9,764	47,702	25,478	139,562	92,199
Jefferson	47,755	1,484	10,375	1,194	35,251	22,581
Lafayette	18,160	3,579	2,282	643	12,182	7,914

See footnote at end of table.   Continued . . .

Table 23.08. FEDERAL GOVERNMENT FINANCE: EXPENDITURE BY TYPE IN THE UNITED STATES AND IN THE STATE AND COUNTIES OF FLORIDA, FISCAL YEAR 1995-96 (Continued)

(in thousands of dollars, except where indicated)

County	Direct expenditure Total	Department of Defense	Grants	Wages and salaries	Direct payment to individuals Total	Retirement and disability
Lake	973,459	49,906	55,926	23,198	883,395	614,689
Lee	1,896,395	70,618	142,571	81,583	1,623,469	1,115,432
Leon	2,391,739	185,562	1,686,252	84,084	467,784	322,309
Levy	126,863	6,581	14,008	3,093	106,878	73,804
Liberty	22,048	925	5,322	1,464	15,031	10,259
Madison	68,220	1,938	13,011	1,875	51,781	32,977
Manatee	1,087,695	42,556	84,692	58,143	921,734	628,648
Marion	1,104,779	37,905	92,619	28,309	967,133	679,067
Martin	611,668	32,707	42,559	13,338	531,276	364,116
Monroe	380,943	100,207	30,043	93,596	231,237	154,396
Nassau	209,329	19,272	25,581	48,006	133,630	97,483
Okaloosa	2,045,309	1,405,397	65,372	799,752	676,248	558,834
Okeechobee	141,205	3,992	15,339	3,092	121,185	71,508
Orange	4,012,211	1,541,129	339,634	452,067	2,055,899	1,366,458
Osceola	424,464	24,170	47,633	11,948	359,572	227,328
Palm Beach	6,445,755	1,625,648	403,390	259,487	4,123,861	2,578,849
Pasco	1,590,600	87,099	106,651	31,747	1,441,267	895,152
Pinellas	5,532,464	825,018	382,251	293,184	4,081,549	2,651,580
Polk	1,751,217	70,754	190,230	67,556	1,466,224	1,021,495
Putnam	294,787	13,925	40,767	6,814	245,509	160,562
St. Johns	451,682	66,857	51,202	20,159	351,818	252,769
St. Lucie	856,978	24,269	79,275	22,433	746,425	503,172
Santa Rosa	490,439	160,990	49,045	74,417	321,517	251,143
Sarasota	1,854,688	68,012	96,515	40,515	1,686,150	1,151,708
Seminole	953,141	98,226	112,051	69,782	738,478	519,225
Sumter	214,405	7,523	20,540	33,945	154,903	105,229
Suwannee	143,265	8,603	21,183	5,235	115,315	78,501
Taylor	98,017	28,770	11,181	1,899	58,615	37,181
Union	26,198	1,389	4,227	921	20,776	13,632
Volusia	1,989,636	123,757	191,779	63,459	1,678,366	1,143,911
Wakulla	59,096	5,430	9,769	2,694	43,160	29,912
Walton	165,725	21,229	22,886	9,387	110,237	79,653
Washington	88,129	5,621	14,403	2,435	70,331	44,780
Undistributed	3,091,072	0	345,877	0	2,209,983	64,148

1/ Rounded to millions of dollars.

Source: U.S., Department of Commerce, Bureau of the Census, *Consolidated Federal Funds Report: County Areas, Fiscal Year 1996.*

University of Florida   **Bureau of Economic and Business Research**

Table 23.15. DEFENSE CONTRACTS: AWARDS AND PAYROLL IN FLORIDA, OTHER SUNBELT
STATES, OTHER POPULOUS STATES, AND THE UNITED STATES, SPECIFIED
FISCAL YEARS ENDING SEPTEMBER 30, 1992 THROUGH 1996

(in millions of dollars)

State	Contract awards 1/			Payroll 2/		
	1991-92	1993-94	1995-96	1991-92	1993-94	1995-96
Sunbelt states						
Florida	4,995	5,910	5,863	6,277	6,164	6,670
Alabama	1,949	1,673	1,838	2,139	2,320	2,183
Arizona	1,946	1,975	2,911	1,658	1,642	1,865
Arkansas	288	374	249	703	701	730
California	23,843	22,573	18,230	14,202	13,467	12,332
Georgia	3,796	4,121	3,966	4,234	4,273	4,332
Louisiana	1,204	2,148	1,078	1,358	1,355	1,333
Mississippi	2,567	1,855	1,912	1,079	1,246	1,301
New Mexico	728	658	676	1,019	1,056	1,168
North Carolina	1,540	1,163	1,421	4,041	4,186	4,259
Oklahoma	759	759	771	2,035	2,015	2,172
South Carolina	756	998	1,012	2,699	2,529	2,263
Tennessee	1,262	1,173	1,137	984	1,068	1,072
Texas	8,672	8,145	8,819	7,016	7,201	8,383
Virginia	6,571	8,017	9,563	11,157	11,483	11,356
Other populous states						
Illinois	1,354	1,256	1,256	1,775	1,810	1,988
Indiana	1,517	1,319	1,552	1,095	1,170	1,022
Massachusetts	5,686	5,106	4,675	993	1,081	843
Michigan	1,568	1,602	1,241	904	878	764
New Jersey	3,319	3,034	2,564	1,601	1,524	1,419
New York	5,430	3,629	3,501	1,810	1,894	1,688
Ohio	3,033	2,966	2,733	2,182	2,215	2,337
Pennsylvania	3,065	2,760	3,687	2,605	2,646	2,218
United States	112,285	110,316	109,408	99,250	99,822	99,794

1/ State data include net value of contracts over $25,000 for military awards for
supplies, services, and construction.

2/ Data are estimates and cover active duty military and direct hire civilian personnel, including Army Corps of Engineers.

Note: Data refer to awards in year specified and to state in which prime contrac-
tor is located. Expenditure may extend over several years and work may be performed
by a subcontractor in another state.

Source: U.S., Department of Commerce, Bureau of the Census, *Statistical Abstract
of the United States, 1997,* and previous editions.

Table 23.20.   VETERANS' ADMINISTRATION: VETERAN POPULATION AND VETERANS'
ADMINISTRATION (VA) EXPENDITURE BY PROGRAM IN THE STATE
AND COUNTIES OF FLORIDA, FISCAL YEAR 1995-96

		Expenditure (amounts rounded to $1,000)				
County	Veteran population 1/	Total	Compensation and pension	Readjustment and vocational rehabilitation	Insurance and indemnities	Construction medical services and related costs 2/
Florida	1,709,060	2,544,360	1,364,183	90,703	179,583	909,891
Alachua	18,346	178,151	18,678	3,530	1,917	154,026
Baker	1,848	4,546	3,864	480	202	0
Bay	19,247	31,578	27,149	2,401	2,029	0
Bradford	3,100	3,797	3,304	167	326	0
Brevard	65,983	75,300	64,252	3,933	7,096	19
Broward	140,750	112,151	92,984	3,994	15,173	0
Calhoun	1,412	1,847	1,653	50	144	0
Charlotte	25,638	20,401	17,490	332	2,579	0
Citrus	22,518	8,759	6,445	86	2,228	0
Clay	16,816	17,916	14,762	1,405	1,749	0
Collier	25,411	15,378	12,485	298	2,595	0
Columbia	5,737	74,107	6,700	175	603	66,629
Dade	103,934	278,380	78,719	5,139	11,510	183,011
De Soto	3,124	3,270	2,902	34	334	0
Dixie	1,835	2,589	2,370	29	189	0
Duval	77,023	92,851	74,157	10,126	8,567	0
Escambia	35,780	60,563	49,162	6,853	3,908	639
Flagler	6,747	1,551	877	6	668	0
Franklin	1,345	1,618	1,458	18	142	0
Gadsden	2,994	4,391	3,879	179	332	0
Gilchrist	1,249	2,026	1,828	62	136	0
Glades	1,226	1,031	887	13	131	0
Gulf	1,477	2,019	1,778	82	158	0
Hamilton	993	1,674	1,545	26	104	0
Hardee	1,981	2,031	1,782	37	212	0
Hendry	1,928	2,057	1,811	41	205	0
Hernando	25,018	22,246	19,292	514	2,440	0
Highlands	13,972	12,319	10,682	246	1,391	0
Hillsborough	99,082	308,215	97,517	8,142	10,673	191,883
Holmes	1,891	4,394	4,073	115	207	0
Indian River	19,996	12,840	10,578	310	1,953	0
Jackson	4,424	6,889	6,138	269	482	0
Jefferson	1,176	1,715	1,535	54	126	0
Lafayette	641	1,051	944	38	69	0

See footnotes at end of table.   Continued . . .

Table 23.20.   VETERANS' ADMINISTRATION: VETERAN POPULATION AND VETERANS'
ADMINISTRATION (VA) EXPENDITURE BY PROGRAM IN THE STATE
AND COUNTIES OF FLORIDA, FISCAL YEAR 1995-96 (Continued)

County	Veteran population 1/	Total	Compensation and pension	Readjustment and vocational rehabilitation	Insurance and indemnities	Construction medical services and related costs 2/
				Expenditure (amounts rounded to $1,000)		
Lake	27,468	20,931	17,399	666	2,866	0
Lee	60,221	44,739	37,119	1,456	6,163	0
Leon	21,006	19,831	13,977	3,684	2,171	0
Levy	4,244	5,423	4,865	118	441	0
Liberty	662	880	801	9	70	0
Madison	1,507	2,008	1,780	66	162	0
Manatee	35,322	28,207	23,837	733	3,638	0
Marion	33,350	17,312	13,723	119	3,470	0
Martin	20,751	13,430	11,119	267	2,045	0
Monroe	13,790	10,916	9,112	366	1,438	0
Nassau	5,651	5,338	4,482	242	614	0
Okaloosa	23,398	51,410	42,504	6,392	2,514	0
Okeechobee	4,157	3,357	2,878	48	431	0
Orange	84,858	85,119	69,758	6,556	8,805	0
Osceola	15,306	3,970	2,379	21	1,569	0
Palm Beach	126,641	193,347	70,751	2,112	12,930	107,553
Pasco	61,807	52,814	45,049	1,742	6,023	0
Pinellas	130,876	355,563	133,929	5,700	13,945	201,988
Polk	54,644	53,524	45,996	1,710	5,818	0
Putnam	9,864	4,633	3,503	85	1,045	0
St. Johns	12,720	10,291	8,517	409	1,344	22
St. Lucie	22,871	20,048	17,074	555	2,419	0
Santa Rosa	12,079	19,452	15,635	2,526	1,291	0
Sarasota	51,304	38,378	32,202	893	5,283	0
Seminole	38,290	40,108	33,136	3,013	3,959	0
Sumter	5,469	15,815	10,806	329	560	4,121
Suwannee	3,163	5,954	5,456	157	341	0
Taylor	1,870	2,445	2,199	41	205	0
Union	1,222	1,194	973	87	134	0
Volusia	59,884	33,395	26,229	871	6,295	0
Wakulla	1,810	2,325	2,007	121	197	0
Walton	5,891	8,295	7,439	278	578	0
Washington	2,334	4,258	3,871	146	241	0

1/ Data as of June 1995.
2/ Includes administrative.

Source: U.S., Veterans' Administration, Internet site http://www.va.gov/.

Table 23.29. STATE GOVERNMENT FINANCE: REVENUE, EXPENDITURE, DIRECT EXPENDITURE INDEBTEDNESS, AND CASH AND SECURITY HOLDINGS IN FLORIDA, 1995

Item	Total ($1,000)	Percentage change 1994 to 1995	Per capita 1/ (dollars)
Revenue, total	37,359,429	7.3	2,637
General revenue	31,012,552	5.2	2,189
Intergovernmental	7,972,736	7.6	563
Taxes	18,564,650	4.2	1,311
General sales	10,656,548	6.1	752
Selective sales	3,670,398	4.6	259
License taxes	1,299,716	-0.1	92
Corporation net income	944,969	-0.6	67
Other taxes	1,993,019	-0.6	15
Current charges	1,696,889	5.4	120
Miscellaneous	2,778,277	4.5	196
Utility	4,737	-12.9	0
Insurance trust	6,342,140	19.3	448
Expenditure, total	34,749,505	7.6	2,453
Intergovernmental	10,949,733	7.0	773
Direct	23,799,772	8.0	1,680
Current operation	16,028,427	8.7	1,131
Capital outlay	3,281,512	16.4	232
Insurance benefits and repayments	2,547,236	13.1	180
Assistance and subsidies	1,070,009	-21.3	76
Interest on debt	872,588	1.0	62
Exhibit: salaries and wages	5,946,865	5.8	420
Expenditure, total	34,749,505	7.6	2,453
General expenditure	32,168,304	7.3	2,271
Intergovernmental	10,949,733	7.0	773
Direct	21,218,571	7.4	1,498
General expenditure by function			
Education	10,845,537	6.0	766
Public welfare	7,046,459	4.8	497
Hospitals	507,404	4.2	36
Health	1,943,154	5.5	137
Highways	2,995,462	10.5	211
Police protection	280,926	27.8	20
Correction	1,599,259	28.3	113
Natural resources	1,091,848	1.6	77
Parks and recreation	106,257	35.6	8
Governmental administration	1,224,385	5.7	86
Interest on general debt	872,588	1.0	62
Other and unallocable	3,655,025	9.0	258
Utility	33,965	-13.6	2
Insurance trust	2,547,236	13.1	180
Debt at end of fiscal year	15,369,609	5.5	1,085
Cash and security holdings	52,464,253	5.5	3,704

1/ Based on U.S. Bureau of the Census population estimates.

Source: U.S., Department of Commerce, Bureau of the Census, Internet site http://www.census.gov/.

University of Florida   **Bureau of Economic and Business Research**

Table 23.31. STATE TREASURER'S REPORT: RESOURCES AND LIABILITIES
FISCAL YEAR 1995-96

(in dollars)

	Balance sheet for fiscal year ending June 30, 1996
Item	Resources
Office cash	
Currency and coin	300,000.00
Bank deposits	
U.C. benefit investment account 1/	1,982,153,163.71
Demand accounts	A/ 251,918,177.27
Time deposit account	662,175,000.00
Total bank deposits	2,234,071,340.98

(The above does not include dollars held in clearing and/or revolving
accounts outside the State Treasury.)

Total all securities held by treasury	7,659,483,088.67

(The above does not include money invested for Treasurer's Special
Purpose Investment Fund, merged October 1993.)

Total state-owned resources in treasurer's custody	10,556,029,429.65
	Liabilities
State Funds subject to Comptroller's warrants	
General revenue fund	1,493,320,497.46
Trust fund	8,697,570,033.05
Working capital fund 2/	1,250,000.00
Budget stabilization fund	260,790,000.00
Total four funds	10,452,930,530.51
Adjustments 3/	103,098,899.14
Total liabilities	10,556,029,429.65

A/ Includes per reconciled cash balance of $277,617,427.71, a difference of
$25,699,250.44 which represents items that have cleared at the bank but have not been
posted to the state ledger.
1/ Represents U.C. benefit funds held and invested by the federal government,
administered by the Treasury.
2/ Working capital funds are invested within the Trust Fund Investment Program.
3/ Represents a $300.23 posting discrepancy within Comptroller's records, cor-
rected July 1996, and $16,039,519.99 interest not yet receipted to state accounts.
Note:　Total market value of all securities held by Treasury $8,116,180,694.38.

Source:　State of Florida, *Annual Report of the State Treasurer for the Fiscal
Year Ending June 30, 1996.*

Table 23.40. STATE GOVERNMENT FINANCE: REVENUE, EXPENDITURE, AND CHANGE
IN FUND BALANCE BY FUND TYPE IN FLORIDA, FISCAL YEAR 1995-96

(in thousands of dollars)

Item	Total 1/	General	Special revenue	Expendable trust
Beginning fund balance, July 1, 1995	7,406,785	1,761,857	4,328,121	481,388
Revenue, total	34,066,635	14,606,358	17,422,395	1,963,925
Taxes 2/	20,352,955	14,245,249	5,232,728	874,978
Licenses and permits	826,009	52,154	773,855	0
Fees and charges	2,230,024	141,101	1,374,961	663,035
Grants and donations	9,246,985	733	9,215,132	30,764
Investment earnings	726,524	157,381	249,398	298,893
Fines, forfeits, and judgments	214,526	782	132,771	80,973
Refunds	468,731	8,958	442,675	15,276
Other	881	0	875	6
Expenditure, total	32,708,022	13,079,153	17,342,405	1,265,837
Current				
Economic opportunities, agriculture and employment	1,942,502	73,820	879,817	988,865
Public safety	2,515,430	2,017,138	498,292	0
Education	8,215,301	5,689,402	2,525,004	895
Health and social concerns	12,273,168	4,381,599	7,891,561	8
Housing and community development	222,890	15,199	207,691	0
Natural resources and environmental management	523,894	138,978	384,916	0
Recreational and cultural opportunities	138,279	59,694	78,584	1
Transportation	813,394	0	813,125	269
Government direction and support services	2,998,832	639,463	2,065,027	275,634
Capital outlay	2,317,418	60,546	1,990,860	162
Debt service				
Principle retirement	260,444	2,765	6,444	0
Interest and fiscal charges	486,470	549	1,084	3
Excess (deficiency) of revenues over expenditures	1,358,613	1,527,205	79,990	698,088
Other financing sources (uses)	-221,820	-996,873	-129,868	-51,143
Excess (deficiency) of revenues and other financing sources over expenditures and other financing uses	1,136,793	530,332	-49,878	646,945
Change in reserve for inventories	9,333	2,988	6,345	0
Ending Fund Balance, June 30, 1996	8,552,951	2,295,177	4,043,222	1,726,787

1/ Total presented only to facilitate financial analyses. Includes fund types and account groups that use differing basis of accounting, restricted and unrestricted amounts, and interfund transactions which have not been eliminated. Excludes community water management districts, community college and university direct-support organizations, transportation/expressway authorities, and other component units.

2/ Florida levies neither a personal income tax nor an ad valorem tax on real or tangible personal property. Taxes are, however, the principal means of financing state operations.

Source: State of Florida, Office of the Comptroller, *Florida Comprehensive Financial Report,* Fiscal Year Ended June 30, 1996.

Table 23.41. STATE GOVERNMENT FINANCE: TAX COLLECTIONS BY TYPE OF TAX COLLECTED IN FLORIDA AND THE UNITED STATES, 1996

	Florida		United States 1/	
Type of tax	Amount ($1,000)	Per capita 2/ (dollars)	Amount ($1,000)	Per capita 2/ (dollars)
Total	19,699,256	1,368.00	418,606,087	1,581.19
Property	754,482	52.39	9,972,851	37.67
Sales and gross receipts	15,240,514	1,058.37	205,580,502	776.53
General sales	11,428,999	793.68	139,306,575	526.20
Selective sales	3,811,515	264.69	66,273,927	250.33
Alcoholic beverage	542,130	37.65	3,666,689	13.85
Amusement	599	0.04	1,774,035	6.70
Insurance premium	482,053	33.48	9,053,346	34.20
Motor fuels	1,337,982	92.92	25,997,902	98.20
Pari-mutuels	81,639	5.67	443,458	1.68
Public utilities	542,993	37.71	8,581,355	32.41
Tobacco sales	458,234	31.82	7,337,771	27.72
Other	365,885	25.41	9,419,371	35.58
License	1,315,384	91.35	26,988,158	101.94
Alcoholic beverage	31,599	2.19	307,059	1.16
Amusement	8,041	0.56	240,919	0.91
Corporation	123,420	8.57	5,195,623	19.63
Hunting and fishing	14,007	0.97	990,170	3.74
Motor vehicle	786,039	54.59	12,677,256	47.89
Motor vehicle operators	93,887	6.52	1,160,698	4.38
Public utility	25,661	1.78	344,879	1.30
Occupation and business	222,771	15.47	5,623,873	21.24
Other	9,959	0.69	447,681	1.69
Other taxes	2,388,876	165.89	176,064,576	665.04
Individual income	(X)	(X)	134,309,097	507.32
Corporation net income	1,007,556	69.97	29,425,386	111.15
Death and gift	406,611	28.24	5,306,218	20.04
Documentary and stock transfer	909,277	63.14	2,267,214	8.56
Severance	65,432	4.54	4,433,707	16.75
Other, NEC	(X)	(X)	322,954	1.22

NEC Not elsewhere classified.
(X) Not applicable.
1/ Excludes the District of Columbia and territories.
2/ Per capita amounts are based on a Bureau of the Census estimate of 14,400,000 in Florida and 264,741,000 in the United States.

Source: U.S., Department of Commerce, Bureau of the Census, Internet site http://www.census.gov/.

University of Florida   **Bureau of Economic and Business Research**

Table 23.43. STATE GOVERNMENT FINANCE: SALES AND USE TAX COLLECTIONS BY TRADE
CLASSIFICATION IN FLORIDA, FISCAL YEARS 1994-95 AND 1995-96

(amounts rounded to thousands of dollars)

Group	1994-95	1995-96	Per- centage change
All classifications, total	10,550,860	11,362,706	7.7
Food and beverage group	1,471,567	1,558,803	5.9
Grocery stores	482,906	515,919	6.8
Meat markets	894	1,037	16.0
Seafood dealers	1,030	1,117	8.4
Vegetables and fruit markets	1,976	2,735	38.4
Bakeries	4,719	4,986	5.6
Delicatessens	8,129	8,208	1.0
Candy, confectionery, concession stands	23,549	25,770	9.4
Restaurants, lunchrooms, catering services	838,030	885,102	5.6
Taverns, night clubs, bars, liquor stores	110,334	113,930	3.3
Apparel group	332,837	352,642	6.0
Clothing stores	281,573	295,450	4.9
Shoe stores	48,580	54,069	11.3
Hat shops	2,684	3,122	16.3
General merchandise group	1,561,901	1,677,628	7.4
Department stores	545,728	578,273	6.0
Variety stores	409,666	528,603	29.0
Drug stores	127,094	125,857	-1.0
Jewelry, leather, and sporting goods	136,949	146,172	6.7
Feed, seed, fertilizer stores	6,269	6,371	1.6
Hardware, paints, and machinery	110,326	116,608	5.7
Farm implements and supplies	19,696	21,192	7.6
General merchandise stores	169,413	116,360	-31.3
Second-hand stores, antique shops, flea markets	20,001	22,253	11.3
Dry goods stores	16,759	15,939	-4.9
Automotive group	1,991,147	2,182,426	9.6
Motor vehicle dealers, trailers, campers	1,562,524	1,728,617	10.6
Auto accessories, tires, and parts	137,945	144,402	4.7
Filling and service stations, car wash	59,344	61,029	2.8
Garage and repair shops	134,494	144,567	7.5
Aircraft dealers	16,355	17,450	6.7
Motorboat and yacht dealers	80,484	86,361	7.3
Furniture and appliances group	658,503	728,289	10.6
Furniture stores, new and used	214,375	230,837	7.7
Household appliances, dinnerware, etc.	76,425	79,131	3.5
Store and office equipment	115,572	128,811	11.5
Music stores, radios, and televisions	252,131	289,510	14.8
Lumber, builders, and contractors group	595,112	613,699	3.1
Building contractors	27,880	30,470	9.3
Heating and air conditioning	32,697	36,308	11.0
Electrical and plumbing	70,588	73,308	3.9
Decorating, painting, and papering	35,585	37,072	4.2
Roofing and sheet metal	10,827	11,131	2.8
Lumber and building materials	417,535	425,410	1.9
General classification group	3,939,793	4,249,218	7.9
Hotels, apartment houses, etc.	458,357	519,683	13.4
Auctioneers and commission dealers	26,834	29,891	11.4
Barber and beauty shops	34,121	36,128	5.9
Book stores	35,894	38,620	7.6
Cigar stands and tobacco shops	1,899	2,543	33.9

Continued . . .

Table 23.43. STATE GOVERNMENT FINANCE: SALES AND USE TAX COLLECTIONS BY TRADE
CLASSIFICATION IN FLORIDA, FISCAL YEARS 1994-95 AND 1995-96 (Continued)

(amounts rounded to thousands of dollars)

Group	1994-95	1995-96	Percentage change
General classification group (Continued)			
Florists	17,209	17,838	3.7
Fuel dealers, L.P. gas dealers	28,158	25,714	-8.7
Funeral directors monuments	5,904	4,402	-25.4
Scrap metal and junk yards	2,822	3,078	9.1
Itinerant vendors	15,714	16,508	5.1
Laundry, cleaning services, alterations	11,809	12,913	9.3
Machine shops and foundries	11,637	12,865	10.5
Horse, cattle, and pet dealers	67,682	67,575	-0.2
Photographers, photo supplies, art galleries	51,342	53,982	5.1
Shoe repair shops	1,019	986	-3.3
Storage and warehousing	7,117	7,675	7.8
Gift, card, and novelty stores, taxidermy	100,324	107,426	7.1
Newsstands	3,520	3,655	3.9
Social clubs and associations	25,827	26,698	3.4
Industrial machinery equipment	120,969	135,015	11.6
Admissions	207,793	225,421	8.5
Holiday season vendors, Christmas trees	527	573	8.6
Rental of tangible property	178,111	193,283	8.5
Fabrication and sales of cabinets, etc.	47,511	49,882	5.0
Manufacturing and mining	316,600	339,918	7.4
Bottlers (beer and softdrinks)	5,770	6,136	6.4
Pawn shops	5,427	5,786	6.6
Communications	449,540	499,102	11.0
Transportation	16,198	15,979	-1.4
Graphic arts and printing	94,237	98,343	4.4
Insurance, banking, information services, etc.	25,763	18,465	-28.3
Sanitary and industrial supplies	30,197	30,296	0.3
Packaging materials and paper boxes	8,915	9,530	6.9
Repair of tangible personal property	62,075	63,168	1.8
Advertising	17,875	18,236	2.0
Topsoil, clay, sand, and fill dirt	19,271	21,210	10.1
Trade stamp redemption centers	9	18	107.9
Nurseries and landscaping	24,955	26,804	7.4
Vending machines	21,465	22,532	5.0
Importing and exporting	10,694	11,985	12.1
Medical, dental, surgical, hospital supplies	33,658	38,212	13.5
Wholesale dealers	289,353	289,957	0.2
Schools and educational institutions	3,499	3,551	1.5
Office space and commercial rentals	587,960	618,450	5.2
Parking lots, boat docking, and storage	16,767	17,858	6.5
Utilities, electric or gas	266,095	279,920	5.2
Dual users of special fuels	1,132	1,191	5.2
Public works, government contractors	1,030	4,577	344.6
Flea market vendors	7,862	8,272	5.2
Carnival concessions	468	447	-4.6
Other professional services	1,975	2,099	6.3
Other personal services	71,222	77,977	9.5
Other industrial services	5,348	5,625	5.2
Commercial fisherman	128	129	0.9
Miscellaneous	82,207	121,092	47.3

Source: State of Florida, Department of Revenue, Internet site http://fcn.state.
fl.us/dor/.

University of Florida   **Bureau of Economic and Business Research**

Table 23.45.   STATE GOVERNMENT FINANCE: TAX COLLECTIONS BY OR WITHIN COUNTIES
BY TYPE OF TAX COLLECTED IN THE STATE AND COUNTIES OF FLORIDA
FISCAL YEAR 1995-96

(rounded to thousands of dollars)

County	Total 1/	Sales and use taxes	Motor vehicle tags	Pari-mutuel wagering taxes	Docu-mentary stamp tax
Florida	12,544,876	11,362,706	412,823	88,788	680,558
Alachua	144,007	133,158	4,401	0	6,448
Baker	5,725	4,842	566	0	317
Bay	125,104	115,655	3,662	0	5,787
Bradford	9,883	8,917	634	0	331
Brevard	281,335	254,865	10,856	530	15,084
Broward	1,278,889	1,156,008	30,319	14,089	78,474
Calhoun	4,143	3,717	249	0	177
Charlotte	81,273	72,283	3,445	0	5,544
Citrus	52,135	44,721	2,828	0	4,587
Clay	76,025	64,091	3,163	3,878	4,894
Collier	230,307	195,643	5,978	0	28,686
Columbia	32,884	30,468	1,305	0	1,110
Dade	1,585,023	1,424,962	57,164	19,784	83,114
De Soto	11,254	9,857	786	0	612
Dixie	3,158	2,547	327	0	284
Duval	635,434	586,464	18,158	4,119	26,692
Escambia	209,462	191,871	6,605	1,733	9,253
Flagler	18,918	15,176	1,107	0	2,636
Franklin	5,415	4,098	237	0	1,080
Gadsden	13,358	11,450	820	0	1,088
Gilchrist	2,516	1,895	339	0	282
Glades	1,441	1,093	170	0	179
Gulf	6,123	4,675	337	0	1,111
Hamilton	6,982	6,254	235	0	493
Hardee	9,530	8,422	691	0	417
Hendry	15,062	12,578	1,162	0	1,321
Hernando	49,888	43,680	2,707	0	3,501
Highlands	41,421	37,092	2,284	0	2,045
Hillsborough	858,877	787,285	25,308	8,659	37,625
Holmes	4,443	3,835	400	0	208
Indian River	73,239	63,771	2,827	0	6,641
Jackson	21,030	19,203	1,056	0	770
Jefferson	5,211	3,136	301	1,438	335
Lafayette	1,062	743	142	0	177
Lake	101,751	89,182	5,164	0	7,405
Lee	345,988	306,971	10,750	4,078	24,190
Leon	173,452	159,158	5,068	0	9,226

See footnotes at end of table.   Continued . . .

Table 23.45.   STATE GOVERNMENT FINANCE: TAX COLLECTIONS BY OR WITHIN COUNTIES
BY TYPE OF TAX COLLECTED IN THE STATE AND COUNTIES OF FLORIDA
FISCAL YEAR 1995-96 (Continued)

(rounded to thousands of dollars)

County	Total 1/	Sales and use taxes	Motor vehicle tags	Pari-mutuel wagering taxes	Docu-mentary stamp tax
Levy	12,629	10,864	1,001	0	764
Liberty	1,493	1,194	187	0	112
Madison	4,934	4,226	403	0	306
Manatee	170,204	144,801	14,360	0	11,043
Marion	149,603	135,923	6,626	53	7,001
Martin	105,575	93,835	3,654	0	8,086
Monroe	107,359	96,993	2,246	0	8,119
Nassau	30,234	26,415	1,289	0	2,530
Okaloosa	128,888	116,335	4,171	0	8,381
Okeechobee	17,382	15,438	1,101	0	843
Orange	1,132,130	1,066,553	23,167	0	42,410
Osceola	125,160	114,183	3,344	0	7,634
Palm Beach	931,631	828,062	24,522	9,266	69,781
Pasco	149,328	131,022	8,423	0	9,883
Pinellas	646,715	579,188	20,395	8,438	38,694
Polk	303,878	276,849	13,005	0	14,024
Putnam	31,013	27,967	1,653	0	1,392
St. Johns	76,467	64,326	2,783	2,178	7,180
St. Lucie	97,925	86,547	4,368	117	6,895
Santa Rosa	39,513	32,548	2,434	0	4,531
Sarasota	262,688	231,045	8,507	1,243	21,893
Seminole	266,144	238,186	8,512	4,700	14,746
Sumter	13,825	11,347	986	0	1,492
Suwannee	12,920	11,515	841	0	564
Taylor	10,948	10,139	490	0	319
Union	2,540	2,133	297	0	109
Volusia	271,703	243,292	10,005	3,580	14,827
Wakulla	4,835	3,834	448	0	553
Walton	29,266	24,626	659	0	3,981
Washington	7,168	5,504	417	907	340
Out-of-state	827,437	827,437	0	0	0
Other	20,615	20,615	A/ 30,975	0	0

A/ Includes refunds.
1/ Does not include gasoline taxes.

Source: Columns 2, 5, State of Florida, Department of Revenue, unpublished data;
Column 3, State of Florida, Department of Highway Safety and Motor Vehicles, Division
of Motor Vehicles, *Revenue Report, July 1, 1995-June 30, 1996;* Column 4, State of
Florida, Department of Business and Professional Regulation, Division of Pari-Mutuel
Wagering, *65th Annual Report for the Fiscal Year Ending on June 30, 1996.*

University of Florida   **Bureau of Economic and Business Research**

Table 23.46. STATE GOVERNMENT FINANCE: GASOLINE AND GASOHOL TAX COLLECTIONS IN FLORIDA, FISCAL YEARS 1969-70 THROUGH 1994-95

Fiscal year	Gallons sold	Tax rate (cents)	Tax collected 1/ (dollars)
		Gasoline	
1969-70	3,054,891,901.3	7	213,842,433.12
1970-71	3,341,148,943.8	7	233,880,426.09
1971-72	3,685,131,310.5	7/8	291,484,318.30
1972-73	4,080,699,270.9	8	326,454,941.67
1973-74	4,157,754,572.7	8	332,617,165.82
1974-75	4,243,123,105.1	8	339,449,848.41
1975-76	4,326,195,422.0	8	346,095,633.76
1976-77	4,483,397,014.2	8	358,671,761.14
1977-78	4,721,812,693.4	8	377,745,015.47
1978-79	4,961,448,003.1	8	396,915,840.25
1979-80	4,765,935,970.1	8	381,274,877.61
1980-81	4,681,857,035.4	8	374,548,562.90
1981-82	4,746,090,470.3	8	379,687,237.63
1982-83	4,686,388,610.8	5.7/8/9.7	387,286,074.47
1983-84	4,709,246,332.0	5.7/8/9.7	455,678,899.26
1984-85	4,739,366,278.0	5.7/9.7	458,188,999.77
1985-86	5,003,004,954.0	5.7/9.7	483,953,518.77
1986-87	5,493,474,844.7	5.7/9.7	484,754,881.20
1987-88	5,869,584,946.8	5.7/9.7	569,328,353.84
1988-89	5,995,884,170.5	5.7/9.7	581,596,538.65
1989-90	6,087,306,071.0	5.7/9.7	590,082,229.69
1990-91	5,985,729,187.8	9.7/10.9/11.2	653,943,345.04
1991-92	6,065,182,815.5	9.7/10.9/11.2/11.6	689,690,791.78
1992-93	6,279,687,903.2	9.7/10.9/11.2/11.6/11.8	723,722,832.76
1993-94	6,451,928,258.1	10.9/11.2/11.6/12.1	765,014,400.64
1994-95	6,560,589,349.5	11.6/11.8/12.1/12.3	802,201,952.42
		Gasohol	
1980-81	40,041,320.0	3	1,201,239.60
1981-82	70,917,324.0	3	2,127,519.72
1982-83	174,716,609.0	3	5,241,498.27
1983-84	450,407,246.3	3/5.7	24,795,573.66
1984-85	580,254,644.0	5.7	32,540,874.16
1985-86	502,585,415.4	5.7/7.7	37,559,028.18
1986-87	216,061,242.3	7.7	16,636,263.27
1987-88	90,593,367.2	7.7/9.7	8,494,772.51
1988-89	83,299,691.4	9.7	8,081,088.78
1989-90	72,191,842.3	9.7	7,027,562.96
1990-91	84,213,028.6	9.7/10.9/11.2	9,177,965.47
1991-92	99,594,325.4	9.7/10.9/11.2/11.6	11,317,423.38
1992-93	104,007,445.0	11.6/11.8	12,162,419.87
1993-94	13,688,278.1	10.9/11.8/12.1	5,806,630.60
1994-95	20,384,143.0	12.1/12.3	2,791,240.05

1/ Includes collection fees.
Note: Some data may be revised.

Source: State of Florida, Department of Revenue, *Report of Fuel Tax Collections and Distributions, Fiscal Year 1994-95,* and unpublished data.

University of Florida   **Bureau of Economic and Business Research**

Table 23.48. STATE FUNDS TO LOCAL GOVERNMENT: DISTRIBUTION OF SHARED TAXES BY THE
FLORIDA DEPARTMENT OF REVENUE TO COUNTY AND CITY GOVERNMENTS BY MAJOR
SOURCE IN THE STATE AND COUNTIES OF FLORIDA
FISCAL YEAR 1995-96

(rounded to thousands of dollars)

County	Total DOR distri- bution	Half-cent sales tax distributed to-- County govern- ments	City govern- ments	Emer- gency and supple- mental	Revenue sharing County	Munici- pal	County tax on motor fuel
Florida	1,524,941	647,357	322,596	5,470	292,949	200,300	56,269
Alachua	19,787	7,268	5,022	0	3,660	3,024	813
Baker	1,445	365	101	303	348	119	209
Bay	16,449	6,069	4,515	0	2,774	2,425	666
Bradford	1,792	632	224	189	404	194	149
Brevard	38,686	13,031	10,205	0	7,691	6,131	1,628
Broward	161,496	47,258	59,321	0	22,311	28,340	4,266
Calhoun	1,000	293	88	142	209	92	177
Charlotte	10,468	6,046	601	0	3,037	205	579
Citrus	7,156	3,709	400	0	2,376	238	432
Clay	9,501	5,157	746	0	2,746	369	483
Collier	24,966	16,357	1,978	0	5,136	476	1,019
Columbia	4,609	2,292	521	0	1,093	272	430
Dade	234,464	83,291	46,313	0	41,247	57,677	5,935
De Soto	2,089	774	228	181	502	183	222
Dixie	988	210	46	206	217	92	216
Duval 1/	89,624	51,526	3,025	0	16,282	16,257	2,534
Escambia	26,972	14,330	3,494	0	6,465	1,639	1,044
Flagler	2,612	1,187	231	99	762	106	228
Franklin	984	266	129	84	179	112	214
Gadsden	3,502	757	364	701	771	652	258
Gilchrist	781	156	41	227	208	43	107
Glades	776	101	20	194	159	44	258
Gulf	1,130	284	182	144	207	123	190
Hamilton	1,136	425	158	0	225	127	201
Hardee	1,745	585	206	110	411	207	225
Hendry	2,520	880	328	154	552	211	395
Hernando	7,272	3,781	262	0	2,605	185	439
Highlands	6,120	2,741	727	0	1,654	496	501
Hillsborough	105,078	51,082	21,724	0	20,671	8,552	3,049
Holmes	1,202	294	80	231	306	113	180
Indian River	9,217	4,219	1,739	0	2,061	746	452
Jackson	3,828	1,283	507	233	847	513	446
Jefferson	1,043	261	63	197	241	70	211
Lafayette	488	73	14	126	98	33	145
Lake	14,000	5,321	2,875	0	3,265	1,763	775
Lee	40,769	19,407	8,369	0	8,538	3,087	1,368

See footnotes at end of table.   Continued . . .

Table 23.48. STATE FUNDS TO LOCAL GOVERNMENT: DISTRIBUTION OF SHARED TAXES BY THE
FLORIDA DEPARTMENT OF REVENUE TO COUNTY AND CITY GOVERNMENTS BY MAJOR
SOURCE IN THE STATE AND COUNTIES OF FLORIDA
FISCAL YEAR 1995-96 (Continued)

(rounded to thousands of dollars)

County	Total DOR distri- bution	Half-cent sales tax distributed to-- County govern- ments	City govern- ments	Emer- gency and supple- mental	Revenue sharing County	Munici- pal	County tax on motor fuel
Leon	22,652	8,132	6,481	0	3,974	3,251	814
Levy	2,483	779	241	303	570	209	381
Liberty	613	113	22	120	105	33	220
Madison	1,445	316	99	288	311	147	283
Manatee	20,785	10,081	3,326	0	5,090	1,460	828
Marion	19,885	10,102	2,486	0	4,975	1,138	1,184
Martin	12,431	7,546	1,172	0	2,865	354	494
Monroe	12,547	6,469	2,447	0	2,196	687	748
Nassau	4,076	1,874	560	0	1,032	275	334
Okaloosa	16,575	7,274	3,597	0	3,325	1,629	749
Okeechobee	2,675	1,225	201	0	730	176	343
Orange	129,176	69,798	28,303	0	20,910	7,435	2,729
Osceola	15,643	7,352	3,252	0	2,982	1,255	802
Palm Beach	112,149	46,625	30,430	0	20,063	11,843	3,188
Pasco	20,746	10,916	1,257	0	6,829	760	984
Pinellas	85,485	28,207	25,417	0	15,220	14,226	2,416
Polk	41,130	17,646	7,913	0	9,171	4,447	1,953
Putnam	4,847	2,098	501	0	1,444	403	401
St. Johns	9,216	5,031	931	0	2,296	421	537
St. Lucie	13,712	4,423	3,560	0	2,800	2,269	660
Santa Rosa	5,880	2,600	413	0	1,996	320	551
Sarasota	31,169	16,024	5,238	0	6,988	1,970	949
Seminole	32,826	13,767	8,215	0	6,420	3,494	930
Sumter	2,689	832	229	290	686	257	395
Suwannee	2,384	850	230	197	603	220	284
Taylor	1,876	651	312	0	358	218	337
Union	764	163	55	210	156	88	92
Volusia	36,957	12,129	10,247	0	7,179	5,964	1,438
Wakulla	1,207	360	15	260	356	19	196
Walton	3,670	1,871	448	0	737	217	397
Washington	1,555	393	150	282	324	202	205

DOR Department of Revenue.
1/ Duval County is the consolidated city of Jacksonville.
Note: Detail may not add to totals due to rounding.

Source: State of Florida, Department of Revenue, Internet site http://fcn.state.
fl.us/dor/.

Table 23.50. STATE LOTTERY: SALES IN THE STATE AND COUNTIES OF FLORIDA
FISCAL YEARS 1991-92 THROUGH 1996-97

(rounded to thousands of dollars)

County	1991-92	1992-93	1993-94	1994-95	1995-96	1996-97
Florida	2,227,202	2,169,700	2,208,088	2,303,486	2,117,085	2,159,669
Alachua	22,207	22,922	23,428	25,103	23,734	24,166
Baker	2,310	2,255	2,504	2,501	2,303	2,262
Bay	26,498	24,721	23,504	24,939	21,866	21,868
Bradford	2,641	2,770	3,038	3,422	3,152	3,193
Brevard	69,147	67,290	69,882	71,821	68,880	70,103
Broward	227,822	225,594	228,624	231,817	209,958	213,034
Calhoun	1,166	1,140	1,159	1,312	1,227	1,180
Charlotte	17,795	17,661	18,222	19,528	17,900	18,906
Citrus	15,070	14,657	15,897	16,784	15,713	16,279
Clay	12,809	12,610	12,691	13,114	12,353	12,911
Collier	22,314	22,232	23,335	24,182	22,357	23,401
Columbia	8,127	8,371	8,268	8,790	8,424	8,796
Dade	378,322	362,759	374,679	375,442	354,696	351,789
De Soto	3,203	3,168	3,061	3,105	2,858	2,848
Dixie	1,015	895	1,120	1,305	1,348	1,326
Duval	107,895	108,200	109,681	115,885	106,516	109,163
Escambia	77,186	70,616	67,172	72,207	62,131	62,689
Flagler	5,136	5,175	5,724	6,397	6,234	6,417
Franklin	1,525	1,645	1,655	1,629	1,442	1,487
Gadsden	7,771	7,892	7,069	7,593	6,671	6,763
Gilchrist	821	961	950	932	1,152	1,306
Glades	1,098	1,223	901	953	907	689
Gulf	1,620	1,582	1,676	1,739	1,551	1,590
Hamilton	18,650	16,542	8,662	8,521	4,892	3,990
Hardee	2,088	1,967	1,998	2,238	1,982	2,024
Hendry	4,396	4,337	4,506	4,629	4,122	4,291
Hernando	17,112	17,765	19,443	20,285	19,531	20,858
Highlands	10,105	9,971	10,375	10,879	9,821	10,047
Hillsborough	120,136	117,110	120,124	128,350	117,034	119,728
Holmes	6,198	6,015	5,740	6,031	5,556	5,529
Indian River	13,596	13,226	14,718	15,783	14,626	14,953
Jackson	23,820	22,387	17,337	19,368	15,299	14,446
Jefferson	9,109	8,231	5,314	5,432	3,379	2,739
Lafayette	499	435	448	444	413	453
Lake	25,706	24,666	26,197	28,555	27,696	29,716
Lee	49,795	49,446	50,867	52,317	49,074	50,732

See footnote at end of table.   Continued . . .

University of Florida   **Bureau of Economic and Business Research**

Table 23.50.   STATE LOTTERY: SALES IN THE STATE AND COUNTIES OF FLORIDA
FISCAL YEARS 1991-92 THROUGH 1996-97 (Continued)

(rounded to thousands of dollars)

County	1991-92	1992-93	1993-94	1994-95	1995-96	1996-97
Leon	25,505	24,074	23,366	25,641	21,986	22,503
Levy	4,521	4,679	4,697	5,191	5,024	4,909
Liberty	701	693	710	831	691	822
Madison	4,502	4,182	3,401	3,507	2,761	2,932
Manatee	30,324	29,701	31,558	33,011	29,786	30,189
Marion	33,229	33,466	35,926	38,014	35,354	37,627
Martin	16,659	17,112	17,589	18,486	17,284	18,281
Monroe	13,807	13,554	13,527	14,049	13,320	13,907
Nassau	26,051	24,298	16,554	16,425	11,390	10,386
Okaloosa	25,371	24,281	23,867	25,640	22,545	22,545
Okeechobee	5,008	5,132	5,494	5,644	5,136	5,307
Orange	111,963	107,891	110,261	118,085	110,784	116,775
Osceola	20,125	20,298	22,523	24,215	22,785	24,084
Palm Beach	142,399	138,584	144,989	151,562	140,687	142,100
Pasco	42,451	42,918	46,409	48,002	44,548	46,521
Pinellas	131,667	126,447	133,874	139,180	127,057	129,920
Polk	63,371	62,771	64,416	69,925	63,533	66,542
Putnam	10,239	10,334	10,763	11,468	10,675	10,662
St. Johns	11,988	12,043	12,574	13,397	12,391	12,721
St. Lucie	25,837	26,662	26,870	28,718	26,251	25,921
Santa Rosa	11,340	11,005	10,926	11,399	10,691	11,184
Sarasota	38,060	36,533	38,334	40,452	36,372	36,732
Seminole	33,633	32,073	33,491	35,889	33,927	35,898
Sumter	5,064	5,274	5,257	5,474	5,076	5,473
Suwannee	3,329	3,536	3,747	3,782	3,601	3,727
Taylor	2,506	2,402	2,563	2,751	2,463	2,584
Union	1,124	1,081	1,104	1,177	1,058	1,117
Volusia	61,749	60,556	63,699	67,907	63,640	66,693
Wakulla	1,750	1,856	1,931	2,112	1,895	1,984
Walton	6,173	5,935	5,841	6,267	5,712	5,965
Washington	2,047	1,888	1,861	1,950	1,867	1,988

Note: Data are unaudited gross sales amounts.

Source: State of Florida, Department of the Lottery, unpublished data.

Table 23.52. ALCOHOLIC BEVERAGE AND TOBACCO LICENSES: NUMBER OF LICENSES
ISSUED IN THE STATE AND COUNTIES OF FLORIDA, FISCAL YEAR 1995-96

County	Alcoholic beverages licenses Number	Per-entage change 1/	Tobacco licenses Number	Per-entage change 1/	County	Alcoholic beverages licenses Number	Per-entage change 1/	Tobacco licenses Number	Per-entage change 1/
Florida	39,931	3.9	32,241	10.2	Lafayette	13	18.2	15	25.0
					Lake	467	0.2	374	12.3
Alachua	469	2.4	374	5.9	Lee	1,229	6.3	871	12.2
Baker	54	1.9	55	7.8	Leon	488	0.4	376	6.8
Bay	570	-1.4	418	1.0	Levy	116	-3.3	100	12.4
Bradford	60	-9.1	56	-6.7	Liberty	17	-15.0	21	-4.5
Brevard	1,325	6.2	984	13.5	Madison	46	-8.0	49	6.5
Broward	3,959	8.1	2,896	13.3	Manatee	615	4.6	474	11.3
Calhoun	37	-2.6	41	10.8	Marion	579	0.2	465	0.9
Charlotte	333	6.4	222	7.8	Martin	425	5.5	251	11.6
Citrus	289	-2.0	216	5.4	Monroe	731	9.6	504	15.3
Clay	227	-3.8	189	4.4	Nassau	156	2.0	139	11.2
Collier	744	-1.1	472	10.3	Okaloosa	479	0.6	329	6.5
Columbia	157	6.1	147	12.2	Okeechobee	116	4.5	96	4.3
Dade	5,700	11.3	5,406	16.3	Orange	2,021	-1.4	1,696	8.9
De Soto	67	8.1	55	10.0	Osceola	482	-0.2	391	5.4
Dixie	46	-4.2	44	12.8	Palm Beach	2,887	10.7	2,035	13.6
Duval	1,784	-1.5	1,554	4.2	Pasco	644	0.3	520	6.3
Escambia	731	-2.4	588	2.1	Pinellas	2,341	0.6	1,932	9.8
Flagler	143	5.9	104	18.2	Polk	1,111	5.4	960	11.2
Franklin	68	-2.9	49	8.9	Putnam	175	-4.4	164	2.5
Gadsden	130	-8.5	128	0.8	St. Johns	370	-2.9	241	3.9
Gilchrist	26	-7.1	26	-3.7	St. Lucie	494	12.3	367	7.6
Glades	45	-2.2	36	5.9	Santa Rosa	156	-4.9	147	0.7
Gulf	56	5.7	50	22.0	Sarasota	877	2.1	568	10.5
Hamilton	48	-7.7	43	4.9	Seminole	699	-1.5	519	5.5
Hardee	42	7.7	39	0.0	Sumter	101	-2.9	97	4.3
Hendry	100	-4.8	99	3.1	Suwannee	77	-1.3	74	2.8
Hernando	251	-6.7	176	1.1	Taylor	74	-8.6	69	3.0
Highlands	217	2.4	159	7.4	Union	17	-5.6	24	14.3
Hillsborough	2,107	1.0	2,019	11.0	Volusia	1,290	3.0	1,049	9.0
Holmes	53	1.9	57	16.3	Wakulla	64	4.9	48	-2.0
Indian River	322	4.5	216	13.1	Walton	182	2.8	129	5.7
Jackson	135	1.5	133	0.0	Washington	47	0.0	53	8.2
Jefferson	50	-3.8	43	0.0					

1/ Percentage change from previous fiscal year.

Source: State of Florida, Department of Business and Professional Regulation,
1995-1996 Annual Report. Data from Division of Alcoholic Beverages and Tobacco.

University of Florida   **Bureau of Economic and Business Research**

Table 23.53. ALCOHOLIC BEVERAGE LICENSES: NUMBER OF LICENSES ISSUED BY TYPE
OF LICENSE IN THE STATE AND COUNTIES OF FLORIDA, LICENSE YEAR
OCTOBER 1, 1995 THROUGH SEPTEMBER 30, 1996

County	Total	Clubs enter-tain-ment and tracks 1/	Package sales only 2/	Package and on-premises sales 3/	Dis-tribu-tors 4/	Manu-factur-ers 5/	Import/ export 6/	Broker sales agent (BSA)
Florida	38,887	1,611	17,271	11,247	8,609	44	87	18
Alachua	473	11	236	111	115	0	0	0
Baker	52	2	36	10	4	0	0	0
Bay	589	19	222	207	141	0	0	0
Bradford	59	2	36	15	6	0	0	0
Brevard	1,240	65	499	388	284	3	0	1
Broward	3,699	104	1,645	1,039	897	1	10	3
Calhoun	35	0	24	11	0	0	0	0
Charlotte	323	25	126	77	95	0	0	0
Citrus	290	27	125	85	53	0	0	0
Clay	232	13	126	49	43	0	1	0
Collier	711	60	236	225	190	0	0	0
Columbia	164	6	103	29	26	0	0	0
Dade	5,177	95	2,335	1,767	926	2	47	5
De Soto	65	6	30	18	11	0	0	0
Dixie	43	0	24	14	5	0	0	0
Duval	1,827	62	925	517	315	5	2	1
Escambia	742	27	343	181	191	0	0	0
Flagler	126	8	39	56	23	0	0	0
Franklin	69	2	24	20	23	0	0	0
Gadsden	132	1	79	39	13	0	0	0
Gilchrist	25	0	15	3	7	0	0	0
Glades	40	2	17	11	10	0	0	0
Gulf	50	2	23	15	10	0	0	0
Hamilton	53	0	33	20	0	0	0	0
Hardee	41	0	28	13	0	0	0	0
Hendry	99	7	51	26	15	0	0	0
Hernando	269	20	119	84	46	0	0	0
Highlands	205	18	97	45	44	0	1	0
Hillsborough	2,180	81	1,041	519	530	5	4	0
Holmes	55	1	41	13	0	0	0	0
Indian River	314	29	134	79	72	0	0	0
Jackson	142	1	100	41	0	0	0	0
Jefferson	46	3	30	10	3	0	0	0
Lafayette	13	0	10	3	0	0	0	0
Lake	471	29	233	119	89	1	0	0
Lee	1,195	83	463	353	293	1	1	1
Leon	508	12	242	139	114	0	0	1
Levy	116	6	67	23	20	0	0	0
Liberty	17	0	14	3	0	0	0	0
Madison	47	0	34	13	0	0	0	0

See footnotes at end of table.   Continued . . .

Table 23.53. ALCOHOLIC BEVERAGE LICENSES: NUMBER OF LICENSES ISSUED BY TYPE
OF LICENSE IN THE STATE AND COUNTIES OF FLORIDA, LICENSE YEAR
OCTOBER 1, 1995 THROUGH SEPTEMBER 30, 1996 (Continued)

County	Total	Clubs enter-tain-ment and tracks 1/	Package sales only 2/	Package and on-premises sales 3/	Dis-tribu-tors 4/	Manu-factur-ers 5/	Import/export 6/	Broker sales agent (BSA)
Manatee	586	24	254	163	145	0	0	0
Marion	593	27	314	157	95	0	0	0
Martin	418	37	155	140	85	1	0	0
Monroe	669	29	204	224	211	1	0	0
Nassau	162	7	83	36	35	1	0	0
Okaloosa	486	27	174	141	144	0	0	0
Okeechobee	115	10	63	30	12	0	0	0
Orange	2,105	54	907	629	510	3	2	0
Osceola	513	15	217	162	119	0	0	0
Palm Beach	2,680	138	1,063	728	736	1	11	3
Pasco	659	55	295	180	129	0	0	0
Pinellas	2,403	100	990	692	613	2	4	2
Polk	1,030	46	566	235	169	14	0	0
Putnam	176	9	92	41	34	0	0	0
St. Johns	393	25	132	143	91	1	1	0
St. Lucie	476	25	263	119	69	0	0	0
Santa Rosa	166	0	106	60	0	0	0	0
Sarasota	833	56	272	266	238	0	1	0
Seminole	717	28	311	206	169	0	2	1
Sumter	99	6	64	15	14	0	0	0
Suwannee	80	1	51	28	0	0	0	0
Taylor	76	4	44	12	16	0	0	0
Union	18	0	10	3	5	0	0	0
Volusia	1,199	50	482	369	298	0	0	0
Wakulla	65	3	35	16	11	0	0	0
Walton	190	6	84	52	47	1	0	0
Washington	46	0	35	10	0	1	0	0

1/ Beer, wine, and/or all alcoholic beverages sold in clubs (including bottle
clubs), civic and performing arts centers, at race tracks and from golf carts. Licenses included in this category are: 11C, 11CS, 11PA, 12RT, 14BC, and GC.

2/ Beer, wine, and/or all alcoholic beverages sold by the package only. Licenses
included in this category are 1APS, 2APS, 3APS, 3BPS, 3CPS, and 3PS.

3/ Beer, wine, and/or all alcoholic beverages to consume on premises and by the
package. Establishments with three are more bars (such as hotels) are included. Licenses included in this category are: 1COP, 2COP, COP, and 3M.

4/ Distributors of beer, wine, and/or liquor (including wine distributed to
churches). Licenses included in this category are: 4COP, 5COP, 6COP, 7COP, 8COP,
JDBW, and KLD.

5/ Manufacturers of beer, wine, and/or liquor. Licenses included in this category
are: AMW, BMWC, CMB, CMBP, DD, and ERB.

6/ Licenses included in this category are: IMPR and MEXP.

Source: State of Florida, Department of Business and Professional Regulation, Division of Alcoholic Beverages and Tobacco, *Number and Series of Beverage Licenses Issued by County,* October 1996.

University of Florida   **Bureau of Economic and Business Research**

Table 23.54. PARI-MUTUEL WAGERING: PERFORMANCES, ATTENDANCE, AND REVENUE
BY TYPE OF EVENT IN FLORIDA, FISCAL YEARS 1991-92 THROUGH 1995-96

Item	Number of-- Days	Per- form- ances	Paid attendance	Pari-mutuel handle (dollars)	Revenue to state (dollars)
All tracks and frontons					
1991-92	5,321	7,282	14,109,252	1,734,102,853	100,647,639
1992-93	5,074	7,009	12,620,914	1,693,636,924	106,762,525
1993-94	5,169	7,121	11,428,607	1,639,598,007	102,137,962
1994-95	4,845	6,681	10,285,062	1,582,305,874	93,536,408
1995-96	4,692	6,616	9,403,703	1,525,851,211	88,788,492
Thoroughbred tracks					
1991-92	375	375	2,097,759	523,246,855	14,095,538
1992-93	372	372	1,908,066	521,495,616	14,004,011
1993-94	374	374	1,800,911	521,266,989	14,884,209
1994-95	379	379	1,789,908	516,739,403	14,503,157
1995-96	380	380	1,678,460	533,743,649	15,341,989
Harness tracks					
1991-92	161	161	481,854	71,574,323	1,035,561
1992-93	177	177	469,981	75,112,688	2,247,224
1993-94	196	196	451,965	76,342,577	1,221,611
1994-95	195	195	418,225	74,200,943	1,609,622
1995-96	176	176	368,770	66,139,058	1,450,038
Quarter horse tracks					
1991-92	20	20	35,755	2,654,959	25,576
1992-93	0	0	0	0	0
1993-94	0	0	0	0	0
1994-95	0	0	0	0	0
1995-96	0	0	0	0	0
Greyhound tracks					
1991-92	3,302	4,632	8,320,731	896,340,416	68,834,464
1992-93	3,223	4,487	7,371,852	862,232,223	71,945,550
1993-94	3,227	4,466	6,617,587	831,076,473	70,631,583
1994-95	3,045	4,240	5,897,749	800,744,617	67,797,851
1995-96	2,963	4,204	5,395,716	745,215,792	63,310,564
Jai Alai frontons					
1991-92	1,463	2,094	3,173,153	240,286,300	16,656,500
1992-93	1,302	1,973	2,871,015	234,796,397	18,565,740
1993-94	1,372	2,085	2,558,144	210,911,968	15,400,559
1994-95	1,226	1,867	2,179,180	190,620,911	9,625,778
1995-96	1,173	1,856	1,960,757	180,752,712	8,685,901

Note: These data represent the distribution of revenue derived from pari-mutuel
performances and do not represent the total revenue received by the Division of Pari-
Mutuel Wagering. Excluded are such items as licenses, fees, escheated tickets, char-
ity, scholarship performances, and other miscellaneous items.

Source: State of Florida, Department of Business and Professional Regulation,
Division of Pari-Mutuel Wagering, *65th Annual Report for the Fiscal Year Ending on
June 30, 1996*.

University of Florida   **Bureau of Economic and Business Research**

Table 23.58. STATE RETIREMENT SYSTEM: MEMBERSHIP, PAYROLL, CONTRIBUTIONS ANNUITANTS, AND BENEFITS IN FLORIDA, JUNE 30, 1996

System	Active member- ship	Annual payroll ($1,000)	Accu- mulated contri- butions ($1,000)	Annu- itants	Annual benefits Total paid ($1,000)	Annual benefits Average (dol- lars)
Total	586,796	15,880,654	376,013	148,877	1,447,391	(X)
Average salary (dollars)	(X)	27,063	(X)	(X)	9,722	9,722
Florida retirement system	584,423	15,764,187	176,490	136,743	1,342,902	(X)
Regular members	525,123	13,794,770	156,099	128,218	1,208,930	9,429
Senior management members	1,232	96,983	2,941	198	6,333	31,984
Special risk members	53,971	1,703,106	12,706	7,272	99,868	13,733
Administrative support	259	9,257	244	56	1,048	18,715
Elected state officer class members	1,914	122,515	4,500	999	26,723	26,750
Renewed membership	1,924	37,556	0	(X)	(X)	(X)
Teachers retirement system	2,267	113,684	197,597	7,474	85,096	11,386
Survivors' benefits	(X)	(X)	(X)	1,096	2,060	1,880
State and county officers and employees retirement system	106	2,783	1,926	3,435	15,419	4,489
Highway patrol pension trust fund	0	0	0	103	1,355	13,154
Judicial retirement system	0	0	0	26	559	21,490

(X) Not applicable.

Table 23.59. STATE RETIREMENT SYSTEM: ANNUITANTS AND BENEFITS BY AGE OF RETIREMENT IN FLORIDA, JUNE 30, 1996

Retirement age	Retirees Number	Retirees Annualized benefits (dollars)	Joint annuitants Number	Joint annuitants Annualized benefits (dollars)
Total	133,946	1,344,081,428	13,835	101,249,064
Under age 50	4,350	29,554,347	1,106	7,041,789
50-54	10,908	116,308,340	1,596	10,923,057
55-59	26,375	292,946,419	2,786	21,400,128
60-64	54,638	547,268,036	4,477	34,919,817
65-69	30,721	294,961,586	2,916	20,480,467
70-74	5,446	51,779,838	703	5,148,174
75-79	1,207	9,312,903	188	1,069,739
Age 80 and over	301	1,949,960	63	265,893

Note: Annuitants include all retired persons or survivors of retired persons who are receiving monthly benefits. Does not include 1,096 persons receiving monthly benefits from the survivors' benefit trust fund or the 694 annuitants under various general revenue pensions.

Source for Tables 23.58 and 23.59: State of Florida, Department of Management Services, Division of Retirement, *Florida Retirement System: July 1, 1995-June 30, 1996 Annual Report.*

Table 23.60. STATE RETIREMENT SYSTEM: REVENUE, EXPENDITURE, AND BALANCES OF THE FLORIDA RETIREMENT SYSTEM, FISCAL YEARS 1994-95 AND 1995-96

Item	1994-95	1995-96
Revenue, total	5,907,568,360	8,240,667,000
Contributions	2,928,863,876	3,016,363,949
Investment earnings	1,954,815,363	2,191,758,335
Earnings from other trust funds 1/	253,999	257,520
Gain/loss on sale of investments	1,023,496,886	3,032,206,020
Other revenue	138,237	81,176
Expenditure, total	1,469,702,924	1,719,085,417
Benefit payments	1,266,903,642	1,417,634,446
Refund of contributions	2,508,704	2,133,106
Operating expenses	11,350,876	13,202,002
Administrative assessment	207,562	25,444
Contractual investment commissions and fees	32,955,086	86,465,247
Interest expense for repurchase agreements	155,424,015	199,625,172
Other expenses	353,039	0
Excess of revenue over expenditure	4,437,865,436	6,521,581,583
Beginning fund balance	33,111,194,879	37,549,060,315
Adjustment to increase beginning fund balance	0	322,595,853
Year-end fund balance (June 30)	37,549,060,315	44,393,237,751

1/ Includes social security and savings bonds.

Table 23.61. STATE RETIREMENT SYSTEM: RETIREMENT TRUST FUND BALANCES OF THE FLORIDA RETIREMENT SYSTEM, FISCAL YEARS 1994-95 AND 1995-96

Trust fund	1994-95	1995-96
Total	37,580,419,615	44,439,643,360
Florida Retirement System	37,549,060,315	44,393,237,751
Health Insurance Subsidy	21,838,313	35,913,093
Institute of Food and Agricultural Sciences (IFAS) Supplemental Retirement Program	9,239,643	10,175,833
Optional Retirement Program	281,077	316,683

Source for Tables 23.60 and 23.61: State of Florida, Department of Management Services, Division of Retirement, *Florida Retirement System: July 1, 1995-June 30, 1996 Annual Report.*

University of Florida   **Bureau of Economic and Business Research**

Table 23.70. FEDERAL GOVERNMENT: AVERAGE MONTHLY EMPLOYMENT COVERED
BY UNEMPLOYMENT COMPENSATION LAW BY INDUSTRY
IN FLORIDA, 1996

SIC code	Industry	Number of employees
01-99	All industries	120,154
27	Printing, publishing, and allied industries	0
37	Transportation equipment	146
43	U.S. postal service	44,535
53	General merchandise stores	3,938
531	Department stores	3,933
59	Miscellaneous retail	4
61	Nondeposit credit institutions	155
63	Insurance carriers	82
65	Real estate	42
70	Hotels, rooming houses, camps, and other lodging places	645
79	Amusement and recreation services	2,090
80	Health services	12,981
801	Offices and clinics of doctors of medicine	866
802	Offices and clinics of dentists	46
806	Hospitals	12,069
83	Social services	18
84	Museums, art galleries, and botanical and zoological gardens	6
87	Engineering, accounting, research, management, and related services	854
89	Services, NEC	500
91	Executive, legislative, and general government, except finance	1,795
92	Justice, public order, and safety	6,828
921	Courts	1,610
922	Public order and safety	5,218
93	Public finance, taxation, and monetary policy	5,284

See footnotes at end of table.   Continued . . .

University of Florida   **Bureau of Economic and Business Research**

Table 23.70. FEDERAL GOVERNMENT: AVERAGE MONTHLY EMPLOYMENT COVERED
BY UNEMPLOYMENT COMPENSATION LAW BY INDUSTRY
IN FLORIDA, 1996 (Continued)

SIC code	Industry	Number of employees
94	Administration of human resource programs	2,932
941	Administration of educational programs	12
943	Administration of public health programs	66
944	Administration of social, human resource, and income maintenance programs	2,273
945	Administration of veterans' affairs, except health and insurance	582
95	Administration of environmental quality and housing programs	1,557
951	Administration of environmental quality programs	1,273
953	Administration of housing and urban development programs	284
96	Administration of economic programs	7,555
961	Administration of general economic programs	362
962	Regulation and administration of transportation programs	2,992
963	Regulation and administration of communications, electric, gas, and other utilities	42
964	Regulation of agricultural marketing and commodities	1,564
965	Regulation, licensing, and inspection of miscellaneous commercial sectors	393
966	Space research and technology	2,203
97	National security and international affairs	28,209
971	National security	26,846
972	International affairs	1,363

NEC Not elsewhere classified.
Note: Data are preliminary. Detail may not add to totals due to disclosure editing and/or rounding.

Table 23.71. INTERNATIONAL GOVERNMENT: AVERAGE MONTHLY EMPLOYMENT COVERED
BY UNEMPLOYMENT COMPENSATION LAW BY INDUSTRY IN FLORIDA, 1995

SIC code	Industry	Number of employees
01-99	All industries	823
40-49	Transportation, communications, and public utilities	805
45	Transportation by air	803

Note: Data are revised.

Source for Tables 23.70 and 23.71: State of Florida, Department of Labor and Employment Security, Bureau of Labor Market Information, "Employment and Wages"
(ES-202), unpublished data.

Table 23.72.   STATE GOVERNMENT: AVERAGE MONTHLY EMPLOYMENT COVERED BY UNEMPLOYMENT
COMPENSATION LAW BY INDUSTRY IN FLORIDA, 1996

SIC code	Industry	Number of employees
01-99	All industries	200,966
08	Forestry	1,085
16	Heavy construction other than building construction-- contractors	7,184
61	Nondeposit credit institutions	75
73	Business services	276
79	Amusement and recreation services	1,254
80	Health services	7,104
82	Educational services	62,544
821	Elementary and secondary schools	745
822	Colleges, universities, professional schools, and junior colleges	61,657
823	Libraries	142
83	Social services	4,728
832	Individual and family social services	525
836	Residential care	4,203
84	Museums, art galleries, and botanical and zoological gardens	60
91	Executive, legislative, and general government, except finance	6,436
911	Executive offices	501
912	Legislative bodies	1,545
919	General government, NEC	4,391
92	Justice, public order, and safety	45,437
921	Courts	1,691
922	Public order and safety	43,747
93	Public finance, taxation, and monetary policy	4,750
94	Administration of human resource programs	40,327
941	Administration of educational programs	1,278
943	Administration of public health programs	30,277
944	Administration of social, human resource, and income maintenance programs	8,490
945	Administration of veterans' affairs, except health and insurance	283
95	Administration of environmental quality and housing programs	5,064
951	Administration of environmental quality programs	4,839
953	Administration of housing and urban development programs	225
96	Administration of economic programs	14,387
961	Administration of general economic programs	295
962	Regulation and administration of transportation programs	5,498
963	Regulation and administration of communications, electric, gas, and other utilities	387
964	Regulation of agricultural marketing and commodities	2,466
965	Regulation, licensing, and inspection of miscellaneous commercial sectors	5,742
97	National security and international affairs	254

NEC Not elsewhere classified.
   Note: Data are preliminary. Detail may not add to totals due to disclosure edit-
ing and/or rounding.
   Source: State of Florida, Department of Labor and Employment Security, Bureau of
Labor Market Information, "Employment and Wages" (ES-202), unpublished data.

Table 23.73. LOCAL GOVERNMENT: AVERAGE MONTHLY EMPLOYMENT COVERED BY UNEMPLOYMENT COMPENSATION LAW BY INDUSTRY IN FLORIDA, 1995 and 1996

SIC code	Industry	Number of employees 1995 A/	1996 B/
01-99	All industries	582,980	587,079
07	Agricultural services	1	1
16	Heavy construction other than building construction--contractors	10	9
41	Passenger transportation	1,167	1,262
44	Water transportation	30	26
45	Transportation by air	1,308	1,297
47	Transportation services	24	25
49	Electric, gas, and sanitary services	5,861	5,833
491	Electric services	2,377	2,385
492	Gas production and distribution	191	196
493	Combination electric and gas, and other utility services	1,601	1,572
494	Water supply	371	366
495	Sanitary services	1,321	1,314
58	Eating and drinking places	704	604
62	Security and commodity brokers and services	(NA)	4
63	Insurance carriers	26	59
637	Pension, health, and welfare funds	2	3
639	Insurance carriers, NEC	24	56
65	Real estate	2,190	2,134
73	Business services	64	69
734	Services to dwellings and other buildings	35	35
737	Computer programming, data processing, and other computer-related services	30	34
75	Automotive repair services, and parking	196	190
79	Amusement and recreation services	793	850
792	Theatrical producers (except motion picture), bands, orchestras, and entertainers	60	63
794	Commercial sports	300	344
799	Miscellaneous amusement and recreation services	433	444
80	Health services	35,637	33,513
801	Offices and clinics of doctors of medicine	1	0
805	Nursing and personal care facilities	233	475
806	Hospitals	35,403	32,928
82	Educational services	307,433	309,128
821	Elementary and secondary schools	275,858	278,470
822	Colleges, universities, professional schools, and junior colleges	30,988	30,056
823	Libraries	587	602
83	Social services	92	44
832	Individual and family services	5	5
833	Job training and vocational rehabilitation services	73	(NA)
839	Social services, NEC	14	(NA)
86	Membership organizations	129	137
861	Business associations	2	2
864	Civic, social, and fraternal associations	126	134
865	Political organizations	0	0
869	Membership organizations, NEC	1	(NA)

See footnotes at end of table.   Continued . . .

Table 23.73.   LOCAL GOVERNMENT: AVERAGE MONTHLY EMPLOYMENT COVERED BY UNEMPLOYMENT
COMPENSATION LAW BY INDUSTRY IN FLORIDA, 1995 and 1996 (Continued)

SIC code	Industry	Number of employees 1994 A/	1995 B/
87	Engineering, accounting, research, management and related services	6	3
89	Services, NEC	49	46
91	Executive, legislative, and general government, except finance	178,957	182,342
911	Executive offices	428	1,379
912	Legislative bodies	56,200	58,503
913	Executive and legislative offices combined	121,934	122,061
919	General government, NEC	394	398
92	Justice, public order, and safety	36,586	37,584
921	Courts	7,002	7,254
922	Public order and safety	29,584	30,331
93	Public finance, taxation, and monetary policy	5,736	5,685
94	Administration of human resource programs	257	253
943	Administration of public health programs	14	18
944	Administration of social, human resource, and income maintenance programs	238	231
945	Administration of veterans' affairs, except health and insurance	5	5
95	Administration of environmental quality and housing programs	4,785	5,143
951	Administration of environmental quality programs	3,937	3,988
953	Administration of housing and urban development programs	848	1,155
96	Administration of economic programs	943	842
961	Administration of general economic programs	163	114
962	Regulation and administration of transportation programs	765	710
964	Regulation of agricultural marketing and commodities	11	15
965	Regulation, licensing, and inspection of miscellaneous commercial sectors	4	4

NEC Not elsewhere classified.
(NA) Not available.
A/ Revised.
B/ Preliminary.
Note: Detail may not add to totals due to disclosure editing and/or rounding.

Source: State of Florida, Department of Labor and Employment Security, Bureau of
Labor Market Information, "Employment and Wages" (ES-202), unpublished data.

University of Florida   **Bureau of Economic and Business Research**

Table 23.74. GOVERNMENT EMPLOYMENT: AVERAGE MONTHLY EMPLOYMENT COVERED
BY UNEMPLOYMENT COMPENSATION LAW BY LEVEL OF GOVERNMENT IN THE STATE
AND COUNTIES OF FLORIDA, 1995 AND 1996

County	1995 A/			1996 B/		
	Federal	State	Local	Federal	State	Local
Florida	119,427	199,223	582,980	120,154	200,966	587,079
Alachua	2,962	25,660	9,779	2,879	25,753	9,831
Baker	70	1,694	787	71	1,671	815
Bay	3,460	1,122	7,030	3,354	1,161	7,202
Bradford	33	1,488	892	34	1,474	919
Brevard	5,912	2,153	16,280	5,630	2,199	16,345
Broward	6,804	7,718	61,415	6,876	7,810	62,439
Calhoun	33	441	448	30	461	445
Charlotte	234	722	3,683	240	730	3,760
Citrus	180	385	3,083	192	388	3,224
Clay	326	414	3,558	329	401	3,746
Collier	547	781	6,514	549	761	6,968
Columbia	1,118	1,535	2,196	1,109	1,549	2,147
Dade	17,666	16,857	95,714	17,871	17,079	96,030
De Soto	50	2,038	1,050	52	1,963	1,037
Dixie	20	462	547	16	461	554
Duval	16,355	7,075	27,957	16,855	7,189	26,384
Escambia	6,749	4,670	10,384	6,378	4,697	10,743
Flagler	74	136	1,479	81	138	1,654
Franklin	30	222	409	26	222	412
Gadsden	116	3,739	1,717	121	3,922	1,769
Gilchrist	24	482	494	25	493	522
Glades	12	36	303	12	37	304
Gulf	17	539	590	16	544	619
Hamilton	29	630	658	30	736	680
Hardee	48	597	1,058	48	590	1,090
Hendry	111	625	1,558	110	643	1,621
Hernando	264	587	3,828	269	598	3,948
Highlands	293	403	3,000	291	398	3,070
Hillsborough	10,615	14,732	40,316	10,839	14,986	40,040
Holmes	56	545	647	55	540	662
Indian River	348	518	3,736	354	502	3,747
Jackson	492	2,688	2,564	501	2,791	2,670
Jefferson	31	389	525	31	409	544
Lafayette	15	404	229	16	400	237
Lake	479	1,040	5,879	484	1,034	5,973
Lee	1,709	3,127	18,029	1,696	3,284	18,169
Leon	1,662	39,290	10,584	1,666	39,265	10,766
Levy	67	283	1,229	68	319	1,282
Liberty	53	419	254	50	421	263
Madison	45	527	870	46	516	851

See footnotes at end of table.   Continued . . .

Table 23.74. GOVERNMENT EMPLOYMENT: AVERAGE MONTHLY EMPLOYMENT COVERED
BY UNEMPLOYMENT COMPENSATION LAW BY LEVEL OF GOVERNMENT IN THE STATE
AND COUNTIES OF FLORIDA, 1995 AND 1996 (Continued)

County	1995 A/			1996 B/		
	Federal	State	Local	Federal	State	Local
Manatee	1,045	967	8,070	1,058	979	8,680
Marion	631	2,050	10,045	640	2,115	10,260
Martin	275	910	3,536	282	860	3,673
Monroe	1,283	761	3,471	1,254	757	3,538
Nassau	621	272	1,922	614	266	2,032
Okaloosa	6,269	972	5,761	6,276	966	5,877
Okeechobee	72	254	1,163	73	459	1,194
Orange	6,997	10,657	33,136	6,840	10,657	34,448
Osceola	244	483	5,363	250	492	5,960
Palm Beach	5,207	8,113	38,217	5,629	8,228	37,940
Pasco	612	1,248	9,212	620	1,264	9,335
Pinellas	5,879	4,523	31,322	5,776	4,555	30,679
Polk	1,396	4,416	18,914	1,403	4,410	18,882
Putnam	147	599	3,643	152	596	3,705
St. Johns	353	1,347	3,454	345	1,355	3,661
St. Lucie	472	1,277	6,720	479	1,255	6,941
Santa Rosa	706	540	3,432	706	629	3,489
Sarasota	852	1,697	10,837	844	1,652	8,931
Seminole	1,330	883	11,055	1,354	886	11,208
Sumter	303	779	1,144	762	735	1,172
Suwannee	107	294	1,104	106	399	1,126
Taylor	35	460	897	32	432	927
Union	19	1,834	422	18	1,504	447
Volusia	1,256	3,375	15,900	1,257	3,017	16,369
Wakulla	70	190	690	70	1,030	759
Walton	81	584	1,212	80	513	1,252
Washington	52	870	1,066	51	858	1,124
Multicounty 1/	3,667	1,318	(NA)	3,591	1,155	(NA)
Out-of-state 2/	343	382	(NA)	299	532	(NA)

(NA) Not available.
A/ Revised.
B/ Preliminary.
1/ Reporting units without a fixed location within the state or of unknown county
location.
2/ Employment based in Florida, but working out of the state or country.
Note: Not shown separately are public international government employment for the
state and Dade County. Those figures are: 1995, Florida 823 and Dade County 589.
Detail may not add to totals due to rounding.

Source: State of Florida, Department of Labor and Employment Security, Bureau of
Labor Market Information, "Employment and Wages" (ES-202), unpublished data.

Table 23.75. STATE AND LOCAL GOVERNMENT: OPTIONAL GAS TAX RATES AND COLLECTIONS
IN THE STATE AND COUNTIES OF FLORIDA, FISCAL YEAR 1995-96

(rounded to thousands of dollars)

County	Esti-mated gallons	Total collec-tions	Service charge 1/	County	Esti-mated gallons	Total collec-tions	Service charge 1/
Florida	7,765,311	459,308	27,558	Lafayette	2,855	171	10
				Lake	96,229	5,774	346
Alachua	104,127	6,248	375	Lee	207,452	12,447	747
Baker	14,415	865	52	Leon	114,725	6,884	413
Bay	85,669	5,140	308	Levy	23,534	1,412	85
Bradford	15,265	916	55	Liberty	6,686	334	20
Brevard	237,134	14,228	854	Madison	52,329	1,570	94
Broward	722,746	43,365	2,602	Manatee	115,278	6,917	415
Calhoun	8,204	492	30	Marion	162,563	9,754	585
Charlotte	78,314	4,699	282	Martin	62,504	3,750	225
Citrus	47,683	2,861	172	Monroe	54,199	3,252	195
Clay	60,435	3,626	218	Nassau	31,929	1,916	115
Collier	105,193	6,312	379	Okaloosa	94,635	4,732	284
Columbia	51,381	3,083	185	Okeechobee	28,573	1,714	103
Dade	889,018	53,341	3,200	Orange	493,956	29,637	1,778
De Soto	12,726	764	46	Osceola	97,932	5,876	353
Dixie	7,857	471	28	Palm Beach	461,076	27,665	1,660
Duval	424,576	25,475	1,528	Pasco	144,813	8,689	521
Escambia	151,642	9,098	546	Pinellas	375,241	22,514	1,351
Flagler	21,396	1,284	77	Polk	285,980	17,159	1,030
Franklin	1,334	80	5	Putnam	37,376	2,243	135
Gadsden	22,823	1,369	82	St. Johns	76,775	4,606	276
Gilchrist	4,609	277	17	St. Lucie	100,201	6,012	361
Glades	5,341	320	19	Santa Rosa	57,126	3,428	206
Gulf	6,309	379	23	Sarasota	138,558	8,313	499
Hamilton	24,081	722	43	Seminole	152,845	9,171	550
Hardee	14,010	841	50	Sumter	77,572	3,103	186
Hendry	28,007	1,120	67	Suwannee	27,023	1,621	97
Hernando	61,764	3,706	222	Taylor	22,028	881	53
Highlands	44,618	2,677	161	Union	7,094	355	21
Hillsborough	503,997	30,240	1,814	Volusia	211,700	12,702	762
Holmes	12,845	642	39	Wakulla	10,684	641	38
Indian River	61,865	3,712	223	Walton	23,872	1,432	86
Jackson	55,369	2,768	166	Washington	11,613	697	42
Jefferson	13,602	816	49				

(X) Not applicable.
1/ Six percent charge imposed on collections for state general revenue fund.
Note: Detail may not add to totals because of rounding.

Source: State of Florida, Department of Revenue, Internet site http://sun6.dms.
state.fl.us/dor/.

Table 23.76. STATE AND LOCAL GOVERNMENT: EMPLOYMENT BY FUNCTION AND PAYROLL
OF STATE AND LOCAL GOVERNMENTS IN FLORIDA AND THE UNITED STATES
OCTOBER 1995

Item	Florida State and local	Florida State only	United States State and local	United States State only
Full-time equivalent employees, all functions	708,937	174,717	14,090,531	3,971,208
Government administration	56,765	21,166	925,710	339,586
Financial	21,112	7,249	353,922	163,995
Judicial and legal	22,799	11,934	331,196	127,637
Other	12,854	1,983	240,592	47,954
Police protection	48,669	3,808	778,756	89,564
Police officers only	32,156	2,177	585,156	54,704
Other police protection	16,513	1,631	193,600	34,860
Fire protection	18,188	0	A/	A/
Correction	44,315	31,062	614,975	409,208
Streets and highways	24,143	10,558	543,143	253,256
Air and water transportation	4,269	2	47,823	7,448
Air transportation	3,296	A/	36,114	2,752
Water transportation/terminals	973	2	11,709	4,696
Public welfare	17,022	11,203	491,813	226,755
Health	20,480	14,701	368,619	160,061
Hospitals	53,261	16,438	1,047,555	496,191
Social insurance administration	4,519	4,519	93,783	93,783
Solid waste management	6,981	A/	108,770	1,552
Sewerage	7,662	A/	124,739	1,378
Parks and recreation	16,634	1,080	245,875	38,575
Housing and community development	4,286	A/	124,279	A/
Natural resources	11,621	7,319	188,265	152,141
Public utilities	22,481	470	451,373	26,623
Water supply	10,919	A/	152,933	935
Electric power	5,046	A/	80,544	5,739
Gas supply	589	A/	10,476	A/
Transit	5,927	470	207,420	19,949
Education	316,598	42,208	7,087,888	1,468,716
Elementary and secondary schools	253,038	A/	5,382,644	41,449
Higher education	60,971	39,619	1,608,794	1,330,817
Other education	2,589	2,589	96,450	96,450
Libraries 1/	4,564	A/	103,370	579
State liquor stores	0	A/	7,963	7,963
Other and unallocable	26,479	10,183	461,506	197,829
October payroll, total ($1,000)	1,727,865	422,890	37,713,627	10,926,502

A/ Local government only.
1/ United States totals include state government amounts for some states.

Source: U.S., Department of Commerce, Bureau of the Census, Internet site http://www.census.gov/.

Table 23.81. COUNTY FINANCE: REVENUE AND EXPENDITURE AND PER CAPITA AMOUNTS
IN THE STATE AND COUNTIES OF FLORIDA, FISCAL YEARS ENDING
SEPTEMBER 30, 1994 and 1995

(amounts in dollars)

County	Revenue				Expenditure			
	Total ($1,000)		Per capita (dollars)		Total ($1,000)		Per capita (dollars)	
	1994	1995	1994	1995	1994	1995	1994	1995
Florida	17,563,541	19,570,686	1,265	1,383	17,229,083	19,006,014	1,241	1,343
Alachua	136,406	146,157	704	737	142,346	146,705	734	740
Baker	12,910	15,713	655	775	13,233	13,116	672	647
Bay	96,492	232,443	708	1,670	84,597	217,359	621	1,562
Bradford	26,968	21,538	1,114	885	18,662	29,664	771	1,219
Brevard	378,302	317,984	867	715	368,085	326,296	844	733
Broward	1,380,256	1,584,591	1,030	1,162	1,327,575	1,569,135	991	1,150
Calhoun	8,267	5,975	715	498	8,019	5,366	693	448
Charlotte	151,454	167,717	1,213	1,314	145,041	159,034	1,161	1,246
Citrus	76,914	83,264	748	789	72,468	86,618	705	821
Clay	93,280	92,066	792	762	103,013	87,985	875	728
Collier	285,084	287,018	1,579	1,539	258,118	256,085	1,430	1,373
Columbia	42,483	44,990	869	893	39,934	35,934	817	713
Dade	4,363,928	4,602,455	2,192	2,285	4,272,881	4,757,612	2,147	2,362
De Soto	24,619	21,213	938	796	25,101	22,275	956	836
Dixie	13,800	15,235	1,136	1,227	13,348	15,608	1,099	1,257
Duval 1/	1,336,741	2,317,324	1,881	3,226	1,233,054	2,047,555	1,735	2,850
Escambia	222,000	205,605	801	727	195,561	184,113	706	651
Flagler	32,822	37,595	930	1,016	32,967	33,497	934	905
Franklin	9,579	9,741	958	952	9,383	8,801	939	860
Gadsden	21,841	24,515	487	548	19,848	22,938	443	513
Gilchrist	8,791	9,065	763	763	9,202	9,358	798	787
Glades	11,548	11,657	1,380	1,363	10,731	11,740	1,283	1,373
Gulf	11,641	19,201	878	1,447	11,037	15,213	832	1,146
Hamilton	11,983	14,930	1,005	1,196	12,893	13,407	1,082	1,074
Hardee	33,198	24,285	1,478	1,061	32,002	22,733	1,425	993
Hendry	30,810	31,273	1,074	1,060	31,965	31,182	1,114	1,057
Hernando	106,549	104,887	928	890	98,309	108,368	856	919
Highlands	55,640	54,626	733	707	47,611	54,583	628	706
Hillsborough	1,197,406	1,325,802	1,362	1,485	1,219,242	1,308,269	1,387	1,465
Holmes	6,628	6,811	392	392	6,620	6,902	391	397
Indian River	117,937	130,752	1,211	1,304	117,296	104,703	1,204	1,044
Jackson	17,303	24,098	381	517	16,539	22,914	364	492
Jefferson	8,895	14,151	680	1,048	10,361	13,189	792	976
Lafayette	5,218	6,102	896	936	4,984	5,797	856	890
Lake	97,198	112,912	568	638	97,587	100,393	570	567

See footnotes at end of table.   Continued . . .

Table 23.81. COUNTY FINANCE: REVENUE AND EXPENDITURE AND PER CAPITA AMOUNTS
IN THE STATE AND COUNTIES OF FLORIDA, FISCAL YEARS ENDING
SEPTEMBER 30, 1994 and 1995 (Continued)

(amounts in dollars)

	Revenue				Expenditure			
	Total ($1,000)		Per capita (dollars)		Total ($1,000)		Per capita (dollars)	
County	1994	1995	1994	1995	1994	1995	1994	1995
Lee	655,632	777,167	1,784	2,063	674,285	639,373	1,835	1,697
Leon	146,619	130,799	691	601	116,094	125,765	547	578
Levy	23,074	24,795	793	831	24,775	24,344	851	816
Liberty	7,906	10,727	1,209	1,561	6,044	12,972	924	1,887
Madison	14,507	14,836	816	809	15,438	14,590	869	795
Manatee	311,314	290,300	1,364	1,245	339,793	279,370	1,488	1,198
Marion	140,459	132,599	645	590	130,515	124,628	599	555
Martin	142,695	146,641	1,295	1,309	131,064	143,545	1,189	1,281
Monroe	167,998	179,047	2,042	2,147	175,011	178,725	2,128	2,143
Nassau	34,774	38,942	734	793	32,684	34,870	690	710
Okaloosa	101,919	124,055	644	762	100,044	119,575	632	735
Okeechobee	29,252	30,632	905	932	30,024	31,409	929	956
Orange	1,005,383	1,109,920	1,358	1,462	955,593	1,074,042	1,291	1,415
Osceola	180,148	97,405	1,374	713	240,323	135,808	1,833	994
Palm Beach	1,385,398	1,444,117	1,478	1,500	1,343,218	1,374,728	1,433	1,428
Pasco	215,129	235,015	720	769	225,059	234,634	753	768
Pinellas	847,613	929,392	973	1,061	852,915	867,259	980	990
Polk	314,007	292,591	718	660	357,751	271,908	818	614
Putnam	53,970	61,743	782	888	52,528	59,456	762	855
St. Johns	122,881	326,433	1,297	3,325	306,208	120,721	3,231	1,229
St. Lucie	167,931	320,157	1,007	1,871	206,030	136,207	1,235	796
Santa Rosa	58,025	71,475	619	744	132,260	68,866	1,410	717
Sarasota	313,190	135,003	1,058	448	189,542	320,906	640	1,064
Seminole	225,837	71,054	713	219	52,292	312,798	165	965
Sumter	53,285	32,200	1,514	883	42,425	37,971	1,206	1,042
Suwannee	24,211	25,616	826	839	23,962	24,174	818	792
Taylor	15,830	14,832	907	809	11,817	12,013	677	656
Union	5,470	7,598	436	601	5,437	6,592	434	521
Volusia	312,801	304,464	789	756	297,864	302,185	751	750
Wakulla	15,103	17,033	919	1,002	15,480	16,547	942	973
Walton	26,404	38,492	829	1,152	24,166	32,865	758	984
Washington	9,882	11,919	546	627	8,829	12,720	487	669

1/ Duval County is the consolidated city of Jacksonville.

Note: Per capita figures computed using Bureau of Economic and Business Research
April 1, 1994 and 1995 population estimates.

Source: State of Florida, Department of Banking and Finance, Office of the Comptroller, unpublished data.

University of Florida   **Bureau of Economic and Business Research**

Table 23.83. COUNTY FINANCE: REVENUE BY SOURCE OF COUNTY GOVERNMENTS IN FLORIDA
FISCAL YEAR ENDING SEPTEMBER 30, 1995

(rounded to thousands of dollars)

County	Total	Taxes and impact fees	Federal grants	State and other govern- ments	Charges for services	Fines and forfeits	Other sources and transfers
Florida	19,570,686	5,986,811	639,583	1,633,331	5,594,883	152,806	5,563,272
Alachua	146,157	57,845	1,099	17,161	24,840	1,838	43,374
Baker	15,713	4,586	1,037	2,296	1,483	336	5,976
Bay	232,443	40,134	837	13,495	137,801	1,103	39,071
Bradford	21,538	4,149	186	2,730	1,565	350	12,559
Brevard	317,984	126,146	8,385	38,250	101,028	3,234	40,941
Broward	1,584,591	496,049	26,884	127,526	434,525	12,801	486,806
Calhoun	5,975	2,400	560	2,443	154	98	321
Charlotte	167,717	70,592	1,733	13,783	52,496	1,478	27,634
Citrus	83,264	38,712	1,880	13,200	11,391	727	17,353
Clay	92,066	32,929	60	15,671	10,432	1,306	31,667
Collier	287,018	110,788	1,300	26,949	76,385	3,817	67,780
Columbia	44,990	14,504	603	5,804	4,155	718	19,206
Dade	4,602,455	1,188,050	370,244	253,594	1,720,400	31,697	1,038,470
De Soto	21,213	9,058	41	3,560	2,397	272	5,885
Dixie	15,235	3,936	733	3,752	810	338	5,666
Duval 1/	2,317,324	361,588	35,148	162,838	979,592	9,135	769,023
Escambia	205,605	94,030	9,113	34,734	31,779	4,107	31,842
Flagler	37,595	16,554	649	3,921	3,949	377	12,147
Franklin	9,741	4,220	1,087	2,501	922	146	866
Gadsden	24,515	8,579	314	4,708	1,655	457	8,802
Gilchrist	9,065	2,935	41	1,703	929	195	3,263
Glades	11,657	3,968	611	2,197	622	446	3,813
Gulf	19,201	5,157	790	2,292	671	155	10,135
Hamilton	14,930	6,348	442	2,789	921	289	4,141
Hardee	24,285	9,281	529	2,860	2,635	442	8,539
Hendry	31,273	12,348	307	5,607	3,475	470	9,067
Hernando	104,887	42,882	21	9,632	22,987	784	28,581
Highlands	54,626	31,344	201	8,295	5,522	1,041	8,222
Hillsborough	1,325,802	401,034	42,008	100,920	220,079	3,749	558,013
Holmes	6,811	2,746	996	1,893	829	25	322
Indian River	130,752	59,783	1,543	10,025	26,874	928	31,600
Jackson	24,098	10,882	803	3,333	2,921	349	5,810
Jefferson	14,151	4,209	2,216	2,802	405	270	4,249
Lafayette	6,102	1,771	41	2,202	268	95	1,725

See footnote at end of table.   Continued . . .

University of Florida   **Bureau of Economic and Business Research**

Table 23.83.   COUNTY FINANCE: REVENUE BY SOURCE OF COUNTY GOVERNMENTS IN FLORIDA
FISCAL YEAR ENDING SEPTEMBER 30, 1995 (Continued)

(rounded to thousands of dollars)

County	Total	Taxes and impact fees	Federal grants	State and other govern-ments	Charges for services	Fines and forfeits	Other sources and transfers
Lake	112,912	45,011	1,600	13,371	23,696	1,536	27,699
Lee	777,167	171,178	8,905	53,450	174,544	2,949	366,141
Leon	130,799	69,500	2,242	20,320	19,889	1,139	17,709
Levy	24,795	9,533	437	3,817	2,419	716	7,873
Liberty	10,727	1,015	746	2,388	727	190	5,660
Madison	14,836	4,266	283	5,277	882	895	3,232
Manatee	290,300	88,698	2,682	29,836	106,734	1,992	60,358
Marion	132,599	69,448	1,060	24,799	21,070	3,203	13,019
Martin	146,641	68,531	335	15,736	36,134	1,923	23,981
Monroe	179,047	74,952	6,534	15,846	32,342	2,487	46,885
Nassau	38,942	18,066	145	7,328	5,227	541	7,636
Okaloosa	124,055	26,814	2,345	15,260	36,576	1,682	41,377
Okeechobee	30,632	9,944	406	5,391	4,050	360	10,481
Orange	1,109,920	431,467	19,609	112,953	215,017	11,525	319,349
Osceola	97,405	42,240	160	11,653	10,555	174	32,624
Palm Beach	1,444,117	443,935	25,619	89,175	349,277	8,324	527,787
Pasco	235,015	100,933	6,362	26,050	59,458	1,007	41,205
Pinellas	929,392	302,784	6,853	63,357	231,795	6,361	318,242
Polk	292,591	119,784	9,004	44,059	79,160	3,738	36,846
Putnam	61,743	23,428	60	6,546	9,320	710	21,678
St. Johns	71,475	35,840	215	8,021	19,840	1,030	6,529
St. Lucie	135,003	69,725	1,133	17,620	32,585	2,459	11,481
Santa Rosa	71,054	25,677	3,079	8,885	19,172	901	13,340
Sarasota	326,433	150,406	3,941	33,283	85,928	2,585	50,290
Seminole	320,157	129,775	3,887	26,057	45,002	3,148	112,289
Sumter	32,200	10,077	861	4,684	2,897	510	13,171
Suwannee	25,616	7,254	54	4,582	2,801	1,049	9,875
Taylor	14,832	8,514	403	3,652	1,108	345	810
Union	7,598	1,913	38	1,805	414	185	3,244
Volusia	304,464	119,071	13,809	40,077	74,005	4,247	53,254
Wakulla	17,033	5,220	1,541	2,719	2,299	298	4,955
Walton	38,492	17,406	1,959	8,334	2,643	720	7,431
Washington	11,919	4,872	837	1,535	418	306	3,951

1/ Duval County is the consolidated city of Jacksonville.

Source: State of Florida, Department of Banking and Finance, unpublished data.

University of Florida   **Bureau of Economic and Business Research**

Table 23.84. COUNTY FINANCE: EXPENDITURE BY FUNCTION OF COUNTY GOVERNMENTS
IN FLORIDA, FISCAL YEAR ENDING SEPTEMBER 30, 1995

(rounded to thousands of dollars)

County	Total	General govern- ment	Public safety	Physical and eco- nomic environ- ment	Trans- porta- tion	Human services cultural and re- creation	Debt service and other uses and interfund transfers
Florida	19,006,014	2,805,654	3,339,659	4,168,161	2,330,634	2,472,643	4,839,563
Alachua	146,705	29,732	46,309	15,759	10,261	5,431	42,684
Baker	13,116	1,919	2,904	759	2,016	520	4,032
Bay	217,359	16,520	20,902	142,674	5,134	111,881	27,723
Bradford	29,664	2,959	8,266	1,577	3,083	817	13,088
Brevard	326,296	79,130	57,459	65,686	34,200	38,692	55,433
Broward	1,569,135	191,267	284,832	250,922	175,770	155,173	568,578
Calhoun	5,366	1,479	1,372	564	967	811	86
Charlotte	159,034	28,893	31,511	35,275	21,917	13,405	34,192
Citrus	86,618	20,667	24,536	13,952	18,048	8,727	4,173
Clay	87,985	13,453	22,198	9,073	11,847	4,826	28,983
Collier	256,085	47,744	59,540	51,283	23,131	25,009	53,741
Columbia	35,934	5,178	7,974	4,468	4,408	1,848	11,661
Dade	4,757,612	502,361	662,389	1,343,409	786,588	987,331	926,782
De Soto	22,275	4,785	9,906	2,050	3,164	817	1,843
Dixie	15,608	1,727	2,612	2,014	4,357	378	3,800
Duval 1/	2,047,555	258,857	238,276	733,847	223,306	264,427	345,422
Escambia	184,113	43,099	58,433	14,214	26,091	8,839	28,205
Flagler	33,497	6,845	7,776	1,508	4,203	1,336	11,821
Franklin	8,801	902	549	1,064	1,955	461	3,316
Gadsden	22,938	4,017	5,525	1,642	2,547	1,710	8,370
Gilchrist	9,358	1,975	2,267	649	721	422	3,206
Glades	11,740	2,294	2,714	1,545	1,318	771	3,694
Gulf	15,213	2,452	2,759	1,283	1,124	399	7,364
Hamilton	13,407	2,021	2,814	1,733	1,577	1,278	4,071
Hardee	22,733	4,435	4,740	1,437	2,461	1,028	8,729
Hendry	31,182	6,083	7,229	2,882	5,206	1,437	8,791
Hernando	108,368	28,786	29,488	13,740	7,925	6,227	24,402
Highlands	54,583	14,227	18,165	10,104	8,716	3,376	1,188
Hillsborough	1,308,269	184,389	208,920	259,462	64,950	195,182	493,188
Holmes	6,902	1,385	1,534	569	1,243	395	1,101
Indian River	104,703	18,200	30,561	24,881	12,185	11,386	11,402
Jackson	22,914	4,473	5,784	1,382	3,114	1,285	6,620
Jefferson	13,189	1,590	3,011	2,943	1,438	305	1,578
Lafayette	5,797	807	1,071	1,290	431	166	1,771

See footnote at end of table.   Continued . . .

Table 23.84. COUNTY FINANCE: EXPENDITURE BY FUNCTION OF COUNTY GOVERNMENTS
IN FLORIDA, FISCAL YEAR ENDING SEPTEMBER 30, 1995 (Continued)

(rounded to thousands of dollars)

County	Total	General govern- ment	Public safety	Physical and eco- nomic environ- ment	Trans- porta- tion	Human services cultural and re- creation	Debt service and other uses and interfund transfers
Lake	100,393	27,950	26,445	11,567	9,926	5,319	20,233
Lee	639,373	91,117	67,428	77,981	136,528	45,310	227,094
Leon	125,765	29,987	32,318	13,324	17,001	9,539	23,385
Levy	24,344	4,966	6,572	2,198	2,427	1,000	7,608
Liberty	12,972	1,167	987	1,351	2,474	861	6,880
Madison	14,590	1,830	3,143	1,798	1,866	496	5,359
Manatee	279,370	64,271	53,534	70,212	24,397	22,559	53,404
Marion	124,628	29,977	43,788	12,917	22,296	9,363	10,895
Martin	143,545	38,818	37,080	28,750	11,346	12,863	18,819
Monroe	178,725	30,571	46,712	20,225	9,103	12,328	55,745
Nassau	34,870	5,127	9,208	5,335	4,068	4,966	6,831
Okaloosa	119,575	22,974	20,494	20,545	10,582	5,760	40,417
Okeechobee	31,409	4,570	8,238	1,988	4,163	2,126	11,167
Orange	1,074,042	140,728	237,716	153,320	104,911	86,756	377,869
Osceola	135,808	13,978	3,502	8,614	48,008	9,636	56,074
Palm Beach	1,374,728	228,345	251,205	217,811	120,597	114,587	475,334
Pasco	234,634	50,760	52,796	46,334	26,089	17,584	45,698
Pinellas	867,259	160,058	171,340	146,623	70,153	65,170	281,184
Polk	271,908	61,904	78,847	83,703	23,245	56,801	12,675
Putnam	59,456	12,699	12,907	8,372	5,101	3,154	18,984
St. Johns	120,721	16,841	25,423	22,179	9,720	11,099	40,479
St. Lucie	136,207	37,833	33,011	13,728	19,674	16,424	20,335
Santa Rosa	68,866	15,215	24,504	8,848	7,270	3,259	11,311
Sarasota	320,906	55,032	62,483	71,211	48,314	30,473	60,657
Seminole	312,798	45,860	54,383	37,218	51,389	11,510	114,437
Sumter	37,971	7,230	6,039	2,357	6,279	1,198	14,929
Suwannee	24,174	3,806	5,497	2,526	2,084	1,915	8,758
Taylor	12,013	770	1,326	3,556	1,286	990	4,804
Union	6,592	1,187	1,154	684	426	249	2,674
Volusia	302,185	55,330	74,903	47,935	42,420	49,481	43,454
Wakulla	16,547	2,245	4,027	1,885	1,461	1,331	4,920
Walton	32,865	5,530	6,026	6,430	7,936	1,569	2,494
Washington	12,720	2,329	2,293	998	2,690	875	3,618

1/ Duval County is the consolidated city of Jacksonville.

Source: State of Florida, Department of Banking and Finance, unpublished data.

University of Florida   **Bureau of Economic and Business Research**

Table 23.85. MUNICIPAL FINANCE: REVENUE AND EXPENDITURE PER CAPITA, PERSONAL
SERVICES EXPENDITURE, AND BONDED INDEBTEDNESS OF CITY GOVERNMENTS
SERVING A 1995 POPULATION OF 45,000 OR MORE IN FLORIDA
FISCAL YEAR ENDING SEPTEMBER 30, 1995

(in dollars)

County	Revenue		Expenditure	
	Total	Per capita	Total	Per capita
Jacksonville (Duval) 1/	1,937,918	2,864	2,047,555	3,026
Miami	506,777	1,387	577,382	1,580
Tampa	560,807	1,967	525,781	1,844
St. Petersburg	383,856	1,589	416,816	1,725
Hialeah	184,617	905	160,545	787
Orlando	405,355	2,380	406,578	2,387
Ft. Lauderdale	300,939	2,013	287,903	1,926
Tallahassee	465,216	3,394	479,311	3,497
Hollywood	187,011	1,492	170,761	1,362
Clearwater	195,546	1,933	199,791	1,975
Gainesville	258,700	2,693	274,476	2,858
Coral Springs	69,287	742	81,504	872
Miami Beach	350,403	3,818	385,081	4,196
Pembroke Pines	86,364	982	89,032	1,012
Cape Coral	96,712	1,127	101,455	1,182
West Palm Beach	174,488	2,283	181,311	2,373
Plantation	72,161	960	85,210	1,133
Lakeland	306,477	4,107	333,460	4,468
Pompano Beach	126,165	1,706	108,325	1,465
Sunrise	113,281	1,542	112,630	1,533
Palm Bay	51,876	709	48,259	660
Port St. Lucie	54,162	755	57,629	803
Largo	62,209	922	58,594	869
Boca Raton	175,078	2,623	178,351	2,672
Melbourne	70,457	1,062	69,610	1,049
Daytona Beach	99,683	1,575	101,149	1,598
Pensacola	124,227	2,058	131,311	2,175
Davie	45,831	839	44,231	810
Sarasota	109,225	2,136	108,650	2,124
North Miami	65,984	1,300	63,775	1,256
Delray Beach	93,287	1,858	95,649	1,906
Lauderhill	29,934	598	27,895	558
Boynton Beach	75,376	1,536	76,176	1,552
Tamarac	37,401	767	35,386	726
Deerfield Beach	6,009	124	5,764	119
Bradenton	43,909	921	63,105	1,324
Margate	35,084	742	35,121	743
Ft. Myers	97,310	2,094	123,117	2,649

1/ Consolidated Duval County.
Note: Per capita figures computed using Bureau of Economic and Business Research
April 1, 1995 population estimates.

Source: State of Florida, Department of Banking and Finance, and unpublished data.

University of Florida   **Bureau of Economic and Business Research**

Table 23.86. MUNICIPAL FINANCE: REVENUE BY SOURCE OF CITY GOVERNMENTS SERVING
A 1995 POPULATION OF 45,000 OR MORE IN FLORIDA, FISCAL YEAR ENDING
September 30, 1995

(rounded to thousands of dollars)

City	Total	Taxes and impact fees	Federal grants	State and other govern- ments	Charges for services	Fines and for- feits	Other sources and trans- fers
Jacksonville							
(Duval) 1/	1,937,918	231,651	139,749	35,148	162,838	979,592	388,941
Miami	506,777	145,168	63,487	13,715	36,250	77,818	170,339
Tampa	560,807	65,083	76,380	50,842	40,573	156,264	171,665
St. Petersburg	383,856	56,779	37,167	4,173	38,332	153,812	93,593
Hialeah	184,617	33,818	42,899	12,178	6,774	47,672	41,276
Orlando	405,355	48,021	52,449	5,073	62,625	137,048	100,138
Ft. Lauderdale	300,939	56,300	37,838	14,140	16,601	100,234	75,827
Tallahassee	465,216	13,427	32,757	3,320	11,149	329,581	74,982
Hollywood	187,011	29,615	26,505	3,062	13,651	75,074	39,104
Clearwater	195,546	23,188	29,333	1,610	11,809	88,965	40,640
Gainesville	258,700	10,472	12,847	3,776	8,602	189,749	33,254
Coral Springs	69,287	16,559	19,129	63	7,079	15,178	11,279
Miami Beach	350,403	52,491	45,233	4,089	18,375	55,906	174,308
Pembroke Pines	86,364	10,966	22,342	753	6,249	25,892	20,162
Cape Coral	96,712	22,931	8,263	603	10,939	27,646	26,330
West Palm Beach	174,488	34,287	17,621	3,993	9,829	62,117	46,642
Plantation	72,161	14,615	16,000	0	5,805	28,847	6,894
Lakeland	306,477	8,779	12,817	2,838	7,451	220,115	54,478
Pompano Beach	126,165	29,096	17,470	1,646	6,554	44,555	26,843
Sunrise	113,281	17,179	17,210	126	6,234	48,573	23,960
Palm Bay	51,876	9,207	12,014	569	4,906	15,590	9,590
Port St. Lucie	54,162	8,306	7,201	764	4,147	23,723	10,021
Largo	62,209	6,314	13,977	900	10,405	22,200	8,413
Boca Raton	175,078	27,626	20,416	2,548	14,129	36,033	74,327
Melbourne	70,457	7,996	13,169	1,035	5,924	32,515	9,818
Daytona Beach	99,683	13,965	12,070	3,568	6,736	48,230	15,115
Pensacola	124,227	8,397	18,810	8,028	7,572	53,099	28,320
Davie	45,831	11,553	11,714	205	4,624	12,977	4,759
Sarasota	109,225	17,708	18,159	1,328	6,010	46,184	19,837
North Miami	65,984	10,015	7,359	1,468	5,914	27,271	13,957
Delray Beach	93,287	20,182	11,150	1,048	5,464	32,809	22,635
Lauderhill	29,934	4,380	7,917	0	4,245	10,901	2,492
Boynton Beach	75,376	16,256	8,535	254	7,088	28,743	14,500
Tamarac	37,401	8,208	5,568	23	3,703	16,651	3,248
Deerfield Beach	6,009	2,228	1,336	0	365	1,915	165
Bradenton	43,909	3,088	10,674	1,925	5,500	15,393	7,329
Margate	35,084	6,977	8,431	0	4,260	13,996	1,420
Ft. Myers	97,310	10,703	13,096	6,972	4,972	36,133	25,434

1/ Consolidated Duval County.

Source: State of Florida, Department of Banking and Finance, unpublished data.

University of Florida   **Bureau of Economic and Business Research**

Table 23.87. MUNICIPAL FINANCE: EXPENDITURE BY FUNCTION OF CITY GOVERNMENTS SERVING A 1995 POPULATION OF 45,000 OR MORE IN FLORIDA, FISCAL YEAR ENDING SEPTEMBER 30, 1995

(rounded to thousands of dollars)

City	Total	General govern- ment	Public safety	Physical and eco- nomic envi- ronment	Trans- porta- tion	Human ser- vices, cultur- al, and recrea- tion	Debt service and other uses and inter- fund trans- fers
Jacksonville (Duval) 1/	2,047,555	258,857	238,276	717,267	223,306	264,427	345,422
Miami	577,382	257,281	132,703	32,139	23,224	36,940	95,095
Tampa	525,781	35,059	130,511	175,096	28,654	33,727	122,734
St. Petersburg	416,816	81,754	77,583	89,330	21,961	45,262	100,926
Hialeah	160,545	40,169	44,172	52,172	3,818	7,396	12,818
Orlando	406,578	67,575	86,768	79,929	36,309	46,693	89,303
Ft. Lauderdale	287,903	45,994	75,051	76,643	12,489	19,485	58,241
Tallahassee	479,311	29,704	40,306	261,604	45,779	17,079	84,839
Hollywood	170,761	48,182	55,009	33,982	9,116	7,928	16,544
Clearwater	199,791	44,036	33,852	64,439	12,973	17,981	26,511
Gainesville	274,476	28,431	26,414	156,955	12,223	4,840	45,613
Coral Springs	81,504	15,214	21,890	12,884	3,985	10,899	16,631
Miami Beach	385,081	48,716	54,886	74,672	15,150	27,659	163,997
Pembroke Pines	89,032	11,354	26,926	16,097	2,285	26,181	6,190
Cape Coral	101,455	11,696	19,143	27,527	12,352	8,234	22,504
West Palm Beach	181,311	29,024	37,073	52,916	7,387	8,863	46,047
Plantation	85,210	15,244	20,615	16,730	2,150	6,426	24,046
Lakeland	333,460	23,513	22,247	174,114	26,823	31,270	55,494
Pompano Beach	108,325	25,232	36,643	29,862	4,204	6,994	5,390
Sunrise	112,630	10,334	24,138	30,546	1,905	14,193	31,514
Palm Bay	48,259	4,627	14,880	9,641	4,780	1,965	12,367
Port St. Lucie	57,629	5,328	9,859	24,169	4,638	4,453	9,183
Largo	58,594	12,463	15,577	17,388	1,672	8,774	2,720
Boca Raton	178,351	12,251	25,958	32,209	5,931	28,021	73,982
Melbourne	69,610	8,958	17,307	17,921	10,028	6,043	9,353
Daytona Beach	101,149	16,229	23,496	30,229	9,377	11,117	10,701
Pensacola	131,311	15,328	17,739	27,449	14,849	8,107	47,839
Davie	44,231	8,159	16,219	3,883	2,742	3,683	9,545
Sarasota	108,650	26,477	26,940	25,390	8,197	10,226	11,419
North Miami	63,775	19,778	10,547	20,487	2,166	5,897	4,899
Delray Beach	95,649	17,055	23,217	22,851	5,171	11,334	16,021
Lauderhill	27,895	5,081	9,701	7,653	653	3,557	1,251
Boynton Beach	76,176	12,965	18,312	21,680	1,293	7,743	14,184
Tamarac	35,386	9,223	9,833	10,554	1,528	1,684	2,563
Deerfield Beach	5,764	689	2,368	1,493	856	110	248
Bradenton	63,105	6,157	8,161	15,340	1,409	5,348	26,691
Margate	35,121	7,357	9,746	11,118	974	1,066	4,860
Ft. Myers	123,117	10,838	18,295	28,067	6,732	10,069	49,115

1/ Consolidated Duval County.

Source: State of Florida, Department of Banking and Finance, unpublished data.

Table 23.89. PROPERTY VALUATIONS: NET ASSESSED VALUES OF REAL, PERSONAL, AND RAILROAD PROPERTY IN FLORIDA, JANUARY 1, 1960 THROUGH 1996

(amounts rounded to thousands of dollars)

Year	Total Amount	Percentage change from previous year	Real property Amount	Percentage of total	Personal property Amount	Percentage of total	Railroad and private car lines Amount	Percentage of total
1960	14,789,849	21.55	12,945,632	87.53	1,686,093	11.40	158,124	1.07
1961	16,678,864	12.77	14,659,588	87.89	1,855,228	11.12	164,049	0.99
1962	18,354,359	10.05	16,157,399	88.03	2,030,580	11.06	166,381	0.91
1963	19,210,827	4.67	16,890,665	87.92	2,152,967	11.21	167,195	0.87
1964	23,994,036	24.90	21,140,438	88.11	2,674,478	11.14	179,121	0.75
1965	29,760,016	24.03	26,233,082	88.15	3,321,356	11.16	205,578	0.69
1966	36,253,654	21.82	31,943,021	88.11	4,036,480	11.13	274,153	0.76
1967	40,606,927	12.01	35,154,260	86.57	5,162,026	12.71	290,640	0.72
1968	42,060,610	3.58	36,637,166	87.10	5,125,541	12.19	297,903	0.71
1969	45,180,722	7.42	39,697,479	87.86	5,187,897	11.48	295,346	0.66
1970	51,247,667	13.43	45,066,274	87.94	5,915,000	11.54	266,393	0.52
1971	59,967,320	17.01	51,822,900	86.42	7,845,286	13.08	299,134	0.50
1972	67,053,619	11.82	56,610,767	84.43	10,134,332	15.11	308,520	0.46
1973	82,146,275	22.51	69,936,535	85.14	11,870,966	14.45	338,774	0.41
1974	107,894,309	31.34	92,979,953	86.18	14,570,730	13.50	343,627	0.32
1975	120,558,360	11.74	103,460,245	85.82	16,690,698	13.84	407,417	0.34
1976	128,700,512	6.75	109,217,279	84.86	19,072,710	14.82	410,523	0.32
1977	139,650,757	8.51	118,232,881	84.66	20,925,041	14.98	492,835	0.35
1978	151,271,654	8.24	129,382,344	85.53	21,393,945	14.14	495,365	0.33
1979	159,642,320	5.53	135,705,468	84.38	24,422,967	15.30	513,884	0.32
1980	187,750,045	17.61	164,755,192	87.75	22,480,384	11.97	514,470	0.27
1981	237,140,341	26.31	211,148,696	89.04	25,579,874	10.79	411,772	0.17
1982	272,997,005	15.12	244,424,808	89.53	28,194,359	10.53	377,839	0.14
1983	298,583,050	9.37	266,304,607	89.19	31,858,923	10.67	419,519	0.14
1984	323,647,775	8.39	288,392,562	89.11	34,820,448	10.76	434,765	0.13
1985	356,061,973	10.02	317,508,051	89.17	38,100,514	10.70	453,408	0.13
1986	385,126,891	8.16	343,168,089	89.11	41,389,766	10.75	569,036	0.15
1987	417,508,830	8.41	372,504,470	89.22	44,326,033	10.62	678,327	0.16
1988	446,103,804	6.80	398,216,681	89.27	47,192,039	10.58	695,085	0.16
1989	485,766,305	8.90	434,583,860	89.46	50,554,052	10.41	628,394	0.13
1990	524,248,524	7.92	469,498,829	89.56	54,114,754	10.32	634,941	0.12
1991	553,456,777	5.57	496,581,168	89.72	56,260,942	10.17	614,667	0.11
1992	560,820,605	1.33	501,638,271	89.45	58,586,918	10.45	595,416	0.11
1993	570,341,544	1.70	509,360,697	89.31	60,380,135	10.59	600,712	0.11
1994	595,216,496	4.36	530,408,830	89.11	62,835,320	10.56	1,972,345	0.33
1995	623,757,999	4.80	556,091,584	89.15	67,006,163	10.74	660,252	0.11
1996	654,348,604	4.90	582,263,148	88.98	71,396,841	10.91	688,615	0.11

Note: Net assessed value is total assessed or just value less nontaxable value of property having a classified use value. Classified use value is the value at which agricultural land and certain privately owned park and recreation land is assessed for tax purposes. The "highest and best" use principle is relaxed and assessment is based on current use only. Some data may be revised.

Source: State of Florida, Department of Revenue, *Florida Property Valuations and Tax Data, December 1996.*

University of Florida   **Bureau of Economic and Business Research**

Table 23.90. PROPERTY VALUATIONS: ASSESSED AND TAXABLE VALUES BY CATEGORY
OF REAL PROPERTY IN FLORIDA, JANUARY 1, 1995 AND 1996

(rounded to thousands of dollars)

Category	Just value 1/		Taxable value 2/	
	1995	1996	1995	1996
Total 3/	657,498,950	682,857,889	468,232,996	488,172,278
Residential				
Vacant	25,713,955	25,549,327	25,325,758	25,162,299
Single-family	269,806,345	285,678,147	202,939,860	215,711,368
Mobile homes	10,527,464	10,859,557	5,803,069	5,953,766
Multifamily				
9 units or less	12,070,654	12,125,086	10,987,121	11,035,999
10 units or more	18,050,678	18,955,462	17,754,951	18,634,621
Condominiums	83,135,132	87,428,185	69,611,105	73,231,268
Cooperatives	3,007,595	3,175,278	2,205,351	2,300,437
Retirement homes	1,901,581	1,951,019	1,621,186	1,659,844
Commercial				
Vacant	7,701,612	7,684,825	7,588,992	7,537,836
Improved	81,499,670	83,813,889	80,091,183	82,358,817
Industrial				
Vacant	2,483,456	2,491,044	2,430,487	2,437,523
Improved	19,547,120	20,215,777	19,247,464	19,866,848
Agricultural	35,800,496	35,754,561	9,078,435	8,972,541
Institutional	17,166,367	17,938,948	4,005,866	4,292,918
Government	57,220,862	58,126,725	486,096	524,054
Leasehold	850,447	849,900	337,455	333,125
Miscellaneous	4,955,513	4,546,994	3,245,860	3,044,300
Nonagricultural	5,945,014	5,614,355	5,428,207	5,085,067

1/ The value of property for tax purposes as determined by the elected county property appraiser. Value is determined at the highest and best use of property, except
for special classes provided for in Florida Statutes.
   2/ The value against which millage rates are applied to compute the amount of tax
levied. Total taxable value makes up the ad valorem tax base for units of government
in Florida.
   3/ Totals include centrally assessed values not shown elsewhere.

   Source: State of Florida, Department of Revenue, *Florida Property Valuations and
Tax Data, December 1996,* and previous edition.

University of Florida   **Bureau of Economic and Business Research**

Table 23.91. PROPERTY VALUATIONS: ASSESSED, EXEMPT, AND TAXABLE VALUES
OF REAL PROPERTY IN THE STATE AND COUNTIES OF FLORIDA
JANUARY 1, 1995 AND 1996

(rounded to thousands of dollars)

County	Just values 1/		Exempt and immune values		Taxable values 2/	
	1995	1996	1995	1996	1995	1996
Florida	657,359,556	684,459,338	185,619,324	189,300,132	467,798,964	488,968,851
Alachua	7,113,800	7,681,044	3,500,643	3,822,973	3,564,471	3,785,532
Baker	595,598	607,632	408,250	412,550	185,018	193,641
Bay	6,019,973	6,117,389	2,412,906	2,457,551	3,599,983	3,653,357
Bradford	647,262	664,084	363,525	366,349	281,906	295,910
Brevard	21,728,287	20,496,484	9,341,819	7,929,060	12,372,735	12,539,198
Broward	62,835,007	66,102,835	14,095,821	14,424,632	48,036,889	50,753,809
Calhoun	344,585	350,428	210,819	212,931	133,720	137,030
Charlotte	7,307,792	7,623,289	1,617,425	1,687,916	5,654,146	5,796,065
Citrus	4,289,215	4,448,002	1,395,649	1,435,389	2,887,865	3,004,719
Clay	3,989,575	4,201,178	1,422,154	1,458,914	2,564,500	2,720,965
Collier	19,283,826	20,527,067	3,201,953	3,302,566	16,038,210	17,146,476
Columbia	1,426,218	1,503,980	785,934	803,476	637,971	684,175
Dade	87,955,575	92,613,462	20,855,043	21,094,274	66,676,675	70,522,772
De Soto	1,251,313	1,353,096	707,184	804,796	543,646	547,418
Dixie	445,385	451,167	286,476	292,048	158,707	158,847
Duval	26,580,793	28,525,439	9,092,731	9,420,358	17,318,517	18,560,523
Escambia	8,753,827	8,907,368	4,384,311	4,433,935	4,339,301	4,447,188
Flagler	2,671,731	2,759,705	627,788	655,738	2,040,714	2,101,587
Franklin	1,270,749	1,390,165	831,824	877,016	436,490	503,306
Gadsden	901,492	985,888	484,125	542,100	412,704	437,459
Gilchrist	396,677	472,286	245,531	315,434	151,146	156,484
Glades	874,752	894,780	588,639	597,639	284,741	296,027
Gulf	636,522	655,143	314,809	323,389	321,713	331,136
Hamilton	426,397	459,783	219,774	245,117	206,315	214,246
Hardee	1,486,842	1,501,143	1,010,704	1,027,205	474,187	469,815
Hendry	2,398,657	2,320,506	1,515,352	1,460,637	883,252	859,607
Hernando	4,606,117	4,736,579	1,550,607	1,617,081	3,038,351	3,111,083
Highlands	3,127,874	3,152,687	1,146,997	1,144,798	1,979,732	2,004,854
Hillsboroug	31,754,541	32,969,504	10,077,975	10,535,576	21,474,535	22,194,461
Holmes	452,966	458,583	297,211	300,805	155,755	157,778
Indian Rive	7,300,027	7,582,875	1,959,755	2,060,396	5,313,363	5,501,276
Jackson	1,274,202	1,301,877	774,540	786,285	499,631	515,202
Jefferson	421,233	446,407	256,111	270,057	164,864	176,034
Lafayette	227,459	236,533	148,340	155,078	79,087	81,186
Lake	6,363,572	6,711,435	1,919,268	2,062,059	4,423,650	4,627,450
Lee	24,122,483	24,981,235	4,923,580	5,101,884	19,085,834	19,715,198

See footnotes at end of table.   Continued . . .

Table 23.91. PROPERTY VALUATIONS: ASSESSED, EXEMPT, AND TAXABLE VALUES
OF REAL PROPERTY IN THE STATE AND COUNTIES OF FLORIDA
JANUARY 1, 1995 AND 1996 (Continued)

(rounded to thousands of dollars)

County	Just values 1/ 1995	1996	Exempt and immune values 1995	1996	Taxable values 2/ 1995	1996
Leon	10,250,111	10,710,374	4,801,928	4,856,173	5,328,947	5,673,884
Levy	1,029,429	1,182,522	438,180	566,217	591,035	615,131
Liberty	237,714	240,076	177,967	179,651	58,351	59,087
Madison	487,054	499,429	286,430	291,160	200,515	207,868
Manatee	10,667,348	11,221,013	2,678,686	2,720,699	7,914,378	8,344,853
Marion	8,028,659	8,274,381	3,323,265	3,417,031	4,694,574	4,833,847
Martin	9,315,256	9,417,551	2,317,525	2,121,326	6,965,860	7,188,409
Monroe	9,825,408	9,988,131	2,909,511	2,938,953	6,853,531	6,970,686
Nassau	2,169,794	2,268,492	636,456	664,347	1,532,838	1,601,535
Okaloosa	6,222,180	6,371,281	1,701,061	1,889,513	4,486,337	4,451,590
Okeechobee	1,353,922	1,374,063	645,284	657,580	707,224	711,904
Orange	39,905,552	41,852,451	10,107,654	10,298,347	29,701,996	31,328,887
Osceola	6,941,773	7,286,801	2,062,840	2,163,318	4,863,673	5,113,629
Palm Beach	64,079,053	66,863,533	13,265,879	13,868,273	50,329,078	52,409,037
Pasco	9,630,181	9,952,848	3,334,345	3,395,196	6,265,816	6,477,573
Pinellas	37,901,306	39,118,948	10,053,090	10,354,693	27,637,296	28,395,811
Polk	13,264,905	13,518,642	4,497,968	4,612,258	8,759,180	8,893,153
Putnam	2,122,863	2,176,076	888,871	905,708	1,226,884	1,256,489
St. Johns	5,694,627	5,983,394	1,278,800	1,317,603	4,336,130	4,597,640
St. Lucie	8,596,767	8,560,726	2,290,345	2,305,030	5,882,862	6,020,857
Santa Rosa	3,774,124	4,090,485	1,356,482	1,397,729	2,373,507	2,591,129
Sarasota	19,808,707	20,950,707	3,758,953	3,836,742	15,870,789	16,832,255
Seminole	12,831,323	13,431,336	2,781,584	2,842,272	10,033,515	10,557,730
Sumter	996,498	1,062,031	543,057	564,894	453,359	496,804
Suwannee	856,498	907,017	478,053	484,922	378,443	398,624
Taylor	791,433	805,807	436,991	441,145	353,843	361,000
Union	241,262	269,714	170,387	192,863	70,839	76,634
Volusia	15,598,653	16,196,095	4,242,458	4,362,105	11,267,736	11,659,044
Wakulla	585,101	619,212	344,535	359,617	232,622	253,905
Walton	2,330,403	2,510,776	546,660	563,993	1,768,503	1,927,909
Washington	539,327	564,372	288,507	292,758	238,978	260,134

1/ The value of property for tax purposes as determined by the elected county property appraiser before deduction of exemptions and immunities. Value is determined at the highest and best use of property, except for special cases provided for in Florida Statutes.

2/ The value against which millage rates are applied to compute the amount of tax levied. The tax base of a unit of local government also includes the taxable value of personal property and centrally assessed property.

Note: Data for 1995 are revised.

Source: State of Florida, Department of Revenue, *Florida Property Valuations and Tax Data, December 1996*.

University of Florida   **Bureau of Economic and Business Research**

Table 23.92. PROPERTY VALUATIONS AND TAXES: ASSESSED, EXEMPT, AND TAXABLE
VALUES, MILLAGE RATES, AND TAXES ON MUNICIPAL REAL, PERSONAL, AND
RAILROAD PROPERTY IN THE STATE, COUNTIES, AND SELECTED
MUNICIPALITIES OF FLORIDA, 1996

(rounded to thousands of dollars, except where indicated)

County and municipality 1/	Total assessed value	Exemption value Homestead	Exemption value Other 2/	Taxable Value	Oper- ating mill- age rate	Taxes
Florida TMP	376,626,747	38,369,792	58,013,543	280,243,412	4.9249	1,380,183
Alachua TMP	6,003,900	497,512	3,165,043	2,341,346	4.9712	11,639
Gainesville	5,407,243	399,628	2,976,496	2,031,119	4.9416	10,037
Baker TMP	116,702	23,340	18,044	75,318	3.5855	270
Bay TMP	3,317,804	455,421	592,995	2,269,388	2.4416	5,541
Panama City	768,102	44,638	35,105	688,358	0.0000	0
Bradford TMP	221,748	34,896	69,960	116,892	3.6199	423
Brevard TMP	11,410,247	1,767,818	1,481,482	8,160,948	3.7779	30,832
Cocoa	567,727	87,296	146,292	334,140	4.2000	1,403
Melbourne	2,949,374	388,589	587,039	1,973,746	4.1606	8,212
Palm Bay	2,411,578	479,172	190,785	1,741,621	3.2942	5,737
Rockledge	745,600	130,888	105,687	509,025	5.2900	2,693
Titusville	1,424,448	258,195	204,339	961,915	4.2745	4,112
Broward TMP	64,862,366	7,987,854	5,316,143	51,558,369	5.1583	265,953
Coconut Creek	1,539,539	274,137	141,778	1,123,624	4.6573	5,233
Cooper City	1,220,791	193,699	103,704	923,389	4.9570	4,577
Coral Springs	4,574,027	481,657	247,932	3,844,437	3.4011	13,075
Dania	1,049,325	93,420	117,084	838,821	5.8000	4,865
Davie	2,966,915	346,063	383,110	2,237,742	5.1086	11,432
Deerfield Beach	2,838,394	396,105	139,176	2,303,114	5.6144	12,931
Ft. Lauderdale	11,999,410	808,815	1,469,428	9,721,167	5.2570	51,104
Hallandale	1,604,369	223,642	53,989	1,326,738	6.7214	8,918
Hollywood	6,408,714	789,163	602,634	5,016,917	5.9999	30,101
Lauderdale Lakes	835,221	155,052	71,590	608,580	5.9500	3,621
Lauderhill	1,520,601	271,298	48,377	1,200,926	4.1000	4,924
Margate	1,754,893	367,827	71,804	1,315,262	6.4766	8,518
Miramar	1,763,084	305,816	164,932	1,292,336	6.9226	8,946
North Lauderdale	744,956	147,561	100,648	496,747	4.6871	2,328
Oakland Park	1,383,714	137,935	145,151	1,100,629	5.5145	6,069
Pembroke Pines	4,538,101	750,441	328,507	3,459,153	3.9034	13,502
Plantation	4,643,408	514,147	342,267	3,786,994	3.8360	14,527
Pompano Beach	4,868,456	440,232	328,373	4,099,850	6.0506	24,807
Sunrise	3,266,794	540,106	207,295	2,519,392	6.4000	16,124
Tamarac	2,101,447	469,309	72,089	1,560,049	4.9999	7,800
Calhoun TMP	70,632	15,280	15,829	39,523	1.3528	53
Charlotte TMP	1,267,126	109,172	99,752	1,058,202	3.2369	3,425
Citrus TMP	583,670	66,495	102,909	414,267	6.1417	2,544
Clay TMP	687,271	94,476	115,893	476,901	3.8032	1,814
Collier TMP	5,155,433	173,116	475,964	4,506,353	1.2091	5,448
Naples	5,121,865	170,922	470,312	4,480,632	1.1800	5,287
Columbia TMP	460,671	45,453	158,192	257,026	3.5556	914
Dade TMP	50,814,880	3,651,700	7,516,501	39,646,679	7.2937	289,171
Aventura	2,841,043	185,473	41,134	2,614,436	2.2270	5,822
Coral Gables	5,549,473	238,394	553,775	4,757,303	5.3650	25,523
Hialeah	5,886,448	786,279	622,942	4,477,226	7.9840	35,746

See footnotes at end of table.   Continued . . .

Table 23.92. PROPERTY VALUATIONS AND TAXES: ASSESSED, EXEMPT, AND TAXABLE
VALUES, MILLAGE RATES, AND TAXES ON MUNICIPAL REAL, PERSONAL, AND
RAILROAD PROPERTY IN THE STATE, COUNTIES, AND SELECTED
MUNICIPALITIES OF FLORIDA, 1996 (Continued)

(rounded to thousands of dollars, except where indicated)

County and municipality 1/	Total assessed value	Exemption value Homestead	Other 2/	Taxable Value	Oper- ating mill- age rate	Taxes
Dade TMP (Continued)						
Homestead	829,460	71,457	204,947	553,055	8.6816	4,801
Miami	16,786,629	1,010,736	4,206,025	11,569,869	9.5995	111,065
Miami Beach	7,332,958	335,423	868,723	6,128,812	7.4990	45,960
North Miami	1,649,407	227,666	238,515	1,183,226	7.9350	9,389
North Miami Beach	1,381,513	195,172	169,510	1,016,830	7.7000	7,830
Opa-locka	489,246	38,447	65,029	385,770	9.8000	3,781
De Soto TMP	212,948	30,784	66,206	115,958	8.2732	959
Dixie TMP	54,203	10,948	22,274	20,980	0.8651	18
Duval TMP	8,325,347	763,486	2,355,155	5,206,706	1.4366	7,480
Jacksonville	6,346,244	505,424	2,201,427	3,639,393	0.5551	2,020
Jacksonville Beach	972,512	122,542	81,481	768,489	3.9071	3,003
Escambia TMP	2,348,493	367,231	448,579	1,532,683	5.0038	7,669
Pensacola	2,311,073	359,944	439,347	1,511,782	5.0570	7,645
Flagler TMP	403,302	44,509	54,760	304,033	2.9717	903
Franklin TMP	197,941	38,069	38,481	121,392	5.1649	627
Gadsden TMP	485,140	78,131	202,777	204,232	1.3921	284
Gilchrist TMP	49,950	11,173	10,823	27,953	0.3377	9
Glades TMP	38,841	7,113	11,215	20,514	4.6380	95
Gulf TMP	362,358	37,120	20,275	304,963	5.2448	1,599
Hamilton TMP	98,149	16,439	26,355	55,355	3.0141	167
Hardee TMP	184,453	36,447	56,029	91,976	5.8202	535
Hendry TMP	409,747	46,225	124,045	239,477	4.1859	1,002
Hernando TMP	361,979	27,510	118,156	216,313	7.5780	1,639
Highlands TMP	645,322	93,495	136,196	415,631	7.9968	3,324
Hillsborough TMP	17,454,709	1,749,866	4,213,993	11,490,850	6.2686	72,031
Plant City	1,110,736	137,980	179,726	793,030	4.7000	3,727
Tampa	15,390,606	1,497,103	3,970,269	9,923,234	6.5390	64,888
Temple Terrace	953,366	114,783	63,998	774,586	4.4100	3,416
Holmes TMP	110,458	20,046	28,150	62,261	0.0687	4
Indian River TMP	3,289,049	267,628	307,185	2,714,237	2.6333	7,147
Vero Beach	1,514,527	114,768	224,115	1,175,644	2.2645	2,662
Jackson TMP	373,484	67,478	114,282	191,724	2.0609	395
Jefferson TMP	76,164	13,990	16,666	45,508	9.3829	427
Lafayette TMP	18,986	4,248	6,481	8,257	1.9999	17
Lake TMP	3,289,286	510,277	501,360	2,277,649	4.5051	10,261
Leesburg	802,431	71,099	178,712	552,620	4.5000	2,487
Lee TMP	10,490,854	895,590	958,583	8,636,681	4.1161	35,549
Cape Coral	4,576,330	649,082	295,238	3,632,010	5.4298	19,721
Ft. Myers	2,519,175	150,862	564,830	1,803,483	5.6600	10,208
Leon TMP	9,043,725	599,585	4,173,490	4,270,650	3.2000	13,666
Tallahassee	9,043,725	599,585	4,173,490	4,270,650	3.2000	13,666
Levy TMP	331,218	51,377	35,349	244,492	3.5772	875
Liberty TMP	20,315	4,374	5,841	10,100	1.0000	10

See footnotes at end of table.   Continued . . .

Table 23.92. PROPERTY VALUATIONS AND TAXES: ASSESSED, EXEMPT, AND TAXABLE VALUES, MILLAGE RATES, AND TAXES ON MUNICIPAL REAL, PERSONAL, AND RAILROAD PROPERTY IN THE STATE, COUNTIES, AND SELECTED MUNICIPALITIES OF FLORIDA, 1996 (Continued)

(rounded to thousands of dollars, except where indicated)

County and municipality 1/	Total assessed value	Exemption value Homestead	Other 2/	Taxable Value	Oper- ating mill- age rate	Taxes
Madison TMP	107,456	20,493	23,795	63,168	5.3981	341
Manatee TMP	3,885,376	397,223	389,448	3,098,706	2.2819	7,071
Bradenton	1,955,036	268,892	235,338	1,450,805	2.1601	3,134
Marion TMP	2,384,717	252,939	344,723	1,787,055	5.2203	9,329
Ocala	2,172,879	214,907	323,909	1,634,063	5.2237	8,536
Martin TMP	2,090,478	104,697	279,470	1,706,312	3.2076	5,473
Monroe TMP	3,943,237	101,553	1,713,672	2,128,011	3.8247	8,139
Key West	3,693,458	93,153	1,707,755	1,892,549	4.1097	7,778
Nassau TMP	994,673	77,304	267,449	649,920	6.4734	4,207
Okaloosa TMP	3,506,292	411,006	366,983	2,728,304	2.8700	7,830
Ft. Walton Beach	866,533	129,264	103,410	633,859	4.9700	3,150
Okeechobee TMP	220,978	27,106	40,441	153,432	3.9400	605
Orange TMP	23,962,618	1,283,069	5,406,991	17,272,558	3.9230	67,760
Apopka	862,329	123,816	93,271	645,242	3.7619	2,427
Ocoee	824,393	123,647	119,132	581,613	4.0000	2,326
Orlando	13,185,679	679,693	4,483,159	8,022,827	6.0666	48,671
Winter Park	2,278,458	154,983	303,713	1,819,762	3.8930	7,084
Osceola TMP	1,949,303	231,941	258,954	1,458,408	4.4477	6,487
Kissimmee	1,381,642	131,616	180,180	1,069,846	4.5453	4,863
St. Cloud	567,661	100,324	78,774	388,562	4.1790	1,624
Palm Beach TMP	44,219,408	3,523,206	4,462,095	36,234,107	5.1036	184,925
Belle Glade	289,135	41,032	79,569	168,534	9.1648	1,545
Boca Raton	9,101,407	508,205	836,474	7,756,728	3.1848	24,704
Boynton Beach	2,812,532	377,946	287,264	2,147,322	7.9251	17,018
Delray Beach	3,253,172	385,495	236,126	2,631,550	6.9500	18,289
Greenacres City	784,278	150,491	33,459	600,328	5.9000	3,542
Jupiter	3,130,164	238,362	320,276	2,571,526	2.2680	5,832
Lake Worth	953,136	152,909	151,753	648,474	8.1928	5,313
Palm Beach Gardens	3,553,259	231,507	422,365	2,899,386	3.9147	11,350
Riviera Beach	1,801,012	130,219	323,572	1,347,221	8.9997	12,125
Royal Palm Beach	774,917	140,336	56,738	577,843	6.9800	4,033
Wellington	1,857,609	188,969	105,701	1,562,939	1.7800	2,782
West Palm Beach	5,075,973	352,795	1,080,349	3,642,830	8.8747	32,329
Pasco TMP	1,404,198	194,859	267,342	941,997	5.7644	5,430
Pinellas TMP	29,688,599	3,938,909	3,803,425	21,946,265	5.0618	111,089
Clearwater	5,884,592	606,291	901,742	4,376,559	5.1158	22,390
Dunedin	1,599,916	258,805	315,822	1,025,288	4.5740	4,690
Largo	2,412,669	358,268	238,426	1,815,974	3.4000	6,174
Pinellas Park	1,916,046	294,722	162,503	1,458,821	4.3808	6,391
Safety Harbor	796,842	129,512	101,399	565,932	3.7527	2,124
St. Petersburg	9,871,474	1,527,511	1,477,532	6,866,431	7.4620	51,237
Tarpon Springs	965,267	133,778	121,854	709,635	5.4541	3,870
Polk TMP	6,617,147	833,066	1,586,421	4,197,660	4.3107	18,095
Bartow	486,976	80,689	151,507	254,779	0.7820	199

See footnotes at end of table.   Continued . . .

University of Florida   **Bureau of Economic and Business Research**

Table 23.92. PROPERTY VALUATIONS AND TAXES: ASSESSED, EXEMPT, AND TAXABLE VALUES, MILLAGE RATES, AND TAXES ON MUNICIPAL REAL, PERSONAL, AND RAILROAD PROPERTY IN THE STATE, COUNTIES, AND SELECTED MUNICIPALITIES OF FLORIDA, 1996 (Continued)

(rounded to thousands of dollars, except where indicated)

County and municipality 1/	Total assessed value	Exemption value Homestead	Other 2/	Taxable Value	Operating millage rate	Taxes
Polk TMP (Continued)						
Lakeland	3,420,959	359,234	957,031	2,104,694	2.9950	6,304
Winter Haven	1,058,282	126,173	222,053	710,056	6.3750	4,527
Putnam TMP	582,402	70,557	210,304	301,541	7.4473	2,246
St. Johns TMP	866,531	94,375	156,920	615,235	5.3865	3,314
St. Lucie TMP	4,606,912	705,202	541,533	3,360,177	4.7675	16,020
Ft. Pierce	1,407,757	152,654	343,496	911,607	7.3305	6,683
Port St. Lucie	3,171,393	548,020	197,285	2,426,088	3.8400	9,316
Santa Rosa TMP	723,751	83,689	178,601	461,461	2.1098	974
Sarasota TMP	7,720,170	586,492	1,093,779	6,039,899	3.3995	20,533
North Port	696,774	135,483	57,538	503,753	5.0000	2,519
Sarasota	3,923,732	287,126	791,826	2,844,779	3.7105	10,556
Venice	1,449,243	125,682	208,350	1,115,210	3.4060	3,798
Seminole TMP	7,291,136	917,293	574,049	5,799,795	4.8442	28,095
Altamonte Springs	1,973,132	165,923	166,898	1,640,311	4.9500	8,120
Casselberry	783,223	124,427	27,842	630,954	3.8000	2,398
Oviedo	854,260	141,385	73,384	639,490	4.9950	3,194
Sanford	1,284,614	157,032	195,726	931,856	6.8759	6,407
Winter Springs	1,019,158	182,874	37,357	798,928	3.6083	2,883
Sumter TMP	179,945	33,580	20,583	125,782	3.9324	495
Suwannee TMP	144,307	29,577	34,866	79,863	4.9046	392
Taylor TMP	229,932	36,384	64,768	128,779	4.7300	609
Union TMP	49,636	7,869	18,845	22,922	3.0235	69
Volusia TMP	25,163,160	3,611,668	2,610,151	18,941,341	4.4839	84,931
Daytona Beach	2,946,538	286,747	563,218	2,096,573	6.5920	13,821
DeLand	832,305	84,712	181,628	565,965	5.9500	3,367
Edgewater	542,399	131,188	27,450	383,761	6.5900	2,529
New Smyrna Beach	1,275,232	142,982	98,614	1,033,635	5.4869	5,671
Ormond Beach	1,826,003	240,940	143,224	1,441,839	3.0544	4,404
Port Orange	1,392,404	274,271	113,557	1,004,577	4.5281	4,549
Wakulla TMP	96,565	15,015	46,856	34,694	1.0061	35
Walton TMP	187,744	36,095	34,195	117,453	4.2638	501
Washington TMP	161,208	28,953	35,474	96,781	4.8291	467

TMP Total municipal property.
1/ Only municipalities with a 1996 population of 15,000 or more are shown. Refer to the source for data for other municipalities.
2/ Includes governmental, institutional, and miscellaneous other exempt properties.

Source: State of Florida, Department of Revenue, *Florida Property Valuations and Tax Data, December 1996.*

Table 23.93. COUNTY MILLAGE: AD VALOREM MILLAGE RATES IN THE COUNTIES
OF FLORIDA, JANUARY 1, 1996

County	Total county-wide millage	County government Oper-ating millage	Debt service millage	District school board Oper-ating millage	Debt service millage	Other mill-age 1/
Alachua	23.4980	9.2500	0.0310	9.2880	2.8890	2.0400
Baker	22.9944	9.1100	0.0000	9.8100	0.0000	4.0744
Bay	14.9080	5.6320	0.0000	7.2260	2.0000	0.0500
Bradford	17.4924	7.3770	0.0000	9.6240	0.0000	0.4914
Brevard	15.8909	4.3081	0.0000	9.6620	0.0000	1.9208
Broward 2/	18.4020	7.0250	0.7270	9.3820	0.5580	0.7100
Calhoun	16.7270	10.0000	0.0000	6.6770	0.0000	0.0500
Charlotte	14.8299	4.5278	0.0000	9.3060	0.5552	0.4409
Citrus	18.3877	7.2430	0.0000	9.8160	0.0000	1.3287
Clay	17.8150	8.0000	0.0000	9.3330	0.0000	0.4820
Collier	12.9410	3.7241	0.0000	8.6860	0.0000	0.5309
Columbia	20.3154	8.7260	0.0000	9.4600	0.0000	2.1294
Dade 2/	18.2190	6.4690	0.7740	9.3560	1.0100	0.6100
De Soto	17.8200	8.4800	0.0000	8.7230	0.0000	0.6170
Dixie	19.9984	10.0000	0.0000	9.5070	0.0000	0.4914
Duval	21.7028	11.0866	0.0292	9.2300	0.8370	0.5200
Escambia	18.4220	8.7560	0.0000	9.6160	0.0000	0.0500
Flagler	16.7114	4.6274	0.2200	9.3660	1.6330	0.8650
Franklin	16.4610	8.7570	0.0000	7.6540	0.0000	0.0500
Gadsden	19.2830	10.0000	0.0000	9.2330	0.0000	0.0500
Gilchrist	20.2784	10.0000	0.0000	9.7870	0.0000	0.4914
Glades	19.3630	10.0000	0.0000	8.6910	0.0000	0.6720
Gulf	15.6680	7.6000	0.0000	8.0180	0.0000	0.0500
Hamilton	19.7424	10.0000	0.0000	9.2510	0.0000	0.4914
Hardee	20.5280	10.0000	0.0000	9.2350	0.0000	1.2930
Hendry	23.8370	8.9500	0.0000	9.7150	2.0000	3.1720
Hernando	20.1730	8.8580	0.1000	10.7930	0.0000	0.4220
Highlands	18.3650	8.5000	0.0000	9.2480	0.0000	0.6170
Hillsborough	19.2584	7.9163	0.2389	9.5180	0.4362	1.1490
Holmes	16.8590	8.1150	0.0000	8.6940	0.0000	0.0500
Indian River	16.5084	4.2999	0.2897	9.1090	1.2100	1.5998
Jackson	15.5520	8.2740	0.0000	7.2280	0.0000	0.0500
Jefferson	18.3624	9.5000	0.0000	8.3210	0.0000	0.5414
Lafayette	20.1014	10.0000	0.0000	9.6100	0.0000	0.4914
Lake	15.0028	4.9090	0.0000	9.2280	0.0000	0.8658
Lee	14.7860	4.7471	0.0000	9.3480	0.0000	0.6909

See footnotes at end of table.   Continued . . .

Table 23.93. COUNTY MILLAGE: AD VALOREM MILLAGE RATES IN THE COUNTIES
OF FLORIDA, JANUARY 1, 1996 (Continued)

County	Total county-wide millage	County government		District school board		Other mill-age 1/
		Oper-ating millage	Debt service millage	Oper-ating millage	Debt service millage	
Leon	19.1730	8.6200	0.0000	9.2370	1.2660	0.0500
Levy	19.3904	9.0000	0.0000	9.8990	0.0000	0.4914
Liberty	17.9090	10.0000	0.0000	7.8590	0.0000	0.0500
Madison	17.7684	10.0000	0.0000	7.2770	0.0000	0.4914
Manatee	18.1198	7.3808	0.4142	9.3620	0.1534	0.8094
Marion	16.1840	5.7100	0.0000	8.8720	1.1200	0.4820
Martin 2/	15.8270	5.1300	0.5120	9.3570	0.1180	0.7100
Monroe	13.6867	6.0857	0.0000	6.2530	0.0000	1.3480
Nassau	16.6221	6.7321	0.0000	9.4080	0.0000	0.4820
Okaloosa	13.1500	4.5280	0.0000	8.5720	0.0000	0.0500
Okeechobee	19.7578	8.6463	0.6565	9.4630	0.0000	0.9920
Orange	14.9479	5.2889	0.0000	9.1770	0.0000	0.4820
Osceola	16.2305	5.9945	0.0000	8.7870	0.6650	0.7840
Palm Beach	16.5927	4.2358	0.2833	9.2520	0.5360	2.2856
Pasco	19.9370	8.9530	0.4050	9.2280	0.9290	0.4220
Pinellas	17.0831	6.2510	0.0000	9.1760	0.0000	1.6561
Polk	17.7950	7.9770	0.0000	9.3360	0.0000	0.4820
Putnam	20.0450	8.4000	0.0000	10.1930	0.9700	0.4820
St. Johns	16.5058	6.0930	0.2750	9.2200	0.8520	0.0658
St. Lucie 2/	20.9408	7.4829	0.0000	9.6740	0.0000	3.7839
Santa Rosa	16.0720	6.9720	0.0000	9.0500	0.0000	0.0500
Sarasota	14.0886	3.8424	0.1884	9.0940	0.0000	0.9638
Seminole	16.1789	5.1638	0.2251	9.3880	0.9200	0.4820
Sumter	20.0870	10.0000	0.0000	9.3670	0.0000	0.7200
Suwannee	19.1064	9.0500	0.0000	9.5650	0.0000	0.4914
Taylor	17.5464	8.0760	0.0000	8.9790	0.0000	0.4914
Union	20.3534	10.0000	0.0000	9.3620	0.0000	0.9914
Volusia	17.5580	6.2170	0.0000	10.8210	0.0000	0.5200
Wakulla	20.9560	9.2500	0.0000	9.5560	2.1000	0.0500
Walton	16.4690	6.8500	0.0000	9.1190	0.0000	0.5000
Washington	17.6370	10.0000	0.0000	7.5870	0.0000	0.0500

1/ Includes county government special service districts and independent special
service districts.
2/ Proposed millage used.

Source: State of Florida, Department of Revenue, *Florida Property Valuations and
Tax Data, December 1996.*

Table 23.94. LOCAL GOVERNMENT FINANCE: AD VALOREM TAXES IN THE STATE AND COUNTIES OF FLORIDA, JANUARY 1, 1996

(in millions, rounded to hundred thousands of dollars)

County	Total taxes levied Amount	Percentage change 1995-1996	Municipal taxes	Total	County-wide County government Operating levy	County-wide County government Debt service	County-wide District school board Operating levy	County-wide District school board Debt service	County-wide Special service districts	County-wide Independent service districts	Less than county-wide County government special services districts	Less than county-wide Independent special services districts
Florida	12,294.5	6.75	1,389.1	9,726.6	3,487.2	192.0	5,282.7	269.5	29.7	465.6	148.3	385.7
Alachua	125.3	15.50	11.6	104.1	41.3	0.1	41.5	12.9	0.0	8.2	0.0	2.2
Baker	6.5	3.53	0.3	6.2	2.5	0.0	2.7	0.0	A/	1.0	0.0	0.0
Bay	72.6	8.67	5.5	65.0	24.4	0.0	31.7	8.8	0.0	0.2	1.7	0.0
Bradford	7.1	5.90	0.4	6.5	2.8	0.0	3.7	0.0	0.0	0.0	0.0	0.2
Brevard	287.0	5.28	38.4	226.6	61.3	0.0	137.4	0.0	20.5	7.4	1.0	0.9
Broward	1,505.6	5.38	287.1	1,067.1	406.4	42.1	544.7	32.3	0.0	41.7	10.5	140.9
Calhoun	3.3	12.75	0.1	3.2	1.9	0.0	1.3	0.0	0.0	A/	0.0	0.0
Charlotte	107.8	5.61	3.4	91.5	28.7	0.0	59.1	3.5	0.0	0.1	0.0	4.1
Citrus	84.9	4.90	2.5	79.1	31.2	0.0	42.2	0.0	1.4	4.3	1.9	1.4
Clay	57.6	4.39	1.8	55.8	25.0	0.0	29.2	0.0	0.0	1.5	0.0	0.0
Collier	272.3	12.10	5.5	237.5	67.4	0.0	157.2	0.0	0.9	12.0	0.0	14.7
Columbia	18.6	6.47	0.9	17.6	7.6	0.0	8.2	0.0	0.1	1.7	0.0	0.0
Dade	2,020.8	4.65	311.2	1,466.6	510.3	103.7	726.8	78.5	0.0	47.4	0.0	0.0
De Soto	12.3	31.45	1.0	11.4	5.4	0.0	5.6	0.0	0.0	0.4	0.0	0.0
Dixie	4.3	0.99	A/	3.7	1.9	0.0	1.8	0.0	0.0	0.1	0.0	0.0
Duval	510.5	5.41	7.5	482.1	237.8	0.7	212.4	19.3	0.0	12.0	0.1	7.5
Escambia	118.1	1.41	7.7	108.3	50.6	0.7	57.3	0.0	0.0	0.4	0.0	0.0
Flagler	40.2	1.64	0.9	37.1	10.5	0.5	21.2	3.7	0.0	1.2	1.5	0.7
Franklin	9.7	16.12	0.6	8.8	4.7	0.0	4.1	0.0	0.0	A/	0.0	0.2
Gadsden	12.5	6.13	0.3	12.3	6.0	0.0	5.5	0.0	0.7	A/	0.0	0.0
Gilchrist	4.3	8.49	A/	4.2	2.0	0.0	2.0	0.0	0.0	A/ 0.1	0.1	0.0

Continued . . .

See footnote at end of table.

Table 23.94. LOCAL GOVERNMENT FINANCE: AD VALOREM TAXES IN THE STATE AND COUNTIES OF FLORIDA, JANUARY 1, 1996 (Continued)

(in millions, rounded to hundred thousands of dollars)

| | Total taxes levied | | | County taxes | | | | | | | | Less than county-wide | |
| | | | | | | County-wide | | | | | | | |
County	Amount	Per-cent-age change 1995-1996	Munic-ipal taxes	Total	County government Operat-ing levy	County Debt ser-vice	District school board Operat-ing levy	District school board Debt ser-vice	Spe-cial ser-vice dis-tricts	Inde-pendent ser-vice dis-tricts	County govern-ment special services dis-tricts	Inde-pendent special ser-vices dis-tricts
Glades	6.9	4.84	0.1	6.7	3.4	0.0	3.0	0.0	0.0	0.2	0.0	0.1
Gulf	11.0	2.68	1.6	9.3	4.5	0.0	4.7	0.0	0.0	A/	0.1	0.0
Hamilton	9.2	8.98	0.2	9.0	4.6	0.0	4.2	0.0	0.0	0.2	0.0	0.0
Hardee	16.5	8.49	0.5	15.9	7.3	0.0	7.6	0.0	0.0	1.1	0.0	0.0
Hendry	25.5	-2.14	1.0	24.3	10.0	0.0	10.8	0.0	0.0	3.5	0.0	0.1
Hernando	80.5	7.67	1.6	73.3	32.2	0.4	39.2	0.0	0.0	1.5	0.0	5.2
Highlands	46.9	1.82	3.3	42.1	20.2	0.0	21.9	0.0	0.0	0.0	0.0	1.5
Hillsborough	715.6	3.50	72.3	525.6	215.8	7.2	259.4	11.9	0.0	31.3	16.5	21.6
Holmes	3.5	17.37	A/	3.5	1.7	0.0	1.8	0.0	0.0	A/	0.0	0.0
Indian River	122.3	1.70	7.3	88.6	25.5	1.7	54.1	7.2	0.0	0.0	11.3	9.9
Jackson	11.0	3.77	0.4	10.3	5.5	0.0	4.8	0.0	0.0	A/	0.4	0.0
Jefferson	4.8	9.22	0.4	4.4	2.3	0.0	2.0	0.0	0.0	A/	0.0	0.0
Lafayette	2.3	14.86	A/	2.3	1.1	0.0	1.1	0.0	0.0	0.1	0.0	0.0
Lake	99.7	1.42	10.3	79.5	26.9	0.0	50.5	0.0	0.0	2.1	0.7	9.3
Lee	479.2	22.15	35.5	371.7	101.2	0.0	255.8	0.0	0.0	14.7	0.0	42.3
Leon	135.3	4.75	13.7	121.7	54.7	0.0	58.6	8.0	0.0	0.3	0.0	A/
Levy	15.5	10.94	0.9	14.1	6.7	0.0	7.4	0.0	0.0	0.0	0.0	0.5
Liberty	2.3	34.69	A/	2.3	1.4	0.0	1.0	0.0	0.0	A/	0.0	0.0
Madison	5.3	4.66	0.3	5.0	2.8	0.0	2.0	0.0	0.0	0.1	0.0	0.0
Manatee	188.4	2.43	7.1	176.4	71.6	4.0	90.9	1.5	0.0	8.4	0.0	A/
Marion	160.0	46.74	9.3	131.8	32.2	0.0	93.3	6.3	0.0	0.0	1.5	3.3
Martin	159.3	12.13	5.5	137.6	44.0	4.4	80.2	1.0	0.0	8.0	0.0	1.2
Monroe	115.8	1.54	8.1	98.8	44.6	0.0	45.8	0.0	0.0	8.4	0.0	0.0

See footnote at end of table.

Continued . . .

Table 23.94. LOCAL GOVERNMENT FINANCE: AD VALOREM TAXES IN THE STATE AND COUNTIES OF FLORIDA, JANUARY 1, 1996 (Continued)

(in millions, rounded to hundred thousands of dollars)

| | Total taxes levied | | | | County taxes | | | | | | Less than county-wide | |
| | | | | | County-wide | | | | | | | |
County	Amount	Per-cent-age change 1995-1996	Munic-ipal taxes	Total	County government Operat-ing levy	County government Debt ser-vice	District school board Operat-ing levy	District school board Debt ser-vice	Spe-cial ser-vice dis-tricts	Inde-pendent ser-vice dis-tricts	County govern-ment special services dis-tricts	Inde-pendent special ser-vices dis-tricts
Nassau	37.4	5.40	4.2	32.2	13.0	0.0	18.2	0.0	0.0	0.9	0.0	0.6
Okaloosa	76.4	0.51	7.8	64.6	22.2	0.0	42.1	0.0	0.0	0.2	0.0	4.0
Okeechobee	17.3	2.26	0.6	16.2	7.3	0.6	8.0	0.0	0.0	0.3	0.0	0.6
Orange	745.0	4.36	67.8	538.2	196.8	0.0	341.4	0.0	0.0	0.0	0.8	27.1
Osceola	108.8	6.51	6.5	97.4	37.9	0.0	55.6	3.9	0.0	0.0	0.0	3.9
Palm Beach	1,236.6	4.54	199.1	948.2	242.0	16.2	528.8	30.6	0.0	130.6	78.2	11.1
Pasco	167.5	1.34	5.4	151.7	68.1	3.1	70.2	7.1	0.0	3.2	6.9	3.6
Pinellas	721.2	2.21	111.1	547.6	198.6	0.0	295.7	0.0	0.7	52.7	0.0	24.4
Polk	244.5	3.78	18.0	217.1	100.0	0.0	117.1	0.0	0.0	0.0	0.0	9.2
Putnam	43.4	0.68	2.2	39.1	17.7	0.0	21.4	0.0	0.0	0.0	0.0	1.0
St. Johns	69.6	-22.88	3.3	61.0	6.3	1.4	45.8	4.2	0.0	3.3	3.3	1.5
St. Lucie	177.0	8.04	16.0	157.1	56.0	0.0	72.5	0.0	3.7	25.0	2.1	1.0
Santa Rosa	49.5	9.22	1.0	48.1	20.8	0.0	27.2	0.0	0.0	0.2	0.0	0.4
Sarasota	256.6	-5.88	0.0	255.9	69.8	3.4	165.2	0.0	1.6	15.9	0.0	0.0
Seminole	233.6	-2.69	28.8	188.7	60.2	2.6	109.5	10.7	0.0	5.6	0.0	0.0
Sumter	13.6	7.24	0.5	12.6	6.5	0.0	6.1	0.0	0.0	0.0	0.0	0.5
Suwannee	11.1	-0.88	0.4	10.7	5.1	0.0	5.3	0.0	0.0	0.3	0.0	0.0
Taylor	12.4	4.74	0.6	11.1	5.1	0.0	5.7	0.0	0.0	0.3	0.6	0.0
Union	2.2	2.35	A/	2.1	1.0	0.0	1.0	0.0	0.1	0.1	0.0	0.0
Volusia	324.2	2.90	48.3	231.1	81.8	0.0	125.0	17.4	0.0	6.8	9.1	29.3
Wakulla	6.7	6.51	A/	6.7	3.0	0.0	3.1	0.7	0.0	A/	0.0	0.0
Walton	35.0	8.06	0.5	33.7	14.4	0.0	19.2	0.0	0.0	0.1	0.2	0.6
Washington	6.9	12.98	0.5	6.4	3.6	0.0	2.8	0.0	0.0	A/	0.0	0.0

A/ Less than $50,000.
Source: State of Florida, Department of Revenue, *Florida Property Valuations and Tax Data*, December 1996.

Table 23.95. LAND USE: ASSESSED VALUE AND PROPORTION OF LAND BY USE IN THE STATE AND COUNTIES OF FLORIDA, 1996

County	Residential Value (million dollars)	Residential Percentage of total value	Commercial Value (million dollars)	Commercial Percentage of total value	Industrial Value (million dollars)	Industrial Percentage of total value	Agricultural Value (million dollars)	Agricultural Percentage of total value	Institutional Value (million dollars)	Institutional Percentage of total value	Miscellaneous 1/ Value (million dollars)	Miscellaneous 1/ Percentage of total value
Florida	450,115.89	69.00	88,353.19	13.50	20,927.68	3.20	10,045.23	1.50	16,553.19	2.50	66,323.27	10.20
Alachua	3,621.19	50.80	871.16	12.20	122.90	1.70	187.32	2.60	164.56	2.30	2,158.02	30.30
Baker	170.91	39.70	28.21	6.60	7.11	1.70	86.98	20.20	12.65	2.90	124.77	29.00
Bay	3,471.99	62.30	742.05	13.30	96.25	1.70	62.97	1.10	130.75	2.30	1,069.77	19.20
Bradford	283.06	59.10	47.58	9.90	9.51	2.00	69.30	14.50	20.21	4.20	49.29	10.30
Brevard	12,448.50	61.40	2,356.65	11.60	495.25	2.40	111.55	0.50	567.21	2.80	4,305.84	21.20
Broward	47,727.37	73.70	8,437.95	13.00	2,822.96	4.40	121.36	0.20	1,202.22	1.90	4,408.94	6.80
Calhoun	93.22	40.90	17.64	7.70	3.90	1.70	76.75	33.60	7.21	3.20	29.39	12.90
Charlotte	5,826.46	80.40	805.30	11.10	73.92	1.00	59.71	0.80	148.27	2.00	331.81	4.60
Citrus	2,923.54	67.90	456.72	10.60	28.72	0.70	42.43	1.00	108.58	2.50	744.29	17.30
Clay	2,809.01	71.60	490.76	12.50	70.84	1.80	65.45	1.70	130.89	3.30	355.72	9.10
Collier	15,454.30	78.30	1,981.82	10.00	295.02	1.50	231.35	1.20	356.76	1.80	1,409.80	7.10
Columbia	583.62	47.60	167.16	13.60	26.14	2.10	126.81	10.30	37.21	3.00	285.37	23.30
Dade	59,302.39	65.40	14,371.33	15.80	5,239.45	5.80	699.51	0.80	2,390.09	2.60	8,708.35	9.60
De Soto	344.61	42.20	75.02	9.20	11.02	1.30	242.95	29.70	24.83	3.00	118.87	14.50
Dixie	143.55	50.00	12.14	4.20	3.21	1.10	62.42	21.70	3.65	1.30	62.40	21.70
Duval	15,578.73	56.70	4,867.84	17.70	1,822.24	6.60	92.01	0.30	1,350.33	4.90	3,742.85	13.60
Escambia	4,626.51	53.40	1,016.40	11.70	253.98	2.90	65.12	0.80	336.19	3.90	2,363.95	27.30
Flagler	2,011.79	77.80	228.04	8.80	28.76	1.10	53.25	2.10	38.59	1.50	226.46	8.80
Franklin	497.74	39.90	42.72	3.40	7.63	0.60	15.75	1.30	12.60	1.00	670.91	53.80
Gadsden	430.80	52.00	63.77	7.70	40.96	4.90	115.50	14.00	32.40	3.90	144.38	17.40
Gilchrist	142.57	55.10	8.47	3.30	1.40	0.50	72.33	27.90	5.86	2.30	28.20	10.90
Glades	176.74	36.30	42.82	8.80	1.84	0.40	120.72	24.80	5.81	1.20	138.58	28.50
Gulf	311.38	58.80	22.36	4.20	20.44	3.90	27.41	5.20	12.22	2.30	136.00	25.70

See footnote at end of table.

Continued . . .

Table 23.95. LAND USE: ASSESSED VALUE AND PROPORTION OF LAND BY USE IN THE STATE AND COUNTIES OF FLORIDA, 1996 (Continued)

County	Residential Value (million dollars)	Residential Per-cent-age of total value	Commercial Value (million dollars)	Commercial Per-cent-age of total value	Industrial Value (million dollars)	Industrial Per-cent-age of total value	Agricultural Value (million dollars)	Agricultural Per-cent-age of total value	Institutional Value (million dollars)	Institutional Per-cent-age of total value	Miscellaneous 1/ Value (million dollars)	Miscellaneous 1/ Per-cent-age of total value
Hamilton	108.98	35.10	27.90	9.00	61.71	19.90	61.95	20.00	5.75	1.90	44.09	14.20
Hardee	200.33	28.40	44.57	6.30	67.93	9.60	237.55	33.70	23.67	3.40	131.87	18.70
Hendry	447.04	37.30	102.48	8.50	40.28	3.40	381.06	31.80	23.18	1.90	205.21	17.10
Hernando	3,180.36	70.80	435.89	9.70	67.65	1.50	84.08	1.90	101.79	2.30	624.56	13.90
Highlands	1,777.15	61.50	382.31	13.20	52.86	1.80	263.41	9.10	128.41	4.40	284.56	9.90
Hillsborough	19,497.47	62.20	5,254.15	16.80	1,552.41	5.00	425.91	1.40	1,103.76	3.50	3,502.00	11.20
Holmes	125.37	37.80	22.28	6.70	3.50	1.10	101.53	30.60	17.73	5.40	60.85	18.40
Indian River	4,832.77	73.70	708.14	10.80	125.96	1.90	237.96	3.60	179.51	2.70	469.55	7.20
Jackson	439.70	43.90	105.27	10.50	26.94	2.70	153.78	15.40	48.86	4.90	226.50	22.60
Jefferson	79.37	27.80	24.66	8.70	2.29	0.80	124.86	43.80	13.56	4.80	40.37	14.20
Lafayette	41.78	30.30	2.95	2.10	0.71	0.50	64.20	46.60	3.21	2.30	24.97	18.10
Lake	4,567.71	70.60	660.95	10.20	135.94	2.10	221.03	3.40	182.38	2.80	698.38	10.80
Lee	18,402.61	77.00	2,937.50	12.30	514.37	2.20	142.74	0.60	521.43	2.20	1,395.70	5.80
Leon	5,182.71	50.60	1,323.11	12.90	178.63	1.70	95.99	0.90	240.16	2.30	3,215.54	31.40
Levy	501.30	54.80	83.81	9.20	6.72	0.70	155.35	17.00	22.10	2.40	146.13	16.00
Liberty	45.15	24.00	3.77	2.00	1.65	0.90	31.27	16.70	4.01	2.10	101.91	54.30
Madison	138.16	39.70	25.49	7.30	10.47	3.00	113.06	32.50	18.02	5.20	43.05	12.40
Manatee	7,513.38	71.30	1,329.46	12.60	385.62	3.70	279.62	2.70	325.16	5.20	700.89	6.70
Marion	4,478.04	60.80	852.39	11.60	289.69	3.90	401.33	5.50	185.30	2.50	1,154.64	15.70
Martin	6,608.68	75.80	817.83	9.40	176.55	2.00	168.17	1.90	127.30	1.50	819.34	9.40
Monroe	5,919.08	59.70	1,393.35	14.10	67.79	0.70	0.02	0.00	139.07	1.40	2,390.54	24.10
Nassau	1,464.31	68.30	253.15	11.80	66.19	3.10	125.42	5.90	47.74	2.20	186.59	8.70
Okaloosa	4,442.31	71.30	750.56	12.00	101.06	1.60	54.18	0.90	145.75	2.30	735.75	11.80
Okeechobee	585.97	59.80	115.13	11.70	15.24	1.60	130.90	13.30	30.93	3.20	102.46	10.40
Orange	30,924.64	76.40	7,343.98	18.20	8.57	0.00	201.44	0.50	6.09	0.00	1,969.22	4.90

See footnote at end of table.

Continued . . .

Table 23.95. LAND USE: ASSESSED VALUE AND PROPORTION OF LAND BY USE IN THE STATE AND COUNTIES OF FLORIDA, 1996 (Continued)

County	Residential Value (million dollars)	Residential Per-cent age of total value	Commercial Value (million dollars)	Commercial Per-cent age of total value	Industrial Value (million dollars)	Industrial Per-cent age of total value	Agricultural Value (million dollars)	Agricultural Per-cent age of total value	Institutional Value (million dollars)	Institutional Per-cent age of total value	Miscellaneous 1/ Value (million dollars)	Miscellaneous 1/ Per-cent age of total value
Osceola	4,023.04	62.60	1,395.56	21.70	106.02	1.70	186.91	2.90	156.14	2.40	555.71	8.70
Palm Beach	49,172.61	76.50	7,635.38	11.90	1,469.65	2.30	740.21	1.20	1,310.73	2.00	3,987.66	6.20
Pasco	7,013.26	75.00	1,237.49	13.20	129.46	1.40	173.56	1.90	268.49	2.90	528.88	5.70
Pinellas	26,739.93	69.10	5,582.63	14.40	1,396.55	3.60	15.53	0.00	1,706.43	4.40	3,241.01	8.40
Polk	7,660.52	61.00	1,677.58	13.40	638.08	5.10	457.29	3.60	436.12	3.50	1,688.88	13.40
Putnam	1,282.01	64.40	154.59	7.80	77.75	3.90	55.25	2.80	72.60	3.60	347.89	17.50
St. Johns	4,519.97	79.00	541.56	9.50	63.06	1.10	76.62	1.30	163.44	2.90	355.61	6.20
St. Lucie	5,351.16	69.10	756.46	9.80	167.72	2.20	301.70	3.90	138.63	1.80	1,032.37	13.30
Santa Rosa	2,847.59	76.00	295.05	7.90	40.40	1.10	102.74	2.70	88.99	2.40	370.84	9.90
Sarasota	15,963.54	78.10	2,403.62	11.80	445.21	2.20	51.65	0.30	586.77	2.90	988.59	4.80
Seminole	9,936.71	75.40	2,057.76	15.60	465.80	3.50	25.44	0.20	240.34	1.80	446.27	3.40
Sumter	499.70	60.80	83.54	10.20	16.94	2.10	107.02	13.00	4.92	0.60	109.95	13.40
Suwannee	352.12	51.90	50.98	7.50	12.59	1.90	155.56	22.90	28.03	4.10	79.47	11.70
Taylor	247.18	44.90	51.61	9.40	59.30	10.80	95.95	17.40	19.87	3.60	76.56	13.90
Union	50.26	26.20	5.97	3.10	3.44	1.80	53.53	27.90	4.23	2.20	74.35	38.80
Volusia	11,623.79	73.80	2,080.07	13.20	355.80	2.30	139.28	0.90	518.59	3.30	1,038.09	6.60
Wakulla	288.08	51.70	23.87	4.30	8.69	1.60	37.53	6.70	7.18	1.30	192.12	34.50
Walton	1,852.93	76.90	134.64	5.60	14.11	0.60	102.52	4.30	40.30	1.70	264.18	11.00
Washington	207.09	48.80	29.82	7.00	12.96	3.10	101.20	23.80	17.43	4.10	56.25	13.20

1/ Includes lease hold interests, utilities, mining, petroleum and gas lands, subsurface rights, right-of-ways, sub-merged lands, sewage disposal, borrow pits, wastelands, outdoor recreational/park lands, and governmental lands.

Source: State of Florida, Department of Revenue, unpublished data. Compiled by Armasi, Inc.

ECONOMIC INDICATORS AND PRICES

Estimates of Gross State Product in Florida, Other Sunbelt States, and Other Populous States, 1994
(millions of current dollars)

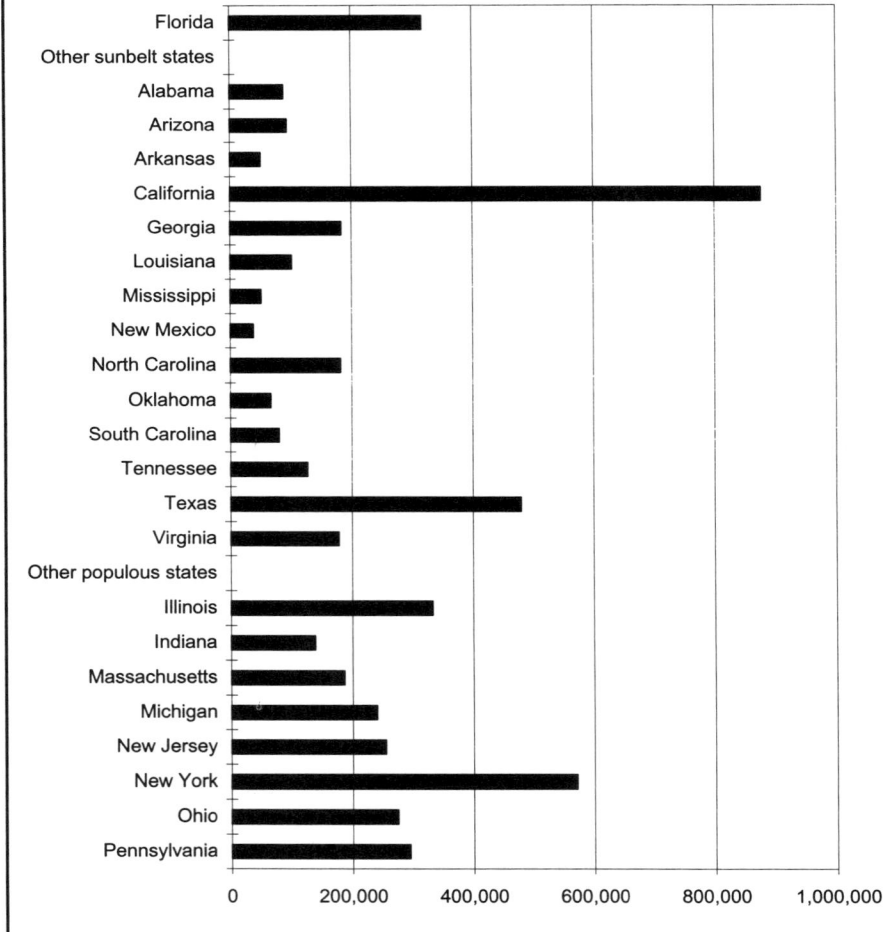

SECTION 24.00
ECONOMIC INDICATORS AND PRICES

TABLES LISTED BY MAJOR HEADINGS

Table 24.12. ECONOMIC INDICATORS: SPECIFIED INDICATORS OF THE FLORIDA ECONOMY
JANUARY 1991 THROUGH DECEMBER 1996

(not adjusted for seasonal variation)

Month and year	Unem- ploy- ment rate	Nonfarm wage and salary employ- ment 1/ (1,000)	Sales and use tax collec- tions 2/	Month and year	Unem- ploy- ment rate	Nonfarm wage and salary employ- ment 1/ (1,000)	Sales and use tax collec- tions 2/
1991				**1994**			
January	6.9	5,301.7	729.8	January	7.3	5,657.6	915.6
February	6.8	5,323.2	651.5	February	6.5	5,724.8	796.5
March	6.8	5,355.3	676.0	March	6.4	5,788.3	841.4
April	7.0	5,316.8	719.4	April	6.4	5,799.2	931.2
May	7.1	5,318.0	676.9	May	6.5	5,801.7	845.3
June	7.8	5,294.5	663.7	June	7.0	5,806.5	825.0
July	7.9	5,193.2	644.7	July	7.2	5,708.6	832.8
August	7.7	5,207.1	651.7	August	6.9	5,713.7	813.0
September	7.8	5,260.0	654.8	September	6.8	5,828.0	825.8
October	7.6	5,271.6	628.8	October	6.3	5,836.3	822.1
November	7.6	5,332.6	655.8	November	6.0	5,947.6	841.7
December	7.7	5,357.5	717.7	December	5.5	5,979.9	913.8
1992				**1995**			
January	8.8	5,277.3	756.2	January	6.2	5,882.0	991.7
February	8.4	5,313.0	685.0	February	5.3	5,956.3	856.1
March	8.1	5,390.9	713.7	March	5.0	6,019.6	898.1
April	8.1	5,357.0	749.4	April	5.1	5,981.6	962.1
May	8.1	5,363.5	707.8	May	5.3	5,996.9	887.5
June	8.9	5,353.4	685.6	June	5.8	6,003.8	906.2
July	9.0	5,267.5	691.9	July	5.9	5,905.1	902.0
August	8.9	5,257.8	709.4	August	5.7	5,910.3	871.1
September	8.8	5,346.0	674.5	September	5.9	6,022.0	878.1
October	7.8	5,398.6	731.5	October	5.5	6,043.3	878.1
November	7.5	5,462.1	771.2	November	5.3	6,113.8	893.9
December	7.0	5,516.8	808.4	December	4.9	6,169.7	993.5
1993				**1996**			
January	7.8	5,434.6	887.7	January	5.7	6,051.3	1,034.9
February	6.9	5,507.6	781.7	February	4.9	6,127.7	936.6
March	6.6	5,558.4	798.3	March	4.7	6,217.6	1,004.7
April	6.7	5,587.3	851.2	April	4.8	6,166.0	1,035.9
May	6.8	5,580.4	808.1	May	4.9	6,189.2	971.0
June	7.4	5,580.9	781.8	June	5.3	6,177.6	963.0
July	7.5	5,492.9	795.8	July	5.4	6,093.5	933.0
August	7.3	5,491.7	781.8	August	5.2	6,095.6	940.7
September	7.2	5,576.2	773.4	September	5.4	6,189.2	945.5
October	7.0	5,625.4	772.7	October	5.0	6,223.2	915.4
November	6.9	5,678.6	784.6	November	4.9	6,299.7	984.9
December	6.5	5,743.2	866.0	December	4.5	6,359.2	1,038.6

1/ Data are for employment covered by unemployment compensation.
2/ Data are in millions, rounded to thousands of dollars.
Note: Some data are revised.

Source: State of Florida, Department of Labor and Employment Security, and State of Florida, Department of Revenue, unpublished data.

University of Florida   **Bureau of Economic and Business Research**

Table 24.14. GROSS STATE PRODUCT: ESTIMATES IN FLORIDA, OTHER SUNBELT STATES
OTHER POPULOUS STATES, AND THE UNITED STATES, SPECIFIED YEARS
1987 THROUGH 1994

(in millions of current dollars)

State	1987	1990	1991	1992	1993	1994
			Sunbelt states			
Florida	205,436	254,993	265,948	279,781	298,452	317,829
Alabama	60,609	71,090	75,008	79,706	82,632	88,661
Arizona	58,909	68,410	70,972	78,449	84,478	94,093
Arkansas	32,252	37,850	40,559	44,214	46,666	50,575
California	620,346	794,397	810,323	826,532	842,068	875,697
Georgia	116,625	140,093	147,205	158,770	170,102	183,042
Louisiana	76,536	91,360	91,897	90,788	94,292	101,101
Mississippi	33,111	37,964	40,066	43,318	46,062	50,587
New Mexico	22,783	26,655	30,222	31,771	34,380	37,832
North Carolina	116,357	143,512	150,114	161,432	169,612	181,521
Oklahoma	48,190	57,048	58,974	61,357	63,949	66,189
South Carolina	53,197	65,434	67,892	71,132	75,060	79,925
Tennessee	81,122	94,218	100,313	109,113	115,341	126,539
Texas	303,157	390,221	404,460	425,824	448,439	479,774
Virginia	120,896	147,998	152,914	160,558	169,431	177,708
			Other populous states			
Illinois	230,030	273,387	281,942	298,370	312,582	332,853
Indiana	91,406	108,769	112,492	120,286	127,398	138,190
Massachusetts	138,973	159,254	160,284	165,805	174,826	186,199
Michigan	166,367	188,397	190,501	202,630	217,082	240,390
New Jersey	175,060	214,799	220,212	231,489	244,767	254,945
New York	420,175	497,547	501,386	525,555	542,833	570,994
Ohio	192,138	226,855	232,355	245,032	256,050	274,844
Pennsylvania	204,910	245,420	255,993	269,359	282,044	294,431
United States	4,651,838	5,661,950	5,837,351	6,135,028	6,430,519	6,835,641

Source: U.S., Department of Commerce, Bureau of Economic Analysis, Economics *and*
Statistics Administration, *News: Gross State Product, New Estimates for 1993-94 and
Revised Estimates for 1977-92.* Release of June 3, 1997.

University of Florida   **Bureau of Economic and Business Research**

Table 24.15. GROSS STATE PRODUCT: ESTIMATES OF GROSS STATE PRODUCT (GSP) BY COMPONENT AND MAJOR INDUSTRIAL GROUP IN FLORIDA, SPECIFIED YEARS 1977 THROUGH 1994

(in millions of dollars)

Item	1977	1982	1987	1991	1992	1993	1994
Components of GSP							
Total	66,189	125,121	205,436	265,948	279,781	298,452	317,829
Compensation	38,223	72,906	119,459	154,146	163,302	173,682	182,606
Indirect business taxes and nontax liability	6,128	10,820	19,193	27,649	29,193	31,046	33,650
Other gross state product	21,838	41,394	66,784	84,153	87,286	93,724	101,574
GSP by major industry							
Farms	1,518	2,682	3,383	3,720	3,802	3,480	3,399
Agriculture forestry, and fisheries	2,135	3,628	5,072	5,985	6,195	6,015	6,134
Mining	546	1,867	847	850	798	692	711
Construction	3,441	7,378	12,430	12,210	12,201	13,477	14,592
Manufacturing	7,060	13,757	21,213	24,123	24,550	25,578	26,612
Durable goods	3,607	8,023	12,615	13,583	14,054	14,431	15,079
Nondurable goods	3,452	5,733	8,598	10,540	10,496	11,147	11,533
Transportation, communications, and public utilities	6,798	12,060	18,614	23,737	24,820	27,542	29,914
Wholesale trade	5,055	8,587	13,471	18,203	19,423	20,596	22,644
Retail trade	7,804	14,014	24,221	29,652	31,104	33,283	35,783
Finance, insurance, and real estate	12,524	25,204	43,483	55,911	59,730	64,289	68,123
Services	10,661	21,765	39,809	58,208	62,988	67,742	72,639
Government	10,165	16,862	26,276	37,068	37,972	39,236	40,677
Federal civilian	1,787	2,938	4,188	5,888	6,228	6,430	6,669
Federal military	1,785	2,955	4,433	5,153	5,269	4,913	4,573
State and local	6,593	10,969	17,655	26,027	26,475	27,894	29,435

Note: Data for earlier years are revised. See Appendix for discussion of Gross State Product (GSP) estimates.

Source: U.S., Department of Commerce, Bureau of Economic Analysis, Regional Economic Information System, CD-ROM, August 1997.

Table 24.20. BUILDING PERMIT ACTIVITY: NUMBER OF PUBLIC AND PRIVATE RESIDENTIAL
HOUSING UNITS AUTHORIZED BY BUILDING PERMITS IN FLORIDA AND
THE UNITED STATES, 1984 THROUGH 1995

Month	1984	1985	1986	1987	1988	1989
Florida						
Annual total 1/	204,925	202,615	195,525	178,764	170,597	164,985
January	15,622	14,750	14,708	15,005	11,786	13,582
February	16,967	13,311	18,168	13,279	12,243	13,404
March	19,856	17,981	15,592	17,625	15,721	14,163
April	17,198	19,752	16,562	16,006	13,935	14,593
May	19,643	18,892	16,043	14,580	14,918	17,165
June	18,187	17,388	18,817	16,843	19,255	17,454
July	16,763	17,196	19,131	15,522	13,523	11,756
August	16,483	15,538	14,278	15,895	15,656	13,657
September	13,882	19,278	15,678	15,541	14,614	12,393
October	14,508	16,660	15,809	13,779	13,578	12,754
November	14,019	13,563	12,282	10,794	13,239	11,483
December	15,703	20,150	14,060	13,077	12,911	11,279
United States						
Annual total	1,664,663	1,733,266	1,769,443	1,534,772	1,455,623	1,338,423

	1990	1991	1992	1993	1994	1995
Florida						
Annual total 1/	126,347	95,308	102,022	115,103	128,602	122,903
January	14,982	7,141	7,103	7,438	11,166	9,940
February	9,318	7,025	6,974	8,604	9,962	8,166
March	12,228	7,485	9,707	9,810	12,164	10,677
April	12,314	8,697	8,870	10,226	11,766	9,686
May	11,836	9,986	8,093	10,893	11,658	10,038
June	12,078	9,773	9,776	11,052	12,077	11,208
July	11,113	9,372	9,853	10,118	11,825	10,101
August	10,667	8,063	8,009	10,119	13,369	10,577
September	8,700	7,246	8,689	11,517	12,136	10,368
October	8,622	7,440	8,972	8,940	11,002	9,266
November	8,592	6,378	7,337	9,333	10,284	9,891
December	6,933	8,458	8,887	12,875	10,483	9,668
United States						
Annual total	1,110,766	948,794	1,094,933	1,199,063	1,371,637	1,332,549

1/ Annual total reflects revisions not distributed to months.
Note: To arrive at state totals, data for metropolitan areas (MSAs and PMSAs)
were taken from reports submitted by all places within these areas. Estimates for
nonmetropolitan areas in Florida and the United States were based on a sample of the
data 16,000 places for 1984, 17,000 places for 1985 through 1993, and 19,000 for 1994
and 1995. Beginning with January 1986, data exclude public housing units. See Glossary for metropolitan area definitions and see map at the front of the book for area
boundaries.

Source: U.S., Department of Commerce, International Trade Administration, *Construction Review, Spring 1996,* and previous editions.

Table 24.30. GROSS AND TAXABLE SALES: SALES REPORTED AND SALES AND USE TAXES
COLLECTED BY THE DEPARTMENT OF REVENUE IN FLORIDA, 1963 THROUGH 1996

(sales and taxes rounded to dollars)

Year	Gross sales	Taxable sales	Net sales taxes paid	Number of reports
1963	16,103,205,516	7,470,457,359	207,577,878	1,375,162
1964	18,243,239,834	8,680,873,802	245,010,164	1,795,111
1965	20,159,138,762	9,306,446,815	270,654,499	1,822,855
1966	22,070,877,464	10,052,183,902	292,635,382	1,848,519
1967	23,523,783,328	10,738,028,301	314,139,054	1,868,644
1968	28,188,063,900	13,361,484,763	467,573,056	2,102,650
1969	33,441,677,220	16,246,816,932	616,919,658	2,324,350
1970	36,834,259,466	18,339,123,013	681,920,445	2,394,366
1971	41,255,223,174	20,272,358,516	784,708,762	2,528,429
1972	49,280,284,464	23,884,881,400	947,086,120	2,508,097
1973	59,294,867,904	28,264,125,745	1,136,864,712	2,495,557
1974	65,887,520,411	29,785,250,309	1,216,071,766	2,689,313
1975	66,764,958,864	29,329,230,180	1,197,020,925	2,845,986
1976	73,791,141,256	32,215,852,176	1,323,271,879	2,962,711
1977	82,783,600,922	36,274,024,296	1,500,074,880	2,788,578
1978	98,227,927,655	43,640,280,027	1,816,192,620	2,844,083
1979	114,373,759,327	50,555,056,774	2,074,119,153	3,005,717
1980	136,318,330,861	58,177,097,809	2,383,348,768	3,177,162
1981	156,619,282,052	66,750,301,522	2,691,772,260	3,214,217
1982	161,796,458,854	66,663,022,175	3,143,878,949	3,451,004
1983	168,492,566,327	73,906,494,761	4,035,324,107	3,632,967
1984	195,758,800,411	84,639,051,288	4,498,315,417	3,735,161
1985	210,089,814,330	89,673,013,371	4,874,199,447	3,887,677
1986	223,601,586,263	98,612,192,144	5,304,286,552	4,249,174
1987	259,753,403,821	113,379,458,921	6,053,620,606	5,054,411
1988	277,485,847,435	119,103,871,758	7,299,532,184	5,115,463
1989	289,076,440,275	122,788,168,387	7,834,635,188	5,101,085
1990	303,464,877,632	127,283,343,961	8,242,720,563	5,177,182
1991	310,147,685,581	126,648,591,209	8,181,744,259	5,505,665
1992	330,770,069,551	135,959,144,438	8,778,486,852	5,747,984
1993	360,267,713,516	150,592,943,893	9,582,751,878	6,091,241
1994	385,110,859,523	159,956,354,846	10,008,966,792	5,837,879
1995	423,309,073,509	171,551,704,651	10,975,746,043	(NA)
1996	451,962,590,686	182,140,968,692	11,461,076,497	5,569,874

Note: These sales were reported to the Department of Revenue for the 5 percent
regular sales tax, the 5 percent use tax, and the 3 percent vehicle and farm equipment sales tax from January to December of each year. The sales occurred, for the
most part, from December of the previous year through November of the posted year.
In February 1988 the regular sales and use tax increased to 6 percent; this increase
is reflected in the collections from March 1988. These data are not comparable with
retail sales figures reported by the Bureau of the Census because of differences in
definitions of retailers and retail sales. At various times, changes in the rate of
the taxes or in the items to be taxed or excluded have been made. Data prior to 1993
are unaudited and are not comparable to later years.

Source: State of Florida, Department of Revenue, unpublished data. Data from 1987
to present are prepared by the University of Florida, Bureau of Economic and Business
Research.

University of Florida   **Bureau of Economic and Business Research**

Table 24.72. CONSUMER AND PRODUCER PRICE INDEXES: ANNUAL AVERAGES AND PERCENTAGE CHANGES FOR ALL URBAN CONSUMERS INDEX AND PRODUCER PRICE INDEX IN THE UNITED STATES, 1979 THROUGH 1996

	Consumer prices 1/					
	All items		Commodities		Services	
Year	Index	Percentage change	Index	Percentage change	Index	Percentage change
1979	72.6	11.3	76.6	11.3	67.5	11.0
1980	82.4	13.5	86.0	12.3	77.9	15.4
1981	90.9	10.3	93.2	8.4	88.1	13.1
1982	96.5	6.2	97.0	4.1	96.0	9.0
1983	99.6	3.2	99.8	2.9	99.4	3.5
1984	103.9	4.3	103.2	3.4	104.6	5.2
1985	107.6	3.6	105.4	2.1	109.9	5.1
1986	109.6	1.9	104.4	-0.9	115.4	5.0
1987	113.6	3.6	107.7	3.2	120.2	4.2
1988	118.3	4.1	111.5	3.5	125.7	4.6
1989	124.0	4.8	116.7	4.7	131.9	4.9
1990	130.7	5.4	122.8	5.2	139.2	5.5
1991	136.2	4.2	126.6	3.1	146.3	5.1
1992	140.3	3.0	129.1	2.0	152.0	3.9
1993	144.5	3.0	131.5	1.9	157.9	3.9
1994	148.2	2.6	133.8	1.7	163.1	3.3
1995	152.4	2.8	136.4	1.9	168.7	3.4
1996	156.9	3.0	139.9	2.6	174.1	3.2

	Producer prices 2/					
	All commodities		Farm products		Industrial commodities	
Year	Index	Percentage change	Index	Percentage change	Index	Percentage change
1979	78.7	12.6	99.6	13.6	75.7	12.8
1980	89.8	14.1	102.9	3.3	88.0	16.2
1981	98.0	9.1	105.2	2.2	97.4	10.7
1982	100.0	2.0	100.0	-4.9	100.0	2.7
1983	101.3	1.3	102.4	2.4	101.1	1.1
1984	103.7	2.4	105.5	3.0	103.3	2.2
1985	103.1	-0.6	95.1	-9.9	103.7	0.4
1986	100.2	-2.8	92.9	-2.3	99.9	-3.7
1987	102.8	2.6	95.5	2.8	102.6	2.7
1988	106.9	4.0	104.9	9.8	106.3	3.6
1989	112.2	5.0	110.9	5.7	111.6	5.0
1990	116.3	3.7	112.2	1.2	115.8	3.8
1991	116.5	0.2	105.7	-5.8	116.5	0.6
1992	117.2	0.6	103.6	-2.0	117.4	0.8
1993	118.9	1.5	107.1	3.4	119.0	1.4
1994	120.4	1.3	106.3	-0.7	120.7	1.4
1995	124.7	3.6	107.4	1.0	125.5	4.0
1996	127.6	2.3	122.3	13.9	127.2	1.4

1/ 1982-84 = 100.
2/ 1982 = 100.
Note: See Appendix for discussion of consumer and producer price indexes.

Source: U.S., Department of Labor, Bureau of Labor Statistics, *CPI Detailed Report*, January 1997, and Internet site http://stats.bls.gov:80/.

Table 24.73. CONSUMER PRICE INDEXES: INDEXES BY COMMODITY IN THE UNITED STATES
1995 AND 1996

(1982-84 = 100, except where indicated)

Index expenditure category and commodity	Relative importance December 1996	Annual average index 1995	Annual average index 1996	Percentage change 1995 to 1996
Wage earners and clerical workers index (CPI-W), all items	100.0	149.8	154.1	2.9
All urban consumers index (CPI-U), all items	100.0	152.4	156.9	3.0
Food and beverages	17.5	148.9	153.7	3.2
Food	15.9	148.4	153.3	3.3
Food at home	10.0	148.8	154.3	3.7
Cereals and bakery products	1.5	167.5	174.0	3.9
Meats, poultry, fish, and eggs	3.0	138.8	144.8	4.3
Dairy products 1/	1.2	132.8	142.1	7.0
Fruits and vegetables	2.0	177.7	183.9	3.5
Other food at home	2.3	140.8	142.9	1.5
Sugar and sweets	0.3	137.5	143.7	4.5
Fats and oils	0.2	137.3	140.5	2.3
Nonalcoholic beverages	0.7	131.7	128.6	-2.4
Other prepared food	1.0	151.1	156.2	3.4
Food away from home	5.9	149.0	152.7	2.5
Alcoholic beverages	1.6	153.9	158.5	3.0
Housing	41.2	148.5	152.8	2.9
Shelter	28.2	165.7	171.0	3.2
Renters' costs 2/	8.0	174.3	180.2	3.4
Rent, residential	5.7	157.8	162.0	2.7
Other renters' costs	2.3	204.3	214.7	5.1
Homeowners' costs 2/	20.0	171.0	176.5	3.2
Owners' equivalent rent 2/	19.6	171.3	176.8	3.2
Household insurance 2/	0.4	157.4	161.0	2.3
Maintenance and repairs 1/	0.2	135.0	139.0	3.0
Maintenance and repair services 1/	0.1	139.8	145.5	4.1
Maintenance and repair commodities 1/	0.1	128.5	130.2	1.3
Fuel and other utilities	7.1	123.7	127.5	3.1
Fuels	3.9	111.5	115.2	3.3
Fuel oil and other household fuel commodities	0.4	88.1	99.2	12.6
Gas (piped) and electricity	3.5	119.2	122.1	2.4
Other utilities and public services	3.2	152.8	157.2	2.9
Household furnishings and operation	5.9	123.0	124.7	1.4
Housefurnishings	3.3	111.2	111.3	0.1
Housekeeping supplies	1.1	137.1	141.1	2.9
Housekeeping services 3/	1.5	143.7	148.0	3.0
Apparel and upkeep	5.3	132.0	131.7	-0.2
Apparel commodities	4.8	128.7	128.2	-0.4
Men's and boys' apparel	1.3	126.2	127.7	1.2
Women's and girls' apparel	2.1	126.9	124.7	-1.7
Infants' and toddlers' apparel 1/	0.2	127.2	129.7	2.0
Footwear	0.7	125.4	126.6	1.0
Other apparel commodities	0.5	152.4	150.6	-1.2
Apparel services 1/ 4/	0.5	157.3	159.8	1.6

See footnotes at end of table.   Continued . . .

Table 24.73. CONSUMER PRICE INDEXES: INDEXES BY COMMODITY IN THE UNITED STATES
1995 AND 1996 (Continued)

(1982-84 = 100, except where indicated)

Index expenditure category and commodity	Relative importance December 1996	Annual average index 1995	1996	Percentage change 1995 to 1996
All urban consumers index (CPI-U) (Continued)				
Transportation	17.1	139.1	143.0	2.8
Private transportation	15.5	136.3	140.0	2.7
New vehicles	5.0	141.0	143.7	1.9
New cars	4.0	139.0	141.4	1.7
Used Cars	1.3	156.5	157.0	0.3
Motor fuel	3.2	100.0	106.3	6.3
Gasoline	(NA)	99.8	105.9	6.1
Maintenance and repair	1.5	154.0	158.4	2.9
Other private transportation	4.6	170.6	173.9	1.9
Other private transportation commodities 5/	0.6	104.8	105.1	0.3
Other private transportation services 6/	4.0	186.0	190.1	2.2
Public transportation	1.6	175.9	181.9	3.4
Medical care	7.3	220.5	228.2	3.5
Medical care commodities	1.3	204.5	210.4	2.9
Medical care services 7/	6.1	224.2	232.4	3.7
Professional medical services	3.5	201.0	208.3	3.6
Entertainment 8/	4.4	153.9	159.1	3.4
Entertainment commodities	2.0	138.7	143.0	3.1
Entertainment services	2.4	172.0	178.1	3.5
Other goods and services	7.1	206.9	215.4	4.1
Tobacco and smoking products	1.6	225.7	232.8	3.1
Personal care 1/	1.1	147.1	150.1	2.0
Toilet goods and personal care appliances 1/	0.6	143.1	144.3	0.8
Personal care services 1/	0.6	151.5	156.6	3.4
Personal and educational expenses	4.4	235.5	247.5	5.1
School books and supplies	0.3	214.4	226.9	5.8
Personal and educational services	4.1	237.3	249.3	5.1
Commodity and service group, all items	100.0	152.4	156.9	3.0
Commodities	42.9	136.4	139.9	2.6
Food and beverages	17.5	148.9	153.7	3.2
Commodities less food and beverages	25.4	128.9	131.5	2.0
Nondurables less food and beverages	15.1	129.5	133.0	2.7
Apparel commodities	4.8	128.7	128.2	-0.4
Nondurables less food, beverages, and apparel	10.4	132.9	138.6	4.3
Durables	10.2	128.0	129.4	1.1
Services	57.1	168.7	174.1	3.2
Rent of shelter 2/	27.6	172.4	178.0	3.2
Household services less rent of shelter 2/	8.7	138.3	142.0	2.7
Transportation services	7.1	175.9	180.5	2.6
Medical care services	6.1	224.2	232.4	3.7
Other services	7.6	193.3	201.4	4.2

See footnotes at end of table.   Continued . . .

Table 24.73.   CONSUMER PRICE INDEXES: INDEXES BY COMMODITY IN THE UNITED STATES
1995 AND 1996 (Continued)

(1982-84 = 100, except where indicated)

Index expenditure category and commodity	Relative impor- tance December 1996	Annual average index 1995	Annual average index 1996	Per- centage change 1995 to 1996
Special indexes				
All items less food	84.1	153.1	157.5	2.9
All items less shelter	71.8	148.6	152.8	2.8
All items less homeowners' costs 2/	80.0	153.5	157.9	2.9
All items less medical care	92.7	148.6	152.8	2.8
Commodities less food	27.0	129.8	132.6	2.2
Nondurables less food	16.7	130.9	134.5	2.8
Nondurables less food and apparel	11.9	134.1	139.5	4.0
Nondurables	32.6	139.3	143.5	3.0
Services less rent of shelter 2/	29.6	176.8	182.5	3.2
Services less medical care	51.1	163.5	168.7	3.2
Energy	7.0	105.2	110.1	4.7
All items less energy	93.0	158.7	163.1	2.8
All items less food and energy	77.0	161.2	165.6	2.7
Commodities less food and energy	23.4	139.3	141.3	1.4
Energy commodities	3.6	98.8	105.7	7.0
Services less energy	53.7	173.7	179.4	3.3
Purchasing power of the consumer dollar (1982-84=$1.00; data in dollars)	(NA)	0.656	0.638	-2.7

(NA) Not available.
1/ Not seasonally adjusted.
2/ Indexes on a December 1982 = 100 base.
3/ Includes postage, moving and storage, household laundry and dry cleaning services, and appliance and furniture repair.
4/ Apparel laundry and dry cleaning services.
5/ Includes motor oil, coolants, tires, and auto parts.
6/ Includes insurance, finance charges, registration and license fees, and auto
rental.
7/ Includes professional services and hospital charges.
8/ Includes newspapers, magazines, books, sporting goods and equipment, toys, hob-
bies, music and photographic equipment, and pet supplies; also fees and admission to
sporting events and other entertainment.
Note: See Appendix for explanation of CPI-W and CPI-U.

Source: U.S., Department of Labor, Bureau of Labor Statistics, *CPI Detailed Re-*
port, January 1997.

University of Florida   **Bureau of Economic and Business Research**

Table 24.74. CONSUMER PRICE INDEXES: INDEXES FOR ALL URBAN CONSUMERS BY CATEGORY
AND COMMODITY IN MIAMI-FT. LAUDERDALE AND TAMPA-ST. PETERSBURG-CLEARWATER
FLORIDA, ANNUAL AVERAGE, 1996, AND MIAMI-FT. LAUDERDALE, FLORIDA
JANUARY 1995, 1996, AND 1997

(1982-84 = 100, except where indicated)

Expenditure category and commodity	Annual average			
	Miami-Ft. Lauderdale		Tampa-St. Petersburg-Clearwater 1/	
	1996	Percentage change 1995 to 1996	1996	Percentage change 1995 to 1996
All items	153.7	3.2	131.6	1.5
Food and beverages	161.4	2.7	129.1	2.9
Food	161.4	2.7	128.3	2.6
Food at home	159.3	3.5	127.9	3.1
Cereals and bakery products	162.2	5.1	146.0	7.2
Meats, poultry, fish, and eggs	142.0	4.3	121.8	-0.7
Meats, poultry, and fish	143.4	4.0	121.1	-1.3
Dairy products	147.8	8.2	129.4	10.9
Fruits and vegetables	231.3	1.6	140.1	1.6
Other foods at home	133.7	0.8	119.4	4.7
Food away from home	166.6	2.1	128.7	2.7
Alcoholic beverages	158.8	3.3	134.9	4.3
Housing	145.1	3.7	126.6	2.3
Shelter	153.6	3.2	134.3	2.9
Renters' costs 2/	156.3	3.0	121.7	2.9
Rent, residential	145.6	3.2	129.1	2.3
Other renters' costs	215.2	2.7	99.5	5.3
Homeowners' costs 2/	158.0	3.3	139.1	2.9
Owners' equivalent rent 2/	155.6	3.0	139.4	3.0
Fuel and other utilities	118.2	4.5	118.2	1.5
Fuels	109.7	4.3	110.5	-0.2
Fuel oil and other household fuel commodities	159.0	2.6	118.4	1.8
Gas (piped) and electricity	108.9	4.3	110.1	-0.4
Household furnishings and operation	140.4	5.1	112.3	0.9
Apparel and upkeep	146.0	-0.7	115.1	-14.2
Apparel commodities	137.8	-1.4	113.0	-15.4
Men's and boys' apparel	137.7	-2.3	121.9	2.3
Women's and girls' apparel	147.0	-2.3	110.9	-25.0
Footwear	139.5	0.9	95.9	4.1
Transportation	144.3	3.2	127.3	1.9
Private transportation	144.1	3.4	128.9	2.6
Public transportation	143.6	-0.4	105.2	-9.2
Medical care	214.4	5.6	188.7	4.0
Entertainment	146.1	4.1	121.9	4.9
Other goods and services	175.0	3.1	156.1	5.8
Personal care	100.0	-4.2	160.4	8.9

See footnotes at end of table.   Continued . . .

Table 24.74. CONSUMER PRICE INDEXES: INDEXES FOR ALL URBAN CONSUMERS BY CATEGORY
AND COMMODITY IN MIAMI-FT. LAUDERDALE AND TAMPA-ST. PETERSBURG-CLEARWATER
FLORIDA, ANNUAL AVERAGE, 1996, AND MIAMI-FT. LAUDERDALE, FLORIDA
JANUARY 1995, 1996, AND 1997 (Continued)

(1982-84 = 100, except where indicated)

Expenditure category and commodity	Miami-Ft. Lauderdale			Percentage change 1996 to 1997
	January			
	1995	1996	1997	
All items	147.3	152.0	158.1	4.0
Food and beverages	156.2	158.9	163.9	3.1
Food	156.2	158.8	164.1	3.3
Food at home	154.5	156.0	161.7	3.7
Cereals and bakery products	154.2	155.9	170.4	9.3
Meats, poultry, fish, and eggs	131.4	143.3	148.7	3.8
Meats, poultry, and fish	133.2	144.7	150.2	3.8
Dairy products	140.1	141.8	148.4	4.7
Fruits and vegetables	237.2	223.1	227.4	1.9
Other foods at home	132.7	130.8	132.7	1.5
Food away from home	160.9	164.7	169.5	2.9
Alcoholic beverages	153.6	157.2	160.1	1.8
Housing	138.5	143.8	149.7	4.1
Shelter	146.9	153.0	157.5	2.9
Renters' costs 2/	152.2	156.6	163.8	4.6
Rent, residential	139.4	143.8	147.7	2.7
Other renters' costs	223.1	227.4	254.4	11.9
Homeowners' costs 2/	150.0	157.2	160.4	2.0
Owners' equivalent rent 2/	148.3	154.8	157.3	1.6
Fuel and other utilities	112.6	116.8	121.2	3.8
Fuels	104.0	109.0	112.8	3.5
Fuel oil and other household fuel commodities	154.6	158.8	173.0	8.9
Gas (piped) and electricity	103.1	108.2	111.7	3.2
Household furnishings and operation	133.4	136.8	149.6	9.4
Apparel and upkeep	148.2	149.8	163.0	8.8
Apparel commodities	141.1	142.2	156.1	9.8
Men's and boys' apparel	141.6	141.5	136.9	-3.3
Women's and girls' apparel	150.9	155.0	194.6	25.5
Footwear	148.3	139.0	149.0	7.2
Transportation	138.0	141.4	146.8	3.8
Private transportation	137.7	140.8	147.0	4.4
Public transportation	138.0	146.7	141.5	-3.5
Medical care	196.6	212.8	215.1	1.1
Entertainment	140.5	142.5	155.1	8.8
Other goods and services	166.5	173.2	177.9	2.7
Personal care	104.5	101.0	101.8	0.8

1/ Indexes are on a 1987 = 100 base.
2/ Indexes on a November 1982 = 100 base for Miami-Ft. Lauderdale.
Note: The Miami-Ft. Lauderdale and Tampa-St. Petersburg-Clearwater areas are two
of several metropolitan areas for which a consumer price index is issued bimonthly.

Source: U.S., Department of Labor, Bureau of Labor Statistics, *CPI Detailed Report*, January 1997.

University of Florida   **Bureau of Economic and Business Research**

Table 24.75. PRODUCER PRICE INDEXES: INDEXES BY STAGE OF PROCESSING, BY DURABILITY
OF PRODUCT, AND BY COMMODITY IN THE UNITED STATES, ANNUAL AVERAGES
1994, 1995, AND 1996, AND JUNE 1997

(1982 = 100, not seasonally adjusted)

| Item | Annual average | | | June |
	1994	1995	1996	1997
All commodities	120.4	124.7	127.6	127.2
By stage of processing				
Crude materials for further processing	101.8	102.7	113.5	107.2
Intermediate materials, supplies, etc.	118.5	124.9	125.7	125.7
Finished goods 1/	125.5	127.9	131.3	131.6
Finished consumer goods	123.3	125.6	129.5	130.1
Capital equipment	134.1	136.7	138.3	138.1
By durability of product				
Durable goods	130.0	133.9	133.7	134.1
Nondurable goods	113.6	118.1	123.0	122.1
Manufactures, total	123.8	128.9	130.5	130.6
Durable manufactures	129.6	133.2	133.3	133.6
Nondurable manufactures	118.2	124.6	127.4	127.3
Farm products, processed foods and feeds				
Farm products	106.3	107.4	122.3	111.7
Foods and feeds, processed	125.5	127.0	133.4	134.4
Industrial commodities				
Chemical and allied products	132.1	142.5	142.1	143.7
Fuels and related products and power	77.8	78.0	85.6	84.4
Furniture and household durables	126.1	128.2	130.3	131.1
Hides, skins, and leather products	148.5	153.7	150.3	154.6
Lumber and wood products	180.0	178.1	176.1	185.2
Machinery and equipment	125.1	126.6	126.5	125.9
Metals and metal products	124.8	134.5	131.0	132.7
Nonmetallic mineral products	124.2	129.0	131.0	133.4
Pulp, paper, and allied products	152.5	172.2	168.6	166.4
Rubber and plastics products	117.6	124.3	123.8	123.0
Textile products and apparel	118.3	120.8	122.4	122.6
Transportation equipment 1/	137.2	139.7	141.7	141.2
Motor vehicles and equipment	131.4	133.0	134.1	132.4

1/ Includes data for items not shown separately.
Note: See Appendix for discussion of producer price indexes.

Source: U.S., Department of Labor, Bureau of Labor Statistics, Internet site
http://stats.bls.gov/.

Table 24.76. ENERGY PRICES: NATURAL GAS, ELECTRICITY, FUEL OIL, AND GASOLINE PRICES, U.S. CITY AVERAGE AND MIAMI-FT. LAUDERDALE, FLORIDA JUNE 1996 THROUGH MAY 1997

(amounts in dollars)

Month and year	Piped gas per 40 therms U.S. city average	Piped gas per 40 therms Miami-Ft. Lauderdale	Electricity per 500 kilowatt-hours U.S. city average	Electricity per 500 kilowatt-hours Miami-Ft. Lauderdale	#2 fuel oil per gallon-- U.S. city average	All types gasoline per gallon U.S. city average	All types gasoline per gallon Miami-Ft. Lauderdale
1996							
June	30.614	45.908	49.178	43.886	0.969	1.354	1.391
July	30.641	45.500	50.483	43.886	0.935	1.328	1.372
August	30.571	45.500	50.753	43.886	0.934	1.298	1.361
September	30.539	45.500	50.789	43.886	0.980	1.293	1.359
October	30.092	45.330	49.913	45.791	1.063	1.287	1.356
November	30.676	45.635	49.181	45.791	1.097	1.308	1.378
December	31.438	46.261	49.231	45.791	1.121	1.318	1.380
1997							
January	32.904	46.261	49.245	45.791	1.136	1.318	1.377
February	32.974	46.794	49.434	45.791	1.127	1.312	1.368
March	31.587	47.067	49.516	45.791	1.079	1.293	1.357
April	30.512	46.867	49.271	45.446	1.046	1.288	1.347
May	30.383	46.867	49.399	45.446	1.031	1.284	1.329

Source: U.S., Department of Labor, Bureau of Labor Statistics, *CPI Detailed Report*, monthly releases.

Table 24.77. ELECTRICITY PRICES: COST PER KILOWATT-HOUR OF ELECTRICITY BY CLASS OF SERVICE OF THE FLORIDA ELECTRIC UTILITY INDUSTRY, 1983 THROUGH 1995

(in cents)

Year	Total	Resi-dential	Com-mercial	Indus-trial	Other public author-ities
1983	6.98	7.69	5.95	6.71	7.37
1984	7.91	8.81	7.00	6.79	9.85
1985	7.63	8.42	7.38	6.02	7.22
1986	7.23	7.98	6.83	5.74	7.06
1987	7.06	7.91	6.45	5.03	10.34
1988	7.04	7.80	6.71	5.31	6.81
1989	7.05	7.74	6.58	5.51	8.20
1990	7.03	7.77	6.82	5.10	6.92
1991	7.15	7.89	6.88	5.29	6.95
1992	6.90	7.75	6.41	5.36	6.59
1993	7.21	7.99	6.43	6.18	7.37
1994	6.95	7.78	6.33	5.56	6.43
1995	7.04	7.76	6.42	5.42	9.06

Note: Cost by class of service is defined as revenue by class of service/kilowatt-hour consumption by class of service. Some data are revised.
Source: State of Florida, Public Service Commission, Division of Research and Regulatory Review, *Statistics of the Florida Electric Utility Industry, 1995*.

Table 24.78. INDUSTRIAL AND COMMERCIAL FAILURES: NUMBER IN FLORIDA AND NUMBER
AND LIABILITIES IN THE UNITED STATES, 1990 THROUGH 1995

	Florida		United States		
					Failures
	Business	Fail-	Business	Num-	Current li-abilities 2/
Year	starts	ures 1/	starts	ber 1/	$1,000,000)
1990	(NA)	3,655	158,930	60,747	56,130
1991	(NA)	5,229	155,672	88,140	96,825
1992	(NA)	5,375	164,086	97,069	94,318
1993	(NA)	5,091	166,154	86,133	47,755
1994	13,997	3,609	188,387	71,558	28,978
1995	12,344	2,906	168,158	71,194	37,507

(NA) Not available.
1/ Includes firms discontinuing following assignment, voluntary or involuntary pe-
tition in bankruptcy, attachment, execution, foreclosure, etc.; voluntary withdrawals
from business with known loss to creditors; also enterprises involved in court action,
such as receivership and reorganization or arrangement which may or may not lead to
discontinuance; and business making voluntary compromise with creditors out of court.
2/ Liabilities exclude long-term publicly held obligations; offsetting assets are
not taken into account.
Note: Some data are revised.
Source: Dun & Bradstreet Corporation, New York, NY, *New Business Incorporations,*
monthly, and *Business Failure Report*, annual, (copyright).

Table 24.79. PRICE LEVEL INDEX: RELATIVE WEIGHTS ASSIGNED TO SELECTED ITEMS
PRICED FOR THE FLORIDA PRICE LEVEL INDEX, 1996

Item	Number of items	Weight	Item	Number of items	Weight
Apparel	17	6.460	Housing	28	38.236
Women's shirtwaist dress		1.010	Apartment rent,		
Food	32	21.860	monthly		4.144
Beer		1.542	Electricity		
Cup of coffee		1.475	500 kilowatt-hours		1.531
Ground Chuck		1.030	1,000 kilowatt-hours		1.531
Soft drink, served		1.475	Hotel-motel rate 1/		1.386
Wine		1.001	House purchase price		19.165
Health, recreation, and			Property Taxes		1.008
personal services	25	15.541	Transportation	14	17.903
College tuition 1/		2.314	Auto insurance		
Extraction		1.130	Liability		1.276
Dental filling		1.130	Physical damage		1.276
Hospital lab fee		1.202	Auto repair charge		1.155
Movie rental		1.316	Chevrolet Cavalier 1/		3.988
Safety deposit box			Ford Escort 1/		3.988
fee		1.242	Gasoline, unleaded		
Semi-private room			self-service		3.266
rate		1.168	Nonlocal travel 1/		1.046

1/ Constant price for all counties.
Note: Items weighted one percent or more are included. See also note on Table
24.80 and discussion under this section in the Appendix.
Source: State of Florida, Department of Education, Office of Education Budget and
Management, *The 1996 Florida Price Level Index.*

University of Florida   **Bureau of Economic and Business Research**

Table 24.80. PRICE LEVEL INDEX: TOTAL INDEX AND INDEXES OF PRICES OF MAJOR ITEMS
IN THE COUNTIES OF FLORIDA, 1996

(population-weighted state average = 100)

County	Florida Price Level Index - Index	Rank among coun-ties	Food	Housing	Apparel	Transpor-tation	Health recrea-tion, and personal services
Alachua	97.04	17	101.98	92.05	103.58	97.27	98.45
Baker	91.92	53	102.68	83.54	91.03	97.93	89.38
Bay	95.28	30	105.09	89.57	93.64	95.60	94.60
Bradford	92.13	51	95.51	85.97	93.07	96.95	95.62
Brevard	96.67	22	96.73	96.94	88.12	97.50	98.56
Broward	105.42	3	102.96	108.50	108.62	102.22	104.15
Calhoun	90.93	62	98.92	81.38	92.33	98.26	92.61
Charlotte	96.59	23	98.75	90.66	99.29	96.84	105.70
Citrus	91.71	56	96.36	87.06	91.08	95.90	91.27
Clay	94.99	31	95.40	90.90	99.59	96.74	99.93
Collier	101.00	6	103.43	104.76	103.84	98.44	90.55
Columbia	90.86	63	100.73	81.64	89.73	97.33	91.08
Dade	107.13	2	101.84	111.71	105.26	107.92	104.11
De Soto	91.57	57	94.78	84.39	89.92	98.50	96.41
Dixie	90.82	64	93.57	84.48	95.86	95.72	93.90
Duval	95.91	26	97.11	93.33	98.40	97.13	97.73
Escambia	93.83	38	93.99	89.16	94.64	97.71	99.66
Flagler	94.53	35	98.22	91.45	89.47	96.53	96.13
Franklin	95.67	27	103.09	91.01	96.46	97.58	93.24
Gadsden	94.29	36	98.60	86.17	96.38	96.84	103.01
Gilchrist	92.08	52	99.02	82.89	98.57	97.22	94.80
Glades	97.92	14	98.40	94.82	95.66	99.94	103.03
Gulf	93.46	42	99.62	84.91	104.11	98.92	93.74
Hamilton	92.49	50	102.72	81.90	92.13	98.81	95.22
Hardee	91.43	59	96.06	84.19	91.73	98.52	93.35
Hendry	96.21	25	99.34	91.68	92.97	97.77	101.69
Hernando	93.56	40	95.19	88.94	96.33	96.64	97.22
Highlands	93.12	46	100.32	85.58	92.26	97.05	96.04
Hillsborough	100.82	8	97.94	102.85	101.40	100.27	100.67
Holmes	91.40	60	101.42	79.65	91.48	98.98	95.45
Indian River	98.55	12	101.24	96.88	91.61	98.51	101.40
Jackson	90.82	64	99.49	83.54	93.67	96.60	87.46
Jefferson	94.87	33	99.12	85.74	101.63	99.55	101.72
Lafayette	91.47	58	101.11	83.65	92.83	96.32	89.57
Lake	95.45	29	99.41	94.42	91.78	96.46	92.48
Lee	97.49	15	95.83	97.01	97.08	98.66	99.83
Leon	96.79	20	98.01	91.48	102.09	98.41	103.25
Levy	91.74	55	96.95	85.53	94.40	96.42	92.19

See footnote at end of table.   Continued . . .

Table 24.80. PRICE LEVEL INDEX: TOTAL INDEX AND INDEXES OF PRICES OF MAJOR ITEMS IN THE COUNTIES OF FLORIDA, 1996 (Continued)

(population-weighted state average = 100)

County	Florida Price Level Index — Index	Florida Price Level Index — Rank among counties	Food	Housing	Apparel	Transportation	Health recreation, and personal services
Liberty	93.25	44	104.25	82.66	94.96	95.93	98.05
Madison	92.66	47	98.74	82.87	97.51	99.27	97.03
Manatee	98.88	11	102.95	98.90	93.50	96.19	98.21
Marion	92.56	49	101.75	85.95	88.37	96.17	92.18
Martin	100.00	9	98.62	102.20	101.78	98.81	97.49
Monroe	108.40	1	101.33	121.67	107.27	99.58	98.45
Nassau	93.23	45	100.53	91.07	94.45	96.23	83.86
Okaloosa	96.26	24	98.74	91.74	104.19	96.96	98.99
Okeechobee	94.22	37	94.15	87.33	97.19	99.55	103.00
Orange	99.42	10	99.91	99.03	98.30	98.67	100.90
Osceola	97.03	18	101.50	93.68	96.51	97.29	98.20
Palm Beach	104.00	4	98.57	105.84	107.40	102.09	108.30
Pasco	94.54	34	95.29	88.03	94.08	98.71	103.93
Pinellas	100.91	7	102.58	105.08	101.80	98.07	91.75
Polk	96.68	21	101.02	93.99	97.87	97.29	95.46
Putnam	91.78	54	98.45	88.26	79.50	95.39	91.32
St. Johns	97.00	19	100.16	96.57	86.82	97.80	96.74
St. Lucie	95.51	28	100.42	90.63	94.47	97.58	97.75
Santa Rosa	92.60	48	96.32	88.94	80.56	95.79	97.05
Sarasota	102.98	5	101.86	104.57	115.23	96.01	103.64
Seminole	98.09	13	98.84	95.87	92.65	99.02	103.32
Sumter	91.29	61	95.34	86.18	82.67	95.88	95.61
Suwannee	90.57	66	94.27	83.42	90.41	97.60	93.92
Taylor	93.72	39	102.57	84.39	96.23	98.67	95.88
Union	93.45	43	100.04	84.75	97.48	99.24	95.80
Volusia	97.30	16	104.02	95.51	89.25	98.01	94.27
Wakulla	94.94	32	99.42	87.45	95.96	97.59	102.31
Walton	93.55	41	98.49	89.99	86.85	95.88	94.78
Washington	89.03	67	95.50	81.11	85.67	96.52	90.96

Note: The Florida Price Level Index is a set of numbers which reflects the price level in each county relative to population-weighted statewide average (100 for each category) for a particular point in time, 1996. It measures price level differences from place to place in contrast to the consumer price index prepared by the U.S. Bureau of Labor Statistics, which measures price level changes from month to month. The basis for these comparisons is one of fixed standard of living which represents the consumption pattern of a typical wage earner or clerical worker. The index measures in each county the relative cost of living by this standard. See Table 24.79 for relative weights of items priced.

Source: State of Florida, Department of Education, Office of Education Budget and Management, *The 1996 Florida Price Level Index.*

Table 24.85. CONSUMER CONFIDENCE INDEX: TOTAL INDEX AND COMPONENTS OF THE FLORIDA CONSUMER CONFIDENCE INDEX BY MONTH, JULY 1994 THROUGH JUNE 1997

(1966 = 100)

Year	Month	Index 1/	Current personal 2/	Future personal 3/	U.S. one year 4/	U.S. five years 5/	House-hold purchases 6/
1994	7	87.00	85.00	100.00	79.00	67.00	105.00
	8	87.00	81.00	97.00	80.00	69.00	109.00
	9	88.00	84.00	98.00	81.00	67.00	111.00
	10	90.00	82.00	99.00	86.00	75.00	110.00
	11	93.00	84.00	100.00	92.00	77.00	110.00
	12	91.00	82.00	100.00	86.00	75.00	110.00
1995	1	94.00	85.00	102.00	93.00	79.00	110.00
	2	93.00	88.00	103.00	89.00	76.00	109.00
	3	91.00	86.00	103.00	85.00	72.00	109.00
	4	90.00	81.00	99.00	87.00	72.00	111.00
	5	88.00	87.00	96.00	79.00	66.00	111.00
	6	91.00	91.00	102.00	82.00	67.00	113.00
	7	91.00	88.00	101.00	89.00	68.00	111.00
	8	92.00	87.00	103.00	88.00	68.00	113.00
	9	92.00	88.00	99.00	88.00	70.00	114.00
	10	90.00	86.00	100.00	85.00	67.00	110.00
	11	89.00	86.00	99.00	87.00	70.00	105.00
	12	87.00	87.00	98.00	84.00	68.00	98.00
1996	1	88.00	91.00	102.00	81.00	68.00	100.00
	2	89.00	89.00	99.00	85.00	67.00	106.00
	3	91.00	87.00	99.00	86.00	71.00	112.00
	4	91.00	88.00	102.00	84.00	71.00	111.00
	5	88.00	86.00	100.00	84.00	71.00	102.00
	6	90.00	89.00	102.00	84.00	69.00	104.00
	7	91.00	86.00	100.00	85.00	72.00	109.00
	8	91.00	85.00	103.00	87.00	73.00	109.00
	9	92.00	83.00	101.00	91.00	76.00	107.00
	10	94.00	87.00	102.00	91.00	78.00	111.00
	11	93.00	87.00	100.00	94.00	78.00	107.00
	12	92.00	82.00	102.00	94.00	77.00	104.00
1997	1	95.00	89.00	102.00	98.00	75.00	111.00
	2	96.00	88.00	104.00	100.00	80.00	110.00
	3	97.00	95.00	102.00	94.00	79.00	112.00
	4	95.00	89.00	102.00	92.00	79.00	113.00
	5	97.00	90.00	101.00	100.00	80.00	114.00
	6	99.00	95.00	106.00	103.00	79.00	112.00

1/ Based on a monthly telephone survey of approximately 1,000 randomly selected Florida households. Compiled from survey responses giving views of personal financial and general business conditions.

2/ Personal financial conditions at time of survey as compared to previous year.

3/ Personal financial conditions anticipated a year from time of survey.

4/ U.S. business conditions anticipated a year from time of survey.

5/ U.S. business conditions anticipated five years from time of survey.

6/ Perception that the time of survey is a good time to buy major household items.

Source: University of Florida, Bureau of Economic and Business Research, Survey Program, *Florida Economic and Consumer Survey,* July 1997.

University of Florida   **Bureau of Economic and Business Research**

STATE
COMPARISONS

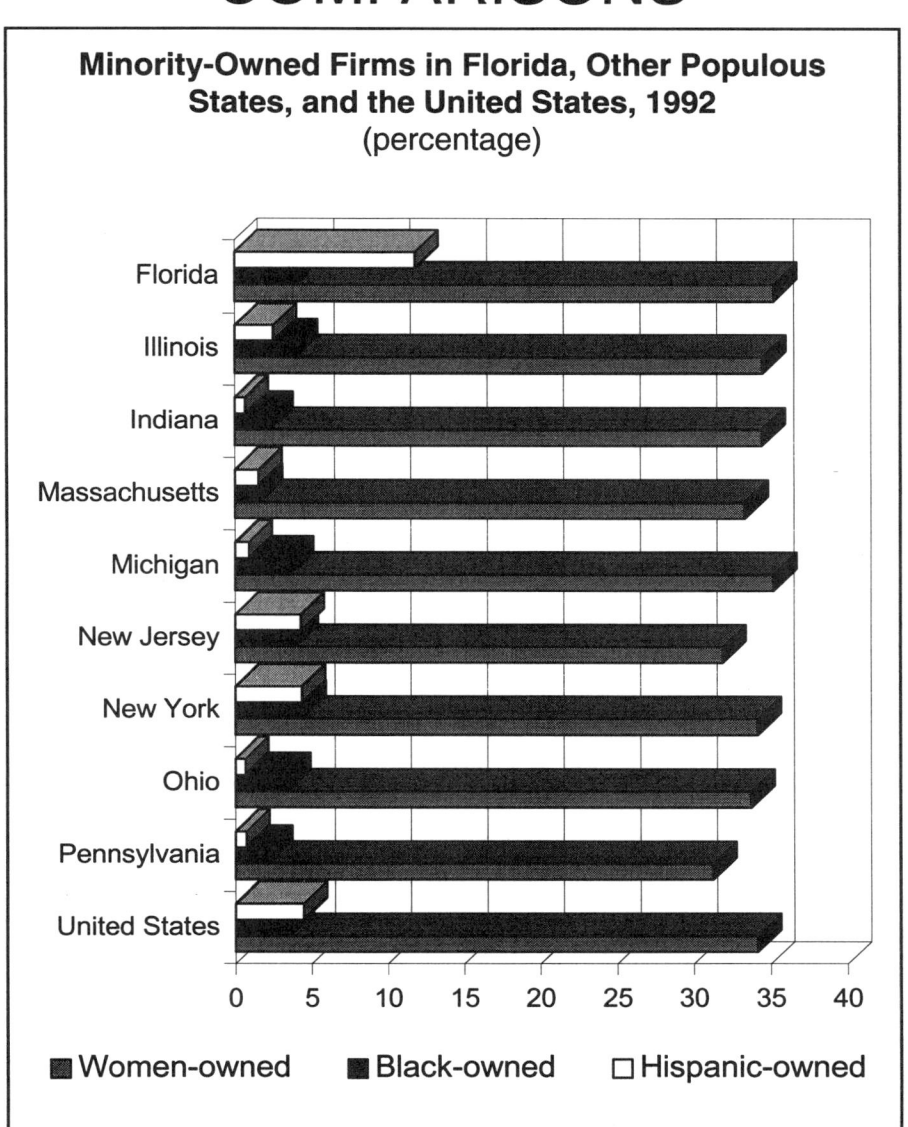

**Minority-Owned Firms in Florida, Other Populous
States, and the United States, 1992**
(percentage)

Source: Table 25.01

SECTION 25.00
STATE COMPARISONS

TABLES LISTED BY MAJOR HEADINGS

Table 25.01. SOCIAL STATISTICS AND INDICATORS: DEMOGRAPHIC, ECONOMIC, SOCIAL, AND PHYSICAL CHARACTERISTICS OF FLORIDA, OTHER SUNBELT STATES, OTHER POPULOUS STATES, AND THE UNITED STATES

State	Total April 1 1990 (1,000)	Population July 1, 1996 A/				
		Total (1,000)	Percent-age of population aged 65 and over	Rank among states	Persons per square mile of land area	Per-centage change 1990 to 1996
Sunbelt states						
Florida	12,938	14,400	18.5	4	267.0	11.3
Alabama	4,040	4,273	13.0	23	84.2	5.8
Arizona	3,665	4,428	13.2	21	39.0	20.8
Arkansas	2,351	2,510	14.4	33	48.2	6.8
California	29,758	31,878	11.0	1	204.4	7.1
Georgia	6,478	7,353	9.9	10	127.0	13.5
Louisiana	4,220	4,351	11.4	22	99.9	3.1
Mississippi	2,575	2,716	12.3	31	57.9	5.5
New Mexico	1,515	1,713	11.0	36	14.1	13.1
North Carolina	6,632	7,323	12.5	11	150.3	10.4
Oklahoma	3,146	3,301	13.5	27	48.1	4.9
South Carolina	3,486	3,699	12.1	26	122.8	6.1
Tennessee	4,877	5,320	12.5	17	129.1	9.1
Texas	16,986	19,128	10.2	2	73.0	12.6
Virginia	6,189	6,675	11.2	12	168.6	7.9
Other populous states						
Illinois	11,431	11,847	12.5	6	213.1	3.6
Indiana	5,544	5,841	12.6	14	162.8	5.3
Massachusetts	6,016	6,092	14.1	13	777.3	1.3
Michigan	9,295	9,594	12.4	8	168.9	3.2
New Jersey	7,730	7,988	13.8	9	1,076.7	3.3
New York	17,991	18,185	13.4	3	385.1	1.1
Ohio	10,847	11,173	13.4	7	272.8	3.0
Pennsylvania	11,883	12,056	15.9	5	269.0	1.5
United States	248,718	265,284	12.8	(X)	75.0	6.7

(X) Not applicable.
A/ Provisional.

Source: U.S., Department of Commerce, Bureau of the Census, Internet site http://www.census.gov/.

University of Florida   **Bureau of Economic and Business Research**

Table 25.01. SOCIAL STATISTICS AND INDICATORS: DEMOGRAPHIC, ECONOMIC, SOCIAL, AND
PHYSICAL CHARACTERISTICS OF FLORIDA, OTHER SUNBELT STATES, OTHER POPULOUS
STATES, AND THE UNITED STATES (Continued)

State	Population (Continued) July 1, 1995 A/ (Continued) Age (1,000)					
	Under 5	5-17	18-24	25-44	45-64	65 and over
Sunbelt states						
Florida	956	2,467	1,167	4,200	2,952	2,657
Alabama	296	780	436	1,300	904	557
Arizona	343	807	429	1,381	882	586
Arkansas	175	484	249	710	530	362
California	2,736	6,131	3,003	10,660	5,832	3,516
Georgia	552	1,401	733	2,467	1,472	730
Louisiana	328	906	460	1,293	868	497
Mississippi	204	552	300	792	534	333
New Mexico	136	365	171	508	344	189
North Carolina	513	1,321	703	2,338	1,532	917
Oklahoma	228	653	330	951	694	445
South Carolina	254	684	378	1,162	774	447
Tennessee	364	958	511	1,665	1,153	667
Texas	1,583	3,869	1,970	6,065	3,691	1,951
Virginia	455	1,177	649	2,257	1,390	747
Other populous states						
Illinois	915	2,241	1,098	3,736	2,371	1,486
Indiana	410	1,089	573	1,823	1,212	735
Massachusetts	391	1,031	515	2,063	1,233	859
Michigan	672	1,865	904	3,010	1,951	1,193
New Jersey	572	1,415	665	2,547	1,689	1,100
New York	1,322	3,219	1,605	5,800	3,804	2,434
Ohio	759	2,089	1,051	3,456	2,321	1,497
Pennsylvania	761	2,133	1,041	3,668	2,541	1,912
United States	19,286	49,762	24,882	83,762	53,731	33,861

A/ Provisional.

Source: U.S., Department of Commerce, Bureau of the Census, Internet site http://
www.census.gov/.

University of Florida   **Bureau of Economic and Business Research**

Table 25.01. SOCIAL STATISTICS AND INDICATORS: DEMOGRAPHIC, ECONOMIC, SOCIAL, AND
PHYSICAL CHARACTERISTICS OF FLORIDA, OTHER SUNBELT STATES, OTHER POPULOUS
STATES, AND THE UNITED STATES (Continued)

State	Median age July 1 1996 A/	Projections, July 1, 2005				Living in metro-politan areas 1992 B/
		White	Black	Other	Hispanic origin 1/	
			Race			
			Sunbelt states			
Florida	37.6	13,332	2,573	374	2,845	92.9
Alabama	34.9	3,391	1,183	58	42	67.5
Arizona	34.4	4,623	203	406	1,269	87.2
Arkansas	35.2	2,286	423	38	40	45.0
California	32.7	26,583	2,511	5,347	12,268	96.8
Georgia	33.3	5,713	2,515	186	226	68.1
Louisiana	33.0	2,923	1,521	92	138	75.1
Mississippi	32.9	1,826	1,049	31	24	35.0
New Mexico	33.3	1,737	56	221	821	56.3
North Carolina	34.7	6,160	1,857	211	139	66.6
Oklahoma	34.9	2,825	311	353	143	60.2
South Carolina	34.4	2,781	1,205	46	50	70.1
Tennessee	35.3	4,887	999	80	67	67.8
Texas	32.6	17,916	2,797	774	6,624	83.9
Virginia	34.5	5,457	1,526	339	322	77.7
			Other populous states			
Illinois	34.3	9,839	1,914	512	1,450	84.0
Indiana	34.8	5,599	530	88	162	71.7
Massachusetts	35.6	5,534	461	317	524	96.1
Michigan	34.6	8,024	1,486	253	289	82.6
New Jersey	36.0	6,465	1,328	601	1,196	100.0
New York	35.3	13,567	3,416	1,267	3,071	91.8
Ohio	35.3	9,852	1,386	190	206	81.2
Pennsylvania	36.9	10,725	1,279	280	391	84.6
United States	34.6	232,463	37,734	15,784	36,057	79.8

Population (Continued)

A/ Provisional.
B/ Population in Metropolitan Statistical Areas July 1, as defined through June
30, 1993, as a percentage of resident population. See Glossary for definition.
1/ Persons of Hispanic origin may be of any race.

Source: Columns 1-5, U.S., Department of Commerce, Bureau of the Census, Internet
site http://www.census.gov/; Column 6, U.S., Department of Commerce, Bureau of the
Census, *Statistical Abstract of the United States, 1996.*

Table 25.01. SOCIAL STATISTICS AND INDICATORS: DEMOGRAPHIC, ECONOMIC, SOCIAL, AND PHYSICAL CHARACTERISTICS OF FLORIDA, OTHER SUNBELT STATES, OTHER POPULOUS STATES, AND THE UNITED STATES (Continued)

		Housing				New privately-owned units permitted 1996 A/ (1,000)
		Households, July 1, 1996				
		Persons per house-hold	Age of householder			
State	Total		15-44	45-64	65 and over	
		Sunbelt states				
Florida	5,648	2.45	41.7	29.2	29.0	125.0
Alabama	1,624	2.56	45.6	31.3	22.6	19.9
Arizona	1,687	2.61	48.4	32.2	21.7	53.7
Arkansas	951	2.51	43.7	31.8	24.8	11.1
California	11,101	2.79	50.8	31.8	19.4	92.1
Georgia	2,723	2.65	51.5	31.4	17.1	74.9
Louisiana	1,572	2.67	47.3	32.4	20.6	18.0
Mississippi	979	2.66	45.9	31.5	22.7	10.4
New Mexico	619	2.64	48.1	32.1	19.7	10.2
North Carolina	2,796	2.53	47.6	31.4	21.1	67.0
Oklahoma	1,265	2.50	45.7	30.6	23.0	10.6
South Carolina	1,376	2.64	46.7	29.8	21.0	29.4
Tennessee	2,041	2.52	46.6	32.1	21.1	40.5
Texas	6,894	2.69	51.4	29.9	18.0	118.8
Virginia	2,511	2.61	49.6	31.8	18.7	45.9
		Other populous states				
Illinois	4,352	2.65	47.1	31.1	21.6	49.6
Indiana	2,209	2.57	47.4	31.3	21.4	37.2
Massachusetts	2,322	2.61	46.6	30.4	23.1	17.3
Michigan	3,576	2.66	47.3	31.3	21.4	52.4
New Jersey	2,889	2.75	43.8	32.9	23.3	24.2
New York	6,737	2.65	44.9	32.5	22.6	34.9
Ohio	4,260	2.54	46.4	31.3	22.5	49.3
Pennsylvania	4,594	2.58	42.5	31.1	26.4	37.9
United States	98,751	2.62	47.3	31.1	21.7	1,425.6

1/ April 1, 1990 to July 1, 1995.

Source: Columns 1-5, U.S., Department of Commerce, Bureau of the Census, *Estimates of Housing Units and Households of States: 1990 and 1996,* Series PPL-73; Column 6, U. S., Department of Commerce, Bureau of the Census, Internet site http://www.census.gov/.

Table 25.01. SOCIAL STATISTICS AND INDICATORS: DEMOGRAPHIC, ECONOMIC, SOCIAL, AND PHYSICAL CHARACTERISTICS OF FLORIDA, OTHER SUNBELT STATES, OTHER POPULOUS STATES, AND THE UNITED STATES (Continued)

	Vital statistics					
	Rate per 1,000 persons				Suicides per 100,000 persons	Per-centage of total births to teenage mothers
State	Live births 1996 A/	Deaths 1996 A/	Marriages 1996 B/	Divorces 1996 B/	1994 C/	1995 D/
	Sunbelt states					
Florida	13.2	10.7	10.4	5.6	14.9	13.7
Alabama	14.4	10.0	11.1	6.0	12.6	18.5
Arizona	18.0	8.8	8.9	5.8	18.8	15.2
Arkansas	14.3	10.2	14.4	6.1	14.8	19.6
California	17.1	7.3	6.9	(NA)	11.8	12.4
Georgia	15.6	8.0	8.2	4.9	11.8	16.3
Louisiana	15.2	9.3	8.9	(NA)	12.8	19.2
Mississippi	15.3	9.9	7.9	5.8	11.8	22.2
New Mexico	15.9	7.2	9.4	6.4	18.3	18.4
North Carolina	14.5	9.1	8.5	4.9	12.7	15.2
Oklahoma	13.7	10.1	8.1	5.8	13.8	17.0
South Carolina	13.7	9.4	11.7	4.1	12.8	17.3
Tennessee	13.8	9.4	15.4	6.5	12.8	16.9
Texas	16.5	7.1	9.4	(NA)	12.7	16.6
Virginia	13.4	7.9	9.8	4.3	12.5	11.4
	Other populous states					
Illinois	15.6	9.0	7.6	3.4	9.1	12.8
Indiana	14.3	9.3	8.4	(NA)	12.5	14.6
Massachusetts	13.2	9.1	6.7	2.0	8.5	7.5
Michigan	14.3	8.8	7.2	4.0	10.9	12.4
New Jersey	14.2	9.0	6.5	3.1	7.3	8.0
New York	14.9	9.0	8.4	3.3	8.2	9.3
Ohio	13.6	9.4	7.4	4.0	9.9	13.7
Pennsylvania	12.4	10.7	5.8	3.2	11.0	10.8
United States	14.7	8.7	8.8	4.3	12.0	13.2

(NA) Not available.

A/ Preliminary. Birth and death rates are by place of residence and exclude non-residents of the United States and members of the armed forces abroad.

B/ Preliminary. Marriage and divorce rates are by place of occurrence. Divorces include annulments.

C/ Place of residence and excludes nonresidents of the United States.

D/ Resident female population aged 15-19 years.

Source: Columns 1-4, U.S., Department of Health and Human Services, Centers for Disease Control and Prevention, *Monthly Vital Statistics Report,* Volume 45, No. 12, July 17, 1997; Columns 5, 6, U.S., Department of Commerce, Bureau of the Census, *Statistical Abstract of the United States, 1996.*

Table 25.01. SOCIAL STATISTICS AND INDICATORS: DEMOGRAPHIC, ECONOMIC, SOCIAL, AND PHYSICAL CHARACTERISTICS OF FLORIDA, OTHER SUNBELT STATES, OTHER POPULOUS STATES, AND THE UNITED STATES (Continued)

State	Community hospital beds per 1,000 population 1994 A/	Hospital care expenditure, 1993 (million dollars)	Number of AIDS cases per 100,000 population 1996 B/	Active physicians per 100,000 population 1995 C/	Percentage of persons not covered by health insurance 1994 D/	Education Enrollment rate fall 1995 E/
			Health			
			Sunbelt states			
Florida	3.7	17,131	54.7	220	17.2	90.4
Alabama	4.3	5,301	15.7	184	19.2	94.4
Arizona	2.4	3,999	15.7	198	20.2	91.5
Arkansas	4.2	2,723	11.5	171	17.4	95.3
California	2.5	34,827	33.5	241	21.1	91.0
Georgia	3.8	8,704	34.8	196	16.2	95.5
Louisiana	4.4	5,956	31.6	222	19.2	86.5
Mississippi	4.7	2,897	15.4	138	17.8	91.0
New Mexico	2.5	1,848	6.7	199	23.1	90.8
North Carolina	3.3	7,801	13.6	214	13.3	90.7
Oklahoma	3.6	3,329	8.5	160	17.8	95.2
South Carolina	3.2	4,221	26.4	190	14.2	93.5
Tennessee	4.3	7,208	17.2	226	10.2	93.2
Texas	3.2	21,592	23.5	189	24.2	97.9
Virginia	3.0	7,031	22.9	227	12.0	94.0
			Other populous states			
Illinois	3.7	15,621	18.2	244	11.4	87.4
Indiana	3.5	6,998	11.4	180	10.5	90.8
Massachusetts	3.3	10,034	21.3	387	12.5	89.3
Michigan	3.3	11,711	10.9	210	10.8	89.5
New Jersey	3.9	10,312	50.3	276	13.0	86.4
New York	4.2	28,001	73.1	361	16.0	89.1
Ohio	3.6	14,305	10.0	219	11.0	88.1
Pennsylvania	4.2	19,540	18.8	273	10.6	84.8
United States	3.5	323,919	26.7	236	15.2	90.9

AIDS Acquired Immunodeficiency Syndrome.
A/ Data are for civilian population based on reporting by facilities.   B/ Data for the 12 months ending June 30, 1996, using 1995 resident population estimates. C/ Excludes federal physicians and the doctors of osteopathy. Rates are per 100,000 civilian population.   D/ Based on civilian noninstitutional population benchmarks established by the 1990 census.   E/ Public elementary and secondary school enrollment, fall 1995, as a percentage of persons 5-17 on July 1, 1995.

Source: Columns 1 - 3, U.S., Department of Health and Human Services, National Center for Health Statistics, *Health United States, 1996-97, and Injury Chartbook;* Column 4, American Medical Association, Chicago, IL, *Physician Characteristics and Distribution in the U.S.,* annual, (copy-right); Column 5, U.S., Department of Commerce, Bureau of the Census, *Current Population Reports: Health Insurance Coverage, 1994.* Series P60-190; Column 6, U.S., Department of Commerce, Bureau of the Census, *Statistical Abstract of the United States, 1997.*

Table 25.01. SOCIAL STATISTICS AND INDICATORS: DEMOGRAPHIC, ECONOMIC, SOCIAL, AND
PHYSICAL CHARACTERISTICS OF FLORIDA, OTHER SUNBELT STATES, OTHER POPULOUS
STATES, AND THE UNITED STATES (Continued)

| State | Education (Continued) | | | Climate | | Personal finances |
| | Public elementary and secondary schools | | | | | |
	Average salary of teachers 1995-96 ($1,000)	Current expenditure per pupil in ADA 1995-96 (dollars)	Number of higher education institutions 1995 A/	Average annual days with rainfall .01 inch or more 1/	Normal seasonal heating degree days 65 degrees base 2/	Average revenue per KWH of electricity sold to residences 1995 (cents)
			Sunbelt states			
Florida	33.3	5,983	114	116	1,434	7.8
Alabama	31.3	4,479	82	122	1,702	6.6
Arizona	32.5	4,332	45	36	1,350	9.1
Arkansas	29.3	4,353	38	105	3,155	8.1
California	43.1	4,977	348	35	1,458	11.6
Georgia	34.1	5,852	120	115	2,991	7.8
Louisiana	26.8	4,844	36	114	1,513	7.2
Mississippi	27.7	4,185	46	109	2,467	6.9
New Mexico	29.6	5,655	35	61	4,425	8.9
North Carolina	30.4	5,147	121	112	3,457	8.1
Oklahoma	28.4	4,523	45	83	3,659	6.7
South Carolina	31.6	5,140	59	110	2,649	7.5
Tennessee	33.1	4,717	76	107	3,082	5.9
Texas	32.0	5,593	179	79	2,407	7.7
Virginia	35.0	6,072	89	113	3,963	7.9
			Other populous states			
Illinois	40.9	5,530	169	126	6,536	10.4
Indiana	37.7	6,222	78	126	5,615	6.8
Massachusetts	42.9	7,385	118	127	5,641	11.4
Michigan	44.8	7,090	109	136	6,569	8.4
New Jersey	47.9	9,967	61	112	5,169	12.0
New York	48.1	9,535	311	121	4,805	14.0
Ohio	37.8	5,749	156	137	5,708	8.6
Pennsylvania	46.1	7,411	217	116	4,954	9.7
United States	37.7	6,103	3,706	(X)	(X)	8.4

ADA Average daily attendance.
KWH Kilowatt-hour.
(X) Not applicable.
A/ Includes universities, colleges, professional schools, junior and teachers colleges, both public and private. Branch campuses count as separate institutions.
1/ Period of record through 1995.
2/ Sums of the negative departures of the average daily temperature from 65 degrees Fahrenheit. Period of record is 1961-90.
Note: Climate data are for a major city in each state.

Source: Columns 1, 2, National Education Association. 1997 Estimates of School Statistics Database. Washington, D. C.: NEA. Used by permission; Column 3 - 5, U.S., Department of Commerce, Bureau of the Census, *Statistical Abstract of the United States, 1997*; Column 6, U.S., Department of Energy, Energy Information Administration *Electric Sales and Revenue, 1995*. Internet site http://www.eia.doe.gov/.

Table 25.01. SOCIAL STATISTICS AND INDICATORS: DEMOGRAPHIC, ECONOMIC, SOCIAL, AND
PHYSICAL CHARACTERISTICS OF FLORIDA, OTHER SUNBELT STATES, OTHER POPULOUS
STATES, AND THE UNITED STATES (Continued)

State	Average amount of life insurance in force per household 1995 A/ (dollars)	Auto-mobile regis-trations per 1,000 persons 1995 B/	State gasoline tax rate December 31, 1995 (cents per gallon)	Income and wealth		
				Median family income 1995 C/ (dollars)	Persons in poverty 1995 (percent-age)	Average adjusted gross income 1995 D/ (dollars)
			Sunbelt states			
Florida	102,700	536	12.3	44,626	16.2	29,585
Alabama	119,300	433	18.0	42,617	20.1	32,486
Arizona	97,800	446	18.0	44,526	16.1	30,196
Arkansas	96,300	325	18.7	38,520	14.9	35,522
California	114,900	470	18.0	51,519	16.7	26,939
Georgia	143,500	587	7.5	48,850	12.1	29,234
Louisiana	107,900	451	20.0	41,442	19.7	33,745
Mississippi	99,100	522	18.4	37,328	23.5	37,470
New Mexico	107,900	494	18.0	37,365	25.3	35,406
North Carolina	126,500	512	21.6	47,367	12.6	31,020
Oklahoma	91,800	497	17.0	42,124	17.1	34,774
South Carolina	121,200	508	16.0	44,048	19.9	33,241
Tennessee	115,400	749	20.0	44,312	15.5	31,300
Texas	119,400	460	20.0	43,977	17.4	30,410
Virginia	139,800	601	17.5	50,032	10.2	26,626
			Other populous states			
Illinois	137,200	559	19.0	53,807	12.4	25,779
Indiana	116,800	581	15.0	47,465	9.6	29,783
Massachusetts	140,800	577	21.0	59,191	11.0	24,407
Michigan	120,600	557	15.0	52,955	12.2	27,232
New Jersey	178,300	590	10.5	61,409	7.8	22,688
New York	136,100	437	21.9	50,672	16.5	24,855
Ohio	122,500	645	22.0	50,893	11.5	30,728
Pennsylvania	131,900	498	22.4	50,884	12.2	28,856
United States	124,100	518	E/ 19.3	49,687	(NA)	28,398

(NA) Not available.
A/ See Glossary for definition of "household."
B/ Based on resident population as of July 1.
C/ Median income for 4-person families.
D/ Preliminary data from a sample of individual income tax forms.
E/ Average rate.

Source: Column 1, American Council of Life Insurance, *1996 Life Insurance Fact
Book;* Columns 2, 3, U.S., Department of Transportation, Federal Highway Administration, *Highway Statistics, 1995;* Columns 4, 5, U.S., Department of Commerce, Bureau of
the Census, Internet site http://www.census.gov/; Column 6, U.S., Department of the
Treasury, Internal Revenue Service, *Statistics of Income: SOI Bulletin, Spring 1997.*

University of Florida   **Bureau of Economic and Business Research**

Table 25.01. SOCIAL STATISTICS AND INDICATORS: DEMOGRAPHIC, ECONOMIC, SOCIAL, AND PHYSICAL CHARACTERISTICS OF FLORIDA, OTHER SUNBELT STATES, OTHER POPULOUS STATES, AND THE UNITED STATES (Continued)

State	Income and wealth (Continued) Average total income tax 1995 B/ (dollars)	Loan growth rates 1994-95 C/	Business climate Total	Firms, 1992 A/ Women-owned (percent-age)	Black-owned (percent-age)	Hispanic-owned (percent-age)
			Sunbelt states			
Florida	6,615	15.8	1,000,542	35.2	4.0	11.8
Alabama	5,373	12.7	227,119	31.5	6.5	0.5
Arizona	5,764	14.2	248,337	37.6	1.2	7.2
Arkansas	4,702	6.9	159,820	31.6	3.6	0.4
California	6,984	15.0	2,259,327	35.5	3.1	11.1
Georgia	6,038	12.0	425,118	33.6	9.0	1.3
Louisiana	5,471	19.5	236,589	32.5	8.6	2.1
Mississippi	4,545	10.8	135,497	30.2	10.4	0.5
New Mexico	4,734	10.3	107,377	37.8	0.9	20.1
North Carolina	5,292	14.4	439,301	32.4	6.7	0.6
Oklahoma	4,774	12.0	246,936	33.6	1.9	1.2
South Carolina	4,902	19.6	197,330	32.8	9.3	0.5
Tennessee	5,817	15.4	325,371	31.1	4.6	0.5
Texas	6,469	14.7	1,256,121	33.0	4.0	12.4
Virginia	6,323	21.4	391,451	35.4	6.7	2.0
			Other populous states			
Illinois	7,382	14.0	726,974	34.5	3.9	2.5
Indiana	5,713	11.7	364,253	34.4	2.3	0.7
Massachusetts	7,525	11.8	442,848	33.3	1.6	1.6
Michigan	6,600	14.5	551,091	35.2	3.6	0.9
New Jersey	8,279	4.0	517,204	31.9	3.9	4.3
New York	7,636	11.7	1,159,700	34.1	4.4	4.4
Ohio	5,428	15.1	666,183	33.7	3.4	0.6
Pennsylvania	6,098	2.7	728,063	31.2	2.2	0.7
United States	6,364	12.3	17,253,143	34.1	3.6	4.5

A/ Data from the 1992 economic census.
B/ Preliminary data from a sample of individual income tax forms.
C/ Rates for commercial and industrial loans from December 31, 1994 through December 31, 1995.

Source: Column 1, U.S., Department of the Treasury, Internal Revenue Service, *Statistics of Income: SOI Bulletin,* Spring 1997; Column 2, Federal Deposit Insurance Corporation, *Quarterly Banking Profile,* Fourth Quarter 1995; Columns 3, 5, U.S., Department of Commerce, Bureau of the Census, *1992 Black-owned Businesses,* MB92-1; Column 4, U.S., Department of Commerce, Bureau of the Census, *1992 Women-owned Businesses,* WB92-1; Column 6, U.S., Department of Commerce, Bureau of the Census, Internet site http://www.census.gov/.

Table 25.01. SOCIAL STATISTICS AND INDICATORS: DEMOGRAPHIC, ECONOMIC, SOCIAL, AND
PHYSICAL CHARACTERISTICS OF FLORIDA, OTHER SUNBELT STATES, OTHER POPULOUS
STATES, AND THE UNITED STATES (Continued)

		Social insurance and welfare				
State	Households in the federal food stamp program 1996 ($1,000)	Average monthly social security benefits 1996 A/ (dollars)	Average weekly state unemploy- ment bene- fits 1995 (dollars)	Public aid recip- ients 1994 B/ (per- centage)	Average monthly AFDC pay- ment per family 1996 (dollars)	Average Medicaid benefits per re- cipient 1994 (dollars)
			Sunbelt states			
Florida	590	685.52	172	6.8	267.21	2,470
Alabama	204	614.45	139	6.8	147.65	2,414
Arizona	159	686.59	149	6.5	300.09	390
Arkansas	109	604.14	168	6.6	187.53	3,687
California	1,169	686.78	154	11.7	549.46	1,995
Georgia	323	628.87	162	8.2	245.71	2,623
Louisiana	256	601.36	121	9.7	153.55	3,449
Mississippi	179	574.27	134	10.9	117.86	2,030
New Mexico	87	648.25	153	8.7	375.97	2,380
North Carolina	265	639.30	190	7.2	220.64	2,726
Oklahoma	147	642.66	173	6.2	261.65	2,494
South Carolina	140	632.52	162	6.7	183.65	2,871
Tennessee	274	628.62	150	9.0	159.58	2,093
Texas	885	642.38	187	6.3	161.78	2,443
Virginia	235	647.72	170	4.8	255.67	2,680
			Other populous states			
Illinois	470	717.74	208	8.3	309.67	3,349
Indiana	155	706.23	179	5.2	241.87	3,721
Massachusetts	163	689.76	244	7.5	528.03	4,296
Michigan	409	740.36	221	9.1	363.26	2,759
New Jersey	233	756.15	253	6.0	262.14	4,573
New York	984	723.79	208	10.0	565.45	6,441
Ohio	459	688.37	197	8.1	307.50	3,279
Pennsylvania	493	707.16	219	7.2	359.88	3,365
United States	10,537	672.79	187	7.7	374.56	3,167

AFDC Aid to Families with Dependent Children.   SSI Supplemental Security Income.
A/ Data are for December 1996 and include retired workers, disabled workers, sur-
vivors, and children.
B/ June recipients of AFDC and federal SSI as a percentage of resident population,
July 1.
C/ Data for persons with federal SSI payments only; state has state-administered
supplementation.
D/ Data for persons with federal SSI payments only; state supplementary payments
not made.
Source: Columns 1, 3, 4, U.S., Department of Health and Human Services, Social
Security Administration, *Social Security Bulletin: Annual Statistical Supplement,*
1996, prepublication release; Columns 2, 6, U.S., Department of Commerce, Bureau
of the Census, *Statistical Abstract of the United States, 1997* and previous edition;
Column 5, U.S., Department of Health and Human Services, *Medicaid Statistics: Program and Financial Statistics, Fiscal Year 1994.*

University of Florida   **Bureau of Economic and Business Research**

Table 25.01.　SOCIAL STATISTICS AND INDICATORS:　DEMOGRAPHIC, ECONOMIC, SOCIAL, AND PHYSICAL CHARACTERISTICS OF FLORIDA, OTHER SUNBELT STATES, OTHER POPULOUS STATES, AND THE UNITED STATES (Continued)

| | Employment | | | | | |
State	Labor force participation rate, 1996 A/ Male	Female	Average annual pay 1995 B/ (dollars)	Average weekly earnings for manu- facturing 1996 C/ (dollars)	Annual average unemployment rate, 1996 A/ Male	Female
		Sunbelt states				
Florida	4.8	5.4	24,710	437.41	69.9	54.8
Alabama	4.9	5.4	24,396	480.80	71.9	56.3
Arizona	5.3	5.8	25,324	490.62	75.3	58.2
Arkansas	5.4	5.4	21,590	432.02	71.7	58.4
California	7.2	7.2	30,716	532.45	75.0	56.4
Georgia	4.0	5.3	26,303	472.49	76.4	60.2
Louisiana	5.6	8.0	23,894	603.77	70.0	55.2
Mississippi	5.2	7.2	21,120	420.85	70.9	54.7
New Mexico	8.4	7.6	22,960	440.99	71.3	55.2
North Carolina	4.3	4.5	24,402	442.78	76.1	61.5
Oklahoma	3.6	4.6	22,671	494.34	72.9	55.8
South Carolina	5.8	6.2	23,292	428.87	73.3	58.2
Tennessee	4.9	5.4	25,046	456.84	73.8	60.8
Texas	5.3	6.1	26,900	508.26	79.0	59.7
Virginia	4.2	4.6	26,894	505.89	74.5	60.8
		Other populous states				
Illinois	5.3	5.2	30,099	543.35	77.1	60.7
Indiana	3.9	4.4	25,571	613.32	76.9	61.9
Massachusetts	4.9	3.7	32,352	545.07	74.0	61.5
Michigan	5.1	4.6	30,543	731.81	74.8	58.6
New Jersey	6.0	6.4	34,534	579.35	75.6	59.5
New York	6.5	5.9	34,938	521.42	70.5	53.9
Ohio	5.0	4.8	26,867	636.08	74.6	58.6
Pennsylvania	5.9	4.6	27,904	551.67	72.4	55.6
United States	5.4	5.4	27,845	(NA)	74.9	59.3

(NA) Not available.

A/ Percentage of civilian noninstitutional population of each specified group in the civilian labor force.　Includes persons 16 years old and over.

B/ Data are for workers covered by state and federal unemployment insurance programs and are preliminary.

C/ Average weekly earnings of production workers on manufacturing payrolls.

Source:　Columns 1, 2, 5, 6, U.S., Department of Commerce, Bureau of the Census, *Statistical Abstract of the United States, 1997*; Column 3, U.S., Department of Labor, Bureau of Labor Statistics, *News:　Average Annual Pay by State and Industry, 1995*; Column 4, U.S., Department of Labor, Bureau of Labor Statistics, *Employment and Earnings*, May 1997.

University of Florida　　　　　　　　　　　**Bureau of Economic and Business Research**

Table 25.01. SOCIAL STATISTICS AND INDICATORS: DEMOGRAPHIC, ECONOMIC, SOCIAL, AND PHYSICAL CHARACTERISTICS OF FLORIDA, OTHER SUNBELT STATES, OTHER POPULOUS STATES, AND THE UNITED STATES (Continued)

State	Construc-tion	Manu-facturing	Whole-sale and retail trade	Finance insurance and real estate	Services	Govern-ment
			Employment (Continued)			
		Percentage distribution of nonagricultural employment, 1996 A/				
			Sunbelt states			
Florida	6.0	2.7	5.7	5.6	6.2	4.8
Alabama	1.7	2.1	1.5	1.2	1.2	1.8
Arizona	2.3	1.1	1.7	1.6	1.6	1.6
Arkansas	0.9	1.4	0.9	0.6	0.7	0.9
California	9.4	10.1	10.5	10.5	11.4	10.9
Georgia	3.0	3.2	3.2	2.6	2.6	2.9
Louisiana	2.1	1.0	1.5	1.2	1.4	1.9
Mississippi	0.9	1.3	0.8	0.6	0.7	1.1
New Mexico	0.8	0.3	0.6	0.5	0.6	0.9
North Carolina	3.5	4.6	2.9	2.2	2.4	2.9
Oklahoma	0.9	0.9	1.1	1.0	1.1	1.4
South Carolina	1.7	2.0	1.4	1.0	1.1	1.5
Tennessee	2.1	2.9	2.1	1.7	1.9	2.0
Texas	8.1	5.8	7.1	6.4	6.5	7.5
Virginia	3.2	2.2	2.5	2.3	2.7	3.1
			Other populous states			
Illinois	4.1	5.3	4.6	5.5	4.8	4.2
Indiana	2.4	3.7	2.4	1.9	1.9	2.0
Massachusetts	1.7	2.4	2.5	3.0	3.1	2.1
Michigan	3.1	5.3	3.6	2.9	3.4	3.3
New Jersey	2.3	2.7	3.0	3.3	3.3	2.9
New York	4.7	5.0	5.8	10.3	7.6	7.1
Ohio	3.9	6.0	4.6	4.0	4.1	3.9
Pennsylvania	3.7	5.1	4.3	4.4	4.8	3.7
United States	4.8	16.2	25.0	6.2	30.5	17.3

A/ Does not include mining and transportation, communications, and public utilities.

Source: U.S., Department of Labor, Bureau of Labor Statistics, *Employment and Earnings,* May 1997.

Table 25.01. SOCIAL STATISTICS AND INDICATORS: DEMOGRAPHIC, ECONOMIC, SOCIAL, AND PHYSICAL CHARACTERISTICS OF FLORIDA, OTHER SUNBELT STATES, OTHER POPULOUS STATES, AND THE UNITED STATES (Continued)

| | Manufacturing | | | | Agriculture | |
| | | | | | Farm cash receipts 1995 A/ | |
State	Jobs won/lost 1994 to 1996 (1,000)	Rank among states in employment 1996	Average annual rate of change in real gross state product 1987-94 B/	Farm acreage 1996 C/ (1,000)	Amount (million dollars)	Rank among states
			Sunbelt states			
Florida	6.4	13	0.0	10,300	5,849	9
Alabama	-3.8	19	2.4	9,800	2,908	26
Arizona	13.1	28	3.6	35,400	2,256	29
Arkansas	-0.5	24	3.5	15,000	5,065	13
California	75.9	1	1.7	30,000	22,261	1
Georgia	7.4	11	3.4	11,800	5,166	11
Louisiana	60.9	31	0.9	8,700	2,025	32
Mississippi	-15.3	26	3.0	12,600	3,126	24
New Mexico	1.2	43	4.6	43,700	1,415	35
North Carolina	-13.1	8	3.1	9,200	6,987	8
Oklahoma	3.8	33	1.7	34,000	3,705	19
South Carolina	-12.2	20	2.9	5,000	1,441	34
Tennessee	-16.7	12	3.2	11,800	2,127	31
Texas	45.3	3	3.7	127,000	13,288	2
Virginia	-5.8	18	2.1	8,600	2,248	30
			Other populous states			
Illinois	19.9	4	2.2	28,100	7,887	5
Indiana	9.3	9	2.9	15,900	4,981	14
Massachusetts	-3.1	15	0.9	570	430	45
Michigan	15.4	5	2.0	10,600	3,521	20
New Jersey	-24.0	14	2.1	840	773	38
New York	-34.3	7	1.1	7,700	2,877	27
Ohio	3.8	33	2.0	15,100	4,576	15
Pennsylvania	-12.9	6	1.9	7,700	3,738	18
United States	-18,239.1	(X)	2.3	968,048	185,750	(X)

(X) Not applicable.
A/ Includes net commodity credit loans.
B/ Percentage based on chain-type quantity indexes (1992=100).
C/ As of June 1.

Source: Columns 1, 2, U. S., Department of Labor, Bureau of Labor Statistics, *Employment and Earnings,* May 1997; Column 3, U.S., Department of Commerce, Bureau of Economic Analysis, Economics and Statistics Administration, *News: Gross State Product, New Estimates for 1993-94 and Revised Estimates for 1977-92.* Release of June 3, 1997. Columns 4, 5, 6, U.S., Department of Agriculture, National Agricultural Statistics Service, Internet site http://usda.mannlib.cornell.edu/.

Table 25.01. SOCIAL STATISTICS AND INDICATORS: DEMOGRAPHIC, ECONOMIC, SOCIAL, AND PHYSICAL CHARACTERISTICS OF FLORIDA, OTHER SUNBELT STATES, OTHER POPULOUS STATES, AND THE UNITED STATES (Continued)

	Elections			Public safety		
State	Percentage of voting-age population voting in 1994	Women in state legislatures, 1997 (percentage)	Hispanic elected officials 1994 A/	Adults on probation per 100,000 resident adults 1996	Inmates enrolled in education programs 1993 B/	Fatal motor vehicle accident rate 1995 C/
			Sunbelt states			
Florida	42.3	23.1	64	2,273	2,919	1.99
Alabama	45.8	4.3	0	1,213	2,500	1.96
Arizona	41.6	37.8	341	1,318	(NA)	2.30
Arkansas	41.6	17.0	2	1,299	(NA)	2.02
California	45.0	22.5	796	1,269	4,814	1.33
Georgia	35.4	16.5	0	2,669	2,928	1.56
Louisiana	34.2	11.1	12	1,135	1,155	1.99
Mississippi	44.3	11.5	0	510	350	2.50
New Mexico	46.8	26.8	716	737	456	2.01
North Carolina	35.7	17.1	0	1,867	2,598	1.72
Oklahoma	46.8	10.1	1	1,161	869	1.55
South Carolina	45.2	12.9	0	1,524	4,346	2.02
Tennessee	43.0	13.6	0	936	1,275	2.01
Texas	37.6	18.2	2,215	3,113	11,976	1.54
Virginia	45.7	15.0	0	587	951	1.18
			Other populous states			
Illinois	42.8	26.0	881	1,329	5,294	1.49
Indiana	38.7	18.6	8	2,294	(NA)	1.33
Massachusetts	51.6	23.0	1	960	2,981	0.87
Michigan	52.2	23.0	8	2,106	5,935	1.61
New Jersey	40.3	15.8	37	2,098	5,240	1.18
New York	44.6	18.5	83	1,323	10,007	1.36
Ohio	46.6	22.0	4	1,234	11,250	1.21
Pennsylvania	42.7	12.3	8	1,206	3,100	1.41
United States	44.6	21.5	5,459	1,621	9,036	1.54

(NA) Not available.
A/ Persons of Hispanic origin may be of any race.
B/ Enrollment in Adult Basic Education (A.B.E.) and/or General Education Development (G.E.D.) programs as reported by the Federal Bureau of Prisons.
C/ Rate per 100 million vehicle-miles of travel.

Source: Columns 1 and 3, U.S., Department of Commerce, Bureau of the Census, *Statistical Abstract of the United States, 1996*; Column 2, Center for the American Woman and Politics (CAWP), National Information Bank on Women in Public Office, Eagleton Institute of Politics, Rutgers University, (copyright), Internet site http://www-rci.rutgers.edu/~cawp/; Column 4, U.S. Bureau of Justice Statistics, release of August 14, 1997. Column 5, U.S., Bureau of Justice Statistics, *Sourcebook of Criminal Justice Statistics, 1994*. Column 6, U.S., Department of Transportation, Federal Highway Administration, *Highway Statistics, 1995*.

University of Florida   **Bureau of Economic and Business Research**

Table 25.01. SOCIAL STATISTICS AND INDICATORS: DEMOGRAPHIC, ECONOMIC, SOCIAL, AND
PHYSICAL CHARACTERISTICS OF FLORIDA, OTHER SUNBELT STATES, OTHER POPULOUS
STATES, AND THE UNITED STATES (Continued)

| | | | Governmental expenditure | | | |
| | | | State and local government direct general expenditure, per capita, 1993-94 (dollars) | | | |
State	Total	Educa-tion	Public welfare	Health and hospitals	Highways	Police protec-tion
			Sunbelt states			
Florida	3,740.66	1,073.87	426.38	386.09	283.03	187.85
Alabama	3,506.06	1,151.93	525.15	659.80	268.44	109.86
Arizona	3,689.16	1,296.51	591.80	202.99	267.12	162.01
Arkansas	3,036.78	1,125.74	568.15	309.95	281.20	83.84
California	4,407.36	1,235.38	744.52	453.78	196.47	199.76
Georgia	3,697.25	1,259.48	600.87	526.96	216.28	117.97
Louisiana	3,905.47	1,181.16	660.62	559.07	270.13	142.40
Mississippi	3,230.37	1,142.83	548.24	483.03	273.40	82.12
New Mexico	4,168.59	1,400.47	575.14	417.18	542.06	147.67
North Carolina	3,524.28	1,277.33	531.92	453.14	259.38	120.01
Oklahoma	3,244.65	1,288.92	468.29	351.01	240.89	101.33
South Carolina	3,772.19	1,261.34	630.37	706.51	193.93	103.17
Tennessee	3,325.85	1,074.54	604.32	432.01	249.93	104.15
Texas	3,477.29	1,333.14	497.93	338.70	244.34	120.92
Virginia	3,585.59	1,345.05	437.00	306.77	285.91	126.02
			Other populous states			
Illinois	3,771.70	1,232.15	603.12	261.03	293.05	169.25
Indiana	3,701.29	1,414.86	691.01	381.38	232.11	91.13
Massachusetts	4,658.58	1,221.06	937.47	412.01	314.84	149.22
Michigan	4,146.00	1,581.72	732.00	416.79	227.00	143.97
New Jersey	4,825.07	1,711.16	727.83	240.18	309.26	205.57
New York	6,242.04	1,743.32	1,317.17	617.85	313.19	217.75
Ohio	3,786.57	1,314.15	760.26	330.09	238.70	129.12
Pennsylvania	3,885.93	1,309.66	802.52	236.79	234.73	109.31
United States	4,125.42	1,357.02	690.75	385.76	276.82	148.44

Note: Data are preliminary.

Source: U.S., Department of Commerce, Bureau of the Census, Internet site http://
www.census.gov/.

University of Florida   **Bureau of Economic and Business Research**

Table 25.01. SOCIAL STATISTICS AND INDICATORS: DEMOGRAPHIC, ECONOMIC, SOCIAL, AND PHYSICAL CHARACTERISTICS OF FLORIDA, OTHER SUNBELT STATES, OTHER POPULOUS STATES, AND THE UNITED STATES (Continued)

	Governmental expenditure (Continued)					
	Federal government expenditure per capita, 1994-95 (dollars)					
State	Total	Grants to state and local govern- ments	Salaries and wages	Direct payments to indivi- duals	Pro- cure- ments	Other
	Sunbelt states					
Florida	5,497.62	586.22	531.97	3,704.79	564.28	110.37
Alabama	5,478.43	778.04	678.12	3,186.57	687.25	148.46
Arizona	4,927.48	698.90	569.82	2,770.85	787.13	100.78
Arkansas	4,810.98	849.07	413.32	3,180.80	180.49	187.30
California	4,939.02	828.58	565.84	2,523.13	869.68	151.80
Georgia	4,723.35	728.76	802.96	2,438.84	644.77	108.01
Louisiana	5,083.27	1,088.12	478.87	2,890.04	479.54	146.69
Mississippi	5,590.55	1,013.98	578.59	3,015.73	856.48	125.78
New Mexico	7,047.97	1,133.50	984.48	2,585.55	2,146.08	198.36
North Carolina	4,475.11	713.71	668.90	2,656.41	313.16	122.92
Oklahoma	5,054.63	737.55	824.15	2,993.16	365.12	134.64
South Carolina	4,974.69	819.72	595.63	2,794.35	677.08	87.91
Tennessee	5,179.92	841.28	507.93	2,912.96	811.52	106.24
Texas	4,521.82	695.13	588.09	2,390.34	723.56	124.69
Virginia	7,535.71	509.83	1,845.99	2,780.77	2,176.57	222.56
	Other populous states					
Illinois	4,324.26	779.03	459.19	2,679.46	267.17	139.40
Indiana	4,145.67	626.01	337.26	2,584.56	357.86	239.98
Massachusetts	5,984.29	1,118.40	468.92	3,074.66	998.13	324.17
Michigan	4,094.80	749.89	289.58	2,729.08	228.15	98.10
New Jersey	4,800.49	814.48	445.22	2,990.57	469.50	80.73
New York	5,205.77	1,350.54	393.56	2,971.38	347.53	142.76
Ohio	4,487.83	785.45	412.78	2,789.42	410.21	89.97
Pennsylvania	5,322.31	839.15	466.58	3,398.53	458.76	159.29
United States 1/	5,179.84	845.47	630.66	2,784.05	745.15	174.52

1/ Average.

Source: U.S., Department of Commerce, Bureau of the Census, *Federal Expenditures by State for Fiscal Year 1996.*

University of Florida   **Bureau of Economic and Business Research**

APPENDIX. EXPLANATORY NOTES AND SOURCES

SECTION 1.00. POPULATION

EXPLANATORY NOTES. The University of Florida Bureau of Economic and Business Research Population Program prepared a revised series of intercensal population estimates for the 1980s in 1991 that appears in Table 1.20. Extreme caution must be exercised when deriving annual changes from successive estimates. Calculating such changes can lead to inaccurate conclusions regarding population growth, especially for small places. The best base of any estimate of population change is generally the most recent census enumeration.

Counties and municipalities are legal and political entities, but, from a sociological point of view the community of which a person considers himself or herself to be a part may not correspond to such an entity. Terms like "Greater Jacksonville" or "the Miami area" are used to indicate the real community. People do not hesitate to cross city or county limits or even state lines to work, to buy or sell, or to seek cultural, medical, recreational, or social services. For this reason, the U.S. Office of Management and Budget has designated areas known as Metropolitan Statistical Areas (MSAs). An MSA is a geographic area with a large population nucleus together with adjacent communities having a high degree of economic and social integration with that nucleus. These areas were designated as Standard Metropolitan Statistical Areas (SMSAs) before January 1983. New MSA designations were announced effective June 1983 and more recently, December 31, 1992.

Generally an area qualifies for recognition as an MSA in one of two ways: if there is a city of at least 50,000 population or an urbanized area of at least 50,000 with a total metropolitan population of at least 100,000. An MSA may include a single county or several counties that have close economic and social ties to a central city or urban area. In metropolitan complexes of one million or more population, separate component areas (previously MSAs or SMSAs) are defined if specified criteria are met. Such areas are designated Primary Metropolitan Statistical Areas (PMSAs) and any area containing PMSAs is designated as a Consolidated Metropolitan Statistical Area (CMSA).

In Florida, MSAs are defined in terms of entire counties. Population living in MSAs may be referred to as the metropolitan population. Nineteen MSAs were designated in Florida effective June 1983 and a twentieth was designated in June 1984. The two areas redefined as PMSAs together comprise the Miami-Ft. Lauderdale CMSA. On December 31, 1992, new MSA designations went into effect (see map on page vii). Florida's total remained twenty although several areas were redefined, two were combined and one was added. Table 1.65 contains population figures for Florida's current MSAs.

Agencies of the state government have grouped counties into different districts. There are eleven planning districts, each containing several counties that have common interests and needs for planning community development. A map on page 45 shows the counties by planning districts. Florida Department of Health districts are mapped on page 227, water management districts are on page 249, crop-reporting-district boundaries are on page 303, and Community Health Purchasing Alliance regions are on page 552.

SOURCES. The Census of Population taken once every ten years by the U.S. Bureau of the Census provides basic statistics about population. Selected Florida data from the 1990 census are included in this *Abstract*. Table 1.19 contains a historical population series for counties beginning with the 1940 census.

At the back of this volume is an index of the most recent census information appearing in previous editions. In 1994, the Bureau of Economic and Business Research (BEBR), University of Florida, published a collection of county 1990 census data titled *1990 Census Handbook - Florida*. This volume also includes some 1980 data for comparison and information on how to use census data, primary census sources, and census definitions.

In addition to the decennial censuses, the Census Bureau issues a series of *Current Population Reports*, known as P-Series. These contain national, regional, and sometimes state population statistics resulting from periodic surveys, special censuses, and cooperative estimation and projection efforts between the individual states and the Census Bureau. Many of these reports can be found on the Census Bureau's worldwide web Internet site, www.census.gov/.

Between census years, estimates of the population of the state, counties, and municipalities of Florida are made by the BEBR Population Program. These are released annually in *Florida Estimates of Population*.

The *Abstract* contains estimates and projections of population by age, race, and sex. Benchmark data are from the 1990 census. The age, race, and sex estimates and projections are developed by BEBR and released in the *Florida Population Studies* series. Table 1.36 highlights much requested Hispanic population estimates by sex and age for Florida and its counties as published in a recent BEBR special population report. BEBR also provides unpublished median age, projections, and elderly population statistics and data on total net migration and migration of persons aged 65 and over to Florida. Voting-age population estimates and projections are presented in Section 21.00.

Data on veterans come from the U.S. Department of Veterans Affairs in Washington, which releases reports on the age, location, and period of service of veterans. Financial information about veterans at the county level can be found in Section 23.00. Data on immigrants are from the U.S. Immigration and Naturalization Services. Data on intercounty migration in Table 1.74 are from the Internal Revenue Service.

SECTION 2.00. HOUSING

SOURCES. The decennial Census of Housing is taken simultaneously with the Census of Population and provides basic information about people in their living arrangements. Extensive data from the 1990 Census of Housing can be found in previous *Abstracts* (refer to the census index at the back of this volume) and in the *1990 Census Handbook - Florida.*

The Census Bureau also issues the *Current Housing Reports* series, which provide statistics compiled on subjects from the decennial or special censuses and surveys such as the American Housing Survey. Estimates of housing units and households in every state are now available as unpublished data on the Internet and appear in Table 2.01. Data on homeownership rates in Table 2.02 are from the Census Bureau's *Housing Vacancy Survey* and are also available on the Internet.

The Bureau of Economic and Business Research (BEBR), University of Florida, makes annual estimates of the number of households and average household size for intercensal years. These are published in the series, *Florida Population Studies*. Average apartment rent and number of units by age of unit and by county are provided by BEBR's survey research program and are published in a new BEBR publication, *Florida Business Briefs*.

Three agencies of the State of Florida provide information relating to housing. The Division of Motor Vehicles of the Department of Highway Safety and Motor Vehicles annually publishes the number of tags sold to owners of mobile homes and recreational vehicles. The Division of Hotels and Restaurants of the State Department of Business and Professional Regulation publishes statistics on apartment houses, rooming houses, and licensed lodgings. The Office of Education Budget and Management, Department of Education provides prices of average housing by county and the Florida Price Level Index, which includes a housing component.

The Florida Association of Homes for the Aging provides a list of homes with locations, number of units and beds in the annual *Directory of Members*. Data on home sales and median sales prices in metropolitan areas, are provided in unpublished form by the Florida Association of Realtors and the University of Florida's Real Estate Research Center.

SECTION 3.00. VITAL STATISTICS AND HEALTH

EXPLANATORY NOTES. Vital statistics usually include data on births, infant deaths, abortions, teenage pregnancies, illegitimate births, marriages, divorces, annulments, and deaths by cause. For births and deaths, "resident" is the term indicating births or deaths among residents of a specified area regardless of where the event occurred. "Recorded" is the term used to identify births or deaths occurring in a specified area regardless of the usual residence of the person counted. The birth and death figures in this section are resident data. Marriages and dissolutions of marriage are reported by place of occurrence. Cases of Acquired Immunodeficiency Syndrome (AIDS) in Table 3.28 of this *Abstract* are diagnosed cases and reported cases. There is a time lag—occasionally as much as several years—between diagnosis of a case according to national Centers for Disease Control criteria and the case's entry into the Florida Department of Health's AIDS Reporting System.

    SOURCES. The Public Health Statistics Section of the Department of Health is the principal source of vital statistics data for Florida and its counties. Data are released monthly in *Vital News* and later accumulated in an annual report, *Florida Vital Statistics*.

    Death rates by leading cause are provided by the Florida Agency for Health Care Administration in cooperation with Local Health Councils of Florida. Their publication, *Florida 1997 Health Data SourceBook*, profiles general health care in the state and counties. Other tables from this source can be found in Sections 7.00 and 20.00.

    Statistics on AIDS are available from the State Health Office of the Florida Department of Health. Data on child and teen deaths, children affected by divorce, and runaways are used with permission from a copyrighted publication, Volume VI of *The 1996 Florida Kids Count Data Book* produced by the University of South Florida, Florida Mental Health Institute, and the Florida Center for Children and Youth, published every two years.

SECTION 4.00. EDUCATION

EXPLANATORY NOTES. In census counts and estimates of population, persons of Hispanic origin are considered to be of any race. Some duplication of data results when persons of Hispanic origin are summed with race data. The Florida Department of Education, on the other hand, reports persons of Hispanic origin as a separate racial category. Therefore, totals are not complete unless persons of Hispanic origin are included. Every effort has been made to individually note the differences on the education tables where this occurs.

    SOURCES. The principal sources of information on education in Florida include the annual *Profiles of Florida School Districts*, reports from the Bureau of Education Information and Accountability Services of the Division of Administration, various *Statistical Briefs* released by both the Division of Administration and the Division of Public Schools, other publications, and unpublished data from the Florida Department of Education. Dropout rates, gruaduation rates, and readiness for college data can be found on the Department's worldwide website www.firn.edu/doe/.

    Enrollment information about the State University System is available in the *Fact Book* published by the Florida Board of Regents. Accredited colleges and universities enrollment data are published by the Office of Educational Research and Improvement of the National Center for Education Statistics,

U.S. Department of Education in the *Directory of Postsecondary Institutions*. Data on public community colleges come from reports of the State Division of Community Colleges, Florida Department of Education.

Data on the extent of public and private education, exceptional programs, the level achieved by the pupils, and the availability and enrollments of schools, colleges, and universities are all included in Section 4.00. Employment and finances of educational institutions and data on educational services are in Section 20.00. Additional information on the public funding of education is in Section 23.00.

SECTION 5.00. INCOME AND WEALTH

EXPLANATORY NOTES. The earnings components of personal income are allocated on a place-of-work basis. These earnings are converted to a place-of-residence basis by means of a residence adjustment factor. Property income and transfer payments are then added to earnings, resulting in total income on a place-of-residence basis. This conversion is illustrated in Table 5.14. The first basis, earnings by place of work, is useful in the analysis of the income structure of a given area in terms of industrial markets and purchasing power. Expressed per capita, the latter basis, earnings by place of residence, is an indicator of living standards and welfare level. See Section 9.00 for estimates of farm income.

Families and unrelated individuals are classified as being above or below the poverty level by comparing their calendar-year money income to an income cutoff or "poverty threshold." The income cutoffs vary by family size, number of children, and age of the family householder or unrelated individual. Poverty status is determined for all families (and, by implication, all family members). Poverty status is also determined for persons not in families, except for inmates of institutions, members of the Armed Forces living in barracks, college students living in dormitories, and unrelated individuals under 15 years old.

The poverty thresholds are revised annually to reflect changes in the Consumer Price Index. The poverty threshold for a family of four in 1996 was $16,029, as shown on Table 5.46. Poverty thresholds are computed on a national basis only. No attempt has been made to adjust these thresholds for regional, state, or other local variations in the cost of living.

The Statistics of Income series data published by the U.S. Internal Revenue Service are based on the tax-defined concept, adjusted gross income (AGI), which excludes certain types of income. Caution should be exercised in comparing these data over time as annual changes in tax law will continue to affect the definition of AGI.

State data showing distribution of income by income class are no longer published by the U.S. Internal Revenue Service. Table 5.03 presents percentage of income in the state distributed by household size and income class based on results from the Florida Economic and Consumer Survey, Bureau of Economic and Business Research (BEBR), University of Florida.

SOURCES. The source for statistics on personal income in Florida is the U.S. Department of Commerce, Bureau of Economic Analysis (BEA). The BEA has made comprehensive estimates of personal income, by type and industrial source, covering all metropolitan areas and counties in the nation for selected years from 1969 through 1995. Annual estimates are published in *Survey of Current Business*. Data in this *Abstract* are from the BEA's Regional Economic Information System (REIS) CD-ROM for August 1997.

Updated estimates of national poverty thresholds are published annually in the *Statistical Abstract of the United States* and can be found on the Internet. Poverty thresholds based on money income are published annually by the U.S. Bureau of the Census in *Current Population Reports*, Series P60 and are also on the Bureau's Internet site, www.census.gov/. Median household income, the number of poor persons, and the number of poor related children can also be found on the Internet site.

The income of military retirees appears in the Department of Defense publication *DOD Statistical Report on the Military Retirement System.*

A source for income data is the U.S. Internal Revenue Service. Data such as income sources, tax deductions, and credits are from statistical samplings of individual tax returns and are reported in the series *Statistics of Income*.

The data on income distribution for the state by income class are derived from the BEBR Florida Economic and Consumer Survey.

SECTION 6.00. LABOR FORCE, EMPLOYMENT, AND EARNINGS

EXPLANATORY NOTES. Tables of employment and payroll devoted to individual industries and nonprofit organizations are presented in this section and in other sections of *Abstract*. Data are defined by the State Unemployment Insurance Program and are often termed "covered employment" or "ES-202" data. Any firm or nonprofit establishment whose employees are covered by state and federal unemployment laws must submit monthly reports on the number of persons on its payroll and the amount employees were paid. The data generated from these reports provide useful measures of the impact of various industries, firms, or other organizations on the economies of the state and its counties. The Bureau of Labor Market Information of the Florida Department of Labor and Employment Security compiles these statistics. Many tables in this *Abstract* include revised data for 1995 as well as unpublished figures for 1996.

Covered employment data include most employed persons in Florida, but certain workers are specifically excluded from coverage. These are some agricultural and domestic employees, self-employed workers, and elected officials. Among the excluded self-employed are such occupations as insurance or real estate agents whose earnings are from commissions. Certain nonprofit organizations such as churches may elect to participate in the program.

Also missing from the tables are data for the state or counties in which there were so few units that the information for an individual establishment might be made public or estimated by competitors. In these instances and when one firm in a specific category or county has 80 percent of the employment of all the business in that category or county, no data are reported. Often data may be undisclosed at the level of the county or 3-digit SIC industry group but are reported in aggregate at the state level. Disclosure guidelines adopted by the Department of Labor and Employment Security in keeping with federal rules prevent publication of reporting units and employment ranges for undisclosed establishments.

The derivation and meaning of SIC codes are briefly discussed in the Preface and the Glossary, which lists the major industrial groups and codes. Table 6.03 presents data for all covered employees by industry and Tables 6.04 and 6.05 present employment data by county. Tables in various sections present state and county data by major industries and industry subgroupings, such as Tables 12.50, 12.51, 12.52, and 12.53, 13.36 and 13.37, etc.

Detailed employment data for governments appear in Section 23.00.

SOURCES. The basis of statistics on the employment status of the population is a monthly Current Population Survey (CPS) conducted by the U.S. Bureau of the Census and detailed data (e.g., employment by occupation, labor force status by age, race, sex) are available from the decennial censuses. The U.S. Bureau of Labor Statistics publishes monthly data from the CPS in *Employment and Earnings* and other related publications listed below. The Bureau of Labor Market Information (BLMI), Department of Labor and Employment Security of the State of Florida has the responsibility of preparing estimates of employment status following procedures developed in cooperation with the U.S. Bureau of Labor Statistics (BLS). The BLMI publishes information about Florida, its counties, metropolitan areas, and cities in *Florida Labor Force Summary*, and releases special reports on small counties. Different samples are used to prepare these sets of employment and unemployment estimates. Its *Florida Industry and Occupational Employment Projections* is published annually by the BLMI.

The U.S. BLS compiles statistics and publishes data on nonagricultural employment in Florida and its metropolitan areas. Its publications include monthly *Employment and Earnings* and *Geographic Profile of*

Employment and Unemployment. It also publishes a series of bulletins or releases under the title *News.* Much of the BLS published data are also available on the Internet.

The U.S. Equal Opportunity Commission publishes the occupational distribution data in *Job Patterns for Minorities and Women in Private Industry.*

The recently dissolved Florida Department of Commerce, Bureau of Economic Analysis published *Florida Facts: Florida's Fifty Largest Private Employers.* Data on Florida's largest employers in 1995 have been repeated on Table 6.30.

Annual manufacturing pay and manufacturing jobs in the state shown on new Table 6.55 are provided by BEBR's *Florida Business Briefs* utilizing data from the U.S. Department of Commerce, Bureau of the Census' *County Business Patterns.*

The U.S. Bureau of Economic Analysis provides data on farm proprietors and wage and salary workers. Farm employment data appear in Section 9.00.

SECTION 7.00. SOCIAL INSURANCE AND WELFARE

EXPLANATORY NOTES. For purposes of managing state-administered public assistance programs, the state has been divided into fifteen Depatment of Health districts; a map showing these districts appears on page 244.

SOURCES. The source of statistics on Social Security programs is the U.S. Department of Health and Human Services, Social Security Administration *Social Security Bulletin*, published monthly with an annual statistical supplement. The department also publishes data on state programs in *OASDI Beneficiaries by State and County* and *SSI Recipients by State and County*, and releases unpublished data.

Specified characteristics about unemployment insurance are published in the *Social Security Bulletin: Annual Statistical Supplement.* Historical average weekly wages and unemployment insurance contribution and disbursement data are provided by the Florida Department of Labor and Employment Security. County data on injuries and cost by industry and accident type are reported in the Florida Department of Labor and Employment Security, Division of Workers' Compensation *Report on Occupational Injuries.*

The Health Care Financing Administration in the U.S. Department of Health and Human Services provides unpublished data on Medicare.

Four public assistance programs—for the aged, the blind, the permanently and totally disabled, and dependent children—are administered by the state but are financed in part by the federal government in grants to states under the Social Security Act. The principal source of state and national data on these programs is the U.S. Department of Health and Human Services, Social Security Administration *Social Security Bulletin: Annual Statistical Supplement.*

The principal source of data on Florida and its counties is the Florida Agency for Health Care Administration. The agency also provides unpublished data on Medicaid recipients and expenditures by county. Published statistics on persons eligible for Medicaid are found in *Florida 1997 Health Data SourceBook* produced in cooperation with Local Health Councils of Florida. Food stamp data are provided in *Florida Food Stamp Program Participation Statistics* by the state Department of Health.

SECTION 8.00. PHYSICAL GEOGRAPHY AND ENVIRONMENT

SOURCES. Tables in this section containing information relating to temperature, precipitation, and other climatic phenomena present data supplied by the Environmental Satellite, Data, and Information Service of the National Oceanic and Atmospheric Administration (NOAA), U.S. Department of Commerce. Their publications are issued both annually and monthly under the title, *Climatological Data: Florida.* A map of National Weather Station Offices appearing on Table 8.70 is on page 272. Hurricane data are published in periodic NOAA technical memoranda.

The Geography Division of the Bureau of the Census, U.S. Department of Commerce provides revised data on the land and water area of the state and counties of Florida based on TIGER mapping files from the 1990 Census of Population and Housing.

The Division of Air Resources Management, Florida Department of Environmental Protection provides information on air pollution in the report *Comparison of Air Quality Data with the National Ambient Air Quality Standards.*

Data on water use are collected by the United States Geological Survey, five water management districts in the state, and the Florida Department of Environmental Regulation. A map of the water management districts with district headquarters is on page 266. Some water-use data are obtained from utilities and information on agricultural irrigation is collected by the Institute of Food and Agricultural Sciences at the University of Florida and the State of Florida Department of Agriculture and Consumer Services. The water-use data were compiled from these various sources by the United States Geological Survey, Water Resource Division in cooperation with the Florida Department of Environmental Protection.

Solid waste data are published by the Bureau of Solid and Hazardous Waste, Florida Department of Environmental Protection in the annual report *Solid Waste Management in Florida.*

SECTION 9.00. AGRICULTURE

EXPLANATORY NOTES. Since 1840 a Census of Agriculture has been taken every five years. Congress authorized agricultural censuses to be taken in 1978 and 1982 to coincide with the quinquennial economic censuses. After 1982, the agricultural census again reverted to a five-year cycle to be taken in years ending in "2" and "7." Some parts of the 1992 Economic Census are included in this *Abstract.* An index at the back of this book lists recent census tables appearing in previous *Abstracts.* As defined since the 1978 census, a farm is "any place from which $1,000 or more of agricultural products were sold or normally would have been sold during the census year." Because data for selected items are collected from a sample of operators, the results are subject to sampling variability. Dollar values have not been adjusted for changes in price levels between census years.

When comparisons are made between Florida and other states, the other states selected either have a similar climate (the southern tier of Sunbelt states) or produce similar crops (citrus in Arizona and California, sugarcane in Hawaii and Louisiana, etc.).

SOURCES. Timely and detailed data on farm receipts, income, taxes, and value of farm marketings are provided in tables based on annual publications of the U.S. Department of Agriculture, *Agricultural Statistics,* and from the Department's Economic Research Service on Internet site www.econ.ag.gov/. The U.S. Department of Commerce, Bureau of Economic Analysis provides additional farm-income data. Some data on farm income also appear in Section 5.00.

Data primarily covering characteristics of farms and farm operators are from the *1992 Census of Agriculture* published by the U.S. Department of Commerce, Bureau of the Census.

Agricultural employment information comes from the Bureau of Economic Analysis, U.S. Department of Commerce and from the Bureau of Labor Market Information, Florida Department of Labor and Employment Security. (See discussion under Section 6.00 of this Appendix.)

Water use for agricultural irrigation data are from the U.S. Geological Survey. (See discussion under Section 8.00 of this Appendix).

Information about citrus production, cash receipts, other crop cultivation, and livestock is from the Florida Agricultural Statistics Service, Florida Department of Agriculture and Consumer Services. A map of counties in crop-reporting districts appears on page 323. A complete series of crop estimates for the state dating back to 1919 is available from the reporting service upon request. The Florida Department of Citrus provides information on orange juice sales from A. C. Nielsen market research reports. The Florida Department of Business and Professional Regulation has data on veterinarians licensed in the state.

The Agricultural Stabilization and Conservation Service, U.S. Department of Agriculture provides state and county estimates of nonresident alien ownership of agricultural land in their publication *Foreign Ownership of U.S. Agricultural Land.*

SECTION 10.00 FORESTRY, FISHERIES, AND MINERALS

SOURCES. Forestry employment and payroll data come from the Bureau of Labor Market Information, Florida Department of Labor and Employment Security, as does similar information for fishing and mining. (See discussion under Section 6.00 of this Appendix.) The Division of Forestry of the Florida Department of Agriculture and Consumer Services provides data on the harvest of forest products. The Forest Service, U.S. Department of Agriculture publishes data on national forests in *Land Areas of the National Forest System.*

The Marine Fisheries Information System, Florida Department of Natural Resources provides unpublished data on fish landings. The National Marine Fisheries Service of the National Oceanic and Atmospheric Administration, U.S. Department of Commerce publishes data on fishery products, plants, and cooperatives in its annual *Fisheries of the United States.* Table 19.45 in Section 19.00 gives information on the number of commercial boats registered in the state and counties of Florida.

Basic data on the production of minerals are from *The Minerals Yearbook,* produced by the U.S. Geological Survey in the U.S. Department of the Interior, and the *1992 Census of Mineral Industries.*

SECTION 11.00. CONSTRUCTION

SOURCES. Statistics on building construction activity and characteristics of that industry (SIC codes 15-17) are in this section. The principal sources of building permit data for Florida are the Bureau of Economic and Business Research (BEBR), University of Florida, and the U.S. Bureau of the Census. The BEBR publishes monthly and annual summaries on the type and value of building permits for construction issued by local administrative offices throughout Florida in *Building Permit Activity in Florida.* The BEBR compiles, and makes available in unpublished form, data on construction starts. Building permit data for states can be found on the Census Bureau's website on the Internet at www.census.gov/. Mobile home data are from the U.S. Bureau of the Census publication *Current Construction Reports: Housing Starts.*

Producer prices of materials used in construction in the U.S. are from *Construction Review* published by the International Trade Administration of the U.S. Department of Commerce.

Data on employment and payrolls are supplied by the Bureau of Labor Market Information, Florida Department of Labor and Employment Security. (See discussion under Section 6.00 of this Appendix.)

SECTION 12.00. MANUFACTURING

SOURCES. Major industry divisions for manufacturing comprise SIC codes 20-39. Data on the number of units, employees, and payroll for these establishments were obtained from the Bureau of Labor Market Information, Florida Department of Labor and Employment Security. A number of industries are detailed in tables in this section and many include county breakdowns.

The U.S. Bureau of the Census conducts a complete count of manufactures every five years as part of its comprehensive economic census. The latest is the *1992 Census of Manufactures.* The Bureau of the Census also conducts, in intervening years, a sample survey called the *Annual Survey of Manufactures.*

Unpublished data on the value of Florida products are made available by the Enterprise Florida using the University of Massachusetts Institute for Social and Economic Research (MISER) program.

SECTION 13.00. TRANSPORTATION

SOURCES. The U.S. Department of Transportation provides data on roads and highways, tax receipts, bridges, and vehicles in *Highway Statistics*, a publication of the Federal Highway Administration. Information about licenses, drivers of motor vehicles, and motor vehicle registrations comes from the Florida Department of Highway Safety and Motor Vehicles. The same department publishes accident data in *Florida Traffic Crash Facts* and automobile tag and revenue data in *Revenue Report*.

Every five years the Bureau of the Census conducts an economic census that includes a *Census of Transportation Industries*. Table 13.01 provides establishment, revenue, and annual payroll data for the transportation, communications, and public utilities industries in the state. An index at the back of the book lists tables from recent censuses appearing in previous editions of *Abstract*.

Employment and payroll figures for all modes of transportation except interstate railroads are supplied by the Bureau of Labor Market Information, Florida Department of Labor and Employment Security. Interstate railroads are not included because their employees are not covered by the same unemployment law as workers in other industries.

Data on miles of track in the state's rail system are from the Office of Planning, Florida Department of Transportation publication, *Florida Rail System Plan*.

Water transportation (SIC code 44) includes both the movement of vessels through Florida waterways and the volume of commodities shipped into and out of Florida ports. The authorities of the various ports in the state have supplied data on their activities.

Unpublished data on exports and imports through Florida customs are provided by Enterprise Florida's Department of Research.

Unpublished air traffic information comes from the Federal Aviation Administration of the U.S. Department of Transportation's Internet site, www.apo.data.faa.gov/, and from *Airport Activity of Certificated Route Air Carriers*.

SECTION 14.00. COMMUNICATIONS

EXPLANATORY NOTES. Newspaper publishing and other print media (SIC code 27) are considered to be manufacturing by the U.S. Bureau of the Census as well as the Office of Management and Budget, which establishes the Standard Industrial Classification. Since newspapers, periodicals, and books compete with electronic media in providing communications, data are repeated in this section. Table 12.50 in Section 12.00 shows newspapers as a component of the manufacturing industry. Also included in Section 14.00 are data on telephones (SIC code 481), telegraph (SIC code 482), radio and television broadcasting (SIC code 483), and cable and other pay TV services (SIC code 484).

SOURCES. Postal revenue data are provided by the U.S. Postal Service. The Florida Public Service Commission supplies data on telephone companies servicing Florida, including the data on number of calls and billed minutes. Employment and payroll data are from the Bureau of Labor Market Information, Florida Department of Labor and Employment Security. (See discussion under Section 6.00 of this Appendix.)

SECTION 15.00. POWER AND ENERGY

SOURCES. Data in this section have been selected to describe the status of the electric, gas, and sanitary service industries, and the consumption and production of electricity, gas, gasoline, fuel oil, and nuclear power. Energy information is supplied in various publications by the Energy Information Administration, U.S. Department of Energy. .

A major source of data on electrical energy in Florida is *Statistics of the Florida Electric Utility Industry* published by the Florida Public Service Commission. Natural gas statistics for the state are found in the Commission's *Annual Report* and on the Energy Information Administration, U.S. Department of Energy website, www.eia.doe.gov/, or in *Historical Natural Gas Annual.*

The Florida Department of Community Affairs (DCA) publishes *Florida Energy Data Report* and the *Florida Motor Gasoline and Diesel Fuel Report.* The DCA also compiled and provided information from U.S. Department of Energy published and unpublished data on energy consumption, pricing, and production along with state and county data on motor fuel consumption. Another source of state motor fuel data is *Highway Statistics*, published by the Federal Highway Administration.

The Bureau of Labor Market Information of the State Department of Labor and Employment Security supplies information on employment and payroll in the utility industry. (See discussion under Section 6.00 of this Appendix.)

Information on consumer prices of energy as measured by the Consumer Price Index is reported in Section 24.00.

SECTION 16.00. WHOLESALE AND RETAIL TRADE

SOURCES. Covered employment and payroll information by kind of business and county comes from the Bureau of Labor Market Information (BLMI), Florida Department of Labor and Employment Security. (See the discussion under Section 6.00 of this Appendix.) Since there are some differences in coverage and classification, BLMI figures are not necessarily comparable with those from the economic censuses conducted by the Bureau of the Census every five years. Data from the *1992 Census of Wholesale Trade* and *1992 Census of Retail Trade* comprise several tables in this section (An index of recent census tables appearing in previous *Abstracts* is at the back of this edition.) Number of establishments, employment, payroll, and sales are presented both by kind of business and by county in which the establishments are located.

The Florida Department of Revenue is the source for information on sales reported by firms in connection with the sales and use tax laws. In addition to the data presented in this section, printouts of county gross and taxable sales by business category are available from the Bureau of Economic and Business Research (BEBR), University of Florida on a subscription basis. These business categories vary in coverage and classification from the Bureau of the Census and the Florida Department of Commerce figures. Data on retail sales tax collections may be found in Table 23.43. A time series of gross and taxable sales is in Table 24.30.

Health professionals who operate at the retail level and are required to have a license such as dispensing opticians or pharmacists are reported by the Florida Department of Business and Professional Regulation. These data are presented in Section 20.00.

SECTION 17.00. FINANCE, INSURANCE, AND REAL ESTATE

EXPLANATORY NOTES. Industries covered in this section are those SIC codes numbered 60 through 67, including banking and other credit agencies, establishments dealing in securities and commodities, insurance and real estate offices, and investment firms.

SOURCES. Historical and recent summaries of banking data for Florida may be found in the *Annual Report of the Division of Banking*, published by the state Office of the Comptroller. Another major source of banking data is the Federal Deposit Insurance Corporation, which issues *Statistics on Banking* and *Data Book: Operating Banks and Branches.*

Figures on number of establishments, employment, and payroll for banking and credit, insurance, real estate and investment industries come from the Florida Department of Labor and Employment Security, Bureau of Labor Market Information. (See the discussion in Section 6.00 of this Appendix.)

A source of information on savings institutions is *Summary of Deposits in SAIF-Insured OTS Regulated Associations*. The mortgage loan activity data are presented in Table 17.33 by permission of Experian, Anaheim, CA. This firm collects loan activity data in forty counties and provides reports by subscription.

Data on homeowner and rental vacancy rates are from the Bureau of the Census, U.S. Department of Commerce annual publication *Housing Vacancy Survey*. These data may also be found on the Internet at www.census.gov/.

A basic source of information on activities of insurance companies in Florida is the *Annual Report of the Florida Department of Insurance*. Data on life insurance are from the American Council of Life Insurance in its *Life Insurance Fact Book*.

Information on licensed persons who handle real estate transactions is reported by the Florida Department of Business and Professional Regulation.

SECTION 18.00. PERSONAL AND BUSINESS SERVICES

EXPLANATORY NOTES. The Standard Industrial Classification System lists services from SIC code 70 to SIC code 89. A county-level aggregate of establishments with these codes appears in Table 18.28. Other tables in this section based on the establishments covered by the unemployment insurance law show data on personal services (SIC code 72), business services (SIC code 73), automotive repair, services, and parking (SIC code 75), miscellaneous repair services (SIC code 76), engineering, accounting, research, management and related services (SIC code 87), private household services (SIC code 88), and services not elsewhere classified (SIC code 89). Information about establishments with other service SIC codes are to be found in Sections 19.00, 20.00, and 22.00.

The U. S. Bureau of the Census has taken a Census of Services Industries as part of the economic census every five years since 1967. In 1977, coverage of service industries broadened from "selected services" to "all services except religious organizations and private households." Data on selected industries from the *1992 Census of Service Industries* are reported in Table 18.01. An index of recent census tables appearing in previous *Abstracts* is at the back of this edition.

SOURCES. Data on establishments, employment, and payroll of service establishments whose employees are covered by the unemployment insurance law are provided by the Bureau of Labor Market Information, Florida Department of Labor and Employment Security. (See the discussion under Section 6.00 of this Appendix.) Data for the same area and industry from the *Census of Service Industries* are not necessarily comparable because of differences in procedures, definitions, and establishments covered.

Many service establishments are operated by professional individuals who are licensed by the state. Data on these professionals have been supplied from the Florida Department of Business and Professional Regulation.

Information on health, educational, and cultural services is reported in Section 20.00.

SECTION 19.00. TOURISM AND RECREATION

EXPLANATORY NOTES. Estimates of the number of tourists entering Florida by automobile are made by the Florida Division of Tourism using traffic counts and information from welcome stations. Tourist arrivals by air are based on arrivals at major airports. Individual visitors are interviewed on a randomly selected basis about expenditures and length of stay. Sample results are expanded to the total visitor population.

SOURCES. The Office of Tourism Research, Florida Department of Commerce issues quarterly and county reports of tourist information and an annual report, *Florida Visitor Study*. The Transportation Statistics Office of the Florida Department of Transportation records traffic counts at strategic highway locations around the state. Data on tourist facilities (hotels, motels, and food service establishments) that are regulated by the Division of Hotels and Restaurants of the Florida Department of Business and Professional Regulation are available from the department's *Master File Statistics*. The Florida Department of Revenue provides information on the gross and taxable sales of businesses. Some businesses have been classified for purposes of presenting data in this section as "tourist- and recreation-related" businesses. The Department of Revenue also provides information on the tourist-development or local option tax collected in several counties.

Data on employment in tourist- and recreation-related industries come from the Bureau of Labor Market Information, Florida Department of Labor and Employment Security. (See discussion under Section 6.00 of this Appendix.)

Data on boats registered by county in Florida are provided by the Bureau of Vessel Titles and Registrations, Florida Department of Highway Safety and Motor Vehicles. Data on recreational boating and personal watercraft accidents are from the Office of Waterway Management, Division of Law Enforcement, Florida Department of Environmental Protection. The Recreation and Parks Management Information System, Florida Department of Environmental Protection issues information on the nature, size, and popularity of state parks. Data on national parks in Florida were taken from the *National Park Service Statistical Abstract*, published by the National Park Service, U.S. Department of the Interior.

SECTION 20.00. HEALTH, EDUCATION, AND CULTURAL SERVICES

SOURCES. Data on establishments, receipts and payroll in Table 20.01 are from the *1992 Census of Service Industries* conducted by the U.S. Bureau of the Census in years ending in 2 and 7. Data on employment are from the covered employment and payroll figures supplied by the Bureau of Labor Market Information, Florida Department of Labor and Employment Security. (See discussion under Section 6.00 of this Appendix.)

Information on physicians, dentists, nurses, opticians, pharmacists, and other licensed health service practitioners and professionals comes from the Florida Department of Business and Professional Regulation.

General, short-term acute care hospital data are from the Florida Agency for Health Care Administration publication *Guide to Hospitals in Florida*. A map of Community Health Purchasing Alliance (CHPA) regions is on page 552. The agency, in cooperation with Local Health Councils of Florida, also provided enrollment data for licensed Health Maintenance Organizations (HMOs) in the *Florida 1997 Health Data SourceBook*.

Library information is supplied by the Division of Library and Information Services, Florida Department of State in *Florida Library Directory with Statistics*.

Data on veterans hospitals come from the U.S. Department of Veterans Affairs, *Annual Report of the Secretary of Veterans Affairs*.

Educational establishment information comes from the Florida Department of Education: *Profiles of Florida School Districts*; *Statistical Briefs*; and unpublished data sources.

Federal aid data are from the *Statistical Abstract of the United States*. Information on arts grants to Florida groups and individuals by county is from *Florida Funding for Culture and the Arts* issued by the Division of Cultural Affairs, Florida Department of State.

SECTION 21.00. GOVERNMENT AND ELECTIONS

SOURCES. Every five years since 1957, the U.S. Bureau of the Census has conducted a Census of Governments. This census covers four major subject areas: governmental organization, taxable property values, public employment, and governmental finances. Table 21.01 presents information from Volume 1 of the 1992 census about governmental units by type in Florida and the United States. Table 21.07 shows numbers of local governments and elected officials in Florida by county and by type of government. An index of recent census tables appearing in previous *Abstract*s is at the back of this edition.

The Division of Elections in the Florida Department of State provides information on registered voters and numbers of votes cast in given elections. The U.S. Bureau of the Census provides voting-age population estimates. Estimates and projections on voting-age population, released annually by the Bureau of Economic and Business Research (BEBR), University of Florida, appear in tables 21.25 and 21.26.

Several private sources have granted permission to include data in this section. The Joint Center for Political and Economic Studies publishes the annual *Black Elected Officials: A National Roster*. The Council of State Governments publishes information on the composition of state legislatures in *State Elective Officials and the Legislature* and 1996 National Conference of State Legislatures unpublished data. Data on female officials may be found in copyrighted information releases from the Center for the American Woman and Politics, Eagleton Institute of Politics, Rutgers University found on Internet site www.rei.rutgers.edu/~cawp/.

Apportionment data are from the Bureau of the Census, U.S. Department of Commerce *1990 Census Profile: Population Trends and Congressional Apportionment*.

SECTION 22.00. COURTS AND LAW ENFORCEMENT

EXPLANATORY NOTES. Data on criminal offenses are subject to certain limitations. Many crimes are not reported to law enforcement agencies and hence are not counted in preparing crime statistics. Victims may report crimes to prosecuting authorities rather than to law enforcement agencies or for various reasons may not report at all.

An additional factor to consider when studying crime rates in Florida is the presence of large numbers of tourists. The crime rates in this section are based on resident population. When adjustments are made for the tourist presence, the crime rate in Florida drops.

SOURCES. The principal source of data on crimes and criminals in Florida is *Crime in Florida*, the annual report of the state Department of Law Enforcement, and other FDLE unpublished data.

Other sources on the criminal justice system include publications of two divisions of the U.S. Department of Justice: the annual *Crime in the United States* (www.fbi.gov/) from the Federal Bureau of Investigation, and reports and bulletins from the Bureau of Justice Statistics.

Data on county jails are from *Florida County Detention Facilities* issued by the Bureau of Planning, Research, and Statistics in the state Department of Corrections. Prison and prisoner information is made available by the Department of Corrections in its *Annual Report: The Guidebook to Corrections in Florida*.

Juvenile delinquency data are from the Bureau of Data and Research, Florida Department of Juvenile Justice, *Profile of Delinquency Cases and Youths Referred at each Stage of the Juvenile Justice System*.

Victim compensation data are from the *Annual Report* of the state Division of Victim Services, Office of the Attorney General, which also publishes *Hate Crimes in Florida* on their worldwide web Internet site legal.firn.edu/justice/.

Data on legal services come from the Florida Bar and the Bureau of Labor Market Information, Florida Department of Labor and Employment Security.

SECTION 23.00. GOVERNMENT FINANCE AND EMPLOYMENT

EXPLANATORY NOTES. A number of tables in the Health, Education, and Cultural Services section (20.00) contain data on property valuations, revenue, expenditure, and taxes for education by public agencies. In Section 19.00, Table 19.54 provides figures on the tourist-development/local option tax and Table 19.70 provides information about tax collections from tourist- and recreation-related businesses.

Although the official records of the Comptroller are used by the Bureau of the Census in its compilations on state and local government finances, the Bureau of the Census has found it necessary at times to classify and present the government financial statistics in terms of its own system of uniform concepts and categories rather than according to the diverse terminology and structure of individual governments. This procedure explains the differences that may be found between similar data from the two sources.

Public government employment data by industry and county are from the Bureau of Labor Market Information (BLMI), Florida Department of Labor and Employment Security.

International government employment is shown in Table 23.71 and in a footnote on Table 23.74.

SOURCES. The U.S. Bureau of the Census publishes a number of annual series and increasingly is providing data on the Internet (www.census.gov/). Users should contact the bureau for a list of current publications. It also conducts a Census of Governments every five years, coincident with the economic censuses. (An index of recent census tables in previous *Abstracts* appears at the end of this book).

Veterans' Administration expenditures shown on new Table 23.20 can be downloaded from their website, www.va.gov/.

Official records and reports of the Comptroller of the State of Florida comprise the basic source of information about government finances in Florida and are published in the *Florida Comprehensive Financial Report* and in unpublished form. Other State of Florida sources of data on government finances and employment include the Department of Revenue, *Florida Property Valuations and Tax Data*; the Department of Business and Professional Regulation, data on pari-mutuel wagering and beverage and tobacco licenses; Department of the Lottery for ticket sales; the Department of Highway Safety and Motor Vehicles for motor vehicle licenses; *The Report of the State Treasurer*; the Bureau of Labor Market Information on employment and payroll; the Division of Retirement, *Annual Report*; and the Florida Department of Banking and Finance. Due to governmental reorganization and financial cut-backs, some state publications are no longer being produced. Users are encouraged to search government agency web sites on the Internet.

The Florida Department of Revenue annually reviews the ad valorem tax rolls submitted by county property appraisers and Armasi, Inc., compiles data from the tax rolls, making the data available with software that displays data geographically by county. Table 23.95 presents assessed land use values by county summarized by Armasi, Inc., from the Department of Revenue files.

SECTION 24.00. ECONOMIC INDICATORS AND PRICES

EXPLANATORY NOTES. Tables in the first twenty-three sections of the *Abstract* are primarily cross-sectional or "snapshot" portrayals of a set of circumstances or a situation existing at any one time. Because many readers are interested in charting trends over time, most tables in Section 24.00 contain data over several years.

Consumer price indexes are developed by the Bureau of Labor Statistics (BLS) of the U.S. Department of Labor and appear in the monthly *CPI Detailed Report* and Internet site stats.bls.gov:80/. The BLS publishes two indexes: one reflecting the buying habits of all urban households (CPI-U) and one reflecting the buying habits of urban wage earners and clerical workers (CPI-W). Both indexes are comparable with historical CPI figures; the index for all urban households is used in tables in this section (except for the entry of the CPI-W index in Table 24.73). The CPI-U is based on information reflecting the buying habits of about 80 percent of the U.S. population and represents all urban residents, including professional workers, the self-employed, the poor, the unemployed, and retired persons. Not included are persons living outside urban areas, farm families, persons in military services, and those in institutions. The Bureau of Labor Statistics issues a bimonthly CPI for the Miami-Ft. Lauderdale CMSA and Tampa-St. Petersburg-Clearwater MSA. (See Table 24.74.)

University of Florida   **Bureau of Economic and Business Research**

Both the CPI-U and the CPI-W use updated expenditure weights based on data tabulated from the consumer expenditure surveys. Also, the rental equivalence measures of home ownership costs in both the CPI-U and the CPI-W were improved to better represent both owners' and renters' shelter costs.

The series of producer prices appears in Tables 24.72 and 24.75. According to the BLS, the series measures the average changes in prices received in primary markets of the United States by producers of commodities in all stages of processing. The sample used for calculating the indexes contains nearly 2,800 commodities and about 10,000 quotations selected to represent the movement of prices of all commodities produced in the agriculture, forestry, fishing, mining, manufacturing, gas, electric, and all public utilities sectors.

The *Florida Price Level Index* (FPLI) is prepared by the Office of Education Budget and Management, Florida Department of Education. The FPLI measures relative price levels across counties. Items representative of the expenditure categories used by the BLS in the CPI are surveyed in each county. Table 24.79 shows the relative weights of selected items in the survey; Table 24.80 compares the index and subindexes for major items across counties.

Data on price trends in construction are in Section 11.00. Section 15.00 contains additional information on energy prices.

The Bureau of Economic Analysis, U.S. Department of Commerce introduced estimates of Gross State Product (GSP) by state, by component, and by industry for each state for the period 1936-1986. GSP is the gross market value of goods and services attributable to labor and property located in the state. It is the state counterpart to national Gross Domestic Product (GDP). These estimates have been updated through 1994 (see Table 24.14 and 24.15), and are available on CD-ROM from the Regional Economic Information System.

SOURCES. Extensive series of economic indicators for the United States, Florida, and its counties are maintained in the BEBR Data Base, Bureau of Economic and Business Research, University of Florida. Data surveying consumer confidence is presented in the BEBR monthly publication, *Florida Economic and Consumer Survey.*

The Bureau of Labor Statistics, U.S. Department of Labor prepares consumer and producer price indexes and publishes them in detailed monthly reports and on the Internet.

The Department of Revenue of the State of Florida has data on sales and use tax collections. The Department of Labor and Employment Security provided employment data.

The International Trade Administration, U.S. Department of Commerce reports building permit activity in the states in *Construction Review.* Table 24.20 presents data from current and previous editions of this publication back to 1984.

Data on new incorporations and failures of industrial and commercial establishments shown in Table 24.78 are available by permission from the copyrighted reports, *New Business Incorporations* and *Business Failure Report*, published by Dun & Bradstreet.

The Florida Public Service Commission provides electricity price data in *Statistics of the Florida Electric Utility Industry.*

SECTION 25.00. STATE COMPARISONS

SOURCES. Both economic and noneconomic factors are listed in Table 25.01 to permit the reader to compare aspects of life in Florida to similar living conditions in other Sunbelt and populous states. There are numerous sources to this table, most of which have been discussed in previous sections. The *Statistical Abstract of the United States* published by the Bureau of the Census is a primary source as is census bureau information on the Internet (www.census.gov/). Sources not previously mentioned are the Federal Deposit Insurance Corporation, *Quarterly Banking Profile;* Bureau of the Census, *Black-owned Businesses, Women-owned Businesses;* and *Federal Expenditures by State*, U.S. Department of Health and Human Services,

Monthly Vital Statistics Report and *Medicaid Statistics: Program and Financial Statistics*; National Center for Health Statistics, *Health United States and Injury Chartbook;* U.S. Department of Energy, Energy Information Administration, *Electric Sales and Revenue; Sourcebook of Criminal Justice Statistics* from the U.S. Department of Justice, Bureau of Justice Statistics, and the copyrighted report *Physicians Characteristics and Distributions in the U.S.* published by the American Medical Association.

SUMMARY OF SOURCES

STATE SOURCES. Most of the state publications are available free of charge from the agency issuing the report. Supplies are frequently limited and sometimes requests cannot be honored unless they come from other state agencies. Increasingly, publication reproductions and/or unpublished data can be retrieved from the Internet. The state has a system of state depository libraries, coordinated by the Division of Library Services, Florida Department of State, R.A. Gray Building, Tallahassee. All state agency publications are supposed to be on file in depository libraries or available for interlibrary loan. The reference departments of most libraries are willing to answer questions about data in these publications if the requests are not too time-consuming. The Florida Division of State Library Services issues a monthly and annual summary of state agency publications called *Florida Public Documents*.

Depository libraries of the State of Florida include the public libraries of Bay, Broward, and Orange counties, Cocoa, Jacksonville, Miami Beach, Miami-Dade, Ocala, St. Petersburg, Tampa-Hillsborough, and West Palm Beach. University libraries designated as depositories are those at Central Florida, Florida Atlantic, Florida (Gainesville), Florida International, Florida State, Miami, North Florida, South Florida, West Florida, Jacksonville, and Stetson. The State Library of Florida in the R.A. Gray Building in Tallahassee also is a depository.

FEDERAL SOURCES. Some federal reports are available without charge from the agency issuing the information, but most federal publications must be purchased from the Superintendent of Documents, U.S. Government Printing Office (GPO), Washington, D.C. 20402 (phone 202/783-3238) or from a local Government Printing Office bookstore. Publications purchased from the GPO must be prepaid. As noted throughout this edition, agencies are making use of the Internet to provide easy access to publications and free data to users. The *Statistical Abstract of the United States* is similar in purpose to the *Florida Statistical Abstract* and much more comprehensive. Readers interested in information about the nation, its regions, and states are referred to it.

The federal government also maintains a system of depository libraries in all fifty states, usually the same libraries as state depositories. The University of Florida is designated as a regional depository library and is required to receive and retain one copy of all depository government publications made available to depository libraries either in print or on microfiche. Many of the libraries listed above as state depositories are also federal depositories and some are not listed. Refer to the annual directory printed by the University of Florida Libraries, *Federal Document Depositories and Resource Information for Florida and Puerto Rico.*

PRIVATE SOURCES. A number of private agencies and associations issue publications or reports which have been used in this and recent editions of *Abstract.* Some are copyrighted and have been used with permission. Several have additional information which can be obtained for a fee.

American Council of Life Insurance, Washington, D.C.
American Medical Association, Chicago, Illinois
Center for the American Woman and Politics (CAWP), Eagleton Institute of Politics, Rutgers University
Council of State Governments, Lexington, Kentucky
Dun & Bradstreet Corporation, New York, New York
Enterprise Florida, Orlando, Florida

Federal Deposit Insurance Corporation, Washington, D.C.
Florida Association of Homes for the Aging, Tallahassee, Florida
Joint Center for Political and Economic Studies, Washington, D.C.
National Conference of State Legislatures, Denver, Colorado
Experian, Anaheim, California

COMPUTER TAPES. The University of Florida Library in Gainesville maintains an extensive collection of information about Florida in books and files and on computer tapes. All the data from the population, housing and economic censuses can be accessed from their computer tapes. Data from the 1990 census and the Bureau of Labor Statistics are also available on CD-ROM. Many agencies make data available through the Internet worldwide computer network; this source may eventually replace many printed publications.

BUREAU PUBLICATIONS. The Bureau of Economic and Business Research (BEBR) at the University of Florida can supply a variety of detailed information about Florida:

Florida Estimates of Population. Intercensal estimates of the population of Florida, its counties, cities, and unincorporated areas. Also includes components of population change and density figures. Published annually. A summary of census results is published in census years.

Florida Population Studies. Bulletins providing information on age, race, and sex components of Florida's population, household numbers and average household size, projections of population, discussions of estimation and projection methodology, and other topics related to population. Published three times a year.

Special Population Reports. 1995 estimates of Hispanic population with age and sex detail is the most recent of these four releases. Also include revised 1980-90 population estimates by county, an evaluation of population projection errors for Florida counties and an evaluation of 1990 population estimation. Published periodically.

Florida and the Nation. Comparison statistics and ranked data for Florida, the other 49 states, and the United States.

Florida Business Briefs. A monthly publication targeted toward organizations and individuals who do business in Florida. Each issue features a current business topic, results from our monthly household survey, and items of local interest.

The Florida Long-term Economic Forecast. A two-volume long-range economic forecast of income, employment, construction, and population for the State of Florida, its metropolitan areas, and counties. Volume One focuses on the state and MSAs and Volume Two on the state and counties. Published annually.

Florida County Rankings. At-a-glance ranked data for more than 400 current data topics for all Florida counties, with a state comparison for each topic and pertinent data maps.

County Perspective. Individual ranking reports for each of Florida's 67 counties in the same categories used in *Florida County Rankings*, with historical data summaries.

Building Permit Activity in Florida. Monthly comparisons with year-to-date data, with an annual summary, of the value and number of units permitted in the state, counties, cities, and unincorporated areas of Florida.

The Economy of Florida. Twenty-three experts explore the many sectors of Florida's economy, including international trade, telecommunications, regions, health care, the labor market, housing, banking, military bases and defense manufacturing, and tourism.

1990 Census Handbook: Florida. Over 600 pages of census information for Florida, its counties, congressional districts and most populous cities and comparisons of Florida with the other forty-nine states.

Gross and taxable sales information. Printouts of sales information from the Florida Department of Revenue reports of gross and taxable sales for the sales and use taxes. Available by county and by kind-of-business category. Issued monthly and annually.

Florida Economic and Consumer Survey. Monthly survey data on Florida consumers' confidence in the national and local economies, buying plans, personal financial condition, and special topics.

University of Florida   **Bureau of Economic and Business Research**

BEBR Monographs. In-depth analyses of topics relevant to an understanding of the Florida economic and business climate. Issued periodically. Current titles include *Population Projections: What Do We Really Know?*; *Local Government Economic Analysis Using Microcomputers*; *Cuban Immigration and Immigrants in Florida and the United States: Implications for Immigration Policy*; *Urban Development Issues: What is Controversial in Urban Sprawl?*; *Preparing the Economic Element of the Comprehensive Plan*; *Concurrency Management Systems in Florida: A Catalog and Analysis*; and *The Economic Impact of Local Government Comprehensive Plans.*

BEBR Data Base. A computerized data management system containing extensive economic data for the United States, Florida, and all counties. Provides PC access to current and historical data for Florida, any of its counties and Metropolitan Statistical Areas, and for the United States. Continuously updated.

Migration releases. Based on data collected by the U.S. Bureau of the Census and Internal Revenue Service these BEBR-prepared reports include state and county migration flows with age, sex, and race detail. Updated as data becomes available.

For pricing and ordering information, please contact:
Bureau of Economic and Business Research
221 Matherly Hall
P. O. Box 117145
University of Florida
Gainesville, Florida 32611-7145
Phone: 352/392-0171   FAX: 352/392-4739
The Internet: http://www.cba.ufl.edu/bebr/
E-mail: bebr@bebr.cba.ufl.edu

GLOSSARY

ALIEN. Person who is not a citizen of the United States whether or not he/she is a resident, legally or illegally.

AMERICAN INDIAN, ESKIMO, OR ALEUT POPULATION. See Race.

ANCESTRY. A person's nationality group, lineage, or the country in which the person or the person's parents or ancestors were born before their arrival in the U.S. Different from other indicators of ethnicity, such as country of birth and language spoken in home and is a separate characteristic from race.

ASIAN OR PACIFIC ISLANDER POPULATION. See Race.

BLACK POPULATION. See Race.

BUSINESS ESTABLISHMENT. A commercial enterprise.

CHILDREN. Sons and daughters classified as "own child of householder," including stepchildren and adopted children, who have never been married and are under age 18.

CIVILIAN LABOR FORCE. See Labor Force.

CLASS OF WORKERS. Private wage and salary workers who work for a private employer for wages, salary, commission, tips, pay-in-kind, or at price rates. Private employers include churches and other nonprofit organizations. Also includes persons who consider themselves self-employed but who work for corporations where in most cases these persons own or are a part of a group that owns controlling interest in the corporation.
Government workers who work for a governmental unit, regardless of the activity of the particular agency.
Self-employed workers who work for profit or fees in their own unincorporated business, profession, or trade, or who operate a farm. Includes owner-operators of large stores and manufacturing establishments, as well as small merchants, independent craft-persons and professionals, farmers, peddlers, and other persons who conduct enterprises of their own.
Unpaid family workers who work without pay on a farm or in a business operated by a person to whom they are related by blood or marriage.

COLLEGE STUDENTS. See Residency.

COMMUNITY HEALTH PURCHASING ALLIANCE (CHPA). Authorized by the 1993 Florida legislature to assist members of the alliance in securing the highest quality health care at the lowest possible price. Membership is voluntary and available primarily to businesses that have 50 or fewer employees. CHPAs are state-chartered, not-for-profit, private purchasing organizations and have exclusive territories.

COMMUTE. Travel back and forth regularly, usually between place of residence and place of work.

CONSOLIDATED METROPOLITAN STATISTICAL AREA (CMSA). A large metropolitan complex with a population over one million in which individual metropolitan components, Primary Metropolitan Statistical Areas (PMSAs), have been defined.

CONSUMER PRICE INDEX (CPI). A measure of the average level of prices over time in a fixed market collection of goods and services. The index is intended to represent prices of most items and services that people purchase in daily living, and is calculated to represent purchases by urban wage earners and clerical workers or by all urban consumers.

CONTRACT RENT. See Rent.

COUNTY. An administrative subdivision of a state; a local government organization and political jurisdiction authorized and designated by a state's constitution or statutes.

DROPOUT. A student over the age of compulsory school attendance (16) who has voluntarily removed himself from the school system before graduation; or who has not met attendance requirements; or who has withdrawn from school but has not transferred to another public or private school or enrolled in any other educational program; or has withdrawn from school due to hardship without official granting of such withdrawal; or is not eligible to attend school because of reaching the maximum age for an exceptional student program.

EARNINGS. Sum of wage and salary income and net income from farm and nonfarm self-employment. Reported before deductions for personal income taxes, social security, bond purchases, union dues, and other deductions.

EDUCATIONAL ATTAINMENT. Years of school completed.

EMPLOYED PERSONS. All civilians 16 years of age and over that work at all as paid employees for an employer, or in their own business or profession, on their own farm, or who work 15 hours or more as unpaid workers in an enterprise operated by a family member and all those temporarily absent from their jobs due to such factors as illness or vacation (during a given reference week).

ENERGY. The ability to do work; can exist in many forms such as chemical, light, heat, etc.
Primary energy is energy available from conversion of original fuel rather than from a secondary form such as electricity.
Renewables are energy sources that can be used continuously or regenerated quickly such as wind, sunlight, wood, and solid waste.

FAMILY HOUSEHOLD. A householder and one or more other person(s) living in the same household who are related to the householder by birth, marriage, or adoption. All persons in a household who are related to the householder and are regarded as members of his or her family.

FAMILY HOUSEHOLD INCOME. See Income.

FARM. For the 1990 census, property of one acre or more where $1,000 or more of agricultural products were sold from the property in 1989.

FARM POPULATION. See Rural farm population.

FIRM. A business organization or entity consisting of one or more establishment(s) under common owner-ship or control; a commercial partnership of two or more persons.

GENERAL, SHORT-TERM ACUTE CARE HOSPITAL. Establishment that offers services more in-tensive than those required for room, board, personal services, and general nursing care. Offers facilities and beds for use beyond 24 hours by individuals requiring diagnosis, treatment, or care for illness, injury, deformity, infirmity, abnormality, disease, or pregnancy. Regularly makes available at least clinical laboratory services, diagnostic radiology services, and treatment facilities for surgery, medical, or obstetrical care, or other definitive medical treatment of similar extent.

GROSS STATE PRODUCT (GSP). The gross market value of the goods and services attributable to labor and property located in a state.

GROUP QUARTERS. All persons not living in households are classified by the Census Bureau as living in group quarters—institutional and noninstitutional. Institutional group quarters are all institutions offering care or custody, e.g., prisons, mental hospitals, nursing homes, juvenile institutions. Noninstitutional quarters include workers' dormitories, monasteries, convents, large rooming houses or boarding houses or communes having at least ten persons unrelated to the resident who maintains the living quarters. Noninstitutional quarters also cover certain living arrangements regardless of the number or relationship of the people in the unit such as military barracks, college dormitories, missions and emergency shelters for the homeless. Data on the homeless also include visible in street locations or predesignated street sites, (e.g., bridges, parks, bus depots) where the homeless congregate.

HISPANIC ORIGIN. Persons who classified themselves in one of the Hispanic-origin categories listed on the census questionnaire—Mexican, Puerto Rican, Cuban, or other Spanish/Hispanic origin. This latter category includes those whose origins are from Spain or the Spanish-speaking countries of Central or South America, or the Dominican Republic, or they are Hispanic-origin persons identify-ing themselves generally as Spanish, Spanish-American, Hispanic, Latino, etc. Origin can be viewed as the ancestry, nationality group, lineage or country in which the person or person's parents or ancestors were born before their arrival in the U.S. Persons of Hispanic origin may be of any race. Households and families are classified by the Hispanic origin of the householder.

HOMELESS POPULATION. See Group quarters.

HOMEOWNER VACANCY RATE. The proportion of the homeowner inventory which is vacant for sale. Rates are computed by dividing the vacant year-round units for sale only by the sum of the number of owner-occupied units, vacant year-round units sold but awaiting occupancy, and vacant year-round units for sale only.

HOMEOWNER VACANCY RATE. The proportion of the homeowner inventory which is vacant for sale. Rates are computed by dividing the vacant year-round units for sale only by the sum of the number of owner-occupied units, vacant year-round units sold but awaiting occupancy, and vacant year-round units for sale only.

HOUSEHOLD. The person or persons occupying a housing unit. Designation of a household as "family" or "nonfamily" is based on the householder. If the household has family members of the house-holder, then it is classified as a family household. If the householder is an individual unrelated to other household members, lives alone, or is living in group quarters (not institutionalized), then the household is classified as a nonfamily household.

HOUSEHOLD INCOME. See Income.

HOUSEHOLDER. Person, or one of the persons, in whose name the home is owned or rented and who is listed in column one of the census questionnaire. If there is no such person in the household, any adult household member could be designated as "householder."
Family householder is a householder living with one or more person(s) related to him or her by birth, marriage, or adoption.
Nonfamily householder is a householder living alone or with nonrelatives only.

HOUSING UNIT. A house, an apartment, a group of rooms, or a single room occupied as a separate living quarters, or if vacant, intended for occupancy as a separate living quarters.
Occupied housing unit is the usual place of residence of the person or group of persons living there at the time of the census enumeration, or the unit from which the occupants are only temporarily absent (away on vacation, etc.).
Owner-occupied housing unit is one in which the owner or co-owner lives, whether the unit is owned without lien or mortgaged.
Renter-occupied unit is any unit not classified as owner-occupied, including a unit rented for cash rent or one occupied without payment of cash rent.
Vacant housing unit has no one living in it at the time of census enumeration, unless the occupants are only temporarily absent. May be classified as "seasonal and migratory," or "year-round." Seasonal unit is intended for occupancy during only certain seasons of the year. Migratory unit is held for occupancy for migratory labor employed in farm work during crop season. Year-round vacant unit is available or intended for occupancy at any time of the year.

IMMIGRANTS. Aliens admitted for legal permanent residence in the United States, including persons who may have entered as nonimmigrants or refugees, but who subsequently changed their status to that of a permanent resident.

INCOME. The amount of money or monetary equivalent received during a specified time period in exchange for work performed, sale of goods or property, or from profits made on financial investments.
Adjusted gross income is a tax-defined concept of income. Certain kinds of income such as some portion of capital gains, social security, and in-kind transfer payments are excluded and certain types of expenses such as some trade and business expenses, alimony payments, and contributions to individual retirement plans are deducted.
Family household income and nonfamily household income are compiled by summing and treating as a single amount the money income of all family or nonfamily household members aged 15 and over. Household income includes the money income of the householder and all other persons aged 15 and over in the household, whether related to the householder or not. Because many households consist of only one person, average household income is usually less than average family income.
Interest, dividend, or net rental income includes interest on savings or bonds, dividends from stockholdings or membership in associations, net royalties, and net income from rental of property to others and receipts from boarders or lodgers.
Labor income is an item generally used for various types of supplemental earnings in cash and in kind.
Mean income is the amount obtained by dividing the total income of a particular statistical universe by the number of units in that universe.
Median income is the amount that divides the income distribution into two equal groups, one having incomes above the median and the other having incomes below the median. For households, families, and unrelated individuals the median income is based on the distribution of the total number of units including those with no income. The median for persons is based on persons with income.

Money income is an income definition of the Census Bureau. It is the sum of amounts reported separately for wage and salary income; net nonfarm self-employment income; net farm self-employment income; interest, dividend, net royalty or rental income; social security or railroad retirement income; public assistance or welfare income; unemployment compensation; alimony; veterans' payments; and all other income. Not included are monies received from the sale of property owned by a recipient; the value of income "in-kind" from food stamps, public housing subsidies, medical care, employer contributions for pensions, etc.; withdrawal of bank deposits; money borrowed; tax refunds; exchanges of money between relatives living in the same household; gifts and lump-sum inheritances, insurance payments, and other types of lump-sum receipts.

Personal income is an income definition of the Bureau of Economic Analysis. It is the sum of current income received by persons from all sources and is measured before deduction of personal contributions to social insurance programs and income and other personal taxes. It is reported in current dollars and includes the following categories of earnings: private and governmental wages and salaries; labor income; farm and nonfarm proprietors' income; property income; and government and business transfer payments, but excludes transfers among persons. (Also, includes some nonmonetary income such as estimated net rental values—to owner—of owner-occupied homes, and the value of services furnished without payment, and food and fuel produced and consumed on farms.)

Disposable personal income is personal income less personal tax and nontax payments. Personal taxes include income, estate, gift, personal property and license taxes. Nontax payments include fines and penalties, tuition, and donations.

Property income is net rental income, dividends, and interest.

Proprietors' income is net income of owners of unincorporated businesses (farm and nonfarm, with the latter including the income of independent professionals).

Public assistance income includes three items: supplementary security income payments made by federal or state welfare agencies to low-income persons aged 65 or over, blind, or disabled; aid to families with dependent children; and general assistance. Separate payments received for hospital or other medical care are excluded.

Social security income includes social security pensions and survivors' benefits and permanent disability insurance payments made by the Social Security Administration prior to deductions. Medicare reimbursements are not included.

INDUSTRIAL CLASSIFICATION SYSTEM, STANDARD. Industrial classification system for classifying establishments by type of economic activity. Developed and published in a manual by the Executive Office of the President, Office of Management and Budget, and revised and published in 1987 (which supersedes the 1972/77 edition). Major industries are assigned two-digit SIC codes: 01 through 99; subdivisions are classified by three- and four-digit codes. The major industry groups and their SIC codes are as follows:

Agriculture (01, 02, 07)
Forestry and fisheries (08, 09)
Mining (10-14)
Construction (15-17)
Manufacturing (20-39)
Transportation, communications, and public utilities (40-49)
Wholesale trade (50-51)
Retail trade (52-59)
Finance, insurance, and real estate (60-67)
Services (70-89)
Public administration (91-97)
Nonclassifiable establishments (99)

An example of SIC coding is the construction industry, which is divided into major group SIC 15, "building construction—general contractors and operative builders"; group SIC 16, "heavy construction other than building construction"; and group SIC 17, "construction—special trade contractors." Group 15 is in turn divided into group 152, "general building contractors, residential buildings," group 153, "operative builders," and 154, "general building contractors, nonresidential buildings." Group 152 is subdivided into 1521, "general contractors, single-family houses," and 1522, "general contractors, residential buildings, other than single-family."

INMATES OF INSTITUTIONS. See Group quarters.

INTEREST, DIVIDEND, OR NET RENTAL INCOME. See Income.

LABOR FORCE. Includes the civilian labor force, which comprises all civilians in the noninstitutional population 16 years and over classified as "employed" or "unemployed" and members of the Armed Forces stationed in the United States.

MANUFACTURED HOUSING. Any prefabricated dwelling such as a mobile home or modular housing.

MANUFACTURING ESTABLISHMENT. An enterprise usually consisting of a single physical location where raw materials are transformed into new products.

MARITAL STATUS. Classification refers to the status of persons aged 15 and over at the time of census enumeration. Couples who live together (unmarried persons, common-law marriages) were allowed to report the marital status they considered the most appropriate. Persons reported as separated are those living apart because of marital discord, with or without a legal separation. Persons in common-law marriages are classified as now married, except separated if they consider this category most appropriate; persons whose only marriage has been annulled are classified as never married; persons married at the time of enumeration (including those separated), widowed, or divorced are classified as ever married. Persons whose current marriage has not ended by widowhood or divorce are classified as now married. This category includes married persons whose spouse may have been (1) temporarily absent for such reasons as travel or hospitalization; (2) absent, including all married persons living in group quarters, employed spouses living away from home or in an institution, or absent in the Armed Forces; and (3) those who are separated.

MARKET VALUE. Amount a seller reasonably expects to obtain in a market for commodities, merchandise, services, or whatever is being sold.

MEDICAID. A jointly funded state and federal health care program for low-income persons. States establish their own eligibility criteria and may set benefits above the minimum established by federal law.

MEDICARE. Federal health insurance program for people aged 65 and over. Also covers (since 1973) eligible disabled persons of any age and persons with chronic kidney disease.

METROPOLITAN POPULATION. Population living inside Metropolitan Statistical Areas (MSAs) or Consolidated Metropolitan Statistical Areas (CMSAs).

METROPOLITAN STATISTICAL AREA (MSA). A geographic area with a large population nucleus together with adjacent communities, which has a high degree of economic and social integration with the nucleus. An MSA may include entire counties and generally has a city of at least 50,000 population or an urbanized area of at least 50,000 with a total metropolitan population of at least 100,000. This term replaces the term Standard Metropolitan Statistical Area, which was used prior to January 1983. See map at front of the book for list of counties in MSAs.

MOBILE HOME. Movable dwelling, ten or more feet wide and thirty-five or more feet long (a movable dwelling of less than these dimensions is considered to be a travel trailer or a motor home), designed to be towed on its own chassis and without need of a permanent foundation. Does not include prefabricated or modular housing, travel trailers, and other self-propelled vehicles such as motor homes. Mobile homes or trailers to which one or more permanent rooms have been added or built are classified by the Census Bureau as single-unit, detached housing.

MILITARY PERSONNEL. See Labor force and Residency.

MILL. Unit of monetary value equal to 1/1000 of a U.S. dollar.

MILLAGE RATE. Tax rate stated in mills where one mill produces one dollar of tax for every $1,000 of taxable property.

MONEY INCOME. See Income.

MUNICIPALITY. Political subdivision within which a municipal corporation has been established to provide a general local government for a specific population concentration in a defined area. In Florida, municipalities may be called cities, towns, or villages and have been established either by special acts of the legislature or by general law.

NONFAMILY HOUSEHOLDER. See Householder.

NONMETROPOLITAN POPULATION. Population living outside of metropolitan areas (as defined by the U.S. Office of Management and Budget).

NONPUBLIC SCHOOL. See Private school.

NONRELATIVES. Any persons in the household not related to the householder by birth, marriage, or adoption. Includes roomers, boarders, partners, roommates, paid employees, wards, and foster children.

OCCUPATIONAL LICENSING. Required operational licenses for professional persons who operate at the retail level such as dispensing opticians or pharmacists.

OCCUPIED HOUSING UNIT. See Housing unit.

OWNER-OCCUPIED HOUSING UNIT. See Housing unit.

PER CAPITA. A per capita (per person) figure is defined by taking the total for some item (e.g., government expenditures, income) and dividing it by the number of persons in the specified population.

PERSONAL INCOME. See Income.

PERSONS PER FAMILY. Number of persons living in families divided by the number of families.

PERSONS PER HOUSEHOLD. Number of persons living in households divided by the number of households.

PLACE OF BIRTH. For census enumeration, the mother's usual state or country of residence at the time of birth. Native-born persons are those born in the U.S., Puerto Rico, or an outlying area of the U.S. Includes a small number of persons born at sea or in a foreign country but with at least one American parent. Foreign-born persons are those not classified as native born.

PLACE OF WORK. Geographic location at which workers carry out their occupational activities.

POVERTY STATUS. In census publications, based on a definition developed by the Social Security Administration in 1964 and revised by a federal interagency committee in 1969 and 1980. Defined by income levels that (depending on family or household size) describe a family or household as being in extreme want of necessities. Income cutoffs or poverty thresholds used by the Bureau of the Census to determine the poverty status of families and individuals are defined by family size and by presence and number of family members aged 18 and under. Unrelated individuals and two-person families are differentiated by age of householder. If total income of a family or individual is less than the corresponding threshold, the family or individual is classified as below the poverty level. Poverty thresholds are adjusted annually to allow for changes in the cost of living as reflected in the Consumer Price Index and are computed on a national basis only. The poverty index is based on money income and does not take into account noncash benefits, such as food stamps, Medicaid, and public housing. Differences in poverty thresholds based on farm-nonfarm residence have been eliminated. Nonfarm thresholds now apply to all families. Beginning in 1987, poverty thresholds are based on revised processing procedures and are not directly comparable with prior years.

POVERTY THRESHOLD. See Poverty status.

PRIMARY METROPOLITAN STATISTICAL AREA (PMSA). A Metropolitan Statistical Area which is part of a larger urban complex with a population over one million and is designated as a Consolidated Metropolitan Statistical Area (CMSA).

PRIVATE SCHOOL. Any individual, association, co-partnership, or corporation which designates itself an education center and which includes kindergarten or a higher grade below college level. Primarily supported by private funds.

PROPERTY INCOME. See Income.

PROPRIETORS' INCOME. See Income.

PUBLIC ASSISTANCE INCOME. See Income.

PUBLIC SCHOOL. Any school controlled and supported primarily by a local, state, or federal agency.

RACE. In census enumeration, reflects self-identification by respondents and does not necessarily denote a scientific definition of biological stock.
American Indian, Eskimo, or Aleut includes persons who are classified in one of these specific categories or who entered the name of a specific Indian tribe.
Asian or Pacific Islander includes persons who indicated their race as Japanese (also Nipponese and Japanese American), Chinese (also Cantonese, Tibetan, Chinese American, Taiwanese, and Formosan),

Cambodian, Hmong, Filipino, Korean, Thai, Vietnamese, Asian Indian, Hawaiian, Guamanian, Samoan, Laotian, or entered responses classified as other Asian or other Pacific Islander.

Black includes those who indicated their race as Black or Negro, or who classified themselves as African American, Afro-American, Jamaican, Black Puerto Rican, West Indian, Haitian, or Nigerian.

White includes those who indicated their race as "white," as well as persons who entered a response such as Canadian, German, Italian, Arab, Near Easterner, Lebanese, or Polish.

The other race category includes all persons not listed in the race categories described above. Persons reporting in the "other race" category and providing write-in entries such as multiracial, multiethnic, mixed, interracial, Wesort, or Spanish/Hispanic origin group (such as Mexican, Cuban, or Puerto Rican) are included here.

RENT. Contract (cash) rent is the monthly rent agreed to, or contracted for, regardless of any furnishings, utilities, fees, meals, or services that may be included. For vacant units, it is the monthly rent asked at the time of enumeration. In some tabulations, contract rent is presented for all renter-occupied housing units, as well as for "specified renter-occupied" housing units and for "specified vacant-for-rent" housing units which include renter units except one-family houses or mobile homes on 10 or more acres. Respondents were asked to exclude any rent paid for additional units or for business premises. Gross rent is the contract rent plus the estimated average monthly cost of utilities if these are paid by the renter. Renter units occupied without payment of cash rent are shown separately as no cash rent.

RENTAL VACANCY RATE. The proportion of the rental inventory which is vacant for rent. Rates are computed by dividing the vacant year-round units for rent by the sum of the number of renter-occupied units, vacant year-round units rented by awaiting occupancy, and vacant year-round units for rent.

RENTER-OCCUPIED HOUSING UNIT. See Housing unit.

RESIDENCY. The place where a person lives and sleeps most of the time is the usual residence. It may not be the person's legal or voting residence. College students are considered residents of the community in which they live while attending college. Military personnel (persons in the Armed Forces) are counted as residents of the area in which their installations are located. Persons staying only temporarily away from their usual residence (e.g., migrant workers, vacationers) are considered to have a usual home elsewhere in which they are counted for census purposes.

RETAIL TRADE. Businesses primarily engaged in selling merchandise for personal, household, or farm consumption.

RURAL FARM POPULATION. Only in rural areas and includes all persons living on places of one acre or more from which at least $1,000 worth of agricultural products were sold during 1989.

RURAL POPULATION. Population not classified as urban.

SCHOOL DISTRICT. A political organization and jurisdiction that supports and administers local public schools. There is an independent school district in each Florida county and there are 28 community college districts in the state.

SCHOOL MEMBERSHIP (ENROLLMENT). Cumulative number of students registered during a school year.

SERVICE INDUSTRIES. Establishments primarily engaged in rendering a wide variety of services to individuals and to business establishments.

SIC. Abbreviation of Standard Industrial Classification. See Industrial Classification System, Standard.

SOCIAL SECURITY INCOME. See Income.

SPANISH ORIGIN. See Hispanic origin.

SPECIAL DISTRICT. A local government entity established to provide one or more specific function(s) such as fire protection, public transit, water management, libraries, or hospitals. About one-third of Florida's special districts have taxing power.

TENURE OF HOUSING UNIT. See Housing unit.

TRANSFER PAYMENTS. General disbursements to persons for which they do not render current services. These include payments by government and business to individuals and nonprofit institutions.

UNEMPLOYED PERSONS. All civilians 16 years of age and over who do not work and who actively seek employment, and who are available to work except for temporary illness (during a given reference week).

UNRELATED INDIVIDUAL. Householder living alone or with nonrelatives or household member who is not related to the householder by blood, marriage, or adoption, or person living in group quarters who is not an inmate of an institution.

URBAN POPULATION. Comprises all persons living in urbanized areas and in places (incorporated and unincorporated) of 2,500 or more inhabitants outside urbanized areas.

URBANIZED AREA. Incorporated place and adjacent densely settled surrounding area that together have a minimum population of 50,000.

VACANT HOUSING UNIT. See Housing unit.

WHITE POPULATION. See Race.

WHOLESALE TRADE. Establishments primarily engaged in selling merchandise to retailers, to institutions, to industrial, commercial, and professional users, or to other wholesalers.

WORKERS. See Labor force and Class of workers.

WORKERS' COMPENSATION. State-administered medical care payments and income maintenance. Benefits are granted for work-caused disability, illness, injury, or death.

INDEX OF CENSUS TABLES

The U.S. Bureau of the Census conducts various censuses at regular intervals. This index lists tables that include data from the most recent of these censuses published in the 1990 through 1996 editions of the *Florida Statistical Abstract*. Only tables that cite Census publications and/or Census Summary Tape Files (STF) as the primary source are listed here. The Bureau of the Census is used frequently as a secondary source on tables throughout the *Abstract*. The user is encouraged to refer to the index at the back of the book for aid in locating additional census-related data. No tables from the 1997 edition are included here. A more complete index of census tables may be found in *Abstracts* from 1994 and earlier. Users are also directed to the *1990 Census Handbook - Florida* published in 1994 by the Bureau of Economic and Business Research. It contains the most-used state and county data from the decennial census.

CENSUS OF AGRICULTURE
(Conducted approximately every 5 years)

AREA AND DEMOGRAPHIC CHARACTERISTIC INCLUDED	FLORIDA CENSUS YEAR	STATISTICAL ABSTRACT YEAR	TABLE
FLORIDA, STATE ONLY			
SPECIFIED CHARACTERISTICS	1987-1992	1994-1996	9.34
STATE AND COUNTIES			
CHARACTERISTICS OF OPERATORS	1987	1990-1993	9.38
DITTO..	1992	1994-1995	9.38
DITTO..	1992	1996	9.39
FARM ACREAGE BY USE	1987	1990-1992	9.36
DITTO..	1992	1994-1996	9.36
FARMS, SIZE, AND VALUE OF LAND AND BUILDINGS	1987-1992	1994-1996	9.35
MARKET VALUE OF AGRICULTURAL PRODUCTS SOLD	1987-1992	1994	9.37
DITTO..	1992	1995-1996	9.38

CENSUS OF GOVERNMENTS
(Conducted every 5 years)

AREA AND DEMOGRAPHIC CHARACTERISTIC INCLUDED	FLORIDA CENSUS YEAR	STATISTICAL ABSTRACT YEAR	TABLE
FLORIDA AND UNITED STATES			
NUMBER OF GOVERNMENTAL UNITS BY TYPE	1987	1990-1993	21.01
DITTO..	1992	1994-1996	21.01
STATE AND COUNTIES			
NUMBER AND TYPE OF GOVERNMENT UNIT	1987	1990-1994	21.07
DITTO..	1992	1995-1996	21.07
SCHOOL SYSTEMS	1987	1990-1994	21.07
DITTO..	1992	1995-1996	21.07

CENSUS OF HOUSING
(Conducted every 10 years)

AREA AND DEMOGRAPHIC HARACTERISTIC INCLUDED	FLORIDA CENSUS YEAR	STATISTICAL ABSTRACT YEAR	TABLE
FLORIDA, SELECTED STATES, AND UNITED STATES			
UNITS IN STRUCTURE, PERCENTAGE AND MEDIAN VALUE			
OF OCCUPIED UNITS	1990*	1992-1994	25.01
STATE AND COUNTIES			
MOBILE HOMES BY HOUSING CHARACTERISTICS	1990	1992-1995	2.35
OCCUPIED HOUSING UNITS AND PERCENTAGE OWNER-			
AND RENTER-OCCUPIED	1990*	1992-1994	2.06
DITTO..	1990*	1995	2.06
OCCUPIED HOUSING UNITS BY NUMBER OF UNITS IN			
STRUCTURE BY TENURE	1990	1992-1994	2.08
OCCUPIED HOUSING UNITS BY RACE AND HISPANIC ORIGIN OF			
HOUSEHOLDER	1990	1992-1994	2.07
BY TENURE	1990	1992-1994	2.07
OWNER-OCCUPIED HOUSING UNITS BY VALUE	1990*	1992-1995	2.09
RENTER-OCCUPIED HOUSING UNITS BY AMOUNT OF RENT	1990	1992-1994	2.10
DITTO..	1990	1995	2.11
TOTAL, VACANT AND OCCUPIED HOUSING UNITS, AND			
VACANCY RATES	1990*	1991-1993	2.01
DITTO..	1990*	1994-1995	2.02
TYPE AND PURPOSE OF FUEL USED	1990	1992-1994	15.05

CENSUS OF MANUFACTURES
(Conducted every 5 years)

AREA AND DEMOGRAPHIC CHARACTERISTIC INCLUDED	FLORIDA CENSUS YEAR	STATISTICAL ABSTRACT YEAR	TABLE
STATE AND SMSAS			
CHARACTERISTICS	1972-1982	1990	12.01
DITTO..	1972-1987	1991-1996	12.01
ESTABLISHMENTS, EMPLOYMENT, VALUE ADDED BY			
MANUFACTURE, AND NEW CAPITAL EXPENDITURE	1972-1982	1990	12.01
DITTO..	1972-1987	1991-1996	12.01
VALUE ADDED BY MANUFACTURE	1972-1982	1990	12.01
DITTO..	1972-1987	1991-1996	12.01
STATE AND COUNTIES			
ESTABLISHMENTS, EMPLOYMENT, VALUE ADDED BY			
MANUFACTURE, VALUE OF SHIPMENTS, AND NEW			
CAPITAL EXPENDITURE	1987	1991-1994	12.06
DITTO..	1992	1996	12.06

*1990 Census of Population and Housing.

University of Florida   **Bureau of Economic and Business Research**

CENSUS OF POPULATION
(Conducted every 10 years)

AREA AND DEMOGRAPHIC CHARACTERISTIC INCLUDED	FLORIDA CENSUS YEAR	STATISTICAL ABSTRACT YEAR	TABLE
FLORIDA, SELECTED STATES, AND UNITED STATES			
EDUCATIONAL ATTAINMENT, HIGH SCHOOL AND COLLEGE			
GRADUATES	1990*	1992-1994	25.01
FAMILY HOUSEHOLD MEDIAN INCOME	1990	1992-1993	25.01
MOBILITY STATUS	1990*	1992-1994	25.01
PERCENTAGE OF PERSONS BELOW POVERTY LEVEL	1990*	1992-1993	25.01
FLORIDA AND UNITED STATES			
RACE AND HISPANIC ORIGIN	1990*	1992-1994	1.25
FLORIDA, STATE ONLY			
POPULATION, TOTAL	1830-1990	1991-1996	1.10
URBAN AND RURAL POPULATION	1830-1990	1991-1996	1.10
STATE AND COUNTIES			
AGE	1990*	1991	1.35
EDUCATIONAL ATTAINMENT	1990	1992-1995	4.01
EMPLOYMENT	1990	1992-1994	6.09
FAMILY HOUSEHOLD MEDIAN INCOME	1990	1992-1995	5.58
DITTO..	1990	1992-1995	5.56
FAMILY HOUSEHOLDS BY SEX OF HOUSEHOLDER	1990	1992-1995	5.51
FAMILY HOUSEHOLDS BY INCOME LEVEL	1990	1992-1995	5.56
HIGH SCHOOL GRADUATES	1980-1990	1992-1995	4.01
HISPANIC ORIGIN	1990	1992-1995	1.26
HOUSEHOLD MEDIAN INCOME	1980-1990	1992-1994	5.58
DITTO..	1990	1995	5.58
DITTO..	1990	1992-1995	5.55
HOUSEHOLDS BY INCOME LEVEL	1990*	1992-1995	5.55
LABOR FORCE PARTICIPATION OF WOMEN AND WOMEN BY			
PRESENCE OF CHILDREN	1980-1990	1992-1995	6.13
LANGUAGE SPOKEN AT HOME	1990	1992-1995	1.92
MARITAL STATUS	1990	1992-1995	1.95
MEDIAN AGE	1970-1990	1995	1.38
DITTO..	1990	1996	1.39
NONFAMILY HOUSEHOLD MEDIAN INCOME	1990	1992-1995	5.58
DITTO..	1990	1992-1995	5.57
NONFAMILY HOUSEHOLDS BY INCOME LEVEL	1990*	1992-1995	5.57
PERSONS BY OCCUPATION	1990*	1992-1994	6.24
PERSONS IN GROUP QUARTERS	1990*	1992-1995	2.16
POVERTY STATUS OF PERSONS, FAMILY HOUSEHOLDS, AND			
UNRELATED INDIVIDUALS	1990	1992-1995	5.50
POVERTY STATUS OF MALE HOUSEHOLDER FAMILIES AN			
FEMALE HOUSEHOLDER FAMILIES BY PRESENCE OF			
CHILDREN	1990	1992-1995	5.51
RACE	1990	1992-1995	1.26
RESIDENCE IN 1985 OF 1990 POPULATION	1990*	1992-1994	1.73
SEX	1990*	1991	1.35
TRANSPORTATION TO WORK	1990	1992-1995	13.01
URBAN AND RURAL POPULATION, AND RURAL FARM	1990*	1992-1995	1.11

*1990 Census of Population and Housing.

CENSUS OF POPULATION (CONTINUED)
(Conducted every 10 years)

CENSUS OF RETAIL TRADE
(Conducted approximately every 5 years)

CENSUS OF SERVICE INDUSTRIES
(Conducted every 5 years)

CENSUS OF WHOLESALE TRADE
(Conducted approximately every 5 years)

Index of Tables

Table   Table

Table   Table

University of Florida   **Bureau of Economic and Business Research**

Table   Table

Table

Table

Table   Table

University of Florida   **Bureau of Economic and Business Research**

University of Florida   **Bureau of Economic and Business Research**

Table

Table

Table

Table

Table

Table

Table

Table

Table   Table

University of Florida   **Bureau of Economic and Business Research**

Table   Table

NEW FROM BEBR

Florida and the Nation 1997 has comparison statistics and ranked data for Florida, the other 49 states, and the United States. There are 102 tables and 70 data maps in this volume. Tables cover a wide range of topics: minority-, women-, black-, and Hispanic-owned firms, bankruptcy, home-ownership and vacancy rates, indicators of child safety, teen and single-parent births, current educational attainment, poverty status, and income data to name a few.

There are 14 sections: Population; Housing and Construction; Vital Statistics and Health; Education; Income; Labor Force, Employment, and Earnings; Business Climate; Personal and Business Services; Agriculture; Motor Vehicle Transportation; Tourism, Recreation, and Leisure; Social Programs and Services; Crime, Corrections, and Legal Services; and Government Elections, Finance, and Employment.

ORDER NOW

221 Matherly Hall
PO Box 117145, Gainesville FL 32611-7145
Phone (352) 392-0171   Fax (352) 392-4739
bebr@bebr.cba.ufl.edu and http://www.cba.ufl.edu/bebr/

 **UNIVERSITY OF FLORIDA**   **Warrington College of Business Administration**
Bureau of Economic and Business Research